NOV   2012

gettyimages

PHOTO JOURNALISM
PHOTO JOURNALISMUS
PHOTOJOURNALISME

Nick Yapp and

Amanda Hopkinson

*h.f.*ullmann

(FRONTISPIECE) STEPHANIE STEPHENS AS PETER PAN IN 1915.

© h.f.ullmann publishing GmbH
Photographs © 2006/2012 Getty Images

Special edition

This book was produced in cooperation with Endeavour London Limited.

Publishing concept: Charles Merullo
Production manager: Mary Osborne
Design: Paul Welti
Picture editors: Ali Khoja, Tea Aganovic
Picture researchers: Sue Percival, Leon Meyer, Jennifer Jeffrey
Project editors: Elisabeth Ingles, Mark Fletcher
German translation: Birgit Herbst (part I) and Manfred Allié (part II); Kirsten Lehmann and Katrin Höller (updates)
French translation: Sylvie Adam-Kuenen, Michèle Schreyer; Jean-Luc Lesouëf and Chantal Mitjaville for InTexte (updates)
Proofreader: Liz Ihre
Indexer: Jennifer Jeffrey
Cover design: Simone Sticker

Overall responsibility for production: h.f.ullmann publishing GmbH, Potsdam, Germany

Printed in China

ISBN 978-3-8480-0062-3
ISBN 978-3-8480-0154-5
ISBN 978-3-8480-0038-8

10 9 8 7 6 5 4 3 2 1
X IX VIII VII VI V IV III II I

www.ullmann-publishing.com
newsletter@ullmann-publishing.com

Contents

Inhalt

Sommaire

Part I

1850–1918

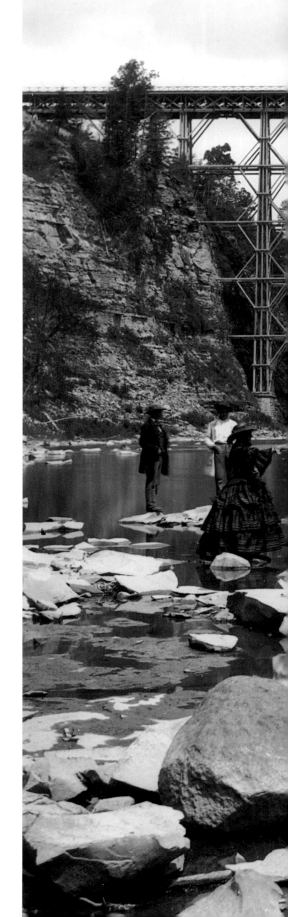

HIGH BRIDGE, GENESEE RIVER, NEAR ROCHESTER,
NEW YORK.

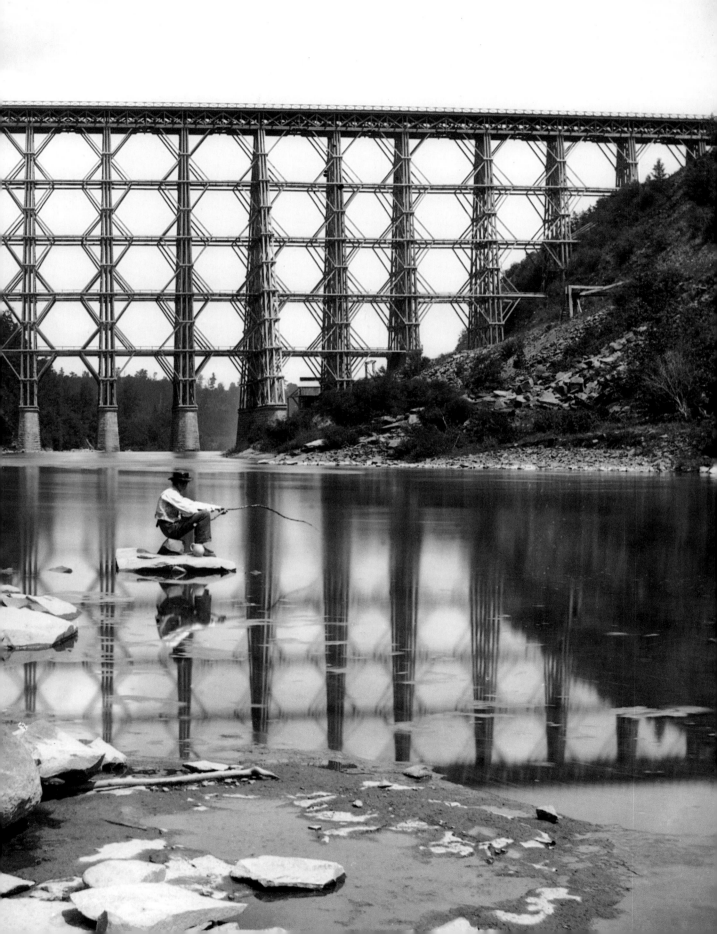

Introduction

LIFE was a lottery in the mid-19th century. Whether rich or poor, mother and baby both needed luck to survive the perils of childbirth. Infant mortality rates were terrifyingly high, and cholera, typhus, diphtheria and a dozen other diseases were in constant brooding attendance. Of those who did survive into infancy, childhood and adulthood, the rich lived longer, ate better, had more to enjoy. The poor struggled to exist in bad housing, worked exhausting hours, ailed and died, often in their thirties and forties. The average expectation of life in the industrial world varied from country to country as well as from class to class. In the slums and sweatshops it could be as low as thirty-five; in villas and offices it could be as high as sixty. For white men and women in the ever-extending colonies it could be little more than forty. Death seemed always near at hand and people fervently prayed for a longer, as well as a better, life hereafter.

But if you won the lottery, what a time it was to be alive! Those born in 1850 who were granted their threescore years and ten witnessed a transformation of life on earth hitherto unknown. They entered a world where most people travelled only as fast as a horse could carry them – though steam locomotives were already rattling along at 45 miles an hour (72kph), shocking Queen Victoria, but delighting many. To sail to another land meant a voyage of considerable discomfort, often prolonged by the vagaries of the wind. Most people still lived, worked and died on the land. Anaesthetics were unknown. Family planning was unheard of. Open sewers ran along the centres of even the most fashionable streets in the smartest cities. There was no electricity, and gas, as a fuel for light or heat, was still something of a novelty.

In Europe there was a sprinkling of insecure republics, but in most countries, king or emperor sat firmly on his throne and all was, on the face of it, right with the world. The indigenous North Americans hunted buffalo on the central plains; the interiors of Africa, Australia and South America were unknown to white people; Japan and China were closed communities. The old order prevailed. Dukes and princes, bishops and cardinals hunted for sport and oppressed for a living. To the vast majority, the deliberations of central government were of far less concern than the whims of the local lord. If you were a poor male and wanted to travel, you joined the army. If you were a poor female and wanted to travel, you couldn't.

A lifetime later, so much had changed. A succession of wars had redrawn the frontiers of Europe. Italy and Germany had both forged painful unification. Russia had given birth to a revolution that was to bring hope and terror to millions in almost equal shares. The great empires of Austro-Hungary and Turkey had collapsed. The bitter fight to win the endless arms race had led to breathtaking developments of plane, submarine, machine gun, tank and a multitude of other toys of war. Colonial greed had hacked and dug its way through most of Africa, India and America, and invaded the far-flung islands of the Pacific Ocean. Custer's Last Stand had proved to be the native Americans' last victory, and train excursions of sharpshooters from the Eastern States had all but removed the buffalo from the plains. Scott and Amundsen had raced to the South Pole. To the Norwegian victor had been immediate glory: to the English loser, fame as lasting as his own body in the frozen wastes of that terrible land.

There was electricity, the gramophone, the cinema. Thomas Crapper had invented the flush lavatory, bringing at first disease and dread to those who used it, but, later, hope and health. The internal combustion engine was shunting the horse off the road: the steam traction engine was driving horses from the land. There was town planning. There were underground sewers and underground railways. There were suburbs, skyscrapers, department stores, millionaires, strikes and cheap newspapers. There was mass production and mass consumption. Women had the vote. Men were conscripted into monster armies. Children received education, whether they liked it or not. International sport had been revived – the first time tribes had met in playful rivalry since the ancient Olympic Games. There was the telephone and the telegraph. In 1919, when those born in 1850 would have been venerable, and quite possibly exhausted, Alcock and Brown flew a Vickers Vimy bi-plane across the Atlantic at 100 miles an hour (160kph), just beating the arrival of the Original Dixieland Jazz Band in Europe. The world had shrunk. The 20th century had arrived.

It was the high-water mark of European domination. The United States was rapidly becoming the richest country in the world, but was still looking inwards on itself, pursuing a policy of isolation and loath to become involved in foreign affairs. Europeans constructed the railways that crossed South America and Africa; engineered the canals that joined oceans; and even built an opera house 3,000 miles up the Amazon River.

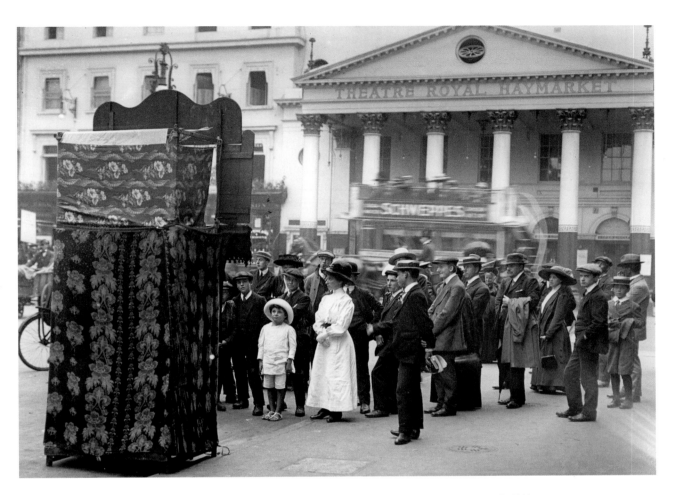

A PUNCH AND JUDY SHOW IN THE HAYMARKET, LONDON, AROUND 1900.

PUPPENTHEATER AUF DEM HAYMARKET, LONDON, UM 1900.

THÉÂTRE DE MARIONNETTES SUR LE HAYMARKET, LONDRES, VERS 1900.

Wherever they went, the French took with them the Code Napoléon: the British took a few foxes and packs of hounds. The ports of Europe filled with the riches of the present: cotton, wool, manganese, copper, rubber, tea and coffee, meat and grain. The museums of Europe filled with the riches of the past: gongs, temple bells, statues, jewellery, fossils, amulets, skeletons, whole tombs. In exchange, entire continents received beads, guns and Bibles – and a second-hand language and culture.

But millions benefited from the advance of science and learning, from better housing, from education. Life was still harsh and brutish for many, but at least fewer people risked losing everything in the lottery. More babies survived. Children were healthier. The poor were a little less poor; the rich, for the most part, a little less rich. Some women had professional and social freedom. People ate better food, but probably breathed worse air. The future seemed to hold much.

On pages 16 and 17 is a gallery of some of the most famous – or notorious – figures of the seventy-year period.

Towards the end of this lifetime of achievement, Europe tore itself apart in the worst war in history, a war that nobody wanted. When the guns finally stopped, an exhausted continent had lost its grip on the world. Germany was crippled, defeated, bankrupt. France and Britain had lost a generation of hope and promise. Russia was emerging from the pangs of revolution into the searing pain of civil war. Serbia, Macedonia and Bosnia had disappeared from the map.

President Woodrow Wilson of the United States laid the ground rules for the Treaty of Versailles and then withdrew his troops and his involvement. But the United States had accumulated a massive self-confidence during the war, and was poised for its turn to plunder the rest of the world – including Europe.

Einleitung

IN der Mitte des 19. Jahrhunderts war das Leben ein Glücksspiel. Ob reich oder arm, Mutter und Kind brauchten Glück, um die Gefahren der Geburt zu überleben. Die Kindersterblichkeitsrate war erschreckend hoch, und Cholera, Typhus, Diphtherie und ein Dutzend anderer Krankheiten grassierten. Von denen, die bis zum Erwachsenenalter durchhielten, konnten sich die Reichen, nicht zuletzt aufgrund einer besseren Ernährung, eines längeren und angenehmeren Lebens erfreuen. Die Armen kämpften in schlechten Unterkünften um ihre Existenz, arbeiteten bis zur Erschöpfung, wurden krank und starben häufig schon zwischen dem dreißigsten und vierzigsten Lebensjahr. Die durchschnittliche Lebenserwartung in der industrialisierten Welt war sowohl von Land zu Land als auch von Klasse zu Klasse verschieden. In den Slums und den Ausbeuterbetrieben wurden die Menschen oft nur 35, in den Villen und Büros jedoch bis zu 60 Jahre alt. Weiße Männer und Frauen, die in den ständig wachsenden Kolonien lebten, hatten eine Lebenserwartung von knapp über 40 Jahren. Der Tod schien überall zu lauern, und die Menschen beteten für ein längeres und besseres Leben im Jenseits.

Wenn man jedoch das große Los gezogen hatte, konnte das Leben herrlich sein. Jene, die 1850 geboren wurden und das siebzigste Lebensjahr erreichten, erlebten bis dahin ungekannte Veränderungen. Sie traten ein in eine Welt, in der die meisten Menschen nur so schnell reisten, wie ein Pferd sie tragen konnte, obwohl die Dampflokomotiven – zum Schrecken von Königin Victoria, aber zur Freude vieler – bereits mit 70 Stundenkilometern dahinratterten. In ein anderes Land zu segeln bedeutete, eine mit beträchtlichen Unannehmlichkeiten verbundene Reise anzutreten, die häufig durch die Unberechenbarkeit des Windes noch verlängert wurde. Die meisten Menschen lebten, arbeiteten und starben noch immer auf dem Land. Betäubungsmittel kannte man nicht, und von Familienplanung hatte man ebenfalls noch nichts gehört. Die Abwässer flossen offen durch die Straßen in den Zentren selbst der elegantesten Städte. Es gab keine Elektrizität, und Gas für Lampen oder Heizungen war noch immer etwas Neues.

In Europa gab es ein paar vereinzelte ungefestigte Republiken, aber in den meisten Ländern saßen Könige oder Kaiser fest auf ihrem Thron, und nach außen hin hatte alles seine Ordnung. In den Ebenen Nordamerikas jagten die Eingeborenen Büffel; das Innere von Afrika, Australien und Südamerika hatte noch kein Weißer gesehen; Japan und China waren geschlossene Gemeinschaften. Die alte Ordnung blieb vorherrschend. Herzöge und Prinzen, Bischöfe und Kardinäle jagten zum Vergnügen und unterdrückten zur Bereicherung. Für die große Mehrheit der Bevölkerung waren die Entscheidungen der zentralen Landesregierung von weitaus geringerer Bedeutung als die Launen ihres Gutsherrn. Mittellose Männer, die reisen wollten, gingen in die Armee, für mittellose Frauen gab es keine solche Möglichkeit.

Eine Generation später hatte sich sehr viel verändert. Eine Reihe von Kriegen hatte die Grenzen Europas verschoben. Sowohl Italien als auch Deutschland hatten einen schmerzhaften Vereinigungsprozeß erlebt. In Rußland hatte sich eine Revolution vollzogen, die für Millionen von Menschen fast ebensoviel Hoffnung wie Schrecken bedeuten sollte. Die großen Reiche Österreich-Ungarn und Türkei waren zusammengebrochen. Der bittere Kampf um den Sieg im Rüstungswettlauf hatte zur atemberaubend schnellen Entwicklung von Flugzeugen, Unterseebooten, Maschinengewehren, Panzern und einer Vielzahl anderer »Kriegsspielzeuge« geführt. Die Gier der Kolonialmächte hatte sich einen Weg durch den größten Teil von Afrika, Indien und Amerika geschlagen und war über die entlegenen Inseln des Pazifischen Ozeans hergefallen. General Custers letztes Gefecht hatte sich als letzter Sieg der amerikanischen Ureinwohner erwiesen, und Trupps von Scharfschützen aus den Oststaaten hatten die Büffel fast vollständig von den Ebenen verschwinden lassen. Scott und Amundsen hatten sich ein Wettrennen zum Südpol geliefert. Dem norwegischen Sieger wurde unmittelbarer Ruhm zuteil, während der britische Verlierer im ewigen Eis dieses grausamen Landes zurückblieb.

Es gab nun Elektrizität, das Grammophon, das Kino. Thomas Crapper hatte das Wasserklosett erfunden und seinen ersten Benutzern Krankheit und Schrecken gebracht, später jedoch Hoffnung und Gesundheit. Der Verbrennungsmotor verdrängte das Pferd von den Straßen, der dampfbetriebene Traktor vertrieb es vom Land. Man betrieb Stadtplanung. Es gab unterirdische Abwasserkanäle und unterirdische Züge. Es gab Vororte, Hochhäuser, Kaufhäuser, Millionäre, Streiks und billige Zeitungen, Massenproduktion und Massenkonsum. Frauen erhielten das Wahlrecht. Männer wurden in Schreckensarmeen eingezogen. Kinder erhielten Erziehung und Ausbildung, ob sie wollten oder nicht. Der internationale Sport war wiederbelebt worden; zum ersten Mal seit den Olympischen Spielen der Antike hatten sich wieder Völker zum spielerischen Wettkampf zusammen-gefunden. Es gab das Telephon und den Fernschreiber. Im Jahre 1919, in dem die 1850 Geborenen mit großer Wahrscheinlichkeit alt und verbraucht gewesen wären, flogen Alcock und Brown in einem Vickers-Vimy-Doppeldecker mit einer Geschwindigkeit von 160 Stundenkilometern über den Atlantik und erreichten Europa kurz vor der Ankunft der Original Dixieland Jazz Band. Die Welt war kleiner geworden. Das zwanzigste Jahrhundert hatte begonnen.

Die europäische Vorherrschaft hatte mittlerweile ihren Höhepunkt erreicht. Die Vereinigten Staaten von Amerika wurden schnell zur reichsten Nation der Welt, waren jedoch noch immer äußerst selbstbezogen und verfolgten eine Politik der Isolation, mit dem erklärten Ziel der Nichteinmischung in fremde Angelegenheiten. Die Europäer bauten Eisenbahnen in Südamerika und in Afrika, sie konstruierten Kanäle, die Ozeane miteinander verbanden, und mitten im Urwald, am Oberlauf des Amazonas, errichteten sie sogar ein Opernhaus. Wo immer sie auch hinkamen, brachten die Franzosen den Code Napoléon und die Briten ein paar Füchse und Jagdhunde mit. Die Häfen Europas füllten sich mit den Reichtümern der Gegenwart: mit Baumwolle, Wolle, Mangan, Kupfer, Kautschuk, Tee und Kaffee, mit Fleisch und Getreide. Die Museen Europas hingegen füllten sich mit den Reichtümern der Vergangenheit: riesige Gongs, Tempelglocken, Statuen, Juwelen, Fossilien, Amulette, Skelette, sogar vollständige Grabanlagen. Im Gegenzug erhielten ganze Kontinente Perlenketten, Gewehre und Bibeln sowie eine Sprache und eine Kultur sozusagen aus zweiter Hand.

Millionen Menschen jedoch profitierten vom Fortschritt der Wissenschaft und den neuen Erkenntnissen, von besserer Unterkunft, Erziehung und Ausbildung. Für viele war das Leben noch immer schwer, aber zumindest liefen weniger Menschen Gefahr, alles in der Lebenslotterie zu verlieren. Mehr Babies überlebten, und die Kinder waren gesünder. Die Armen waren ein bißchen weniger arm und die meisten Reichen ein bißchen weniger reich. Einige Frauen genossen berufliche und soziale Freiheit. Die Menschen ernährten sich besser, atmeten aber schlechtere Luft. Die Zukunft schien vieles bereit-zuhalten.

Auf den Seiten 16 und 17 finden Sie eine Porträtgalerie einiger der berühmtesten – berüchtigtsten – Persönlichkeiten jener fast 70 Jahre zwischen 1850 und 1918.

Gegen Ende dieser Zeit der bahnbrechenden Errungenschaften zerriß sich Europa im verheerendsten Krieg der Geschichte, einem Krieg, den niemand gewollt hatte. Als die Gewehre endlich schwiegen, hatte ein erschöpfter Kontinent seine Macht über die Welt verloren. Deutschland war geschunden, geschlagen und bankrott. Frankreich und Großbritannien hatten eine hoffnungsvolle und vielversprechende Generation verloren. Rußland war dabei, die Schrecken der Revolution gegen die des Bürgerkrieges einzutauschen. Serbien, Mazedonien und Bosnien waren von der Landkarte verschwunden.

Nachdem der Präsident der Vereinigten Staaten, Woodrow Wilson, die Statuten des Versailler Vertrages festgelegt hatte, zog er seine Truppen zurück und überließ Europa seinem Schicksal. Aber die Vereinigten Staaten hatten während des Krieges großes Selbstvertrauen gewonnen und waren bereit, den Rest der Welt – einschließlich Europa – zu plündern.

Introduction

LA vie, au milieu du XIXe siècle, était un événement aléatoire. Riches ou pauvres, mères et enfants devaient avoir de la chance pour survivre à l'épreuve de l'accouchement. La mortalité infantile était terriblement élevée à une époque où le choléra, le typhus, la diphtérie et une dizaine d'autres maladies sévissaient. Parmi ceux qui survivaient à la petite enfance et à l'enfance pour atteindre l'âge adulte, c'était les riches qui vivaient le plus longtemps, grâce à une meilleure alimentation et à des avantages plus nombreux. Les pauvres luttaient pour survivre dans de méchants logements, s'échinaient au travail, étaient en mauvaise santé et mourraient souvent avant d'atteindre 50 ans, voire la quarantaine. L'espérance de vie moyenne dans le monde industriel variait aussi bien d'un pays à l'autre que d'une classe à l'autre. Dans les bidonvilles et les ateliers où la main-d'œuvre se faisait exploiter, elle pouvait être de 35 ans seulement. Dans les villas et dans les bureaux, elle pouvait monter jusqu'à 60 ans. Pour les hommes et les femmes de race blanche, dans les colonies en expansion, elle pouvait légèrement dépasser 40 ans. On priait avec ferveur pour une vie plus longue et meilleure après la mort qui semblait toujours rôder.

Mais si vous étiez chanceux, quelle époque bénie ! Ceux qui naquirent en 1850 et eurent la bonne fortune de vivre jusqu'à 70 ans furent témoins d'une transformation sans précédent de leur existence ici-bas. Ils pénétraient dans un monde où la plupart des gens ne voyageaient pas plus loin qu'un cheval pouvait les porter, même si les locomotives à vapeur roulaient déjà, dans un vacarme strident, à 70 km/h, choquant la reine Victoria mais ravissant le plus grand nombre. Les voyages à l'étranger en bateau étaient synonymes de bien des désagréments qu'aggravaient souvent les vents capricieux. La plupart des gens continuaient à vivre, travailler et mourir à la campagne. Les anesthésiques étaient inconnus, tout comme le planning familial. Les collecteurs d'eaux usées étaient disposés à ciel ouvert au beau milieu des rues, même dans les plus élégantes des villes les plus pimpantes. Il n'y avait pas d'électricité ; quant au gaz, pour s'éclairer ou se chauffer, il faisait encore figure de nouveauté.

En Europe, il y avait bien ici et là quelques républiques peu stables, mais dans la majorité des pays régnait un roi ou un empereur fermement assis sur son trône. Tout était pour le mieux dans le meilleur des mondes ; l'ordre établi prévalait. Les ducs et les princes, les évêques et les cardinaux avaient fait de la chasse un sport, et de l'oppression un moyen d'existence. Pour l'immense majorité des gens, les délibérations du gouvernement central étaient bien moins préoccupantes que les caprices du seigneur local. L'homme pauvre qui voulait voyager entrait dans l'armée. Pour la femme pauvre, c'était impossible.

Que de changements en l'espace d'une vie. Une cascade de guerres avait redessiné les frontières en Europe. L'Italie et l'Allemagne avaient toutes deux forgé une unification douloureuse. La Russie avait enfanté une révolution qui allait être synonyme d'espoir et de terreur pour des millions de personnes. Les grands empires d'Autriche-Hongrie et de Turquie s'étaient effondrés. La bataille acharnée en vue de remporter l'interminable course aux armements avait abouti à des progrès stupéfiants : l'avion, le sous-marin, la mitrailleuse, le char d'assaut et tant d'autres engins de guerre étaient apparus. La cupidité coloniale s'était frayée un chemin par la violence à travers la plus grande partie de l'Afrique, de l'Inde et de l'Amérique, jusqu'aux îles qui fourmillaient dans l'océan Pacifique. Le massacre des hommes de Custer fut la dernière victoire des Amérindiens. Les chasseurs des états de l'Est, venus par trains, firent peu à peu disparaître les bisons de la prairie. Scott et Amundsen s'étaient lancés dans une course au pôle Sud. Le vainqueur norvégien en avait tiré une gloire immédiate ; son malheureux concurrent anglais une popularité qui devait durer aussi longtemps que son propre corps pris dans la glace.

Il y avait l'électricité, le gramophone et le cinéma. Thomas Crapper avait inventé la chasse d'eau qui commença par répandre la maladie parmi ses utilisateurs avant d'apporter l'hygiène. Le moteur à combustion interne était en passe de supplanter le cheval ; la traction à vapeur sur le point d'éliminer les chevaux des campagnes. On urbanisait. Il y avait les collecteurs de déchets et les chemins de fer souterrains. Il y avait les banlieues, les gratte-ciel, les grandes surfaces, les millionnaires, les grèves et les journaux bon marché. Il y avait la production en série et la consommation de

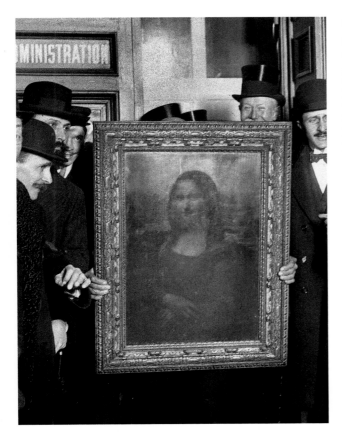

THE MONA LISA ARRIVING AT THE
ÉCOLE DES BEAUX-ARTS, PARIS.

DIE ANKUNFT DER MONA LISA IN DER
ÉCOLE DES BEAUX-ARTS, PARIS.

LA JOCONDE ARRIVE À
L'ÉCOLE DES BEAUX-ARTS, PARIS.

masse. Les femmes votaient. Les hommes devaient s'enrôler dans des armées gigantesques. Les enfants étaient instruits, quel qu'en fût leur désir. Le sport international avait été remis à l'honneur : c'était la première fois que des tribus rivalisaient dans des joutes amicales depuis les Jeux olympiques de l'Antiquité. Il y avait le téléphone et le télégraphe. En 1919, alors que ceux qui avaient vu le jour en 1850 étaient normalement devenus de vénérables vieillards vraisemblablement fatigués, Alcock et Brown traversaient l'Atlantique à 160 km/h dans un biplan, le Vickers Vimy, précédant de peu l'arrivée en Europe de l'Original Dixieland Jazz Band. Le monde avait rapetissé. Le XXe siecle était là.

La domination de l'Europe était à son apogée. Les États-Unis, en passe de devenir le pays le plus riche du monde, continuaient à faire de l'introspection et à poursuivre leur politique d'isolement, répugnant à s'engager dans les affaires des autres nations. Les Européens avaient construit des chemins de fer pour traverser l'Amérique du Sud et l'Afrique, des canaux pour relier les océans et même un opéra à quelque 48 000 kilomètres en amont de l'Amazone. Partout où ils allaient, les Français emportaient avec eux le code Napoléon, les Britanniques quelques renards et des meutes de chiens de chasse. Les ports d'Europe s'emplissaient de coton, de laine, de manganèse, de cuivre, de caoutchouc, de thé, de café, de viande et de céréales. Les musées d'Europe accumulaient les richesses du passé : gongs, cloches de temples, statues, joyaux, fossiles, amulettes, squelettes et tombes intactes. En échange, des continents entiers recevaient des colliers de perles, des armes à feu, des canons, des bibles, ainsi qu'une langue et une culture importées.

Mais ils furent des millions à profiter des progrès de la science et des nouvelles connaissances, à bénéficier de meilleures conditions de logement et de l'instruction. Si la vie restait dans l'ensemble âpre et brutale, moins nombreux étaient les perdants. Davantage de bébés survivaient. Les enfants étaient en meilleure santé. Les pauvres étaient un peu moins pauvres et les riches, en majorité, un peu moins riches. Certaines femmes jouissaient d'une liberté dans le domaine social et professionnel. La qualité des aliments s'était améliorée, et bien que celle de l'air eût certainement empiré, l'avenir semblait riche de promesses.

Vous trouverez aux pages 16 et 17 une galerie de portraits de quelques – unes des personnalités les plus célèbres et les plus considérées durant ces presque 70 années de 1850 à 1918.

Après cette période faste, l'Europe connut la pire guerre de son histoire. Lorsque les armes se turent enfin, un continent exsangue avait perdu son emprise sur le monde. L'Allemagne était vaincue et ruinée. La France et la Grande-Bretagne avaient perdu une génération pleine d'espoir et de promesses. La Russie émergeait des convulsions de la révolution pour plonger dans une guerre civile douloureuse. La Serbie, la Macédoine et la Bosnie avaient été rayées de la carte.

Le président américain Woodrow Wilson jeta les bases du traité de Versailles, puis retira ses troupes et se désengagea. Toutefois, les États-Unis avaient fait preuve d'une immense assurance au cours de la guerre, et ils étaient bien décidés à accroître leur hégémonie économique.

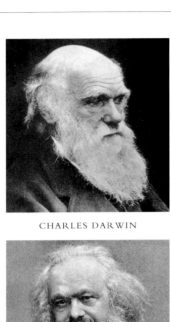

CHARLES DARWIN

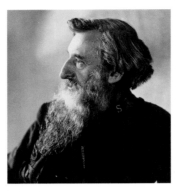

GENERAL WILLIAM BOOTH

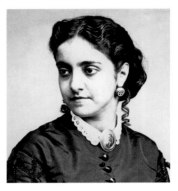

ADELINA PATTI

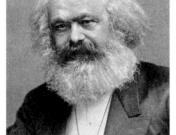

KARL MARX

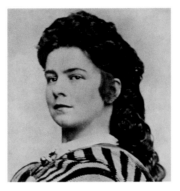

EMPRESS ELISABETH

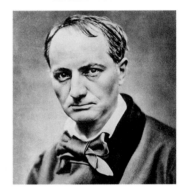

CHARLES BAUDELAIRE

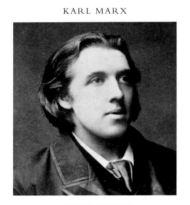

OSCAR WILDE

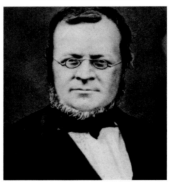

CAMILLO CAVOUR

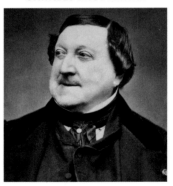

GIOACCHINO ROSSINI

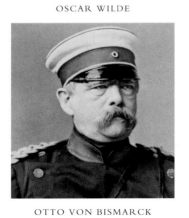

OTTO VON BISMARCK

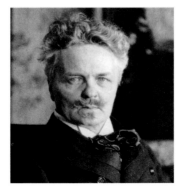

AUGUST STRINDBERG

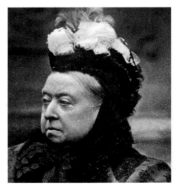

QUEEN VICTORIA

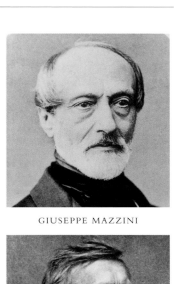

GIUSEPPE MAZZINI

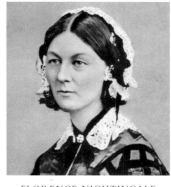

FLORENCE NIGHTINGALE

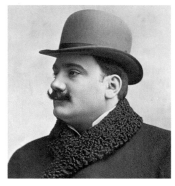

ENRICO CARUSO

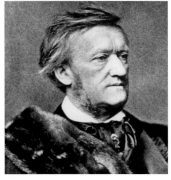

RICHARD WAGNER

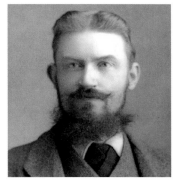

GEORGE BERNARD SHAW

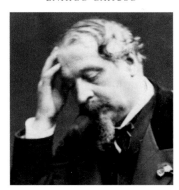

NAPOLÉON III

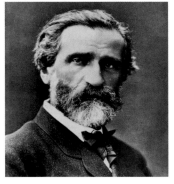

GIUSEPPE VERDI

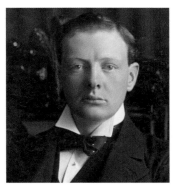

WINSTON CHURCHILL

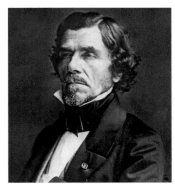

EUGÈNE DELACROIX

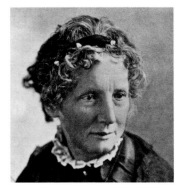

HARRIET BEECHER STOWE

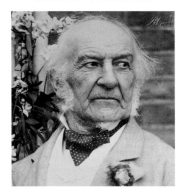

WILLIAM GLADSTONE

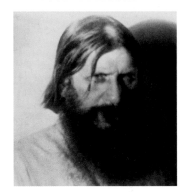

GRIGORI RASPUTIN

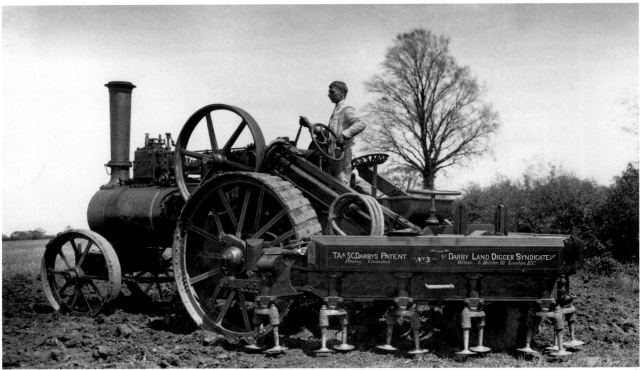

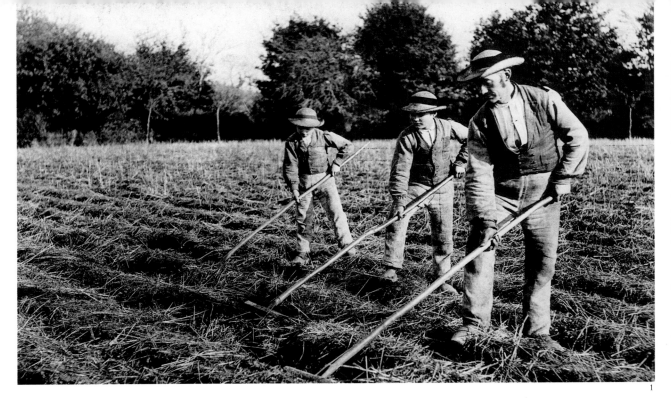

STEAM traction engines first appeared in the 1860s (2). They were cumbersome, but powerful and reliable for ploughing, harrowing, reaping, threshing. On smaller farms, man still provided much of the power – father and son moved in line to rake the hay (1). Much of the work on this English turkey farm would have been seasonal (5), and plucking poultry was traditionally a woman's job (3). There was still plenty of wildlife to be stalked and shot (4), and conservation never entered anyone's head.

DAMPFBETRIEBENE Traktoren tauchten zum ersten Mal in den 1860er Jahren auf (2). Sie waren schwer zu manövrieren, aber leistungsstark und verläßlich und konnten für viele Aufgaben eingesetzt werden – zum Pflügen, Eggen, Mähen und Dreschen. Auf kleineren Farmen bewältigte noch immer der Mensch den größten Teil der Arbeit; Vater und

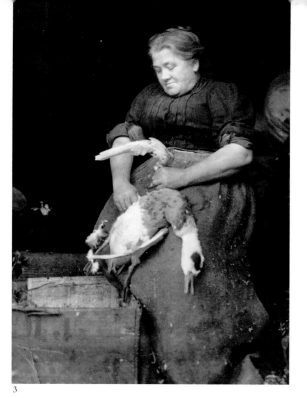

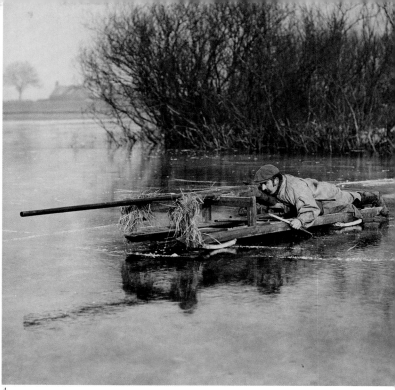

3

4

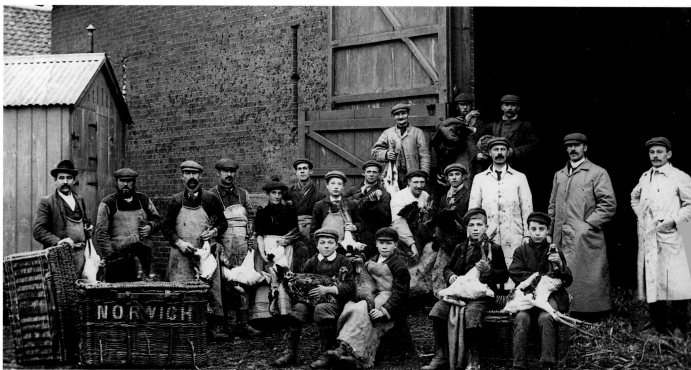

5

Sohn bewegten sich in einer Reihe und harkten das Heu (1). Ein Großteil der Arbeit auf dieser englischen Truthahnfarm war saisonbedingt (5), und das Rupfen des Geflügels war traditionsgemäß Aufgabe der Frauen (3). Es gab noch immer viele wilde Tiere, auf die man Jagd machen konnte (4), und niemand dachte an Naturschutz.

LES premières machines à traction à vapeur firent leur apparition dans les années 1860 (2). Quoique encombrantes, elles étaient puissantes et fiables, et pouvaient remplir de multiples tâches : le labourage, l'hersage, le moissonnage et le battage. Sur les petites exploitations, l'homme fournissait encore une grosse partie de l'énergie : père et fils râtelant le foin en ligne (1). Lorsque

c'était possible, les exploitants se spécialisaient. Une grosse partie du travail dans cet élevage de dindes en Angleterre avait très certainement un caractère saisonnier (5). Plumer la volaille était traditionnellement un travail de femme (3). Le gibier restait abondant pour la chasse à l'approche (4), et défendre l'environnement ne venait à l'idée de personne.

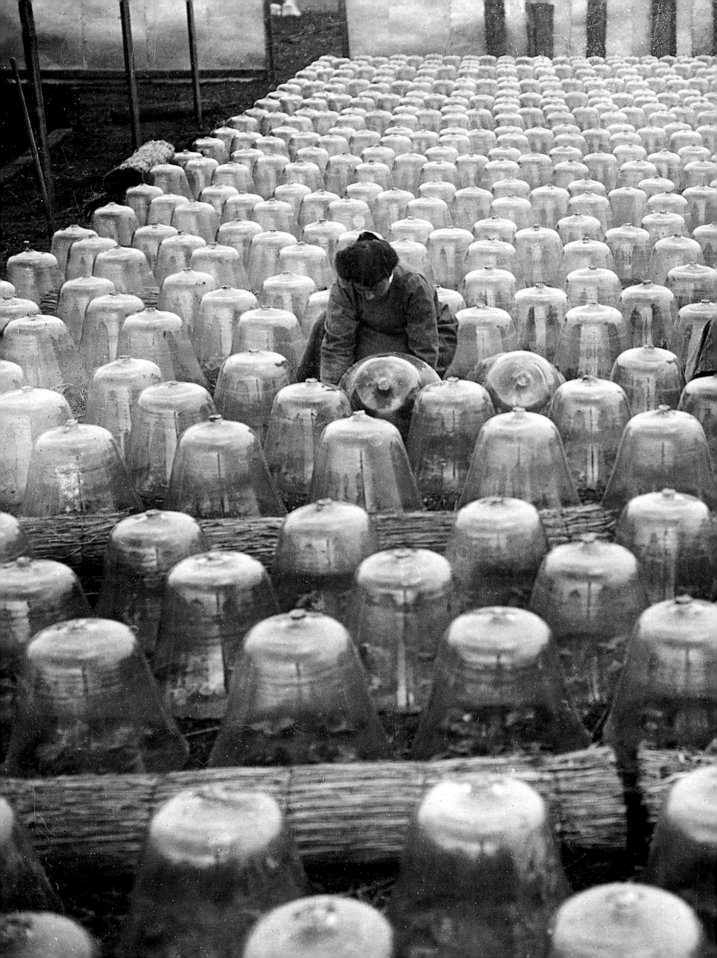

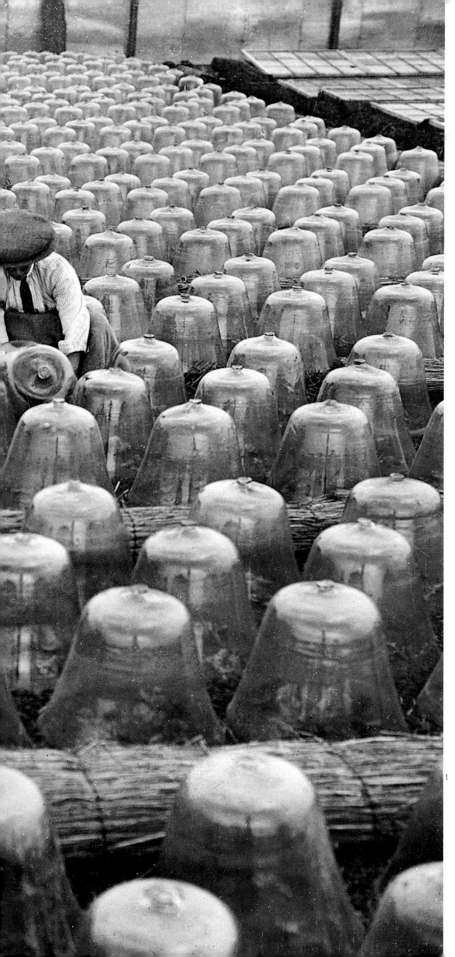

2

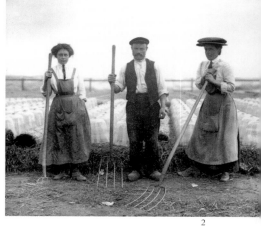

1

BY the second half of the 19th century fruit and vegetable growers used cloches (1) to lengthen the growing season. Regular train services ensured that the crops reached market while still fresh. This changed people's tastes – and in the boom years of the 1860s, 1870s, and 1890s there was more money to spend on food. Scratching a living from the land had become a little less back-breaking (2).

IN der zweiten Hälfte des 19. Jahrhunderts verwendeten Obst- und Gemüsezüchter Glasglocken (1), um die Reifezeit zu verlängern. Regelmäßige Bahntransporte sorgten dafür, daß die Ernte den Markt erreichte, solange sie frisch war. Dieser Umstand hatte Einfluß auf den Geschmack der Menschen, und in der Blütezeit der 60er, 70er und 90er Jahre des 19. Jahrhunderts gab man mehr Geld für Essen aus. Sich seinen Lebensunterhalt auf dem Land zu verdienen war etwas weniger anstrengend geworden (2).

DÈS la seconde moitié du XIXe siècle, les maraîchers utilisèrent des cloches (1) pour allonger la période de maturation. Grâce aux liaisons ferroviaires régulières, les produits arrivaient frais sur le marché. Les goûts s'en trouvèrent modifiés. Pendant les années de prospérité que furent les années 1860, 1870 et 1890, on consacra davantage d'argent à l'alimentation. Tirer sa subsistance de la terre n'avait jamais été facile ; c'était tout de même devenu un peu moins éreintant (2).

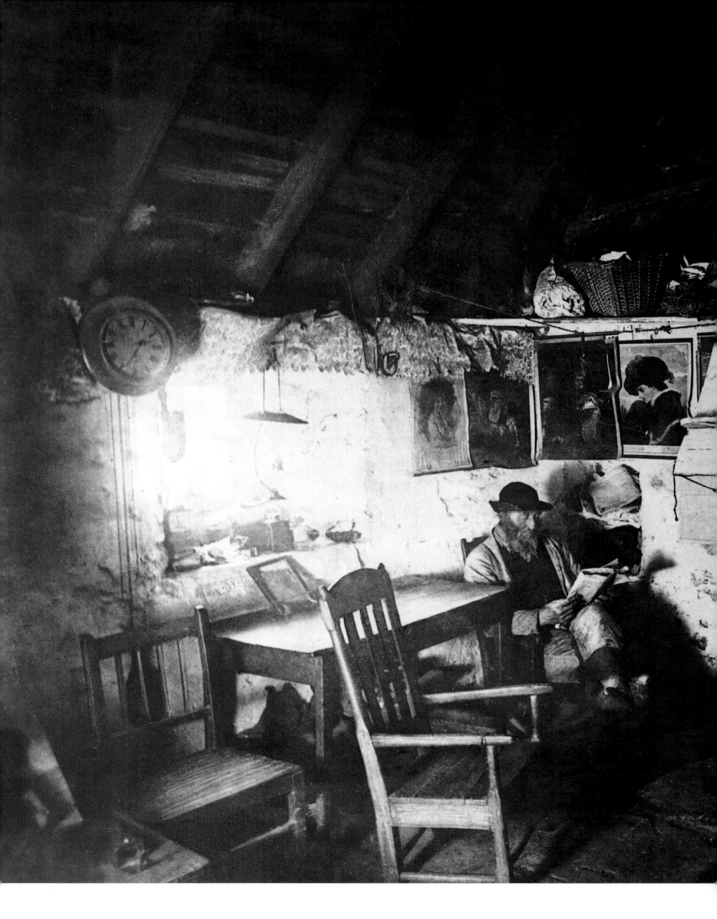

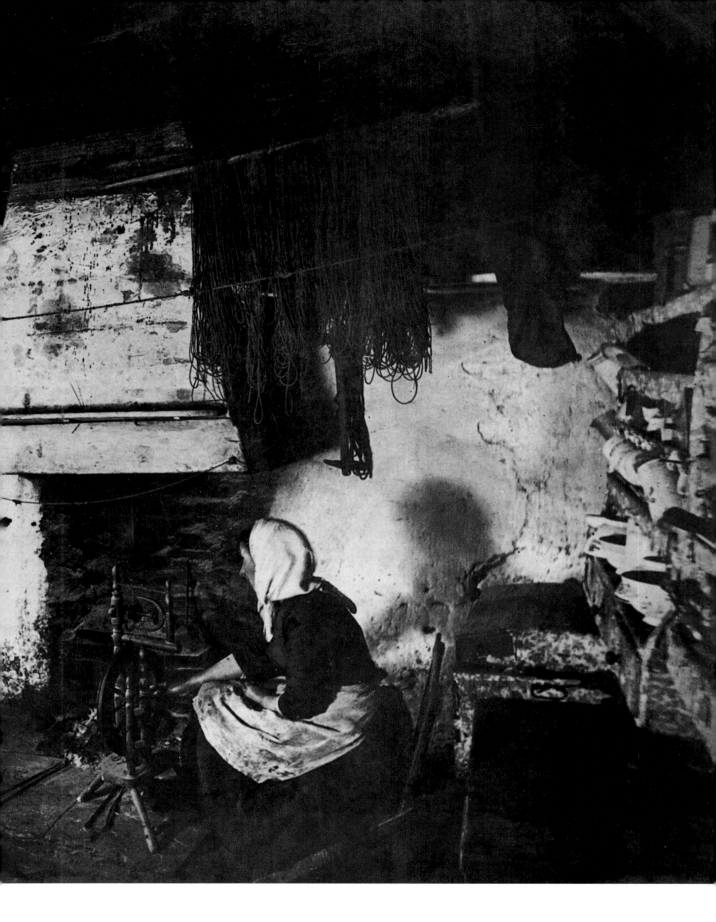

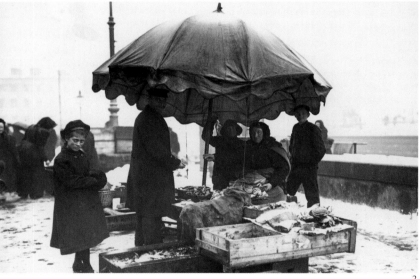

1

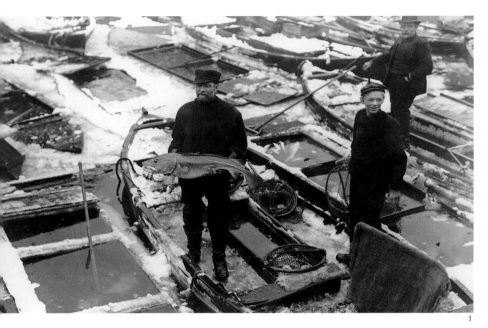

2

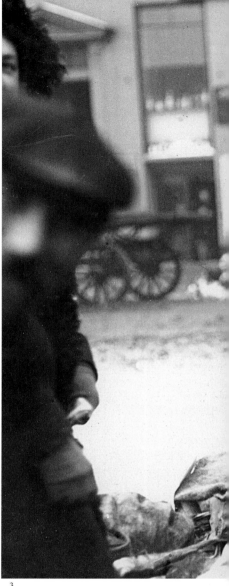

3

(Previous pages)

T HE scene is peaceful enough: a crofter's house on the Shetland Isles. This was the romantic view of rural life in the late 19th century. The reality was less idyllic. Many farmworkers faced redundancy and eviction from their tied cottages. This photograph was probably taken within a few years of the Crofters' War, when police and soldiers fought men and women on these remote Scottish islands.

(Vorherige Seiten)

D IESE idyllische Szene zeigt das Haus eines Kleinpächters auf den Shetlandinseln. Dies war die romantische Sicht des Landlebens im späten 19. Jahrhundert. Aber die Realität war weniger idyllisch. Viele Bauern sahen sich mit Arbeitslosigkeit und der anschließenden Vertreibung aus ihren gepachteten Hütten konfrontiert. Diese Photographie wurde vermutlich wenige Jahre vor dem »Crofters' War«, dem Krieg der Kleinpächter, aufgenommen, als Polizei und Soldaten gegen die Männer und Frauen auf diesen fernen schottischen Inseln kämpften.

(Pages précédentes)

C E tableau de la maison en pierre d'un petit fermier des îles Shetland ne manque pas de sérénité. Telle était la vision romantique qu'on se faisait de la vie rurale à la fin du XIXe siècle. La réalité était moins rose. Le travail se faisait rare dans la plupart des campagnes européennes. Nombreux étaient les ouvriers agricoles que menaçait le licenciement, inévitablement suivi par l'expulsion de leur logement de fonction. Cette photographie a vraisemblablement été prise durant les quelques années de résistance menée par ces petits fermiers contre les forces de police et les soldats qui combattaient les hommes et les femmes de ces îles situées au fin fond de l'Écosse.

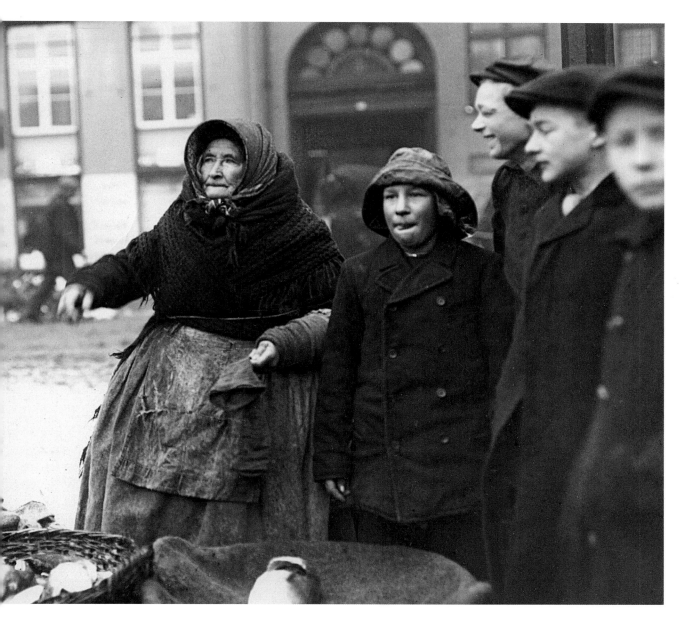

FOR centuries before these photographs were taken, the people of Copenhagen had hauled a living from the North Sea. Catches were loaded into tanks (1), to keep them fresh until they reached the old port. The fish were then gutted on the quayside, and loaded into boxes or baskets for sale (2, 3). It was good food, but prices were as low as the market could force them, and the men who went to sea and the women who sold what they caught earned barely enough to survive.

BEREITS Jahrhunderte bevor diese Aufnahmen gemacht wurden, hatten die Einwohner von Kopenhagen von der Nordsee gelebt. Die Fänge wurden in Wasserbecken (1) verladen, um sie so bis zur Ankunft im alten Hafen frisch zu halten. Der Fisch wurde dann am Kai ausgenommen und zum Verkauf in Kisten oder Körbe gefüllt (2, 3). Fisch war ein gutes Nahrungsmittel, aber die Preise waren so niedrig, wie der Markt sie drücken konnte, und die Männer, die zur See fuhren, und die Fischverkäuferinnen verdienten kaum genug, um zu überleben.

DEPUIS des siècles, bien avant que ces photographies n'aient été prises, les habitants de Copenhague tiraient leur sub-sistance de la mer du Nord. Ils hissaient à bord leur pêche qu'ils entreposaient à l'intérieur de réservoirs (1), de manière à la conserver fraîche jusqu'à l'arrivée dans le vieux port. Le poisson était ensuite vidé à quai avant d'être chargé dans des caisses ou dans des paniers pour être vendu (2 et 3). Le produit était de bonne qualité, mais les prix étaient maintenus aussi bas que possible par le marché. De telle sorte que les marins-pêcheurs et les femmes qui vendaient leurs prises gagnaient tout juste de quoi vivre.

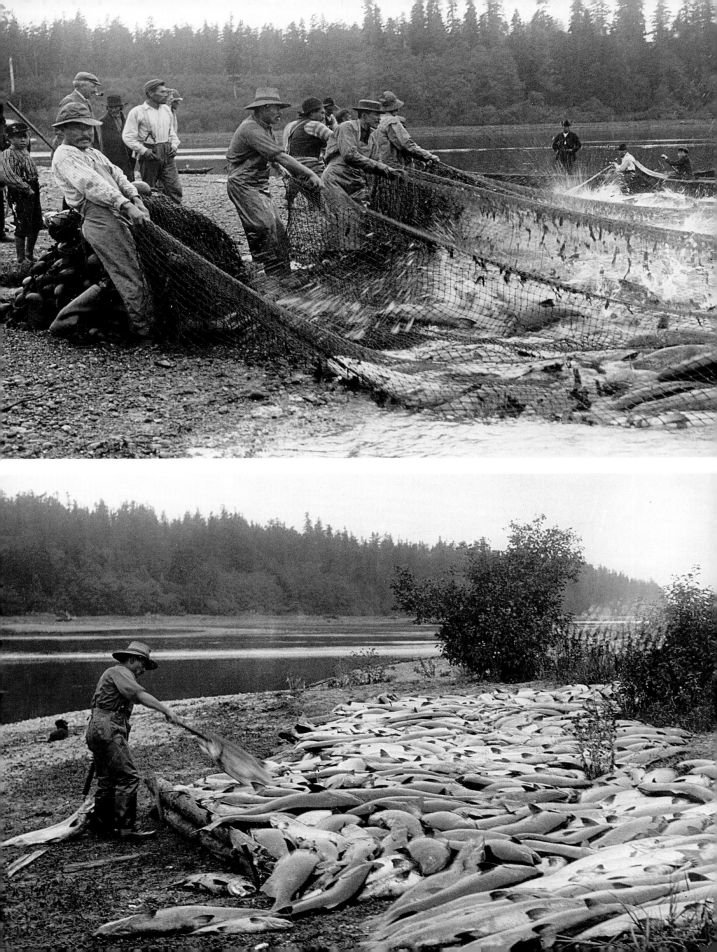

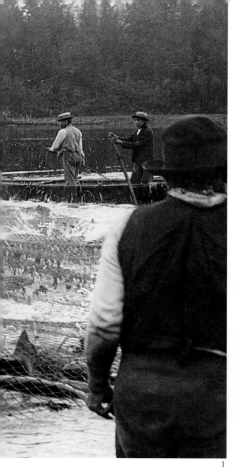

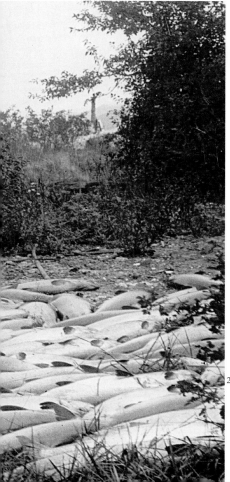

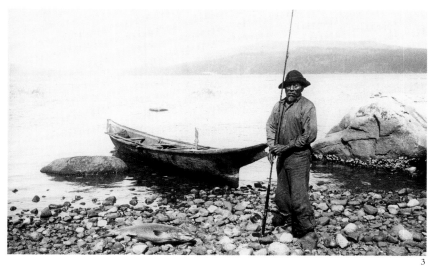

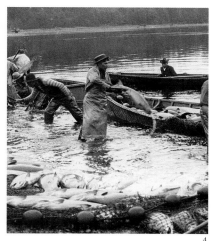

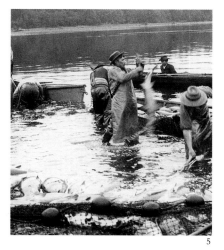

B Y the 1870s the process of preserving food by canning was well established, and the entire economic system of food production and trade was never the same again. The salmon rivers of British Columbia, Canada (photographed by Todd in the 1890s) were abundant larders. Hauling 30 lb (15 kg) salmon from the cold, clear, clean water was as easy as shelling peas. Salmon was the staple food of the Indian tribes indigenous to the region.

I N den 1870er Jahren hatte sich die Haltbarmachung von Lebensmitteln in Konserven durchgesetzt und das gesamte System von Nahrungsmittelherstellung und -handel revolutioniert. Die Lachsflüsse von British Columbia in Kanada (in den 1890er Jahren von Todd photographiert) waren übervolle Speisekammern. Fünfzehn Kilogramm Lachs aus dem kalten, klaren

und sauberen Wasser zu fangen war so einfach wie Erbsenschälen. Lachs war das Grundnahrungsmittel der in dieser Region lebenden Indianerstämme.

D ÈS les années 1870, le procédé de mise en conserve des aliments était bien établi. Le système économique qui réglait la production et le commerce des denrées alimentaires allait changer du tout au tout. Les rivières à saumon de la Colombie-Britannique, au Canada (photo-graphiées par Todd dans les années 1890), se transformèrent en un garde-manger qui approvisionnait abondamment une grande partie du monde. Remonter 15 kg de saumon des eaux froides et cristallines était aussi aisé qu'écosser des petits pois. Le saumon constituait la nourriture de base des tribus indigènes de la région.

Street Life

I<small>T</small> was always cheaper to sell on the street than to rent a shop. Cities were crowded with all kinds of tinkers, pedlars and wandering traders who had lost their country customers as people moved from the land. Hours were long. 'Why, I can assure you,' said one London street trader, 'there's my missus – she sits at the corner of the street with fruit... she's out from ten in the morning till ten at night.' Earnings were poor for the army of knife-grinders, shrimp-sellers, old-clothes dealers, window-menders, boot-blacks and flower-sellers.

For the old blind beggar, with his tray of almanacs, bootlaces, brushes and pencils (1), life was a desperate struggle, with only his dog for support. 'We must either go to the workhouse or starve. If we go to the workhouse, they'll give us a piece of dry bread and abuse us worse than dogs.'

At the top end of the scale was Cast-Iron Billy (3, overleaf), one of the most famous omnibus drivers in London in the 1870s, portrayed in neat billycock hat and shining shoes in John Thomson's photograph. Near the bottom of the scale was the match-seller (4, overleaf), who relied as much on charity as on custom. The flower-sellers (2) probably had their pitch in the middle of the road to avoid being charged by the police with obstructing the pavement.

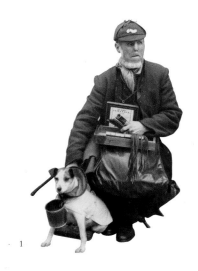

1

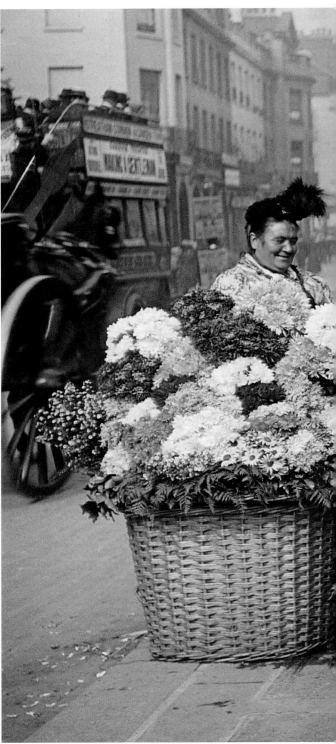

2

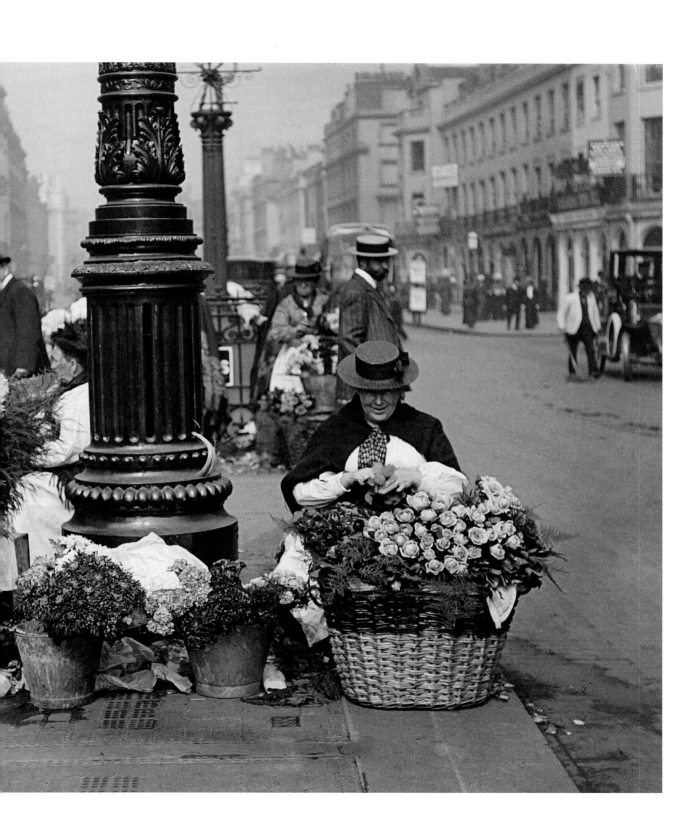

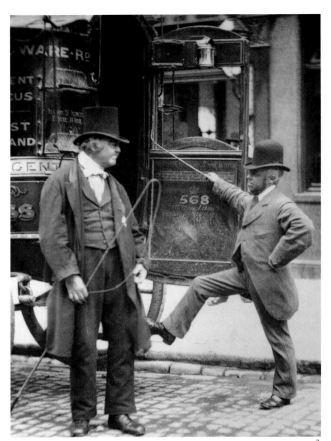

3

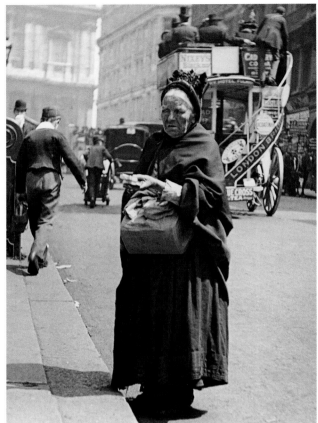

4

Es war stets billiger, seine Waren auf der Straße zu verkaufen, als einen Laden zu mieten. Die Städte waren überfüllt mit Kesselflickern, Hausierern und fahrenden Händlern, die ihre Kundschaft auf dem Land verloren hatten, als die Menschen in die Städte zogen. Die Tage waren lang. »Sie können mir glauben«, sagte ein Londoner Straßenhändler, »meine Frau dort drüben sitzt an der Straßenecke und verkauft Obst … sie ist von morgens um zehn bis abends um zehn draußen.« Die unzähligen Scherenschleifer, Krabbenverkäufer, Altkleiderhändler, Schuhputzer und Blumenverkäufer verdienten wenig.

Für den blinden alten Bettler mit seinem Bauchladen voller Kalender, Schnürsenkel, Bürsten und Bleistifte (1) war das Leben ein bitterer Kampf, in dem ihm nur sein Hund zur Seite stand. »Wir müssen entweder ins Armenhaus oder verhungern. Wenn wir ins Armenhaus gehen, geben sie uns ein Stück trockenes Brot und behandeln uns schlimmer als Hunde.«

Am obersten Ende der sozialen Leiter stand Cast-Iron Billy (3), einer der berühmtesten Omnibusfahrer im London der 1870er Jahre, der in dieser Photographie von John Thomson mit feiner Melone und blankpolierten Schuhen zu sehen ist. Am unteren Ende der Leiter stand die Zündholzverkäuferin (4), die ebensosehr auf Almosen wie auf zahlende Kunden angewiesen war. Die Blumenverkäuferinnen (2) hatten ihren Stand vermutlich auf dem Mittelstreifen der Straße, um eine Geldstrafe wegen Blockierung des Gehsteigs zu vermeiden.

Il était toujours plus avantageux de vendre dans la rue que de payer un bail. Les villes étaient pleines de rétameurs, camelots et marchands ambulants de toutes sortes ayant perdu leur clientèle campagnarde à la suite de l'exode rural. Les heures étaient longues. « En tous les cas, je peux vous assurer, déclarait un marchand de rue à Londres, que ma bourgeoise qui est assise au coin de la rue avec ses fruits … est dehors de dix heures du matin à dix heures du soir. » Les revenus étaient maigres pour cette armée de rémouleurs, vendeurs de crevettes, fripiers, réparateurs de fenêtres, cireurs de chaussures et vendeurs de fleurs. Quant au vieux mendiant aveugle qui offrait sur son plateau des almanachs, des lacets, des brosses et des crayons (1), sa vie était un combat désespéré avec son chien pour seul soutien. « Nous avons le choix entre la maison des pauvres ou mourir de faim. Si nous allons dans la maison des pauvres, nous recevrons un morceau de pain sec et serons traités pire que des chiens. »

Tout en haut de l'échelle se trouvait « l'inflexible » Billy (3), l'un des conducteurs d'omnibus les plus célèbres de Londres dans les années 1870 et que le photographe John Thomson a pris en chapeau melon et chaussures étincelantes. La vendeuse d'allumettes (4), au bas de l'échelle, comptait autant sur la charité que sur la fidélité de sa clientèle. Les vendeuses de fleurs (2) avaient placé leur éventaire au beau milieu de la chaussée, vraisemblablement pour éviter d'être accusées par les forces de l'ordre d'obstruer le trottoir.

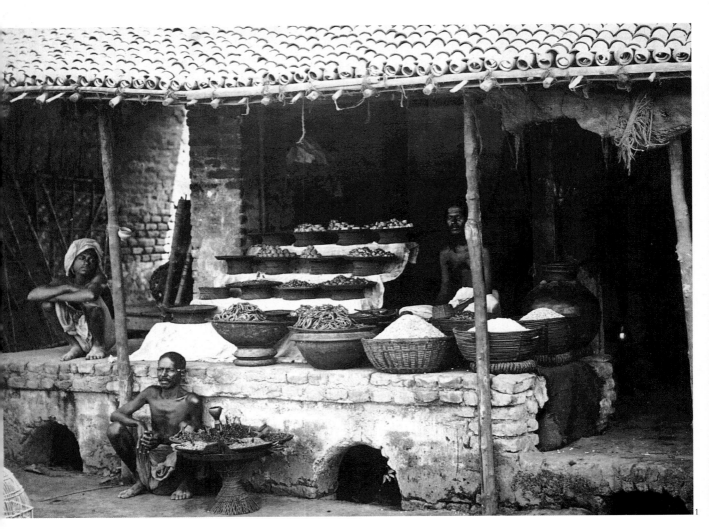

INDIA was repeatedly plagued by famine. British officials there took it as a fact of life. But there was always food to be found in luckier parts of the sub-continent. An Indian sweet-seller's shop (1), open to the street, might be plagued with flies, but there were plenty of tempting sweetmeats, biscuits and nuts. In Egypt, shoe-pedlars (2) trudged the dusty streets, their wares slung round their necks.

INDIEN wurde wiederholt von Hungersnöten heimgesucht. Für die britischen Beamten dort gehörte das zum Leben. In den gesegneteren Teilen des Subkontinents jedoch gab es immer etwas zu essen. Der zur Straße hin offene Laden eines indischen Süßwarenverkäufers (1) mochte zwar voller Fliegen sein, aber es gab viele verlockende Leckereien, Kekse und Nüsse. In Ägypten durchstreiften Schuhverkäufer (2) mit ihren um den Hals gehängten Waren die staubigen Straßen.

L'INDE était régulièrement frappée par la famine. Les Britanniques qui s'y trouvaient en poste officiel jugeaient la chose normale. Pourtant les régions plus chanceuses du sous-continent avaient souvent de quoi manger. Le magasin du confiseur indien (1), ouvert sur la rue, était infesté de mouches mais regorgeait de sucreries, de biscuits, d'arachides, toutes choses bien tentantes. En Égypte, les marchands de chaussures ambulants (2) allaient pesamment le long des routes poussiéreuses, portant leurs marchandises autour du cou.

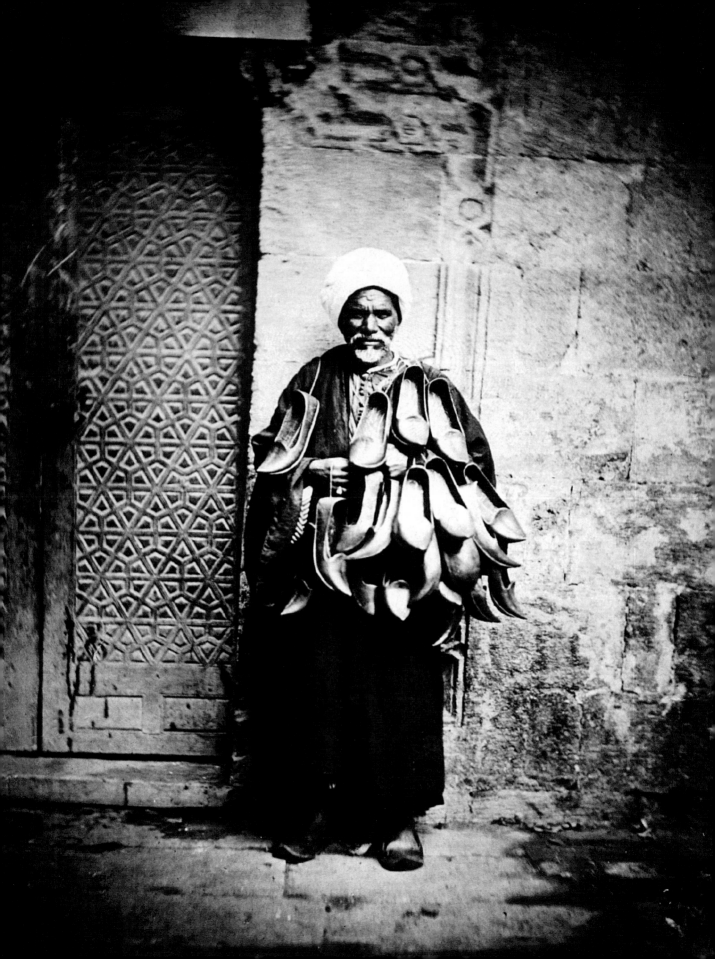

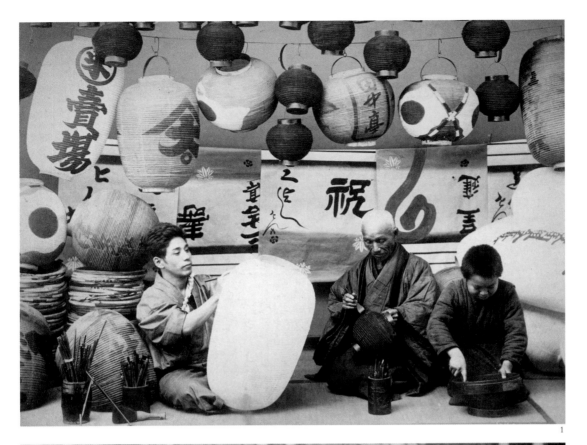

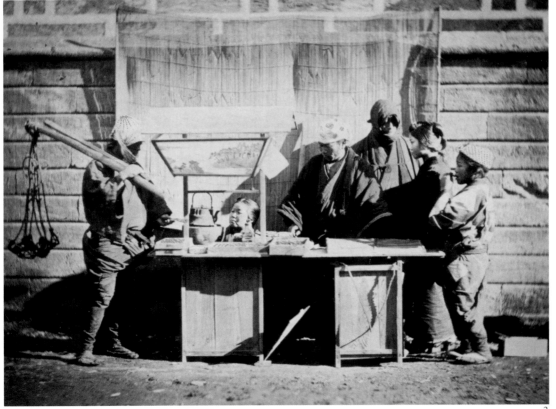

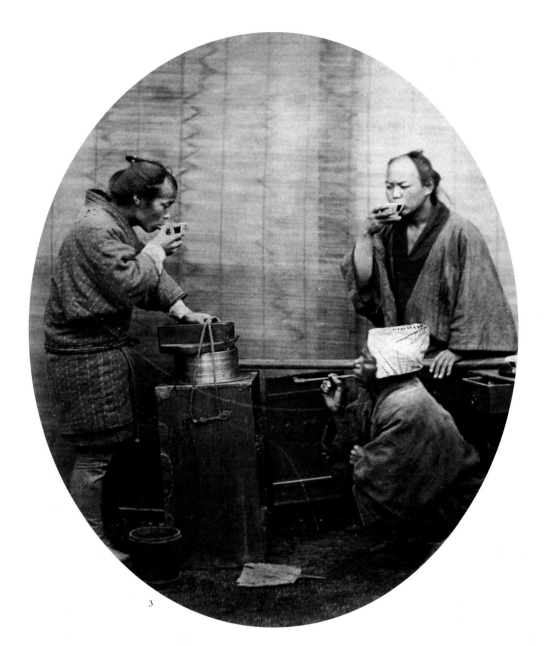

3

WHILE some moved from house to house, other traders had permanent shops, open to the street. Lanterns were made of split bamboo cane and thin paper, painted by hand (1). Ya-tai-mise (2) were refreshment stalls, set up at busy street corners, with small charcoal fires over which tea was prepared and a little cooking done. No respectable Japanese patronized these street-traders, who supplied the working coolies. The saki-seller (3) was an itinerant trader providing weak, sweet rice beer, flavoured with mint or salt.

WÄHREND einige japanische Händler von Haus zu Haus zogen, besaßen andere feste, zur Straße hin offene Läden. Laternen wurden aus gespaltenen Bambusrohren und dünnem Papier gefertigt und von Hand bemalt (1). An geschäftigen Straßenecken wurden die Ya-tai-mise (2) aufgestellt, Erfrischungsstände, in denen kleine Holzkohlefeuer brannten, auf denen man Tee und kleine Mahlzeiten zubereitete. Kein angesehener Japaner behandelte diese Straßenhändler, die die Tagelöhner versorgten, mit Herablassung. Der Sakeverkäufer (3) war ebenfalls ein umherziehender Händler, der dünnen, süßen, mit Minze oder Salz aromatisierten Reiswein feilbot.

ALORS que certains Japonais faisaient du porte à porte, d'autres avaient un fonds de commerce ouvert sur la rue. Les lanternes, fabriquées avec des cannes de bambou fendues et du papier fin, étaient peintes à la main (1). Le «Ya-tai-mise » (2) était un étal placé au coin des rues très passantes où l'on pouvait se restaurer en prenant du thé ou des plats légers préparés sur des braises. Aucun Japonais respectable ne patronnait ces marchands de rue, dont les coolies étaient les clients. Le vendeur de saké (3) était un autre de ces marchands ambulants ; sa bière légère et douce, parfumée à la menthe ou salée, était très appréciée.

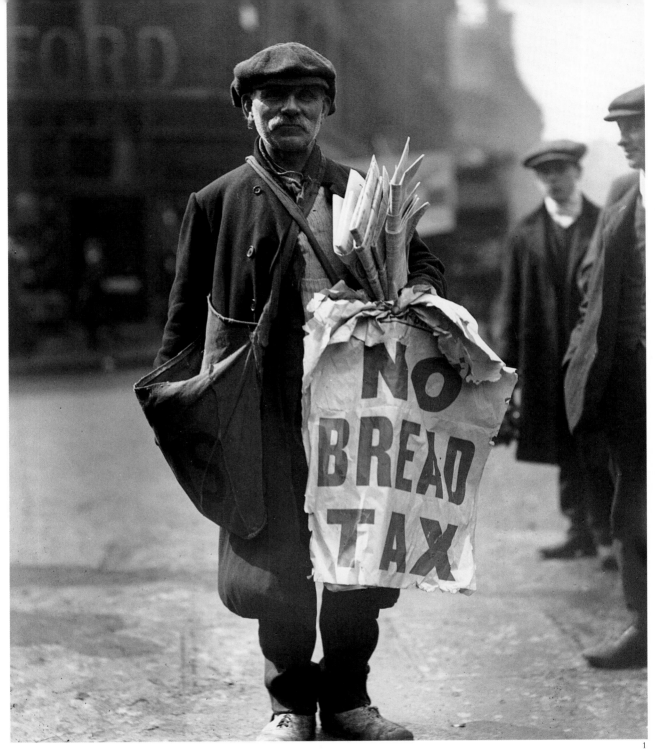

1

SELLING papers (1) provided a regular, if scant, living. The first cheap mass-circulation newspapers were founded in the 1890s. Toys (2) were a more seasonal trade, and the streets at Christmas were thronged with toy-sellers. In the 1860s eggs used to be suspended in these wire baskets in huge jars of preservative (3).

DER Verkauf von Zeitungen (1) sicherte ein zwar mageres, aber regelmäßiges Einkommen. Die ersten billigen Massen-zeitungen wurden in den 1890er Jahren gegründet. Der Handel mit Spielzeug (2) war dagegen eher ein saisonbedingtes Geschäft, und in der Weihnachtszeit waren die Straßen überfüllt von Spielzeugver-käufern. In den 1860er Jahren war es üblich, Eier in solchen Drahtkörben in große Frischhaltegläser zu hängen (3).

LA vente des journaux (1) fournissait régulièrement, quoique chichement, de quoi vivre. Les premiers journaux bon marché à grande circulation furent fondés dans les années 1890. Les jouets (2) avaient un caractère plus saisonnier, de sorte qu'à Noël les rues étaient encombrées de ven-deurs de jouets. La vendeuse de paniers à œufs (3) existait dans les années 1860, à l'époque où les œufs se conservaient dans ces immenses casiers en fer suspendus.

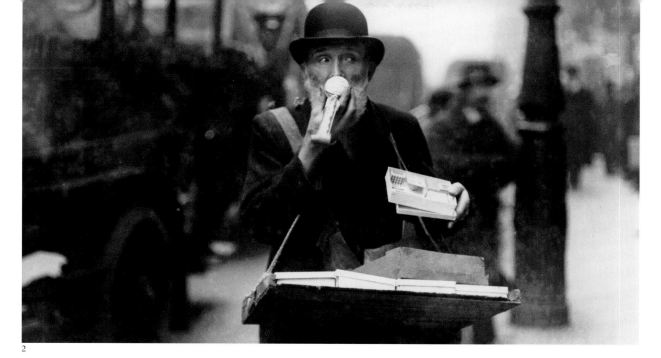

2

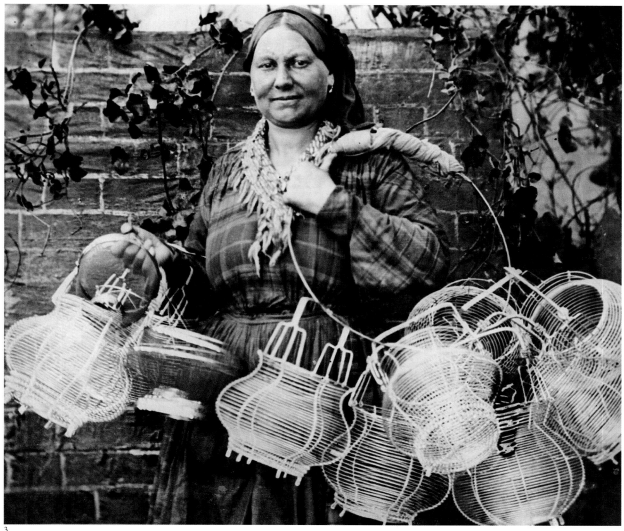

3

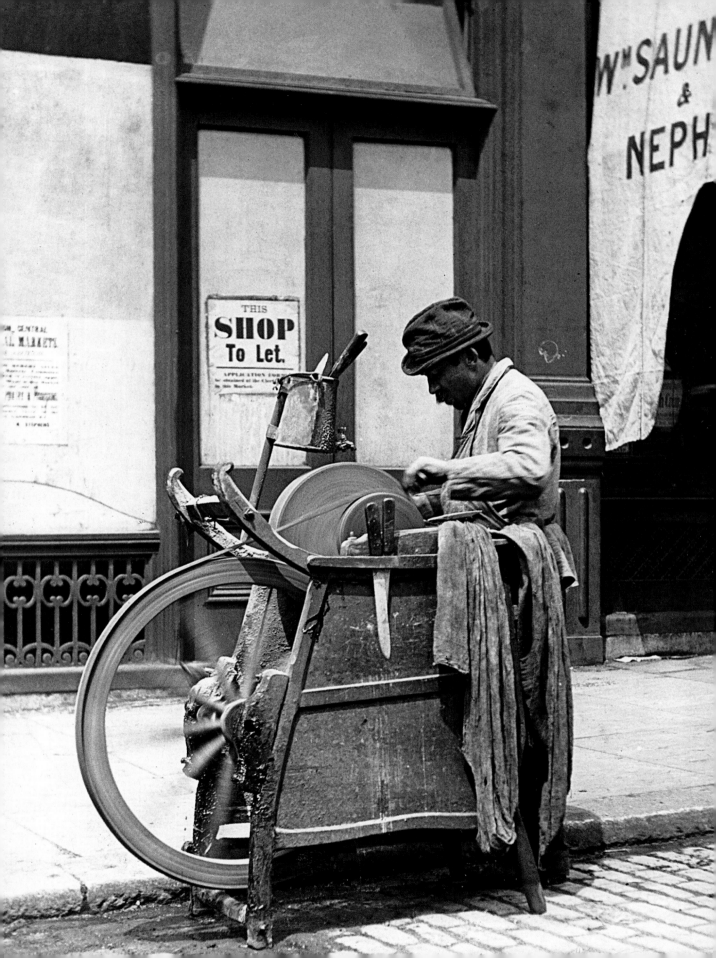

FOR the knife-grinder (1) trade was regular – meat was tough. By 1912, the motor car would have destroyed much of the whip-minder's trade (2). The cat-and-dog meat man (3) could always attract customers.

FÜR den Scherenschleifer (1) lief das Geschäft recht gut, denn das Fleisch war meist zäh. Die Existenz der Peitschen-hüterin (2) war um 1912 durch die zunehmende Motorisierung bedroht. Der Fleischer für Hunde und Katzen (3) zog dagegen immer Kunden an.

LE rémouleur (1) avait un travail régulier – la viande était dure. L'automobile avait en 1912 enlevé une grande partie de la clientèle aux cochers. Le boucher pour chats et chiens (3) était toujours sûr d'attirer les clients.

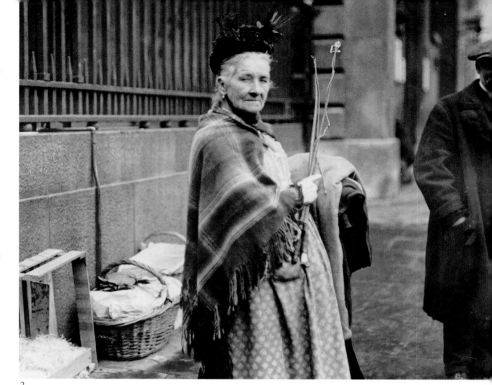

1

2

3

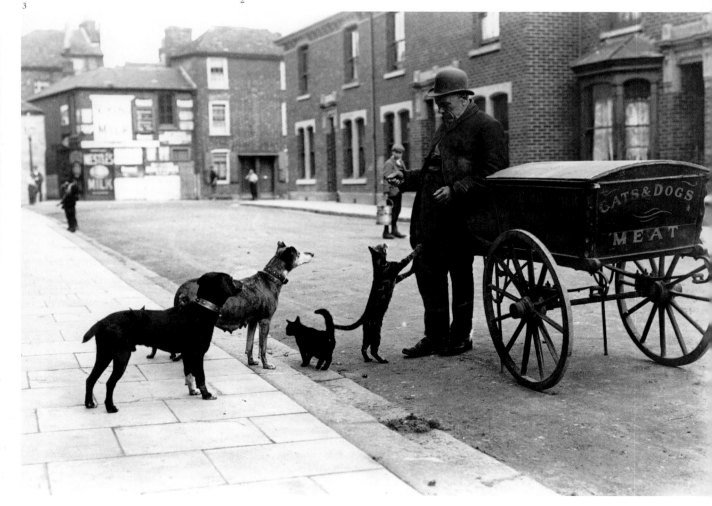

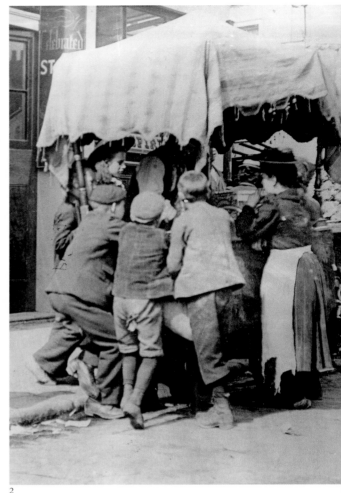

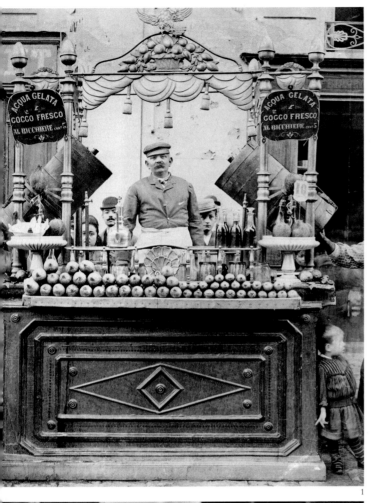

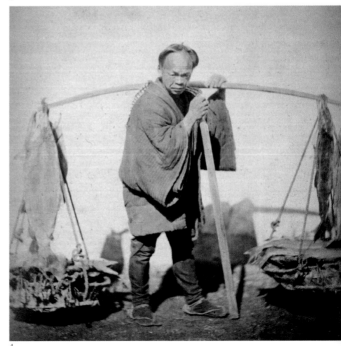

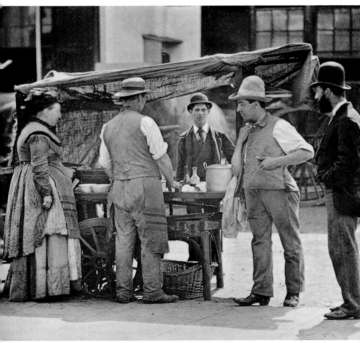

1 2

3 4

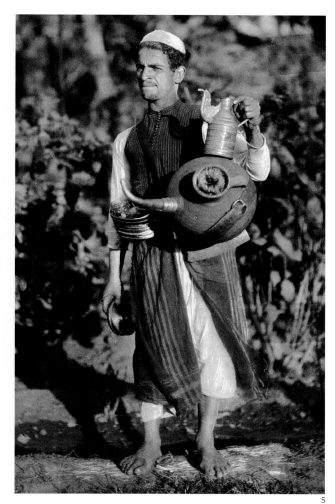

THE Neapolitan lemonade and ice-cream seller (1) had a stall that was both sturdy and ornate – the pride and joy and the living of the entire family, and an impressive contrast to the humble barrow of his London counterpart (2). The shellfish stall holder (3) told the photographer (Thomson): 'Find out a prime thirsty spot, which you know by the number of public houses it supports. Oysters, whelks and liquor go together invariable.' The Japanese fishmonger (4) carried dried or salted salmon and tuna fish tied to his long bamboo pole. In Cairo, the lemonade seller (5) offered refreshing glasses on small brass trays, while his London counterpart (6) sold a mixture of sherbet and water.

DER neapolitanische Limonaden- und Eiscremeverkäufer (1) besaß einen Stand, der nicht nur stabil, sondern auch reich verziert war. Er war der Stolz, die Freude und der Lebensunterhalt der ganzen Familie und stand in beeindruckendem Kontrast zu seinem bescheidenen Londoner Pendant (2). Der Inhaber des Schalentierstandes (3) empfahl dem Photographen (Thomson): »Suchen Sie sich einen Platz, wo die Leute ihren Durst löschen, dort, wo es viele Pubs gibt. Austern, Wellhornschnecken und Alkohol gehören einfach zusammen.« Der japanische Fischhändler (4) trug getrockneten oder gesalzenen Lachs und Thunfisch in Schalen, die an einem langen Bambusstab hingen. In Kairo bot der Limonadenverkäufer (5) erfrischende Getränke auf kleinen Messingtabletts an, während sein Londoner Kollege (6) eine Mischung aus Brause und Wasser verkaufte.

LE vendeur napolitain de limonade et de glaces (1) avait une échoppe à la fois solide et bien décorée : elle était l'orgueil, la joie et la source de revenus de toute la famille, et contrastait de manière impressionnante avec l'humble voiture de quatre saisons de son homologue londonien (2). Le propriétaire de l'étal de coquillages et de fruits de mer (3) expliqua au photographe (Thomson) : « Repérez un endroit où l'on boit bien au nombre de bars qu'il accueille. Les huîtres, les buccins et la liqueur vont toujours de compagnie. » Le poissonnier japonais (4) portait ses saumons et ses thons, séchés ou salés, attachés à une longue tige de bambou. Au Caire, le vendeur de limonade (5) offrait ses boissons rafraîchissantes dans des verres présentés sur des petits plateaux en laiton, tandis que son homologue londonien (6) proposait un mélange de jus de fruits glacés et d'eau.

5

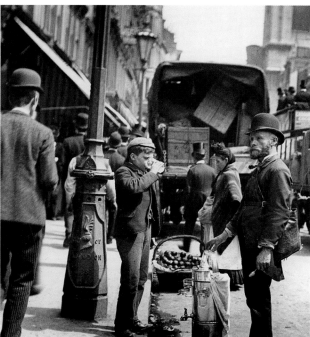

6

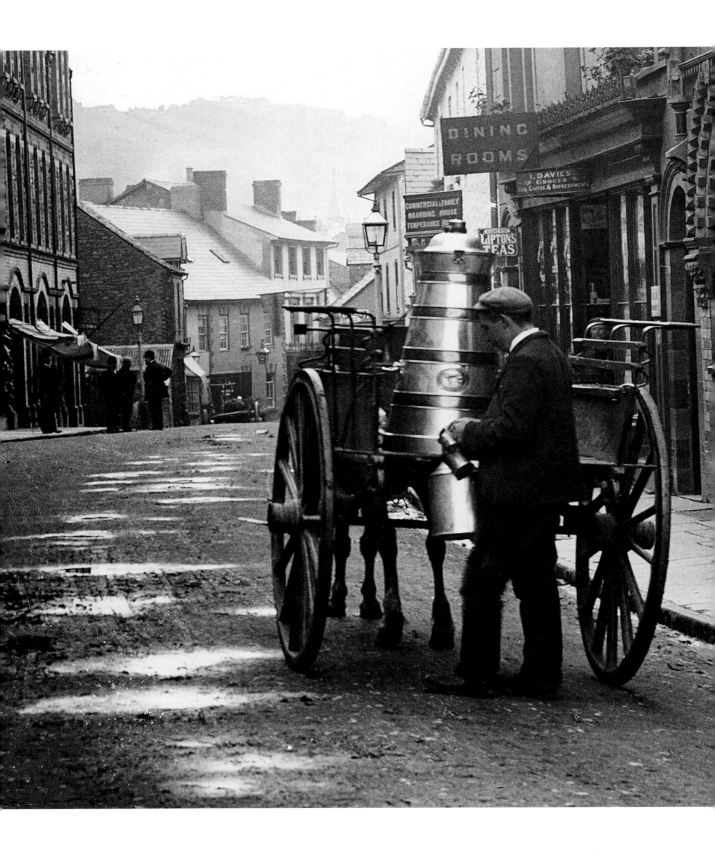

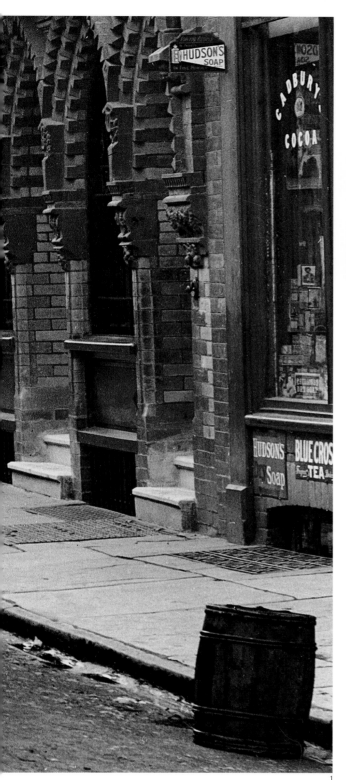

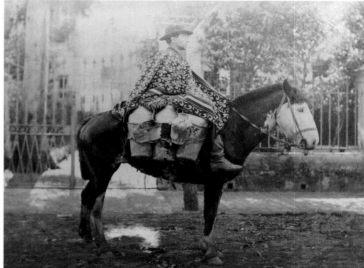

WATER from the well, milk from the cart. All over the world milk was brought to the customer. Fresh, it was claimed, and unadulterated and undiluted. There were always rumours of what could be done with chalk and water, but the real danger came more from the unhygienic circumstances in which cows were milked than from fraudulent practices. Regular customers had their own jugs and measures, filled straight from the churn – in the case of this Welsh supplier (1) – or from jars – in the case of the Argentinian milkman (2).

WASSER aus der Quelle, Milch vom Karren. In der ganzen Welt wurde die Milch zum Kunden gebracht. Frisch mußte sie sein, nicht gepanscht und nicht verdünnt. Es kursierten immer Gerüchte, was man mit Kalk und Wasser alles machen könne, aber die wirkliche Gefahr waren eher die unhygienischen Bedingungen, unter denen die Kühe gemolken wurden, als betrügerische Machenschaften. Stammkunden hatten ihre eigenen Kannen und Meßbecher und füllten diese, wie bei dem walisischen Lieferanten (1), direkt aus der Milchkanne oder, wie bei diesem argentinischen Milchmann, vom Faß (2).

L'EAU venait du puits, le lait de la carriole. Dans le monde entier on livrait le lait au client. On le prétendait frais, pur et non dilué. Des bruits couraient sans cesse sur ce qu'on pouvait faire avec de la craie et de l'eau ; mais le véritable danger venait davantage des conditions peu hygiéniques dans lesquelles on trayait les vaches que des pratiques frauduleuses. Les chalands se servaient de leurs propres récipients et mesures, remplis directement au bidon de ce fournisseur gallois (1) ou à la jarre de ce laitier argentin (2).

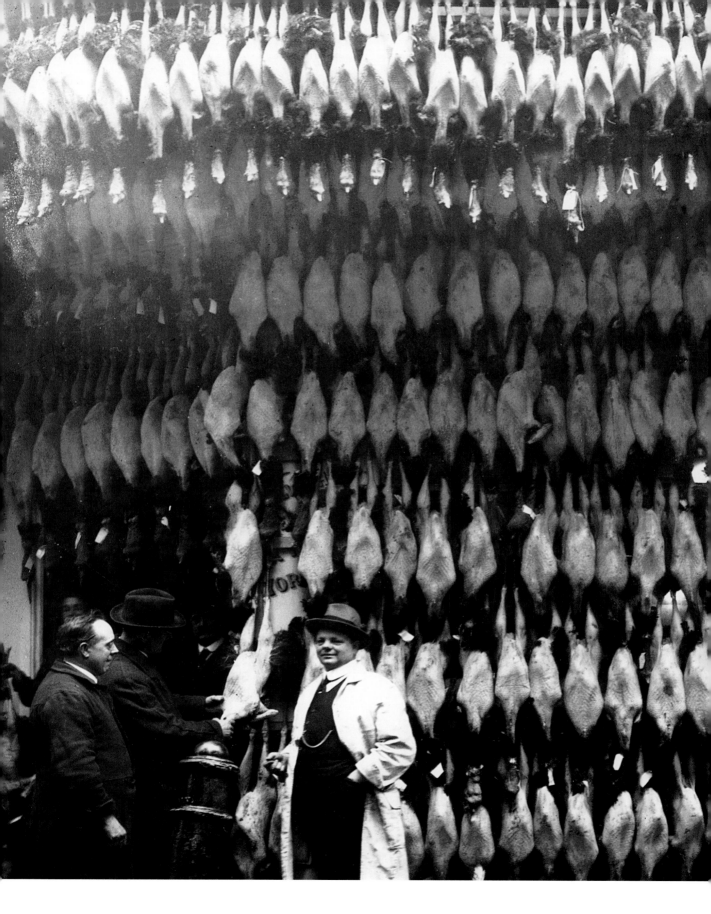

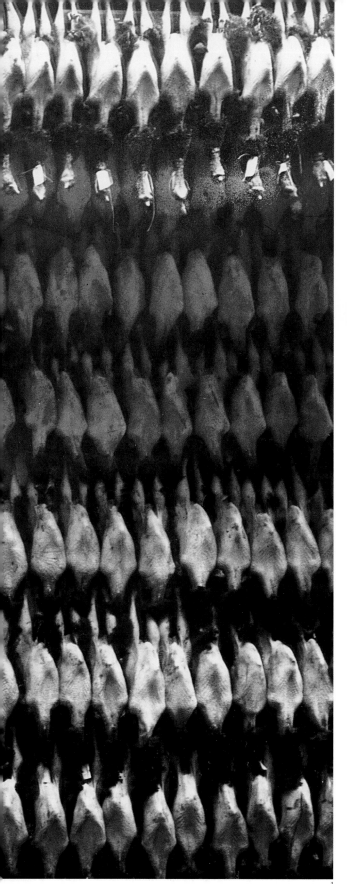

2

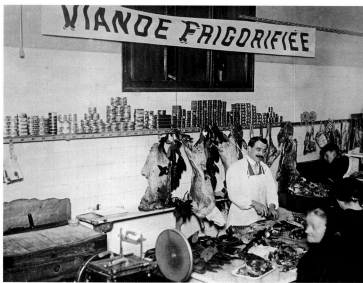

AFTER the pre-war years of plenty, most Europeans had to tighten their belts during the First World War. The governments of the major powers all imposed restrictions and controls. In 1916 the first supplies of meat under municipal control went on sale in Paris (2). Unlike the austere aftermath of the Second World War, once hostilities came to an end, however, supplies returned in plenty to much of Europe – as this poulterer's display of 1919 shows (1).

NACH den goldenen Vorkriegsjahren mußten viele Europäer im Ersten Weltkrieg ihren Gürtel enger schnallen. Die Regierungen der Großmächte verordneten Restriktionen und Kontrollen. Im Jahre 1916 wurden in Paris die ersten Fleisch-lieferungen unter städtischer Kontrolle verkauft (2). Anders als in den mageren Jahren nach dem Zweiten Weltkrieg, füllten sich nach dem Ende des Ersten Weltkriegs die Läden rasch wieder, wie diese Auslage eines Geflügelhändlers aus dem Jahre 1919 zeigt (1).

APRÈS les années d'abondance, la plupart des Européens durent se serrer la ceinture pendant la Première Guerre mondiale. Les gouvernements des grandes puissances imposèrent des restrictions et des contrôles. En 1916 eut lieu à Paris la première vente de viande sous la surveillance des autorités de la ville (2). Contrairement à l'époque d'austérité qui succéda à la Deuxième Guerre mondiale, en 1919, une fois les hostilités terminées, presque toute l'Europe se retrouva abondamment réapprovisionnée comme le montre l'étal de ce marchand de volailles et de gibier (1).

1

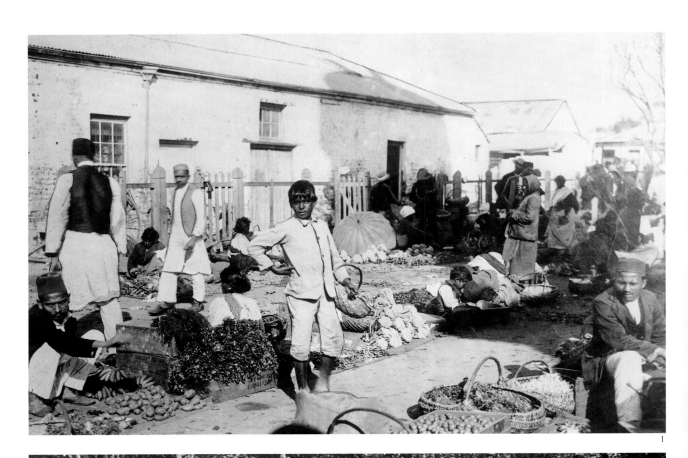

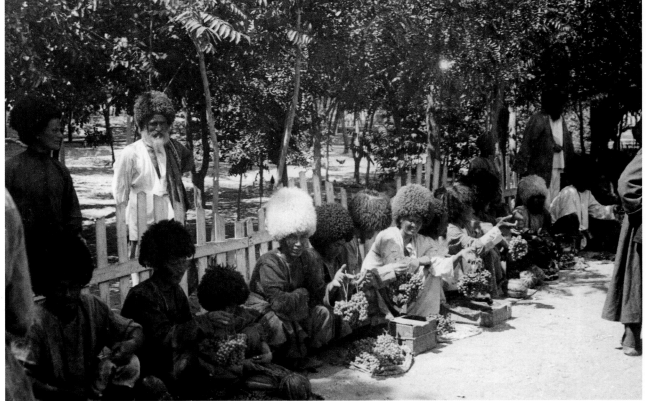

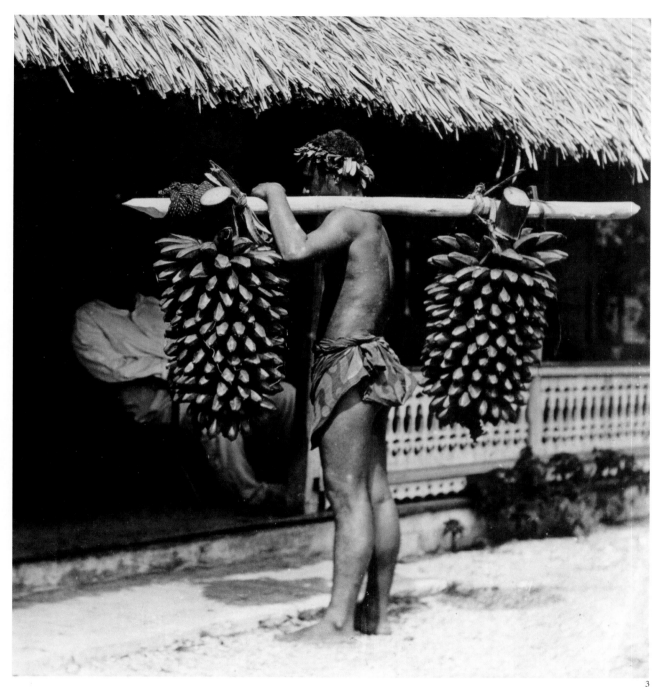

3

IN little-known regions, adventurers, explorers and fortune hunters stopped to photograph local markets and buy supplies. In South Africa, many market traders were Indian immigrants (1). In Russian Kirghizia, peasants offered grapes to members of the Tien-Shan Expedition of the 1890s (2). In Tahiti, 50 kg of plantain were painfully hauled to the white man's veranda (3).

IN den weniger bekannten Regionen der Welt machten Abenteurer, Entdecker und Globetrotter halt, um einheimische Märkte zu photographieren und einheimische Waren zu kaufen. Viele der Markthändler in Südafrika waren indische Einwanderer (1). Im russischen Kirgisien boten Bauern den Mitgliedern der Tien-Shan-Expedition in den 1890er Jahren Weintrauben an (2). In Tahiti wurden 50 Kilogramm Bananen mühsam zur Veranda des weißen Mannes geschleppt (3).

LES aventuriers, les explorateurs et les coureurs de dots s'arrêtaient dans des régions peu connues, le temps de photographier les marchés locaux et d'y acheter des produits. En Afrique du Sud, les commerçants du marché étaient souvent d'origine indienne (1). En Géorgie, les paysans offrirent des raisins aux membres de l'expédition de Tien-Shan dans les années 1890 (2). À Tahiti, 50 kg de bananes sont péniblement hissées jusqu'à la véranda de l'homme blanc (3).

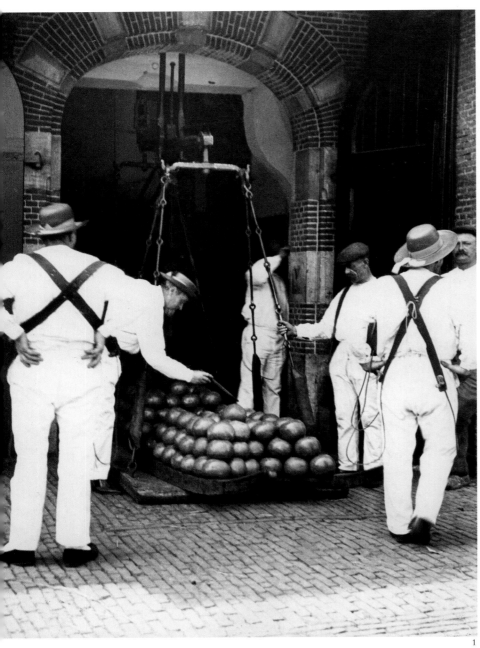

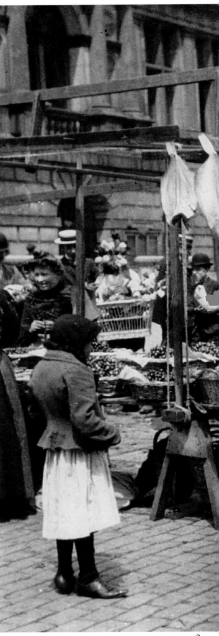

TRADITIONAL markets still flourished in Europe. The cheese-market in Alkmaar, Noord Holland (1), had been set up every Friday from May to October for hundreds of years when this photograph was taken in 1910. Dried fish, as on this stall in a Belgian market (2), had been part of the staple diet of North Europeans for a long time. Catholic restrictions on the eating of meat had made fish a popular substitute on fast days, and had brought prosperity to many great fish merchants over the centuries.

IN Europa florierten noch immer die traditionellen Märkte. Als diese Photographie 1910 aufgenommen wurde, fand der Käsemarkt in Alkmaar, Nord-holland (1), bereits seit Hunderten von Jahren von Mai bis Oktober jeden Freitag statt. Getrockneter Fisch, wie er an diesem Stand auf einem belgischen Markt verkauft

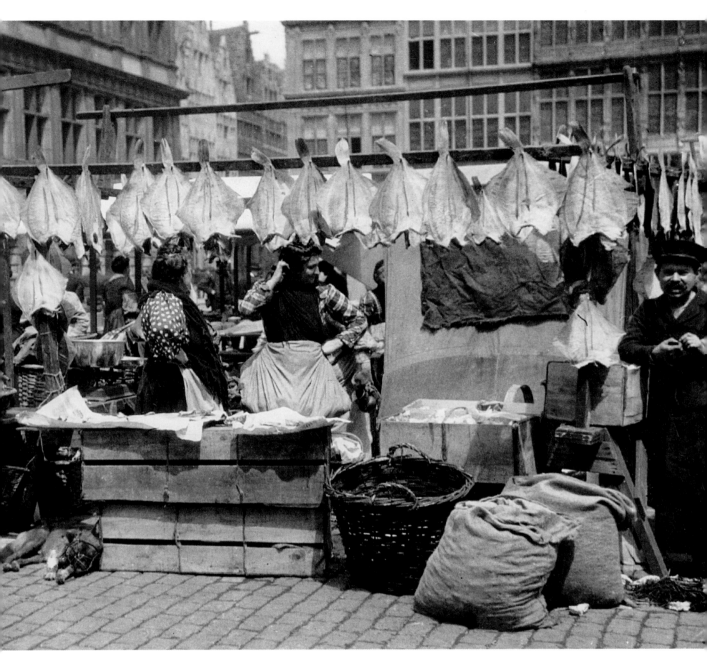

wurde (2), hatte lange Zeit zu den Grundnahrungsmitteln der Nordeuropäer gehört. Restriktionen der katholischen Kirche bezüglich des Verzehrs von Fleisch hatten Fisch zu einem beliebten Ersatz an Fastentagen gemacht und im Laufe der Jahrhunderte vielen Fischhändlern zu großem Reichtum verholfen.

En Europe, les marchés traditionnels étaient toujours aussi florissants. Le marché aux fromages d'Alkmaar, en Hollande septentrionale (1), se tenait chaque vendredi de mai à octobre depuis déjà des siècles lorsque, en 1910, cette photographie a été prise. Le poisson séché, comme sur cet étal d'un marché belge (2), constituait depuis

longtemps l'aliment de base des Européens du Nord. La consommation de viande étant limitée par les catholiques, le poisson était devenu un aliment populaire de remplacement les jours de jeûne et faisait depuis des siècles la fortune de bien des grands marchands de poissons.

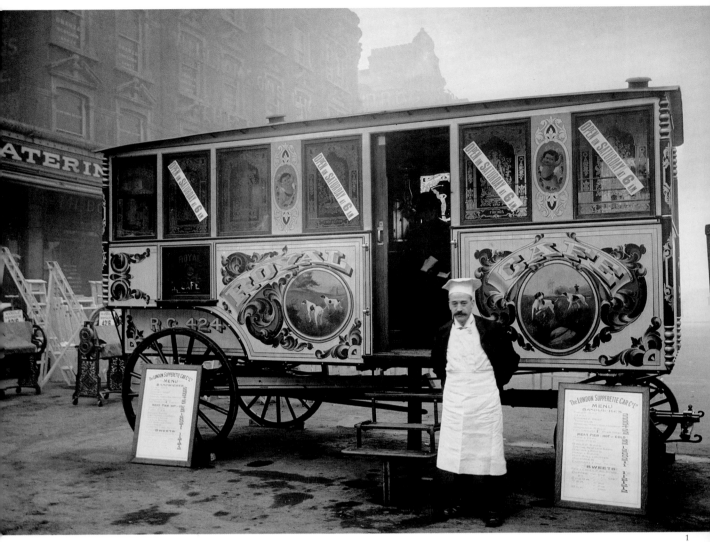

THE Royal Café and Night Lunch (1) was the first open-air car-restaurant in Britain. 'The car-restaurant,' boasted its manager, 'is a place into which a man may safely bring his wife or his sweetheart.' The hotel kitchen (2) was a place of toil and trouble, and sweated labour: 'a stifling, low-ceilinged inferno of a cellar... deafening with oaths and the clanging of pots and pans... In the middle were furnaces, where twelve cooks skipped to and fro, their faces dripping with sweat in spite of their white caps.' But the customer, quietly dining in Baker's Chop House, London (3), would have seen and heard none of this.

DAS Royal Café and Night Lunch (1) war das erste mobile Freiluft-Restaurant in Großbritannien. Das »Wagen-Restaurant«, prahlte sein Manager, »ist ein Ort, an den ein Mann sicher seine Frau oder seine Geliebte führen kann.« Die Hotelküche (2) war ein Ort des Chaos, der Hektik und der schweißtreibenden Arbeit: »Eine stickige, niedrige Kellerhölle mit ohrenbetäubendem Lärm aus Flüchen und dem Scheppern von Töpfen und Pfannen ... In der Mitte Öfen, an denen zwölf Köche hantierten, die Gesichter schweiß-überströmt, trotz ihrer weißen Mützen.« Aber der Gast, der in aller Ruhe in Baker's Chop House in London (3) dinierte, sah und hörte von all dem nichts.

LE Royal Café and Night Lunch (1) fut la première voiture-restaurant en plein air en Grande-Bretagne. « La voiture-restaurant », proclamait le gérant, « est un endroit dans lequel un homme peut en toute sécurité amener son épouse ou sa petite amie ». La cuisine de l'hôtel (2) n'était pas de tout repos, c'était plutôt un lieu de labeur : « Un enfer étouffant au plafond bas dans une cave ... où retentissaient les jurons, les bruits des marmites et des casseroles s'entrechoquant ... Au milieu se trouvaient les fourneaux autour desquels s'affairaient douze cuisiniers, aux visages dégoulinant de sueur malgré leurs toques blanches. » Toutefois le client qui dînait tranquillement au Baker's Chop House à Londres (3) n'en avait certainement jamais entendu parler.

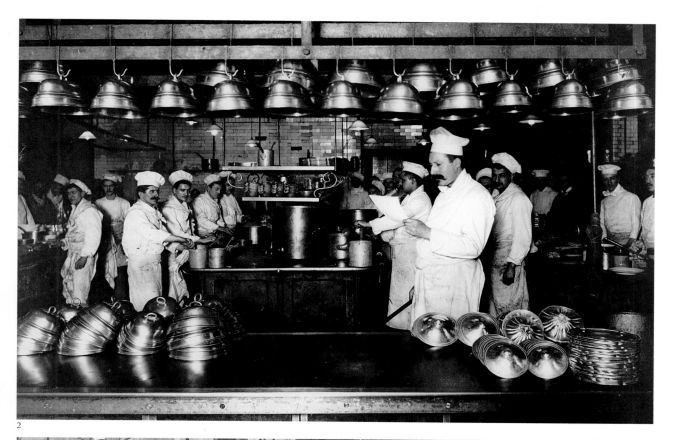

2

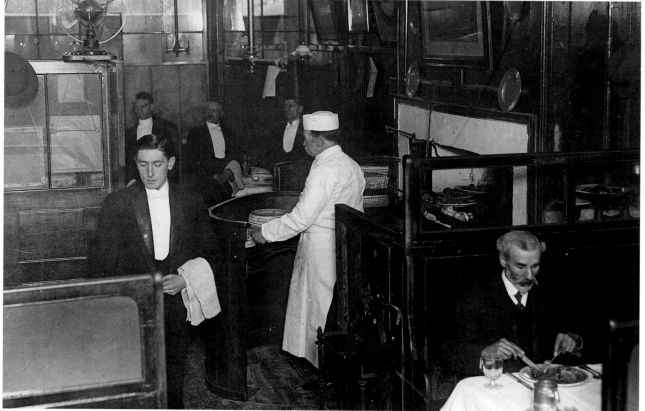

3

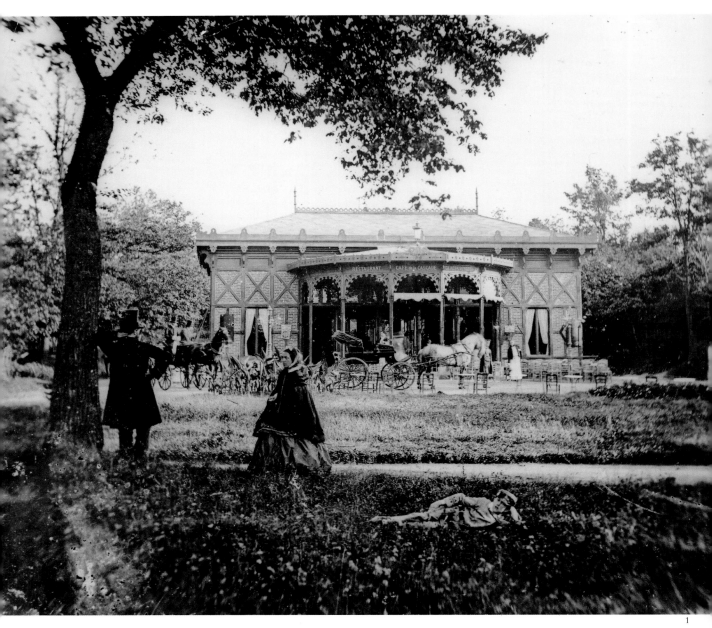

IT was a pleasure to eat where everything was so tidy, the food so well cooked, the waiters so polite, and the coming and departing company so moustached, so frisky, so affable, so fearfully and wonderfully Frenchie!' wrote Mark Twain of his visit to a Paris restaurant in 1866. The Café de la Cascade, in the Bois de Boulogne (1), certainly had an air of calm and order as it awaited custom on a summer day in 1859. Eating out was a feature of 19th-century life, and every hotel, every railway terminus and exhibition hall had its own fully equipped dining room – like this at the London International Exhibition in 1862 (2).

Es war ein Vergnügen, dort zu speisen, wo alles so sauber, das Essen so gut zubereitet, die Kellner so höflich, die kommende und gehende Gesellschaft so schnurrbärtig, so verspielt, so freundlich, so schrecklich und wunderbar französisch war!« schrieb Mark Twain 1866 nach seinem Besuch in einem französischen Restaurant. Im Café de la Cascade im Bois de Boulogne (1) herrschte gewiß eine

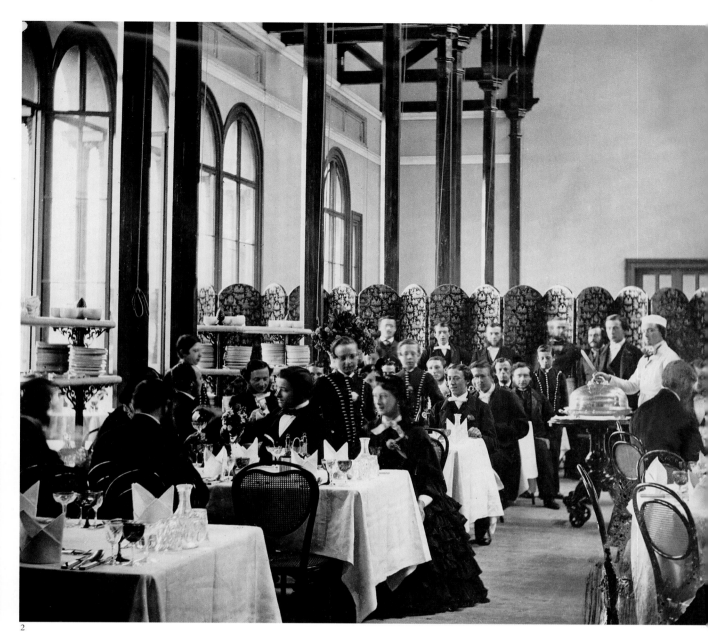

2

ruhige und gesittete Atmosphäre, wenn an einem Sommertag des Jahres 1859 die Gäste erwartet wurden. Auswärts zu essen war typisch für das Leben im 19. Jahrhundert, und jedes Hotel, jeder Bahnhof und jedes Museum besaßen einen eigenen, komplett ausgestatteten Speisesaal wie z. B. diesen, den man 1862 auf der Londoner internationalen Ausstellung besuchen konnte (2).

C'ÉTAIT un plaisir de manger dans un endroit où tout était si propre, où la nourriture était si bien cuisinée, où les garçons étaient si polis et où entraient et sortaient des clients si moustachus, si enjoués, si affables, si épouvantablement et merveilleusement typiquement français ! » écrivait Marc Twain relatant ses souvenirs d'un restaurant parisien en 1866. Le Café de la Cascade au Bois de Boulogne (1) dégageait certainement cette impression de calme et d'ordre avant l'arrivée des clients en ce jour d'été 1859. Manger à l'extérieur était très prisé au XIXᵉ siècle. De plus, chaque hôtel, chaque terminus de train et chaque salon d'exposition disposaient d'une salle à manger aménagée, semblable à celle de l'Exposition internationale à Londres en 1862 (2).

Industry

IN 1852, a factory inspector reported to the British government: 'I believe the work people never were so well off as they are at present; constant employment, good wages, cheap food, and cheap clothing; many cheap, innocent and elevating amusements brought within their reach... the greater proportion of all the operatives in mills have at length time for some mental improvement, healthful reaction, and enjoyment of their families and friends.'

It was an assertion reiterated often in the next 60 years. The workers had never had it so good, were they black cotton pickers in the American south (1), or mill workers in cotton factories in Europe (2, 3). Shorter hours, improved conditions, better pay – all fought for by the newly legitimized unions – freed most factory hands from the conditions of near-slavery in which their grandparents had toiled.

But life in the average industrial town was still ugly and foul: '... a town of machinery and tall chimneys, out of which interminable serpents of smoke trailed themselves for ever and ever, and never got uncoiled. It had a black canal in it, and a river than ran purple with ill-smelling dye, and vast piles of building... where the piston of a steam engine ran monotonously up and down, like an elephant in a state of melancholy madness' (Charles Dickens).

The workers may never have had it so good – before the end of the century they showed they wanted it a good deal better.

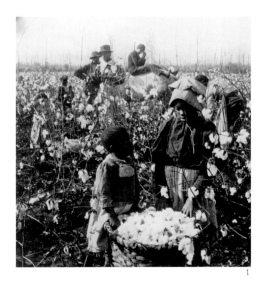

1

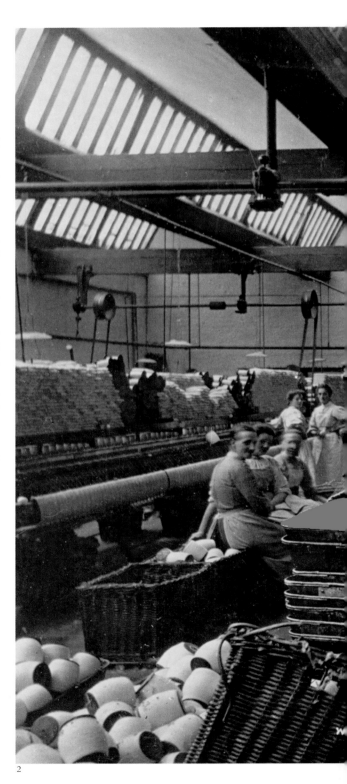

2

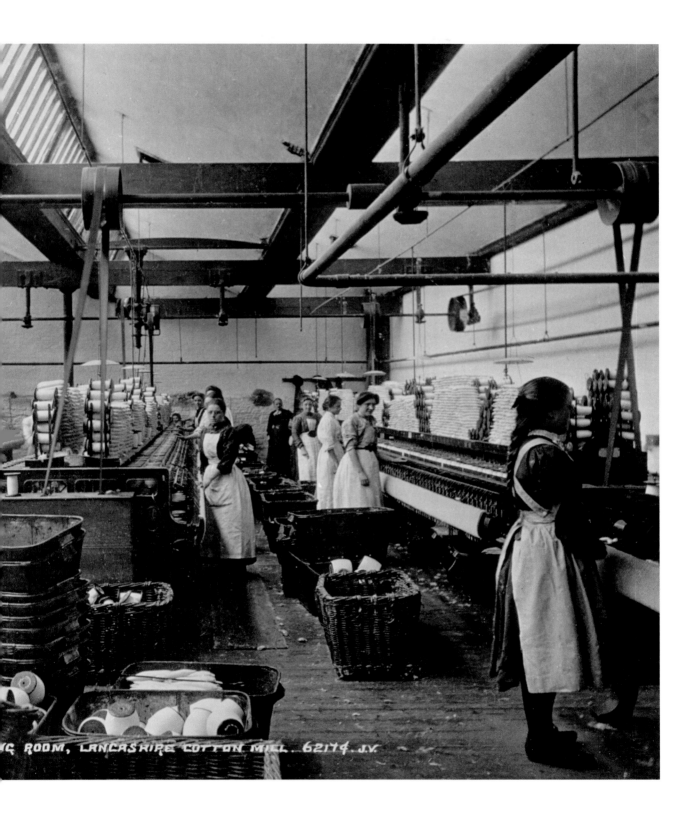

...NG ROOM, LANCASHIRE COTTON MILL. 62174. J.V.

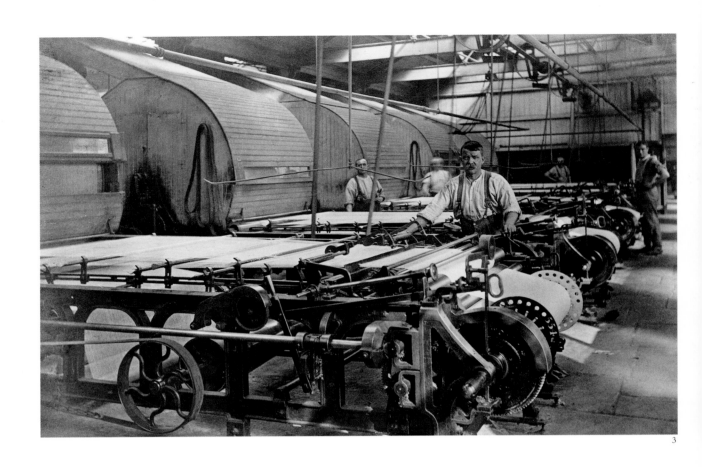

3

IM Jahre 1852 berichtete ein Fabrikinspektor der britischen Regierung: »Ich bin der Ansicht, daß es den Arbeitern noch nie so gut ging wie heute; dauerhafte Beschäftigung, gute Löhne, billiges Essen und billige Kleidung, harmlose und erheiternde Unterhaltung stehen ihnen zur Verfügung ..., die meisten der Fabrikarbeiter haben genügend Zeit für geistige Fortbildung, gesunde Körperertüchtigung und vergnügliches Zusammensein mit Freunden und Familie.«

Diese Behauptung wurde in den folgenden sechzig Jahren ständig wiederholt. Die Arbeiter hatten es niemals so gut gehabt, ob es sich nun um schwarze Baumwollpflücker im Süden der Vereinigten Staaten (1) oder um Arbeiter in europäischen Baumwollfabriken (2, 3) handelte. Die von den wieder legitimierten Gewerkschaften erkämpften kürzeren Arbeitszeiten, verbesserten Arbeitsbedingungen und besseren Löhne befreiten die meisten Fabrikarbeiter von Zuständen, die fast an Sklaverei gegrenzt und unter denen ihre Großväter noch gelitten hatten.

Aber das Leben in einer durchschnittlichen Industriestadt war noch immer öde und grau: »... eine Stadt von Maschinen und hohen Schornsteinen, aus denen ohne Unterlaß endlos lange Rauchschlangen stiegen. In ihr wanden sich ein schwarzer Kanal und ein Fluß, in dem rote, stinkende Farbe floß, und es gab große Gebäudeberge ..., in denen der Kolben einer Dampfmaschine monoton auf und ab stampfte, wie ein Elefant im Zustand melancholischen Wahnsinns.« (Charles Dickens)

Den Arbeitern mochte es niemals so gut gegangen sein, aber vor dem Ende des Jahrhunderts machten sie deutlich, daß sie es in der Zukunft noch viel besser haben wollten.

EN 1852, un inspecteur d'usine signalait au gouvernement britannique : « Je suis convaincu que les travailleurs n'ont jamais été aussi bien qu'aujourd'hui ; l'emploi ne manque pas et il est bien payé, la nourriture est bon marché et les vêtements de prix modiques ; de nombreux amusements innocents qui élèvent l'esprit sont mis à leur portée... la très grande majorité des ouvriers dans les fabriques ont tout le temps de perfectionner leur entendement, de prendre soin de leur santé et d'apprécier la compagnie de leurs familles et de leurs amis. »

On répéta cette affirmation tout au long des soixante années qui suivirent. La condition des travailleurs n'avait jamais été aussi bonne, qu'il s'agît des cueilleurs de coton noirs du sud des États-Unis (1) ou des ouvriers dans les filatures de coton européennes (2 et 3). La diminution des horaires, l'amélioration des conditions de travail et la revalorisation des salaires arrachés par les syndicats fraîchement légitimés libérèrent la plupart des ouvriers travaillant en usine du quasi-esclavage qui avait été le lot de leurs grands-parents.

La vie dans la ville industrielle moyenne n'en restait pas moins laide et insalubre : « ... une ville de machines et de hautes cheminées desquelles s'échappaient continuellement d'interminables serpents de fumées qui ne déroulaient jamais leurs anneaux. Elle possédait un canal noir et une rivière aux eaux violettes qui empestaient la teinture, ainsi que de vastes empilements de constructions ... où le piston d'un moteur à vapeur montait et descendait à la façon monotone d'un éléphant pris de folie mélancolique. » (Charles Dickens)

Même si la condition des travailleurs n'avait jamais été aussi bonne, ceux-ci montrèrent avant la fin du siècle qu'ils la voulaient meilleure encore.

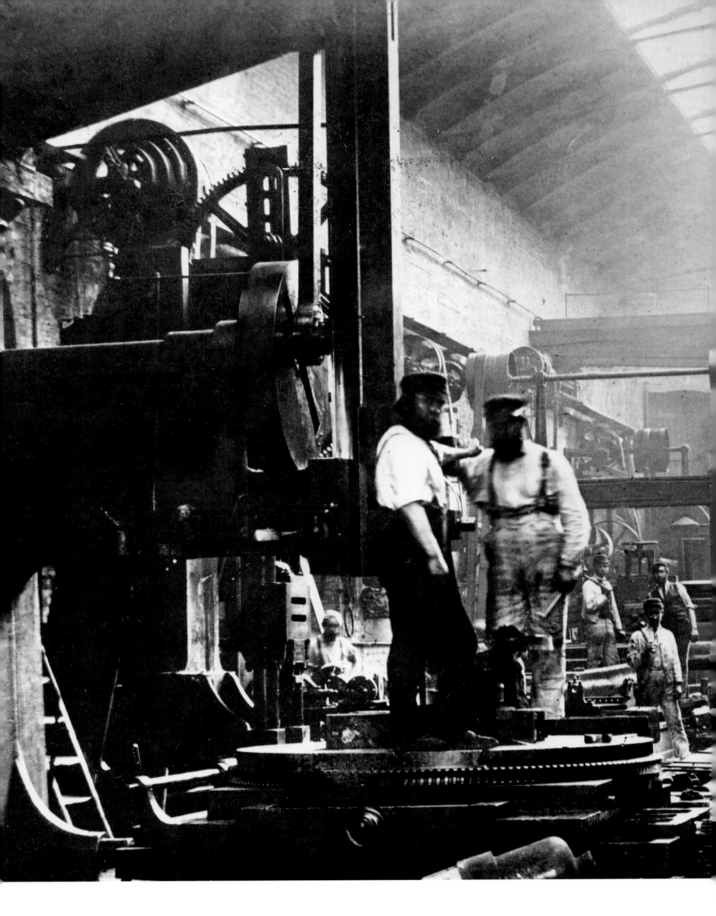

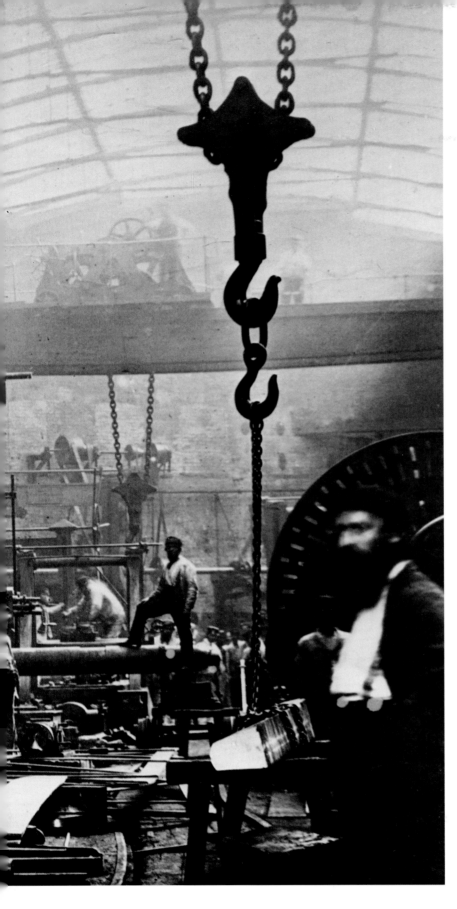

For all the faults and horrors of industrialization, the 19th century was in love with machines and the vast edifices that housed them. A visit to a factory or workshop was as exciting as a trip to a leisure park may be to us today. An engineering shed, such as this at the Thomas Ironworks, London, in 1867, echoed to the ringing blows of the workmen's hammers, and throbbed with the mighty machinery that had harnessed the power of steam.

Any major construction site – bridge, tunnel, railway, dock or building – could expect a visit from a photographer, and the men and women would pause from their labour and pose for a moment of eternity.

Trotz aller Mißstände und Schrecken der Industrialisierung war man im 19. Jahrhundert vernarrt in Maschinen und in die riesigen Gebäude, in denen sie untergebracht waren. Der Besuch in einer Fabrik oder Werkstatt war ebenso aufregend wie heutzutage ein Ausflug in einen Vergnügungspark. In einer Maschinenhalle wie dieser der Thomas Eisenwerke in London ertönte 1867 das Echo der Hammerschläge der Arbeiter und die Vibration der Maschinen, die die Kraft des Dampfes zügelten.

Jede Großbaustelle, ob Brücke, Tunnel, Eisenbahn, Dock oder Gebäude, war bei Photographen beliebt, und Männer und Frauen unterbrachen ihre Arbeit, um für einen Moment der Ewigkeit zu posieren.

Malgré toutes les fautes et les horreurs de l'industrialisation, le XIXᵉ siècle était amoureux des machines et des vastes édifices qui les abritaient. Pour les nantis, la visite d'une usine ou d'un atelier était tout aussi excitante que le serait peut-être pour nous aujourd'hui le parc de loisirs. Un hangar de construction tel que celui de Thomas Ironworks à Londres en 1867 résonnait des coups assénés par les marteaux des ouvriers et des puissantes machines qui exploitaient à l'unisson le pouvoir de la vapeur.

N'importe quel site de construction, pont, tunnel, chemin de fer, chantier – naval ou non – pouvait compter sur la visite du photographe, ce qui permettait à ces hommes et à ces femmes d'interrompre leur travail, le temps de poser pour un moment d'éternité.

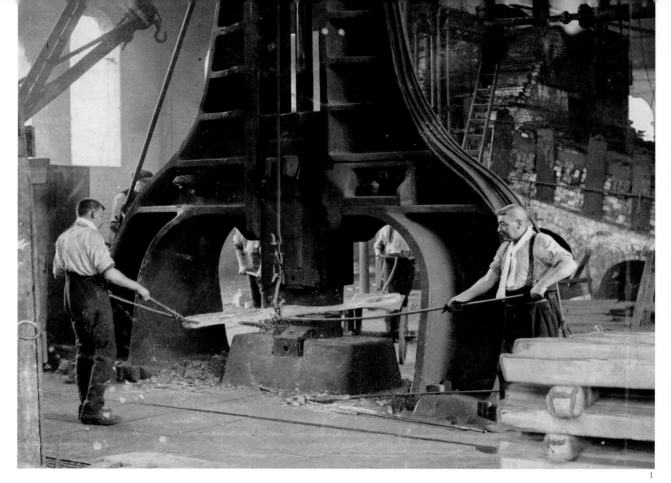

1

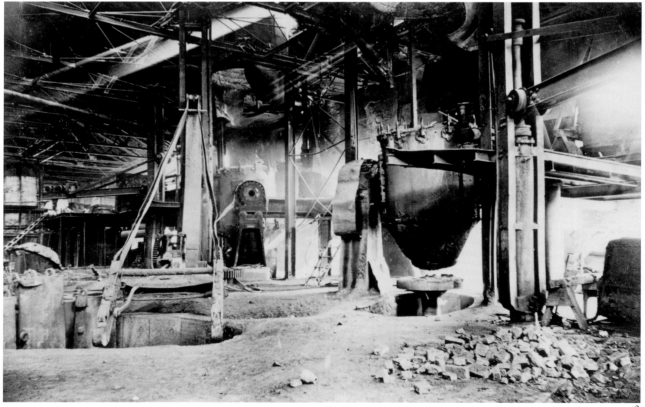

2

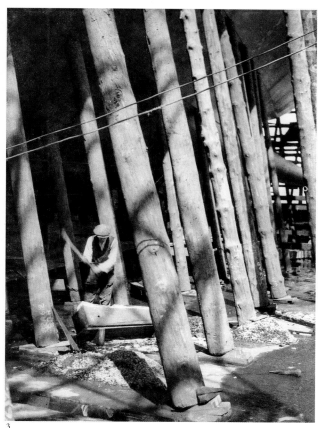

IN the great industrial race it was the United States that eventually emerged the winner. The Bessemer Converter, introduced in 1856, revolutionized steel production, as in the Otis Steel Works in Pittsburgh, USA (1, 2). Krupps of Essen (4) was the biggest works in Europe, and employed over 16,000 people when this photograph was taken in 1870. Harland and Wolff's shipyard in Belfast was hard at work in 1910 on perhaps the most famous liner of all – the *Titanic* (3).

IM großen Wettlauf der Industrialisierung machten schließlich die Vereinigten Staaten das Rennen. Der Bessemer Konverter, 1856 erfunden, revolutionierte die Stahlproduktion, beispielsweise in den Otis Stahlwerken in Pittsburgh, USA (1, 2). Krupp in Essen (4) war die größte Stahlfabrik Europas und beschäftigte über 16 000 Menschen, als diese Photographie im Jahre 1870 aufgenommen wurde. In der Werft von Harland und Wolff in Belfast wurde im Jahre 1910 hart gearbeitet, und zwar am vielleicht berühmtesten Ozeanriesen aller Zeiten, der *Titanic* (3).

LES États-Unis sortirent vainqueurs de la formidable course industrielle. Le procédé de Bessemer, introduit en 1856, révolutionna la sidérurgie, comme ici dans les usines Otis Steel Works de Pittsburg (1 et 2). Les usines Krupp, à Essen, (4) étaient les plus importantes d'Europe et elles employaient plus de 16 000 personnes, en 1870, à l'époque où cette photographie fut prise. Les chantiers navals d'Harland and Wolff à Belfast travaillaient d'arrache-pied en 1910 à la construction de ce qui restera peut-être le paquebot le plus fameux de tous les temps, le *Titanic* (3).

3

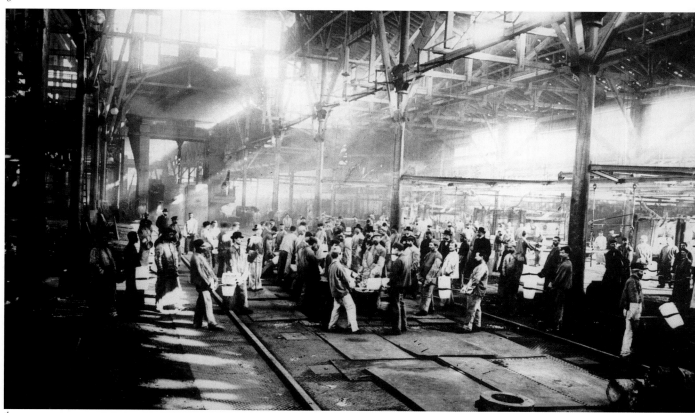

4

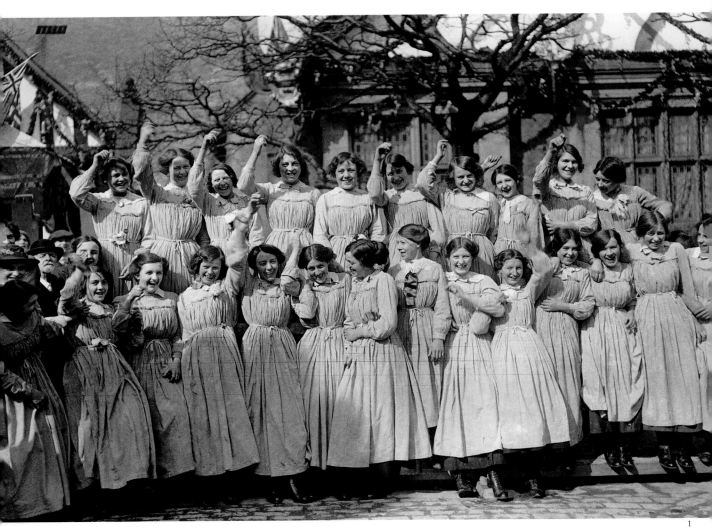

1

NEW machines demanded new skills. The typewriter, patented by C. L. Sholes in 1868, became the means by which women entered the office world, as evidenced by the British House of Commons type-writing staff in 1919 (3). But more traditional industries, like hatting in this Manchester factory (2), also required nimble fingers. It was hard work, poorly paid, and there were many who were forced into prostitution for better pickings. Occasionally, however, young women took to the streets for happier reasons. These English workers from Port Sunlight were setting out to welcome the King and Queen on an official visit in 1914 (1).

NEUE Maschinen erforderten neue Fertigkeiten. Die Schreibmaschine, 1868 von C. L. Sholes patentiert, wurde für Frauen zum Schlüssel zur Bürowelt, wie es die 1919 photographierten Schreibkräfte des britischen Unterhauses zeigen (3). Aber auch traditionellere Industriezweige, wie diese Hutfabrik in Manchester (2), verlangten geschickte Finger. Es war harte, schlecht bezahlte Arbeit, und es gab viele Frauen, die zur Prostitution gezwungen waren, um ihren Lebensunterhalt zu verdienen. Zuweilen gingen die Frauen jedoch auch aus erfreulicheren Gründen auf die Straße. Diese englischen Arbeiterinnen aus Port Sunlight machten sich 1914 auf, um den König und die Königin bei ihrem offiziellen Besuch zu begrüßen (1).

À nouvelles machines nouvelles qualifications. La machine à écrire, brevetée par C. L. Sholes en 1868, ouvrit aux femmes le monde des bureaux, comme en témoignent les dactylographes de la Chambre des Communes britannique en 1919 (3). Cependant des industries plus traditionnelles comme la confection de chapeaux dans cette chapellerie de Manchester (2) avaient besoin, elles aussi, de doigts agiles. Le travail était dur et mal payé. Beaucoup de femmes devaient se prostituer pour arrondir leurs fins de mois. De temps à autre, cependant, des raisons plus gaies amenaient les jeunes femmes dans les rues. Ces ouvrières anglaises à Port Sunlight s'apprêtent à accueillir le roi et la reine en visite officielle en 1914 (1).

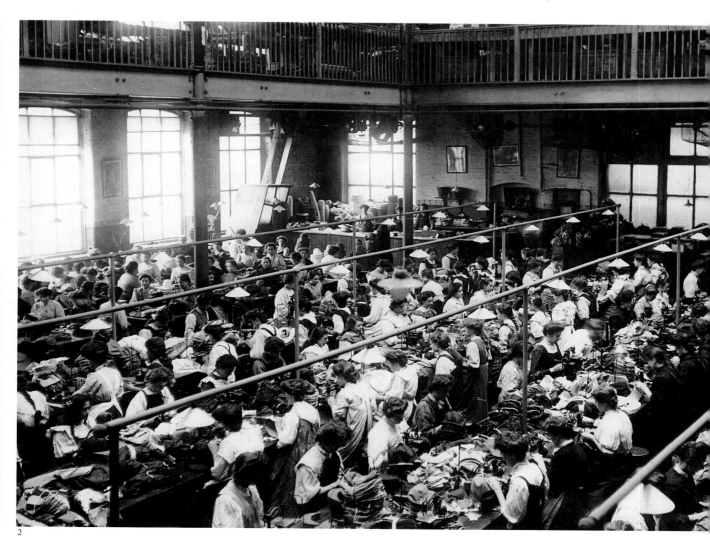

2

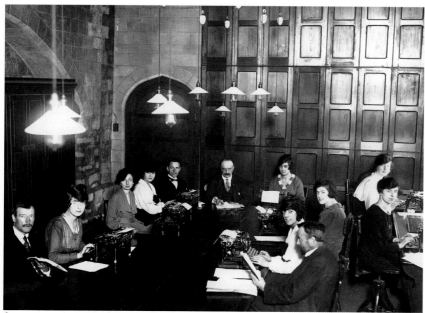

3

Home and Transport

I N 1865 John Ruskin, the artist and critic, described what he believed was the true nature of the 19th-century home: 'It is a place of Peace; the shelter, not only from all injury, but from all terror, doubt and division…' Many would have agreed – home was a refuge from the turmoil and frenzy of work and the wider world. But home was also a prison – for many women, for the poor, and for anyone unhappy with the stifling conventions of family life.

Home could be anything from a hollow in a mud bank for an evicted Irish family, to the palatial mansion staffed by a hundred servants and stuffed with the plunder of centuries. It could be epitomized by the splendid mantelpiece of a suburban villa (1), or by the opulence of the second-floor salon in Castle Konopischt (see pages 86–87), now in the Czech Republic, one of the retreats of the Archduke Franz Ferdinand.

Whatever the splendour or the squalor, in most homes more attention was paid to public display than to private comfort. Bedrooms were unheated, plainly furnished, often poorly decorated. The front room or the parlour was the showpiece – crammed with knick-knacks and crowded with furniture, a haven for dust, a nightmare to clean. But then, in a well regulated home, cleaning was someone else's problem. After all, what were servants for?

'Prompt notice,' wrote Mrs Beeton, 'should be taken of the first appearance of slackness, neglect, or any faults in domestic work, so that the servant may know that the mistress is quick to detect the least disorder, and will not pass unsatisfactory work.'

1

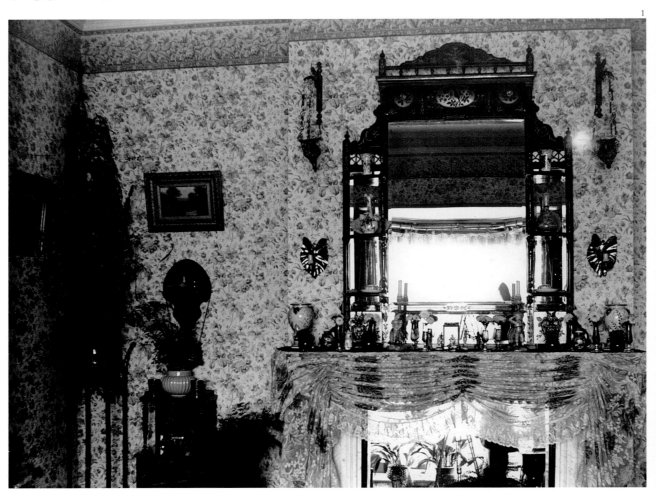

DER Künstler und Kritiker John Ruskin beschrieb 1865, was er für das wahre Wesen des Heims des 19. Jahrhunderts hielt: »Es ist ein Ort des Friedens, des Schutzes nicht nur vor Verletzungen, sondern vor allen Schrecken, Zweifeln und Konflikten ...« Dem hätten viele zugestimmt – das Heim bot eine Zuflucht vor dem Chaos und der Hektik der Arbeit und des Lebens. Aber für viele Frauen, für die Armen und für jeden, der sich in den Konventionen der Familie unwohl fühlte, war das Heim auch ein Gefängnis.

Zuhause konnte alles sein, von der Mulde im Moor für eine vertriebene irische Familie bis zum palastartigen Herrenhaus mit hundert Bediensteten, vollgestopft mit Requisiten der Jahrhunderte. Das Heim konnte durch den herrlichen Kaminsims einer Vorortvilla (1) verkörpert werden oder durch einen Salon im zweiten Stock der Burg Konopischt in der heutigen tschechischen Republik (siehe S. 86–87), eines der Refugien der Erzherzogs Franz Ferdinand.

Egal wie prächtig oder wie elend, in den meisten Heimen legte man mehr Wert auf Zurschaustellung als auf privaten Komfort. Die Schlafzimmer waren nicht beheizt, einfach und sparsam eingerichtet. Das Schaustück war das Wohnzimmer oder der Salon. Überladen mit Nippes und Möbeln, glich er einem riesigen Staubfänger, in dem Putzen zum Alptraum wurde. Aber in den besseren Häusern war Putzen das Problem anderer; wozu gab es schließlich Bedienstete?

»Bei den ersten Anzeichen von Nachlässigkeit und jeder Art von Fehlern bei der Hausarbeit ist sofort Meldung zu machen, damit der Bedienstete weiß, daß die Hausherrin die geringste Unordnung schnell entdecken und schlampige Arbeit nicht dulden wird«, schrieb Mrs. Beeton.

EN 1865, le critique d'art John Ruskin décrivait ce qu'il estimait être la nature véritable du foyer au XIXᵉ siècle : « C'est un endroit de paix, l'abri non seulement contre toutes les blessures mais aussi contre toute terreur, doute et division ... » Ils étaient certainement nombreux à convenir que le foyer était un refuge contre la tourmente et la folie du travail et du monde extérieur. Mais le foyer était aussi une prison pour bien des femmes, pour les pauvres et pour quiconque souffrait des conventions de la vie familiale.

Le foyer pouvait être un trou creusé dans la boue pour une famille irlandaise expulsée de son domicile ou une demeure somptueuse peuplée d'une centaine de serviteurs et regorgeant des pillages accumulés pendant des siècles. Il pouvait être symbolisé par le splendide manteau de cheminée d'une villa de banlieue (1), ou par l'opulence d'un salon au deuxième étage du château de Konopischt (République tchèque; voir p. 86–87), une des retraites de l'archiduc François-Ferdinand.

Quelle qu'en fût la splendeur ou la laideur, la plupart des foyers témoignaient davantage du souci de paraître que de celui du confort privé. Les chambres à coucher n'étaient pas chauffées, elles étaient sobrement meublées et médiocrement décorées. L'antichambre ou le parloir étaient par excellence les pièces que l'on montrait, et dans lesquelles s'entassaient les bibelots et les meubles : une aubaine pour la poussière et un cauchemar à nettoyer. De toute façon, dans une maison digne de ce nom, le nettoyage était le souci de quelqu'un d'autre.

Madame Beeton écrivait : « Il convient de relever immédiatement le plus petit signe de relâchement, négligence ou toute autre faute dans le service des domestiques de manière à faire connaître aux serviteurs que la maîtresse est prompte à détecter le moindre désordre et qu'elle ne tolèrera pas le travail mal fait. »

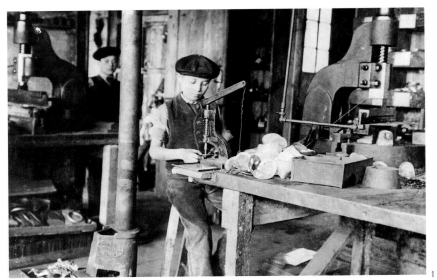

WHERE they could, children like these 'mudlarks' on the Yorkshire sands in 1880 (2) snatched moments of play and rest from their day's work. The lad working in a factory in 1908 (1) may have been as young as 12. Further up the social scale, there were many hours to spend on a home-made seesaw (4). And, at the Richmond Regatta of 1917 (3), privileged children twirled their parasols in a life of ease.

JEDE freie Minute nutzten arbeitende Kinder, wie diese »Schmutzfinken« am Strand der Grafschaft Yorkshire im Jahre 1880 (2), um zu spielen oder sich auszuruhen. Der Junge, der 1908 in einer Fabrik arbeitete (1), war wohl kaum älter als zwölf Jahre. Diejenigen, die höher auf der sozialen Leiter standen, verbrachten viele Stunden, auf selbstgezimmerten

1

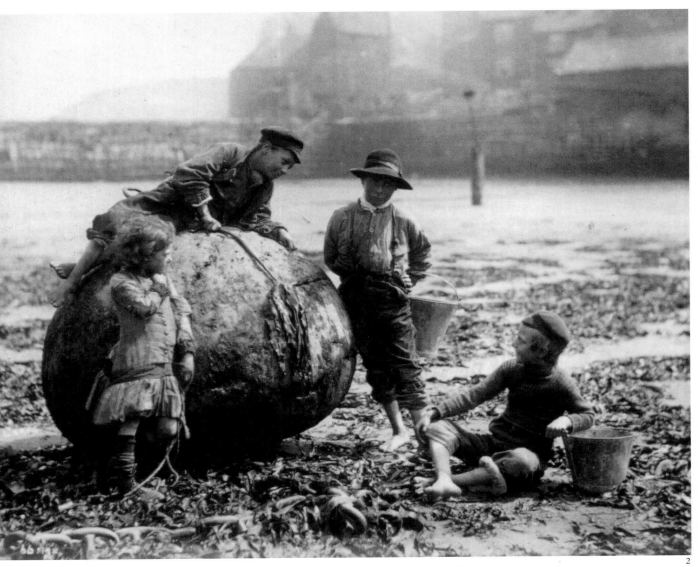

2

Wippen (4). Und bei der Richmond Regatta im Jahre 1917 (3) ließen privilegierte Kinder ihre Sonnenschirme kreisen und genossen ein unbeschwertes Leben.

Chaque fois qu'ils le pouvaient, les enfants, comme ces « fouilleurs de boue » sur les plages du Yorkshire en 1880 (2), dérobaient à leur travail quotidien des moments de jeu et de repos. Ce jeune garçon en 1908 (1) pouvait, bien qu'il n'eût que douze ans, travailler à l'usine en toute légitimité. Plus haut, dans l'échelle sociale, on jouait à loisir de nombreux après-midi durant sur une balançoire faite à la maison (4). À la régate de Richmond en 1917 (3), les enfants privilégiés faisaient tourner leurs parasols et s'exerçaient à une vie aisée.

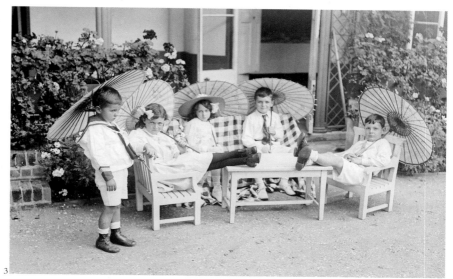

3

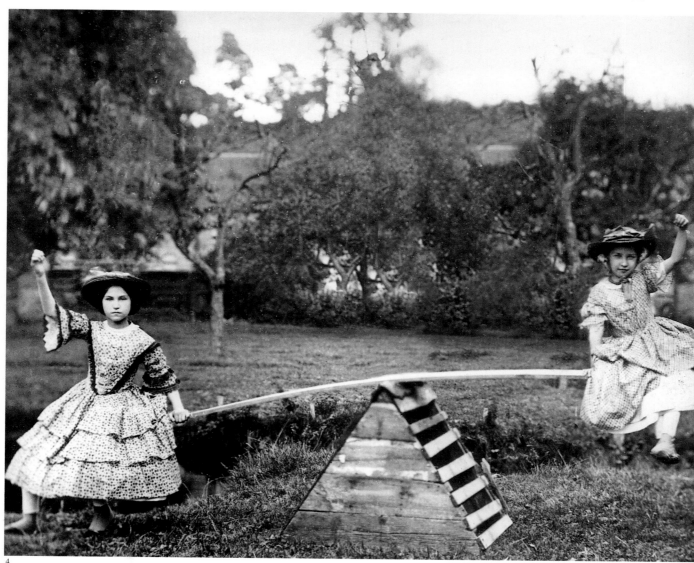

4

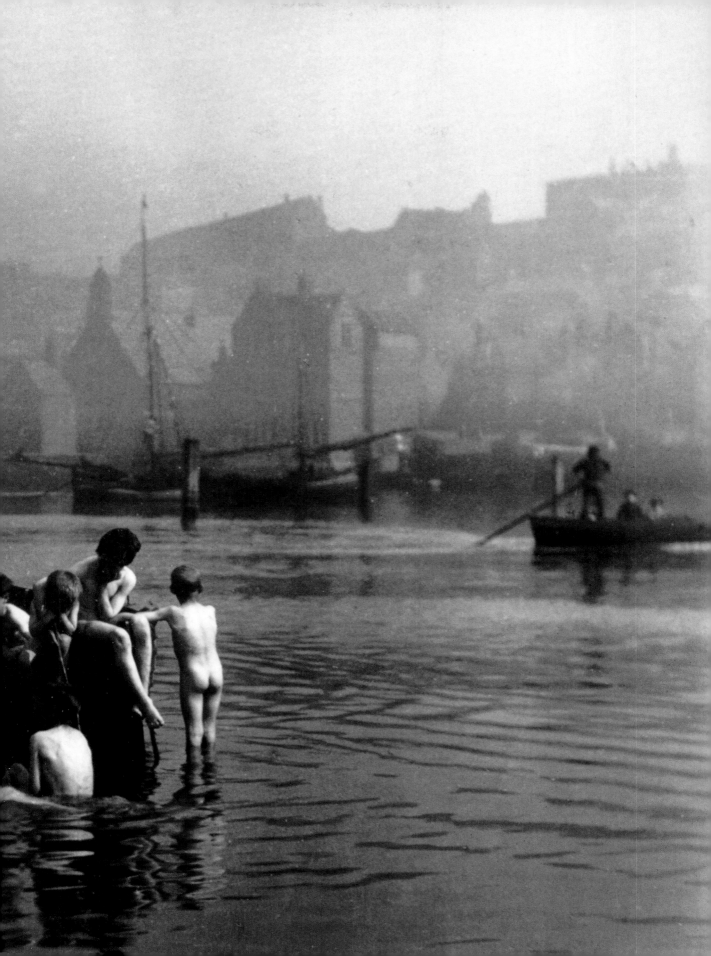

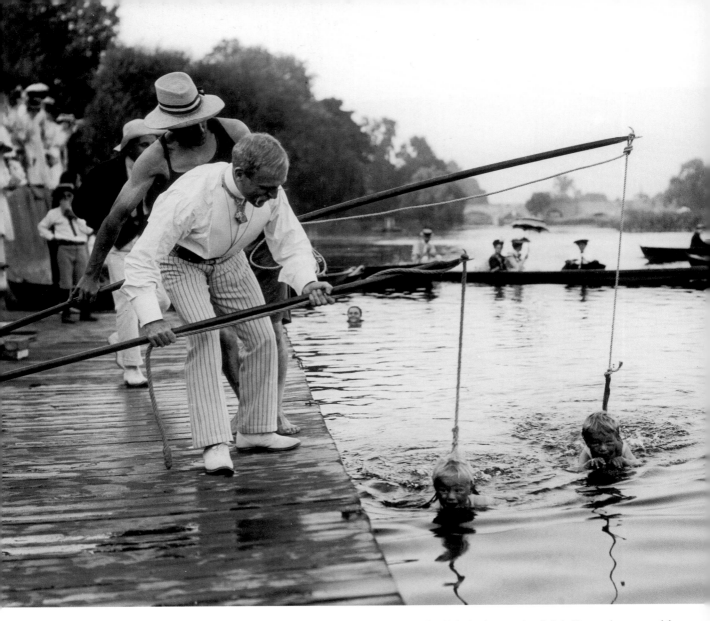

IT was a great age for messing about in boats, and, consequently, for drowning. Some parents went to ingenious lengths to teach their children how to swim (1). Others preferred to stay at home and have their portrait taken for the family album (2). Cameras became more and more portable, and studies more informal (3). And, early in the 20th century, another wonderful gadget was at hand to amuse and entertain – Thomas Edison's Phonograph, the hi-fi of 1908 (4).

(*Previous pages*)
A study of childhood innocence – Frank Meadow Sutcliffe's beautiful 'Water Rats', taken at Whitby in Yorkshire, England, some time in the late 1870s.

ES war eine Zeit, in der man herrlich in Booten herumgondeln und folglich auch ertrinken konnte. Einige Eltern scheuten keine Mühen, um ihren Kindern das Schwimmen beizubringen (1). Andere zogen es vor, zu Hause zu bleiben und sich für das Familienalbum porträtieren zu lassen (2). Die Photoapparate wurden immer handlicher und die Aufnahmen immer ungezwungener (3). Und zu Beginn des 20. Jahrhunderts gab es einen weiteren wunderbaren Apparat zur Belustigung und Unterhaltung, Thomas Edisons Phonograph, die Hifi-Anlage des Jahres 1908 (4).

(*Vorherige Seiten*)
EINE Studie der unschuldigen Kindheit; Frank Meadow Sutcliffes herrliche »Wasserratten«, gegen Ende der 1870er Jahre bei Whitby in Yorkshire, England, aufgenommen.

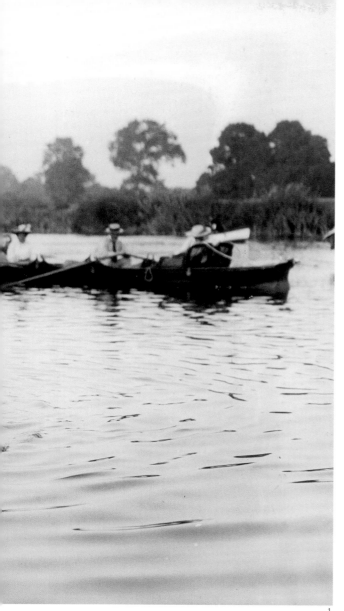

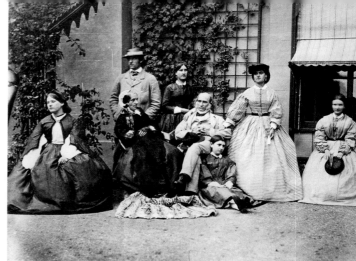

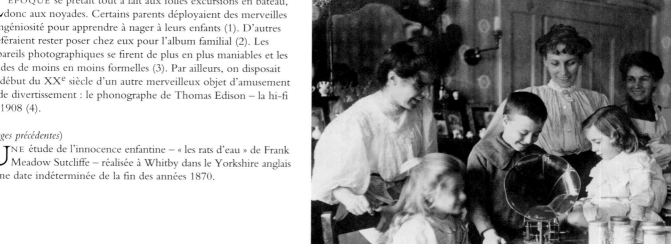

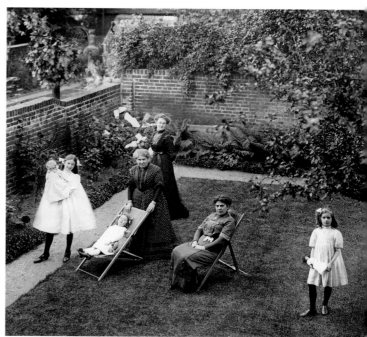

L'ÉPOQUE se prêtait tout à fait aux folles excursions en bateau, donc aux noyades. Certains parents déployaient des merveilles d'ingéniosité pour apprendre à nager à leurs enfants (1). D'autres préféraient rester poser chez eux pour l'album familial (2). Les appareils photographiques se firent de plus en plus maniables et les études de moins en moins formelles (3). Par ailleurs, on disposait au début du XXᵉ siècle d'un autre merveilleux objet d'amusement et de divertissement : le phonographe de Thomas Edison – la hi-fi de 1908 (4).

(*Pages précédentes*)
UNE étude de l'innocence enfantine – « les rats d'eau » de Frank Meadow Sutcliffe – réalisée à Whitby dans le Yorkshire anglais à une date indéterminée de la fin des années 1870.

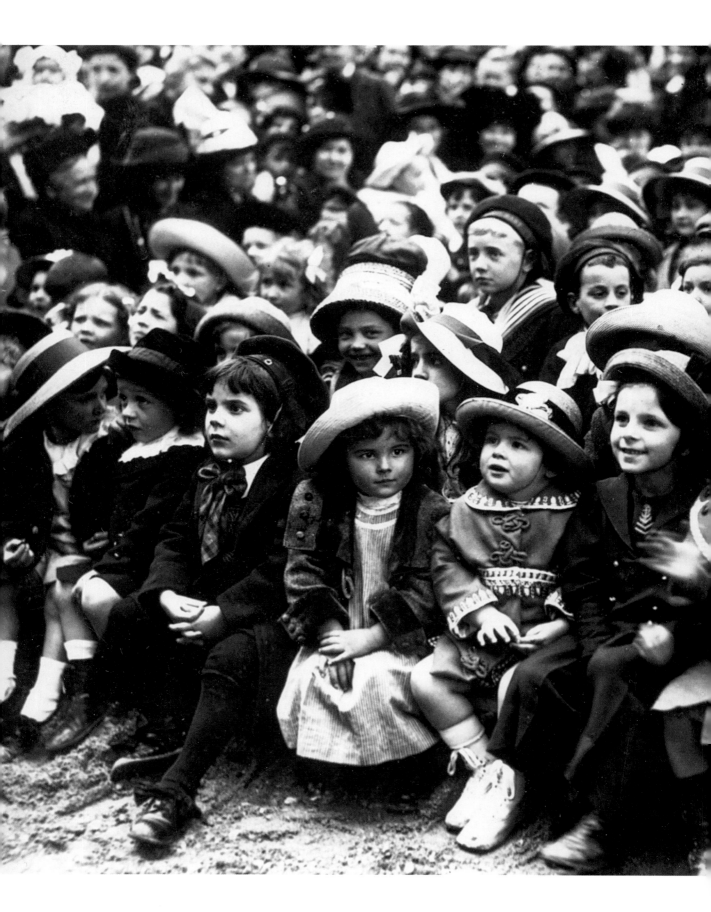

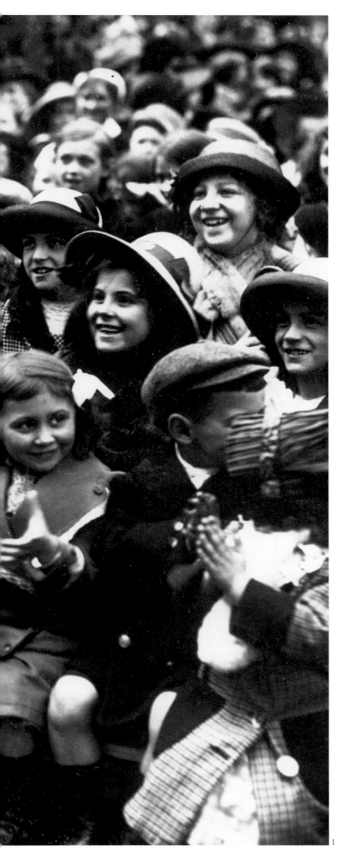

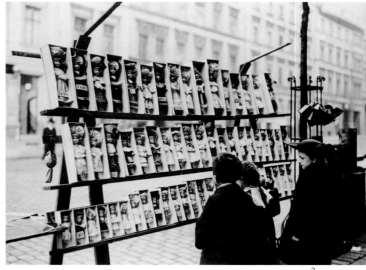

It was the heyday of the Punch and Judy Show, of the marionette theatre, of puppets and puppetry. Crowds gathered in parks and piazzas to see the traditional children's shows that had delighted their parents and grandparents (1). And, if you had enough pfennigs in your pocket, maybe you could buy a doll from this Berlin stall (2), and produce your own puppet play at home.

Es war die Blütezeit des Kasperletheaters, des Marionetten-theaters, der Puppen und Puppenspiele. In Parks und auf Plätzen versammelten sich die Kinder, um die traditionellen Vorführungen zu sehen, an denen sich bereits ihre Eltern und Großeltern erfreut hatten (1). Und wenn man genügend Pfennige in der Tasche hatte, konnte man an diesem Berliner Stand eine Puppe kaufen (2) und zu Hause sein eigenes Puppenspiel aufführen.

Le spectacle de Punch et de Judy, le théâtre de marionnettes, la production et la création de celles-ci, étaient en plein triomphe. On se pressait dans les parcs et sur les places publiques pour assister aux traditionnels spectacles pour enfants qui avaient fait le ravissement des parents et des grands-parents (1). Et si vous aviez suffisamment de pfennigs en poche, vous pouviez acheter une poupée dans cette boutique à Berlin (2) afin de monter votre propre spectacle de marionnettes à domicile.

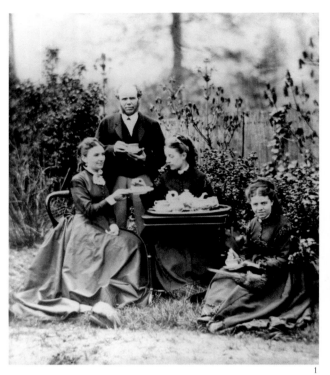

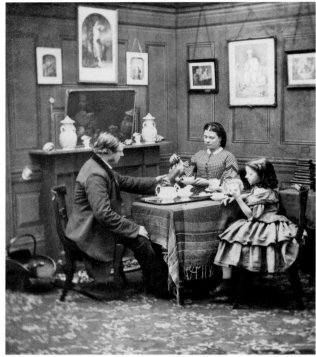

1

2

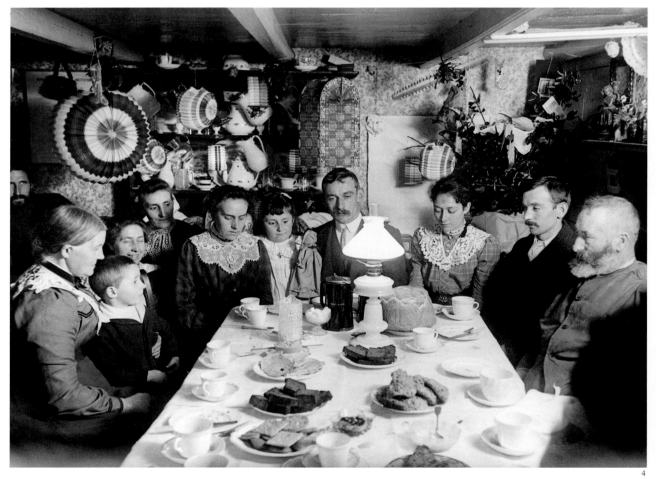

4

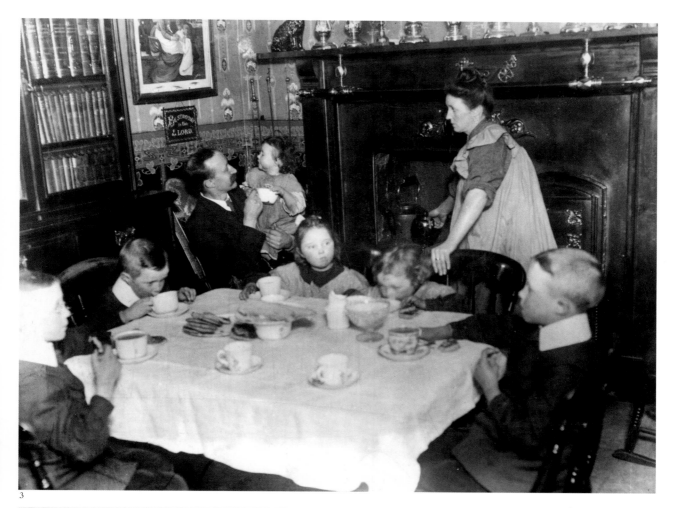

3

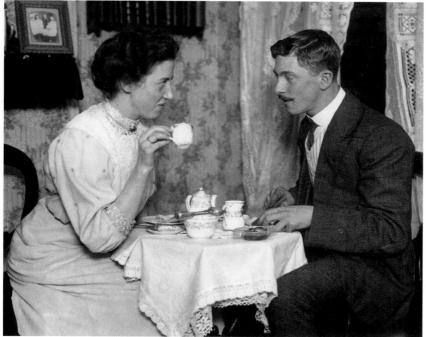

5

Teatime was part of the domestic ideal (3 and overleaf), when the husband returned from the office to hear the daily report on the family (1, 2). For the working class, it was the one chance to entertain guests (4). And it was a chance for a romantic *tête à tête* (5).

Die Teestunde war Teil des häuslichen Ideals (3 und folgende Seiten), wenn der Herr des Hauses aus dem Büro nach Hause kam und sich von seiner Frau berichten ließ, was die Familie den Tag über getan hatte (1, 2). Für die Arbeiterklasse war es die einzige Möglichkeit, gelegentlich Gäste einzuladen (4). Und sie bot Gelegenheit zu einem romantischen Tête-à-tête (5).

Le thé faisait partie du rite domestique (3 et pages suivantes), tandis que l'époux, rentrant du bureau, écoutait le rapport quotidien de sa femme (1 et 2). Dans les couches populaires il s'agissait du seul repas au cours duquel on était susceptible d'avoir des invités (4). Et c'était l'occasion d'un tête-à-tête romantique (5).

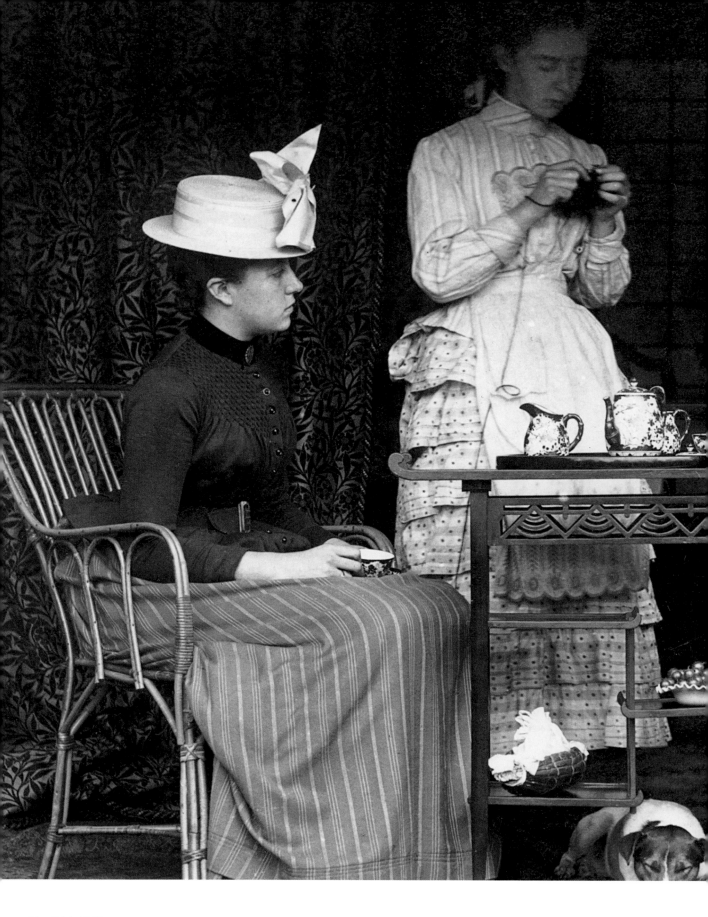

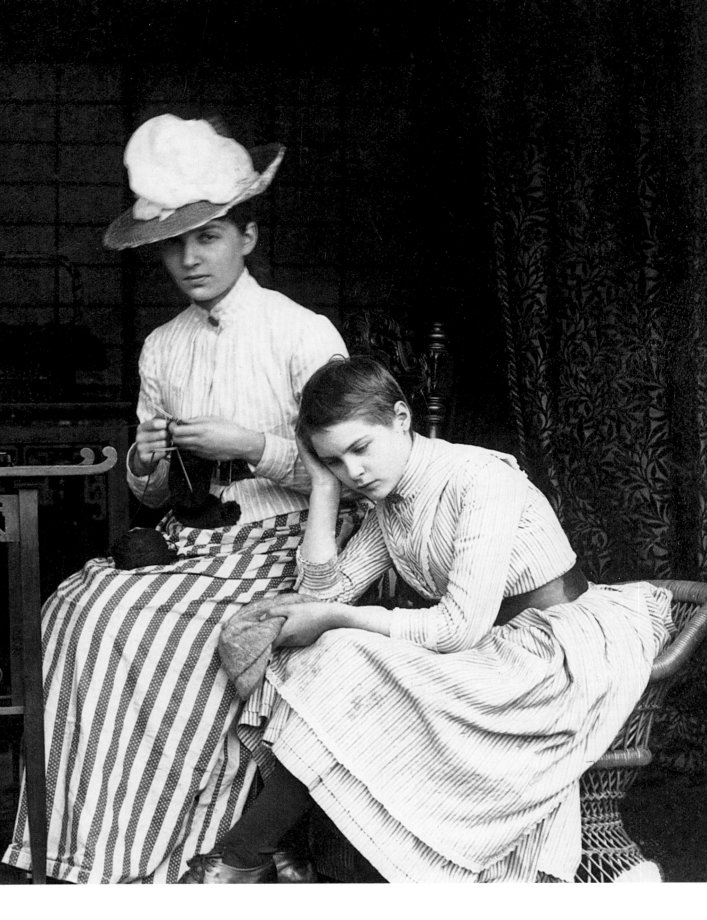

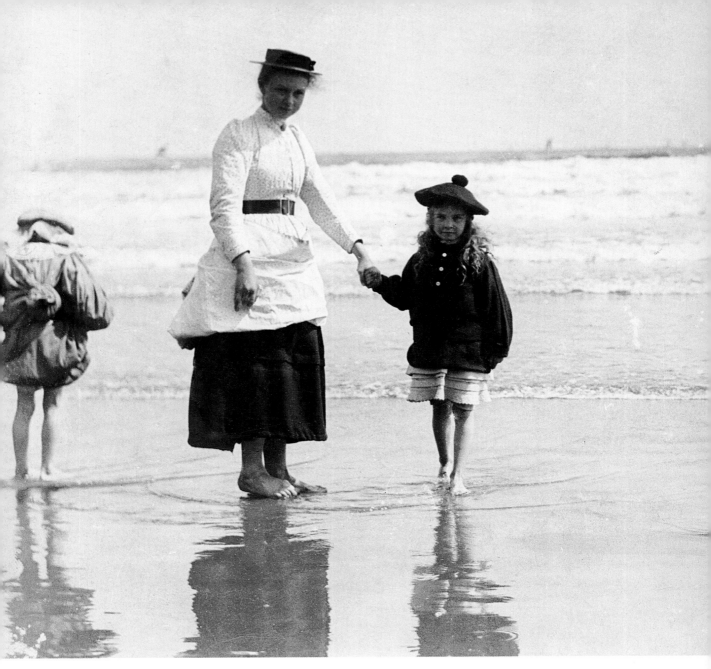

ACROSS Northern Europe and the eastern seaboard of the United States, resorts for the masses were crowded in the summer months. For the price of a cheap rail or charabanc ticket, families could enjoy a day by the sea (1) – an escape from the grim grind of the workplace and the foul smoke of the city. A week in a modest boarding house allowed leisurely enjoyment of the delights of bathing (3) and the promenade (5). Decorum fought decadence (2) under the watchful eye of the bathing machine attendant (4).

IN Nordeuropa und an der Ostküste der Vereinigten Staaten waren die Erholungsorte während der Sommermonate überfüllt. Zum Preis einer billigen Fahrkarte für den Zug oder den offenen Omnibus konnten Familien einen Tag am Meer verbringen (1) und sich vom monotonen Fabrikalltag und von der verpesteten Stadtluft erholen. Ein einwöchiger Aufenthalt in einer bescheidenen Pension bot die Möglichkeit, die Freuden des Badens (3) und Promenierens (5) zu genießen. Unter dem wachsamen Auge der Wärterin der transportablen Umkleidekabinen (4) lagen Anstand und Dekadenz dicht nebeneinander (2).

DANS toute l'Europe septentrionale et sur toute la côte est des États-Unis, on s'entassait pendant les mois d'été dans les stations ouvertes au public. Pour le prix d'un ticket de train ou d'autocar bon marché, on pouvait s'offrir une journée à la mer en famille (1), loin des corvées, de l'austérité du travail et des fumées pestilentielles de la ville. L'excursion d'un jour permettait une rapide partie de canotage, alors qu'une semaine entière dans une modeste pension donnait le temps de s'adonner aux plaisirs de la baignade (3) et de la promenade (5). Les convenances rivalisaient avec la décadence (2) sous l'œil vigilant de la surveillante des cabines de bains roulantes (4).

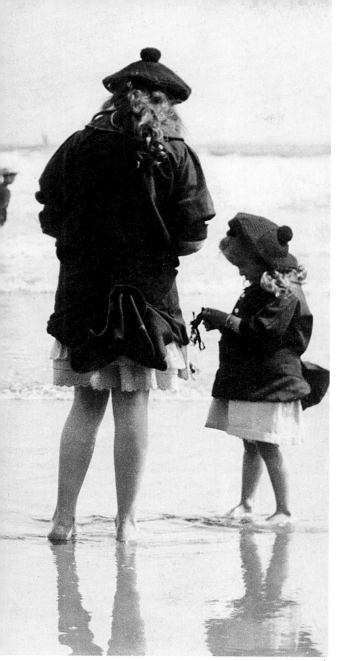

1

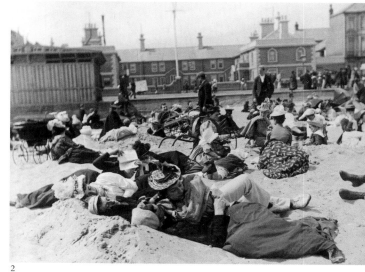

2

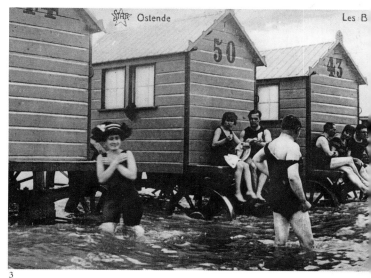

3

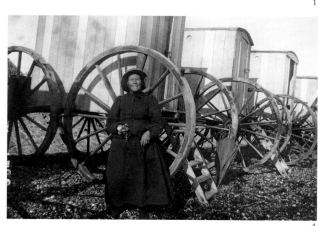

4

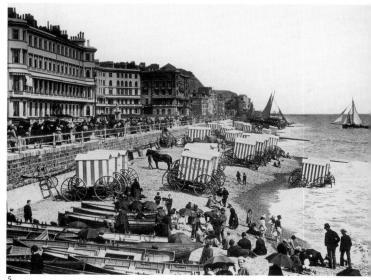

5

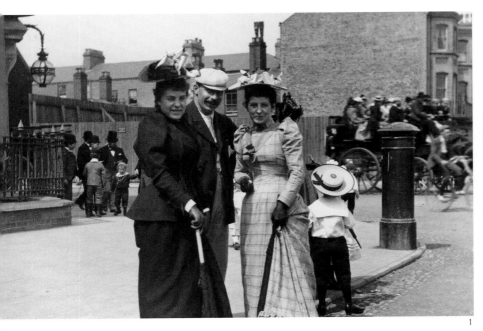

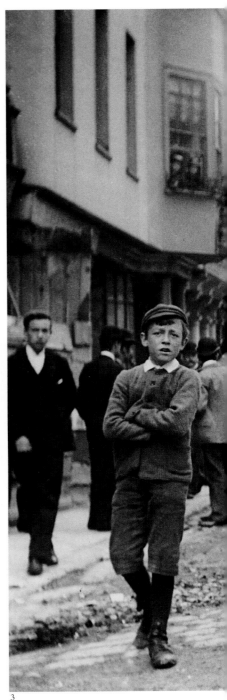

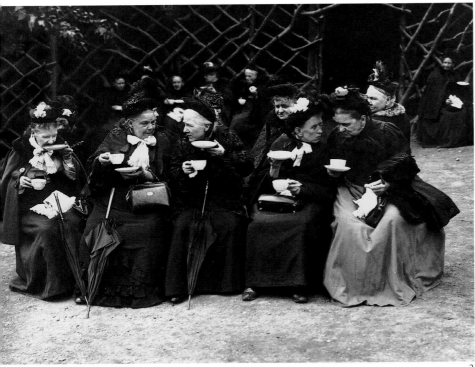

DESPITE the long hours demanded by the factory boss, the master or the mistress, there were Sundays and bank holidays when there was the chance of a day out – a visit to the park, the fair, the circus, the local menagerie, the country-side, friends and relations, the river or the races. Some put on their finest clothes (1). Others wore the uniform of their old age or institution, while they took a refreshing cup of tea (2). And those with a little spare cash to risk on a flutter set off to double it, treble it, or lose all at Goodwood Races (3).

AUCH wenn die Fabrikbesitzer wie der Herr und die Herrin viele Arbeits-stunden von ihren Beschäftigten verlangten, gab es Sonn- und Feiertage, die Gelegenheit zu Ausflügen boten – in den Park, zum Jahrmarkt, zum Zirkus, zum Tierpark, aufs Land, zu Freunden und Verwandten, zum Fluß oder zum Pferderennen. Einige zogen

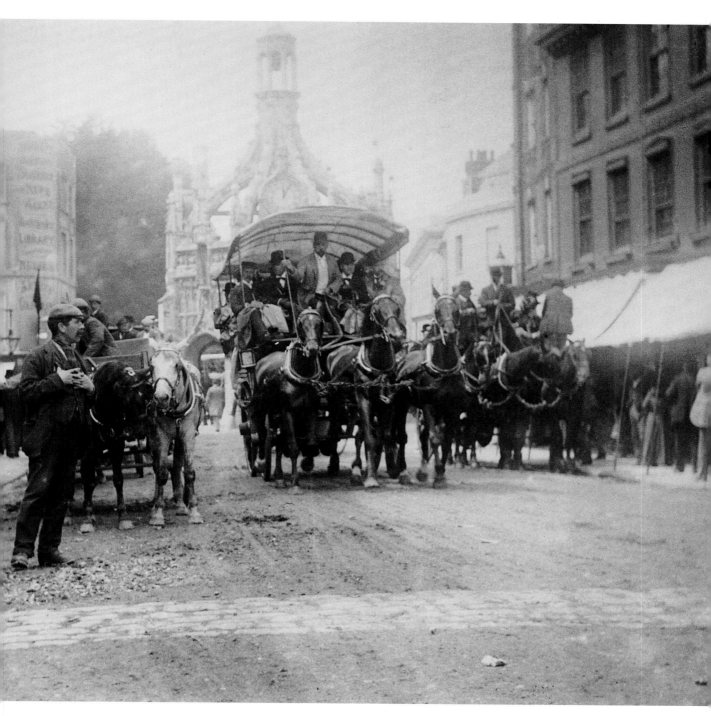

ihre besten Kleider an (1). Andere trugen ihrem Alter oder ihrer Stellung gemäße Kleidung, während sie sich bei einer Tasse Tee erfrischten (2). Und jene, die ein wenig Geld zum Wetten übrig hatten, machten sich zum Pferderennen nach Goodwood auf, um es zu verdoppeln, zu verdreifachen, oder aber alles zu verlieren (3).

Eɴ dépit des longues heures exigées par le patron de l'usine, le maître ou la maîtresse, il y avait les dimanches et les jours fériés qui permettaient d'aller au parc, à la foire, au cirque, à la ménagerie du coin, à la campagne, chez les amis et les parents, à la rivière ou aux courses. Certains met-

taient leurs plus beaux habits (1). D'autres arboraient leur vieil uniforme ou celui de leur institution tout en prenant une tasse de thé (2). Et ceux qui avaient mis quelque argent de côté pour parier s'en allaient le doubler, le tripler ou tout perdre aux courses à Goodwood (3).

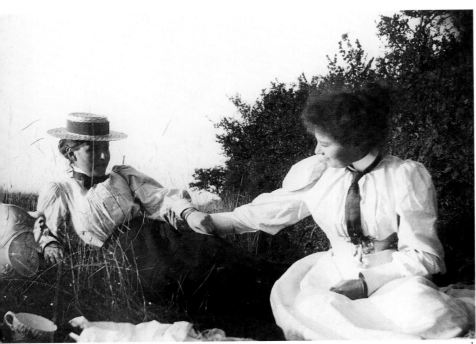

THE French invented the picnic in the mid-18th century. A hundred years later it had become a craze – a symbolic return to the simpler way of life that had existed before the industrial revolution. Some picnics were very private affairs (1), others hearty celebrations of friendship (2). Sometimes they were more formal luncheons – as in this outing to Netley Abbey, Hampshire, in 1900 (4). Best of all was a picnic on the river – the flat punt gently rocking under the willows (3) on the Sunday before Ascot Races, in 1912.

MITTE des 18. Jahrhunderts erfanden die Franzosen das Picknick. Hundert Jahre später kam es groß in Mode – eine symbolische Rückkehr zur einfacheren Lebensart der Zeit vor der industriellen Revolution. Einige Picknicks waren eine sehr private Angelegenheit (1), bei anderen wurde in geselliger Runde gefeiert (2). Manchmal war es ein eher formelles Mittagessen, wie dieser

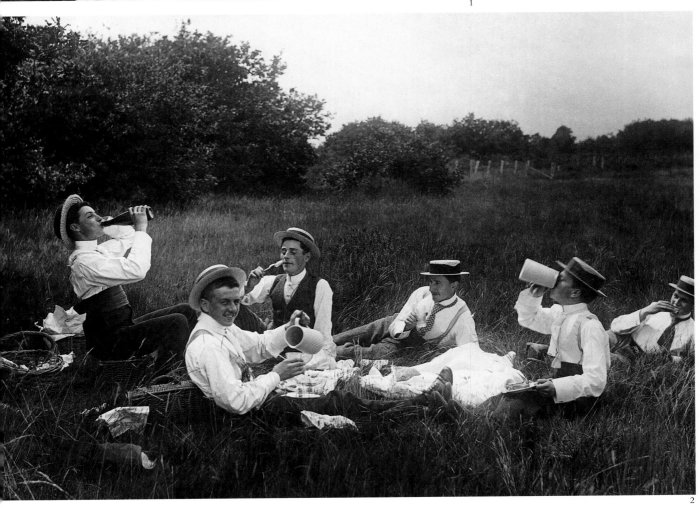

Ausflug zur Netley Abbey in Hampshire im Jahre 1900 (4). Am schönsten war wohl das Picknick auf dem Fluß, bei dem die flachen Kähne sanft unter den Weiden schaukelten (3), bevor es im Jahre 1912 zum Pferderennen von Ascot ging.

L ES Français inventèrent le pique-nique au milieu du XVIIIᵉ siècle. Une centaine d'années plus tard, c'était devenu une folie, un retour symbolique au mode de vie plus simple qui prévalait avant la révolution industrielle. Certains pique-niques étaient très intimes (1), d'autres l'occasion de bonnes et franches agapes (2). Il s'agissait parfois de déjeuners plus formels, tels que cette visite à l'abbaye de Netley dans le Hampshire en 1900 (4). Le summum était peut-être le pique-nique sur la rivière, tandis que le fond plat de la barque se balançait doucement sous les saules pleureurs (3), le dimanche qui précédait les courses à Ascot en 1912.

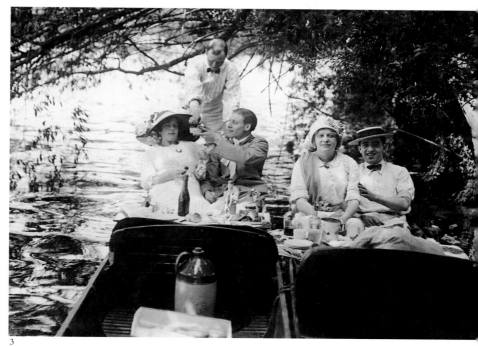

3

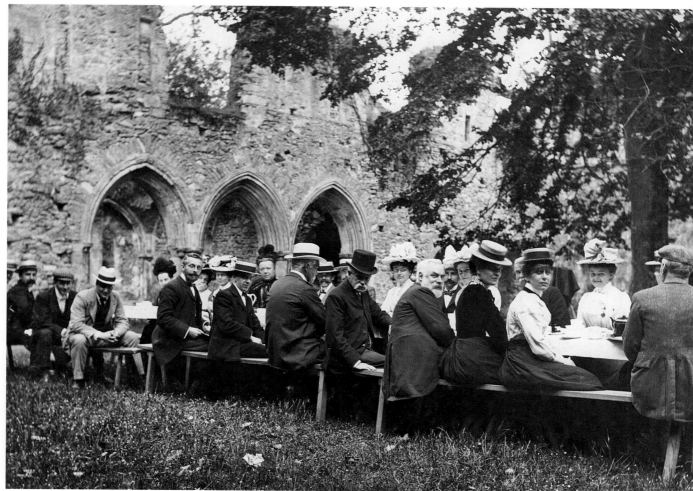

4

THE rich picnicked at the races (1), at the Bournemouth Aviation Show (2), at the Hurlingham Balloon Contest (3). At Stonehenge in 1877 the party included the Queen's son Prince Leopold (4).

DIE Reichen picknickten während der Pferderennen (1), der Flugschau in Bournemouth (2), beim Fesselballonwettbewerb von Hurlingham (3). In Stonehenge war 1877 auch der Sohn der Königin, Leopold, mit von der Partie (4).

LES riches pique-niquaient aux courses (1), au meeting aérien de Bournemouth (2), à la compétition de ballons à Hurlingham en 1909 (3). La partie de campagne à Stonehenge en 1877 incluait le prince Léopold, fils de la reine Victoria (4).

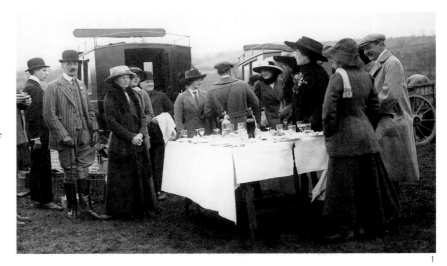

1

2

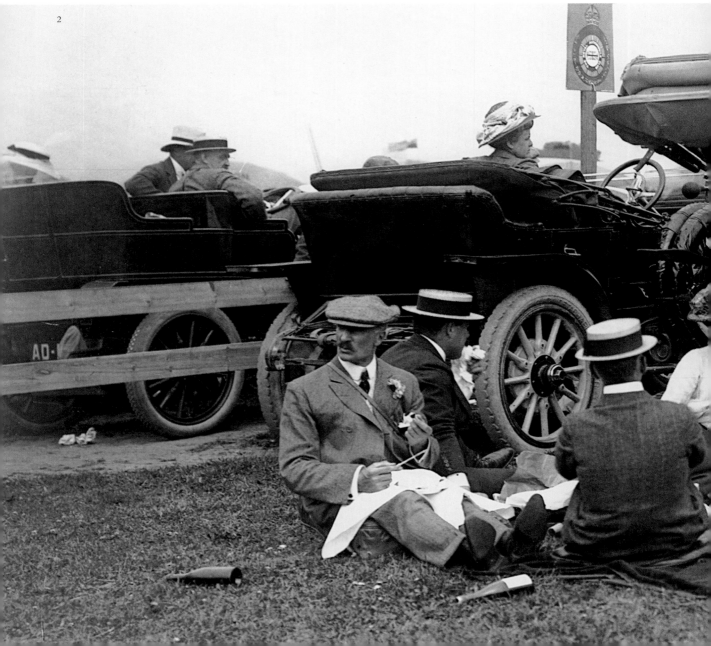

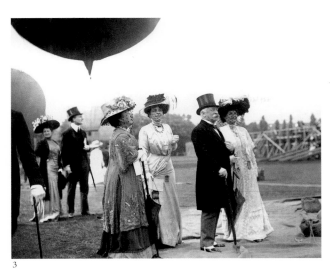

3

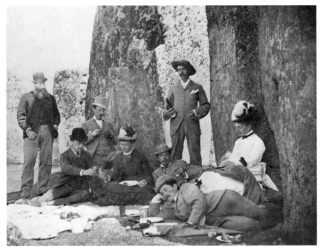

4

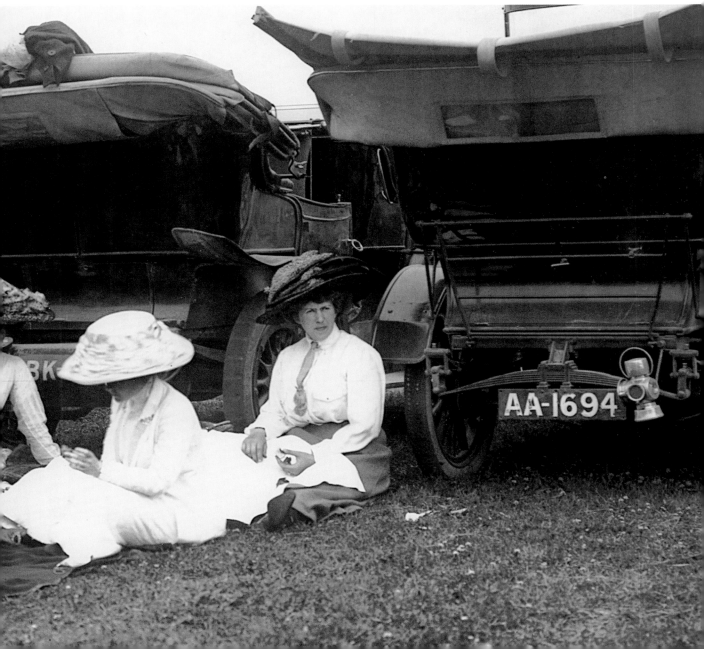

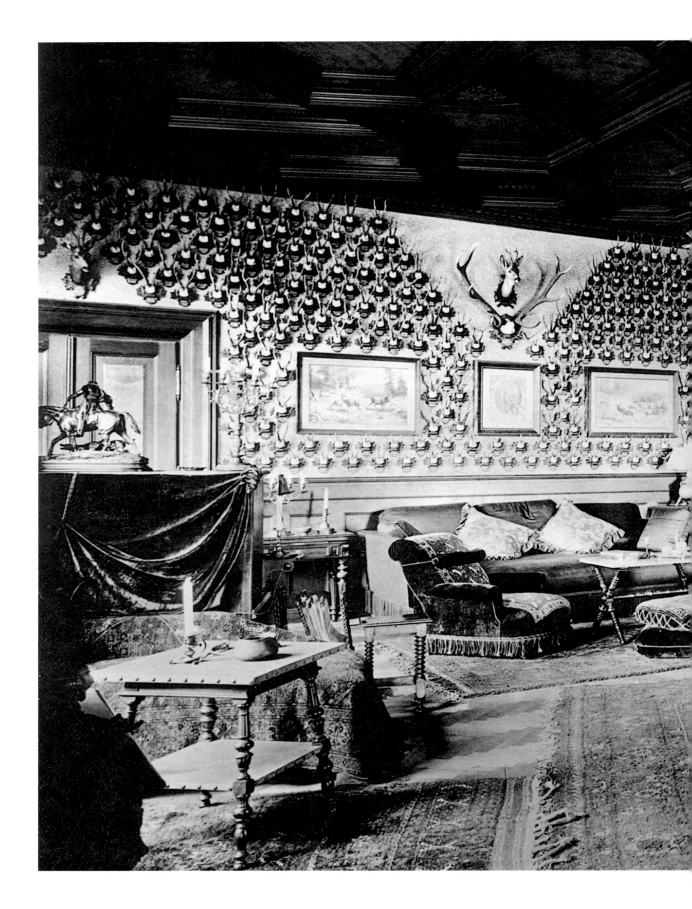

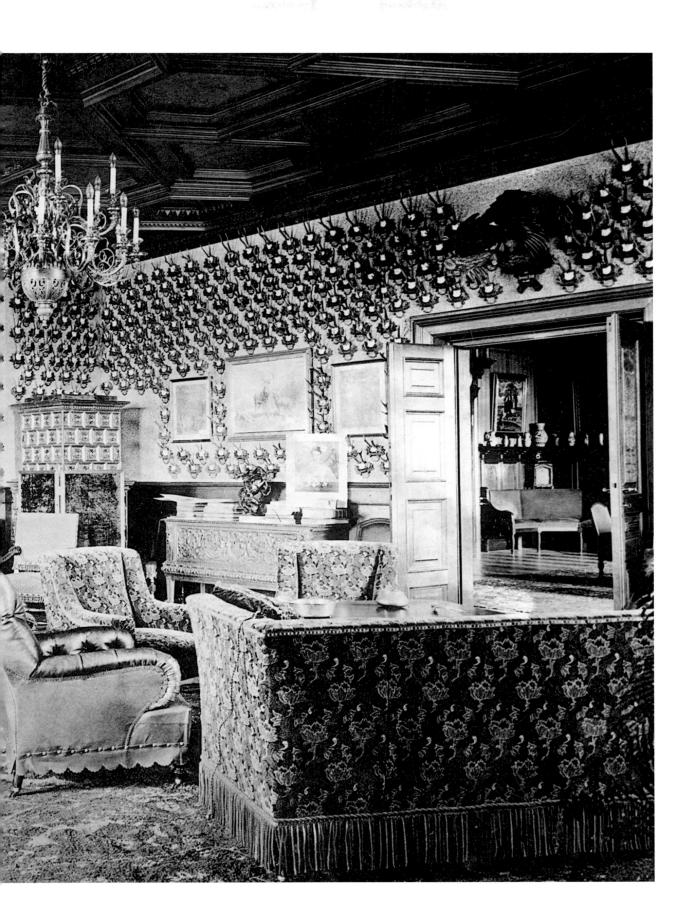

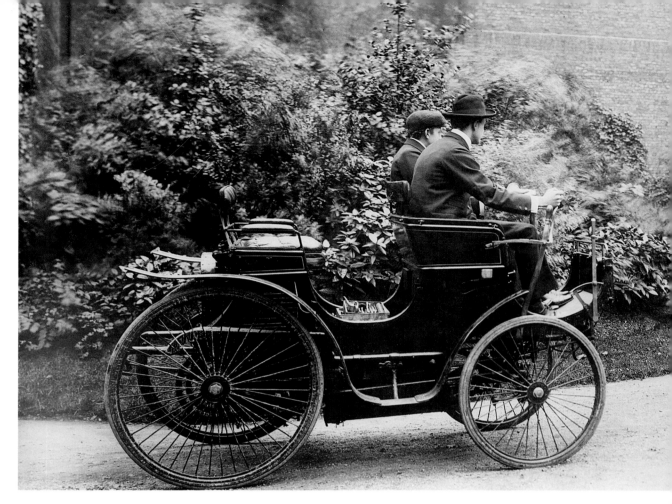

GOTTLIEB Daimler's invention spread rapidly. Like all English motorists, C. S. Rolls (1), driving his first car, an 1896 Peugeot, was preceded by a pedestrian carrying a red flag, for safety's sake. Henry Ford's first car (2) was steered by tiller. Thomas Edison patented an early electric car in the 1890s, the Baker (3). Daimler's son Paul drove one of the earliest four-wheeled cars (4). The designs may have appeared flimsy by modern standards, but at Achères, on l May 1899, Jenatzy drove his electric car, 'Jamais Contente', at a speed of over 100 kph (5).

GOTTLIEB Daimlers Erfindung verbreitete sich schnell. Wie vor allen englischen Autofahrern, lief auch vor C. S. Rolls (1), hier in seinem ersten Automobil, einem Peugeot aus dem Jahre 1896, aus Sicherheitsgründen ein Mann mit einer roten Fahne her. Henry Fords erster Wagen (2) wurde mit einer Ruderpinne gesteuert. Thomas Edison ließ in den 1890er Jahren eines der ersten Elektroautos, den Baker (3), patentieren. Daimlers Sohn Paul fuhr eines

der ersten Modelle mit Vierradantrieb (4). Gemessen an heutigen Standards mögen die Karosserien zerbrechlich wirken, aber am 1. Mai 1899 brachte Jenatzy sein Elektroauto »Jamais Contente« bei Achères auf eine Geschwindigkeit von über 100 Stundenkilometern (5).

L'INVENTION de Gottlieb Daimler se répandit rapidement. Comme tous les automobilistes anglais, C. S. Rolls (1), lorsqu'il était au volant de sa première voiture, la Peugeot de 1896, se faisait précéder d'un piéton portant un drapeau rouge par mesure de sécurité. La première voiture d'Henry Ford (2) était équipée d'un gouvernail. Thomas Edison breveta très tôt dans les années 1890 une voiture électrique, la Baker (3). Paul, le fils de G. Daimler, conduisit une des premières voitures à quatre roues (4). Même si, par rapport aux normes modernes, leurs lignes ne payent pas de mine, cela n'empêcha pas Jenatzy de rouler à plus de 100 km/h dans sa voiture électrique « Jamais Contente » à Achères, le 1er mai 1899 (5).

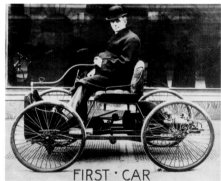

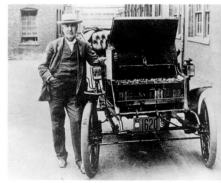

FIRST · CAR

2

3

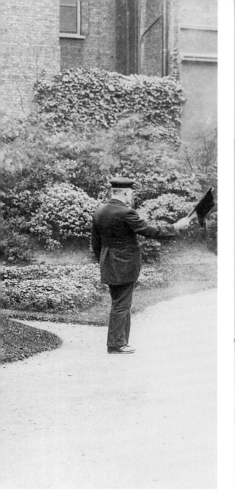

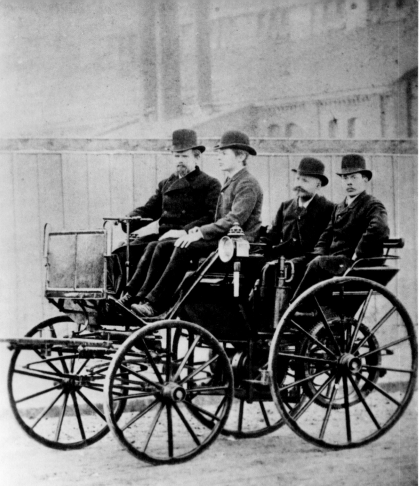

1   4

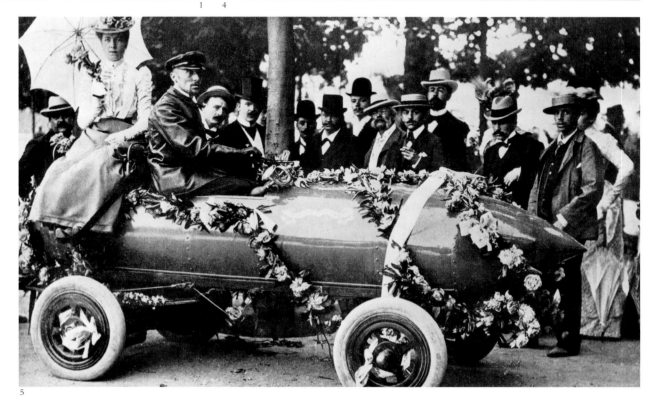

5

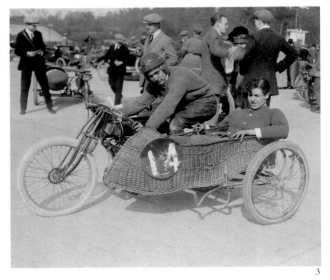

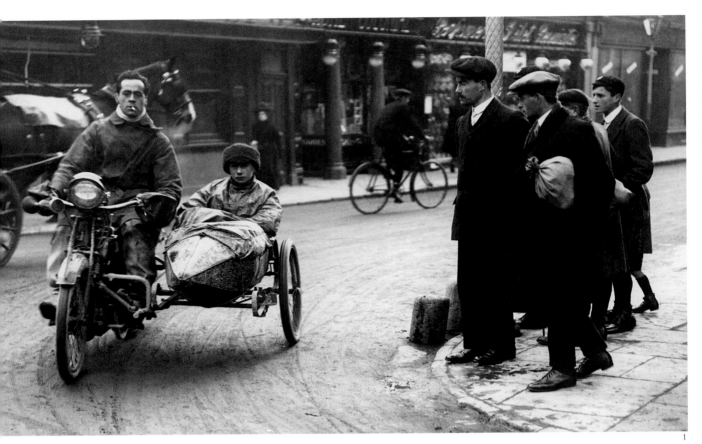

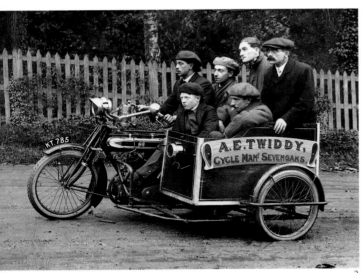

By 1913 a Premier motor cycle (1) was powerful enough to carry six people up a steep gradient (2). A year later, A. J. Luce and H. Zenith won three races at Brooklands (3). Harley Davidsons were as powerful and as sought-after then as now – this one is rearing up a steep gradient on a cross-country run (4).

Ein Premier-Motorrad (1) war 1913 leistungsstark genug, um sechs Leute eine steile Steigung hinaufzubefördern (2). Ein Jahr später gewannen A. J. Luce und H. Zenith drei Rennen in Brooklands (3). Harley-Davidson-Motorräder waren ebenso schnell und begehrt wie heute; diese Harley kämpft sich in einem Geländerennen eine Steigung hinauf (4).

Dès 1913, la motocyclette Premier (1) était suffisamment puissante pour monter avec six personnes une pente très inclinée (2). Un an plus tard, A. J. Luce et H. Zenith remportaient trois courses à Brooklands (3). Les Harley Davidson étaient alors aussi puissantes et recherchées qu'aujourd'hui : celle-ci attaque une pente raide dans une épreuve sur terrain accidenté (4).

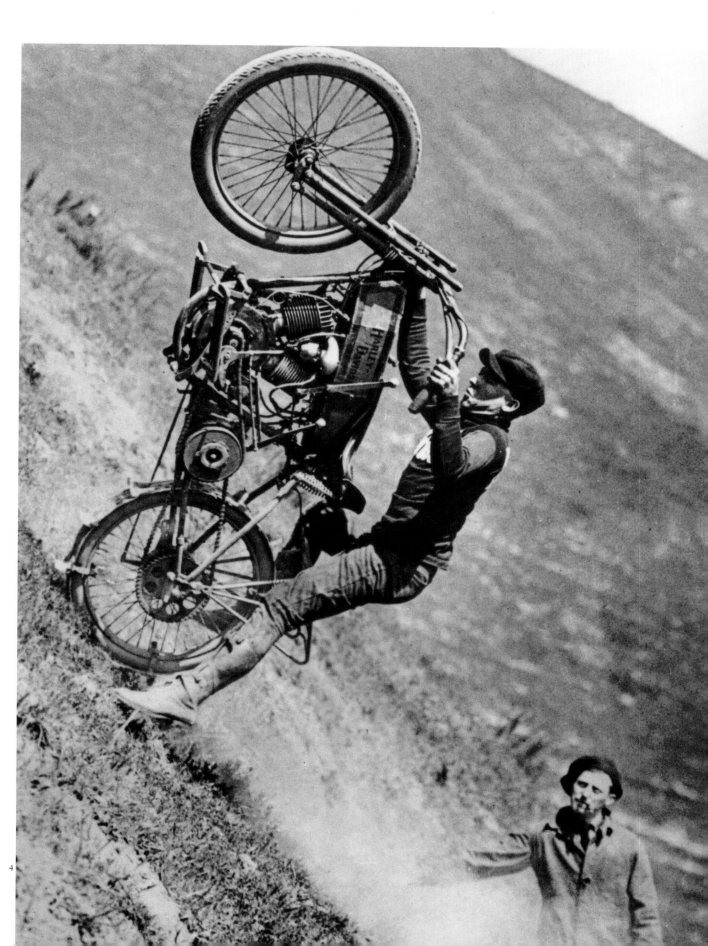

Sport

THE 19th-century bicycle was a comparatively slow developer. It started life as the 'boneshaker', a wheeled hobby-horse with solid tyres, no pedals and no brakes. In the 1840s pedals and pneumatic tyres were added, giving much improved comfort and efficiency. The Penny Farthing (1), with its enormous front wheel, made getting on and off something of a circus trick, but gave a great return in ground covered for each revolution of the pedals fixed to it. With the invention of the safety cycle in the middle of the century, cycling became a craze, a mania. Cycling clubs were formed all over the world. The cycle was used for military purposes, for recreation, even for ceremony – Berlin cyclists take part in an historical pageant for the Gymnastics and Sports Week in the 1900s (2 overleaf).

Quiet rural areas were invaded by weekend tours and daily dashes. At first cycling was considered suitable for men only, but women rapidly caught up. 'Ten years ago,' wrote Jerome K. Jerome in 1900, 'no German woman caring for her reputation, hoping for a husband, would have dared to ride a bicycle; today they spin about the country in their thousands. The old folks shake their heads at them; but the young men, I notice, overtake them, and ride beside them' (*Three Men on a Bummel*).

They were pleasant days for cyclists. The motor car was still something of a noisy freak – rare and unreliable. Road surfaces were adequate, though thorns from hedgerows still produced many a puncture. Lanes smelt of honeysuckle or new-mown hay, there was the sound of birdsong, the skies above were blue and empty. 'One skimmed along,' wrote one early cyclist, 'almost without effort; one coasted downhill and even on the flat when speed had been attained, and later one free-wheeled. One was carefree, death did not lurk at every corner, at every crossing. There was space, there was room, there was freedom. You rang your bell, a musical enough little chime, when you went round a corner and only the very careless pedestrian who had not yet got bicycle-conscious or a yapping dog who had aversions for bicycles, or had been taught to attack them, could do you any damage' (W. MacQueen Pope).

Indeed, the only real danger came from other carefree road users, from other cyclists, or from the groups of children who had not yet learned that the road was not a playground. It was a good time, a gentle time – but Henry Ford and the conveyor belt and the mass-produced motor car were about to bring it all to a swift and noisy and smelly and dangerous end.

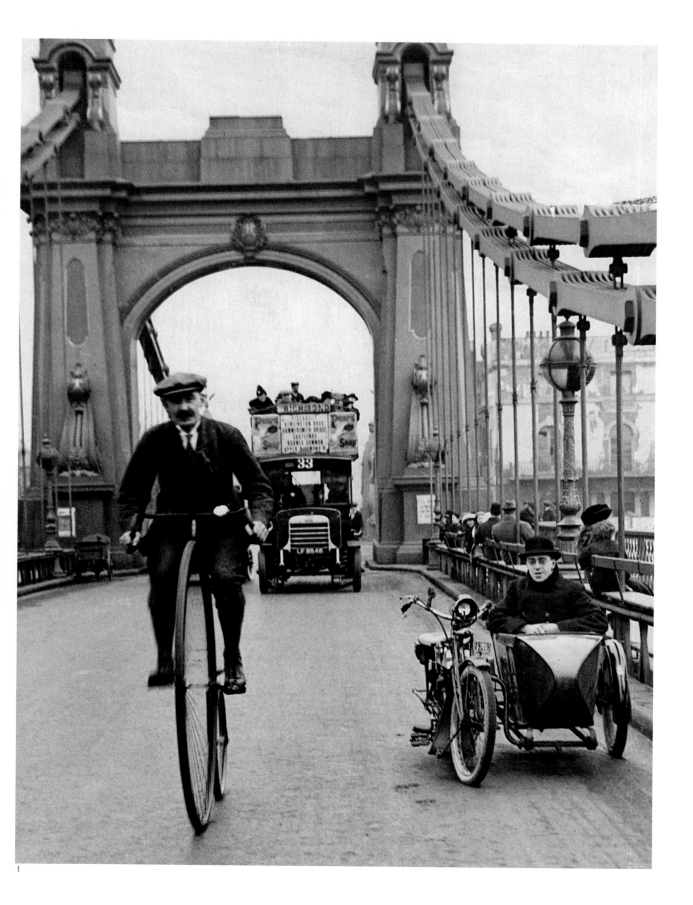

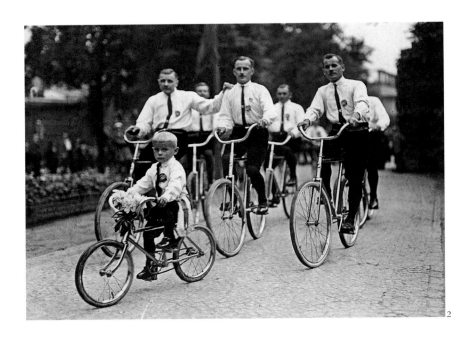

DAS Fahrrad des 19. Jahrhunderts war ein relativer Spätentwickler. Die ersten Modelle waren Klappergestelle, Drahtesel ohne Gummireifen, ohne Pedalen und ohne Bremsen. In den 1840er Jahren stattete man es mit Pedalen und Gummireifen aus und machte es so schneller und bequemer. Durch sein riesiges Vorderrad machte das Hochrad (1, vorherige Seite) das Auf- und Absteigen zu einer Art Zirkusnummer, aber mit jeder Umdrehung der daran befestigten Pedale konnte man sehr viel Boden gutmachen. Mit der Erfindung des Niederrades wurde Radfahren zur großen Mode, beinahe zur Manie. Überall auf der Welt wurden Fahrradclubs gegründet. Das Fahrrad wurde auch für militärische Zwecke genutzt, es diente der Freizeitgestaltung und wurde sogar bei Feierlichkeiten eingesetzt – Berliner Radfahrer nehmen im Jahre 1900 an einem historischen Umzug im Rahmen der Woche der Gymnastik und des Sports teil (2).

Fahrradfahrer störten die Ruhe ländlicher Gegenden nicht nur am Wochenende. Am Anfang war man der Ansicht, Radfahren sei nur für Männer geeignet, aber die Frauen holten schnell auf. »Vor zehn Jahren«, schrieb Jerome K. Jerome 1900, »hätte keine deutsche Frau, die um ihren Ruf besorgt war und auf einen Ehemann hoffte, gewagt, Fahrrad zu fahren; heute schwirren sie zu Tausenden durchs Land. Alte Leute schütteln bei ihrem Anblick den Kopf; aber junge Männer, so konnte ich beobachten, holen sie ein und fahren neben ihnen her.« (aus: *Three Men on a Bummel*)

Es war eine angenehme Zeit für Radfahrer. Das Auto war noch immer ein lärmendes Ungetüm, selten und unzuverlässig. Der Zustand der Straßen war gut, auch wenn die Dornen der Heckenreihen für so manchen platten Reifen sorgten. Auf den Wegen duftete es nach Geißblatt oder frisch gemähtem Gras, die Vögel zwitscherten, und der Himmel war blau und wolkenlos.

»Man glitt fast mühelos dahin«, schrieb einer der ersten Radfahrer, »man rollte spielend den Berg hinab und sogar über ebene Straßen, wenn man die richtige Geschwindigkeit erreicht hatte, und dann fuhr man im freien Lauf dahin. Man war sorglos, der Tod lauerte nicht an jeder Ecke, an jeder Kreuzung. Es gab Platz, es gab Raum, es gab Freiheit. Man klingelte, und es ertönte ein fast musikalisches Glockenspiel, wenn man um eine Ecke fuhr. Nur sehr unvorsichtige Fußgänger, die dem Fahrrad noch nicht genügend Respekt schenkten, oder ein kläffender Hund, der etwas gegen Fahrräder hatte oder dem man beigebracht hatte, sie anzugreifen, konnten einem gefährlich werden.« (W. MacQueen Pope)

Die einzige wirkliche Gefahr waren sorglose Fußgänger, andere Radfahrer oder Gruppen von Kindern, die noch nicht gelernt hatten, daß die Straße kein Spielplatz ist. Es war eine gute Zeit – aber Henry Ford, das Fließband und die Massenfertigung von Autos sollten sie zu einem schnellen, lauten, stickigen und gefährlichen Ende bringen.

LA bicyclette du XIXᵉ siècle mit, en comparaison, du temps à évoluer. Elle s'apparenta au début plutôt au « tapecul », sorte de cheval à roues doté de solides pneus, sans pédales ni freins. Dans les années 1840 vinrent s'y ajouter les pédales et les pneumatiques qui en améliorèrent nettement le confort et l'efficacité. Enfourcher le grand Bi (1) qui était monté sur une énorme roue frontale, ou en descendre, tenait plus ou moins de l'acrobatie, mais cela était compensé par l'énorme distance parcourue à chaque coup de pédale. Avec l'invention de la bicyclette, au milieu du siècle, le cyclisme devint à la mode et dégénéra en manie. Des clubs de cyclisme se constituèrent un peu partout dans le monde. La bicyclette servait à des fins militaires, récréatives et même cérémonielles : les cyclistes de Berlin participèrent à la reconstitution historique de la Semaine de la gymnastique et du sport dans les années 1900 (2).

Les paisibles zones rurales étaient envahies en fin de semaine par les cyclistes et secouées par les collisions quotidiennes. On considéra d'abord que le cyclisme ne convenait qu'aux hommes. Cependant les femmes s'y mirent rapidement. Jerome K. Jerome écrivait en 1900 : « Il y a dix ans, aucune Allemande soucieuse de sa réputation ou de trouver un mari n'aurait osé monter sur une bicyclette. Aujourd'hui elles sont des milliers à pédaler dans tout le pays. Les vieilles personnes hochent la tête sur leur passage, tandis que les jeunes gens, je l'ai remarqué, les rattrapent pour pédaler à leurs côtés. » (*Three Men on a Bummel*)

C'était les beaux jours du cyclisme. L'automobile restait une sorte d'extravagance bruyante, rare et peu fiable. Les revêtements des routes lui convenaient même si, malgré tout, les épines des haies provoquaient bien des crevaisons. Les allées sentaient bon le chèvrefeuille ou le foin fraîchement coupé, on entendait les oiseaux chanter, les cieux étaient bleus et vides. Comme l'écrivait un de ces premiers cyclistes :

« On filait presque sans effort ; on descendait les pentes en roue libre en maintenant sur le plat la vitesse acquise, qui vous emportait sans que vous eussiez besoin de pédaler. On était insouciant. La mort ne guettait pas à chaque coin de rue ou à chaque carrefour. On avait de l'espace, on avait de la place, on avait la liberté. Vous actionniez votre timbre avertisseur, au doux carillon musical, en abordant un tournant, et seul le piéton le plus inattentif qui n'avait pas encore pris conscience de l'importance de la bicyclette, ou un chien glapissant qui exécrait les bicyclettes, ou dressé pour les attaquer, pouvaient vous faire courir un risque quelconque. » (W. MacQueen Pope)

En fait, le seul véritable danger provenait des usagers de la route, eux aussi insouciants, des autres cyclistes ou des groupes d'enfants qui n'avaient pas encore appris à la distinguer d'un terrain de jeux. C'était le bon temps – un temps bon enfant qui allait bien vite s'achever avec les inventions de Henry Ford : le tapis roulant et l'automobile fabriquée en série.

(*Overleaf*)
THE remarkable penny-farthing bicycle made its first appearance in the 1880s (2). Its enormous front wheel meant that a single turn of the pedals enabled the cyclist to advance a considerable distance. Cycling clubs were popular (1). Seaside towns were invaded by swarms of healthy young athletes demanding lemonade, tea, coffee, and refreshing sherbet.

(*Folgende Seiten*)
IN den 1880er Jahren tauchte das bemerkenswerte Hochrad auf (2). Durch sein riesiges Vorderrad konnte man durch eine einzige Umdrehung der Pedale eine beträchtliche Wegstrecke zurücklegen. Fahrradclubs waren sehr populär (1). In die Küstenorte fielen Schwärme kräftiger junger Athleten ein und verlangten Limonade, Tee, Kaffee und Brause zur Erfrischung.

(*Pages suivantes*)
L'extraordinaire grand Bi fit son apparition dans les années 1880 et remporta immédiatement un succès total (2). Son énorme roue frontale permettait au cycliste de couvrir en un seul coup de pédale une distance considérable. Les clubs de cyclisme étaient populaires (1). Les villes en bord de mer étaient envahies par des athlètes réclamant de la limonade, du thé, du café et des jus de fruits glacés.

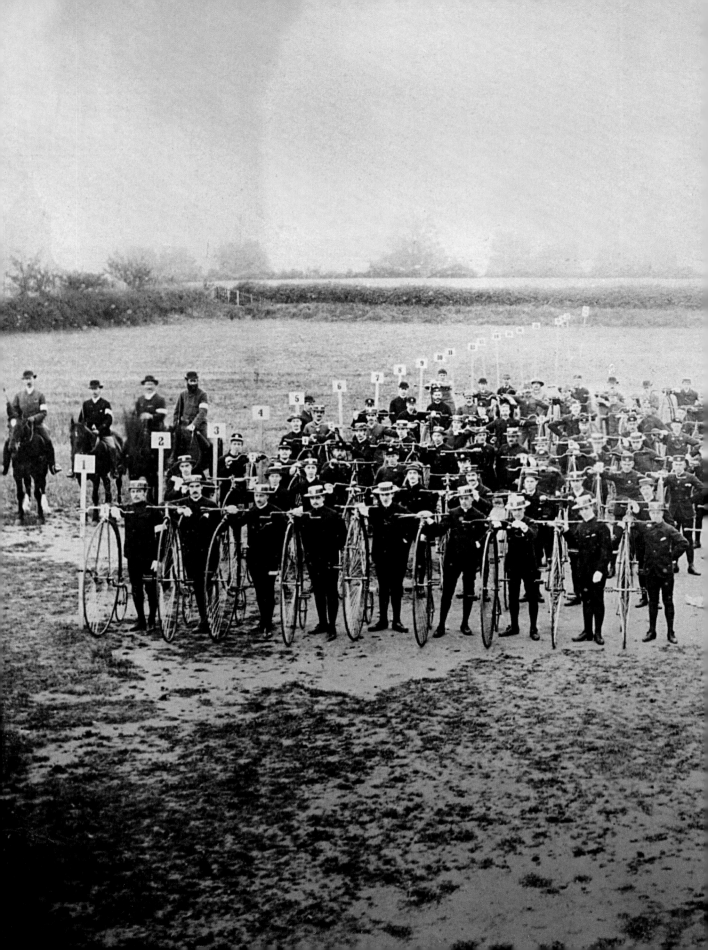

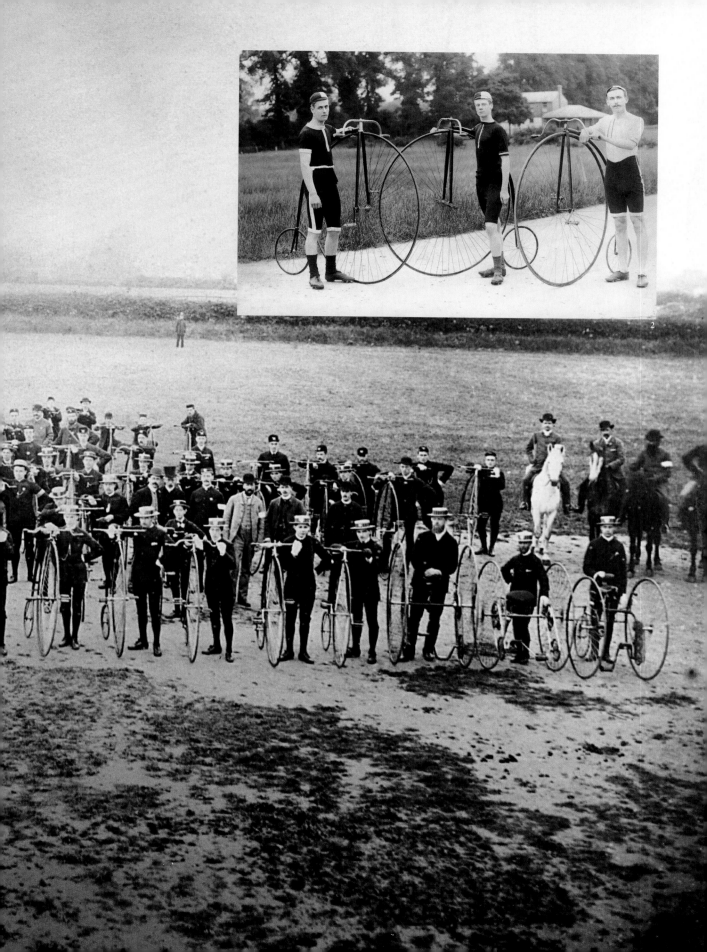

2

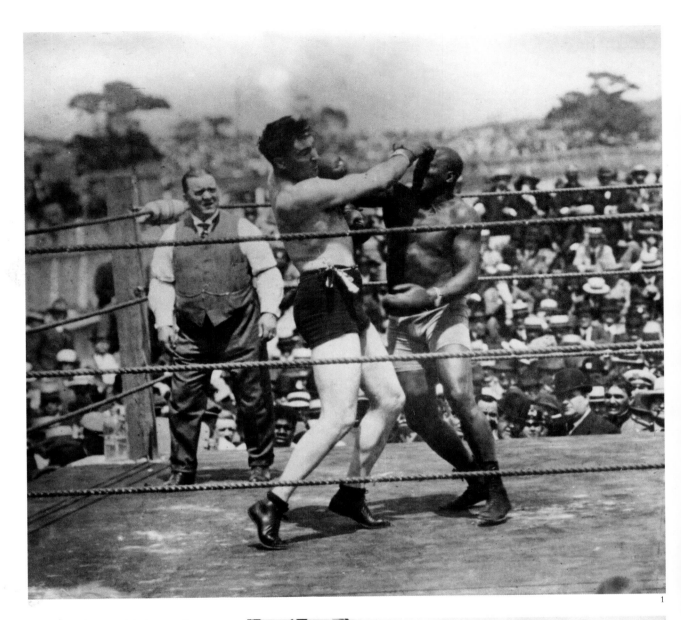

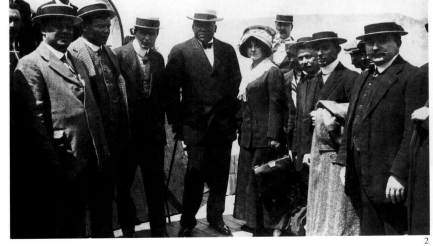

GREAT heavyweight boxers: Jim Jeffries (right) and Tom Sharkey (3); Jack Johnson (2), the first black World Heavyweight Champion, here fighting Jess Willard (1) in 1915.

GROSSE Schwergewichtsboxer: Jim Jeffries (rechts) und Tom Sharkey (3). Jack Johnson (2), der erste schwarze Schwergewichtsweltmeister, hier 1915 in einem Kampf gegen Jess Willard (1).

LES plus fameux poids lourds furent Jim Jeffries (à droite) et Tom Sharkey (3). Jack Johnson (2), le premier Noir à devenir champion du monde dans la catégorie des poids lourds, défend ici son titre contre Jess Willard en 1915 à Cuba (1).

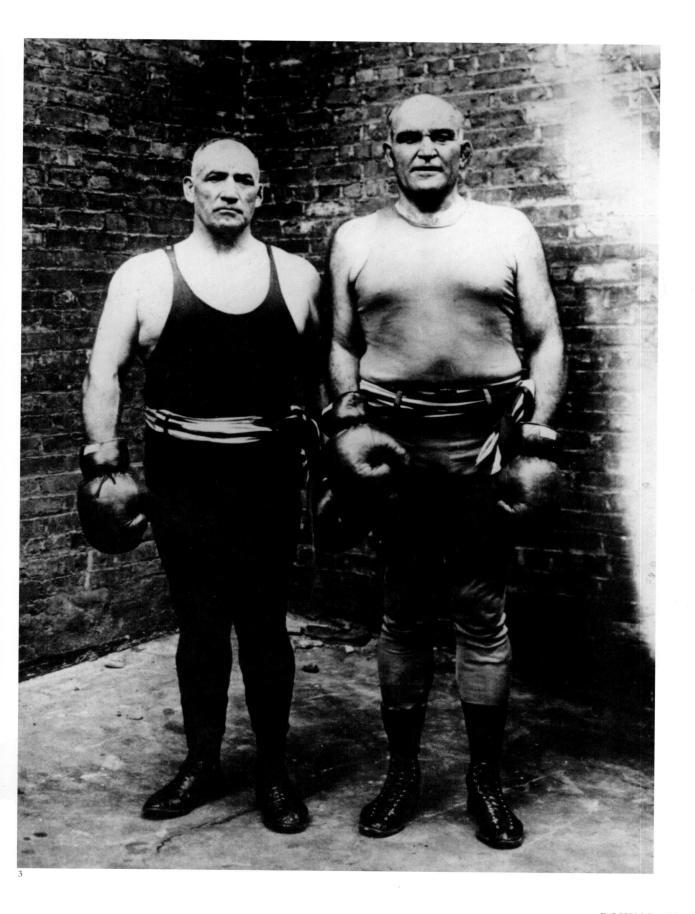

3

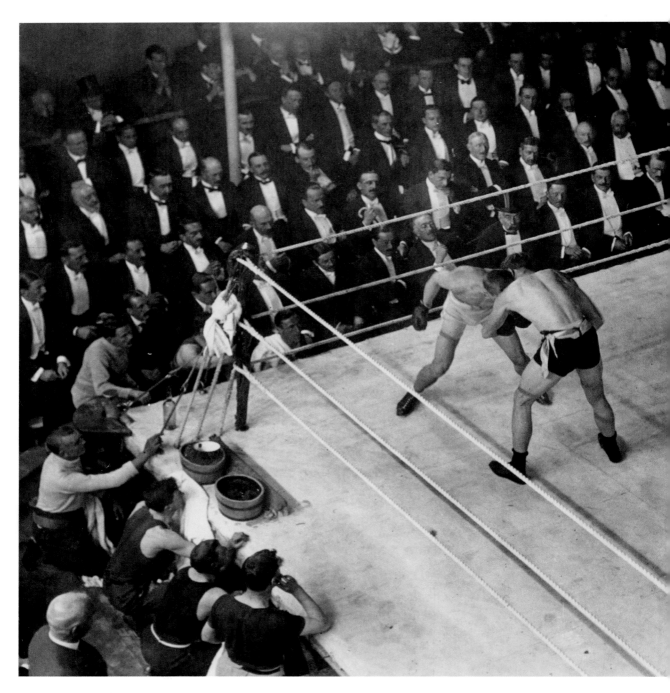

IF not the Sport of Kings, boxing was certainly the sport of gentlemen, given the sartorial elegance of the crowd watching the fight between Bombardier Billy Wells and Georges Carpentier (1) in December 1913. Matt Wells (2) held the World and Empire Welterweight titles 1914-1919. One of the greatest fighters of all was John L. Sullivan (3), the last bare-knuckle heavyweight champion. One of the most elegant was Gentleman Jim Corbett (4), who won the championship from Sullivan in 1892.

BOXEN war zwar nicht der Sport der Könige, aber wohl der der Gentlemen, wenn man nach dem eleganten Aussehen der Zuschauer urteilt, die im Dezember 1913 den Kampf zwischen »Bombardier« Billy Wells und Georges Carpentier (1) sahen. Matt Wells (2) war von 1914 bis 1919 Empire- und Weltmeister im Weltergewicht. Einer der größten Kämpfer von allen war John L. Sullivan (3), der letzte Schwergewichtschampion, der ohne Handschuhe boxte. Einer der elegantesten

war der Gentleman Jim Corbett (4), der Sullivan 1892 den Titel abnahm.

LA boxe était, sinon le sport des rois, en tout cas celui de la bonne société si on en juge par la tenue élégante du public qui suit le combat opposant Bombardier Billy Wells à Georges Carpentier (1) en décembre 1913. Matt Wells (2) conquit le monde et l'empire des titres mi-moyens de 1914 à 1919. John L. Sullivan (3), un des plus grands boxeurs, fut le dernier champion

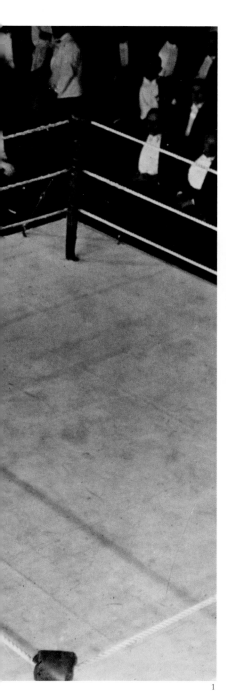

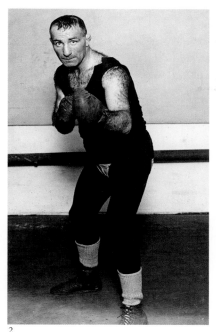

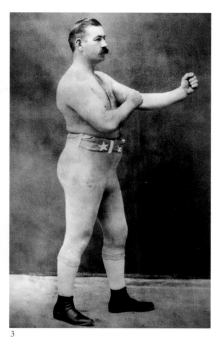

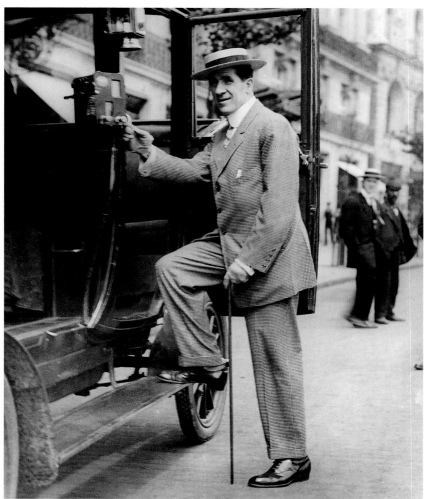

à combattre à poings nus dans la catégorie
des poids lourds. L'un des plus élégants
était Gentleman Jim Corbett (4), qui conquit son titre de champion aux dépens de
Sullivan en 1892.

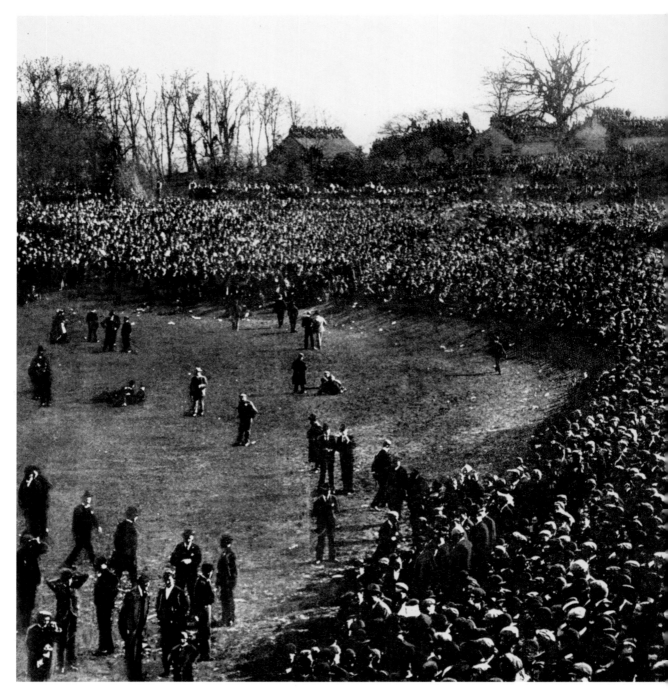

CUP FINALS and international football matches were first played in the 1870s. In 1906 vast crowds jolted their way to Crystal Palace in South London (2) to see Everton defeat Newcastle by a goal to nil in the FA Cup. Five years later Newcastle again lost by the single goal in a Cup Final, this time to Bradford City (3, 4). Tottenham Hotspurs' triumph over Sheffield United by three goals to one was said to be one of the best performances in a Cup Final (1).

POKALENDSPIELE und internationale Fußballspiele wurden zum ersten Mal in den 1870er Jahren ausgetragen. Die Massen strömten 1906 zum Crystal Palace im Süden Londons (2), um den 1:0-Sieg von Everton über Newcastle im Spiel um den englischen Meisterpokal zu sehen. Fünf Jahre später verlor Newcastle erneut mit 1:0 in einem Meisterschaftsspiel, diesmal gegen Bradford City (3, 4). Der 3:0-Triumph der Tottenham Hotspurs über Sheffield United gilt als eines der besten Pokal-Endspiele aller Zeiten (1).

LES matchs en coupe finale et les internationaux de football furent disputés pour la première fois dans les années 1870. En 1906 des foules immenses se

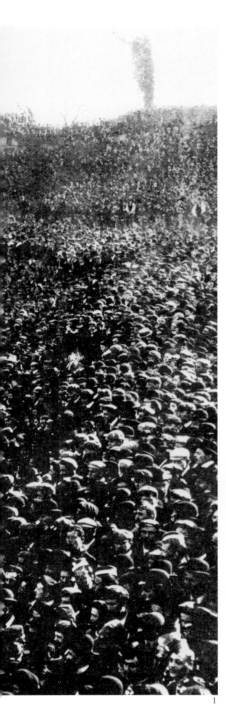

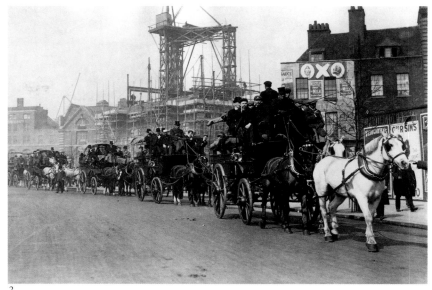

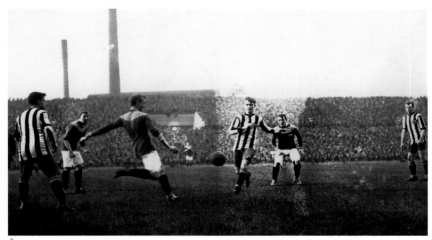

bousculaient pour aller assister à Crystal Palace, dans le sud de Londres (2), à la victoire par 1 but à 0 d'Everton sur Newcastle dans le match de la Coupe de la FA. Cinq années plus tard, Newcastle perdit de nouveau d'un but en finale, cette fois-ci contre Bradford City (3 et 4). La victoire éclatante de Tottenham Hotspur par 3 buts à 1 sur Sheffield United est considérée comme l'un des plus beaux matchs jamais disputés en coupe finale (1).

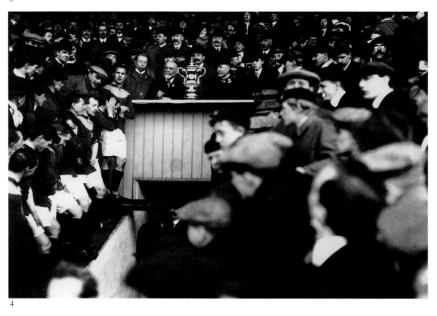

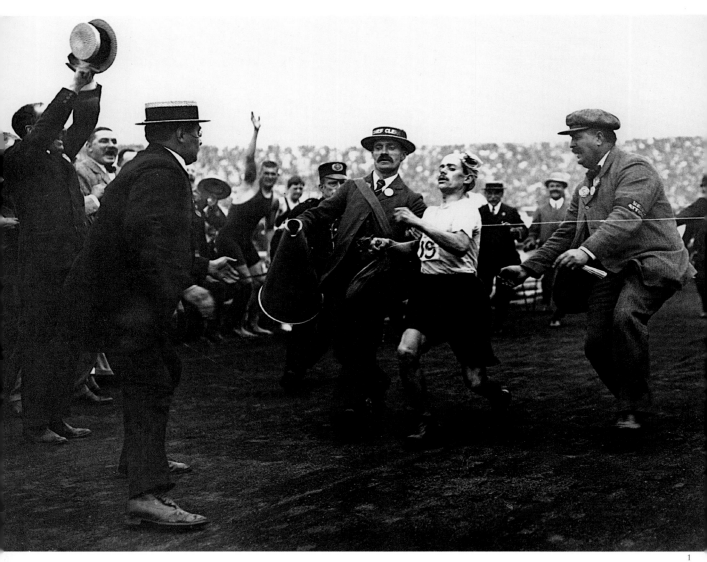

1

Pierre de Fredi, Baron de Coubertin, inaugurated the modern Olympic Games in 1896. Early Olympic Games included some sports no longer covered (such as cricket) or no longer practised (like the Standing Long Jump, 3). Clothes were generally modest and cumbersome, though swimming trunks were brief, if not symmetrical (2).

The 1908 Marathon ended in high drama. The course had been lengthened by over a mile, at the request of the British Royal family, who wished it to start beneath Princess Mary's bedroom window at Windsor Castle. Towards the end of the race, Dorando Pietri of Italy was first into the stadium, leading by a considerable distance. He stumbled and fell, probably as a result of having to change direction – he had thought he should turn right on to the track, officials pointed to the left. Pietri fell four more times in the next 250 metres, the last time opposite the Royal Box. He struggled to his feet but was helped across the finishing line (1) by, among others, Sir Arthur Conan Doyle (right, in cap). For this, poor Pietri was disqualified, and the gold medal went to an American, Johnny Hayes.

Im Jahre 1896 weihte Pierre de Fredi, Baron de Coubertin, die modernen Olympischen Spiele ein. Bei den frühen Olympischen Spielen gab es Disziplinen, die heute nicht mehr zugelassen (Kricket) oder ausgeübt werden (der Weitsprung aus dem Stand, 3). Die Sportkleidung war meist züchtig und deshalb hinderlich, abgesehen von den knappen, fast symmetrischen Badehosen (2).

Der Marathonlauf bei den Olympischen Spielen von 1908 endete äußerst dramatisch. Die Strecke war auf Bitten des Königshauses um mehr als eine Meile verlängert worden, denn man wünschte, daß der Lauf unter dem Schlafzimmerfenster von Prinzessin Mary in Windsor Castle beginnen sollte. Der Italiener Dorando Pietri lief mit deutlichem Vorsprung als erster ins Stadion ein. Er stolperte und fiel, vermutlich weil er die Richtung wechseln mußte; er hatte geglaubt, er müsse nach rechts laufen, aber die Offiziellen zeigten nach links. Pietri fiel auf den nächsten 250 Metern noch viermal hin, das letzte Mal vor der königlichen Loge. Er rappelte sich wieder hoch, aber über die Ziellinie half ihm unter anderen Sir Arthur Conan Doyle (1, rechts, mit Kappe). Dafür wurde Pietri disqualifiziert, und die Goldmedaille ging an den Amerikaner Johnny Hayes.

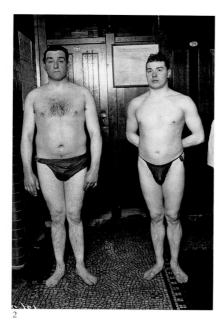

2

PIERRE de Fredi, baron de Coubertin, inaugura en 1896 les Jeux olympiques modernes. Les premiers Jeux olympiques comprenaient des sports dont on ne parlait plus (tel le cricket) ou qui ne se pratiquaient plus, tel le saut en longueur à pieds joints (3). Les tenues étaient en général pudiques et encombrantes, même si les maillots de bain étaient courts, à défaut d'être symétriques (2).

En 1908, le marathon se termina sur un drame poignant. La course avait été rallongée de plus d'un kilomètre et demi sur les instances de la famille royale britannique qui souhaitait la faire débuter sous les fenêtres de la chambre à coucher de la princesse Mary, au château de Windsor. Vers la fin de la course, l'Italien Dorando Pietri fit le premier son entrée dans le stade en disposant d'une avance considérable. Il trébucha et tomba, probablement quand il lui fallut changer de direction : il croyait devoir tourner à droite sur la piste, mais les officiels lui indiquaient la gauche. Pietri tomba encore quatre fois au cours des 250 mètres suivants, la dernière chute eut lieu devant la loge royale. Il se releva péniblement et franchit la ligne d'arrivée (1), aidé notamment par Sir Arthur Conan Doyle (en casquette à droite). Cela valut au pauvre Pietri d'être disqualifié, tandis que la médaille d'or revenait à l'Américain Johnny Hayes.

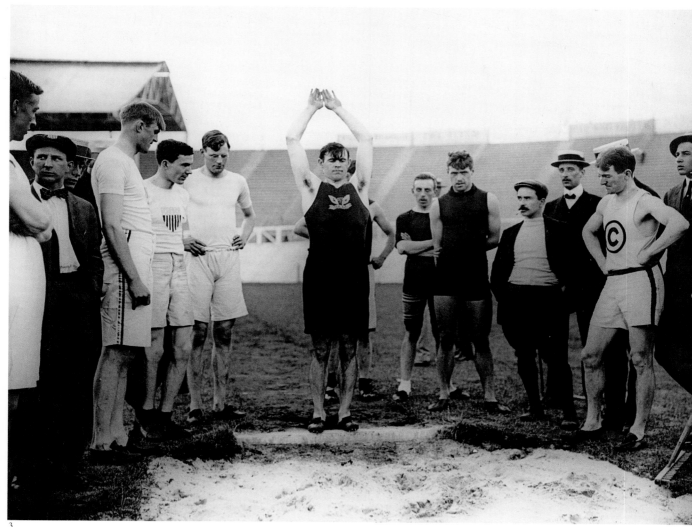

3

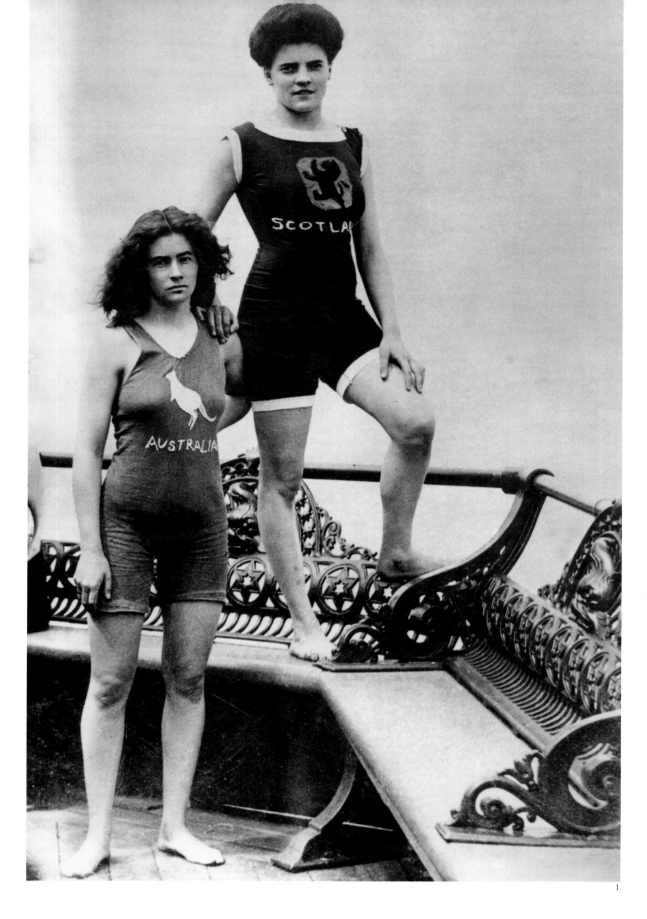

1

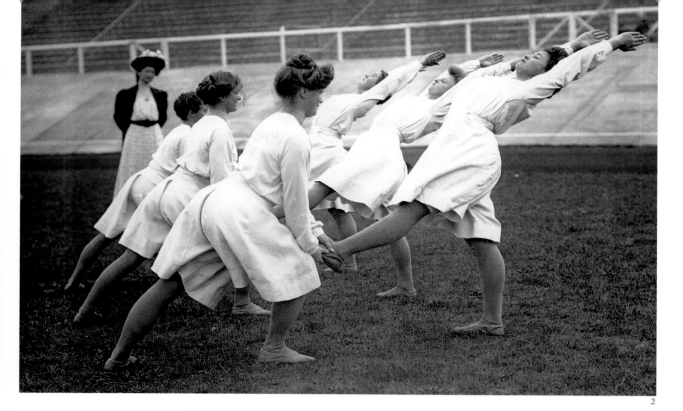

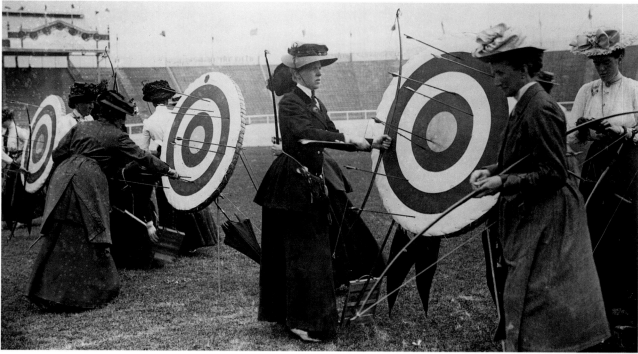

For women, sports costume appeared designed to maintain modesty and impede performance: one-piece bathing costumes in 1907 (1). Danish women gymnasts at the 1908 Olympics (2). Lady archers, sensibly wrapped against the cold of an English July (3).

Sportkleidung für Frauen schien dafür gemacht, den Anstand zu wahren und die Bewegungsfreiheit einzuschränken: einteilige Badeanzüge aus dem Jahre 1907 (1). Die dänischen Gymnastinnen bei der Olympiade von 1908 (2). Weibliche Bogenschützen, gut gegen die Kälte des englischen Juli geschützt (3).

Chez les femmes, le vêtement de sport paraissait conçu pour protéger la pudeur et empêcher toute performance. Pour preuve ces maillots de bain une pièce en 1907 (1). Des gymnastes danoises aux Jeux olympiques de 1908 (2). Ces dames tirant à l'arc étaient judicieusement emmitouflées contre la froidure du mois de juillet en Angleterre (3).

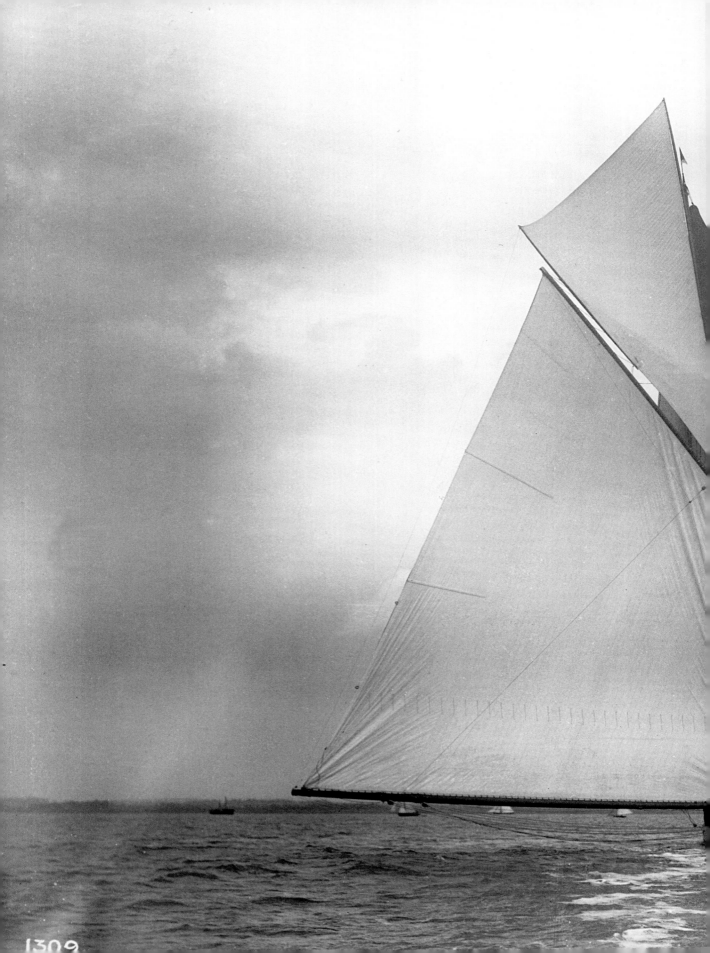

ONE of the highlights of the English 'season' was Cowes
Week, held every August on the Isle of Wight. It was –
and still is – part regatta, part ritual, part opportunity for the
rich to show off (2). Crowds gathered (3) to watch the races
between the graceful yachts, such as *Navahoe* in the 1890s (1).

EINER der Höhepunkte der englischen »Saison« war die
Cowes Week, die jedes Jahr im August auf der Isle of
Wight stattfand. Sie war und ist noch immer zum Teil Regatta,
zum Teil Ritual und zum Teil eine Gelegenheit für die
Reichen, ihren Wohlstand zu zeigen (2). Menschentrauben
bildeten sich (3), um das Rennen der prächtigen Jachten zu
sehen, beispielsweise die *Navahoe* in den 1890er Jahren (1).

L'UN des grands événements de la « saison » anglaise était
la Cowes Week qui se tenait chaque année au mois d'août
sur l'Île de Wight. Il s'agissait, et il s'agit toujours, à la fois
d'une régate, d'un rituel et d'une occasion de se montrer pour
les riches (2). La foule s'entassait sur la plage (3) pour suivre la
course que se livraient les gracieux yachts, tel le *Navahoe* ici au
cours d'une régate dans les années 1890 (1).

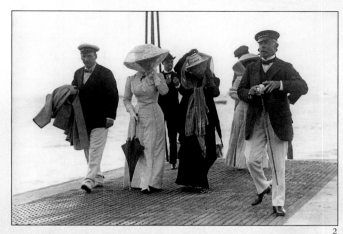

2

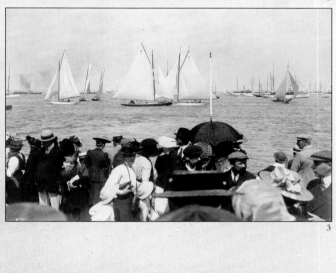

3

Entertainment

'THERE is a range of imagination in most of us,' wrote Charles Dickens, 'which no amount of steam engines will satisfy; and which The-great-exhibition-of-the-works-of-industry-of-all-nations will probably leave unappeased.'

High and low, rich and poor, at home and abroad – what people wanted was fun. And mass migration to towns and cities created lucrative markets for any showman, impresario or theatrical entrepreneur with a few fancy costumes, a portable stage and a voice loud enough to drum up an audience. Crowds flocked to theatres, music halls, cabarets, concerts in the park, and, later, the new bioscopes and cinemas. Top performers earned fortunes, were courted by kings and princes, commanded adoring devotion. Those at the foot of the bill raced from one venue to another, performing six, seven, eight shows a night, until their throats were hoarse and their feet bled. The show had to go on – somehow, somewhere – though audiences were too often crushed or choked or burnt to death in appalling blazes when gaslit theatres caught fire, or killjoy authorities fought bitter rearguard actions to outlaw the wild abandonment of the Can-Can or the shattering insights of an Ibsen play.

In major cities centres of pleasure evolved – Montmartre, Schwabing, Soho – bohemian quarters frequented by the artistic and the raffish, by socialites, intellectuals and tourists, rambling 'up and down the boulevards without encountering anything more exciting than the representatives of loitering and licensed vice' (Guy de Maupassant, *An Adventure in Paris*). Much popular entertainment sprang from poor country roots – the Neapolitan *canzone*, the Spanish *flamenco*, the Argentinian *tango*, the Wild West show. Some had a veneer of glib sophistication, of city slickness – the music hall, the burlesque theatre, the cabaret. All attracted audiences of all classes: from the nobs, swells and mashers who could afford to turn the pretty heads of chorus girls with champagne suppers, and of leading ladies with a good deal more, to the scruffy hecklers who could scarcely afford the cheapest seats in the house.

Ancient forms of entertainment received new leases of life. P. T. Barnum, the American showman, revived the circus with a mixture of magic and hokum, proving that you could fool most of the people most of the time. Zoos and menageries became more popular than ever before, their exotic exhibits augmented by the plunder of jungle and steppe, veldt and prairie. Travelling fairs brought a diet of sword-swallowing and fire-eating, and the wonders of the bearded lady, the mermaid and Siamese twins to the gullible of town and country alike. Jules Léotard extended the art of tightrope-walking, and gave his name to the figure-hugging garment, while Blondin walked further and higher, even crossing the mighty Niagara Falls.

The musical comedy was invented in the late 19th century, a popular if initially down-market development from the Savoy light operas of Gilbert and Sullivan. The musical revue was the lavish brainchild of Florence Ziegfeld, an American showman with more money than taste. For the discerning, the highbrow, or the plain snooty, there was a constant supply of new operas. Wagner, the boldest composer the world has known, wrote *The Flying Dutchman* in Paris, fled from Dresden, where he had flirted with revolution and had written *Tannhäuser* and *Lohengrin*, and began work on the *Ring* cycle in Switzerland. Famous and forgiven, he returned to Germany, settled in Ludwig II's Bavaria and staged the first full *Ring* at his new Festival Theatre in Bayreuth. In Italy, the no less revolutionary Verdi composed *Rigoletto*, *Il Trovatore*, *La Traviata*, *Otello* and his swansong comedy *Falstaff*. Less revolutionary, but as popular, were the offerings of Puccini: *Manon Lescaut*, *La Bohème*, *Tosca* and *Madame Butterfly*.

Theatres prospered as never before. It was the era of the great actor-managers – Belasco, Terry, Hicks, Beerbohm Tree, Komisarjevskaya – men and women with big dreams and large voices, who toured from town to town with their own companies of actors, scenery, props and costumes, doing flamboyant justice to anything from Shakespeare to Cinderella. It was the age of Ibsen, Strindberg, the young George Bernard Shaw, the precocious Oscar Wilde, Hauptmann and Hofmannsthal, Chekhov, Echegaray, Feydeau, Lopez de Ayala and Tamayo y Baus, Gorky, Hallstrom and dozens of other great playwrights.

Actors became stars, household names, gods and goddesses – the Divine Sarah, Adelaide Ristori, Mrs Patrick Campbell, Lily Langtry, Charles Fechter, Josef Kainz. And there was one actor who became the devil incarnate in his most famous role – John Wilkes Booth, who crashed into a box at the Ford Theatre in Washington DC, to interrupt a performance of Tom Taylor's *Our American Cousin* and assassinate the President of the United States.

Until 1850, the Romantic movement in art, literature and music had imposed restrictions on ballet.

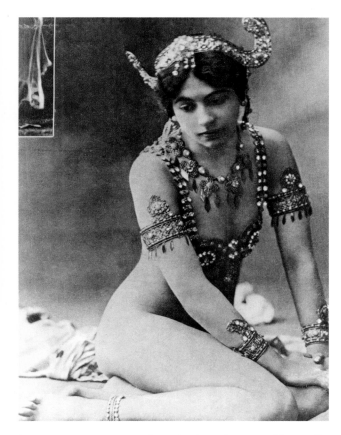

Dancers were expected to look and move like well-drilled sylphs or phantoms. After 1850, costumes became shorter, music more exciting, choreography bolder. Ballet became more athletic and dramatic, fuelled by the music of Delibes, Tchaikovsky and later Stravinsky. Dancers such as Pavlova, Karsavina, Nijinsky, Massine and Isadora Duncan leapt and pirouetted their way into international fame.

Mass education led to a rapidly growing appetite for literature. There was a huge market for the novels of Dickens and Thackeray, Freytag, Zola, the brothers Goncourt, Dumas *père et fils*, Hugo, Henry James and Thomas Hardy. Sir Arthur Conan Doyle created the greatest fictional detective of all time in 1887, when Sherlock Holmes first appeared in *A Study in Scarlet*. Robert Louis Stevenson unleashed *The Strange Case of Dr Jekyll and Mr Hyde* in 1886, and Alice disappeared down the rabbit hole into Wonderland for the first time in 1865.

Finally, it was also the age when the sensuality of Delacroix and the convention of massive historical paintings gave way to the bright purity of the Pre-Raphaelites and the shimmering beauty of the Impressionists. In 1894, Don Jose Ruiz handed his paints and brushes to his son Pablo Picasso, and the world was never quite the same again. And, all the while, the camera captured the world's beauties, its freaks and horrors, its bizarre and wonderful happenings.

»Es gibt einen Bereich der Phantasie in den meisten von uns«, schrieb Charles Dickens, »den noch so viele Dampfmaschinen nicht zufriedenstellen können und den Die-große-Ausstellung-der-Industrieprodukte-aller-Nationen vermutlich kaltläßt.«

Von hoher oder niedriger Geburt, arm oder reich, zu Hause oder im Ausland – die Menschen wollten sich amüsieren. Und mit der Abwanderung der Massen in die Großstädte entstanden lukrative Märkte für Schausteller, Impresarios und Theaterbesitzer, die ein paar verrückte Kostüme, eine transportable Bühne und eine Stimme besaßen, die laut genug war, das Publikum neugierig zu machen. Die Menschen strömten in die Theater, Musikhallen, Kabaretts, Konzerte im Park und später in die neuen Bioskope und Lichtspieltheater. Die Stars dieser Veranstaltungen verdienten ein Vermögen, wurden von Königen und Prinzen verehrt und von den Massen bewundert. Die weniger Berühmten eilten von einer Veranstaltung zur nächsten und traten in sechs, sieben oder acht Vorführungen pro Abend auf, bis ihre Kehlen rauh waren und ihre Füße bluteten. Die Show mußte irgendwie und irgendwo weitergehen, obwohl das Publikum nur allzuoft zerquetscht wurde, erstickte oder verbrannte, wenn in mit Gas beleuchteten Theatern Feuer ausbrach. Gefahr ging auch von der Obrigkeit aus, die keinen Spaß verstand und sich in erbitterte Kämpfe stürzte, um den wilden, hemmungslosen Cancan oder die erschütternde Botschaft eines Ibsen-Stückes zu unterbinden.

In den großen Städten entstanden Vergnügungszentren – Montmartre, Schwabing, Soho – Künstlerviertel, die von den Schöngeistern, der Bohème, der feinen Gesellschaft, von Intellektuellen und Touristen aufgesucht wurden, die »die Boulevards entlangschlenderten, ohne auf etwas Aufregenderes zu stoßen als auf die herumstehenden Vertreter und Vertreterinnen des lizensierten Lasters« (Guy de Maupassant, *Une aventure parisienne*). Viele der populären Veranstaltungen hatten ihre Wurzeln in armen, ländlichen Regionen, z. B. die neapolitanische *Canzone*, der spanische *Flamenco*, der argentinische *Tango* oder die Wild-West-Show. Einige wiesen eine gewisse Eleganz und die Gewandtheit der Großstadt auf, wie beispielsweise das Varietétheater und das Kabarett. Sie alle zogen Zuschauer aller Klassen an: von »hohen Tieren« mit Rang und Namen, oder Frauenhelden, die es sich leisten konnten, den schönen Revuegirls den Kopf mit Champagner-Soupers und den der Damen der Gesellschaft mit weit Kostbarerem zu verdrehen, bis zu den verwegenen Schreihälsen, die kaum die billigsten Plätze des Hauses bezahlen konnten.

Frühe Formen des Entertainments erlebten einen neuen Aufschwung. P. T. Barnum, der amerikanische Schausteller, belebte den Zirkus mit einer Mischung aus Zauberei und Hokuspokus und zeigte, daß man die

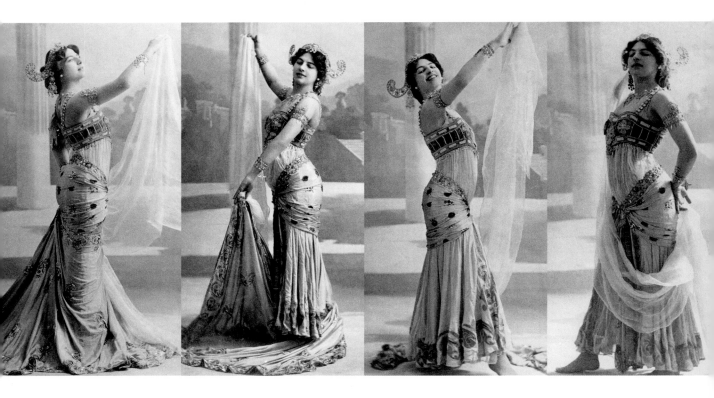

MATA HARI WAS THE DAUGHTER OF A PROSPEROUS HATTER. HER REAL NAME WAS MARGARETHA GEERTRUIDA ZELLE. HER *DANCE OF THE SEVEN VEILS* WAS A SENSATIONAL SUCCESS, BUT HER CAREER IN ESPIONAGE WASN'T. SHE WAS SHOT AS A SPY IN OCTOBER 1917.

MATA HARI WAR DIE TOCHTER EINES WOHLHABENDEN HUTMACHERS. SIE HIESS EIGENTLICH MARGARETHA GEERTRUIDA ZELLE. IHR *TANZ DER SIEBEN SCHLEIER* WAR EIN SENSATIONELLER ERFOLG, GANZ IM GEGENSATZ ZU IHRER KARRIERE ALS SPIONIN. OB SIE DEN DEUTSCHEN VON NUTZEN GEWESEN IST, BLEIBT UNGEWISS. SIE WURDE IM OKTOBER 1917 ALS SPIONIN ERSCHOSSEN.

MATA HARI ÉTAIT LA FILLE D'UN CHAPELIER PROSPÈRE. ELLE SE NOMMAIT EN FAIT MARGARETHA GEERTRUIDA ZELLE. SI SA *DANSE DES SEPT VOILES* REMPORTA UN VIF SUCCÈS, CE NE FUT GUÈRE LE CAS DE SA CARRIÈRE D'ESPIONNE. ELLE FUT EN EFFET FUSILLÉE POUR ESPIONNAGE EN OCTOBRE 1917.

meisten Leute fast immer an der Nase herumführen kann. Zoos und Menagerien wurden beliebter als jemals zuvor, und ihre exotischen Ausstellungsstücke vermehrten sich durch die Plünderung der Urwälder, Steppen und Prärien. Fahrende Jahrmärkte zeigten den Leichtgläubigen von Stadt und Land Schwert- und Feuerschlucker, das Wunder der bärtigen Jungfrau, Nixen und siamesische Zwillinge. Jules Léotard perfektionierte die Kunst des Seiltanzes und gab dem figurbetonten Anzug seinen Namen, während sein Kollege Blondin immer weiter und immer höher kletterte und sogar die Niagarafälle überquerte.

Das Musical wurde gegen Ende des 19. Jahrhunderts erfunden, eine populäre, wenn auch anfänglich weniger anspruchsvolle Weiterentwicklung der leichten Opern von Gilbert und Sullivan aus dem Savoy. Die musikalische Revue war der lebhaften Phantasie von Florence Ziegfeld entsprungen, einem amerikanischen Showman mit mehr Geld als Geschmack. Für die Anspruchsvolleren, die Intellektuellen und die Hochnäsigen gab es ein reichhaltiges Angebot an Opern. Wagner, der kühne Komponist, schrieb den *Fliegenden Holländer* in Paris, floh aus Dresden, wo er mit der Revolution geliebäugelt, den *Tannhäuser* und den *Lohengrin* geschrieben hatte, und begann seine Arbeit am *Ring des Nibelungen* in der Schweiz. Dem berühmten Mann war vergeben worden, und er kehrte nach Deutschland zurück, ließ sich im Bayern Ludwigs II. nieder und führte erstmals den kompletten *Ring* in seinem neuen Bayreuther Festspieltheater auf. In Italien komponierte der nicht weniger revolutionäre Verdi *Rigoletto, Il Trovatore, La Traviata, Otello* und *Falstaff*. Nicht so revolutionär, aber ebenso populär waren die Werke von Puccini: *Manon Lescaut, La Bohème, Tosca* und *Madame Butterfly*.

Die Theater florierten wie niemals zuvor. Es war die Zeit der großen Schauspieler-Manager wie Belasco,

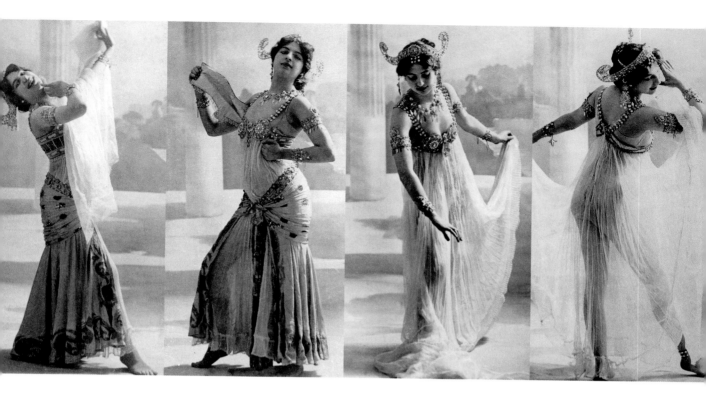

Terry, Hicks, Beerbohm Tree, Komisarjewskaja — Männer und Frauen mit großen Träumen und vollen Stimmen, die mit ihren eigenen Ensembles, Bühnendekorationen und Kostümen von Stadt zu Stadt zogen und alles von Shakespeare bis Cinderella aufführten. Es war die Zeit von Ibsen, Strindberg, dem jungen George Bernard Shaw, dem frühreifen Oscar Wilde, Hauptmann, Hofmannsthal, Tschechow, Echegaray, Feydeau, Lopez de Ayala und Tamayo y Baus, Gorki, Hallstrom und unzähliger anderer großer Dramatiker.

Schauspieler wurden zu Stars, zu Inbegriffen, zu Göttern und Göttinnen — die göttliche Sarah, Adelaide Ristori, Mrs. Patrick Campbell, Lily Langtry, Charles Fechter und Josef Kainz. Und es gab einen Schauspieler, der in seiner berühmtesten Rolle zum Teufel in Person wurde: John Wilkes Booth stürmte bei einer Aufführung von Tom Taylors *Our American Cousin* in eine Loge des Ford Theatres in Washington D. C. und tötete den Präsidenten der Vereinigten Staaten.

Bis 1850 hatte die romantische Bewegung in Kunst, Literatur und Musik dem Ballett Beschränkungen auferlegt. Die Tänzer sollten wie gedrillte Nymphen und Phantome aussehen und sich auch so bewegen. Nach 1850 wurden die Kostüme kürzer, die Musik aufregender und die Choreographie gewagter. Zu den Klängen der Musik von Delibes, Tschaikowsky und später Strawinsky wurde das Ballett athletischer und dramatischer. Tänzer wie Pawlowa, Karsawina, Nijinsky, Massine und Isadora Duncan bahnten sich mit ihren Sprüngen und Pirouetten den Weg zu internationalem Ruhm.

Ein allen zugängliches Bildungs- und Erziehungswesen führte bald zu einem wachsenden Hunger nach Literatur. Es gab eine große Nachfrage nach den Romanen von Dickens und Thackeray, Freytag, Émile Zola, der Brüder Goncourt, von Vater und Sohn Dumas, Victor Hugo, Henry James und Thomas Hardy. Sir Arthur Conan Doyle schuf 1887 den größten Romandetektiv aller Zeiten: sein Sherlock Holmes trat erstmals in *A Study in Scarlet* auf. Robert Louis Stevenson gab 1886 *The Strange Case of Dr Jekyll and Mr Hyde* heraus, und Alice verschwand zum ersten Mal 1865 durch den Hasenbau ins Wunderland.

Es war auch die Zeit, da die Sinnlichkeit eines Delacroix und die Konventionen der gewaltigen Historiengemälde der strahlenden Reinheit der Präraffaeliten und der glänzenden Schönheit der Impressionisten wichen. Im Jahre 1894 übergab Don José Ruiz Farben und Pinsel seinem Sohn Pablo Picasso, und die Welt war seitdem nicht mehr dieselbe. In dieser Zeit fing der Photoapparat mehr und mehr die Schönheiten der Welt ein, ihre Absonderlichkeiten und Schrecken, ihre bizarren und wunderbaren Begebenheiten.

CHARLES Dickens écrivait : « La plupart d'entre nous ont une imagination effrénée que ne sauraient satisfaire les engins à vapeur, aussi nombreux soient-ils, et que la-fabuleuse-exposition-des-œuvres-de-l'industrie-de-toutes-les-nations laissera sans doute sur sa faim. »

Quelle que fût leur condition, qu'ils fussent riches ou pauvres, dans leur pays natal ou à l'étranger, les gens voulaient s'amuser. D'autre part, les grandes migrations vers les villes et les cités ouvraient des perspectives lucratives à n'importe quel forain, impresario ou entrepreneur de théâtre possédant quelques costumes, une scène portative et une voix suffisamment forte pour faire accourir les foules. On se précipitait au théâtre, aux variétés, au cabaret, aux concerts du parc, et plus tard dans les salles de projection assister aux balbutiements du cinéma. Les meilleurs artistes gagnaient des fortunes, étaient courtisés par les rois et les princes, objets d'adoration et de dévotion. Les gagne-petit couraient d'un spectacle à l'autre, exécutant six, sept, huit représentations dans la même nuit jusqu'à en avoir la voix enrouée et les pieds en sang. Le spectacle devait continuer quelque part, d'une manière ou d'une autre, même si pour cela le public devait trop souvent se retrouver entassé, voire écrasé ou encore risquer de périr brûlé dans les effroyables incendies qui éclataient dans les théâtres éclairés au gaz. Les pouvoirs publics livraient des batailles perdues d'avance pour interdire le cancan et ses débordements licencieux ou encore une pièce d'Ibsen bouleversante de lucidité.

Dans les grandes villes s'épanouissaient les centres de plaisirs – Montmartre, Schwabing, Soho – quartiers de bohème fréquentés par les artistes et les libertins, les gens de la haute, les intellectuels et les touristes parcourant « ...les boulevards sans rien voir, sinon le vice errant et numéroté ». (Guy de Maupassant, *Une aventure parisienne*). Bien des divertissements populaires étaient originaires des pays pauvres : le *canzone* napolitain, le *flamenco* espagnol, le *tango* argentin, le spectacle de l'Ouest sauvage. Certains avaient le vernis de l'improvisation nonchalante et de la superficialité citadine comme les variétés, le théâtre burlesque et le cabaret. Leur point commun était d'attirer les publics de toutes classes : des sommités, des élégants et des don juans – qui se proposaient de tourner les jolies têtes des filles de la troupe par des soupers au champagne, et celles des actrices principales en y mettant déjà de plus gros moyens – jusqu'aux gêneurs sans-le-sou qui pouvaient tout juste s'offrir une place bon marché.

D'anciennes formes de divertissement étaient remises à l'honneur. P. T. Barnum, un forain américain, ranima le cirque en lui conférant un mélange de magie et de niaiserie, prouvant ainsi que l'on peut presque toujours faire prendre aux gens des vessies pour des lanternes. Les zoos et les ménageries connaissaient un succès sans précédent et présentaient de plus en plus d'attractions exotiques grâce au pillage de la jungle et de la steppe, du veldt et de la prairie. Les fêtes foraines servaient des avaleurs de sabres et des cracheurs de feu, d'« incroyables » femmes à barbe, sirènes et sœurs siamoises aux gogos des villes et des campagnes. Jules Léotard perfectionna l'art du funambule en donnant son nom au maillot moulant, pendant que Blondin allait plus loin, plus haut et traversait même les puissantes chutes du Niagara. Céline Celeste ouvrit la voie au mime moderne.

La comédie musicale fut inventée à la fin du XIXe siècle. C'était une variante très appréciée, bien qu'au départ d'origine populaire, des opéras légers de Gilbert et Sullivan au Savoy. La revue musicale était la somptueuse trouvaille de Florence Ziegfeld, forain américain qui possédait plus d'argent que de goût. Pour ceux qui faisaient des manières, pour les intellectuels ou les snobs, les nouveaux opéras ne manquaient pas. Wagner, le compositeur le plus hardi que le monde ait connu, écrivit *Le Vaisseau fantôme* à Paris, s'enfuit de Dresde où il avait flirté avec la révolution, écrivit *Tannhäuser* et *Lohengrin* et entama son cycle de *L'Anneau* en Suisse. Célèbre et pardonné, il retourna s'établir en Allemagne dans la Bavière de Louis II où il monta, dans le nouveau théâtre de Bayreuth consacré au festival de ses œuvres, la première représentation complète de *L'Anneau*. En Italie, le non moins révolutionnaire Verdi composait *Rigoletto*, *Il Trovatore*, *La Traviata*, *Othello* ainsi que la comédie qui fut son chant du cygne, *Falstaff*. Moins révolutionnaires mais tout aussi populaires étaient les offrandes de Puccini : *Manon Lescaut*, *La Bohème*, *Tosca* et *Madame Butterfly*.

Les théâtres prospéraient comme jamais auparavant. C'était l'époque des grands directeurs de compagnie – Belasco, Terry, Hicks, Beerbohm Tree, Komisarjevskaya – d'hommes et de femmes qui avaient de grands rêves et de puissantes voix, qui partaient faire la tournée des villes avec leurs propres troupes de comédiens, leurs décors, leurs accessoires et leurs costumes, et qui rendaient brillamment justice à tout, de Shakespeare à Cendrillon. C'était l'époque d'Ibsen, de Strindberg, du jeune George Bernard Shaw, du précoce Oscar Wilde, d'Hauptmann et d'Hofmannsthal, de Tchekhov, d'Echegaray, de Feydeau, de Lopez de Ayala et de Tamayo y Baus, de Gorki, de Hallstrom et de dizaines d'autres grands dramaturges.

Les comédiens devenaient des vedettes, des noms familiers, des dieux et des déesses, tels la divine Sarah, Adelaide Ristori, Madame Patrick Campbell, Lily Langtry, Charles Fechter et Josef Kainz. Un comédien s'incarna lui-même en démon dans son rôle le plus fameux. Il s'agit de John Wilkes Booth qui se rua dans une loge au Ford Theatre de Washington DC en inter-

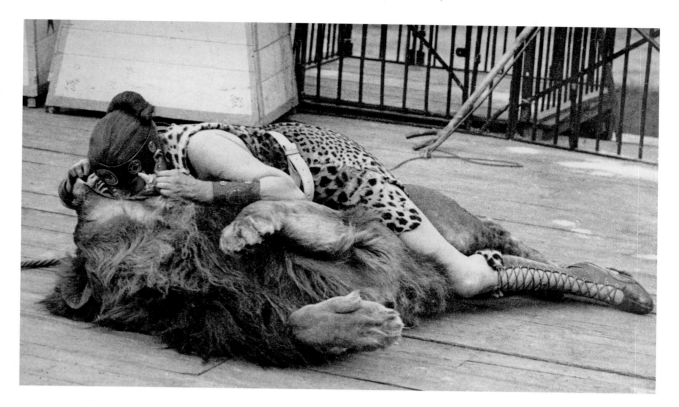

CIRCUS ACT. CIRCUSES WERE EXTREMELY POPULAR.
DER ZIRKUS WAR ÄUSSERST BELIEBT.
LES CIRQUES CONNAISSAIENT UNE TRÈS GRANDE POPULARITÉ.

rompant la représentation du *Our American Cousin* de Tom Taylor pour assassiner le président des États-Unis.

Jusqu'en 1850, le mouvement romantique illustré dans l'art, dans la littérature et dans la musique avait imposé des contraintes au ballet. On attendait des danseurs qu'ils ressemblent à des sylphes ou des fantômes exercés qui se déplacent à l'avenant. Après 1850, les costumes raccourcirent, la musique s'emporta et la chorégraphie s'enhardit. Le ballet devenait plus athlétique et plus dramatique sur des musiques de Delibes, Tchaïkovski et plus tard Stravinski. Les sauts et les pirouettes de Pavlova, Karsavina, Nijinski, Massine et Isadora Duncan valurent à ces danseurs une renommée internationale.

L'instruction populaire entraîna un appétit de littérature qui grandit rapidement. Il existait un énorme marché pour les romans de Dickens et de Thackeray, de Freytag, de Zola, des frères Goncourt, des Dumas père et fils, d'Hugo, d'Henry James et de Thomas Hardy. Sir Arthur Conan Doyle créa en 1887 la plus grande figure de détective de tous les temps lorsque Sherlock Holmes

apparut pour la première fois dans *A Study in Scarlet*. Robert Louis Stevenson dévoila *The Strange case of Dr Jekyll and Mr Hyde* en 1886, tandis qu'Alice disparaissait pour la première fois en 1865 dans le trou de lapin qui allait la mener au Pays des merveilles.

Enfin, ce fut aussi à cette époque que la sensualité de Delacroix et les vastes fresques historiques conventionnelles cédèrent la place à la pureté brillante du mouvement des préraphaélites et à la beauté scintillante des impressionnistes. En 1894, don José Ruiz passait ses tubes de peinture et ses pinceaux à son fils, Pablo Picasso : après lui, le monde ne serait plus jamais le même. Pendant ce temps, l'appareil photographique ne cessait de capter les beautés du monde, ses extravagances et ses horreurs, ses bizarreries et ses merveilles.

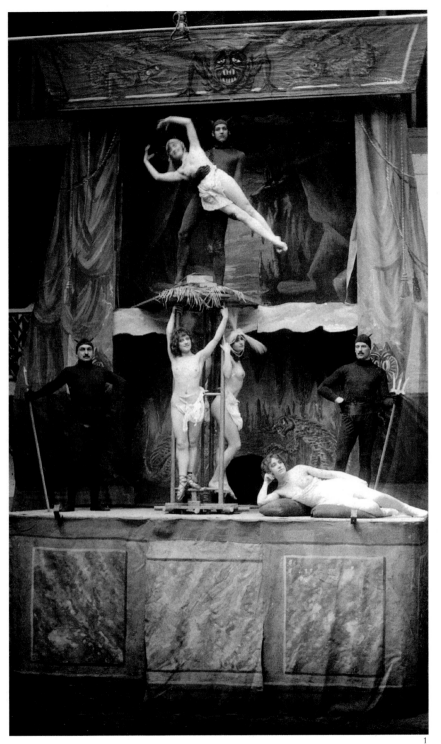

1

BY reputation the most shocking city in the world was Paris, and its decadent focus was Montmartre (1). The daring of *fin-de-siècle* Paris was typified by the Moulin Rouge, home of the infamous, noisy, brash Can-Can (2, 4). Dancers at the Moulin Rouge became celebrities in their own right, their fame spreading through the posters and paintings of Henri de Toulouse-Lautrec (3, with Tremolada, the Director of the Moulin Rouge). Some Can-Can dancers made wealthy marriages. One of the most famous, La Goulue (5), was reduced to opening her own fairground booth as her talents faded.

PARIS stand in dem Ruf, die berüchtigste Stadt der Welt zu sein, und das Zentrum ihrer Dekadenz war Montmartre (1). Die Verkörperung des aufregenden Paris des *Fin de siècle* war das Moulin Rouge, die Heimat des berüchtigten, lauten Cancan (2, 4). Die Tänzerinnen des Moulin Rouge wurden zu Berühmtheiten, und ihr Ruhm vermehrte sich durch die Plakate und Gemälde von Henri de Toulouse-Lautrec (3, mit Tremolada, dem Direktor des Moulin Rouge). Einige Cancan-Tänzerinnen heirateten reiche Männer. Eine der berühmtesten, La Goulue (5), war gezwungen, eine Jahrmarktsbude zu eröffnen, als ihr Talent nachließ.

PARIS avait la réputation d'être la cité la plus choquante du monde, et Montmartre son centre décadent (1). Les audaces de ce Paris-là se retrouvaient toutes entières au Moulin-Rouge qui popularisait l'infâme cancan, si bruyant et fripon (2 et 4). Les danseuses du Moulin-Rouge jouissaient d'une célébrité qu'elles ne devaient qu'à elles-mêmes, propagée par les affiches et les tableaux d'Henri de Toulouse-Lautrec (3, en compagnie de Tremolada, le directeur du Moulin-Rouge). Certaines danseuses de cancan épousèrent des hommes très riches. Une des plus célèbres, La Goulue (5) en fut pourtant réduite, après avoir brûlé les planches, à ouvrir son propre stand sur un champ de foire.

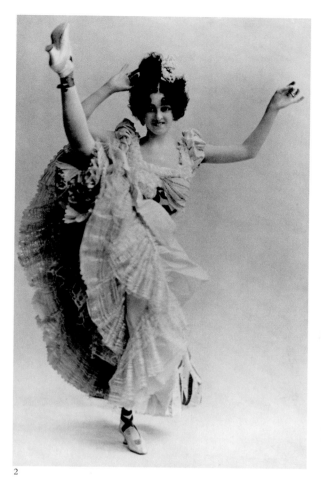

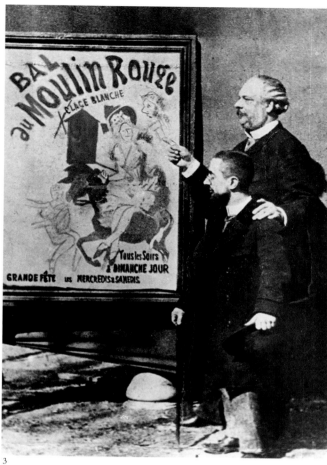

2

3

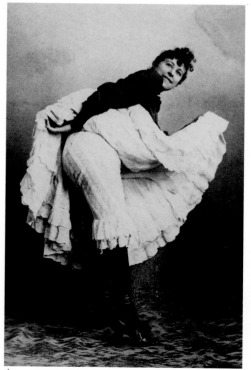

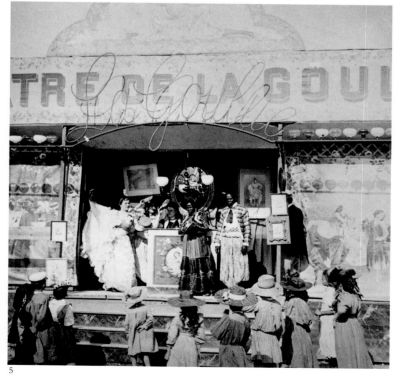

4

5

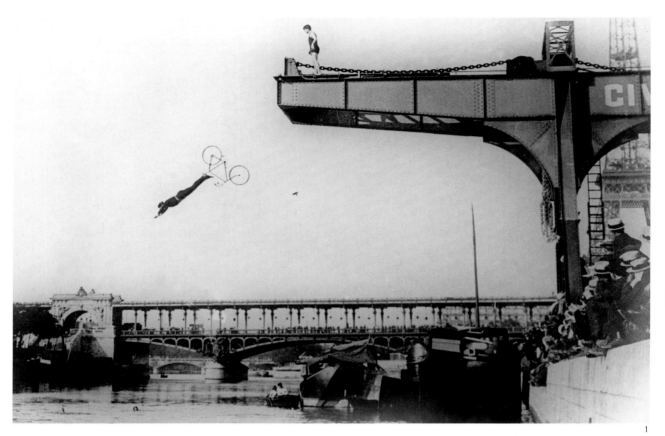

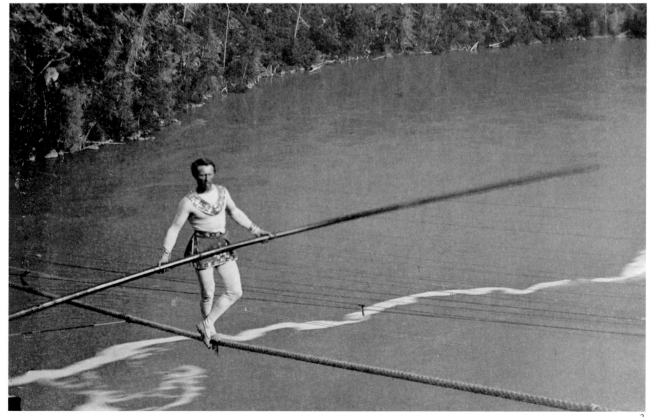

MANY acrobats – as these in London (3) – performed in the streets, a thin mat marking out their stage on the rough pavement. In Mexico (4) the Strong Señorita and the Clown's Baby Act would have had a softer landing in the sand. The greater the novelty, the bigger the crowd – hundreds of Parisians watched Gaston Mourand dive on his bicycle into the Seine at 'Swan's Island' (1). Perhaps the most famous circus performer of all time, Blondin was photographed by William England crossing Niagara Falls in 1859 (2).

WIE diese Londoner Akrobaten (3) führten viele ihre Kunststücke auf der Straße auf, wobei ihnen eine dünne Matte als Bühne auf dem harten Gehsteig diente. Die starken Señoritas und das kleine Mädchen in Mexiko (4) hatten vermutlich eine weichere Landung im Sand. Je größer die Sensation, desto größer die Zuschauermenge; Hunderte von Parisern sahen zu, wie Gaston Mourand mit seinem Fahrrad in der Nähe der »Schwaneninsel« in die Seine eintauchte (1). Der vielleicht berühmteste Zirkusartist aller Zeiten war Blondin, hier auf einer Photographie von William England beim Überqueren der Niagarafälle im Jahre 1859 (2).

DE nombreux acrobates, tels ceux-ci à Londres, (3) exécutaient leurs numéros dans les rues sur un mince paillasson qui délimitait la scène au milieu du trottoir. Au Mexique (4), Madame Muscle et Bébé clown faisaient un atterrissage plus moelleux dans le sable. Plus la nouveauté était grande et plus elle attirait de monde : des centaines de Parisiens regardent Gaston Mourand plonger dans la Seine sur sa bicyclette du haut de l'Île au Cygne (1). Le plus grand artiste de cirque de tous les temps fut peut-être Blondin, photographié ici en 1859 par William England en train de traverser les chutes du Niagara (2).

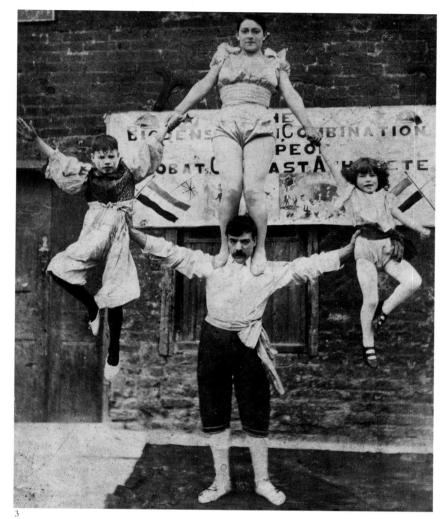

3

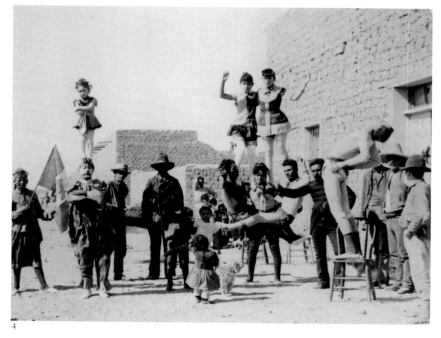

4

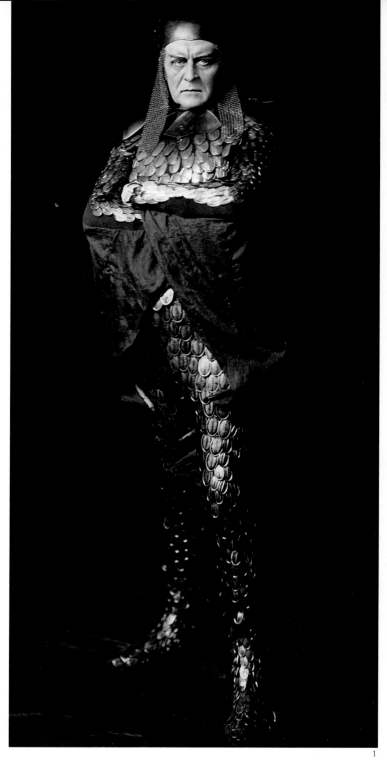

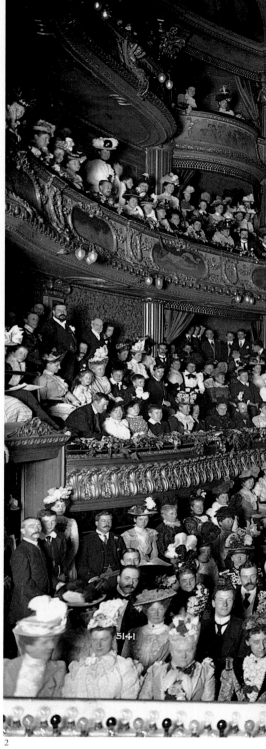

1   2

Sir Herbert Draper Beerbohm Tree was one of the greatest of all actor-managers. He staged lavish and spectacular productions of most of Shakespeare's plays, as well as the first performances of Wilde's *A Woman of No Importance* (1893) and Shaw's *Pygmalion* (1914), in which Tree created the part of Professor Higgins. His most fearsome role was that of Mephis-topheles in Marlowe's *Doctor Faustus* (1). Many of his greatest successes were staged at the Haymarket Theatre (2), though by 1899, when this photograph was taken, Tree had moved to Her Majesty's.

Sir Herbert Draper Beerbohm Tree war einer der berühmtesten Schauspieler-Manager. Er inszenierte spektakuläre Aufführungen der meisten Shakespeare-Stücke sowie die erste Aufführung von Oscar Wildes *A Woman of No Importance* (1893) und Shaws *Pygmalion* (1914), in der Tree

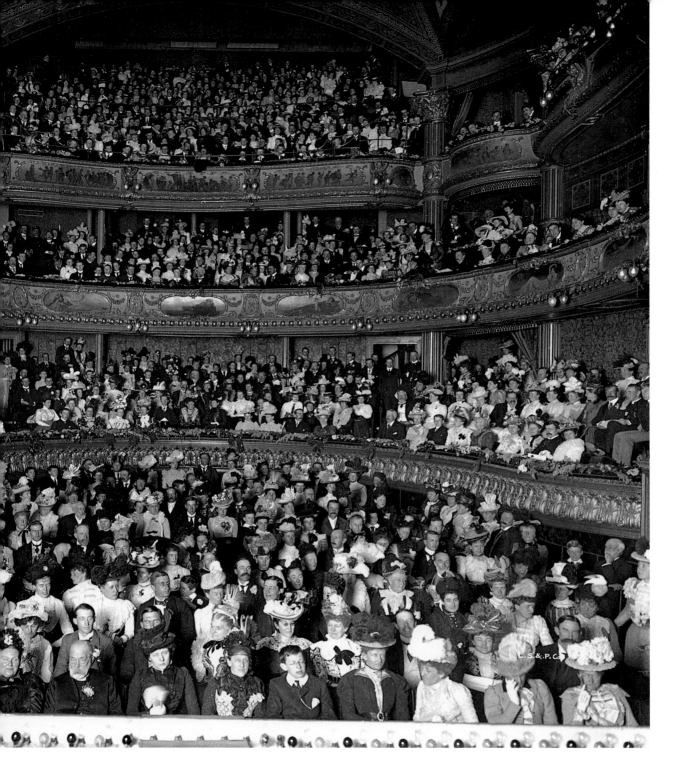

selbst die Rolle des Professor Higgins spielte. Seine furchterregendste Rolle war jedoch die des Mephistopheles in Marlowes *Doctor Faustus* (1). Viele seiner großen Erfolge feierte er im Haymarket Theatre (2). 1899, als diese Aufnahme gemacht wurde, hatte er bereits zum königlichen Theater gewechselt.

SIR Herbert Draper Beerbohm Tree était un des plus grands directeurs de compagnie. Il monta des productions somptueuses et spectaculaires de la plupart des pièces de Shakespeare, ainsi que les premières représentations de *A Woman of No Importance* (1893) d'Oscar Wilde et du *Pygmalion* de Shaw (1914), dans lequel

il créa le personnage du professeur Higgins. Son rôle le plus effrayant fut celui de Méphistophélès dans le *Doctor Faustus* de Marlowe (1). Beaucoup de ses plus grands succès furent montés au théâtre de Haymarket (2), bien qu'en 1899, Tree eût déjà déménagé au Her Majesty's Theatre.

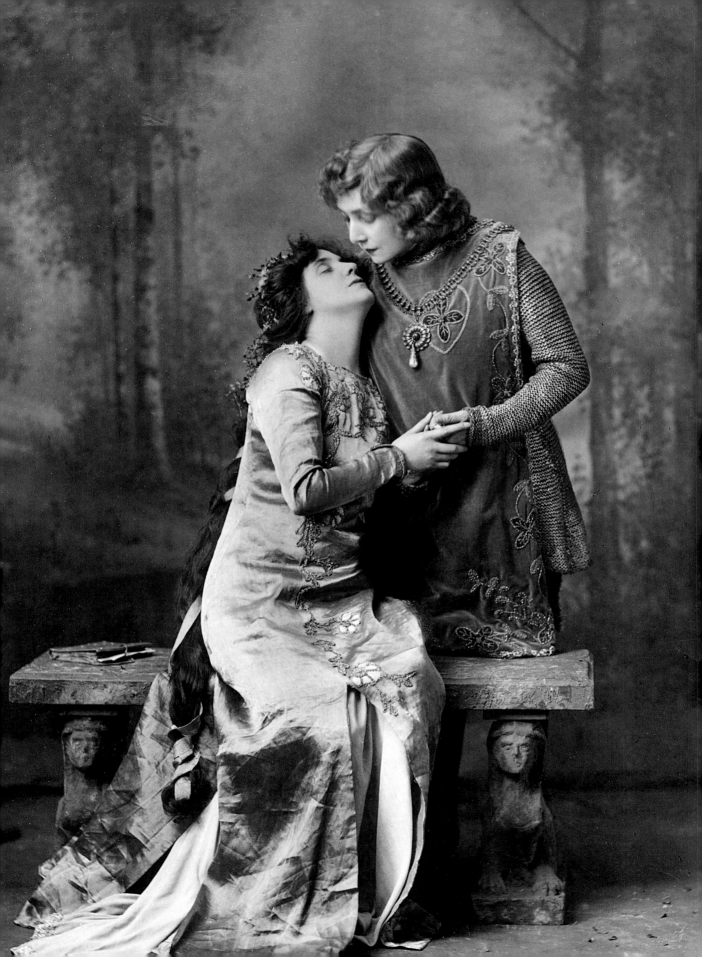

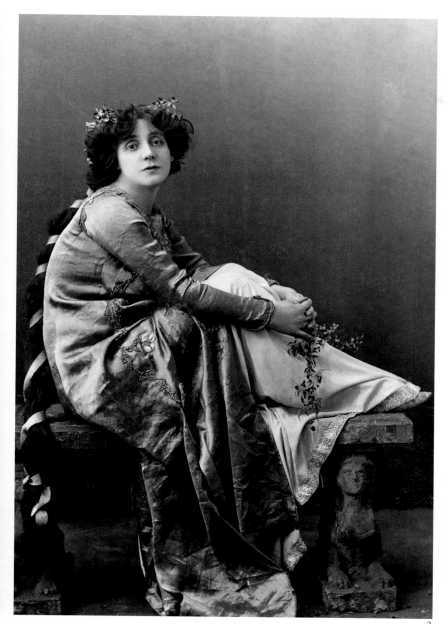

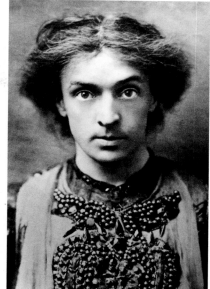

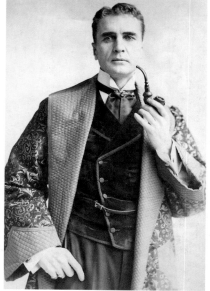

IN 1904 the 60-year-old Sarah Bernhardt went to London to play Pelléas opposite Mrs Patrick Campbell's Mélisande (1) – a romantic duo with the combined age of 99 years. Campbell (2) once described her then recent marriage as: 'the deep, deep peace of the double bed after the hurly-burly of the chaise-longue'. Martin Harvey (3), possibly a more likely Pelléas, was another famous actor-manager. William Gillette (4), an American, adapted and took the lead in the first stage production of *Sherlock Holmes*.

IM Jahre 1904 kam die sechzigjährige Sarah Bernhardt nach London, um an der Seite von Mrs. Patrick Campbell als Mélisande den Pelléas zu spielen (1) – ein romantisches Paar, das zusammen 99 Jahre zählte. Mrs. Campbell (2) beschrieb ihre damals noch junge Ehe als »den tiefen, tiefen Frieden des Ehebetts nach der Hektik der Chaiselongue«. Martin Harvey (3), vermutlich ein geeigneterer Pelléas, war ebenfalls ein bekannter Schauspieler-Manager. Der Amerikaner William Gillette (4) adaptierte den *Sherlock Holmes* erstmals für die Bühne und spielte selbst die Hauptrolle.

EN 1904, Sarah Bernhardt âgée de 60 ans se rendit à Londres pour jouer Pelléas, avec Madame Campbell dans le rôle de Mélisande (1) pour lui donner la réplique. Elles totalisaient 99 ans à elles deux. Campbell (2) avait un jour décrit son mariage alors récent comme « la profonde, profonde paix du grand lit après les tumultes de la chaise longue ». Martin Harvey (3), un Pelléas certainement plus vraisemblable, était lui aussi un directeur de compagnie célèbre. L'Américain William Gillette (4) adapta au théâtre les premiers *Sherlock Holmes*, dans lesquels il joua le rôle principal.

Arts

BALLET had shaken off the restraints and stiff formality of its courtly origins in the early 19th century. Dancing became more ethereal, and yet also more gymnastic, with the focus very much on the female dancer. Emma Pitteri (1) was the most fêted ballerina of the 1860s, though destined to die in squalid obscurity many years later while appearing in a dance hall on the Marseilles dockside.

From the middle of the century to the First World War, ballet employed huge forces. There were spectacular new works, new companies, new choreographers. Delibes, Tchaikovsky and Stravinsky wrote the most famous ballet scores of all time. Fokine, Bolm and Nijinsky brought new athleticism to ballet and restored the role of the male dancer; Duncan eschewed the style of dancing on points epitomized by the classical ballerina (2). It was a far cry from the quaint rigidity of the two dancers photographed by the London Stereoscopic Company in the 1860s (3) to Nijinsky's spectacular leap in *Spectre de la Rose*.

The finest dancing and the finest dancers came from the Russian Imperial School of Ballet in St Petersburg. Graduates toured Europe and the Americas, and found dancing standards considerably lower than those in Russia. Like missionaries of old, they brought their ideals (and, unlike missionaries, their genius) to companies all over the world.

ZU Beginn des 19. Jahrhunderts hatte das Ballett die Zurückhaltung und die steife Förmlichkeit seiner höfischen Ursprünge abgelegt. Die Tänze wurden ätherischer, aber gleichzeitig auch akrobatischer, und der männliche Tänzer stand deutlich im Mittelpunkt. Emma Pitteri (1) war die meistgefeierte Ballerina der 1860er Jahre; viele Jahre später sollte sie bei einem Auftritt in einem schäbigen Tanztheater im Hafen von Marseille sterben.

Von der Mitte des 19. Jahrhunderts bis zum Ersten Weltkrieg waren beim Ballett sehr viele Menschen beschäftigt. Es gab spektakuläre neue Werke, neue Truppen, neue Choreographen. Delibes, Tschaikowsky und Strawinsky schrieben die berühmteste Ballettmusik aller Zeiten. Fokine, Bolm und Nijinsky führten neue athletische Bewegungen ein und verliehen der Rolle des männlichen Tänzers ein neues Gesicht; Duncan verabscheute es, wie die klassische Ballerina (2) auf der Spitze zu tanzen. Die seltsame Steifheit der in den 60er Jahren von der London Stereoscopic Company photographierten Tänzer (3) war weit entfernt von Nijinskys spektakulären Sprüngen in *Spectre de la Rose*.

Die besten Tänze und Tänzer kamen aus der Kaiserlichen Russischen Ballettschule in St. Petersburg. Ihre Absolventen gastierten in Europa und Amerika, wo das Ballett ihrer Meinung nach ein weitaus niedrigeres Niveau als in Rußland hatte. Wie Missionare früherer Zeiten vermittelten sie ihre Ideale (und, anders als die Missionare, ihr Genie) den Tänzern in der ganzen Welt.

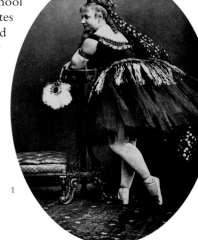

1

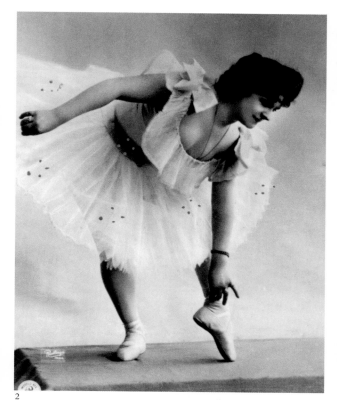

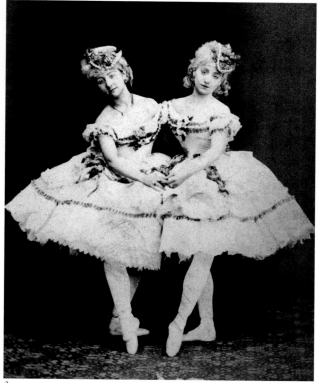

2

3

LE ballet s'était débarrassé des contraintes et de la formalité rigide qu'il devait à ses origines de cour du début du XIXᵉ siècle. La danse se fit plus éthérée tout en se rapprochant aussi davantage de la gymnastique, et mit en valeur la danseuse. Emma Pitteri (1), qui fut la plus fêtée des ballerines des années 1860, devait mourir dans un sordide anonymat quelques années plus tard, alors qu'elle dansait dans un cabaret du port de Marseille.

À partir du milieu du siècle et jusqu'à la Première Guerre mondiale, le ballet mit en branle des forces prodigieuses. Il y eut un nombre spectaculaire de nouvelles œuvres, de compagnies et de chorégraphes. Delibes, Tchaïkovski et Stravinski écrivirent les orchestrations pour ballet les plus célèbres de tous les temps.

Fokine, Bolm et Nijinski donnèrent au ballet un aspect plus physique et rétablirent le rôle du danseur. Duncan évita le style de la danse sur pointe que la ballerine classique incarnait (2). Il y a tout un monde entre la rigidité curieusement démodée des deux danseuses photographiées par la London Stereoscopic Company dans les années 1860 (3) et le spectaculaire bond de Nijinski dans le *Spectre de la rose*.

La plus belle danse et les plus beaux danseurs venaient de l'École du ballet impérial russe de Saint-Pétersbourg. Ses diplômés parcouraient l'Europe et les Amériques et constataient que les normes de danse y étaient bien inférieures à celles en vigueur en Russie. Tels des missionnaires du temps passé, ils apportaient leurs idéaux aux compagnies de danse du monde entier.

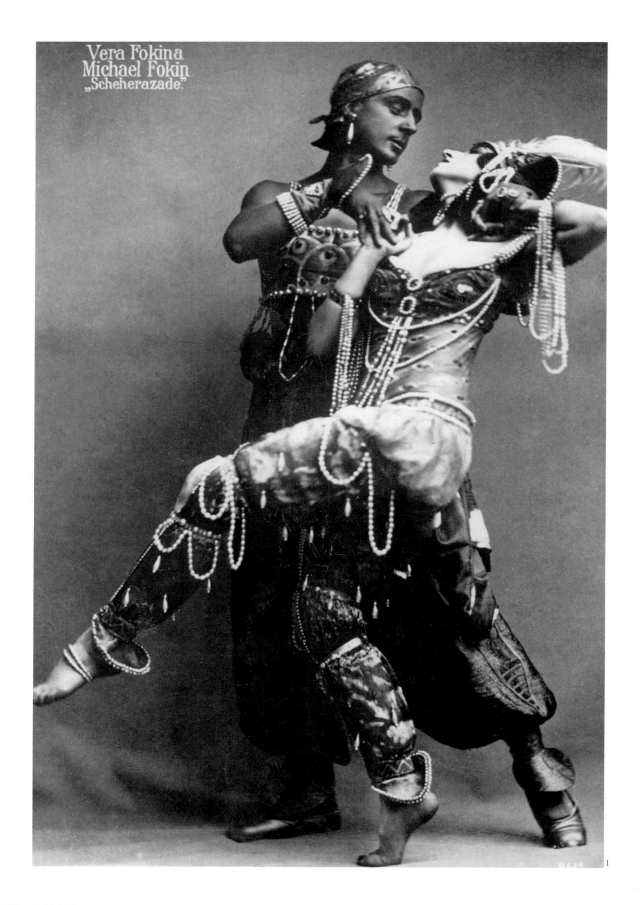

Vera Fokina
Michael Fokin
„Scheherazade.“

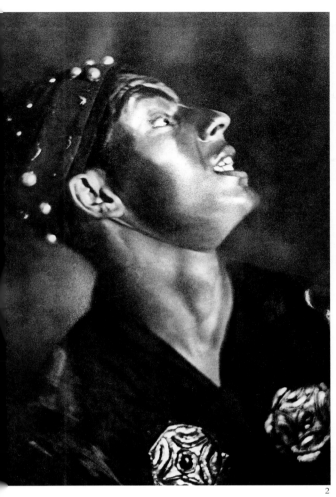
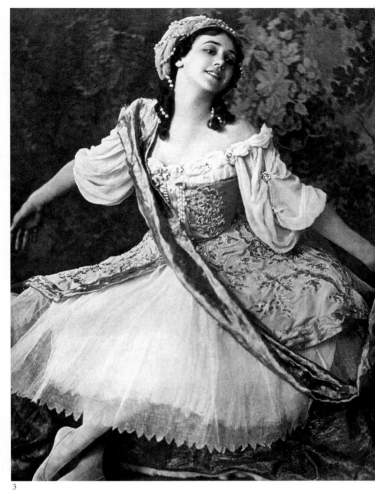

2   3

THE most explosively exciting dance company was Diaghilev's Ballets Russes, formed in 1909 originally as a touring troupe of the Russian Imperial Ballet. It attracted the talents of the finest composers, painters and designers, as well as the leading choreographers and dancers. Those lucky enough to see them in Paris could thrill to Mikhail Fokine and Vera Fokina in Rimsky-Korsakov's *Scheherazade* (1), Adolphe Bolm in the Polovtsian Dances from Borodin's *Prince Igor* (2), and Tamara Karsavina (3), one of the first Russian dancers to be seen in the West.

DAS faszinierendste aller Tanzensembles waren Diaghilews Ballets Russes, die 1909 ursprünglich als Tourneetruppe des Kaiserlichen Russischen Balletts entstanden waren. Sie zogen die besten Komponisten, Maler und Designer sowie führende Choreographen und Tänzer an. Wer das Glück hatte, das Ensemble in Paris zu sehen, konnte sich von Michail Fokine und Vera Fokina in Rimski-Korsakows *Scheherazade* (1), Adolphe Bolm in Borodins *Prinz Igor* (2) und Tamara Karsawina (3), eine der ersten russischen Tänzerinnen, die im Westen auftrat, verzaubern lassen.

LA compagnie de danse la plus explosive et la plus excitante était celle des Ballets russes de Diaghilev. Initialement créée en 1909 pour servir de troupe itinérante au ballet impérial russe, elle attirait les talents des compositeurs, des peintres et des créateurs les plus brillants ainsi que les meilleurs chorégraphes et les meilleurs danseurs. Ceux qui avaient la chance de pouvoir assister à leurs spectacles à Paris pouvaient palpiter en regardant Michel Fokine et Vera Fokina danser dans *Schéhérazade* de Rimski-Korsakov (1), Adolphe Bolm dans les danses polovtsiennes du *Prince Igor* (2) de Borodine et Tamara Karsavina (3), qui fut l'une des premières danseuses russes à se produire en Occident.

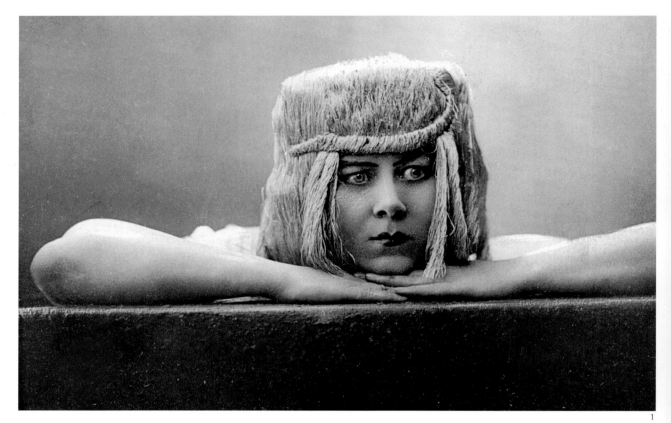

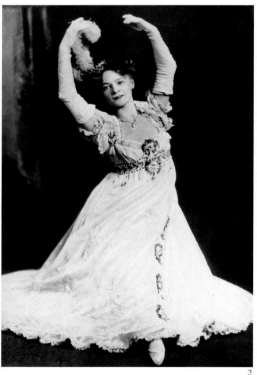

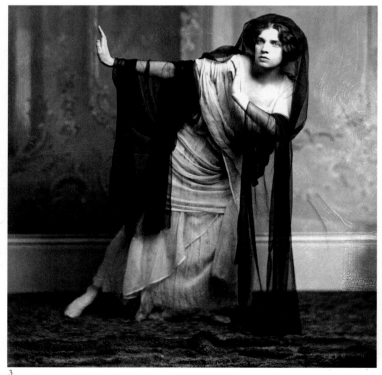

1

2   3

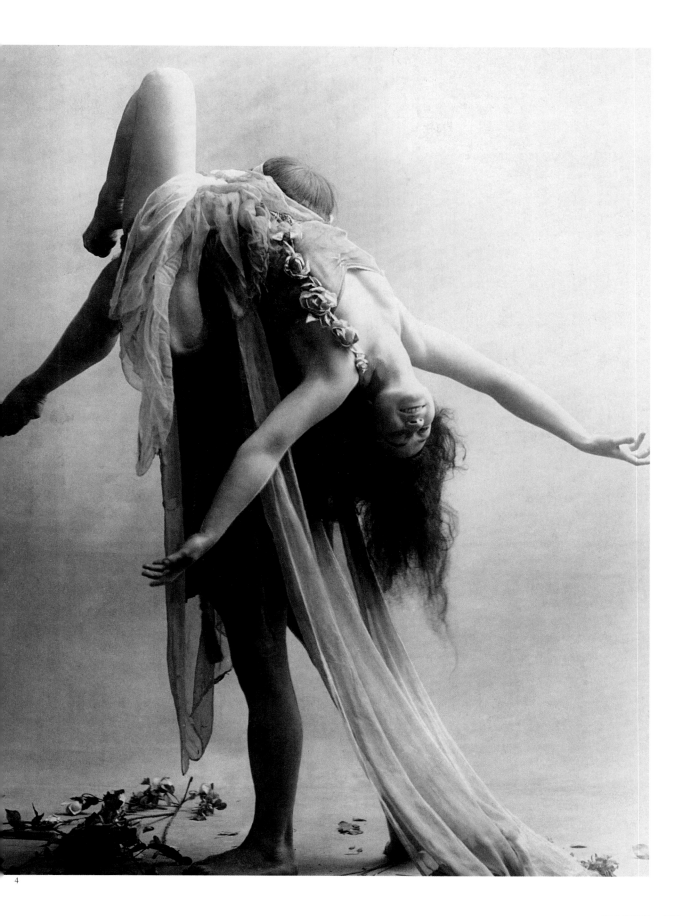

4

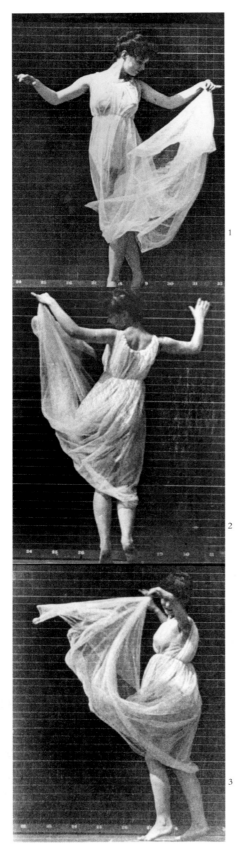

EADWEARD Muybridge used his series of cameras to capture the flowing movements of the dancer Isadora Duncan (1, 2 and 3). Duncan (6, in later life) founded her own ballet company, inspired by the ancient Greek approach to art. 'I am inspired by the movement of the trees, the waves, the snows,' she wrote, 'by the connection between passion and the storm, between the breeze and gentleness…'. Among her pupils was her sister Erika (4). Duncan was 27 when her portrait was taken in 1905 (5). Her last words, before her long scarf caught in a car wheel in 1927 and broke her neck, were: 'Farewell, my friends. I am going to glory.'

EADWEARD Muybridge verwendete mehrere Kameras, um die fließenden Bewegungen der Tänzerin Isadora Duncan einzufangen (1, 2 und 3). Duncan (6, in reiferem Alter) gründete ihr eigenes Ballettensemble, inspiriert von der Kunstauffassung der alten Griechen. »Ich werde von der Bewegung der Bäume, der Wellen und der Schneeflocken inspiriert«, schrieb sie, »von der Verbindung zwischen der Leidenschaft und dem Sturm, zwischen der Brise und der Sanftheit …« Zu ihren Schülerinnen gehörte ihre Schwester Erika (4). Duncan war 27 Jahre alt, als dieses Portrait im Jahre 1905 aufgenommen wurde (5). Ihre letzten Worte, bevor sich der lange Schal, den sie trug, 1927 in einem Autoreifen verfing und ihr das Genick brach, waren: »Lebt wohl, meine Freunde, ich gehe in die Ewigkeit.«

EADWEARD Muybridge se servit d'une batterie d'appareils photographiques pour capter la fluidité des mouvements de la danseuse Isadora Duncan (1, 2 et 3). Duncan (6, plus âgée) fonda sa propre compagnie de ballets en s'inspirant de l'attitude de la Grèce antique vis-à-vis de l'art. Elle notait : « Je m'inspire du mouvement des arbres, des vagues et des neiges, du lien qui unit la passion et l'orage, la brise et la caresse… » Elle comptait au nombre de ses élèves sa propre sœur Erika (4). Duncan avait 27 ans en 1905 (5). Ses dernières paroles avant que sa longue écharpe ne lui rompît la nuque en se prenant dans la roue d'une voiture en 1927 ont été : « Adieu, mes amis. Je vais à la gloire. »

(Previous pages)
THE American Loie Fuller (1) was described by critics as 'less a dancer than a magician of light', an actress who turned to ballet and made astounding use of pieces of cheesecloth. She created a sensation on her début at the Folies Bergère. Adeline Genée (2) was Danish, enchantingly pretty and adored by audiences the world over. Maud Allen (3) was billed as a 'speciality dancer', and was famous for her reportedly scandalous Vision of Salome. There was a wealth of Russian talent (4) which failed to gain international fame but delighted Imperial audiences with technique and artistry of a high order.

(Vorherige Seiten)
IN der Amerikanerin Loie Fuller (1) sahen die Kritiker »weniger eine Tänzerin als eine Zauberin des Lichts«. Sie war ursprünglich Schauspielerin, bevor sie zum Ballett überwechselte und dort erstaunlichen Gebrauch von Baumwollstoff machte. Ihr Debut bei den Folies Bergère machte sie zur Sensation. Die hübsche Dänin Adeline Genée (2) wurde vom Publikum in der ganzen Welt bewundert. Maud Allen (3) wurde als »Spezialtänzerin« bezeichnet und war berühmt für ihre skandalösen Auftritte in Vision of Salome. Es gab viele russische Talente (4), die zwar keinen internationalen Ruhm erlangten, jedoch das Publikum der Kaiser- und Königshäuser mit ihrer Technik und ihrer hohen Kunst erfreuten.

(Pages précédentes)
L'AMÉRICAINE Loïe Fuller (1), selon les critiques « moins une danseuse qu'une magicienne de la lumière », était une comédienne venue au ballet ; elle faisait une utilisation étonnante des voiles de gaze. Elle fit sensation à ses débuts aux Folies Bergère. Adeline Genée (2) était danoise, jolie comme un cœur et adorée par les publics du monde entier. Maud Allen (3), qu'on présentait à l'affiche comme une « danseuse de fantaisie », avait été rendue célèbre par sa Vision de Salomé que l'on disait scandaleuse. Il existait une profusion de talents russes (4) que la renommée internationale boudait, mais qui ravissaient les cours impériales par leur virtuosité technique et artistique.

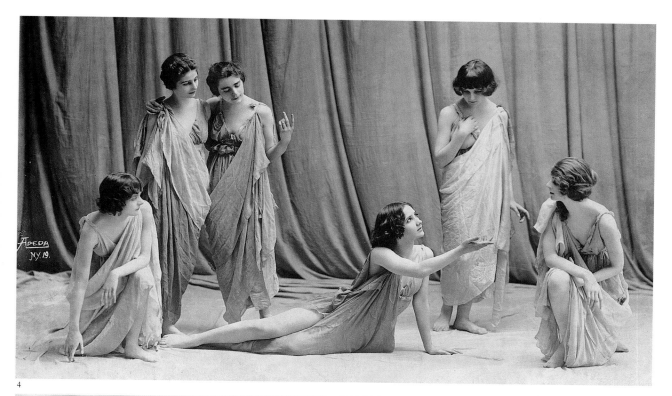

4

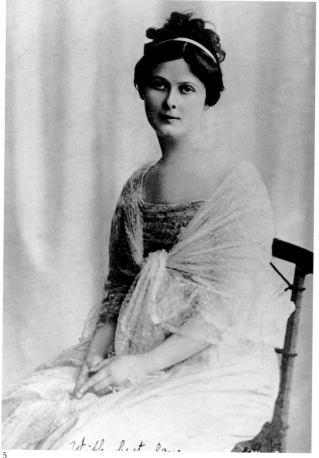

5

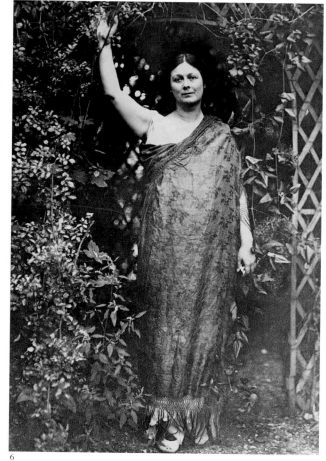

6

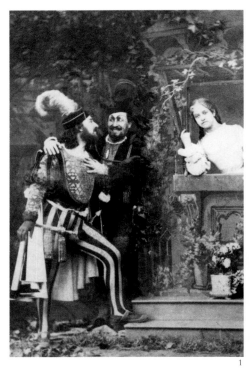

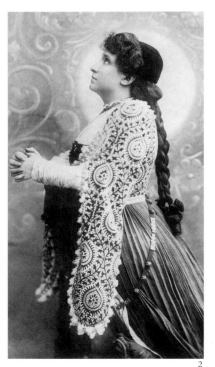

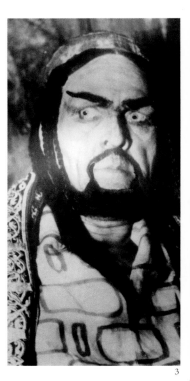

1

2

3

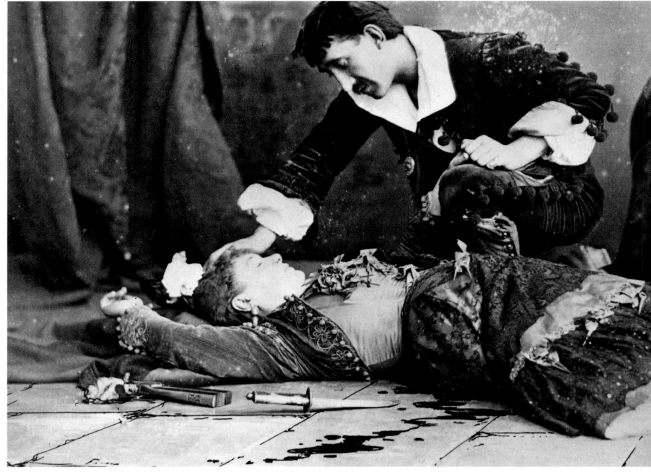

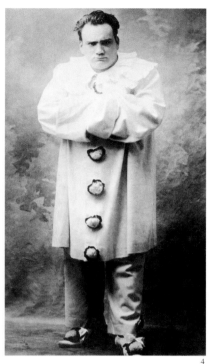

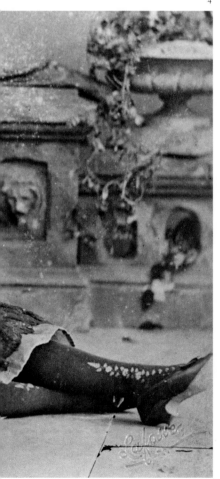

BIZET'S *Carmen* had its première in Paris in 1875. Emmy Soldene was an early Carmen – dead (5), and very much alive and smoking (6). From 1860 to 1905, the most celebrated soprano was Adelina Patti (1) – here as Marguerite in Gounod's *Faust*, with Mario. At the other end of several scales was the Russian baritone Feodor Chaliapin as Prince Igor (3). Enrico Caruso was perhaps the greatest tenor of all time, in his most famous role as Canio in *Pagliacci* (4). Another great soprano, and rival for the part of Marguerite, was Nellie Melba (2).

BIZETS *Carmen* hatte 1875 in Paris Premiere. Emmy Soldene spielte als eine der ersten die Carmen, tot (5) und sehr lebendig rauchend (6). Von 1860 bis 1905 war Adelina Patti (1), hier als Marguerite in Gounods *Faust* mit Mario, der meistgefeierte Sopran. Am anderen Ende der Tonleiter befand sich der russische Bariton Fjodor Schaljapin, hier als Prinz Igor (3). Enrico Caruso, der wohl größte Tenor aller Zeiten, hier in seiner bekanntesten Rolle als Canio in *Pagliacci* (4). Ein weiterer großer Sopran und Rivalin für die Rolle der Marguerite war Nellie Melba (2).

LA première du *Carmen* de Bizet eut lieu à Paris en 1875. Emmy Soldene incarna une des premières Carmen : morte (5) et bien vivante en train de fumer (6). Entre 1860 et 1905, Adelina Patti (1) était la soprano la plus célébrée : ici en Marguerite dans le *Faust* de Gounod où elle partageait la vedette avec Mario. À l'autre extrémité et plusieurs gammes au-dessous, le baryton russe Fedor Chaliapine dans le rôle du prince Igor (3). Enrico Caruso fut peut-être le plus grand ténor de tous les temps, et son rôle le plus célèbre celui de Canio dans le *Pagliacci* de Leoncavallo (4). L'autre grande soprano, une rivale dans le personnage de Marguerite, était Nellie Melba (2).

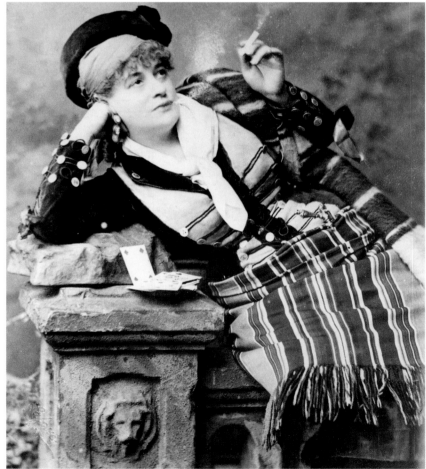

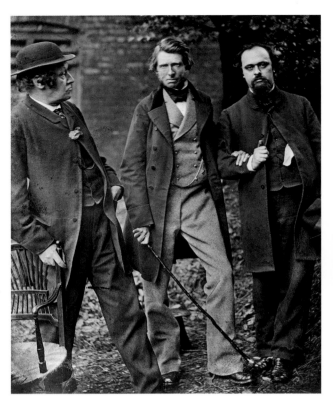

JOHN RUSKIN *(centre)* WITH D. G. ROSSETTI *(right)*

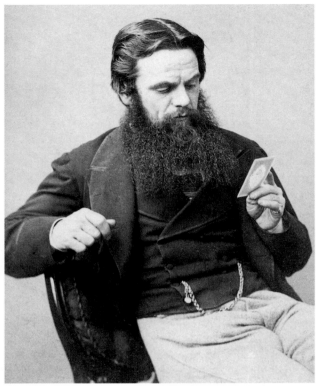

WILLIAM HOLMAN HUNT

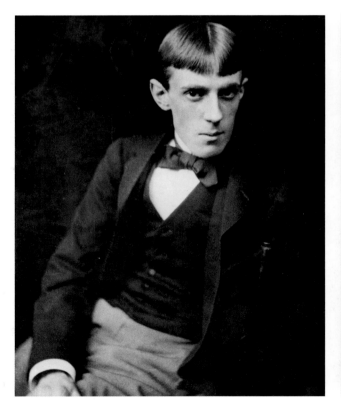

AUBREY BEARDSLEY

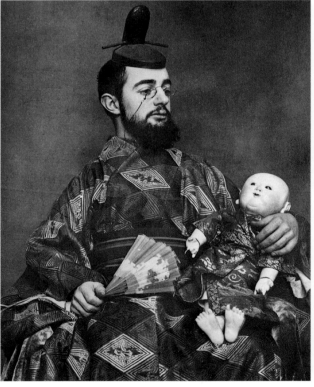

HENRI DE TOULOUSE-LAUTREC

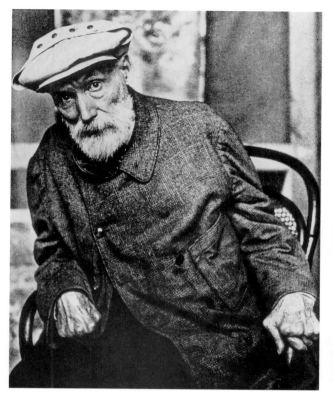

AUGUSTE RENOIR

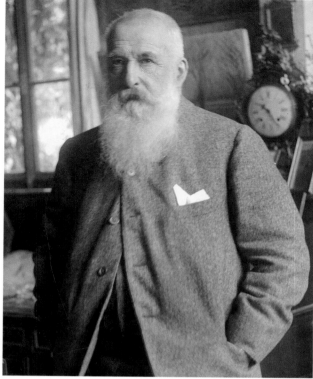

CLAUDE MONET

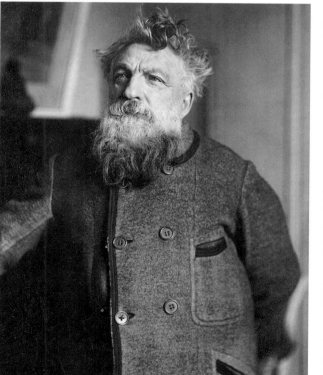

AUGUSTE RODIN

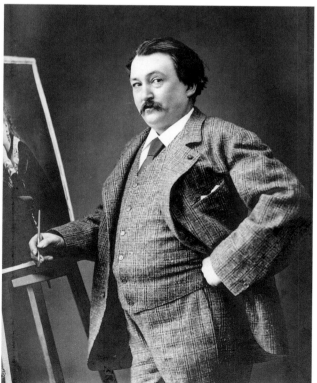

GUSTAVE DORÉ

Empire

BY the end of the 19th century, the European powers directly ruled almost half the world's land-mass and half the world's population. From Germany, France, Spain, Britain, Portugal, Belgium and the Netherlands thousands of young men and women sailed by steamship to colonies that stretched from New Guinea in the South Pacific to Newfoundland and St Pierre et Miquelon in the North Atlantic. In the entire African continent, only Abyssinia and Liberia retained their independence. Most of the Indian sub-continent was under British rule. In the Far East, Laos, Cambodia and Indo-China belonged to France, and much of Japan and mainland China was under European influence, if not control, as a result of major financial investment. Between 1871 and 1914 the French Empire grew by nearly 4 million square miles and 47 million people, the German Empire by 1 million square miles and 14 million people.

But the greatest Imperial power of them all was Great Britain. In 1897, the year of Queen Victoria's Diamond Jubilee, Britain had the largest empire in the history of the world; vigorous, fertile, hard-working, ordered and exploited. To celebrate the Jubilee, every tenth convict was set free in Hyderabad, a week's free food was distributed to all the poor families in Jamaica. There was free travel on the state railways of Baroda for 24 hours, a Grand Ball in Rangoon, a dinner at the Sultan's Palace in Zanzibar, a performance of the Hallelujah Chorus in Hong Kong. Troops from Canada, South Africa, Australia, India, North Borneo, Cyprus and a dozen other subject states came to London to take part in the Jubilee procession. The *Kreuz Zeitung* in Berlin reported that the British Empire was 'practically unassailable'. The *New York Times* was a little more enthusiastic, declaring: 'We are a part, and a great part, of the Greater Britain which seems so plainly destined to dominate this planet.'

Europe brought the light of Christianity and civilization to heathen and savage swathes of darkness. Drew Gay of the *Daily Telegraph* described the Hindus as 'the worst washed men I ever saw'. 'The only people who have a right to India are the British,' wrote one outraged correspondent. 'The so-called Indians have no right whatsoever.' H. M. Stanley, the man who 'discovered' Dr Livingstone, wrote that the Congo was 'a murderous world, and we feel for the first time that we hate the filthy, vulturous ghouls who inhabit it'. The photographer John Thomson described the Chinese as 'revolting, diseased and filthy objects'. Less brutally, Mary Fitzgibbon, an engineer's wife, concluded that the native Icelanders were 'teachable servants, neat, clean and careful, but have not constitutional strength to endure hard work'.

No races, it seemed, matched the European, for ingenuity, hard work, honesty, invention and guts. When Imperial adventurers got themselves into diffi-culties and were surrounded by 'murdering native hordes', they shook hands with each other, sang their national anthem, and resolutely faced their own imminent massacre.

The young men and women who served as agents of the European powers in huts and cabins and bungalows and villas from Surinam to Singapore were undeniably brave. They risked their health and their sanity, clustered in expatriot ghettos where only bridge or the piano could relieve the monotony of life. They wrote long letters home, and sent them with their own children back to Europe, back to the 'old country', back to family, friends and the old familiarity. Left alone, they drank, tried to cultivate European-style gardens, and died before their time − to be buried in some parched cemetery or a rough clearing in the thick vegetation, or at sea when only a few weeks away from home.

For all the fine sentiments, the real aim of colonization was, of course, financial gain. The world was sacked by Europe for its metals, rubber, coffee, tea, oil, lumber, gold and diamonds, fruit and fish. White hunters trekked with gun and camera into the bush of East Africa, or the foothills of the Himalayas, or the Argentinian pampas, returning with bales of horn and skins and plenty of tales to tell. Colonies produced vast wealth of many sorts, little of which found its way back to its land of origin. Labour was cheap, and untouched by the impertinent arguments of trade unions back home. So African and Burmese, Cuban and Maori toiled for their white masters, accepting harsh discipline, long hours and the lowest of wages. If they were lucky, they were invited to join the lower ranks of white society − as soldiers, porters, servants, gardeners. If they were unlucky, they were cast aside, with their traditional way of life destroyed. Edmond La Meslée described what was left of aborigine society in Australia when the white man had finished with it: 'Men and women, barely covered in veritable rags and tatters of decomposing woollen blankets, wandered about the camp. In the shelter of the huts, half enveloped in an ancient rag some old hag gnawed away at a kangaroo bone… never had I seen such a degrading spectacle, and I would never have believed that there were human beings capable of living in such a state of nastiness and misery.' Small wonder, perhaps, that a couple of decades later such people would be shot for sport by offspring of the original white settlers.

Chancellor Bismarck of Germany offered a novel solution to the problem of Ireland, Britain's nearest and most troublesome colony. He suggested that the Dutch and the Irish should change places. The industrious Dutch would soon turn Ireland into a thriving country, and the Irish would fail to maintain the dykes, and so be rapidly swept away. The lives of the indigenous populations of the colonies were always held very cheap.

But there was another side. There were those European settlers who fell in love with new worlds and new peoples; who devoted their lives to protecting and preserving traditional ways of life; who brought comfort and understanding, alternative medicine and alternative knowledge; who admired and did not ravage; who cried out, as Florence Nightingale did for the people of India: 'Have we no voice for these voiceless millions?'

GEGEN Ende des 19. Jahrhunderts beherrschten die Geuropäischen Mächte fast die Hälfte der Landmasse und die Hälfte der Weltbevölkerung. Aus Deutschland, Frankreich, Spanien, Großbritannien, Portugal, Belgien und den Niederlanden brachen Männer und Frauen in Dampfschiffen in die Kolonien auf, die sich von Neuguinea im Südpazifik bis nach Neufundland und St. Pierre et Miquelon im Nordatlantik erstreckten. Von den Ländern des afrikanischen Kontinents behielten nur Abessinien und Liberia ihre Unabhängigkeit. Der größte Teil des indischen Subkontinents stand unter britischer Herrschaft. Im Fernen Osten gehörten Laos, Kambodscha und Indochina zu Frankreich, und weite Teile Japans sowie das Kernland Chinas standen als Folge umfangreicher finanzieller Investitionen unter dem Einfluß, wenn nicht der Kontrolle Europas. Zwischen 1871 und 1914 wuchs das französische Reich um fast vier Millionen Quadratmeilen und 47 Millionen Menschen an, das Deutsche Reich um eine Million Quadratmeilen und 14 Millionen Menschen.

Die größte Kolonialmacht jedoch war Großbritannien. Im Jahre 1897, dem Jahr, in dem Königin Victoria ihr 60. Amtsjubiläum feierte, besaß Großbritannien das größte Reich in der Geschichte der Welt; kraftvoll, fruchtbar, hart arbeitend, geordnet und ausgebeutet. Zur Feier des Jubiläums wurde in Hyderabad jeder zehnte Häftling freigelassen; eine Woche lang wurde kostenloses Essen an arme Familien in Jamaika verteilt. Für die Dauer von 24 Stunden konnte man mit der staatlichen Eisenbahn von Baroda umsonst reisen, es gab einen großen Ball in Rangoon, ein Abendessen im Palast des Sultans von Sansibar und eine Aufführung des Halleluja-Chors in Hongkong. Truppen aus Kanada, Südafrika, Australien, Indien, Nord-Borneo, Zypern und einem Dutzend anderer Staaten des Empire kamen nach London, um an den Jubiläumsfeierlichkeiten teilzunehmen. Die Berliner *Kreuz Zeitung* berichtete, das britische Empire sei »praktisch unbezwingbar«. Die *New York Times* zeigte etwas mehr Begeisterung und erklärte: »Wir sind Teil, und zwar ein großer Teil des britischen Empire, dem es so deutlich bestimmt zu sein scheint, den gesamten Planeten zu beherrschen.«

Europa brachte den in Dunkelheit lebenden Heiden und Wilden das Licht des Christentums und der Zivilisation. Drew Gay vom *Daily Telegraph* beschrieb die Hindus als »die schmutzigsten Menschen, die ich je sah«. »Das einzige Volk, das ein Recht auf Indien besitzt, sind die Briten«, schrieb ein aufgebrachter Korrespondent. »Die sogenannten Inder haben nicht das geringste Recht.« H. M. Stanley, der Mann, der Dr. Livingstone »entdeckte«, schrieb, der Kongo sei »eine mörderische Welt, und wir spüren zum ersten Mal, daß wir die schmutzigen, vulgären Ghule hassen, die sie bewohnen«. Der Photograph John Thomson beschrieb die Chinesen als »aufsässige, verseuchte und dreckige Subjekte«. Weniger brutal war das Urteil von Mary Fitzgibbon, der Frau eines Ingenieurs, die zu dem Schluß kam, die Bewohner Islands seien »gelehrige Diener, sauber und umsichtig, aber ohne die nötige körperliche Konstitution für harte Arbeit«.

Keine Rasse, so schien es, konnte sich mit der europäischen messen, wenn es um Genialität, harte Arbeit, Ehrlichkeit, Erfindungsreichtum und Mut ging. Wenn Abenteurer des Empire in Schwierigkeiten gerieten und von »blutrünstigen Eingeborenenhorden« umzingelt waren, gaben sie einander die Hand, sangen ihre Nationalhymne und sahen entschlossen ihrem eigenen Tod ins Auge.

Die jungen Männer und Frauen, die als Vertreter der europäischen Mächte von Surinam bis Singapur in Hütten, Bungalows und Villen lebten, waren zweifelsohne tapfere Menschen. Sie setzten ihre körperliche und geistige Gesundheit aufs Spiel und lebten zusammengedrängt in Ghettos fernab der Heimat, wo nur Bridge und Klavierspiel eine Abwechslung zur Monotonie des Lebens boten. Sie schrieben lange Briefe nach Hause und schickten sie zusammen mit den eigenen Kindern nach Europa, zurück in das alte Land, zurück zu Familie, Freunden und den alten, vertrauten Verhältnissen. Alleingelassen verfielen sie dem Alkohol, versuchten, europäische Gärten anzulegen und starben früh, um auf einem verdorrten Friedhof, einer Lichtung in der üppigen Vegetation oder nur wenige Wochen von der Heimat entfernt auf See beigesetzt zu werden.

Aber trotz all der beschönigenden Worte war das wirkliche Ziel der Kolonisation natürlich finanzielle Bereicherung. Die Welt wurde von den Europäern wegen ihrer Metalle, wegen Kautschuk, Kaffee, Tee, Öl, Holz, Gold und Diamanten, Früchten und Fisch regelrecht geplündert. Weiße Jäger zogen, mit Flinte und Kamera bewaffnet, in den ostafrikanischen Busch, in die Ausläufer des Himalaja oder in die argentinischen Pampas und kehrten mit Bündeln von Hörnern, Häuten und vielen abenteuerlichen Geschichten zurück. Die Kolonien produzierten große Reichtümer aller Art, von denen nur wenige den Weg zurück in ihr Ursprungsland fanden. Arbeitskräfte waren billig und unbeeinflußt von den »unverschämten« Forderungen der heimischen Gewerkschaften. So plagten sich Afrikaner und Burmesen, Kubaner und Maori für ihre weißen Herren, sie akzeptierten strenge Disziplin, lange Arbeitszeiten und niedrigste Löhne. Wenn sie Glück hatten, wurden sie als Soldaten, Pförtner, Diener oder Gärtner in die niedrigeren Ränge der weißen Gesellschaft aufgenommen. Wenn sie aber Pech hatten, wurden sie fallengelassen und fanden ihre traditionellen Lebensformen zerstört. Edmond La Meslée beschrieb, was von der Gesellschaft der australischen Ureinwohner übrigblieb, als der weiße Mann mit ihr fertig war: »Männer und Frauen, nur spärlich bekleidet mit regelrechten Lumpen und Fetzen aus zerfressenen Wolldecken, zogen durch das Lager. Im Schutz der Hütten nagte ein altes Weib, halb eingehüllt in einen alten Teppich, an einem Känguruhknochen … ich habe niemals ein solch erniedrigendes Schauspiel gesehen, und ich hätte niemals geglaubt, daß es Menschen gibt, die es ertragen, in solch abscheulichen und elenden Verhältnissen zu leben.« So verwundert es wohl kaum, daß sich ein paar Jahrzehnte später die Nachkommen der ersten weißen Siedler einen Sport daraus machten, diese Menschen abzuschießen.

Der deutsche Reichskanzler Bismarck schlug eine neuartige Lösung für das Problem Irland, Großbritanniens nächstgelegene und schwierigste Kolonie, vor. Er regte an, die Holländer und die Iren sollten ihre Plätze tauschen. Die fleißigen Holländer würden Irland schnell zu einem aufstrebenden Land machen, und weil die Iren es wohl kaum schaffen würden, die Deiche instandzuhalten, würden sie bald fortgespült werden. Das Leben der einheimischen Bevölkerung der Kolonien galt zu keiner Zeit viel.

Aber es gab auch eine andere Seite. Es gab jene Europäer, die sich in die neue Welt und ihre Menschen verliebten, die ihr Leben dem Schutz und der Bewahrung der traditionellen Lebensformen widmeten, die Trost und Verständnis aufbrachten, alternative Medizin und alternatives Wissen vermittelten, die bewun-

derten, statt zu plündern, und ihre Stimme erhoben, wie es Florence Nightingale für das indische Volk tat: »Haben wir keine Stimme für diese stummen Millionen?«

DÈS la fin du XIXᵉ siècle, les puissances européennes détenaient sous leur autorité directe près de la moitié de la masse terrestre du globe et la moitié de sa population. Partant d'Allemagne, de France, d'Espagne, de Grande-Bretagne, du Portugal, de Belgique et des Pays-Bas, des bateaux à vapeur emportaient à leur bord des milliers de jeunes gens et de jeunes femmes vers les colonies qui s'étendaient de la Nouvelle-Guinée dans le sud du Pacifique jusqu'à Terre-Neuve et Saint-Pierre-et-Miquelon dans le nord de l'Atlantique. Sur le continent africain, seuls l'Abyssinie et le Liberia conservèrent leur indépendance. La plus grande partie du sous-continent indien se trouvait sous la domination britannique. En Extrême-Orient, le Laos, le Cambodge et l'Indochine appartenaient à la France, tandis qu'une grande partie du Japon et de la Chine continentale se retrouvait sous l'influence européenne, pour ne pas parler de surveillance, à la suite de très gros investissements financiers. Entre 1871 et 1914, l'empire français avait gagné près de 4 millions de kilomètres carrés et 47 millions d'habitants, et l'empire allemand 1 million de kilomètres carrés et 14 millions d'habitants.

La Grande-Bretagne était cependant la plus grande puissance impériale. En 1897, l'année du soixantième anniversaire de la reine Victoria, elle possédait le plus vaste empire de l'Histoire : vigoureux, fertile, travaillant dur, dirigé et exploité. À l'occasion de cet anniversaire, on libéra un condamné sur dix à Hyderabad et on distribua l'équivalent d'une semaine de nourriture à toutes les familles pauvres de la Jamaïque. On put circuler gratuitement 24 heures durant dans les trains publics de la ville de Baroda ; on organisa un grand bal à Rangoon, un dîner dans le palais du sultan à Zanzibar et une représentation du Hallelujah Chorus à Hong Kong. Des troupes débarquèrent du Canada, d'Afrique du Sud, d'Australie, d'Inde, du Bornéo septentrional, de Chypre ainsi que d'une dizaine d'autres États sujets pour prendre part au défilé du cortège d'anniversaire à Londres. Le *Kreuz Zeitung* à Berlin écrivit que l'empire britannique était « pratiquement inattaquable ». Le *New York Times* se montra un peu plus enthousiaste : « Nous sommes une partie, et une grande, de la plus grande Bretagne qui semble destinée si naturellement à dominer cette planète. »

L'Europe apportait la lumière de la chrétienté et de la civilisation au sein des forces obscures, païennes et sauvages. Drew Gay du *Daily Telegraph* disait des Hindous qu'ils étaient « les hommes les plus mal lavés qu'il m'ait été donné de voir ». « Les seuls à posséder un droit sur l'Inde sont les Britanniques », écrivait un correspondant maltraité, « les *prétendus* Indiens n'ont absolument aucun droit ». H. M. Stanley, l'homme qui « découvrit » le Dr Livingstone, consignait dans son journal que le Congo était « un monde de meurtriers, et pour la première fois nous ressentons de la haine envers les démons sales et les charognards qui le peuplent ». Le photographe John Thomson qualifiait les Chinois « d'objets révoltants, souffreteux et sales ». Mary Fitzgibbon, l'épouse d'un ingénieur, en concluait avec moins de brutalité que les natifs Islandais étaient des « serviteurs éducables, ordonnés, propres et soigneux mais que leur constitution physique rend inaptes aux durs travaux ».

Aucune race, semblait-il, n'égalait les Européens pour ce qui était de l'ingéniosité, du labeur, de l'honnêteté, de l'inventivité et du cran. Lorsque les aventuriers impériaux étaient encerclés par des « hordes indigènes sanguinaires », ils se serraient la main entre eux, entonnaient leur hymne national et affrontaient résolument leur propre massacre.

Les jeunes gens et jeunes femmes qui servaient les puissances européennes en vivant dans des cabanes, des bungalows ou des villas du Surinam à Singapour étaient sans conteste courageux. Regroupés avec leurs compatriotes dans des ghettos, avec le bridge et le piano pour toute distraction, ils risquaient leur santé physique et mentale. Ils écrivaient de longues lettres qu'ils expédiaient avec les enfants en Europe, « au pays », dans leur famille, chez les amis et vers tout ce qu'ils avaient laissé là-bas. Restés seuls, ils buvaient, essayaient de cultiver des jardins à l'européenne et mouraient prématurément ; on les inhumait dans quelque cimetière desséché ou vague clairière creusée dans l'épaisse végétation, ou bien en mer, parfois quelques semaines seulement avant qu'ils ne rentrent dans leurs foyers.

Quoi qu'en dît Ruskin en évoquant la « lumière » et la « paix », le véritable but de la colonisation était bien entendu le gain financier. Le monde était pillé par l'Europe pour ses métaux, son caoutchouc, son café, son thé, son huile, son bois d'œuvre, son or et ses diamants, ses fruits et ses poissons. Les chasseurs blancs armés de fusils et d'appareils photographiques progressaient péniblement dans la brousse de l'Afrique de l'Est, au pied de l'Himalaya ou dans la pampa argentine et en revenaient chargés de ballots de cornes, de peaux et pleins d'histoires. Les colonies produisaient toutes sortes de richesses, mais peu d'entre elles profitaient à leur pays d'origine. La main-d'œuvre bon marché n'avait pas été pervertie par les arguments oiseux des syndicats. Aussi les Africains et les Birmans, les Cubains et les Maoris s'échinaient-ils pour leurs maîtres blancs, acceptant la dure discipline, les longues heures de travail et les salaires de misère. S'ils avaient de

la chance ils étaient invités à rejoindre les rangs inférieurs de la société blanche comme soldats, porteurs, serviteurs et jardiniers. Sinon on s'en défaisait après avoir détruit leur mode de vie traditionnel. Edmond La Meslée décrivit ce qui restait de la société des Aborigènes d'Australie une fois que le Blanc en eut fini avec elle : « Des hommes et des femmes que couvraient à peine de véritables lambeaux de couvertures en laine tombant en loques erraient à travers le camp. À l'abri des cabanes et à moitié enveloppée dans son antique guenille, une vieille sorcière mâchonnait obstinément un os de kangourou … Jamais je n'avais assisté à un spectacle aussi dégradant ni n'aurais cru possible que des êtres humains puissent vivre dans un tel état de saleté et de misère. » Il ne faut donc peut-être pas s'étonner si, une vingtaine d'années plus tard, la progéniture des premiers colons blancs leur tirait dessus pour la beauté du sport.

Le chancelier allemand Bismarck suggéra une nouvelle solution au problème de l'Irlande, la plus proche et la plus remuante des colonies de la Grande-Bretagne. Il proposa que les Néerlandais et les Irlandais permutassent. Les Néerlandais industrieux ne tarderaient pas à rendre l'Irlande prospère, et les Irlandais à se noyer faute d'entretenir les digues. Les vies des populations indigènes des colonies étaient toujours tenues pour négligeables.

Mais il y eut des colons européens qui tombèrent amoureux des nouveaux mondes et des nouveaux peuples, qui consacrèrent leurs vies à protéger et à préserver les modes de vie traditionnels, qui réconfortaient et comprenaient, qui délivraient une autre médecine et un autre enseignement, qui admiraient sans dévaster, qui, comme le fit Florence Nightingale en faveur du peuple indien, criaient : « N'aurons-nous pas de voix pour ces millions de sans-voix ? »

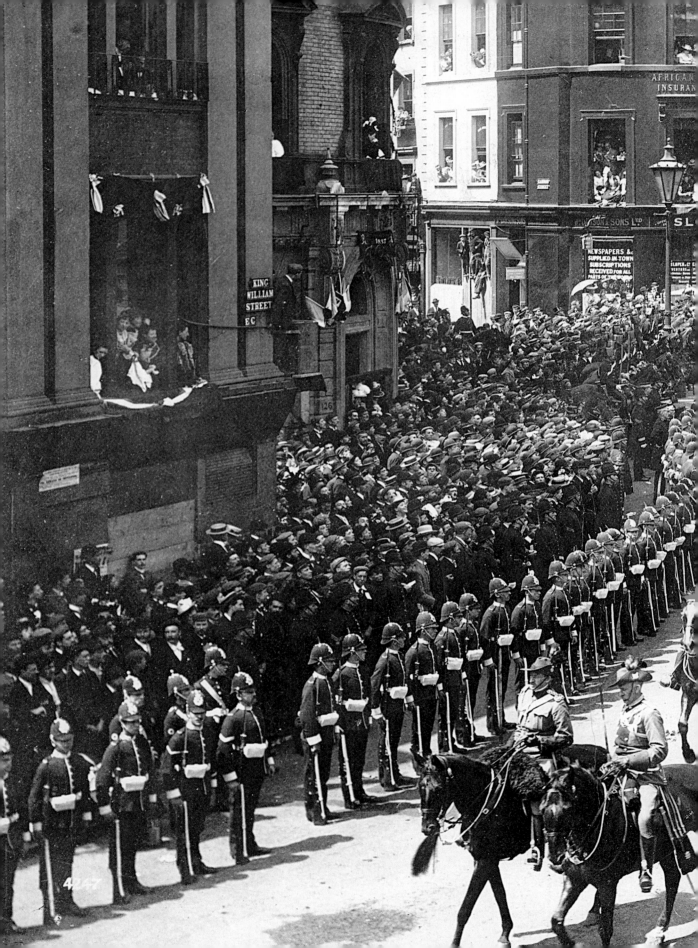

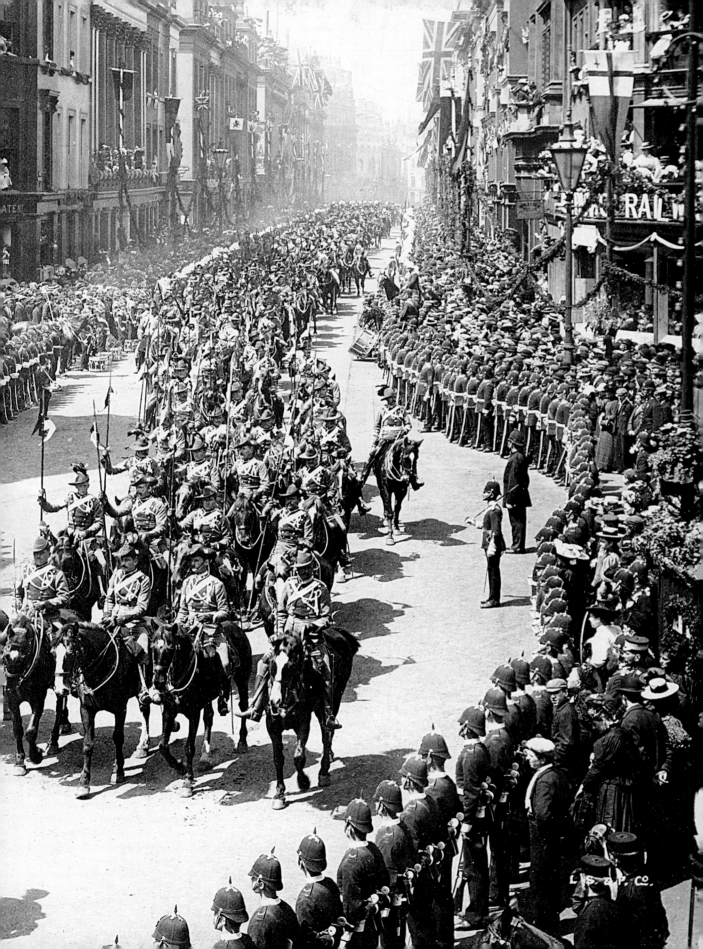

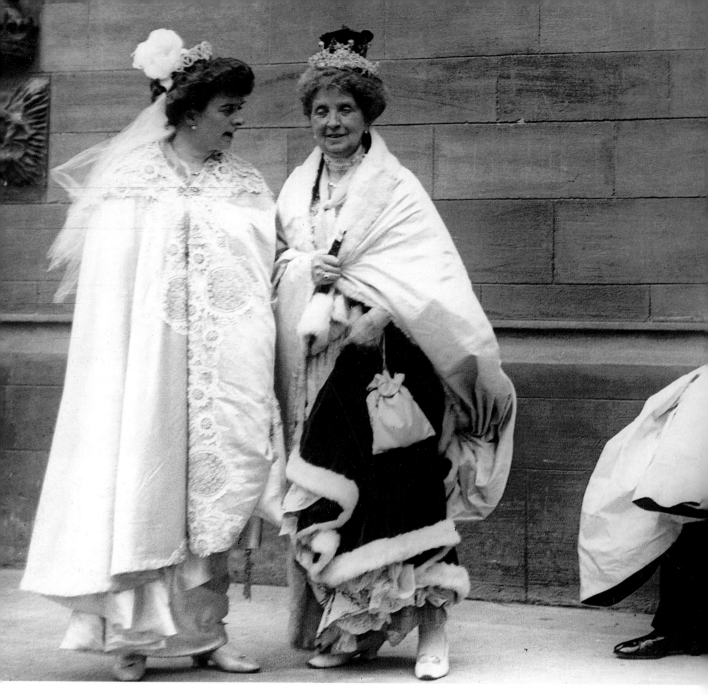

THE greatest moment in the history of the British Empire was the Diamond Jubilee of Queen Victoria on 22 June 1897 (previous pages). The Coronation of Edward VII had originally been scheduled for 26 June 1902, but the new King was ill, so the Coronation feast was given away to the poor. The Coronation took place on 9 August (2). 'When the King entered the Abbey, the huge congregation watched anxiously to see if he would falter because of his recent illness. But the King – I learned later that he had been laced into a metal girdle – walked confidently to the throne' (Dorothy Brett, an eyewitness).

Nine years later, the streets of London were once again decorated when Edward's son was crowned George V (3). The King's diary recorded: 'The service in the Abbey was most beautiful, but it was a terrible ordeal…Worked all the afternoon answering telegrams and letters, of which I have had hundreds … May and I showed ourselves again to the people. Bed at 11.45. Rather tired.' He wasn't the only one (1).

DAS 60jährige Amtsjubiläum von Königin Victoria am 22. Juni 1897 wurde zum größten Augenblick in der Geschichte des britischen Empire (vorherige Seiten). Die Krönung von Edward VII. war ursprünglich für den 26. Juni 1902 vorgesehen, aber der neue König war krank, so daß das Festmahl an die Armen verteilt wurde. Die Krönung fand schließlich am 9. August des Jahres statt (2). »Als der König die Abtei betrat, waren die versammelten Gäste besorgt, daß er wegen seiner Krankheit ins Stocken geraten könnte. Aber der König trug, wie ich später erfuhr, ein metal-

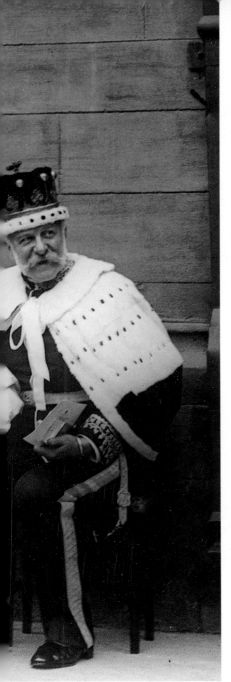

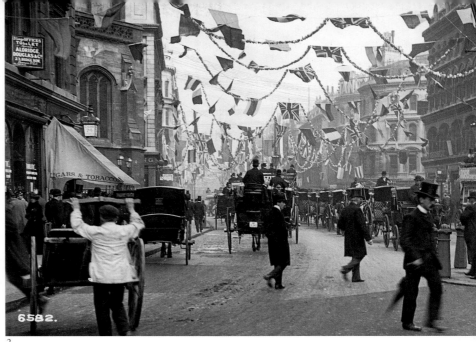

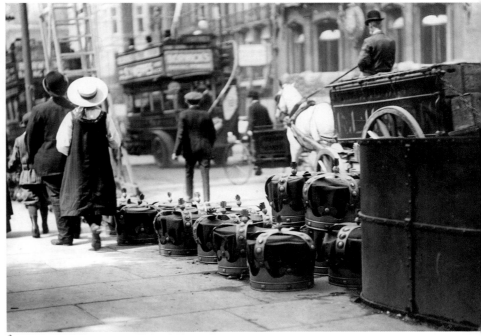

lenes Korsett und schritt zuversichtlich zum Thron.« (Dorothy Brett, eine Augenzeugin)

Neun Jahre später waren die Straßen von London anläßlich der Krönung von Edwards Sohn, George V., erneut geschmückt (3). Der König schrieb in sein Tagebuch: »Der Gottesdienst in der Abtei war wundervoll, aber es war eine fürchterliche Tortur … Habe den ganzen Nachmittag gearbeitet und Hunderte von Telegrammen und Briefen beantwortet … May und ich zeigten uns noch einmal dem Volk. Zu Bett um 23.45 Uhr. Ziemlich müde.« Er war nicht der einzige (1).

LE plus grand moment dans l'histoire de l'Empire britannique a été le Jubilée de diamant de la Reine Victoria, le 22 juin 1897 (pages précédentes). Le couronnement d'Édouard VII devait à l'origine avoir lieu le 26 juin 1902. Il fut différé en raison de la maladie du nouveau roi, et le festin prévu fut distribué aux pauvres. Le couronnement eut lieu le 9 août (2). « Lorsque le roi pénétra dans l'Abbaye, toute l'assemblée le suivit d'un regard anxieux craignant de le voir trébucher après sa récente maladie. Mais le roi, je devais par la suite apprendre qu'il avait été enserré dans un corset en métal, marcha d'un pas assuré jusqu'au trône. » (Dorothy Brett, témoin oculaire)

Neuf ans plus tard, les rues de Londres furent à nouveau décorées à l'occasion du couronnement de George V, fils d'Édouard (3). Le roi note dans son journal : « Le service à l'Abbaye était magnifique, mais quelle épreuve … Me suis employé toute l'après-midi à répondre aux télégrammes et aux lettres que j'avais reçus par centaines … May et moi nous sommes de nouveau montrés au peuple. Couché à 23 h 45. Plutôt fatigué. » Il n'était pas le seul (1).

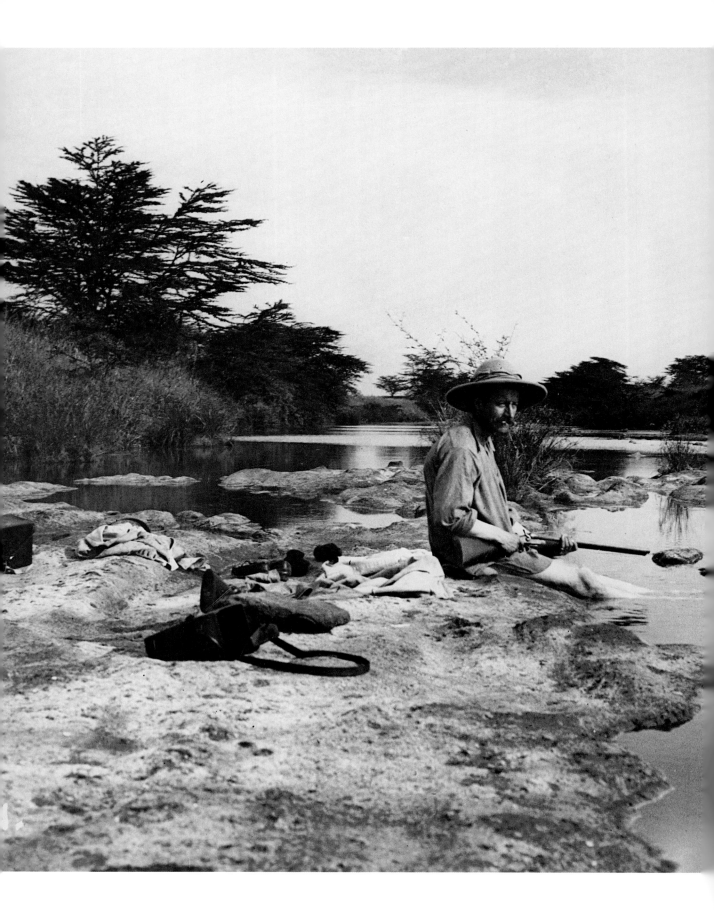

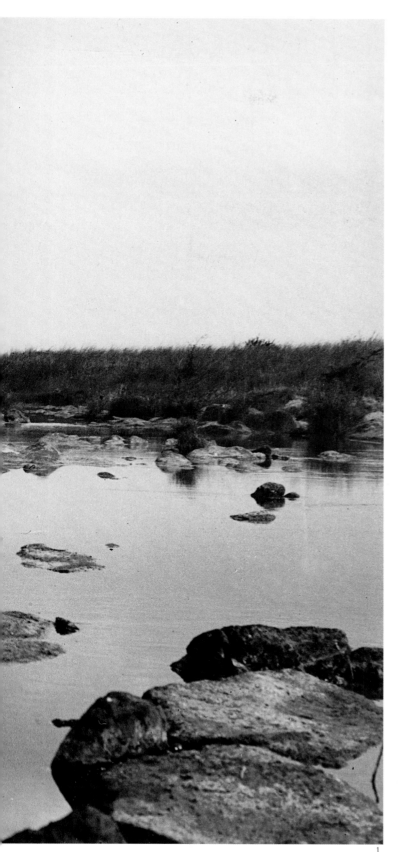

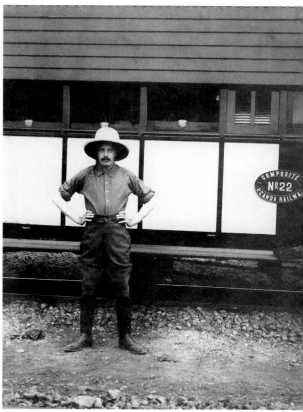

IN the 1880s, Lord Salisbury, the Prime Minister, said of Africa, 'British policy is to drift lazily downstream, occasionally putting out a boathook.' Also drifting lazily downstream were the crocodiles and hippopotamuses hunted by white settlers and incautious visitors alike (1). T. E. Todd (2) photographed them on his visit in 1879.

PREMIERMINISTER Lord Salisbury sagte in den 1880er Jahren über Afrika: »Britische Politik bedeutet, gemächlich flußabwärts zu gleiten und von Zeit zu Zeit einen Bootshaken auszuwerfen.« Ebenso gemächlich glitten die Krokodile und Nilpferde flußabwärts, die von weißen Siedlern und waghalsigen Touristen gejagt wurden (1). T. E. Todd (2) photographierte sie bei seinem Besuch im Jahre 1879.

DANS les années 1880, le Premier ministre Lord Salisbury disait en parlant de l'Afrique : « La politique britannique consiste à se laisser aller paresseusement au fil du courant en se servant de temps à autre de la gaffe. » Se laissaient aussi paresseusement aller au fil du courant les crocodiles et les hippopotames pourchassés par les colons blancs et les visiteurs imprudents (1). T. E. Todd (2) les a photographiés pendant sa visite en 1879.

TODD returned several times to Africa, taking a unique series of photographs. It may appear artificially staged, but this photograph (1) is probably genuine. One of the native bearers or porters attached to the hunting party has climbed a pole to scan the landscape for game. Sadly, the picture of the hunter with a dead rhinoceros (2) is certainly not staged. No tally was ever kept in those days of the number of animals in any species that were left alive – all that mattered was the trophy count.

TODD reiste mehrere Male nach Afrika und machte einzigartige Aufnahmen. Diese Photographie (1) mag gestellt wirken, ist aber vermutlich natürlich. Einer der eingeborenen Träger der Jagdgesellschaft ist an einem Stab hinaufgeklettert, um nach Wild Ausschau zu halten. Leider ist das Bild des Jägers mit dem toten Rhinozeros (2) mit Sicherheit nicht gestellt. Niemand zählte in jenen Tagen die Tiere all der verschiedenen Arten, die am Leben gelassen wurden; worauf es ankam, war einzig die Zahl der Trophäen.

TODD retourna plusieurs fois en Afrique où il prit une série unique de photographies. Même si la photographie semble mise en scène ici, tel n'a probablement pas été le cas (1). L'un des porteurs indigènes de la partie de chasse s'est perché tout en haut d'un poteau pour scruter le paysage à la recherche du gibier. Malheureusement la photographie montrant un chasseur à côté d'un rhinocéros mort (2) n'est, elle, certainement pas une mise en scène. On ne faisait jamais à l'époque le compte des animaux laissés en vie, quelle qu'en soit l'espèce. Seul comptait le nombre des trophées.

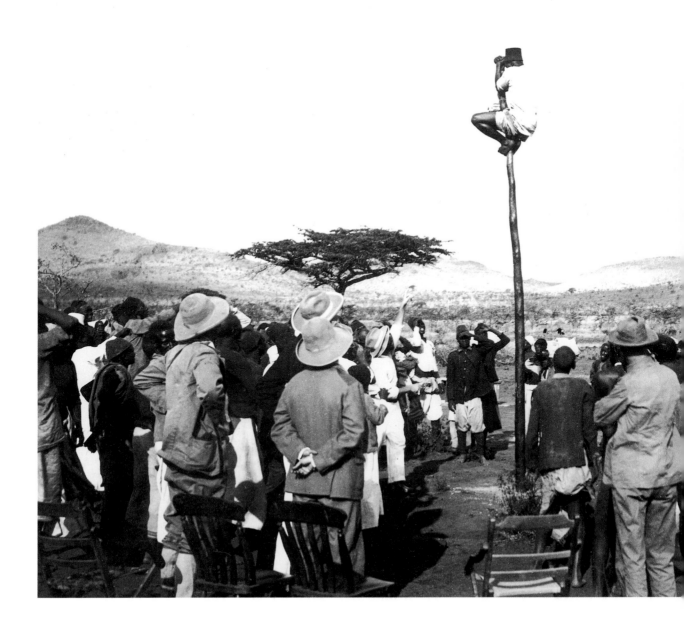

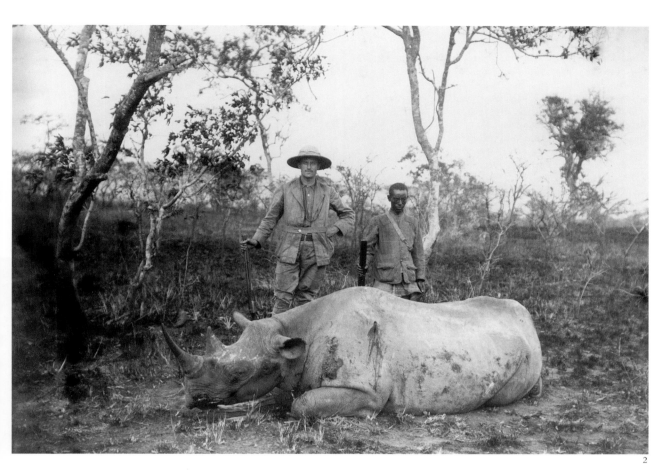

2

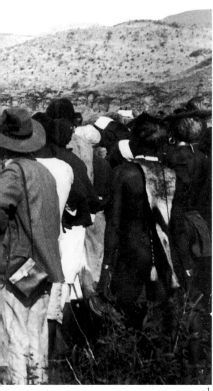

1

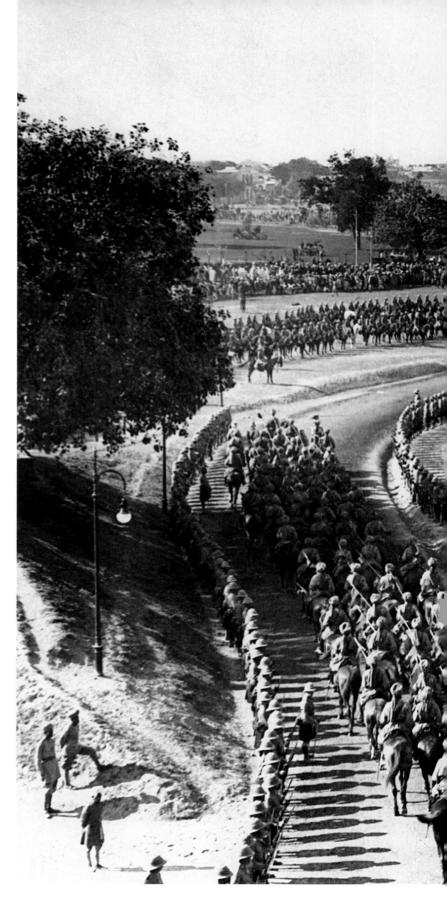

THREE times during the British Raj in India the notables of that vast subcontinent were summoned to Delhi, for an Imperial Durbar, or 'court'. The grandest was the last, in 1911, to celebrate the accession of George V. The King was most impressed: 'The weather was all that could be wished, hot sun, hardly any wind, no clouds… I wore a new crown made for India which cost £60,000 which the Indian Government is going to pay for…' The ceremonies lasted three and a half hours. 'Rather tired,' wrote the King at the end of the day, 'after wearing the crown… it hurt my head, as it is pretty heavy.'

DREIMAL während der britischen Oberherrschaft in Indien wurden die bedeutenden Persönlichkeiten dieses großen Subkontinents zu einem Durbar oder »Hof« des Empires nach Delhi zitiert. Der prächtigste war auch der letzte und fand im Jahre 1911 anläßlich der Thronbesteigung von George V. statt. Der König zeigte sich sehr beeindruckt: »Das Wetter hätte nicht besser sein können, heiße Sonne und kaum Wind, keine Wolken … Ich trug eine neue, für Indien angefertigte Krone im Wert von £ 60 000, die die indische Regierung zahlen wird…« Die Zeremonie dauerte dreieinhalb Stunden. »Ziemlich müde«, schrieb der König am Ende des Tages, »vom Tragen der Krone … sie drückte auf meinen Kopf, denn sie ist sehr schwer.«

TROIS fois pendant tout le temps que s'exerça la souveraineté britannique sur l'Inde, les notables de ce vaste sous-continent furent sommés de se rendre à Delhi pour assister à la réception offerte par l'empire britannique. La dernière, qui célébrait l'accession au trône de George V en 1911, fut la plus grandiose. Le roi était impressionné : « Le beau temps était au rendez-vous : soleil chaud, vent quasiment inexistant, aucun nuage … Je portais une nouvelle couronne faite exprès pour l'Inde et qui avait coûté £ 60 000 que le gouvernement indien payera … » Les cérémonies durèrent trois heures et demie. Le roi nota à la fin de cette journée : « Plutôt fatigué d'avoir porté la couronne … elle m'a donné mal à la tête, tant elle était lourde. »

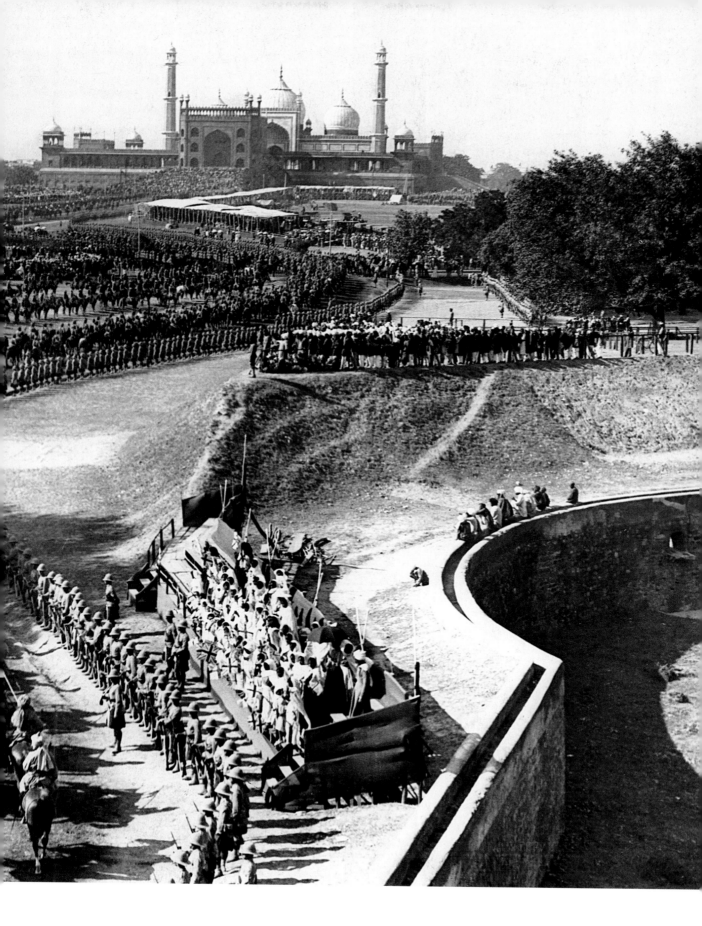

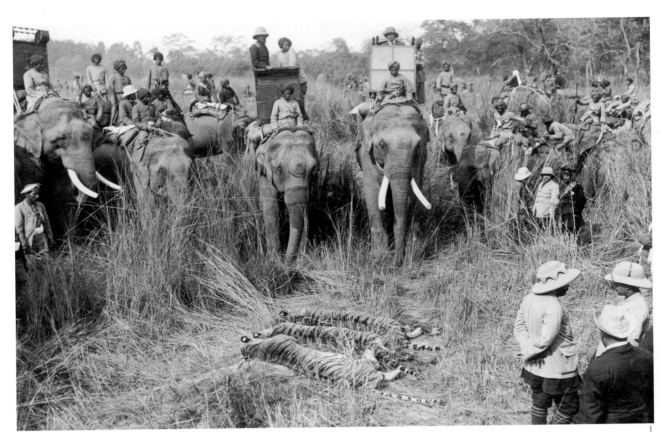

1

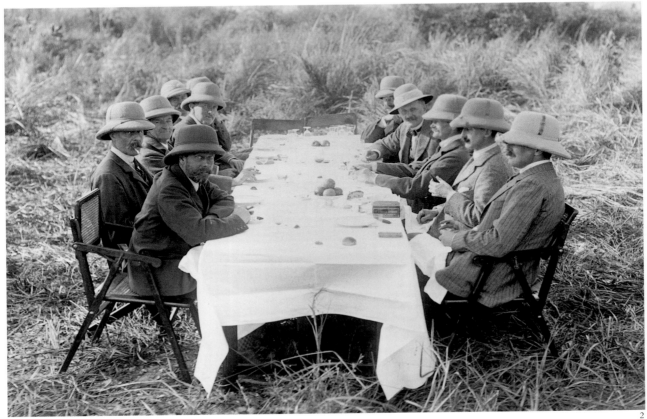

2

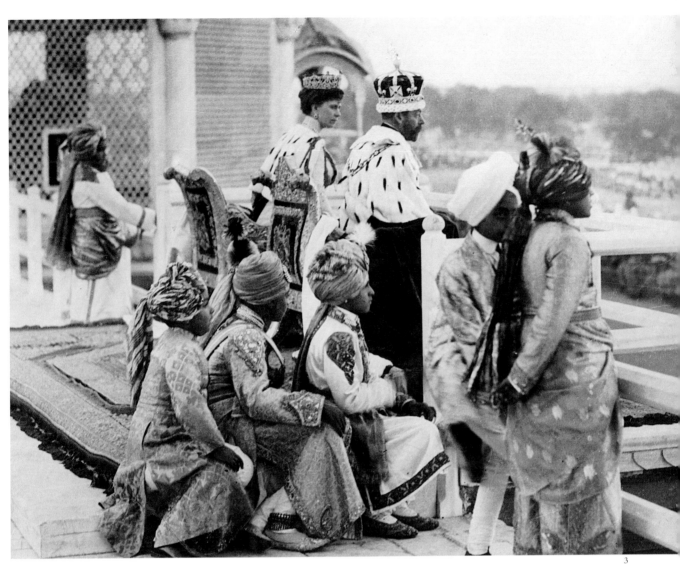

3

DURING the Durbar celebrations the itinerary included the customary tiger hunt (1) – the wholesale and much vaunted slaughter of what was then considered a ferocious predator rather than, as now, an endangered species. Less violent was the picnic that refreshed the men of the royal party (2) – George V is nearest the camera, on the left of the table. At the Durbar itself, King George and Queen Mary were attended by a clutch of young Indian princes (3).

WÄHREND der Durbar-Feiern fand auch die traditionelle Tigerjagd (1) statt, das vielgepriesene Abschlachten eines Tieres, das man damals als bösartiges Raubtier sah, und nicht, wie heute, als Vertreter einer gefährdeten Spezies. Weniger gewaltsam war das Picknick zur Erfrischung der königlichen Gesellschaft (2). George V. sitzt vorne links am Tisch. Beim Durbar selbst warteten King George und Queen Mary junge indische Prinzen auf (3).

LE programme des festivités prévoyait l'inévitable chasse au tigre (1), massacre en série tant exalté de ce que l'époque considérait être un prédateur féroce et non, comme aujourd'hui, une espèce menacée. Dans un registre moins violent, voici le pique-nique au cours duquel se restaurèrent les hommes de la suite royale (2). George V est le plus proche de nous, à gauche. Au cours de la réception même, le roi George et la reine Marie bénéficiaient des soins attentifs d'un essaim de jeunes princes indiens (3).

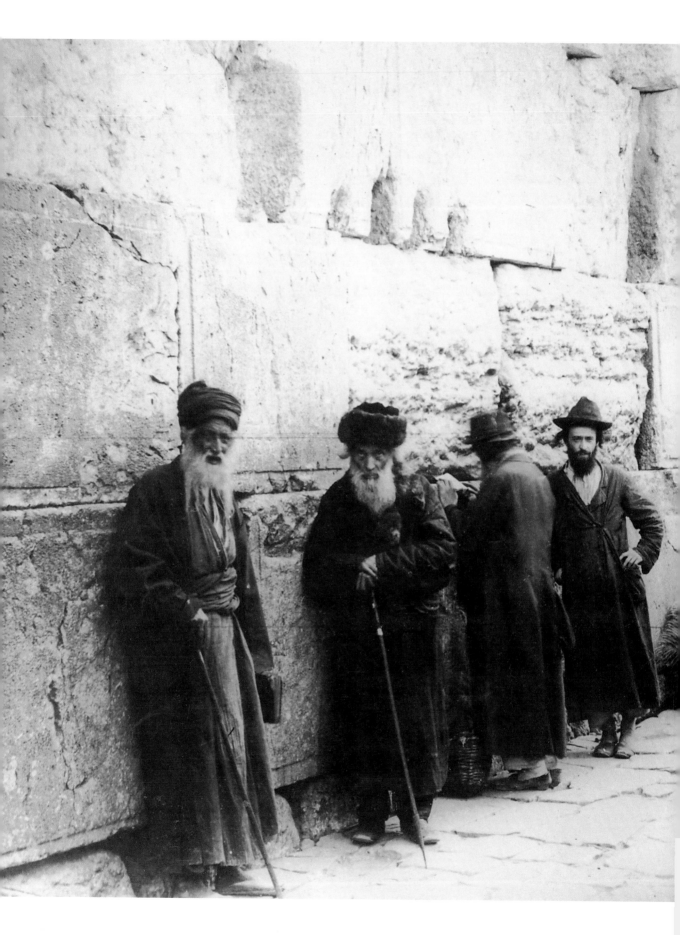

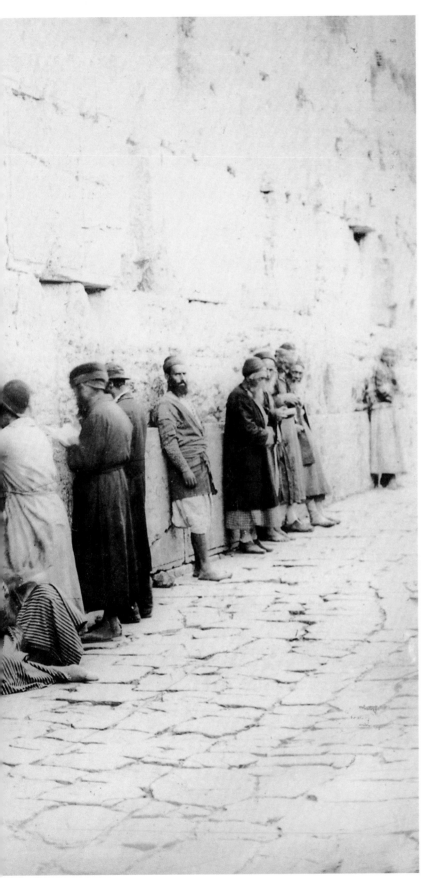

SLOWLY and cautiously, religious toleration was creeping across the world. No one could see evil in a group of old men leaning against a wall, as in the case of these elderly Jews at the Wailing Wall in Jerusalem. Protestants and Catholics began to allow each other the right to hold high office, to become members of government, to gain important posts in military and civil service. Christians and Jews began to trust each other. Hindus and Moslems lived in comparative peace in India.

Perhaps a reason for all this was that new enemies of religion and faith had emerged: Darwinism, free-thinking, Marxism. In industrial societies, churchgoing decreased dramatically.

ALLMÄHLICH und behutsam setzte sich religiöse Toleranz in der Welt durch. Niemand konnte etwas Böses in einer Gruppe alter Männer sehen, die sich an eine Mauer lehen, wie in dieser Aufnahme älterer Juden an der Klagemauer in Jerusalem. Protestanten und Katholiken begannen, einander das Recht zu gewähren, hohe Ämter zu bekleiden, Mitglieder der Regierung zu werden und wichtige Positionen im militärischen und öffentlichen Dienst zu bekleiden. Christen und Juden vertrauten sich allmählich, und in Indien lebten Hindus und Moslems relativ friedlich zusammen.

Der Grund für all diese Entwicklungen lag auch darin, daß neue Feinde der Religion und des Glaubens aufgetaucht waren: Darwinismus, Freidenkertum und Marxismus. In den Industrieländern gingen immer weniger Menschen zum Gottesdienst.

LENTEMENT et précautionneusement, la tolérance religieuse se répandait à travers le monde. Il faut être bien fou pour voir le mal dans un groupe de vieillards appuyés contre un mur, tels ces vieux juifs près du mur des Lamentations à Jérusalem. Les protestants et les catholiques se mettaient à s'accorder réciproquement le droit d'occuper des fonctions élevées, d'obtenir des portefeuilles, d'accéder à des postes importants dans la fonction militaire ou civile. Les chrétiens et les juifs commençaient à se faire confiance. En Inde, les hindous et les musulmans vivaient relativement en paix.

Une des raisons en était peut-être que des nouveaux ennemis de la religion et de la foi avaient surgi : le darwinisme, la libre pensée et le marxisme. Dans les sociétés industrielles, la fréquentation des églises diminuait de façon dramatique.

WISDOM and holiness were still almost synonymous with old age. The camera respectfully recorded a Samaritan High Priest, displaying the Pentateuch Roll said to have been written by Eleazar (1); three aged Jews reflecting beneath a fig tree (2); and a Georgian Jew wearing a phylactery on his forehead (3).

WEISHEIT und Heiligkeit waren noch immer nahezu gleichbedeutend mit hohem Alter. Respektvoll nahm die Kamera einen Samariter-Priester auf, der die angeblich von Eleazar verfaßte Pentateuch-Rolle hält (1); drei alte Juden in Andacht unter einem Feigenbaum (2) und ein georgischer Jude mit einem Phylakterion auf der Stirn (3).

LA sagesse et la sainteté demeuraient synonymes, ou presque, de grand âge. L'appareil photographique a respectueusement pris un haut dignitaire samaritain présentant le rouleau du pentateuque supposé avoir été écrit par Eléazar (1) ; trois juifs âgés réfléchissent sous un figuier (2) ; ici un juif géorgien portant un phylactère sur le front (3).

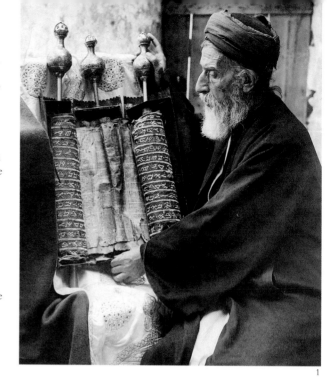

1

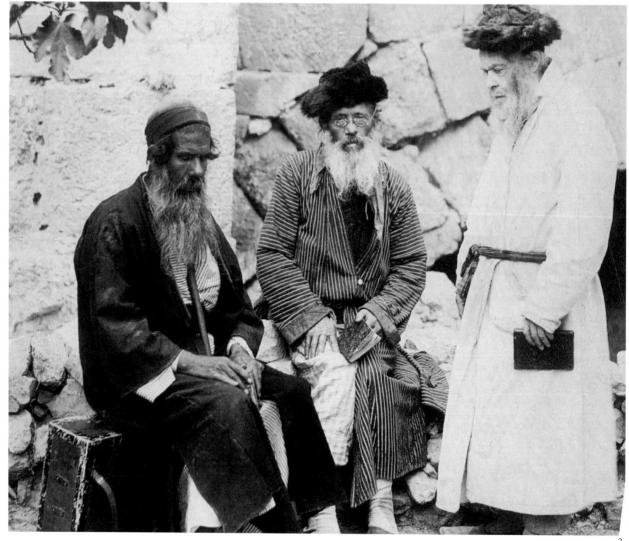

2

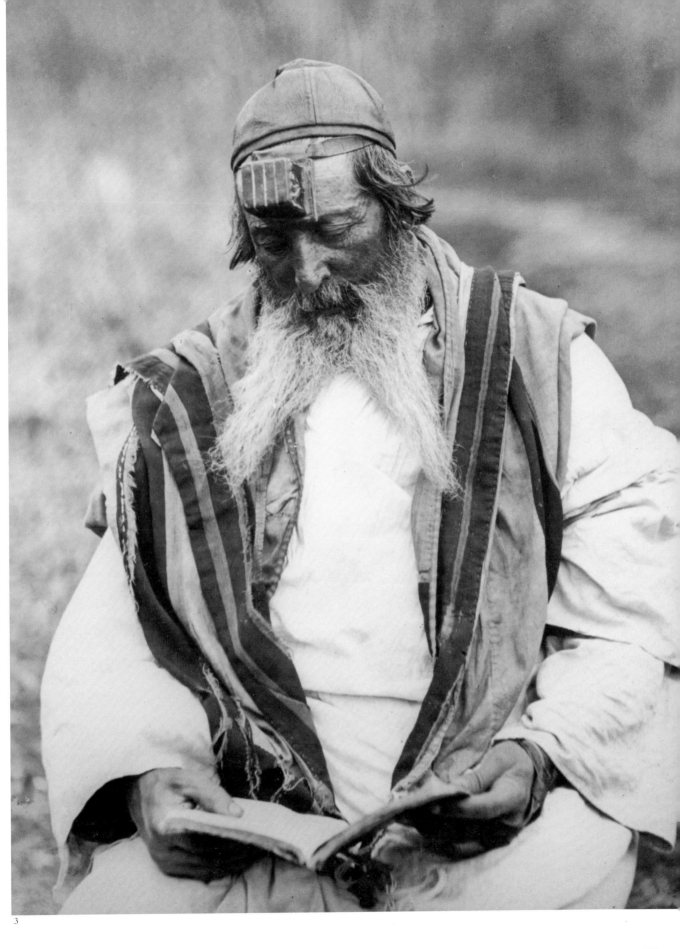

3

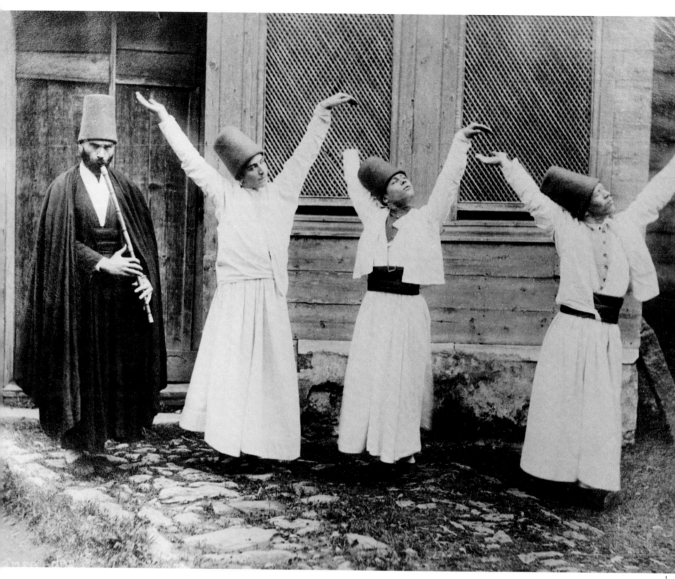

1

MARK Twain was impressed by the whirling Dervishes he came across in Constantinople in 1869. To induce a trance-like state, 'they spun on the left foot, and kept themselves going by passing the right rapidly before it and digging it against the floor. Most of them spun around 40 times in a minute, and one averaged about 61 times to the minute, and kept it up for 25 minutes... They made no noise of any kind, and most of them tilted their heads back and closed their eyes, entranced with a sort of devotional ecstasy... Sick persons came and lay down... and the patriarch walked upon their bodies. He was supposed to cure their diseases by trampling upon their breasts or backs or standing on the backs of their necks.'

MARK Twain zeigte sich beeindruckt von den wirbelnden Derwischen, die er 1869 in Konstantinopel sah. Um einen tranceartigen Zustand zu erreichen, »drehten sie sich auf dem linken Fuß, wobei sie sich schnell mit dem rechten Fuß abstießen. Die meisten von ihnen drehten sich vierzigmal in der Minute, und einer brachte es für die Dauer von fast einer halben Stunde sogar auf 61 Umdrehungen pro Minute ... Sie machten keinerlei Geräusche, und die meisten warfen ihre Köpfe zurück, schlossen die Augen und brachten sich in einen Zustand hinge-bungsvoller Ekstase ... Kranke Menschen kamen und legten sich auf den Boden ... und der Älteste der Derwische ging über ihre Körper. Er sollte sie von ihren Krank-heiten heilen, indem er ihnen auf die Brust oder auf den Rücken sprang oder sich auf ihren Nacken stellte.«

MARK Twain fut impressionné par les derviches tourneurs qu'il découvrit à Constantinople en 1869. « Ils induisaient leur état de transe en pivotant rapidement sur leur pied gauche, et pour conserver leur élan donnaient de petits coups rapides sur le sol en faisant passer leur pied droit devant celui de gauche. La plupart d'entre eux faisaient 40 tours à la minute, tandis que l'un d'entre eux tournait en moyenne 61 fois dans la minute et cela pendant 25 minutes ... Ils ne faisaient absolument aucun bruit, la plupart renversaient la tête en arrière et fermaient les yeux en pleine transe de dévotion et d'extase ... Les mala-des venaient s'allonger ... et le patriarche des derviches leur marchait sur le corps. Il était censé soigner leurs maladies en leur piétinant la poitrine, le dos ou encore en se tenant debout sur leur nuque. »

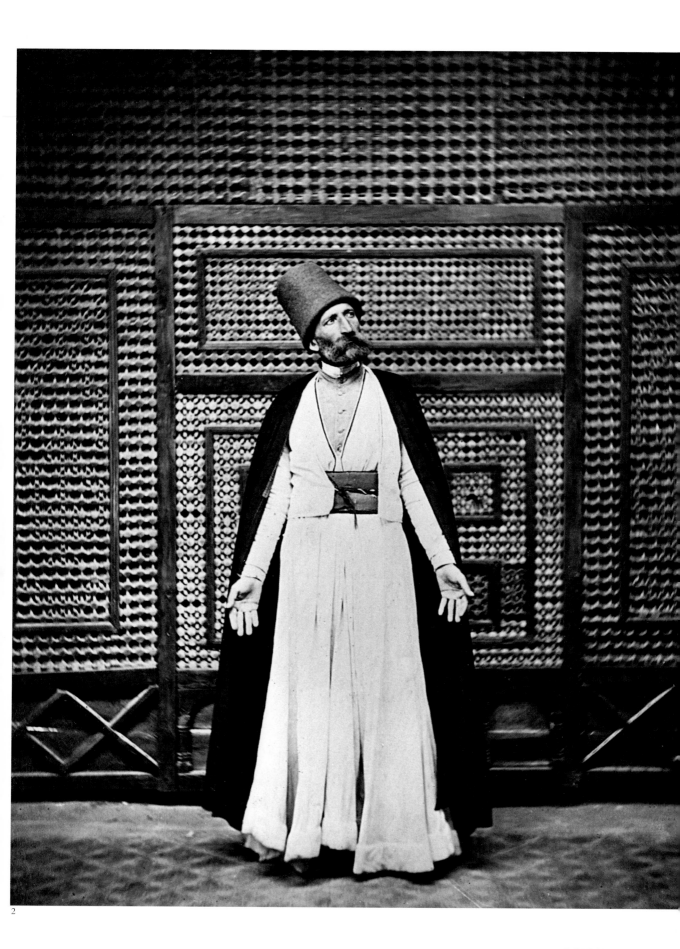

2

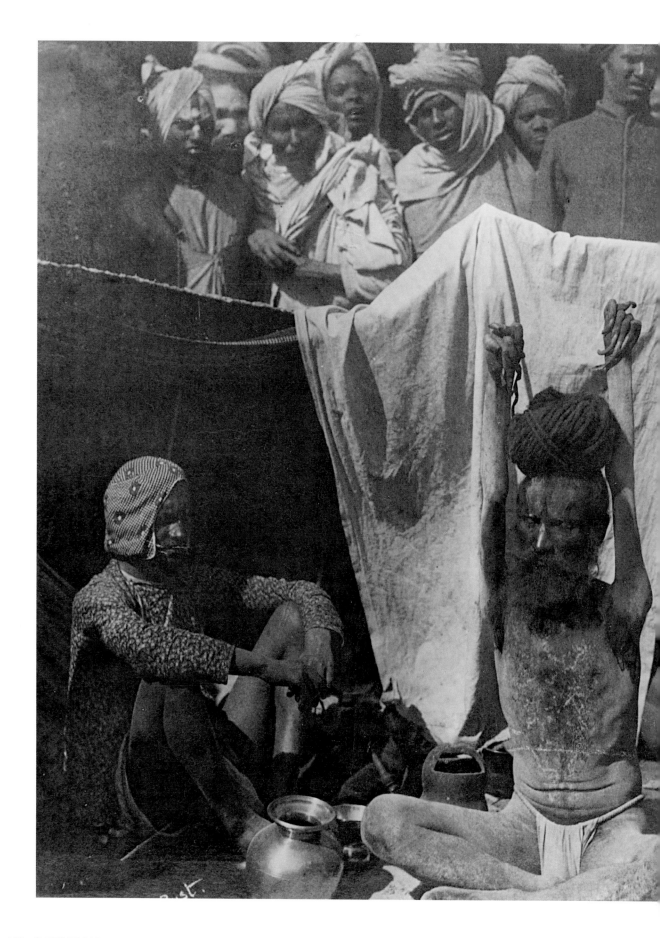

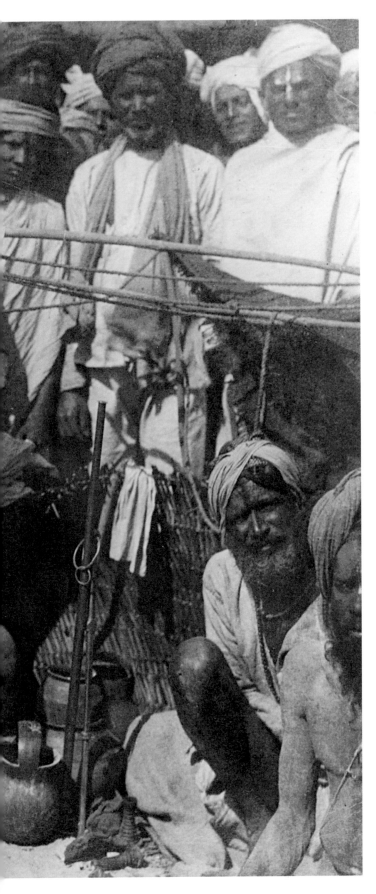

THE wandering mendicants known as fakirs were to be found all over India. They were common to many religions, practising several forms of self-mortification – lying on beds of nails, walking over hot coals. Fakirs took vows of poverty, and poverty originally meant 'need of God'. The origin of the word *fakir* comes from a saying of Muhammad: 'al-faqr-fakhri', meaning 'poverty is my pride'.

DIE als Fakire bekannten wandernden Bettelmönche der verschiedensten Religionen konnte man in ganz Indien antreffen. Sie praktizierten viele Formen der Selbstkasteiung, legten sich auf Nagelbetten oder liefen über glühende Kohlen. Fakire legten Armutsgelübde ab, denn Armut bedeutete ursprünglich »Notwendigkeit Gottes«. Das Wort *Fakir* entstammt einem Ausspruch Mohammeds: »al-faqr-fakhri«, was soviel heißt wie »Armut ist mein Stolz«.

LES mendiants itinérants connus sous le nom de fakirs étaient répandus à travers toute l'Inde. Ils étaient communs à de nombreuses religions et pratiquaient diverses formes de mortification : s'étendre sur des lits de clous ou marcher sur des braises incandescentes. Les fakirs faisaient vœu de pauvreté, laquelle signifie à l'origine « besoin de Dieu ». Le mot *fakir* vient d'une parole de Mahomet : « Al-faqr-fakhri » qui signifie « la pauvreté est ma fierté ».

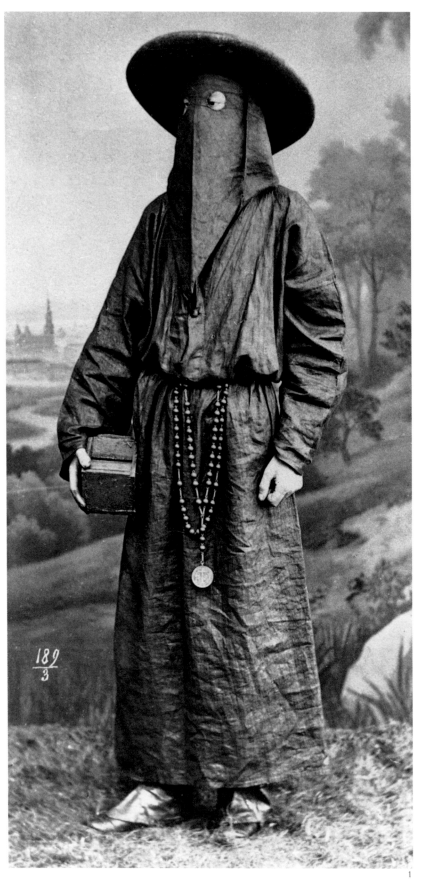

EARER home, the Fratelli della Misericordia (1) were a radical spiritual branch of the Franciscan Order, originally strongly anti-clerical, and regarded by some as heretics. Like the nuns of Biarritz (2), they kept their faces well hidden from camera and public. The monks of St Bernard in Switzerland (3) were more outgoing – the pose here seems to suggest an early all-male version of *The Sound of Music*.

IN heimatlichen Gefilden gab es die Fratelli della Misericordia (1), ein radikaler spiritueller Zweig des Franziskanerordens, der ursprünglich äußerst antiklerikal war und von manchen als ketzerisch betrachtet wurde. Wie die Nonnen von Biarritz (2) verhüllten sie ihre Gesichter vor der Kamera und der Öffentlichkeit. Die Mönche von St. Bernhard (3) in der Schweiz waren der Welt mehr zugewandt; diese Pose hier erinnert an eine frühe, rein männliche Version von *Meine Lieder, meine Träume*.

PLUS proches de nous, les Fratelli (1) della Misericordia composaient une branche spirituelle radicale de l'ordre des franciscains et, en raison de leur origine fortement anticléricale, passaient aux yeux de certains pour des hérétiques. De même que les nonnes de Biarritz (2), ils tenaient soigneusement leurs visages à l'abri des appareils photographiques et du public. Les moines de Saint-Bernard, en Suisse (3), étaient plus extravertis. Leur pose évoque ici une version précoce et entièrement masculine de *The Sound of Music*.

(Overleaf)
IN 1858 Bernadette Soubirous and her sister reported their vision of the Virgin Mary in a cave near Lourdes. Within a few years it had become a major shrine and Lourdes itself had become a pilgrim centre (1). If the people didn't come to God, however, in 1911 the Motor Mission Van brought God to the people (2). But the Catholic Church still had a firm hold on the souls of many in Europe, and a religious procession (3) was sure to bring out the crowds.

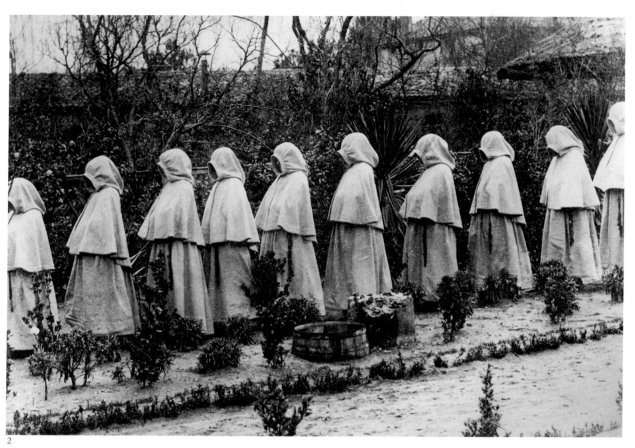

2

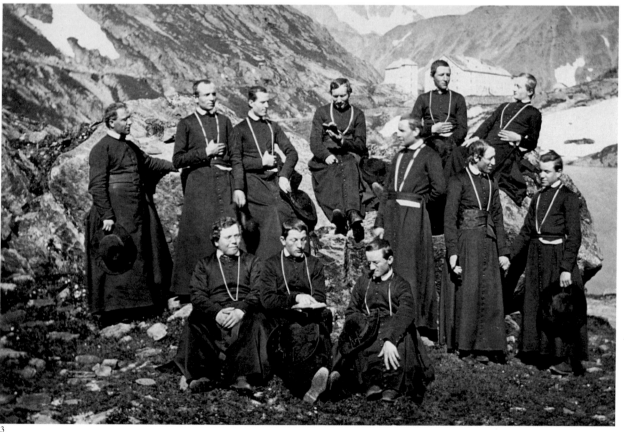

3

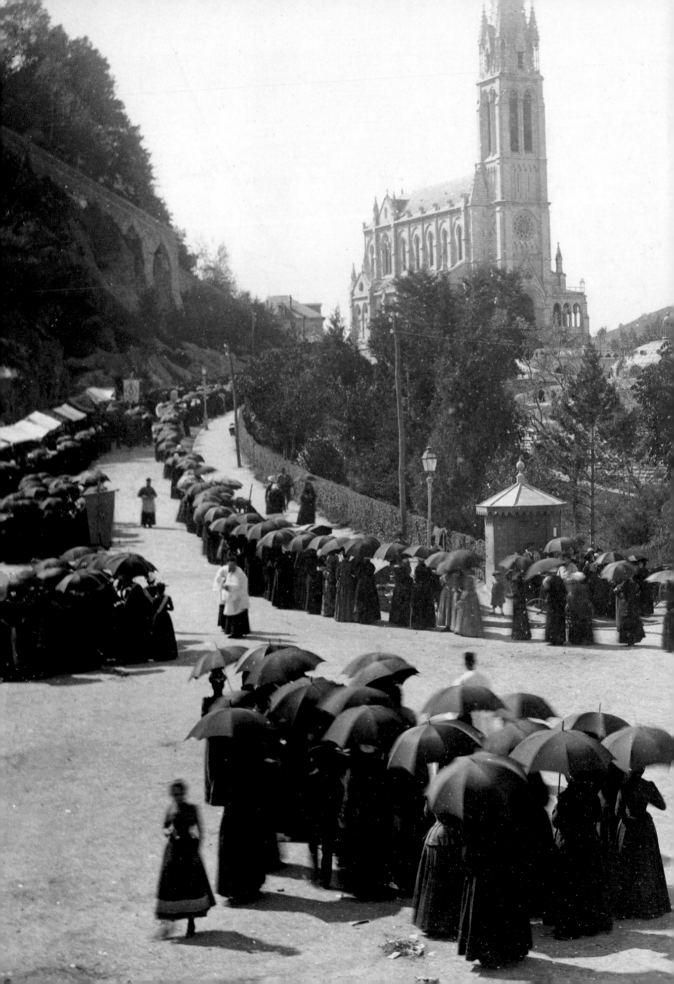

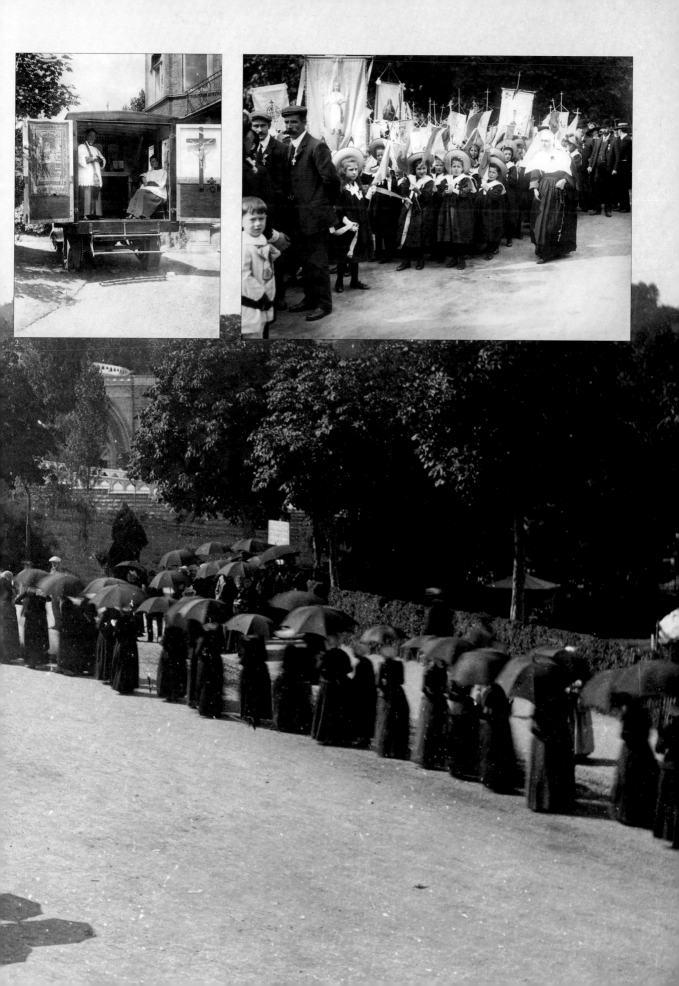

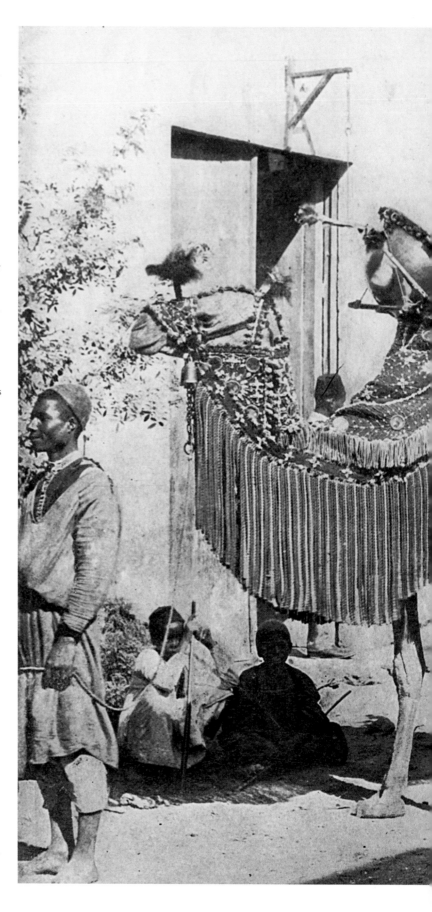

Few European weddings could rival those of more exotic cultures in the lavishness of costume and decoration. This Arab procession in Cairo could almost be a scene from *Kismet*. Hired musicians preceded the bridal party to the house of the bridegroom. The European writer of the caption to this photograph described the camels as being 'decked in gaudy trappings'.

Wenn es um prachtvolle Kostüme und Dekorationen ging, konnten nur wenige europäische Hochzeiten mit denen exotischerer Kulturen mithalten. Diese arabische Prozession in Kairo mutet an wie eine Szene aus *Kismet*. Gemietete Musikanten geleiteten die Braut und ihre Gesellschaft zum Haus des Bräutigams. Der europäische Verfasser der Unterschrift zu dieser Photographie beschrieb die Kamele als »in leuchtend bunten Schmuck gehüllt«.

Peu de mariages européens pouvaient rivaliser en faste avec ceux des cultures plus exotiques. Cette procession arabe au Caire pourrait presque sortir d'une scène de *Kismet*. Des musiciens avaient été engagés pour précéder le cortège de la mariée jusqu'à la maison du futur époux. L'européen qui a rédigé la légende de cette photographie a écrit que les chameaux étaient « recouverts d'ornements criards ».

(*Vorherige Seiten*)
Im Jahre 1858 berichteten Bernadette Soubirous und ihre Schwester, in einer Grotte in der Nähe von Lourdes sei ihnen die Jungfrau Maria erschienen. Innerhalb weniger Jahre war die Grotte zum Schrein und Lourdes zu einem Wallfahrtsort geworden (1). Wenn die Menschen im Jahre 1911 jedoch nicht zu Gott kamen, brachte der Missionswagen Gott zu den Menschen (2). Aber die katholische Kirche hatte noch immer großen Einfluß auf das Seelenleben vieler Europäer, und eine religiöse Prozession (3) lockte die Menschen in Scharen auf die Straße.

(*Pages précédentes*)
En 1858, Bernadette Soubirous et sa sœur racontèrent avoir eu une vision de la Vierge Marie dans une grotte de Lourdes. En l'espace de quelques années, celle-ci et la ville de Lourdes elle-même devinrent un haut lieu de pélerinage (1). Si les gens n'allaient pas à Dieu, en 1911 la mission motorisée le leur amenait dans un fourgon (2). Du reste l'Église catholique conservait une solide emprise sur de nombreuses âmes en Europe, et toute procession religieuse (3) était assurée d'attirer du monde.

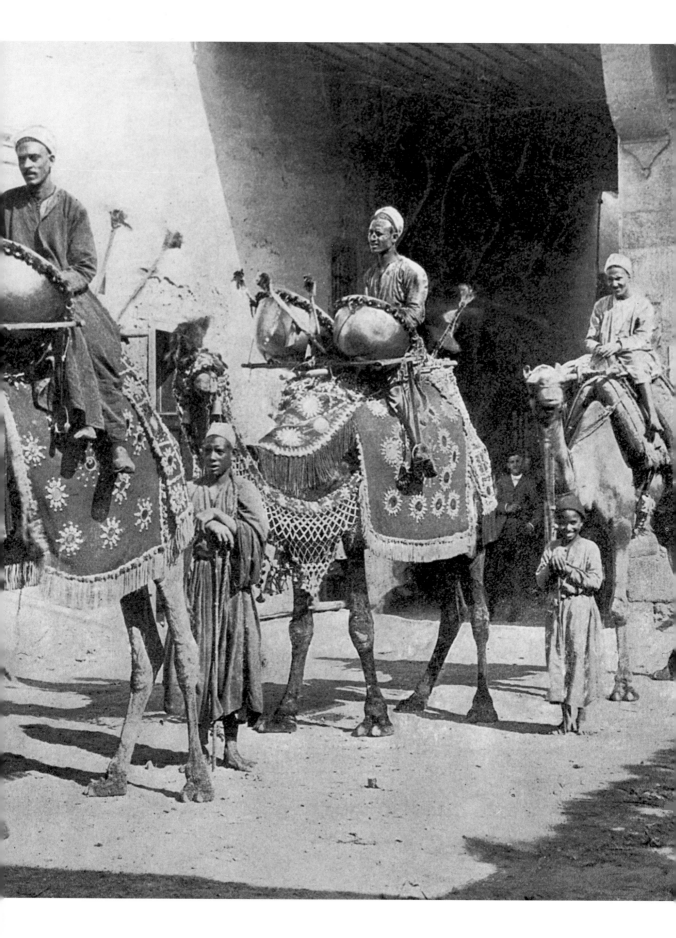

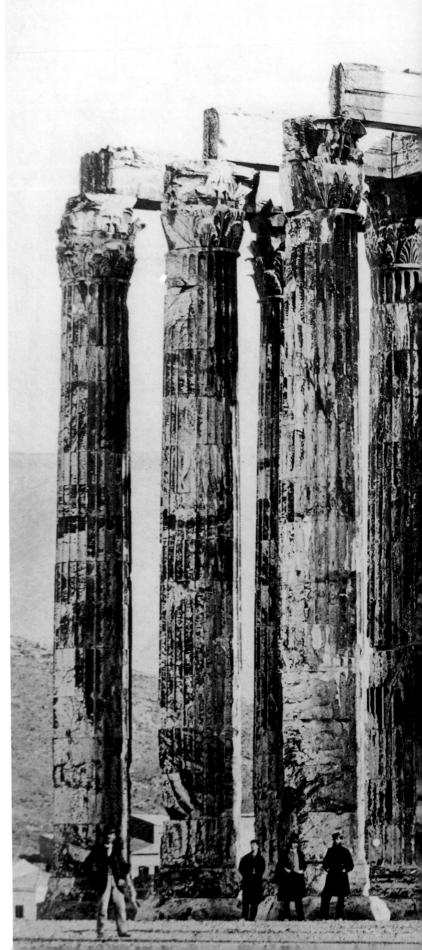

UNTIL the 19th century, the Grand Tour of Europe and the Near East had been a privilege enjoyed only by the rich, an adventure for the bold or desperate. But by 1850 tourism had become a well established industry in Europe. Mark Twain sailed from New York in 1867 with a party of American tourists, to visit Paris, Heidelberg, Rome, Constantinople and the Holy Land. At the end of his tour he wrote: 'I have no fault to find with the manner in which our excursion was conducted. It would be well if such an excursion could be gotten up every year and the system regularly inaugurated.' A fellow American writer, Henry James, was less complimentary about the average British tourist – such as these at Athens in 1860. 'They are always and everywhere the same,' he wrote, 'carrying with them in their costume and physiognomy, that indefinable expression of not considering anything out of England worth making, physically or morally, a toilet for.' William Howard Russell, a newspaper correspondent, disliked all tourists: 'They fill hotels inconveniently, they crowd sites which ought to be approached in reverential silence… The very haggling and bargaining which accompany their ways makes one feel uncomfortable.'

BIS zum 19. Jahrhundert war die »Grand Tour« durch Europa und in den Nahen Osten ein Privileg der Reichen, ein Abenteuer für Mutige und Verzweifelte. Aber um 1850 war der Tourismus in Europa zu einem etablierten Industriezweig geworden. Mark Twain bestieg 1867 zusammen mit anderen amerikanischen Touristen in New York ein Schiff und besuchte Paris, Heidelberg, Rom, Konstantinopel und das Heilige Land. Am Ende seiner Reise schrieb er: »Ich habe nichts auszusetzen an der Art, wie unsere Exkursion geführt wurde. Es wäre schön, wenn eine solche Reise jedes Jahr veranstaltet und das System zur festen Einrichtung würde.« Ein amerikanischer Schriftstellerkollege, Henry James, war weniger gut auf englische Touristen, wie diese 1860 in Athen, zu sprechen: »Sie sind immer und überall gleich…und tragen in ihrer Kleidung und ihrer Physiognomie diesen undefinierbaren Ausdruck, daß es außerhalb von England nichts gibt, das es wert wäre, sich körperlich oder moralisch herzurichten.« William Howard Russell, ein Zeitungskorrespondent, verabscheute alle Touristen: »Sie füllen rücksichtslos die Hotels, scharen sich um Sehenswürdigkeiten, denen man sich in respektvoller Stille nähern sollte … Durch ihr ständiges Handeln und Feilschen fühlt man sich äußerst unbehaglich.«

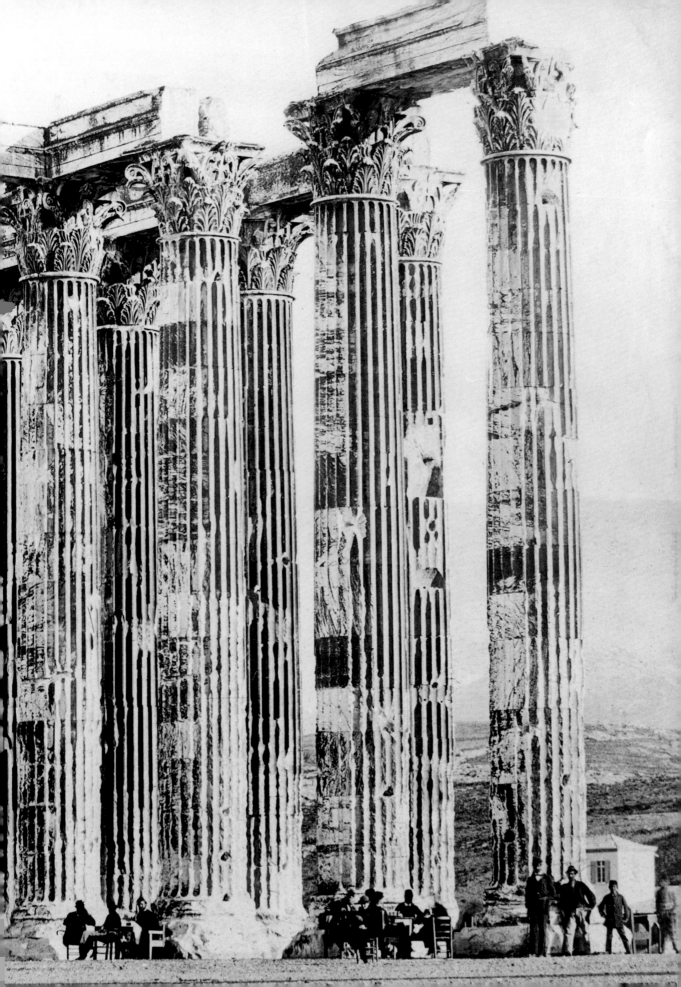

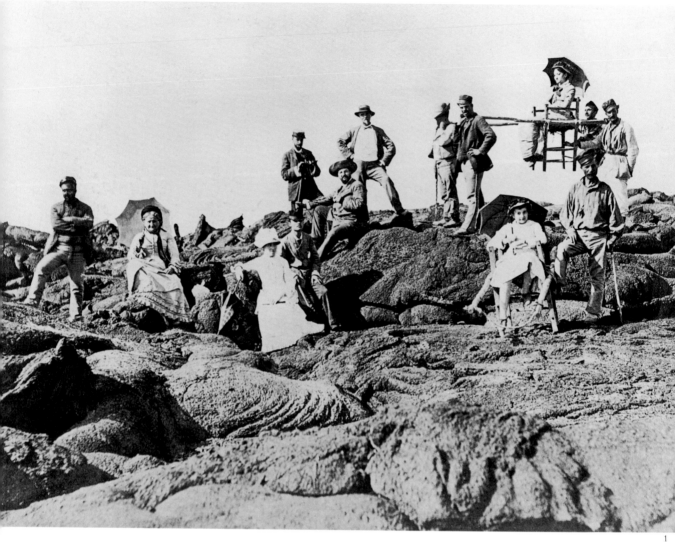

1

(*Pages précédentes*)

Jusqu'au XIXe siècle, le grand circuit
européen et le Proche-Orient étaient
un privilège réservé aux seuls riches, une
aventure pour les téméraires ou les déses-
pérés. Mais dès 1850, l'industrie touristique
était bien implantée en Europe. Mark Twain
s'embarqua à New York en 1867 en compagnie d'un groupe de touristes américains
pour visiter Paris, Heidelberg, Rome,
Constantinople et la Terre Sainte. Au terme
du circuit il nota : « Je n'ai rien à redire de
la manière dont s'est déroulée notre excursion. Ce serait bien qu'une excursion
comme celle-ci soit mise sur pied chaque
année et que sa pratique en soit institution-
nalisée. » Un écrivain de ses compatriotes,

Henry James, parlait en termes moins
élogieux du touriste britannique moyen,
tels ceux-ci en 1860 : « Ils sont toujours et
partout les mêmes, arborant sur toute leur
personne et leur physionomie cet air
indéfinissable de ne rien trouver hors de
l'Angleterre qui vaille le dérangement, ni
physique ni mental. » William Howard
Russell, qui était correspondant de presse,
détestait tous les touristes : « Ils encombrent
fâcheusement les hôtels, envahissent les
sites qui devraient être approchés dans un
silence révérencieux … La seule vision des
chipotages et des marchandages auxquels
ils se livrent vous met horriblement mal à
l'aise. »

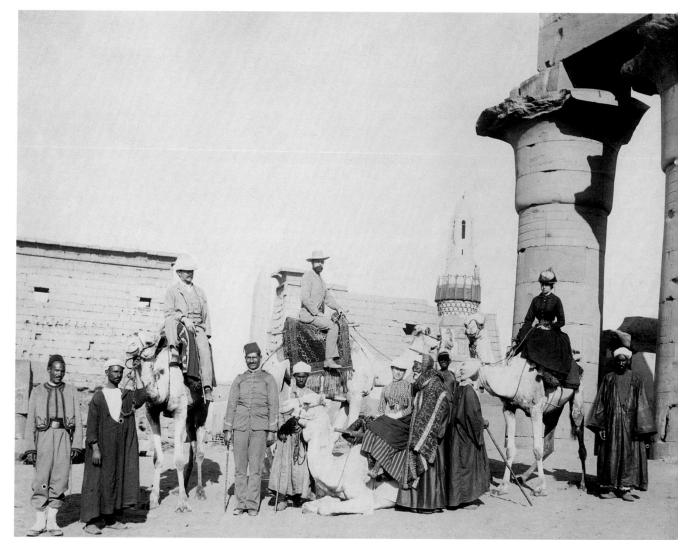

2

IT took Mark Twain an hour and a quarter to climb up the rough narrow trail over the old lava bed from Annunziata to the summit of Mount Vesuvius. Other tourists, like these in 1880 (1), had the services of local porters. 'They crowd you, infest you, swarm about you, and sweat and smell offensively, and look sneaky and mean and obsequious.' At the summit Twain recorded: 'Some of the boys thrust long strips of paper down into the holes and set them on fire, and so achieved the glory of lighting their cigars by the flames of Vesuvius.' Others cooked eggs.

At Luxor (2) tourists could enjoy the wonders of the Temple of Karnak, picnic in the Valley of the Kings, or inhale the putrefying stink that arose from pits of imperfectly preserved mummies.

MARK Twain brauchte eineinviertel Stunden, um über den rauhen, schmalen Pfad des Lavabetts von Annunziata zum Gipfel des Vesuv zu gelangen. Andere Touristen, wie diese im Jahre 1880 (1), nahmen die Dienste einheimischer Träger in Anspruch. »Sie umzingeln einen, fallen über einen her, schwirren um einen herum, sie schwitzen und stinken fürchterlich und sehen verschlagen, böse und unterwürfig aus.« Auf dem Gipfel notierte Twain: »Einige der Jungen warfen lange Papierstreifen in Löcher und steckten sie in Brand, so daß sie ruhmreich behaupten konnten, ihre Zigarren mit den Flammen des Vesuv angezündet zu haben.« Andere kochten Eier.

In Luxor (2) konnten sich Touristen am Wunder des Karnak-Tempels erfreuen, im Tal der Könige picknicken oder den Verwesungsgestank einatmen, der schlecht konservierten Mumien entströmte.

MARK Twain dut grimper une heure et quart durant l'étroit et rude sentier qui mène au-dessus de l'ancien lit de lave de l'Annunziata jusqu'au sommet de la montagne du Vésuve. D'autres touristes, comme ceux-ci en 1880 (1), faisaient appel aux services des porteurs locaux. « Ils vous envahissent, vous infestent, grouillent autour de vous, transpirent de manière malodorante, et ont des allures de serpents mesquins et obséquieux. » Au sommet Twain nota: « Des garçons lançaient de longues bandes de papier à l'intérieur des trous qu'ils enflammaient, se couvrant ainsi de la gloire d'allumer leurs cigares aux flammes du Vésuve. » D'autres se faisaient cuire des œufs.

À Louxor (2), les touristes pouvaient s'émerveiller devant le temple de Karnak, pique-niquer dans la vallée des Rois ou inhaler les odeurs putrides qui s'élevaient des fosses où finissaient de se décomposer des momies mal conservées.

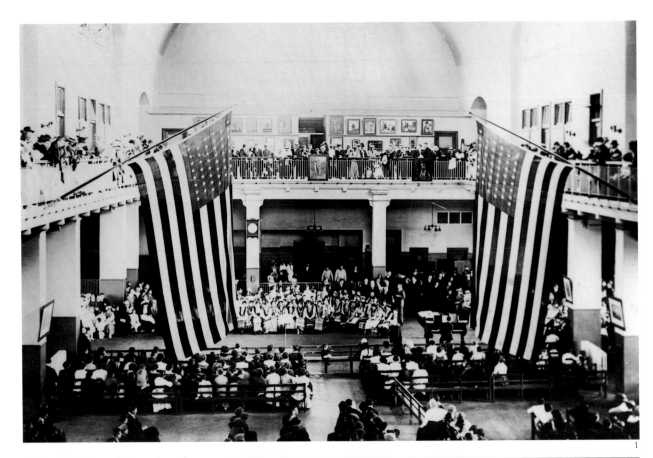

E LLIS Island wasn't just a place of
educational tests, physical examinations
and disinfectant baths. Immigrants
occasionally had the chance to celebrate
the culture they brought with them – this
Ukrainian concert took place in 1916 (1).
But bureaucracy was strict – all arrivals
were labelled – and there was an overall
atmosphere of a cattle market about many
of the proceedings (2). The journey itself
was long and hard – thousands of miles
across Europe to the coast, and then the
wait for a boat (3). It took these Norwegian
immigrants up to two weeks to sail across
the Atlantic in 1870 (4).

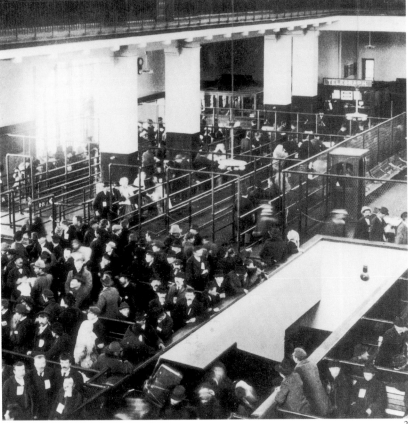

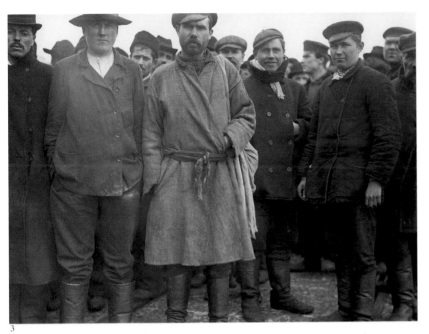

3

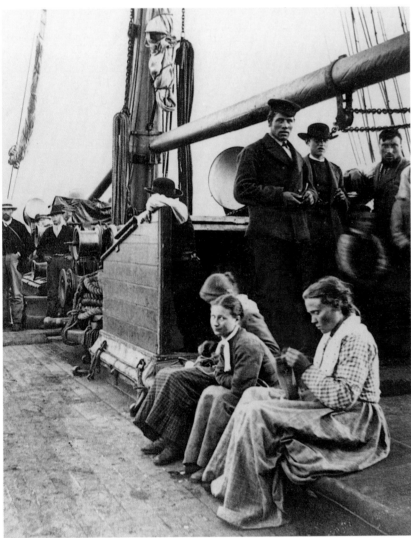

4

ELLIS Island war nicht nur ein Ort für Schulprüfungen, ärztliche Untersuchungen und Desinfektionsbäder. Gelegentlich hatten Immigranten die Möglichkeit, die Kultur zu feiern, die sie mitgebracht hatten – dieses ukrainische Konzert fand im Jahre 1916 statt (1). Aber die Bürokratie war streng. Alle Ankömmlinge wurden registriert, und bei vielen Prozeduren herrschte die Atmosphäre eines Viehmarktes (2). Die Reise selbst war lang und strapaziös; Tausende von Kilometern mußten durch Europa bis zur Küste zurückgelegt werden, bevor das Warten auf ein Schiff begann (3). Diese norwegischen Immigranten brauchten 1870 fast zwei Wochen, um den Atlantik zu überqueren (4).

ELLIS Island n'était pas seulement un endroit où étaient vérifiés le niveau d'instruction et la condition physique ni où l'on prenait des bains désinfectants. Les immigrants avaient de temps à autre l'occasion de célébrer la culture qu'ils emportaient avec eux : concert ukrainien en 1916 (1). Mais la bureaucratie était rigoureuse ; toute arrivée était étiquetée, et bien des procédures se déroulaient dans une ambiance générale évoquant le marché aux bestiaux (2). Le voyage lui-même, long et pénible, imposait de parcourir des milliers de kilomètres à travers l'Europe jusqu'à la côte, et pour finir d'attendre avant de pouvoir embarquer (3). Ces immigrants norvégiens ont mis deux semaines à traverser l'Atlantique en 1870 (4).

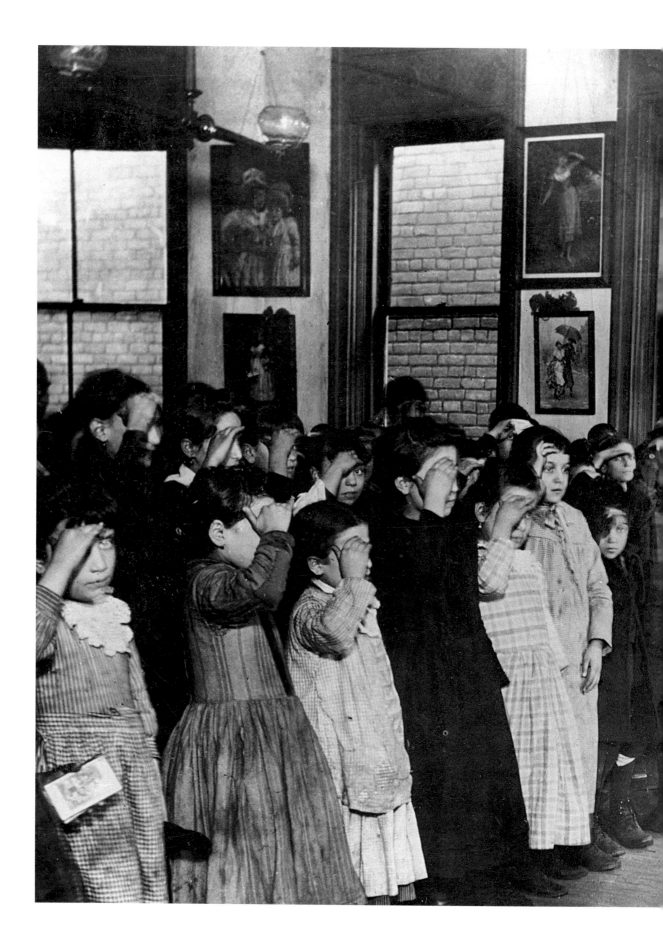

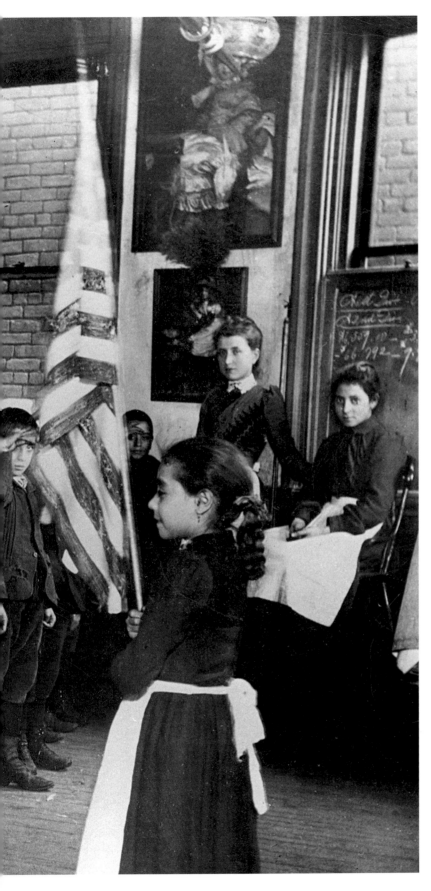

IN 1887, a police reporter for the New York *Daily Tribune* took some of the earliest flashlight photographs, to record the lives and hard times of refugees from Europe. His name was Jacob Riis, and he was himself from Denmark. His most lasting work was the series of hundreds of pictures he took in the slums of New York. The pictures were lost for nearly 60 years, but were rediscovered in 1947 and presented to the Museum of the City of New York. Describing the children saluting the flag and repeating the oath of allegiance at the Mott Street Industrial School, Riis wrote: 'No one can hear it and doubt that the children mean every word and will not be apt to forget that lesson soon.'

IM Jahre 1887 machte ein Polizeireporter der New Yorker *Daily Tribune* einige der ersten Blitzlichtaufnahmen und photographierte das harte Leben europäischer Flüchtlinge. Er hieß Jacob Riis und war selbst ein Immigrant, aus Dänemark. Seine beeindruckendste Arbeit waren die vielen hundert Photographien, die er in den Slums von New York gemacht hatte. Die Bilder waren fast sechzig Jahre lang verschollen, sie tauchten 1947 jedoch wieder auf und wurden dem Museum der Stadt New York übergeben. Über die Kinder, die vor der Flagge salutieren und den Treueeid in der Erziehungsanstalt für verwahrloste Kinder in der Mott Street sprechen, schrieb Riis: »Niemand, der es hört, kann daran zweifeln, daß diese Kinder jedes Wort, das sie sagen, ernst meinen und diese Lektion so bald nicht vergessen werden.«

EN 1887, un reporter chargé de couvrir les affaires policières pour le *Daily Tribune* new-yorkais prenait quelques-unes des toutes premières photographies au flash, sauvant ainsi de l'oubli la vie et les durs moments des réfugiés venus d'Europe. Il s'appelait Jacob Riis et il était lui-même immigré du Danemark. Les centaines de photos qu'il a prises des bidonvilles de New York restent son œuvre la plus marquante. Ces images avaient été perdues pendant près de soixante ans, avant d'être redécouvertes en 1947 et offertes au musée de la ville de New York. Décrivant la cérémonie de l'allégeance au drapeau des enfants de l'Industrial School à Mott Street, Riis écrit : « Quiconque les entend ne peut être que convaincu que ces enfants croient chacun de leurs mots et qu'ils ne sont pas prêts d'oublier cette leçon de si tôt. »

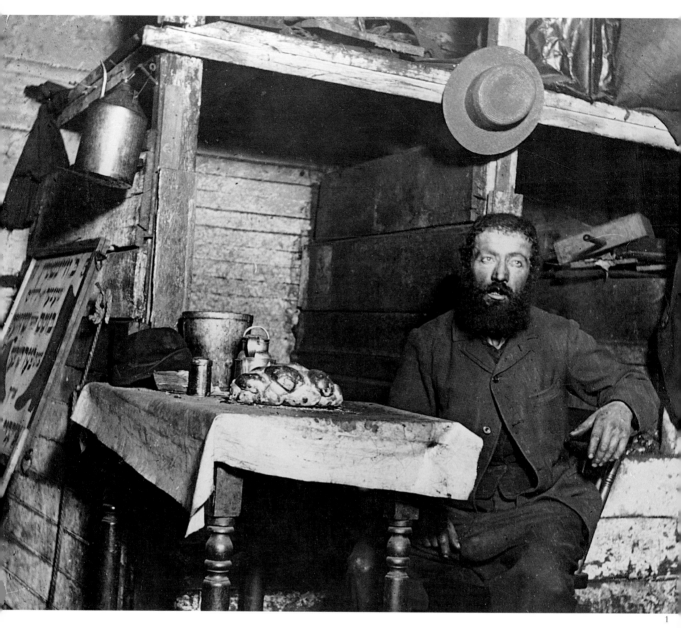

1

RIIS captioned the picture of the poor Jewish cobbler (1): 'Ready for the Sabbath Eve in a coal-cellar ... The Board of Health has ordered the family out... but it will require the steady vigilance of the police for many months to make sure that the cellar is not again used for a living room. Then it will be turned into a coal cellar or a shoe-shop by a cobbler of old boots, and the sanitary police in their midnight tours will find it a bedroom for mayhaps half a dozen lodgers, all of whom "happened in", as the tenant will swear the next day, and fell asleep here.' The family of Jewish tailors (2) fared better – at least they were working above ground.

ZUM Bild des armen jüdischen Schusters (1) schrieb Riis: »Fertig für den Abend des Sabbat im Kohlenkeller ... Das Gesundheitsamt hat die Familie ausgewiesen ... aber es wird vieler Monate der ständigen Überwachung durch die Polizei bedürfen, um sicherzustellen, daß der Keller nicht wieder als Wohnraum genutzt wird. Dann wird daraus ein Kohlenkeller oder das Geschäft eines

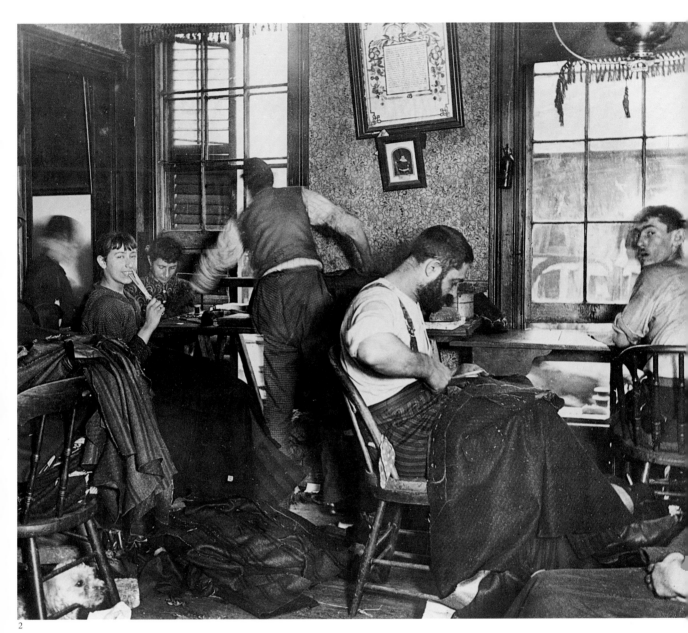

2

Flickschusters, und die Gesundheitspolizei wird auf ihren nächtlichen Kontrollgängen darin ein Schlafzimmer für etwa ein halbes Dutzend Untermieter vorfinden, die alle ›zufällig vorbeigekommen‹ und dort eingeschlafen sind, wie der Hauptmieter am nächsten Tag beteuern wird.« Der Familie des jüdischen Schneiders (2) erging es besser, zumindest arbeitete sie nicht unter der Erde.

RIIS a rédigé la légende de la photographie du pauvre savetier juif : « Préparatifs de Sabbat dans une cave à charbon … Les services sanitaires ont ordonné l'expulsion de la famille … cependant il faudra une vigilance soutenue de la police des mois durant pour empêcher que la cave ne serve à nouveau d'habitation. Elle sera ensuite transformée en cave à charbon ou en magasin de chaussures par un savetier faisant le commerce de vieux souliers, jusqu'à ce qu'un jour la police sanitaire au cours d'une ronde de nuit n'y découvre une chambre à coucher contenant peut-être six occupants qui tous, en jurera le locataire le lendemain, ‹ passant par là › s'y étaient endormis. » La famille de tailleurs juifs (2) était mieux lotie, au moins elle ne travaillait pas sous terre.

Peoples

For centuries, the advance of European civilization had posed a major threat to the indigenous people of many parts of the world. In the 16th century, Spanish conquistadores under Cortés had not only conquered Mexico, but had completely destroyed the Aztec culture they found there. The Aztecs believed that, for their society to continue, the sun and the earth had to be nourished with human blood and human hearts. In the heyday of their empire, the Aztecs had sacrificed 10,000 victims a year to appease their principal god, Huitzilopochtli. By the time this photograph was taken (1), some 350 years later, the Aztec couple in it were among the last survivors of this warlike race that had once been the most powerful in Central America. Their numbers had dwindled to a pitiful few.

For, wherever they went, the Europeans brought with them a mixture of blessings and curses. They abolished slavery in Africa but plundered most of the continent for its raw materials and cheap labour. They abolished Thuggee in India, where for hundreds of years travellers had feared this secret society of stranglers – but denied the citizens of India any say in their own government. They helped put an end to the time-honoured system of binding a young girl's feet in China, but greatly increased the trade in and consumption of opium, so that millions became addicts.

In some cases the blessings are hard to discern. Australian aborigines had lived contentedly for thousands of years, before settlers and farmers brought fever, greed and an inexhaustible supply of cheap alcohol. For centuries, the Plains Indians of North America had prospered as nomadic hunters over millions of square miles. They were proud people who respected the earth and even the buffalo that they killed for food, clothing, tools and shelter. Within a few decades of the coming of the white man they had been driven into reservations, slaughtered in their thousands and weakened by disease. In the 1880s George Augustus Sala saw once great warriors begging at railroad stations. 'The white post-traders sell them poisonous whisky and cheat them in every conceivable manner, while the white squatters crowd them out by stealing the land assigned for Indian occupancy by the United States.' The inhabitants of Tasmania were rounded up en masse and shipped off to tiny Flinders Island by British government agents. 'When they saw from shipboard the splendid country which they were promised,' wrote an eye-witness of this appalling genocide, 'they betrayed the greatest agitation, gazing with strained eyes at the

sterile shore, uttering melancholy moans, and, with arms hanging beside them, trembling with convulsive feeling. The winds were violent and cold, the rain and sleet were penetrating and miserable… and this added to their foreboding that they were taken there to die.' Many died from chest and stomach complaints. Most died from homesickness. Not one survived.

But wherever they went, the Europeans also took their cameras and their notebooks, and maybe we should be grateful that they recorded the very people, places and cultures that they were about to destroy. In 1874 Viscountess Avonmore saw – from the safety of a train – 'a number of Indians on the war-path, dressed in all the glory of feathers, skins and scarlet blankets, leading their horses in single file over a frozen stream.' The same year the explorer John Forrest faced the terror of an aborigine attack in Australia: 'I saw from fifty to sixty natives running towards the camp, all plumed up and armed with spears and shields… One advanced to meet me and stood twenty yards off; I made friendly signs; he did not appear very hostile. All at once the whole number made a rush towards us, yelling and shouting with their spears shipped…' Forrest survived to tell the tale.

Among the most inflexible Christian interlopers were the Afrikaaners of South Africa. Theirs was a harsh, unforgiving God, who they believed approved their treatment of Hottentot and Bushman, whom they almost completely exterminated. Not for them the mealy-mouthed British insistence that black and white were equal before the law. More than any other group of European descent, the Boers of South Africa embodied the deafness and blindness of colonization and commerce to the values of other societies and cultures.

The problem was, of course, that Europeans saw themselves as superior to all other people, and therefore had a right to be in charge of the world. They had more advanced industries, weapons, ideas, commercial know-how, and public health. They were more inventive, better governed, better educated. And, above all, Europe was the workshop of Christianity, the faith that could save the heathen hordes from eternal damnation, whether they wanted it or not.

It was a two-way process. Europeans gained new markets and bigger dividends on their shares: everyone else gained the chance of life everlasting. It was God's will. The working millions of Africa, India, Asia had not come under European management 'merely that we might draw an annual profit from them, but that we

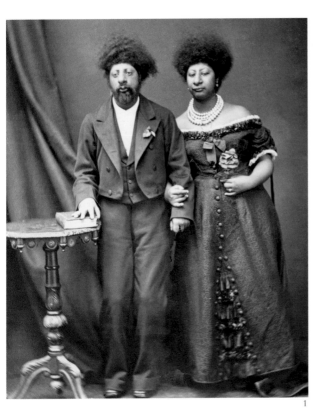

1

might diffuse among [these] inhabitants the light and the benign influence of the truth, the blessings of well-regulated society, the improvements and comforts of active industry.'

The tragedy was that these noble sentiments arose from an utter disregard for the older civilizations that were being swept aside. The people of Hindustan were 'lamentably degenerate and base'. The Africans were 'cannibal butchers'. The Chinese were 'revolting, diseased and filthy objects'. So it was small wonder that the Bushman and the Tasmanian disappeared, and the Sioux and the Cheyenne were herded into reservations. As for the Aztecs – well, they hadn't even managed to invent the wheel; they simply passed away, and only their language remained.

JAHRHUNDERTELANG hatte der Fortschritt der europäischen Zivilisation eine große Bedrohung für die Ureinwohner vieler Länder dieser Erde bedeutet. Im 16. Jahrhundert hatten die spanischen Conquistadores unter Cortéz nicht nur Mexiko erobert, sondern auch die aztekische Kultur, die sie dort vorfanden, völlig zerstört. Die Azteken glaubten, zur Erhaltung ihrer Gesellschaft die Sonne und die Erde mit menschlichem Blut und menschlichen Herzen speisen zu müssen. In der Blütezeit ihres Reiches hatten sie jährlich 10 000 Menschenopfer dargebracht, um ihren Hauptgott Huitzilopochtli zufriedenzustellen. Zu der Zeit, als obenstehende Aufnahme (1) gemacht wurde,

etwa 350 Jahre später, gehörte das abgebildete aztekische Paar zu den letzten Überlebenden dieses kriegerischen Volkes, einst das mächtigste in Zentralamerika.

Denn wo die Europäer auch hinkamen, brachten sie eine Mischung aus Segnungen und Flüchen mit. Sie schafften zwar die Sklaverei in Afrika ab, beuteten aber fast den gesamten Kontinent wegen seiner Bodenschätze und billigen Arbeitskräfte aus. In Indien beseitigten sie die Thug, eine Raubmörderbande, die Reisende seit Hunderten von Jahren gefürchtet hatten, verweigerten den Bürgern von Indien aber jedes Mitspracherecht in ihrer eigenen Regierung. In China trugen sie zwar zur Beendigung des althergebrachten Brauchs bei, die Füße junger Mädchen zusammenzuschnüren, sie förderten aber auch Handel und Konsum von Opium, so daß Millionen von Menschen süchtig wurden. Der Photograph John Thomson beschrieb die Freuden einer eleganten Opiumhöhle in den 1870er Jahren: »... mit Mädchen, die sich stets bereithalten, einige, um die Pfeife vorzubereiten und mit Opium zu stopfen, andere, um süße Lieder zu singen, und den Schlafenden in das Reich der Träume zu geleiten.«

In einigen Fällen sind die Segnungen nur schwer auszumachen. Australische Aborigines hatten Tausende von Jahren zufrieden gelebt, bevor Siedler und Farmer das Fieber, Habgier und unerschöpfliche Vorräte billigen Alkohols brachten. Jahrhundertelang hatten die Indianer der nordamerikanischen Prärie als jagende Nomaden ein Gebiet von Millionen Quadratkilometern bevölkert. Sie waren stolze Menschen, die nicht nur die Erde respektierten, sondern auch den Büffel, den sie töteten, um Essen, Kleidung, Werkzeuge und Zelte von ihm herzustellen. Innerhalb weniger Jahrzehnte nach der Ankunft des weißen Mannes waren sie in Reservate getrieben, zu Tausenden abgeschlachtet und durch Krankheiten geschwächt worden. In den 1880er Jahren sah George Augustus Sala einst große Krieger, die auf Bahnhöfen bettelten. »Die weißen Händler verkaufen ihnen schädlichen Whisky und machen sich auf jede nur erdenkliche Art über sie lustig, während die illegalen weißen Siedler sie von dem Land verdrängen, das ihnen von den Vereinigten Staaten zugewiesen wurde.« Die Bewohner von Tasmanien wurden in Massen zusammengetrieben und von britischen Regierungsvertretern auf das winzige Flinders Island verschifft. »Als sie von Bord des Schiffes aus das ›herrliche‹ Land sahen, das man ihnen versprochen hatte«, schrieb ein Augenzeuge dieses entsetzlichen Völkermords, »zeigten sie große Aufregung, starrten mit aufgerissenen Augen auf die karge Küste und stießen melancholische Seufzer aus; ihre Arme hingen kraftlos herab, und sie wurden von Krämpfen geschüttelt. Der Wind war rauh und kalt, Regen und

Graupelschauer durchnäßten sie bis auf die Haut … und ihre Vorahnung, daß man sie zum Sterben hierhergebracht hatte, wurde bestätigt.« Viele starben an inneren Krankheiten, die meisten jedoch an Heimweh. Nicht ein einziger überlebte.

Aber wohin die Europäer auch reisten, sie nahmen ihre Kameras und Notizbücher mit, und vielleicht sollten wir dankbar dafür sein, daß sie Berichte über die Menschen, Orte und Kulturen verfaßten, die sie dann zerstören sollten. Im Jahre 1874 sah die Viscountess Avonmore vom sicheren Eisenbahnabteil aus »einige Indianer auf dem Kriegspfad, die prächtige Federn, Häute und rote Decken trugen und ihre Pferde in einer Reihe über einen zugefrorenen Fluß führten«. Im selben Jahr erlebte der Forscher John Forrest in Australien die Schrecken eines Angriffs der Aborigines: »Ich sah zwischen fünfzig und sechzig Eingeborene auf das Lager zurennen, alle mit Federn geschmückt und mit Speeren und Schilden bewaffnet … Einer lief auf mich zu und blieb etwa zwanzig Meter vor mir stehen; ich machte ihm freundschaftliche Zeichen; er machte keinen sehr feindseligen Eindruck. Plötzlich rannten alle auf uns zu, schrien und schleuderten ihre Speere …« Forrest überlebte, um die Geschichte zu erzählen.

Zu den verbohrtesten christlichen Eindringlingen gehörten die Afrikaaner in Südafrika. Ihr Gott galt als streng und unversöhnlich, und sie waren überzeugt, er billige ihre Behandlung der Hottentotten und Buschmänner, die sie fast vollständig auslöschten. Die heuchlerische Behauptung der Briten, der schwarze und der weiße Mann seien vor dem Gesetz gleich, galt für sie nicht. Mehr als jede andere Gruppe von Europäern verkörperten die Buren Südafrikas die Taubheit und Blindheit von Kolonisation und Kommerz für die Werte anderer Gesellschaften und Kulturen.

Das Problem bestand natürlich darin, daß die Europäer glaubten, allen anderen Völkern überlegen zu sein, und daher das Recht und die Pflicht zu besitzen, die Verantwortung für die Welt zu übernehmen. Sie verfügten über besser entwickelte Industrien, bessere Waffen und Erfindungen, besseres kommerzielles Know-how und ein besseres Gesundheitswesen. Auch ihre Kultur war weiter entwickelt, was sie jedoch nicht daran hinderte, den Rest der Welt seiner Kunstschätze zu berauben. Die Europäer waren erfindungsreicher, besser regiert sowie besser erzogen und ausgebildet. Vor allem war Europa die Heimat des Christentums, jenes Glaubens, der die heidnischen Horden vor ewiger Verdammnis bewahren konnte, ob sie es nun wollten oder nicht.

Es war ein Prozeß des Gebens und Nehmens: Europäer erschlossen neue Märkte und erzielten höhere Dividenden auf ihre Aktien, während alle anderen die Aussicht auf das ewige Leben erhielten. Es war Gottes Wille. Die Millionen arbeitender Menschen in Afrika, Indien und Asien unterstanden der europäischen Verwaltung nicht »nur, damit wir einen jährlichen Gewinn durch sie erzielen, sondern damit wir unter diesen Einwohnern das Licht und das Gute der Wahrheit, die Segnungen einer gut organisierten Gesellschaft und die Annehmlichkeiten einer aktiven Industrie verbreiten können«.

Das Tragische war, daß diese ehrenwerten Absichten einer krassen Mißachtung der älteren Zivilisationen entsprangen, die verdrängt wurden. Die Menschen aus Hindustan waren »beklagenswert degeneriert und niederträchtig«. Die Afrikaner waren »kannibalistische Metzger«. Die Chinesen waren »aufsässige, verseuchte und dreckige Subjekte«. In den Augen eines britischen Premierministers waren selbst die Iren »wild, gefährlich, faul, unzuverlässig und abergläubisch«.

Kein Wunder also, daß der Buschmann und der Tasmane verschwanden und die Sioux und Cheyenne in Reservate getrieben wurden. Was die Azteken betraf, so hatten sie es ja noch nicht einmal geschafft, das Rad zu erfinden; sie verschwanden einfach, und nur ihre Sprache blieb übrig.

L'EXPANSION de la civilisation européenne avait représenté pendant des siècles une très grosse menace pour les peuples indigènes de bien des régions du monde. Au XVIᵉ siècle, les conquistadors espagnols dirigés par Cortès avaient non seulement conquis le Mexique, mais en plus anéanti la culture aztèque. Les Aztèques croyaient qu'il leur fallait nourrir le soleil et la terre de sang et de cœurs humains pour que leur société perdure. À l'apogée de leur empire, ils sacrifiaient 10 000 victimes chaque année pour apaiser leur dieu principal, Huitzilopochtli. Le couple aztèque que l'on voit sur cette photographie (1, page précédente) prise environ 350 ans plus tard faisait partie des derniers survivants de cette race guerrière, jadis la plus puissante de l'Amérique centrale.

En effet, partout où ils allaient, les Européens faisaient tout à la fois le bien et le mal. Ils abolirent certes l'esclavage en Afrique, mais pillèrent la plupart des matières premières du continent et en exploitèrent la main-d'œuvre. En Inde, ils interdirent les thugs, cette société secrète d'étrangleurs qui avaient fait vivre les voyageurs dans la terreur pendant des siècles, mais refusèrent aux citoyens le droit d'intervenir dans la façon dont on les gouvernait. En Chine, ils contribuèrent aussi bien à la disparition de la pratique traditionnelle du bandage des pieds des fillettes qu'à la formidable expansion du commerce et de la consommation d'opium qui fit des millions de drogués. Le photographe John Thomson décrivant les plaisirs d'une fumerie d'opium fréquentée par la haute société dans les années 1870 : «... entourés par des filles attentives, les unes à préparer l'opium pour en remplir le fourneau de la pipe, les autres à accompagner en douceur le fumeur dans le royaume des rêves de leurs chants mélodieux ».

Il est dans certains cas difficile de parler de bienfaits. Les Aborigènes australiens avaient vécu heureux pendant des milliers d'années jusqu'au jour où les colons et les fermiers étaient arrivés avec leurs maladies, leur cupidité et leurs provisions inépuisables de mauvais alcool. Pendant des siècles, les Indiens des prairies de l'Amérique du Nord avaient mené une existence prospère de chasseurs nomades sur un territoire couvrant des millions de kilomètres carrés. C'était un peuple fier qui respectait la terre et même le bison qu'ils tuaient pour se nourrir, s'habiller, fabriquer leurs outils et leurs abris. En l'espace de quelques décennies après l'arrivée de l'homme blanc, ils se retrouvèrent parqués dans des réserves, massacrés par milliers et affaiblis par les maladies. Dans les années 1880, George Augustus Sala voyait mendier dans les gares des Indiens qui autrefois avaient été de grands guerriers. « Les fournisseurs blancs de l'armée leur vendent un whisky empoisonné et les trompent de toutes les manières imaginables, pendant que les squatters blancs les envahissent de plus en plus en volant les terres que les États-Unis ont assignées aux Indiens. » Les habitants de Tasmanie étaient heureux, affectueux et primitifs ; tous furent rassemblés puis expédiés sur l'île Flinders par les agents du gouvernement britannique. C'était un marché de dupes. La Tasmanie s'étend sur approximativement 68 000 kilomètres carrés, alors que l'île Flinders en couvre tout juste 1 800. Les Tasmaniens, cependant, partirent sans faire trop d'histoires. « Lorsqu'ils aperçurent du bateau le pays splendide qui leur avait été promis », rapporte un témoin de cet effroyable génocide, «... ils manifestèrent une agitation extrême, s'usant les yeux à fixer la plage stérile, poussant des grognements mélancoliques, le corps parcouru de convulsions tandis que leurs bras pendaient ballants. Les vents étaient violents et froids, la pluie mêlée à la bruine tombait sale et pénétrante ... ce qui venait s'ajouter au pressentiment qu'ils avaient d'être amenés là-bas pour y mourir. » Beaucoup moururent d'affections de la poitrine et de l'estomac. La plupart du mal du pays. Pas un seul ne survécut.

Mais partout où ils allaient, les Européens prenaient aussi leurs appareils photographiques et leurs carnets, et ils ont enregistré précisément les gens, les lieux et les cultures qu'ils s'apprêtaient à détruire. En 1874, l'explorateur John Forrest faisait face, terrorisé, à une attaque des Aborigènes en Australie : « Je vis cinquante à soixante indigènes courir en direction du camp, tous recouverts de plumes et armés de lances et de boucliers... L'un se porta à ma rencontre et s'arrêta à environ 18 mètres de moi. Je lui adressai des gestes amicaux : il n'avait pas l'air très hostile. Soudain, ils se ruèrent sur nous comme un seul homme en poussant des hurlements et en projetant leurs lances ... » Forrest survécut pour le raconter.

Certains se référaient à des principes chrétiens. Les Afrikaners furent les plus inflexibles et les plus dénués de scrupules. C'était un Dieu dur et impitoyable que le leur, censé approuver leur façon de traiter les Hottentots et les Bochimans, qu'ils exterminèrent presque complètement. Ce n'est pas eux qui auraient réclamé, à l'instar de ces timorés de Britanniques, l'égalité des Noirs et des Blancs devant la loi. Plus que tout autre groupe d'ascendance européenne, les Boers personnifièrent l'aveuglement colonial et commercial face aux valeurs des autres sociétés et cultures.

Le problème était bien sûr que les Européens se considéraient supérieurs à tous les autres peuples, et de ce fait en droit de diriger le monde. Ils possédaient des industries, des armes, des idées, un savoir-faire commercial et un système de santé public plus avancés. Leur culture était supérieure, ce qui ne les empêchait pas de piller avec fébrilité les richesses artistiques du reste du monde. Ils étaient plus inventifs, mieux gouvernés et plus instruits. Et surtout, l'Europe était l'atelier de la chrétienté, de la foi qui pouvait sauver les hordes païennes de la damnation éternelle, avec ou sans leur consentement. L'Afrique, l'Inde et l'Asie et les millions de personnes qui y travaillaient n'étaient pas passés sous administration européenne « uniquement afin que nous en tirions un profit annuel, mais pour que nous puissions répandre parmi leurs habitants la lumière et l'influence bénéfique de la vérité, les bienfaits d'une société bien ordonnée, ainsi que les améliorations et agréments d'une industrie active ».

Hélas, ces nobles sentiments allaient de pair avec un manque absolu de considération pour les civilisations plus anciennes qu'on était ainsi en train de balayer. Le peuple de l'Hindoustan était « lamentablement dégénéré et vil », les Africains étaient « des bouchers anthropophages » et les Chinois « des objets révoltants, souffreteux et sales ». Aux yeux d'un des premiers ministres britanniques, les Irlandais eux-mêmes étaient « sauvages, impulsifs, indolents, incertains et superstitieux ».

Qui s'étonnera, dans ces conditions, de la disparition des habitants de la brousse et des Tasmaniens ou des réserves dans lesquelles on parqua les Sioux et les Cheyennes. Quant aux Aztèques, dont une terrible prophétie prédisait une bataille à l'issue fatale, ils disparurent purement et simplement. Tous ces peuples ne laissèrent derrière eux que leur langue.

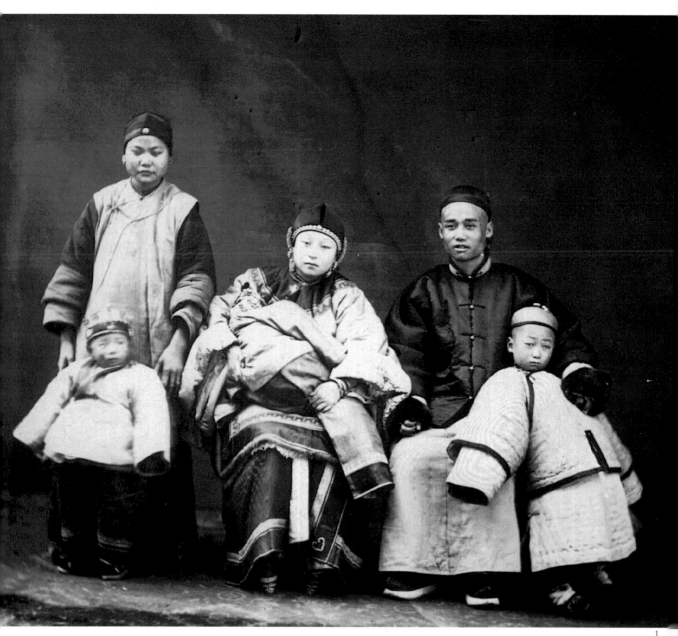

'Not one Chinaman in ten thousand knows anything about the foreigner,' reported the (European) Chief Inspector of the Chinese Customs Service in the late 19th century. 'Not one Chinaman in a hundred thousand knows anything about foreign inventions and discoveries; and not one in a million acknowledges any superiority in either the condition or the appliances of the West.' These Manchu families followed the old teachings of Confucius, which stressed the responsibilities of parents to children, and the duties of children to parents.

Nicht einer von zehntausend Chinesen weiß etwas über Fremde«, berichtete der (europäische) Oberinspektor des chinesischen Zollwesens Ende des 19. Jahrhunderts. »Nicht einer von hunderttausend Chinesen weiß irgend etwas über ausländische Erfindungen und Entdeckungen, und nicht einer von einer Million erkennt die Überlegenheit westlicher Verhältnisse und Errungenschaften an.« Diese Familien aus der Mandschurei folgten den alten Lehren des Konfuzius, der die Verantwortung der Eltern für ihre Kinder und die Pflichten der Kinder gegenüber ihren Eltern betonte.

Pas un Chinois sur dix mille ne sait la moindre chose de l'étranger » rapportait l'inspecteur en chef (européen) du service des douanes chinoises à la fin du XIXe siècle. « Pas un Chinois sur une centaine de mille n'a la moindre idée de ce qui a été inventé ou découvert par des étrangers ; et pas un sur un million ne dit trouver aux conditions ou aux techniques occidentales la moindre supériorité. » Ces familles mandchoues suivaient les anciens enseignements de Confucius qui soulignaient les responsabilités des parents envers leurs enfants et les devoirs des enfants vis-à-vis des parents.

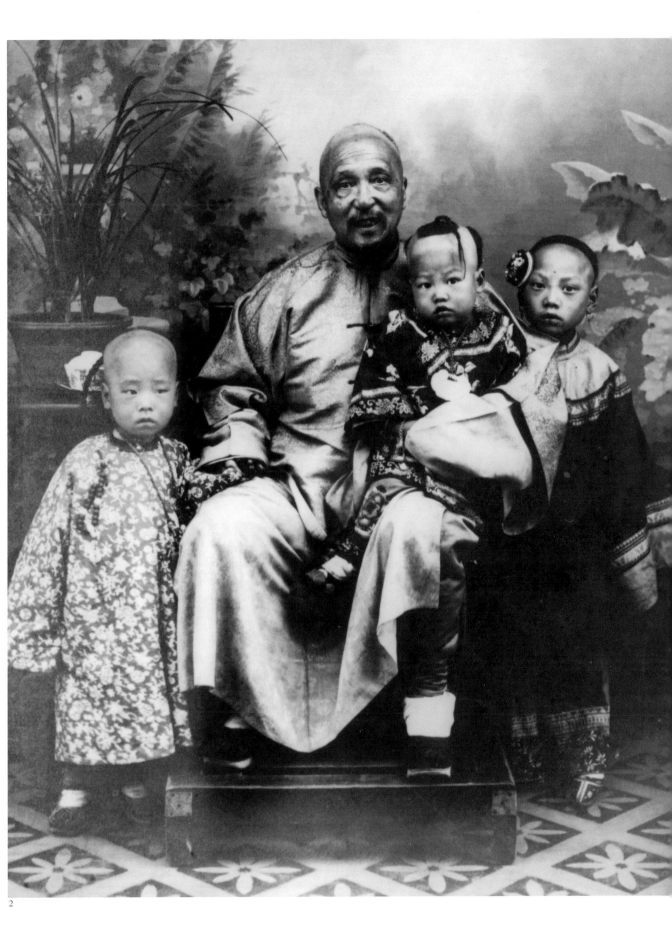

2

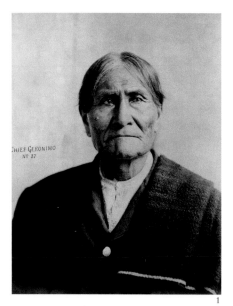

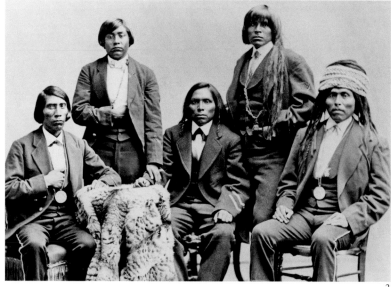

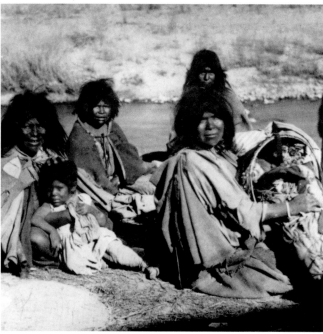

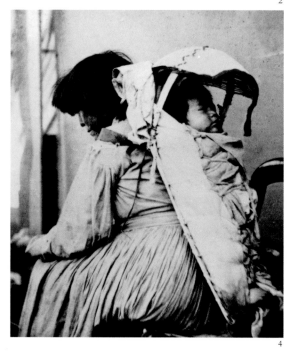

THE Indian wars ended: the chiefs lived on. Geronimo (1) ended his days on an Apache reservation. The Shoshone (3 and 4) stayed in Utah, and were westernized for the camera by the Mormons (2). These Fraser River Indians in British Columbia (5) had to scratch for the poorest of livings. The Blackfoot stayed on the Plains, but fighting days were over for this warrior (6), and for Red Cloud and American Horse (7). By 1891 'The Home of Mrs American Horse' (8) in South Dakota had a forlorn look to it, although it had once been a chief's lodge.

DIE Indianerkriege waren zu Ende, aber die Häuptlinge lebten weiter. Geronimo (1) verbrachte seine letzten Tage in einem Apachenreservat. Die Shoshonen (3, 4) blieben in Utah und wurden von Mormonen für die Kamera westlich zurechtgemacht (2). Diese Indianer vom Fraser River in British Columbia (5) mußten um ihren kargen

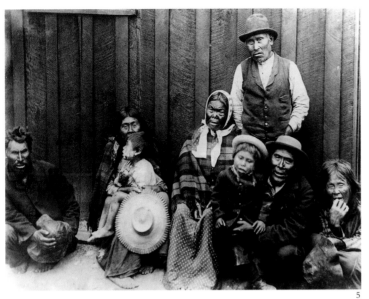

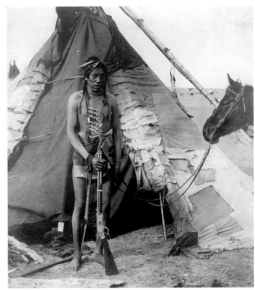

5

6

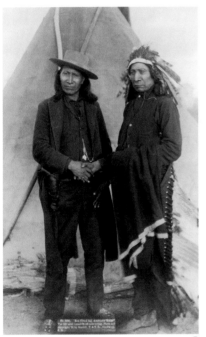

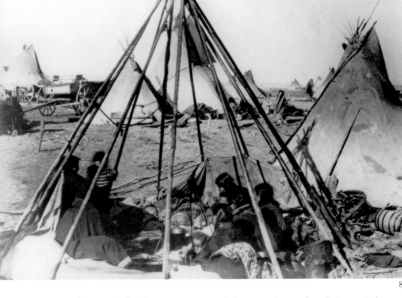

7

8

Lebensunterhalt kämpfen. Die Blackfoot blieben in der Prärie, aber für diesen Krieger (6), für Red Cloud und American Horse (7) waren die Tage des Kampfes vorbei. »The Home of Mrs American Horse« (8) in South Dakota sah 1891 heruntergekommen und verlassen aus, obwohl es einst Wohnsitz eines Häuptlings gewesen war.

LES guerres indiennes s'achevèrent. Geronimo (1) finit ses jours dans une réserve apache. Les Shoshones (3 et 4) demeurèrent en Utah où l'appareil photographique des Mormons les occidentalisa (2). Ces Indiens du Fraser menaient une existence misérable en Colombie-Britannique (5). Les Blackfoot restèrent dans les prairies, mais le temps des combats était terminé pour ce guerrier (6), comme pour Red Cloud et American Horse (7). En 1891, « la maison de Madame American Horse » (8) dans le Dakota du Sud avait un air de solitude délabrée ; et pourtant elle avait été autrefois le camp d'un chef.

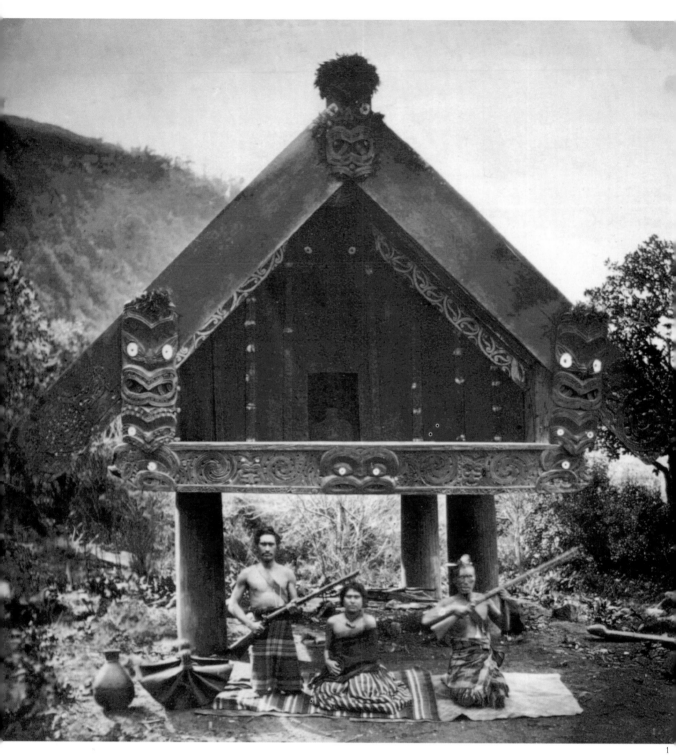

UNTIL 1871, the Maoris (1) were
frequently at war with the British,
though they were more likely to shoot
each other in wars of blood-vengeance
than to kill white settlers. The Ashanti (2)
were also an aggressive people. 'If power is
for sale,' ran one of their proverbs, 'sell
your mother to buy it – you can always
buy her back again.' Life was more relaxed
in Freetown (3), capital of Sierra Leone
on the West Africa coast, and a haven for
thousands of freed slaves. It was a town
of 'civilization, Christianity and the
cultivation of the soil.'

BIS zum Jahre 1871 führten die Maori
(1) häufig Krieg gegen die Briten,
obwohl es wahrscheinlicher war, daß
sie sich gegenseitig in Blutfehden
erschossen, als weiße Siedler zu töten.
Die Ashanti (2) waren ebenfalls ein
aggressives Volk. »Wenn man Macht
kaufen kann«, so lautete eines ihrer
Sprichwörter, »dann verkauf deine

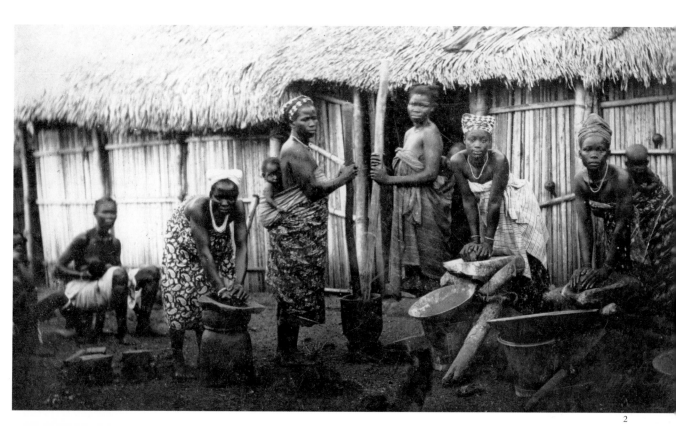

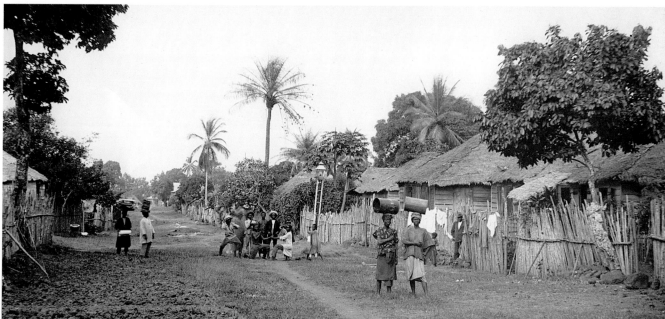

Mutter, um sie dir zu kaufen, du kannst deine Mutter ja jederzeit zurückkaufen.« Entspanntere Verhältnisse herrschten in Freetown (3), der Hauptstadt von Sierra Leone an der afrikanischen Westküste, einem Zufluchtsort für Tausende befreite Sklaven. Es war eine Stadt der »Zivilisation, des Christentums und der Kultivierung des Bodens«.

J USQU'EN 1871 les Maoris (1) étaient souvent en lutte contre les Britanniques. Il était cependant plus courant de les voir s'entre-tuer que supprimer les colons blancs. Les Ashanti (2) étaient eux aussi un peuple agressif. Un de leurs proverbes disait : « Si le pouvoir est à vendre, vends ta mère et

achète-le. Tu pourras toujours la racheter. » La vie était plus tranquille à Freetown (3), la capitale du Sierra Leone, située sur la côte de l'Afrique de l'Ouest, qui accueillit des milliers d'esclaves affranchis. C'était une ville de « civilisation, de chrétienté et de culture du sol. »

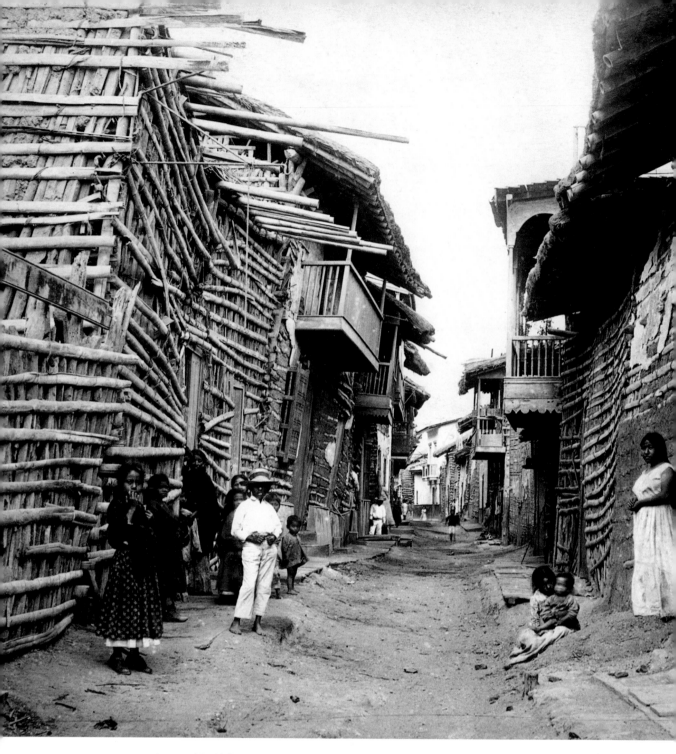

EUROPEANS were interested in Chile for two reasons: nitrates and manganese. For the inhabitants of a run-down street (1) the best that life could offer was a ticket to sail a few thousand miles up the Pacific coast to California. Life was better on Bermuda (2), a coaling station for the ubiquitous British fleet, blessed with its own Constituent Assembly and a railway line – although the island is only twenty miles long. The black workers who lived in log huts at Thomasville, Georgia, in the USA (3), were also near a railway – the Florida and Western Railroad – but they had little occasion to use it on the wages they were paid.

DIE Europäer waren an Chile aus zwei Gründen interessiert: Nitrate und Mangan. Für die Bewohner eines Slums (1) war das Beste, was ihm das Leben bieten konnte, eine Schiffspassage einige Tausend Meilen die Pazifikküste hinauf nach Kalifornien. Auf Bermuda (2) war das Leben besser; dort befand sich ein Kohlenlager der allgegenwärtigen britischen Flotte, die über

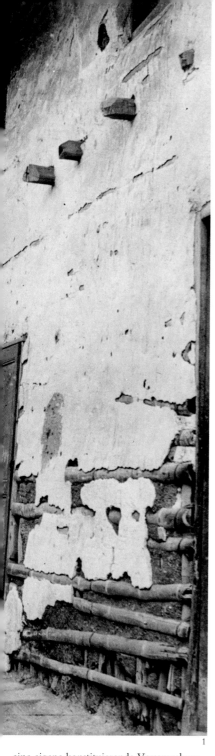

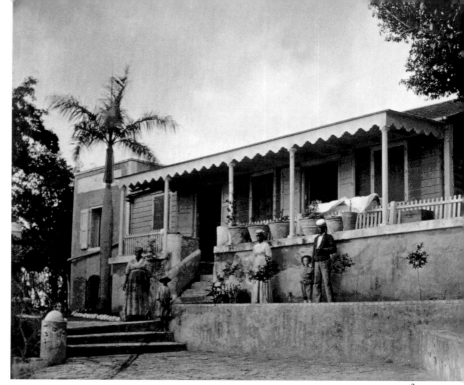

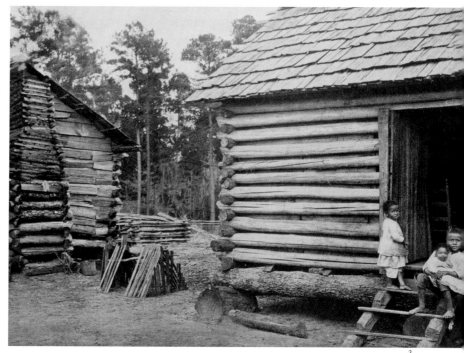

eine eigene konstituierende Versammlung und eine Eisenbahnlinie verfügte, obwohl die Insel nur 32 Kilometer lang ist. Die schwarzen Arbeiter, die in Holzhütten in Thomasville, Georgia, USA, lebten (3), waren auch in der Nähe einer Eisenbahn, der Florida and Western Railroad, aber angesichts ihrer niedrigen Löhne hatten sie kaum Gelegenheit, sie zu benutzen.

LES Européens s'intéressaient au Chili pour deux raisons : les nitrates et le manganèse. Pour les habitants de cette rue délabrée (1), ce qui pouvait leur arriver de mieux était de se voir offrir un billet de bateau pour remonter le littoral du Paci-fique jusqu'à la Californie. On vivait mieux aux Bermudes (2), qui servaient de dépôt de charbon à l'omniprésente flotte britannique et bénéficiaient de leur propre assemblée constituante ainsi que d'une voie de chemin de fer alors que l'île ne fait que 32 kilomè-tres de long. Les ouvriers noirs vivant dans des cabanes en rondins à Thomasville, en Géorgie, aux États-Unis (3), se trouvaient eux aussi près d'une ligne de chemin de fer – the Florida and Western Railroad – qu'ils n'avaient cependant guère l'occasion d'utiliser étant donné leurs salaires.

Aviation and Railways

THE world was turned upside down by changes in transport during the latter half of the 19th century. Bus rides across cities, train journeys across continents, voyages by steamship across oceans – all were faster, cheaper, safer, more reliable. The Duke of Wellington had grumpily declared that he saw no reason to suppose that steam trains 'would ever force themselves into general use', but His Grace was profoundly wrong. By 1850 there were 1870 miles (3,000 km) of railway in France, 3,735 miles (6,000 km) in Germany and 6,621 miles (10,500 km) in Britain. There were railways in North America, China, Japan, India, Africa, and Australia. Along the sea lanes of the world steamships huffed and puffed their prosperous way transporting hundreds of thousands of tons of pig-iron – the basic ingredient of any railway system.

There were underground railways (the first in 1865), electric railways (the first main line service in 1895), rack-and-pinion mountain railways (Thomas Cook owned the funicular up Mount Vesuvius), and luxury railways (the *Orient Express* was inaugurated on 4 October 1883). In 1891 Tsar Alexander gave the go-ahead for the Trans Siberian Railway to the Tsarevich in bold and imperious words:

'Your Imperial Highness!
Having given the order to build a continuous line of railway across Siberia… I entrust you to declare My will, upon your entering the Russian dominions after your inspection of the foreign countries of the East.'

And, so there should be no doubt as to the route of this 4,000-mile (6,400 km) undertaking, the Tsar drew a straight line right across the said dominions. Dostoyevsky hated railways. Dickens loved them.

In 1852 Henry Giffard, a French engineer, built an airship driven by a screw-propelled steam engine. It was a success, chugging along at only some five miles (eight km) an hour but staying up in the sky. But this was not enough for the German pioneer Otto Lilienthal. He had spent years studying the principles of flight, watching birds to see how they used air currents and how their wings controlled their speed, their ascent and descent. In 1889 he published *Bird Flight as a Basis of Aviation*. Two years later he built a glider with two wings made from cotton twill stretched over a willow framework (1). By running and leaping from a platform 20 ft (6 m) high, Lilienthal was able to glide for 25 yards (25 m). In 1896 he built a more solid glider (2), with two sets of wings and better controls, allowing him more time in the air, but that same year he was killed in a gliding accident at Stollen.

Others took up where Lilienthal left off. An Englishman, Percy Pilcher, built a glider with an undercarriage, and was experimenting with a powered machine when he, too, was killed. The following year (1900) the American Wright brothers began gliding at Kitty Hawk, North Carolina. They streamlined the gliding process by lying along the lower wing, instead of dangling their bodies from the framework as Lilienthal had done. By 1901 they were able to make flights of some 200 yards. From then on, progress was ridiculously rapid, spurred by much competition and the obvious military advantages to be gained from mastery of the skies.

Within a few years Alcock and Brown flew almost two thousand miles non-stop, at an average speed of 117 mph (184 kph), to cross the Atlantic.

Life was never the same again.

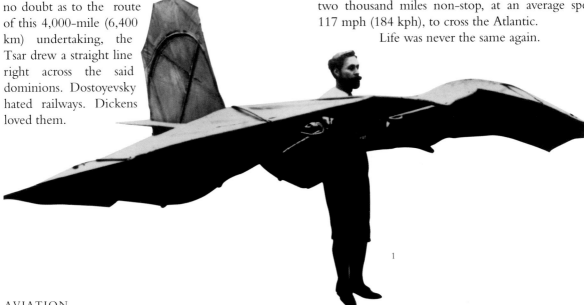

1

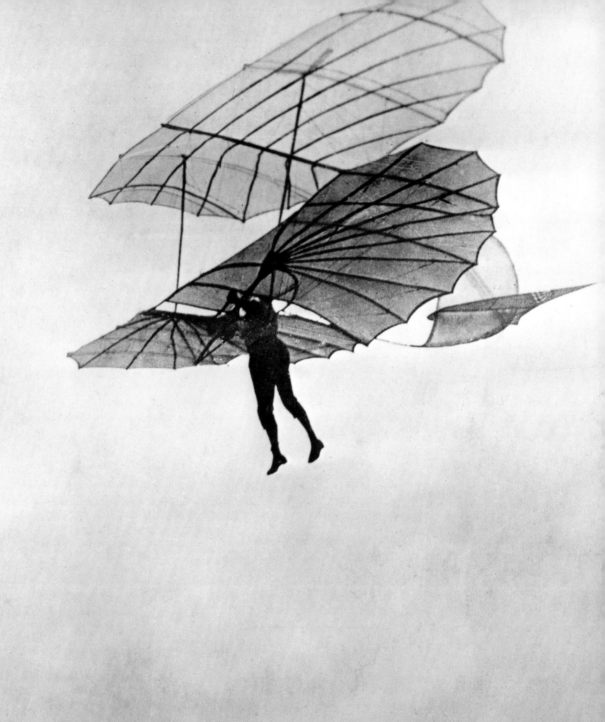

DIE Welt wurde durch die Veränderungen im Transportwesen, die sich in der zweiten Hälfte des 19. Jahrhunderts vollzogen, auf den Kopf gestellt. Busfahrten durch Städte, Zugreisen durch Kontinente, Überquerungen von Ozeanen mit dem Dampfschiff – alles war schneller, billiger, sicherer und zuverlässiger geworden. Der Duke of Wellington hatte mürrisch erklärt, er sehe keinen Grund zu der Annahme, daß Dampflokomotiven »sich jemals durchsetzen werden«, aber Seine Hoheit irrte gewaltig. Im Jahre 1850 zogen sich 3000 Kilometer Gleise durch Frankreich, 6000 Kilometer durch Deutschland und 10500 Kilometer durch Großbritannien. Es gab Eisenbahnen in Nordamerika, China, Japan, Indien, Afrika und Australien. Auf den Seewegen der Welt fuhren rauchende Dampfschiffe und transportierten Hunderttausende Tonnen Roheisen – Grundbestandteil eines jeden Eisenbahnnetzes.

Es gab Untergrundbahnen (die erste im Jahre 1865), elektrische Eisenbahnen (die erste Hauptstrecke wurde 1895 in Betrieb genommen), Zahnradbahnen (Thomas Cook gehörte die Seilbahn, die zum Vesuv hinaufführte) und Luxuseisenbahnen (der *Orient Express* wurde am 4. Oktober 1883 eingeweiht). Im Jahre 1891 gab Zar Alexander dem Zarewitsch grünes Licht für die Transsibirische Eisenbahn – mit den kraftvollen und gebieterischen Worten:

»Eure Kaiserliche Hoheit!
Ich habe den Befehl gegeben, eine Eisenbahnstrecke durch Sibirien zu bauen … und ich beauftrage Sie, nach der Inspektion der fremden Länder des Ostens beim Betreten der russischen Herrschaftsgebiete meinen Willen zu verkünden!«

Und damit es keinen Zweifel über die Route des 6400 Kilometer langen Unternehmens gab, zog der Zar eine gerade Linie durch die besagten Gebiete. Dostojewski haßte die Eisenbahn. Dickens liebte sie.

Im Jahre 1852 konstruierte der französische Ingenieur Henry Giffard ein Luftschiff, das mit einem dampfgetriebenen Schraubenpropeller angetrieben wurde. Ein voller Erfolg: Zwar tuckerte es nur mit acht Stundenkilometern dahin, es blieb aber in der Luft. Für den deutschen Luftfahrtpionier Otto Lilienthal war das jedoch nicht genug. Er hatte jahrelang die Gesetze des Fluges durch Beobachtung der Vögel studiert, um herauszufinden, wie diese die Luftströme nutzten und mit ihren Flügeln Geschwindigkeit, Auf- und Abstieg steuerten. Im Jahre 1889 veröffentlichte er die Schrift *Der Vogelflug als Grundlage der Fliegekunst*. Zwei Jahre später baute er einen Gleiter mit zwei Flügeln aus Baumwollköper, der über einen Rahmen aus Weidenholz gespannt war (1). Nach Anlauf und dem Sprung von einer sechs Meter hohen Plattform konnte Lilienthal 25 Meter weit gleiten. 1896 baute er einen stabileren Gleiter (2) mit zwei Flügelpaaren und verbesserter Steuerung, die es ihm ermöglichte, länger in der Luft zu bleiben, aber noch im selben Jahr verunglückte er tödlich mit dem Gleiter bei Stollen.

Andere setzten fort, was Lilienthal begonnen hatte. Der Engländer Percy Pilcher konstruierte einen Gleiter mit Fahrgestell und experimentierte mit Antriebsmaschinen, bis auch er ums Leben kam. Im darauffolgenden Jahr (1900) begannen die amerikanischen Gebrüder Wright in Kitty Hawk, North Carolina, mit ihren Gleitexperimenten. Sie machten den Gleitvorgang stromlinienförmig, indem sie sich auf den unteren Flügel legten, anstatt sich, wie Lilienthal, an den Rahmen des Gleiters zu hängen. Im Jahre 1901 konnten sie etwa 200 Meter weit fliegen. Seitdem wurden in kürzester Zeit große Fortschritte gemacht, gefördert durch die Konkurrenz und die offensichtlichen militärischen Vorteile, die man durch die Beherrschung der Lüfte gewinnen konnte.

Nur wenige Jahre später überquerten Alcock und Brown mit einer durchschnittlichen Geschwindigkeit von 184 Stundenkilometern den Atlantik im Nonstopflug.

Das Leben sollte nun nicht mehr dasselbe sein.

L'ÉVOLUTION des transports de la deuxième moitié du XIXᵉ siècle avait chamboulé le monde. Les trajets en bus dans les grandes villes, les voyages en train à travers les continents, les traversées des océans en bateau à vapeur, tout était devenu plus rapide, meilleur marché, plus sûr et plus fiable. Le duc de Wellington maugréait qu'il ne voyait aucune raison de supposer que les trains à vapeur « parviennent jamais à s'imposer à l'usage de tous », mais sa Grâce était dans l'erreur. Dès 1850, il y avait 3 000 kilomètres de voies ferrées en France, 6 000 kilomètres en Allemagne et 10 500 en Grande-Bretagne. Il y avait des voies ferrées en Amérique du Nord, en Chine, au Japon, en Inde, en Afrique et en Australie. Sillonnant à coups de sirène les mers du monde, les bateaux à vapeur prospéraient grâce au transport des centaines de milliers de tonnes de saumon de fonte qui constituait la composante de base de tout système de chemin de fer.

Il y avait des voies ferrées souterraines (les premières datant de 1865), ou électriques (la première grande ligne entra en service en 1895), des chemins de fer à crémaillère en montagne (Thomas Cook possédait le funiculaire qui montait jusqu'en haut de la montagne du Vésuve) et des lignes pour trains de luxe (l'*Orient Express* fut inauguré le 4 octobre 1883). En 1891, le tsar Alexandre donna au tsarévitch le feu vert pour le chemin de fer transsibérien en ces termes clairs et impérieux :

« Votre Altesse !
Ayant donné l'ordre de construire une ligne
de chemin de fer continue à travers la Sibérie …
Je vous confie le soin de faire connaître que
telle est Ma volonté lorsque vous pénétrerez dans
les dominions russes une fois que vous en aurez
terminé avec votre inspection des pays étrangers de
l'Est. »

De manière à ne laisser planer aucun doute sur le tracé de ces 6 400 kilomètres d'ouvrage, le tsar traça un trait rectiligne au travers desdits dominions. Dostoïevski détestait les chemins de fer, Dickens les adorait.

En 1852, Henry Giffard, un ingénieur français, construisit un dirigeable mû par une machine à vapeur et une hélice. L'appareil fut un succès : émettant un bruit sourd et haletant, il ne faisait qu'environ huit kilomètres à l'heure, mais au moins il restait dans le ciel. Cela ne suffit cependant pas au pionnier que fut l'Allemand Otto Lilienthal. Il avait passé des années à étudier les principes du vol en observant les oiseaux et comment ceux-ci utilisaient les courants de l'air et leurs ailes pour contrôler leur vitesse, leur ascension ou leur descente. En 1889 il fit paraître *Bird Flight as a Basis of Aviation* (Du vol des oiseaux comme base de l'aviation). Deux ans plus tard, il construisait un planeur équipé de deux ailes en cotonnade de serge tendue sur une armature en saule (1). En s'élançant en courant d'une plateforme placée à une hauteur de six mètres, Lilienthal parvint à planer sur 25 mètres. En 1896 il construisit un planeur plus solide (2) équipé de deux paires d'ailes et de commandes perfectionnées qui lui permettaient de rester plus longtemps dans les airs. Mais il mourut la même année à Stollen dans un accident de planeur.

D'autres reprirent le flambeau. Un Anglais, Percy Pilcher, construisit un planeur muni d'un train d'atterrissage ; lui aussi se tua alors qu'il expérimentait une machine à moteur. L'année suivante (1900) des Américains, les frères Wright, se lancèrent dans les vols en planeur à Kitty Hawk, en Caroline du Nord. Ils en perfectionnèrent la technique en s'allongeant sur l'aile inférieure pour faire corps avec l'ossature, contrairement à ce que faisait Lilienthal. Dès 1901, ils étaient en mesure de planer sur environ 180 mètres. À partir de là, on peut parler de progrès ridiculement rapides, aiguillonnés par une forte concurrence et par les avantages militaires évidents que représentait la maîtrise des cieux.

À peine quelques années plus tard, Alcock et Brown traversaient l'Atlantique à la vitesse moyenne de 184 km/h en volant près de 32 186 kilomètres sans s'arrêter.

La vie avait changé du tout au tout.

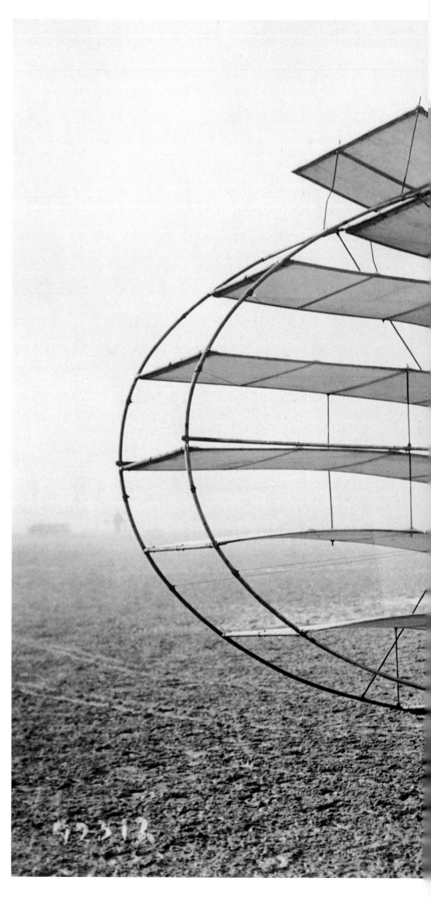

THE French took to aviation like eagles to the air. In the great tradition of the Montgolfier Brothers, they were experimenting with vertical take-off planes in 1907 – Paul Cornu's prototype got a metre and a half off the ground before his brother threw himself on it, fearful that it was going out of control. On 13 January 1908, Henri Farman flew for 88 seconds at a height of 25 metres and a speed of 24 miles per hour (39 kph). Another early enthusiast was the Comte d'Ecquevilly, whose plane, seen here, seemed designed in honour of Chinese lanterns.

DIE Franzosen begeisterten sich für die Luftfahrt wie der Adler für die Lüfte. In der großen Tradition der Gebrüder Montgolfier experimentierten sie 1907 mit Flugzeugen, die senkrecht starteten. Paul Cornus Prototyp erhob sich 1,50 Meter über den Boden, bevor sein Bruder sich darauf warf, weil er befürchtete, das Flugzeug könne außer Kontrolle geraten. Am 13. Januar 1908 flog Henri Farman mit einer Geschwindigkeit von 39 Stundenkilometern 88 Sekunden lang in einer Höhe von 25 Metern. Ein weiterer früher Enthusiast war der Comte d'Ecquevilly, dessen hier abgebildetes Flugzeug von chinesischen Laternen inspiriert zu sein schien.

LES Français se lancèrent dans l'aviation tels des aigles à la conquête des airs. Fidèles à la grande tradition inaugurée par les frères Montgolfier, ils s'essayaient en 1907 au décollage à la verticale. Le prototype de Paul Cornu s'éleva de 150 centimètres au-dessus du sol avant que son frère ne se jetât dessus, craignant que la machine ne répondît plus aux commandes. Le 13 janvier 1908, Henri Farman vola pendant 88 secondes à une hauteur de 25 mètres et à une vitesse de 39 km/h. On voit ici l'avion aux allures de lanterne chinoise du comte d'Ecquevilly, un des enthousiastes de la première heure.

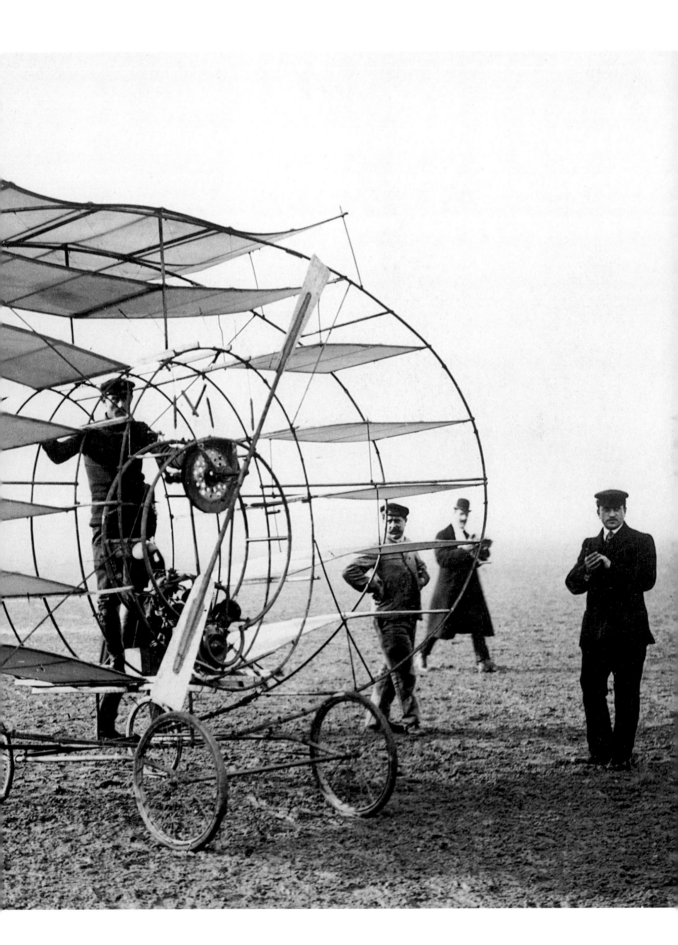

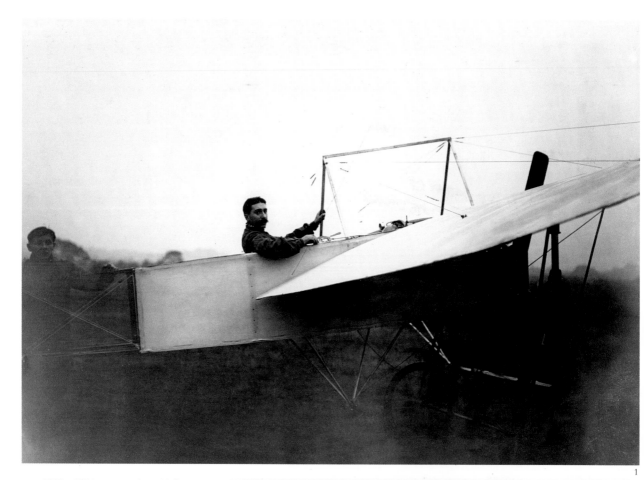

IN 1909 a Blériot monoplane (1) flew
across the Channel in 37 minutes. Wilbur
Wright in 1908 (2): his brother Orville had
made the first ever powered flight in an
aeroplane. Tommy Sopwith (3). Alcock and
Brown's historic Atlantic flight came to an
abrupt end in Ireland on 15 June 1919 (4):
their Vickers Vimy grounded.

IM Jahre 1909 überflog ein Blériot-Ein-
decker (1) den Ärmelkanal in 37 Minuten.
Wilbur Wright (1908, 2): Sein Bruder
Orville steuerte das erste Flugzeug mit
Antriebsmaschine. Tommy Sopwith (3).
Der historische Atlantikflug von Alcock und
Brown kam am 15. Juni 1919 zu einem
abrupten Ende (4): Ihre Vickers Vimy
erhielt Startverbot.

EN 1909, le monoplan de Blériot (1)
traversa la Manche en 37 minutes. Wilbur Wright (1908, 2), l'année précédente.
Orville, son frère, avait effectué le premier
vol de l'histoire dans un aéronef à moteur.
Tommy Sopwith (3). Le vol historique
d'Alcock et de Brown au-dessus de l'océan
Atlantique s'acheva de manière abrupte le
15 juin 1919 (4): leur Vickers Vimy n'obtint
pas l'autorisation de décoller.

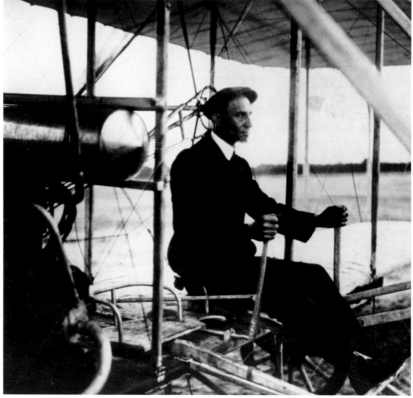

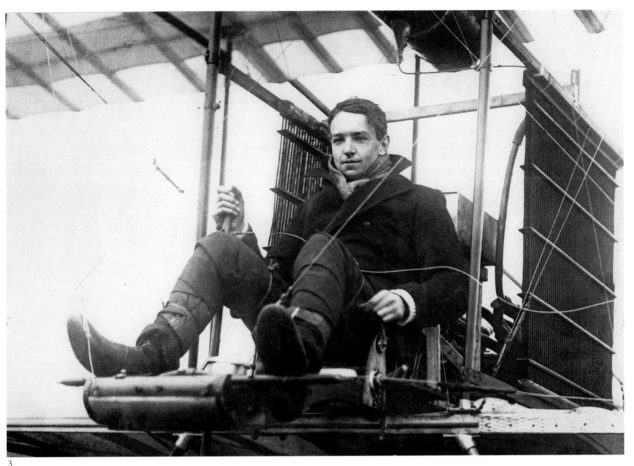

3

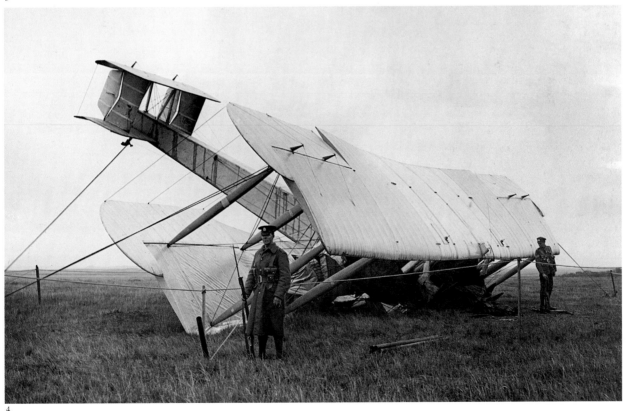

4

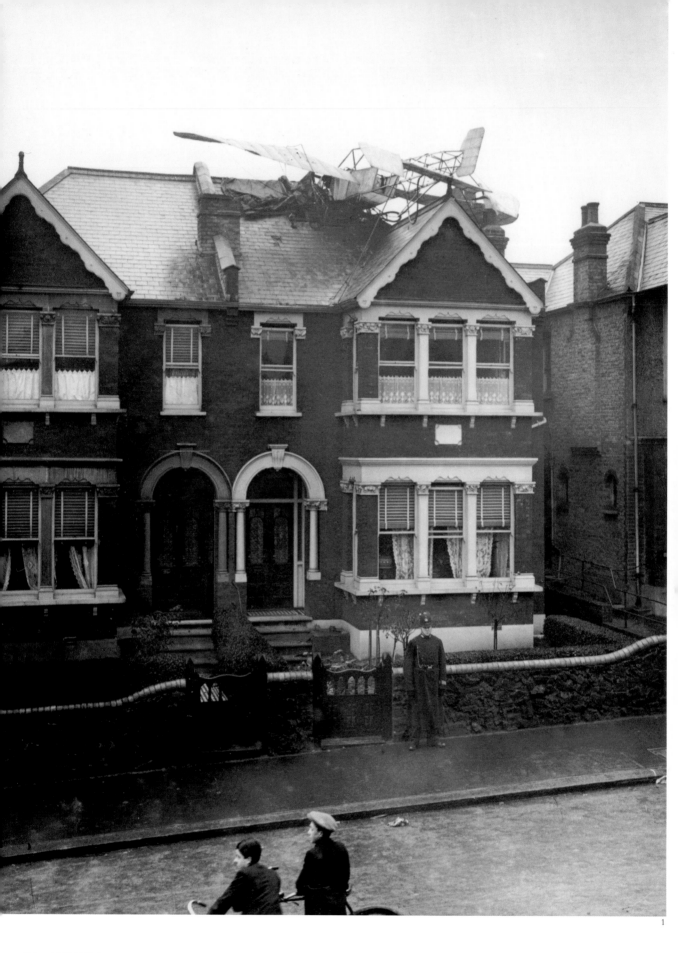

1

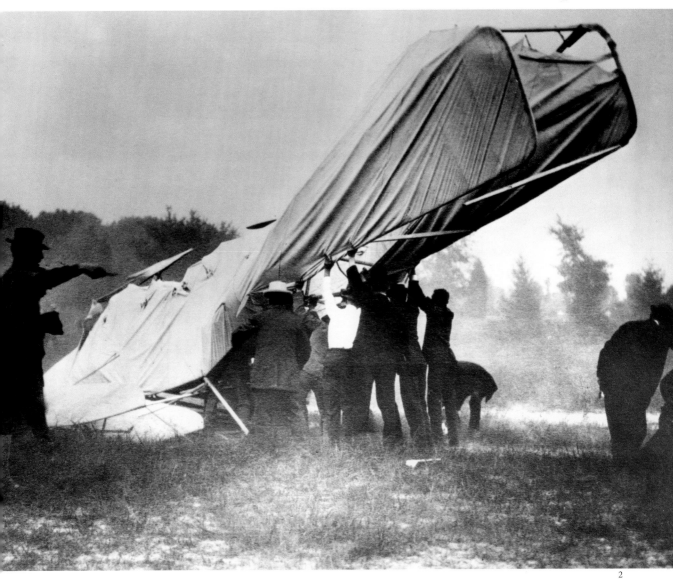

2

EARLY machines were frail, which made some of them unreliable, but at least meant that a minimum of damage was done when they fluttered from the sky, out of control. The roof of this house at Palmers Green, London, needed only a few slates replaced after a monoplane crashed into it in December 1912 (1). Pilots were often less fortunate. When a Wright Brothers plane crash-landed at Fort Meyer, Virginia, in September 1908, Orville Wright was injured and his co-pilot, Lieutenant Selfridge, was killed (2).

DIE ersten Maschinen waren zerbrech-lich und unberechenbar. Deshalb richteten sie auch nur wenig Schaden an, wenn sie außer Kontrolle gerieten und vom Himmel fielen. Beim Dach dieses Hauses in Palmers Green, London, mußten nur ein paar Pfannen erneuert werden, nachdem im Dezember 1912 ein Flugzeug hineingestürzt war (1). Die Piloten hatten oft weniger Glück. Als ein Flugzeug der Gebrüder Wright im September 1908 in Fort Meyer, Virginia, eine Bruchlandung machen mußte, wurde Orville Wright verletzt und sein Kopilot, Lieutenant Selfridge, getötet (2).

LES premières machines étaient frêles, ce qui les rendait parfois peu fiables, mais au moins elles causaient des dégâts minimes quand, ne répondant plus aux commandes, elles venaient s'abattre sur le sol. Il suffit de remplacer quelques ardoises sur le toit de cette maison à Palmers Green à Londres après qu'un monoplan s'y abattit en décembre 1912 (1). Les pilotes avaient souvent moins de chance. Lorsqu'un des avions des frères Wright s'écrasa au sol à Fort Meyer en septembre 1908 en Virginie, Orville Wright fut blessé et son copilote, le Lieutenant Selfridge, tué (2).

AIRSHIPS lacked the manoeuvrability of planes, but were believed to be more reliable, and could carry heavier loads. The Stanley Spencer airship, which made its first flight across London in 1902 (1), appears a direct descendant of the hot-air balloons of the Montgolfier Brothers, a hundred and twenty years earlier. But airships needed vast supplies of gas, such as these cylinders for the British R34 in 1919 (2), and even airships were not totally safe. L2, one of the earliest Zeppelins, crashed near Berlin in October 1913 (3).

LUFTSCHIFFE besaßen nicht die Manövrierfähigkeit von Flugzeugen, aber sie wurden für zuverlässiger gehalten und konnten größere Lasten transportieren. Das Luftschiff von Stanley Spencer, das 1902 seinen ersten Flug über London machte (1), war ein direkter Nachfahre des 120 Jahre zuvor entwickelten Heißluft-ballons der Gebrüder Montgolfier. Aber Luftschiffe brauchten große Mengen Gas, wie diese Zylinder für das britische R34 im Jahre 1919 zeigen (2), und selbst sie waren nicht vollkommen sicher. Der L2, einer der ersten Zeppeline, verunglückte im Oktober 1913 in der Nähe von Berlin (3).

LES dirigeables étaient moins maniables que les avions, mais ils passaient pour plus fiables et pouvaient transporter des charges plus lourdes. Le dirigeable Stanley Spencer, qui effectua son premier survol de Londres en 1902 (1), semble un descendant direct des ballons remplis d'air chaud des frères Montgolfier, quelque 120 ans plus tôt. Mais les dirigeables avaient d'énormes besoins en gaz, comme le montrent ces réservoirs cylindriques destinés au R34 britannique en 1919 (2), et même eux n'étaient pas totalement sûrs. Le L 2, un des premiers Zeppelins, s'écrasa près de Berlin en octobre 1913 (3).

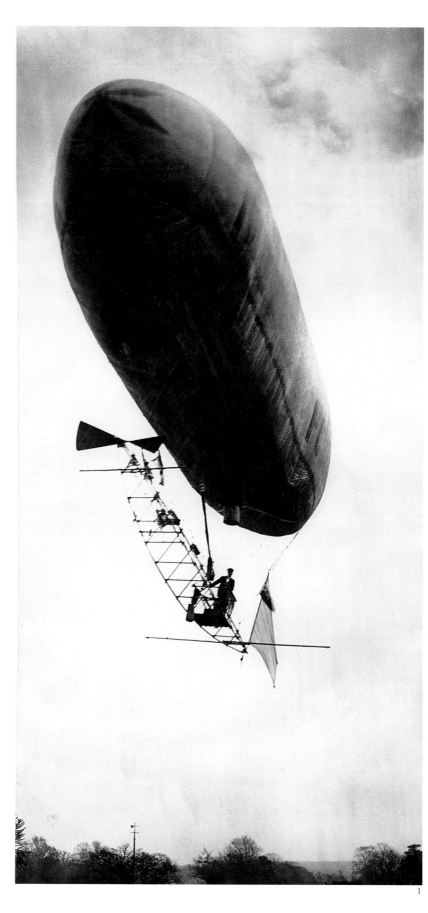

1

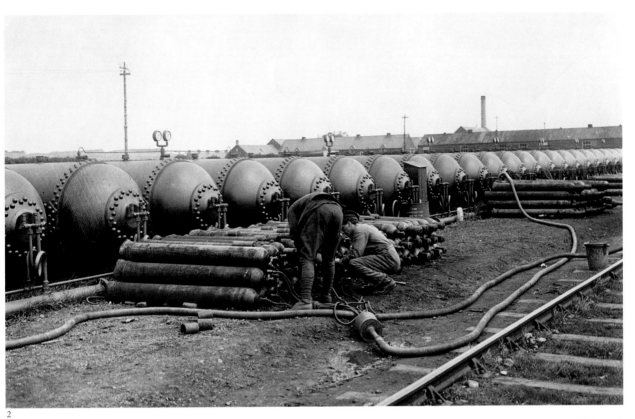

2

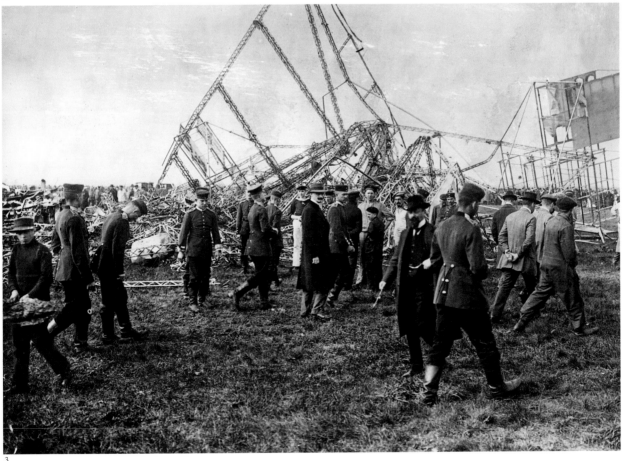

3

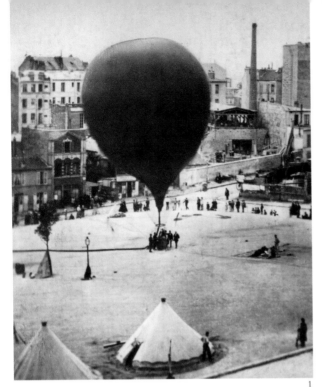

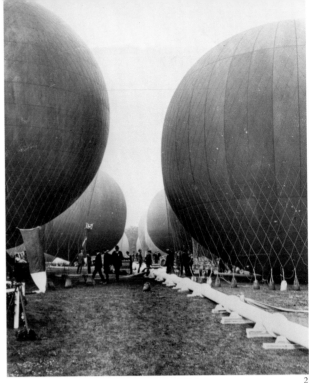

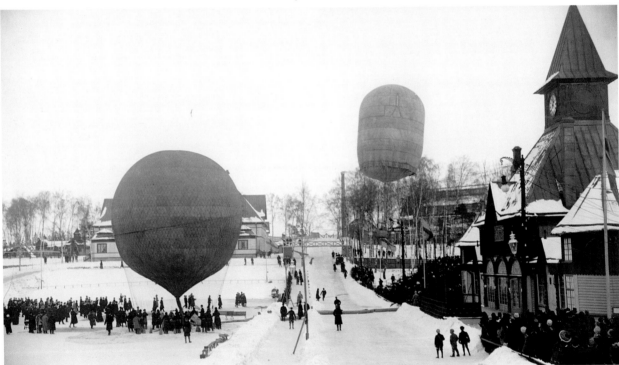

1

2

3

DURING the siege of Paris in 1870, balloons took off each week with official despatches and news of conditions in the city. The most famous flight was that of Gambetta, on a mission to raise a provincial army (1). Massed balloons at Hurlingham in 1908 (2); at the Northern games in 1909 (3); the Berlin Balloon Society's meeting in 1908 (4).

WÄHREND der Belagerung von Paris im Jahre 1870 stiegen in der französischen Hauptstadt regelmäßig Ballons mit offiziellen Depeschen und Berichten über die Zustände in der Stadt in die Höhe. Der berühmteste Flug war der von Gambetta (1), dessen Mission darin bestand, eine Provinzarmee aufzustellen. Eine Ansammlung von Ballons 1908 in Hurlingham (2); 1909 bei den Nordischen Spielen (3); das Treffen der Berliner Ballongesellschaft 1908 (4).

DURANT le siège de Paris en 1870, deux à trois ballons en moyenne quittaient la ville chaque semaine en transportant des dépêches officielles et des nouvelles sur la situation. Le vol le plus fameux fut celui de Gambetta (1) qui avait pour mission de lever une armée en province. Un rassemblement de ballons à Hurlingham en 1908 (2); les jeux nordiques en 1909 (3). Un rassemblement organisé par la société pour la promotion des ballons à Berlin en 1908 (4).

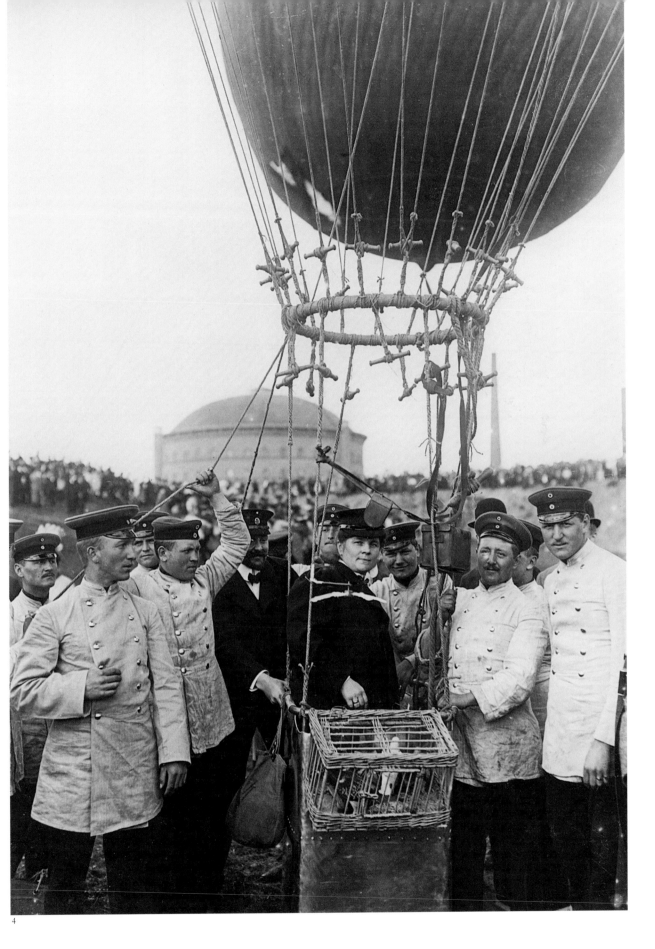

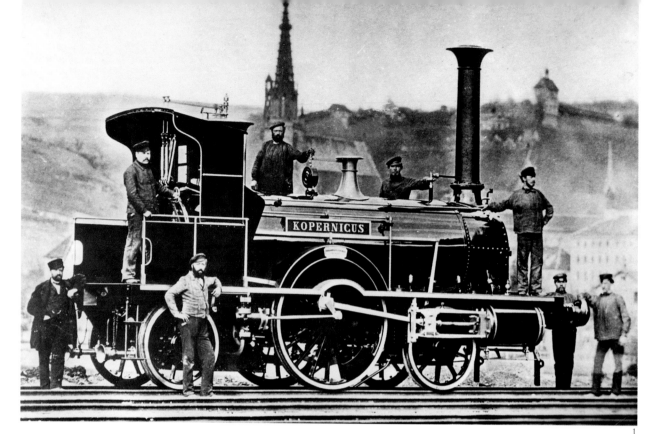

As far back as 1828, Goethe had told his friend Eckermann that Germany would one day be united – its good highways and future railways would make sure of that. Twelve years later, Treitschke wrote: 'It is the railways which first dragged the nation from its economic stagnation.' One machine that helped do the dragging was Kopernicus, a mighty iron monster of 1858 (1). Less impressive but more ingenious was the first electric train, made by Werner Siemens in 1879 (2). The world's first underground railway, between Paddington and the City of London, opened on 24 May 1862: Gladstone was on board (3). In 1860, this locomotive had to be hauled by road from the nearest railhead to its Welsh branch line (4).

BEREITS 1828 hatte Goethe seinem Freund Eckermann gesagt, es bestehe kein Zweifel daran, daß Deutschland eines Tages vereint sein werde, seine guten Straßen und zukünftigen Eisenbahnen würden dafür sorgen. Zwölf Jahre später schrieb Treitschke: »Es war die Eisenbahn, die die Nation aus ihrer wirtschaftlichen Stagnation gezogen hat.« Eine Maschine, die dabei half, war Kopernicus, ein mächtiges eisernes Monster aus dem Jahre 1858 (1). Weniger beeindruckend, aber genialer war die erste Elektrolok von Werner Siemens von 1879 (2). Die erste Untergrundbahn der Welt fuhr zwischen Paddington und London City; sie wurde am 24. Mai 1862 eingeweiht. Gladstone war an Bord (3). Im Jahre 1860 mußte diese Lokomotive auf der Straße zum nächstgelegenen Gleisende des walisischen Schienennetzes gezogen werden (4).

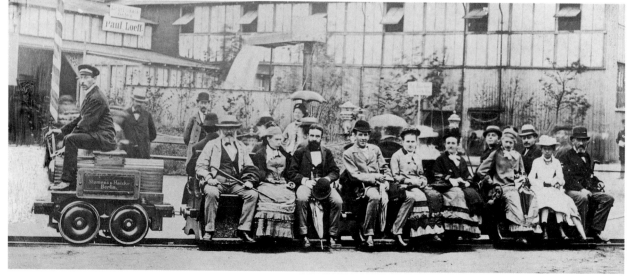

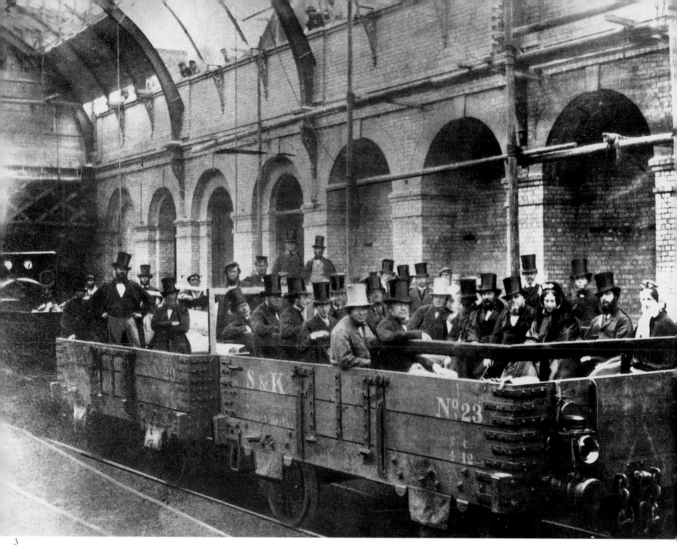

3

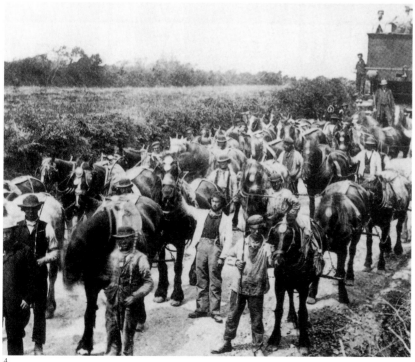

4

Déjà en 1828 Goethe disait à son ami Eckermann qu'il ne faisait aucun doute que l'unité de l'Allemagne se ferait un jour, et cela grâce à son bon réseau routier et à ses futures lignes de chemin de fer. Douze ans plus tard, Treitschke écrivait : « C'est le chemin de fer qui le premier a fait sortir la nation [allemande] de sa stagnation économique. » Une des machines qui y contribua fut le Kopernicus, puissant monstre d'acier apparu en 1858 (1). Moins impressionnant mais plus ingénieux était le premier train électrique fabriqué par Werner Siemens qui fut présenté à la foire commerciale de Berlin en 1879 (2). Le premier métro souterrain du monde reliait Paddington à la city de Londres et fut mis en service le 24 mai 1862. William Gladstone (3) était à bord.

En 1860, cette locomotive devait être remorquée par la route de la tête de ligne la plus proche jusqu'à la station d'embranchement ferroviaire galloise (4).

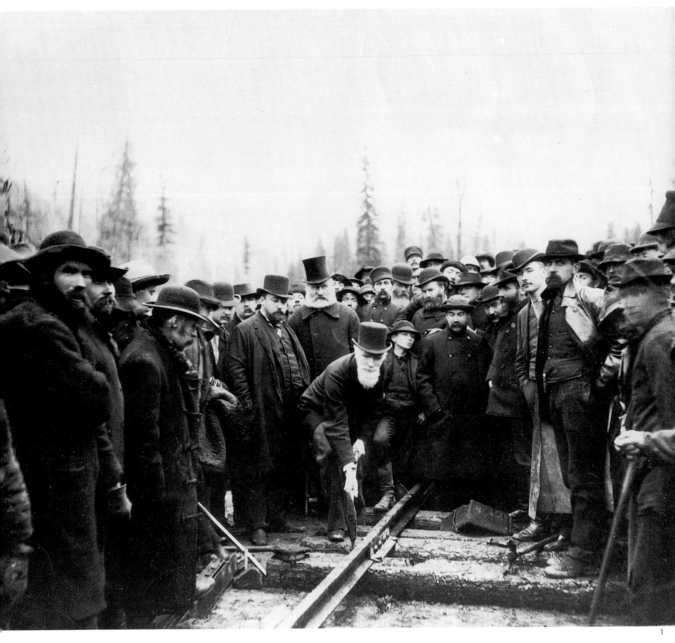

1

A T 9.30 am on 7 November 1885, the Honourable D. A. Smith drove in the silver spike that marked the completion of the Canadian Pacific Railroad, from the eastern seaboard to Vancouver (1). Third-class passengers on the CPR in 1885 were supplied with sleeping cars (2), an early form of the European couchette. Twenty-six years earlier, first-class passengers had more

luxurious sleeping accommodation (3), but sleeping facilities for the men who built the railroads were primitive. These tents were for the engineers of the CPR, at the summit of the Selkirk Mountains in British Columbia (4). For a slightly more comfort-able night, there were the liquors, cigars and beds available at Ed Lawler's Hotel – if the harp didn't keep you awake all night (5).

A M 7. November 1885 um 9.30 Uhr schlug D. A. Smith den silbernen Nagel ein, der die Fertigstellung der Cana-dian Pacific Railroad von der Ostküste nach Vancouver markierte (1). Passagiere der dritten Klasse der CPR konnten 1885 in solchen Liegewagen (2), einer frühen Form der europäischen *Couchette*s, fahren. Sechs-undzwanzig Jahre zuvor hatten die Passagiere der ersten Klasse luxuriösere Schlafmöglich-

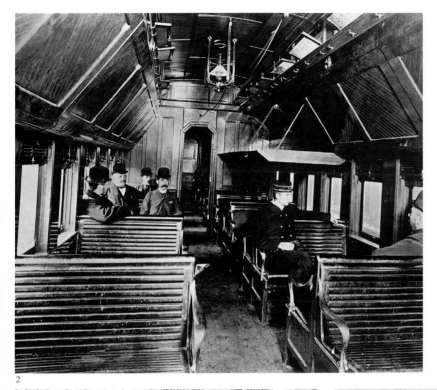

2

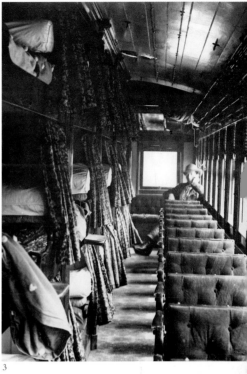

3

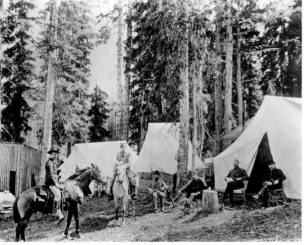

4

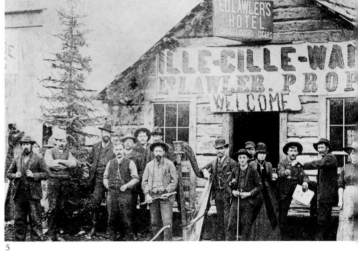

5

keiten (3), aber die Schlafplätze der Gleis-
arbeiter waren primitiv. Die Ingenieure
der CPR waren in diesen Zelten auf dem
Gipfel der Selkirk Mountains in British
Columbia untergebracht (4). Für eine beque-
mere Nacht gab es in Ed Lawlers Hotel
alkoholische Getränke, Zigarren und Betten,
falls die Harfenklänge einem nicht den
Schlaf raubten (5).

À 9 h 30 le 7 novembre 1885,
l'Honorable D. A. Smith marqua
solennellement avec une pointe en argent
l'achèvement de la ligne du chemin de
fer Pacifique canadien (CPR) reliant la
côte est à Vancouver (1). Les passagers
voyageant en troisième classe sur la CPR
en 1885 avaient à leur disposition des
voitures (2) équipées de couchettes qui
rappelaient les toutes premières couchettes
européennes. Vingt-six ans auparavant, les
voyageurs de première classe dormaient

dans des conditions plus luxueuses (3) ; en
revanche, les hommes qui construisaient
les chemins de fer dormaient dans des conditions primitives. Ces tentes-ci étaient
réservées aux ingénieurs du CPR au sommet
des montagnes Selkirk en Colombie-
Britannique (4). Pour une nuit légèrement
plus confortable, il y avait les liqueurs,
les cigares et les lits de l'hôtel d'Ed Lawler,
si toutefois la harpe ne vous empêchait
pas de fermer l'œil de la nuit (5).

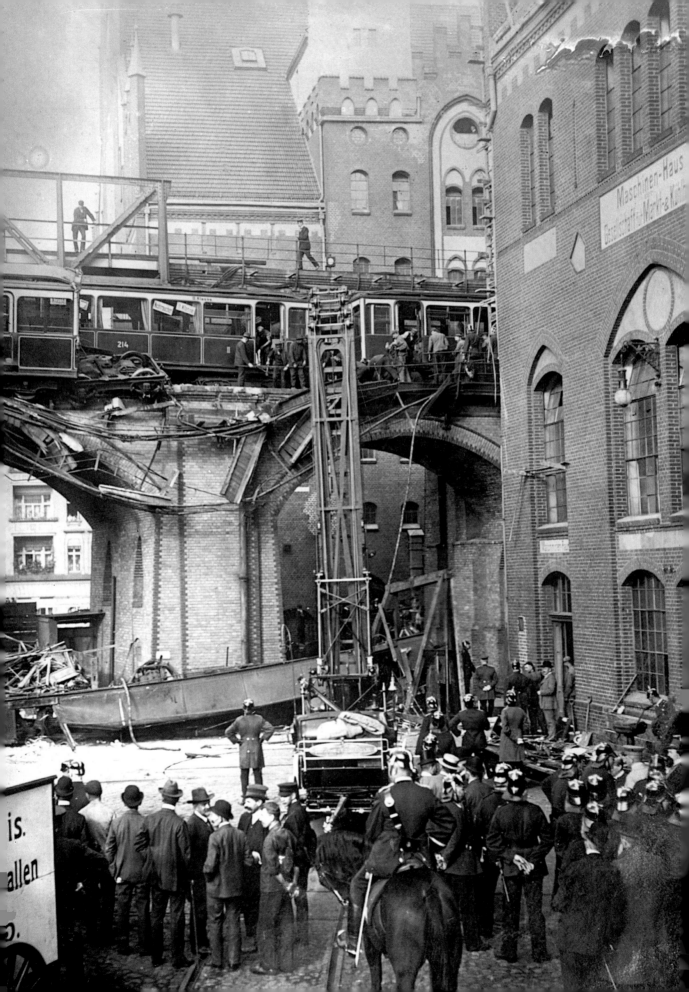

IN September 1908 crowds gathered to
watch the aftermath of a crash on the
Berlin Overhead Railway (1). In India
there were plenty of crashes (2, 3). One of
the most famous disasters in railway
history was in Scotland, the Great Tay
Bridge Disaster of 1879. The locomotive,
recovered from the river bed, survived
surprisingly well (4). The tragedy was
celebrated in the poetic gem of William
McGonagall:

Beautiful Railway Bridge of the Silv'ry Tay!
Alas! I am very sorry to say
That ninety lives have been taken away
On the last Sabbath day of 1879
Which will be remembered for a very long time.

IM September 1908 liefen die Menschen
zusammen, um sich die Folgen eines
Unfalls der Berliner Hochbahn anzusehen
(1). In Indien gab es viele Unfälle (2, 3).
Einer der spektakulärsten Unfälle in der
Geschichte der Eisenbahn ereignete sich
in Schottland, das Great Tay Bridge
Desaster von 1879. Die Tragödie wurde in
dem Gedicht von William McGonagall
verewigt (oben). Die Lokomotive wurde
aus dem Fluß geborgen; sie war in einem
erstaunlich guten Zustand (4).

EN septembre 1908, les gens accoururent
pour regarder ce qui restait d'une
collision survenue sur les voies du métro
aérien à Berlin (1). En Inde les collisions ne
manquaient pas (2, 3). Une des catastrophes
les plus célèbres de l'histoire du chemin de
fer se déroula en Écosse ; il s'agit du grand
désastre du pont Tay de 1879 célébré par
William McGonagall dans une magnifique
poésie :

Beau pont de fer du Tay argenté !
Hélas ! Je dois le dire le cœur serré
Que quatre-vingt-dix vies il fut emporté
Le dernier jour du sabbat de 1879, an
Qui restera dans les mémoires longtemps.

La locomotive qui tirait le train fatal
fut retirée du lit de la rivière : elle avait
étonnamment peu souffert (4).

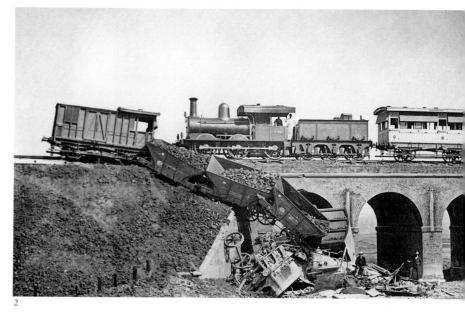

2

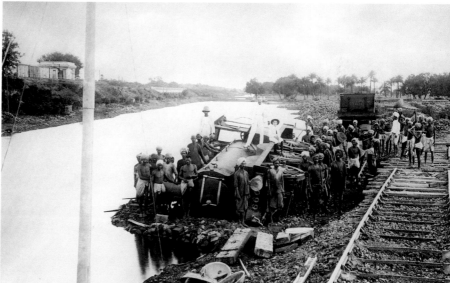

3

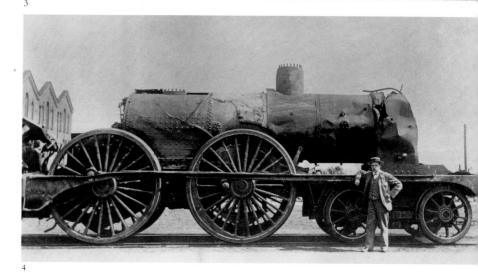

4

Science and Transport

O N 1 November 1895, while experimenting with cathode rays, Wilhelm Konrad Röntgen (1) accidentally stumbled across the greatest discovery of the 1890s: the X-ray – a source of light that penetrated flesh but not bone, as Albert Köllicher's wife's hand bore testimony (2).

It was a typical 19th-century advance, the product of one man (or one woman) working alone in a laboratory, painfully edging his or her way towards new knowledge that we take for granted today, but that changed the lives of ordinary people beyond all recognition: Pasteur and fermentation, Curie and radiation, Lister and antiseptics, Liston and anaesthetics, Bell and the telephone, Parsons and the steam turbine, Benz and the internal combustion engine, Marconi and the telegraph, Edison and electric light.

Public health improved immeasurably. Sewage was no longer pumped raw into the nearest river. Hospitals became places of healing, no longer the hell-holes in which death was likely – even preferable to the mutilated life that formerly had so often resulted. Homes were safer, better built, more comfortable. Buildings were stronger – Monier developed reinforced concrete in 1867. A revolution took place in communication. Journeys that had taken weeks took days. News – good and bad – which had taken days to reach its destination on the other side of the world could be sent thousands of miles in a matter of minutes, thanks to the telegraph.

On the ocean, sail gave way to steam. Paddle steamers plied the Mississippi, ploughed their way across the Atlantic (with library, musical instruments and all luxuries on board); bustled across the North Sea, the Black Sea, the Mediterranean and the Channel. People began to take to the sea for pleasure – a totally novel concept. Just like X-rays.

1

B EI seinem Experimentieren mit Kathodenstrahlen machte Wilhelm Konrad Röntgen (1) am 1. November 1895 zufällig die größte Entdeckung des Jahrzehnts: der Röntgenstrahl, eine Lichtquelle, die durch den Körper, aber nicht durch die Knochen drang, wie die Hand von Albert Köllicher zeigte (2).

Es war eine für das 19. Jahrhundert typische Errungenschaft: das Produkt eines einzigen Mannes (oder einer Frau), der oder die alleine in einem Labor arbeitete und sich mühsam zu neuen Erkenntnissen vortastete, die wir heute als selbstverständlich erachten, das Leben der Menschen damals jedoch entscheidend veränderten – Pasteur und die Fermentation, Curie und die Strahlen, Lister und das Antiseptikum, Liston und die Anästhesie, Bell und das Telephon, Parsons und die Dampfturbine, Benz und der Verbrennungsmotor, Marconi und der Telegraph, Edison und das elektrische Licht.

Die öffentliche Gesundheitsvorsorge verbesserte sich enorm: Abwässer wurden nicht mehr ungefiltert in den nächstgelegenen Fluß gepumpt. Krankenhäuser wurden zu Orten der Heilung und blieben nicht länger jene gräßlichen Anstalten, in denen der Tod regierte und sogar dem elenden Leben vorzuziehen war, das zu früheren Zeiten nach der Behandlung auf einen wartete. Wohnhäuser waren sicherer, besser konstruiert und bequemer, große Gebäude stabiler; Monier entwickelte im Jahre 1867 den verstärkten Beton. Im Kommunikationswesen vollzog sich eine technische Revolution. Reisen, für die man früher Wochen gebraucht hatte, dauerten jetzt nur wenige Tage. Gute und schlechte Nachrichten, die bis dahin Tage gebraucht hatten, bevor sie ihren Bestimmungsort irgendwo am anderen Ende der Welt erreichten, konnten dank des Telegraphen in wenigen Minuten über eine Distanz von bis zu mehreren tausend Meilen übermittelt werden.

Auf den Meeren wichen die Segel dem Dampf. Raddampfer

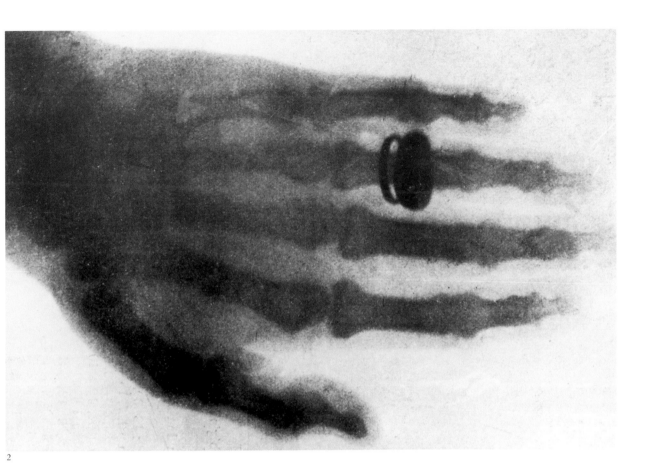

2

durchpflügten den Mississippi, bahnten sich ihren Weg über den Atlantik (mit Bibliotheken, Musikinstrumenten und aller Art von Luxus an Bord) und eilten über die Nordsee, das Schwarze Meer, das Mittelmeer und den Ärmelkanal. Die Menschen begannen, aus Vergnügen zur See zu fahren – ein ebenso neues Phänomen wie die Röntgenstrahlen.

Le 1er novembre 1895, alors qu'il faisait des expériences sur les rayons cathodiques, Wilhelm Konrad Röntgen (1) fit accidentellement la plus grande découverte des années 1890 : les rayons X, une source lumineuse qui traverse la chair mais pas les os, ainsi que la main d'Albert Köllicher en témoigna (2).

Il s'agit d'un progrès typique du XIXe siècle, résultant des travaux isolés d'un seul homme (ou d'une seule femme) s'efforçant péniblement dans son laboratoire d'acquérir des connaissances que nous trouvons aujourd'hui banales, mais qui transformèrent radicalement la vie de tous les jours : Pasteur et la fermentation, Curie et la radiation, Lister et les antiseptiques, Liston et les anesthésiques, Bell et le téléphone, Parsons et la turbine à vapeur, Benz et le moteur à combustion interne, Marconi et le télégraphe sans fil, Edison et la lumière électrique.

La santé publique s'améliora au-delà de toute mesure. Les détritus n'étaient plus déversés tels quels dans la plus proche rivière. Les hôpitaux devenaient des endroits où l'on guérissait et non plus des enfers où la mort était certaine. Les maisons étaient plus sûres, mieux construites et plus confortables. Les édifices étaient plus solides : en 1867, Monier mit au point le béton armé. Les communications connurent une révolution. Les voyages qui avaient exigé des semaines prenaient des journées. Les nouvelles, bonnes ou mauvaises, qui mettaient des jours à parvenir à destination, pour peu que celle-ci se trouvât à l'autre bout du monde, parcouraient des milliers de kilomètres en quelques minutes grâce au télégraphe.

Sur l'océan, la vapeur avait remplacé la voile. Les bateaux à roues faisaient la navette sur le Mississippi, sillonnaient l'Atlantique (avec à leur bord des bibliothèques, des instruments de musique et autres luxueux agréments) ; ils fourmillaient dans la mer du Nord, la mer Noire, la Méditerranée et la Manche. On commençait à assimiler la mer au plaisir, ce qui, à l'instar des rayons X, était entièrement nouveau.

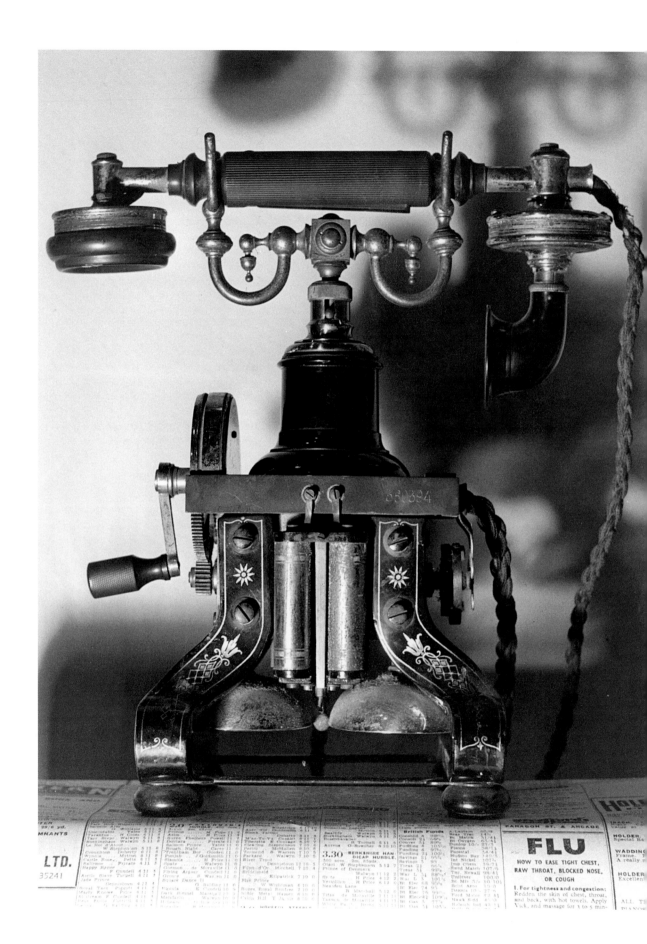

IN 1876 the telephone was invented by Alexander Graham Bell (2 – seated at desk), a Scotsman who had emigrated to the United States five years earlier. Bell was greatly interested in oral communication (and lack of it – he devoted much of his life to the education of deaf-mutes). The first telephone service between London and Paris was opened in 1891. At first, telephones were used almost entirely for commercial purposes, and by 1900 there were enough in use to warrant large switchboards, like this of the National Telephone Company (3). The early hand-crank set (1) was used at the Hull Exchange – the only local-authority-owned service in Britain.

IM Jahre 1876 erfand der Schotte Alexander Graham Bell (2, am Tisch sitzend), der fünf Jahre zuvor in die Vereinigten Staaten emigriert war, das Telephon. Bell war sehr an mündlicher Kommunikation interessiert (und an ihrem Fehlen; er widmete viele Jahre seines Lebens der Arbeit mit Taubstummen). Die erste Telephonverbindung zwischen London und Paris wurde 1891 in Betrieb genommen. Zunächst wurde das Telephon fast ausschließlich für kommerzielle Zwecke genutzt, aber bereits im Jahre 1900 gab es so viele Anschlüsse, daß große Schaltzentralen erforderlich waren, wie die der National Telephone Company (3). Das frühe Telephon mit Handkurbel (1) wurde bei der Börse in Hull verwendet, der einzigen Telephongesellschaft in Großbritannien, die sich im Besitz einer Gemeinde befindet.

EN 1876, Alexander Graham Bell (2, assis à sa table de travail) inventa le téléphone. Cet Écossais était arrivé aux États-Unis cinq ans auparavant. Bell s'intéressait beaucoup à la communication orale (et à son absence ; il consacra une grande partie de sa vie à l'éducation des sourds-muets). La première ligne téléphonique fut mise en service entre Londres et Paris en 1891. Au départ, les téléphones servaient presque uniquement à des fins commerciales, et dès 1900 leur nombre suffisait à justifier l'installation de vastes standards comme celui de la Compagnie nationale de téléphone (3). Le premier combiné (1) fut utilisé au Hull Exchange, le seul service téléphonique municipal de Grande-Bretagne.

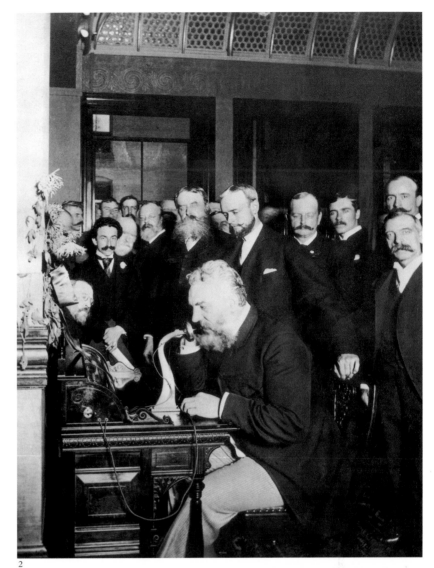

2

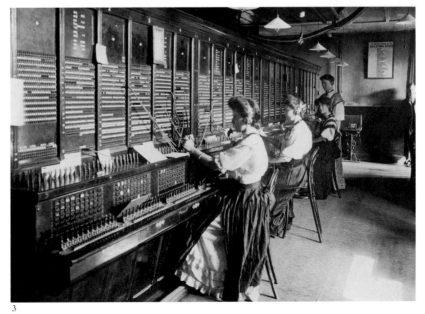

3

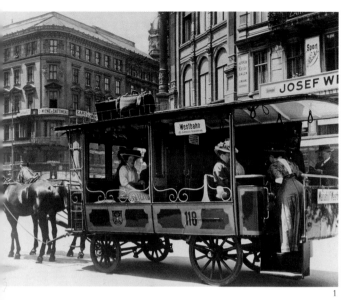

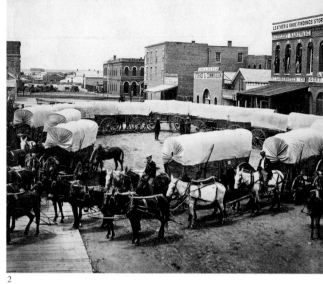

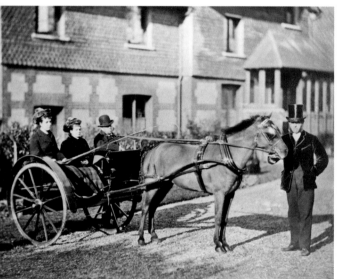

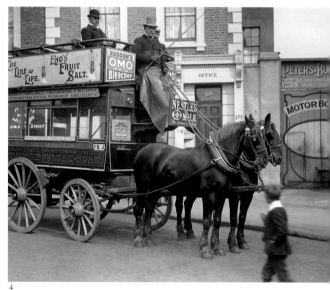

HORSE-DRAWN buses were still being used in Vienna in 1904 (1), and in London in 1911 (4). Outside Europe, heavy freight was carried on mule trains – Denver, Colorado, in 1870 (2). In Europe, the smart trap was the forerunner of the family car (3). In city centres, traffic moved as slowly as it does now – London Bridge was congested daily in the 1890s (5). With a little decoration, such as a painting of a battle, the family cart could become a vehicle of individual beauty – though six people might have been a tough load for one horse in Palermo (6). The London Hansom cab (7) was such as Sherlock Holmes would have hailed when he and Dr Watson went sleuthing.

PFERDEBUSSE gab es noch 1904 in Wien (1) und 1911 in London (4). Außerhalb Europas wurden schwere Frachten mit von Maultieren gezogenen Planwagen-Konvois befördert, wie hier 1870 in Denver, Colorado (2). In Europa war der flotte zweirädrige Pferdewagen der Vorläufer des Familienautos (3). Der Verkehr in den Stadtzentren bewegte sich so schnell oder so langsam wie heute – die London Bridge war in den 1890er Jahren täglich verstopft (5). Durch ein wenig Verzierung, beispielsweise mit einem Schlachtengemälde, konnte man aus dem Familienwagen ein Gefährt von individueller Schönheit machen – obwohl sechs Personen vielleicht eine etwas schwere Last für dieses Pferd in Palermo waren (6). Der Londoner Hansom (7) war ein Einspänner, wie ihn Sherlock Holmes benutzt haben mag, wenn er zusammen mit Dr. Watson seine Nachforschungen anstellte.

LES omnibus tirés par des chevaux étaient encore utilisés à Vienne en 1904 (1), et à Londres en 1911 (4). Hors d'Europe, les lourdes charges étaient transportées par des convois de mulets : à Denver dans le Colorado, en 1870 (2). En Europe, cette élégante charrette anglaise précéda la voiture familiale (3). Dans le centre des grandes villes, la circulation était aussi rapide ou aussi lente qu'aujourd'hui : le pont de Londres était congestionné tous les jours dans les années 1890 (5). Décoré, par exemple d'une scène guerrière, l'attelage familial se transformait en véhicule doté d'une beauté individuelle, quand bien même six personnes pouvaient se révéler une lourde charge à tirer pour un cheval de Palerme (6). Ce fiacre londonien (7) ressemble à l'un de ceux que Sherlock Holmes aurait hélés pour se lancer, avec le docteur Watson, dans une de leurs enquêtes.

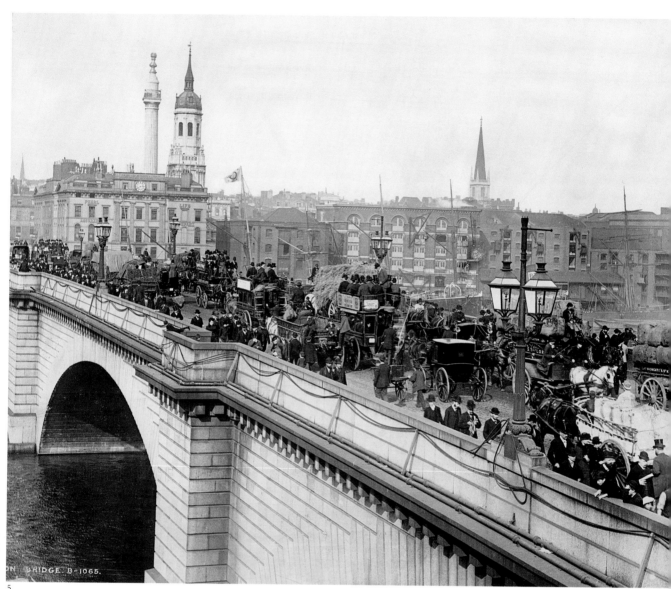

5

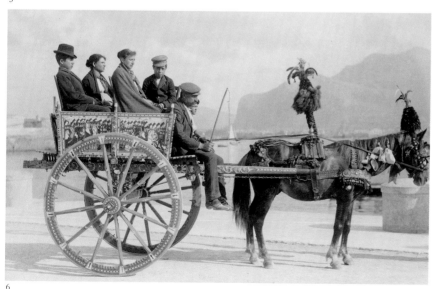

6

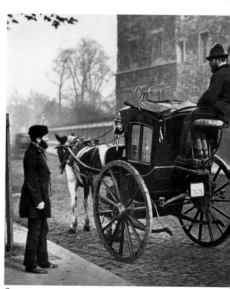

7

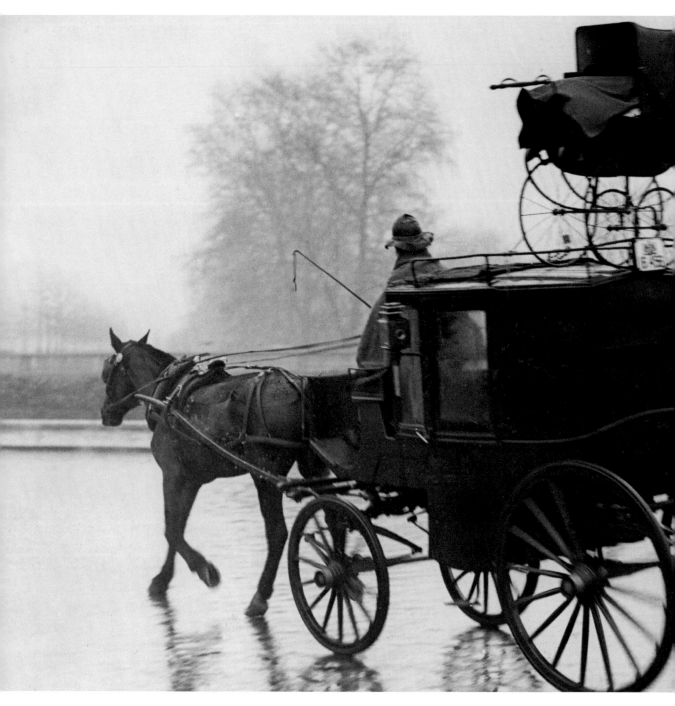

FEW sensations evoke an image of 19th-century city life more strongly than the sound of horses' hooves rattling over cobblestones (1). Vast stables were needed on the outskirts of Berlin, Madrid, Rome, Paris and other capitals to supply the tens of thousands of horses needed to pull public conveyances. A popular London cab was the Growler (2), first put in service in 1865. Fifty years later, horse-drawn traffic was in decline, but this smart little zebra was still trotting along London streets (3).

Es gibt nur wenige Geräusche, die stärker an das Stadtleben im 19. Jahrhundert erinnern als das Geklapper von Pferdehufen auf Kopfsteinpflaster (1). Am Stadtrand von Berlin, Madrid, Rom, Paris und anderen Metropolen befanden sich große Ställe, um die vielen tausend Pferde unterzubringen, die man für den öffent-

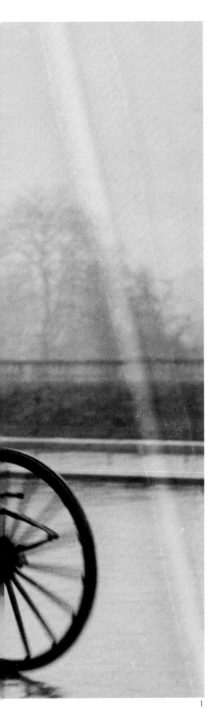

2

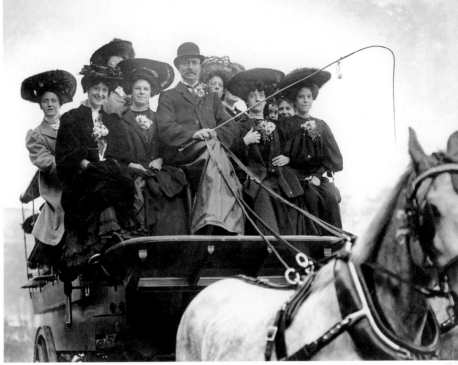

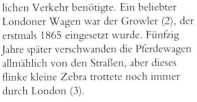

1

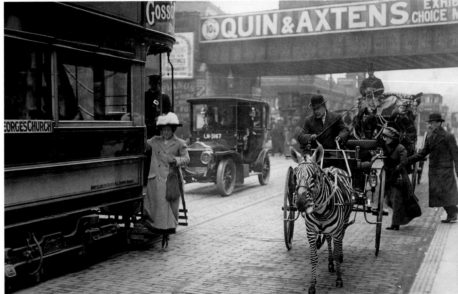

3

lichen Verkehr benötigte. Ein beliebter Londoner Wagen war der Growler (2), der erstmals 1865 eingesetzt wurde. Fünfzig Jahre später verschwanden die Pferdewagen allmählich von den Straßen, aber dieses flinke kleine Zebra trottete noch immer durch London (3).

Peu de sensations évoquent avec plus de force la vie dans les grandes villes au XIXe siècle que le claquement des sabots des chevaux sur les pavés ronds (1). Aux abords de Berlin, de Madrid, de Rome, de Paris et des autres capitales, il fallait prévoir de vastes étables pour fournir les dizaines de milliers de chevaux nécessaires aux attelages publics. Un fiacre était populaire à Londres : le Growler (2), mis en service pour la première fois en 1865. Cinquante ans après, les voitures tirées par les chevaux disparaissaient, à l'exception de ce charmant petit zèbre qui continuait à trotter dans les rues de Londres (3).

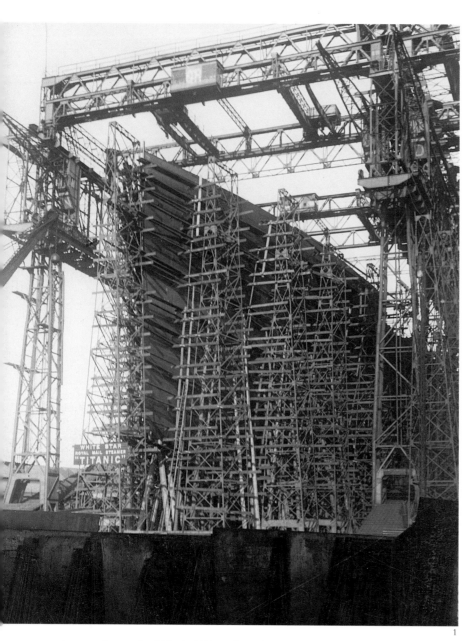

Ce fut une carrière brève et dramatique. En 1910 commençait la construction dans les chantiers navals d'Harland and Wolff à Belfast (1) du puissant *Titanic*, pesant 46 000 tonnes, fierté de la White Star Line. Le capitaine Smith (2) avait été nommé pour en prendre le commandement pendant sa première traversée de l'Atlantique. En 1912 le *Titanic* est remorqué au large pour ses premières manœuvres en mer (3). Il était énorme, superbe, puissant et luxueux : on le disait insubmersible.

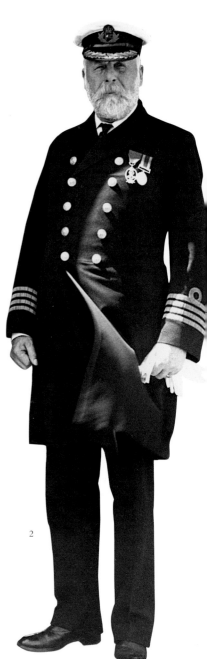

It was a short and sad life. In 1910 work began at Harland and Wolff's shipyard in Belfast (1) on the mighty 46,000-ton *Titanic*, the pride of the White Star Line. Captain Smith (2) was appointed captain for her maiden voyage across the Atlantic. The *Titanic* was towed out for her sea trials early in 1912 (3). She was huge, superb, powerful, luxurious, and, so it was said, unsinkable.

Es war ein kurzes und trostloses Leben: 1910 begann auf der Schiffswerft von Harland und Wolff in Belfast (1) die Arbeit an der 46 000 Tonnen schweren *Titanic*, dem Stolz der White Star Line. Kapitän Smith (2) erhielt das Kommando für die Jungfernfahrt über den Atlantik. Die *Titanic* wurde zu Beginn des Jahres 1912 zur Erprobung ihrer Seetüchtigkeit aus dem Hafen geschleppt (3). Sie war gewaltig, großartig, kraftvoll, luxuriös und, so behauptete man, unsinkbar.

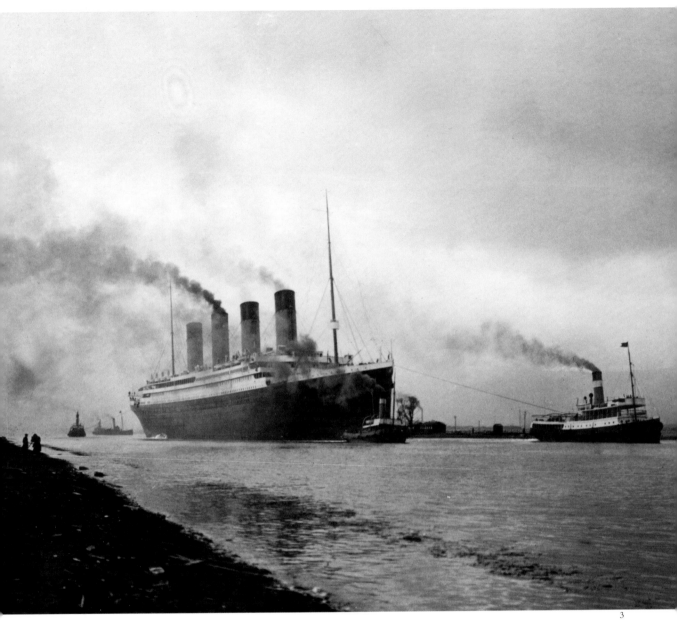

(*Overleaf*)

IT was a proud but empty boast. On 12 April 1912, on that maiden voyage, the *Titanic* hit an iceberg in the North Atlantic and sank with the loss of 1 513 lives out of the 2 224 on board. There were not enough lifeboats (1). Other ships were said to have ignored *Titanic*'s calls for help. Understandably, many panicked. When the survivors reached safety, they were dazed and bewildered by their ordeal (2). Relatives who greeted them were more obviously emotional (3). The disaster shocked Britain and the United States, and

men, women and children contributed to the appeal fund set up to aid the families of those who had drowned (5). Survivors became short-term celebrities – crowds queued for their autographs (4).

(*Folgende Seiten*)

DER Stolz war groß, aber nicht berechtigt. Am 12. April 1912 rammte die *Titanic* auf ihrer Jungfernfahrt einen Eisberg im Nordatlantik und ging mit 1 513 der 2 224 Passagiere unter. Es gab nicht genügend Rettungsboote (1). Andere Schiffe hatten angeblich die Hilferufe der

Titanic ignoriert. Verständlicherweise gerieten viele Passagiere in Panik. Als sich die Überlebenden in Sicherheit befanden, waren sie von den schrecklichen Erlebnissen benommen und wie gelähmt (2). Ihre Angehörigen, die auf sie warteten, zeigten mehr Emotionen (3). Die Katastrophe schockierte Großbritannien und die Vereinigten Staaten, und Männer, Frauen und Kinder spendeten für den Hilfsfonds, der den Familien der Ertrunkenen zugute kommen sollte (5). Die Überlebenden waren für kurze Zeit Berühmtheiten, und ihre Autogramme sehr begehrt (4).

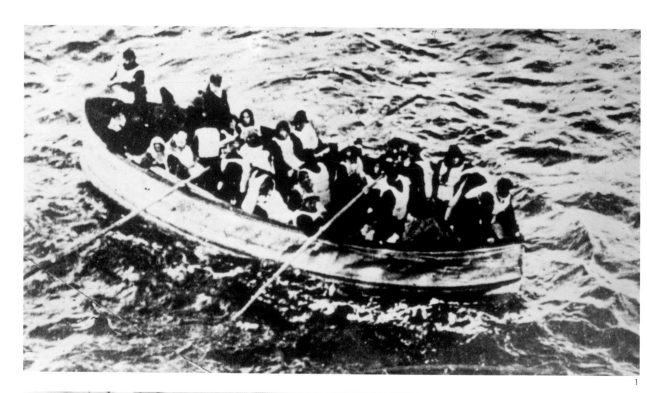

1

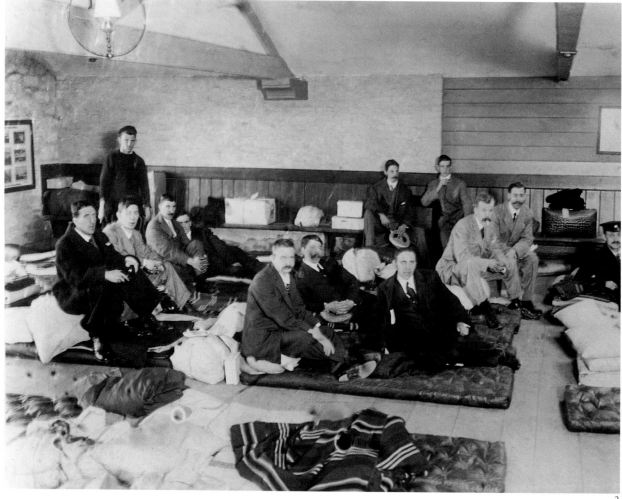

2

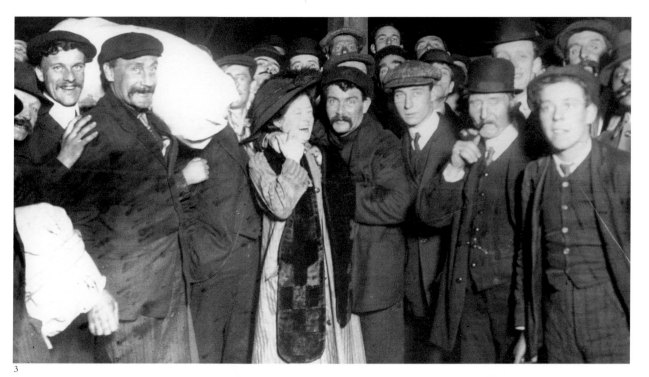

3

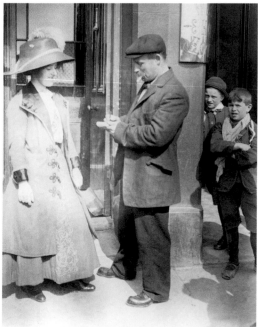

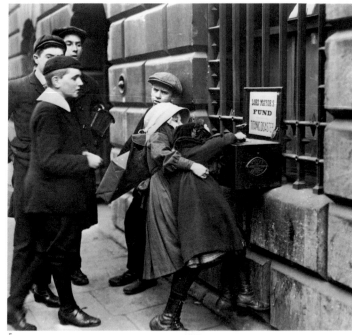

4   5

UNE vanité sans fondement. Le 12
avril 1912, au cours de cette première
traversée, le *Titanic* heurta un iceberg au
nord de l'Atlantique et sombra. Il avait à
son bord 2 224 personnes: 1 513 moururent.
Les canots de sauvetage n'étaient pas assez
nombreux (1). On a dit que les autres

navires n'avaient pas répondu aux appels de
détresse du *Titanic*. On comprendra que
beaucoup furent pris de panique. Les
rescapés étaient hébétés et en plein désarroi
à la suite de leur épreuve (2). Leurs parents,
en les accueillant, se montraient plus
démonstratifs (3). Ce désastre secoua la

Grande-Bretagne et les États-Unis: hommes,
femmes et enfants versèrent des dons au
fonds de secours qui avait été constitué pour
venir en aide aux familles des noyés (5).
Les survivants jouirent d'une célébrité sans
lendemain et l'on faisait la queue pour
obtenir d'eux des autographes (4).

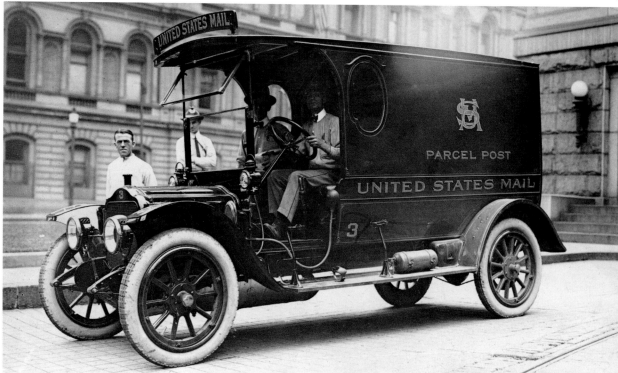

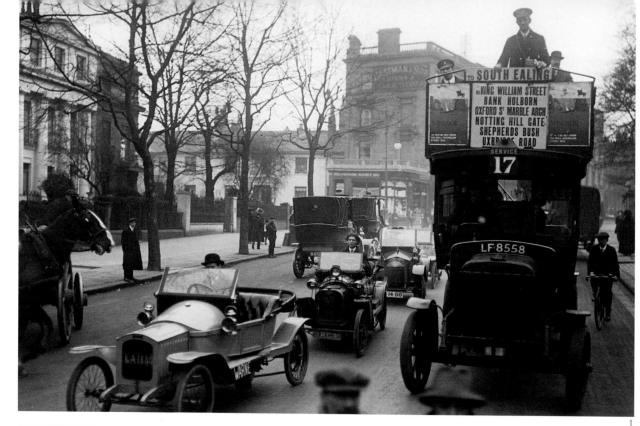

LANE discipline was a thing unknown in the early days of motoring (1). The volume of commercial road transport grew rapidly – this US mail truck (2) was a far cry from the Pony Express of a generation or two earlier. Rehearsals began for an airmail service at Hendon, near London, in 1911. The plane was named *Valkyrie* (4). Horse buses disappeared for ever – they could not compete with the power and increasing reliability of motorbuses (3).

IN den ersten Tagen des Autoverkehrs war eine disziplinierte Fahrweise noch unbekannt (1). Der kommerzielle Transport auf den Straßen wuchs schnell an – dieses amerikanische Postauto (2) hatte mit dem Ponyexpress früherer Generationen nichts mehr zu tun. In Hendon in der Nähe von

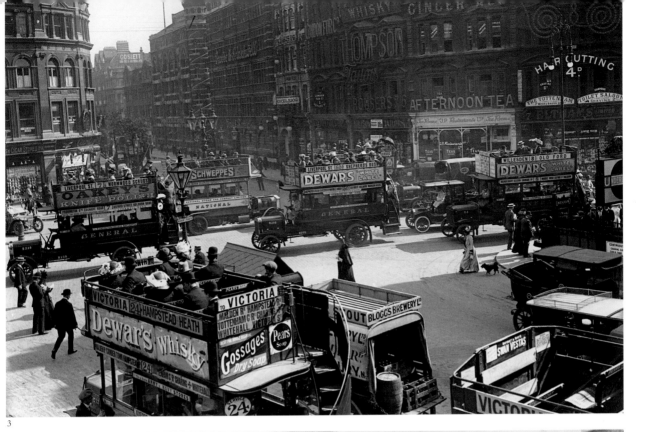

3

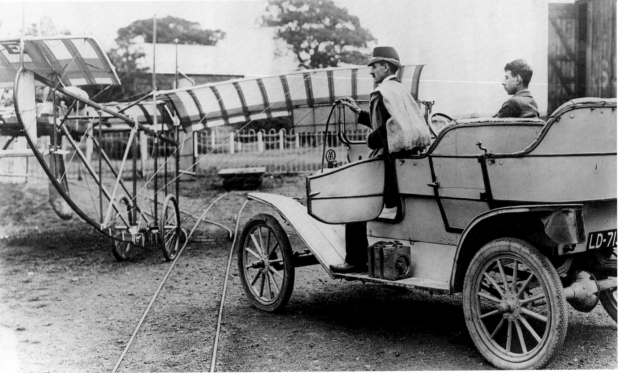

4

London begann man 1911 mit der Erprobung eines Luftpostdienstes. Das Flugzeug hieß *Valkyrie* (4). Pferdebusse verschwanden für immer aus dem Straßenbild, denn sie konnten mit der Leistung und der zunehmenden Sicherheit der Motorbusse nicht konkurrieren (3).

Rester dans sa voie était une règle inconnue des premiers temps de l'automobile (1). Le volume des transports commerciaux par la route augmentait rapidement. Ce fourgon postal aux États-Unis (2) n'a plus rien de commun avec le Pony Express qui existait une ou deux générations auparavant.

On commençait à faire des tentatives de courrier aérien à Hendon, près de Londres, en 1911. L'avion avait été baptisé *Valkyrie* (4). Les voitures publiques hippo-mobiles disparurent à jamais, faute de pouvoir soutenir la comparaison avec la fiabilité toujours plus grande des omnibus à moteur (3).

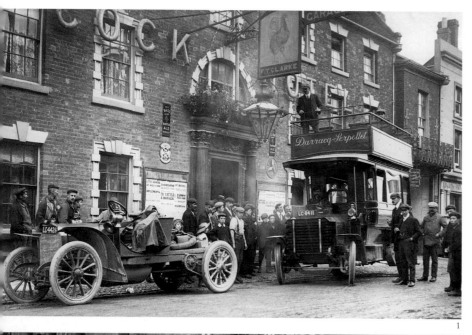

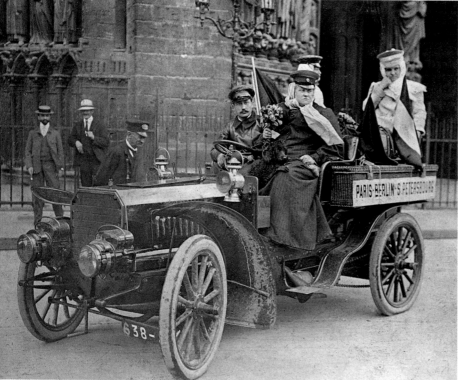

1

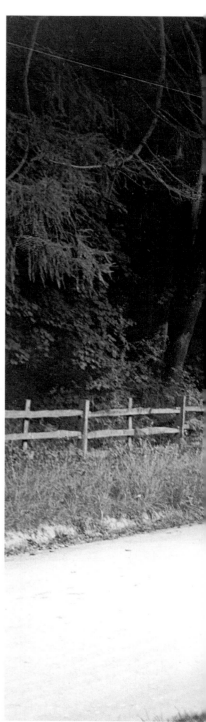

THE charabanc (3) was one of the most popular motor vehicles for a day out. It was noisy, a little slow, and open to the elements, but with its raked seats it gave everyone on board a good view of whatever troubles or delights lay ahead. Bolder motorists dressed for longer journeys. In 1903 Madame Lockart and her daughter set off from Notre Dame in Paris (2). They were bound for St Petersburg, over 1,800 miles (3,000 km) away.

Motor cars, buses and charabancs brought a new lease of life to the old coaching inns. Enthusiasts off to the Blackpool Motor Races in 1906 in the Serpollet bus paused for refreshment at the Cock Hotel, Stratford (1).

DER Charabanc (3) war eines der beliebtesten Motorfahrzeuge für einen Ausflug ins Grüne. Er war zwar laut, ein wenig langsam und offen, aber mit seinen ansteigenden Sitzen bot er allen Passagieren an Bord einen guten Ausblick auf all die Schrecken und Freuden, die auf sie zukamen. Kühnere Autofahrer unternahmen längere Fahrten. Im Jahre 1903 starteten Madame Lockart und ihre Toch-

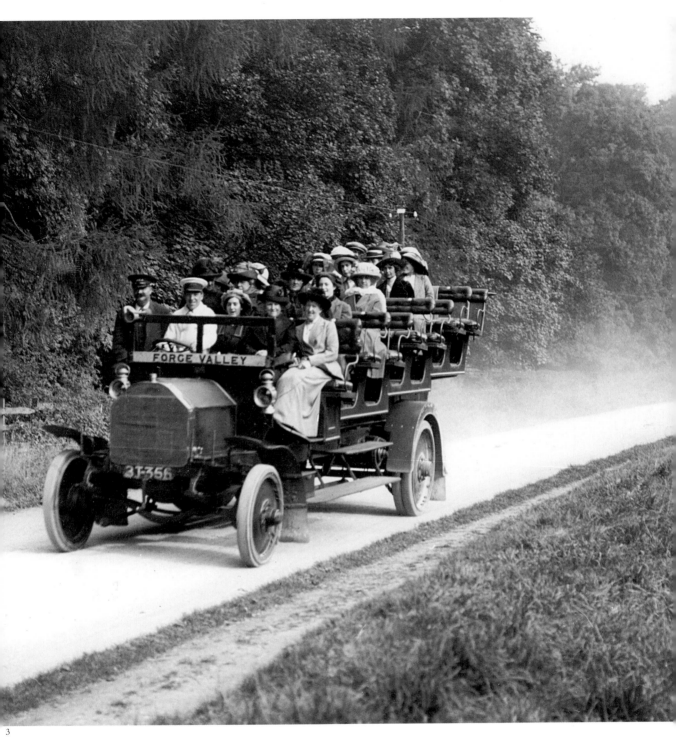

3

ter von Notre Dame in Paris (2). Ihr Ziel war das 3.000 Kilometer entfernte St. Petersburg.

Autos, Busse und Charabancs brachten den alten Rasthäusern neuen Aufschwung. Anhänger des Motorsports, die 1906 in diesem Serpollet-Bus auf dem Weg zum Autorennen in Blackpool waren, machten im Cock Hotel in Stratford Rast, um sich zu erfrischen (1).

Le char à bancs motorisé (3) était l'un des véhicules automobiles les plus prisés pour une journée d'excursion. Il était bruyant, un peu lent et ouvert à tous les éléments, mais aussi garni de rangs superposés qui permettaient à leurs occupants d'apprécier pleinement les inconvénients et les plaisirs que leur réservait le trajet. Les plus hardis s'habillaient en prévision de voyages plus longs. Madame Lockart

et sa fille en 1903 prenant le départ à Notre-Dame-de-Paris (2). Leur voyage devait les mener jusqu'à Saint-Pétersbourg, à plus de 3 000 kilomètres de distance.

Les automobiles, les omnibus et les chars à bancs remirent en activité les anciens relais de poste. Les enthousiastes, se rendant aux courses automobiles à Blackpool en 1906 en bus Serpollet, descendaient se restaurer au Cock Hotel à Stratford (1).

Social Unrest

For some, the world was beginning to spin a little too fast. The established order found itself giddy, perplexed, outraged as new ideas threatened to take over. Darwin's theories challenged the literal truth of the Old Testament story of the Creation. Freud suggested that all men and women possessed dark unexplored regions of the subconscious far more terrifying than anywhere that Livingstone or Stanley had visited. Marx informed the workers that they had nothing to lose but their chains, and a whole world to gain – however fast it was spinning.

Trade unions were becoming more vociferous, encouraging people to demand better pay, better protection, better conditions, shorter hours. The suffragists were demanding votes for women. Married women had the impertinence to suggest that they should have the right to own property. The unemployed were demanding work and shattering the windows of the rich to show the strength of their feeling. Nationalists in Africa and India were demanding independence, or at least a say in how they were governed.

There was a disturbing amount of talk about 'rights' – to education, to better housing, to better medical care. There was open discussion of such heresies as birth control, homosexuality, free love, republicanism, atheism, socialism, anarchy. Students were questioning their teachers, servants arguing with their masters. Children, it was said, were disobeying their parents.

What had happened? A hundred years later it may be impossible to tell, but the words of a German worker early in the 20th century may hold a clue: 'I got to know a shoemaker called Schröder… Later he went to America… he gave me some newspapers to read and I read a bit before I was bored, and then I got more and more interested… They described the misery of the workers and how they depended on the capitalists and landlords in a way that was so lively and true to nature that it really amazed me. It was as though my eyes had been closed before. Damn it, what they wrote in those papers was *the truth*. All my life up to that day was proof of it.'

People's lives were undergoing a faster and more profound change than at any other time in history. They lived in different places in different conditions under different rules from those that had ordered the lives of generations before. The rhythm of rural life had been broken. When they trudged to the cities, seeking work, they were transported to another world. And one of the first things they wanted to do in this new world was to try to understand it, to make sense of it. A sleeping curiosity had been awakened. People looked about them – saw, compared, contrasted, drew conclusions. 'Only connect,' wrote the novelist E. M. Forster in 1910, 'and the beast and the monk, robbed of the isolation that is life to either, will die.'

Many may have drawn the wrong conclusions, but many made the right connections. Ideas poured forth in plays, books, newspapers, even paintings and cartoons – about the subjugation of woman to man; about the right of the Church to have a monopoly on morality; about equality before the law; about the tyranny of privilege; about the power of the masses.

No new idea can exist without threatening someone, and there was an almighty backlash. The established order sent its army and its police force to the front line. Revolutionaries were bundled away, to exile if they were lucky. Suffragettes were bound and forcibly fed. Socialists were hunted down. Homosexuals were imprisoned. Nationalists were whipped, and their ideas temporarily stifled.

But the old system of unquestioning obedience to orders was on its way out. It had one last grossly triumphant chance to show what it was capable of – in the slaughter of the First World War.

1

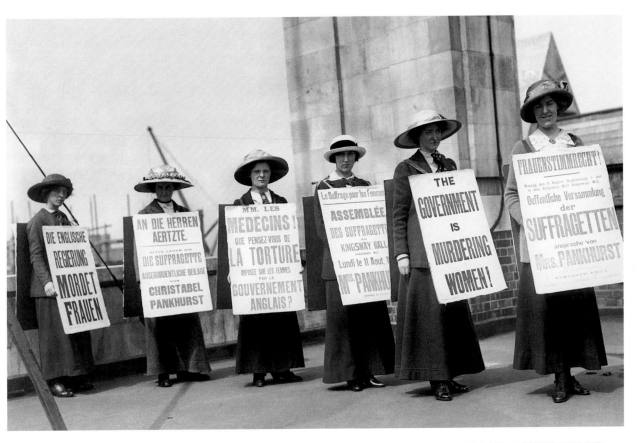

THE VICTIM OF AN ANCIENT ANTI-SEMITISM: ALFRED DREYFUS (1). AN INTERNATIONAL RESPONSE TO BRITISH PERSECUTION OF SUFFRAGETTES (2).

DAS OPFER EINES URALTEN ANTISEMITISMUS: ALFRED DREYFUS (1). EINE INTERNATIONALE ANTWORT AUF DIE VERFOLGUNG DER SUFFRAGETTEN IN GROSSBRITANNIEN (2).

ALFRED DREYFUS (1): UNE VICTIME DE L' ANTISÉMITISME AMBIANT ET DE L'AVEUGLEMENT NATIONALISTE. RÉACTION INTERNATIONAL DEVANT LA PERSÉCUTION DES SUFFRAGETTES PAR LES BRITANNIQUES (2).

FÜR einige drehte sich die Welt ein wenig zu schnell. Die etablierte Ordnung geriet ins Wanken, war verwirrt und zum Teil schockiert, als neue Ideen sich durchzusetzen drohten. Darwins Theorien stellten die Wahrheit der Schöpfungsgeschichte des Alten Testaments in Frage. Freud behauptete, der Mensch berge dunkle, unentdeckte Bereiche des Unterbewußten in sich, die weitaus erschreckender seien als all die Orte, die Livingstone oder Stanley besucht hatten. Marx sagte den Arbeitern, daß sie außer ihren Ketten nichts zu verlieren und eine ganze Welt zu gewinnen hätten – so schnell sie sich auch drehen mochte.

Die Gewerkschaften wurden immer energischer und ermutigten die Menschen, höhere Löhne, besseren Schutz, bessere Bedingungen und kürzere Arbeitszeiten zu fordern. Die Suffragetten verlangten das Wahlrecht für Frauen. Verheiratete Frauen besaßen die Unver-schämtheit, das Recht auf eigenen Besitz einzufordern. Die Arbeitslosen wollten Arbeit und warfen die Fenster der Reichen ein, um ihren Gefühlen Nachdruck zu verleihen. Nationalisten in Afrika und Indien forderten die Unabhängigkeit, oder zumindest ein Mitspracherecht in Regierungsfragen.

Überall gab es Diskussionen um »Rechte« auf Erziehung und Ausbildung, auf bessere Wohnungen, bessere medizinische Versorgung. Man diskutierte offen über solche Ketzereien wie Geburtenkontrolle, Homosexualität, freie Liebe, Republikanismus, Atheismus, Sozialismus und Anarchie. Studenten zweifelten ihre Professoren an, Diener stritten sich mit ihren Herren, und Kinder gehorchten ihren Eltern nicht mehr.

Was war passiert? Hundert Jahre später ist es vielleicht nicht mehr möglich, darauf eine Antwort zu finden, aber die Worte eines deutschen Arbeiters vom Beginn des 20. Jahrhunderts könnten einen Hinweis enthalten: »Ich lernte einen Schuhmacher namens Schröder kennen ... Er ging später nach Amerika ... er gab mir ein paar Zeitungen zu lesen, und ich las ein bißchen darin, bevor sie mich langweilten, aber dann interessierten sie mich immer mehr ... Sie be-schrieben das Elend der Arbeiter und ihre Abhängigkeit von den Kapitalisten und Grundbesitzern auf eine so lebendige und wirklichkeitsnahe Art, daß es mich völlig erstaunte. Es war, als hätte ich meine Augen vorher geschlossen gehabt. Verdammt, was sie in diesen Zeitungen schrieben, war *die Wahrheit*. Mein ganzes Leben bis zu diesem Tag war der Beweis dafür.«

Das Leben der Menschen veränderte sich schneller und grundlegender als zu jeder anderen Zeit in der Geschichte. Sie lebten an anderen Orten, unter anderen Bedingungen und anderen Gesetzen als denen, die das Leben früherer Generationen bestimmt hatten. Der Rhythmus des Landlebens war zerstört. Als die Menschen in die Städte zogen, um Arbeit zu suchen, wurden sie in eine andere Welt katapultiert. Und vor allem wollten sie diese neue Welt verstehen, ihr einen Sinn geben. Eine schlafende Neugier war geweckt worden. Die Menschen sahen sich um, erkannten, verglichen, unterschieden, zogen Schlüsse. »Sobald man Verbindungen herstellt«, schrieb der Romancier E. M. Forster 1910, »werden das Tier und der Mönch ihrer Isolation, die für beide das Leben bedeutet, beraubt und sterben.«

Sehr viele haben die falschen Schlüsse gezogen, aber viele haben die richtigen Verbindungen hergestellt. Theaterstücke, Bücher, Zeitungen und sogar Gemälde und Karikaturen steckten voller Ideen – über die Unterwerfung der Frau durch den Mann, über das Recht der Kirche auf ein Monopol in Fragen der Moral, über die Gleichheit vor dem Gesetz, über die Tyrannei der Privilegien, über die Macht der Massen.

Es gab keine neuen Ideen, die nicht die bestehende Ordnung bedrohen würden, und es kam zu einer heftigen Gegenreaktion. Das etablierte System schickte seine Armee und seine Polizei an die Front. Revolutionäre ließ man verschwinden – ins Exil, wenn sie Glück hatten. Suffragetten wurden gefesselt und zwangsernährt, Sozialisten wurden gejagt, Homosexuelle verhaftet. Nationalisten peitschte man aus und machte sie vorübergehend mundtot.

Aber das alte System des blinden Gehorsams gegenüber der Obrigkeit verschwand allmählich. Es hatte eine letzte, schrecklich triumphale Chance zu zeigen, wozu es fähig war – im Gemetzel des Ersten Weltkriegs.

L E monde commençait à tourner un peu trop vite pour certains. Les gens bien pensants se sentaient étourdis, embarrassés, malmenés par les idées nouvelles qui menaçaient l'ordre établi. Les théories de Darwin remettaient en cause la vérité de l'histoire de la Création telle qu'elle est racontée dans l'Ancien Testament. Freud laissait entendre que les hommes et les femmes possédaient une région sombre et inexplorée, le subconscient, plus terrifiant encore que les endroits visités par Livingstone et Stanley. Marx disait aux travailleurs n'avoir rien à perdre que leurs chaînes, et tout un monde à conquérir.

Les syndicats élevaient la voix, encourageant les travailleurs à exiger de meilleurs salaires, une meilleure protection, de meilleures conditions de travail et des horaires plus courts. Les suffragettes exigeaient le droit de vote pour les femmes. Les femmes mariées avaient l'impertinence de revendiquer la possession de biens en propre. Les chômeurs exigeaient du travail en cassant les fenêtres des riches pour faire savoir leur détermination. En Afrique et en Inde les nationalistes réclamaient l'indépendance, ou du moins la mise en œuvre de réformes.

On parlait avec une fréquence alarmante de « droits » à l'instruction, à un meilleur logement et à de meilleurs soins médicaux. On débattait sur la place publique d'hérésies telles que la limitation des naissances, l'homosexualité, l'amour libre, le républicanisme, l'athéisme, le socialisme et l'anarchie. Les étudiants remettaient leurs professeurs en question, les serviteurs discutaient les ordres de leurs maîtres. On prétendait que les enfants désobéissaient à leurs parents.

Que s'était-il passé ? Il est difficile de répondre à cette question une centaine d'années après. Cependant les paroles d'un ouvrier allemand du début du XXe siècle peuvent fournir une réponse : « J'ai rencontré un cordonnier nommé Schröder ... Après il est parti en Amérique ... il m'avait donné des journaux à lire, ce que j'ai fait un peu puis cela m'a ennuyé. Mais après ils m'ont intéressé de plus en plus. Ils décrivaient la condition misérable des travailleurs et leur dépendance par rapport aux capitalistes et aux propriétaires terriens d'une façon si vivante et si réaliste que j'en ai été absolument abasourdi. C'était comme si mes yeux avaient été fermés jusqu'alors. Nom d'une pipe ! Ce que ces journaux disaient, c'était *la vérité*. Toute ma vie jusqu'à ce jour était là pour en témoigner. »

L'existence des gens changeait avec rapidement et profondément, comme jamais auparavant. Ils vivaient dans des lieux différents, dans des conditions différentes et selon des règles différentes de celles des générations précédentes. Les rythmes de la vie rurale avaient été cassés. Lorsque ces gens gagnaient la ville à la recherche d'un travail, ils se transportaient dans un autre monde. Et ils voulaient avant tout essayer de comprendre ce nouveau monde, lui trouver un sens. Une curiosité s'était éveillée. Les gens regardaient autour d'eux, voyaient, comparaient, relevaient les différences et tiraient des conclusions. Le romancier E. M. Forster écrivait en 1910 : « Faites seulement des associations, et la bête et le moine dérobés à l'isolement qui est leur vie mourront. »

D'aucuns s'adaptèrent et la moitié échouèrent. Les idées se déversaient dans les pièces de théâtre, les livres et les journaux. Même les tableaux et les dessins humoristiques n'échappaient pas aux idées : ils traitaient de la soumission de la femme ; de l'Église en tant que gardienne de l'ordre moral ; de l'égalité devant la loi ; des privilèges et du pouvoir ouvrier.

Une nouvelle idée représente toujours une menace, et le retour de flamme fut puissant. Les bien-pensants firent monter en ligne l'armée et la police. Les révolutionnaires furent retirés de la circulation, exilés pour les plus chanceux. Les suffragettes furent enchaînées et alimentées de force. Les socialistes furent traqués sans merci et les homosexuels emprisonnés. Les nationalistes furent fouettés et leurs idées temporairement étouffées.

Cependant le vieux système de l'obéissance inconditionnelle aux ordres était condamné. Il triompha une dernière fois en montrant brutalement de quoi il était capable en provoquant la boucherie de la Première Guerre mondiale.

(*Overleaf*)

THE Dreyfus Affair lasted twelve years, and almost brought about the collapse of France. The Jewish Dreyfus (1 – sixth from left in top row) graduated from the Polytechnic in Paris in 1891 and entered the French General Army Staff. He was wrongly accused of selling military secrets to Germany, and became the centre of a war of words between royalists, militarists and Catholics on one side, and republicans, socialists and anti-clerics on the other. Dreyfus was found guilty and sent to Devil's Island, but his case was reopened in Rennes in 1899. Members of the court (2) were divided in opinion. Journalists flocked to the town for the retrial (3), among them Bernard Lazare, who had long campaigned on Dreyfus's behalf (4 – centre). Colonel Picquart (5 – left) was one of the few Army officers who backed Dreyfus. Even after the retrial had established Dreyfus's innocence, the Army turned their backs on him (6), for the verdict was 'guilty – with extenuating circumstances'.

(*Folgende Seiten*)

DIE Dreyfus-Affäre dauerte zwölf Jahre und führte fast zum Niedergang Frankreichs. Der Jude Alfred Dreyfus (1, sechster von links in der obersten Reihe) absolvierte 1891 die Technische Hochschule in Paris und trat in den Generalstab der französischen Armee ein. Die zu Unrecht erhobene Beschuldigung, er habe militärische Geheimnisse an die Deutschen verkauft, lieferte den Anlaß für erbitterte Auseinandersetzungen zwischen Royalisten, Militaristen und Katholiken auf der einen, und Republikanern, Sozialisten und Antiklerikalen auf der anderen Seite. Dreyfus wurde schuldig gesprochen und auf die Teufelsinsel verbannt, aber sein Verfahren wurde 1899 in Rennes wiederaufgenommen. Das Gericht (2) teilte sich in zwei Lager. Journalisten strömten in die Stadt, um über das Wiederaufnahmeverfahren zu berichten (3), unter ihnen Bernard Lazare, der sich lange für Dreyfus eingesetzt hatte (4, Mitte). Colonel Picquart (5, links) war einer der wenigen Armeeoffiziere, die Dreyfus unterstützten. Selbst nachdem im Wiederaufnahmeverfahren die Unschuld von Dreyfus bewiesen worden war, wandte sich die Armee von ihm ab (6), denn das Urteil lautete »schuldig – mit mildernden Umständen«.

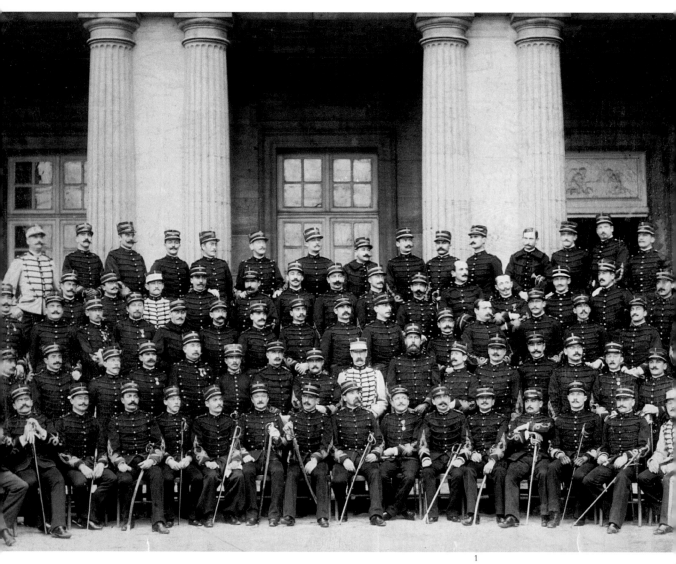

L'AFFAIRE Dreyfus dura douze ans et marqua profondément la France. Dreyfus (1, le sixième au dernier rang à gauche), d'obédience juive, sortit diplômé de l'école Polytechnique de Paris en 1891 et entra à l'état-major général de l'armée française. Il fut accusé à tort de vendre des secrets militaires à l'Allemagne, et se retrouva au centre d'une polémique révélant de profonds clivages entre d'un côté les royalistes, les militaristes et l'opinion catholique, et de l'autre les républicains, les socialistes et les anticléricaux. Dreyfus fut déclaré coupable et déporté à l'île du Diable. Cependant

l'affaire fut réexaminée à Rennes en 1899. Les membres du tribunal (2) avaient des opinions divergentes. Les journalistes affluèrent dans la ville pour le deuxième procès (3), et parmi eux Bernard Lazare qui avait mené une longue campagne en faveur de Dreyfus (4, au centre). Le colonel Picquart (5, à gauche) fut un des rares officiers de l'armée à soutenir Dreyfus. Même après que son innocence fut rétablie à l'issue du deuxième procès, l'armée lui tourna le dos (6) parce que les termes du jugement prononcé déclaraient Dreyfus coupable avec des circonstances atténuantes.

1

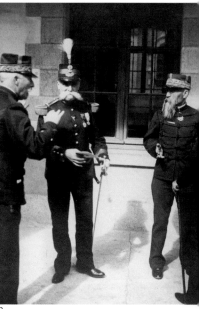

2

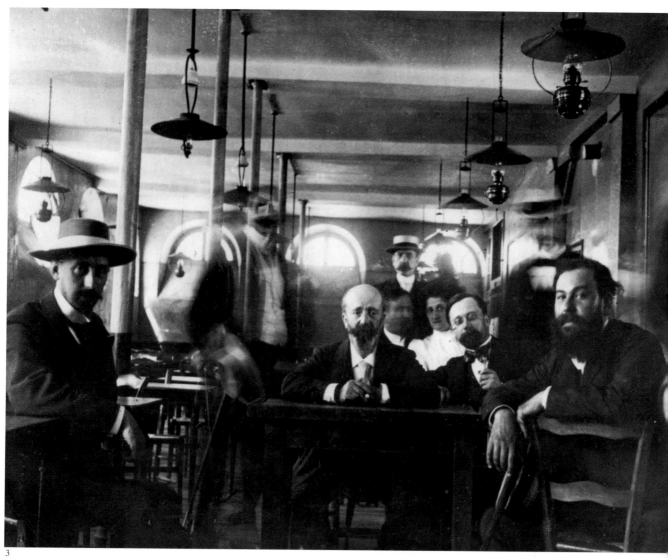

3

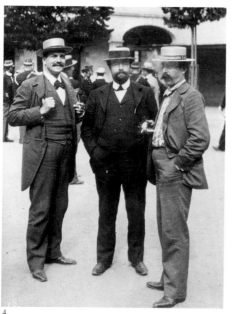

4

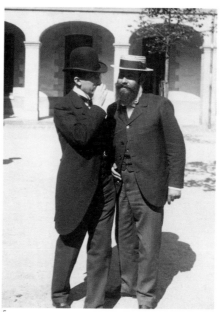

5

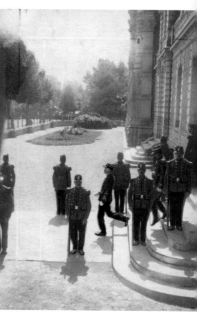

6

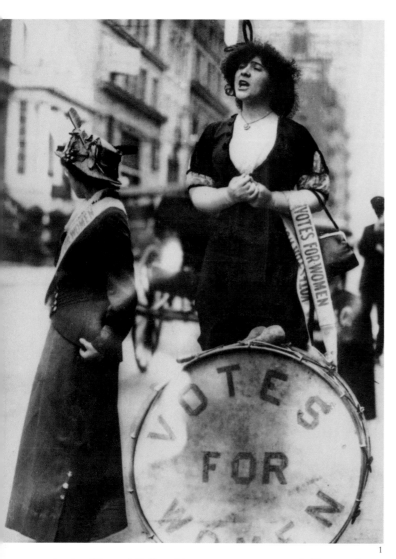

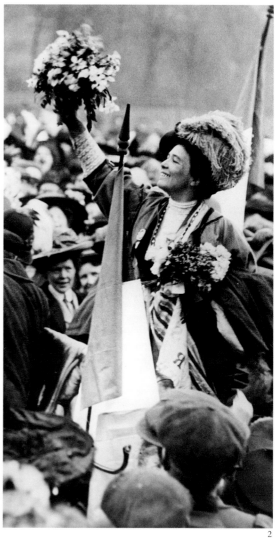

THE Women's Suffrage Movement
began in 1865 in Manchester, and was
largely limited to Britain and North
America (1). It sprang from, and appealed
largely to, the middle classes – though
there were plenty of active members of
the aristocracy, such as Lady Emmeline
Pethwick-Lawrence (2). The militant
Women's Social and Political Union
(WSPU) was formed in 1903 by Emmeline
Pankhurst. It used arson and bombing as
weapons in its campaign to get Votes for
Women. In quieter moments, Emmeline's
daughter Sylvia, also an activist, painted
the Women's Social Defence League shop-
front in 1912 (3).

DIE Suffragetten-Bewegung entstand
1865 in Manchester und blieb weitgehend auf Großbritannien und Nordamerika beschränkt (1). Sie war von Frauen
aus der Mittelklasse ins Leben gerufen
worden und zielte auch überwiegend auf
diese ab, aber es gab auch zahlreiche aktive
Mitglieder aus der Aristokratie, darunter
Lady Emmeline Pethwick-Lawrence (2).
Die militante Women's Social and Political
Union (WSPU), 1903 von Emmeline
Pankhurst gegründet, setzte in ihrem Kampf
für das Frauenwahlrecht auch Brandstiftung
und Bomben ein. In ruhigeren Zeiten,
1912, bemalte Emmelines Tochter Sylvia,
ebenfalls eine Aktivistin, die Fassade
des Büros der Women's Social Defence
League (3).

LE mouvement en faveur du suffrage des
femmes naquit en 1865 à Manchester
et se limitait principalement à la Grande-
Bretagne et à l'Amérique du Nord (1). Il
provenait des classes populaires et bénéficiait
d'un très large écho, bien qu'il comptât aussi
énormément de membres actifs au sein
de l'aristocratie tels que Lady Emmeline
Pethwick-Lawrence (2). L'Union féminine
sociale et politique (WSPU) fondée en
1903 par Emmeline Pankhurst, utilisa les
incendies et les grenades dans sa campagne
en faveur du droit de vote des femmes.
Dans des moments plus calmes, en 1912,
Sylvia, la fille d'Emmeline et activiste
comme elle, peignait la devanture du local
de la Ligue pour la défense sociale des
femmes (3).

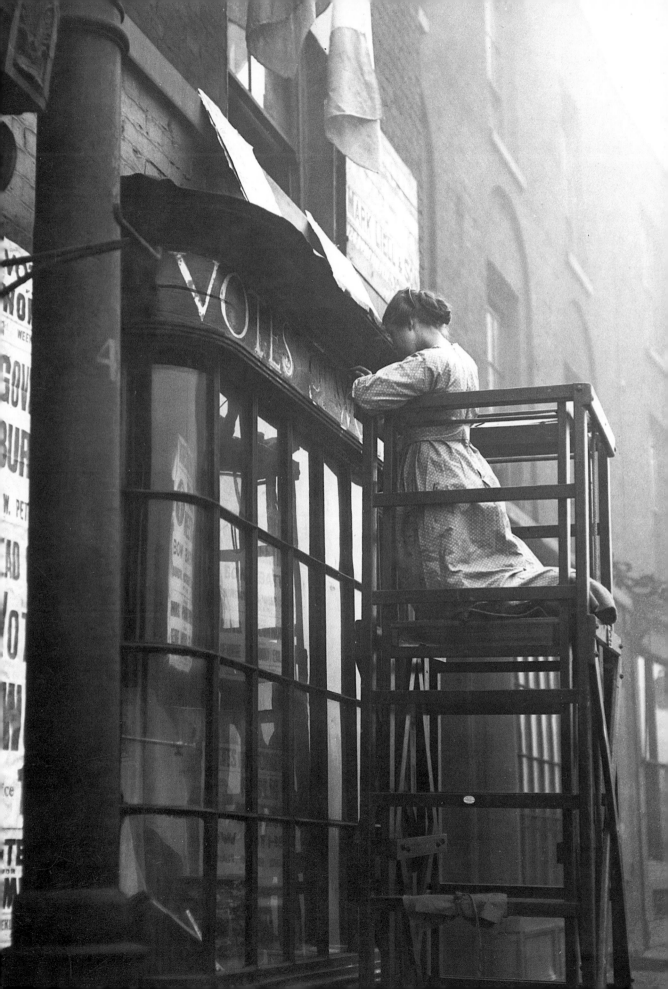

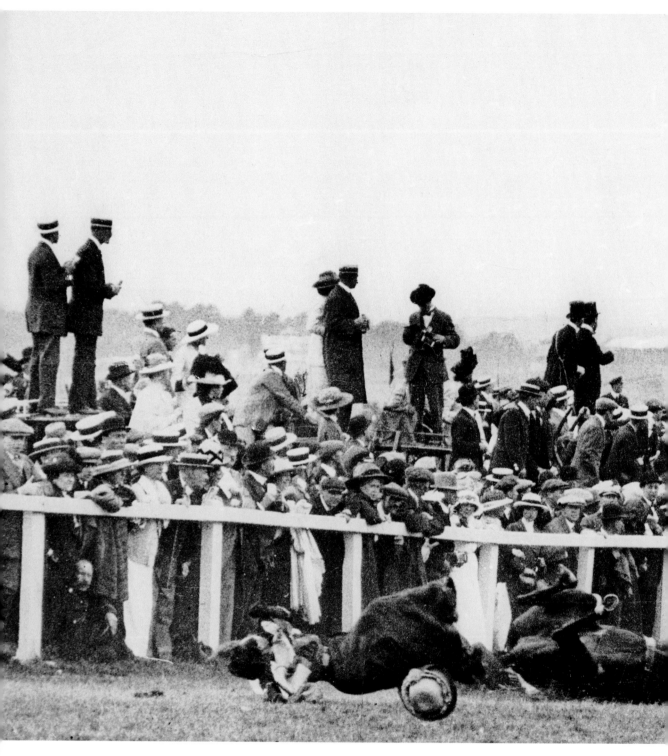

THERE were many men and women
who decried the actions of the
suffragettes – there still are. But most
were shocked at the death of Emily
Davison, who threw herself in front of
the King's horse in the 1913 Derby (1).
The campaign of direct action also
included window smashing (3) and setting
fire to the churches of unsympathetic
ministers (2).

DIE Aktionen der Suffragetten wurden
und werden noch immer von vielen
Frauen und Männern verurteilt. Trotzdem
waren die meisten über den Tod Emily
Davisons schockiert, die sich beim Derby

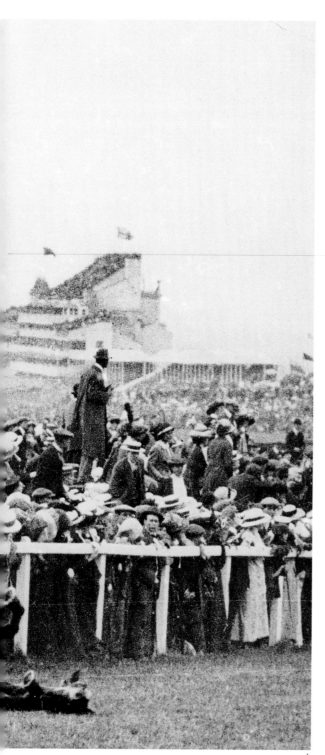

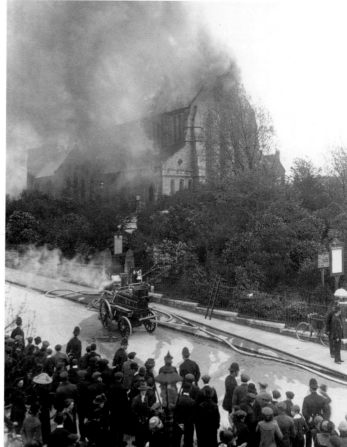

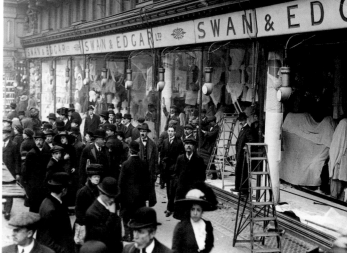

1913 vor das Pferd des Königs warf (1).
Die Kampagne direkter Aktionen umfaßte
auch das Einwerfen von Fensterscheiben (3)
und das Anzünden der Kirchen verständnis-
loser Priester (2).

LES hommes et les femmes qui décriaient
les agissements des suffragettes étaient
nombreux – et ils le sont toujours. La plupart furent cependant choqués par la mort
d'Emily Davison qui se jeta devant le cheval
du roi au cours du Derby de 1913 (1). La
campagne d'action directe consistait aussi à
casser les fenêtres (3) et incendier les églises
des pasteurs et des ministres de culte hostiles
au progrès (2).

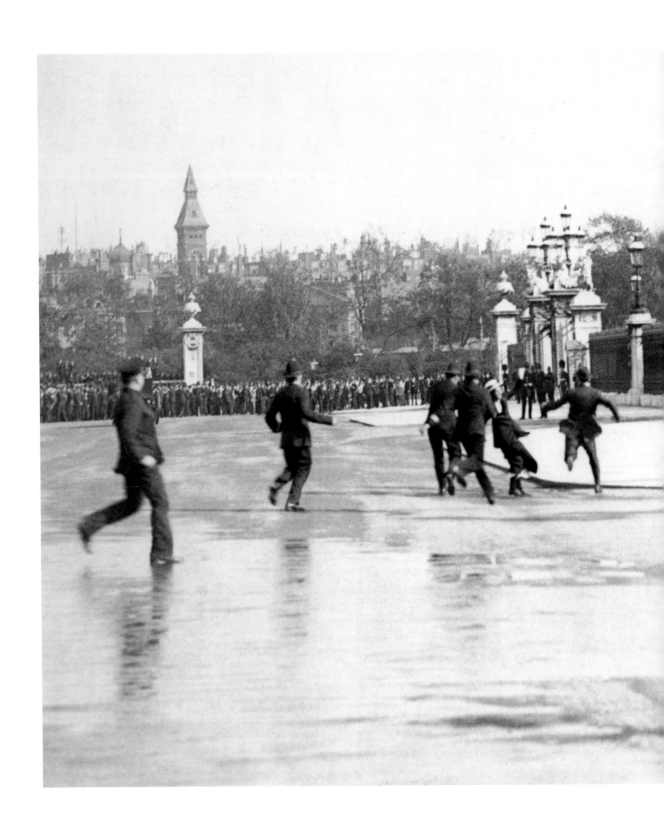

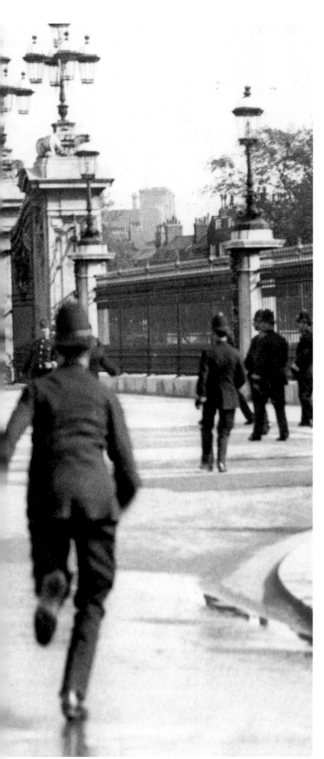

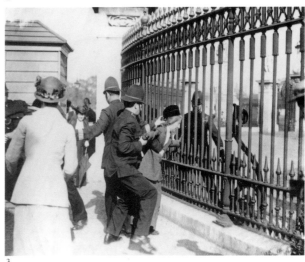

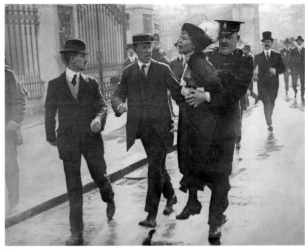

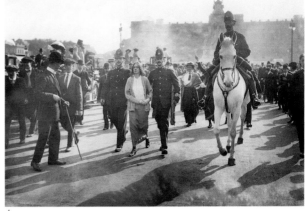

One of the suffragettes' most effective moves was to chain themselves to the railings of Buckingham Palace (1, 3). The founder of the WSPU, Emmeline Pankhurst (2), and many others were arrested on this occasion (4).

EINE der wirksamsten Aktionen der Suffragetten bestand darin, sich an das Gitter vor dem Buckingham Palace anzuketten (1, 3). Die Gründerin der WSPU, Emmeline Pankhurst (2), und viele andere wurden bei dieser Gelegenheit verhaftet (4).

UNE des actions les plus efficaces des suffragettes consistait à s'enchaîner aux grilles du palais de Buckingham (1 et 3). La fondatrice de la WSPU, Emmeline Pankhurst (2), et beaucoup d'autres furent arrêtées à cette occasion (4).

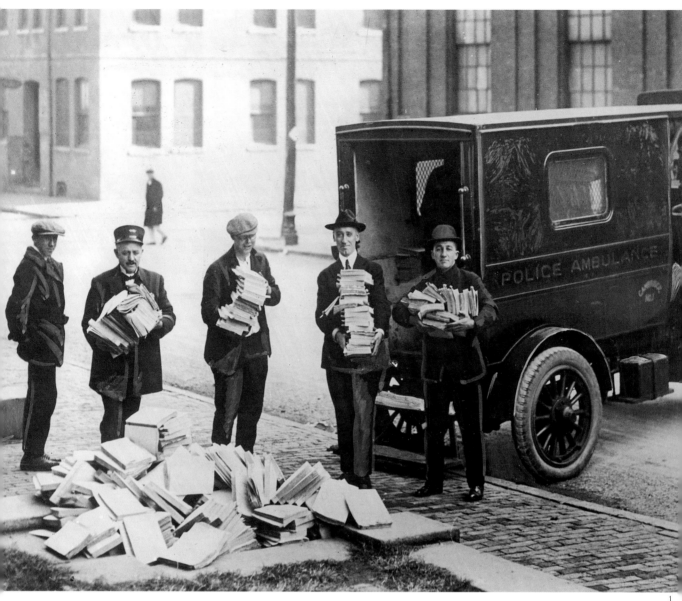

1

UNREST was not confined to the industrial front. The rumblings of revolution in Russia had shocked and inspired the rest of the world in equal parts. To poor people in rich countries socialism brought hope. To rich people in rich countries it brought fear. 'Revolution in Boston nipped in the bud' was the caption to this photograph in 1919 (1). Presumably, once these few dozen books had been destroyed all would be safe for the onward march of capitalism. In Paris in 1911 students clashed with police outside the Faculty of Justice (2, 3).

DIE Unruhen beschränkten sich aber nicht nur auf die Industrie. Die Erschütterungen der Revolution in Rußland hatten den Rest der Welt ebenso schockiert wie inspiriert. Für die armen Menschen der reichen Länder brachte der Sozialismus Hoffnung. Für die reichen Menschen der reichen Länder brachte er Angst. »Revolution in Boston im Keim erstickt«, lautete 1919 die Bildzeile zu dieser Photographie (1). Wenn diese Bücher erst einmal verbrannt waren, würde dem Vormarsch des Kapitalismus vermutlich nichts mehr im Wege stehen. In Paris lieferten sich Studenten 1911 vor der Juristischen Fakultät Kämpfe mit der Polizei (2, 3).

L'AGITATION ne se limitait pas au hair front industriel. Les échos de la révolution en Russie avaient, à parts égales, offensé et inspiré le reste du monde. Pour les pauvres vivant dans les pays riches, le socialisme apportait l'espoir. Pour les riches desdits pays, la peur. « La révolution étouffée dans l'œuf à Boston » titrait cette photographie en 1919 (1). Il est à présumer qu'une fois détruits ces quelques dizaines de livres, la marche en avant du capitalisme n'aura plus rien à craindre. À Paris en 1911 : des étudiants en prise avec les forces de police à l'extérieur de la faculté de droit (2 et 3).

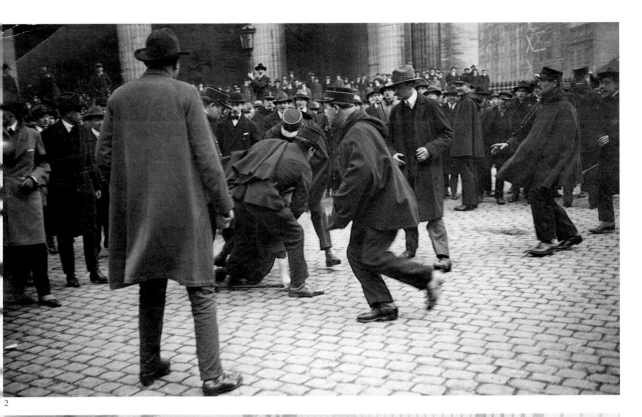

2

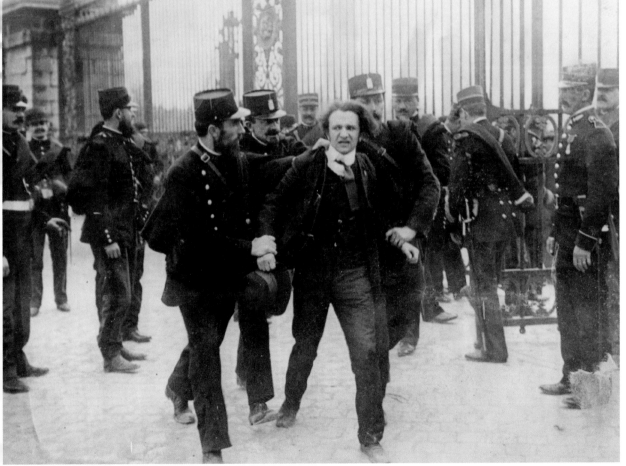

3

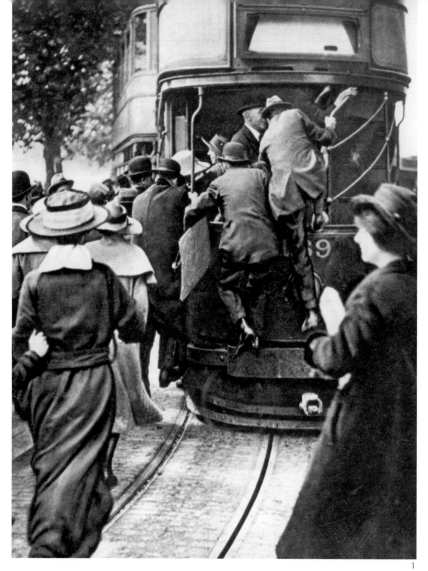

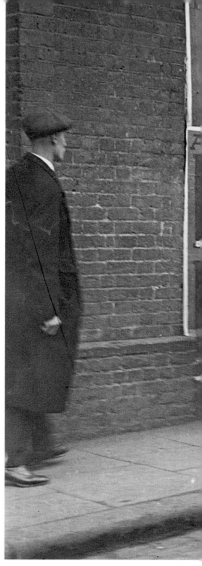

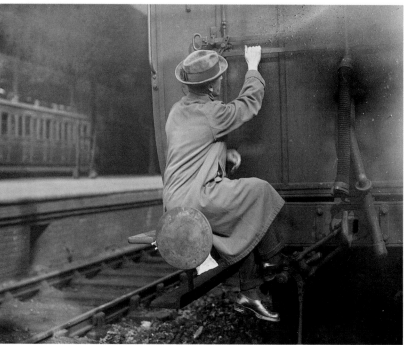

THROUGHOUT Europe, the most
powerful workers were the dockers,
miners and railway workers. The Great
Railway Strike of 1919 in Britain was
triggered by the threat of a reduction in
wages. Office workers fought to get on
trams as alternative transport (1). Where
trains did run, seats were scarce and
passengers sat wherever they could (2).
'Blacklegs' provoked fights in the streets
(3). Supplies were brought in by road.
The food depot in London's Hyde Park
was guarded by troops (4) – but the
strike was successful.

IN ganz Europa waren Dockarbeiter,
Bergarbeiter und Eisenbahner die
wichtigsten und daher mächtigsten
Arbeiter. Der große Eisenbahnerstreik
in Großbritannien wurde 1919 durch die
Ankündigung von Lohnkürzungen aus-
gelöst. Büroangestellte aus der Mittel-
schicht erkämpften sich einen Platz in
der Straßenbahn (1). Dort, wo die Züge
fuhren, waren Sitzplätze rar, und die

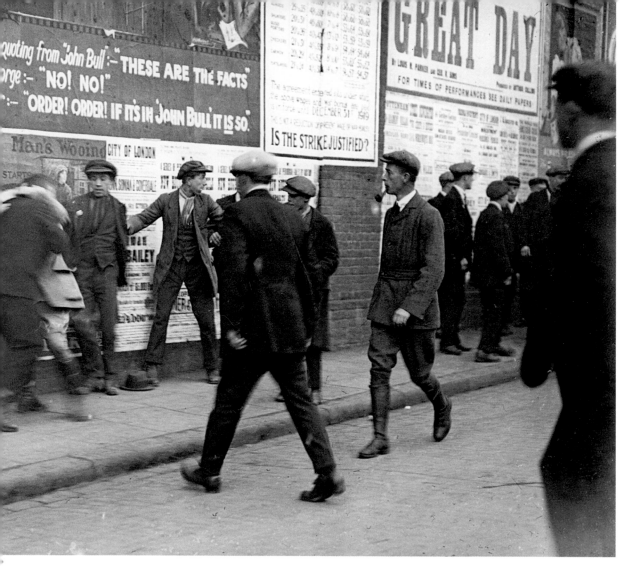

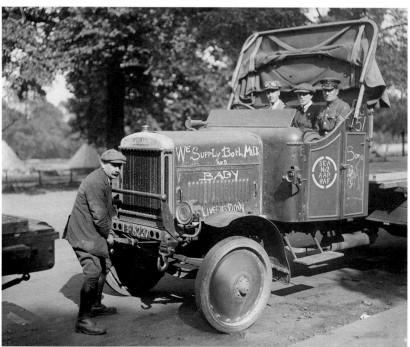

Passagiere setzten sich hin, wo sie konnten (2). Streikbrecher provozierten Kämpfe auf den Straßen (3). Lieferungen wurden über die Straßen transportiert. Das Lebensmitteldepot im Londoner Hyde Park wurde von Truppen bewacht (4) – aber der Streik war erfolgreich.

En Europe, les travailleurs les plus puissants étaient les dockers, les mineurs et les cheminots. La grève générale des cheminots en 1919 en Grande-Bretagne s'était déclenchée à la suite d'une menace de réduction des salaires. Les classes moyennes se battaient pour monter dans les trams, l'autre moyen d'aller et de revenir du travail (1). Dans les trains qui circulaient, les places étaient rares et les passagers s'asseyaient là où ils pouvaient (2). Les « briseurs de grève » provoquaient des combats dans les rues (3). L'approvisionnement se faisait par la route. Les dépôts de vivres de Hyde Park, à Londres, étaient gardés par les troupes (4). La grève fut malgré tout couronnée de succès.

4

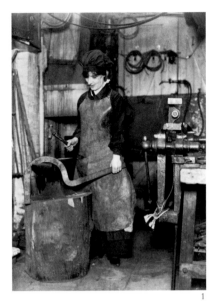

1

WOMEN left the prison of home or
service in increasing numbers. As far
as possible, the male establishment kept
them from positions of power or authority,
but they were prepared to allow women
the more menial or less prestigious jobs
available. Some became blacksmiths (1),
others coal heavers (2).

IMMER mehr Frauen brachen aus dem
Gefängnis ihres Heims oder ihrer
Stellung aus. Das männliche Establishment
schloß Frauen so weit wie möglich von
Machtpositionen aus, aber man war bereit,
ihnen die niedrigeren und weniger
prestigeträchtigen Arbeiten zu überlassen.
Einige wurden Schmied (1), andere
lieferten Kohle aus (2).

DE plus en plus de femmes quittaient
leur foyer-prison ou la maison où elles
servaient. Le monde masculin les écartait
autant que faire se peut des positions de
pouvoir ou d'autorité ; en revanche, il leur
laissait volontiers les emplois moins importants ou moins prestigieux qui étaient dispo-
nibles. Certaines se mettaient à la forge (1),
d'autres au transport du charbon (2).

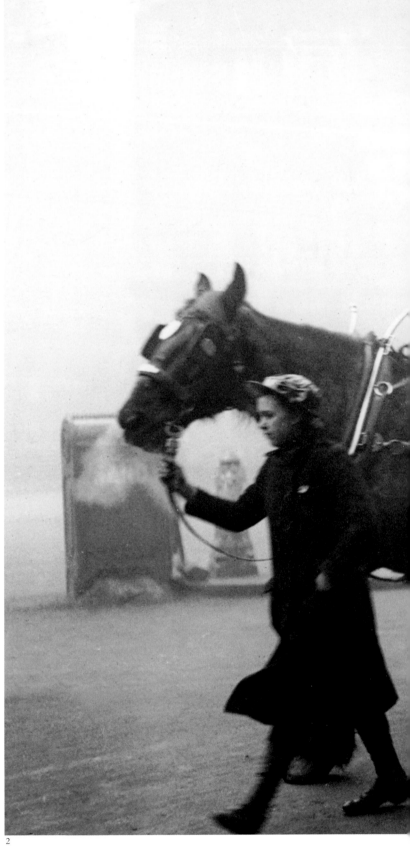

2

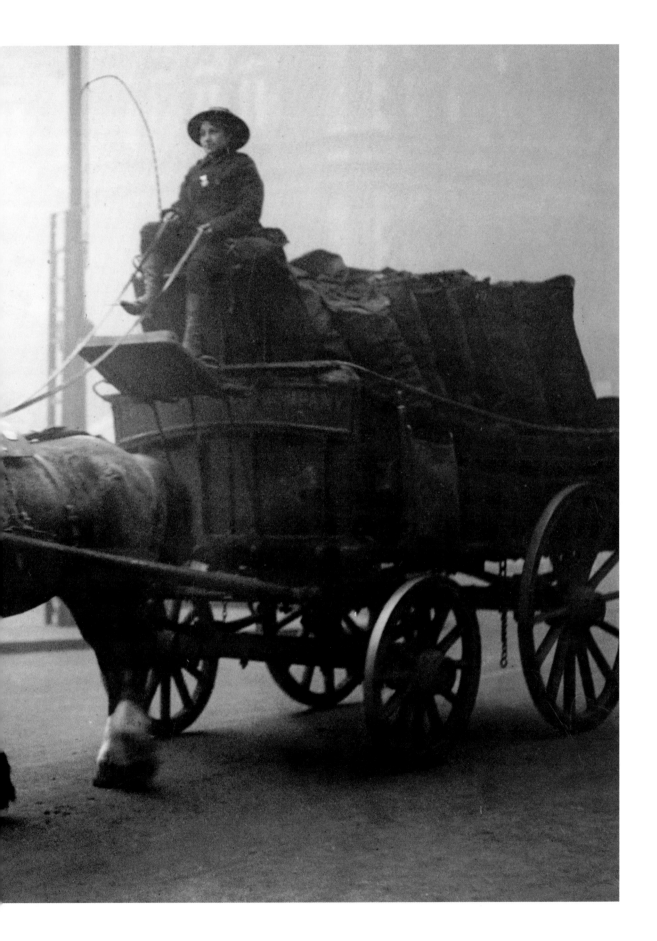

THE First World War deprived labour markets of millions of fighting men, and women were encouraged and ordered to take on many new roles. The Women's Volunteer Reserve ran their own garages and motor workshops (1). Women worked in armament factories in France (2) and all over Europe. The First Aid Yeomanry were forerunners of women's army corps (3). And women found themselves once again working in collieries (4).

DER Erste Weltkrieg beraubte den Arbeitsmarkt vieler kämpfender Männer, und Frauen wurden ermutigt und aufgefordert, viele neue Rollen anzunehmen. Die freiwillige Frauenreserve, Women's Volunteer Reserve, betrieb eigene Garagen und Autowerkstätten (1). In Frankreich (2) und in ganz Europa arbeiteten Frauen in Rüstungsfabriken. Die First Aid Yeomanry war eine Vorläuferin des ersten weiblichen Armeekorps (3). Und erneut arbeiteten Frauen in Bergwerken (4).

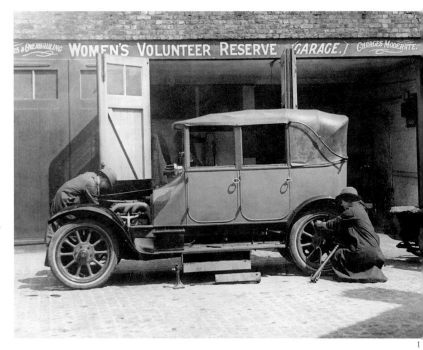

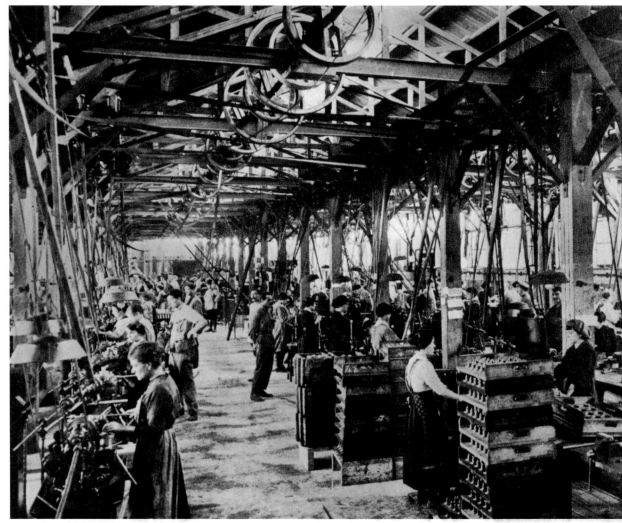

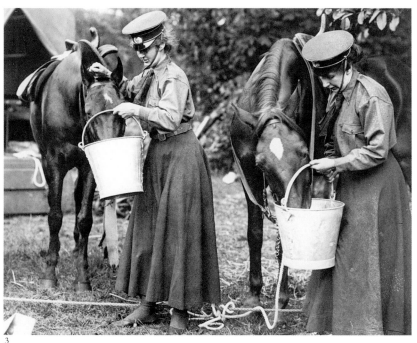

L A Première Guerre mondiale privant
le marché du travail des millions
d'hommes envoyés se battre, encouragea
et contraignit les femmes à assumer un grand
nombre de rôles nouveaux. La réserve des
volontaires féminines exploitait ses propres
garages et ateliers de réparation automobile
(1). Les femmes travaillaient dans les usines
d'armement en France (2) comme dans
le reste de l' Europe. Le First Aid Yeomanry
fut l'ancêtre des corps de volontaires
féminins (3). Et les femmes se retrouvèrent
une fois de plus au fond des houillères (4).

3

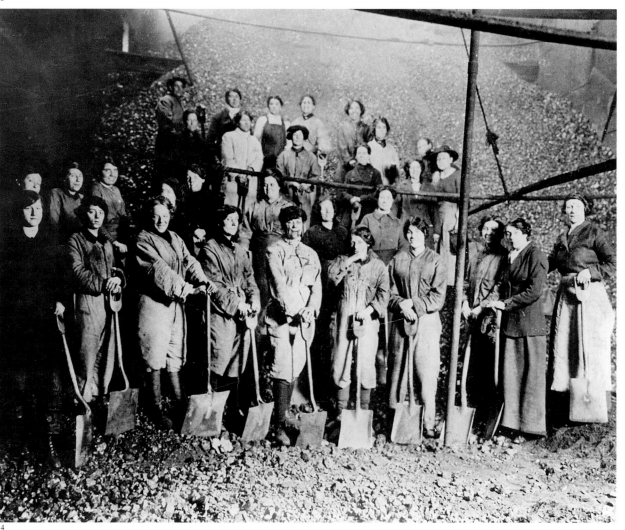

4

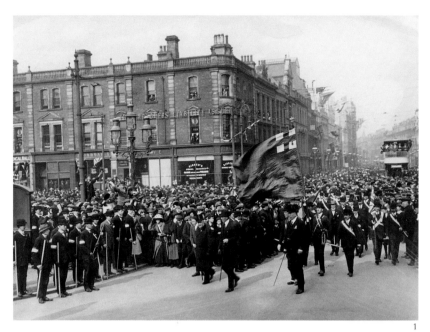

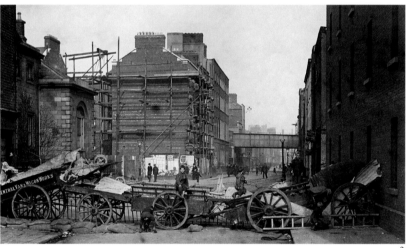

1

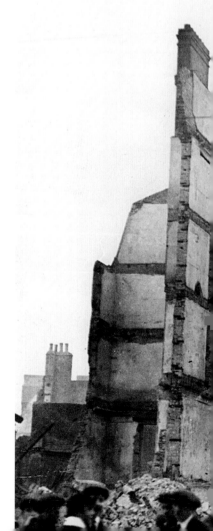

2

BY the 20th century, British governments were seriously negotiating
independence for Ireland. Under the
skilled, not to say cunning, leadership of
Sir Edward Carson, the Unionists sought
to prevent this. They raised the armed
Ulster Volunteer Force and organized
massive rallies against Home Rule, such as
this in 1912, when Carson and others led a
parade to Belfast's City Hall (1). Four years
later, the Irish Volunteers – who supported
Irish independence – rose in open rebellion
against the British. They barricaded the
Dublin streets (2), took possession of key
buildings and held out against British
troops for four days. The General Post
Office was gutted (3), and parts of Sackville
Street looked as though they had been
bombed (4).

IN den ersten Jahrzehnten des 20. Jahrhunderts verhandelten britische Regierungen ernsthaft über die Unabhängigkeit
Irlands. Unter der fähigen, um nicht zu
sagen listigen Führung von Sir Edward
Carson versuchten die Unionisten, dies zu
verhindern. Sie stellten bewaffnete
Truppen auf, die Ulster Volunteer Force,
und organisierten Kundgebungen gegen
die Selbstbestimmung, die Home Rule,
beispielsweise die 1912 von Carson ange-
führte Demonstration zum Belfaster Rat-
haus (1). Vier Jahre später erhoben sich
die Irish Volunteers, die die irische Unabhängigkeit unterstützten, in offener
Rebellion gegen die Briten. Sie errichteten
Barrikaden in den Straßen von Dublin (2),
besetzten wichtige Gebäude und konnten
die Angriffe der britischen Truppen vier

Tage lang abwehren. Die Hauptpost von
Belfast brannte aus (3) und Teile der
Sackville Street sahen aus, als seien sie
bombardiert worden (4).

DÈS le XXᵉ siècle, les autorités
britanniques négociaient sérieuse-
ment l'indépendance de l'Irlande. Sous
la direction habile, pour ne pas dire rusée,
de Sir Edward Carson, les unionistes
essayèrent de s'y opposer. Ils levèrent la
Force armée des volontaires de l'Ulster
et organisèrent d'importantes manifestations populaires contre le mouvement
Home Rule réclamant l'autonomie : on

4

voit ici, entre autres, Carson à la tête d'une manifestation, marchant sur l'hôtel de ville de Belfast en 1912 (1). Quatre ans plus tard, les volontaires irlandais qui soutenaient l'indépendance du pays entrèrent en rébellion ouverte contre les Britanniques. Ils élevèrent des barricades dans les rues de Dublin (2), s'emparèrent de bâtiments-clés et tinrent tête aux troupes britanniques quatre jours durant. L'intérieur de la poste générale fut démoli (3), tandis que la rue de Sackville donnait à certains endroits l'impression d'avoir été bombardée (4).

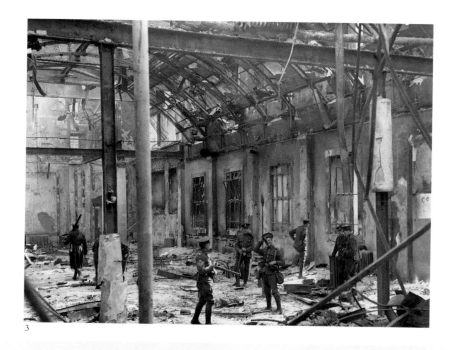

3

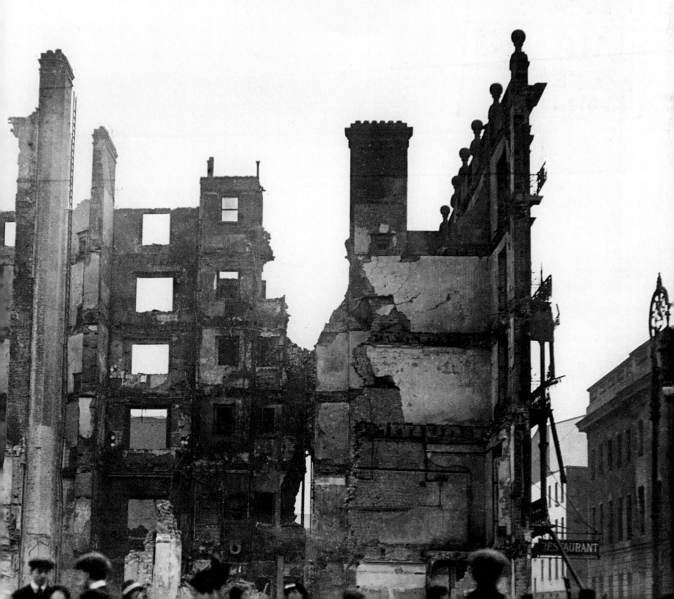

Conflict

War broke out between Russia and Turkey in 1853. France and Britain sided with Turkey, and sent armies to the Crimea. It was nearly 40 years since there had been a major European war, and the generals of both sides were a little rusty. Lord Raglan (1 – on left, in fancy pith helmet), Commander-in-Chief of the British troops, had an unfortunate habit of referring to the enemy as 'the French', a hangover from his last campaign, against Bonaparte. Quite what the French Commander-in-Chief, General Pélissier (1 – on right), thought of this is not recorded.

The Crimean War was the first to be covered by reporters – William Howard Russell (2) was war correspondent of *The Times*. People at home learnt of the appalling blunders made by those in charge. One consignment of woollen underwear, sent to keep troops warm in temperatures that were sometimes 30° below zero, had been made for children under ten.

Inefficiency apart, it was a war of traditional bravado and heroism, run on old-fashioned lines – a war in which cavalry charged artillery, infantries clashed in thick fog, and the *vivandière* revictualled the troops (3).

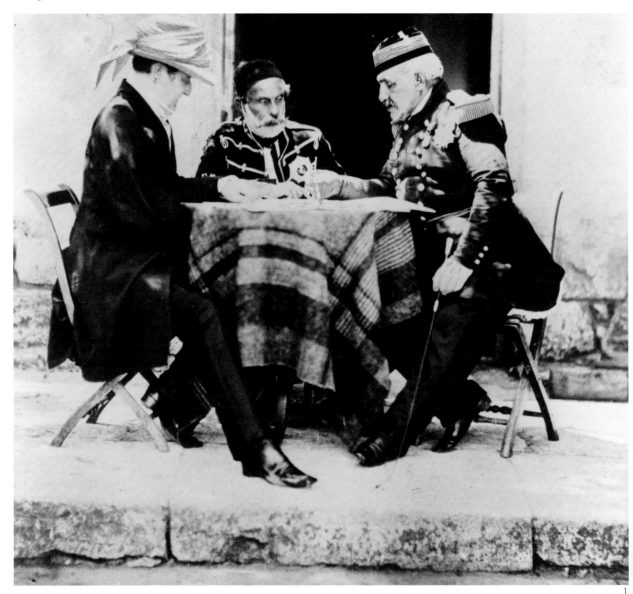

1

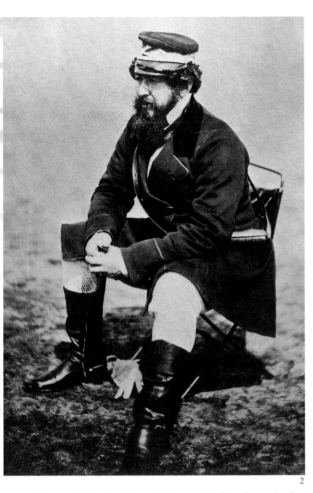

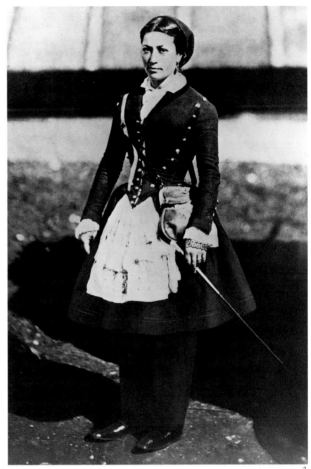

IM Jahre 1853 brach zwischen Rußland und der Türkei Krieg aus. Frankreich und Großbritannien unterstützten die Türkei und schickten Armeen an die Krim. Der letzte große Krieg in Europa lag fast vierzig Jahre zurück, und die Generäle waren ein wenig aus der Übung. Lord Raglan (1, links, mit Tropenhelm), Oberkommandeur der britischen Truppen, hatte die unselige Angewohnheit, den Feind als »der Franzose« zu bezeichnen, wie in seinem letzten Feldzug gegen Bonaparte. Was der französische General Pélissier (1, rechts) davon hielt, ist nicht überliefert.

Der Krimkrieg war der erste, über den Kriegsberichterstatter schrieben. W. H. Russell (2) war Korrespondent der *Times*. Die Menschen zu Hause erfuhren von den Fehlern, die den Verantwortlichen unterliefen. Eine Sendung wollener Unterwäsche, die die Truppen bei Temperaturen von unter minus dreißig Grad warmhalten sollte, war für Kinder unter zehn Jahren gemacht.

Von den Fehlern abgesehen, war es ein Krieg des traditionellen Heldentums, der mit altmodischen Strategien geführt wurde; ein Krieg, in dem die Kavallerie die Artillerie angriff, Infanterien in dichtem Nebel zusammenstießen und die Marketenderin die Truppen mit Proviant versorgte, wohin sie auch gingen (3).

LA guerre éclata entre la Russie et la Turquie en 1853. La France et la Grande-Bretagne épousèrent la cause de la Turquie et envoyèrent leurs armées en Crimée. Lord Raglan (1, à gauche en casque colonial fantaisiste), commandant en chef des troupes britanniques, avait la déplorable habitude d'appeler l'ennemi « les Français », nostalgie de sa dernière campagne contre Bonaparte. L'histoire ne dit pas ce qu'en pensait le commandant en chef, le général Pélissier (1, à droite).

La guerre de Crimée fut la première à être photographiée et couverte sur place par des reporters de presse : William Howard Russell (2) était le correspondant de guerre du journal *The Times*. La population civile entendait parler des effroyables bourdes commises par les responsables : un lot de sous-vêtements en laine pour enfants de moins de dix ans fut expédié aux troupes qui les attendaient par -30°. Cette inefficacité mise à part, c'était une guerre traditionnelle et démodée de bravade et d'héroïsme : une guerre dans laquelle la cavalerie chargeait l'artillerie, les infanteries s'entremêlaient dans un brouillard épais. Les vivandières ravitaillaient les troupes où qu'elles fussent (3).

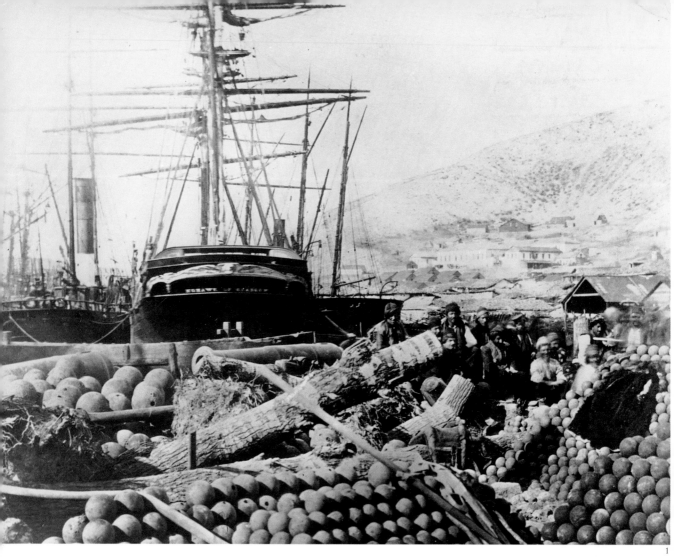

THE French and British base was at
Balaclava (1). Into this small harbour
poured powder, shot, cannonballs, siege
weapons, food, clothing, huts, blankets and
boots. The war centred around the siege
of the Russian stronghold, Sebastopol. Life
in the trenches was boring rather than
dangerous (2). Life inside the Redan, the
inner fortress of Sebastopol, was more
exciting, especially once the French and
British had realized the futility of the siege
and turned instead to a direct assault. The
Russians left little behind (3).

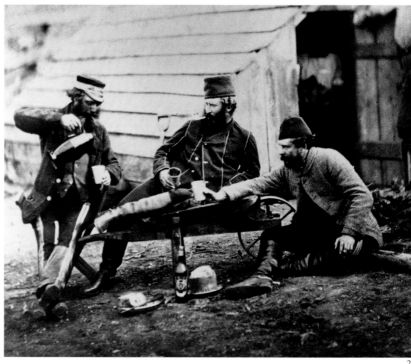

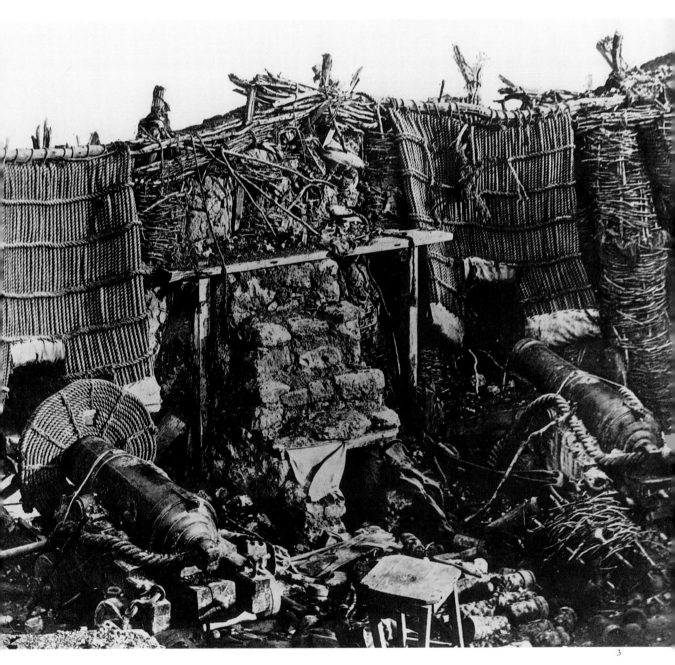

DER Stützpunkt der Briten und Franzosen befand sich in Balaclava (1). In diesen kleinen Hafen wurden Schießpulver, Kanonenkugeln, Belagerungswaffen, Lebensmittel, Kleidung, Zelte, Decken und Stiefel gebracht. Der Krieg konzentrierte sich auf die Belagerung des russischen Stützpunktes Sebastopol. Das Leben in den Schützengräben war eher langweilig als gefährlich (2). In Redan, der Festung im Inneren von Sebastopol, war es aufregender, besonders als die Franzosen und Briten die Sinnlosigkeit der Belagerung erkannt hatten und zum direkten Angriff übergingen. Die Russen ließen nur wenig zurück (3).

LES Français et les Britanniques avaient leur base à Balaklava (1). Dans ce petit port arrivaient la poudre, les balles et autres projectiles, les boulets de canon, les armes destinées aux sièges, les vivres, l'habillement, les baraques, les couvertures et les chaussures. La guerre se concentrait sur le siège de la place forte russe de Sébastopol. La vie dans les tranchées autour de Sébastopol était plus ennuyeuse que dangereuse, et la pause café était la bienvenue (2). La vie à l'intérieur de Redan, ouvrage fortifié dans Sébastopol, était plus excitante, surtout lorsque les Français et les Britanniques, ayant réalisé la futilité du siège, montèrent directement à l'assaut. Les Russes ne laissèrent que peu de choses derrière eux (3).

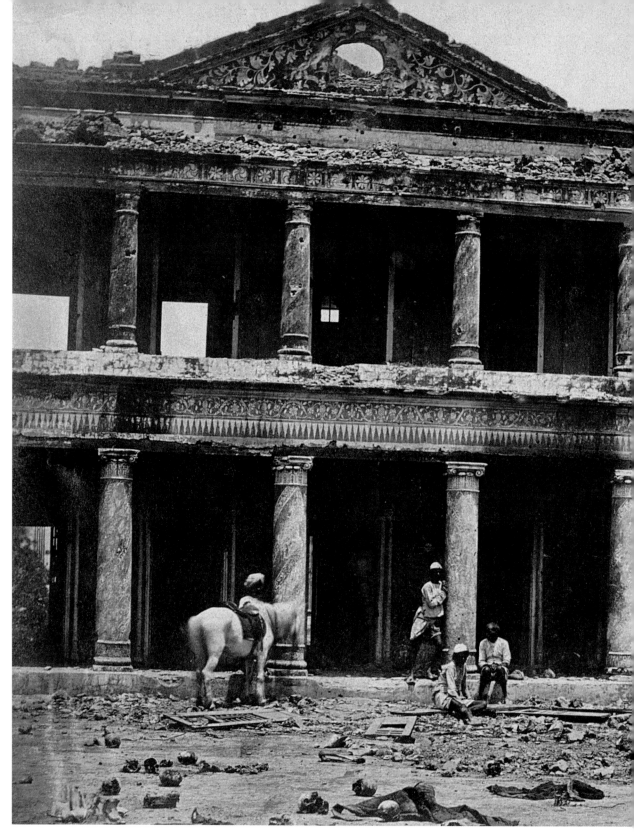

IN 1857, during Ramadan, five English people were murdered in the fortress palace of the Moghul Emperor. It was the start of the Indian Mutiny, a cruel war, with atrocities committed by both sides. During

Sir Colin Campbell's relief of Lucknow, 2,000 rebel sepoys were killed (1). Mutineers (2) were brave but ill-led. Hodson's Horse was a mixed troop of British and Indian officers (3).

WÄHREND des Ramadan im Jahre 1857 wurden fünf Engländer im Palast des Moguls umgebracht. Es war der Beginn des indischen Aufstands, eines brutalen Krieges, der von beiden Seiten mit der gleichen Grausamkeit geführt wurde. Während der Befreiung der Garnison

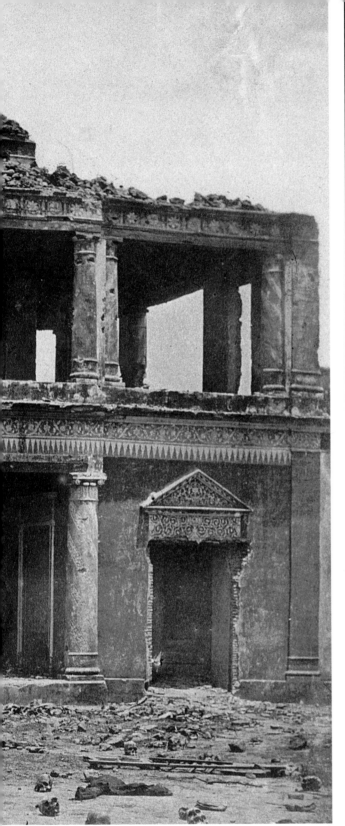

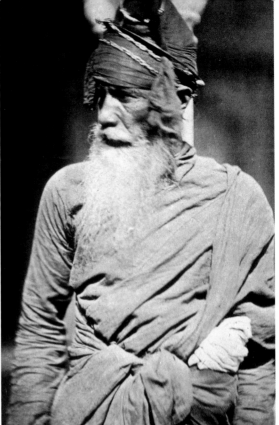

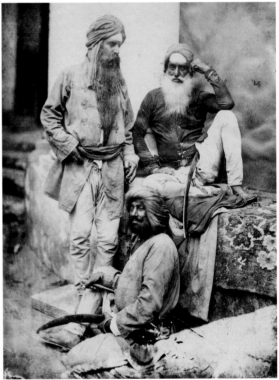

Lucknow durch Sir Colin Campbell wurden 2000 rebellische Sepoys, eingeborene Soldaten der britischen Armee in Indien, getötet (1). Aufständische (2) waren zwar tapfer, aber schlecht organisiert. Hodson's Horse war eine aus Briten und Indern zusammengesetzte Truppe (3).

EN 1857, durant le ramadan, cinq Anglais furent assassinés dans le palais fortifié de l'empereur moghol. Ce fut le départ de la révolte des cipayes, une guerre cruelle avec des atrocités commises des deux côtés. Lorsque Sir Colin Campbell arriva à la rescousse de la garnison assiégée à Lucknow, il laissa ses hommes massacrer 2000 cipayes rebelles à Secundra Bagh (1). Les mutins, comme ce Sikh (2), étaient courageux mais mal commandés. Les troupes irrégulières britanniques incluaient le célèbre Hodson's Horse, un corps mêlé d'officiers britanniques et indiens (3).

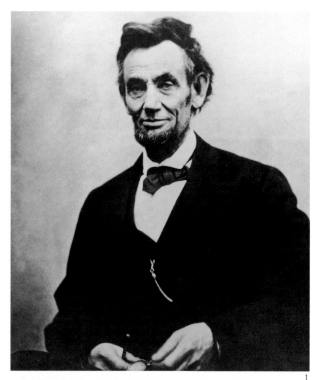

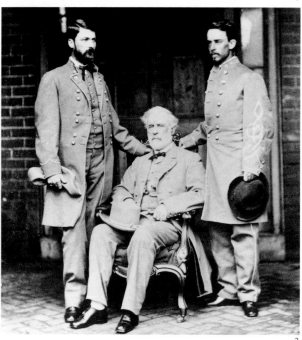

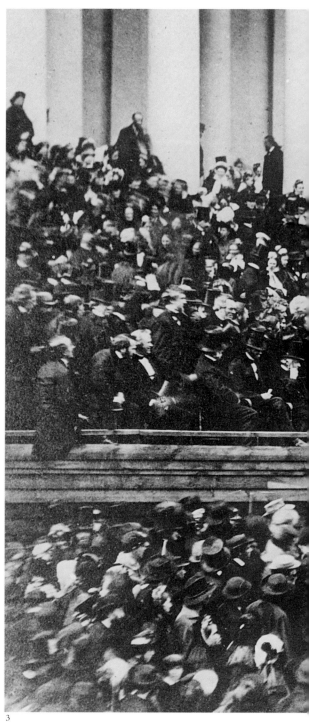

2   3

THE War Between the States was the first truly modern war. It was also the bloodiest conflict in American history. More Americans died in the Civil War than in all the nation's other wars put together. For four years, from 1861 to 1865, father fought son, brother fought brother, and the land east of the Mississippi was torn apart. The issues were a bull-headed mixture of political, economic and moral factors. For the South, secession from the Union was almost inevitable once Abraham Lincoln (1) had been inaugurated as President (3). The champion of the South was General Robert E. Lee (2 – seated centre), brave in battle, gentlemanly in defeat.

DER Amerikanische Bürgerkrieg war der erste wirklich moderne Krieg und zudem der blutigste Konflikt in der amerikanischen Geschichte. Es starben mehr Amerikaner als in den gesamten übrigen Kriegen, die das Land führte. Vier Jahre lang, von 1861 bis 1865, kämpfte Vater gegen Sohn, Bruder gegen Bruder, und das Land östlich des Mississippi wurde zerrissen.

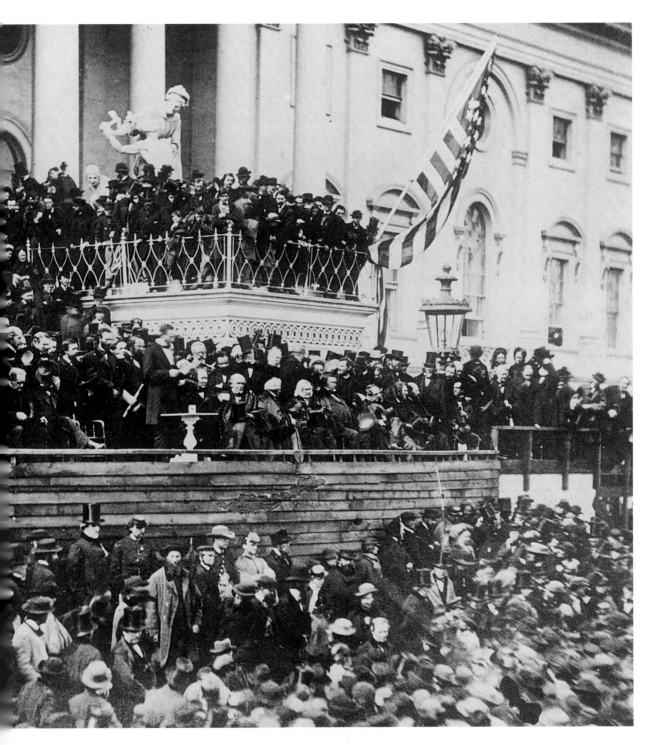

Der Anlaß war eine starrköpfige Mischung aus politischen, wirtschaftlichen und moralischen Faktoren. Für den Süden war die Abspaltung vom Bund fast unvermeidlich, nachdem Abraham Lincoln (1) das Amt des Präsidenten angetreten hatte (3). Der Held des Südens war General Robert E. Lee (2, Mitte), tapfer in der Schlacht und ein Gentleman in der Niederlage.

LA guerre de Sécession fut la première véritable guerre moderne. Ce fut aussi le conflit le plus sanglant de l'histoire d'Outre-Atlantique. Il mourut plus de Nord-Américains durant la guerre civile que pendant toutes les autres guerres livrées par la nation. Quatre années durant, de 1861 à 1865, le père combattit le fils, le frère son frère, et les territoires, à l'est du Mississippi, se déchirèrent.

Les enjeux en résultaient d'un mélange détonant de considérations politiques, économiques et morales. Pour le Sud, sa sortie de l'Union était devenue quasiment inévitable dès lors qu'Abraham Lincoln (1) avait été investi de la présidence (3). Le champion du Sud était le général Robert E. Lee (2, assis au centre), brave sur le champ de bataille et gentilhomme dans la défaite.

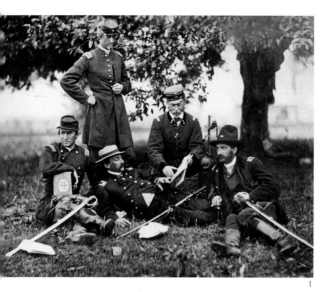

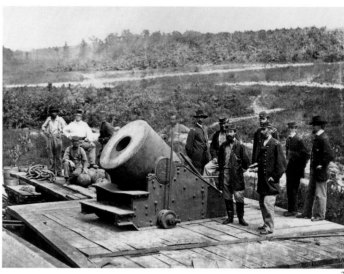

Many nations sent observers to the American Civil War, to study the killing power of modern weapons. Among them was Count Zeppelin from Germany (1, second from right). One of the largest of the new weapons was the giant mortar, 'Dictator' (2), used by the North at the beginning of 1865. The battles were

bloody, and casualties on both sides were heavy. One of the worst was Chancellorsville in May 1863 – here a black soldier tends a wounded comrade (3). It was largely a war of attacks by infantrymen (4) on positions defended by artillery, such as Battery A, Fourth US Artillery, Robertson's Brigade (5).

Viele Nationen sandten Beobachter in den Amerikanischen Bürgerkrieg, um die tödliche Wirkung moderner Waffen zu studieren. Unter ihnen war auch der deutsche Graf Zeppelin (1, zweiter von rechts). Eine der größten neuen Waffen war der gigantische Minenwerfer »Dictator« (2), den die Nordstaaten zu Beginn des Jahres 1865 einsetzten. Die Kämpfe waren blutig und die Verluste auf beiden Seiten

5

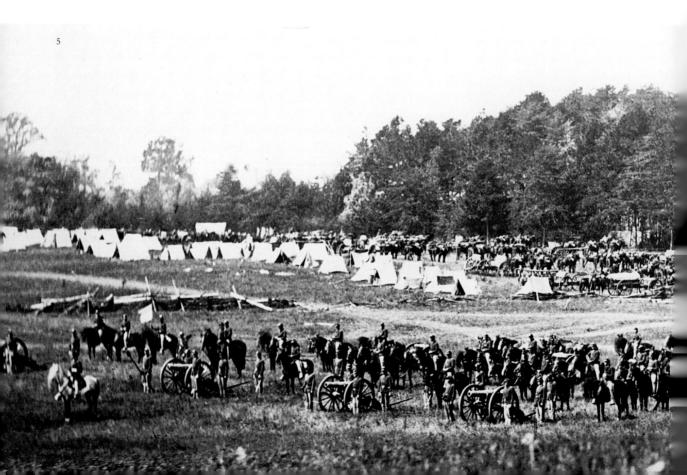

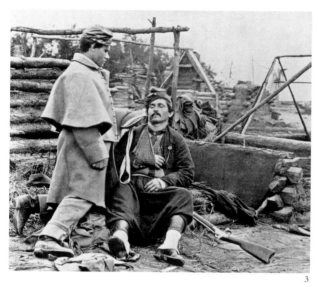

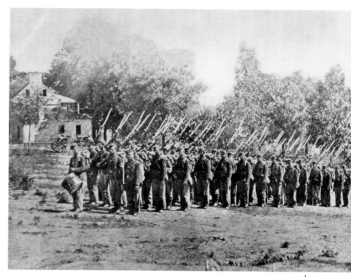

3

4

immens. Eine der schlimmsten Schlachten war die von Chancellorsville im Mai 1863 – hier kümmert sich ein schwarzer Soldat um einen verwundeten Kameraden (3). Dieser Krieg wurde überwiegend mit Angriffen der Infanterie (4) aus Stellungen geführt, die von der Artillerie gedeckt waren, beispielsweise von Robertsons Brigade der vierten US-Artillerie (5).

DE nombreuses nations envoyèrent des observateurs étudier sur place la puissance destructrice des armes modernes. Parmi eux se trouvait le comte allemand Zeppelin (1, deuxième à droite). Une des nouvelles armes les plus impressionnantes par ses dimensions était l'obusier géant, le « Dictateur » (2), que le Nord avait utilisé au début de 1865. Les batailles étaient sanglantes et les morts et

les blessés s'accumulaient des deux côtés. Une des pires fut la bataille de Chancellorsville en mai 1863 : ici un soldat noir s'affaire autour d'un camarade blessé (3). Ce fut en grande partie une guerre où l'infanterie (4) attaquait les positions défendues par l'artillerie : ici la batterie A, quatrième corps d'artillerie des États-Unis, brigade de Robertson (5).

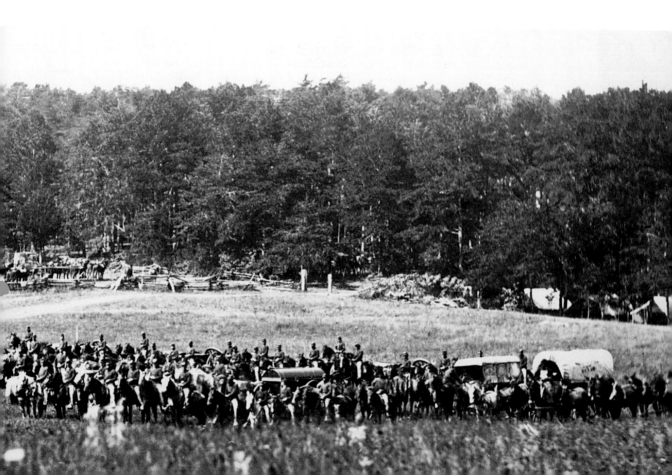

In many ways the American Civil War was a direct forerunner of the First World War. These defensive positions at Fort Sedgewick 1865 in (1) bear a strong resemblance to the trenches on the Western Front 50 years later. The South was finally pounded into surrender in April 1865, after its capital, Richmond, Virginia (3), and many other cities had been razed to the ground. Exactly one week after Lee's surrender at Appomattox, Lincoln was assassinated. There was no mercy for the conspirators responsible. John Wilkes Booth died in a shoot-out with Federal troops. Mrs Surratt and three other conspirators were hanged (2).

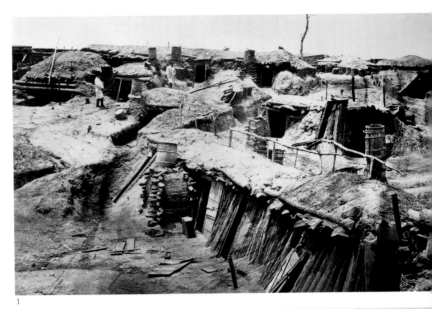

1

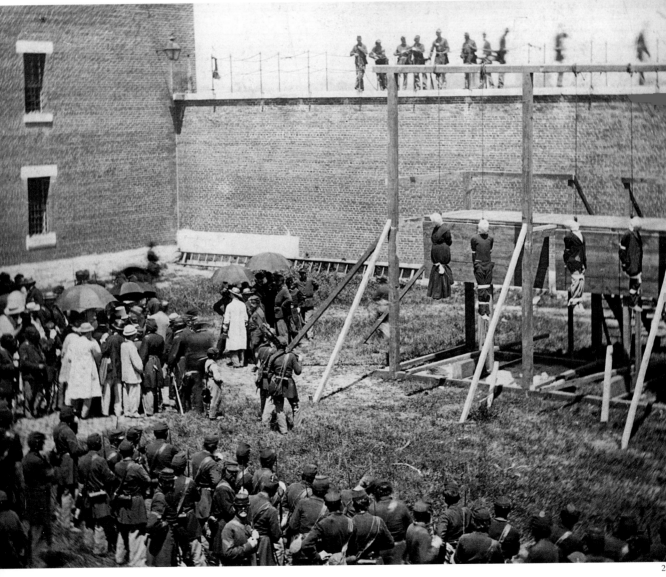

2

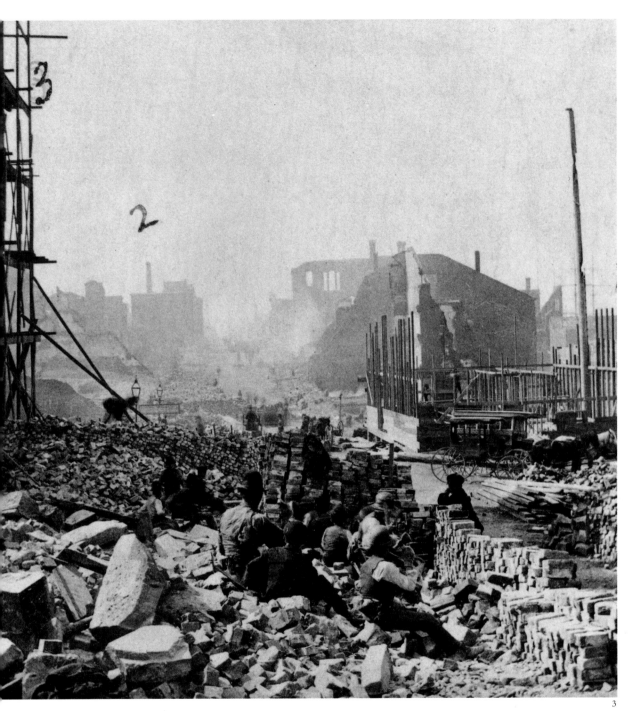

IN vieler Hinsicht war der Amerikanische Bürgerkrieg ein direkter Vorläufer des Ersten Weltkriegs. Die Verteidigungsstellungen in Fort Sedgewick 1865 (1) hatten große Ähnlichkeit mit den Schützengräben an der Westfront fünfzig Jahre später. Der Süden wurde schließlich im April 1865 zur Aufgabe gezwungen, nachdem seine Hauptstadt Richmond in Virginia (3) und viele andere Städte dem Erdboden gleichgemacht worden waren. Genau eine Woche nach Lees Kapitulation bei Appomattox wurde Lincoln durch ein Attentat getötet. Für die Verschwörer gab es keine Gnade. John Wilkes Booth starb in einer Schießerei mit den föderalistischen Truppen. Mrs. Surratt und drei andere Verschwörer wurden gehängt (2).

À bien des égards la guerre civile américaine servit de banc d'essai à la Première Guerre mondiale. Ces positions défensives à Fort Sedgewick en 1865 (1) ressemblent fort aux tranchées du front Ouest cinquante années plus tard. Le Sud fut finalement contraint de se rendre en avril 1865, après que sa capitale, Richmond en Virginie (3), et beaucoup d'autres grandes villes eurent été rasées. Une semaine après la capitulation de Lee à Appomattox, Lincoln était assassiné. Les conspirateurs furent traités impitoyablement. John Wilkes Booth fut tué par les troupes fédérales au cours d'un échange de balles. Madame Surratt et trois autres conspirateurs furent pendus (2).

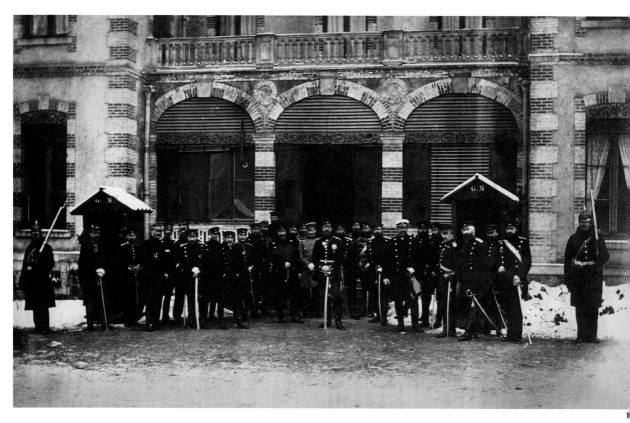

THE Franco-Prussian war was swift and deadly. It was also a war of massive armies and big battles.

For Prussia it was a brilliant success. For the rest of the German Confederation it was proof that unity under Prussian leadership was sound policy. For France it was a humiliating defeat, sowing the seeds of the bitter harvest of the First World War. The trap was laid by the German Chancellor, Bismarck. On 2 June 1870 news reached France that the Spanish throne had been offered to Prince Leopold of Hohenzollern, a relative of the Prussian King. It was unthinkable for France to face potentially hostile regimes on two fronts. The Emperor Napoleon III insisted that Leopold's candidature be withdrawn. It was. But Napoleon went further, and demanded an undertaking that the candidature would never be renewed. Wilhelm of Prussia refused to discuss this with the French Ambassador in Berlin. Bismarck subtly changed the wording of the telegram informing the French Emperor of this sad state of affairs, giving the impression that

the French Ambassador had been summarily dismissed. France declared war.

From then on, in the words of a French commander, the French Army was in a chamber pot, 'about to be shitted upon'. Prussian victories at Woerth, Gravelotte and Sedan, where vast numbers of French artillery pieces were captured (2), led to ignominious French retreat, with worse to follow. 'There was something in the air, a subtle and mysterious emanation, strange and intolerable, which hung about the streets like a smell – the smell of invasion. It filled the houses and the public places, gave to the food an unfamiliar taste, and made people feel as though they were in a distant land among dangerous and barbaric tribes' (Guy de Maupassant, *Boule de Suif*).

They were not barbaric, but they were efficient – Crown Prince Friedrich Wilhelm, Chief of the Prussian Southern Army, with his General Staff at their headquarters, 'Les Ombrages', 13 January 1871, less than two weeks before the surrender of Paris (1).

DER Deutsch-Französische Krieg war kurz und tödlich, ein Krieg der gewaltigen Armeen und großen Schlachten.

Für Preußen war es ein glänzender Erfolg, für den Rest des Deutschen Bundes dagegen der Beweis, daß eine Einheit unter preußischer Führung eine vernünftige Politik war. Für Frankreich bedeutete es eine demütigende Niederlage und die Saat für die bittere Ernte des Ersten Weltkriegs. Die Falle hatte der deutsche Kanzler Bismarck gelegt. Am 2. Juni 1870 traf in Frankreich die Nachricht von der spanischen Thronkandidatur des Prinzen Leopold von Hohenzollern ein, einem Verwandten des preußischen Königs. Für Frankreich war es undenkbar, an zwei Grenzen mit potentiell feindlichen Regimes konfrontiert zu werden. Kaiser Napoleon III. verlangte den Verzicht Leopolds auf die Thronkandidatur. So kam es. Aber Napoleon ging weiter und verlangte die Garantie, daß die Kandidatur nicht erneuert würde. Kaiser Wilhelm weigerte sich, darüber mit dem französischen Botschafter in Berlin zu verhandeln. Bismarck nahm eine subtile Änderung des Wortlauts des Telegramms vor, in dem der französische Kaiser über den traurigen Stand der Verhandlungen informiert wurde, und vermittelte den Eindruck, der französische Botschafter

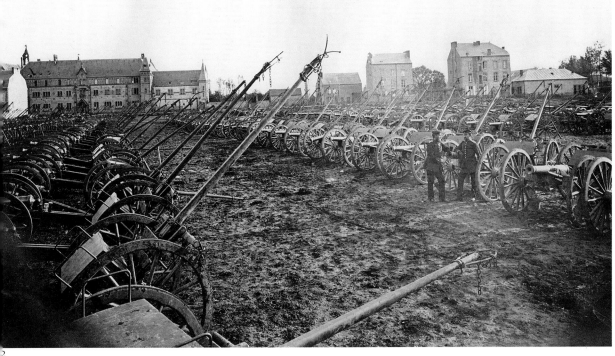

2

sei abgewiesen worden. Daraufhin erklärte Frankreich den Krieg.

Um mit den Worten eines französischen Kommandanten zu sprechen, befand sich die französische Armee von nun an in einem Nachttopf, »kurz davor, vollgeschissen zu werden«. Preußische Siege bei Woerth, Gravelotte und Sedan, bei denen große Mengen französischer Angriffswaffen erobert wurden (2), führten zu einem schmachvollen Rückzug der Franzosen, dem Schlimmeres folgen sollte. »Es lag etwas in der Luft. Eine subtile und mysteriöse Atmosphäre, seltsam und unerträglich, hing wie ein Geruch über den Straßen – der Geruch der Invasion. Er erfüllte die Häuser und die öffentlichen Plätze, verlieh dem Essen einen fremden Geschmack und gab den Menschen das Gefühl, sich in einem fernen Land unter gefährlichen und barbarischen Stämmen zu befinden.« (Guy de Maupassant, *Boule de Suif*)

Sie waren nicht barbarisch, sondern effizient. Kronprinz Friedrich Wilhelm, Oberbefehlshaber der preußischen Armee im Süden, mit seinem Generalstab im Hauptquartier »Les Ombrages« am 13. Januar 1871, weniger als zwei Wochen vor der Kapitulation von Paris (1).

ENTRE la France et la Prusse, ce fut une guerre éclair et mortelle, qui eut aussi ses immenses armées et ses grandes batailles.

Pour la Prusse ce fut un succès éclatant. Pour le reste de la confédération germanique la preuve que la politique de l'unité sous la houlette de la Prusse avait été judicieuse. La France connut une défaite humiliante qui conforta les raisons de la Première Guerre mondiale. Le chancelier allemand Bismarck tendit le piège. Le 2 juin 1870, la France apprenait que le trône d'Espagne avait été offert au prince Léopold de Hohenzollern, parent du roi de Prusse. Pour la France il n'était pas question de se retrouver presque encerclée par deux régimes potentiellement hostiles. L'empereur Napoléon III insista pour que Léopold retirât sa candidature. Ce qui fut fait. Mais Napoléon exigea en plus que cette candidature ne soit plus jamais représentée. Guillaume de Prusse refusa de discuter de la question avec l'ambassadeur de France à Berlin. Bismarck changea subtilement le libellé du télégramme informant l'empereur français du triste état des choses et qui donnait l'impression que l'ambassadeur de France avait été purement et simplement renvoyé. La France déclara alors la guerre.

À partir de là, pour reprendre les termes d'un commandant français, l'armée française se trouvait dans un pot de chambre. Les victoires prussiennes à Woerth, Gravelotte et Sedan au cours desquelles de grandes quantités de pièces d'artillerie française furent saisies (2) forcèrent la France à une retraite ignominieuse, et ce n'était qu'un commencement. « Il y avait cependant quelque chose dans l'air, quelque chose de subtil et d'inconnu, une atmosphère étrangère intolérable, comme une odeur répandue, l'odeur de l'invasion. Elle emplissait les demeures et les places publiques, changeait le goût des aliments, donnait l'impression d'être en voyage, très loin, chez des tribus barbares et dangereuses » (Guy de Maupassant, *Boule de Suif*).

Barbares ou pas, ils étaient efficaces : le prince héritier Frédéric-Guillaume, chef de l'armée prussienne du Sud, entouré de son état-major dans ses propres quartiers, « Les Ombrages », le 13 janvier 1871, moins de deux semaines avant la capitulation de Paris (1).

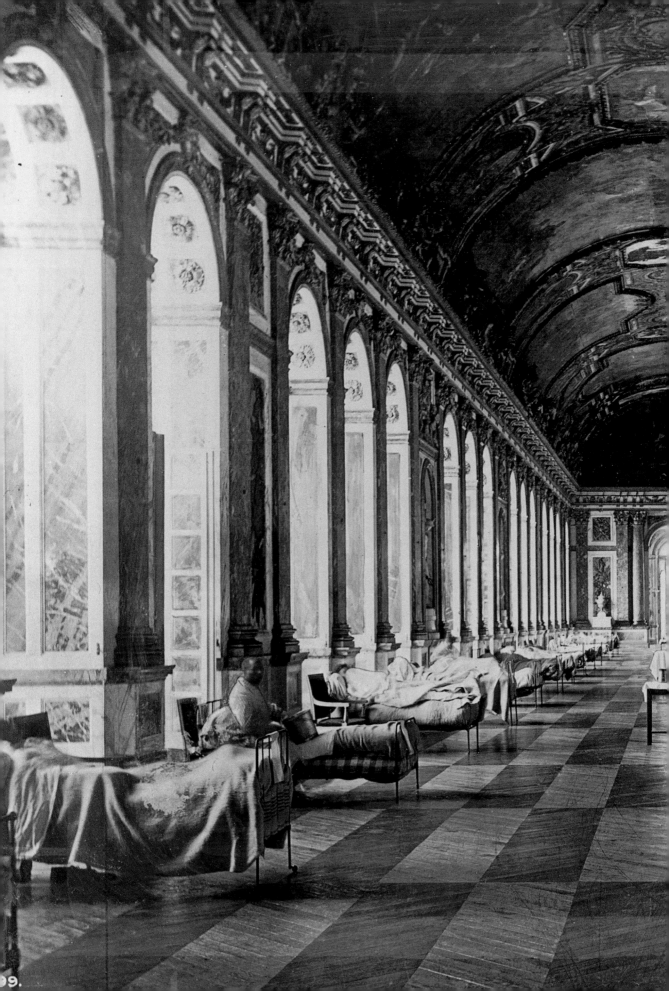

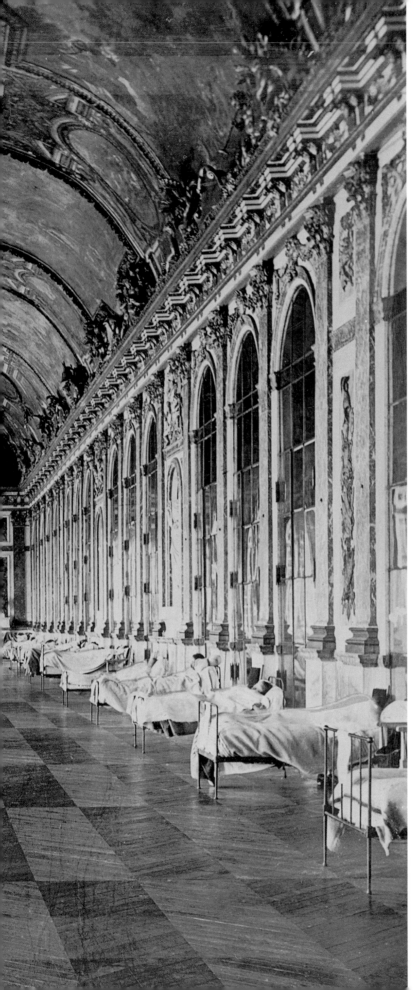

THE German occupation of France, 1870-71: the Gallery of Mirrors, Versailles, converted into a German hospital during the Franco-Prussian War.

DIE deutsche Besatzung Frankreichs, 1870 bis 1871: Der Spiegelsaal in Versailles diente den Deutschen während des Deutsch-Französischen Krieges als Hospital.

L'OCCUPATION de la France par les Allemands de 1870 à 1871 : la Galerie des glaces à Versailles reconvertie en hôpital allemand pendant la guerre entre la France et la Prusse.

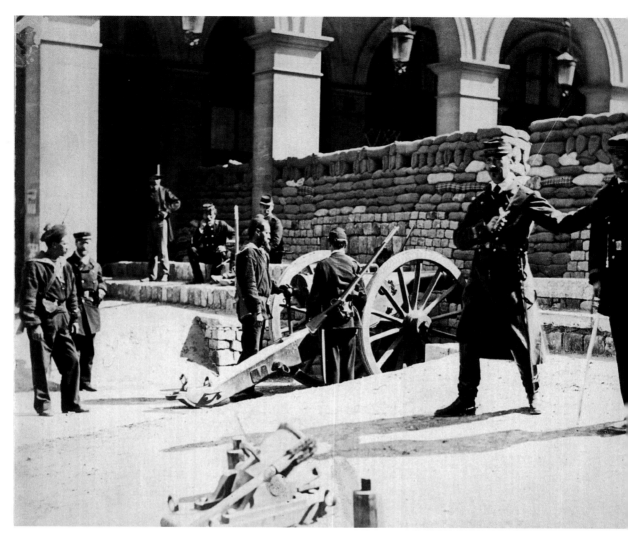

THE Prussians found it easier to defeat
the French Emperor than the French
people. In late September 1870, Paris was
completely encircled, but the city held out
for four months. The people were reduced
to eating sparrows, rats, dogs, cats and all
the animals in the zoo. It was said that only
the French genius for cooking could make
the elephants palatable. Pigeons were
spared – they were needed to take Nadar's
micro-photos out of the city.

After the siege came the Commune.
On 18 March 1871, the red banner flew
over Paris. Barricades were raised by the
Communards and the National Guard in
the Place Vendôme (1), and by opposing
government troops (2). French ingenuity
resulted in mobile barricades (3), which
could be rushed from one part of the city
to another, wherever the action was
hottest.

FÜR die Preußen war es leichter, den
französischen Kaiser zu besiegen als das
französische Volk. Paris war gegen Ende
September 1870 vollständig umzingelt,
aber die Stadt konnte sich vier Monate lang
halten. Die Menschen waren gezwungen,
Spatzen, Ratten, Hunde, Katzen und
alle Tiere aus dem Zoo zu essen. Es hieß,
nur das französische Kochgenie habe es
geschafft, die Elefanten genießbar zu
machen. Tauben blieben verschont, denn
sie wurden benötigt, um Nadars Mikro-
filme aus der Stadt herauszubringen.

Der Belagerung folgte der Aufstand der
Pariser Kommune. Am 18. März 1871
wehte das rote Banner über Paris. Auf der
Place Vendôme (1) wurden sowohl von
Kommunarden und Nationalgardisten als
auch von gegnerischen Regierungstruppen
Barrikaden errichtet (2). Französischer
Erfindungsreichtum brachte mobile Barri-
kaden (3) hervor, die schnell von einem
Kampfschauplatz der Stadt zum anderen
transportiert werden konnten.

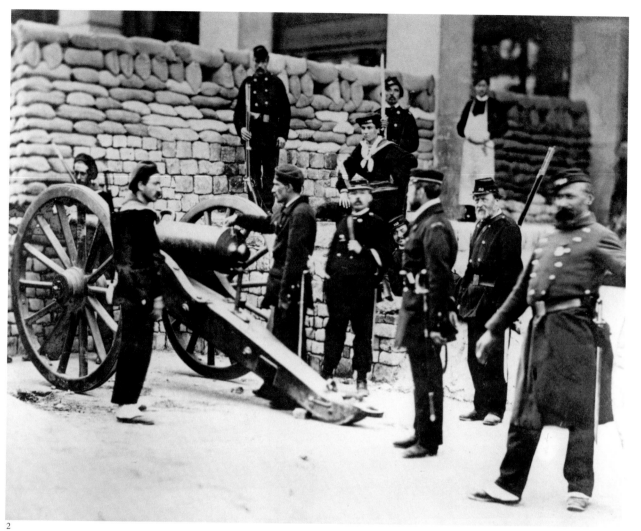

2

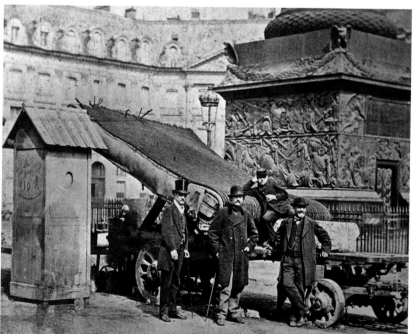

3

LES Prussiens s'aperçurent qu'il était plus facile de battre l'empereur français que le peuple français. Fin septembre 1870, bien qu'encerclé complètement, Paris résista quatre mois durant. La population en était réduite à manger des moineaux, des rats, des chiens, des chats et tous les animaux du Jardin des Plantes. On a dit que seul le génie culinaire français avait pu rendre la viande d'éléphant savoureuse. Les pigeons furent épargnés car on en avait besoin pour faire sortir les microphoto-graphies de Nadar de la ville.

Au siège succéda la Commune. Le 18 mars 1871, la bannière rouge flottait au-dessus de Paris. Des barricades avaient été érigées par les communards et la Garde nationale sur la place Vendôme (1), mais également par les troupes gouvernementales auxquelles ils s'opposaient (2). Les Français firent la preuve de leur ingéniosité en construisant des barricades mobiles (3) que l'on pouvait rapidement déplacer d'un bout à l'autre de la capitale, suivant le lieu des affrontements.

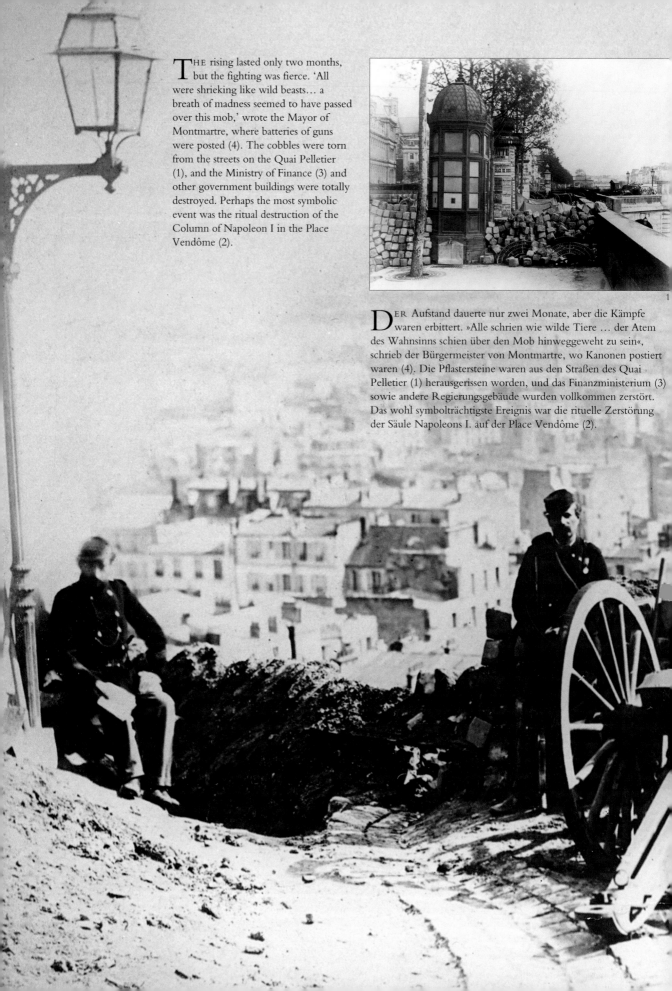

THE rising lasted only two months, but the fighting was fierce. 'All were shrieking like wild beasts… a breath of madness seemed to have passed over this mob,' wrote the Mayor of Montmartre, where batteries of guns were posted (4). The cobbles were torn from the streets on the Quai Pelletier (1), and the Ministry of Finance (3) and other government buildings were totally destroyed. Perhaps the most symbolic event was the ritual destruction of the Column of Napoleon I in the Place Vendôme (2).

1

DER Aufstand dauerte nur zwei Monate, aber die Kämpfe waren erbittert. »Alle schrien wie wilde Tiere … der Atem des Wahnsinns schien über den Mob hinweggeweht zu sein«, schrieb der Bürgermeister von Montmartre, wo Kanonen postiert waren (4). Die Pflastersteine waren aus den Straßen des Quai Pelletier (1) herausgerissen worden, und das Finanzministerium (3) sowie andere Regierungsgebäude wurden vollkommen zerstört. Das wohl symbolträchtigste Ereignis war die rituelle Zerstörung der Säule Napoleons I. auf der Place Vendôme (2).

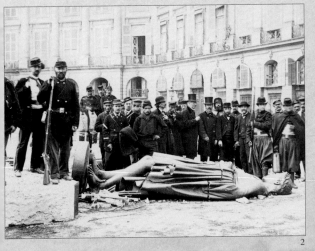

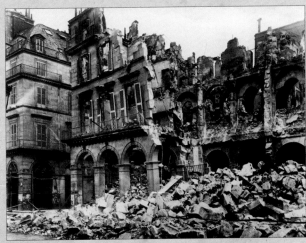

2   3

L E soulèvement ne dura que deux mois, mais les combats furent féroces. Le maire de Montmartre nota l'agressivité de la foule et pensa qu'un vent de folie soufflait sur elle. À Montmartre étaient disposées des batteries de canons (4). Les pavés des rues avaient été arrachés quai Pelletier (1), tandis que le bâtiment du ministère des Finances (3) et ceux d'autres administrations avaient été complètement détruits. L'événement le plus symbolique fut peut-être la destruction rituelle de la colonne de Napoléon Ier sur la place Vendôme (2).

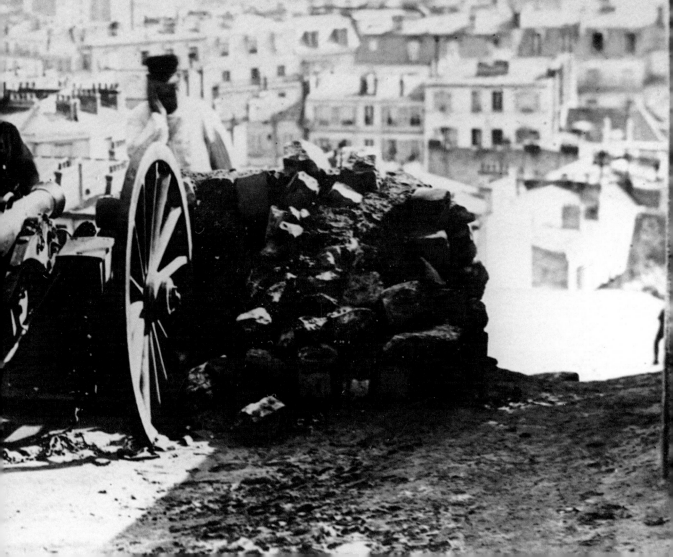

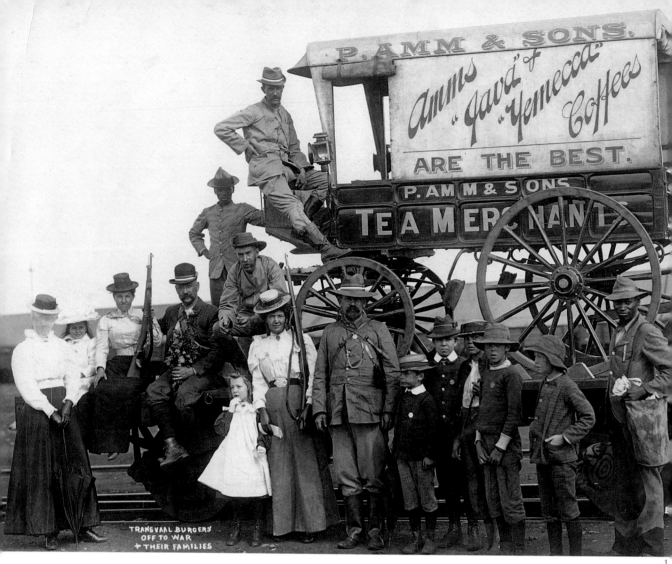

TRANSVAAL BURGERS
OFF TO WAR
+ THEIR FAMILIES

1

For over 80 years the British had ruled South Africa, with ever-increasing friction between them and the Boer descendants (1) of the Dutch settlers in Transvaal and the Orange Free State. In 1899 British avarice provoked a second war with the Boers, and for two months half a million troops of the greatest Imperial power in the world (3) were being contained and besieged by 40,000 guerrillas – while those whose land it had once been scratched for a living, or slaved to bring the white man diamonds from the Big Hole at Kimberley, a mile round at the top and over 200 metres deep (2).

Die seit über achtzig Jahren bestehende Herrschaft der Briten in Südafrika wurde überschattet von immer größeren Spannungen mit den Buren (1), Nachfahren niederländischer Siedler in Transvaal und im Oranje-Freistaat. In Jahre 1899 führte die britische Habgier zu einem zweiten Krieg mit den Buren, und zwei Monate lang wurde eine halbe Million Soldaten der größten imperialen Macht der Welt (3) von 40 000 Guerillas in Schach gehalten und belagert – während jene, denen das Land einst gehört hatte, ums Überleben kämpften oder als Sklaven für den weißen Mann im Big Hole bei Kimberley über 200 Meter tief nach Diamanten gruben (2).

Depuis plus de quatre-vingts ans que les Britanniques étaient les maîtres de l'Afrique du Sud, les frictions n'avaient fait que s'accroître entre eux et les descendants Boers (1) des colons néerlandais installés dans le Transvaal et dans l'État libre d'Orange. En 1899, la progression des Britanniques provoqua une deuxième guerre contre les Boers : pendant deux mois, un demi-million de soldats de la plus grande puissance impériale du monde (3) furent assiégés par 40 000 combattants. Les noirs vivotaient sur leur terre ou travaillaient comme des esclaves dans le Big Hole (le Grand Trou, profond de 200 mètres) à Kimberley pour en rapporter les diamants (2).

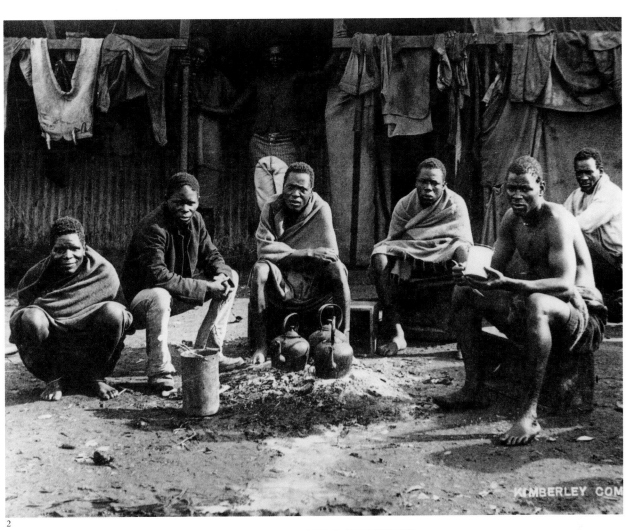

2

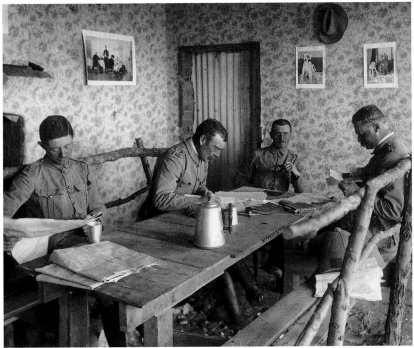

3

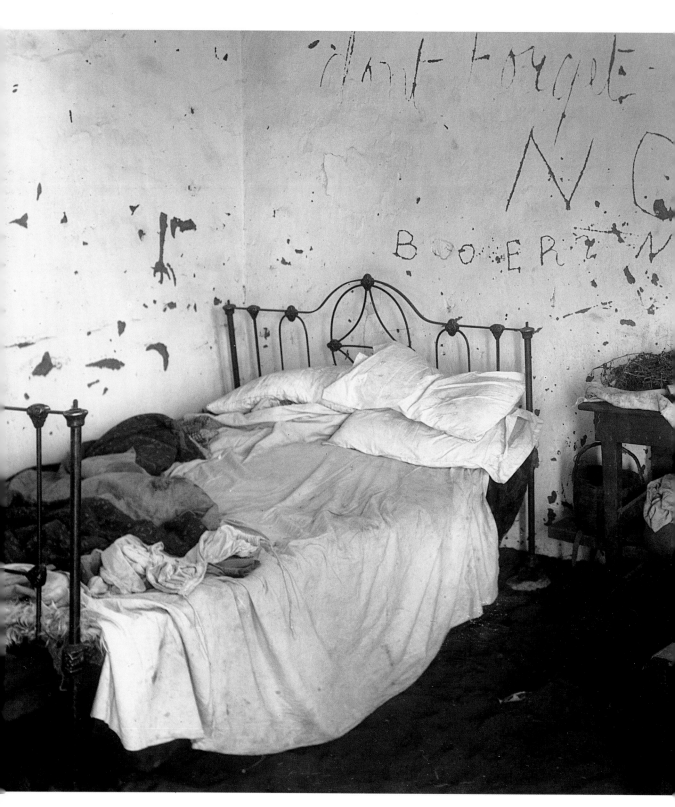

THOUGH outnumbered and outgunned, the Boers knew how to use their terrain, and throughout 1899 the British suffered a series of embarrassing defeats – at Nicholson's Nek, Ladysmith, Stormberg, Magersfontein and Colenso.

Boer morale was high, recalling victories of the war of 1881 – 'don't forget Majuba Boys' was scratched on the wall of a Boer homestead (1). But Britain summoned up fresh resources and appointed new generals. Boer sieges of Ladysmith and Mafeking

were raised, and a combined force of English and Imperial troops defeated the Boers at the battle of Spion Kop, where Canadians drove the Boers at bayonet point from the kopje (2).

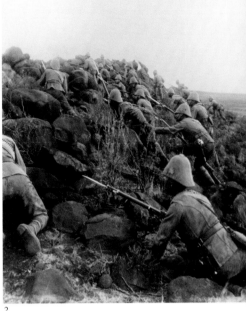

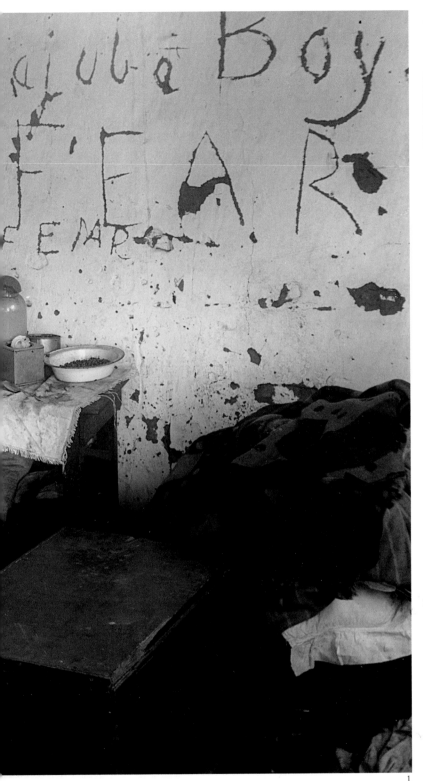

machten neue Reserven mobil und setzten neue Generäle ein. Die von den Buren besetzten Städte Ladysmith und Mafeking wurden zurückerobert, und eine Armee aus britischen Soldaten und Truppen des Empire besiegte die Buren in der Schlacht von Spion Kop, wo Kanadier die Buren mit Bajonetten vom Hügel vertrieben (2).

S'ILS étaient inférieurs en nombre et en armement, les Boers connaissaient bien le terrain ; ils infligèrent ainsi aux Britanniques une série de défaites embarrassantes tout au long de 1899, à Nicholson's Nek, Ladysmith, Stormberg, Magersfontein et Colenso. Le moral des Boers était très bon ; ils se rappelaient les victoires de 1881 : « N'oubliez pas les gars de Majuba », pouvait-on lire sur le mur de la ferme d'un Boer (1). Cependant la Grande-Bretagne rassembla de nouvelles ressources et nomma de nouveaux généraux. Les sièges des Boers à Ladysmith et Mafeking furent levés, tandis que les forces anglaises et impériales combinées aboutirent à la défaite des Boers à la bataille de Spion Kop, où les Canadiens forcèrent ces derniers à redescendre à la pointe de leurs baïonnettes du sommet de Kopje (2).

OBWOHL sie zahlenmäßig unterlegen waren und weniger Waffen besaßen, wußten die Buren ihr Terrain zu nutzen und fügten 1899 den Briten eine Reihe schmachvoller Niederlagen zu, beispielsweise bei Nicholson's Nek, Ladysmith, Stormberg, Magersfontein und Colenso. Die Kampfmoral der Buren war enorm, denn sie erinnerten sich an die Siege über die Briten im Krieg von 1881 – »Denkt an Majuba Boys« war in die Wand eines Buren-Hauses gekratzt (1). Aber die Briten

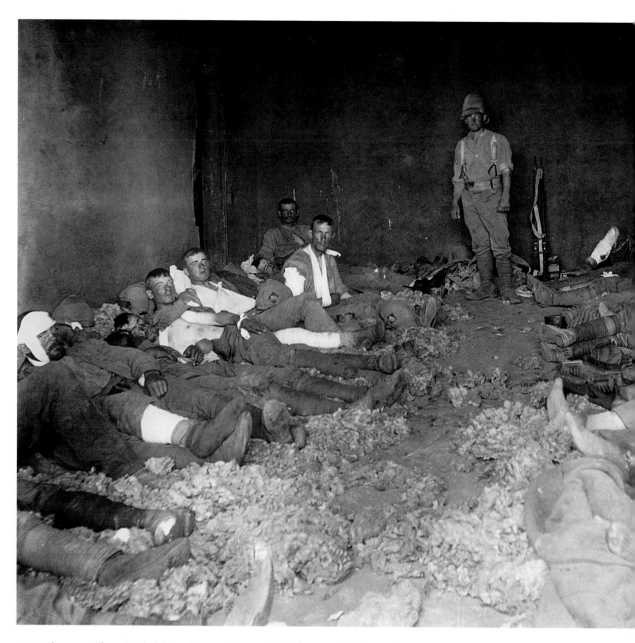

To the reports from South Africa of war correspondents such as Rudyard Kipling, Winston Churchill and Conan Doyle were added the pictures of many war artists, and at least one great photographer – Reinhold Thiele – whose photographs of troops training, marching, resting (3) and recuperating were reprinted in the *London Daily Graphic*. The realism of pictures of British wounded lying in the filth of a wagon house (1) contrasted starkly with propaganda studies taken in a military hospital many miles from the actual fighting (2). But in general it was still the war artists, rather than the photographers, who recorded the battles, and there was no suggestion in their drawings that the British were suffering heavy defeats.

DEN Berichten über den Krieg in Südafrika von Korrespondenten wie Rudyard Kipling, Winston Churchill und Conan Doyle wurden die Bilder vieler Kriegszeichner und zumindest eines bedeutenden Photographen beigefügt, Reinhold Thiele, dessen Aufnahmen von exerzierenden, marschierenden, rastenden (3) und verwundeten Soldaten in der *London Daily Graphic* abgedruckt wurden. Der Realismus der Bilder von britischen Verwundeten im

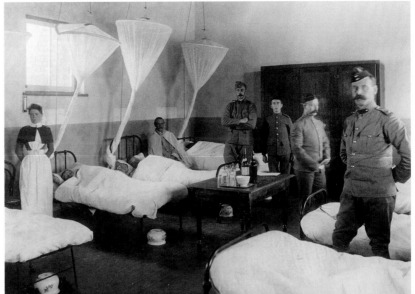

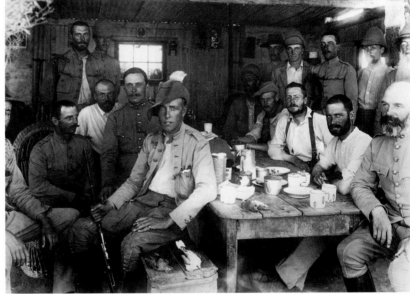

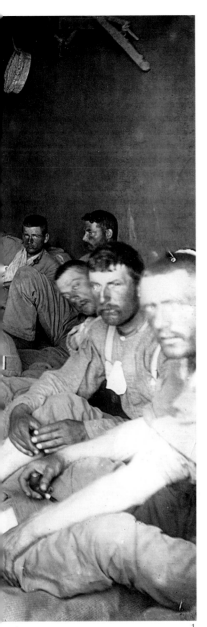

Schmutz eines Schuppens (1) stand in starkem Kontrast zu den Propagandaaufnahmen, die in einem Militärhospital viele Meilen von den Kampfschauplätzen entfernt gemacht wurden (2). Aber im allgemeinen waren es noch immer die Kriegszeichner, und nicht die Photographen, die die Schlachten dokumentierten, und in ihren Zeichnungen gab es keinen Hinweis darauf, daß die Briten große Verluste erlitten hatten.

Aux rapports expédiés d'Afrique du Sud par les correspondants de guerre tels que Rudyard Kipling, Winston Churchill et Conan Doyle, s'ajoutaient les images réalisées par de nombreux artistes de guerre, parmi lesquels un grand photographe – Reinhold Thiele – dont les clichés montrant des troupes à l'entraînement, en marche, au repos (3) et en convalescence furent repris dans le *London Daily Graphic*. Le réalisme des images montrant des Britanniques gisant blessés dans

la saleté d'un wagon aménagé (1) contrastait vivement avec les études de propagande réalisées dans un hôpital militaire situé à plusieurs kilomètres du théâtre même des combats (2). Mais, de façon générale, c'étaient toujours les artistes de guerre, et non les photographes, qui représentaient les batailles, et rien dans leurs dessins ne laissait entrevoir les importants et cuisants revers subis par les Britanniques.

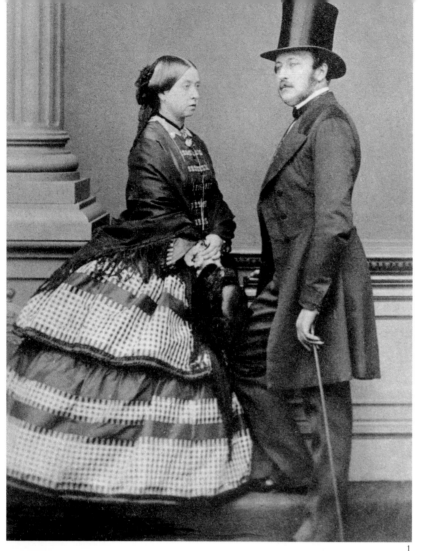

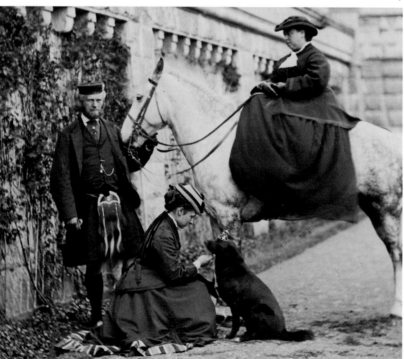

KINGS, emperors, princes and dukes arrived and departed during the 19th century – Queen Victoria went on for ever (3). She was mother or grandmother to most of the royal families of Europe, a matriarchal figure who was never afraid to admonish those whose subjects trembled beneath them. In 1857 her beloved husband, Albert of Saxe-Coburg-Gotha, was made Prince Consort. She was heartbroken when he died in 1861, the year of this photograph (1). It was said that, although she lived a further 40 years, she never loved another – though it was also said that John Brown (2, on left, with Princess Louise, centre) was more to Her Majesty than a mere personal servant.

DAS 19. Jahrhundert sah viele Könige, Kaiser, Prinzen und Herzöge, aber Königin Victoria schien sie alle zu überleben (3). Sie war die Mutter oder Großmutter der meisten königlichen Familien Europas, eine matriarchalische Figur, die niemals davor zurückschreckte, jene zu ermahnen, deren Untertanen unter ihnen litten. 1857 ernannte sie ihren geliebten Mann Albert von Sachsen-Coburg-Gotha zum Prinzgemahl. Unter seinem Tod im Jahre 1861, in dem diese Aufnahme entstand (1), litt sie sehr. Man sagte, sie habe in den vierzig Jahren, die sie ihn überlebte, nie wieder einen anderen geliebt – aber man sagte auch, John Brown (2, links, mit Prinzessin Louise) sei für Ihre Majestät mehr gewesen als nur ein persönlicher Diener.

LES rois, les empereurs, les princes et les ducs défilèrent tout au long du XIXᵉ ; la reine Victoria demeura à jamais (3). Elle était la mère et la grand-mère de la plupart des membres des familles royales d'Europe, un personnage matriarcal qui n'avait jamais craint d'adresser de doux reproches à ceux qui faisaient trembler leurs sujets. En 1857, son époux bien-aimé, Albert de Saxe-Cobourg-Gotha, fut fait prince consort. La mort de celui-ci en 1861, l'année de cette photographie (1), lui brisa le cœur. La rumeur veut que bien qu'elle lui survécût encore quarante années, elle n'en aima jamais d'autre ; toutefois on a aussi dit que John Brown (2, à gauche aux côtés de la princesse Louise au centre) n'était pas seulement le serviteur attitré de Sa Majesté.

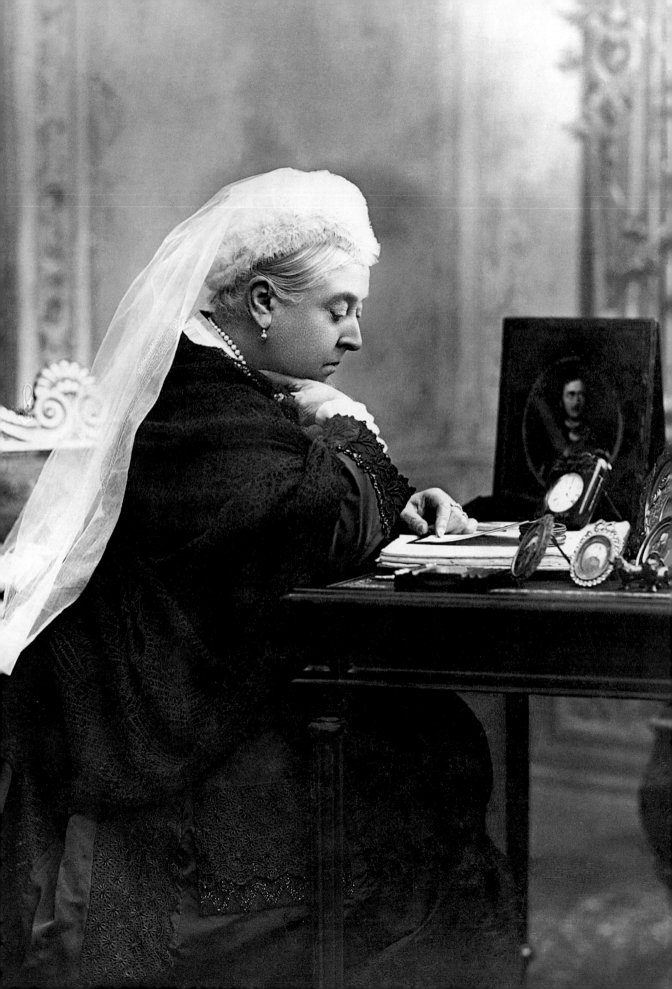

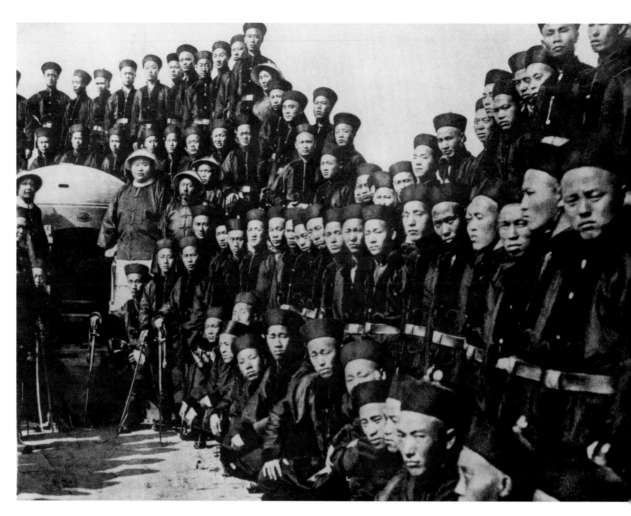

THE Boxer Rising of 1900 was directed against foreign influence in China, and championed the traditional Chinese way of life. There was some support for the insurgents from the Imperial Court and from members of the army, among them cadets at Tientsin (1), but the lead was taken by the Fist-Fighters for Justice and Unity, part of the ancient Buddhist secret society known as the White Lotus. Western powers joined forces to crush the rising: German cavalry occupied the centre of Peking (2).

DER Boxeraufstand von 1900 richtete sich gegen fremde Einflüsse in China und kämpfte für den Erhalt der traditionellen chinesischen Lebensart. Die Aufständischen wurden zum Teil vom kaiserlichen Hof und von Mitgliedern der Armee unterstützt, darunter Kadetten aus Tientsin (1). Die Führung übernahmen aber die »Faust-Rebellen« der Vereinigung für Recht und Eintracht, Teil der alten buddhistischen Geheimgesellschaft, die als Weißer Lotus bekannt war. Die Westmächte entsandten Truppen, um den Aufstand niederzuschlagen: Die deutsche Kavallerie besetzte das Zentrum von Peking (2).

EN 1900, les Boxers se soulevèrent contre l'influence des étrangers en Chine et en faveur du mode de vie traditionnel chinois. Les insurgés bénéficièrent d'un certain soutien auprès des membres de la cour impériale et de l'armée, et parmi celle-ci des cadets de T'ien-tsin (1). Cependant, le soulèvement était dirigé par les « milices combattant à coups de poing pour la justice et l'unité », qui faisaient partie de l'ancienne société secrète bouddhiste connue sous le nom du Lotus blanc. Les puissances occidentales unirent leurs forces pour écraser le soulèvement : la cavalerie allemande occupa le centre de Pékin (2).

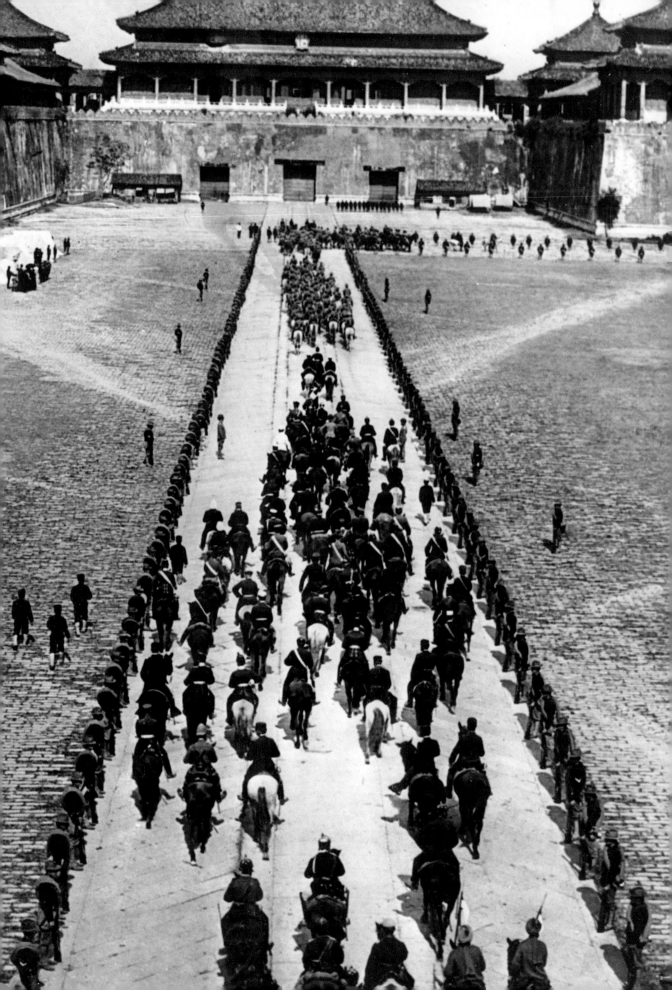

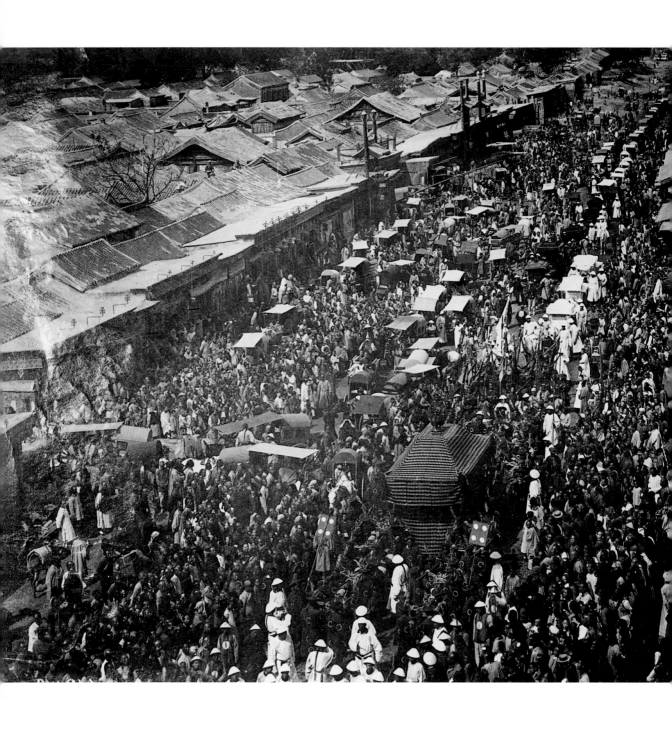

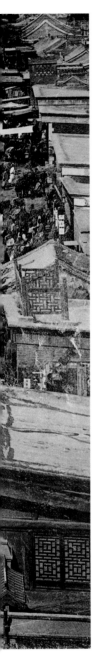

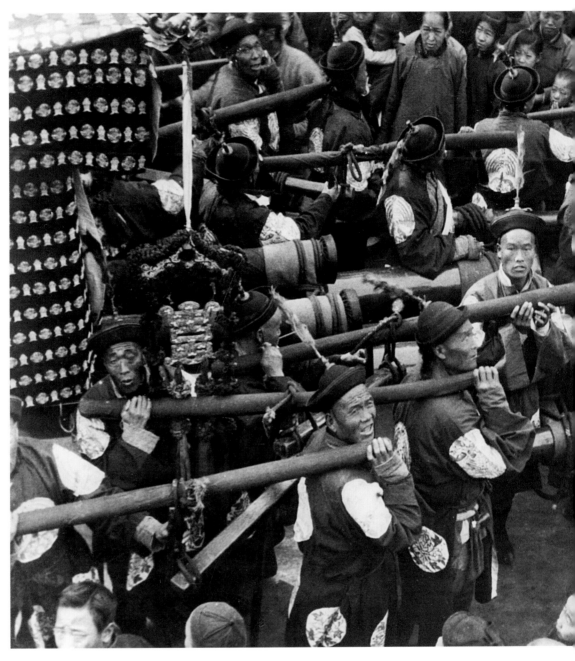

THE funeral of the aged, but feared, Dowager Empress Tz'u-hsi took place in 1908. Born in 1835, she had ruled with a rod of iron since the death of her husband Hsien-feng in 1861. Greedy and unprincipled, she was a powerful figure in a country where women were traditionally subservient, but ultimately she made no positive contribution to China.

DIE alte, aber gefürchtete Kaiserwitwe Tz'u-Hsi wurde 1908 zu Grabe getragen. Sie war 1835 zur Welt gekommen und hatte das Land seit dem Tod ihres Gemahls, Kaiser Hsien-Feng, im Jahre 1861 mit eiserner Hand regiert. Habgierig und skrupellos, war sie eine mächtige Figur in einem Land, in dem Frauen traditionsgemäß unterwürfig waren, aber letztlich tat sie nichts Positives für China.

LES funérailles de l'impératrice douairière Tseu-hi, redoutée en dépit de son grand âge, eurent lieu en 1908. Née en 1835, elle gouvernait d'une main de fer depuis la mort de son époux Hsien-Feng en 1861. Cupide et dénuée de principes, c'était un personnage puissant dans un pays où les femmes étaient traditionnellement dociles et déférentes, mais la période de son règne s'avéra négative pour la Chine.

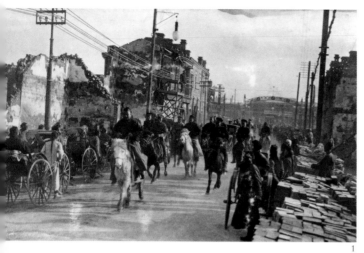

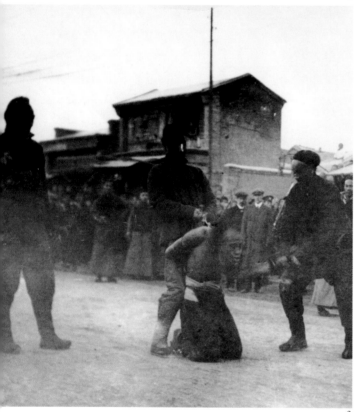

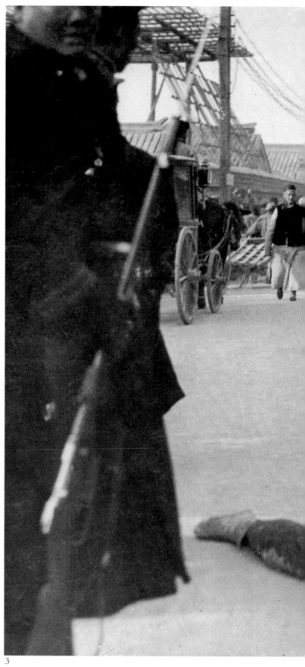

ELEVEN years after the Boxer Rising, a more serious revolution took place in China. Following the death of the Dowager Empress, the Manchu dynasty lost much of its authority in southern China. Imperial officials fled from Tientsin (1) early in 1912, when followers of Sun Yat-sen raised the army of nationalism, republicanism and socialism (a mild form of agrarian reform). Reprisals were swift, and executions summary (2 and 3), but the Empire fell.

ELF Jahre nach dem Boxeraufstand fand in China eine größere Revolution statt. Nach dem Tod der Kaiserwitwe verlor die Mandschu-Dynastie viel von ihrer Autorität in Südchina. Beamte des Hofes flohen zu Beginn des Jahres 1912 aus Tientsin (1), als Anhänger von Sun Yat-Sen eine nationalistische, republikanische und sozialistische Armee aufstellten (eine milde Form der Agrarreform). Vergeltungsmaßnahmen folgten prompt: Hinrichtungen wurden im Schnellverfahren vorgenommen (2, 3), aber das Kaiserreich fiel.

ONZE ans après le soulèvement des Boxers, une révolution autrement plus grave eut lieu en Chine. Dès la mort de l'impératrice douairière, l'autorité de la dynastie mandchoue se mit à faiblir grandement en Chine du Sud. Les officiers impériaux fuirent T'ien-tsin (1) au début de 1912, quand les sympathisants de Sun Yat-Sen levèrent l'armée du Guomintang (pour une forme atténuée de réforme agraire). Les représailles ne se firent pas attendre : on procéda à des exécutions sommaires (2 et 3). L'empire s'effondra tout de même.

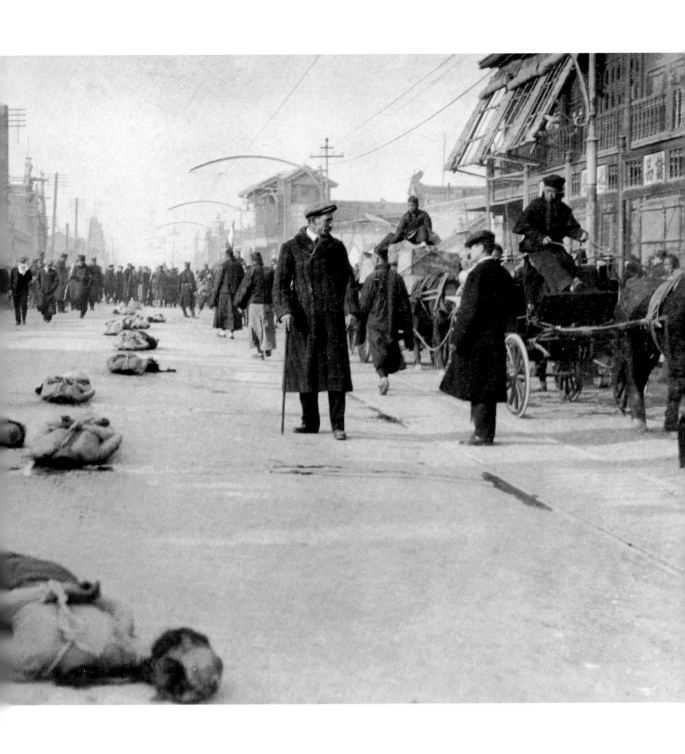

World War I

IN 1909 the Italian futurist F. T. Marinetti wrote: 'We will glorify war – the world's only hygiene – militarism, patriotism, the destructive gesture of freedom-bringers, beautiful ideas worth dying for, and scorn for woman.'

Everyone had wondered when the great conflict was coming, but all professed surprise when it broke out. Many had looked forward to the day: 'In the life of camps and under fire,' wrote one French student, 'we shall experience the supreme expansion of the French force that lies within us.' A cartoon in the British humorous magazine *Punch* in 1909 depicted three cavalry officers discussing the Great War. The caption read:

MAJOR: It's pretty certain we shall have to fight 'em in the next few years.
SUBALTERN: Well, let's hope it comes between the polo and the huntin'.

There were old scores to settle, old rivalries to renew – between France and Germany, Russia and Austria. There were new weapons to be tried, fleets to be matched against each other. A whole new generation of generals needed to be put through their old paces on the battlefield. There were plans, timetables, mobilization orders ready to be put into effect.

But no one wanted it, and no one was prepared to take responsibility for it. Indeed, we shall never know exactly what caused the First World War, for each of the combatants had a different theory. These theories have one thing in common – all nations protested that what they did, they did out of self-defence.

There is, however, general agreement on what precipitated the headlong dash into war. On 28 June 1914, the Archduke Franz-Ferdinand, heir to the great Austro-Hungarian Empire, and his wife visited Sarajevo. They arrived by train and toured the city in an open motor car (1). They were given a mixed reception. Roses were presented, but bombs were thrown. The Archduke decided enough was enough, and headed back to the railway station. But the car took a different route, and made a wrong turning into a cul de sac. The street was narrow. The car stopped to turn round. A Bosnian student named Gavrilo Princip, one of several who had been armed by the Intelligence Bureau of the Serbian General Staff, found himself opposite the man he had sworn to assassinate. He leapt on to the running board of the car and fired his pistol at point-blank range. The Archduke and his wife were both killed.

A month later Austro-Hungary declared war on Serbia. Russia declared war on Austro-Hungary. On 1 August Germany declared war on Russia, and two days later on France. On 4 August Britain declared war on Germany. The cast was almost fully assembled. Turkey joined in 1914, Italy in May 1915. The United States waited until April 1917.

And when that terrible war finally arrived, it was greeted with wild acclaim. 'Now God be thanked who had matched us with His hour, and caught our youth and wakened us from sleeping,' wrote the English poet Rupert Brooke. Enthusiastic crowds gathered in London, Paris, Vienna and on the Unter den Linden in Berlin on the day war was declared. Young men flocked to join the army. Their elders had other priorities – crowds also gathered outside this Berlin bank eager to draw out their savings (overleaf). As in every war, everyone expected to win, and most believed it would all be over by Christmas.

It was not. Four years and three months later the last shots were fired on the Western Front. Millions had been killed, many millions wounded, mutilated, maddened. No army had gained any ground, save a corner of north-eastern France still in German hands. An hour before the Armistice came into force, Canadian troops entered Mons, the site of the first battle of the war in 1914.

Whole empires disappeared, new nations emerged. The German Kaiser abdicated and fled to Holland. The Russian Tsar and most of his family were assassinated. An era ended. Europe was never the same again.

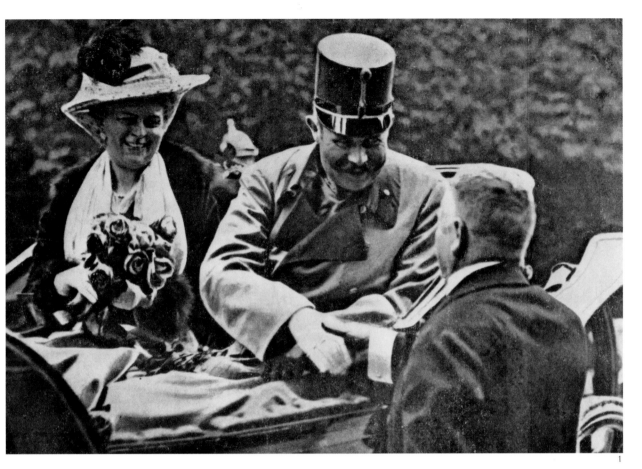

DER italienische Futurist F. T. Marinetti schrieb 1909: »Wir werden den Krieg verherrlichen – diese einzige Hygiene der Welt – Militarismus, Patriotismus, die destruktive Geste der Friedensbringer, wunderschöne Ideen, für die es sich lohnt, zu sterben, und Verachtung für die Frau.«

Jedermann hatte sich gefragt, wann es zum großen Konflikt kommen würde, aber alle waren überrascht, als er dann wirklich ausbrach. Viele hatten sich auf den Tag gefreut: »Beim Leben in Lagern und unter Beschuß«, schrieb ein französischer Student, »werden wir die absolute Ausbreitung der französischen Kraft erfahren, die in uns schlummert.« In einer Karikatur des britischen Satiremagazins *Punch* wurden 1909 drei Kavallerieoffiziere dargestellt, die über den großen Krieg diskutierten. Die Bildunterschrift lautete:

MAJOR: Es ist ziemlich sicher, daß wir in den nächsten paar Jahren gegen sie kämpfen müssen.
UNTERGEBENER: Nun, hoffen wir, daß es zwischen Polo und Jagd staffindet.

Zwischen Frankreich und Deutschland und zwischen Rußland und Österreich gab es alte Rechnungen zu begleichen und alte Rivalitäten zu erneuern. Neue Waffen mußten getestet werden und Flotten mußten gegeneinander antreten. Eine völlig neue Generation von Generälen wurde auf dem Schlachtfeld auf Herz und Nieren geprüft. Es gab Strategien, Zeitpläne und Mobilmachungsbefehle, die jederzeit in die Tat umgesetzt werden konnten.

Aber das wollte niemand, und niemand war bereit, die Verantwortung zu übernehmen. Wir werden die genauen Gründe, die zum Ausbruch des Ersten Weltkriegs führten, wohl niemals erfahren, denn alle Beteiligten hatten eine andere Theorie. Diese Theorien haben jedoch eines gemeinsam: Alle Nationen gaben vor, einzig und allein aus Gründen der Selbstverteidigung gehandelt zu haben.

Über die Ursache des überstürzten Eintritts in den Krieg herrscht jedoch allgemein Einigkeit. Am 28. Juni 1914 besuchten Erzherzog Franz Ferdinand, Thronfolger des großen österreichisch-ungarischen Reiches, und seine Frau Sarajevo. Sie kamen mit dem Zug an und fuhren in einem offenen Automobil durch die Stadt (1). Man bereitete ihnen einen gemischten Empfang. Rosen wurden überreicht, und Bomben wurden geworfen. Der Erzherzog eilte zurück zum Bahnhof.

Aber der Wagen nahm eine andere Route und bog in eine enge Sackgasse ein, wo er anhielt, um zu wenden. Ein bosnischer Student namens Gavrilo Princip, einer der vielen, die vom Geheimdienst des serbischen Generalstabs mit Waffen versorgt worden waren, fand sich plötzlich dem Mann gegenüber, den er geschworen hatte, umzubringen. Er sprang auf das Trittbrett des Autos und feuerte seine Pistole aus kürzester Distanz ab. Der Erzherzog und seine Frau waren sofort tot.

Einen Monat später erklärte Österreich-Ungarn Serbien den Krieg. Rußland erklärte Österreich-Ungarn den Krieg. Am 1. August erklärte Deutschland Rußland den Krieg und zwei Tage später auch Frankreich. Am 4. August erklärte Großbritannien Deutschland den Krieg. Die Teilnehmer waren fast komplett. Die Türkei kam 1914, Italien im Mai 1915 dazu. Die Vereinigten Staaten warteten bis zum April 1917.

Als dieser schreckliche Krieg endlich ausbrach, wurde er stürmisch willkommen geheißen. »Nun danken wir Gott, der uns mit Seiner Stunde gesegnet, unsere Jugend genommen und uns aus dem Schlaf erweckt hat«, schrieb der englische Dichter Rupert Brooke. Am Tag der Kriegserklärung versammelten sich begeisterte Menschenmengen in London, Paris, Wien und Unter den Linden in Berlin. Tausende junger Männer traten freiwillig in die Armee ein. Ihre älteren Zeitgenossen hatten andere Prioritäten; Menschenmengen versammelten sich auch vor dieser Berliner Bank, um ihre Ersparnisse abzuheben (2). Wie in jedem Krieg zeigten sich alle siegessicher, und die meisten glaubten, alles werde bis Weihnachten vorbei sein.

Aber das war nicht der Fall. Vier Jahre und drei Monate später fielen an der Westfront die letzten Schüsse. Millionen von Menschen kamen ums Leben, viele Millionen waren verwundet, verstümmelt oder wahnsinnig geworden. Keine der Armeen hatte Boden gewonnen, außer einer Ecke im Nordosten Frankreichs, die sich noch immer in deutscher Hand befand. Eine Stunde vor Inkrafttreten des Waffenstillstands trafen kanadische Truppen in Mons ein, dem Schauplatz der ersten Schlacht des Krieges im Jahre 1914.

Ganze Reiche verschwanden, und neue Nationen entstanden. Der deutsche Kaiser dankte ab und ging in die Niederlande. Der russische Zar und die meisten seiner Angehörigen wurden ermordet. Eine Ära ging zu Ende. Das alte Europa gehörte der Vergangenheit an.

EN 1909, le futuriste italien F. T. Marinetti écrivait : « Nous glorifierons la guerre, la seule hygiène du monde, le militarisme, le patriotisme, le geste destructeur de ceux qui apportent la paix, les belles idées valant la peine de mourir et le mépris de la femme. »

Chacun s'était demandé quand le grand conflit allait arriver, pourtant tout le monde se montra surpris lorsqu'il éclata. Beaucoup avaient espéré ce jour : « Dans la vie des camps et sous le feu », écrivait un étudiant français, « nous ferons l'expérience de l'expansion suprême de la force française qui est en nous. » Un dessin satirique dans le magazine humoristique *Punch* en 1909 montre trois officiers de cavalerie discutant de la grande guerre. La légende est la suivante :

OFFICIER SUPÉRIEUR : *Il est plus que probable que nous devrons nous battre contre eux dans les toutes prochaines années.*
OFFICIER SUBALTERNE : *Et bien espérons que ça sera entre le polo et la chasse.*

Il y avait de vieux comptes à régler, de vieilles rivalités à réveiller entre la France et l'Allemagne, la Russie et l'Autriche. Il y avait de nouvelles armes à tester, des flottes à comparer sur le terrain. Toute une nouvelle génération de généraux devait faire ses premières armes sur le champ de bataille. Des plans, des calendriers et des ordres de mobilisation attendaient de servir.

Mais nul n'en voulait, et personne n'était prêt à en accepter la responsabilité. En fait nous ne saurons jamais exactement ce qui provoqua la Première Guerre mondiale car chacun des belligérants présenta sa propre théorie. Celles-ci avaient une chose en commun, à savoir que toutes les nations protestèrent avoir agi en situation de légitime défense.

Toutefois l'on s'accorde à dire ce qui précipita cette guerre. Le 28 juin 1914, l'archiduc François-Ferdinand, héritier du grand empire austrohongrois, et son épouse se rendirent à Sarajevo. Ils arrivèrent en train et firent le tour de ville dans une voiture décapotée (1), où on leur fit un accueil mitigé. On leur offrit des roses, mais des grenades furent aussi lancées. L'archiduc en eut assez et reprit le chemin de la gare en sens inverse. Cependant la voiture prit une route différente de celle empruntée à l'arrivée et, après un mauvais tournant, entra dans un cul-de-sac. La rue était étroite et la voiture s'arrêta pour faire demi-tour. Un étudiant bosniaque du nom de Gavrilo Princip, un des nombreux individus armés par les services de renseignements de l'état-major serbe, se retrouva en face de

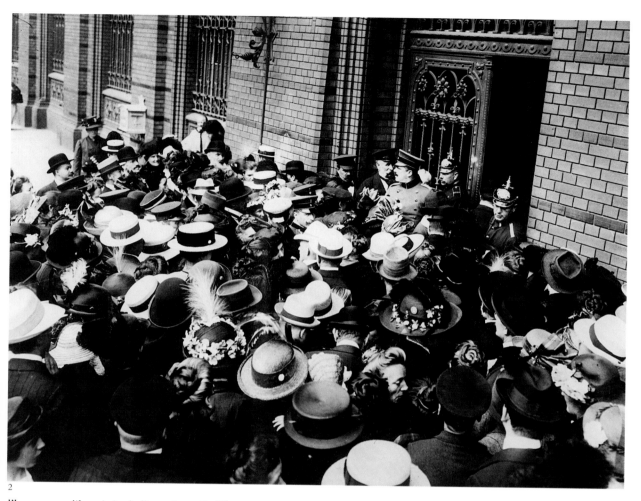

2

l'homme qu'il avait juré d'assassiner. Il s'élança au passage sur le marchepied et tira à bout portant. L'archiduc et son épouse furent tués sur-le-champ.

Un mois plus tard, l'Autriche-Hongrie déclara la guerre à la Serbie. La Russie déclara la guerre à l'Autriche-Hongrie. Le 1er août, l'Allemagne déclara la guerre à la Russie et deux jours plus tard à la France. Le 4 août la Grande-Bretagne déclara la guerre à l'Allemagne. Toutes les forces étaient presque en place. La Turquie entra en guerre en 1914, et l'Italie en mai 1915. Les États-Unis attendirent jusqu'en avril 1917.

Et lorsque cette terrible guerre se déclara enfin, elle fut accueillie par des vivats. « Dieu soit loué de nous avoir confrontés à Son heure, d'avoir pris notre jeunesse et de nous avoir tirés de notre sommeil », écrivait le poète anglais Rupert Brooke. Les foules manifestèrent leur enthousiasme à Londres, Paris, Vienne et sur le Unter den Linden à Berlin le jour où la guerre fut déclarée. Les jeunes gens s'enrôlaient en masse. Leurs aînés avaient d'autres priorités : cette foule impatiente

s'est, elle aussi, assemblée à l'extérieur d'une banque berlinoise pour retirer ses économies (2). Comme c'est le cas dans toutes les guerres, chacun s'attendait à la gagner, et la plupart croyaient que tout serait terminé pour Noël.

Ce ne fut pas le cas. Quatre années et trois mois plus tard, les derniers coups de feu étaient tirés sur le front Ouest. Des millions de personnes avaient été tuées, d'autres blessées, mutilées ou avaient sombré dans la folie. Aucune armée n'avait progressé sur le terrain si ce n'est dans le Nord-Est de la France, demeuré aux mains des Allemands. Une heure avant l'entrée en vigueur de l'armistice, les troupes canadiennes pénétraient dans Mons, qui avait été en 1914 le théâtre de la première bataille.

Des empires entiers avaient disparu, de nouvelles nations virent le jour. L'empereur allemand abdiqua et s'enfuit en Hollande. Le tsar russe et la majorité des membres de sa famille furent assassinés. Une ère prit fin. L'Europe avait changé du tout au tout.

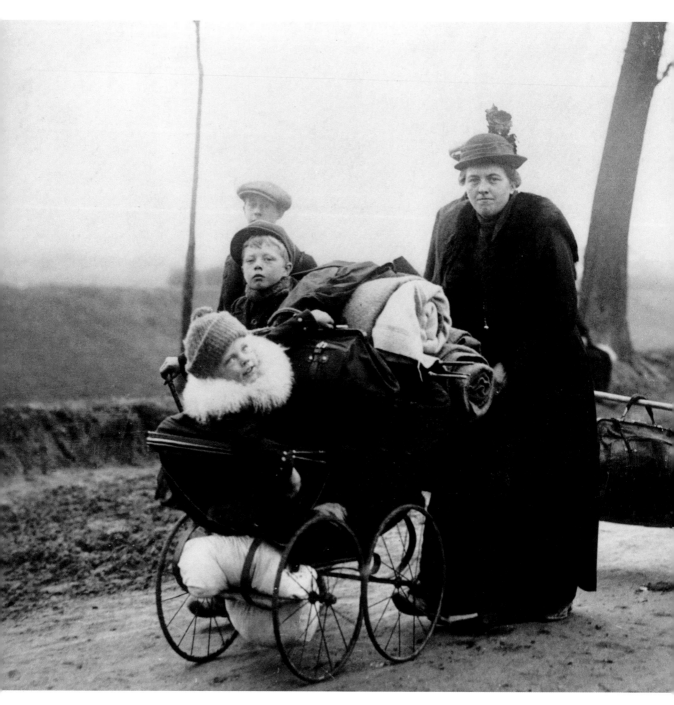

AT first it was a war of movement.
German armies marched westward,
passing through Belgium to strike at Paris.
Belgian refugees trundled their most
precious belongings ahead of the invading
troops (1). In the east, Austrian troops

mobilized, and officers bade farewell to
wives and sweethearts at railheads (2).
Within a few days they, too, were on the
march (3), heading east to meet the vast
Russian army as it headed west. The killing
had begun.

ANFANGS zeichnete sich der Krieg
durch große Mobilität aus. Deutsche
Armeen marschierten westwärts und
durchquerten Belgien, um Paris anzugreifen.
Belgische Flüchtlinge brachten sich vor
den einfallenden Truppen in Sicherheit (1).
Im Osten machten österreichische

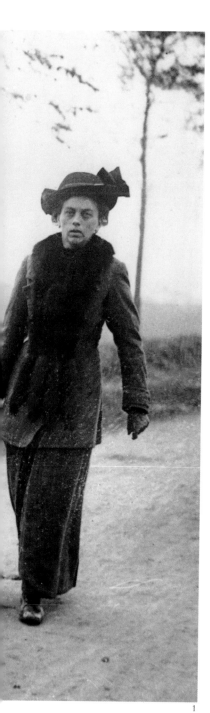

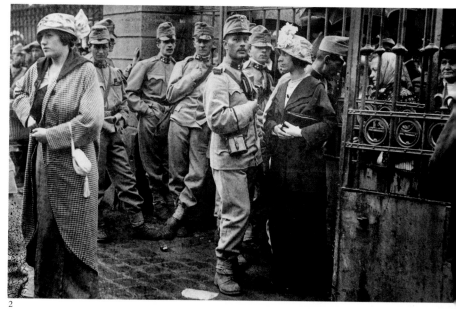

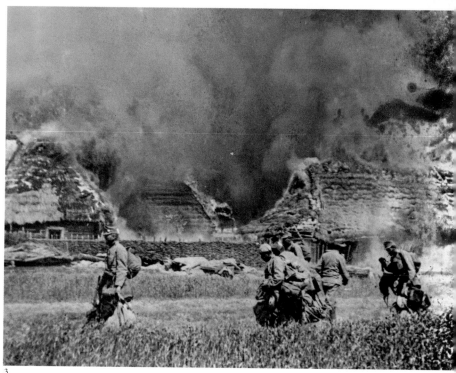

Truppen mobil, und Offiziere sagten an den Bahnhöfen ihren Frauen Lebewohl (2). Innerhalb weniger Tage befanden auch sie sich auf dem Marsch nach Osten (3), um auf die nach Westen vorrückende russische Armee zu treffen. Das Töten hatte begonnen.

Ce fut d'abord une guerre de mouvement. Les armées allemandes marchèrent vers l'ouest, traversant la Belgique pour attaquer Paris. Les réfugiés belges fuirent pour se mettre à l'abri face aux troupes de l'envahisseur (1). À l'est, les troupes autrichiennes étaient mobilisées et les officiers disaient adieu à leurs épouses et petites amies dans les gares de départ menant aux lignes (2). Quelques jours plus tard, ils étaient eux aussi en marche (3) vers l'est pour couper la route à la vaste armée russe en marche vers l'ouest. La tuerie avait commencé.

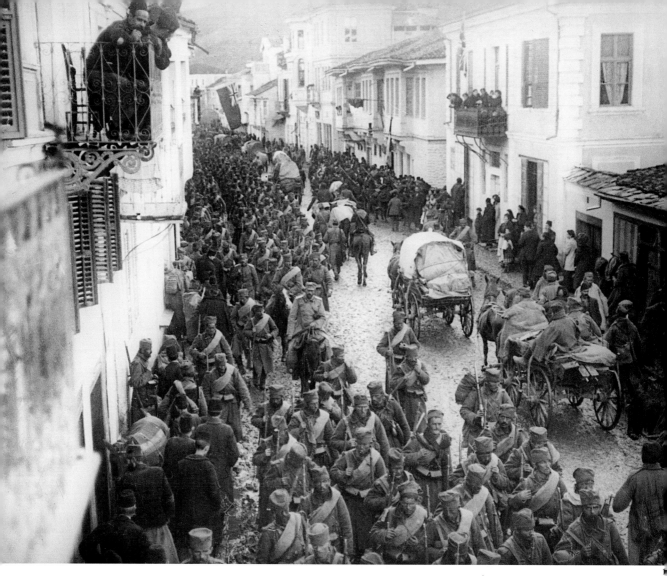

IN the east, the first casualty was Serbia. Austrian and Bulgarian troops inflicted a series of defeats on the Serbian army, which was in retreat by the summer of 1915 (1). As on the Western Front, the war soon became bogged down into one of attrition. Spotter planes, machine guns, artillery and, later, tanks put an end to the old supremacy of cavalry on the battlefield. The Bulgarian trenches on the Macedonian front (2) were every bit as uncomfortable as those in Flanders. After a prolonged spell in them, soldiers could sleep anywhere (3).

IM Osten wurde zuerst Serbien besiegt. Nach einer Reihe vernichtender Niederlagen durch österreichische und bulgarische Truppen trat die serbische Armee im Sommer 1915 den Rückzug an (1). Wie bereits an der Westfront kam es auch hier zu einem Zermürbungskrieg. Aufklärungsflugzeuge, Maschinengewehre, Artillerie und später Panzer machten der alten Vormachtstellung der Kavallerie auf dem Schlachtfeld ein Ende. Die bulgarischen Schützengräben an der mazedonischen Front (2) waren genauso unbequem wie die in Flandern. Nachdem sie viele Stunden darin verbracht hatten, konnten die Soldaten überall schlafen (3).

À l'est, les premières victimes furent serbes. Les troupes autrichiennes et bulgares infligèrent toute une série de défaites à l'armée serbe qui battit en retraite dès l'été 1915 (1). Quant aux opérations sur le front Ouest, elles ne tardèrent pas à s'enliser dans une guerre d'usure. Les avions d'observation, les mitrailleuses, l'artillerie et plus tard les chars d'assaut mirent fin à la vieille suprématie de la cavalerie sur les champs de bataille. Les tranchées bulgares sur le front macédonien (2) étaient tout aussi inconfortables que celles des Flandres. Après un séjour prolongé dans l'une d'entre elles, les soldats pouvaient dormir n'importe où (3).

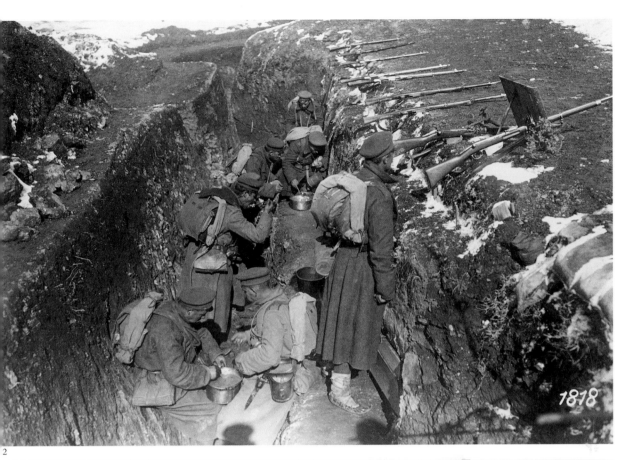

2

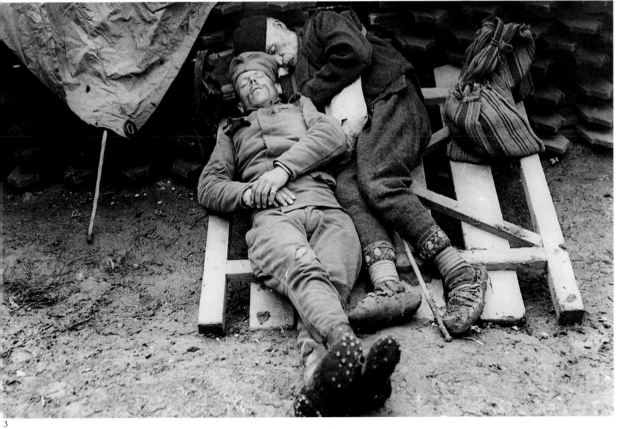

3

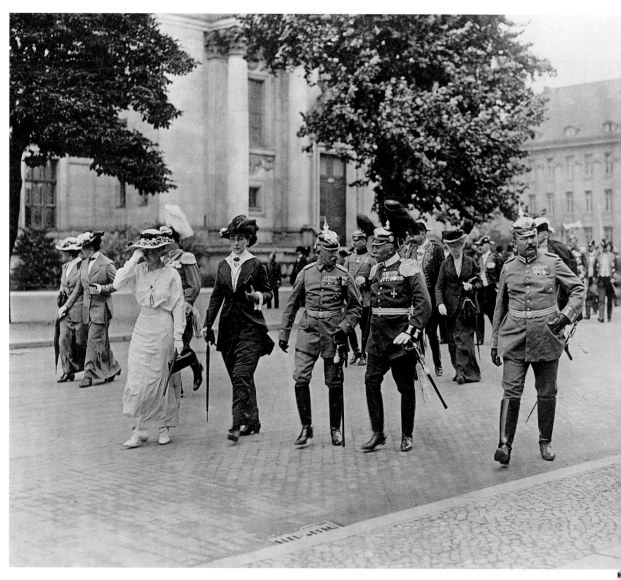

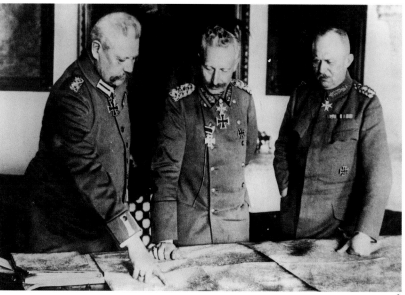

Of all the nations involved, Germany was perhaps the best prepared. God's blessing was sought at the Dom (cathedral) in Berlin (1). Kaiser Wilhelm II (2, centre) had enough sense to leave German strategy in the hands of Generals Ludendorff (2, left) and Hindenburg (2, right). Young Germans were trained in the arts of war, including the maintenance of planes (3). And on the Ruhr, the weapons of war were forged in vast furnaces (4).

Von allen beteiligten Nationen war Deutschland wahrscheinlich am besten vorbereitet. Im Berliner Dom (1) beteten die Menschen um Gottes Segen. Kaiser Wilhelm II. (2, Mitte) war so vernünftig, die deutsche Strategie den Generälen Ludendorff (2, links) und Hindenburg (2, rechts) zu überlassen.

2

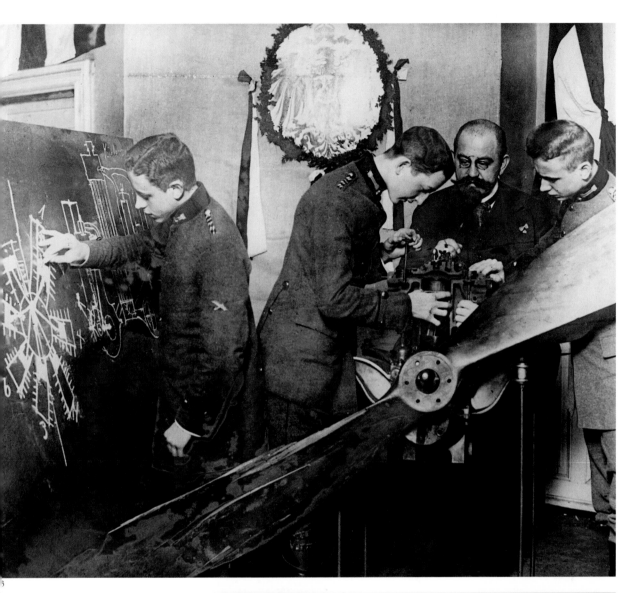

ungen Deutschen wurde die Kriegskunst
beigebracht, einschließlich der Wartung
von Flugzeugen (3). Und an der Ruhr
wurden die Waffen in der Hitze riesiger
Hochöfen geschmiedet (4).

D E toutes les nations, l'Allemagne était
peut-être la mieux préparée. Dieu
fut remercié et prié de bénir les armes allemandes au cours de services spéciaux qui
eurent lieu au Dom (la cathédrale) de
Berlin (1). L'empereur Guillaume II (2, au
centre) eut suffisamment de bon sens pour
laisser les généraux Ludendorff (2, à gauche)
et Hindenburg (2, à droite) conduire la
stratégie allemande. Les jeunes Allemands
furent initiés aux arts de la guerre, notamment à l'entretien des avions (3). Tandis
que dans la Ruhr les armes de guerre
étaient forgées dans la chaleur et la furie
des vastes fourneaux (4).

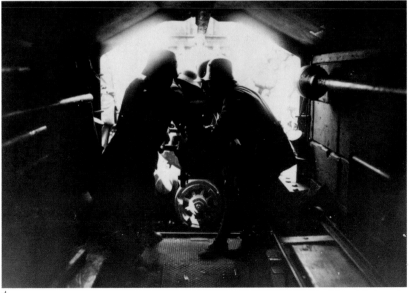

4

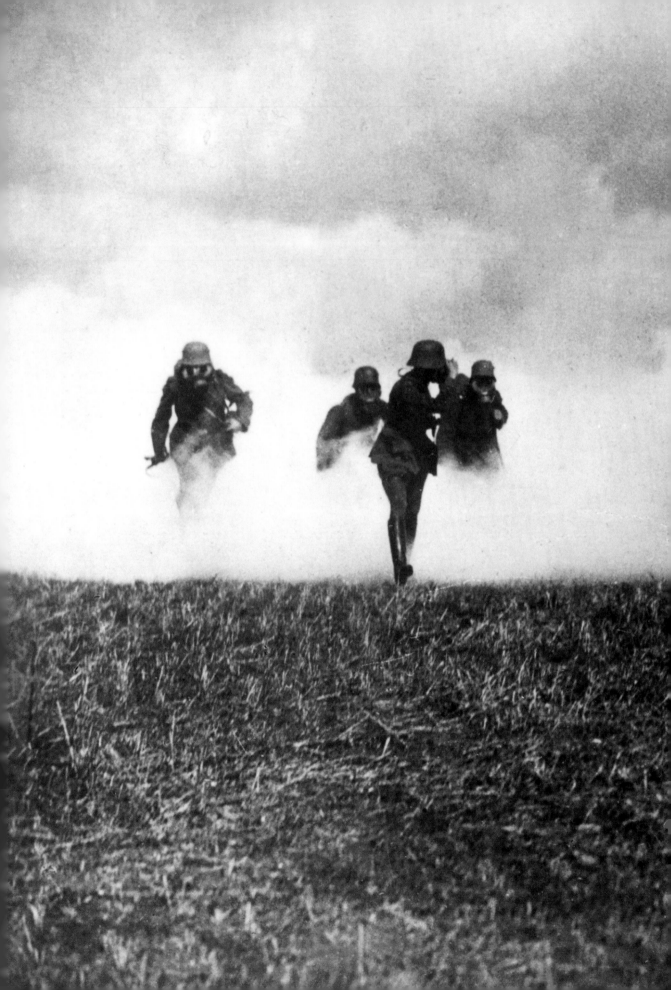

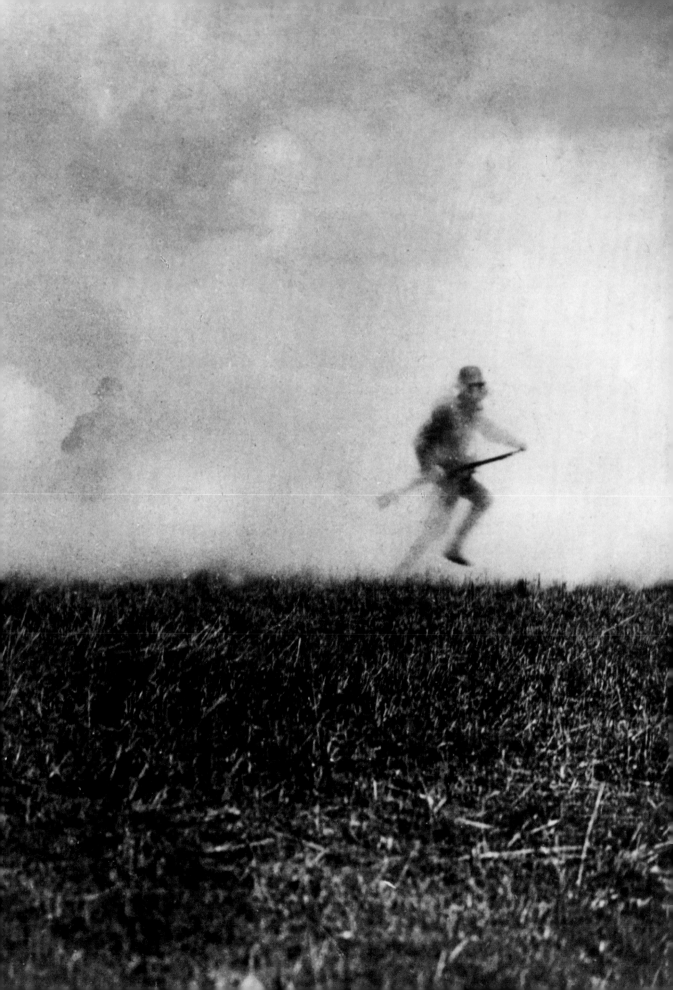

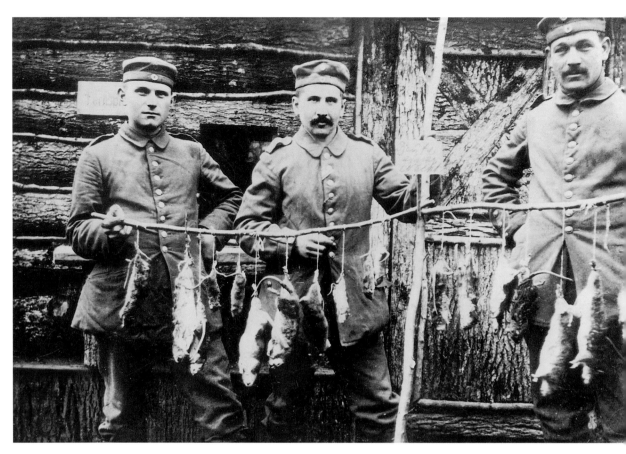

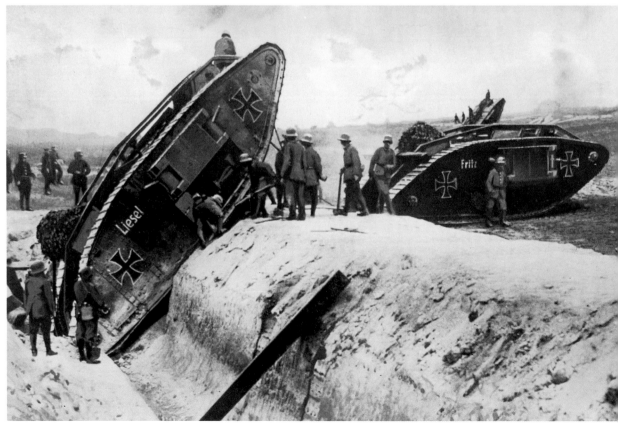

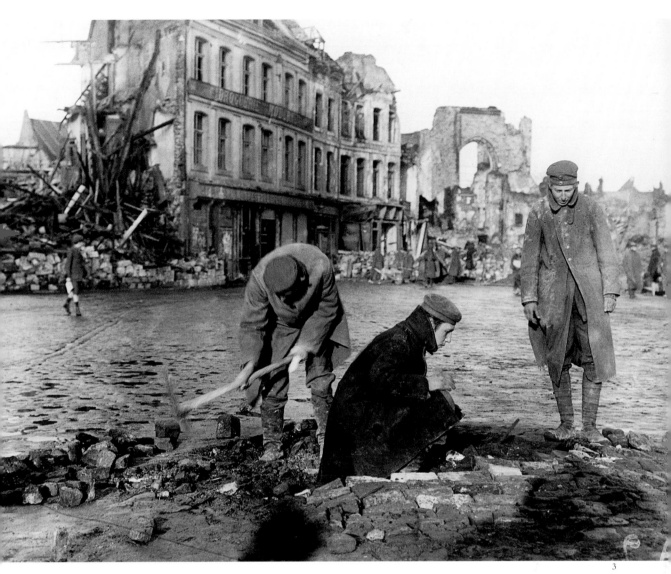

3

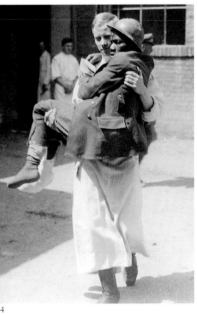

A German officer leads his platoon through a cloud of phosgene gas in an attack on British trenches (previous pages). By March 1916, German troops were stuck in the muddy trenches of Flanders, which crawled with rats. This was just one night's catch (1). A luckier catch were these captured British tanks – the one secret weapon possessed by the British (2). In the ruins of Béthune, German prisoners were made to repair the roads (3). A wounded Senegalese soldier is carried by a German nurse (4).

EIN deutscher Offizier führt in einem Angriff auf britische Schützengräben seine Einheit durch eine Wolke aus dem Giftgas Phosgen (vorherige Seiten). Im März 1916 saßen deutsche Truppen zusammen mit Ratten in den schlammigen Gräben von Flandern fest. Dies war nur der Fang einer Nacht (1). Ein besserer Fang waren diese britischen Panzer, die Geheimwaffe der Briten (2). In den Ruinen von Béthune mußten deutsche Gefangene die Straßen ausbessern (3). Ein verwundeter senegalesischer Soldat wird von einem deutschen Pfleger getragen (4).

UN officier allemand guide son unité à l'assaut des tranchées britanniques à travers un nuage de gaz de phosgène (pages précédentes). Dès mars 1916, les troupes allemandes se retrouvèrent enlisées dans la boue des Flandres, dans des tranchées fourmillant de rats. La prise d'une seule nuit (1). Une prise plus heureuse étant celle de ces chars d'assaut britanniques – l'arme secrète des Britanniques – capturés, repeints et testés sur le terrain (2). Dans les ruines de Béthune, les prisonniers allemands étaient affectés à la réfection des routes (3). Un infirmier allemand emmène un soldat sénégalais blessé à l'infirmerie (4).

4

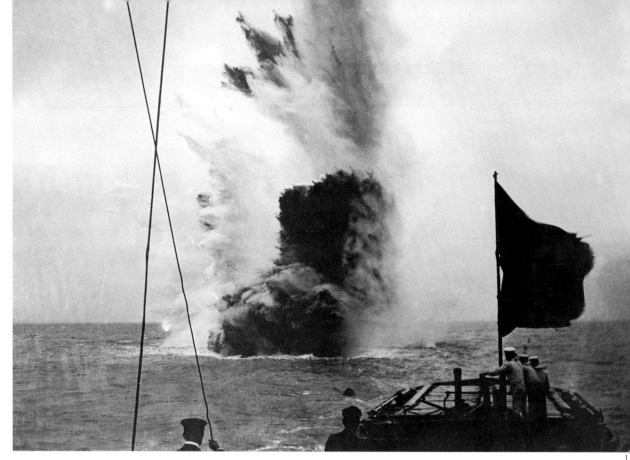

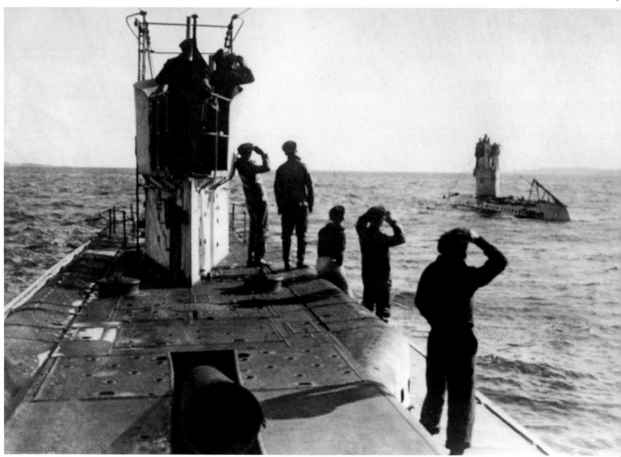

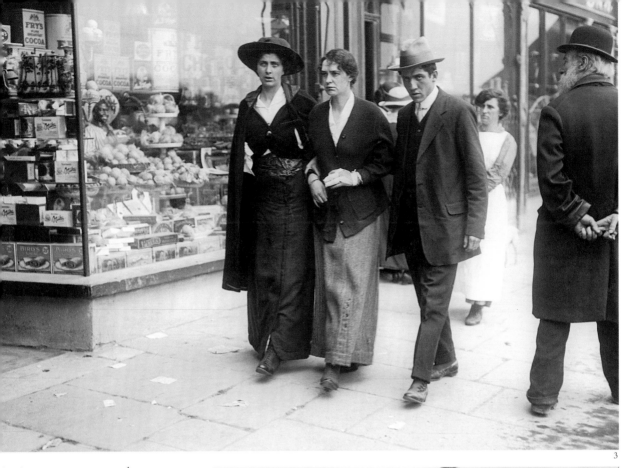

3

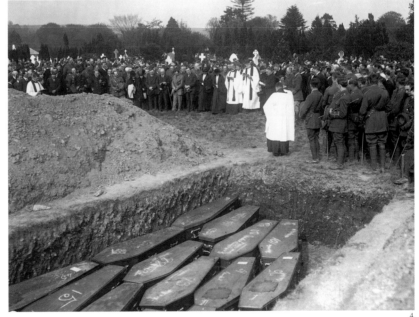

4

THE war at sea was mostly a contest between submarine and merchant ship, or merchant ship and mine (1). Sailors on board the German U35 and U42 must have been relieved when they surfaced within sight of land in the Mediterranean (2). One of the most notorious episodes was the sinking of the *Lusitania*, which was almost certainly carrying war supplies as well as passengers and was thus a legitimate target. Shocked survivors were brought ashore at Queenstown, Ireland (3). Victims were buried in mass graves (4).

DER Seekrieg bestand größtenteils aus Auseinandersetzungen zwischen U-Booten und Handelsschiffen, oder zwischen Handelsschiffen und Minen (1). Matrosen an Bord der deutschen U35 und U42 müssen aufgeatmet haben, als sie beim Auftauchen aus dem Mittelmeer Land sahen (2). Eine der berüchtigtsten Episoden des Krieges war der Untergang der *Lusitania*, ein Passagierschiff, das mit großer Wahrscheinlichkeit auch Kriegsgerät transportierte und daher ein legitimes Angriffsziel war. Die entsetzten Überlebenden wurden bei Queenstown in Irland an Land gebracht (3), die Opfer in Massengräbern beigesetzt (4).

LES batailles navales mettaient principalement aux prises un sous-marin et un navire marchand, ou un navire marchand et une mine (1). Les équipages à bord des U35 et U42 allemands se sont certainement sentis soulagés de refaire surface aux abords de la terre ferme en Méditerranée (2). Un des épisodes notoires de la guerre fut le torpillage du *Lusitania*, un paquebot de ligne transportant très vraisemblablement des fournitures de guerre en même temps que des passagers, et qui en conséquence représentait une cible légitime. Les survivants en état de choc furent ramenés sur la terre ferme à Queenstown en Irlande (3). Les victimes furent enterrées dans des fosses communes (4).

Four years of shot and shell on the Western Front reduced Flanders to a nightmare landscape of water-filled shell holes. Many men went mad. Most shrugged their packs on to their shoulders and did what they were told – crouching in dug-outs while artillery shells rained down, waiting to go 'over the top'. A file of men from the East Yorkshire Regiment, near Frezenburg,
5 September
1917.

Vier Jahre Gewehr- und Granatenfeuer an der Westfront machten Flandern zu einer alptraumhaften Landschaft, durchzogen von wassergefüllten Bombentrichtern und Schlammgruben. Viele Männer wurden verrückt. Die meisten luden sich ihren Tornister auf die Schultern und taten, was

ihnen befohlen wurde; sie krochen durch Schützengräben, während es Granaten regnete, und warteten darauf, »aufzutauchen« und die relative Sicherheit des Lebens unter der Erde zu verlassen, um über Niemandsland ins Mündungsfeuer der Maschinen-

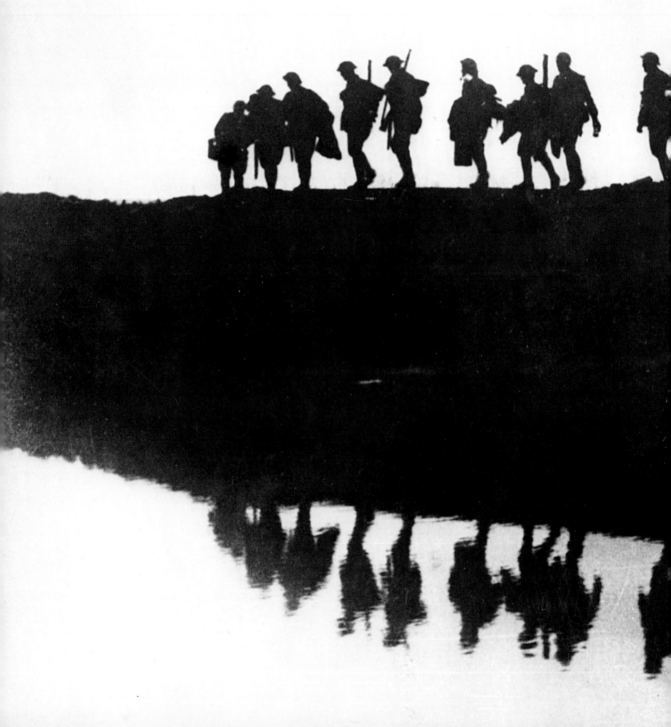

gewehre zu laufen. Wenn sie überlebten, marschierten sie zurück zu den Reserve-gräben, wie diese Männer des East York-shire Regiments am 5. September 1917 in der Nähe von Frezenburg, denn man hatte keinen Boden gewonnen.

QUATRE années de pilonnage du front Ouest transformèrent le paysage des Flandres en un cauchemar de trous d'obus emplis d'eau. Beaucoup perdirent la raison. La plupart réajustant d'un mouvement d'épaule leur paquetage sur leur dos exécu-taient les ordres : ils se terraient dans les tranchées-abris, sous la pluie des obus tirés par l'artillerie, attendant « d'en finir ». S'ils survivaient, ils regagnaient les retranchements de réserve – colonne d'hommes du régiment de l'Est du Yorkshire, près de Frezenbourg le 5 septembre 1917 –, car il était peu pro-bable que le moindre terrain eût été gagné.

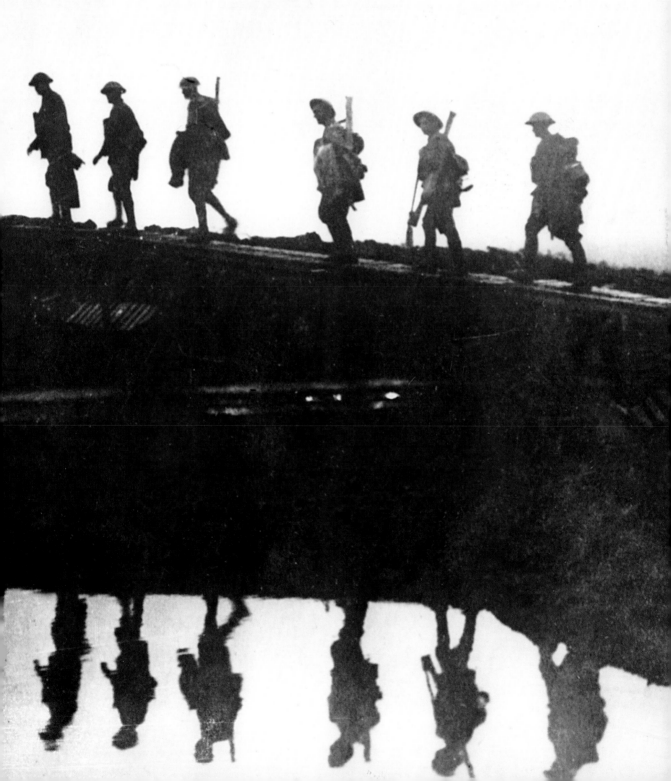

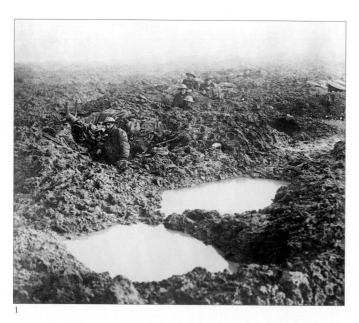

1

SOME died thousands of miles from home – Canadian troops of the 16th Machine Gun Company at Passchendaele, 1917 (1); US 23rd Infantry in action in the Argonne (2). Others died on their native soil, many of the French at Verdun (3).

EINIGE starben Tausende von Kilometern fern der Heimat. Eingegrabene kanadische Soldaten der 16. Machine Gun Company bei Passchendaele Ridge, 1917 (1); die 23. US-Infanterie in Aktion in der Argonne (2). Andere starben auf heimatlichem Boden, viele Franzosen bei Verdun (3).

CERTAINS allaient mourir à des milliers de kilomètres de chez eux : troupes canadiennes de la 16e compagnie de mitrailleurs terrées à Passchendaele Ridge en 1917 (1) ; 23e unité d'infanterie américaine en pleine action dans l'Argonne (2). D'autres mouraient sur le sol natal ; de nombreux Français moururent à Verdun (3).

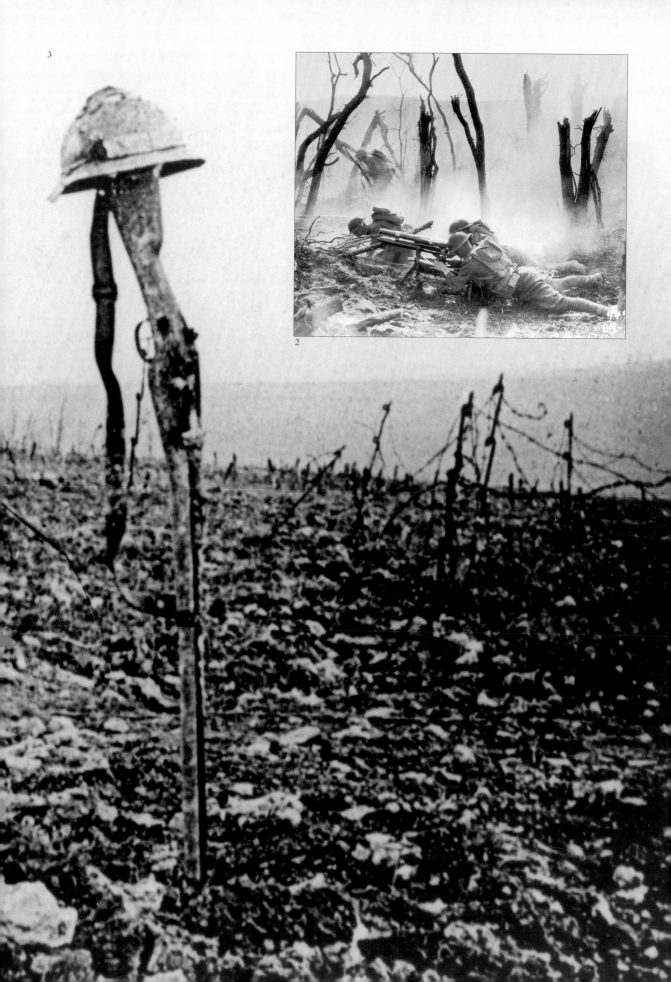

3

2

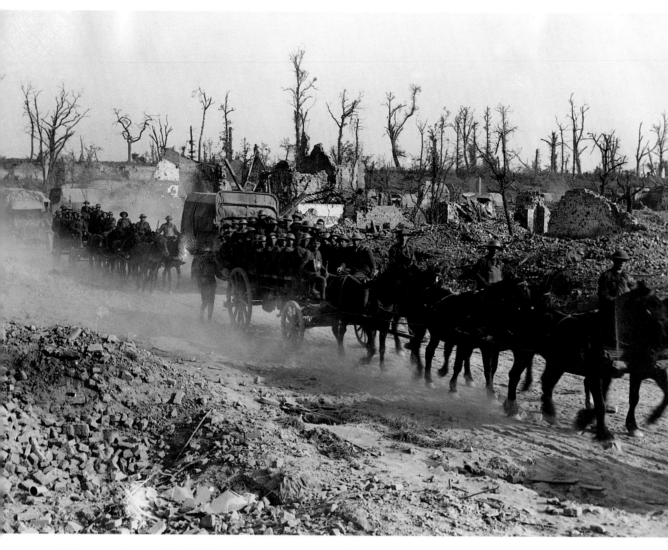

TROOPS often moved up the line towards death (2) and the enemy in greater comfort than they returned – British troops are carried on gun limbers past what was left of Polderhoek during the Battle of Ypres (1).

DER Vormarsch der Truppen auf Tod (2) und Feind war oft bequemer als der Rückzug; britische Truppen fahren auf Geschützwagen an dem vorüber, was von Polderhoek nach der Schlacht von Ypres übriggeblieben war (1).

LES troupes marchaient souvent vers la mort (2) ou l'ennemi dans des conditions plus confortables qu'elles n'en revenaient. Ici des troupes britanniques transportées sur des avant-trains dépassent ce qui reste de Polderhoek au cours de la bataille d'Ypres (1).

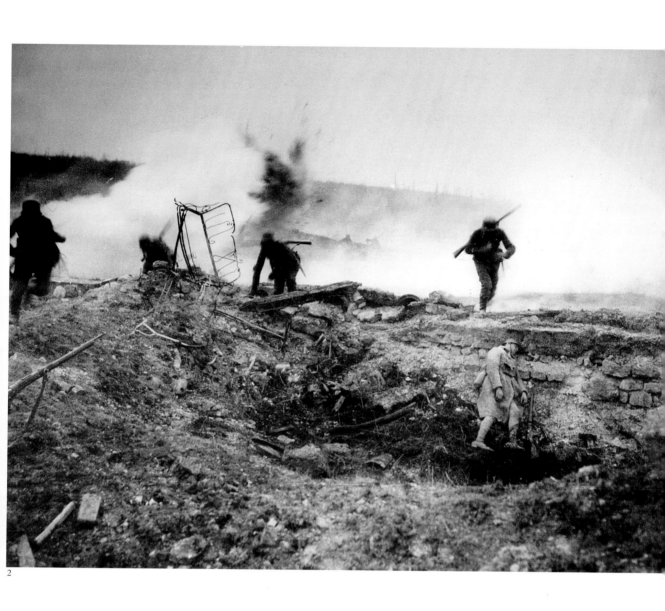

2

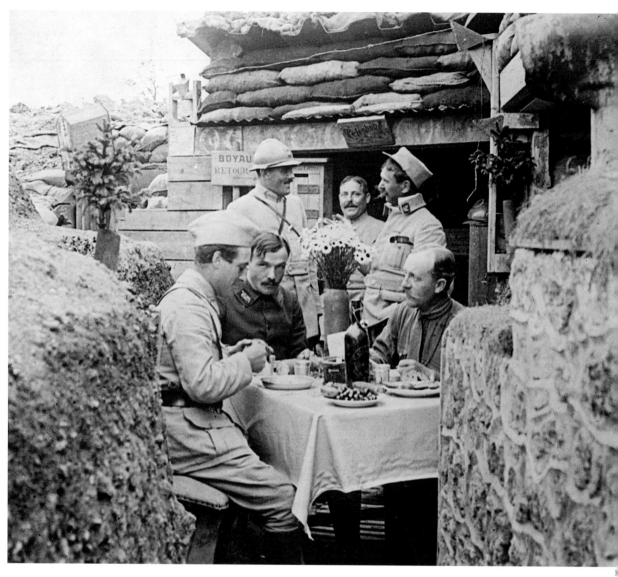

TRENCH life for French officers had a few civilized touches (1). But for others clothing had to be regularly inspected for unwelcome visitors (2).

The following pages show French trenches in 1916 (left) and the devastation wrought by German machine guns in the Italian trenches at Cividale (right).

SOGAR in den Schützengräben gelang es französischen Offizieren, dem Leben etwas Zivilisiertes zu verleihen (1). Andere hingegen mußten die Kleidung regelmäßig nach unwillkommenen Gästen durchsuchen (2).

Die folgenden Seiten zeigen einen französischen Schützengraben im Jahre 1916 (links) und die Verwüstung durch deutsche Maschinengewehre in einem italienischen Schützengraben bei Cividale (rechts).

LES officiers français apportaient quelques touches de civilisation à l'intérieur des tranchées (1). Mais pour les autres l'habillement devait être régulièrement inspecté (2).

Dans les tranchées françaises en 1916 (pages suivantes à gauche), et les ravages des armes allemandes dans les tranchées italiennes à Cividale (pages suivantes à droite).

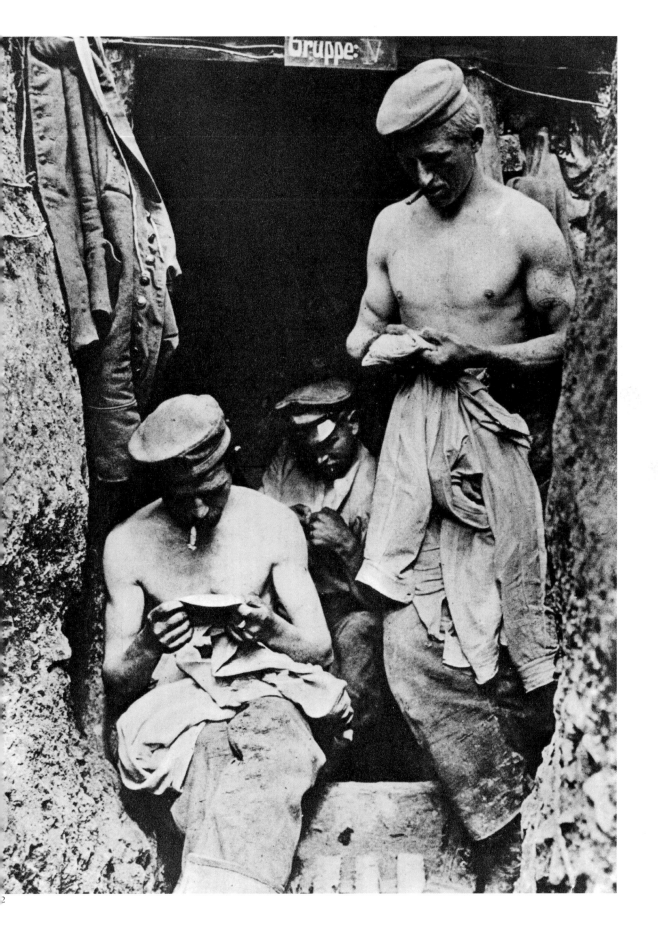

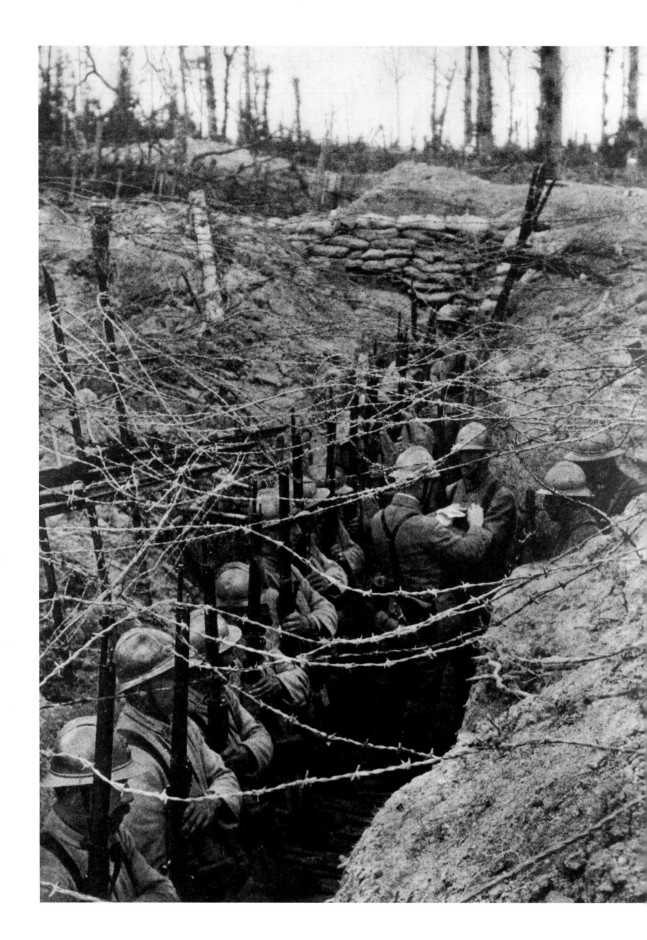

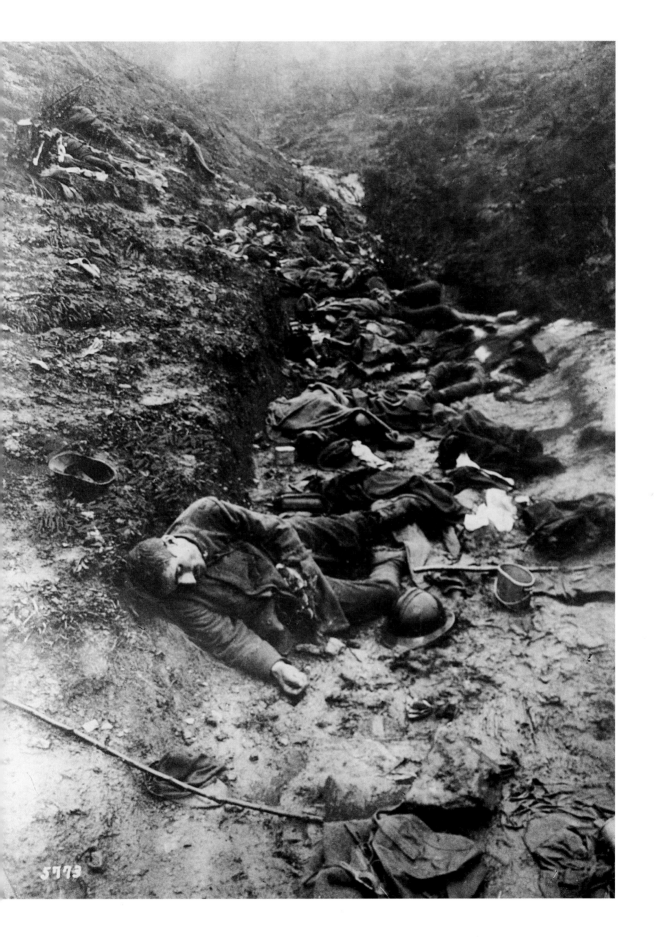

5773

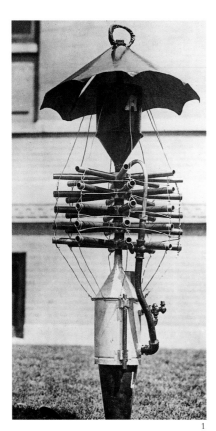

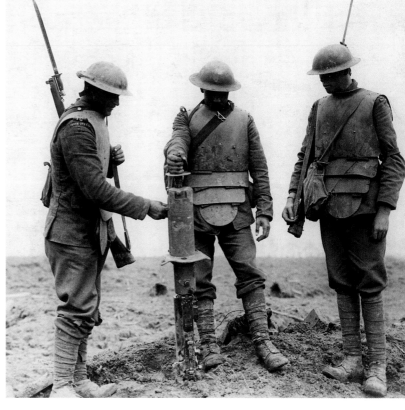

THE ingenuity of the human mind is always well to the fore in any war. One of the problems in the First World War was that of lighting a battlefield after dark. The days of chivalry – when battles ceased at dusk – were long gone, and there was always the fear of a surprise night attack. This flare was fired into the air above No-Man's-Land, where it ignited, and then fluttered slowly down under its parachute, throwing light on the ground below (1). Working parties of British troops wore breastplates of armour to protect them from stray bullets (2). German troops mounted large guns on canal barges in Belgium to transport them more easily to the battlefield (3). Tanks used in the war were descendants of this early caterpillar-track farm machine of 1902, first used in eastern England (4).

DER menschliche Geist vollbringt in jedem Krieg Höchstleistungen. Eines der Probleme im Ersten Weltkrieg bestand darin, ein Schlachtfeld nach Einbruch der Dunkelheit zu beleuchten. Die Tage der Ritter im Mittelalter, als Schlachten in der Abenddämmerung endeten, lagen lange zurück, und es herrschte immer die Angst vor einem nächtlichen Überraschungs-angriff. Diese Leuchtrakete wurde über Niemandsland in die Luft geschossen, wo sie sich entzündete, und dann langsam an einem Fallschirm herabsank und dabei das darunterliegende Gebiet beleuchtete (1). Arbeitstrupps der britischen Armee trugen gepanzerte Brustplatten, um sich vor verirrten Kugeln zu schützen (2). In Belgien luden deutsche Soldaten große Kanonen auf Schleppkähne, um sie einfacher zum Schlachtfeld transportieren zu können (3). Die im Krieg eingesetzten Panzer waren Abkömmlinge dieses landwirtschaftlichen Raupenfahrzeugs aus dem Jahre 1902, das zuerst auf Farmen im Osten Englands verwendet wurde (4).

LES hommes se montrent toujours ingénieux en temps de guerre. Un des problèmes qui se posaient pendant la Première Guerre mondiale était l'éclairage des champs de bataille après la tombée de la nuit. Les temps de la chevalerie où les batailles cessaient au crépuscule étaient révolus depuis longtemps. Chaque camp vivait dans la crainte continuelle de faire le frais d'une attaque-surprise en pleine nuit. Cette fusée éclairante, suspendue à son parachute, tirée au-dessus du no man's land s'est enflammée et redescend en tourbil-lonnant, éclairant le sol au-dessous (1). Les soldats britanniques travaillaient en plastron de cuirasse pour se protéger des balles per-dues (2). En Belgique, les troupes allemandes fixaient sur des barges d'énormes canons qu'elles transportaient ainsi plus facilement jusqu'au champ de bataille par la voie des canaux (3). Les chars d'assaut utilisés pendant la guerre descendaient de cette première machine agricole sur chenilles de 1902, qui fut pour la première fois utilisée dans les fermes de l'est de l'Angleterre (4).

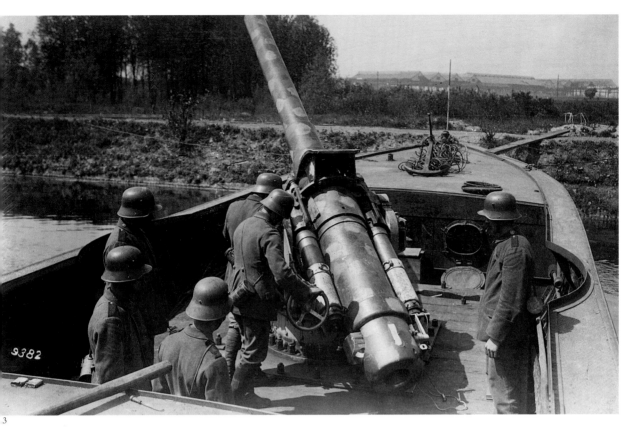

3

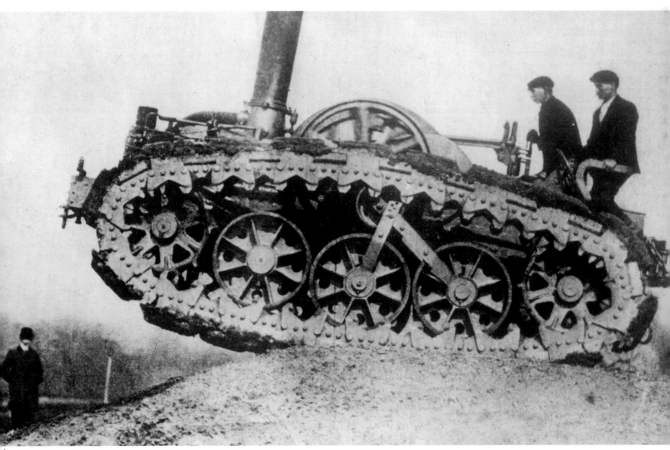

4

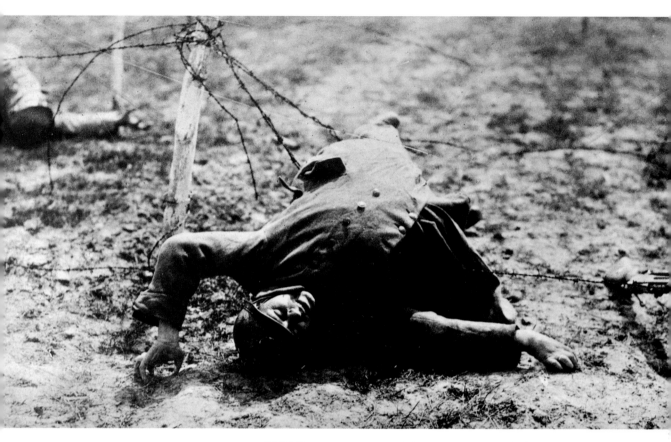

THE poem *The Last Laugh* by Wilfred Owen, provides a poignant commentary on the horror of war as seen in these pictures (1 and 2).

'O Jesus Christ! I'm hit,' he said; and died.
Whether he vainly cursed, or prayed indeed,
The Bullets chirped – In vain! vain! vain!
Machine guns chuckled, – Tut-tut! Tut-tut!
And the Big Gun guffawed.

It was a war of words as well as weapons, and a war of information. All armies feared and loathed spies, and punishment was swift and terrible for anyone convicted, rightly or wrongly, of espionage. The caption on the post reads: 'Spy – traitor to his country' (3). The graffiti painted on this French gate marks the house as the home of a traitor (4) – what happened to the occupant, we can only guess.

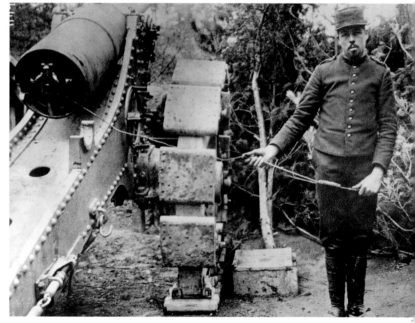

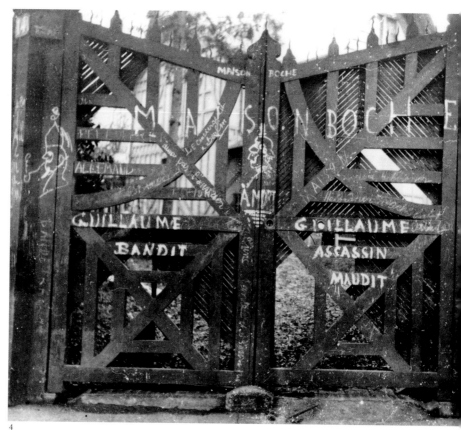

4

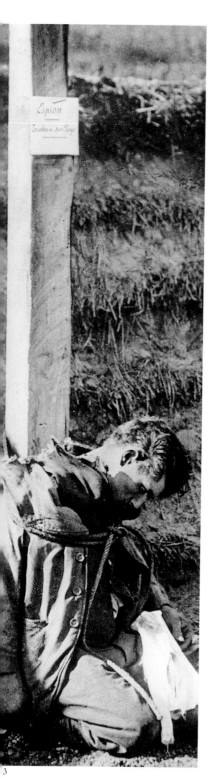

3

DAS Gedicht *The Last Laugh* von Wilfred Owen kommentiert ergreifend den Schrecken des Krieges auf diesen Bildern (1 und 2).

»Oh, mein Gott! Ich bin getroffen«, sagte er und starb.
Ob er vergeblich fluchte, oder tatsächlich betete,
Die Kugeln zwitscherten – umsonst, umsonst!
Maschinengewehre kicherten – Tut-tut! Tut-tut!
Und die große Kanone lachte schallend.

Es war ein Krieg der Worte, der Waffen und der Informationen. Alle Armeen fürchteten und haßten die Spione, und jeden, der zu Recht oder zu Unrecht der Spionage angeklagt wurde, ereilte eine schnelle und schreckliche Strafe. Auf der Karte an diesem Pfahl ist zu lesen: »Spion, Vaterlandsverräter« (3). Die Aufschriften auf diesem französischen Tor brandmarken das Haus als das eines Verräters (4) – was mit seinem Bewohner geschah, läßt sich nur vermuten.

LE poème *The Last Laugh* de Wilfred Owen est un commentaire poignant sur l'horreur de la guerre telle qu'elle apparaît dans ces images (1 et 2).

« Ô Doux Jésus ! Je suis touché », dit-il, et il mourut.
Qu'il maudît en vain ou qu'il criât, ou même qu'il priât,
Les balles chantaient : en vain ! vain ! vain !
Les mitrailleuses gloussaient : Tut-Tut ! Tut-Tut !
Et le gros canon s'esclaffait.

Ce fut une guerre des mots autant que des armes, et une guerre de renseignements. Toutes les armées redoutaient et exécraient les espions : le châtiment de toute personne reconnue coupable d'espionnage, à tort ou à raison, était prompt et terrible. L'inscription sur le poteau est la suivante : « Espion, traître à son pays » (3). Les graffiti peints sur ce portail en France signalent qu'un traître vit dans cette maison (4) ; nous devinons sans peine le sort réservé à son occupant.

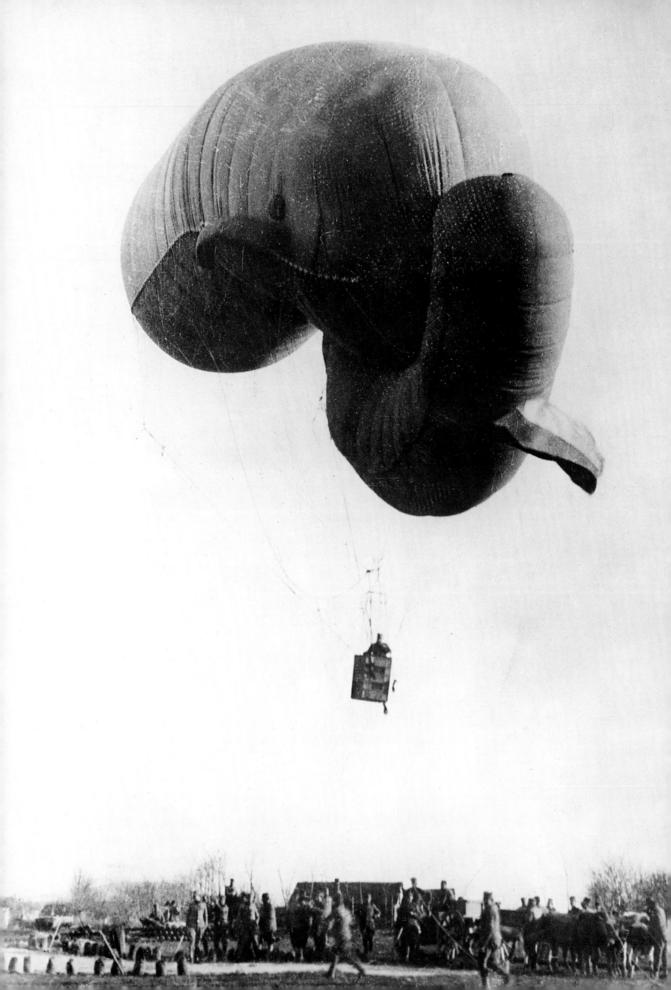

BALLOONS had one main function in the war – as observation posts. Some were of bizarre design, as this Serbian military balloon (1). Maybe the enemy died of laughter. Life in an observation balloon was uncomfortable and exposed. There was always the danger that it would drift within range of enemy guns – this German observer leaps from his gondola after his balloon has been hit (2 – note the primitive parachute). It took a whole team of mechanics to help inflate a balloon with gas (3). Zeppelins had a different use. They were powerful enough to carry a load of bombs from Germany to London, and produce panic in the streets. Not all returned, however. Crowds turned out to see the wreckage of a Zeppelin that crashed at Potters Bar on 2 October 1916 (4).

BALLONS dienten im Krieg hauptsächlich als Beobachtungsposten. Einige hatten eine bizarre Form, beispielsweise dieser serbische Militärballon (1). Vielleicht lachte sich der Feind ja tot. Das Leben in einem Observationsballon war unbequem und gefährlich. Es konnte immer passieren, daß der Ballon in die Schußlinie des Feindes abdriftete; dieser deutsche Späher springt aus der Gondel, nachdem sein Ballon getroffen wurde (2, man beachte den primitiven Fallschirm). Es bedurfte eines ganzen Teams von Mechanikern, um den Ballon mit Gas aufzupumpen (3). Zeppeline wurden für andere Zwecke eingesetzt. Sie waren stark genug, um eine Ladung Bomben von Deutschland nach London zu befördern und für Panik in den Straßen zu sorgen. Aber nicht alle kamen zurück. Die Menschen liefen zusammen, um das Wrack eines Zeppelins zu sehen, der am 2. Oktober 1916 bei Potters Bar abgestürzt war (4).

LES ballons avaient une tâche essentielle pendant la guerre : servir de postes d'observation. Certains étaient de forme bizarre, tel ce ballon militaire serbe (1). L'ennemi en mourut peut-être de rire. La vie dans un ballon d'observation était inconfortable et périlleuse. Il pouvait toujours dériver à portée de tir des canons ennemis : cet observateur allemand saute hors de sa nacelle après que son ballon a été touché (2, on notera le parachute primitif). Il fallait toute une équipe de mécaniciens pour gonfler un ballon au gaz (3). Les zeppelins servaient à autre chose. Leur puissance leur permettait de transporter un chargement de bombes de puis l'Allemagne jusqu'à Londres et de semer ainsi la panique dans les rues. Cependant tous ne revenaient pas. Attroupement autour des débris d'un zeppelin qui s'écrasa à Potters Bar le 2 octobre 1916 (4).

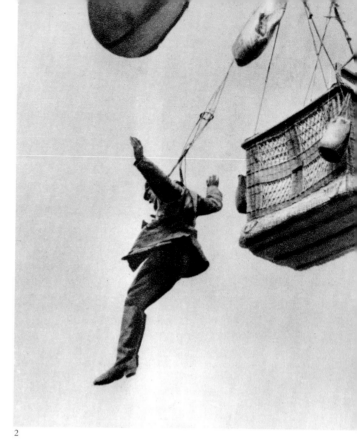

2

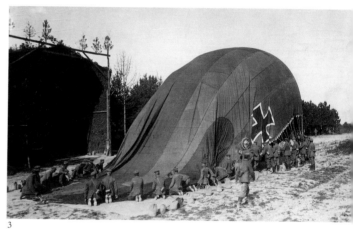

3

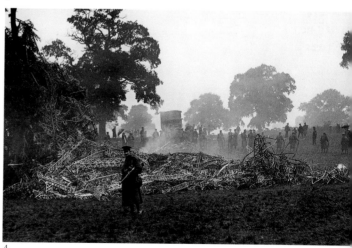

4

SUCH glamour as there was in the First World War came from the war in the air. A new hero was born – the 'air-ace'. Their names were not always household words, for those in command did what they could to keep the names of Ball, Richthofen, and Roland Garros out of the newspapers. There were also those who regarded the single-combat duels between these brave young men as reminiscent of the days of chivalry – though one British airman spat out, on hearing that Richthofen had been shot down and killed: 'I hope he roasted all the way down'. But to the earthbound, the courage and audacity of the men who flew the fragile biplanes – such as this Vickers bomber (2) – became legendary. And they looked so good in propaganda films (1).

BESONDERS die Auseinandersetzungen in der Luft verliehen dem Ersten Weltkrieg seine Brisanz. Ein neuer Heldentypus wurde geboren, das »Luft-As«. Die Namen Ball, Richthofen und Roland Garros waren jedoch nicht immer ein Begriff, denn die Befehlshabenden taten alles, um sie aus den Zeitungen herauszuhalten. Manch einer fühlte sich durch die Luftduelle dieser tapferen jungen Männer an die Tage des Rittertums erinnert, obwohl ein britischer Pilot ausspuckte, als er hörte, daß Richthofen abgeschossen worden war: »Ich hoffe, er hat den ganzen Weg nach unten geschmort.« Aber bei den Menschen am Boden wurden diese mutigen und verwegenen Männer, die fragile Doppeldecker wie den Vickers-Bomber (2) flogen, zu Legenden. Und sie sahen so gut aus in den Propagandafilmen (1).

TOUT l'éclat qu'il put y avoir dans la Première Guerre mondiale doit être attribué à la guerre des airs. Un nouveau héros était né : l'« as des airs ». Leurs noms n'étaient pas toujours familiers à cause de ceux qui, tout en haut, faisaient de leur mieux pour empêcher les noms de Ball, Richthofen et Roland Garros de figurer dans les journaux. D'autres pensaient que les duels que se livraient ces téméraires jeunes gens remémoraient l'époque des chevaliers. Cela n'empêcha pas un aviateur britannique de commenter avec aigreur la nouvelle de la mort de Richthofen en combat aérien par : « J'espère qu'il aura rôti jusqu'au sol. » Quoi qu'il en soit, pour ceux qui restaient sur terre, le courage et l'audace de ces hommes aux commandes des fragiles biplans, comme ce bombardier Vickers (2), devinrent légendaires. Et puis ils avaient si belle allure dans les films de propagande (1).

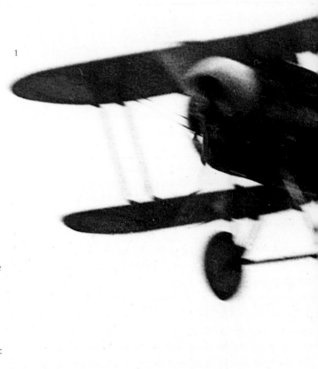

1

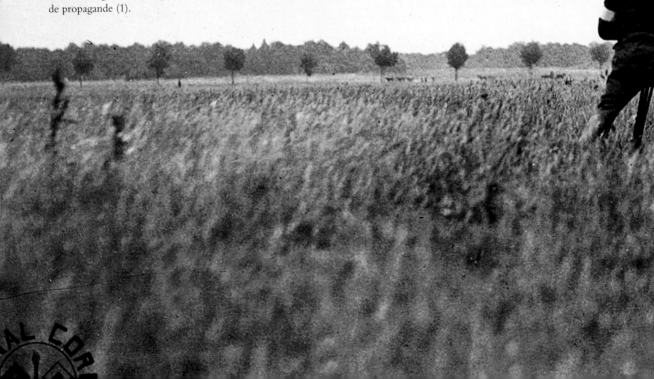

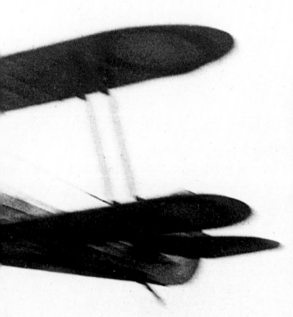

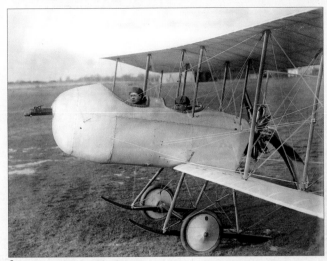

2

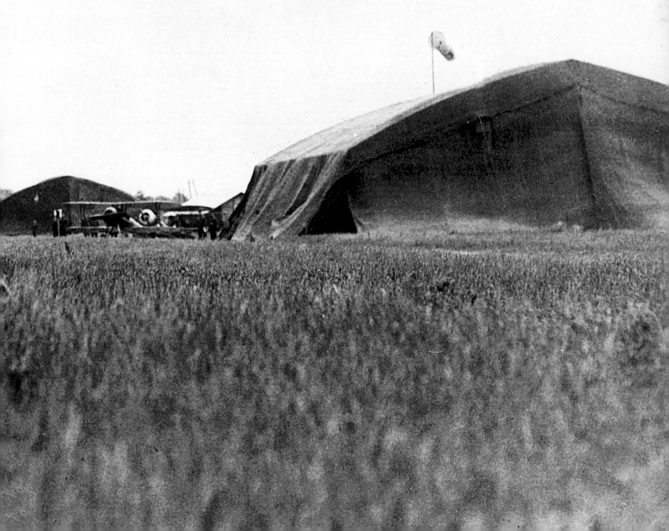

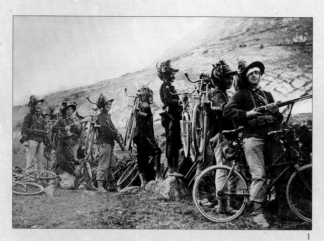

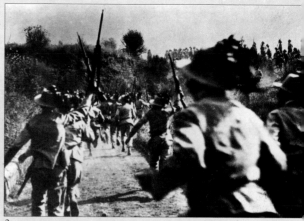

1   2

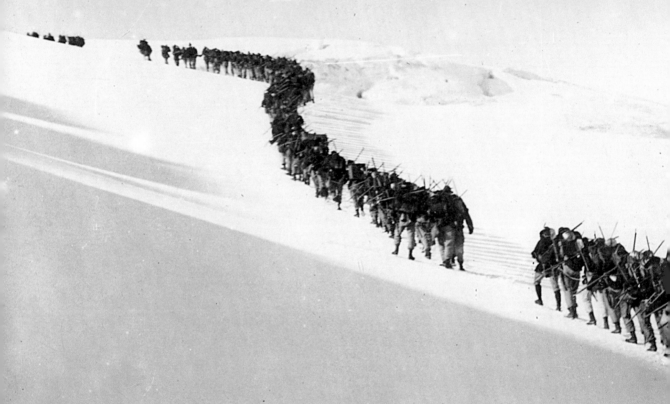

ITALY entered the war on the side of France and Britain on 23 May 1915. For two years there was stalemate between Italian and Austrian troops. The Bersaglieri, or rifle battalions, were clearly ready for a war of movement, whether on bicycle (1) or foot (2). An Italian column trudges slowly up the Rurtor Glacier (3). Eventually, the stalemate was broken by a massive victory for German and Austrian troops at Caporetto in October 1917.

ITALIEN verbündete sich mit Frankreich und Großbritannien und trat am 23. Mai 1915 in den Krieg ein. Zwei Jahre lang herrschte eine Pattsituation zwischen der italienischen und der österreichischen Armee, obwohl die italienischen Bersaglieri oder Scharfschützentruppen eindeutig zu einem mobilen Krieg bereit waren, sei es auf dem Fahrrad (1) oder zu Fuß (2). Eine italienische Kolonne zieht langsam den Rurtor-Gletscher hinauf (3). Im Oktober 1917 wurde die Pattsituation durch einen entscheidenden Sieg deutscher und öster-reichischer Truppen bei Caporetto beendet

L'ITALIE entra en guerre aux côtés de la France et de la Grande-Bretagne le 23 mai 1915. Deux années durant, les armées italiennes et autrichiennes restèrent bloquées face à face le long de l'Isanzo, bien que les bersagliers italiens fussent manifestement prêts pour une guerre de mouvement à bicyclette (1) ou à pied (2). Une colonne italienne escalade ici pénible-ment le glacier de Rurtor (3). Finalement la victoire massive remportée par les troupes allemandes et autrichiennes à Caporetto en octobre 1917 mit fin à la confrontation.

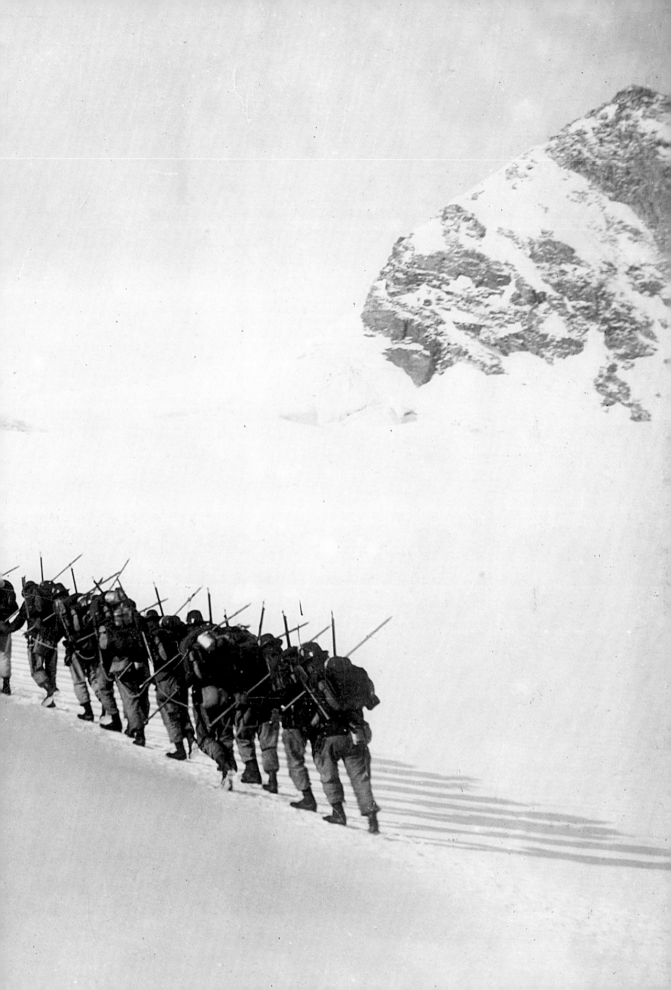

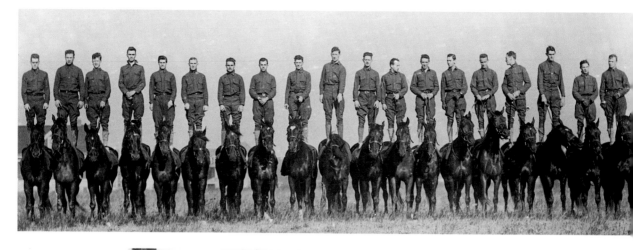

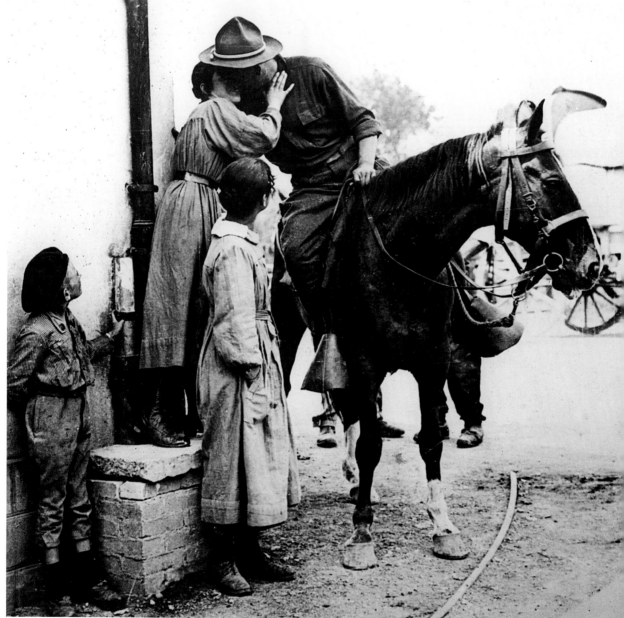

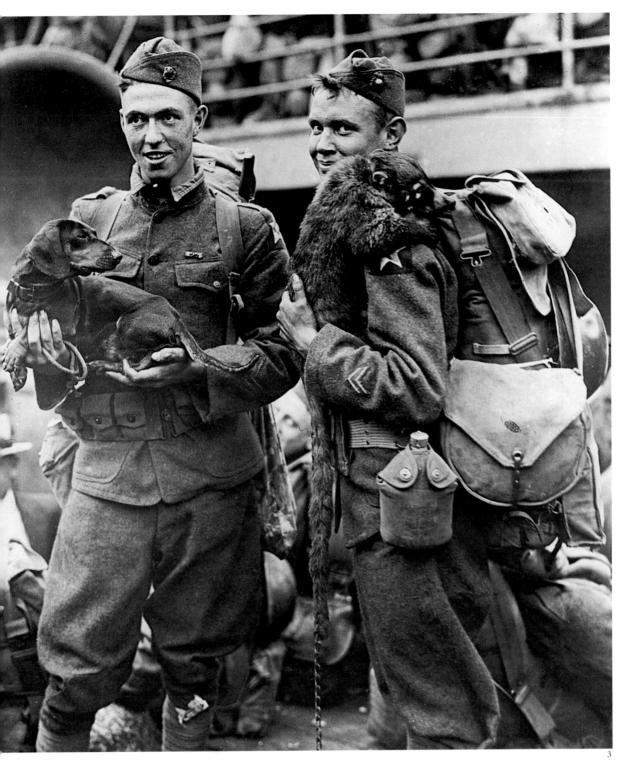

3

LAST into the war were the Americans, who did everything with style and panache, whether fraternizing (2), or displaying cavalry skills of limited use in modern warfare (1). They were young and brave and tough, if sentimentally attached to their pets (3).

ALS letzte traten die Amerikaner in den Krieg ein, und sie taten alles mit Stil und Verve, sei es die Verbrüderung mit den Einheimischen (2) oder die Vorführung von Kavallerie-Kunststücken, für die in moderner Kriegsführung allerdings wenig Bedarf herrschte (1). Sie waren jung, tapfer und hart, mit einem Herz für Tiere (3).

LES derniers à entrer en guerre furent les Américains qui firent tout avec style et panache, qu'il s'agît de fraterniser (2) ou de déployer des qualités de cavalier sans grande utilité dans une guerre moderne (1). Ils étaient jeunes et courageux en dépit de l'attachement qu'ils portaient à leurs animaux familiers (3).

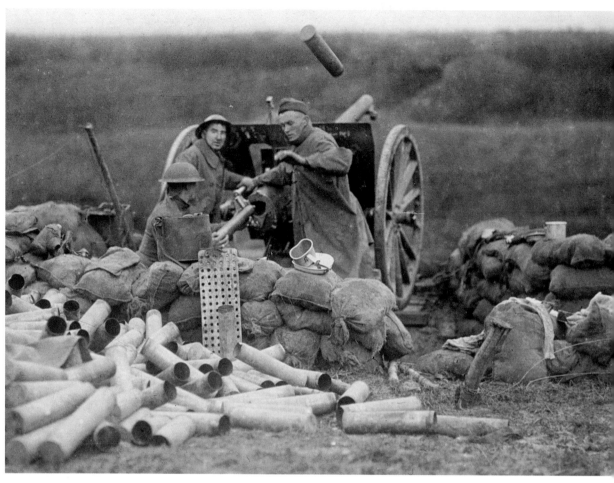

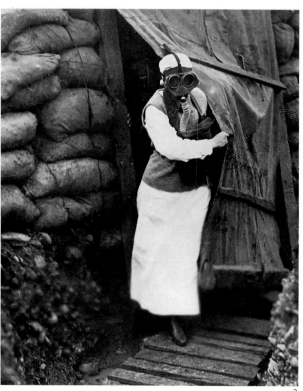

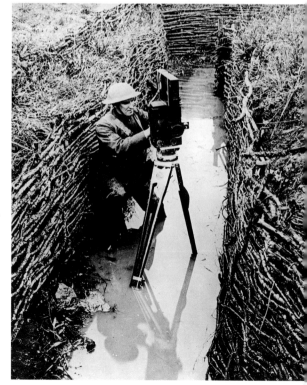

2

THOUGH late into the war, the Americans played a vital role in communiations: a semaphore unit of the U.S. Army (4). Sir Douglas Haig, Commander-in-Chief of the British troops, prayed: 'Give me victory, O Lord, before the Americans arrive', but without their help, defeat would have been a distinct possibility. When the final push came, American gunners were in the thick of it (1). American nurses were near enough to the front lines to need gas masks (2), and American inematographers filmed the Big Parade for the folks back home (3).

OBWOHL sie erst spät in den Krieg eintraten, spielten die Amerikaner eine entscheidende Rolle für die Kommunikation: ein Semaphor der amerikanischen Armee (4). Sir Douglas Haig, Oberbefehlshaber der britischen Truppen, betete: »Schenk' mir den Sieg, O Herr, bevor die Amerikaner kommen«, aber ohne ihre Hilfe wäre eine Niederlage unausweichlich gewesen. Als die letzte Offensive gestartet wurde, kämpften die Amerikaner mittendrin (1). Amerikanische Krankenschwestern waren so nah an der Front, daß sie Gasmasken tragen mußten (2); amerikanische Kameramänner filmten die große Schlacht für die Menschen in der Heimat (3).

BIEN qu'entrés tardivement dans la guerre, les Américains jouèrent un rôle capital dans le domaine des communications : sémaphore de l'armée américaine (4). Sir Douglas Haig, commandant en chef des troupes britanniques priait : « Accorde-moi la victoire, ô Seigneur, avant l'arrivée des Américains. » Mais sans leur aide la défaite aurait été de l'ordre du possible. Lors de l'assaut, les artilleurs américains se retrouvèrent aux premières loges (1). Les infirmières américaines étaient suffisamment proches des lignes de front pour devoir porter des masques à gaz (2), tandis que les cinématographes américains filmaient la grande parade pour leurs compatriotes restés chez eux (3).

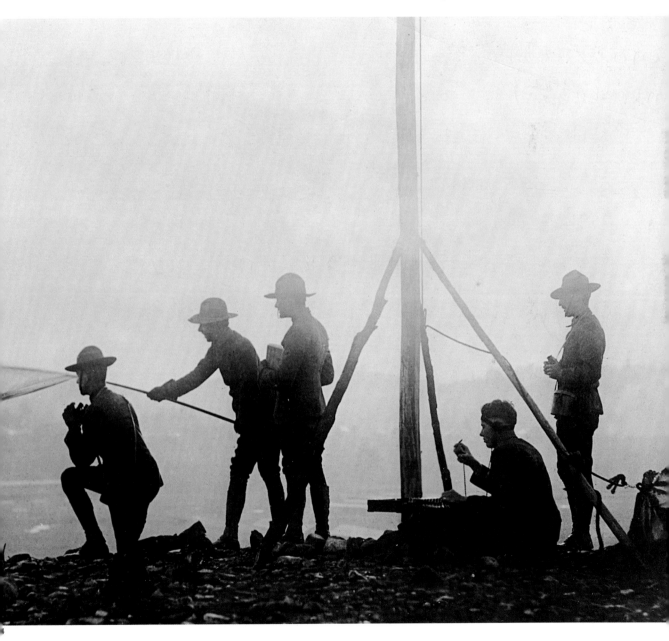

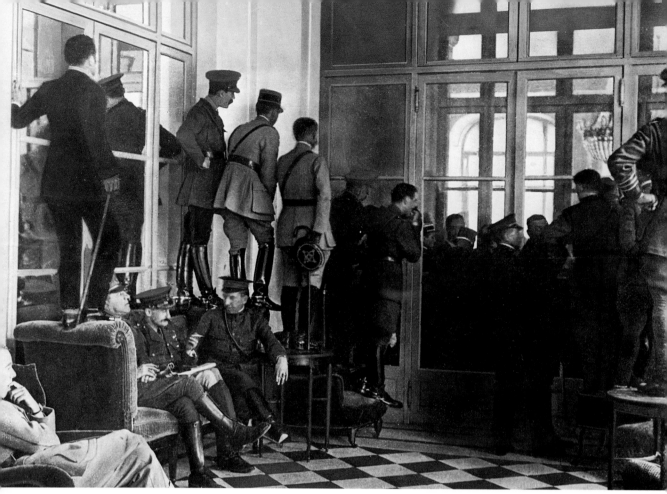

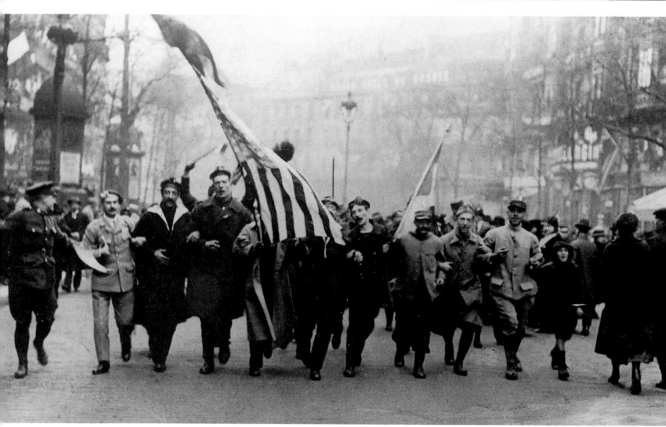

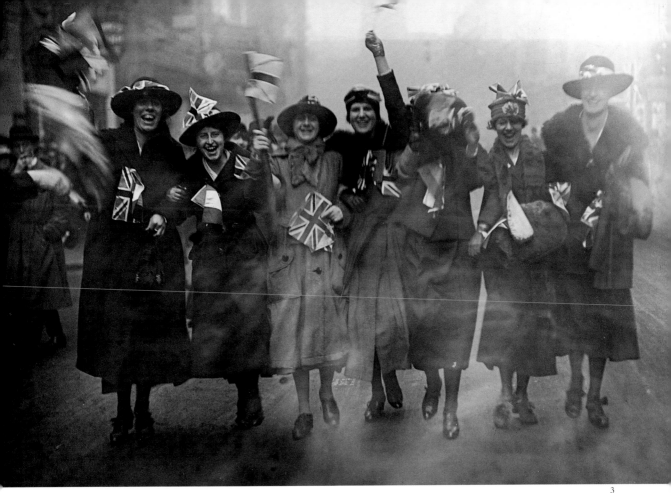

IN September 1918, Lord Northcliffe, an English newspaper tycoon, had prophesied: 'None of us will live to see the end of the war'. But on the eleventh hour of the eleventh day of the eleventh month of that year, the guns finally stopped. Some 14 million people had died – an average of 9,000 every day since the war began. Troops were bewildered; there was no fraternization and little cheering in the trenches. But among those at home there was widespread jubilation. Crowds thronged the boulevards of Paris (2) and the streets of London (3). Couples made love in public, an affirmation of new life after four years of death. There followed a great deal of bickering among the victors, but the Peace Treaty was finally signed at the Palace of Versailles in June 1919. Allied officers stood on chairs and tables to witness the signing (1). Peace was a great relief. The Treaty was a disaster.

IM September 1918 hatte der englische Zeitungsverleger Lord Northcliffe prophezeit: »Niemand von uns wird das Ende des Krieges erleben.« Aber zur elften Stunde des elften Tages im elften Monat jenes Jahres schwiegen die Waffen endlich. Etwa vierzehn Millionen Menschen waren getötet worden – im Durchschnitt 9000 pro Tag seit Kriegsbeginn. Die Soldaten waren verwirrt; es gab keine Verbrüderung und wenig Jubel in den Schützengräben. Aber bei den Menschen zu Hause war die Freude grenzenlos. Sie liefen in Scharen über die Pariser Boulevards (2) und durch die Straßen von London (3). Paare küßten sich in der Öffentlichkeit – ein Ausbruch neuen Lebenswillens nach vier Jahren des Tötens. Die Siegermächte waren sich lange nicht einig, aber schließlich wurde der Friedensvertrag im Juni 1919 im Schloß von Versailles unterzeichnet. Alliierte Offiziere standen auf Stühlen und Tischen, um Zeuge der Unterzeichnung zu werden (1). Der Frieden war eine große Erleichterung. Der Vertrag aber war eine Katastrophe.

EN septembre 1918, Lord Northcliffe, magnat de la presse britannique, avait prophétisé : « Aucun de nous ne verra la fin de la guerre de son vivant. » Pourtant, à la onzième heure du onzième jour du onzième mois de cette année-là, les armes se turent enfin. Environ quatorze millions de personnes avaient péri, soit une moyenne de neuf mille par jour depuis le début de la guerre. Les troupes étaient en plein désarroi. On ne fraternisa pas et on ne s'enthousiasma que très peu dans les tranchées. En revanche, ailleurs l'allégresse était générale. La foule envahit les boulevards de Paris (2) et les rues de Londres (3). Les couples s'embrassaient en public, une nouvelle vie reprenait après quatre années de mort. Les vainqueurs se lancèrent dans des querelles innombrables et futiles, puis finalement le traité de paix fut signé au château de Versailles en juin 1919. Les officiers des forces alliées montèrent sur des chaises et des tables pour être témoins de la signature (1). La paix fut un énorme soulagement, le traité un désastre.

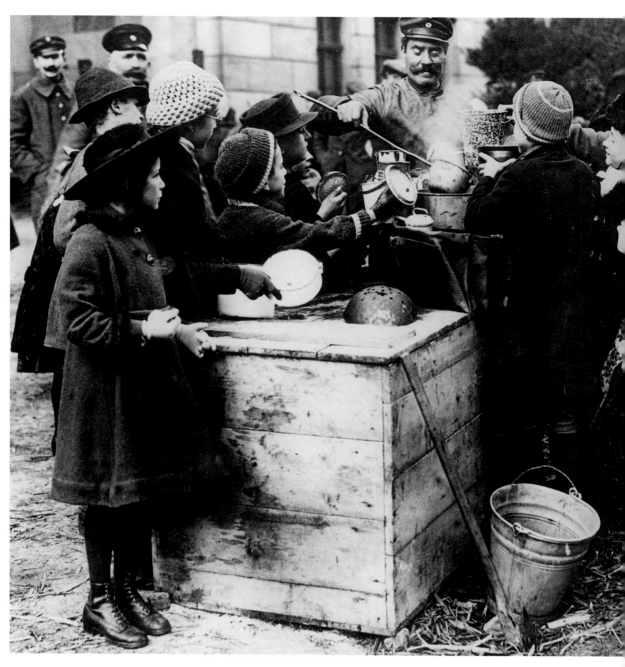

GERMANY had suffered appalling hardship during the war. The Imperial German Navy had made it difficult for Britain, France and Russia to obtain all the supplies they needed, but had been unable to bring any supplies at all to Germany. By 1917 there were queues for food in most German cities (3). Berlin schoolgirls helped clear snow from the streets (2). And even after the war, in December 1918, street kitchens were needed to supply children with a barely adequate diet (1).

DEUTSCHLAND hatte während des Krieges große Not gelitten. Die Kaiserliche Marine hatte es Großbritannien, Frankreich und Rußland zwar schwergemacht, auf dem Seeweg Vorräte und Waffen zu transportieren, sie war aber nicht in der Lage gewesen, Deutschland zu versorgen. In den meisten deutschen Städten standen die Menschen 1917 bei der Verteilung von Lebensmitteln Schlange (3). Berliner Schulmädchen schippten Schnee (2). Und selbst nach dem Krieg, im Dezember 1918, gab es in den Suppenküchen nicht gerade reichhaltige Kost für Kinder (1).

L'ALLEMAGNE avait effroyablement souffert pendant la guerre. La flotte impériale allemande avait rendu difficile l'approvisionnement de la Grande-Bretagne de la France et de la Russie, sans pour autant réussir à approvisionner l'Allemagne Dès 1917, on faisait la queue dans la plupart des grandes villes allemandes afin de recevoir des denrées alimentaires (3). À Berlin, des écolières aident à dégager la neige dans les rues (2). Même après la guerre, en décembre 1918, des cuisines durent être installées dans les rues pour distribuer aux enfants des repas tout juste suffisants (1).

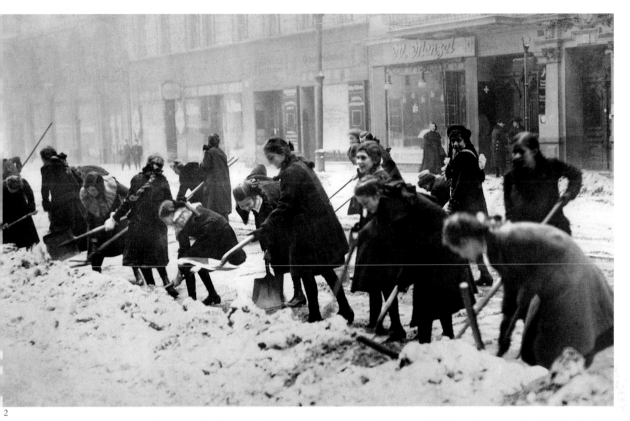

2

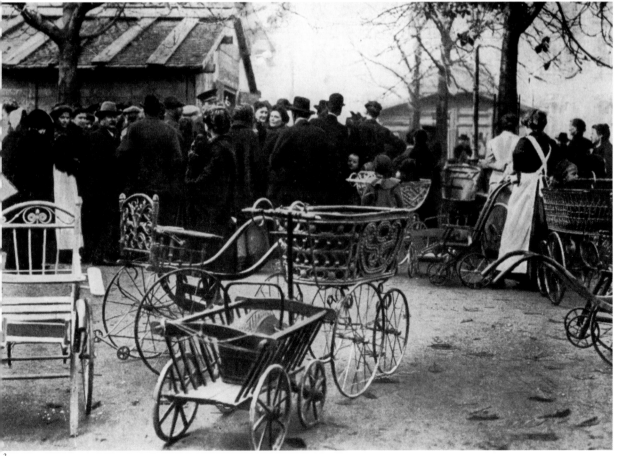

3

Russian Revolution

THOUGH they were perhaps the most autocratic rulers in Europe, life was seldom easy for the Tsars. The role of God as well as Emperor is a difficult one to play. Shot at and bombed, disliked and derided by rich and poor alike, ill-advised and unwise, they pleased practically none of the people most of the time.

Within a year of becoming Tsar in 1855, Alexander II had to face the humiliation of defeat in the Crimea. Although he embarked on a series of progressive reforms, such as freeing Russian serfs, his policies always gave too little, too late. And throughout his reign, the secret police and their activities were hardly secret. In 1881 Alexander was assassinated by a Polish student, who hurled a bomb at him in a St Petersburg street.

He was succeeded by his son, Alexander III. The new Tsar believed in repression. He increased police powers, crushed liberalism where he could, and persecuted the Jews and other minority groups. After the earlier taste of his father's reforms – seen as weaknesses by many – this hardline approach provoked riots throughout Russia. Colonel Wellesley, British Military Attaché in Russia, remarked how 'Curiously enough, the minimum of political liberty and the maximum of social freedom are to be found side by side under this strange Autocratic Government. Although in Russia the press is gagged, obnoxious articles in foreign newspapers are obliterated, and the native dares not even whisper an opinion as to politics, he can have his supper at a restaurant at 1 a.m. if it so pleases him …'

But late-night suppers did little to relieve ever-increasing political frustration, especially among middle-class Russians. When Alexander III died in 1894, ceremoniously mourned by many, sincerely mourned by few, he was succeeded by Nicholas II, doomed to be the last of the Romanov Tsars.

Within two years there were more serious outbreaks of rioting in St Petersburg. For the next twenty years reform and revolution jostled for position as the next obvious step. The crushing military defeat of Russia in the war with Japan (1904-5) led to the establishment of a short-lived Soviet in St Petersburg and the famous mutiny on the battleship *Potemkin*. In 1906 Nicholas summoned the Duma, the Russian parliament, and two years later granted freedom of religious worship to all Russians – but it was again too little, too late. The suffering and defeat of the Russian troops in the First World War merely hastened the end. Reform was swept aside. Revolution carried the day.

OBWOHL sie die wohl autokratischsten Herrscher in Europa waren, hatten die russischen Zaren nur selten ein leichtes Leben. Die Rolle eines Gottkaisers ist schwer zu erfüllen. Sie wurden beschossen und bombardiert, von Reichen und Armen gleichermaßen abgelehnt und verachtet, sie waren schlecht beraten und unklug – das Volk war fast nie mit ihnen zufrieden.

Ein Jahr nach seiner Proklamation zum Zar im Jahre 1855 sah sich Alexander II. mit der demütigenden Niederlage im Krimkrieg konfrontiert. Obwohl er eine Reihe fortschrittlicher Reformen erließ, beispielsweise die Abschaffung der Leibeigenschaft, waren seine politischen Maßnahmen nicht effizient und kamen zu spät. Während seiner Herrschaft konnte man die Geheimpolizei und ihre Aktivitäten kaum als geheim bezeichnen. Im Jahre 1863 brach in Polen eine Rebellion aus, und 1881 wurde Alexander von einem polnischen Studenten durch eine Bombe in St. Petersburg ermordet.

Ihm folgte sein Sohn, Alexander III. Der neue Zar suchte sein Heil in der Unterdrückung. Er verstärkte die Polizeikräfte, bekämpfte den Liberalismus, wo er konnte, und verfolgte Juden und andere Minderheiten. Nach den Reformen seines Vaters, in denen viele eine Schwäche sahen, provozierte diese harte Linie Unruhen im ganzen russischen Reich. Colonel Wellesley, britischer Militärattaché in Rußland, sagte: »Merkwürdigerweise gibt es unter dieser seltsamen autokratischen Regierung gleichzeitig ein Minimum an politischer und ein Maximum an sozialer Freiheit. Obwohl man in Rußland die Presse knebelt, unangenehme Artikel in ausländischen Zeitungen unkenntlich gemacht werden, und die Einheimischen es nicht einmal wagen, eine politische Meinung auch nur zu flüstern, können sie um ein Uhr nachts im Restaurant speisen, wenn es ihnen gefällt …«

Aber nächtliche Mahle änderten wenig an der ständig wachsenden politischen Enttäuschung besonders der russischen Mittelklasse. Als Alexander III. 1894 starb, von vielen im Rahmen der offiziellen Feierlichkeiten betrauert, aber nur von wenigen aufrichtig beweint, folgte ihm Nikolaus II., der letzte der Romanow-Zaren.

Innerhalb von zwei Jahren gab es weitere Unruhen in St. Petersburg. In den folgenden zwanzig Jahren schwankte die Politik zwischen Reform und Revolution. Die vernichtende russische Niederlage im Krieg gegen Japan (1904-1905) führte zur Einrichtung eines kurzlebigen Sowjet in St. Petersburg und zur berühm-

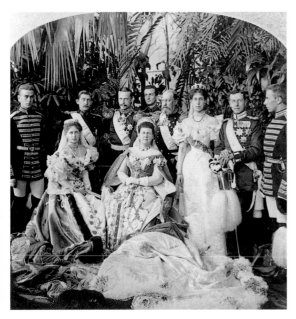

ten Meuterei auf dem Panzerkreuzer *Potemkin*. 1906
berief Nikolaus das russische Parlament, die Duma, ein,
und zwei Jahre später gewährte er allen Russen Reli-
gionsfreiheit, aber auch dies kam zu spät. Das Leid und
die Niederlage der russischen Truppen im Ersten Weltkrieg beschleunigten das Ende nur. Reformen kamen
nicht mehr in Frage, die Revolution flammte auf.

BIEN qu'ils fussent peut-être les dirigeants les plus
autocratiques d'Europe, les tsars russes avaient rarement la tâche facile. Il est difficile d'être à la fois dieu et
empereur. On leur tirait dessus, on leur lançait des
grenades, riches et pauvres les détestaient et les rail-
laient. Ils étaient mal conseillés et dépourvus de sagesse :
ils ne plaisaient pratiquement à personne la majeure
partie du temps.

Dans l'année qui suivit son accession au trône, en
1855, le tsar Alexandre II dut subir une défaite humiliante en Crimée. Bien qu'il eût entamé une série de
réformes progressistes comme l'affranchissement des
serfs russes, ses mesures politiques pesèrent toujours trop
peu. Tout au long de son règne l'existence de la police
secrète et de ses activités n'étaient un secret pour
personne. En 1863 une rébellion éclata en Pologne, et
en 1881 Alexandre fut assassiné par un étudiant polonais
qui lui lança une grenade dans une rue de Saint-
Pétersbourg.

Son fils Alexandre III lui succéda. Le nouveau tsar
croyait en la répression. Il augmenta les pouvoirs de la
police, écrasa le libéralisme partout où il le put et
persécuta les juifs ainsi que les autres minorités. Après
les réformes du père, considérées par beaucoup comme
des faiblesses, cette politique dure provoqua des émeutes
dans tout l'empire russe. Le colonel Wellesley, attaché
militaire britannique en poste en Russie, faisait remar-
quer : « On voit se côtoyer curieusement le minimum
de liberté politique et le maximum de liberté sociale
sous cet étrange régime autocratique. Bien qu'en Russie
la presse soit bâillonnée, les articles désapprobateurs
supprimés dans les journaux étrangers et que les gens ici
n'osent même pas chuchoter une opinion d'ordre
politique, vous pouvez souper dans un restaurant à une
heure du matin si le cœur vous en dit... »

Cependant les soupers tardifs ne contribuèrent guère
à atténuer la frustration politique qui allait croissante,
surtout au sein de la classe moyenne russe. Alexandre III
mourut en 1894 ; il fut solennellement pleuré par beaucoup et sincèrement par peu, et Nicolas II lui succéda :
il devait être le dernier tsar de la lignée des Romanov.

Deux ans plus tard, des émeutes plus graves éclatèrent à Saint-Pétersbourg. Puis pendant vingt ans, réformes
et révolutions s'enchaînèrent tour à tour. La défaite
militaire écrasante de la Russie dans la guerre contre le
Japon (1904) aboutit à la mise en place d'un soviet
éphémère à Saint-Pétersbourg et à la célèbre mutinerie
du cuirassé *Potemkine*. En 1906, Nicolas convoqua la
Douma (le parlement russe), puis accorda deux ans plus
tard la liberté de culte à tous les Russes. Là encore ce
fut trop peu et trop tard. Les souffrances et les défaites
subies par les troupes russes au cours de la Première
Guerre mondiale ne firent que précipiter la fin. Les
réformes furent balayées. La révolution triompha.

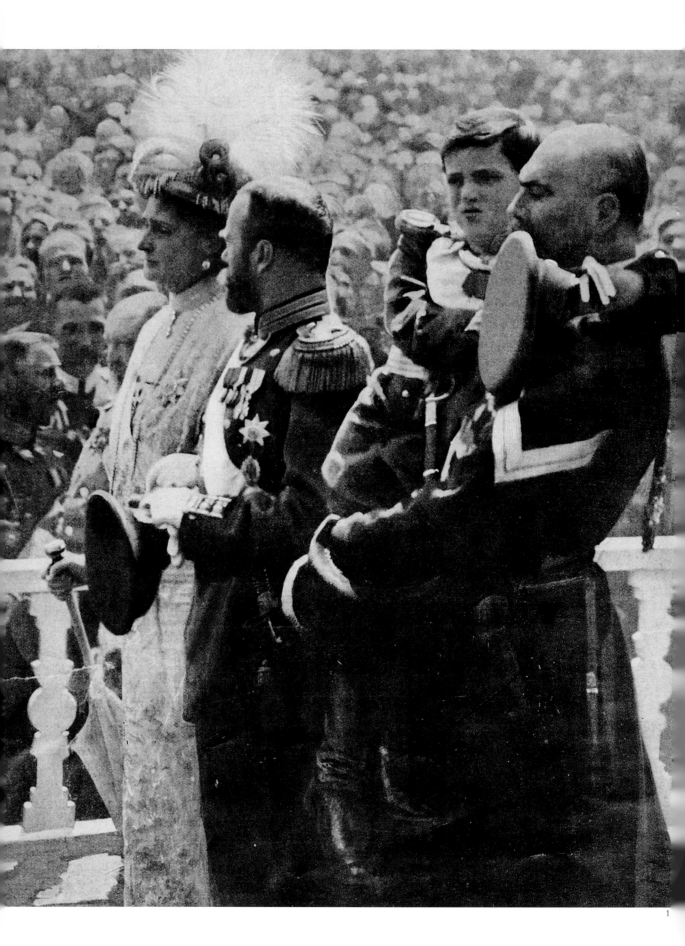

1

IN 1896, Nicholas and his wife Alexandra
– another of Queen Victoria's grand-
daughters – visited the Queen (2) and
Edward, Prince of Wales (right), at Balmoral,
taking with them their bonnie baby, the
Grand Duchess Tatiana. In 1913, Nicholas,
Alexandra and the Tsarevich Alexis (1 –
held by a Cossack) celebrated the centenary
of the Romanov dynasty at the Kremlin.
And in 1916, the Russian Imperial family
posed at Tsarskoe Selo (3, left to right,
back row – the Princes Nikita, Rostislav,
and Dmitri; middle row – an officer, The
Tsar, the Grand Duchesses Tatiana, Olga,
Marie, Anastasia, and the Tsarevich: front –
Prince Vasili).

IM Jahre 1896 besuchten Nikolaus und
seine Frau Alexandra, eine weitere
Enkelin von Königin Victoria, zusammen
mit ihrem wohlgenährten Baby, der Groß-
herzogin Tatjana, die englische Königin (2)
und Edward, Prince of Wales (rechts) auf
Schloß Balmoral. 1913 feierten Nikolaus,
Alexandra und der Zarewitsch Alexis
(1, auf dem Arm eines Kosaken) im Kreml
das hundertjährige Bestehen der Dynastie
der Romanows. Und im Jahre 1916 posier-
te die russische Zarenfamilie bei Zarskoje
Selo (3, von links nach rechts in der hinte-
ren Reihe: die Prinzen Nikita, Rostislaw
und Dimitrij; mittlere Reihe: ein Offizier,
der Zar, die Großherzoginnen Tatjana,
Olga, Marie, Anastasia und der Zarewitsch;
vorne: Prinz Wassilij).

EN 1896, Nicolas et son épouse Alexandra, une des arrière-petites-filles de la
reine Victoria (2), se rendirent à Balmoral
accompagnés d'Édouard, prince de Galles,
(à droite), ainsi que d'un poupon à la mine
plaisante, la grande-duchesse Tatiana. En
1913, Nicolas, Alexandra et le tsarévitch
(1, porté par un cosaque) célébraient le
centenaire de la dynastie des Romanov au
Kremlin. En 1916, la famille impériale
russe posait à Tsarskoïe Selo (3, de gauche
à droite au dernier rang les princes Nikita,
Rostislav et Dmitri ; au milieu, les grandes-
duchesses Tatiana, Olga, Marie, Anastasia
et le tsarévitch ; devant, le prince Vassili).

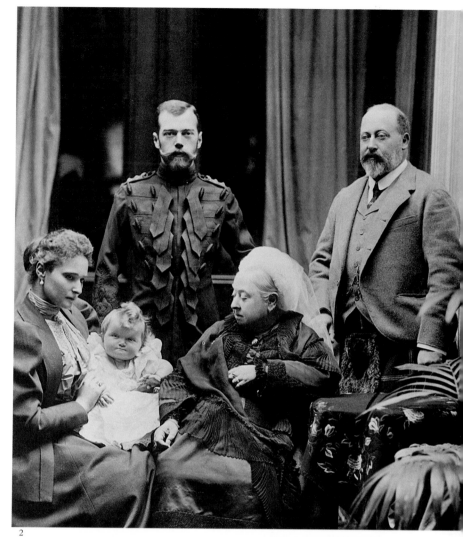

2

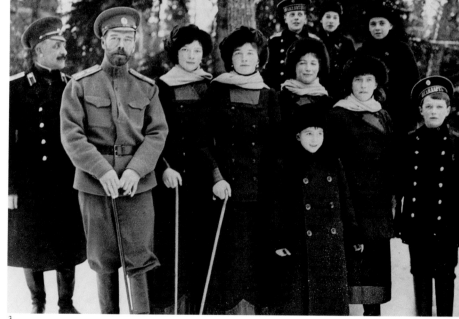

3

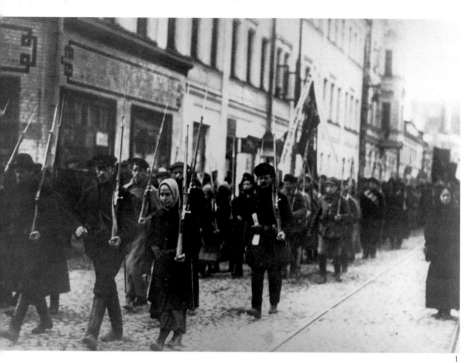

1

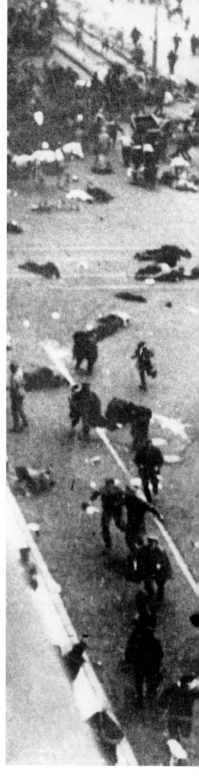

IN March 1917, the English writer Arthur Ransome cabled from Moscow: 'This is not an organized revolution. It will be impossible to make a statue of its organizer… unless it be a statue representing a simple Russian peasant soldier…'. Revolutionary troops marched through Petrograd, March 1917 (1). Four months later, Leninists besieged the Duma, and the provisional government responded with force, producing panic (3). Not all demonstrations were in favour of revolution, however. A patriotic demonstration of blind ex-soldiers marched through Petrograd behind a banner proclaiming: 'Continue the war until victory is complete! Long live liberty!' (2).

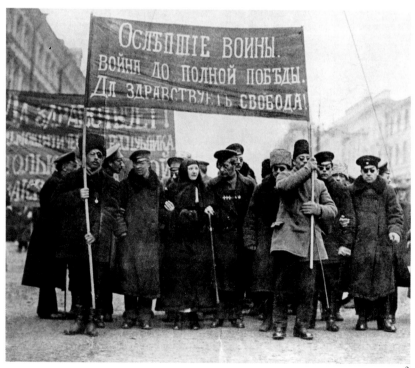

2

IM März 1917 telegraphierte der englische Schriftsteller Arthur Ransome aus Moskau: »Dies ist keine organisierte Revolution Es wird nicht möglich sein, eine Statue ihres Anführers anzufertigen … es sei denn, sie stellt einen einfachen russischen Soldaten dar …« Revolutionstruppen marschierten im März 1917 durch Petrograd (1). Vier Monate später besetzten Leninisten

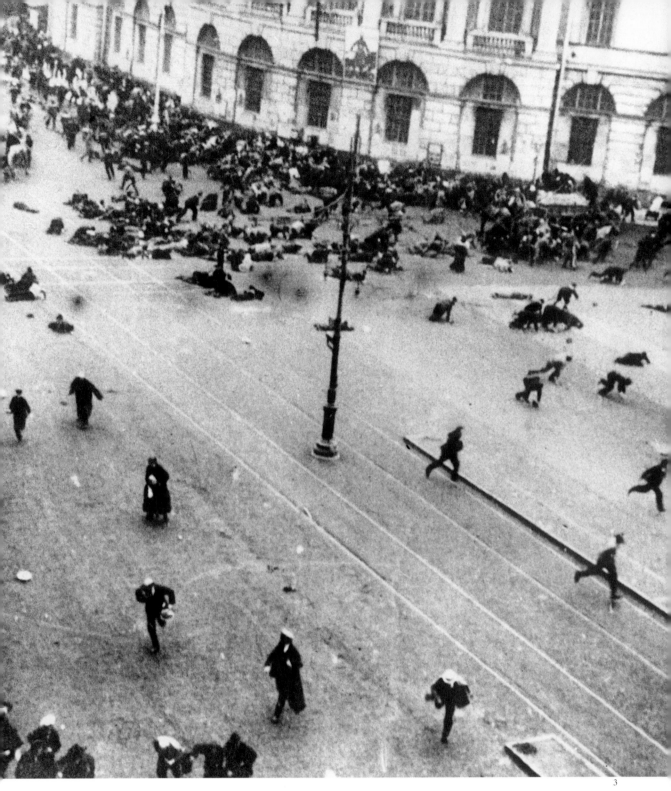

3

die Duma, die provisorische Regierung antwortete mit Gewalt und löste eine Panik aus (3). Aber nicht alle gingen für die Revolution auf die Straße. Patriotische blinde Veteranen marschierten hinter einem Banner durch Petrograd, auf dem zu lesen war: »Kämpft weiter bis zum Sieg! Lang lebe die Freiheit!« (2)

EN mars 1917, l'écrivain anglais Arthur Ransome câblait de Moscou : « Il ne s'agit pas d'une révolution organisée. Il sera impossible d'ériger à son organisateur une statue . . . sauf à représenter un simple Russe à la fois soldat et paysan . . . » Les troupes révolutionnaires défilent dans les rues de Petrograd en mars 1917 (1). Quatre mois plus tard les partisans de Lénine assiégèrent la Douma. Le gouvernement provisoire employa alors la force, provoquant ainsi la panique (3). Toutes les manifestations n'étaient pas en faveur de la révolution. Des anciens combattants aveugles défilent dans Petrograd en proclamant : « Poursuivez la guerre jusqu'à la victoire complète ! Vive la liberté ! » (2).

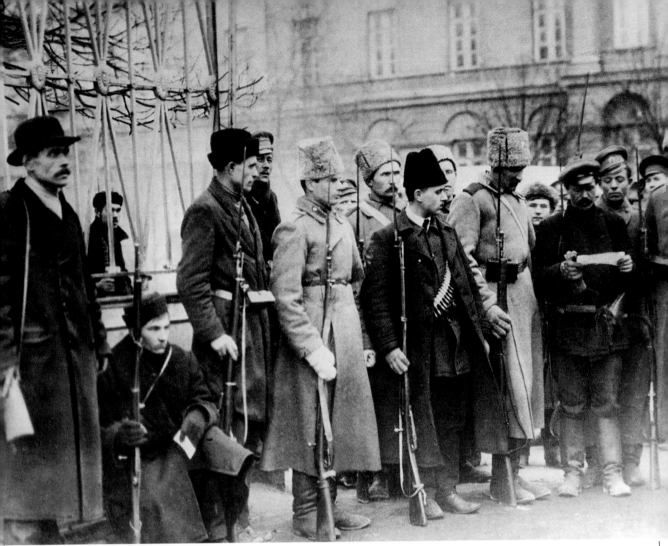

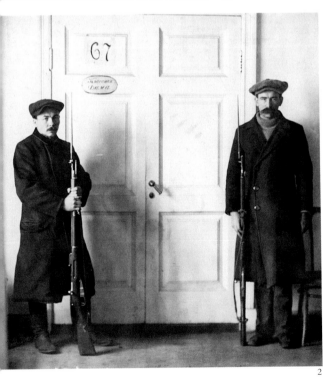

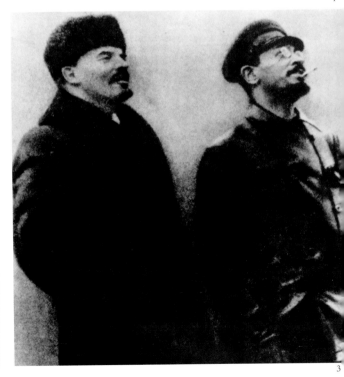

By the autumn of 1917, the Bolsheviks
(4) were increasingly in charge of
Moscow and other major Russian cities. In
Petrograd troops checked the mandates of
Soviet deputies (1). Red Guards protected
Lenin and Trotsky's offices, October 1917
(2). The architects of the Bolshevik
Revolution were Vladimir Ilyich Lenin
and Leon Trotsky (3). The Tsar and his
family posed for one of their last group
photographs while in captivity at Tobol'sk,
during the winter of 1917-18 (5 – left to
right: Olga, Anastasia, Nicholas, the
Tsarevich, Tatiana and Marie).

Im Herbst 1917 hatten die Bolschewiken
(4) Moskau und andere große russische
Städte immer fester im Griff. In Petrograd
überprüften Truppen die Mandate von
Abgeordneten des Sowjets (1). Rotarmisten
bewachten im Oktober 1917 die Büros
von Lenin und Trotzki (2). Die Architek-
ten der bolschewistischen Revolution
waren Wladimir Iljitsch Lenin und Leo
Trotzki (3). Der Zar und seine Familie
posierten für eines der letzten Gruppen-
photos, während sie sich im Winter
1917/18 in Tobolsk in Gefangenschaft
befanden (5, von links nach rechts: Olga,
Anastasia, Nikolaus, der Zarewitsch,
Tatjana und Marie).

Dès l'automne 1917, les bolcheviks (4)
étaient en passe de contrôler Moscou
et les autres principales grandes villes russes.
À Petrograd, les troupes vérifiaient les
mandats des députés soviétiques (1). Les
gardes rouges protégeaient les bureaux de
Lénine et de Trotski en octobre 1917 (2).
Les architectes de la révolution bolche-
vique étaient Vladimir Ilitch Lénine et Lev
Davidovich Bronstein dit Trotski (3). Le
tsar et sa famille posant pour l'une de leurs
dernières photographies de groupe durant
leur captivité à Tobolsk pendant l'hiver
1917 (5, de gauche à droite : Olga, Anastasia,
Nicolas, le tsarévitch, Tatiana et Marie).

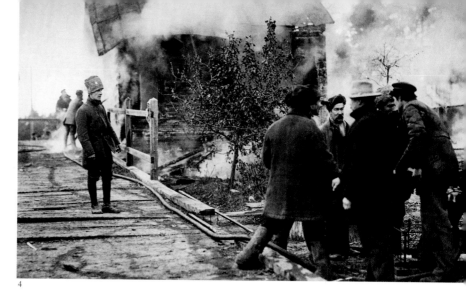

4

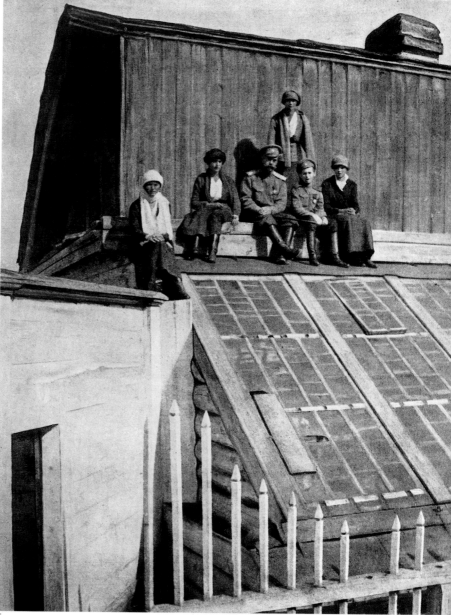

5

Construction

NEVER had the earth been so built upon: houses, hotels, engine-rooms, pumping stations, hospitals, churches, museums, skyscraper office blocks, towers, exhibition halls, factories and workshops, blast furnaces and boiler-houses. Old cities were rebuilt, reshaped, resettled. The cluttered medieval streets, so vividly described in Victor Hugo's *Notre Dame de Paris*, were hacked down and cleared away, and grand avenues, boulevards and Allees were erected in their place. The commercial hearts of London, Paris, Rome, Berlin, Madrid, Vienna, New York, Chicago and many more cities were ringed with new suburbs – orderly, respectable, convenient, scorned by the glitterati of the day.

But the achievements of the great engineers were hailed as modern monuments that rivalled the Wonders of the Ancient World. There was Joseph Paxton's Crystal Palace, home of the Great Exhibition of 1851; Alexandre Gustave Eiffel's extraordinary Tower, for the Paris Exhibition of 1889; the ever-enlarging Krupp works at Essen, and the gloomy two-hundred-room Villa Hügel built for Krupp himself a few miles away; Frédéric Auguste Bartholdi's Statue of Liberty, built in Paris for the people of the United States; the Singer works at Glasgow in Scotland; the Forth, Brooklyn, Niagara and hundreds more bridges. In the last age before mass circulation newspapers and moving pictures, engineers were second only to soldiers as public heroes: Brunel, de Lesseps, Roebling, Vickers, Eiffel (1, in top hat), Rathenau.

Capitalism was enjoying its finest and most lucrative hour. There was always money at hand to back these giant enterprises, and labour was cheap, plentiful and often desperate. The designs may have been the work of individual genius, but the hard work of construction was done by sweating thousands in scruffy trousers, worn waistcoats, shirtsleeves, bowler hats and metal-tipped boots – hammering, digging, quarrying, welding, riveting, fetching and carrying, mixing and shovelling. Many died as tunnels collapsed, scaffolding tumbled, mines exploded. Nobody played for safety, least of all for that of their employees.

Whole new cities appeared, made by the discovery of gold, by the coming of the railway, by military necessity or convenience, by the sheer single-mindedness of a founding figure. In many cases we may have forgotten those responsible for the masterpieces of the late 19th century, but their achievements remain.

NIEMALS wurde auf der Erde soviel gebaut: Häuser, Hotels, Maschinenhallen, Pumpstationen, Krankenhäuser, Kirchen, Museen, Bürohochhäuser, Türme, Ausstellungshallen, Fabriken und Werkshallen, Hochöfen und Kesselhäuser. Alte Städte bekamen so ein neues Gesicht und wurden neu besiedelt. Die überfüllten mittelalterlichen Straßen, die Victor Hugo in *Notre Dame de Paris* so lebhaft beschrieben hat, wurden aufgerissen und machten Platz für große Avenuen, Boulevards und Alleen. Die Stadtzentren von London, Paris, Rom, Berlin, Madrid, Wien, New York, Chicago und vielen anderen Metropolen bekamen neue Vororte – ordentlich, überschaubar, zweckmäßig und von der damaligen Hautevolee verachtet.

Die Errungenschaften der bedeutenden Ingenieure wurden als moderne Bauwerke gepriesen, die die Wunder der alten Welt in den Schatten stellten. Da war Joseph Paxtons Kristallpalast für die Londoner Weltausstellung 1851; Alexandre Gustave Eiffels außergewöhnlicher Turm für die Pariser Weltausstellung 1889; die ständig wachsenden Krupp-Werke in Essen und die prächtige Villa Hügel mit ihren 200 Zimmern, die einige Kilometer entfernt für Krupp selbst gebaut wurde; Frédéric Auguste Bartholdis Freiheitsstatue, für das Volk der Vereinigten Staaten in Paris geschaffen; die Singer-Werke im schottischen Glasgow; die Forth-, die Brooklyn-, die Niagara- und Hunderte anderer Brücken. Im letzten Zeitalter ohne Massenblätter und bewegte Bilder waren Ingenieure fast ebenso große Helden wie die Soldaten: Brunel, de Lesseps, Roebling, Vickers, Eiffel (1, unten) und Rathenau.

Der Kapitalismus erlebte seine beste und lukrativste Zeit. Also war stets Geld vorhanden, um diese gigantischen Unternehmungen zu finanzieren, und Arbeitskräfte waren billig, reichlich vorhanden, und oft genug waren das Verzweifelte. Die Entwürfe mögen das Werk einzelner Genies gewesen sein, aber die harte Arbeit auf den Baustellen wurde von Tausenden schwitzender Männern in abgerissenen Hosen, zerschlissenen Westen, Hemdsärmeln, Melonen und Stiefeln mit Stahlspitzen geleistet: Hämmern, Graben, Schweißen, Vernieten Auf- und Abladen, Mischen und Schaufeln. Viele starben, wenn Tunnel einstürzten, Gerüste zusammenbrachen oder Minen explodierten. Niemand kümmerte sich um Sicherheit, am wenigsten um die der Arbeiter.

Es entstanden neue Städte durch die Entdeckung von Gold, die Verlegung von Eisenbahnschienen, durch

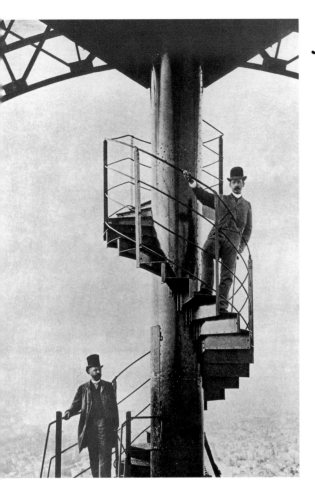

militärische Notwendigkeit oder Willkür und durch die Zielstrebigkeit von Gründerpersönlichkeiten. In vielen Fällen haben wir heute vermutlich vergessen, wer für die Meisterwerke des späten 19. Jahrhunderts verantwortlich war, aber die Errungenschaften dieser Menschen bleiben.

J AMAIS il n'y avait eu autant d'édifices sur la terre : maisons, hôtels, salles des machines, stations de pompage, hôpitaux, églises, musées, gratte-ciel de bureaux, tours, salles d'exposition, usines et ateliers, hauts fourneaux et salles des chaudières. Les vieilles cités étaient reconstruites, remodelées et repeuplées. Les rues médiévales pleines de bruits confus dont Victor Hugo avait donné une description si vivante dans *Notre-Dame de Paris* étaient démolies et rasées pour faire place aux grandes avenues, aux boulevards et aux allées. Les cœurs commerciaux de Londres, Paris, Rome, Berlin, Madrid, Vienne, New York, Chicago et d'un millier d'autres grandes villes se retrouvaient encerclés par des banlieues neuves – ordonnées, respectables, commodes et méprisées par les *célébrités* du jour.

Cependant les exploits des grands ingénieurs étaient salués comme autant de monuments modernes rivalisant avec les merveilles du Vieux Monde. Il y avait le Crystal Palace de Joseph Paxton qui abrita la grande exposition de 1851 ; l'extraordinaire tour de Gustave Eiffel construite pour l'exposition de Paris en 1889 ; les usines Krupp à Essen qui ne cessaient de se développer, et la sinistre villa Hügel de deux cents pièces que Krupp s'était fait bâtir à quelques kilomètres de là ; la statue de la liberté de Frédéric Auguste Bartholdi construite à Paris pour le peuple américain ; les usines Singer à Glasgow en Écosse ; les ponts Forth, Brooklyn, Niagara et des centaines d'autres.

À cette époque, qui a précédé les journaux de grande circulation et les images animées, les ingénieurs ne le cédaient qu'aux soldats comme figures héroïques dans le cœur du public : Brunel, de Lesseps, Roebling, Vickers, Eiffel (1, en chapeau haut de forme) et Rathenau.

Le capitalisme vivait ses heures les plus belles et les plus lucratives. On trouvait toujours de l'argent pour financer ces entreprises géantes, par ailleurs la main-d'œuvre était bon marché, abondante et souvent résignée. Ces constructions sont peut-être les fruits du génie d'une seule personne, mais elles furent exécutées à la sueur de milliers d'autres travaillant dans des pantalons dégoûtants, des gilets élimés, en bras de chemise, chapeaux ronds et chaussures à bouts en métal qui ont martelé, creusé, extrait, soudé, rivé, transporté, mélangé et pelleté. Beaucoup moururent, car personne ne pensait à se protéger.

Des villes entières furent créées à la faveur de la ruée vers l'or, l'arrivée du chemin de fer, la nécessité ou la commodité militaire ou grâce à la pugnacité de leur fondateur. Les chefs-d'œuvre de la fin du XIXe siècle demeurent, mais dans bien des cas nous avons peut-être oublié à qui nous les devons.

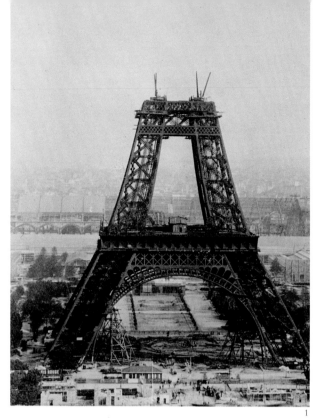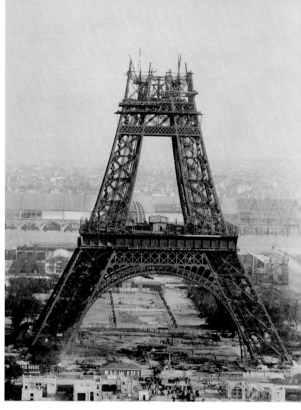

1

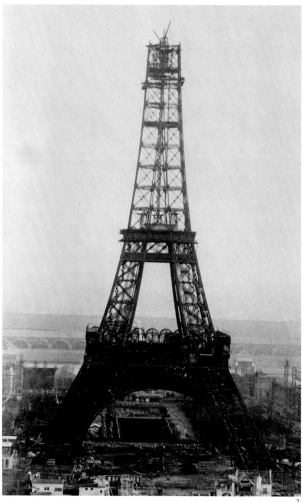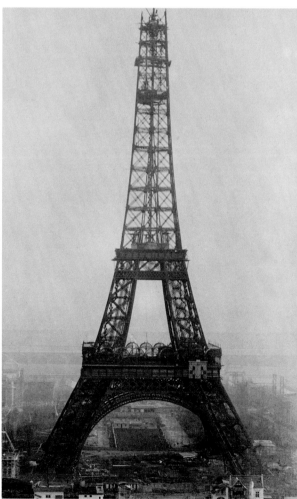

3

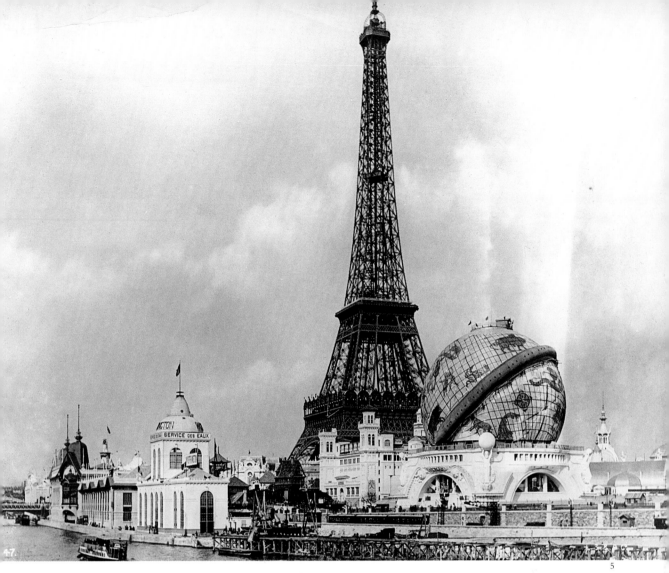

5

IT took almost a year to complete the Eiffel Tower. As it steadily rose above the Paris skyline (1-4), there were those who loved it, those who detested it. The French writer Edouard Drumont, who hated urban life, Dreyfus, the Jews, de Lesseps and almost everything modern, regarded it as a symbol of all that was wrong with France. But once the Tower was finished in 1889, it became the most famous landmark in Paris, outlasting the Globe Céleste, which was dismantled after the Paris Exhibition of 1900 (5).

DIE Fertigstellung des Eiffelturms dauerte fast ein Jahr. Als er sich allmählich immer höher über Paris erhob (1-4), gab es Menschen, die ihn liebten, aber auch solche, die ihn verabscheuten. Der französische Schriftsteller Edouard Drumont haßte das urbane Leben, Dreyfus, die Juden, de Lesseps und fast alles Moderne, denn es war für ihn ein Symbol all dessen, was mit Frankreich nicht stimmte. Aber als der Turm 1889 fertig war, wurde er zum berühmtesten Wahrzeichen von Paris und überragte den Globe Céleste, der nach der Pariser Weltausstellung von 1900 wieder entfernt wurde (5).

IL fallut près d'un an pour terminer la tour Eiffel. Au fur et à mesure qu'elle s'élevait à l'horizon de Paris (1 à 4) – on découvrait ceux qui l'adoraient et ceux qui la détestaient. L'écrivain français Édouard Drumont qui exécrait la vie urbaine, Dreyfus, les juifs, de Lesseps et presque tout ce qui était moderne la considérait comme le symbole de tout ce qui allait de travers en France. Mais une fois que la tour fut achevée en 1889, on l'identifia à Paris, et elle a survécut au Globe Céleste qui fut démonté après l'exposition de Paris en 1900 (5).

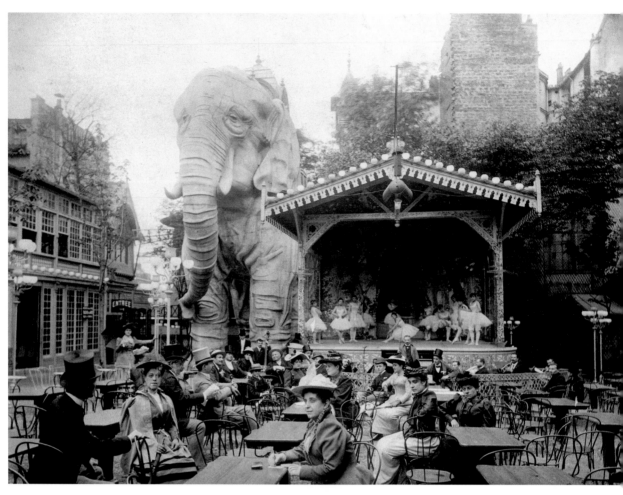

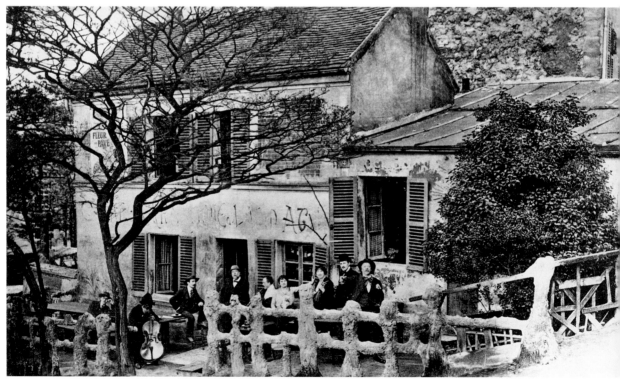

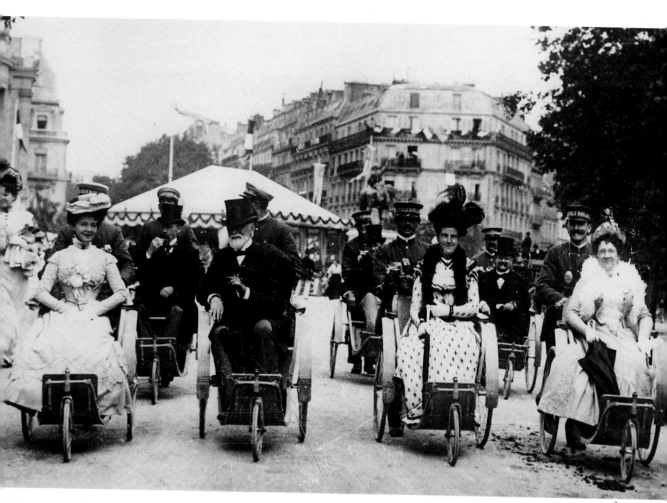

For many, Paris was the one city that symbolized *La Belle Epoque*, with its mixture of excitement and gaiety. The shame of defeat in 1871 and the bitterness left by the aftermath of the Commune were a generation away. The city had been grandly rebuilt. It was a place of passion and beauty, of art and music, of sensual delight and great good humour. In Montmartre, a vast elephant – built for the 1900 Paris Exhibition – dwarfed the famous Moulin Rouge (1), and artists gathered at the Cabaret Artistique du Lapin Agile (2). Visitors to the Exhibition travelled effortlessly in bath-chairs pushed by porters along the boulevards of Baron Haussmann (3).

Mit seiner Mischung aus Aufregung und Fröhlichkeit war Paris für viele die Stadt, die wie keine andere die *Belle Epoque* verkörperte. Die Schande der Niederlage von 1871 und die Verbitterung in der Zeit nach der Kommune lagen eine Generation zurück. Die Stadt war in aller Pracht wiederaufgebaut worden. Sie war ein Ort der Leidenschaft und der Schönheit, der Kunst und der Musik, der Sinnenfreuden und der guten Laune. In Montmartre ließ der riesige Elefant, der für die Pariser Weltausstellung von 1900 gebaut worden war, das Moulin Rouge (1) winzig erscheinen; Künstler trafen sich im Cabaret Artistique du Lapin Agile (2). Besucher der Ausstellung wurden bequem in Rollstühlen über die Boulevards des Baron Haussmann geschoben (3).

Pour beaucoup Paris symbolisait par excellence *La Belle Époque* et offrait un mélange d'effervescence et de gaieté. La honte de la défaite de 1871 et l'amertume laissée par la Commune appartenaient à la génération précédente. La capitale avait été reconstruite de façon grandiose. C'était un lieu de passions et de beauté, d'art et de musique, de plaisirs sensuels et de formidable bonne humeur. À Montmartre, l'éléphant construit pour l'exposition de Paris en 1900 faisait paraître minuscule le célèbre Moulin-Rouge (1), tandis que les peintres se donnaient rendez-vous au Lapin Agile (2). Les visiteurs de l'exposition se déplaçaient dans des fauteuils roulants que poussaient des porteurs le long des boulevards du baron Haussmann (3).

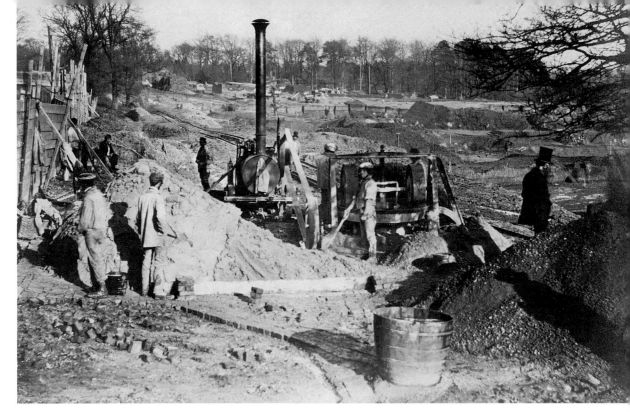

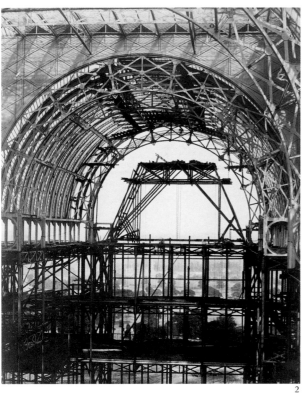

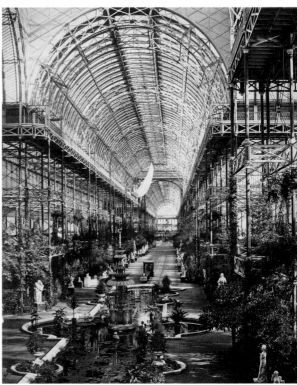

2

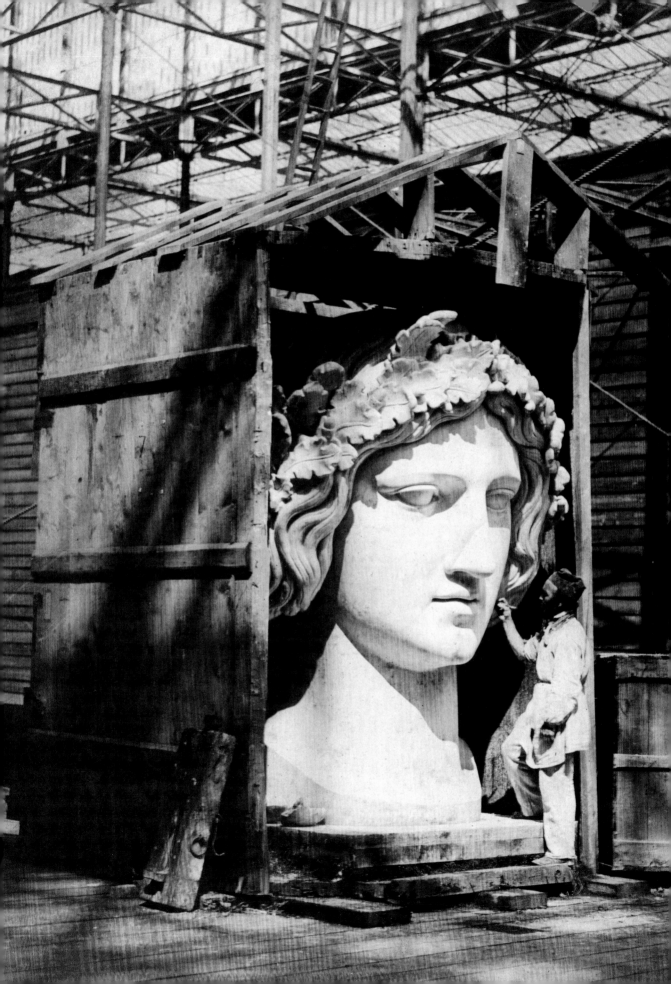

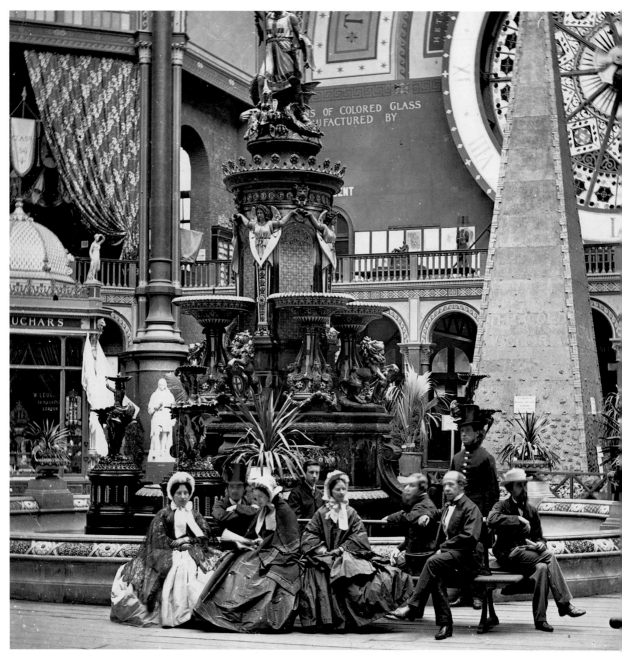

(Previous pages)

THE Great Exhibition of 1851 was
staged in London's Hyde Park. It was
held in the vast Crystal Palace (3), an iron
and glass construction (2) built to house 'the
Works and Industry of all Nations' which
was re-erected in South London in 1854
(1). It was a celebration of modern
achievement, a chance for every country to
show off its accomplishments, in peaceful
competition. National emblems were
proudly displayed – the finishing touches are
put to a plaster head of 'Bavaria' (4).

(Vorherige Seiten)

DIE Weltausstellung von 1851 fand im
Londoner Hyde Park im riesigen
Kristallpalast (3) statt, einer Stahl- und Glas-
konstruktion (2), die gebaut worden war,
um »die Errungenschaften und Industrien
aller Nationen« zu beherbergen und die 1854
im Süden Londons wieder aufgebaut wurde (1).
Die Ausstellung feierte die modernen Errungenschaften und bot jedem Land die Möglichkeit, in einem friedlichen Wettbewerb seine
Leistungen und Fertigkeiten zu demonstrieren.
Nationale Embleme wurden stolz zur Schau
gestellt – hier erhält ein Gipskopf der Bavaria
den letzten Schliff (4).

(Pages précédentes)

LA grande exposition de 1851 avait été
installée à Hyde Park à Londres. Elle
était logée à l'intérieur du Crystal Palace (3
vaste palais en fer et en verre (2) construit
pour abriter les travaux et l'industrie de tout
les nations et qui fut transféré dans le sud d
Londres en 1854 (1). Cette exposition célébrait les réalisations des Temps modernes e
offrant à chaque pays la possibilité de démo
trer ses capacités de façon concrète dans un
esprit de compétition pacifique. Les emblèm
nationaux étaient fièrement exposés : les
dernières touches sont apportées à un plât
représentant la tête de la « Bavière » (4).

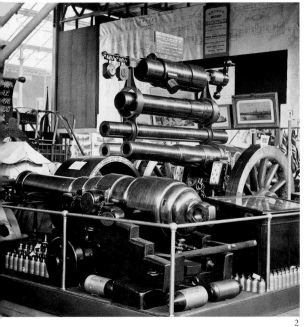

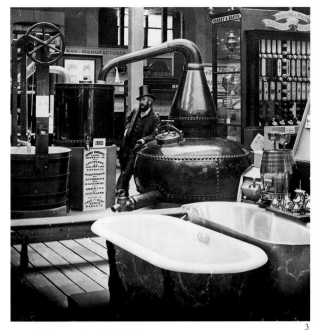

2

3

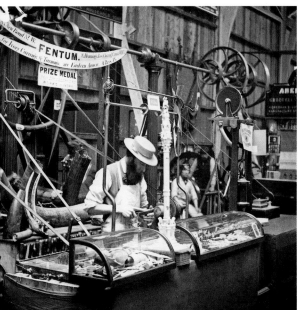

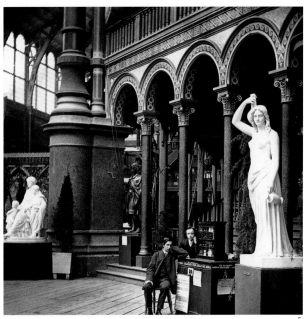

4

5

On the opening day of the International Exhibition of 1862 in South Kensington, the British historian Thomas Macaulay wrote in his diary: 'I was struck by the number of foreigners in the streets. All, however, were respectable and decent people' (1). Though the aim was peaceful, Armstrong guns were prominent in the Exhibition (2). Less warlike were Henry Pontifex's plumbing artefacts (3), Fentum's ivory-turning machines (4), and a number of titillating statues (5).

Am Tag der Eröffnung der Weltausstellung von 1862 in South Kensington schrieb der britische Historiker Thomas Macaulay in sein Tagebuch: »Ich war verblüfft über die vielen Fremden in den Straßen. Aber es waren alles ehrwürdige und anständige Menschen.« (1) Trotz der friedlichen Absichten der Ausstellung sprangen diese Armstrong-Kanonen besonders ins Auge (2). Weniger kriegerisch waren die sanitären Anlagen von Henry Pontifex (3), Fentums Elfenbeinschleifer (4) und eine Reihe aufregender Statuen (5).

Le jour de l'ouverture de l'exposition internationale de 1862 à South Kensington, l'historien britannique Thomas Macaulay notait dans son journal : « J'étais frappé par le nombre des étrangers qu'il y avait dans les rues. Tous, par ailleurs, gens respectables et honnêtes » (1) . Bien que le but en fût pacifique, les canons d'Armstrong étaient bien en vue à l'exposition (2). Moins guerriers étaient les objets de plomberie fabriqués par Henry Pontifex (3), les tours de Fentum pour le façonnage de l'ivoire (4) et un certain nombre de statues émoustillantes (5).

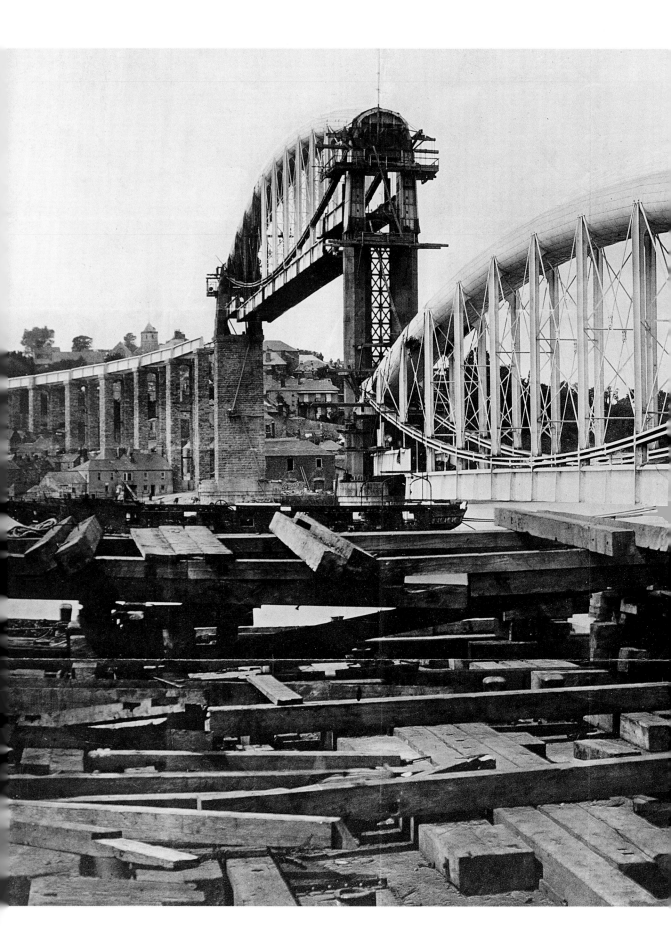

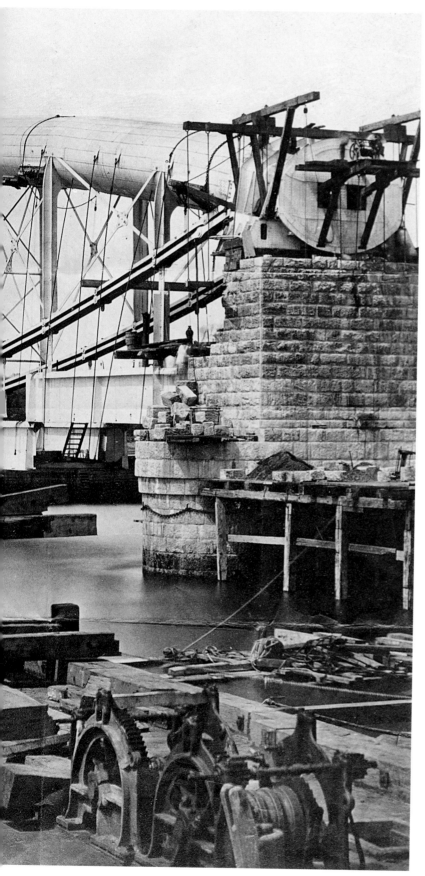

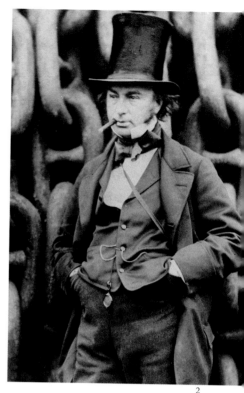

ONE of the finest British engineers of
the 19th century was Isambard
Kingdom Brunel (2 – seen here in front of
the massive chains tethering his steamship
Great Eastern while under construction).
Brunel built ships, railways and bridges,
among them the Royal Albert Bridge over
the River Tamar at Saltash, south-west
England (1).

EINER der bedeutendsten britischen
Ingenieure des 19. Jahrhunderts war
Isambard Kingdom Brunel (2, hier vor den
gigantischen Ketten, die sein Dampfschiff
Great Eastern während des Baus festhielten).
Brunel konstruierte Schiffe, Eisenbahnen
und Brücken, darunter die Royal Albert
Bridge über den Fluß Tamar bei Saltash im
Südwesten Englands (1).

UN des ingénieurs britanniques les plus
brillants du XIXᵉ fut Isambard
Kingdom Brunel (2, ici devant les chaînes
massives retenant son bateau à vapeur, le
Great Eastern, en cours de construction).
Brunel construisit des navires, des chemins
de fer et des ponts, et parmi ces derniers le
Royal Albert Bridge au-dessus de la rivière
Tamar à Saltash dans le sud-ouest de
l'Angleterre (1).

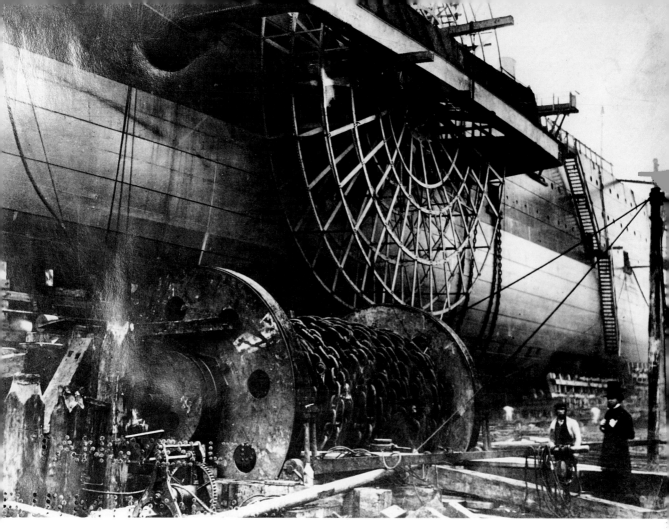

THE *Great Eastern* (1 and 4) was Brunel's masterpiece of engineering – a huge ship weighing 18,915 tons, almost six times the size of any vessel then afloat. She was built with both paddle-wheels (2) and a screw propeller, but had a tragic and haunted history. The first attempted launch was in November 1857 (3, left to right: J. Scott Russell, Henry Wakefield, I. K. Brunel). It was one of the first examples of photo-reporting, though the launch could not be completed. The ship stuck on the slipway for two months. She was eventually launched on 31 January 1858, but on her first trial voyage a boiler burst, killing six men. From then on, there were repeated stories that the ship was cursed. It was said that a riveter working on her had been incarcerated between the plates of her hull, and that ghostly hammerings could be heard.

When she was broken up in 1888, the skeleton of a riveter – with hammer – was found in her bilge.

DIE *Great Eastern* (1, 4) war Brunels technisches Meisterwerk – ein riesiges Schiff mit einem Gewicht von 18 915 Tonnen, fast sechsmal so groß wie die meisten damaligen Schiffe. Es wurde mit Schaufel-rädern (2) und einer Schiffsschraube ausgestattet, es hatte aber eine tragische Geschichte. Der erste Versuch des Stapellaufs fand im November 1857 statt (3, von links nach rechts: J. Scott Russell, Henry Wakefield, I. K. Brunel). Eine der ersten Photoreportagen dokumentierte das Ereignis, auch wenn der Stapellauf nicht durchgeführt werden konnte. Das Schiff steckte zwei Monate lang auf den Gleit-planken fest. Schließlich wurde es am 31. Januar 1858 zu Wasser gelassen, aber auf seiner ersten Probefahrt explodierte ein Kessel und tötete sechs Männer. Von nun an kursierten wiederholt Gerüchte, das Schiff sei verflucht. Man erzählte sich, ein Nieter sei bei der Arbeit zwischen den Platten des Schiffsrumpfes eingekerkert worden, und nun sei sein gespenstisches Hämmern zu hören.

Als das Schiff 1888 zerlegt wurde, fand man in seinem Rumpf das Skelett eines Nieters – mit Hammer!

LE *Great Eastern* (1 et 4) fut le chef-d'œuvre de Brunel. Il s'agissait d'un immense navire de 18 915 tonnes, près de six fois la taille de n'importe quel autre vaisseau navigant à l'époque. Il avait été muni à la fois de grandes roues (2) et d'une hélice. Il eut cependant une histoire tragique. La première tentative de lance-ment eut lieu en novembre 1857 (3) en présence des ingénieurs qui l'avaient construit (de gauche à droite : J. Scott Russell, Henry Wakefield et I. K. Brunel). C'est là un des premiers exemples de repor-tage photographique, même si le lance-ment avorta. Le navire ne quitta pas la cale deux mois durant. Son lancement eut finalement lieu le 31 janvier 1858 ; mais au cours de son premier voyage d'essai une chaudière éclata, tuant six hommes. La rumeur qui court alors prétendait que le navire était maudit. On disait qu'un riveur y travaillant était resté coincé dans le blin-dage de la coque et qu'on pouvait entendre son fantôme donner des coups de marteau.

Lorsque le *Great Eastern* fut mis en pièces en 1888, on trouva dans la sentine le squelette d'un riveur avec son marteau.

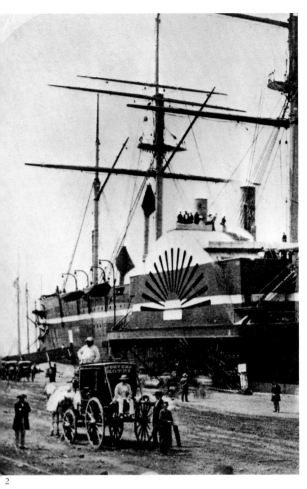

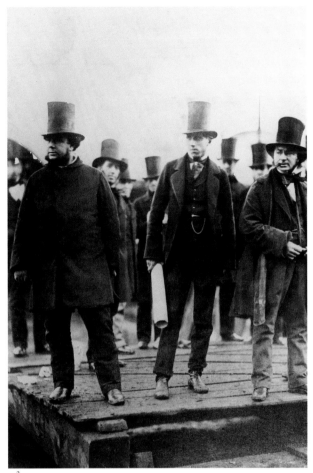

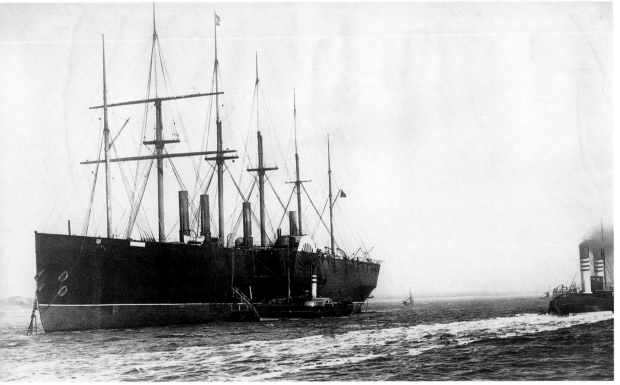

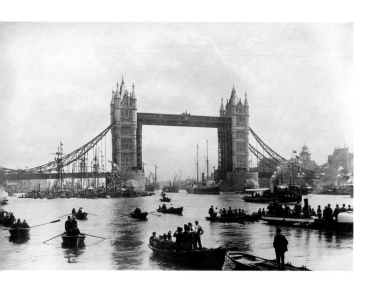

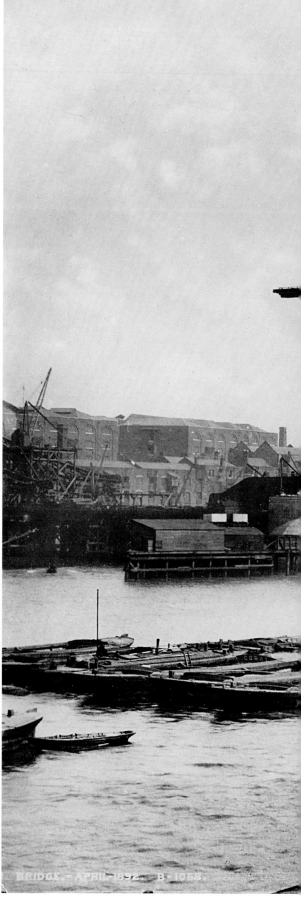

No other people know how to unite with the same harmonious force the cult of the past, the religion of tradition, to an unchecked love of progress and a lively and insatiable passion for the future,' wrote a French enthusiast for London's Tower Bridge. It was completed in 1894, with an opening of 250 ft (76 m), the two ramps being operated by steam-driven hydraulic pumps. It was the last bridge to be built over the Thames before the motor car began to exercise its tyranny.

KEIN anderes Volk versteht es, mit einer solch harmonischen Kraft den Kult der Vergangenheit und die Religion der Tradition mit einer ungezügelten Liebe zum Fortschritt und einer lebendigen und unstillbaren Leidenschaft für die Zukunft zu vereinen«, schrieb ein Franzose voller Begeisterung über die Londoner Tower Bridge. Die Brücke wurde 1894 fertiggestellt; ihr Öffnungswinkel maß 76 Meter, und ihre beiden Rampen wurden durch dampfbetriebene hydraulische Pumpen bewegt. Sie war die letzte Brücke, die über die Themse gebaut wurde, bevor das Auto seine Tyrannenherrschaft antrat.

AUCUN autre peuple ne sait unir avec autant de force har-monieuse le culte du passé et la religion de la tradition à un amour sans faille du progrès et une passion vivante et insatiable pour l'avenir », écrivait un Français enthousiasmé par le pont de la Tour de Londres. Celui-ci fut achevé en 1894, sa portée faisait 76 mètres et ses deux rampes étaient actionnées par des pompes hydrauliques à vapeur. Ce fut le dernier pont construit au-dessus de la Tamise avant que la voiture automobile ne commençât à exercer sa tyrannie.

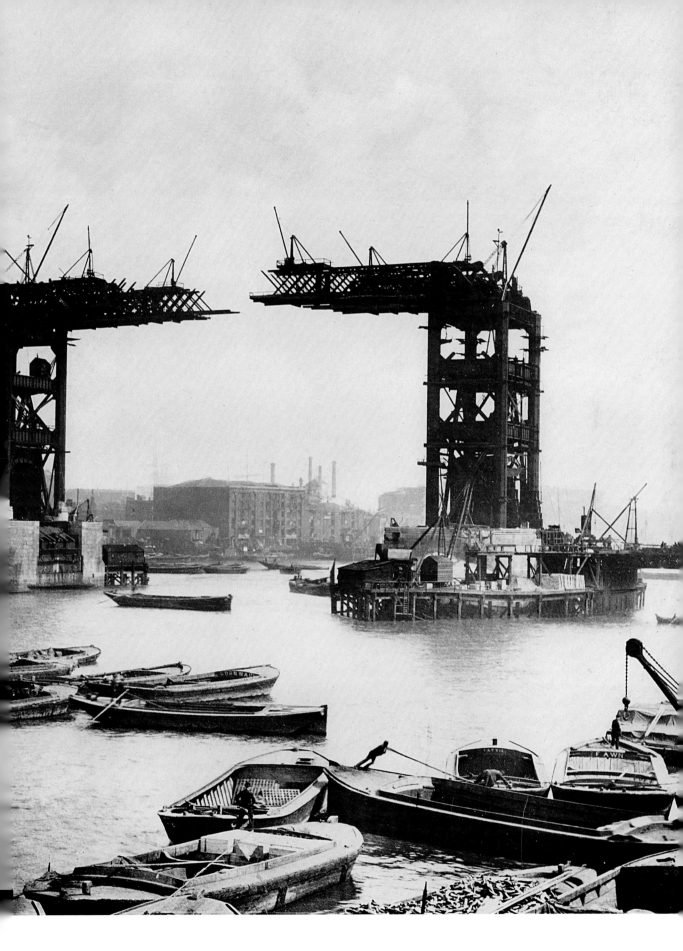

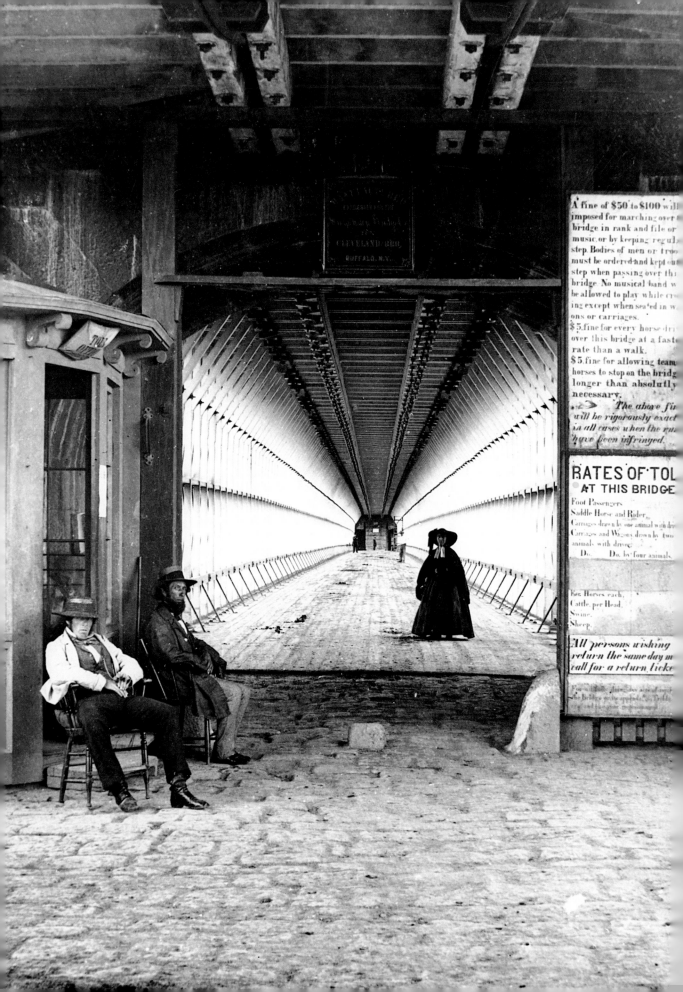

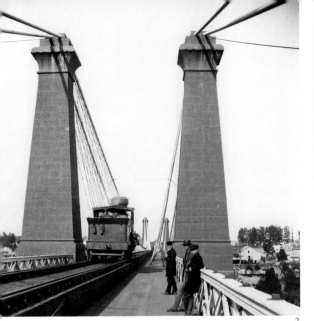

2

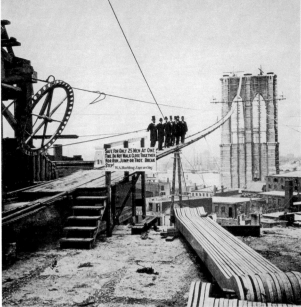

3

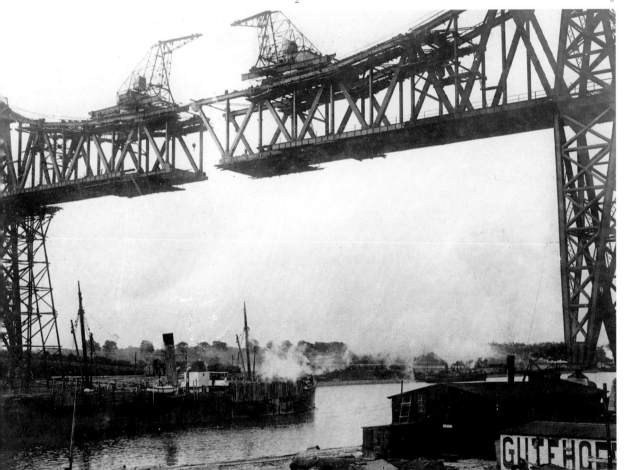

4

THE suspension bridge over the Niagara River was a two-decker (1, 2). The four main cables of the 1,000 yd-long Brooklyn Bridge (3) were each made up of 5,000 strands of steel wire. The bridge over the Kiel canal at Rendsburg in North Germany (4) was the largest bridge in the world when it was built in 1913.

DIE Hängebrücke über den Niagara war zweistöckig (1, 2). Die vier Hauptkabel der knapp 1 000 Meter langen Brooklyn Bridge (3) bestanden jeweils aus 5 000 Stahldrähten. Die 1913 erbaute Brücke über den Nord-Ostee-Kanal bei Rendsburg in Norddeutschland (4) war seinerzeit die größte der Welt.

LE pont suspendu au-dessus du Niagara comprenait deux niveaux (1-2). Les quatre câbles principaux du pont Brooklyn, long de 910 mètres (3), étaient composés chacun de cinq mille fils d'acier. Le pont au-dessus du canal de Kiel à Rendsbourg, dans le nord de l'Allemagne (4), était le plus grand du monde quand il fut construit en 1913.

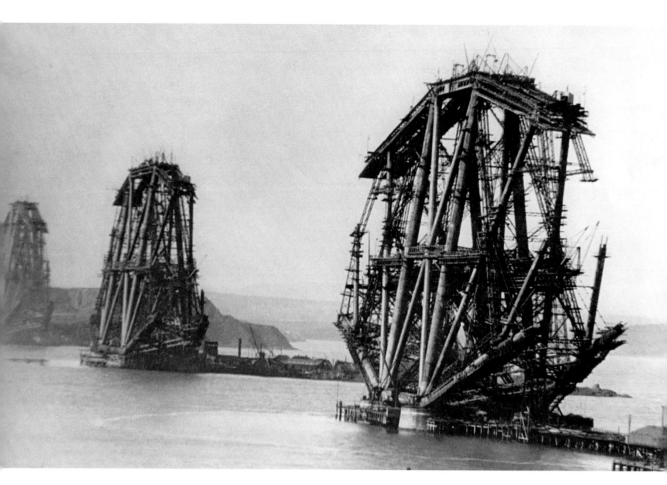

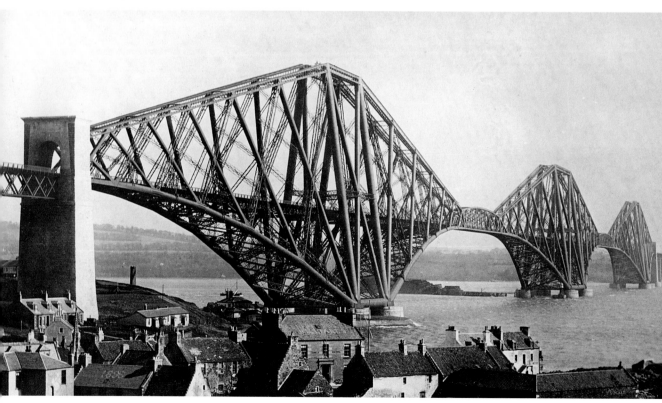

CROSSING water (left) - the Forth Bridge in Scotland was one of the first cantilever bridges and, at the time, the longest bridge in the world. It cost £3 million - an enormous amount of money in the 1880s. Crossing land (right) - US President Teddy Roosevelt (in white suit) makes his mark on the isthmus as he drives one of the giant steam shovels used in the construction of the Panama Canal.

DIE Forth Bridge in Schottland war eine der ersten Auslegerbrücken und bei ihrer Fertigstellung die längste Brücke der Welt. Ihr Bau kostete £ 3 Millionen, in den 1880er Jahren eine gewaltige Summe. William Morris, der britische Künstler, Designer und Schriftsteller, bezeichnete diese Eisenbahnbrücke als »unerreichten Inbegriff aller Häßlichkeit«.

LE pont Forth en Écosse fut un des premiers ponts cantilever construits, et c'était le pont le plus long du monde. Il avait coûté trois millions de livres, ce qui en 1880 représentait une somme gigantesque. William Morris, peintre, artiste et écrivain britannique, qualifiait le pont et son chemin de fer de « spécimen parfait du comble de la laideur ».

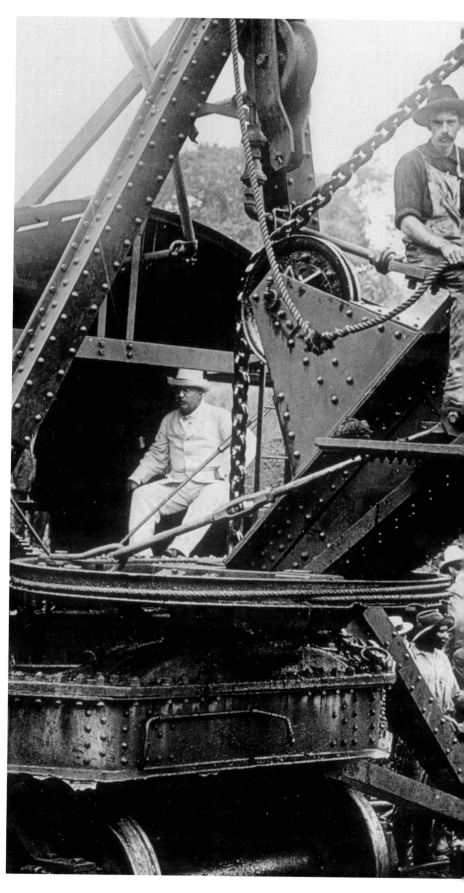

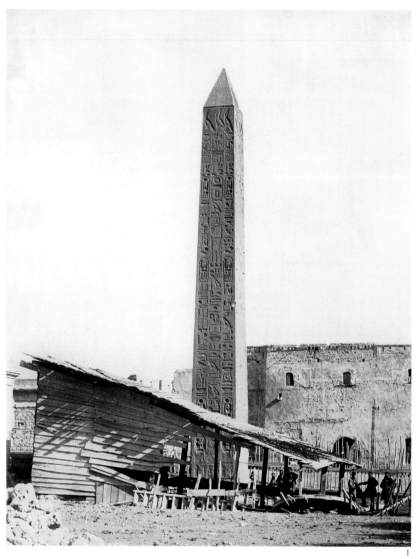

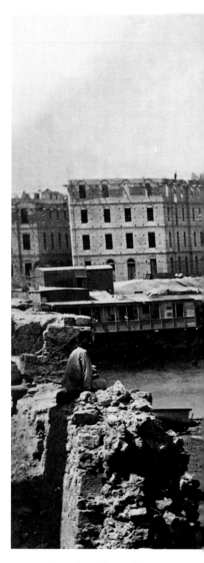

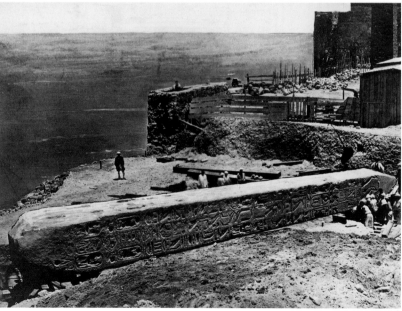

T HE Suez Canal focused European attention on Egypt and made things Egyptian fashionable. For nearly two thousand years, the monolith known as Cleopatra's Needle had stood near Alexandria (1). Now, English archaeologists had their greedy eyes on it, and it was removed from site (2), wrapped in a specially built torpedo-shaped shell (3) – which nearly sank in the Bay of Biscay – and towed to London, where it was reerected on the Thames Embankment (4).

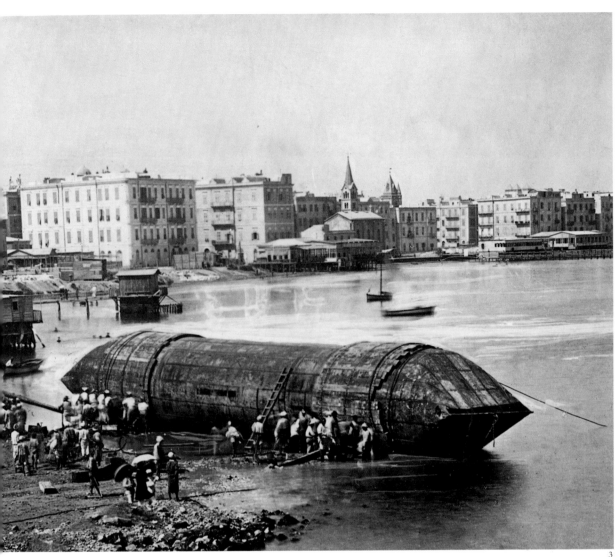

3

D ER Suezkanal lenkte die europäische Aufmerksamkeit nach Ägypten und brachte Ägyptisches in Mode. Fast 2 000 Jahre hatte der als Kleopatras Nadel bekannte Monolith in der Nähe von Alexandria gestanden (1). Jetzt hatten britische Archäologen ein gieriges Auge darauf geworfen. Er wurde von seinem Standort entfernt (2), in eine speziell dafür angefertigte, torpedoförmige Ummantelung verpackt (3), die in der Bucht von Biskaya fast gesunken wäre, und nach London geschleppt, wo man ihn am Ufer der Themse wiederaufstellte (4).

L E canal de Suez concentra l'attention des Européens sur l'Égypte et mit les objets égyptiens à la mode. Depuis près de deux mille ans le monolithe connu sous le nom d'aiguille de Cléopâtre se dressait près d'Alexandrie (1). Et voilà que les archéologues anglais le contemplaient de leurs yeux concupiscents ; il fut retiré du site (2), enveloppé dans une capsule spécialement conçue en forme de torpille (3) – qui faillit bien sombrer dans le golfe de Gascogne – et remorqué jusqu'à Londres pour se dresser de nouveau sur le quai de la Tamise (4).

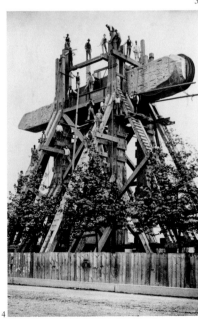

4

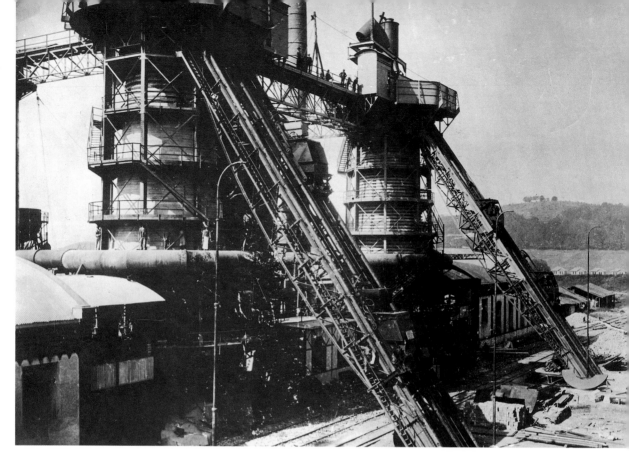

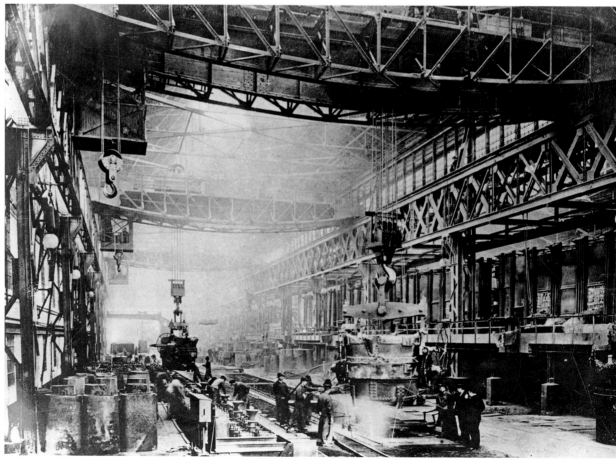

THE Krupp family were the richest in Germany, producing the guns and armaments that made possible implementation of Bismarck's policy of 'blood and iron' in the late 19th century. At the outbreak of the First World War, the Essen works (1 and 2) employed 70,000 workers. In one year alone, Alfred Krupp (3) bought three hundred iron ore mines, to provide the raw material for his colossal foundries. His most famous gun was Big Bertha (4), a monster cannon with a range of 76 miles (122 km) and weighing 200 tons. It fired a shell 12 miles (20 km) high and for twenty weeks in 1918 bombarded Paris.

DIE Krupps waren die reichste Familie Deutschlands. Sie stellten die Waffen für die Umsetzung von Bismarcks Blut-und-Eisen-Politik des ausgehenden 19. Jahrhunderts her. Beim Ausbruch des Ersten Weltkriegs waren in den Essener Werken 70 000 Arbeiter beschäftigt (1, 2). In nur einem Jahr kaufte Alfred Krupp (3) 300 Eisenerzminen, um seine riesigen Gießereien mit Rohstoffen zu versorgen. Seine berühmteste Waffe war die Dicke Bertha (4), eine riesige Kanone mit einer Reichweite von 122 Kilometern und einem Gewicht von 200 Tonnen. Sie feuerte eine Granate 20 Kilometer hoch in die Luft; 1918 bombardierte sie 20 Wochen lang Paris.

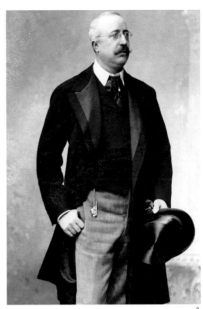

3

LA famille Krupp était la plus riche d'Allemagne ; elle produisit les canons et les armements qui permirent à Bismarck de mettre en œuvre sa politique de « sang et de fer » à la fin du XIXᵉ siècle. Lorsque la Première Guerre mondiale éclata, les usines d'Essen (1 et 2) employaient 70 000 salariés. Alfred Krupp (3) acheta en une seule année trois cents mines de minerai de fer pour fournir la matière première indispensable à ses fonderies colossales. Son canon le plus célèbre fut la Grosse Bertha (4), un canon monstrueux de 200 tonnes qui avait une portée de tir de 122 km. Il tirait des obus qui montaient à 20 km de hauteur. Il pilonna Paris vingt semaines durant en 1918.

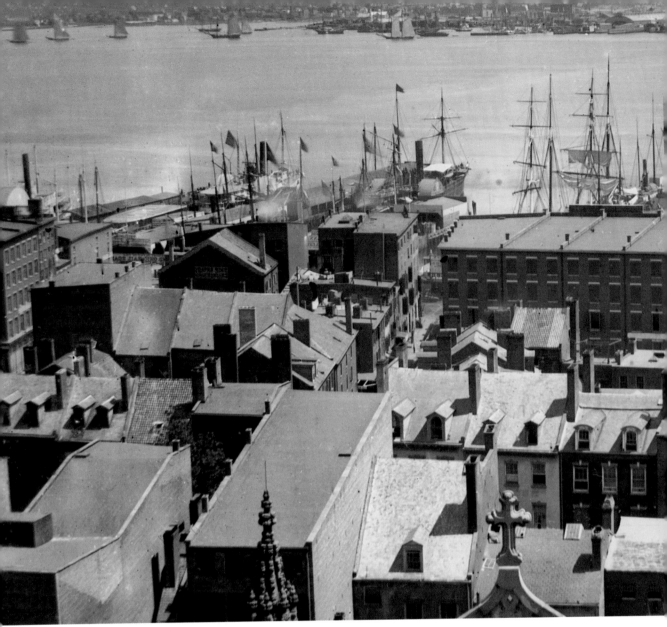

In 1859 William England photographed New York City: the docks (1), the fine brownstone buildings (3), and Wall Street (2), already the financial centre of the city. From the top of the Brandreth Hotel he took pictures of Broadway (overleaf), a street filled with some of the largest shops in the world.

WILLIAM England photographierte New York im Jahre 1859: die Docks (1), die prächtigen Sandsteinhäuser (3) und die Wall Street (2), bereits damals das Finanzzentrum der Stadt. Vom Dach des Brandreth Hotels machte er Aufnahmen vom Broadway (folgende Seiten), einer Straße, in der es einige der größten Geschäfte der Welt gab.

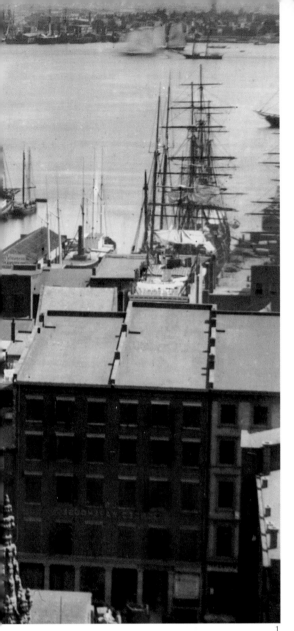

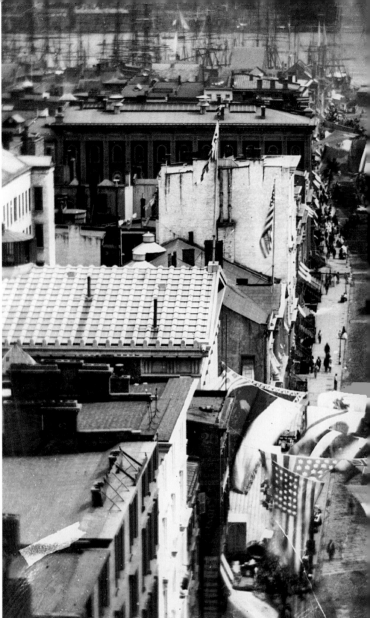

1 2

WILLIAM England photographia New York en 1859 : les quais (1), de beaux bâtiments de grès brun (3), et Wall Street (2), déjà le centre financier de la ville. Il prit du haut de l'hôtel Brandreth des photographies de Broadway (pages suivantes), rue où l'on trouvait quelques-uns des plus vastes grands magasins du monde.

3

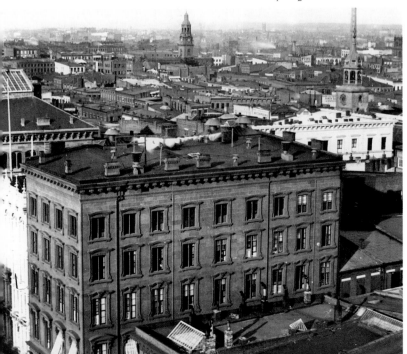

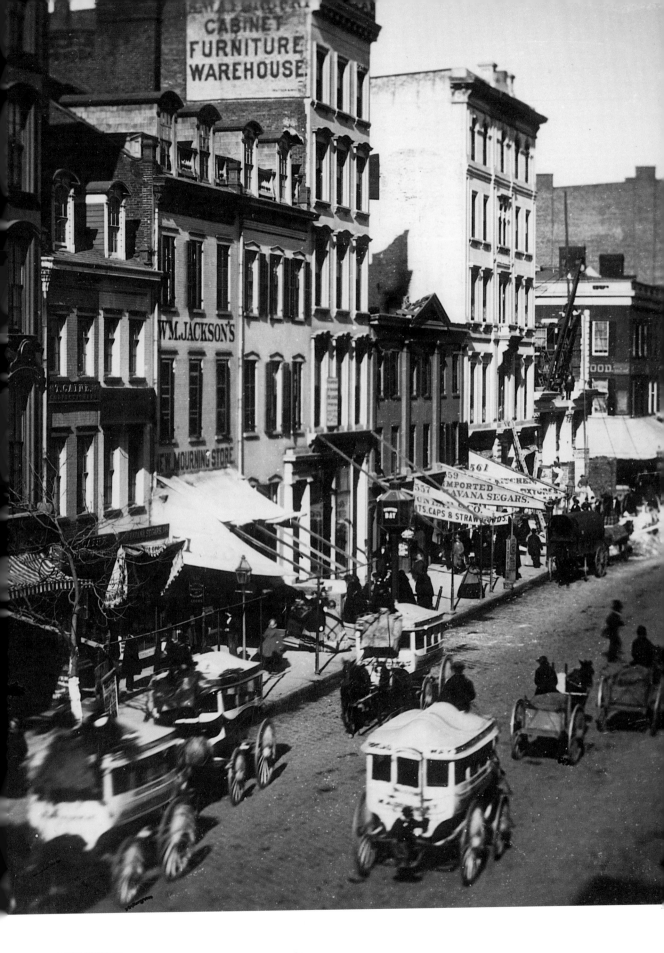

By the mid-1870s, George Augustus Sala, who had last seen Broadway (1) in 1863, was amazed at what had happened: 'Where I remembered wildernesses I now behold terraces after terraces of lordly mansions of brown stone, some with marble façades, others wholly of pure white marble.' By 1890, Fulton's ferries had been superseded by the bold span of the Brooklyn Bridge (2). And by 1917, it took a bold man or woman to build, clean or decorate the towering office and apartment blocks – here Miss Lucille Patterson, an American artist, is painting bills on the side of a skyscraper (3).

MITTE der 1870er Jahre staunte George Augustus Sala, der den Broadway (1) zum letzten Mal im Jahre 1863 gesehen hatte, über die Veränderungen: »Wo damals eine Wildnis war, fand ich jetzt Reihen herrschaftlicher Sandsteinhäuser, einige mit marmornen Fassaden, andere ganz aus weißem Marmor.« In den 1890er Jahren waren Fultons Fähren von der riesigen Brooklyn Bridge (2) verdrängt worden. Und 1917 brauchte es kühne Männer oder Frauen, um die alles überragenden Büro- und Appartementhochhäuser zu bauen, zu reinigen oder zu dekorieren – hier sieht man Miss Lucille Patterson, eine amerikanische Künstlerin, die Werbeanzeigen an die Wand eines Hochhauses malt (3).

DES le milieu des années 1870, George Augustus Sala, dont la dernière visite à Broadway (1) remontait à 1863, était abasourdi par les changements : « Là où dans mes souvenirs se trouvaient des étendues en friche, j'étais frappé de voir se succéder les terrasses d'orgueilleuses demeures en pierre brune, certaines avec une façade en marbre, d'autres entièrement recouvertes d'un marbre blanc et pur. » Dès 1890, les ferry-boats de Fulton avaient été supplantés par la portée hardie du pont Brooklyn (2). En outre, dès 1917, il fallait avoir le cœur bien accroché pour construire, nettoyer ou décorer les bureaux et les immeubles haut perchés : Mademoiselle Lucille Patterson, peintre américain, en train de peindre des affiches sur la face d'un gratte-ciel (3).

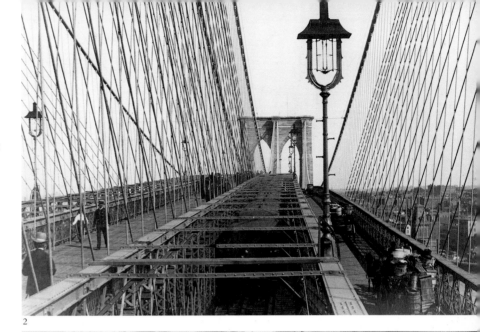

2

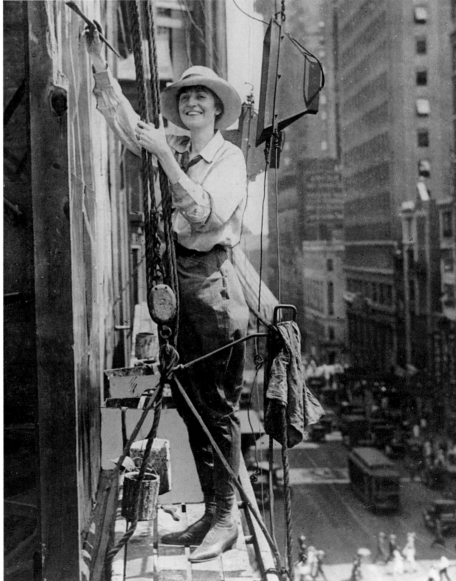

3

New Frontiers

FOR the first time, the camera could capture the glories and eccentricities, the disasters, wonders, heroes and horrors of the age. Early daguerreotypes needed cumbersome equipment and lengthy exposures. It was hardly surprising that most 'sitters' regarded having their photograph taken as more an ordeal than a bit of fun. A good portrait required up to twenty minutes' exposure, during which time the subject must neither move nor blink, while his or her body was fastened into weird metal frameworks that gripped the arms and clamped the neck (1).

By the 1850s, the camera had become more portable, though photographers still travelled with a great deal of heavy apparatus. In 1856 Francis Frith set out on an 800-mile (1,250 km) journey into the Nile Valley with three glass-plate cameras and a complete darkroom. The same year the Bisson brothers of France employed 25 porters to carry their equipment into the Alps. Two years earlier, Roger Fenton had covered the Crimean War from a horse-drawn wagon proudly named 'The Photographic Carriage'. Action pictures were not yet possible, but Fenton was forbidden to photograph death and destruction – even though corpses didn't move during exposures of ten to fifteen seconds.

For a further ten years, photographers toured the world in their vans and wagons, capturing scenes of life in the Far East and the Far West. The Venetian-born Felice Beato visited India to photograph the Mutiny in 1857; he then went on to China, where he took pictures of the rebellion of 1860, before settling in Japan in 1862, where he opened his own photographic business.

In the 1860s the first truly portable cameras appeared on the market, and by the 1880s photography was sufficiently accessible for the general public to become the most popular hobby of the day. Informal 'snapshots' (the word was first used in 1890) preserved for eternity the everyday life of ordinary people. For the first time in history it was possible for one half of the world to see how the other half lived; for the sons and daughters of miners, shopkeepers, parlour-maids, stable-lads, factory hands and chimney-sweeps to know what their parents had looked like when they, too, were young; for stay-at-homes to see the Taj Mahal, the Eiger, the Golden Horn or the Great Wall of China.

And before the century ended, there were pictures that moved.

ZUM ersten Mal konnte die Kamera den Stolz und die Exzentrizität, die Desaster, Wunder, Helden und Schrecken der Zeit einfangen. Für die frühen Daguerrotypien waren eine umfangreiche Ausrüstung und lange Belichtungszeiten erforderlich. Es überraschte kaum, daß die meisten Modelle es eher anstrengend als lustig fanden, eine Photographie von sich machen zu lassen. Ein gutes Portrait mußte bis zu zwanzig Minuten belichtet werden; in dieser Zeit durfte sich das Modell weder bewegen noch blinzeln, und sein oder ihr Körper steckte in einem merkwürdigen Metallrahmen, der die Arme festhielt und das Genick festklammerte (1).

Um die Mitte des 19. Jahrhunderts war die Kamera transportabler geworden, obwohl die Photographen noch immer mit vielen schweren Apparaten herumreisten. Francis Frith begab sich 1856 mit drei Glasplattenkameras und einer kompletten Dunkelkammer auf eine 1 250 Kilometer lange Reise ins Niltal. Im selben Jahr beschäftigten die französischen Bisson-Brüder 25 Träger, um ihre Ausrüstung in die Alpen zu bringen. Zwei Jahre zuvor hatte Roger Fenton den Krimkrieg von einem Pferdewagen aus photographiert, der den stolzen Namen »The Photographic Carriage« trug. Aufnahmen von Bewegungen waren noch nicht möglich, aber Fenton wurde es verboten, Tod und Zerstörung zu photographieren – auch wenn sich Leichen während einer Belichtungszeit von zehn bis fünfzehn Sekunden bestimmt nicht bewegten.

Weitere zehn Jahre bereisten Photographen die Welt in ihren Wagen und Waggons und fingen Szenen des Lebens im Fernen Osten wie im Fernen Westen ein. Der in Venedig geborene Felice Beato besuchte 1857 Indien, um den Aufstand zu photographieren, und fuhr dann nach China, wo er 1860 Aufnahmen von der Rebellion machte, bevor er sich 1862 in Japan niederließ und dort sein eigenes Photoatelier eröffnete.

In den 1860er Jahren erschienen die ersten wirklich tragbaren Kameras auf dem Markt. In den 1880er Jahren hatte fast jedermann Zugang zur Photographie, und sie wurde zum beliebtesten Hobby der Zeit. Zwanglose »Schnappschüsse« (das Wort wurde zum ersten Mal 1890 verwendet) hielten das Alltagsleben der einfachen Menschen für die Ewigkeit fest. Zum ersten Mal in der Geschichte der Menschheit konnte die eine Hälfte der Welt sehen, wie die andere Hälfte lebte, erfuhren die Söhne und Töchter von Bergarbeitern, Ladenbesitzern, Dienstmädchen, Stallburschen, Fabrikarbeitern und

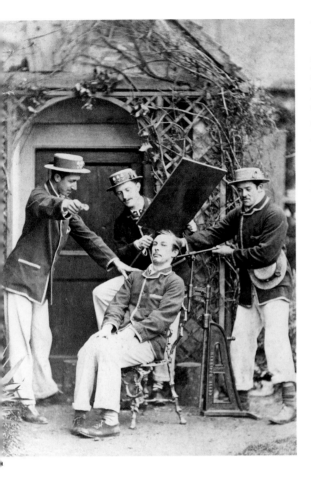

Schornsteinfegern, wie ihre Eltern in jungen Jahren ausgesehen hatten, und konnten die zu Hause Gebliebenen Bilder vom Taj Mahal, dem Eiger, dem Goldenen Horn oder der chinesischen Mauer betrachten.

Und bevor das Jahrhundert zu Ende ging, gab es Bilder, die sich bewegten.

POUR la première fois, l'appareil photographique pouvait capter les gloires et les excentricités, les désastres, les merveilles, les héros et les horreurs de l'époque. Les tout premiers daguerréotypes nécessitaient un équipement encombrant et des temps d'exposition extrêmement longs. Rien d'étonnant donc si la plupart des « modèles » considéraient la séance photographique davantage comme une épreuve que comme une partie de plaisir. Un bon portrait exigeait jusqu'à vingt minutes de pose sans bouger ni ciller, tandis que le corps de la personne photographiée était sanglé dans d'étranges cadres de métal qui enserraient ses bras et son cou (1).

Dès les années 1850, l'appareil photographique devint plus maniable, bien que les photographes continuassent à se déplacer avec un lourd appareillage. En 1856, Francis Frith entreprit un voyage de 1 250 km dans la vallée du Nil en transportant trois appareils photographiques munis de plaques en verre et une chambre noire complète. La même année, des Français, les frères Bisson, employèrent vingt-cinq porteurs pour transporter leur équipement dans les Alpes. Deux ans plus tôt, Roger Fenton avait couvert la guerre de Crimée à partir d'un chariot tiré par des chevaux et fièrement qualifié d' « attelage photographique ». Les photographies animées n'étaient pas encore possibles ; pourtant on avait interdit à Fenton de photographier les morts et les destructions, même si les cadavres ne bougeaient pas pendant les dix à quinze secondes que duraient l'exposition.

Au cours des dix années qui suivirent, les photographes parcoururent le monde dans leurs fourgons et chariots, fixant les scènes de la vie en Extrême-Orient et dans le Far West. Felice Beato, qui était né à Venise, se rendit en Inde pour y photographier la révolte de 1857, puis en Chine la rébellion de 1860, avant de s'installer au Japon en 1862 où il se mit à son propre compte comme photographe.

Dans les années 1860 apparurent sur le marché les premiers appareils photographiques véritablement portables ; dès les années 1880, le grand public avait accès à la photographie de sorte que celle-ci devint le loisir le plus populaire de l'époque. Les « instantanés » (le terme apparut en 1890) informels préservaient pour l'éternité la vie quotidienne des gens ordinaires. Pour la première fois dans l'histoire, une moitié du monde pouvait regarder vivre l'autre ; les fils et filles de mineurs, boutiquiers, femmes de chambre, garçons d'étable, les ouvriers d'usine et les ramoneurs pouvaient voir à quoi avaient ressemblé leurs parents plus jeunes ; les pantouflards avaient la possibilité de voir le Taj Mahal, le mont Eiger, la Corne d'Or ou la Grande Muraille de Chine.

Et le siècle n'était pas achevé que déjà les images s'animaient.

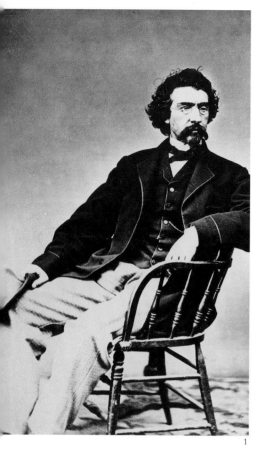

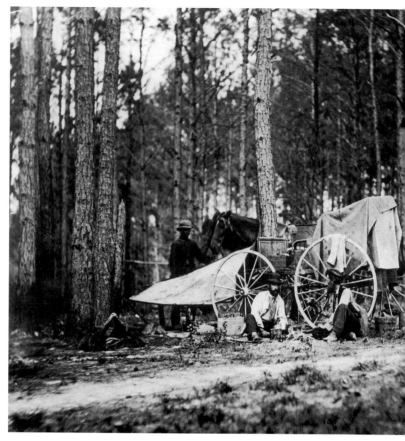

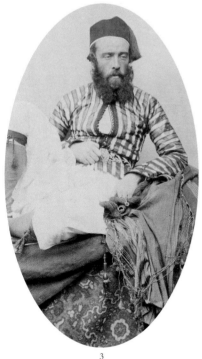

3

MATTHEW Brady (1) was an early travelling photographer who covered the American Civil War. The federal soldiers whom he photographed called the converted buggy in which he had his darkroom 'The Whatisit Wagon' (2). Francis Frith (3) made three journeys into Egypt and opened a photographic printing firm. Eadweard Muybridge (4) was an Englishman who pioneered the technique of using trip wires, taking a series of action pictures to study how humans and animals moved.

MATTHEW Brady (1) war ein früher Reisephotograph, der über den Amerikanischen Bürgerkrieg berichtete. Die von ihm photographierten föderalistischen Soldaten nannten den umgebauten Wagen, in dem er seine Dunkelkammer eingerichtet hatte, »The Whatisit Wagon« (2). Francis Frith (3) unternahm drei Reisen nach Ägypten und gründete ein Unternehmen für Photabzüge. Der Engländer Eadweard Muybridge (4) leistete Pionierarbeit für die Technik der Fernauslöserdrähte, mit denen er eine Serie von Aktionsphotos machte, um die Bewegungen von Mensch und Tier zu studieren.

MATTHEW Brady (1) fut l'un des premiers photographes itinérants à documenter la guerre civile américaine. Le soldats fédéraux qu'il photographiait appelaient le chariot qu'il avait converti pour y placer sa chambre noire « le chariot qu'est-ce-que-c'est » (2). Francis Frith (3) se rendit trois fois en Égypte et monta une entreprise de films photographiques. Eadweard Muybridge (4) fut un pionnier de la technique du déclenchement par fil et fit une série de photographies animées permettant d'étudier les mouvements de l'homme et de l'animal.

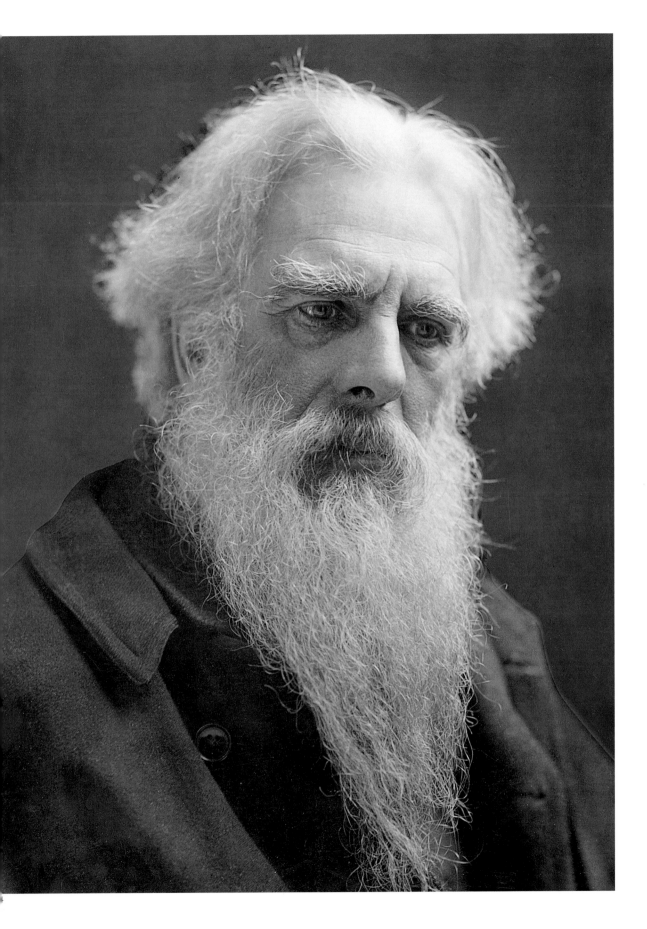

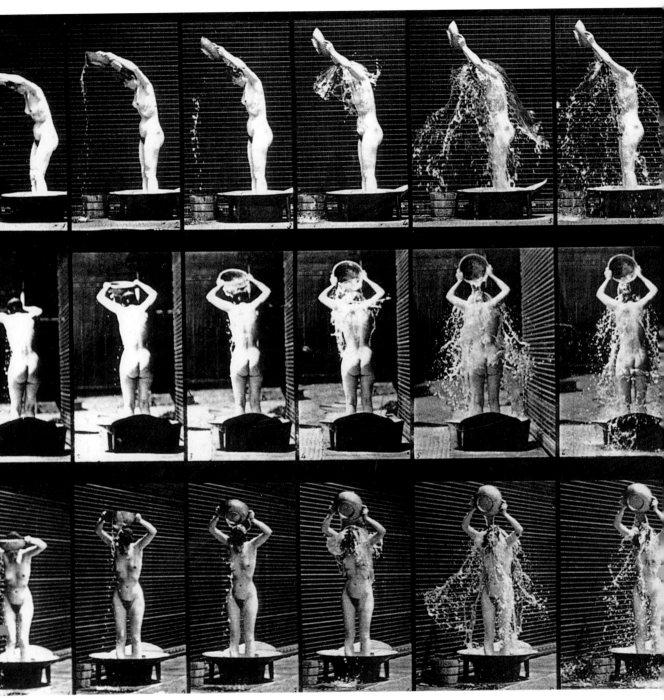

THIS is one of Muybridge's most famous (and most popular) studies of movement – a naked woman dowsing herself with water in a bathtub. There were some who regarded these pictures as shocking, some who considered them delightful, and many who looked on them as both. Among Muybridge's more ridiculous models in the 1880s were a naked cricketer, a naked hurdler, and a naked swordsman. The pictures were taken with a series of 12 to 24 cameras at an exposure of 1/500th of a second and caused a sensation at the Chicago Exhibition of 1893 when projected on a Zoopraxiscope.

DIES ist eine von Muybridges berühmtesten (und beliebtesten) Bewegungsstudien, eine nackte Frau, die sich in einer Badewanne mit Wasser übergießt. Manche fanden diese Bilder schockierend, andere reizend, und für viele waren sie beides. Zu Muybridges eher lächerlichen Modellen gehörten in den 1880ern ein Kricketspieler

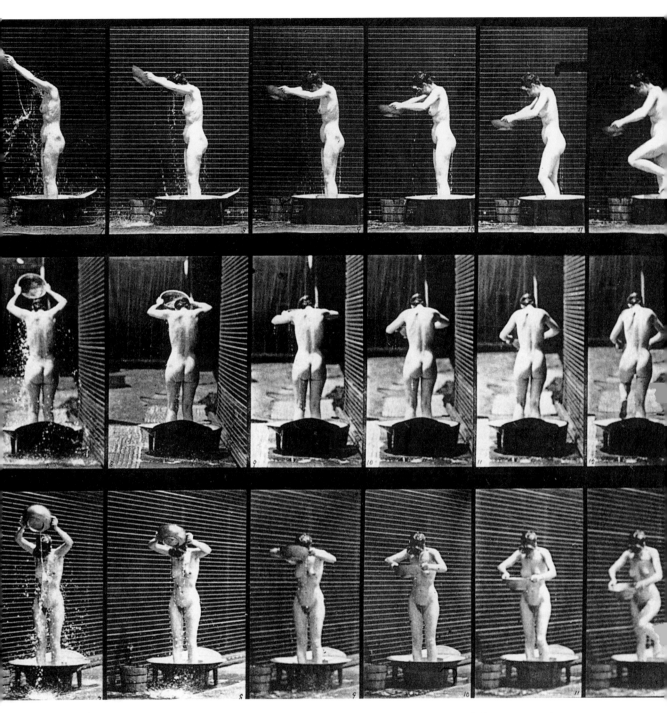

in Hürdenläufer und ein Fechter – alles kte. Die Aufnahmen wurden mit 12 bis 4 Kameras bei einer Belichtungszeit von iner Fünfhundertstelsekunde gemacht und orgten bei der Chicagoer Weltausstellung on 1893 für eine Sensation, als sie auf ein Zoopraxiskop projiziert wurden.

VOICI une des études de mouvement les plus célèbres (et les plus prisées) de Muybridge : une femme nue qui s'asperge d'eau dans une baignoire. Certains trouvèrent ces photos choquantes, d'autres plaisantes et beaucoup les deux à la fois. Parmi les modèles les plus ridicules de Muybridge durant les années 1880 figurent un joueur de cricket,

un sauteur de haies et un escrimeur nus. Les photographies avaient été prises avec une batterie de 12 à 24 appareils photographiques et une exposition de 1/500 de seconde. Elles firent sensation lorsqu'elles furent projetées au moyen de son zoopraxiscope en 1893 à l'exposition de Chicago.

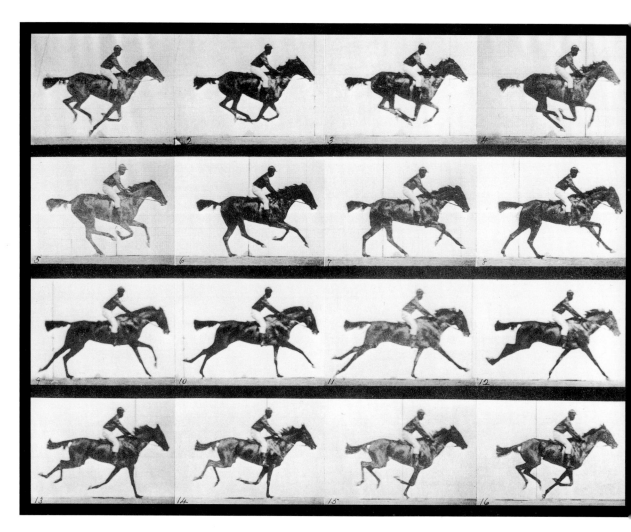

THANKS to Muybridge's action shots of a horse (1), it was possible to establish that the horse did at one time have all four feet off the ground when trotting – news that pleased Governor Leland Stanford of California, who had made a wager to that effect. There were some, however, who claimed that a horse's legs could never assume such unlikely positions. Among others who had experimented with moving action pictures was Dr Jules Marey, with his chronophotograph of a fencer (2). Thomas Edison (3) pioneered micrography – the study of microscopic objects by photography.

DANK Muybridges Bewegungsstudien eines Pferdes (1) konnte man feststellen, daß beim Trab für einen Moment keines seiner vier Beine den Boden berührte – eine Neuigkeit, die dem kalifornischen Gouverneur Leland Stanford sehr gefiel, denn er hatte darauf eine Wette abgeschlossen. Es gab jedoch auch manche, die behaupteten, die Beine eines Pferdes könnten niemals solch unwahrscheinliche Haltungen einnehmen. Zu denen, die ebenfalls mit Bewegungsphotos experimentierten, gehörte Dr. Jules Marey mit seiner Chronophotographie eines Fechters (2). Thomas Edison (3) erfand die Mikrophotographie, das Studium mikroskopisch kleiner Objekte mit Hilfe der Photographie.

GRÂCE aux instantanés animés d'un cheval (1) pris par Muybridge, on pu constater que l'animal au trot avait à un moment donné ses quatre sabots en l'air ; nouvelle réjouit le gouverneur de Californie, Leland Stanford, qui avait parié en ce sens. Certains affirmèrent malgré tout qu'i était tout à fait impossible que les jambes d'un cheval prissent des positions aussi invrai semblables. Parmi ceux qui s'essayèrent à la photographie animée, on trouve Jules Marey et sa chronophoto-graphie d'un escrimeur (2). Thomas Edison (3) fut un pionnier de la micrographie, l'étude des objets microscopiques grâce à la photographie.

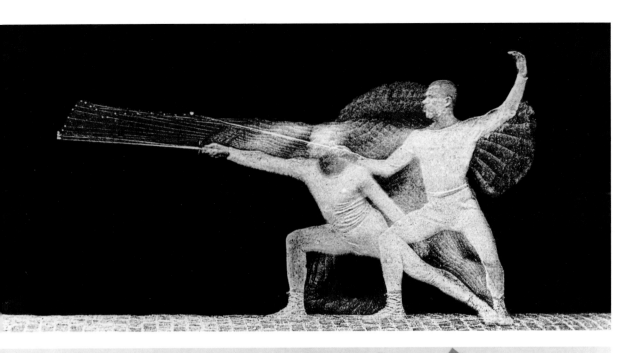

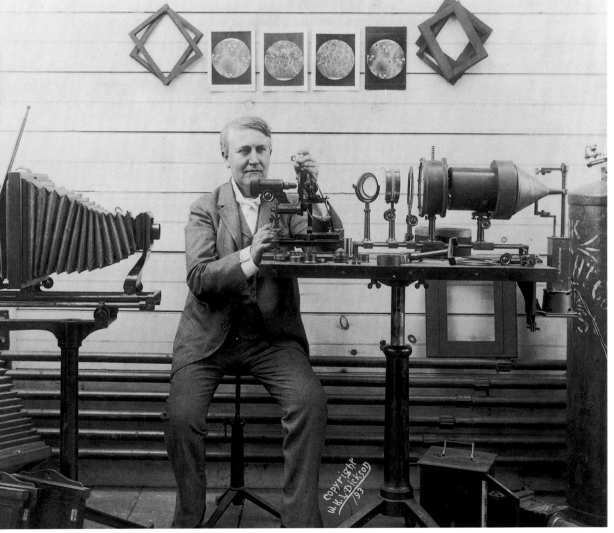

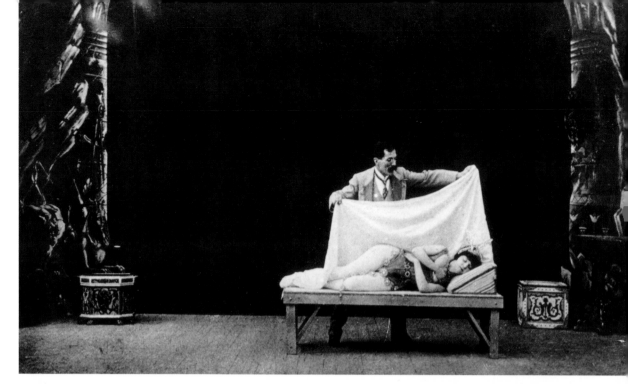

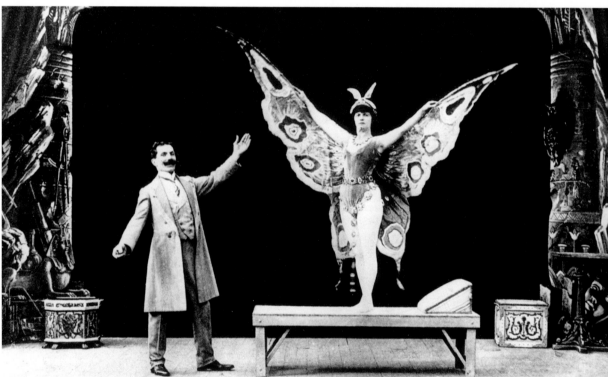

GEORGES Méliès was a French magician, designer, actor and theatre manager. He quickly saw how magic and fantasy could be combined with the new cinematograph cameras. Here he turns a woman into a butterfly (1 and 2). His later films were more lavish and complex, with specially built sets (3) and special effects (4).

DER Franzose Georges Méliès war Magier, Designer, Schauspieler und Theaterdirektor. Er erkannte schnell, daß die neuen kinematographischen Kameras neue Horizonte für Magie und Phantasie eröffneten. Hier verwandelt er eine Frau in einen Schmetterling (1, 2). Seine späteren Filme waren überschwenglicher und komplexer, mit speziellen Dekorationen (3) und Effekten ausgestattet (4).

GEORGES Méliès était un illusionniste français, créateur, comédien et directeur de théâtre. Il comprit rapidement comment combiner et photographier la magie et le fantastique grâce aux nouvelles caméras cinématographiques. Il transforme ici une femme en papillon (1 et 2). Après 1899, ses films se firent complexes et nécessitaient des décors (3) et des effets spéciaux (4).

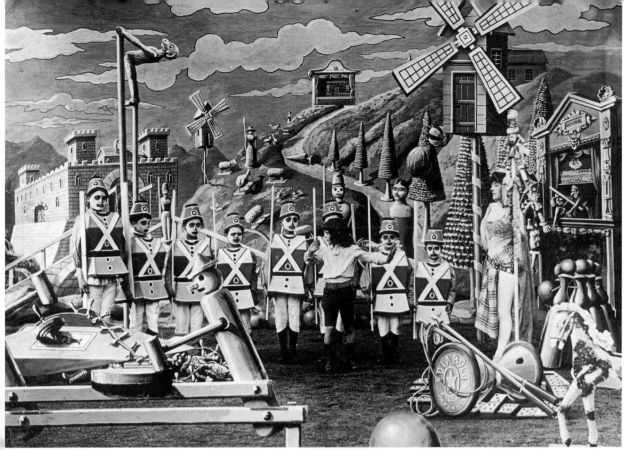

3

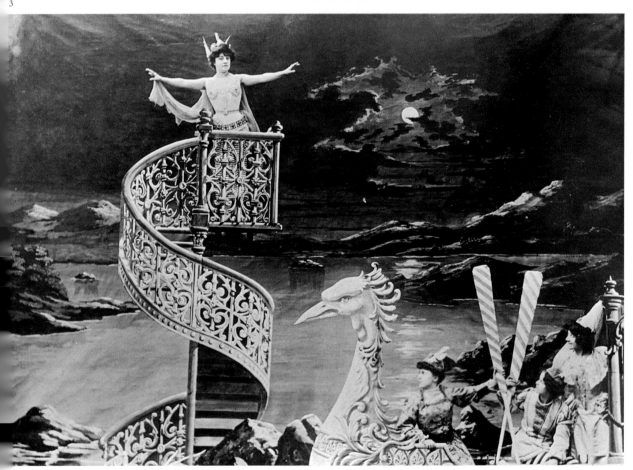

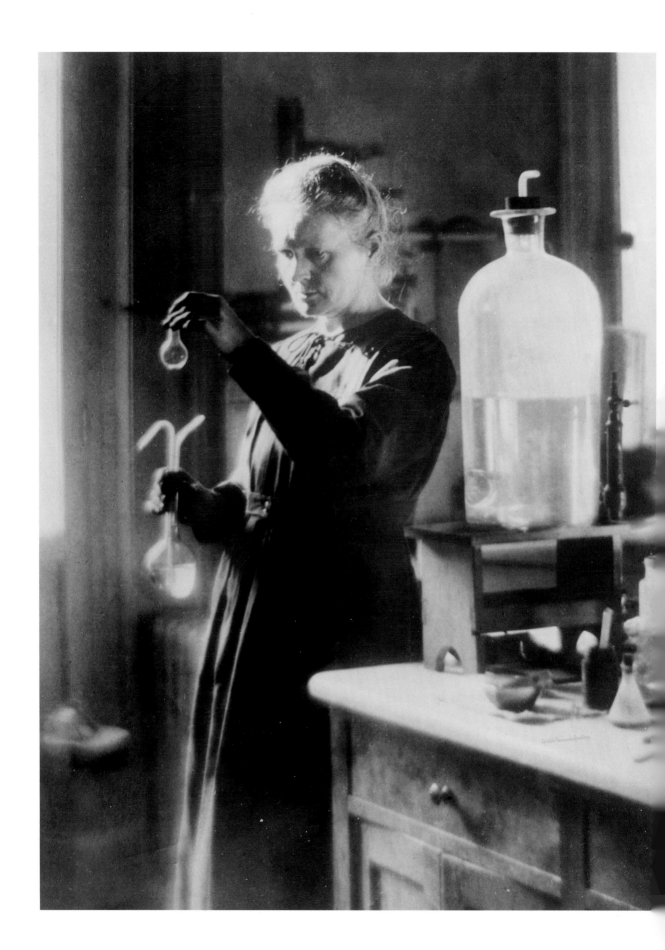

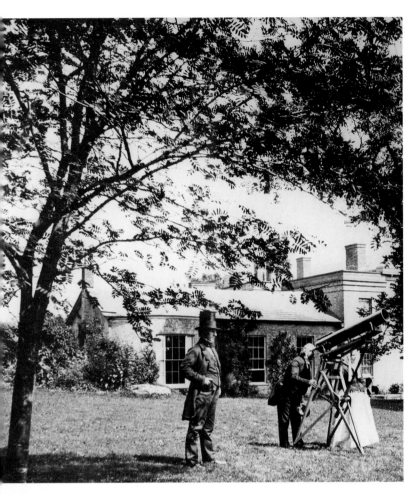

THOMAS Edison and Henry Ford
(3, right and left) examine Edison's
light bulbs. Marie Curie at work in
her laboratory (1). Amateur astronomers
examine the heavens in the days before
flashlight photography (2). The Marchese
Marconi (4, centre) at Signal Hill,
Newfoundland, before receiving the first
trans-Atlantic wireless signal.

THOMAS Edison und Henry Ford
(3, rechts und links) untersuchen
Edisons Glühbirnen. Marie Curie bei der
Arbeit in ihrem Labor (1). In den Tagen
vor der Erfindung der Blitzlichtphotogra-
phie untersuchen zwei Amateurastronomen
den Himmel bei Tag (2). Der Marchese
Marconi (4, Mitte) auf dem Signal Hill in
Neufundland, kurz vor dem Empfang des
ersten transatlantischen Telegraphensignals.

THOMAS Edison et Henry Ford (3, à
droite et à gauche) examinent la première ampoule électrique d'Edison. Marie
Curie au travail dans son laboratoire (1).
Deux astronomes amateurs examinant les
cieux à la lumière du jour avant l'arrivée
de la photographie au flash (2). Le marquis
Marconi (4, au centre) à Signal Hill, Terre-
Neuve, quelques instants avant de recevoir
le premier signal transatlantique par ondes
hertziennes.

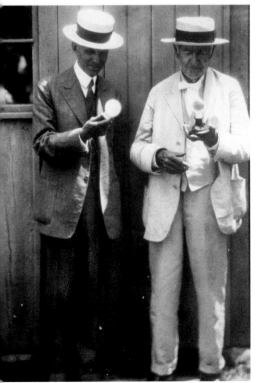

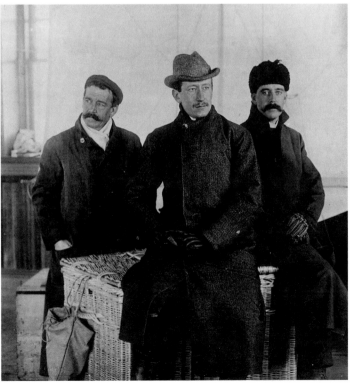

4

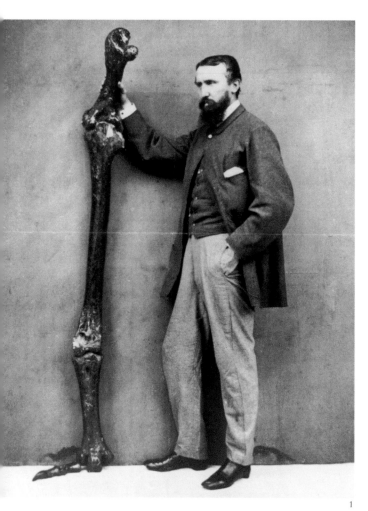

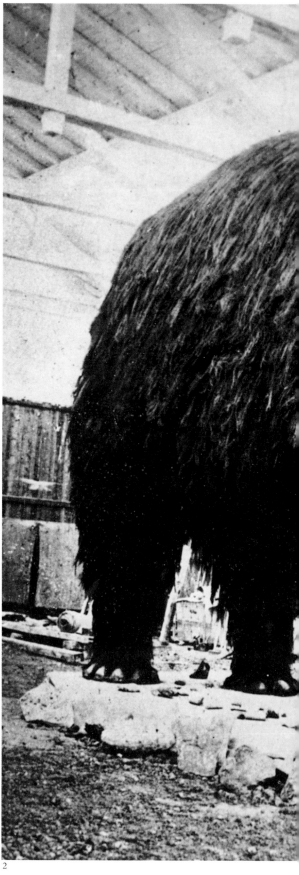

A stuffed mammoth from Siberia is exhibited in the St Petersburg Museum in the 1860s (2), while an unknown archae-
ologist holds a newly discovered fossil of a leg bone from some
colossal animal (1).

EIN ausgestopftes Mammut aus Sibirien wird in den 1860er
Jahren im Museum von St. Petersburg ausgestellt (2). Ein
unbekannter Archäologe hält den jüngst entdeckten versteinerten
Beinknochen eines riesigen Tieres (1).

UN mammouth empaillé en provenance de Sibérie est exposé
au musée de Saint-Pétersbourg dans les années 1860 (2).
Un archéologue inconnu tient un fossile que l'on vient de découvrir :
le tibia d'un animal gigantesque (1).

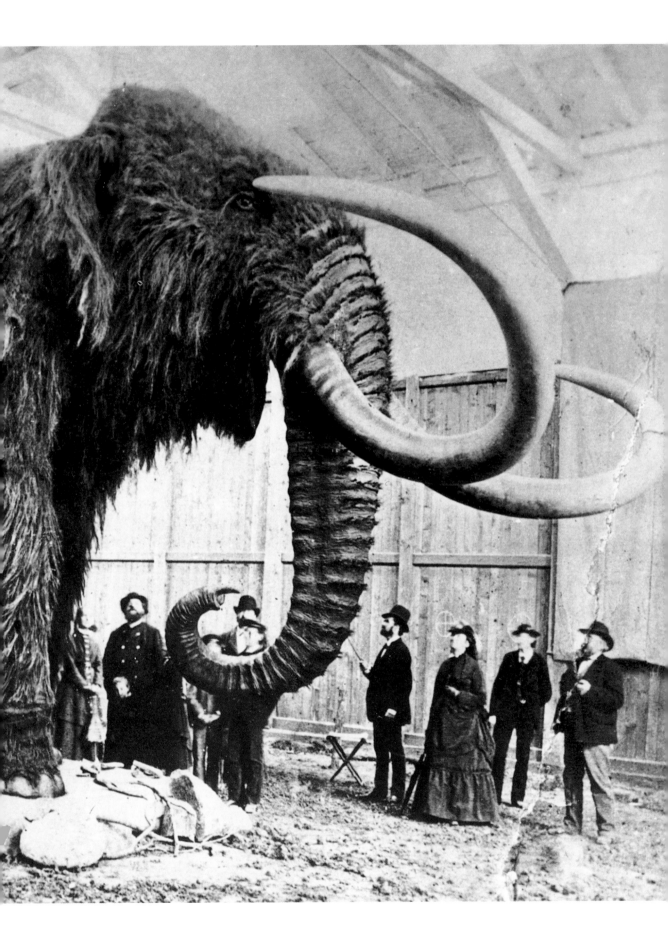

IN 1898 gold was discovered in the Klon
dike in north-west Canada. 22,000 pro-
spectors a year poured in, dragging their
stumbling pack-horses up the ice (1).
In their wake came saloon-keepers and
'actresses' (2, crossing the Dyea River).
Towns like Skagway – the most lawless
place on earth – sprang up overnight (3).
Dawson City (4) was the biggest boom
town.

IM Jahre 1898 wurde im Klondike im
Nordwesten Kanadas Gold gefunden.
Jährlich kamen 22 000 Goldsucher und
zogen ihre stolpernden Packpferde über d
Eis (1). Mit ihnen kamen Saloonbetreiber
und »Schauspielerinnen« (2, beim Überqueren des Flusses Dyea). Städte wie Skag
way, der gesetzloseste Ort der Welt,
entstanden über Nacht (3). Dawson City
war die größte Goldgräberstadt (4).

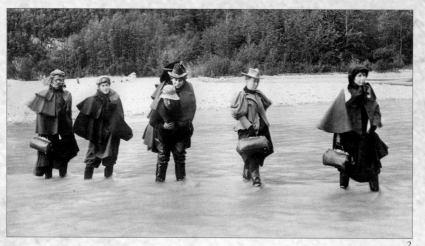

2

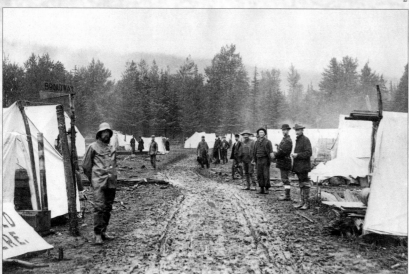

3

En 1898, on découvrit de l'or dans le Klondike, au nord-ouest du Canada. 2 000 chercheurs d'or arrivaient chaque année, tirant leurs chevaux de bât qui trébuchaient sur la glace (1). Dans leur sillage suivaient les tenanciers de tripots et les « actrices » (2, traversant la rivière Dyea). Des villes comme Skagway – l'endroit aux mœurs les plus dissolues de la terre – surgirent en une nuit (3). Dawson City (4) fut la ville qui connut la plus grande prospérité.

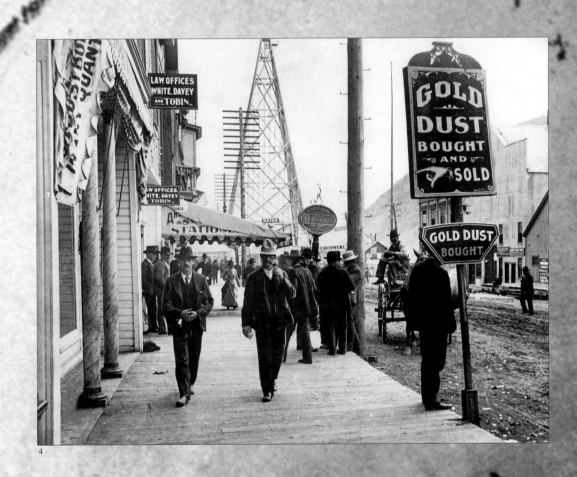

4

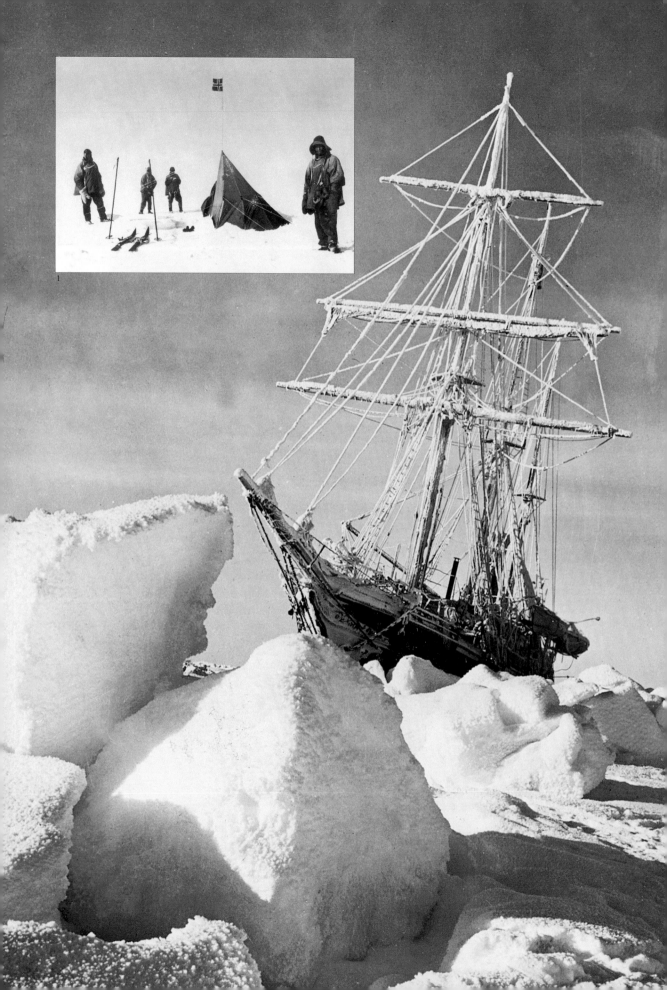

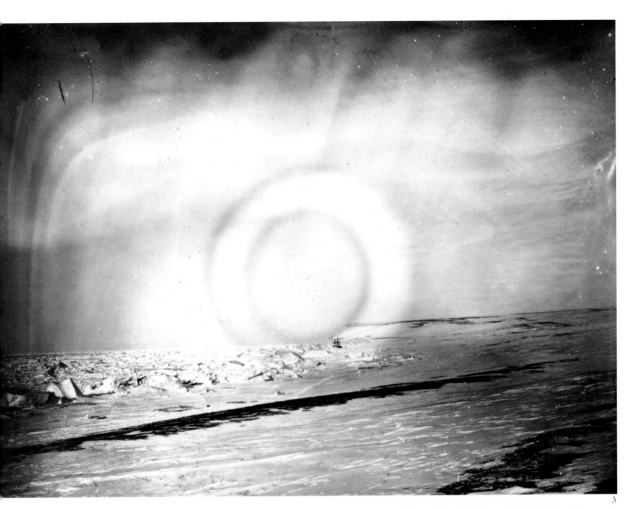

3

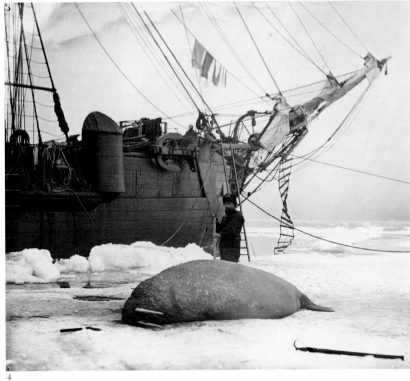

MEMBERS of Scott's last South Polar Expedition outside Amundsen's tent at the Pole, January 1912 (1). Shackleton's *Endurance* caught in the Antarctic ice in 1917 (2) . The Aurora Borealis (3), photographed in 1876 by members of the British Nares Expedition (4 – with dead walrus).

MITGLIEDER der letzten Expedition zum Südpol unter Kapitän Scott stehen im Januar 1912 vor Amundsens Zelt am Pol (1). Shackletons *Endurance* wurde 1917 im antarktischen Eis aufgenommen (2). Die Aurora Borealis am arktischen Himmel (3), 1876 von Mitgliedern der britischen Nares-Expedition photographiert (4, mit totem Walroß).

LES membres de la dernière expédition du capitaine Scott au pôle Sud à côté de la tente d'Amundsen en janvier 1912 (1). L'*Endurance* de Sir Ernest Shackleton pris dans les glaces de l'Antarctique en 1917 (2) ; une aurore boréale dans le ciel de l'Arctique (3) photographiée en 1876 par les membres de l'expédition britannique Nares (4, près d'un morse mort).

4

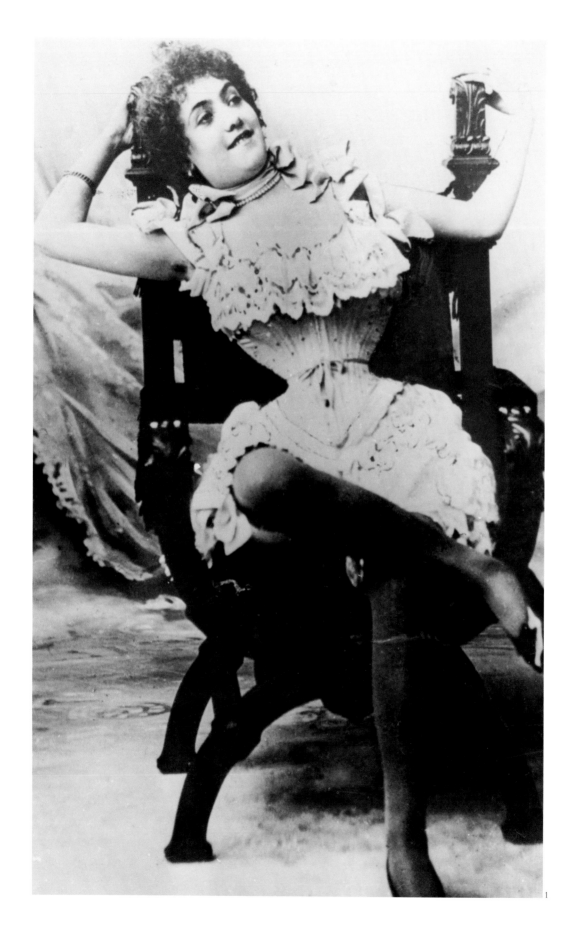

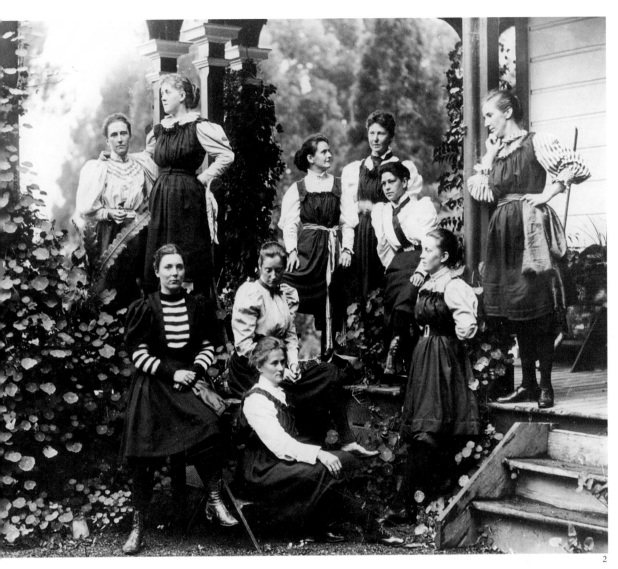

PIN-UP pictures became popular in the early 1900s. Scorning the fashion scene, however, were those who favoured practicality in costume – an afternoon tea party in rational dress in 1895 (2). But some were prepared almost to cut themselves in half to display a wasp waist – the French music-hall singer Polaire in 1890 (1).

DIE beliebtesten Pin-up-Bilder kurz nach 1900 waren die der Gibson Girls. Verachtet wurde die Modeszene von den Befürwortern praktikabler Bekleidung – eine nachmittägliche Teaparty in zweckmäßiger Kleidung im Jahre 1895 (2). Aber es gab auch Frauen, die bereit waren, sich fast in der Mitte durchzutrennen, um eine Wespentaille präsentieren zu können, wie die französische Sängerin Polaire im Jahre 1890 (1).

LES photographies de dames les plus appréciées au début des années 1900 représentaient les Gibson Girls. Il y avait celles qui faisaient fi de la mode et voulaient que le vêtement fût seulement pratique : un goûter dans une robe fonctionnelle en 1895 (2). Mais certaines étaient prêtes à se couper quasiment en deux pour montrer une taille de guêpe – la chanteuse Polaire, en 1890 (1).

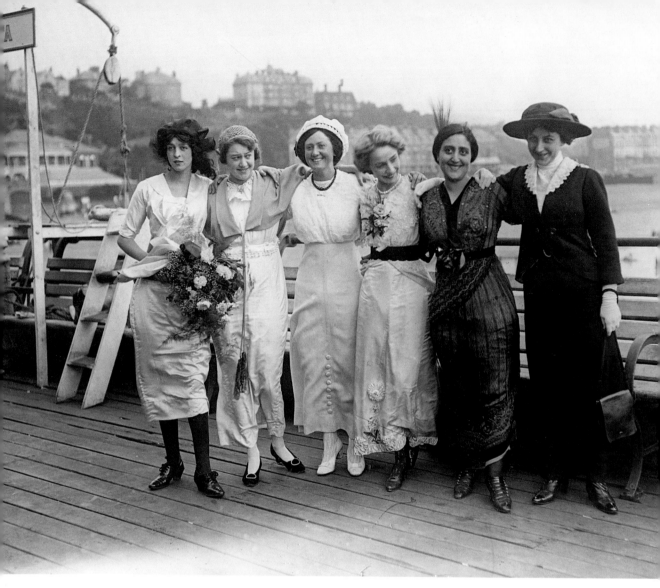

ON Folkestone Pier in August 1913, contestants in an early International Beauty Show parade their smiles (1 – from left to right: England, France, Denmark, Germany, Italy and Spain). The camera played a highly culpable part in popularizing fashion displays and beauty competitions – a prizewinner in a Paris magazine contest in 1902, one of the first 'cover-girls' (2).

Edward VII died on 6 May 1910. A month later, society was still in mourning, but fashionably so for the Ascot Race Meeting (3). At the racecourse at Long-champs, Paris, in 1914, just before the outbreak of war, the fashion of the day was the harem skirt (4).

AM Pier von Folkestone präsentieren die Mitstreiterinnen eines frühen Schönheitswettbewerbs im August 1913 ihr Lächeln (1, von links nach rechts: England, Frankreich, Dänemark, Deutschland, Italien und Spanien). Die Kamera trug dazu bei, daß sich Modenschauen und Schönheitswettbewerbe immer größerer Beliebtheit erfreuten; die Gewinnerin des Wettbewerbs eines Pariser Magazins aus dem Jahre 1902, eines der ersten »Cover-girls« (2).

Edward VII. starb am 6. Mai 1910. Einen Monat später trauerte die Gesellschaft zwar noch immer, für das Pferderennen in Ascot tat sie dies jedoch modebewußt (3). Auf der Rennbahn von Longchamps in Paris waren 1914, kurz vor Ausbruch des Krieges, Haremsröcke der letzte Schrei (4).

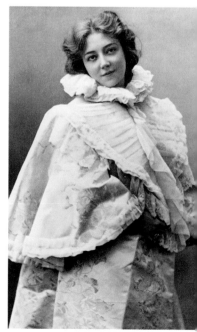

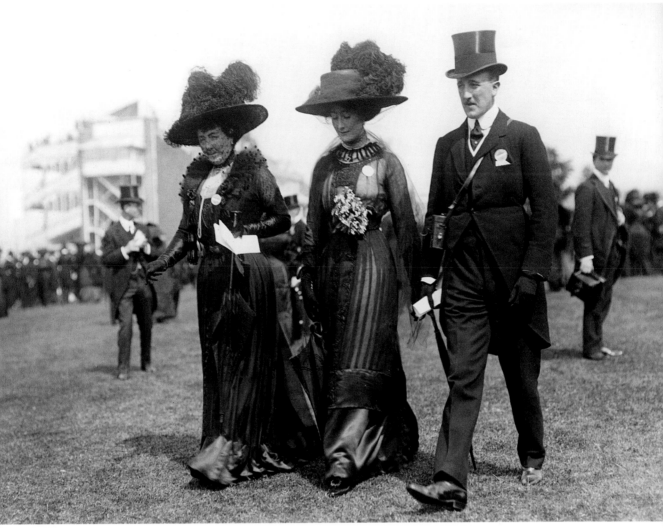

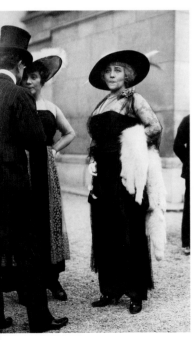

Sur la jetée de Folkestone en août 1913, les concurrentes participent à l'un des premiers concours internationaux de beauté (1, de gauche à droite : Angleterre, France, Danemark, Allemagne, Italie et Espagne). L'appareil photographique a joué ici un rôle extrêmement coupable puisqu'il popularisa les défilés de mode et les concours de beauté. La lauréate du concours organisé par un magazine parisien en 1902, une des premières « cover-girls » (2).

Édouard VII mourut le 6 mai 1910. Un mois plus tard, la haute société le pleurait toujours, sans que la mode ne perdît ses droits aux courses d'Ascot (3). Aux courses de Longchamp à Paris, en 1914, juste avant que n'éclatât la guerre, la jupe « Harem » était alors en vogue (4).

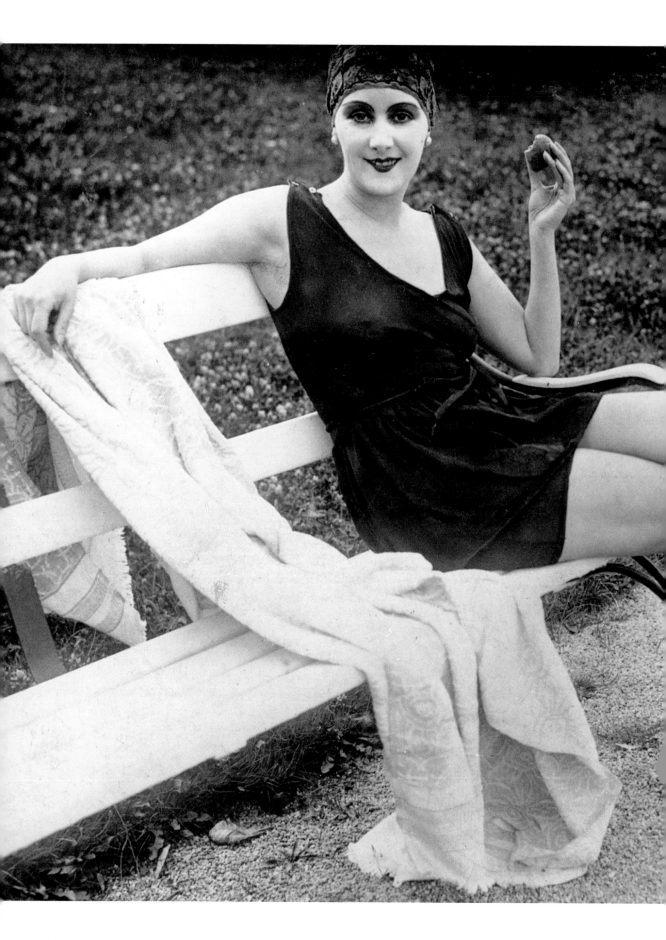

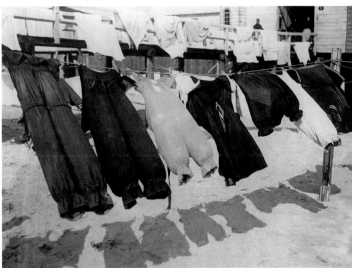

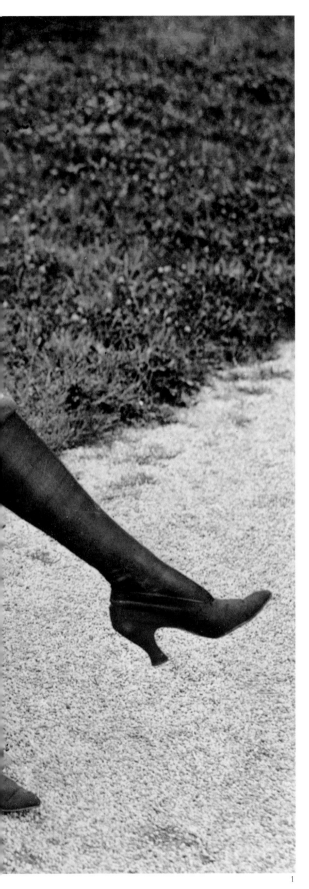

IN sport, education, the arts, society and employment, the New Woman had made considerable progress against enormous opposition. 'They dress … like men. They talk … like men. They live … like men. They don't … like men' was *Punch's* funny little view in 1895. Women now smoked cigarettes in public, took their own lodgings or at least demanded a key to the family home, and challenged outmoded social conventions. By the beginning of the 20th century, all caution – and many swimsuits – had been thrown to the wind (2). Decent folk were outraged by the wanton shamelessness of bathing belles who dared to pose (rather than swim) in the one-piece bathing costume (1).

IM Sport, in der Ausbildung und Erziehung, in der Kunst, der Gesellschaft und der Arbeitswelt hatte die Neue Frau trotz einer äußerst starken Opposition enorme Fortschritte gemacht. »Sie kleiden sich … wie Männer. Sie reden … wie Männer. Sie leben … wie Männer. Sie mögen … keine Männer«, war 1895 *Punchs* Meinung. Frauen rauchten nun in der Öffentlichkeit, hatten ihre eigenen Wohnungen oder verlangten zumindest einen Schlüssel für das Familienheim und stellten überkommene gesellschaftliche Konventionen in Frage.

Zu Beginn des 20. Jahrhunderts war alle Vorsicht – und viele Badeanzüge – über Bord geworfen worden (2). Viele Leute waren entsetzt über die sträfliche Schamlosigkeit von Badeschönheiten, die es wagten, (statt zu schwimmen) in einem einteiligen Badeanzug zu posieren (1).

DANS le monde du sport, de l'éducation, des arts, dans la société et sur le marché du travail, la Femme Nouvelle avait gagné un terrain considérable face à une énorme opposition. « Elles s'habillent … comme les hommes. Elles parlent … comme les hommes. Elles vivent … comme les hommes. Elles ne font pas … comme les hommes. »

Telle était la plaisanterie sans finesse qu'on pouvait lire dans *Punch* en 1895. Les femmes fumaient maintenant des cigarettes en public, avaient leurs propres appartements ou au moins exigeaient de posséder une clé du domicile familial, et défiaient les conventions sociales démodées.

Dès le début du XXᵉ siècle, toute précaution – et bien des maillots de bain – furent mis au vestiaire (2). Les gens honnêtes se sentirent outragés par l'impudeur de ces belles baigneuses qui avaient l'audace de poser (plutôt que de nager) dans un costume de bain une pièce (1).

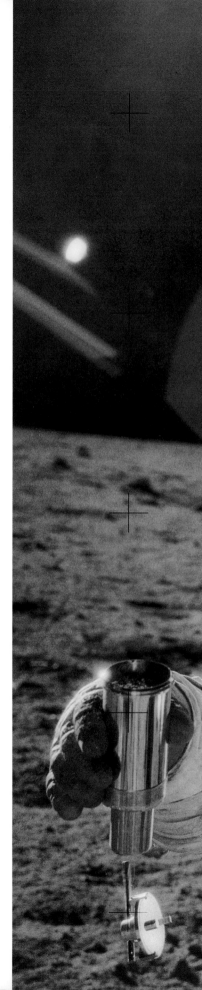

Part II

1918 to the present

ALAN BEAN AND CHARLES CONRAD,
NOVEMBER 1969.

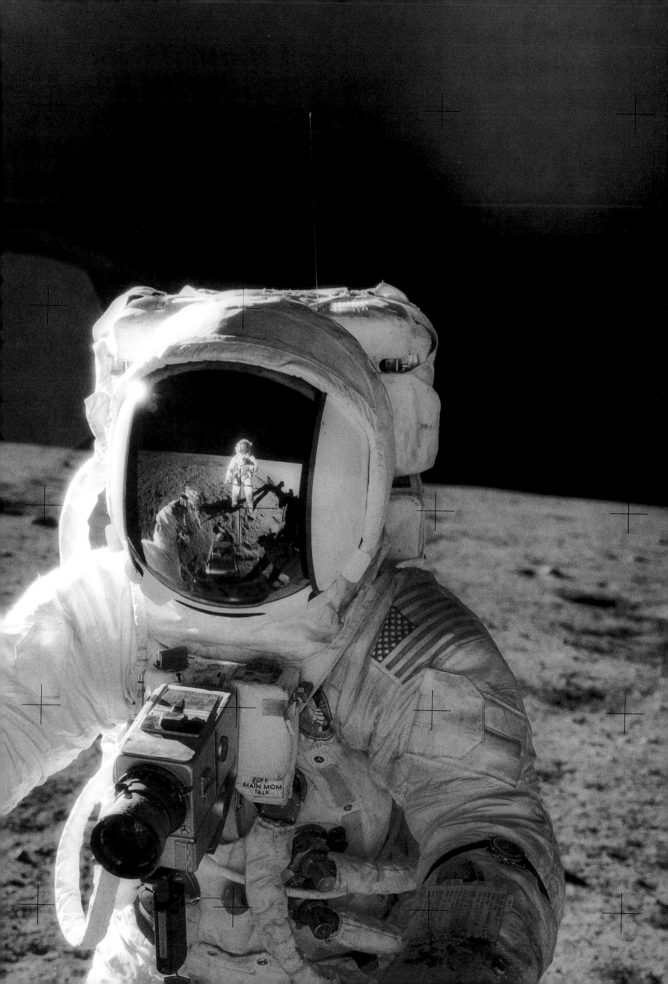

Introduction

WITHIN the span of fifty years this century, Europe was in the eye of two world wars. Thereafter, western powers were increasingly accused of exporting wars overseas, ostensibly on ideological grounds but in reality to protect economic and neo-colonial interests. Whilst the causes of the First World War remain debatably obscure, the Second World War united the Allied against the Axis countries in a battle increasingly portrayed as one against evil. The allegiance forged between Churchill, de Gaulle, Eisenhower and Stalin was soon to falter. The Korean and Vietnam Wars were joined by US forces sent on the pretext of halting the 'tumbling dice' of world Communism.

The Kremlin's determination to maintain control of the satellite states of the Soviet Union led to its much-decried military interventions in Hungary (1956) and Czechoslovakia (1968). Here the crushing was of largely spontaneous populist uprisings. In other countries, politically organized national liberation movements engaged in an armed struggle against the old imperial foreign powers. Erstwhile Commonwealth countries such as Canada won their autonomy without a struggle, although there is still a frustrated secessionist movement among the French-speaking Québecquois. India had blazed an independence trail through Gandhi's massively successful campaign of civil disobedience, only to find itself faced with partition, granting its substantial Moslem minority the northern territories that became known as Pakistan.

It became a hallmark of this allegedly godless century that religious wars were endemic once more. The increasing militance of Islam and the recourse to *jihad* (or holy war against the infidel) divided many countries against themselves, particularly in Balkan Europe and the Middle East. Here, too, the foundation of the state of Israel in 1948 appeared to Palestinians as another way in which Europe sought to displace its own problems. Civil wars erupted in countries overthrowing the ancient systems of oppression, most particularly in China where in 1949 Mao Tse-Tung inaugurated the People's Republic, the world's largest and one of the few continuing Communist countries.

Yet, curiously, the twentieth century has also been characterized by a popular desire and demand for peace. From small organisms of conscientious objectors during the First World War to worldwide Campaigns for Nuclear Disarmament, groups of individuals have grown into mass movements that have insisted on putting the human race first. Partly this is because war increasingly affect civilians as much as or more than armies: according to Red Cross statistics, while 85 per cent of First World War casualties were military, the percentage was inverted (15 per cent military: 85 per cent civilian) during the Gulf War of 1988. While no one would advocate a return to the decimating trench warfare of the former, technological advances also rendered redundant the lining-up of armies for the battlefield slaughter. New technologies brought other sorts of advances too. In medicine, the spread of vaccines brought the eradication of smallpox and scarlet fever worldwide; that of polio, yellow fever and hepatitis in many countries. Life expectancy virtually doubled in 'developed' countries with many living into their eighties and nineties, twice as long as a century earlier. Yet poorer regions remained plagued by avoidable diseases such as cholera and malaria.

Technological advances could also bring many of us culturally closer. Television soap serials have achieved mass popularity. A whole new art form, cinema, advanced to a peak in the Thirties and Forties. Realistic imaging came further within the popular remit through the widespread availability of cheap photo and video cameras. North American films and video games in particular were widely blamed for the promotion of impersonal violence, especially among the young among whom sophisticated weaponry and a 'drug culture' were pervasive.

Fashions in music and clothes became complementary, with many regions abandoning traditional customs. Cheap travel on charter aircraft led to exotic tourist resorts producing interchangeable T shirts and carrier bags worldwide. In turn, western centres of fashion sought inspiration in natural fibre and traditional patterns, particularly with the emergence of Japan on the fashion scene. Other clothes styles mimicked other technological advances: the first moonwalkers of the 1960s generated a rash of space outfits on the catwalks of Paris and Milan. Overall the move was towards more comfortable, wearable clothes and less formality, particularly in women's wear.

The fashionable emaciated look from the 1960s onwards also conflicted with what people increasingly knew about 'slimmer's diseases' such as anorexia and bulimia, and with the extent of world starvation. War that the cynical claimed were promoted more by arms manufacturers than ideological causes led to the number

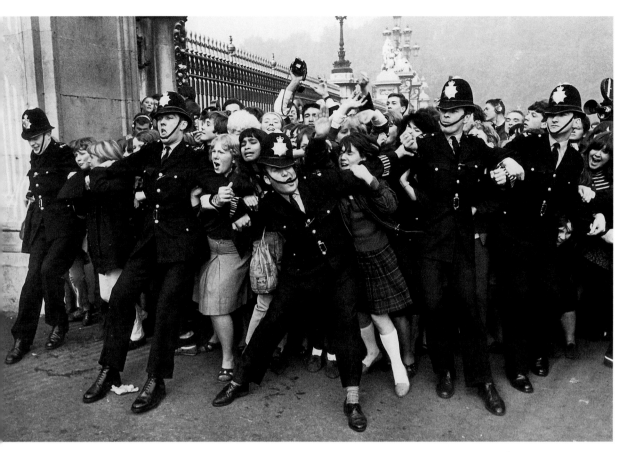

POLICE KEEP BACK BEATLES FANS (AND PRESS CAMERAMEN) OUTSIDE BUCKINGHAM PALACE, LONDON, WHERE THEY WHERE RECEIVING OBE'S (ORDER OF THE BRITISH EMPIRE), OCTOBER 1965.

DIE POLIZEI HÄLT DIE BEATLESFANS UND PRESSEPHOTOGRAPHEN VOR DEM BUCKINGHAM PALAST IN ZAUM, WO DEN BEATLES IM OKTOBER 1965 DER ORDEN DES BRITISCHEN EMPIRES VERLIEHEN WURDE.

LA POLICE EMPÊCHE LES FANS DES BEATLES (ET LES PHOTOGRAPHES) D'ENTRER DANS LE PALAIS DE BUCKINGHAM À LONDRES OÙ L'ORDRE DE L'EMPIRE BRITANNIQUE (OBE) LEUR EST DÉCERNÉ, OCTOBRE 1965.

f migrants doubling in the 1980s alone. Whole peoples moved, fleeing wars and natural catastrophes, but also increasingly as 'economic refugees', seeking to escape living conditions under which they could not survive. While the global shift was from south to north and east to west, a continent such as Australasia became a whole new regional melting pot.

Despite flickering support for a revival of Italian fascism under Mussolini's granddaughter; the neo-Nazis in Germany and Austria; the racist policies of Le Pen's National Party in France and the British Movement, Europe at the close of this century is consolidating its union, finally incorporating the 'guest' populations it invited to immigrate at a time of rising employment following the Second World War. If the nineteenth century saw a net emigration of Europeans to overseas colonies, then the twentieth has witnessed a shift in the reverse direction. South Africa has finally (and relatively peacefully) transferred to majority rule, as has the last outpost of British imperialism, Northern Ireland. A

belated consideration for the situation of indigenous peoples – from the Amazon to Africa to Australia – goes hand-in-hand with a respect for their common understanding of the delicate interrelationship between the species of our planet.

For many of today's young generation, the overriding concern is for the sustainable future of the world as a whole, regardless of boundaries and nationalities. A scientifically raised awareness of the five species that every hour become extinct in this unrenewable world has galvanized the ecological impetus to render the destruction of the jungles of Borneo or Brazil of immediate impact in industrialized North America or Western Europe. The European Union, the Congress of Non-Aligned States, and the Organization of African or American States, are all phenomena that could not have been foreseen at the last century's start. It remains for this century to reveal where present-day global concerns will lead, if the pursuit of harmony will outweigh that of war.

Einleitung

In einem Zeitraum von nur fünfzig Jahren haben in unserem Jahrhundert in Europa zwei Weltkriege getobt. Und seit Ende des letzten wird immer häufiger der Vorwurf laut, daß der Westen Kriege in andere Länder exportiere, unter ideologischem Vorwand, doch in Wirklichkeit aus ökonomischen und neokolonialistischen Motiven. Wie es zum Ersten Weltkrieg kam, ist bis heute umstritten; im Zweiten galt der Krieg der Alliierten gegen die Achsenmächte zusehends als der Kampf gegen das Böse schlechthin. Die Solidarität zwischen Churchill, de Gaulle, Eisenhower und Stalin sollte nicht lange halten – schon bald griffen amerikanische Truppen in den Korea- und den Vietnamkrieg ein, um, wie es hieß, dem Vormarsch des Weltkommunismus Einhalt zu gebieten.

Der Kreml war fest entschlossen, die Satellitenstaaten der Sowjetunion an der kurzen Leine zu halten, daher die militärischen Interventionen in Ungarn (1956) und der Tschechoslowakei (1968), die dem Ansehen der Sowjets sehr schadeten. Wurden hier weitgehend spontane Volksaufstände niedergeschlagen, so kämpften in anderen Ländern politisch organisierte nationale Befreiungsbewegungen mit Waffengewalt gegen die alten Kolonialmächte. Einstige Commonwealth-Staaten wie zum Beispiel Kanada erlangten ihre Unabhängigkeit kampflos, auch wenn im französischsprachigen Québec bis heute eine glücklose Separatistenbewegung tätig ist. In Indien hatte der ungeheure Erfolg von Gandhis Kampagne des zivilen Ungehorsams den Weg zur Unabhängigkeit gebahnt, doch mit ihr kam auch die Zweiteilung des Landes, bei der die bedeutende islamische Minderheit die nördlichen Territorien übernahm, die den Namen »Pakistan« erhielten.

Bezeichnend für dieses angeblich so gottlose Jahrhundert war, daß überall wieder Glaubenskriege aufflammten. Die zunehmende Militanz des Islam und die Rückkehr zum Dschihad (dem »heiligen Krieg« gegen die Ungläubigen) spaltete die Bevölkerung vieler Länder, besonders auf dem Balkan und im Mittleren Osten. Hier hatten die Palästinenser die Gründung des Staates Israel von 1948 als einen weiteren Versuch der Europäer empfunden, ihre eigenen Probleme auf die Einheimischen abzuwälzen. Überall, wo Länder das Joch ihrer alten Unterdrücker abschüttelten, kam es zu Bürgerkriegen, besonders heftig in China, wo Mao Tse-tung 1949 die Volksrepublik ausrief, das größte kommuni-

stische Land der Erde und heute eines der letzten de Kommunismus.

Doch kurioserweise läßt sich das 20. Jahrhunde ebenso als ein Jahrhundert des weltweiten Strebens nac Frieden verstehen. Von einzelnen Kriegsdienstverwe gerern im Ersten Weltkrieg zu weltweiten Kampagne für nukleare Abrüstung sind aus Grüppchen un einzelnen Massenbewegungen geworden, für die di Rechte der Menschheit an erster Stelle stehen. Ei Grund dafür ist sicher, daß Kriege in zunehmenden Maße die Zivilbevölkerung treffen und im Verhältn immer weniger das Militär: Nach Statistiken des Rote Kreuzes waren 85 Prozent der Opfer des Ersten Wel kriegs Soldaten, im Golfkrieg von 1988 war das Verhäl nis umgekehrt (15 Prozent Soldaten gegenüber 85 Proze Zivilisten). Doch niemand wird ernsthaft fordern, z den verlustreichen Stellungskriegen zurückzukehren, un der technische Fortschritt macht den Aufmarsch de Truppen auf dem Schlachtfeld inzwischen ganz übe flüssig. Auch im zivilen Bereich hat die neue Techni viele Schlachten gewonnen. In der Medizin sind durc Fortschritte der Impftechnik Pocken, Scharlach un Lepra weltweit ausgerottet, und Kinderlähmung, Gelb fieber und Hepatitis in vielen Ländern. Die Lebenserwa tung in den Industrieländern verdoppelte sich, vie Menschen werden achtzig und neunzig Jahre, doppe so alt, wie sie vor einem Jahrhundert geworden wäre Doch in den ärmeren Weltgegenden wüten vermeidba re Krankheiten wie Cholera und Malaria nach wie vor

Technische Fortschritte brachten viele von uns auc kulturell näher zusammen. Fernsehserien erreichen ei gewaltiges Publikum. Eine ganz neue Kunstform, da Kino, kam in den 30er und 40er Jahren zur Blüt Abbilder der Wirklichkeit wurden mit billigen Photo apparaten und Videokameras für jedermann erschwing lich. Doch andererseits gelten besonders nordamerikanisch Filme und Videospiele als eine der Hauptursache dafür, daß sinnlose Gewalt überall zunimmt, besonde unter Jugendlichen, die leicht den hochtechnisierte Waffen und der »Drogenkultur« verfallen.

Musik- und Kleidungsmoden wurden weltumspan nend und verdrängten in vielen Gegenden die ei heimischen Traditionen völlig. Billige Charterflüg verbreiteten die immergleichen T-Shirts und Plastik tüten exotischer Reiseziele rund um den Erdball. I Gegenzug suchten die westlichen Modezentren ih

Krankheiten wie Magersucht und Bulimie bekannt wurde, und dem Hunger überall auf der Welt. Kriege, von denen die Zyniker sagten, sie seien eher von den Waffenhändlern als von Ideologien angefacht, sorgten dafür, daß sich allein in den 80er Jahren die Zahl der Flüchtlinge verdoppelte. Ganze Völker waren auf Wanderschaft, flohen vor Kriegen und Naturkatastrophen, waren aber auch in immer stärkerem Maße als »Wirtschaftsflüchtlinge« auf der Flucht vor Verhältnissen, in denen sie nicht überleben konnten. Die globalen Wanderbewegungen verliefen von Süd nach Nord und von Ost nach West, und ein Kontinent wie Australien und Ozeanien wurde zum neuen regionalen Schmelztiegel.

Obwohl noch dann und wann die italienischen Neofaschisten unter Mussolinis Enkeln von sich reden machen, die Neonazis in Deutschland und Österreich, Le Pens Nationalpartei in Frankreich und die britischen Europagegner, steht doch am Ende dieses Jahrhunderts die europäische Einigung bevor, bei der auch die »Gäste« einbezogen werden, die nach dem Zweiten Weltkrieg zu der Zeit, als Arbeitskräftemangel herrschte, in die einzelnen Länder geholt wurden. Im 19. Jahrhundert emigrierten die Europäer in die überseeischen Kolonien, doch im 20. Jahrhundert kehrte sich die Richtung des Stromes um. Südafrika hat nun endlich (und vergleichsweise friedlich) die Regierung der Mehrheit übergeben, und ebenso haben es die Engländer in ihrer letzten Kolonie Nordirland getan. Nun endlich findet auch die Lage der Ureinwohner die Aufmerksamkeit, die sie verdient – vom Amazonas über Afrika bis nach Australien –, und mit dieser Aufmerksamkeit entsteht ein Verständnis des ihnen allen gemeinsamen Sinns für das empfindliche Gleichgewicht der Spezies auf unserem Planeten.

Vielen in der heutigen jüngeren Generation kommt es vor allem darauf an, den Fortbestand der Welt als solcher zu sichern, ohne Rücksicht auf Grenzen und Nationalitäten. In jeder Stunde werden fünf Spezies dieses Planeten für immer ausgelöscht, und ein geschärftes ökologisches Bewußtsein hat uns vor Augen geführt, daß die Zerstörung der Regenwälder von Borneo und Brasilien nicht ohne Folgen für die Industrienationen Nordamerikas und Westeuropas bleiben wird. Die Europäische Union, der Kongreß unabhängiger Staaten, die Organisation afrikanischer oder amerikanischer Staaten – das alles sind Dinge, die zu Anfang dieses Jahrhunderts niemand vorausgesehen hätte. Es bleibt dem nächsten Jahrhundert überlassen zu zeigen, wohin die Sorgen der heutigen Welt führen werden und ob das Streben nach Harmonie den Drang zum Krieg überwinden wird.

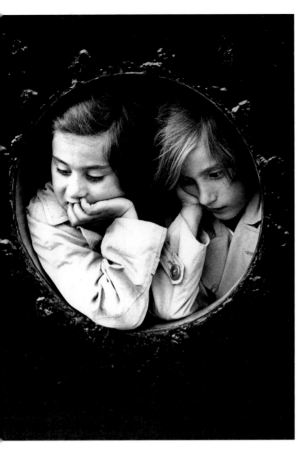

TWO JEWISH GIRL REFUGEES LOOKING THROUGH THE PORTHOLE OF THE HAMBURG-AMERIKA LINER SS. *ST. LOUIS*, WHICH WAS REFUSED ENTRY TO CUBA AND THE USA, ON ARRIVAL BACK IN EUROPE AT ANTWERP, 17 JUNE 1939.

ZWEI JÜDISCHE FLÜCHTLINGSMÄDCHEN SCHAUEN DURCH DAS BULLAUGE DES PASSAGIERSCHIFFS SS. *ST. LOUIS*, DAS NACH AUFNAHMEVERWEIGERUNG IN DEN USA UND KUBA NACH EUROPA ZURÜCKKEHREN MUSSTE, 17. JUNI 1939.

DEUX JEUNES RÉFUGIÉES JUIVES REGARDANT PAR LE HUBLOT DU PAQUEBOT SS. *ST. LOUIS* DE LA LIGNE HAMBOURG-AMÉRIQUE À SON ARRIVÉE À ANVERS. L'ENTRÉE À CUBA ET AUX ÉTATS-UNIS LUI AYANT ÉTÉ REFUSÉE, IL AVAIT DÛ RETOURNER EN EUROPE, 17 JUIN 1939.

Inspiration in Naturfasern und traditionellen Mustern, gerade nachdem die Japaner in der Modeszene Furore machten. Anderswo ahmte die Mode andere technische Fortschritte nach: Als die ersten Menschen auf dem Mond spazierten, sah man in den 60er Jahren auf den Laufstegen von Paris und Mailand eine wahre Flut von Raumanzügen. Insgesamt ging die Tendenz hin zu bequemeren, tragbareren Kleidern, und besonders die Damenmode war weniger formell geworden.

Das Schlankheitsideal der 60er Jahre stand in einem kuriosen Spannungsverhältnis zu dem, was nun über

Introduction

C'EST à deux reprises, au XXᵉ siècle, qu'en l'espace de cinquante ans l'Europe s'est trouvée au cœur d'un conflit mondial. Par la suite, les puissances occidentales furent très vivement accusées d'exporter les guerres dans les régions d'outre-mer, masquant sous de fausses préoccupations idéologiques une défense évidente de leurs intérêts économiques et coloniaux. Alors que les causes de la guerre de 1914-1918 demeurent contestables et obscures, la Seconde Guerre mondiale unit les Alliés contre les pays de l'Axe dans une confrontation qui prendra de plus en plus l'allure d'une croisade contre le Mal. L'entente entre Churchill, De Gaulle, Eisenhower et Staline fut de courte durée. En effet, les États-Unis engagèrent la guerre de Corée puis celle du Viêt-nam sous le prétexte de stopper la progression du communisme dans le monde.

Comme par le passé, le Kremlin, qui était décidé à contrôler les États satellites de l'Union soviétique, intervint militairement en Hongrie (1956) et en Tchécoslovaquie (1968). Dans ces pays, le soulèvement populaire était en grande partie spontané. Dans d'autres, au contraire, ce furent des mouvements de libération nationale politiquement organisés qui engagèrent une lutte armée contre les vieilles puissances impérialistes. Pour la première fois, des pays appartenant au Commonwealth comme le Canada, malgré un mouvement indépendantiste frustré qui perdure chez les Québécois, obtinrent pacifiquement leur indépendance. L'Inde fit office de pionnière avec ses campagnes de désobéissance civile prônées par Gandhi. Elles rencontrèrent un écho favorable et montrèrent une réelle efficacité dans la lutte contre les Anglais. Plus tard, ce grand pays devra accorder les territoires du Nord à sa forte minorité musulmane, lesquels formeront ultérieurement le Pakistan.

Ce siècle, que l'on dit sans Dieu, est paradoxalement caractérisé par les guerres à caractère religieux. La montée en puissance de l'islamisme et le recours au Djihad (la Guerre sainte) divisa de nombreux pays en Europe, particulièrement dans la région des Balkans, mais aussi au Moyen-Orient. En 1948, la création de l'État d'Israël apparut aux Palestiniens comme une façon pour l'Europe de déplacer ses propres problèmes. Des guerres civiles éclatèrent dans des pays qui renversaient les anciens systèmes d'oppression. Ce fut le cas en Chine où, dès 1949, Mao Tsé-Toung inaugura la République populaire, le plus vaste pays communiste du monde.

Paradoxalement, ce XXᵉ siècle s'illustre aussi par une forte aspiration populaire à la paix. Depuis les petits groupes d'objecteurs de conscience contre la Première Guerre mondiale aux campagnes internationales pour le désarmement nucléaire, les individus organisés se sont regroupés au sein de mouvements de masse n'ayant pour autre ambition que de donner à l'être humain une place prépondérante. Il est vrai que, de plus en plus, les guerres modernes affectent tout autant, voire plus, les civils que les militaires. Selon les chiffres fournis par la Croix-Rouge, si 85 % des victimes de la Première Guerre mondiale étaient des militaires, le pourcentage s'était exactement inversé en 1988 pendant le conflit du Golf. Si la guerre meurtrière des tranchées appartient à une époque révolue, les progrès technologiques rendent également caduc l'alignement des armées sur le champ de bataille. Les techniques nouvelles ont généré aussi des progrès d'un autre genre, tout particulièrement dans le domaine médical. En effet, la propagation des vaccins a entraîné la disparition de la variole, de la scarlatine et de la lèpre dans le monde. L'éradication de la poliomyélite, de la fièvre jaune et de l'hépatite virale est en cours dans de nombreux pays. L'espérance de vie dans les nations développées, où l'existence se prolonge souvent entre quatre-vingts et quatre-vingt-dix ans, doublé par rapport au siècle dernier. Néanmoins, les régions plus pauvres sont encore affligées de maladies comme le choléra et le typhus, qu'il serait pourtant possible d'éradiquer.

Culturellement, les progrès technologiques seraient aussi susceptibles de rapprocher les populations. Qu'on le salue ou qu'on le déplore, il est incontestable que les séries télévisées populaires ont conquis de larges secteurs du public planétaire. Une toute nouvelle forme d'art, le cinéma, a connu son apogée durant les années 30 et 40. Puis l'image se popularisa irrésistiblement avec l'accession à la photo bon marché et au caméscope. Dans cette saga moderne, les films américains et les jeux vidéo furent accusés d'avoir servi la promotion de la violence anonyme, en particulier auprès des jeunes.

Dans le domaine de la musique et de la confection, l'apparition de la mode comme un important phéno-

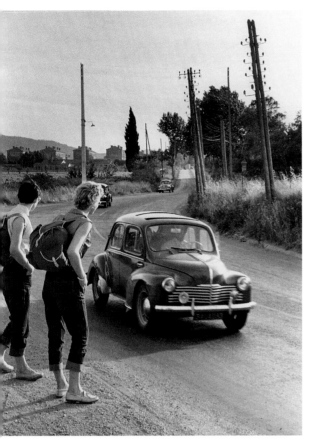

TWO GIRLS HITCHHIKING IN THE SOUTH
OF FRANCE, JULY 1954.

ZWEI MÄDCHEN FAHREN PER AUTOSTOPP DURCH
DEN SÜDEN FRANKREICHS, JULI 1954.

DEUX JEUNES FILLES FAISANT DE L'AUTO-STOP DANS
LE SUD DE LA FRANCE, JUILLET 1954.

mène de société obligea de nombreuses régions à se défaire de leurs habitudes traditionnelles. Des charters se mirent à emmener les touristes, à des prix de plus en plus économiques, pour des destinations exotiques. Ceux-ci en ramenèrent tee-shirts et sacs en matière plastique qui, à leur tour, essaimèrent le globe. L'un après l'autre, les centres occidentaux de la confection cherchèrent l'inspiration dans les fibres naturelles et les modèles traditionnels. Ce mouvement fut surtout sensible après l'entrée du Japon sur la scène de la mode. D'autres styles vestimentaires intégrèrent les progrès scientifiques dans leurs créations : en 1968, les premiers hommes à marcher sur la Lune inspirèrent une série de tenues « spatiales » dans les défilés parisiens et milanais.

En général, la mode s'orientait vers une conception plus confortable et moins formelle de la confection, en particulier pour le vêtement féminin.

Dans les seules années 80, le nombre des émigrants doubla. Si la cause est à chercher dans les conflits où les intérêts des marchands d'armes et des usines d'armement l'emportent sur les motifs purement idéologiques, il n'en demeure pas moins qu'un exode de type nouveau est en train d'apparaître : celui des « réfugiés économiques » cherchant à échapper à des conditions difficiles qui ne permettent plus leur survie.

Tandis qu'on assistait à des transformations globales aussi bien du nord au sud que de l'est à l'ouest, un continent, s'affirma de plus en plus comme un tout nouveau creuset de cultures : l'Australie.

À la fin de ces années 80, en dépit de certains mouvements réactionnaires, l'Europe de cette fin de siècle consolide néanmoins son union, et tente tant bien que mal d'intégrer les travailleurs émigrés appelés à y travailler lors du boom de l'emploi consécutif à la Seconde Guerre mondiale.

Si le XIXe siècle a vu les Européens émigrer vers les colonies d'outre-mer, le XXe siècle fut le témoin du phénomène inverse.

L'Afrique du Sud, à l'instar de l'Irlande du Nord, est enfin (presque pacifiquement) passée à un gouvernement digne des nations démocratiques. Une nouvelle considération, bien que tardive, pour les populations autochtones amazonniennes, africaines et australiennes s'accompagne du respect et de la compréhension communes des relations délicates gouvernant les espèces qui peuplent notre planète.

Aujourd'hui, faisant fi des frontières et des nationalités, le souci primordial d'un grand nombre de jeunes concerne notre avenir commun. La prise de conscience, entretenue par les scientifiques, que chaque heure passée voit disparaître inexorablement cinq espèces dans le monde, a galvanisé l'élan écologique. Hormis une aide efficace en direction des jungles de Bornéo ou du Brésil, cet élan a permis d'avoir un impact immédiat dans les pays industrialisés d'Amérique du Nord et d'Europe de l'Ouest. L'Union européenne, le Congrès des États non alignés, l'Organisation des États africains ou américains sont autant de structures qu'il eût été difficile d'imaginer au début du siècle. Ce qu'il reste présentement à faire, c'est avant tout d'anticiper sur les problèmes actuels et de tout mettre en œuvre afin que la recherche de l'harmonie prenne le pas sur celle de la guerre.

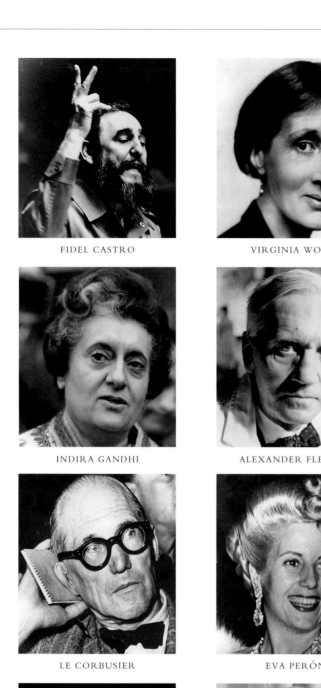

FIDEL CASTRO

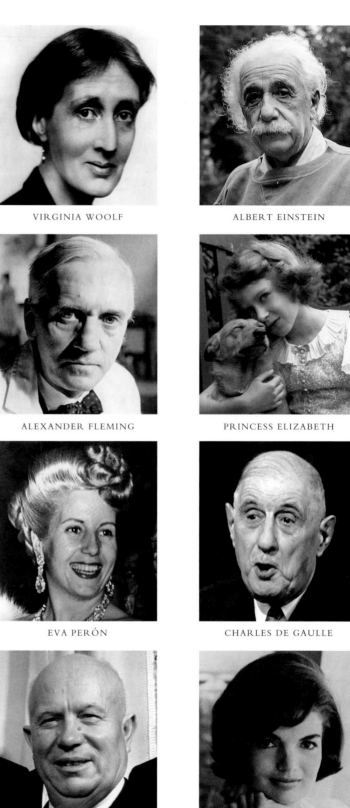

VIRGINIA WOOLF

ALBERT EINSTEIN

INDIRA GANDHI

ALEXANDER FLEMING

PRINCESS ELIZABETH

LE CORBUSIER

EVA PERÓN

CHARLES DE GAULLE

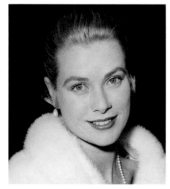

PRINCESS GRACE

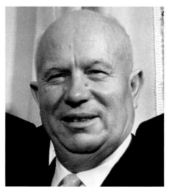

NIKITA KHRUSHCHEV

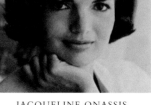

JACQUELINE ONASSIS

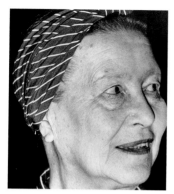

SIMONE DE BEAUVOIR

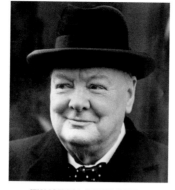

WINSTON CHURCHILL

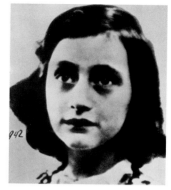

ANNE FRANK

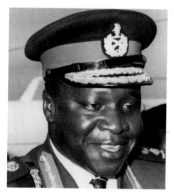

IDI AMIN

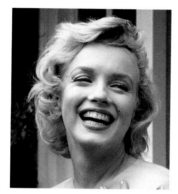

MARILYN MONROE

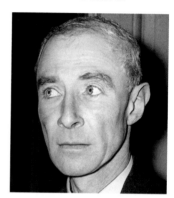

ROBERT OPPENHEIMER

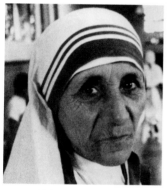

MOTHER TERESA

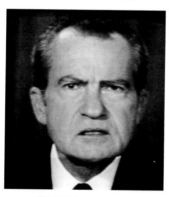

RICHARD NIXON

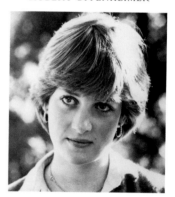

THE PRINCESS OF WALES

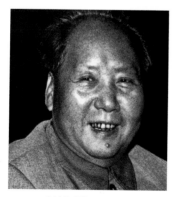

MAO TSE-TUNG

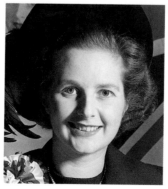

MARGARET THATCHER

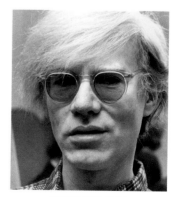

ANDY WARHOL

Aspects of the 1920s and 1930s

UNTIL the twentieth century, fashion concerned men at least as much as women. Concepts such as 'power dressing' and 'dressing to kill' may not have been so labelled, but clothing as an expression of sex and control was a male province.

Fashion in women's attire developed relatively gradually in the nineteenth century, from the smooth sweep of crepe and chiffon in Empire-line gowns to the fussy bustles and lacy overskirts of the Victorian era. Power and sexuality were not yet linked to the role of women, which in the eighteenth and nineteenth centuries was primarily to be demure and obedient. That, at least, was the behaviour expected of upper-class women, those belonging to the only level of society which could afford to follow fashion anyway. Perhaps one of the greatest changes to take place in women's fashions this century is the factor of economic control. No longer attired merely as a delightful ornament displaying her husband's wealth, the twentieth-century woman could dress to please herself at a price she can afford. This has meant two major differences, both closely linked to women's new purchasing power. One is the growth of a medium-price range, independent of either couturier exclusivity or chain-store mass production; the other is a preference for garments practical for work and daily living rather than decoration and ostentation.

The first major shift came in the wake of the Great War. With so many men away, women entered the industrial workplace in considerable numbers. Even after the war the male death toll from the trenches and the aftermath of the 'flu epidemic was so high that women never wholly returned to their home-bound role. The 1920s saw an adaptation of styles – bobbed haircuts, suits and trousers – to new living conditions, coloured by the whole mood of the flappers' jazz era.

The 1930s saw the parallel development of the well-dressed woman, with her fitted bodice,

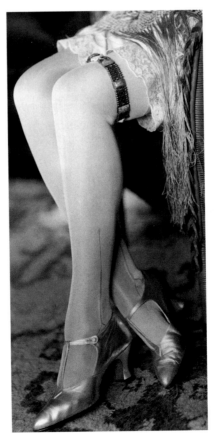

stiletto heels and neat hat, and increasingly frenetic leisure designs to match the mood of the times. Fashion moved with the speed of new transport through increasingly racy styles. The rise of cabaret and film stars began to set the more masculine trends that became common currency in the 1940s: tailored trouser suits demonstrated that women were increasingly wearing the pants and even the top hats of the men, with accessories that stretched to copies of their cigarette holders and briefcases.

Gabrielle Chanel, nicknamed 'Coco', became a byword for neat elegance in the 1920s and '30s (2). She liberated women from corsets and heavy dresses, putting them instead into tailored suits and chemises and bobbed hairstyles. From a poor background, she mingled with the richest and most famous, but claimed never to feel truly at home. She never married. Her first perfume (called No. 5 after her lucky number) became a world best-seller, and her costume jewellery gave the *nouveaux riches* permission to set aside their pearls. There was also plenty of scope for other unorthodox details – like the metal garters and the clocks on these silk stockings (1).

The elegance of Thirties fashion, as epitomized by the films of Myrna Loy, Ginger Rogers and Marlene Dietrich, was in strong contrast to the hard lives of Mid-West American farmers and their families, or the families of the poor and unemployed in Britain. The Depression following the Wall Street Crash of 1929 was a deeper and more far-reaching recession than any before or since. It led to a world slump, beginning with a drastic drop in wheat prices when over-production in the US and Canada flooded markets, and new competition from Soviet timber caused a further collapse. The despair of the Mid-West farmers was documented in the seminal book by Walker Evans and James Agee, *Let Us Now Praise Famous Men* (1930).

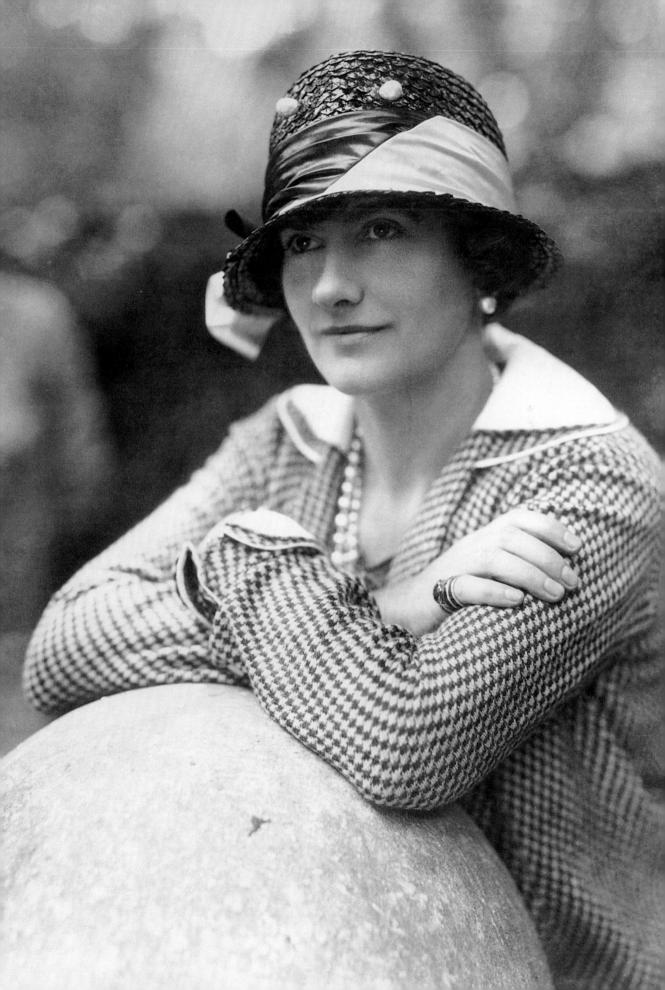

Bis zu unserem Jahrhundert war Mode mindestens ebensosehr eine Sache der Männer wie der Frauen. Zwar diente die Kleidung noch nicht zur Demonstration von »Macht« oder der »Verführung«, doch von jeher kleideten Männer sich, um ihre Überlegenheit und Sexualität zu zeigen.

Die Damenmode des 19. Jahrhunderts entwickelte sich nach und nach vom weichen Fall der Empirekleider aus Crêpe und Chiffon zu den gekünstelten Turnüren und Spitzenüberröcken der viktorianischen Zeit. Macht und Sexualität kamen im Frauenbild dieser Zeit noch nicht vor, denn im 18. und frühen 19. Jahrhundert hatte eine Frau vor allem still und gehorsam zu sein, zumindest eine Frau der Oberschicht, und sie waren die einzigen, die es sich leisten konnten, mit der Mode zu gehen. Darin bestand vielleicht die größte Neuerung der Mode unseres Jahrhunderts – daß sie nun nicht mehr den Wohlhabenden vorbehalten war. Die Frau des 20. Jahrhunderts war nicht mehr nur ein hübsches Zierstück, mit dem ihr Mann seinen Wohlstand demonstrierte, sondern Frauen konnten tragen, was sie wollten, jede nach ihrem Geschmack und ihrem Geldbeutel. Das brachte zwei große Veränderungen mit sich. Zum einen kamen Kleider mittlerer Preislage auf, unabhängig von den exklusiven Modehäusern und den Massenprodukten der Kaufhäuser; zum anderen lag das Schwergewicht nun auf praktischer Kleidung für Alltag und Beruf und nicht mehr auf Prunk und Dekor.

Die ersten grundlegenden Wandlungen kamen im Zuge des Ersten Weltkriegs. Ein Großteil der Männer war im Feld, und ein beträchtlicher Teil der Frauen begann nun in den Fabriken zu arbeiten. Und auf den Schlachtfeldern und anschließend der großen Grippeepidemie kamen so viele Männer um, daß die Frauen nie wieder ganz an ihren alten Platz am heimischen Herd zurückkehrten. In den 20er Jahren paßte sich der Stil den veränderten Lebensumständen an – die Frauen hatten nun kurze Haare, trugen Kostüme und Hosen, und alles war geprägt vom Lebensgefühl des Jazz-Zeitalters.

In den 30er Jahren entwickelten sich nebeneinander das Bild der gut gekleideten Frau mit enger Taille, hohen Absätzen und adrettem Hut und eine immer ausgefallener werdende Freizeitmode, in der die Stimmung der Zeit zum Ausdruck kam. Der Aufstieg von Kabarett- und Filmstars prägte nun den eher maskulin bestimmten Stil der 40er Jahre: Maßgeschneiderte Anzüge zeigten, daß Frauen zusehends die Hosen und sogar die Zylinderhüte der Männer trugen, und zudem schmückten sie sich mit typisch männlichen Accessoires, mit Zigarettenspitzen und Aktentaschen.

Gabrielle Chanel, genannt »Coco«, wurde in den 20er und 30er Jahren zum Inbegriff gepflegter Eleganz (1).

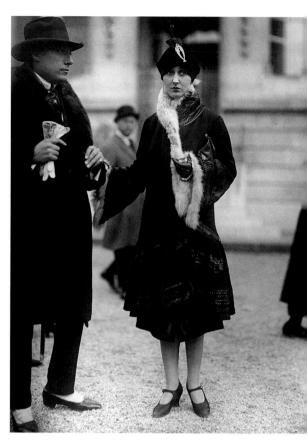

FASHION PHOTOGRAPHS FOR THE HOUSE OF SEEBERGER FRÈRES
MODEPHOTOGRAPHIEN DER GEBRÜDER SEEBERGER

Sie befreite die Frauen von Korsetts und schwere Stoffen und steckte sie statt dessen in Schneiderkostüm und Hemden.

Nirgends kommt die Eleganz der Mode der 30e Jahre besser zum Ausdruck als in den Filmen mit Star wie Myrna Loy, Ginger Rogers und Marlene Dietrich und der Kontrast zum anstrengenden Leben ameri kanischer Farmer im Mittelwesten oder den Armen un Arbeitslosen in England hätte nicht größer sein könner Die Wirtschaftskrise nach dem Schwarzen Freitag 192 brachte tiefgreifendere Veränderungen mit sich als jed andere Krise zuvor oder danach. Die ganze Welt wurd in den Strudel gerissen; die Weizenpreise fielen dra stisch, als die Überproduktion aus den Vereinigten Staa ten und Kanada die Märkte überschwemmte, und di neue Konkurrenz sowjetischer Holzhändler brachte ei nen weiteren Markt zum Zusammenbruch. Walker Evar und James Agee hielten das Elend der Farmer de Mittelwestens 1930 in einem einflußreichen Buch fes *Let Us Now Praise Famous Men*.

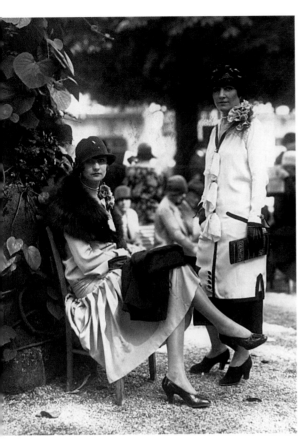

PHOTOGRAPHIES DE MODE POUR
LA MAISON DE SEEBERGER FRÈRES.

USQU'AU XXᵉ siècle la mode était une affaire d'hommes autant que de femmes. Même si l'habit en tant qu'arme de « puissance » et de « séduction » était encore un concept inexistant, il n'en demeurait pas moins à l'usage exclusif des hommes comme l'expression du pouvoir sexuel et de la domination.

La mode s'imposa dans le vêtement féminin plutôt petit à petit au cours du XIXᵉ siècle, évoluant du drapé lisse du crêpe et du chiffon de la ligne Empire jusqu'aux tournures maniérées et aux tabliers en dentelle de l'ère victorienne. Ni le pouvoir ni la sexualité n'étaient encore rattachés au rôle de la femme, qui se devait avant tout, aux XVIIIᵉ et XIXᵉ siècles, d'être grave et obéissante. Tel était du moins le comportement attendu des femmes de la bourgeoisie, seules à pouvoir se permettre le luxe de suivre la mode. La maîtrise du pouvoir économique permettra à la femme du XXᵉ siècle de s'habiller selon ses moyens et ses propres goûts. Deux grands phénomènes sont étroitement liés au nouveau pouvoir d'achat de la femme. L'un est l'apparition d'une gamme de prix moyens indépendants des couturiers exclusifs et des productions en série des grands magasins. L'autre est la préférence donnée aux vêtements de travail ou de tous les jours pour lesquels on privilégie le côté pratique au détriment de la décoration et de l'ostentation.

Le premier grand changement se produisit dans le sillage de la Grande Guerre. À cause du nombre élevé d'hommes absents, les femmes s'engouffrèrent en masse dans l'industrie. Même après la fin de la guerre, où tant d'hommes avaient trouvé la mort dans les tranchées tandis que d'autres avaient été décimés par l'épidémie de grippe, les femmes ne se cantonnèrent plus jamais entièrement à un rôle exclusif de ménagère. Dans les années 20, les styles s'adaptent – coiffures à la Jeanne d'Arc, ensembles et pantalons – aux nouvelles conditions de vie et aux couleurs d'une époque jazzy à l'humeur « garçonne ».

Au cours des années 30, on assiste à une évolution vers la femme bien habillée, au corsage ajusté, aux talons aiguilles et au chapeau coquet, à l'apparition de lignes toujours plus frénétiquement décontractées pour répondre à l'humeur du jour. Le succès grandissant des cabarets et des vedettes de cinéma participe au lancement des tendances plus masculines qui devaient se généraliser durant les années 40 : les femmes portent de plus en plus le pantalon et même le chapeau haut-de-forme agrémentés d'accessoires inspirés de leurs fume-cigarettes et leurs serviettes. Gabrielle Chanel, surnommée « Coco », devint synonyme d'élégance dans les années 20 et 30 (1). Elle débarrassa la femme de ses corsets et de ses lourdes robes qu'elle remplaça par des ensembles sur mesure, des robes-chemisiers et des coiffures courtes. Issue d'un milieu modeste, elle fréquenta les plus riches et les plus célèbres, mais affirma toujours ne pas se sentir vraiment à l'aise en leur compagnie. Elle ne se maria jamais. Son premier parfum (baptisé Nᵒ 5, d'après son chiffre porte-bonheur) remporta un succès commercial mondial, tandis que ses bijoux, en toc, donnaient aux nouveaux riches la permission de laisser leurs perles à la maison. D'autres détails aussi peu orthodoxes étaient admis, telles ces jarretières métalliques et les broderies sur le côté de ces bas en soie (2). L'élégance de la mode des années 30 dont les films de Myrna Loy, Ginger Rogers et Marlène Dietrich se faisaient les ambassadeurs contrastait violemment avec l'existence difficile des pauvres et des chômeurs en Grande-Bretagne. L'effondrement de la bourse de Wall Street en 1929 entraîna une récession d'une ampleur et d'une gravité sans précédent. Elle fut suivie d'un marasme mondial qui commença par la chute brutale des prix du blé. Le désespoir des fermiers du Middle West est décrit dans un ouvrage, écrit par Walker Evans et James Agee, intitulé *Let Us Now Praise Famous Men* (1930).

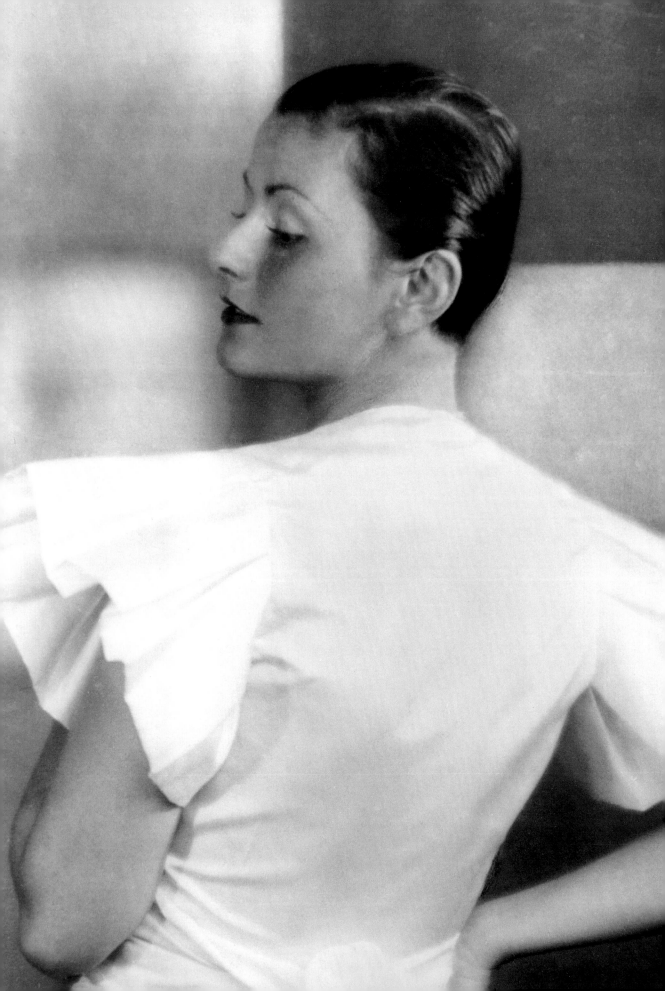

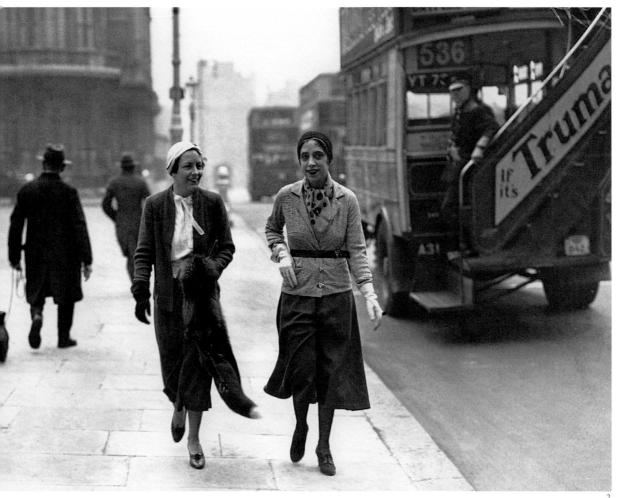

THEATRE had a part to play in a model's training. This German model dramatically posed and lit to make a back view as alluring as a front one, the head tossed to one side like a cabaret singer's (1). Elsa Schiaparelli (2), remarkable for her unexpected plainness in one devoted to beauty, and primarily known for her fashion choice of a shocking pink that came to be called after her, here puts down a further marker. Arriving in London in 1935, she announced 'Trousers for Women' in the same crusading tone as 'Votes for Women'. And to demonstrate that she, too, is on to a winner, she wears them herself, albeit in more restrained form as culottes.

DAS Theater spielte einen wichtigen Part bei der Ausbildung eines Models. Dieses deutsche Mannequin nimmt eine dramatische Pose ein und ist so beleuchtet, daß die Rückenansicht genauso anziehend wirkt wie ein Frontalporträt; den Kopf hat sie zur Seite geworfen wie eine Sängerin im Kabarett (1). Elsa Schiaparelli (2), die sich für eine Modeschöpferin immer betont einfach kleidete, und die vor allem durch den nach ihr benannten schockierenden Pinkton im Gedächtnis geblieben ist, macht hier ein weiteres Mal Geschichte. Bei ihrer Ankunft in London im Jahre 1935 forderte sie »Hosen für die Frau« mit den gleichen flammenden Worten, mit denen zuvor »Wahlrecht für die Frau« gefordert worden war. Und um zu zeigen, daß sie ebenso siegesgewiß ist, trägt sie sie gleich selbst, wenn auch in der gemäßigten Form des Hosenrocks.

L'ART dramatique faisait partie de la formation des mannequins. On a fait prendre à ce mannequin allemand une pose théâtrale sous un éclairage destiné à la rendre aussi aguichante de dos que de face, la tête inclinée sur le côté à la manière d'une chanteuse de cabaret (1). Elsa Schiaparelli (2), remarquable de simplicité, ce qui est inattendu chez quelqu'un qui se consacre à la beauté, était avant tout connue en raison du rose flamboyant, qui reçut son nom, et qu'elle choisit de mettre à la mode. On la voit poser ici un nouveau jalon. Arrivée à Londres en 1935, elle proclama « les femmes en pantalon » sur le même ton revendicatif que « le vote aux femmes ». Elle-même le portait pour se montrer dans le coup, bien que dans sa variante plus modeste de jupe-culotte.

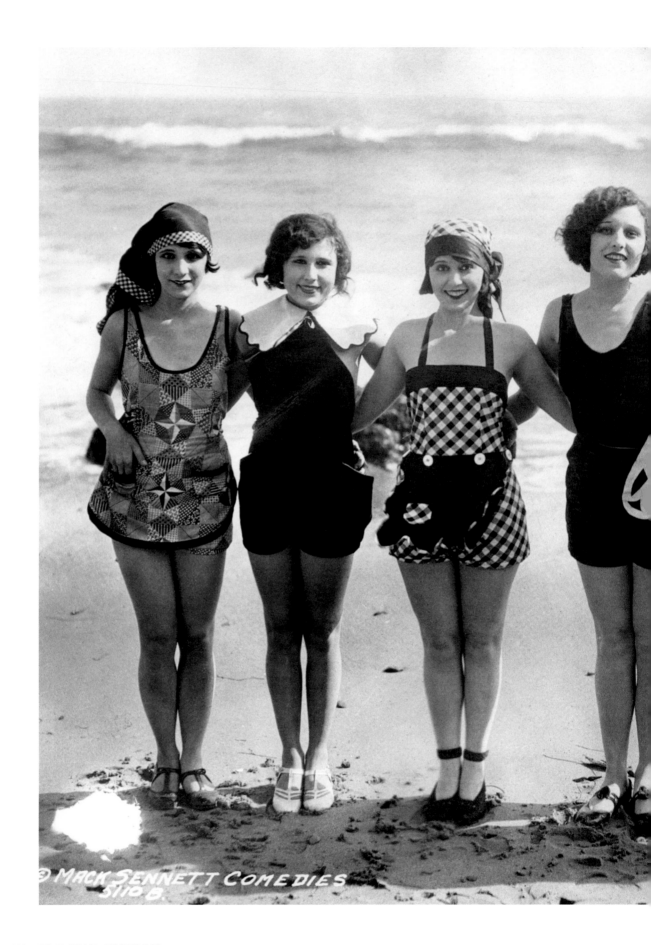

© MACK SENNETT COMEDIES
5110 B.

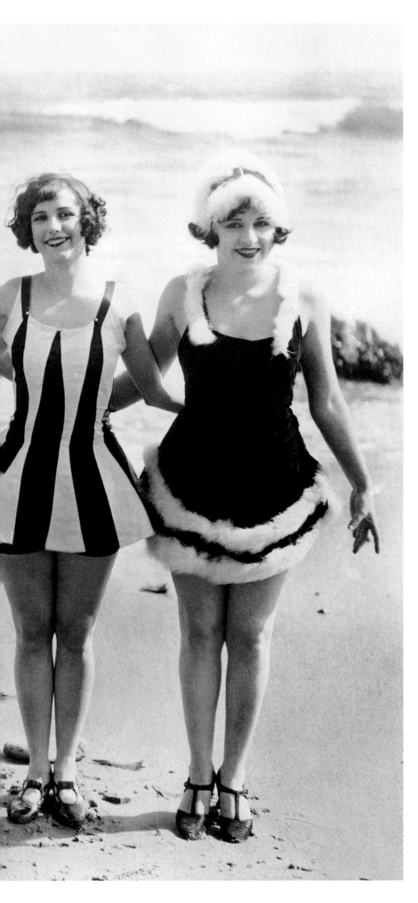

THE cult of the body beautiful, 1925. Suntanned legs might just be coming into fashion but shoes must be worn on the beach at all costs. These bathing belles sport costumes as artificial as their smiles, and what happens to this kind of 'skating skirt' in the salt water doesn't bear thinking about. But perhaps swimming is not too high up on the agenda.

DER Kult des schönen Körpers, 1925. Sonnengebräunte Beine kamen gerade in Mode, doch niemand ging ohne Schuhe an den Strand. Diese Badenixen führen Kleider vor, die genauso unnatürlich sind wie ihr Lächeln, und was aus einem solchen Röckchen, das eher an ein Eislaufkostüm erinnert, wird, wenn es ins Salzwasser kommt, ist gar nicht auszudenken. Doch hatte Badevergnügen wahrscheinlich ohnehin keine Priorität.

LE culte du beau corps, 1925. Les jambes bronzées devenaient peut-être à la mode, mais les chaussures n'en restaient pas moins, quoi qu'il en coûtât, indispensables sur la plage. Ces jolies baigneuses paradent dans des tenues aussi artificielles que leurs sou-rires. En outre, on frémit à la pensée de ce qui pouvait arriver dans l'eau salée avec ce genre de « jupe de patinage ». Mais la nage ne figurait pas forcément au programme.

DEVICES for those loath to undertake serious exercise but prepared to submit to slimming devices. One woman greets the 'first appearance in England of New Gymnastic Apparatus' designed for a confined space by simultaneously somersaulting and cartwheeling (1). Another demonstrates the 'spring leg' which comes with the aim of 'perfecting the limbs' as a 'developing treatment for our athletic ladies' (2). Rosemary Andree straps her high heels and, rather bravely, her neck into a 'slimming exerciser' whose exact function remains a mystery (3).

GERÄTE für alle, die zwar nichts für Sport übrighatten, aber um der Schlankheit willen turnen wollten. Eine Frau begrüßt »das erste Exemplar eines neuartigen Gymnastikapparates in England« mit dem man auf engem Raum gleichzeitig einen Salto machen und radschlagen konnte (1). Eine andere führt die »Beinfeder« vor, die »perfekte Waden« versprach, eine »Trainingshilfe für unsere Athletinnen« (2). Rosemary Andree hat keine Furcht, Stöckelschuhe und Hals in diesen »Schlankheitstrimmer« zu stecken, dessen genaue Funktion rätselhaft bleibt (3).

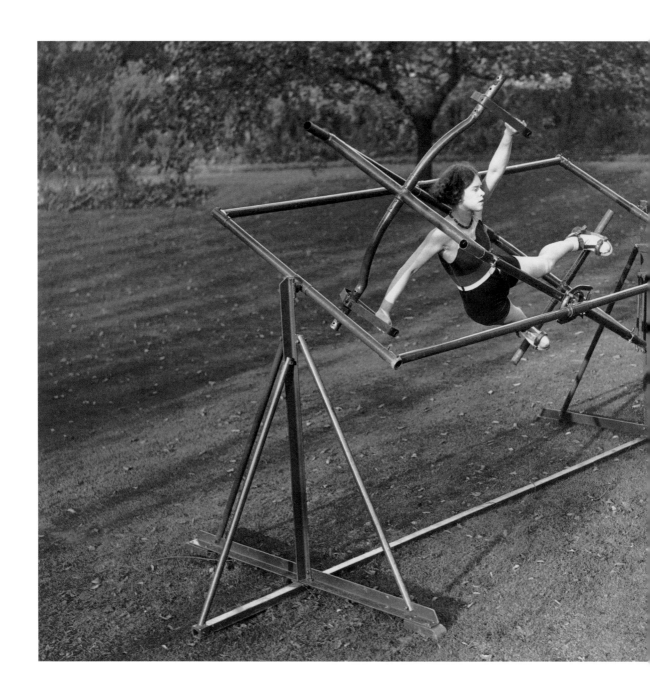

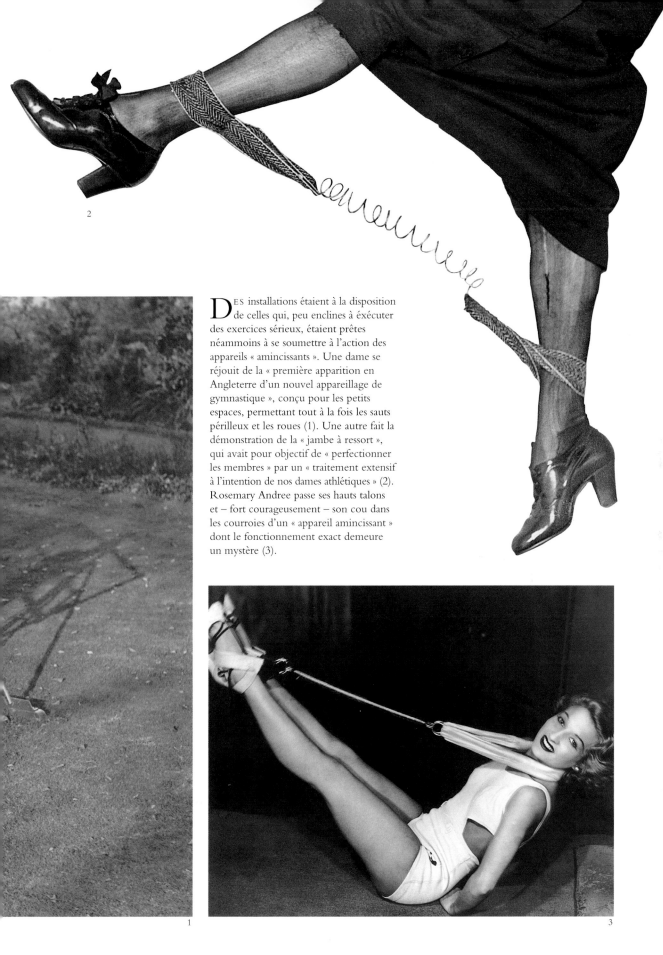

D ES installations étaient à la disposition
de celles qui, peu enclines à éxécuter
des exercices sérieux, étaient prêtes
néammoins à se soumettre à l'action des
appareils « amincissants ». Une dame se
réjouit de la « première apparition en
Angleterre d'un nouvel appareillage de
gymnastique », conçu pour les petits
espaces, permettant tout à la fois les sauts
périlleux et les roues (1). Une autre fait la
démonstration de la « jambe à ressort »,
qui avait pour objectif de « perfectionner
les membres » par un « traitement extensif
à l'intention de nos dames athlétiques » (2).
Rosemary Andree passe ses hauts talons
et – fort courageusement – son cou dans
les courroies d'un « appareil amincissant »
dont le fonctionnement exact demeure
un mystère (3).

PHYSICAL studies, often linked to eurythmics and Isadora Duncan-style 'Greek' dancing, was a part of a whole back-to-nature programme current in the 1920s. In Germany this had a more sinister dimension, working on an assumption of human perfectability that chimed in with Hitlerian notions of higher beings derived from the combination of female spirituality and male superiority.

LEIBESÜBUNGEN, oft verbunden mit Eurhythmie und »griechischen« Tänzen in der Art Isadora Duncans, waren ein wichtiger Teil der Zurück-zur-Natur-Bewegung der 20er Jahre. In Deutschland hatte dies eine unheilvolle Seite, weil dort die Vervollkommnung des Körpers mit der Nazi-Ideologie einherging, nach der die Verbindung weiblicher Spiritualität mit männlicher Überlegenheit Übermenschen hervorbringen sollte.

L'ÉTUDE du corps, souvent liée à la gymnastique rythmique et à la danse d'inspiration « grecque » telle que celle d'Isadora Duncan, faisait partie de tout un programme de retour à la nature alors en vogue dans les années 20. En Allemagne elle avait pris des contours plus sinistres, développant l'affirmation de la perfectibilité de l'homme et popularisant les notions hitlériennes d'êtres supérieurs nés de la combinaison de la spiritualité féminine et de la supériorité masculine aryennes.

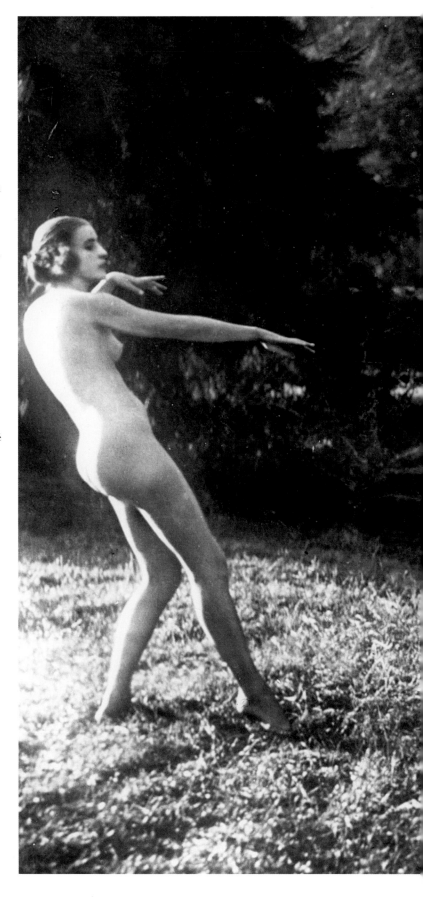

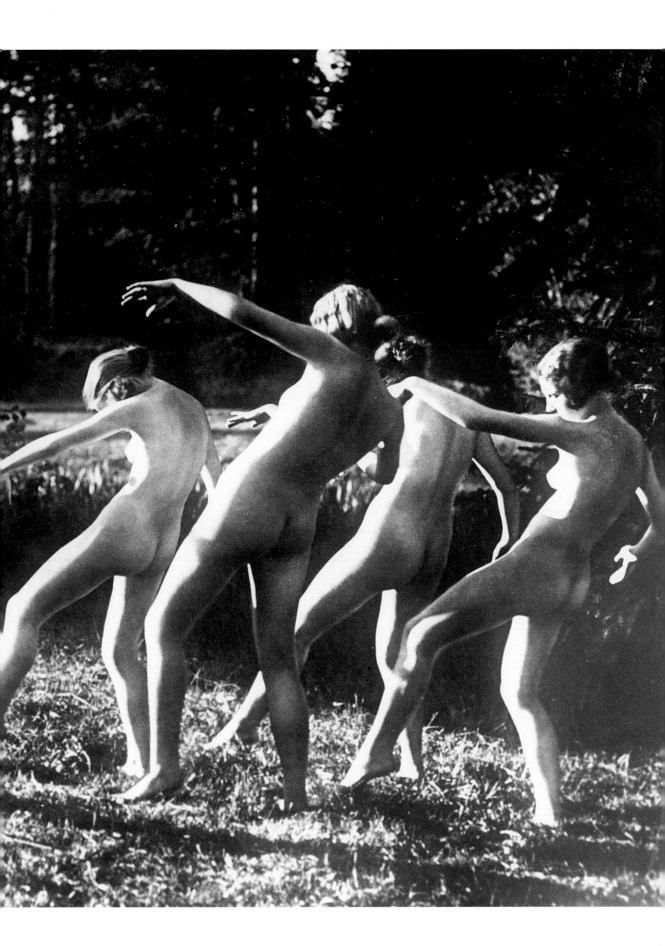

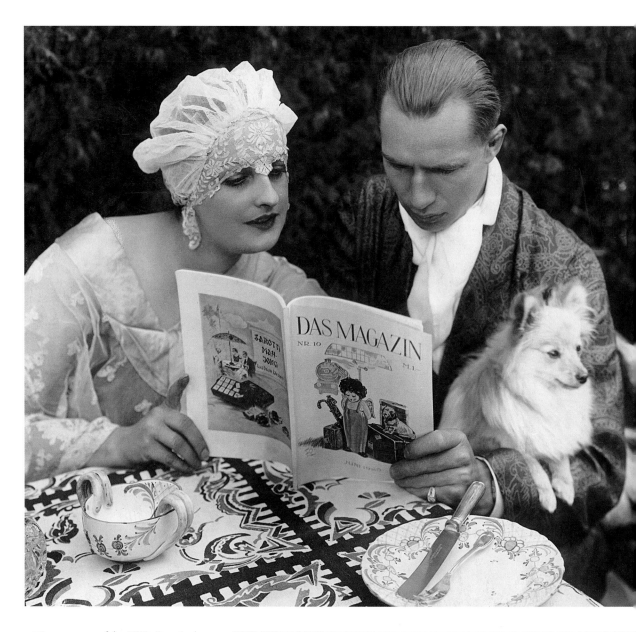

CELEBRITIES of the 1920s Fern Andra and Kurt Prenzel pose at the breakfast table (1). Andra was dubbed 'the Mary Pickford of Germany', Prenzel was German Middleweight Boxing Champion. The two married in 1923 but were soon divorced. Less homely, more 'arty' poses were adopted by German athletes at the Berlin Stadium (2). Technicians put the finishing touches to a giant model camera from the Ernamen works before the start of a photography exhibition in Berlin, 1927 (3). The cutting edge of architectural design was provided by in 1926 Walter Gropius in the Bauhaus Academy, Dessau (4).

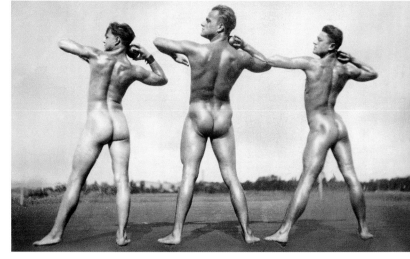

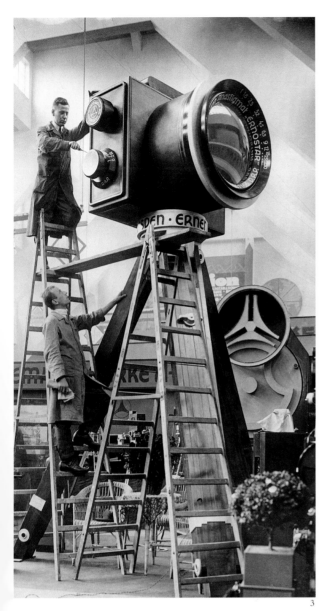

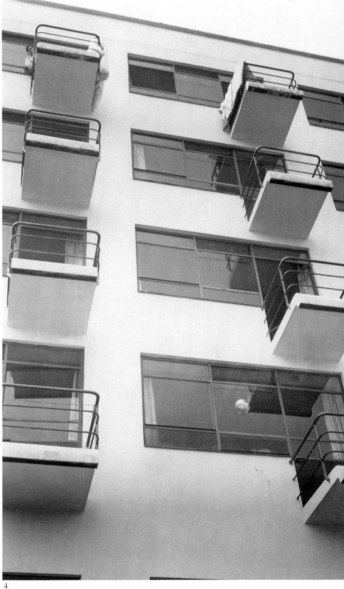

3   4

BERÜHMTHEITEN der 1920er Jahre: Fern Andra und Kurt Prenzel posieren für die Kamera am Frühstückstisch (1): Fern Andra war Produzentin, Regisseurin, Drehbuchautorin und Darstellerin und wirkte allein in Deutschland in über 40 Filmen mit; Kurt Prenzel war Boxmeister im Mittelgewicht. Die beiden heirateten 1923, doch die Ehe hielt nicht lang. Weniger heimelige, dafür um so künstlichere Posen nahmen deutsche Athleten im Berliner Stadion ein (2). Techniker legen letzte Hand an ein überdimensionales Kamera-Modell aus den Ernamen-Werken zur Eröffnung der Photographieausstellung in Berlin 1927 (3). Die klaren Linien eines neuen Architekturdesigns stammten 1926 aus der Feder von Walter Gropius an der Bauhausakademie in Dessau (4).

CÉLÉBRITÉS des années 20 : Fern Andra et Kurt Prenzel posent pour la caméra au petit déjeuner (1) : Fern Andra était productrice, réalisatrice, auteur de scénarii et actrice et, pour la seule Allemagne, a joué dans plus de 40 films ; Kurt Prenzel était champion de boxe en poids moyen. Ils se marièrent en 1923, mais leur couple ne dura pas longtemps. Image moins familiale, mais d'autant plus esthétique, ces athlètes allemands prennent la pose dans un stade berlinois (2). Les techniciens donnent la dernière touche à une maquette géante de caméra des usines Ernamen à l'occasion de l'inauguration du Salon de la Photographie, à Berlin, en 1927 (3). Ces lignes claires d'un nouveau design architectural feront la célébrité, en 1926, de Walter Gropius, de l'Académie du Baushaus, à Dessau (4).

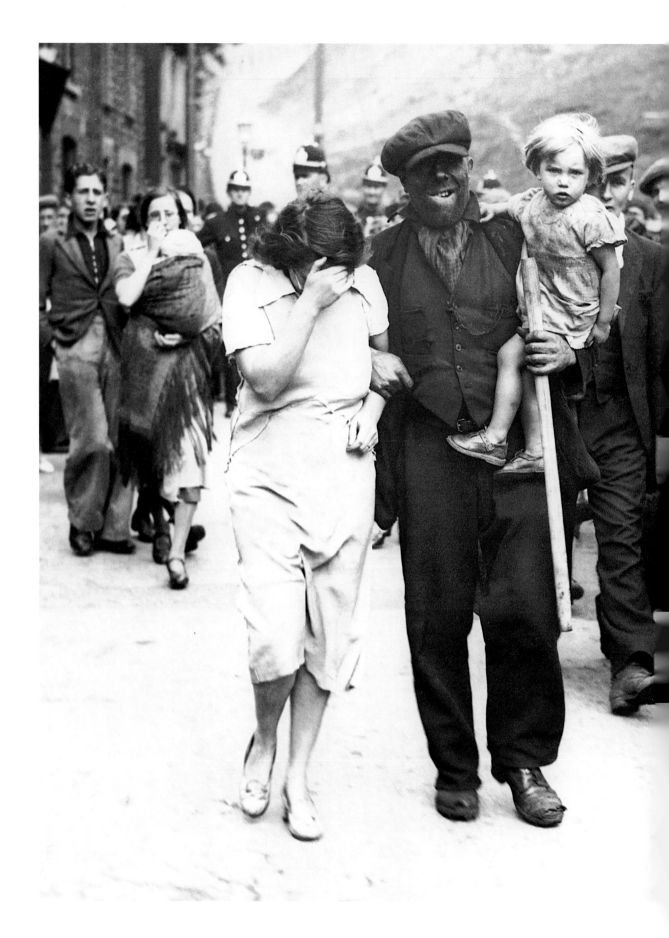

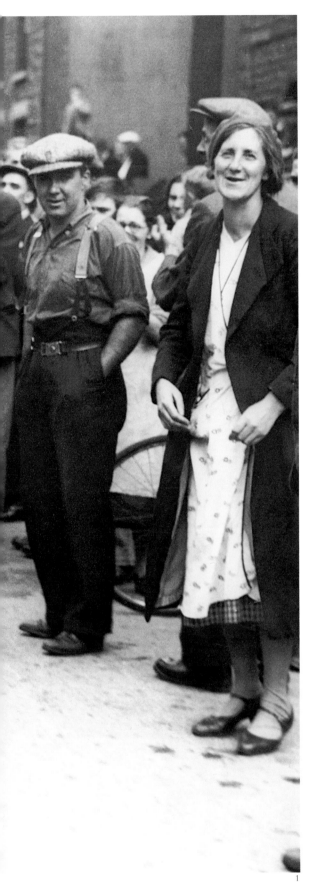

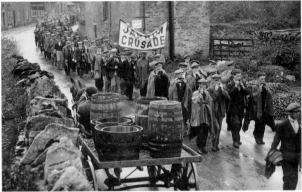

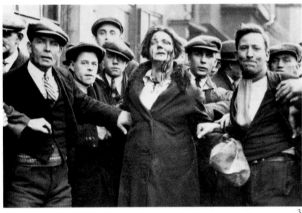

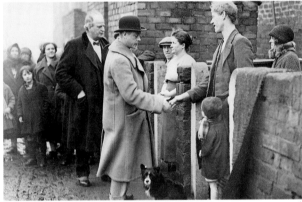

Unemployment in the 1930s: sit-ins at a Welsh colliery (1); the Jarrow Crusade, a march by the jobless from the North (2); riots in Bristol (3); the Prince of Wales visits miners' homes on a tour of the coalfields (4).

Arbeitslosigkeit in den 30er Jahren: Proteste walisischer Bergarbeiter (1); der »Jarrow-Kreuzzug«, ein Hungermarsch der Arbeitslosen aus dem englischen Norden (2); Aufstände in Bristol (3); der Prince of Wales besucht Bergarbeiterhäuser auf seiner Rundfahrt durch die Bergwerksgebiete (4).

Chômage dans les années 30 : occupation d'une houillère dans le Pays de Galles (1) ; la croisade de Jarrow, marche des chômeurs descendus du Nord (2) ; émeutes à Bristol (3) ; le Prince de Galles rendant visite à des familles de mineurs au cours d'une tournée dans les bassins houillers (4).

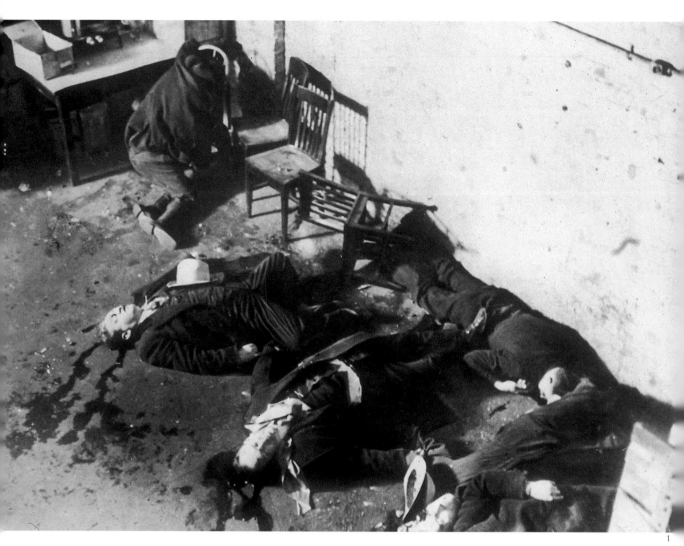

FROM January 1920 until December 1933 'the manufacture, sale or carriage' of alcoholic drink was forbidden by the 18th Amendment to the US Constitution. Kegs of alcohol (2) were destroyed by federal police. 'Bootlegging' (illicit distilling and distribution) fell under the control of criminal gangs who went to war with each other to secure profits. Seven members of the O'Banion-Moran gang were lined up against a Chicago garage wall in 1929 and machine-gunned in what became known as the St Valentine's Day Massacre (1). When the Amendment was finally repealed in May 1933, Sloppy Joe's Bar in Chicago (3) was the scene of wild celebration repeated all over America.

VOM Januar 1920 bis zum Dezember 1933 waren »Herstellung, Verkauf oder Besitz« von Alkohol in den Vereinigten Staaten per Gesetz verboten (18. Zusatz der Verfassung, die Prohibition). Die Bundespolizei zerschlug die Alkoholfässer (2). Das Schwarzbrennen (*bootlegging*) wurde von Verbrecherbanden gesteuert, die sich gegenseitig bekämpften, um sich möglichst hohe Profite zu sichern. Im sogenannten Massaker am Valentinstag wurden 1929 in Chicago sieben Mitglieder der O'Banion-Moran-Bande in einer Garage an die Wand gestellt und mit dem Maschinengewehr erschossen (1). Als die Verfassungsergänzung im Mai 1933 endlich außer Kraft gesetzt wurde, wurde überall in Amerika heftig gefeiert – wie hier in Sloppy Joe's Bar in Chicago (3).

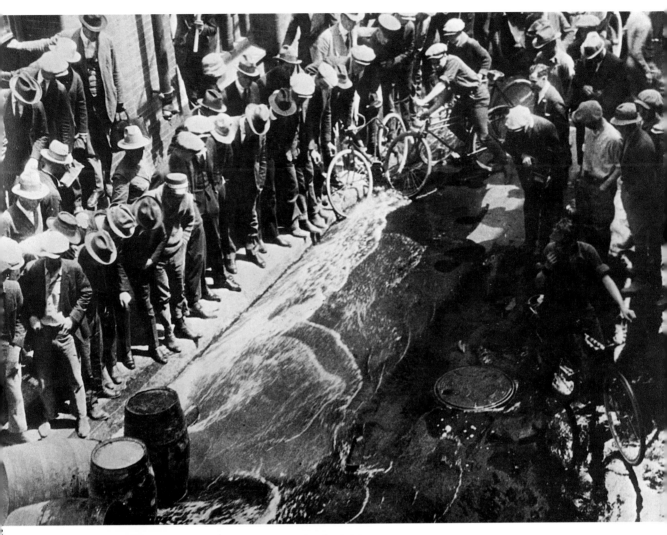

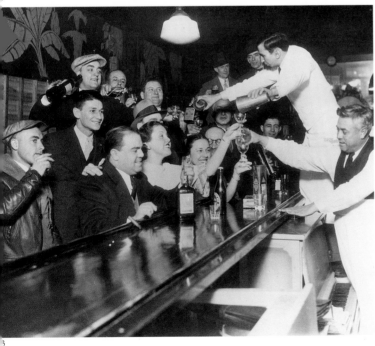

De janvier 1920 à décembre 1933, « la fabrication, la vente ou le transport » de boissons alcoolisées sont interdits en vertu du dix-huitième amendement de la Constitution des États-Unis. La police fédérale détruira les fûts d'alcool (2). La distillation et la distribution illégales sont réglées par les gangs de malfaiteurs qui se font la guerre afin d'en contrôler les bénéfices. Sept membres du gang O'Banion-Moran seront alignés contre un mur de garage à Chicago, en 1929, et abattus d'une salve de mitraillette, forfait devenu célèbre sous le nom de Massacre de la Saint-Valentin (1). Quand l'amendement constitutionnel est finalement aboli, en mai 1933, les Américains laissent éclater leur joie dans tout le pays – comme ici, dans le Sloppy Joe's Bar, à Chicago (3).

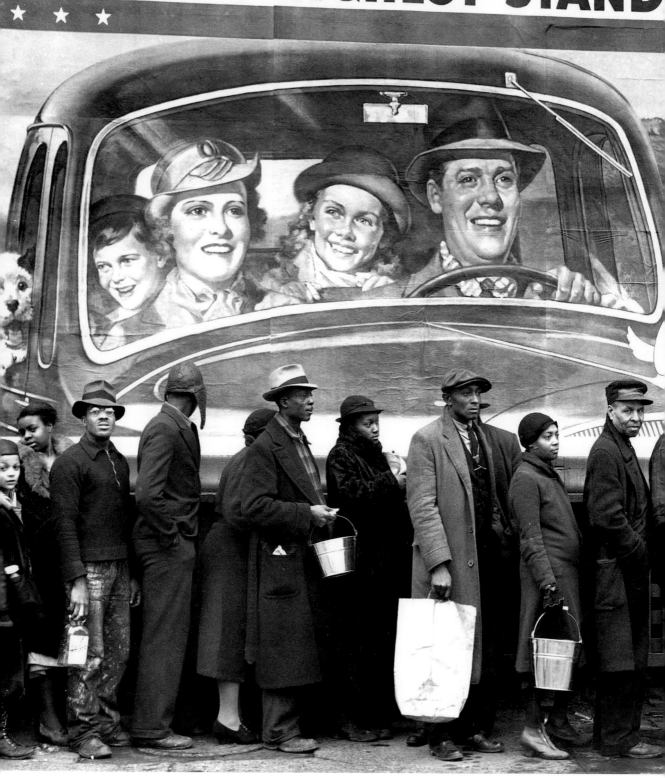

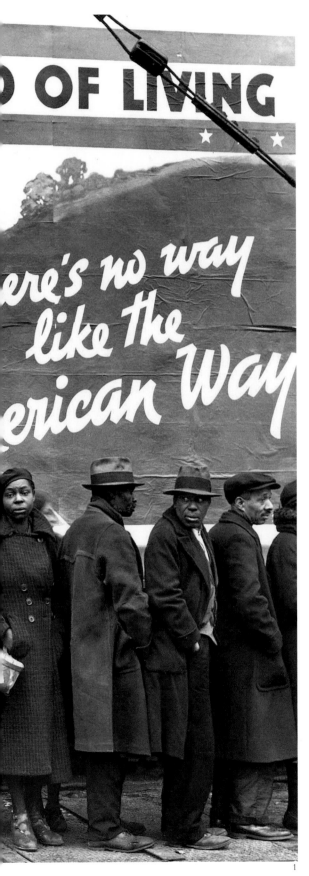

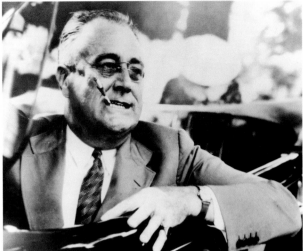

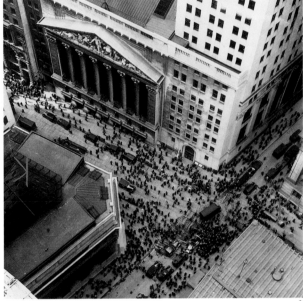

DREAM and nightmare. Crowds scuttle through Wall Street as the market crashes, 29 October 1929 (3). Flood victims in Kentucky queue for Red Cross relief, February 1937 (1). The architect of the New Deal and recovery, Franklin D. Roosevelt drives through New York, 4 July 1937 (2).

TRÄUME und Albträume: Eine Menschenmenge hastet durch die Wall Street, als am 29. Oktober 1929 die Börse zusammenbricht (3). Flutopfer im US-Bundesstaat Kentucky stehen im Februar 1937 für Hilfsgüter des Roten Kreuzes Schlange (1). Der Architekt des »New Deal« – eines Reformprogramms zur Stabilisierung der amerikanischen Wirtschaft – und 32. Präsident der Vereinigten Staaten, Franklin D. Roosevelt, fährt am 4. Juli 1937 durch New York (2).

RÊVE et cauchemar. La foule se masse dans Wall Street lors de l'effondrement de la Bourse, le 29 octobre 1929 (3). Des victimes des inondations au Kentucky font la queue pour les secours de la Croix Rouge, en février 1937 (1). L'architecte du New Deal et de la reconstruction, Franklin D. Roosevelt, circulant dans New York, le 4 juillet 1937 (2).

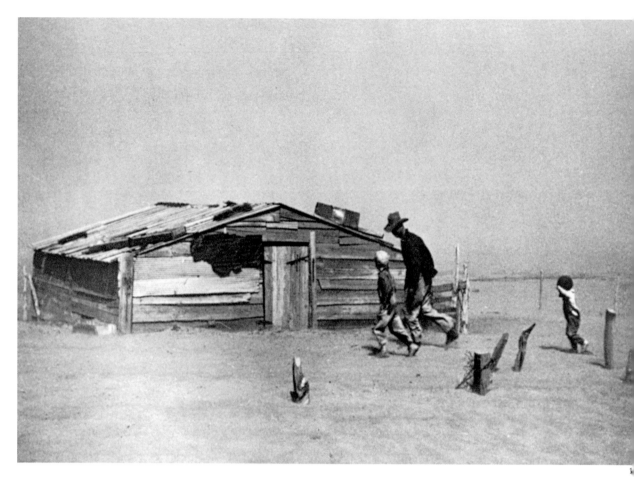

THE Depression that followed the Wall Street Crash led to a world slump. Bad farming methods rapidly turned the US Great Plains bread-basket into a dust bowl where the most primitive existence was only possible thanks to relief. Evicted from their farms, entire families lived in shacks (1) until they died or desperation forced them to hit the road westward. The nightmare lasted right through the 1930s – this young boy (2) was photographed in 1937. The photograph of Florence Thompson, a migrant mother who took her seven children to a camp in Nipomo, California (3), was taken by Dorothea Lange.

DIE Wirtschaftsflaute, die dem Börsenkrach an der Wall Street folgte, führte weltweit zu einem Konjunkturrückgang. Schlechte Erntemethoden führten außerdem dazu, daß die Great Plains – Amerikas Kornkammer im US-Bundesstaat Texas – sich im Handumdrehen in staubige Öden verwandelten, in denen auch die einfachste Lebensweise nur mit staatlichen Hilfslieferungen aufrechterhalten werden konnte. Gezwungen, ihre Farmen zu verlassen, lebten ganze Familien bis zu ihrem Tod in primitiven Holzhütten (1) oder machten sich aus Verzweiflung auf den Weg nach Westen. Dieser Albtraum dauerte die ganzen 1930er Jahre hindurch – dieser Junge (2) wurde 1937 photographiert. Das Photo von Florence Thompson – einer Mutter, die sich mit ihren sieben Kindern auf den Weg in ein Auffanglager nach Nipomo, Kalifornien, machte (3) – hat Dorothea Lange aufgenommen.

LA Dépression qui a suivi le krach de Wall Street a débouché sur un désastre mondial. De mauvaises méthodes d'agriculture ont rapidement transformé les Grandes Plaines, grenier à blé des États-Unis, en un désert de poussière où l'existence la plus rudimentaire n'était possible que grâce aux secours. Evincées de leur ferme, des familles entières végétaient jusqu'à la mort dans des baraques (1) quand le désespoir ne les forçait pas à s'exiler vers l'Ouest. Ce cauchemar a duré durant toutes les années 30 – ce jeune garçon (2) a été photographié en 1937. La photo de Florence Thomson, une mère qui a émigré pour emmener ses enfants dans un camp d'hébergement à Nipomo, en Californie (3), a été prise par Dorothea Lange.

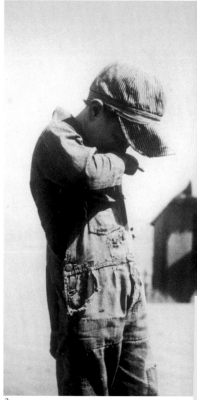

2

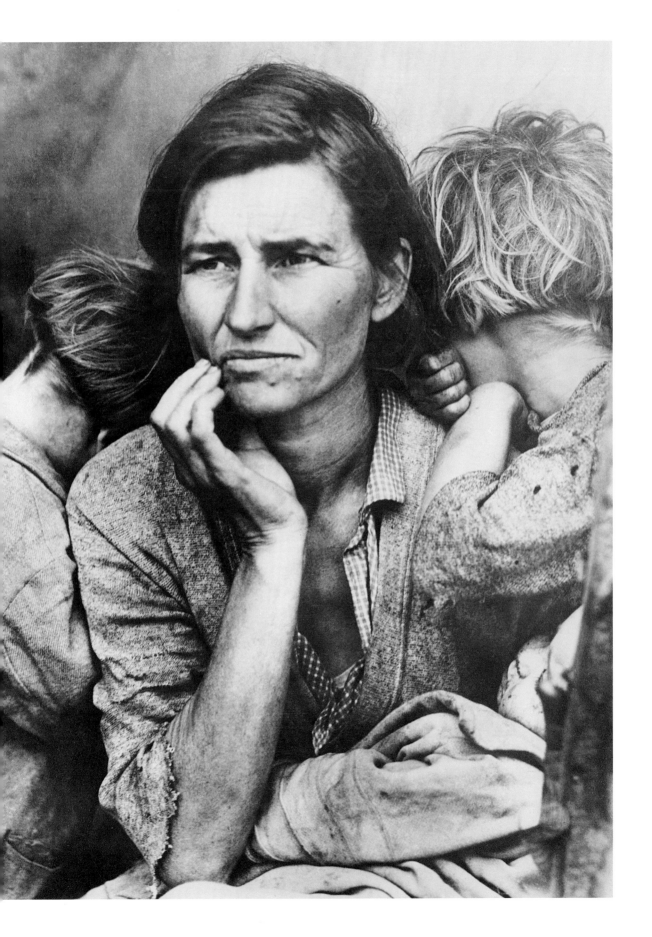

The Rise of Fascism

PERHAPS the most damning feature to emerge from all the books, lectures and opinions about European fascism is that the reasons for its rise were so predominantly negative. Economically, Europe was reeling from crash, depression and slump. To counter the ignominy as well as the poverty wrought by mass unemployment by guaranteeing not only wages and housing but uniforms and status through military conscription was an offer to which there seemed little alternative. Rearmament was also attractive to a Germany that felt herself humiliated by the terms of the Treaty of Versailles at the conclusion of the Great War; one result was a witch-hunt for the 'enemies within' that could be blamed for defeat.

Political enemies at first took precedence over racial ones, in Germany as in Italy. The smashing of the Spartacists and the killing of Rosa Luxemburg and Karl Liebknecht in 1919 failed to unseat a nascent but entrenched Socialist and Communist movement. Fears that the recent Russian Revolution would spread through Europe were in no way allayed by the vacillations of the Weimar régime, apparently as incapable of pursuing a political as an economic programme. If democracy could not deal with the problems, it was argued, then maybe democracy should make way.

The term 'Fascism' originated in Milan in 1919 with the formation of the *Fascio di Combattimento*, an anti-Socialist militia called after the bundle of rods that was the symbol of ancient Roman legislature. It took an authoritarian form under Mussolini in the decade from 1922. Rome in 1932 saw 40,000 Junior Fascists aged between 14 and 18 gather for a rally addressed by him. This very junior Junior Fascist served as a mascot, and is seen here saluting Il Duce (2). A former Socialist himself, Mussolini confusingly boasted: 'We allow ourselves the luxury of being aristocratic and democratic, reactionary and revolutionary'. Unlike Hitler, Mussolini primarily vaunted his pride in the glories of a real imperial past; a wish to destroy both the 'putrefying corpse' of parliamentary democracy and to strangle at birth any attempt at creating a Marxist state. His anti internationalism extended to an insistence that Fascism was an Italian creed 'not for export'. It took until July 1938 and the formation of the Axis alliance for him to renege and become overtly anti-Semitic and to issue a *Manifesto della Razza* in imitation of his German ally.

Meanwhile in Spain, between 1936 and 1939 Franco's Falangist Party fought with German support to unseat the elected Republican government. Civil war erupted when the army rose against the government in July 1936: here, a Republican soldier throws a hand grenade at enemy trenches (1). General Franco, the future dictator who would rule Spain repressively for 35 years, stationed his headquarters in Spanish Morocco. From there he had to ferry insurgents across the Strait of Gibraltar and would have been unable to attain victory without the assistance of Fascist forces from Germany and Italy.

The postwar English historian A. J. P. Taylor has sought to diminish Hitler's role, considering that 'in principle and in doctrine, Hitler was no more wicked and unscrupulous than many other contemporary statesmen'. Few, however, would rush to concur. One has only to take, almost at random, a passage from *Mein Kampf* (My Struggle, 1923) to establish the histrionic fanaticism that swept so much before it, determining the fate of nations and the deaths of 55 millions:

'The adulteration of the blood and racial deterioration conditioned thereby are the only causes that account for the decline of ancient civilizations; for it is never by war that nations are ruined but by the loss of their powers of resistance, which are exclusively a characteristic of pure racial blood. In this world everything that is not of sound stock is like chaff.'

That this reads today as nonsensical rhetoric more appropriate to a stock-breeder's manual than a political manifesto is a measure of the discredit into which the term 'Fascism' has finally fallen.

1

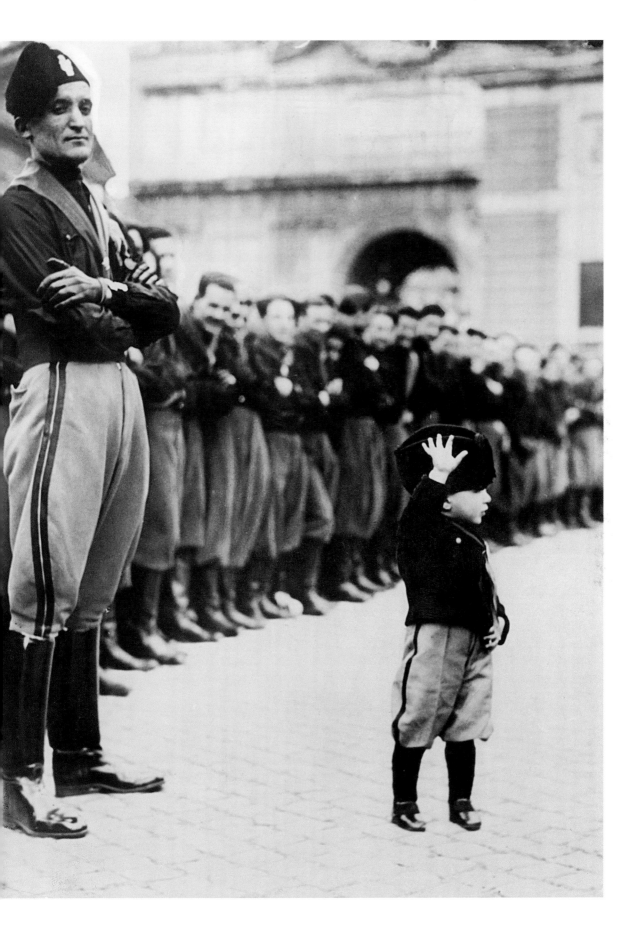

DIE Quintessenz all der Bücher, Vorträge und Meinungen über den europäischen Faschismus ist die Erkenntnis, daß er so große Macht gewinnen konnte, weil die Zeiten so schlecht waren. Europa lag nach der Weltwirtschaftskrise am Boden, und hier wurden nicht nur Arbeit und Unterkunft versprochen, durch die man mit der Schande und Armut der Massenarbeitslosigkeit fertigwerden konnte, sondern auch noch Uniformen und das Ansehen eines militärischen Dienstranges – dazu schien es keine Alternative zu geben. Für die Deutschen, die sich von den Bedingungen des Versailler Vertrages gedemütigt fühlten, war die Aussicht auf Wiederaufrüstung verlockend, und nun konnten sie die Feinde im eigenen Lande gnadenlos verfolgen.

Zunächst stand in Deutschland wie in Italien eher politische Feindschaft im Vordergrund und nicht die Rassenzugehörigkeit. Die Niederwerfung des Spartakistenaufstandes und die Ermordung Rosa Luxemburgs und Karl Liebknechts 1919 konnte die noch junge, aber schon verwurzelte sozialistische und kommunistische Bewegung nicht vernichten. Die Ängste, daß die Russische Revolution auf ganz Europa übergreifen könnte, wurden durch die Schwäche der Weimarer Regierung noch geschürt, die in politischer Hinsicht ebenso orientierungslos wirkte wie in wirtschaftlicher. Wenn die Demokratie nicht mit den Schwierigkeiten fertigwerden konnte, sagten sich die Leute, dann sollte die Demokratie einer anderen Staatsform Platz machen.

Die Bezeichnung »Faschismus« kam 1919 in Mailand auf, wo der *Fascio di Combattimento* gegründet wurde, eine antikommunistische Miliz, die sich nach dem Rutenbündel benannte, das im alten Rom das Symbol der Legislative gewesen war. Seit 1922 nahm er unter Mussolini autoritäre Züge an. 1932 versammelten sich in Rom 40 000 Jungfaschisten zwischen 14 und 18 Jahren, um ihn sprechen zu hören. Dieser sehr junge Juniorfaschist (2) war als Maskottchen dabei, und man sieht, wie eifrig er den Duce begrüßt. Mussolini, der früher selbst Sozialist gewesen war, rühmte sich in Paradoxen: »Wir erlauben uns den Luxus, aristokratisch und demokratisch, reaktionär und revolutionär zugleich zu sein.« Anders als Hitler konnte Mussolini stolz auf die Tradition eines Weltreichs zurückblicken, und er wollte den »stinkenden Leichnam« der Demokratie beiseite räumen und jeglichen Versuch, einen marxistischen Staat zu errichten, im Keime ersticken. Sein

Nationalismus ging so weit, daß er sogar verlauten lie▮ der Faschismus sei eine italienische Weltanschauung, d▮ »nicht für den Export bestimmt« sei. Erst im Juli 193▮ als der Bund der Achsenmächte geschlossen war, gab ▮ sich offen antisemitisch und veröffentlichte ein *Manifes▮ della Razza* nach dem Vorbild seiner deutschen Ve▮ bündeten.

In Spanien bekämpfte derweil 1936 bis 193▮ Francos Falangistenpartei mit deutscher Unterstützun▮ die gewählte republikanische Regierung. Als die Arme▮ sich im Juli 1936 gegen die Regierung erhob, hatte de▮ Bürgerkrieg begonnen: Hier (1) wirft ein republikan▮ scher Soldat eine Handgranate auf feindliche Schützer▮ gräben. General Franco, der künftige Diktator, de▮ 35 Jahre lang über Spanien herrschen sollte, errichte▮ sein Hauptquartier im spanischen Marokko. Von do▮ mußte er seine Aufständischen per Schiff über di▮ Straße von Gibraltar bringen und hätte sich niema▮ durchsetzen können, wenn faschistische Truppen au▮ Deutschland und Italien ihm nicht geholfen hätten.

Der englische Historiker A. J. P. Taylor schrie▮ später, man solle Hitlers Rolle nicht überbewerten: »I▮ seinen Prinzipien und Ansichten war Hitler nich▮ schlechter und gewissenloser als viele andere Politike▮ seiner Zeit.« Doch nur wenige pflichteten ihm bei. Ma▮ muß sich nur eine willkürlich ausgewählte Passage a▮ *Mein Kampf* von 1923 ansehen, dann begreift man, da▮ hier ein größenwahnsinniger Fanatiker das Schicks▮ ganzer Nationen und den Tod von mehr als 55 Mi▮ lionen Menschen besiegelte: »Die Blutsvermischun▮ und das dadurch bedingte Senken des Rassenniveaus i▮ die alleinige Ursache des Absterbens aller Kulture▮ denn die Menschen gehen nicht an verlorenen Kriege▮ zugrunde, sondern am Verlust jener Widerstandskraf▮ die nur dem reinen Blute zu eigen ist. Was nicht gu▮ Rasse ist auf dieser Welt, ist Spreu.« Daß sich das heut▮ als hohle Rhetorik liest, die eher in ein Handbuch f▮ Viehzüchter paßt als in ein politisches Manifest, zeig▮ uns, welcher Verachtung der Begriff »Faschismus« an▮ heimgefallen ist.

Des ouvrages, conférences et opinions qu'inspirèrent le fascisme européen, on retiendra le souci constant de mettre en valeur un contexte essentiellement négatif propice à son essor. Économiquement, l'Europe se trouvait dans un état d'effondrement, de dépression et de marasme. Tant pour échapper à l'angoisse qu'à la pauvreté causées par un chômage massif, il n'y avait guère d'autre choix possible que d'accepter non seulement le salaire et le logement, mais aussi l'uniforme et le statut que garantissait un engagement dans l'armée. Le réarmement séduisait aussi une Allemagne humiliée par les clauses du traité de Versailles qui avait conclu la Grande Guerre. Il en résulta notamment une chasse aux sorcières contre les « ennemis de l'intérieur » rendus responsables de la défaite.

L'Allemagne, à l'instar de l'Italie, s'en prit d'abord aux ennemis politiques avant de s'occuper de la question raciale. L'écrasement des spartakistes, suivi de l'assassinat de Rosa Luxemburg et de Karl Liebknecht en 1919 ne parvinrent pas à déstabiliser un mouvement ouvrier où les communistes jouaient déjà un grand rôle. La crainte de voir la jeune révolution russe se propager en Europe ne se trouvait guère dissipée devant les hésitations du régime de Weimar apparemment incapable de mettre en œuvre un programme économique et politique. Si la démocratie n'était pas en mesure d'affronter les problèmes, disait-on, c'est peut-être qu'elle devait céder la place.

Le terme « Fascisme » prit naissance à Milan en 1919 avec la formation du *Fascio di Combattimento*, milice antisocialiste qui tenait son nom du faisceau de verges servant de symbole à la magistrature romaine dans l'Antiquité. Il incarna dès 1922 le régime autoritaire de Mussolini, et cela pendant dix ans. À Rome, en 1932, ce sont 40 000 jeunes fascistes âgés de 14 à 18 ans qui sont ici rassemblés pour écouter Mussolini. Ce tout petit fasciste servait de mascotte ; on le voit ici saluant *Il Duce* (2). Ancien socialiste lui-même, Mussolini aimait à répéter ces paroles qui rendent perplexes : « Nous nous offrons le luxe d'être aristocratiques et démocratiques, réactionnaires et révolutionnaires ». Contrairement à Hitler, il était animé d'une fierté qui puisait dans un véritable passé impérial : du désir tout à la fois de détruire la « carcasse pourrissante » de la démocratie parlementaire et d'étouffer dans l'œuf toute tentative de créer un état marxiste. Son anti-internationalisme allait jusqu'à souligner que le fascisme était une croyance italienne « non destinée à l'exportation ». Il faut attendre juillet 1938 et la constitution de l'alliance de l'Axe pour qu'il se dédise, se déclare ouvertement antisémite et fasse publier son *Manifesto della Razza* à l'instar de son alliée allemande.

Pendant ce temps, en Espagne, de 1936 à 1939, le parti phalangiste de Franco était soutenu par l'Allemagne dans sa lutte qui visait à confisquer la République. La guerre civile éclata lorsque l'armée entra en Juillet 1936 en rébellion contre le gouvernement : un soldat républicain lance ici une grenade à main vers une tranchée ennemie (1). Le général Franco, candillo d'un régime qui durera trente-cinq ans, établit son quartier général au Maroc espagnol. De là il lui fallut faire traverser aux insurgés le détroit de Gibraltar en bateau: c'est aux forces fascistes venues d'Allemagne et d'Italie qu'il devra en partie la victoire.

L'historien anglais de l'après-guerre, A.J.P. Taylor, s'emploie à minimiser le rôle de Hitler, estimant que « s'agissant du principe et de la doctrine, Hitler ne fut ni plus mauvais ni moins dénué de scrupules que beaucoup d'autres de nos hommes d'État contemporains ». Peu s'empresseront cependant de lui donner raison. Il suffit de prendre, presque au hasard, un passage de *Mein Kampf* (1923), pour se convaincre qu'il s'agit bien là d'un fanatisme orchestré et dévastateur qui devait tracer la destinée de nations entières et décider de la mort de 55 millions de personnes :

« L'adultération du sang et la dégénérescence raciale qui en a résulté sont là les seules causes du déclin des civilisations antérieures ; car ce n'est jamais la guerre qui cause la ruine des nations mais bien la perte de leurs pouvoirs de résistance, qui sont une caractéristique exclusive d'un sang de race pure. Dans ce monde, tout ce qui n'est pas de souche saine est de l'ivraie ».

Aujourd'hui, cette ineptie ampoulée résonne plus comme un manuel destiné aux éleveurs que comme un manifeste politique, à la mesure du discrédit attaché au terme « fascisme ».

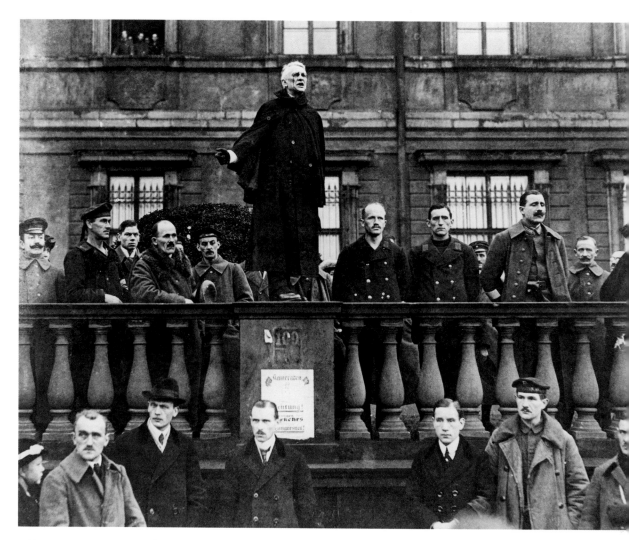

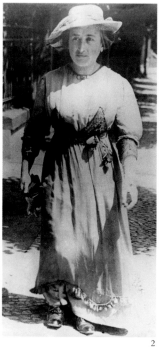

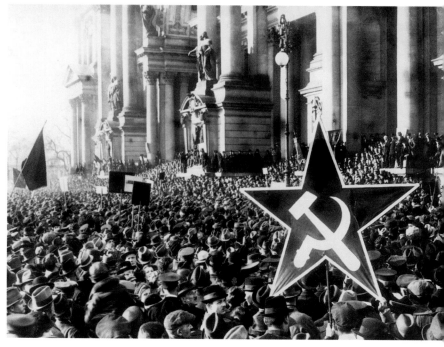

2

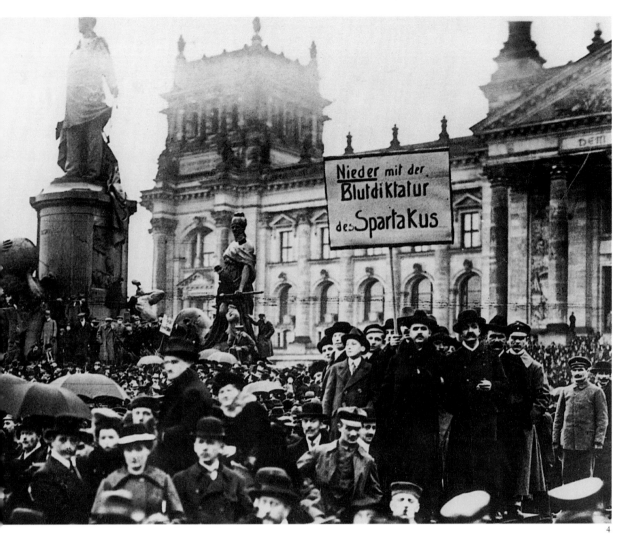

ON 7 January 1919 the Spartacists – their name derived from the slaves who led the last revolt to overthrow Roman rule – took to the streets of Berlin, which they then barricaded. For over a week the battle raged. Fighting deeds and speeches (1) followed; rallies and allegiances blurred – the hammer and sickle (3) v. 'Down with the Spartacists' Dictatorship of Blood!' (4). On 16 January the popular revolutionary leaders 'Red Rosa' Luxemburg (2) and former Reichstag deputy Karl Liebknecht were murdered by officers of the Gardekavallerie-Schützen-Division, an irregular right-wing force officered by professionals from the dissolved army, sent to arrest them. Instead the leaders were tortured, shot and their bodies thrown into a canal. The officers were never brought to trial.

AM 7. Januar 1919 gingen die Sparta-kisten – die sich nach dem Anführer des letzten Sklavenaufstands gegen die Römer benannt hatten – in Berlin auf die Straße und errichteten ihre Barrikaden. Über eine Woche dauerten die Straßen-kämpfe. Kämpfe in Taten und Worten folgten (1); Zugehörigkeit verwischte sich – Hammer und Sichel (3) kontra »Nieder mit der Blutdiktatur des Spartakus!« (4) Am 16. Januar wurden die populäre Revolu-tionsführerin Rosa Luxemburg (die »Rote Rosa«) (2) und der ehemalige Reichstags-abgeordnete Karl Liebknecht von Mitglie-dern der Gardekavallerie-Schützendivision, eines inoffiziellen rechtsgerichteten Frei-korps, dessen Offiziere Berufssoldaten aus der aufgelösten Armee waren, ermordet. Die Männer hatten die beiden Anführer verhaften sollen, doch statt dessen folterten und erschossen sie sie und warfen ihre Leichen in einen Kanal. Die Offiziere wur-den nie vor Gericht gestellt.

LE 7 janvier 1919, les spartakistes, du nom des esclaves qui organisèrent la dernière révolte contre la domination romaine, – entreprirent de barricader les rues de Berlin. Pendant plus d'une semaine la bataille fit rage. Les accords tactiques et les discours suivirent (1) ; les rassemble-ments et les allégeances se déroulèrent dans la confusion. Ici, la faucille et le marteau (3). « À bas la dictature sanguinaire et sparta-kiste » (4). Le 16 janvier, les chefs de file de la révolution populaire « Rosa la rouge » Luxemburg (2) et l'ancien député au Reichs-tag, Karl Liebknecht, sont blessés par des officiers en mission commandée de la Gar-dekavallerie-Schützendivision, une force irrégulière rassemblant des éléments de droite et encadrée par des professionnels issus de l'armée dissoute. En fait de cela, ils furent torturés avant d'être abattus, et leurs cadavres furent jetés dans un canal. Les officiers ne furent jamais traduits en justice.

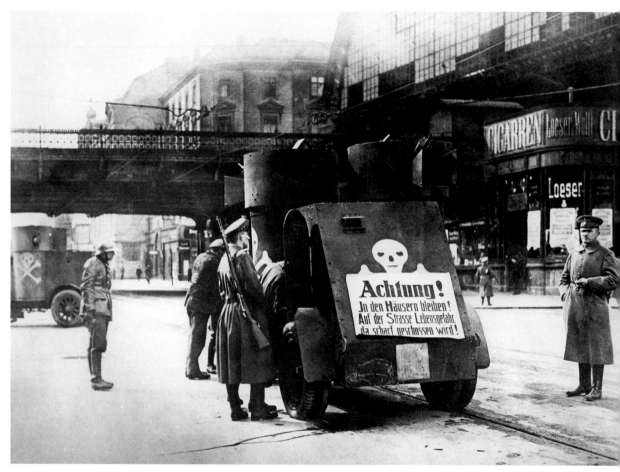

JANUARY 1919 was a time of elections to the National Assembly, which had before it the task of drawing up a new constitution. Because of the disturbances on the streets of Munich and Berlin, much of the business had to be moved to Weimar. In Berlin this quaint-looking government armoured car bears a warning skull and placard: 'Beware! Stay in your homes! Coming onto the streets can put your life at risk: you will be shot!' (1). As though bearing this out, Berlin civilians flee the machine-gun fire from Chancellor Ebert's government troops (2).

IM Januar 1919 wurde die Nationalversammlung gewählt, die eine neue Verfassung ausarbeiten sollte. Wegen der Unruhen in den Straßen von München und Berlin wurden die Amtsgeschäfte größtenteils nach Weimar verlegt. In Berlin warnt dieser kuriose offizielle Panzerwagen unter dem Totenschädel: »Achtung! In den Häusern bleiben! Auf der Straße Lebensgefahr, da scharf geschossen wird!« (1) Wie um dies zu beweisen, fliehen Berliner vor den Maschinengewehren von Reichspräsident Eberts Regierungstruppen (2).

JANVIER 1919 fut l'époque des élection[s] à l'Assemblée nationale, laquelle avait pour tâche d'élaborer une nouvelle Const[i]tution. En raison des troubles qui avaient éclaté dans les rues de Munich et de Berli[n] on transféra presque tout à Weimar. À Berli[n] ce véhicule blindé des autorités publiques offre un bien curieux spectacle avec sa têt[e] de mort et son inscription en guise d'avertissement : « Attention ! Restez chez vous Sortir dans la rue peut vous coûter la vie : vous risquez d'être abattus ! » (1). Comme pour lui donner raison, des civils s'enfuier[t] à Berlin sous les rafales des mitraillettes gouvernementales du chancelier Ebert (2)

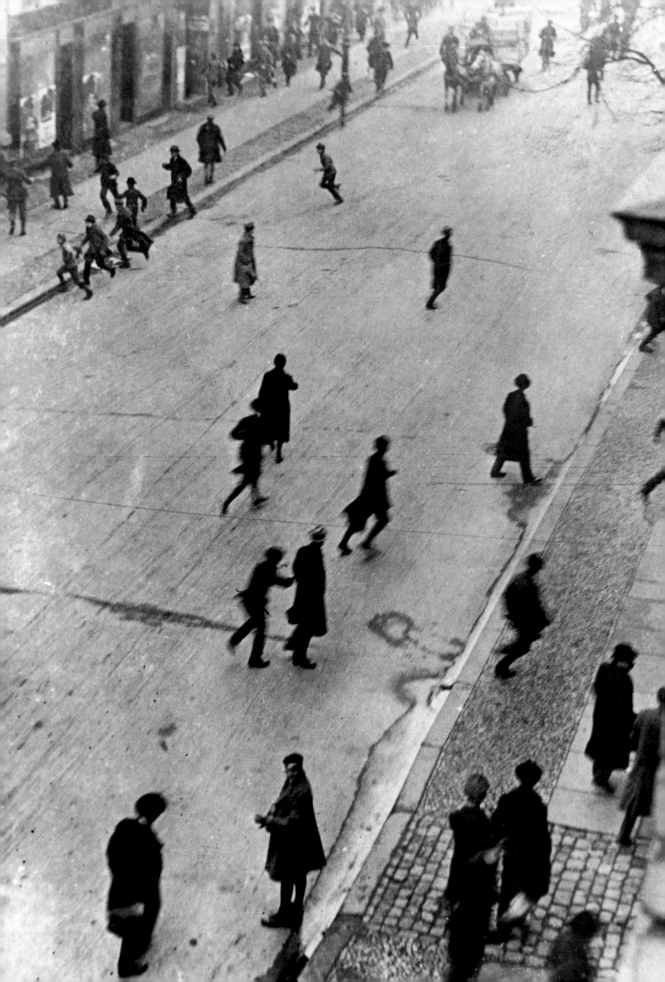

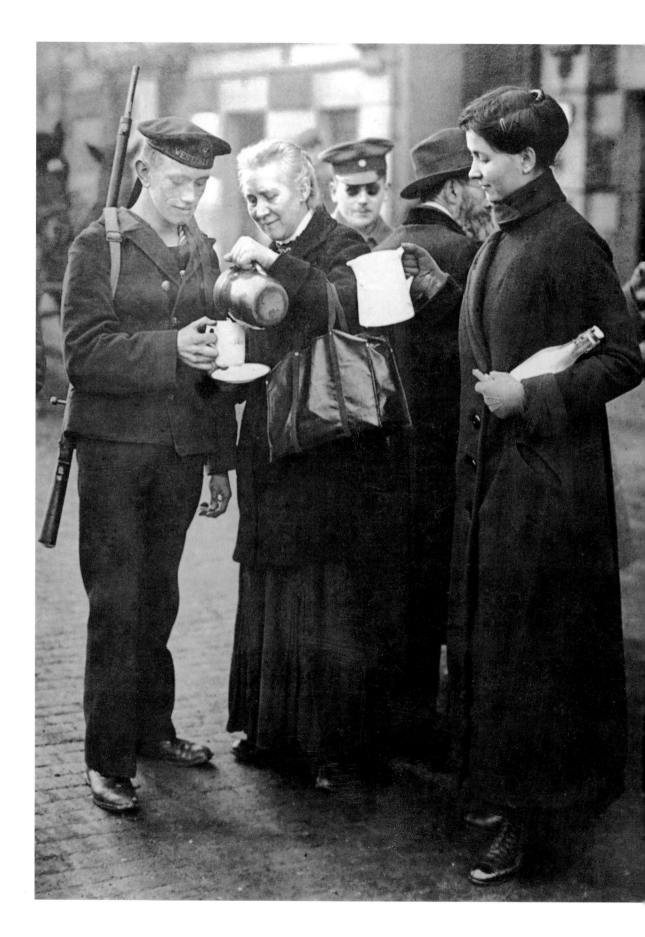

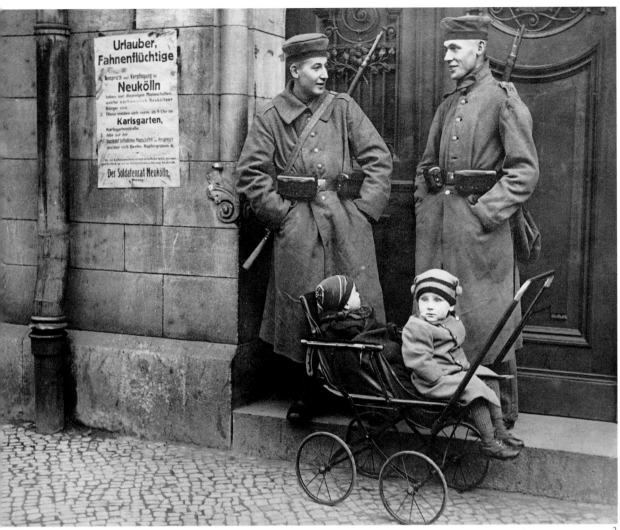

THE confusion caused by circumstances at the war's end led women (1) and even children (2) to fraternize with the military. While the Spartacists looked to nascent workers' soviets to create a 'free socialist republic of Germany', there were rapid and increasing signs that the Socialist People's Militia and *Freikorps* would not fight with the newly created city soviets. The revolution collapsed when the militias threw in their lot with the police and armed forces.

IN den Wirren, die am Ende der deutschen Revolution herrschten, sympathisierten Frauen (1) und sogar Kinder (2) mit den Militärs. Die Spartakisten hofften, daß Arbeiterräte »eine freie sozialistische Republik in Deutschland« schaffen würden, doch bald war offensichtlich, daß die sozialistischen Volksmilizen und Freikorps nicht gegen die neugeschaffenen Stadträte kämpfen würden. Die Revolution war zu Ende, als die Milizen sich auf die Seite der Polizei und der Armee schlugen.

LA confusion qui règne à la fin de la guerre conduisit des femmes (1), voire des enfants (2) à fraterniser avec les militaires. Tandis que les spartakistes comptaient sur les comités ouvriers naissants pour créer la base d'une « République socialiste libre d'Allemagne », il apparut bientôt de plus en plus clairement que la milice du peuple socialiste et les *Freikorps* (volontaires) ne combattraient pas aux côtés des comités tout juste créés dans les villes. La fin de la révolution était scellée lorsque les milices décidèrent de lier leur sort à celui de la police et des forces armées.

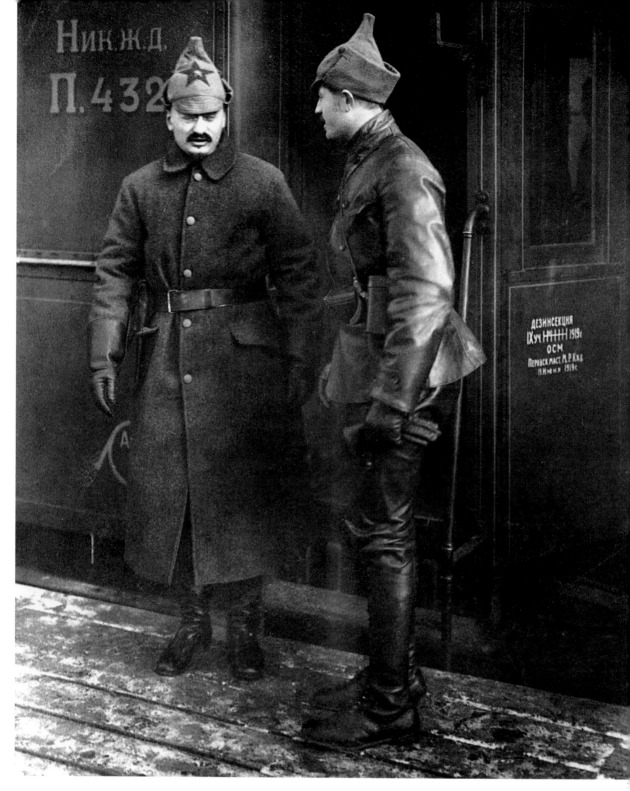

TROTSKY, here at Petrograd (St Petersburg) in 1921 (1), was supposedly 'in
the vanguard of the Revolution, while
Lenin was in the guard's van'. As erstwhile
War Minister and Head of the Red Army,
he paid a visit to the Red Commanders of
the Russian Military Academy at Moscow
(2). From 1917 to 1922, Lenin was
undisputed leader, but from 1922 until his

death in 1924, he suffered three serious
heart attacks and was obliged to retire to the
country (3). His meeting there with Stalin
in the summer of 1922 was a prophetic one
(4). While Trotsky described Stalin as 'the
Party's most eminent mediocrity', Lenin
concluded: 'I am not always sure that he
knows how to use power with caution.' In
1923, he recommended Stalin's dismissal.

TROTZKI, hier 1921 in Petrograd (St.
Petersburg) (1), galt als »der Schaffner
der Revolution, und Lenin war der
Bremser«. Als damaliger Kriegsminister und
Oberbefehlshaber der Roten Armee stattet
er hier (2) den Roten Kommandeuren der
Russischen Militärakademie in Moskau
einen Besuch ab. Von 1917 bis 1922 war
Lenin der unangefochtene Führer der

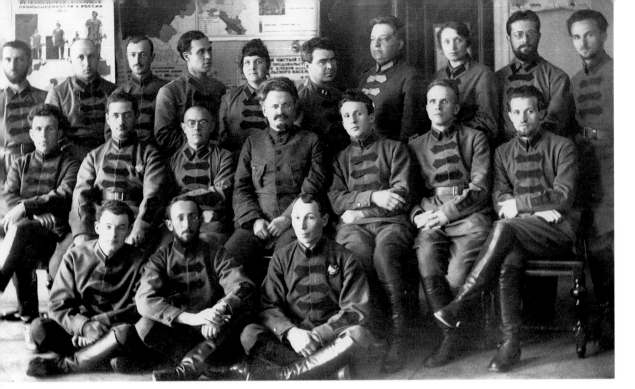

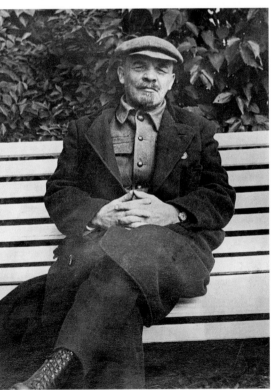

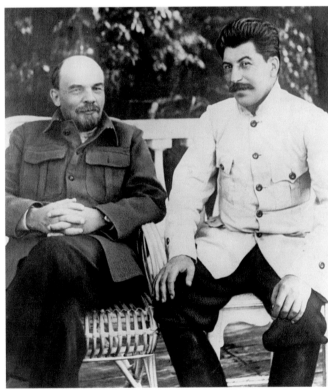

Revolution, doch von 1922 bis zu seinem Tode 1924 erlitt er drei schwere Herzanfälle und mußte sich aufs Land zurückziehen (3). Sein Treffen dort mit Stalin im Sommer 1922 sollte zukunftsweisend sein (4). Lenin kam zu dem Schluß: »Ich bin mir nicht immer sicher, ob er beim Umgang mit der Macht das rechte Maß kennt.« 1923 empfahl er, Stalin zu entlassen.

Trotski, ici à Petrograd (Saint-Péters-bourg) en 1921 (1) était supposé « à l'avant-garde de la Révolution et Lénine sous la garde de celle-ci ». Ancien ministre de la Guerre et de chef de l'Armée rouge, il rendit visite aux commandants commu-nistes à Moscou (2). Lénine régna de 1917 à 1922. Mais, dès 1922 et jusqu'à sa mort en 1924, trois graves attaques cardiaques le

contraignirent à se retirer à la campagne (3), où il eut une entrevue avec Staline au cours de l'été 1922 (4). Alors que Trotski qualifiait Staline de « médiocrité la plus éminente du Parti », Lénine concluait : « Je ne suis pas toujours sûr qu'il sache faire un bon usage du pouvoir. » En 1923, il recom-manda le limogeage de Staline.

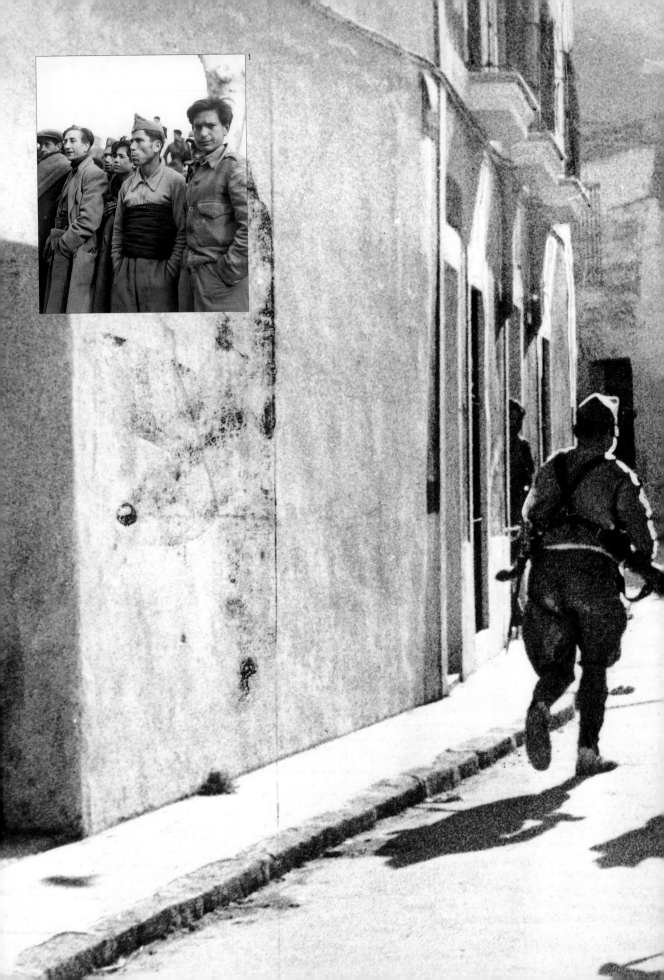

OYAL Republican Spanish troops at
ease in 1936 (1) contrast with jack-
booted Foreign Legionaries on a 'hunt the
eds' mission in Mérida, rifles raised (2).

LOYALE Truppen der spanischen
Republik während einer Pause, 1936
(1), und im Kontrast dazu die Fremden-
legionäre in Mérida, wie sie in ihren
Stiefeln mit erhobenen Gewehren »die
Roten jagen« (2).

LA décontraction des troupes espagnoles
républicaines loyalistes en 1936 (1) contraste
avec la « chasse aux rouges » dans laquelle se
sont lancés les hommes de la légion étrangère,
bottes montantes et fusils brandis à Mérida (2).

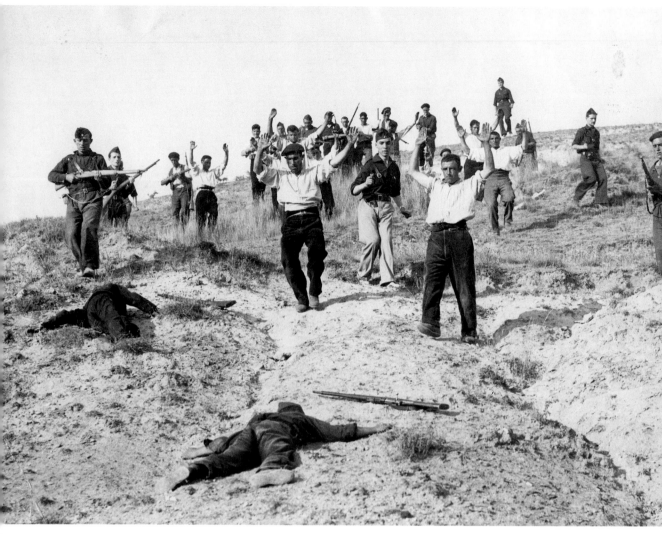

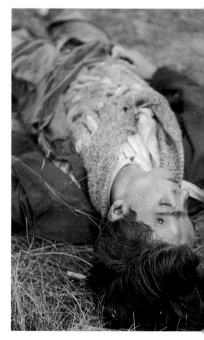

ON 29 August 1936, this group of
Republicans was forced to surrender
by the Nationalist rebels (1). In their ill-
assorted uniforms and weapons, they look
more like a ragtag than a national army,
suggesting how many of the regular troops
were anti-Republican. A 17-year-old lies
dead from a bullet in the head (2). A vivid
account of one man's experience is offered
by George Orwell's *Homage to Catalonia*.
Words were enormously important to
the ideological battle: after all, Franco's
Falangists adopted the Foreign Legionnaires'
war cry 'Death to Intellectuals! Long live
death!' The Republicans responded with
poster propaganda like this Catalan
advertisement post calling women to arms
(4). All the unions, particularly female-
dominated ones such as the
garmentworkers, organized women like
these militia seated wearily at a roadside (3).
Their lack of uniforms, even boots, implies
that this was taken late in the war.

AM 29. August 1936 zwangen die
nationalistischen Rebellen diesen
Trupp Republikaner zur Kapitulation (1).
In ihren verschiedenerlei Uniformen und
Waffen sehen sie eher wie ein bunt zusam-
mengewürfelter Haufen aus als wie eine
Nationalarmee, und man kann ahnen, wie
viele reguläre Truppen sich auf die Seite
der Gegner geschlagen hatten. Ein siebzehn-
jähriger Gefallener mit einer Kugel im
Kopf (2). George Orwell hat in *Mein Kata-
lonien* eindrucksvoll seine Kriegserlebnisse
in Spanien beschrieben. Ideologische
Kriegführung war von großer Bedeutung:
Schließlich hatten Francos Falangisten den
Kampfruf der Fremdenlegion übernommen,
»Tod den Intellektuellen! Lang lebe der
Tod!« Die Republikaner antworteten mit
Plakaten darauf, wie hier an einer Litfaß-
säule in Katalonien, wo Frauen zu den
Waffen gerufen werden (4). Gewerkschaf-
ten, besonders von Frauen beherrschte wie
die Näherinnengewerkschaft, organisierten

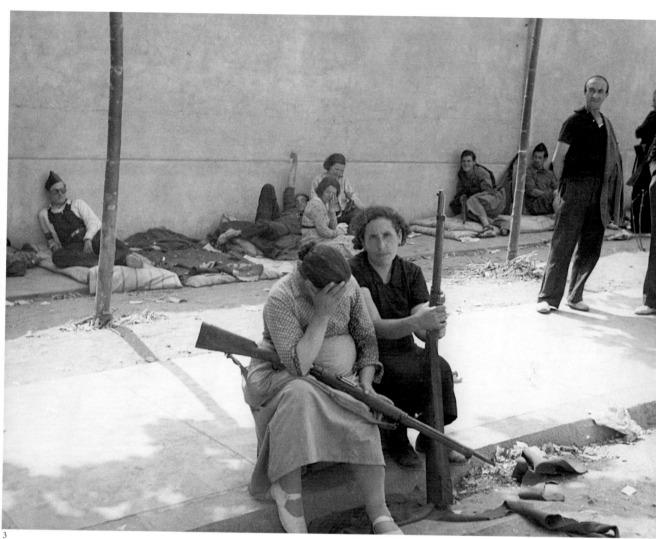

3

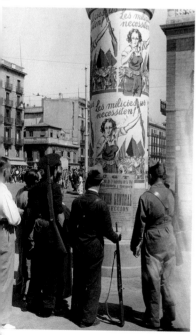

Frauenmilizen; hier (3) sieht man einige Kämpferinnen erschöpft am Straßenrand sitzen. Da sie keine Uniformen tragen, nicht einmal Stiefel, dürfte das Bild gegen Ende des Krieges entstanden sein.

Le 29 août 1936, les insurgés forcent un groupe de républicains à se rendre (1). Leurs uniformes dépareillés et leurs armes leur donnent plus l'allure d'une armée en déroute que d'une armée nationale. Un jeune homme de dix-sept ans tué d'une balle dans la tête (2). George Orwell, dans son *Hommage à la Catalogne*, raconte d'une manière vivante l'expérience d'un homme.

Les mots comptaient énormément : après tout, les phalangistes de Franco n'avaient-ils pas adopté le cri de guerre du *Tercio* (une légion étrangère) : « Vive la mort ! » Les républicains ripostaient par des affiches de propagande pour inviter les femmes à prendre les armes (4). Tous les syndicats, en particulier féminins, comme celui des ouvrières du vêtement, embrigadaient les femmes, comme ces miliciennes assises, épuisées, sur le bord de la route (3). L'absence d'uniforme et de bottes laisse penser que la photographie a été prise vers la fin de la guerre.

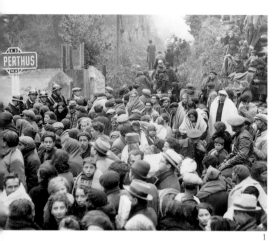

REFUGEES jam the roads into France (1). In January 1939, Franco's victorious troops entered Barcelona supported by General Yague's feared 'Moors', meeting with only sporadic resistance. Here some of the 3,000 Czech, Polish and German members of the International Brigade merge with the retreating Republican army and the mass of refugees fleeing north (2).

FLÜCHTLINGE drängen sich auf den Straßen nach Frankreich (1). Im Januar 1939 marschierten Francos siegreiche Truppen, verstärkt durch General Yagues gefürchtete »Mauren«, in Barcelona ein und trafen nur noch auf vereinzelten Widerstand. Auf diesem Bild (2) schließen sich einige der 3 000 Tschechen, Polen und Deutschen, die mit den Internationalen Brigaden ins Land gekommen waren, der geschlagenen republikanischen Armee und den zahllosen Flüchtlingen im Strom nach Norden an.

LES réfugiés s'amassaient sur les routes en direction de la France (1). En janvier 1939, les troupes victorieuses de Franco entraient dans Madrid appuyées par les redoutés « Maures » du général Yague, où elles ne rencontrèrent qu'une résistance sporadique. Ici quelques-uns des 3 000 Tchèques, Polonais et Allemands, membres des brigades internationales, se mêlent à l'armée républicaine battant en retraite et aux flots de réfugiés qui font route vers le Nord (2).

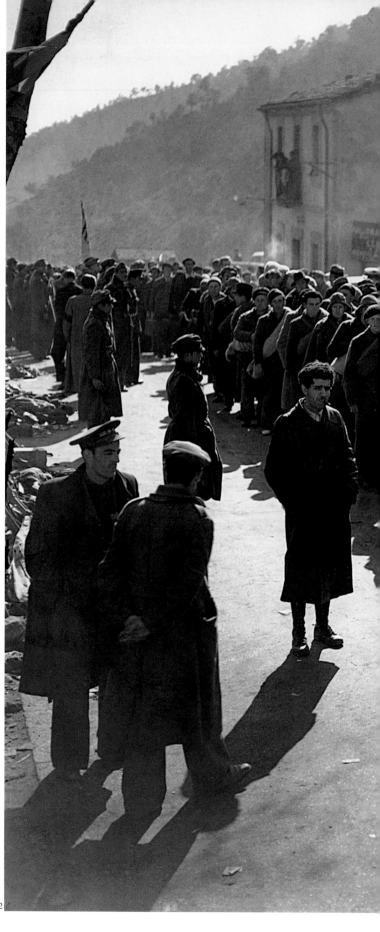

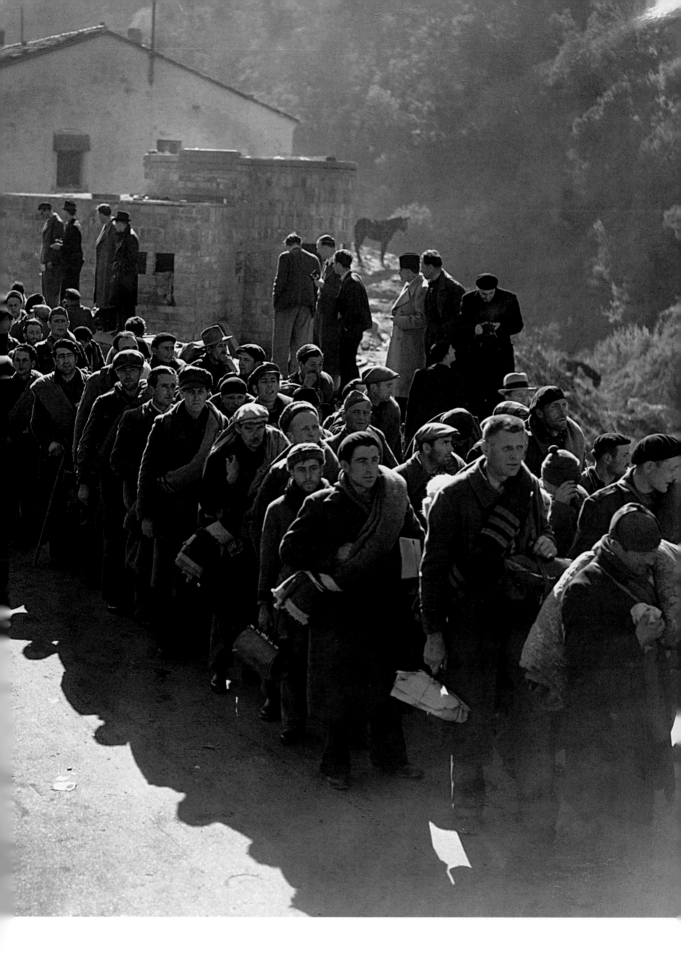

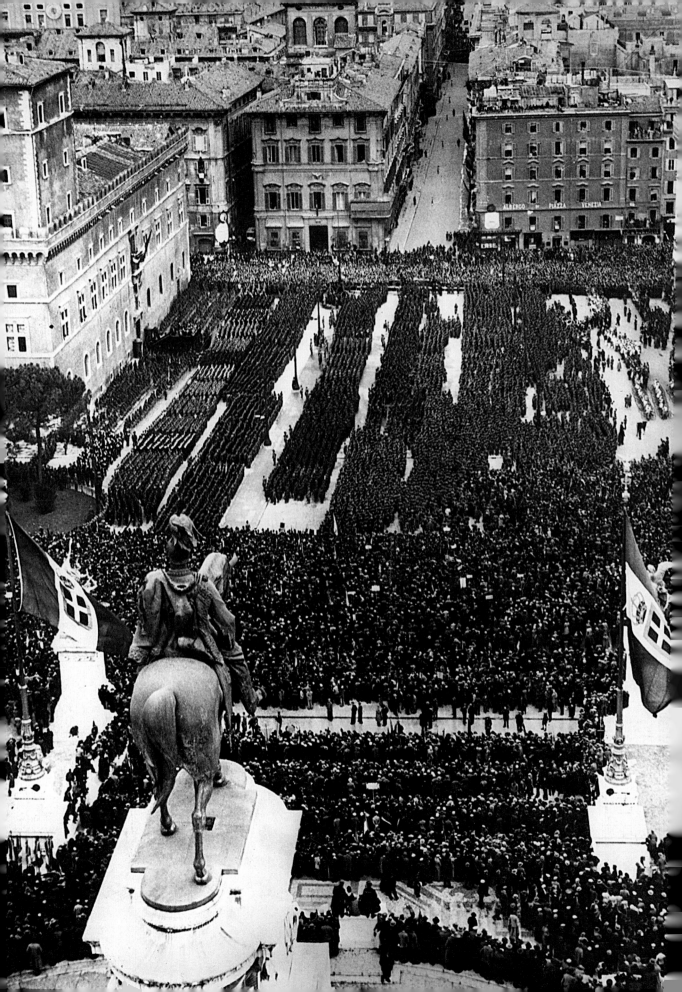

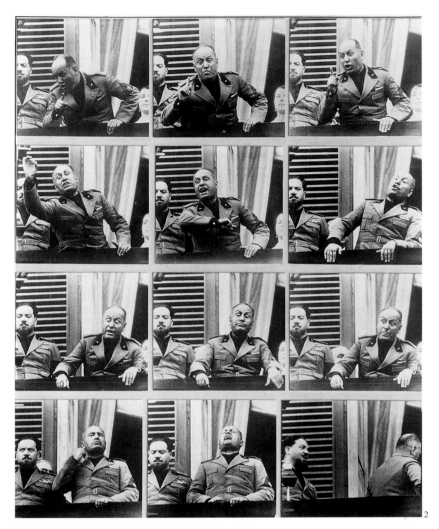

2

THE March on Rome has been called 'the Fascist-inspired myth of the way in which Mussolini came to power in Italy'. In 1922, civil war appeared imminent and the ex-socialist Mussolini demanded the formation of a Fascist government to save the country from socialism. On 29 October, King Victor Emmanuel III invited him to come from Milan to Rome, and Mussolini did so on the overnight express. On 30 October Mussolini formed the government and on the 31st some 25,000 blackshirts were imported, also by train, for a ceremonial parade (1). The 'March on Rome' was as histrionic an exaggeration as the expressions on Il Duce's face as he addresses his marchers', the 'Representatives of National Strengths', from the Palazzo Venezia (2).

DEN Marsch auf Rom hat man den »faschistischen Mythos von Mussolinis Machtergreifung in Italien« genannt. 1922 schien ein Bürgerkrieg unvermeidlich, und der ehemalige Sozialist Mussolini forderte die Bildung einer faschistischen Regierung, um das Land vor dem Sozialismus zu bewahren. Am 29. Oktober lud König Viktor Emmanuel III. ihn ein, von Mailand nach Rom zu kommen, woraufhin Mussolini schon den Nachtexpress nahm. Am 30. Oktober bildete er seine Regierung, und am 31. kamen, ebenfalls per Zug, etwa 25 000 Schwarzhemden zur feierlichen Parade (1). Der »Marsch auf Rom« war eine genauso lächerliche Übertreibung wie der Gesichtsausdruck des Duce, mit dem er die Eintreffenden, die »Vertreter nationaler Stärke«, vom Palazzo Venezia aus begrüßt (2).

LA marche sur Rome a été appelée « l'arrivée au pouvoir de Mussolini en Italie mythifiée par les fascistes ». En 1922, alors que la guerre civile semble imminente, l'ex-socialiste Mussolini réclame la constitution d'un gouvernement fasciste pour sauver le pays du socialisme. Le 29 octobre, le roi Victor Emmanuel III convie à Rome Mussolini, qui se trouvait alors à Milan. Celui-ci arrive par l'express de nuit. Le 30 octobre, il constitue son gouvernement ; le 31 il fait venir quelque 25 000 chemises noires, également par le train, pour participer à une parade solennelle (1). La « marche sur Rome » est une affabulation, tout comme sont volontairement exagérées les mimiques du Duce s'adressant du Palazzo Venezia à ses « marcheurs », aux « représentants des forces nationales » (2).

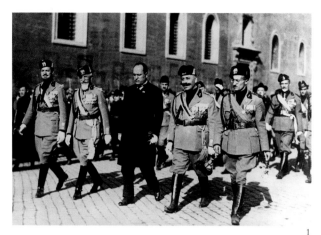

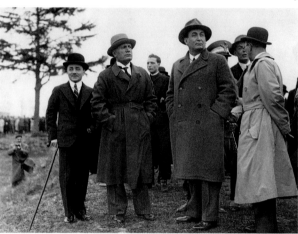

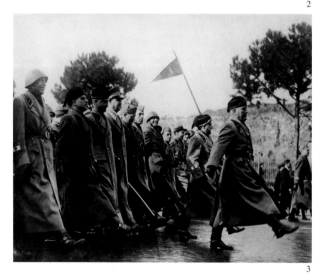

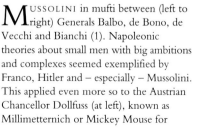

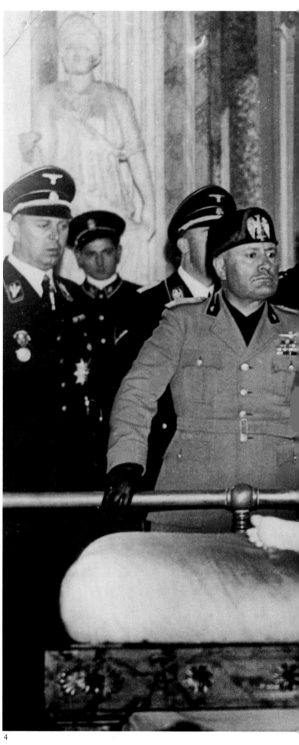

1

2

3   4

MUSSOLINI in mufti between (left to right) Generals Balbo, de Bono, de Vecchi and Bianchi (1). Napoleonic theories about small men with big ambitions and complexes seemed exemplified by Franco, Hitler and – especially – Mussolini. This applied even more so to the Austrian Chancellor Dollfuss (at left), known as Millimetternich or Mickey Mouse for

being under 5 feet tall, here fraternizing with his fellow-dictator shortly before his assassination in 1934 (2). Mussolini brought the Führer to gaze at the hefty white marble nymph Pauline Borghese, Napoleon's sister, at the Villa Borghese (4). He then led the Fascist officials off in a disorderly goose-step during the Roman Parade (3).

MUSSOLINI in Zivil zwischen den Generalen Balbo, de Bono, de Vecch und Bianchi (1, von links nach rechts). Di Idee vom »Napoleonkomplex« – daß klein- wüchsige Männer einen ganz besonderen Ehrgeiz entwickeln – scheint durch Franco, Hitler und ganz besonders durch Mussolin bestätigt zu werden. Noch mehr traf das auf den österreichischen Kanzler Dollfuß zu (links), den man wegen seiner knappen

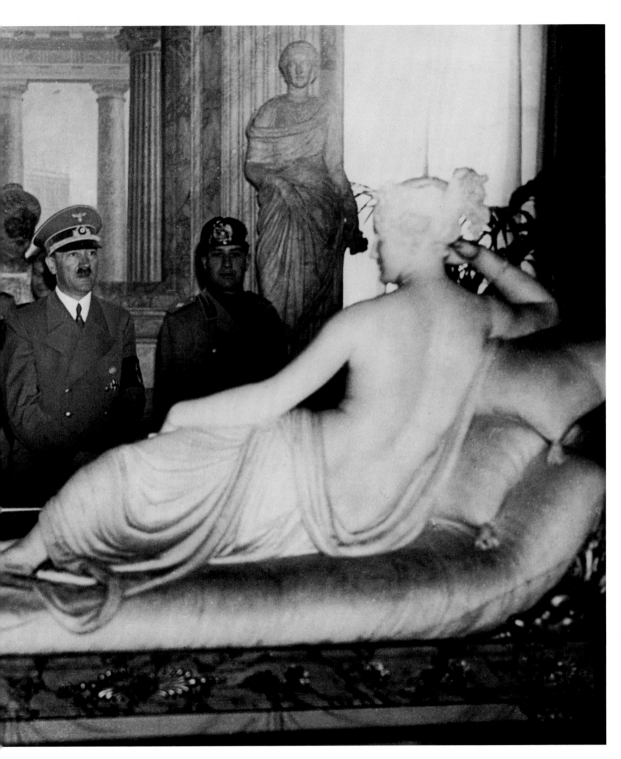

in Meter fünfzig den »Millimetternich«
nnte; hier sieht man ihn in bestem Ein-
ernehmen mit seinem Diktatorkollegen,
urz vor seiner Ermordung 1934 (2). Dem
ührer zeigte Mussolini in der Villa Borghese
e Marmorstatue Venus (4). Er führte die
schistische Prominenz in einem etwas aus
em Takt gekommenen Gänsemarsch zur
ömischen Parade (3).

MUSSOLINI en civil entre (de gauche
à droite) les généraux Balbo, de Bono,
de Vecchi et Bianchi (1). Les théories à propos de Napoléon et des hommes de petite
taille dotés de grandes ambitions et de gros
complexes semblent se vérifier à travers Franco,
Hitler et Mussolini. Elles sont encore plus
vraies dans le cas du chancelier autrichien
Dollfuss (à gauche) surnommé « Mickey la

souris », fraternisant avec un de ses homo-
logues dictateurs peu de temps avant d'être
assassiné en 1934 (2). À la Villa Borghese,
Mussolini conduisit le Führer contempler
la nymphe qui représente Pauline Borghese, sœur de Napoléon (4). Il entraîna
ensuite la délégation fasciste dans un pas de
l'oie désordonné à la Parade romaine (3).

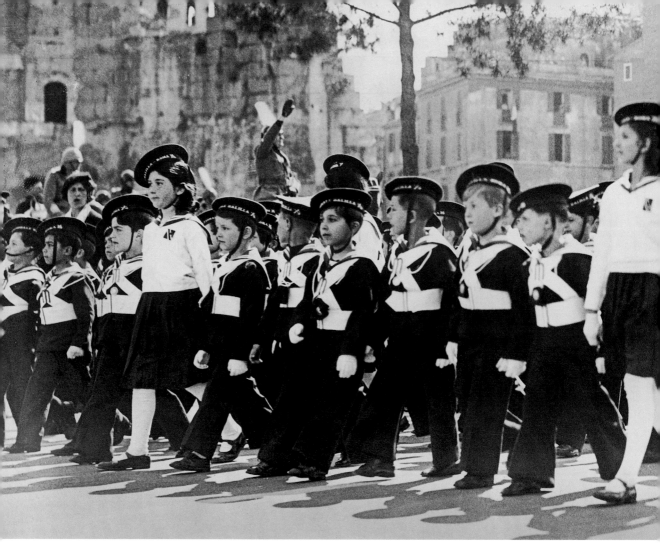

FASCIST march-pasts were intended to
unite the nations and the generations.
In 1936 the Marine branch of the *Figli della
Lupa* (Sons of the She-wolf – presumably a
reference to Romulus, Remus and the
glories of ancient Rome) marched beneath
Mussolini's raised salute (1). In 1945 in
Tripoli Fascist women were organized in
militias, possibly as advance warning of fresh
neo-imperialist intentions in the region, only
months before the invasion of Abyssinia (2).
And secondary schoolboys underwent
military training even when it was too hot to
wear much beyond plimsolls and sunhats (3).

DIE Faschistenaufmärsche sollten die
Nationen und Generationen zusammen-
bringen. 1936 zog die Marineabteilung der
Figli della Lupa (Söhne der Wölfin – eine
Anspielung auf Romulus und Remus und den
Ruhm des alten Rom) an Mussolini vorüber,
der die Hand zum Gruß erhoben hat (1).
1945 werden die Faschistenfrauen in Tripolis
zu Milizen organisiert, möglicherweise ein
Vorzeichen, daß sich neoimperialistische
Ambitionen in der Gegend zu regen begannen,
nur Monate vor der Invasion Abessiniens (2).
Und Schuljungen mußten ihre soldatische
Ausbildung auch dann absolvieren, wenn es
so heiß war, daß man außer Sonnenhut und
Turnschuhen nicht viel tragen konnte (3).

L'IDÉE des défilés fascistes était de
réunir les nations et les générations. E
1936, la section marine des *Figli della Lupa*
(les fils de la louve ; probable référence à
Romulus, Remus et aux gloires de la Rom
antique) défilent au-dessous de Mussolini
qui salue debout (1). En 1945, à Tripoli,
les femmes fascistes sont organisées en
milices, probablement afin de prévenir les
velléités néo-impérialistes qui se font jour
dans la région, à quelques mois seulement
de l'invasion de l'Abyssinie (2). Ailleurs,
des écoliers du secondaire suivent un entraî
nement militaire en dépit d'une chaleur
n'autorisant guére que les sandales et le
chapeau de soleil (3).

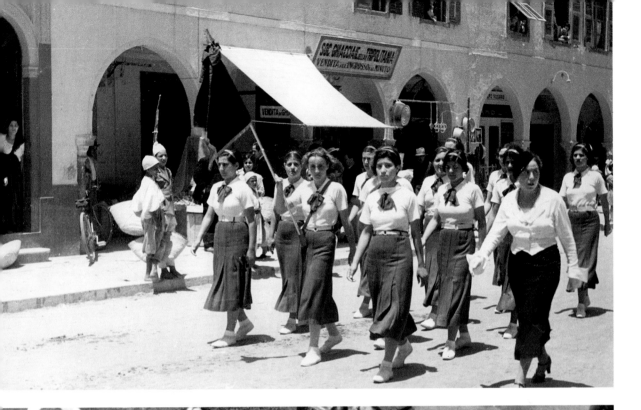

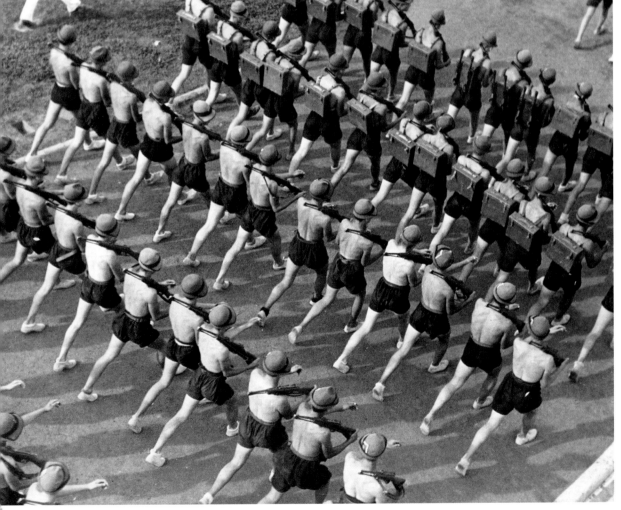

Nazism

ADOLF Hitler was on the face of it perhaps the least likely of Fascist dictators. Non-German and erratically educated, a professional failure in everything he had tried before entering politics, at first he neither looked nor acted the part. Instead of the statuesque physique of a Nordic god, he was small and black-haired and dark-eyed, a vegetarian in a decidedly carnivorous country. Yet his own mixed psychology succeeded in touching a chord that played on both Germans' fears and their pride. By creating an enemy 'other' of mythic dimensions, he could unite the German-speaking peoples in pursuit of his goal, the foundation of the 1000-year Third Reich.

If the enemy did not actually exist, then it would have to be invented. In Central Europe, Ashkenazi Jews had been largely assimilated during their 500-year-long sojourn, many having been known as 'Court Jews' for their sought-after pre-eminence in the arts that sent them from one principality to the next to perform as musicians and artists. Many of these described themselves by nationality rather than religion and thought of themselves as Germans or Austrians before Jews. Ironically, by defining Jews not by their religion but by being even one-eighth of Jewish blood, Hitler was including himself in, by dint of one grandparent. If the stereotype of the grasping miser didn't exist, it would be promoted by scurrilous graffiti and wild accusations. When, after Kristallnacht, Propaganda Minister Goebbels surveyed the mess of shattered glass on the streets of Berlin, he groaned: 'They [the SA/Stormtroopers' mob] should have broken fewer Jewish windows and taken more Jewish lives.'

When the Communists failed to carry out the awaited revolutionary putsch, the burning of the Reichstag was staged as a pretext to clamp down in their suppression. Much blame has been attached to the policy of appeasement pursued by both French and British governments through the 1920s and 30s, though Churchill was the sole politician in favour of a military response when Hitler annexed the Rhineland in 1936. The truth was probably that too much of Europe was preoccupied with licking its own wounds from the Great War and with the shortage of manpower and political will to wish for any further warmongering.

ADOLF Hitler war unter den faschistischen Diktatoren vielleicht derjenige, dem man es am wenigsten zutraute. Als Österreicher mit nur unvollständiger Schulbildung, der in allem, was er versucht hatte, bevor er in die Politik ging, völlig gescheitert war, sah er nicht nur nicht danach aus, sondern benahm sich auch anfangs nicht wie ein Führer. Er hatte nicht die Statur eines nordischen Gottes, sondern war klein und schwarzhaarig mit dunklen Augen, ein Vegetarier im Land der Fleischesser. Und doch rührte er mit seiner konfusen Psyche eine Saite an, die sowohl die Ängste als auch den Stolz der Deutschen erklingen ließ. Er beschwor ein Feindbild von geradezu mythischen Ausmaßen herauf, und damit konnte er die deutschsprachigen Völker vereint für sein großes Ziel gewinnen, die Gründung eines »tausendjährigen Dritten Reichs«.

Wenn es keine Feinde gab, dann mußte man welche erfinden. In Mitteleuropa hatten sich im Laufe ihrer fünfhundertjährigen Wanderschaft zahlreiche Ostjuden niedergelassen, viele davon »Hofjuden«, die als gefragte Musiker oder Miniaturmaler von einem Fürstenhof zum anderen zogen. Viele davon fühlten sich eher einer Nation zugehörig als einer Religionsgemeinschaft und verstanden sich zuerst als Deutsche oder Österreicher und erst dann als Juden. Für Hitler war es nicht die Religion, sondern das Blut, das zählte, und ironischerweise hätte er sich, da auch jemand mit einem Achtel Judenblut noch als Jude galt, selbst dazurechnen müssen, denn dem Vernehmen nach hatte er einen jüdischen Großvater. Wenn die Leute nicht von sich aus das Vorurteil vom »raffgierigen Geizkragen« hatten, bekamen sie es durch verleumderische Wandsprüche und aus der Luft gegriffene Anschuldigungen eingetrichtert. Als nach der »Reichskristallnacht« der Propagandaminister Goebbels das zerschmetterte Schaufensterglas auf den Berliner Straßen musterte, seufzte er: »Ich wünschte nur, [die SA-Männer] hätten weniger jüdische Scheiben und mehr jüdische Schädel eingeschlagen.«

Als der vorausgesagte Kommunistenaufstand auf sich warten ließ, wurde der Brandanschlag auf den Reichstag inszeniert, damit man einen Vorwand für ihre Verfolgung hatte. Vieles ist später der zu nachgiebigen Haltung der französischen und britischen Regierungen der 20er und 30er Jahre angelastet worden, doch im-

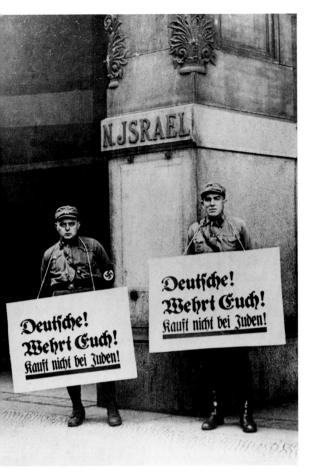

NAZI PICKETS OUTSIDE JEWISH STORE IN BERLIN,
APRIL 1933: 'GERMANS! DEFEND YOURSELVES! DON'T BUY
FROM JEWS!' READ THE PLACARDS.

WACHPOSTEN DER NAZIS VOR EINEM JÜDISCHEN
GESCHÄFT IN BERLIN, APRIL 1933.

DES PIQUETS DE GRÈVE NAZIS DEVANT UN MAGASIN
JUIF À BERLIN, AVRIL 1933 : «ALLEMANDS! DÉFENDEZ-VOUS
MÊMES! N'ACHETEZ PAS CHEZ LES JUIFS!»
PEUT-ON LIRE SUR LES AFFICHES.

ADOLF Hitler était peut-être le plus paradoxal de tous les dictateurs fascistes. Non Allemand, ayant bénéficié d'une éducation disparate et échoué à tous les métiers auxquels il s'était essayé avant de se lancer dans la politique, il n'avait a priori ni le parcours ni le physique de l'emploi. Au lieu d'avoir la stature et l'apparence d'un dieu nordique, sa chevelure était noire et ses yeux foncés. Enfin, il était végétarien dans un pays résolument carnivore. Pourtant, sa psychologie composite sut jouer des peurs et de l'orgueil des Allemands. En créant un ennemi « différent », aux dimensions mythiques, il réussit à unir les peuples de langue allemande derrière lui à la poursuite de son objectif : fonder le Troisième Reich millénaire.

Puisque l'ennemi n'existait pas vraiment, il serait inventé. En Europe centrale, les Juifs ashkénazes étaient largement assimilés depuis leur arrivée, cinq siècles plus tôt. Beaucoup étaient appelés les « Juifs de cour » parce qu'ils excellaient dans les métiers artistiques. Ils étaient de ce fait très recherchés, voyageant d'une principauté à l'autre en tant que musiciens ou portraitistes. Ils se définissaient davantage par rapport à leur nationalité qu'en fonction de leur religion, et se considéraient d'abord allemands ou autrichiens avant d'être juifs. L'ironie voulut qu'en ne définissant pas le Juif par sa religion mais par le fait d'avoir un huitième de sang juif, Hitler s'incluait lui-même. En effet, l'un de ses grands-parents était juif. Le stéréotype du Juif âpre au gain sera accentué par des graffiti injurieux et des accusations insensées. Quand, après la Nuit de cristal, Goebbels, ministre de la Propagande, se rendit sur les lieux, devant le triste état des rues de Berlin jonchées de débris de verre, il gémit : « Ils [les sbires des troupes d'assaut] auraient mieux fait de briser un peu moins de vitres juives et de supprimer plus de Juifs. »

Après l'échec du putsch révolutionnaire tant attendu, l'incendie du Reichstag fut monté de toutes pièces et utilisé comme un prétexte pour réclamer la suppression des activités communistes. On a beaucoup reproché, tant au gouvernement français que britannique, la politique d'apaisement qui fut la leur tout au long des années 20 et 30. C'est oublier que Churchill fut le seul homme politique favorable à une riposte militaire en 1936 après l'annexion de la Rhénanie par Hitler. La vérité était probablement que l'Europe, trop préoccupée de panser ses propres blessures au lendemain de la Grande Guerre, manquait de ressources humaines et de volonté politique pour risquer de s'engager dans une autre guerre.

nerhin war Churchill der einzige Politiker, der sich für einen militärischen Gegenschlag einsetzte, als Hitler 1936 das Rheinland besetzte. In Wahrheit war wohl ganz Europa zu sehr damit beschäftigt, die Wunden des Ersten Weltkriegs zu lecken, mit Massenarbeitslosigkeit und politischer Orientierungslosigkeit, als daß man sich auf einen neuen Krieg hätte einlassen können.

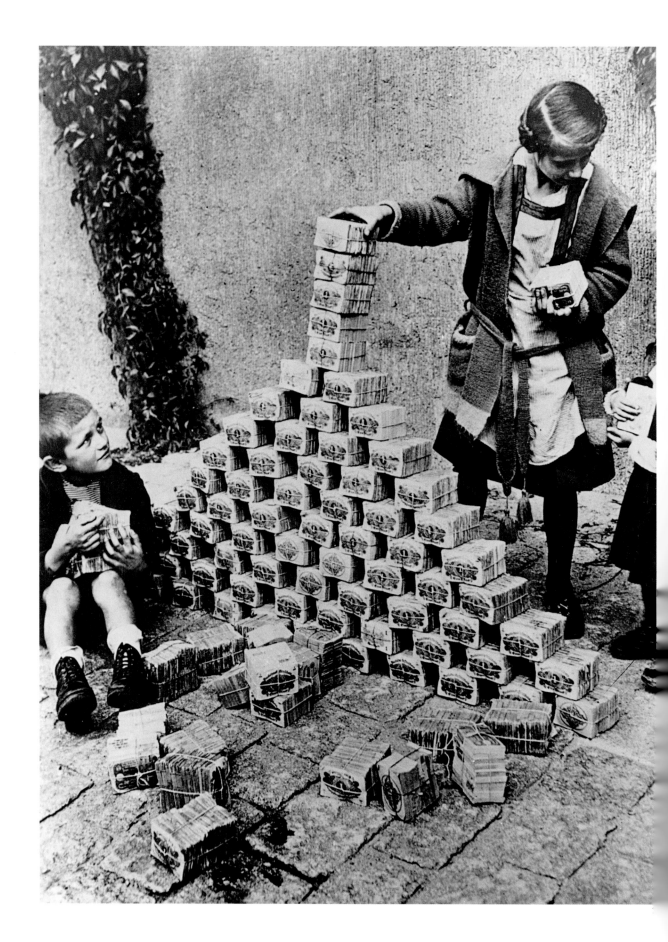

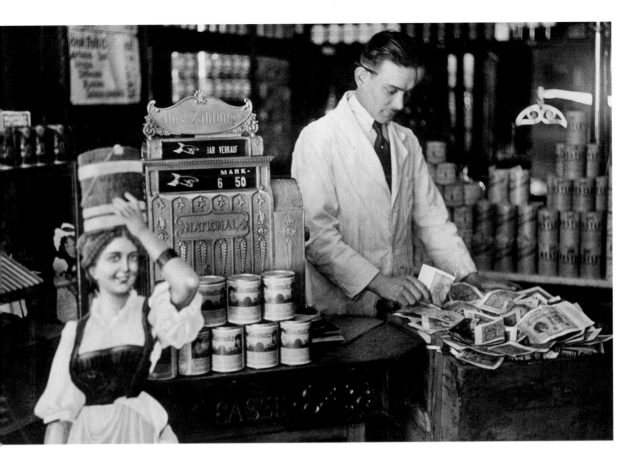

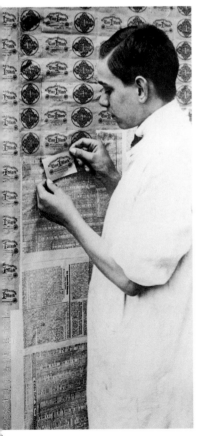

I NFLATION turned to hyperflation in the wake of the Great War. In 1923, one US dollar became worth 4.2 m Reichsmarks; five years later it had doubled its decline. Banknotes became cheaper than toys (1) or wallpaper (3), and this shopkeeper abandoned his till for tea-chests to store the wads (2). Politically, the Reichstag proved itself likewise bankrupt. In the September elections, the Nazi Party increased its own vote from 810,000 to a staggering 6,409,600. Parliamentary democracy was now suspended and parliament became paralysed by the rot within and the threat from without.

D IE Inflation nahm nach dem Ersten Weltkrieg bis dahin ungekannte Ausmaße an. 1923 war ein US-Dollar 4,2 Millionen Reichsmark wert; fünf Jahre darauf war der Wert der Mark auf die Hälfte gesunken. Banknoten waren weniger wert als Bauklötze (1) oder Tapete (3), und hier hat ein Ladenbesitzer es aufgegeben, die Bündel noch in die Kasse zu stopfen, und nimmt statt dessen Teekisten (2). Und der Reichstag erwies sich in politischer

Hinsicht als ebenso bankrott. Bei den Wahlen im September 1930 konnten die Nationalsozialisten ihre Stimmen von 810 000 auf unglaubliche 6 409 600 erhöhen. Damit war die parlamentarische Demokratie am Ende, und das Parlament gelähmt von der Zersetzung im Inneren und der Bedrohung von außen.

L 'INFLATION se changea en hyper-inflation au lendemain de la Grande Guerre. En 1923, un dollar des États-Unis valait 4,2 millions de Reichsmarks, et perdait le double de sa valeur cinq ans plus tard. Les billets de banque valaient moins cher que les jouets (1) ou le papier peint (3). Ce commerçant a délaissé sa caisse pour entreposer ses rouleaux de billets dans des caisses à thé (2). Politiquement le Reichstag s'avérait tout aussi en faillite. Au cours des élections de septembre, le parti nazi augmenta son score, lequel passa de 810 000 voix au chiffre inquiétant de 6 409 600. La démocratie parlementaire se trouva alors suspendue, le Parlement paralysé sous le coup de sa propre déliquescence et de la menace extérieure.

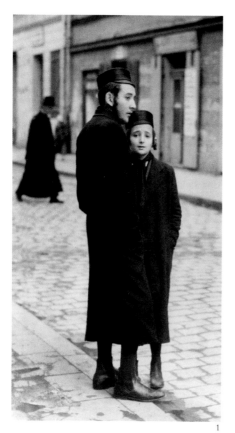

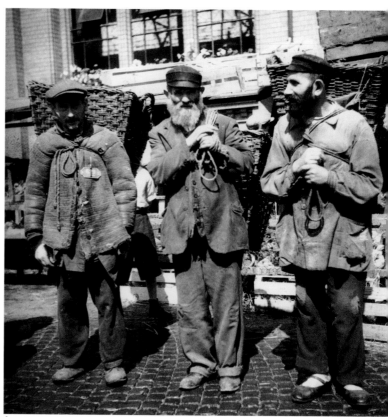

I N the Warsaw ghetto, where this man and
boy are pictured (1), Orthodox Jewish boys
attend Sabbath *schule* (3). The diversity of
Jewish occupations included serving as market
porters (2). Signs from Schwedt an der Oder
in 1935 read 'Jews are not wanted in this place!'
(5), while a Jewish tailor's shop in Vienna (6)
is defaced with graffiti saying, 'If you wash
this off, you can holiday in Dachau!' – this in
1938. Even after the war the legacy of race-
hatred can still be read. This bench says it is
'Not for Jews' (4).

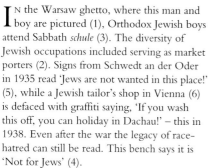

I M Warschauer Ghetto, wo diese Aufnahme
von einem Mann und einem Jungen entstand (1), gingen die orthodoxen jüdischen
Jungen am Sabbatabend zur Schule (3). Juden
waren in den verschiedensten Berufen tätig,
hier als Träger auf dem Markt (2). Schwedt an
der Oder zeigte 1935 deutlich, wo es politisch
stand (5), und einem jüdischen Schneider in
Wien (6) wird Urlaub in Dachau versprochen,
wenn er die Schmierereien übertüncht – und
das schon 1938. Selbst nach dem Krieg blieben
die Zeichen des Rassenhasses noch sichtbar:
Diese Bank ist »nicht für Juden« (4).

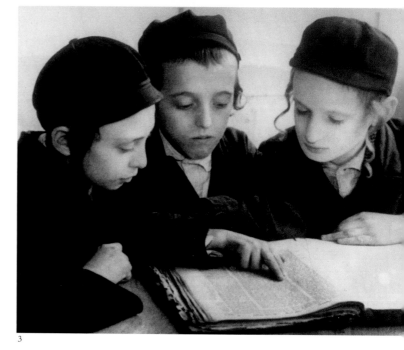

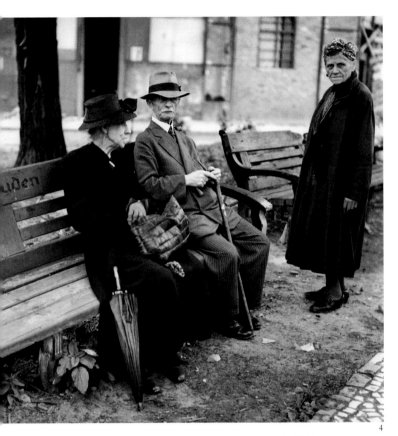

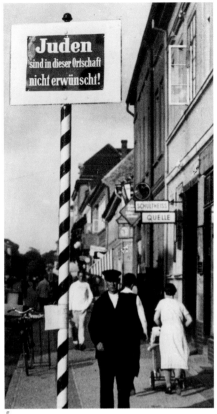

4

5

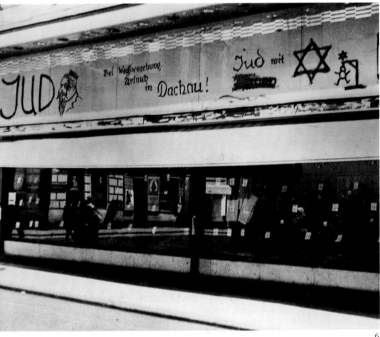

6

Dans le ghetto de Varsovie, où fut prise la photographie de cet homme et de cet enfant (1), les garçonnets juifs orthodoxes allaient à la *Schule* (école) sabbatique (3). Parmi les divers emplois exercés par les Juifs, on trouve celui de porteur sur le marché (2). Les panneaux à Schwedt an der Oder signalaient en 1935 : « Ici on ne veut pas de Juifs ! » (5). Ailleurs, la boutique d'un tailleur juif à Vienne (6) est barbouillée de graffiti prévenant : « Si tu effaces cette inscription, tu es bon pour un petit voyage à Dachau ! » Cela en 1938 ! Même après la guerre, la haine raciste pouvait encore s'affiches dans des inscriptions à l'image de celle figurant sur ce banc : « Pas pour les Juifs » (4).

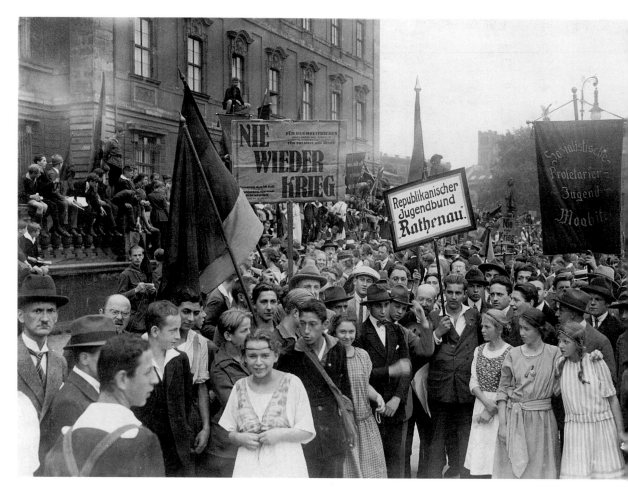

THE aftermath and humiliation of the
Great War took time to dispel. In July
1922 the Rathenau Youth Organization
assembled before the castle on a 'No More
War' demonstration (1). During the so-
called 'Kapp Revolution' of 1920, named
after an obscure provincial official, right-
wingers attempted a *coup d'état* and a
proclamation of a new government led by
Kapp but were swiftly routed by a general
strike of Berlin workers. The rising was
noted, however, for the early use of the
swastika (however amateurishly painted
onto helmets) and for revealing an
embryonic Nazi Party (3). Among a group
of Hitler's stormtroopers who participated
in the Munich putsch of 9 November 1923
is Heinrich Himmler (holding the flag),
later Nazi Gestapo chief (2).

ES dauerte seine Zeit, bis Schrecken und
Erniedrigung des Ersten Weltkriegs
vorüber waren. Im Juli 1922 versammelte
sich der Jugendbund Rathenau zu einer
Demonstration unter dem Motto »Nie wieder Krieg« (1). Beim sogenannten Kapp-
Putsch von 1920, nach einem obskuren
Provinzbeamten benannt, versuchten
rechtsgerichtete Kräfte einen Staatsstreich
und proklamierten eine neue, von Kapp
geführte Regierung, die aber nach einem
Generalstreik der Berliner Arbeiter bald
wieder aufgeben mußte. Bemerkenswert ist
dieser Putsch für den frühen Einsatz von
Hakenkreuzen, wenn auch recht amateur-
haft auf die Stahlhelme gemalt, der erste
größere Auftritt der eben erst gegründeten
NSDAP (3). Zu den SA-Männern, die an
Hitlers Münchner Putsch vom 9. November 1923 beteiligt waren, gehörte auch
Heinrich Himmler (mit Flagge), der spätere
Gestapochef (2).

LES conséquences de la Grande Guerre
et l'humiliation qui s'ensuivit mirent
du temps à disparaître. En juillet 1922,
l'organisation Rathenau de la jeunesse mani
festait devant le château pour qu'il n'y ait
« jamais plus de guerre » (1). En 1920, au
cours de ce qu'on appela la « révolution
Kapp », du nom d'un obscur responsable
provincial, des éléments de droite tentaien
de proclamer par un coup d'État un nouveau gouvernement dirigé pas Kapp. Ils
furent promptement mis en déroute grâce
à la grève générale déclenchée par les ouvrier
berlinois. L'émeute retint cependant l'atten
tion parce qu'à cette occasion la croix
gammée apparut pour la première fois
(même si son dessin laisse à désirer), révélant ainsi l'existence d'un parti nazi à l'état
embryonnaire (3). Au milieu de l'un des
groupes formés par les troupes d'assaut
d'Hitler, qui participa au putsch de Munic
le 9 novembre 1923, on aperçoit Heinrich
Himmler (tenant le drapeau), qui devint
plus tard le responsable de la Gestapo (2).

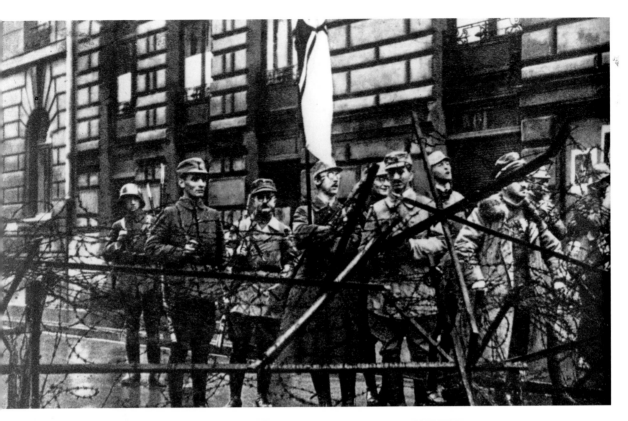

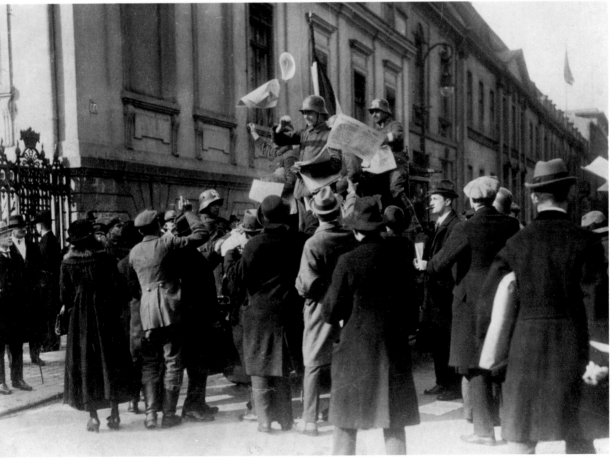

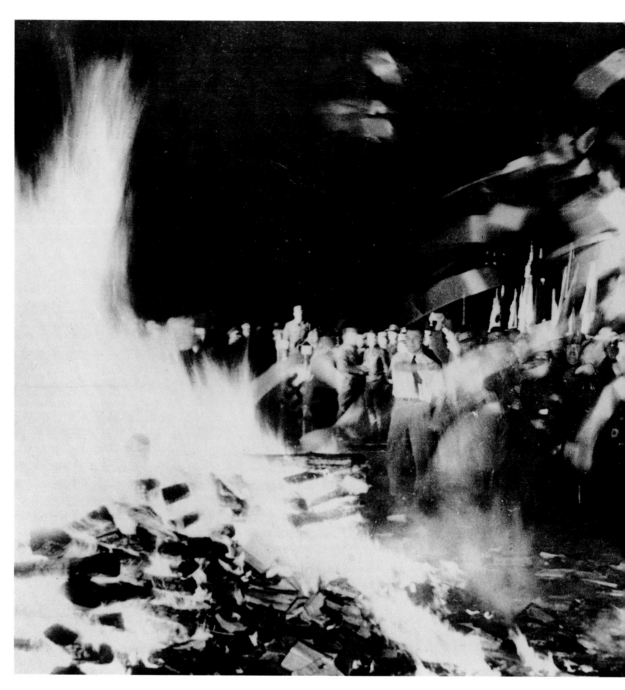

Not since Savonarola had Europe seen such pyres of books. As part of the 1933 bonfire of 'anti-German literature' many of Europe's greatest writers were consigned to the flames in Berlin's Opernplatz (1). Another bonfire in 1933 was that of the Reichstag (2). Goering reached the scene, already proclaiming: 'The Communist Party is the culprit... We will show no mercy. Every Communist must be shot on the spot.'

Seit Savonarola hatte es in Europa keine solche Bücherverbrennung mehr gegeben. Als 1933 auf dem Berliner Opernplatz »undeutsches Schrifttum« in Flammen aufging, waren die Werke vieler der bedeutendsten Schriftsteller Europas dabei (1 Ein anderer großer Scheiterhaufen des

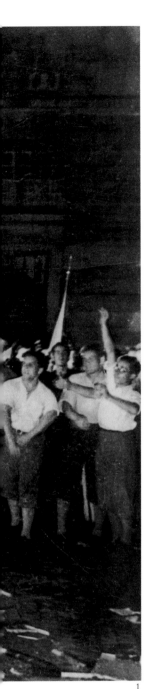

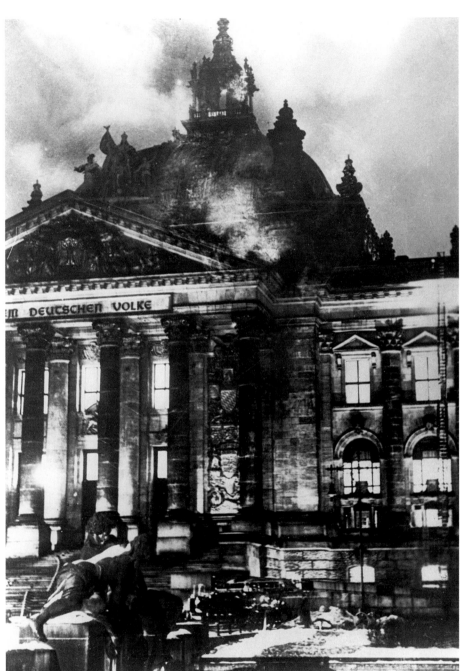

...hres 1933 war der Reichstag (2). Als ...öring am Ort des Geschehens eintraf, ...rüllte er unverzüglich: »Das ist das Werk ...er kommunistischen Partei … Wir wer... ...en keinerlei Gnade walten lassen. Jeder ...ommunist muß auf der Stelle erschossen ...erden.«

Depuis Savonarole, l'Europe n'avait plus jamais connu de tels autodafés. Un grand nombre d'immenses écrivrains européens comptèrent parmi ceux dont les livres brûlèrent sur la Opernplatz à Berlin, en 1933 (1), dans le feu de joie de la « littérature anti-allemande ». L'autre feu de joie fut celui du Reichstag en 1933 également (2). Goering, en arrivant sur les lieux, clama tout de suite : « C'est le parti communiste le coupable … nous ne ferons pas de quartier. Tout communiste doit être abattu sur place. »

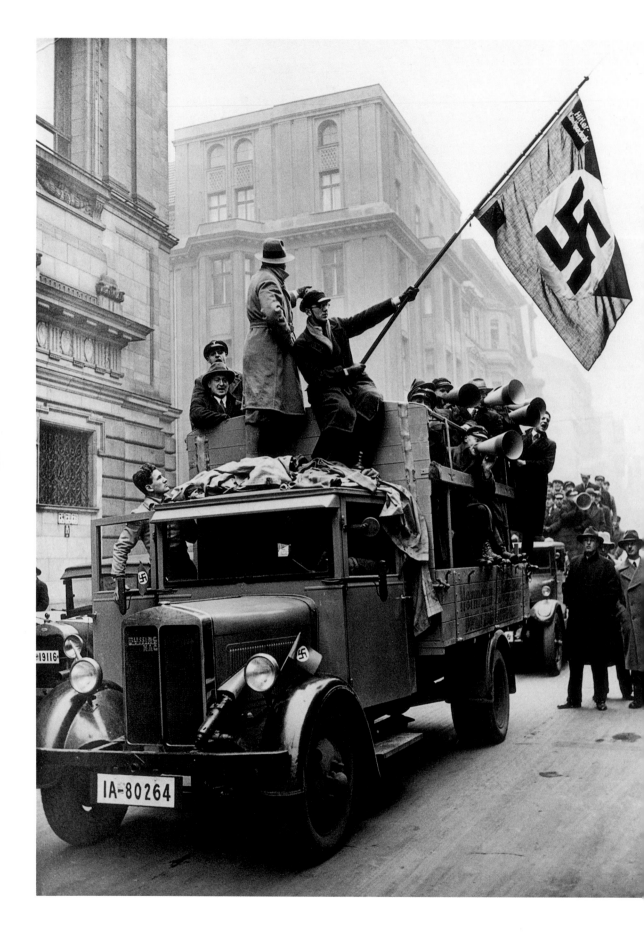

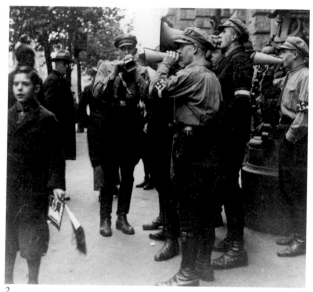

ON 12 November 1933 Berlin streets were packed with flag-waving, megaphone-bearing Nazis, calling out voters for the plebiscite (1). Stormtroopers dispatched to the polling booth anyone who had failed to vote (2). The 1936 anniversary of the 1923 March on Munich was restaged by Hitler and his cohorts from the beer hall where the original putsch was plotted to the Königsplatz (3).

AM 12. November 1933 waren die Berliner Straßen voll von Nazis, die Wähler zu den Urnen nötigten (1). SA-Männer halfen nach, wenn sich jemand der Wahl entziehen wollte (2). 1936 fand zum Jahrestag des Münchner Aufstandes von 1923 eine Parade statt, bei der Hitler und seine Kohorten vom Bürgerbräukeller, in dem sie den Putsch geplant hatten, zum Königsplatz zogen (3).

LE 12 novembre 1933, les nazis envahirent les rues de Berlin pour appeler les électeurs à participer au plébiscite (1). Les troupes d'assaut expédiaient à l'isoloir tous ceux qui n'avaient pas voté (2). L'anniversaire de la marche sur Munich de 1923, célébré en 1936 par Hitler et ses troupes, est organisé depuis la brasserie où le putsch avait été conçu jusqu'à la Königsplatz (3).

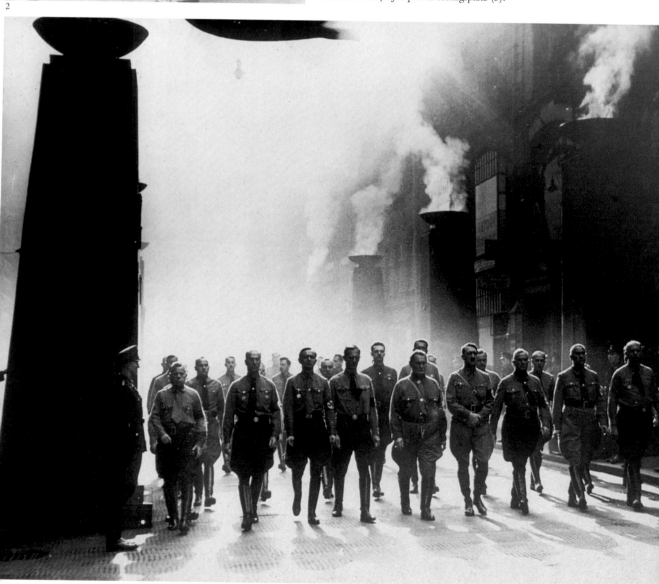

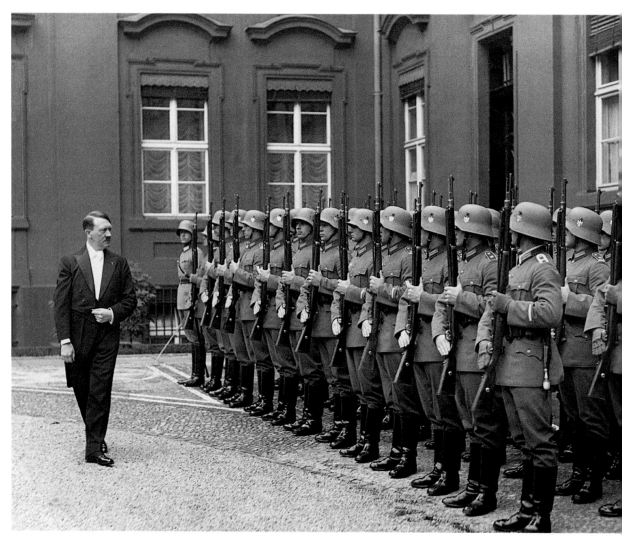

IN 1935 Hitler inspected the guard of honour before receiving the new Spanish Ambassador at the presidential palace (1). Hermann Goering displays an unusually ambiguous response to the attention he and his medals are receiving from his pet lioness, oddly named 'Caesar' (2). Some say this is Hitler's only worthwhile legacy – the Volkswagen, a car tough and reliable as a tank, designed in 1938 and still running (4). This one-theme postcard vendor (3) is clearly a Hitler fan, having adopted his moustache and adapted his clock to suit.

IM Jahre 1935 inspiziert Hitler die Ehrengarde vor dem Empfang des neuen spanischen Botschafters im Präsidentenpalast (1). Hermann Göring ist ausnahmsweise einmal die Aufmerksamkeit, die ihm und seinen Orden entgegengebracht wird, zuviel – von seiner zahmen Löwin, die auf den Namen »Cäsar« hörte (2). Nach Meinung vieler die einzig positive Hinterlassenschaft Hitlers – der Volkswagen, ein Auto so robust wie ein Panzer, 1938 entworfen und noch immer fahrtüchtig (4). Dieser Postkartenverkäufer hat nur ein einziges Bildmotiv für seine Karten und ist offenbar ein Verehrer des Führers, denn er hat nicht nur sein Bärtchen übernommen, sondern besitzt sogar eine passende Wanduhr (3).

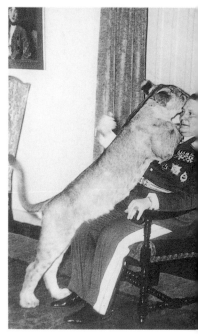

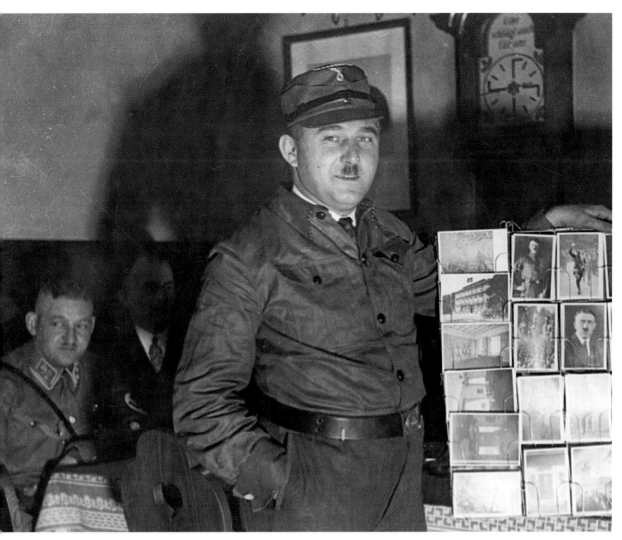

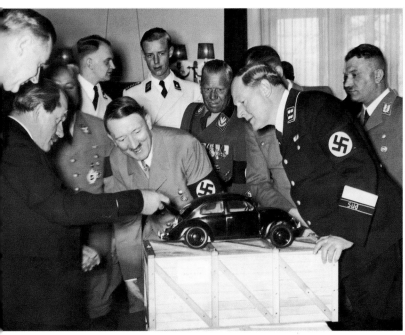

HITLER inspectant en 1935 la garde d'honneur avant d'accueillir le nouvel ambassadeur d'Espagne au palais présidentiel (1). Hermann Goering a un comportement singulièrement ambigu face aux attentions prodiguées sur sa personne et ses médailles par sa lionne apprivoisée répondant au nom de « Caesar » (2). Certains estiment que c'est la seule chose valable léguée sous Hitler: la Volkswagen, une voiture fiable comme un char d'assaut, conçue en 1938 et encore aujourd'hui sur les routes (4). Ce vendeur de cartes postales (3) au thème unique est manifestement un admirateur d'Hitler auquel il emprunte la moustache et en l'honneur duquel il a adapté son horloge.

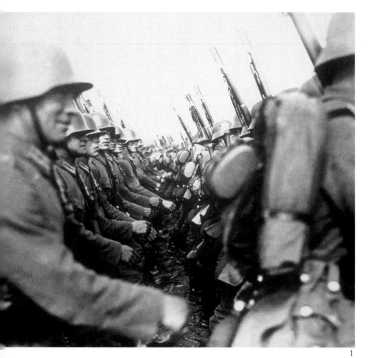

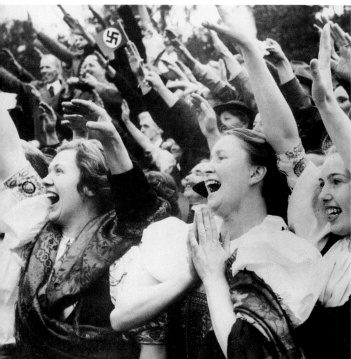

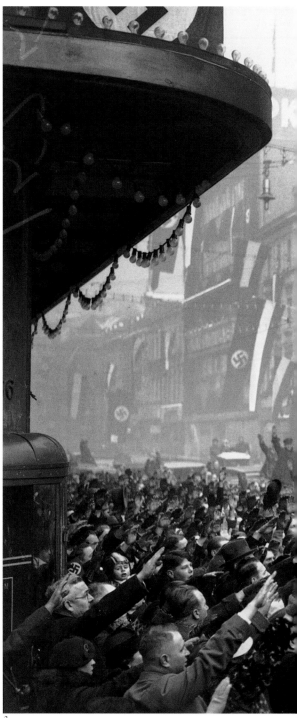

IN 1935 Hitler's army entered the Saarland (3), in 1936 the Rhineland (1); in 1938 it was the Egerland (Bohemia). Female adoration seems to have increased over the period, with 50,000 young women of Carlsbad sporting their best scarves and *dirndln*, their brightest smiles (2). Each step nearer France proved more of a pushover than the Germans anticipated,

it being against the terms of the treaties of Versailles and Locarno. When in 1935 Britain also signed a treaty permitting Germany to rebuld its naval strength, the French press fumed: 'Does London imagine that Hitler has renounced any of the projects indicated in his book *Mein Kampf*? If so, the illusion of our friends across the Channel is complete'.

1935 marschierten Hitlers Armeen im Saarland ein (3), 1936 im Rheinland (und 1938 im Egerland (Böhmen). Schein steigerte sich die Begeisterung der Frauen für die Soldaten zusehends. Hier in Karlsb sind 50 000 Frauen gekommen und zeige ihr schönstes Lächeln (2). Der Vormarsch Richtung Frankreich war für die Deutsch ein Kinderspiel, obwohl jeder Schritt ein Verstoß gegen die Verträge von Versaille

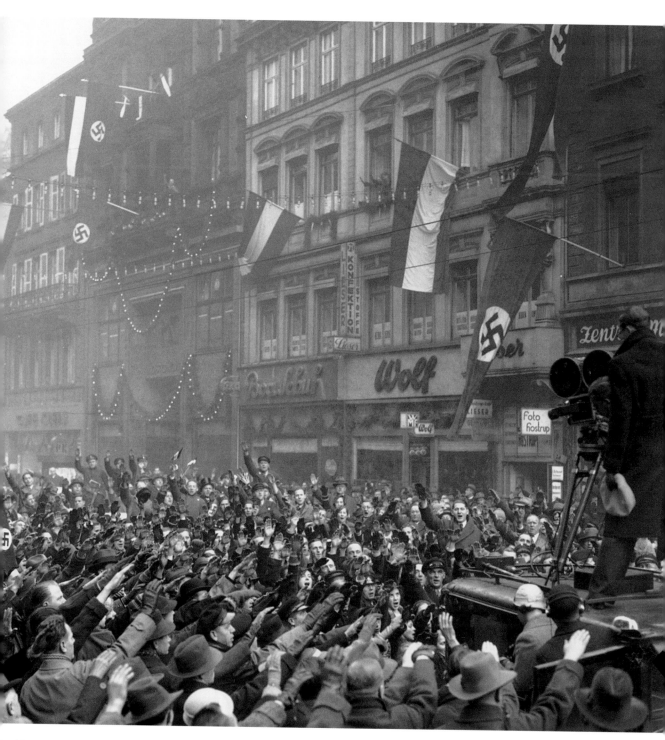

und Locarno war. Als 1935 die Engländer einen Vertrag mitunterzeichneten, der den Deutschen gestattete, ihre Marine wiederaufzubauen, empörte sich die französische Presse: »Glaubt denn die Regierung in London, Hitler habe die Ziele aufgegeben, die er in seinem Buch *Mein Kampf* beschreibt? Wenn ja, dann könnten unsere Freunde jenseits des Ärmelkanals sich nicht schwerer täuschen.«

EN 1935 l'armée d'Hitler pénètre en Sarre (3) et en 1936 en Rhénanie (1) avant d'arriver dans l'Egerland (la Bohême) en 1938. 50 000 jeunes femmes à Carlsbad arborent leurs plus beaux fichus et leur sourire le plus éclatant (2). Au fur et à mesure qu'ils se rapprochaient de la France, sa conquête apparaissait aux Allemands de plus en plus facile, bien qu'elle allât ainsi à l'encontre des clauses stipulées sur les traités de Versailles et de Locarno. Lorsqu'en 1935 la Grande-Bretagne signa à son tour le traité permettant à l'Allemagne de reconstituer sa puissance navale, la presse française fulmina : « Londres s'imagine t-elle qu'Hitler ait renoncé à un seul de ses projets mentionnés dans son livre *Mein Kampf* ? Si oui, nos amis d'Outre-Manche se font bel et bien des illusions ».

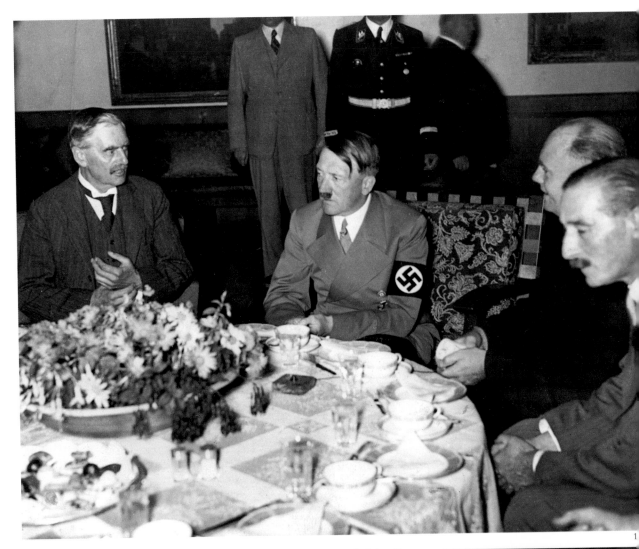

1

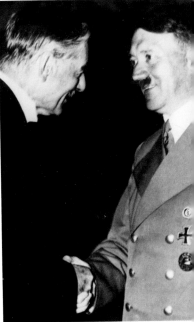

2

CHAMBERLAIN'S policy of appeasing Hitler pleased some, not least, of course, the Führer himself, who fêted him at no fewer than three conferences in September 1938 (1, 2); or the Ludgate Circus florist (4) honouring the British Prime Minister who wanted 'peace at any price'. Unfortunately, appeasement went too far: the Czechs and French felt betrayed by it; many English politicians and commentators mistrusted it; and finally even Hitler turned out to have been keener on invading the Sudetenland than accepting the Czech surrender brokered for him by Chamberlain. On 1 October Hitler occupied the Sudetenland anyway, and Chamberlain waved his famous scrap of white paper (3), announcing that the terms of the Munich agreement spelt the intention of the British and German nations 'never to go to war with one another again'.

CHAMBERLAINS versöhnlicher Kurs gefiel manchem, nicht zuletzt natürlich dem Führer selbst, der ihn auf gleich drei Konferenzen im September 1938 feierte (1, 2), oder auch der Floristin in Ludgate, die ihr Fenster zu Ehren des britischen Premiers dekorierte, der »Frieden um jeden Preis« wollte (4). Leider ging die Appeasement-Politik zu weit: Tschechen und Franzosen fühlten sich betrogen; viele englische Politiker und Kolumnisten trauten ihr nicht; und am Ende stellte sich heraus, daß Hitler es eher auf das Sudetenland abgesehen hatte als auf die tschechische Kapitulation, die Chamberlain für ihn aushandelte. Am 1. Oktober marschierten die deutschen Truppen im Sudetenland ein, und Chamberlain zeigte sein berühmtes Blatt Papier und verkündete, daß gemäß den Münchner Verträgen die britischen und deutschen Nationen »nie wieder gegeneinander Krieg führen werden« (3).

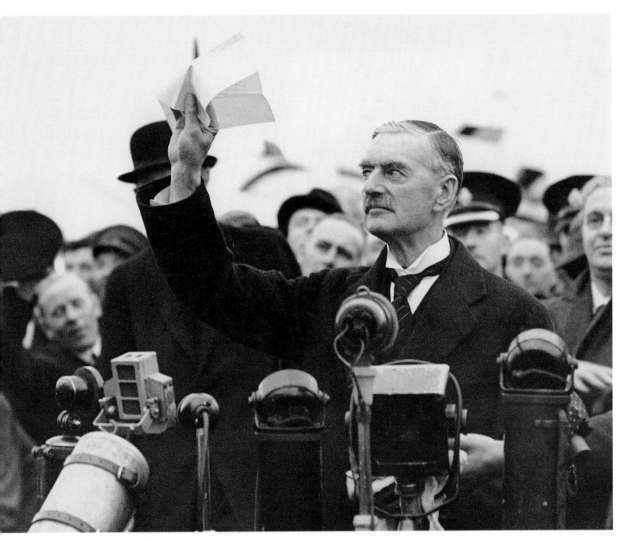

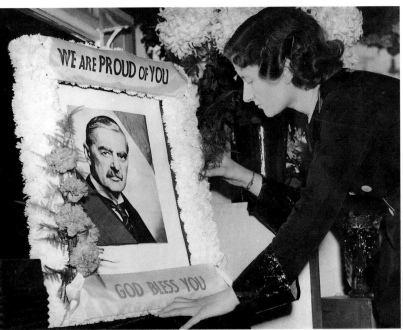

LA politique menée par Chamberlain en vue d'apaiser Hitler plaisait à certains, en premier au Führer, qui le fêta à l'occasion de trois conférences qui se déroulèrent en septembre 1938 (1, 2) ; mais aussi à la fleuriste du cirque Ludgate (4) qui rend hommage au Premier ministre britannique désireux de présenter « la paix à tout prix ». Malheureusement il alla trop loin dans l'apaisement, donnant aux Tchèques et aux Français le sentiment d'être trahis, suscitant la méfiance de bien des hommes politiques et observateurs anglais. Hitler lui-même préféra l'invasion des Sudètes à une capitulation tchèque que Chamberlain lui offrait. Le 1er octobre, Hitler occupait tout de même les Sudètes tandis que Chamberlain annonçait en agitant son célèbre chiffon de papier blanc (3) que les clauses de l'accord de Munich énonçaient l'intention des nations britannique et allemande de « ne plus jamais se livrer la guerre ».

World War II

By the late summer of 1939, appeasement had shot its bolt. When Nazi troops invaded Poland on 1 September, Britain and France at last committed themselves to war. Once the terrible decision had been taken, there was a breathless hush, a phoney war, and then all hell broke out. France was overrun and forced to surrender, though the nation's pride was saved by émigré warriors and a truculent Resistance. The British Expeditionary Force was famously rescued from the beaches of Dunkirk by the Royal Navy and a fleet of 'little ships'. Britain was battered from the skies in what became known as 'the Blitz' (1 and 2). Liverpool, Coventry, Southampton and other major cities were bombed in concentrated raids. Night and day London was a regular target. It was an appalling ordeal, though Churchill's government made excellent propaganda use of the Cockney spirit of resolution and the heroism of the Battle of Britain fighter pilots.

In August 1941, Churchill had the first of his nine meetings with Roosevelt. It was timely, for the war was rapidly spreading. In July 1941, disappointed at a lack of success in Western Europe, Hitler ordered the invasion of the Soviet Union, a 'win-all lose-all' gamble that promised an early victory, but failed to deliver. On 7 December 1941 some 360 planes of the Japanese air force descended on the American fleet in Pearl Harbor. Two months later, advancing at the rate of 30 miles a day across terrain believed impassable by the British, the Japanese army attacked Singapore, the greatest of all naval bases in the Far East and the heart of Britain's Asian empire. The two great Western powers had been caught napping. Singapore fell. In less than a year, the Japanese extended their sphere of influence from the Bering Sea to the southern islands of Melanesia. The British retreated, to keep a precarious hold on western Burma and the southern strip of New Guinea.

The fight back was slow and arduous, with Allied armies pursuing Germans and Italians across North Africa and then gaining a toehold in Sicily. At Stalingrad, citizens and troops of the Soviet Army withstood a bitter siege in freezing temperatures before launching a counter-attack that turned into a rout. Millions of brave soldiers in the German army were killed or captured or simply died in a nightmare retreat that matched that of Napoleon's *Grande Armée* on the same frozen soil 130 years earlier. In one of the best kept secrets of the war, the Allies fixed on Normandy as the site of the greatest seaborne invasion in history, and on D Day (6 June 1944) the liberation of France began. Less than a year later, the fighting ended in Europe; those that had survived the Holocaust were freed from the camps, and victors and vanquished began the long walk home.

In the Pacific, American troops clawed their way back, island by island, until they were at last in a position to attack Japan itself. There had already been air raids on Tokyo and other cities, but the knock-out blows were delivered in August 1945, when atomic bombs were dropped on Hiroshima and Nagasaki. The result was man-made devastation and carnage on a scale that the world had never suffered before. Burnt and poisoned by radiation, choked by smoke and fumes, and blown apart by the sheer force of the explosions, the Japanese surrendered.

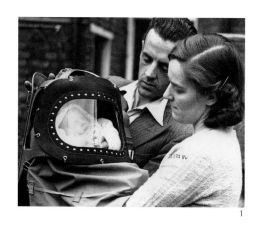

1

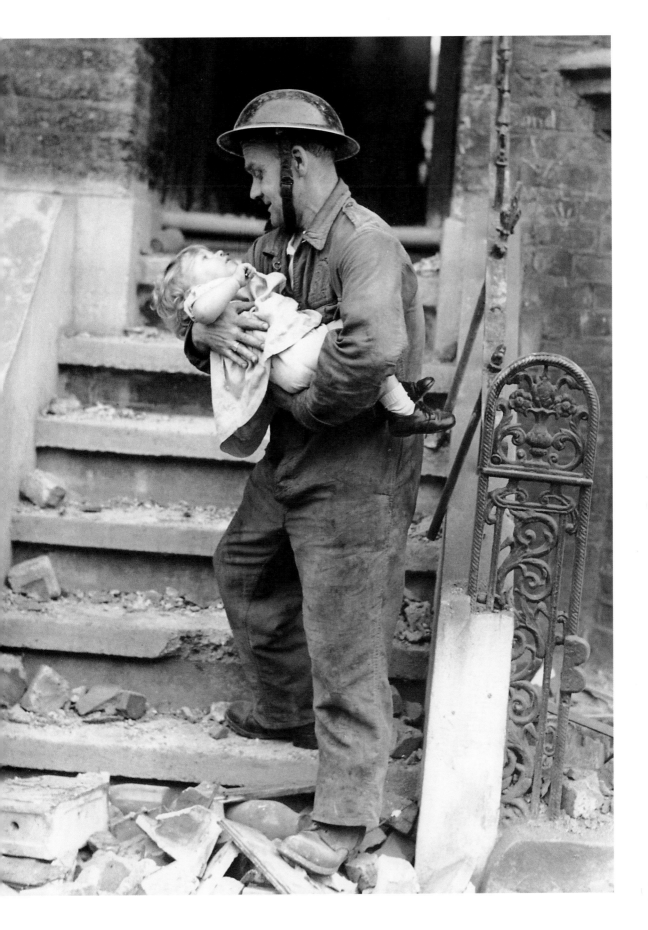

IM Spätsommer 1939 unternahm das Bündnis der Beschwichtigungspolitik einen letzten Versuch; als die deutsche Wehrmacht jedoch am 1. September in Polen einmarschierte, erklärten England und Frankreich schließlich Nazideutschland den Krieg. Nachdem die Entscheidung gefallen war, herrschte zunächst atemloses Schweigen, ein Sitzkrieg. Und dann brach die Hölle los. Frankreich wurde überrannt und gezwungen, sich zu ergeben – auch wenn der Nationalstolz der Franzosen durch eine hartnäckige Widerstandsbewegung und kämpfende Emigranten gerettet wurde. Die britischen Expeditionsstreitkräfte wurden durch die Royal Navy und eine Flotte »kleiner Schiffe« vor Dünkirchen gerettet. Und Großbritannien wurde im sogenannten »Blitzkrieg« angegriffen (1 und 2): Liverpool, Coventry, South-ampton und weitere Städte waren das Ziel konzentrier-ter Bombardements der deutschen Luftwaffe; London blieb Tag und Nacht Ziel ihrer Angriffe. Das waren schlimme Wochen – auch wenn die Regierung Churchills die Entschlossenheit der Londoner Bevölke-rung und den Heroismus der englischen Piloten in der Schlacht um England propagandistisch außerordentlich zu nutzen wußte.

Im August 1941 trafen sich Churchill und Roosevelt zum ersten Mal; es sollten acht weitere Treffen folgen. Der Zeitpunkt war günstig gewählt, zumal sich der Krieg rasant ausweitete. Nach der Enttäuschung über den ausbleibenden Erfolg an der Westfront hatte Hitler im Juli 1941 den Überfall auf die Sowjetunion angeordnet – eine Entscheidung, bei der es um Alles oder Nichts ging und deren Hoffnung auf einen schnellen Erfolg sich nicht erfüllte. Am 7. Dezember 1941 griffen mehr als 350 Flugzeuge der japanischen Luftwaffe den amerikanischen Flottenstützpunkt Pearl Harbour an; zwei Monate später erfolgte der Angriff der japanischen Bodentruppen: Mit einer Geschwindig-keit von nahezu 50 Kilometern pro Tag rückten sie über ein Gelände, das die Engländer für unpassierbar gehalten hatten, bis nach Singapur vor – dem Herz des britischen Empire in Asien und größter Stützpunkt der britischen Flotte im Fernen Osten. Damit waren die

beiden westlichen Großmächte überrumpelt. Singapu fiel. In weniger als einem Jahr erweiterte Japan sei Einflußgebiet vom Beringmeer bis zu den südliche Inseln Melanesiens. Die Engländer zogen sich bis a ihren prekären Stützpunkt in Westbirma und d Südküste Neuguineas zurück.

Der Gegenangriff war mühsam und kam nu schleppend voran; die alliierten Streitkräfte drängten d deutschen und italienischen Truppen durch Nordafrik bis nach Sizilien zurück. In Stalingrad hatte Zivilbevölkerung und Truppen der Sowjetarmee be frostigen Temperaturen erbitterten Widerstand gege die Belagerung geleistet, bis auch sie zum Gegenangri übergingen, der eine wilde Flucht in Gang setzte: De deutsche Rückzug wurde zum Albtraum – in dei Millionen tapferer Soldaten starben oder i Gefangenschaft gerieten – und stand dem der Grand Armée Napoleons 130 Jahre zuvor auf demselbe frostigen Boden in Nichts nach. In einem beispiellose Akt von Geheimhaltung gingen die Alliierten bei de größten über den Seeweg erfolgten Invasion de Geschichte in der Normandie an Land; am 6. Jun 1944 – der als »D-Day« in die Geschichte einging begann die Befreiung Frankreichs. Kaum ein Jahr späte kamen die Kämpfe in Europa zum Erliegen; wer de Holocaust überlebt hatte, wurde aus den Konzen trationslagern befreit, und Sieger wie Besiegte machte sich auf den mühevollen und langen Weg nach Haus.

Im Pazifik eroberten währenddessen die amerikanische Truppen langsam Insel für Insel zurück – bis sie in de Lage waren, Japan direkt anzugreifen. Zuvor hatten si bereits Luftangriffe auf Tokyo und andere japanisch Städte geflogen; doch die endgültige Entscheidung fie mit dem Abwurf der Atombomben auf Hiroshima un Nagasaki im August 1945. Das Ergebnis: eine durc Menschenwerk erzeugte Zerstörung und Vernichtun von bisher nicht gekanntem Ausmaß. Durc Radioaktivität verbrannt und vergiftet, durch Nebe Dämpfe und Rauch erstickt sowie durch zerrissen di schiere Gewalt der Explosion kapitulierte Japan.

A LA fin de l'été 1939, l'alliance pour une politique d'apaisement fait une ultime tentative, mais, quand Wehrmacht allemande, envahit la Pologne, le 1er septembre, l'Angleterre et la France déclarent finalement la Guerre à l'Allemagne nazi. Une fois la décision prise, c'est tout d'abord un silence assourdissant qui règne, une guerre d'attente. Puis l'enfer se déclenche. La France est balayée en quelques jours et contrainte de se rendre – même si la fierté nationale des français est sauvée grâce à un mouvement de résistance infatigable et courageux ainsi que des émigrants qui poursuivent le combat depuis l'étranger. Les forces d'expédition britanniques sont sauvées par la Royal Navy et une armada de petits bateaux devant Dunkerque. Puis c'est la Grande-Bretagne qui est attaquée durant le « Blitz » (1 et 2): Liverpool, Coventry, Southampton et d'autres villes sont la cible de bombardements concentrés de la Luftwaffe allemande ; Londres, quant à elle, reste jour et nuit la cible de leurs attaques. Ce sont des semaines terribles – même si le gouvernement de Winston Churchill sait mettre adroitement à profit – à des fins de propagande – la détermination de la population londonienne et l'héroïsme des pilotes anglais dans la bataille d'Angleterre.

En août 1941, Churchill et Roosevelt se rencontrent pour la première fois ; huit autres rencontres devaient suivre. La date est bien choisie, d'autant plus que les hostilités s'étendent à la vitesse de l'éclair. Après la déception suscitée par l'absence de succès sur le front Ouest, Hitler ordonne, en juillet 1941, l'attaque de l'Union soviétique – une décision dont l'enjeu est « Tout au rien » et dont l'espoir d'un succès rapide ne devait jamais se vérifier. Le 7 décembre 1941, plus de 350 avions de l'armée de l'air japonaise attaquent la base de la marine américaine de Pearl Harbor ; deux mois plus tard, ce sont, cette fois, les troupes terrestres japonaises qui attaquent : à la vitesse de près de cinquante kilomètres par jour, elles conquièrent un terrain que les Anglais avaient jugé infranchissable, jusqu'à Singapour – le cœur de l'Empire britannique en Asie et la plus grande base de sa flotte en Extrême-Orient. En moins d'un an, le Japon étend son hégémonie de la mer de Béring jusqu'aux îles australes de la Mélanésie. Les Anglais se retirent jusqu'à leurs bases, précaire, de Birmanie occidentale et de la côte Sud de la Nouvelle-Guinée.

A l'Ouest, la contre-attaque est laborieuse et n'avance que lentement ; les forces alliées pourchassent les troupes allemandes et italiennes à travers l'Afrique du Nord et jusqu'en Sicile. A Stalingrad, la population civile et des troupes de l'armée soviétique opposent entre temps une résistance acharnée aux Allemands, malgré des températures arctiques, jusqu'à ce que les Soviétiques, eux aussi, contre-attaquent, ce qui déclenche un sauve-qui-peut éperdu : la retraite de l'Allemagne est un cauchemar – des millions de courageux soldats périssent alors ou sont faits prisonniers – qui ne le cède en rien à celle de la Grande Armée de Napoléon, cent trente ans auparavant, sur les mêmes terres gelées. Dans un acte de confidentialité sans précédent, les alliés déclenchent la plus grande invasion par voie maritime de l'histoire en mettant pied à terre en Normandie ; le 6 juin 1944 – qui est entré dans l'histoire sous le nom de « D-Day », le Jour J – commence la libération de la France. A peine un an plus tard, les combats cessent en Europe ; les survivants de l'holocauste sont libérés des camps de concentration, et vainqueurs comme vaincus entament leur pénible et long retour chez eux.

Pendant ce temps, dans le Pacifique, les troupes américaines reprennent lentement île par île – jusqu'au moment où elles sont en mesure d'attaquer directement le Japon. Auparavant, elles ont déjà bombardé Tokyo et d'autres villes japonaises ; mais la décision définitive tombe avec le lancement des bombes atomiques sur Hiroshima et Nagasaki, en août 1945. Résultat : une destruction et une extermination par la main de l'homme d'une ampleur jusqu'ici inconnue. Brûlé et empoisonné par la radioactivité, étouffé par le brouillard, les vapeurs et la fumée et déchiré par la violence inimaginable de l'explosion, le Japon capitule.

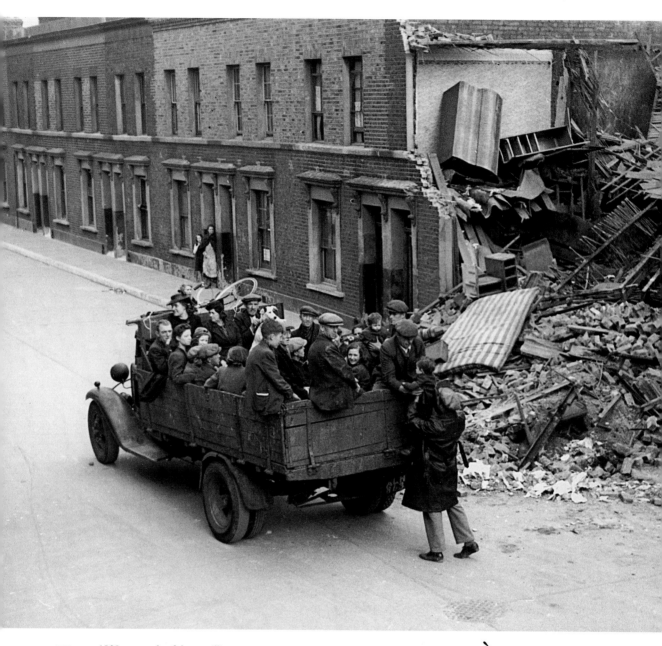

FROM 1939, upwards of three million children, including infants and babes-in-arms with their mothers, were evacuated from the city centres to the countryside to avoid the nightly bombing (1). The Battle of Britain began early in 1940, with daily attacks by the *Luftwaffe* to destroy RAF planes and airfields before Hitler's planned invasion in the autumn. It was fought in the skies above southern England by brave young men on both sides. These two German airmen (2) were among the lucky ones. Their Heinkel HE-111 was shot down and they were captured by the Home Guard near Goodwood, Sussex, 12 September 1940.

VON 1939 an wurden drei Millionen Kinder, darunter Säuglinge und Klein-kinder mit ihren Müttern, aus den Zentren der Großstädte aufs Land evakuiert, wo ihnen weniger Gefahr durch Bomben drohte (1). Die Schlacht um England begann Anfang 1940 mit täglichen Angriffen der deutschen Luftwaffe, die Flugzeuge und Landeplätze der Royal Air Force noch vor Hitlers geplantem Einmarsch im Herbst zerstören sollten. Im Himmel über Süd-england kämpften tapfere junge Männer auf beiden Seiten. Diese beiden deutschen Piloten gehörten zu den Glücklicheren. Ihre Heinkel HE-111 wurde in der Nähe von Goodwood, Sussex, abgeschossen und sie selbst gefangen genommen – 12. September 1940 (2).

À PARTIR de 1939, on évalue à plus de trois millions le nombre des enfants, y compris les tout-petits, les nourrissons et leurs mères, à être évacués des grandes villes pour être amenés dans les campagne (1). La Bataille d'Angleterre commence au début de 1940 par des attaques quotidiennes de la Luftwaffe allemande qui veut détruire les avions et aérodromes de la Royal Air Force avant même l'invasion que projette Hitler pour l'automne. Dans les cieux du Sud de l'Angleterre, de courageux jeunes hommes se battent des deux côtés. Ces deux pilotes allemands figurent parmi les plus chanceux. Leur Heinkel HE-111 a été abattu à proximité de Goodwood, dans le Sussex, et eux-mêmes ont été faits prisonniers – 12 septembre 1940 (2).

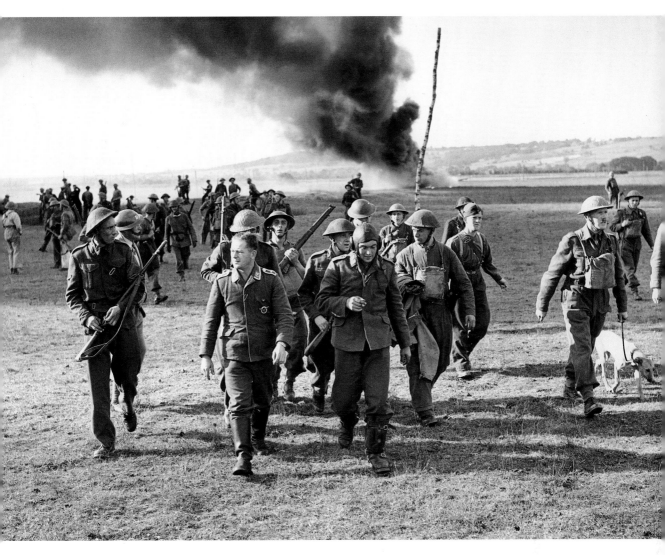

PERHAPS the most famous British picture of the War (overleaf). New Year's Eve 1940 and, two days after the raid, London's East End still burns around St Paul's Cathedral. The cathedral, however, remained standing, a symbol of resistance.

DIES (folgende Seiten) ist vielleicht das berühmteste Kriegsbild aus England überhaupt. Silvester 1940, und zwei Tage nach dem Luftangriff brennt das Londoner East End rund um die St.-Pauls-Kathedrale noch immer. Doch die Kathedrale blieb bestehen, ein Symbol des Widerstands.

VOICI peut-être la photographie la plus célèbre de la guerre en Grande-Bretagne (pages suivantes). C'est le réveillon de l'An 1940; depuis deux jours, l'incendie de l'East End continue de faire rage. La cathédrale Saint Paul demeura toutefois debout, comme le symbole de la résistance.

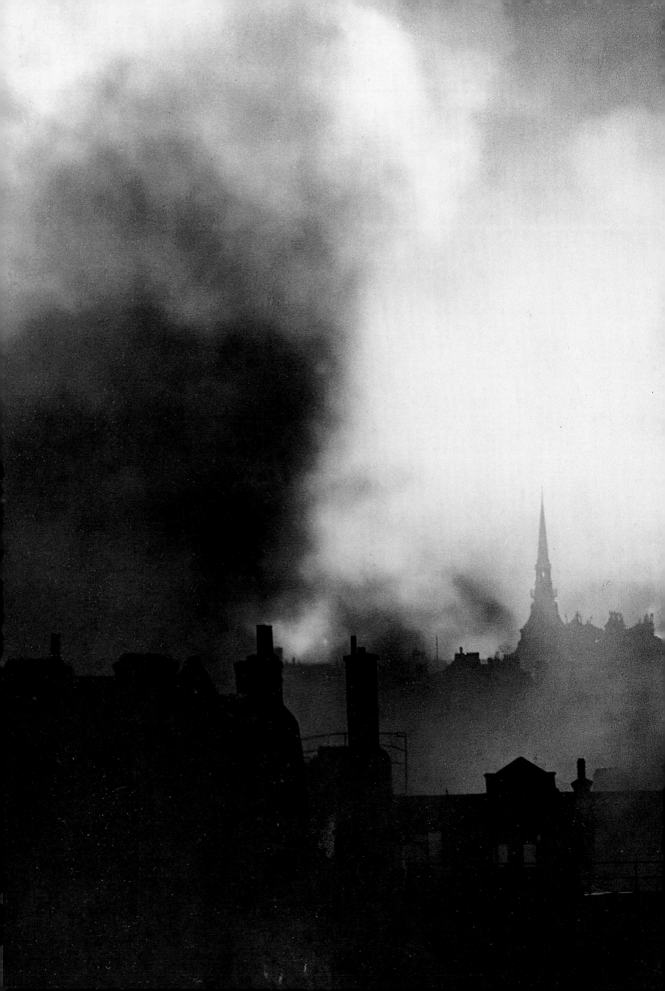

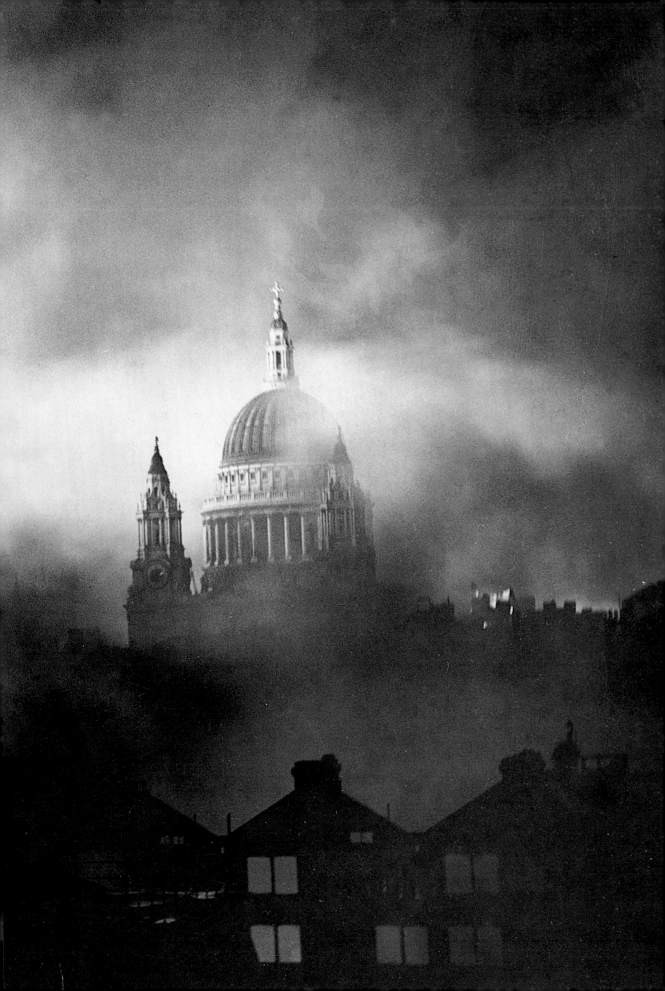

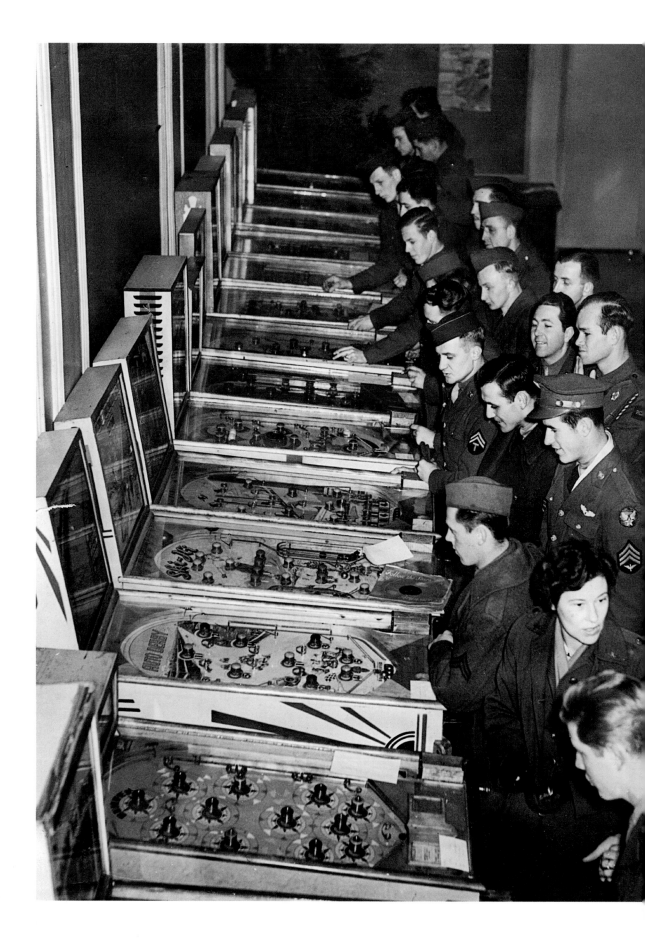

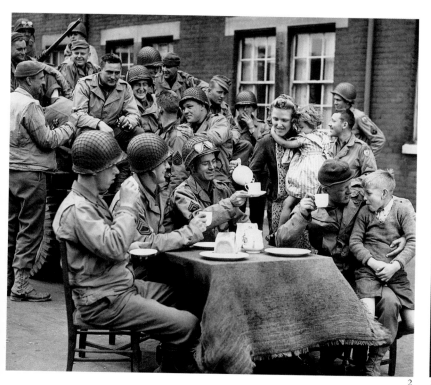

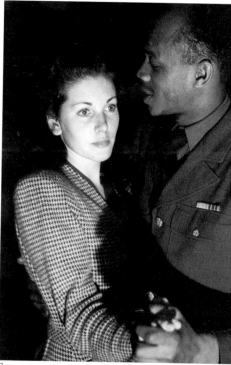

2   3

AMERICAN GIs – Overpaid, Over-sexed and Over Here – brought gloom to British men and a sparkle to the women. Children came fresh to Wrigley's gum and Hershey bars (2); women to tipped Virginia tobacco (3); and the GIs themselves demanded big-band Bourbon-fuelled night clubs to remind them of home (4). Even the American Red Cross got involved in running a 'Coney Island' arcade provided by the Amusement Caterers' Association (1).

DIE amerikanischen GIs waren den englischen Männern ein Dorn im Auge, doch bei den Frauen hochwillkommen. Die Kinder bekamen ihre ersten Wrigley-Kaugummis (2), die Frauen Virginia-Zigaretten mit Filtern (3). Die GIs selbst waren immer auf der Suche nach Nacht-clubs mit Big Bands und Bourbon, damit sie sich wie zu Hause fühlen konnten (4). Selbst das amerikanische Rote Kreuz half mit, den »Coney Island«-Spielsalon zu betreiben (1).

ALORS que les femmes britanniques découvraient l'Amérique par le biais de ses soldats, les enfants découvraient la gomme Wrigley et les barres Hershey (2). Si les Anglaises appréciaient les cigarettes de Virginie (3), les GIs, quant à eux, voulaient reconstituer l'atmosphère de la mère patrie (4). La Croix-Rouge américaine elle-même géra la galerie Coney Island, proposée par l'Association des fournisseurs de distractions (1).

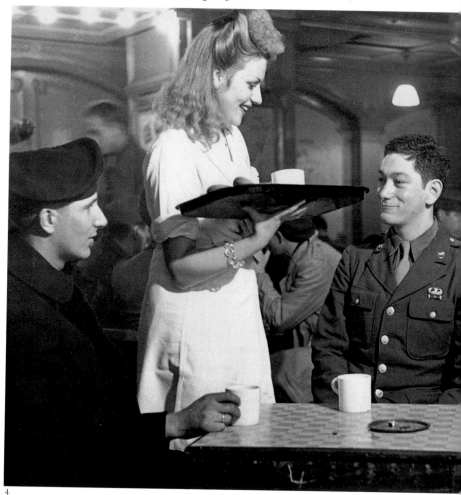

4

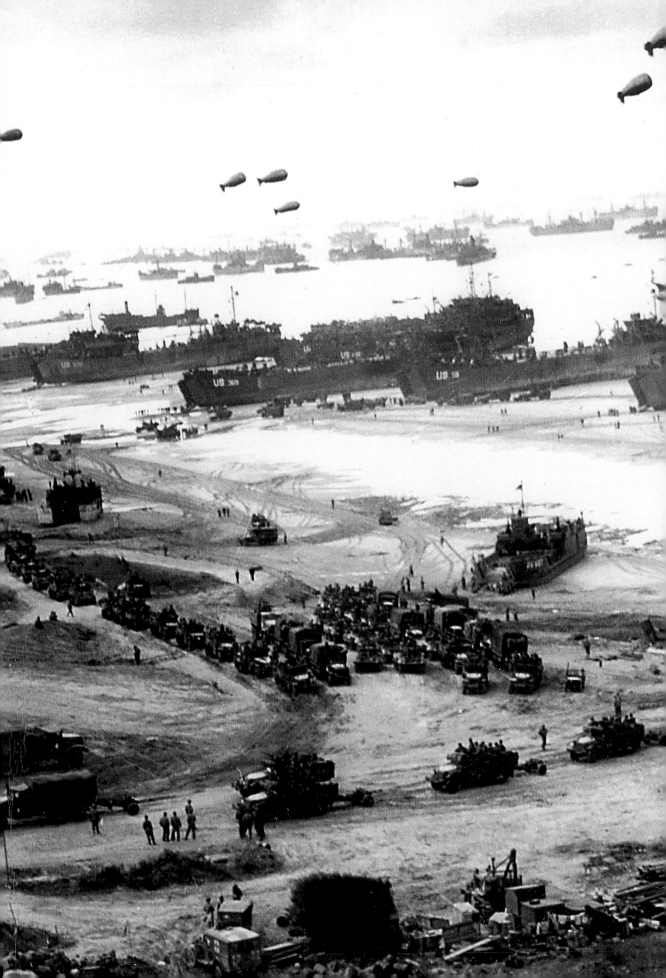

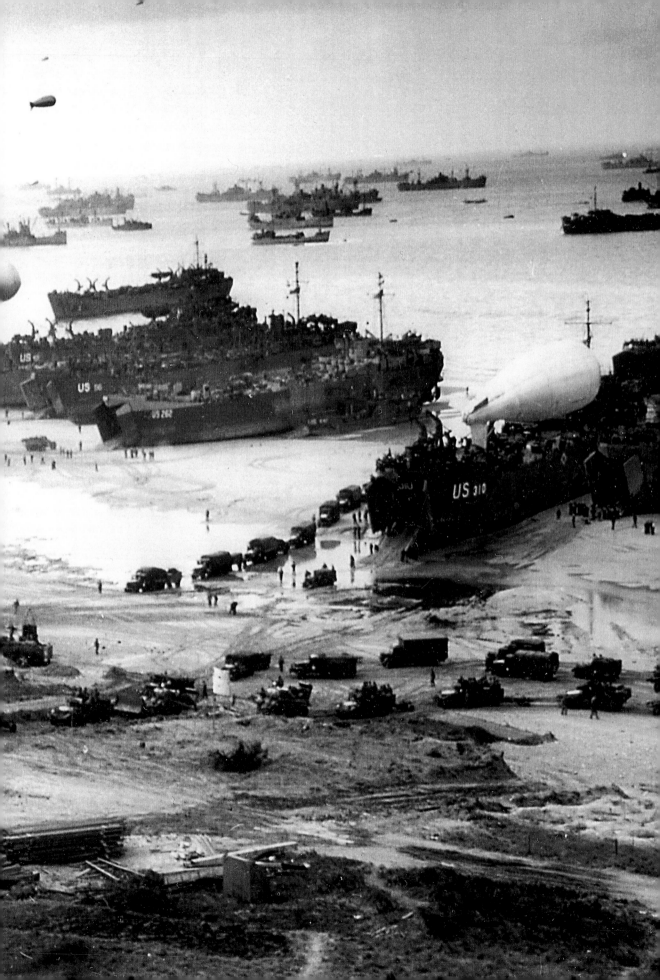

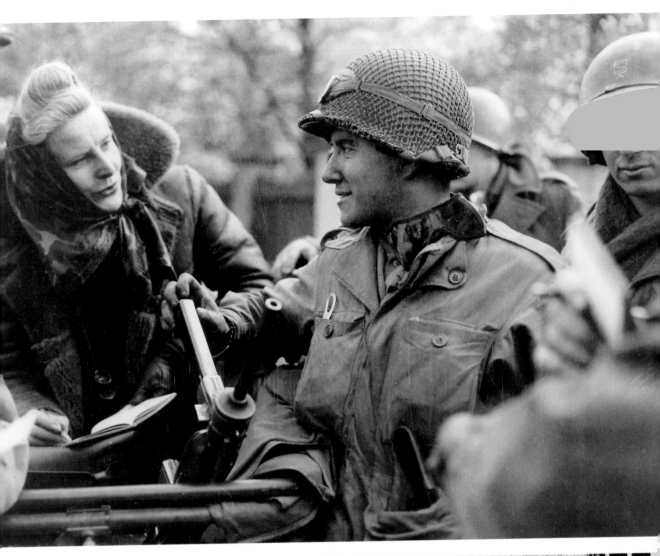

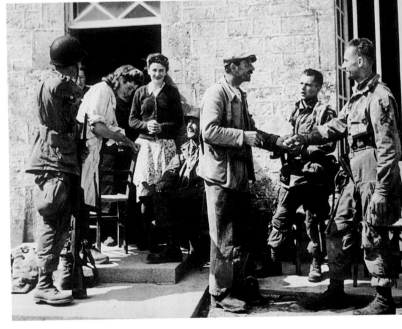

(*Previous pages*)

DAY 2 of the world's greatest seaborne invasion. US ships disgorge tanks, troops and vehicles on Omaha Beach in Normandy, 7 June 1944.

(*Vorherige Seiten*)

TAG Zwei der größten über den Seeweg erfolgten Invasion der Geschichte: Amerikanische Schiffe spucken Panzer, Fahrzeuge und Bodentruppen auf den Strand von Omaha in der Normandie – 7. Juni 1944.

(*Pages précédentes*)

JOUR J plus 1 de la plus grande invasion au monde arrivée par la mer. Les bâtiments américains crachent leurs blindés, hommes de troupes et véhicules sur la plage d'Omaha Beach, en Normandie, le 7 juin 1944.

LANGUAGE is clearly not a necessary means of communication when there is something in common to celebrate. After regaining their country from the German Occupation, French villagers fraternize with GIs of the liberating forces (2, 4), while in the town of Saint-Sauveur-Lendelin residents shower armoured personnel carriers with flowers (3). When, close to the end of the war on the continent (27 April 1945), the US and the Ukraine First Armies met at Torgau on the Elbe, reporter Iris Carpenter of the *Boston Globe* (1) wanted to get her compatriot's first-hand account.

MAN muß nicht unbedingt dieselbe Sprache sprechen, wenn es etwas Gemeinsames zu feiern gibt: Nach der Befreiung von der deutschen Besatzung verbrüdern sich die Bewohner eines französischen Dorfes mit den GIs der Befreiungstruppen (2, 4), und die Frauen des Städtchens Saint-Sauveur-Lendelin werfen den Soldaten in ihren Panzerwagen Blumen zu (3). Als sich am 27. April 1945, kurz vor Ende des Krieges in Europa, die Erste US-Armee und die Erste Armee der Ukraine in Torgau an der Elbe trafen, war Iris Carpenter, Reporterin des *Boston Globe*, dabei, um von ihren Landsleuten einen Bericht aus erster Hand zu bekommen (1).

IL est manifestement possible de comprendre la langue de l'autre lorsqu'on a quelque chose en commun à célébrer. Après la libération des pays, les villageois français fraternisent avec les soldats américains des forces de libération (2 et 4), tandis que dans la ville de Saint-Sauveur-Lendelin, les habitants font pleuvoir des fleurs sur les véhicules blindés transportant les troupes (3). Quand, vers la fin de la guerre sur le continent (le 27 avril 1945), les premières armées américaine et ukrainienne opérèrent leur jonction à Torgau, sur l'Elbe, la journaliste Iris Carpenter du *Boston Globe* (1) voulut obtenir d'un de ses compatriotes un compte rendu de première main.

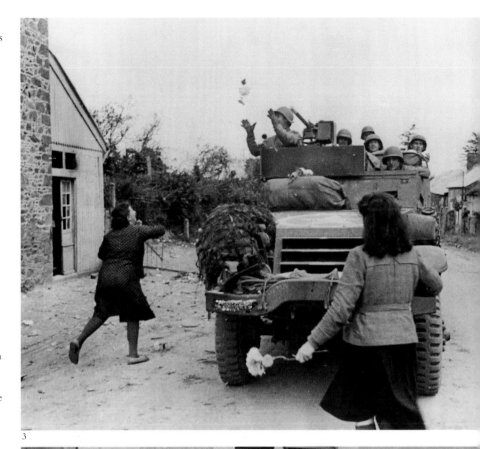

3

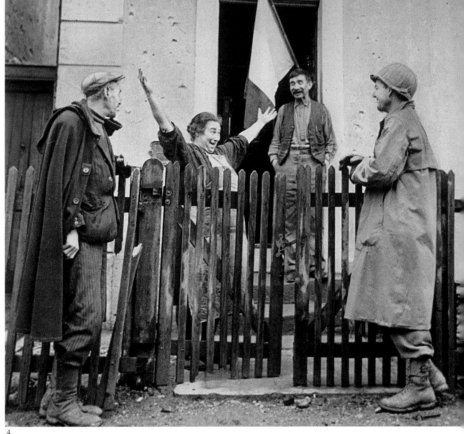

4

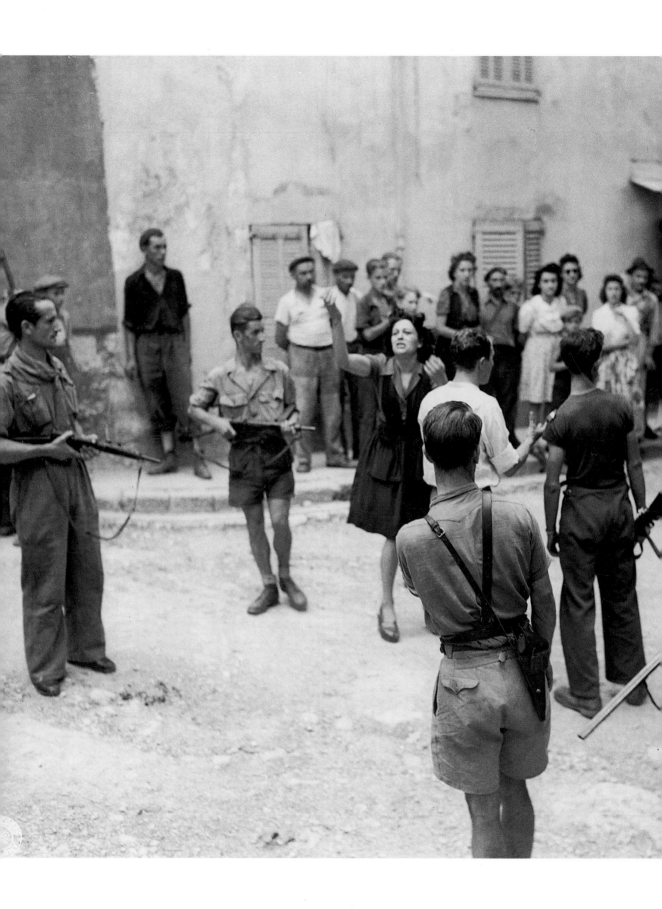

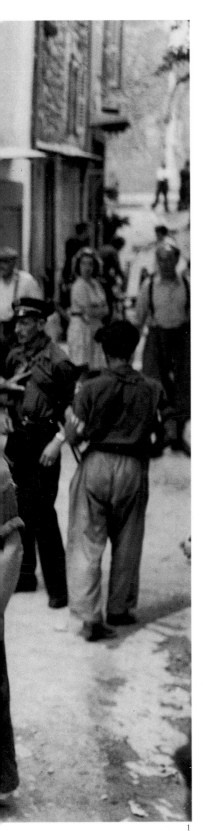

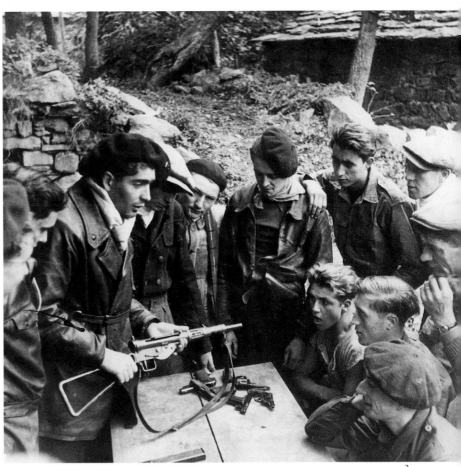

THE end of the German Occupation
brought recriminations for many in
France (1). Here youthful members of the
maquis (Resistance fighters) undergo
weapons training (2) with an international
variety of Sten, Ruby, Mark II and Le
Français pistols, Colt and Bulldog
revolvers, air-dropped by the London-
based Free French, led by General de
Gaulle.

NACH dem Ende der deutschen
Besatzung hatten sich viele Franzosen
wegen Kollaboration zu verantworten (1).
Hier sieht man jugendliche Widerstands-
kämpfer (*maquis*) bei Übungen mit einer
internationalen Mischung an Waffen, mit
Sten-, Ruby-, Mark II- und Le Français-
Pistolen, Colt- und Bulldog-Revolvern,
allesamt von Flugzeugen der Freien Fran-
zösischen Armee abgeworfen, die von
London aus operierte und unter der
Führung von General de Gaulle stand (2).

EN France, avec la fin de l'occupation
allemande, sonna également l'heure des
règlements de comptes (1). Ici, des jeunes
du maquis s'entraînent au maniement des
armes provenant d'un arsenal international
(2) – Sten, Ruby, Mark II, Le Français,
Colt et Bulldog –, parachutées par la France
libre, l'organisation du général de Gaulle,
basée à Londres.

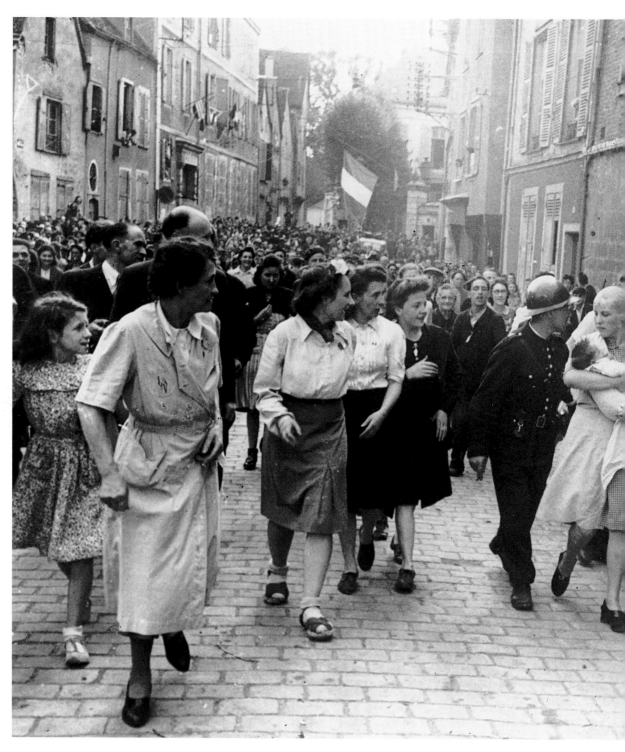

WITH the recapture of Chartres on 18 August 1944, women collaborators suffer the indignities of having their hair publicly shaved and of being jeered and jostled and whistled at by the local population (1, 3). The women (2) are mother and grandmother of this German-fathered baby.

NACH der Rückeroberung von Chartres am 18. August 1944 werden Kollaborateurinnen öffentlich kahlgeschore und dem Spott der Bevölkerung preisgege

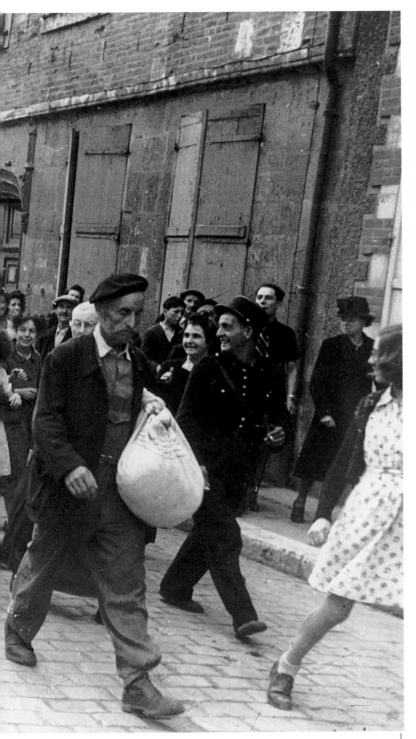

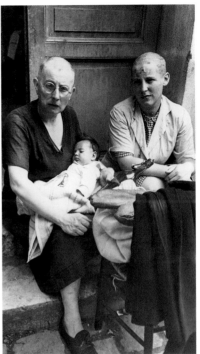

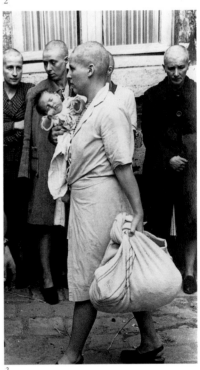

1

2

3

...en (1, 3). Die beiden Frauen (2) sind ...utter und Großmutter des Kindes von ...inem deutschen Vater.

Après la reprise de Chartres le 18 août 1944, les femmes soupgounées d'avoir collaboré avec l'ennemi sont humiliées : rasées en public, raillées, injuriées et sifflées par la population locale (1 et 3). Ces femmes (2) sont respectivement la mère et la grand-mère de ce bébé de père allemand.

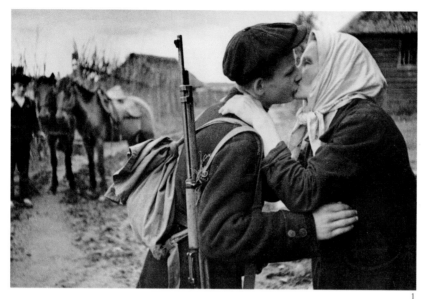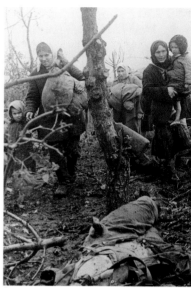

1 2

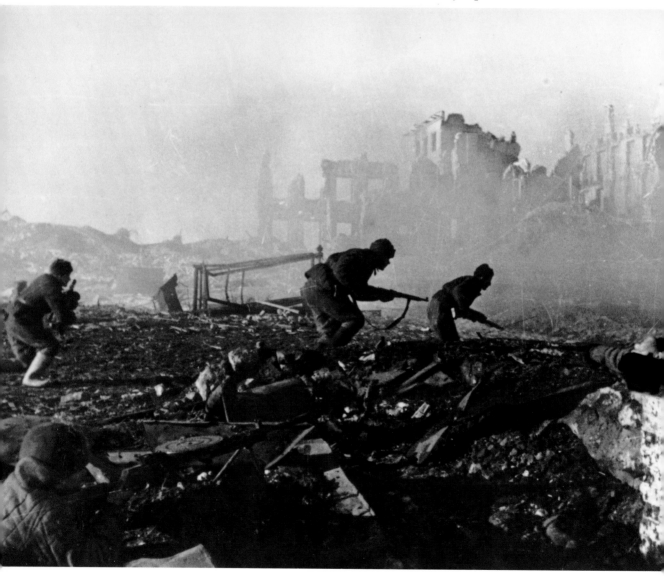

THE Russian people lost more lives than any other nation during the Second World War: over 20 million are estimated to have died. Like Napoleon, Hitler threw division after division into the war on the eastern front, only to see them driven back or, more humiliatingly still, defeated by the Russian winter, an even fiercer enemy than the Russian troops. The fall of Stalingrad in November 1942 (3) was for many the turning-point of the war, while the siege of Leningrad led to starvation for its beleaguered inhabitants. Even youths joined up to fight, like this boy bidding his mother farewell (1), while Russian villagers who had taken to the woods near Orel to flee the German army here pass the corpses of their soldiers on their return home (2).

3

DIE Russen waren das Volk im Zweiten Weltkrieg, das die meisten Toten zu beklagen hatte: vermutlich über 20 Millionen Menschen kamen um. Wie Napoleon schickte auch Hitler Division um Division in den Krieg an der Ostfront, und alle wurden sie vom russischen Winter, einem noch erbitterteren Feind als die russische Armee, zurückgetrieben oder ganz geschlagen. Der Fall Stalingrads im November 1942 (3) war für viele die entscheidende Wende des Krieges; in Leningrad verhungerte die belagerte Bevölkerung. Selbst Kinder kamen an die Front, wie dieser Junge, der sich hier von seiner Mutter verabschiedet (1). Russische Bauern, die bei Orel in die Wälder geflohen waren, als die Deutschen kamen, finden bei ihrer Rückkehr ihre gefallenen Soldaten (2).

LE peuple soviétique fut, au cours de la Seconde Guerre mondiale, de toutes les nations, celui qui paya le plus lourd tribut en vies humaines : on l'estime à plus de 20 millions de morts. Comme Napoléon, Hitler lança ses divisions l'une après l'autre à l'assaut du front est avec pour seul résultat de les voir repoussées ou, plus humiliant encore, tenues en échec par l'hiver russe. La chute de Stalingrad, en novembre 1942 (3), signala pour beaucoup un tournant dans la guerre, alors que le siège de Leningrad affamait les habitants de la ville. Même les jeunes s'enrôlèrent pour combattre, tel ce garçon faisant ses adieux à sa mère (1). Ailleurs, des villageois russes, qui s'étaient réfugiés dans les bois non loin d'Orel pour échapper à l'armée allemande, prennent le chemin du retour au milieu des cadavres de leurs soldats (2).

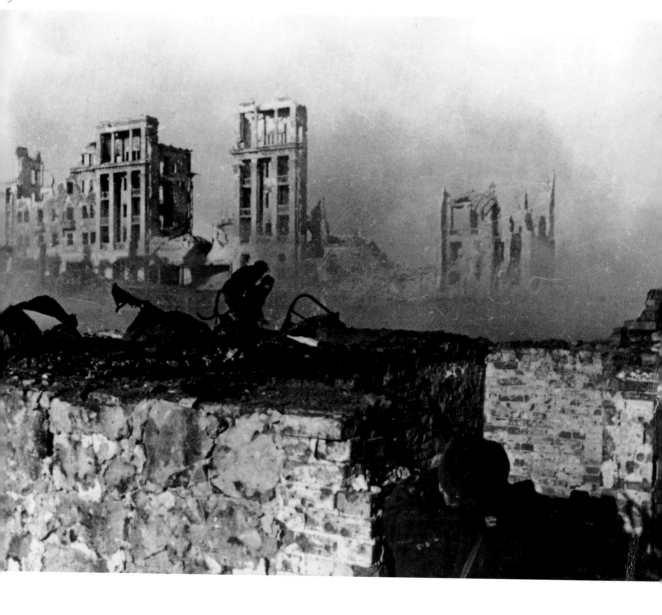

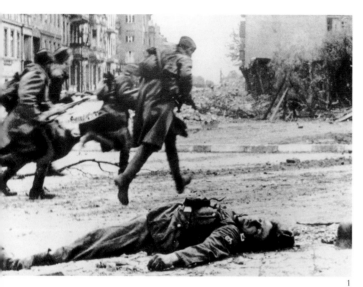

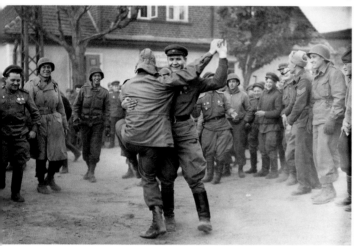

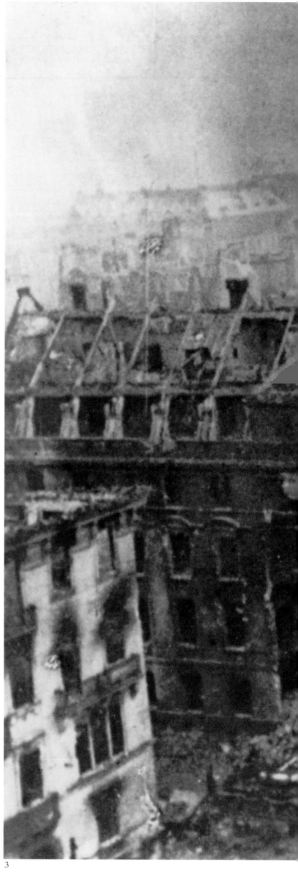

I N April 1945 Berlin was subjected to street-by-street fighting to gain control of the capital (1). Dimitri Baltermants, famous Russian photographer and war hero, took the victory pictures: the Soviet hammer-and-sickle is raised over the Reichstag (3). May Day 1945: the US Ninth Army meets the Russians on the Elbe. Two soldiers celebrate in a dance, watched by their comrades-in-arms (2).

I M April 1945 kämpften sich in Berlin die einrückenden Armeen Straße um Straße vor (1). Dimitri Baltermants, der berühmte russische Photograph und Kriegsheld, hielt den Sieg in Bildern fest: Die sowjetische Flagge mit Hammer und Sichel wird über dem Reichstag gehißt (3). 1. Mai 1945: Die Neunte US-Armee und die russischen Truppen treffen sich an der Elbe. Zwei Soldaten beim Freudentanz, und ihre Waffenbrüder sehen zu (2).

E N avril 1945, Berlin était le théâtre de combats dont l'enjeu était de conquérir la capitale, rue après rue (1). Dimitri Baltermants, célèbre photographe et héros de guerre russe, prit les photographies de la victoire : le marteau et la faucille soviétiques sont hissés au-dessus du Reichstag (3). 1er mai 1945 : la 9e armée des États-Unis rejoint les Russes sur les bords de l'Elbe. Deux soldats dansent de joie sous le regard de leurs compagnons d'armes (2).

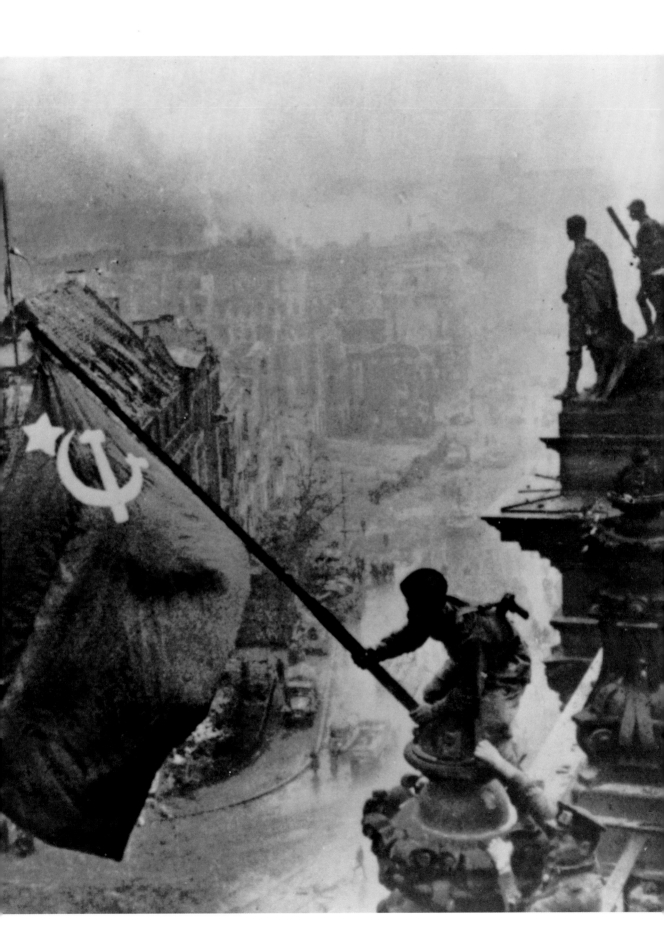

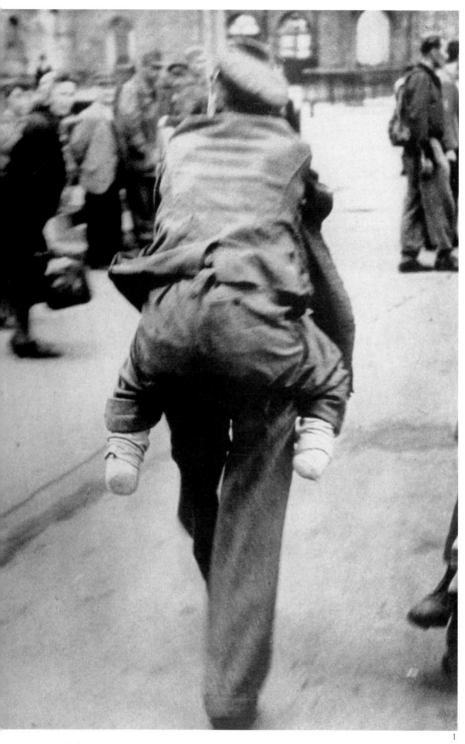

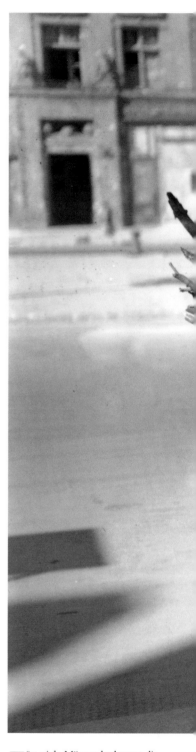

1

FOR many men, coming home meant making your way on foot from battlefront or prison camp. Two German soldiers make their painful way back from a Russian POW camp in October 1945 (1). For many women, maintaining a home meant hunting for food and fuel. This Berlin housewife (2) has raided firewood from a forest eight miles (13 kilometres) away.

FÜR viele Männer bedeutete die Heimkehr, den Weg von der Front oder aus dem Gefangenenlager zu Fuß zurückzulegen: zwei deutsche Soldaten auf dem schmerzvollen Heimweg aus einem russischen Gefangenenlager – im Oktober

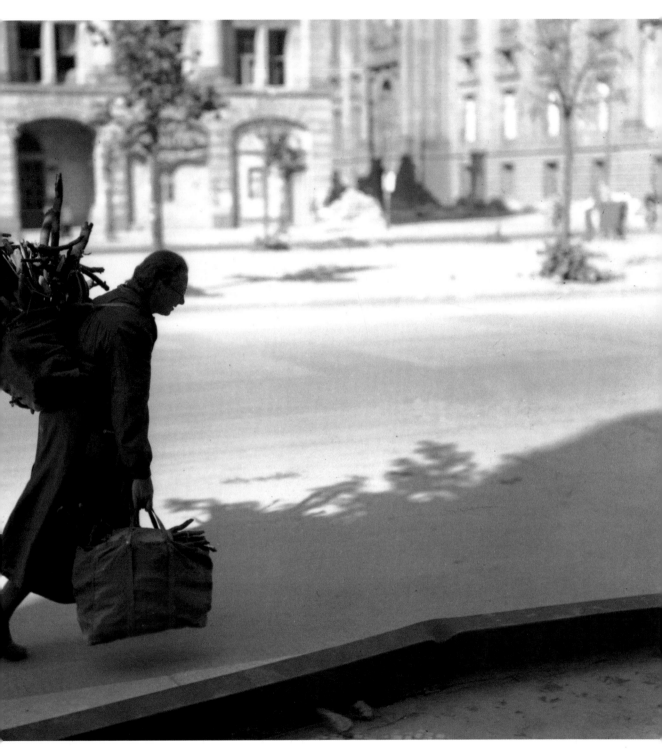

45 (1). Die Haushaltsführung bedeutete
· viele Frauen, sich auf die Jagd nach Essen
d Energiequellen zu machen: Diese
rliner Hausfrau hat in einem mehr als
:ölf Kilometer entfernten Wald Ofenholz
sammelt (2).

Pour beaucoup d'hommes, rentrer chez
soi signifiait couvrir à pied le chemin
depuis le front ou le camp de prisonniers :
deux soldats allemands lors de leur
douloureuse marche de retour depuis un
camp prisonnier russe – en octobre 1945 (1).

Pour beaucoup de femmes, tenir le ménage
équivalait à une véritable chasse à
l'alimentation et aux sources d'énergie : cette
Berlinoise est allée chercher du bois pour sa
cuisinière dans une forêt éloignée de plus de
douze kilomètres (2).

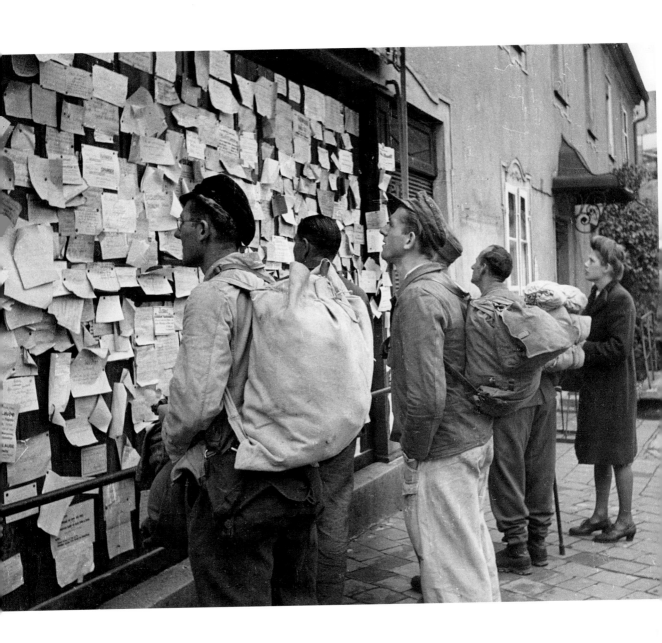

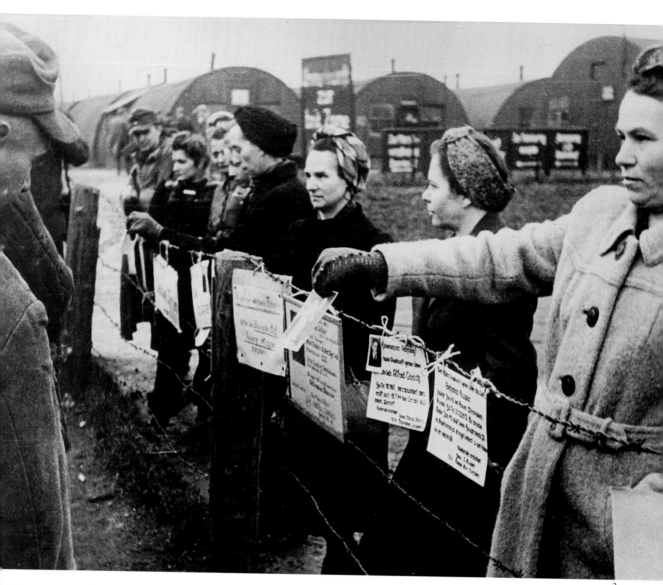

2

NOTICES pasted on trees, boards, railings or strung from barbed wire served multiple functions. A dearth of newspapers led to this means of disseminating information. Specifically in Germany and Austria notes were posted at train stations in an attempt to recover sons and husbands who had failed to return from the eastern front (1). In former POW camps relatives posted faded photographs with the rubric 'Have you seen this man?' beneath (2).

NACHRICHTEN wurden an Bäume, Anschlagtafeln, Geländer oder Drahtzäune geheftet; es war die einzige Möglichkeit, Informationen weiterzugeben, denn Zeitungen gab es kaum. Besonders in Deutschland und Österreich hängten Familien Nachrichten in den Bahnhöfen aus, in der Hoffnung, Männer oder Söhne wiederzufinden, die nicht von der Ostfront zurückgekehrt waren (1). In ehemaligen Kriegsgefangenenlagern hängten die Angehörigen verblaßte Fotografien aus, mit der Frage darunter: »Wer kennt diesen Mann?« (2)

LES bouts de papier collés sur les arbres, les panneaux et les barrières ou accrochés aux fils barbelés servaient à toutes sortes de choses. La pénurie de journaux faisait recourir à ce moyen pour diffuser les nouvelles. En Allemagne et en Autriche, en particulier, on placardait dans les gares ferroviaires des notices pour essayer de retrouver des fils ou des époux qui n'étaient pas revenus du front de l'Est (1). Dans les anciens camps de prisonniers, les parents plaçaient des photos vieillies sur lesquelles on pouvait lire : « Avez-vous vu cet homme ? » (2)

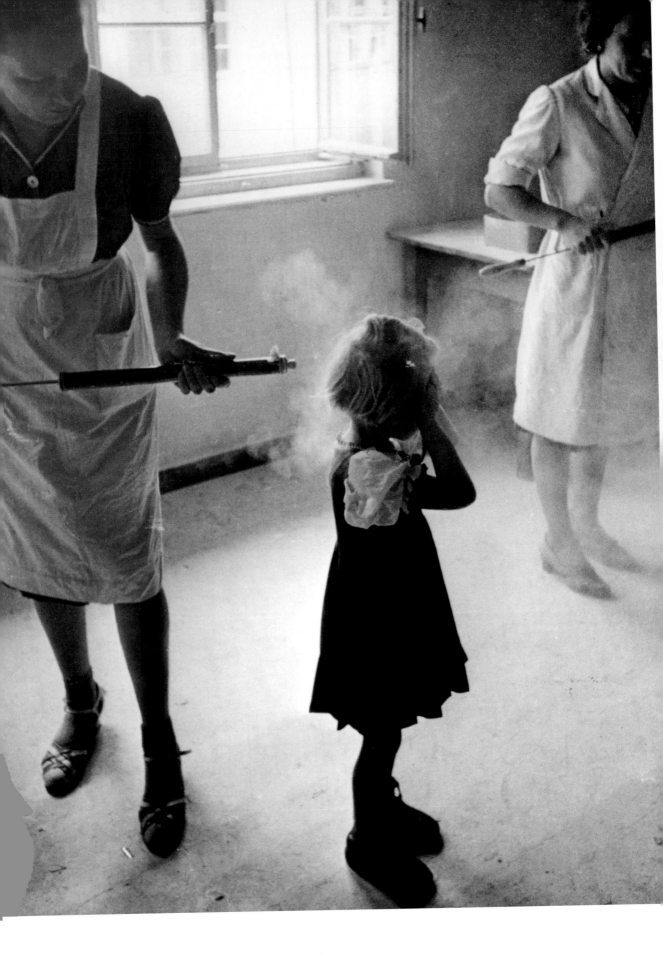

UNESCO supplemented a child health-care programme intended to combat communicable infections. This little refugee from the former Sudetenland (Czechoslovakia) is being deloused (1). At much the same time, UNICEF took on the responsibility of inspecting schools in countries formerly ruled by the Nazis. In this Austrian school the pupils were supplied with basic meals (2).

DIE UNESCO stockte ein Gesundheits-programm für Kinder auf, das ansteckende Krankheiten bekämpfen sollte. Diese kleine Heimatvertriebene aus dem Sudetenland (das nun wieder tschechisch war) wird gerade entlaust (1). Etwa zur gleichen Zeit ließ die UNICEF eine Inspektion an Schulen in ehemals von den Nazis kontrollierten Ländern durchführen. In dieser österreichischen Schule erhielten die Schüler eine Grundversorgung (2).

L'UNESCO a majoré un programme de protection de la santé des enfants, en vue de lutter contre les maladies contagieuses. Cette petite réfugiée, originaire de l'exrégion des Sudètes (Tchécoslovaquie), subit un épouillage (1). A peu près à la même époque, l'UNICEF réalise une inspection dans les écoles de pays jadis contrôlés par les nazis. Dans cette école autrichienne les enfants reçoivent une alimentation de base (2).

(Overleaf)
MARKED with yellow stars (3), deportees were herded onto trains like cattle. At Auschwitz, where this cattle-truck was bound (2), 1.5 million were gassed and incinerated. At Buchenwald these living skeletons (1) were the scant survivors of a further 800,000 who died.

(Folgende Seiten)
DIE mit Judensternen gekennzeichneten Deportierten (3) wurden in Güter-wagen verladen wie Vieh. In Auschwitz, wohin dieser Viehwagen unterwegs ist (2), wurden 1,5 Millionen Menschen vergast und verbrannt. In Buchenwald kamen weitere 800 000 um, und diese bis aufs Skelett Abge-magerten (1) waren die einzigen Überlebenden.

Pages suivantes)
MARQUÉS de l'étoile jaune (3), les déportés étaient parqués comme du bétail dans les trains. À Auschwitz, desti-ation de ce fourgon, qui aurait dû servir ux bestiaux (2), un million et demi de ersonnes furent gazées et précipitées sous rre. À Buchenwald ces hommes et femmes éduits à l'état de squelettes (1) ont à peine rvécu, tandis que 800 000 autres sont morts.

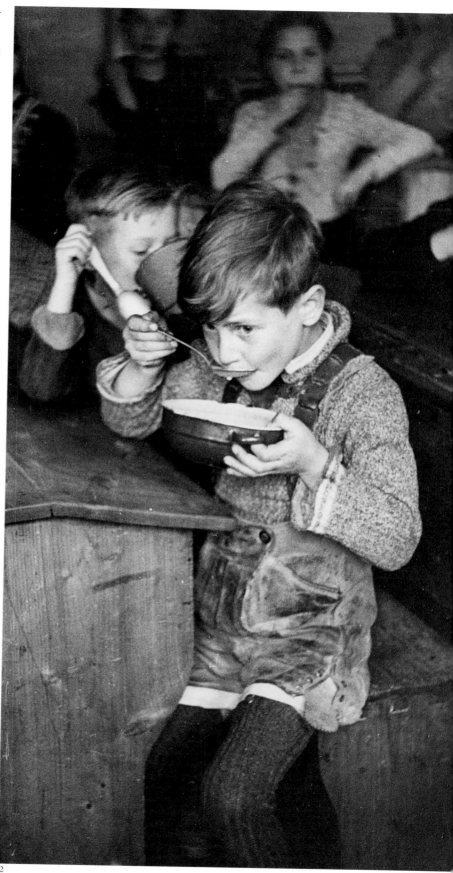

2

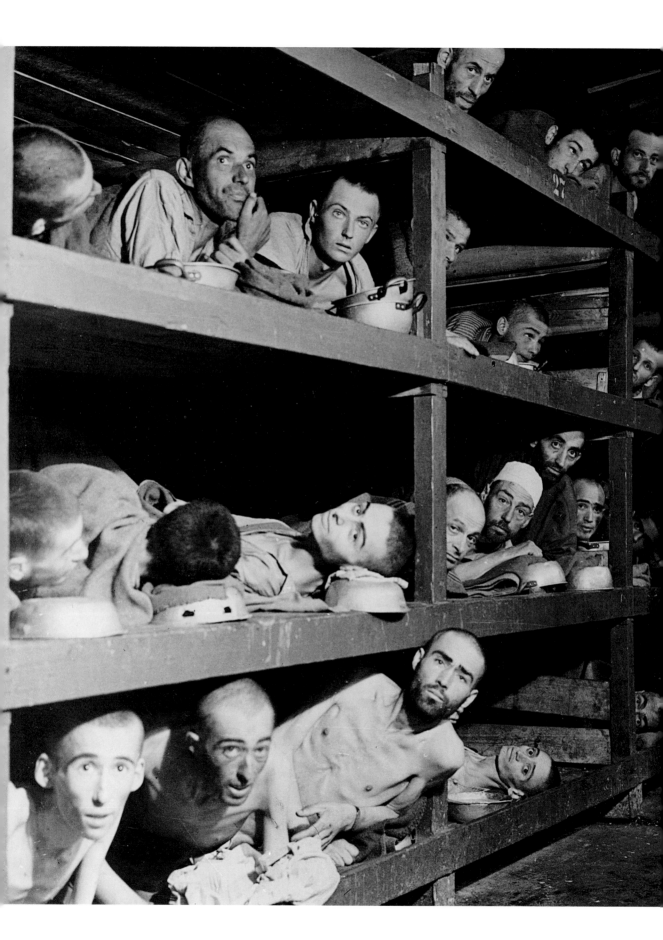

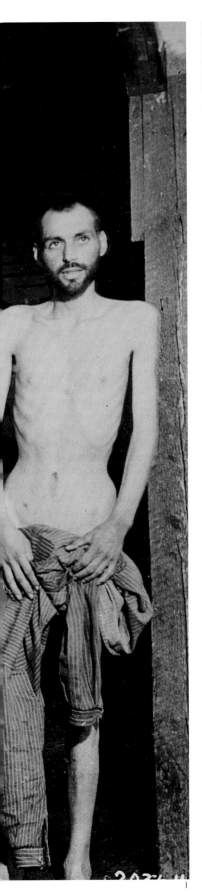

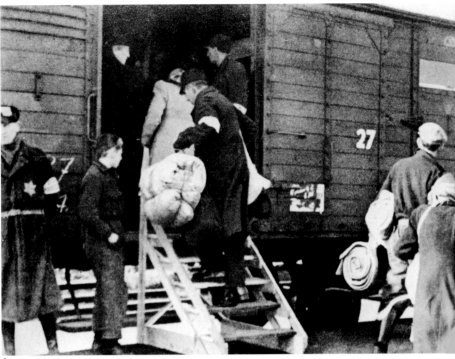

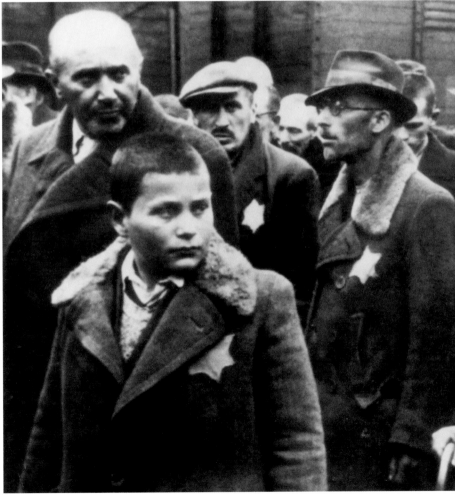

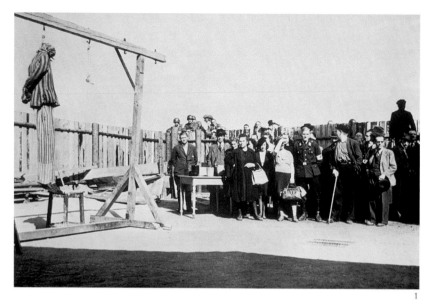

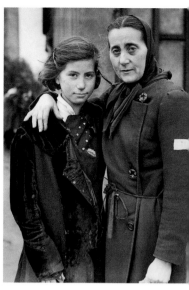

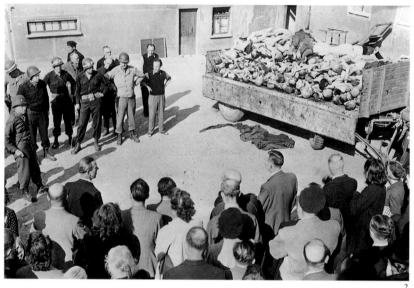

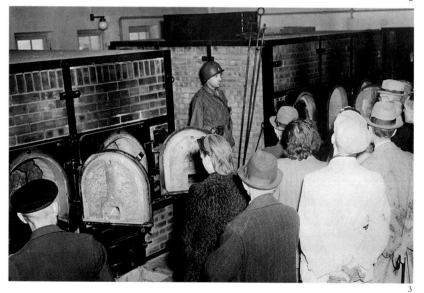

The Allies and then the West German government sought to implement a programme of 're-education', through recognition of what had actually taken place. It began at Buchenwald in April 1945, where local civilians were brought to acknowledge what so many had previously refused to open their eyes to. Some look away before the swinging man (1), and a lorry stacked with corpses, naked and in extreme emaciation (2). Finally, they visit the ovens, whose smoke Weimar townspeople must have witnessed daily (3). A contemporary report noted: 'Many of the witnesses leave the camp in tears. Others appear indifferent and claim they are being subjected to Allied propaganda.'

A few of the sturdiest inmates, brought in as slave-labour from across Europe, survived on minimum rations, working a 12- to 18-hour day. An 11-year-old Czech 'child slave' is reunited with her mother at Kaunitz in 1945 (4). *J'accuse* – a Russian slave labourer singles out a German camp commander notorious for his sadistic brutality (5). At Dachau, some released prisoners rounded on their SS guards in enraged retaliation: soldiers of the US 42nd Division hook out a corpse from the moat round the camp (6).

DIE Alliierten und später die westdeutsche Regierung wollten in einer »Umerziehungskampagne« den Deutschen die Greuel vor Augen führen, die geschehen waren. Sie begann im April 1945 in Buchenwald, wo Einheimische durchs Lager geführt und gezwungen wurden zu sehen, wovor zuvor so viele die Augen verschlossen hatten. Einige wenden den Blick von dem Erhängten (1) und von dem Wagen ab, auf dem die nackten Leichen verhungerter Menschen aufgestapelt liegen (2). Als letztes sehen sie die Verbrennungsöfen, deren aufsteigenden Rauch die Bewohner von Weimar täglich gesehen haben müssen (3). Ein Reporter berichtete seinerzeit: »Viele Zeugen verlassen das Lager mit Tränen in den Augen. Andere machen einen gleichgültigen Eindruck und behaupten, es sei alles alliierte Propaganda.«

Ein paar besonders kräftige Insassen, die als Zwangsarbeiter aus ganz Europa hierher gebracht wurden, überlebten den Hunger und den zwölf- bis achtzehnstündigen Arbeitstag. Ein elfjähriges tschechisches »Sklavenmädchen« findet seine Mutter 1945 in Kaunitz wieder (4). *J'accuse* – ein russischer Zwangsarbeiter klagt einen Lagerkommandanten an, der die Gefangenen besonders brutal und sadistisch behandelte (5). In Dachau nahmen einige befreite Gefangene an ihren SS-Wachen selbst Rache: Soldaten der 42. US-Division holen eine Leiche aus dem Lagergraben (6).

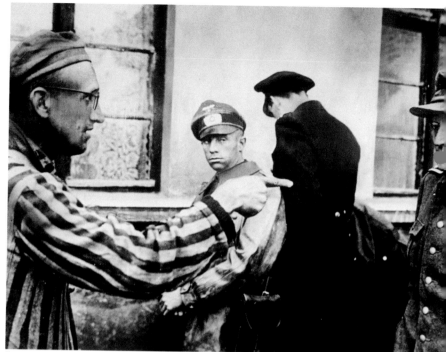

5

LES Alliés et le gouvernement ouest-allemand cherchèrent ensuite à promouvoir un programme de « rééducation » qui impliquait la reconnaissance de la réalité des faits. Il débuta à Buchenwald, en avril 1945, qu'on fit visiter aux populations des alentours pour leur faire reconnaître ce que tant de gens avaient auparavant refusé de voir. Certains détournent les yeux devant le corps qui se balance (1) et le camion où s'empilent les cadavres nus et émaciés (2). La visite se termine devant les fours dont les habitants de la ville de Weimar avaient dû chaque jour apercevoir les fumées (3). Un rapport de l'époque note : « Beaucoup des personnes présentes quittent le camp en larmes. D'autres semblent indifférentes, affirmant subir la propagande des Alliés. »

Un petit nombre de détenus, les plus vigoureux parmi ceux qui furent amenés de toute l'Europe dans les camps de travaux forcés, survécurent aux rations minimales et aux journées de travail de douze à dix-huit heures. Une « enfant des camps », tchèque âgée de onze ans, retrouve sa mère à Kaunitz en 1945 (4). Un prisonnier signale la présence d'un commandant de camp allemand, réputé pour sa brutalité sadique (5). À Dachau, des prisonniers libérés, ivres de revanche, s'en prennent à leurs gardes SS : des soldats de la 42ᵉ division américaine repêchent un cadavre dans les douves entourant le camp (6).

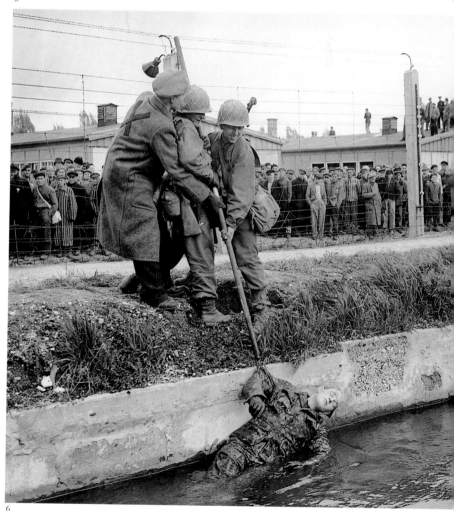

6

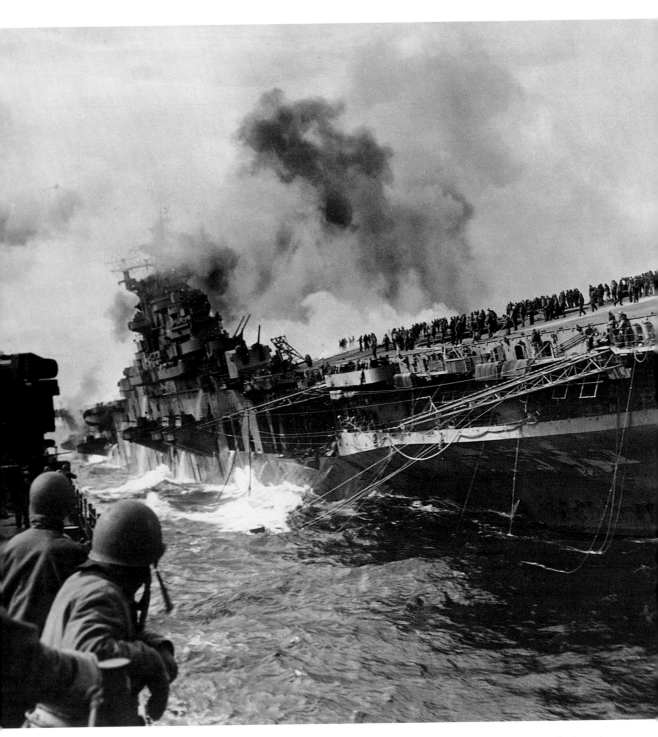

IN the war at sea, the US Navy suffered in the western Pacific. In December 1944, a wounded US soldier under the auspices of a surgical nurse, his arms raised in agony at the bullet wound to his stomach, lies near the baptismal font of Leyte Cathedral in the Philippines (2). The cathedral alternated as hospital and place of worship. And on 17 May 1945,

the cruiser *Santa Fé* pulls away from the burning carrier USS *Franklin*, victim of a Japanese dive-bombing attack (1). Retreating from the flames of exploding bombs and rockets, the ship's crew cluster on the flight deck. Despite a thousand casualties, the *Franklin* eventually limped thousands of miles home to the Brooklyn Navy Yard.

DIE US-Navy erlitt ihre schwersten Verluste im Westpazifik. Im Dezember 1944 hält eine Krankenschwester in der Kathedrale von Leyte auf den Philippinen Wache bei einem verwundeten Soldaten; er liegt am Taufbecken und wirft wegen der Schmerzen seiner Bauchwunde die Arme in die Luft (2). Die Kathedrale wird für Gottesdienste und gleichzeitig als Lazarett genutzt. Und am 17. Mai 1945 legt der

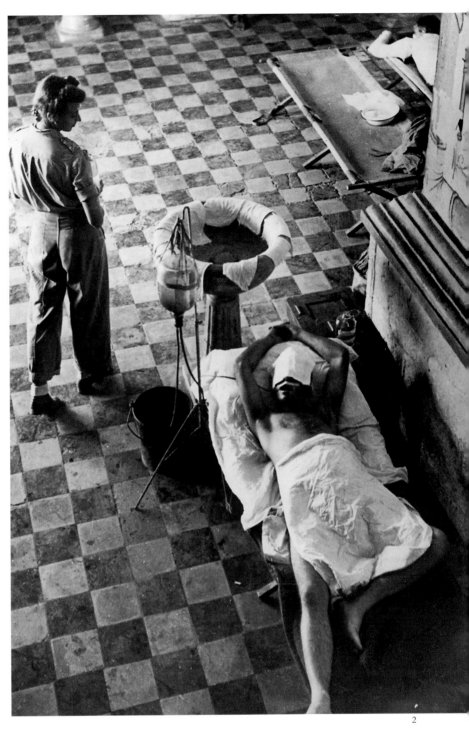

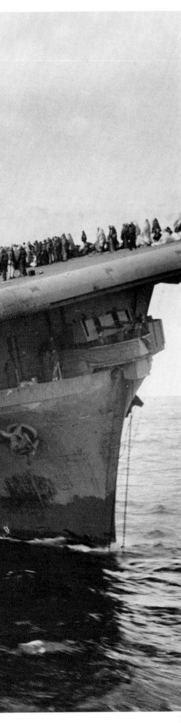

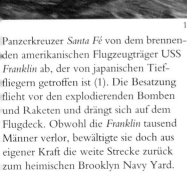

Panzerkreuzer *Santa Fé* von dem brennenden amerikanischen Flugzeugträger USS *Franklin* ab, der von japanischen Tieffliegern getroffen ist (1). Die Besatzung flieht vor den explodierenden Bomben und Raketen und drängt sich auf dem Flugdeck. Obwohl die *Franklin* tausend Männer verlor, bewältigte sie doch aus eigener Kraft die weite Strecke zurück zum heimischen Brooklyn Navy Yard.

A U cours de la guerre navale, la flotte des États-Unis essuya des pertes dans l'Ouest du Pacifique. Décembre 1944 : un soldat américain blessé est pris en charge par une infirmière de l'équipe chirurgicale ; touché au ventre par une balle, il souffre allongé près des fonts baptismaux de la cathédrale de Leyte aux Philippines (2). La cathédrale sert tour à tour d'hôpital et de lieu de culte. 17 mai 1945 : le croiseur

Santa Fé s'éloigne du navire de transport américain en flammes, le USS *Franklin*, atteint par les bombardements japonais (1). Battant en retraite devant les incendies provoqués par les explosions, l'équipage du navire s'est rassemblé sur le pont d'envol. Malgré la perte de mille de ses hommes, le *Franklin* parvint à rentrer tant bien que mal, couvrant les milliers de milles qui le séparaient du centre naval de Brooklyn.

JAPANESE kamikaze pilots were famous for their
resolve during the Pacific War. While European
officers had their cyanide pills to take if captured,
Japanese pilots volunteered to fly suicide missions and
blow themselves up with their bombers. Here one is
helped on with his scarf bearing the Emperor's 'golden
sun' (1); another attempts to manoeuvre his 'Zeke' on to
the deck of a US warship (2). In the event he crashed
into the sea (4), but a neighbouring hospital ship, the
USS *Comfort*, was hit; 29 were killed and 33 injured.
Luck was allied with the skill of this American pilot,
Ensign R. Black: shot up over Palau, he managed to land
on an aircraft carrier with his hydraulic system gone and
one wing and part of the tailplane shorn off (3).

DIE japanischen Kamikazeflieger waren im Pazifik-
krieg berühmt für ihren Mut. Europäische Offiziere
hatten ihre Zyanidkapseln, für den Fall, daß sie in
Gefangenschaft gerieten, doch die japanischen Piloten
meldeten sich freiwillig für Selbstmordflüge. Hier wird
einem der Schal umgebunden, den die »goldene Sonne«
des Kaisers ziert (1); ein anderer versucht, seine »Zeke«
auf dem Deck eines amerikanischen Schlachtschiffs

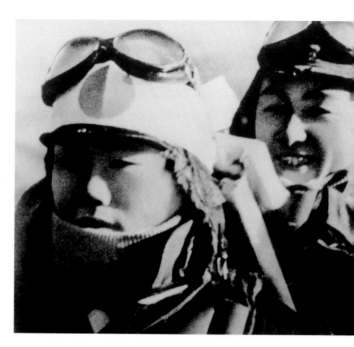

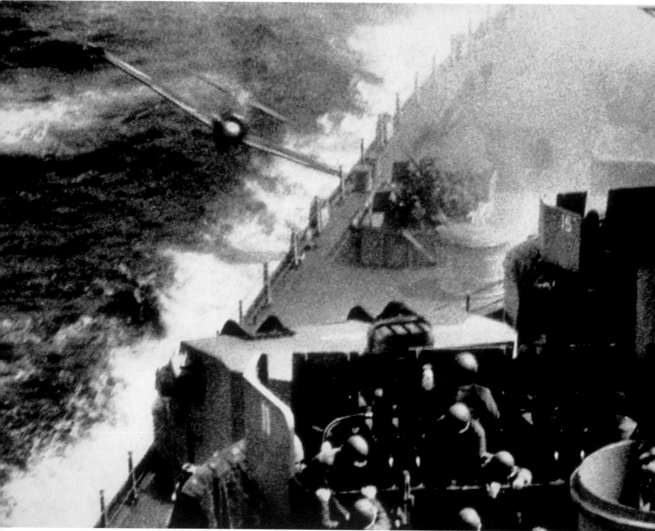

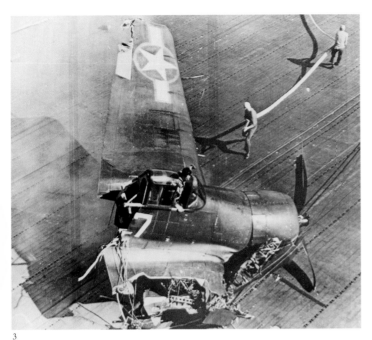

abzusetzen (2). Dieser verfehlte sein Ziel und stürzte ins Meer (4), doch ein benachbartes Hospitalschiff, die USS *Comfort*, wurde getroffen; es gab 29 Tote und 33 Verwundete. Glück im Unglück und viel Geschick hatte der amerikanische Flieger Ensign R. Black: Er wurde über Palau getroffen, und es gelang ihm, mit nur einer Tragfläche auf einem Flugzeugträger zu landen (3).

L ES kamikazes japonais se rendirent célèbres par leur résolution durant la guerre du Pacifique. Tandis que les officiers européens avalaient du cyanure en cas d'interception, les pilotes japonais se portaient volontaires lors des missions suicides à l'aide de leurs avions chargés d'explosifs. On voit ici l'un d'eux se faire nouer son foulard surmonté du « soleil d'or » impérial (1). Un autre tente d'amener son « zeke » sur le pont d'un navire de guerre américain (2). Ce faisant il s'écrase en mer (4), touchant toutefois un navire-hôpital de la marine des États-Unis, le *Comfort* : il y eut 29 morts et 33 blessés. Ce pilote américain réussit à poser son appareil touché au-dessus de Palau sur un navire porte-avions, alors qu'il n'avait plus de système hydraulique, qu'une aile et une partie de la queue de l'avion (3).

3

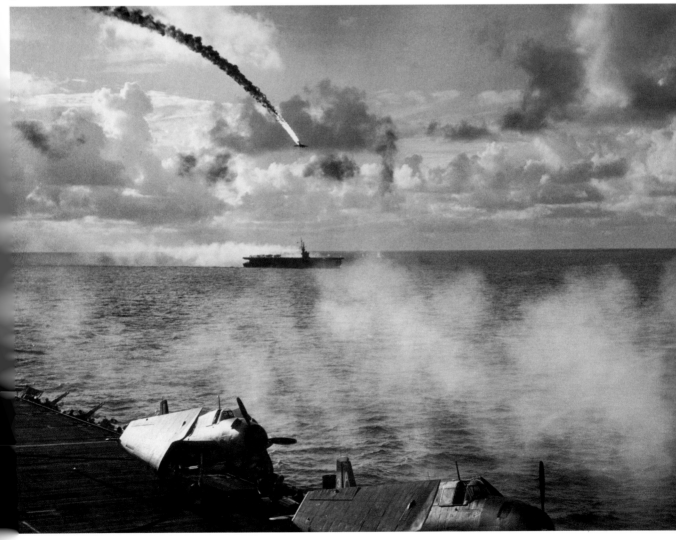

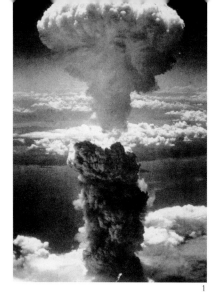

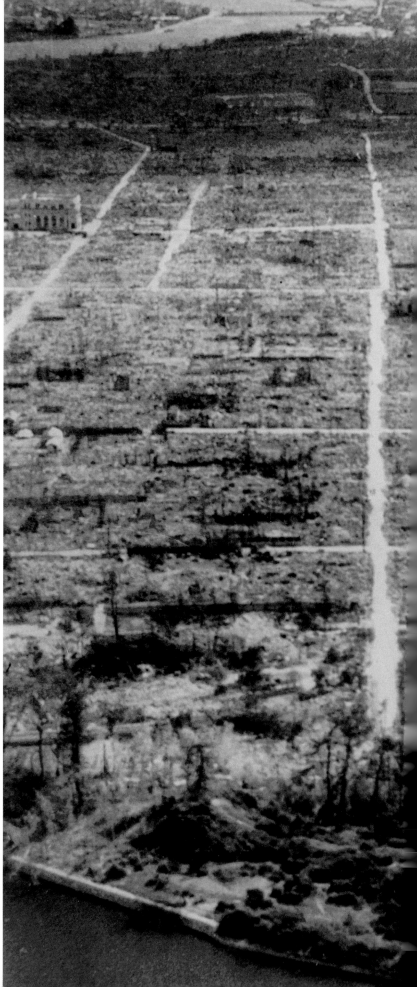

O N 6 August 1945 a first atomic bomb
was unleashed on Hiroshima (2). On
9 August a second landed on Nagasaki (1).
The former killed 100,000 outright; another
100,000 were to die in the ensuing months
from burns and radiation sickness. The latter
killed 75,000 outright. On 10 August, Japan
sued for peace – two days after Russia
had joined the war against her old enemy.
On 14 August President Truman formally
declared the end of the Second World War,
in which 55 million people died.

A M 6. August 1945 ging die erste Atombombe der Welt auf Hiroshima nieder
(2). Am 9. August traf eine zweite Nagasaki
(1). In Hiroshima fanden 100 000 Menschen
sofort den Tod; weitere 100 000 sollten an
den Folgen der Verbrennungen und an
Strahlenschäden sterben. Der zweite Abwurf
forderte 75 000 unmittelbare Opfer. Am
10. August kapitulierte Japan – zwei Tage
nachdem Rußland in den Krieg gegen
seinen alten Feind eingetreten war. Am
14. August verkündete der amerikanische
Präsident Truman offiziell das Ende des
Zweiten Weltkriegs, in dem mehr als
55 Millionen Menschen ihr Leben verloren
hatten.

L E 6 août 1945, une première bombe
atomique fut lâchée sur Hiroshima (2).
Le 9 août, une seconde tomba sur Nagasaki
(1). La première tua instantanément
100 000 personnes, tandis que 100 000 autres
devaient mourir dans les mois qui suivirent
consèquemment aux brûlures et aux radia-
tions. La seconde tua 75 000 personnes
sur le coup. Le 10 août, le Japon abdiquait –
deux jours après que l'URSS lui eut déclaré
la guerre. Le 14 août, le président Truman
annonçait officiellement la fin de la Seconde
Guerre mondiale qui avait coûté la mort à
55 millions de personnes.

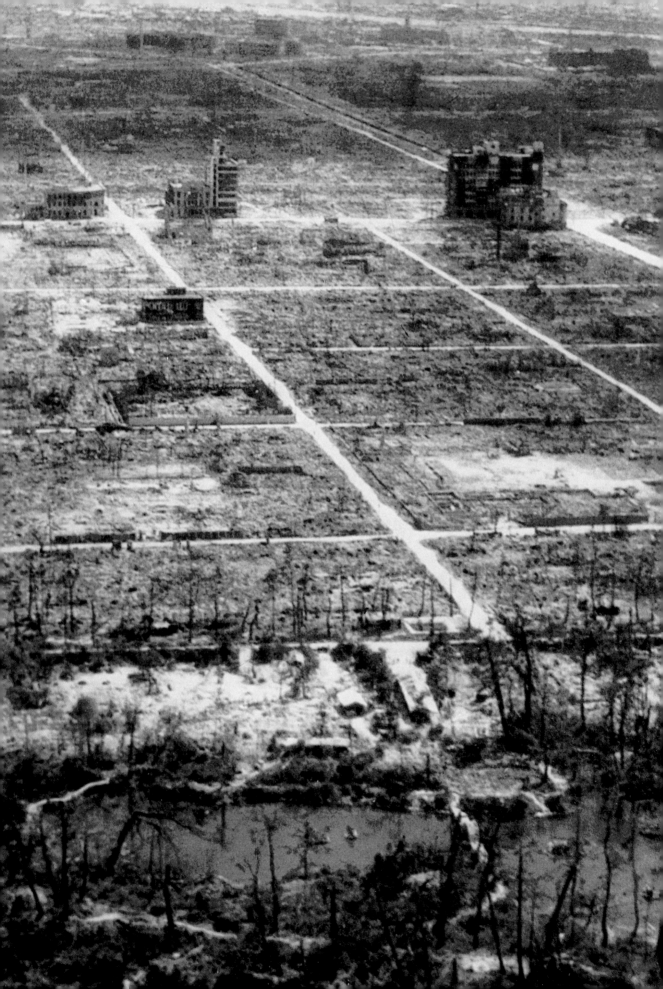

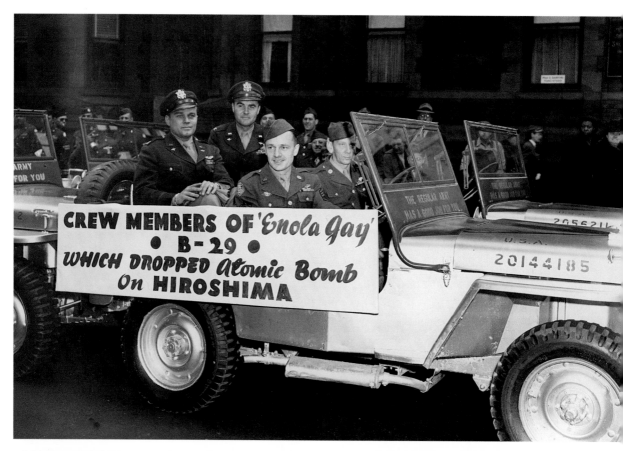

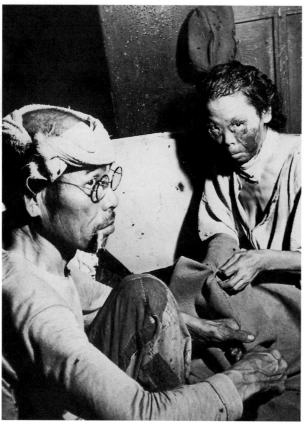

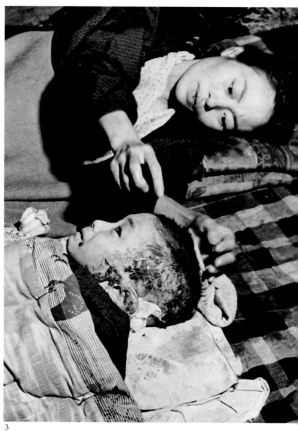

2   3

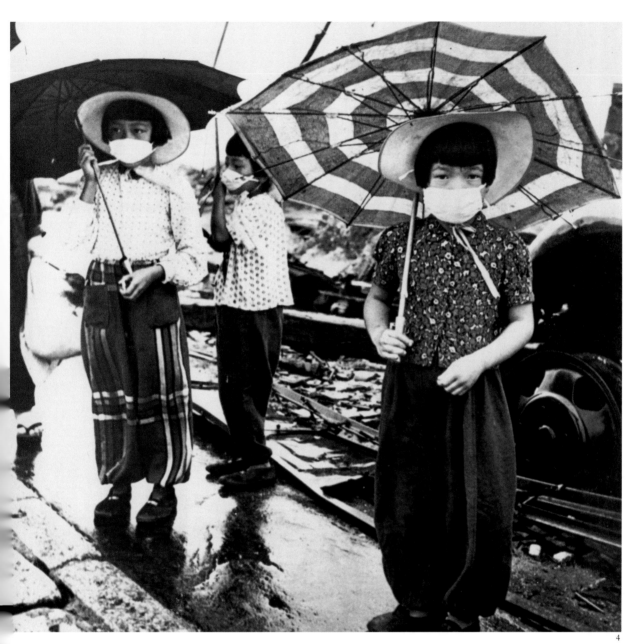

4

DESPITE the devastation wrought on a civilian population, the bomber crew responsible returned home to a tickertape heroes' welcome at New York's Army Day parade (1). Their jeep boasted of their mission and advertised that 'The Regular Army has a Good Job for you'. In Hiroshima, civilian victims were effectively left to care for themselves in a damaged bank near the blasted town centre (2), where burns and injuries were treated by parents substituting for medical staff (3). Those who survived relatively unscathed wore wartime issue long bloomers and masks against the stench of death within their ruined city (4).

TROTZ der verheerenden Auswirkung auf die Zivilbevölkerung wurde der Bombercrew bei der Militärparade in New York ein rauschender Empfang bereitet (1). Auf ihrem Jeep war ihr Auftrag groß zu lesen, und der Werbespruch lautet: »Die Army hat immer einen guten Job für Dich.« In Hiroshima waren die verwundeten Opfer praktisch sich selbst überlassen; in einem halb eingestürzten Bankgebäude der in Trümmern liegenden Innenstadt (2) richteten sie ein Hospital ein, und Eltern statt Sanitäter kümmerten sich um die Verletzungen ihrer Kinder (3). Diejenigen, die vergleichsweise ungeschoren davonkamen, banden sich Masken um gegen den Todesgeruch in ihrer zerstörten Stadt (4).

MALGRÉ les dévastations infligées aux populations civiles, les équipages des bombardiers furent acclamés à New York à l'occasion de la journée de l'Armée (1). Leurs jeeps portaient des inscriptions vantant leur exploit et prévenait que « dans l'armée de métier vous attend un emploi intéressant ». À Hiroshima, les victimes civiles sont abandonnées à leur sort dans une banque du centre ville dévasté par le souffle de l'explosion (2). Leurs brûlures et leurs blessures sont soignées par des parents, à défaut de personnel médical (3). Ceux qui s'en sortirent portaient les longues culottes bouffantes et les masques distribués pendant la guerre afin de se prémunir contre la puanteur des cadavres (4).

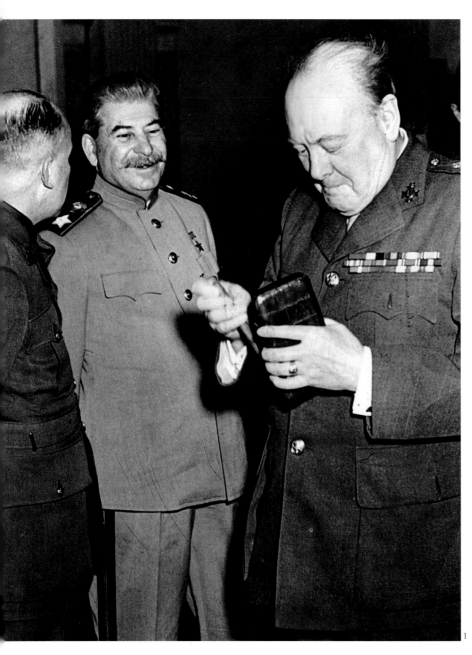

IM Februar 1945 fand im Livadia-Palast in Jalta auf der Krim die Dreimächte-Konferenz zwischen Premierminister Churchill, Präsident Roosevelt und Marschall Stalin statt (2). Roosevelt rang Stalin die Zusage ab, in den Krieg gegen Japan einzutreten und die Gründung der Vereinten Nationen zu unterstützen. Churchill, hier mit Stalin und Zigarren (1), erhielt die russische Unterschrift auf dem Vertrag, der die Teilung Deutschlands in französische, britische, russische und amerikanische Besatzungszonen vorsah. Als Gegenleistung bekam Stalin eine neu festgelegte russisch-polnische Grenze mit polnischer Westgrenze entlang der Oder-Neiße-Linie. Zwar wurde in einer »Erklärung zum befreiten Europa« der Wunsch der drei Staatsmänner nach »freien Wahlen« und »demokratischen Institutionen« in den von Deutschland besetzten Ländern bekräftigt, doch die Vereinbarungen von Jalta erfuhren bittere Kritik auf beiden Seiten. Westliche Kommentatoren beschuldigten Roosevelt, er habe »Rußland das Tor zum Fernen Osten geöffnet« und überlasse Stalin Osteuropa, und in England war die Empörung groß, daß Churchill die kosakischen Soldaten verraten habe, die zurück in die UdSSR verbracht wurden, wo der sichere Tod auf sie wartete. Doch die sowjetisch-amerikanischen Beziehungen waren nie herzlicher als damals in Jalta.

1

THE three-power conference held at Livadia Palace, Yalta, in the Crimea, in February 1945, between Prime Minister Churchill, President Roosevelt and Marshal Stalin (2). Roosevelt succeeded in obtaining Stalin's agreement to enter the war against Japan and to cooperate in the founding of the United Nations Organization. Churchill, here with Stalin and cigars (1), further obtained Stalin's signature to the partition of Germany into French, British, Russian and US-controlled zones. Stalin, in return, achieved recognition of a redrawn Russian-Polish border and a western frontier on the Oder-Neisse Line. Despite a 'Declaration on Liberated Europe', affirming the three leaders' desire for 'free elections' and 'democratic institutions' in lands previously controlled by Germany, the Yalta accords were bitterly criticized on both sides. Western commentators accused Roosevelt of 'bringing Russia into the Far East' and 'handing eastern Europe over to Stalin', whilst Britain's part in betraying the Cossack soldiers, forcibly returned to their death in the USSR, caused a row which still resonates. Soviet-US relations were, however, never more cordial than here.

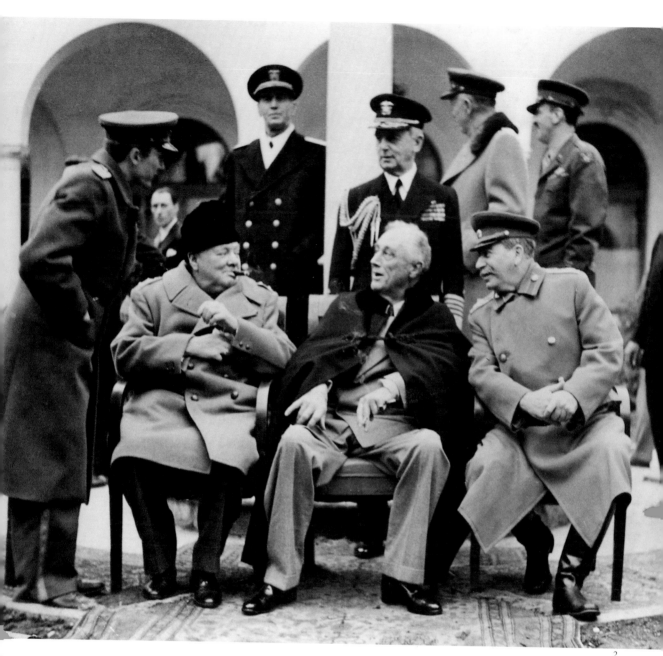

2

LA conférence des trois grandes puissances se déroula au palais de Livadia, à Yalta, en Crimée, dès février 1945. Elle réunit le Premier ministre Churchill, le président Roosevelt et le maréchal Staline (2). Roosevelt obtint de Staline que celui rentrât en guerre contre le Japon et coopérât à la fondation de l'Organisation des Nations Unies. Churchill que l'on voit ici, cigare à la main, en compagnie de Staline (1), obtint en plus de ce dernier qu'il validât la division de l'Allemagne en zones contrôlées par les Français, les Britanniques, les Soviétiques et les Américains. En contrepartie, Staline fit reconnaître le nouveau tracé des frontières séparant l'URSS et la Pologne ainsi que la frontière occidentale de la ligne Oder-Neisse. Malgré une « Déclaration sur l'Europe libérée », formulant le souhait des trois dirigeants de voir s'instaurer des « élections libres » et des « institutions démocratiques » dans les pays auparavant sous domination allemande, les accords de Yalta furent amèrement critiqués de part et d'autre. Les observateurs occidentaux accusèrent Roosevelt d'avoir « ouvert à la Russie la porte de l'Extrême-Orient » et d'avoir « cédé l'Europe orientale à Staline ». La Grande-Bretagne, quant à elle, en trahissant les soldats cosaques qui furent renvoyés de force en URSS où les attendait une mort certaine, provoqua une vive émotion. Les relations soviéto-américaines, toutefois, ne furent jamais plus cordiales qu'à ce moment-là.

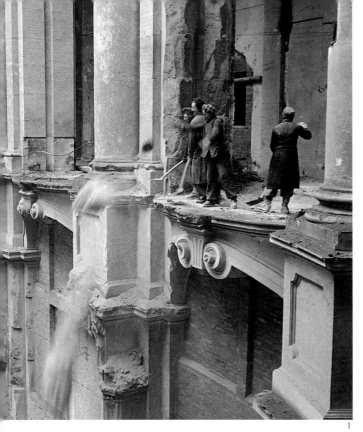
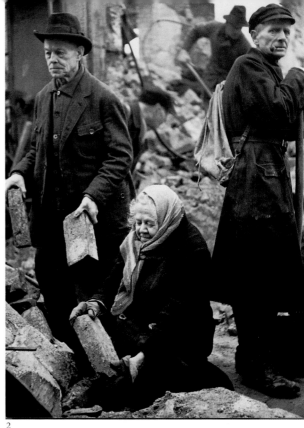

1   2

ON 14 February 1945, the RAF and
USAF started a day and a half of
relentless bombardment that reduced the
German city of Dresden to a smoking ruin.
It remained impossible to ascertain how
many civilians died, since the population
had already doubled to over a million
seeking a 'safe haven'. Estimates of the
death toll swung from 130,000 to 400,000.
In addition to this colossal human cost,
Dresden had been compared to Florence
for its wealth of Baroque and Rococo art
and architecture, its galleries of Dutch and
Flemish paintings. Senior Allied military
officers were tight-lipped about the
diversion of effort away from German
centres of communication and oil
installations to predominantly civilian and
symbolic targets. The Chief of RAF
Bomber Command, Air Marshal Arthur
Harris, vehemently persisted in his
controversial theory that terror bombing
was the way to destroy the enemy's will to
fight. A year later, these Dresden survivors
are still struggling to rebuild their city via
a 'human brick chain' (2) while a women's
squad starts the first stages of rehabilitating
the Zwinger Palace (1). Meanwhile in
Berlin's ruined Nollendorfplatz, a Russian-
language sign and a knocked-out German
tank speak volumes of the city's recent
history, in the wake of which these citizens
are still searching for a home among the
desolation (3).

AM 14. Februar 1945 begannen die
Royal Air Force und die US Air Force
mit einem anderthalbtägigen Bombardement, das die Stadt Dresden in Schutt und
Asche legte. Die Zahl der toten Zivilisten
ließ sich nie genau bestimmen, denn die
Bevölkerung hatte sich durch den Zustrom
von Flüchtlingen auf der Suche nach einem
»sicheren Hafen« auf über eine Million
verdoppelt. Schätzungen variierten zwischen
130 000 und 400 000 Opfern. Es wurde eine
Stadt zerstört, die wegen ihres Reichtums
an Kunst und Architektur als »Florenz des
Nordens« galt. Die Alliierten hüllten sich in
Schweigen, wenn gefragt wurde, warum
sie statt Verkehrsknotenpunkten und petro-
chemischen Einrichtungen nun zivile und
letzten Endes symbolische Ziele bombardierten. Der Chef der britischen Luftwaffe,
General Arthur Harris, verteidigte vehement
seine umstrittene Ansicht, daß Bombardements den Willen der Zivilbevölkerung
brechen. Ein Jahr später versuchen diese
Überlebenden von Dresden noch immer,
ihre Stadt mit einer »menschlichen Back-
steinkette« wiederaufzubauen (2), und ein
Frauentrupp unternimmt erste Anstrengun-
gen, den Zwinger wieder instand zu setzen
(1). Am Nollendorfplatz in Berlin sprechen
derweil russische Hinweisschilder und ein
zerschossener deutscher Panzer Bände über
die jüngste Vergangenheit der Stadt.
Heimatlos gewordene Berliner suchen
zwischen den Trümmern nach einer neuen
Bleibe (3).

LE 14 février 1945, les forces aériennes
britannique et américaine entreprirent
de bombarder sans répit un jour et demi
durant la ville de Dresde, en Allemagne.
Il fut impossible d'établir le nombre des
civils disparus, car la population, grossie
des centaines de milliers de personnes qui
cherchaient à « se mettre à l'abri », comptait
plus d'un million d'habitants. Les estimations oscillaient entre 130 000 et 400 000.
Jadis, on comparait Dresde à Florence pour
ses richesses artistiques. La hiérarchie militaire des troupes alliées se montrait avare de
commentaires sur le fait que son effort
portait moins sur les centres de communications ou les installations pétrochimiques
allemandes que sur les objectifs civils et
symboliques. Le chef de l'aviation britannique, le général Arthur Harris, s'en tenait
énergiquement à sa théorie discutable selon
laquelle la terreur provoquée par les
bombardements brisait la combativité de
l'ennemi. Un an plus tard, ces survivants de
Dresde luttent toujours pour reconstruire
leur ville, recourant à une « chaîne humaine
de briques » (2), et des femmes entrepren-
nent de réhabiliter le palais Zwinger (1).
Ailleurs, dans les ruines de la Nollendorfplatz à Berlin, les panneaux en langue russe
et le char d'assaut allemand mis hors de
combat expliquent à eux seuls que ces
citoyens sont toujours à la recherche d'un
refuge (3).

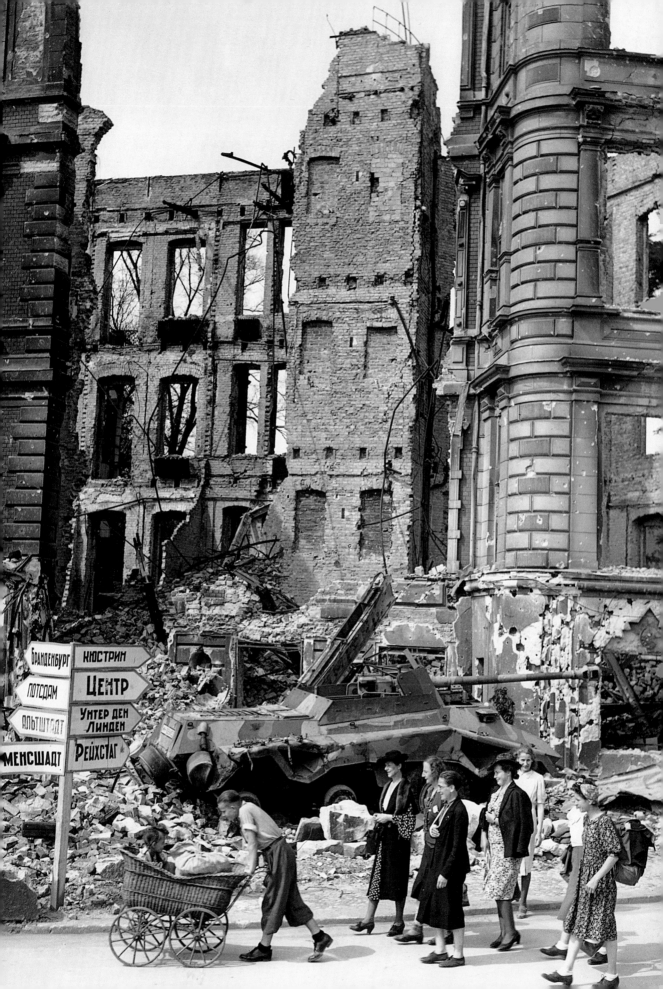

Postwar World

ONLY when the fighting stopped in Europe was it possible to see just what damage had been done – some 13 million dead, and the lives of millions more shattered. Across the continent, from France to the Soviet Union, were huddled bewildered masses of people – in POW camps, in newly liberated concentration camps, in defeated armies, among groups of orphaned children, in makeshift hospitals, and on the now silent battlefields. With the mixture of hope and instinct that marks the human race, these millions now began the long march back – begging, stealing, working casually for a meal or a night's lodging, searching for old friends and relatives, and wondering what they would find when they eventually arrived home.

There were organizations to help them. The United Nations was born in San Francisco on 26 July 1945. 'Oh, what a great day this can be in history,' declared President Truman, and over the next few years there were many whose lives were saved and whose hopes were kept alive by UN agencies. Departments and committees were created to care for refugees and children, and to implement the most ambitious programmes in the world's history to fight disease, poverty and hunger.

Some sought a new life in a new land. Many Jews turned their backs on the continent that had treated them so shamefully, and found their clandestine way to the embryonic new state of Israel. Muslims and Hindus in India clamoured and fought for partition and independence. To Churchill's horror, the new Labour Government in Britain consented, ordering the Raj to pack its bags and depart in August 1947. In China, at last free from Japanese occupation, Mao and his marchers completed their Long March and the Communists took over. The Communists, in the form of the Soviet Empire, also took over in Eastern Europe, but were seen by the West as not so much a liberating force but more a new army of occupation.

Cities were rebuilt. Rubble was cleared away. Cars instead of tanks began to roll off the production lines of Europe. Delicacies returned to the palettes of Europe – bananas, oranges, chocolate. Petrol was available – in limited supplies – for pleasure trips. 'Austerity' and 'Utility' labels disappeared from clothes and items of furniture. Rationing remained, but those with a bit of money could always get whatever they wanted from their friendly, neighbourhood black marketeer (1).

ERST nachdem die Kämpfe in Europa aufgehört hatten, kam das tatsächliche Ausmaß der Schäden zutage: über 13 Millionen Tote und das Leben von weiteren Millionen von Menschen zerstört. Quer über den Kontinent, von Frankreich bis zur Sowjetunion, gab es verwirrte zusammengepferchte Menschenmassen – in Kriegsgefangenen- und seit kurzem befreiten Konzentrationslagern, in besiegten Armeezügen, in Gruppen verwaister Kinder, in Behelfskrankenhäusern sowie auf den nun schweigenden Schlachtfeldern. Getrieben von einer Mischung aus Hoffnung und dem Menschen ureigenen Instinkt machten sich Millionen von Menschen auf den langen Weg nach Hause – sie bettelten, stahlen und arbeiteten für ein Stück Brot oder eine Übernachtung; sie suchten nach Verwandten und alten Freunden und bangten, was sie wohl antreffen würden, wenn sie endlich nach Hause kamen.

Es gab Hilfsorganisationen: Die Vereinten Nationen wurden am 26. Juli 1945 aus der Taufe gehoben. »Was für ein großer Tag in der Geschichte kann dies werden!«, erklärte Präsident Truman, und im Laufe der folgenden Jahre konnte das Leben vieler Menschen, die die Hoffnung nicht aufgegeben hatten, gerettet werden – dank der Hilfsorganisationen der Vereinten Nationen. Abteilungen und Komitees für Flüchtlinge und Kinder wurden gegründet und damit das wohl ambitionierteste Programm zur Bekämpfung von Armut, Hunger und Epidemien ins Leben gerufen.

Manche suchten ein neues Leben in einem neuen Land. Viele Juden kehrten dem Kontinent, der sie so unmenschlich behandelt hatte, den Rücken und fanden heimliche Wege in den Staat, der noch nicht geboren war – Israel. Moslems und Hindus verlangten lautstark nach der Teilung und kämpften für die Unabhängigkeit ihrer Gebiete. Zum Entsetzen Churchills gab die neue Labourregierung in Großbritannien nach und rief den Raj auf, seine Sachen zu packen und im August 1947 das ehemalige Britisch-Indien zu verlassen. In China wo endlich die japanische Besatzung endete, machten sich Mao und seine Genossen auf den Langen Marsch - und bald übernahmen die Kommunisten hier die Macht Kommunisten – in Gestalt des sowjetischen Imperiums - übernahmen auch die Macht in Osteuropa. In der Augen des Westens waren sie jedoch weniger eine Befreiungs- als vielmehr eine neue Besatzungsmacht.

Städte wurden wiederaufgebaut, Trümmer beiseit geräumt. Autos – statt Panzer – verließen die Fließ

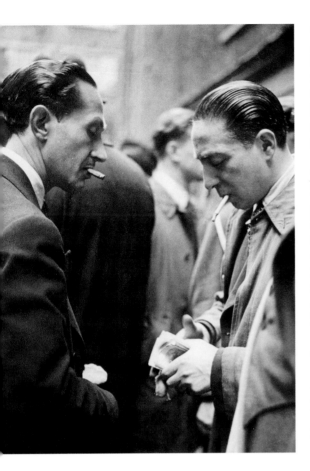

ainsi que sur les champs de bataille maintenant muets. Animés par un mélange d'espoir et de cet instinct intrinsèque à l'homme, des millions de personnes reprirent la route vers leur foyer – mendiant, volant et travaillant pour un morceau de pain ou une nuit à l'abri ; à la recherche de parents et de vieux amis, mais craignant ce qu'elles allaient sans doute découvrir en arrivant enfin chez elles.

Mais il y avait des organisations humanitaires ; le 26 juillet 1945, les Nations unies sont portées sur les fonts baptismaux. « Quelle grande journée de l'histoire cela peut devenir ! », déclara le président Truman et, durant les années qui suivirent, cela permit de sauver la vie de nombreuses personnes qui n'avaient pas perdu tout espoir – grâce aux organisations humanitaires des Nations unies. Des départements et comités pour réfugiés et enfants furent créés, donnant ainsi naissance au programme sans aucun doute le plus ambitieux de lutte contre la pauvreté, la famine et les épidémies.

Beaucoup cherchèrent une nouvelle vie dans un nouveau pays. Beaucoup de juifs tournèrent le dos au continent qui les avait traités de façon si inhumaine et se rendirent par voies clandestines dans l'État qui n'était pas encore né – Israël. Musulmans et Hindous exigèrent à corps et à cri la partition et se battirent pour l'indépendance de leurs territoires. Pour la plus grande fureur de Churchill, le nouveau gouvernement travailliste au pouvoir en Grande-Bretagne céda et ordonna au Raj d'emballer ses affaires et de quitter, en août 1947, l'ancienne Inde britannique. En Chine, où l'occupation japonaise s'était enfin terminée, Mao et ses camarades entamèrent leur Longue Marche et, bientôt, les communistes prirent le pouvoir dans ce pays. Les communistes – sous la forme de l'empire soviétique – prirent aussi le pouvoir en Europe de l'Est. Mais, au yeux de l'Ouest, ils étaient cependant moins une puissance de libération que, bien au contraire, une nouvelle puissance d'occupation.

Les villes seront reconstruites, les ruines, déblayées. Des voitures – et non plus des blindés – sortent alors des chaînes des usines de la nouvelle Europe. Et les produits exotiques font bientôt leur réapparition sur les tables d'Europe – bananes, oranges, chocolat. Bientôt, l'essence est aussi disponible – quoique en quantité encore limitée – et l'on peut de nouveau partir se promener en voiture. Les étiquettes comme « modèle économique » ou « d'occasion » apposées sur les vêtements ou les meubles disparaissent ; certes, les tickets de rationnement restent en vigueur, mais, à condition d'avoir suffisamment d'argent, on peut s'acheter tout ce que l'on désire grâce à ses aimables voisins qui s'adonnent au marché noir (1).

änder im neuen Europa. Und Delikatessen kehrten auf ie Tische Europas zurück – Bananen, Orangen, Schoko-de. Bald war Benzin – wenn auch in begrenztem Jmfang – verfügbar, und damit wurden Spritztouren nd Vergnügungsfahrten möglich. Etikettierungen auf Ĺeidungs- oder Möbelstücken wie »Sparmodell« oder gebraucht« verschwanden; zwar blieben Rationie-ıngsmaßnahmen noch aufrechterhalten, doch wer enügend Geld besaß, der konnte sich, was immer er ∵ünschte, über den freundlichen Schwarzmarkthändler ı seiner Nachbarschaft besorgen (1).

L aura fallu attendre la fin des combats en Europe pour constater quels dommages la guerre avait causés – uelque 13 millions de morts et une vie détruite pour es millions et des millions d'hommes et de femmes. À ravers tout le continent, de la France à l'Union oviétique, des masses d'êtres humains encore dans le ésarroi errent sans but – attendant dans des camps de risonniers, dans les camps de concentration libérés epuis peu, dans les files de soldats de l'armée battue, les roupes d'enfants orphelins, les hôpitaux de fortune

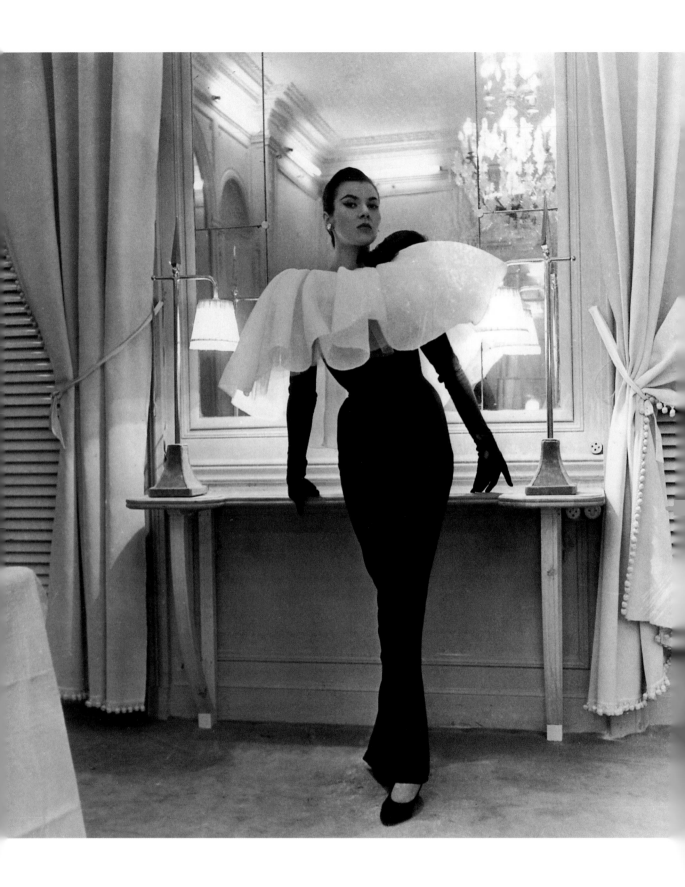

THE 1950s seemed to want to prove
that the years of austerity were forever
behind us. In Britain, Macmillan was
telling the population they had 'never had
it so good', while in Germany Adenauer
promoted economic expansion through
the 'rebuilding' generation. Lashings
of fabric and trimmings spared neither
expense nor fuss – with a certain tongue-
in-cheek mockery in the labels: Jacques
Fath's 'lampshade look' (1) – a bell shape
here (2), a pie frill there.

IN den Fünfzigern wollte offenbar jeder
beweisen, daß die entbehrungsreichen
Jahre für immer vorbei waren. Den Briten
verkündete Macmillan, daß sie es »noch
nie so gut hatten«, und in Deutschland
spornte Adenauer zum Wiederaufbau an.
Bei der Mode wurde an Stoff und Zierat
und damit an den Kosten nicht gespart –
doch immerhin spricht aus den Bezeich-
nungen ein gewisser Humor: Jacques Faths
»Lampenschirm-Look« (1), hier mit
einer Glockenform (2), dort mit einem
Rüschenkragen.

DANS les années 50, on semblait vouloir
prouver que l'époque de l'austérité
était à jamais révolue. En Grande-Bretagne,
Macmillan disait à la population que « ses
conditions n'avaient jamais été aussi bonnes
qu'aujourd'hui », pendant qu' en Allemagne
Adenauer encourageait l'expansion économique portée par la génération de la
« reconstruction ». On n'épargnait ni argent
ni strass dans des modèles où l'abondance
de tissu ne le cédait qu'à celle de l'ornemen-
tation, et auxquels étaient donnés, non sans
un certain humour pince-sans-rire, des
noms de baptême tels que : « Style abat-jour »
(1) de Jacques Fath – ici une forme de
cloche (2), là des fronces.

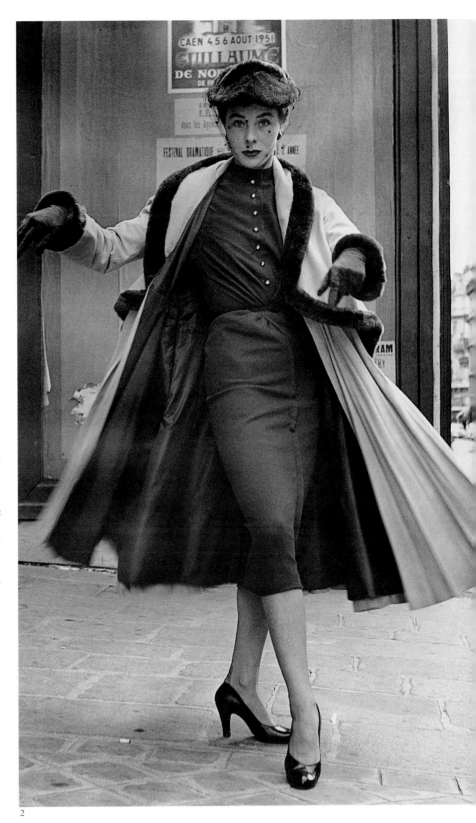

2

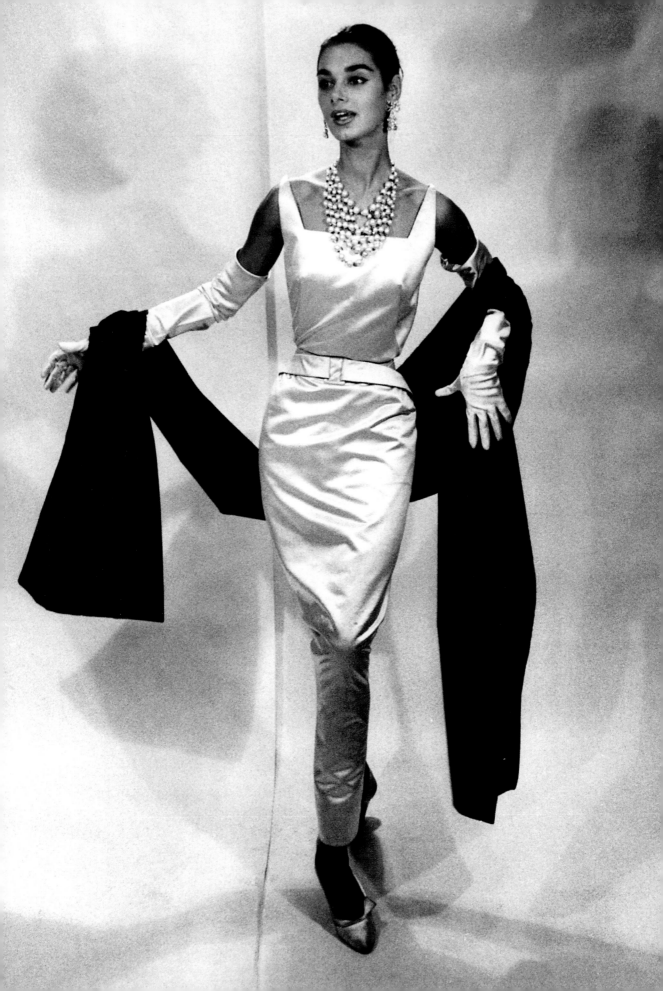

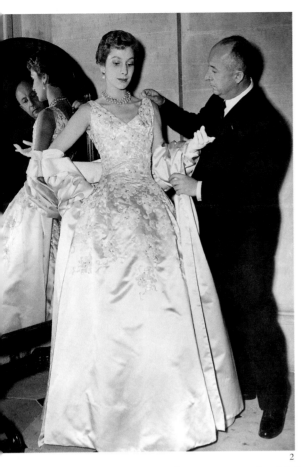
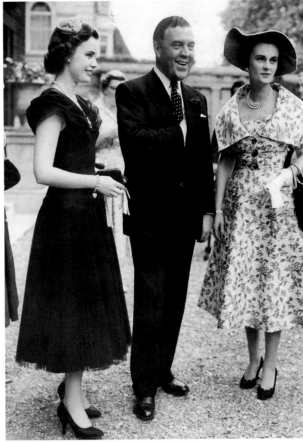

2 3

THE English aristocracy were assumed even by French couturiers to have a certain *je ne sais quoi*. Dior paid his homage to Churchill with *Blenheim*, a wide white satin gown embroidered with flowers (2). Givenchy, a new boy to Paris fashion in 1955, came to Park Lane's grand new Dorchester Hotel to display his 'dazzling white satin dinner dress, slit from calf to ankle, and worn with a crimson velvet stole and pearl and rhinestone bib necklace' (1). And Margaret, Duchess of Argyll (notorious for the slant she gave a favourite good health maxim – 'Go to bed early and often'), here keeps sedate company with her daughter and Norman Hartnell, the Queen's couturier (3).

SELBST französische Couturiers waren überzeugt, daß die englische Aristokratie ein gewisses *je ne sais quoi* hatte. Dior erwies Churchill seine Reverenz, indem er dieses weite, weiße, blumenbestickte Satinkleid *Blenheim* nannte (2). Givenchy, 1955 noch ein junger Spund in der Pariser Modewelt, kam nach London und stellte im exklusiven neuen Dorchester-Hotel in der Park Lane sein »blendend weißes Abendkleid aus Satin« vor, »geschlitzt von der Wade bis zum Knöchel, getragen mit karminroter Samtstola und Kollier aus Perlen und Straß« (1). Und Margaret, die Herzogin von Argyll (berühmt für die neue Wendung, die sie einer altehrwürdigen Gesundheitsregel gab – »Man sollte früh und oft ins Bett gehen«) wird wohlweislich von ihrer Tochter und dem Hofschneider der Königin, Norman Hartnell, begleitet (3).

MÊME les couturiers français prêtaient à l'aristocratie anglaise un certain je ne sais quoi. Dior présenta ses hommages à Churchill avec *Blenheim*, une robe ample de satin blanc brodée de fleurs (2). Givenchy, qui faisait en 1955 figure de nouvel arrivant sur la scène de la mode parisienne, vint montrer dans le nouvel et magnifique hôtel Dorchester, à Park Lane, son « époustouflante robe de dîner de satin blanc, fendue du mollet à la cheville, portée avec une étole de velours cramoisi et un pectoral de perles et de faux diamants » (1). Margaret, duchesse d'Argyll, célèbre pour son détournement de sens d'une maxime très prisée – « Couchez-vous tôt et souvent » – tient ici sagement compagnie à sa fille et à Norman Hartnell, le couturier de la reine (3).

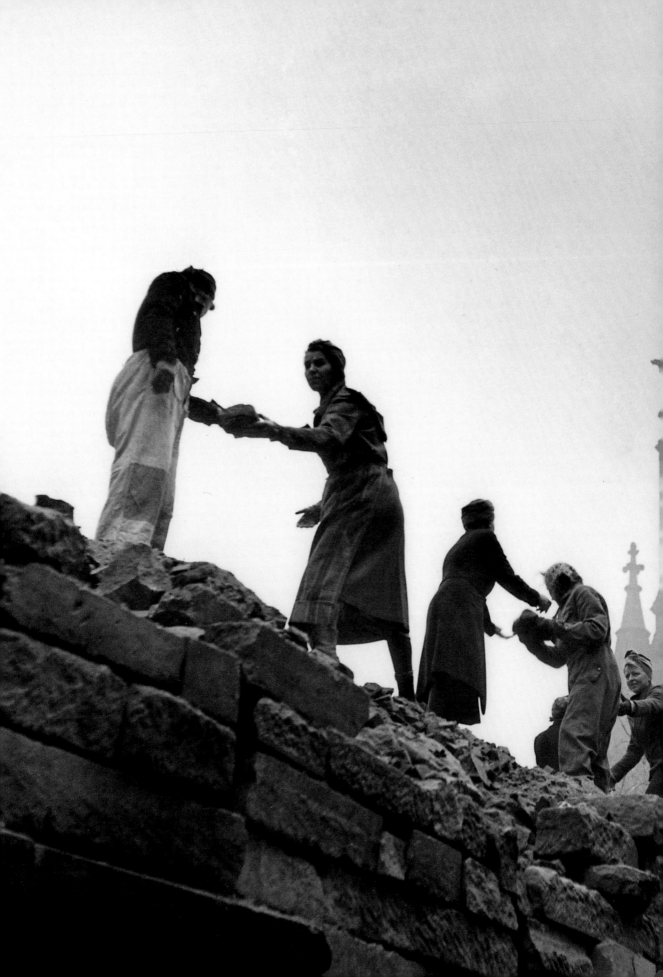

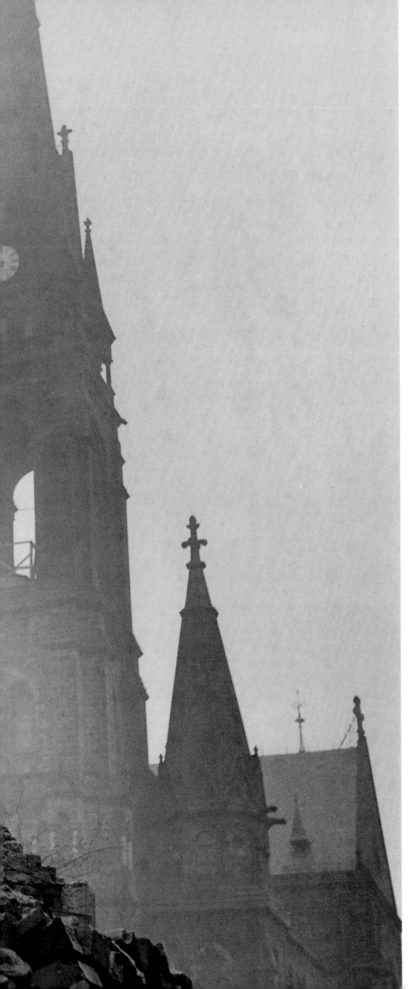

Dresden, March 1946. A human
chain of women workers collects
bricks from the rubble to be used in
rebuilding their   city. In the background
are the remains of the Roman Catholic
cathedral. Until the Allied raid on 14
February 1945, Dresden had been one of
the centres of Baroque beauty in Europe.

Dresden im März 1946:
»Trümmerfrauen« sammeln Steine
und Ziegeln aus den Ruinen, um damit die
Stadt wieder aufzubauen; im Hintergrund
die römisch-katholische Kathedrale. Bis
zum Bombardement durch die Alliierten
am 14. Februar 1945 war Dresden eines
der schönsten Barockzentren Europas.

Dresde, en 1946.
Des « Trümmerfrauen », femmes
travaillant dans les ruines, fouillent les
gravas à la recherche de pierres et briques
utilisables pour reconstruire les maisons ;
à l'arrière-plan, les vestiges de la
Cathédrale. Avant le bombardement par les
alliés, le 14 février 1945, Dresde avait été
l'une des plus belles villes baroques
d'Europe.

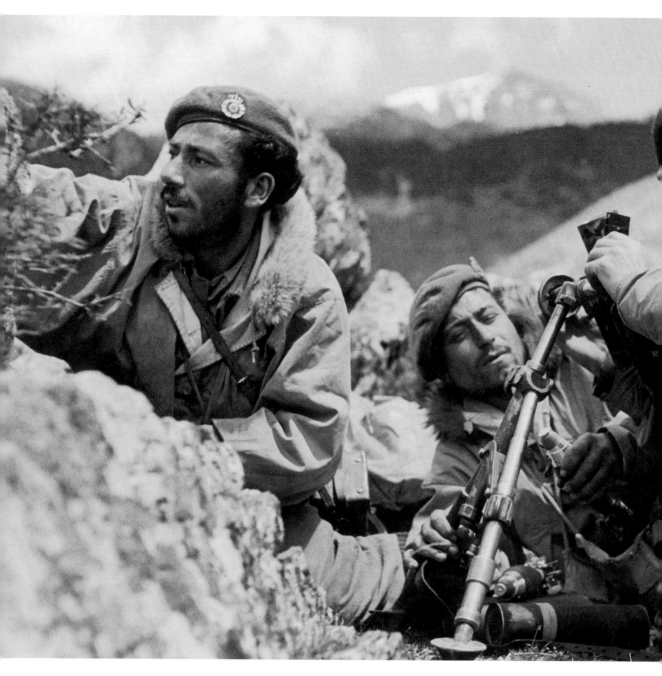

THE seeds of the Greek Civil War of
1944 to 1949 were sown before the
Nazi invasion and occupation in World
War II. At the end of the war, fighting
broke out between Communist guerrillas
and the National Army. The Soviet Union
played no part in the struggle, but Britain
and the US supplied equipment to the

National Army. These NA commandos
(1), fighting near Karpenisi in 1948, wore
British berets and American jackets.
Fighting was intense. Although many of
the 20,000 Communist guerrillas were
forced to surrender (2), when peace came
in 1949 it was for political rather than
military reasons.

DIE Saat für den griechischen Bürger
krieg 1944–1949 wurde bereits vor
der Invasion durch faschistische Verbände
und die anschließende Okkupation
während des Zweiten Weltkrieges gesät.
Zum Ende des Krieges brachen Kämpfe
zwischen kommunistischen Guerillas
(ELAS) und der Nationalen Armee aus.
Die Sowjetunion spielte in dieser Auseinandersetzung keine Rolle, im Gegensatz
zu Großbritannien und den USA, die die
Ausrüstung für die Nationale Armee

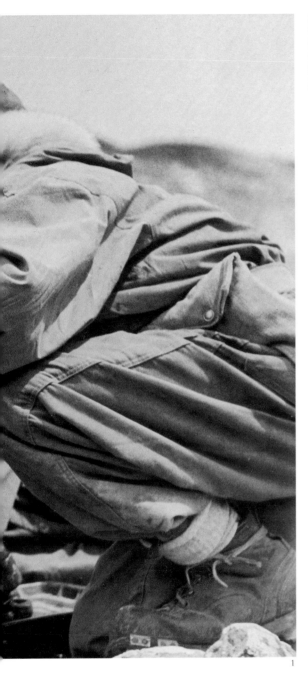
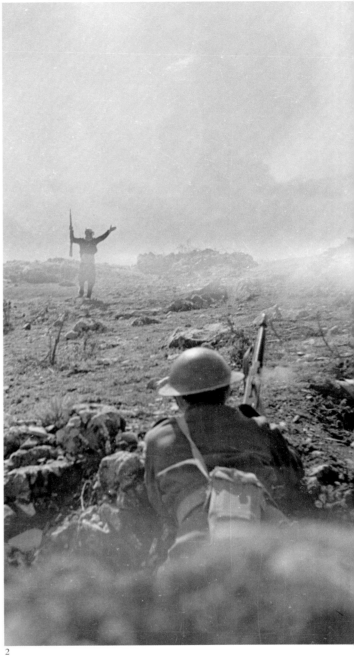

1 2

ereitstellten: Diese NA-Kommandos in
efechtsstellungen nahe Karpenisi im Jahre
948 (1) trugen britische Feldmützen und
merikanische Jacken. Es wurde hart
ekämpft; doch obwohl viele der rund
0.000 kommunistischen Guerillakämpfer
ch am Ende ergeben mußten (2), wurde
er Frieden im Jahre 1949 weniger auf
em Schlachtfeld als vielmehr auf dem
olitischen Parkett entschieden.

L ES graines de la guerre civile grecque,
de 1944 à 1949, ont été semées bien
avant l'invasion nazi et l'occupation durant
la Seconde Guerre mondiale. À la fin de la
guerre, des combats ont éclaté entre les
rebelles communistes et l'Armée nationale,
l'AN. L'Union soviétique n'a joué aucun
rôle dans cette lutte, mais la Grande-
Bretagne et les États-Unis ont fourni des

équipements à l'Armée nationale. Ces
commandos de l'AN (1) qui se battent près
de Karpenisi en 1948 portent des bérets
britanniques et des blousons américains. La
lutte fut acharnée. Bien que beaucoup des
20 000 rebelles communistes aient été
contraints de se rendre (2) au retour de la
paix en 1949, ils l'ont fait pour des motifs
politiques plutôt que militaires.

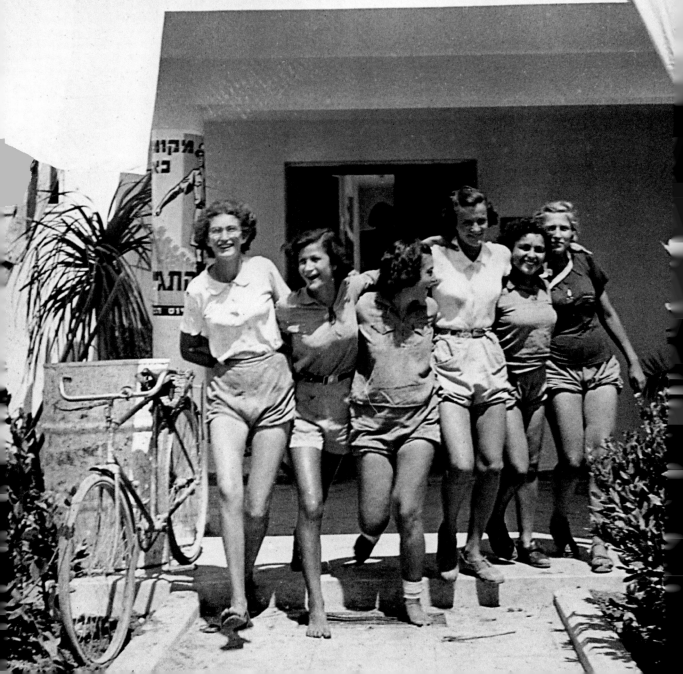

THESE Jewish Palestinian girls are celebrating the successful conclusion to [h]ard day's work signing up some of the [2]5,000 volunteering for National Service [1]. The Hebrew posters over the doorway [are] part of the propaganda that resulted in [th]e Israeli army being among the first to [in]corporate women as regular soldiers. Until [19]48, Britain maintained its Palestinian [ma]ndate, searching both Jews and Arabs (2) [for] weapons and bombs on the streets of [Je]rusalem and imposing a blockade along [th]e coast. To add to the confusion, the [Irg]un 'terrorist' organization (one of whose [lea]ders, David Ben Gurion, became Israel's [fir]st Prime Minister) waged war against the [nex]t Israeli government in 1948. Their arms [shi]p was ignited by government mortar [bo]mbs (3), destroying 600 tons of weapons.

DIESE jüdischen Mädchen in Palästina freuen sich über das Ende eines harten [Ar]beitstages, an dem sie einen Teil der [2]5 000 Freiwilligen für den Militärdienst [ein]geschrieben haben (1). Die hebräischen [Pl]akate gehören zu einer Werbekampagne, [mit] der auch Frauen zum Militärdienst be[ruf]en wurden – die israelische Armee war [ein]e der ersten, die Frauen aufnahm. Bis [19]48 war Palästina britisches Mandatsgebiet, [un]d Juden wie Araber wurden in den Straßen [Je]rusalems nach Waffen und Bomben durch[su]cht (2); zudem gab es eine Seeblockade. [Di]e Lage wurde noch verwirrender da[du]rch, daß die »Terroristen« der Gruppe [Irg]un (einer ihrer Führer war der spätere [isr]aelische Premierminister David Ben [Gu]rion) Krieg gegen die offizielle israelische [R]egierung führten. Das Schiff, das ihnen [W]affen bringen sollte, wurde von Minen[w]erfern der Regierungstruppen beschossen, [un]d 600 Tonnen Waffen und Munition [fl]ogen in die Luft (3).

CES jeunes Juives installées en Palestine célèbrent l'heureuse issue d'une dure [jo]urnée de travail : elles font partie des [2]5 000 volontaires au service national (1). [Le]s affiches en langue hébraïque placées [au-]dessus de la porte aidèrent l'armée israé[lie]nne à intégrer des femmes en service [ré]gulier. Jusqu'en 1948, la Grande-Bretagne, [im]posant un blocus du littoral, maintint son [m]andat palestinien. Elle fouillait Juifs et [A]rabes dans les rues de Jérusalem (2) dans [un]e hypothétique quête d'armes et de bombes. [Po]ur ajouter à la confusion, l'Irgoun, que les [b]ritanniques taxaient de terrorisme – l'un de [se]s chefs, David Ben Gourion, deviendra un [pr]emier ministre israélien – livra une guerre [far]ouche aux autorités. Le bateau qui abritait [le]urs armes fut incendié (3), détruisant pas [m]oins de 600 tonnes d'armes.

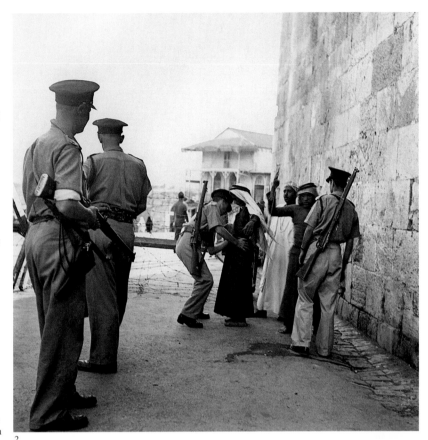

2

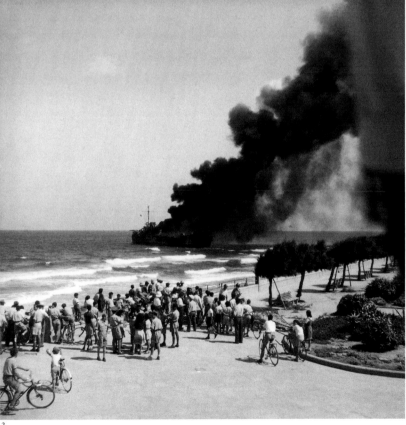

3

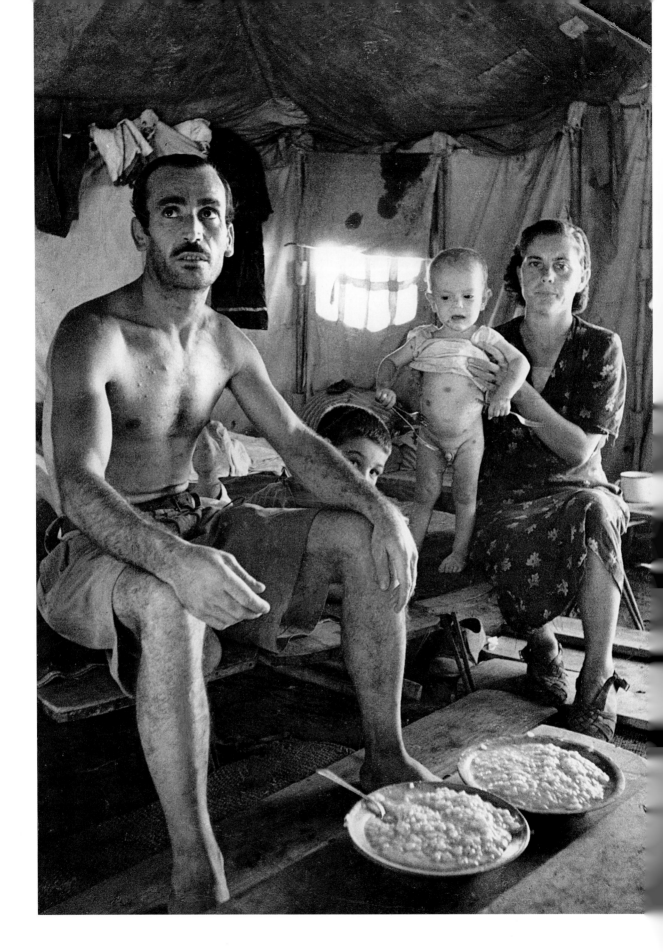

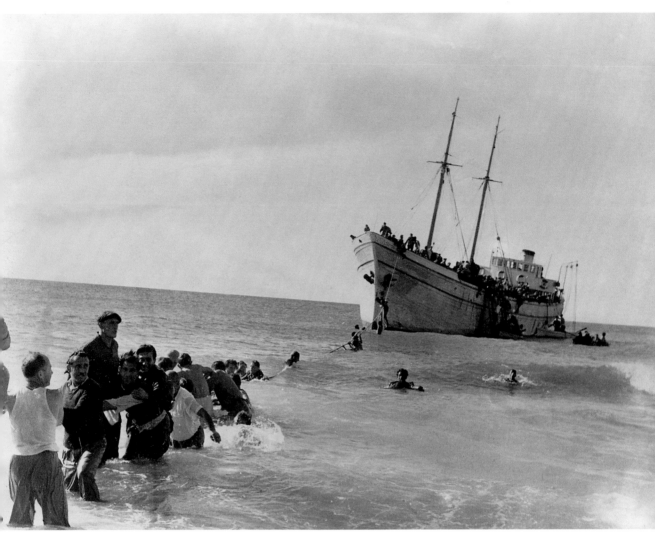

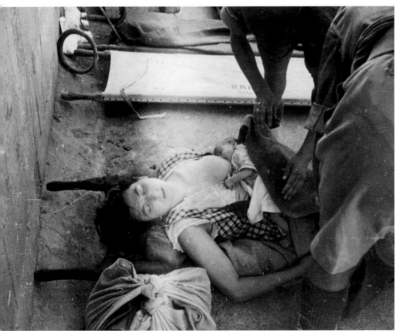

In 1947 some hundreds of Jewish survivors were packed off to a detention camp in Cyprus (1, 3). And in 1948 the *SS United States* deliberately ran aground with 700 Jews on board, at Nahariya, near Haifa in Israel. The local population waded out to help bear the sick and old ashore (2).

Im Jahre 1947 erreichten einige Hundert jüdische Überlebende ein Lager auf Zypern (1, 3). Und 1948 setzte der Kapitän sein Schiff *SS United States*, mit 700 Juden an Bord, ein paar Meilen von dem Badeort Nahariya (nahe bei Haifa in Israel) absichtlich auf Grund; die Einheimischen kamen und holten die Alten und Kranken an Land (2).

En 1947, des centaines de Juifs survivants sont envoyés dans un camp chypriote (1, 3). En 1948, le *SS United States*, avec 700 Juifs européens à son bord, arriva à Nahariya (près de Haïfa). La population locale vint aider à transporter les malades et les personnes âgées (2).

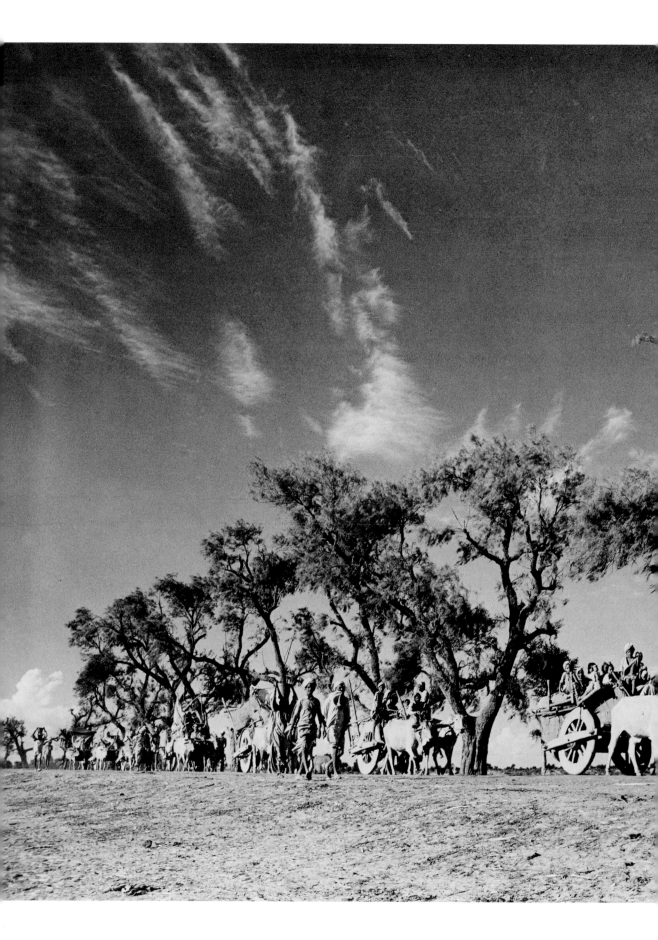

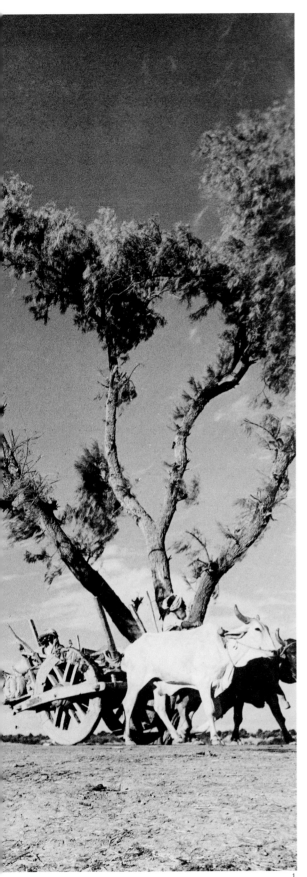

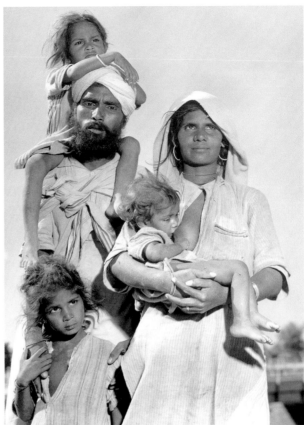

THE British Labour government stuck to its pledge to give independence to India in 1947. The partition of the country into Hindu India and Muslim Pakistan was not achieved without considerable violence, and the migration of millions of people, among them Sikh families (2) who migrated to the Hindu East Punjab (1).

DIE britische Labour-Regierung hielt Wort und entließ 1947 Indien in die Unabhängigkeit. Die Teilung des Landes in ein hinduistisches Indien und ein muslimisches Pakistan kam jedoch nicht ohne ein gehöriges Ausmaß an Gewalt zustande und zog eine Migrationswelle von Millionen von Menschen nach sich – unter ihnen viele Sikh-Familien (2), die sich vor allem im Ostteil der indischen Region Pandschab niederließen.

LE gouvernement travailliste a tenu parole et, en 1947, accorde l'indépendance à l'Inde. La partition du pays en une Inde hindouiste et un Pakistan musulman ne peut cependant pas se faire sans des débordements de violence qui entraînent l'exode de millions de personnes – parmi lesquelles beaucoup de familles sikh (2) qui s'établirent surtout dans la partie orientale de la région indienne du Panjab (1).

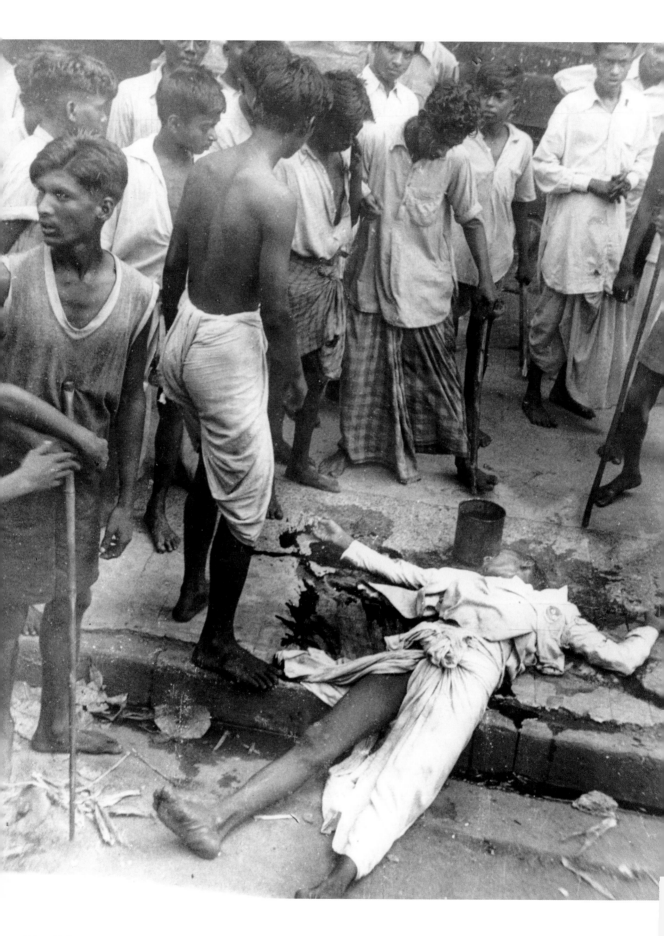

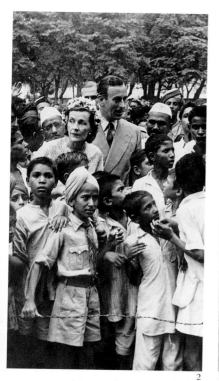

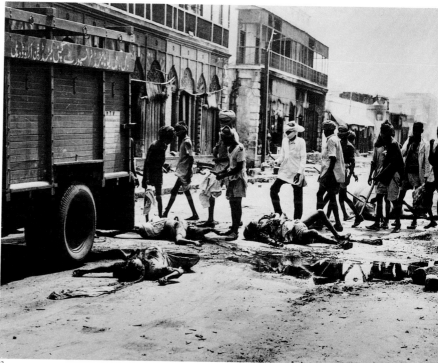

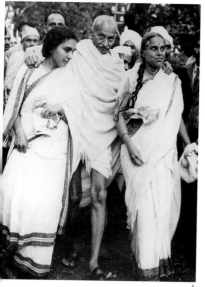

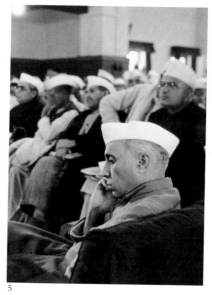

IN April 1946 the British Cabinet dele-gation to India held discussions with the frail Hindu leader Mahatma Gandhi (here assisted by his doctor and helper, 4). The following year Lord Mountbatten (2, with his wife Edwina), last Viceroy of India, ended 150 years of British rule, and on 15 August 1947 Pandit Nehru (5) became first Indian Prime Minister. However, the fighting over Partition into the Moslem state of Pakistan to the north and predom-nantly Hindu India to the south provided violent aftermath: 25,000 dead in New Delhi (3) and Calcutta (1) alone. Nonethe-less, King George VI assured the new Constituent Assembly: 'In thus achieving your independence by agreement, you have set an example to the freedom-loving people throughout the world.'

IM April 1946 verhandelte eine Delegation der britischen Regierung mit dem Hindu-führer Mahatma Gandhi (hier von seiner Ärztin und einer Helferin gestützt, 4) über das Schicksal Indiens. Im folgenden Jahr erklärte der letzte Vizekönig, Lord Mount-batten (2, mit Gattin Edwina), die 150 Jahre britischer Herrschaft über Indien für be-endet, und am 15. August 1947 wurde Pandit Nehru erster indischer Premierminister (5). Doch die Auseinandersetzungen um die Teilung des Landes in einen Moslemstaat Pakistan im Norden und ein hauptsächlich von Hindus bevölkertes Indien im Süden nahm ein blutiges Ende: 25 000 Tote allein in Neu-Delhi (3) und Kalkutta (1). Das hinderte König Georg VI. nicht, dem neuen indischen Parlament zu versichern: »Indem Sie Ihre Unabhängigkeit durch friedliche Verhandlungen errungen haben, haben Sie freiheitsliebenden Völkern überall auf der Welt ein Beispiel gegeben.«

EN avril 1946, la délégation du cabinet britannique en Inde entame des discus-sions avec le frêle leader hindou Mahatma Gandhi (soutenu ici par son médecin et un assistant, 4). L'année suivante, Lord Mountbatten (2, avec son épouse Elvira), le dernier vice-roi de l'Inde, met fin à un siècle et demi de gouvernement britan-nique. Le 15 août 1947, le Pandit Nehru (5) devient Premier ministre de l'ex-empire. Toutefois, le conflit généré lors de la divi-sion en un État musulman du Pakistan au nord et un État à prédominance hindoue au sud sera très violent : 25 000 morts rien qu'à New-Delhi (3) et Calcutta (1). Néan-moins, le roi George VI assure la nouvelle assemblée constituante que : « En obtenant votre indépendance par accord mutuel, vous servirez d'exemple aux gens aimant la paix de par le monde. »

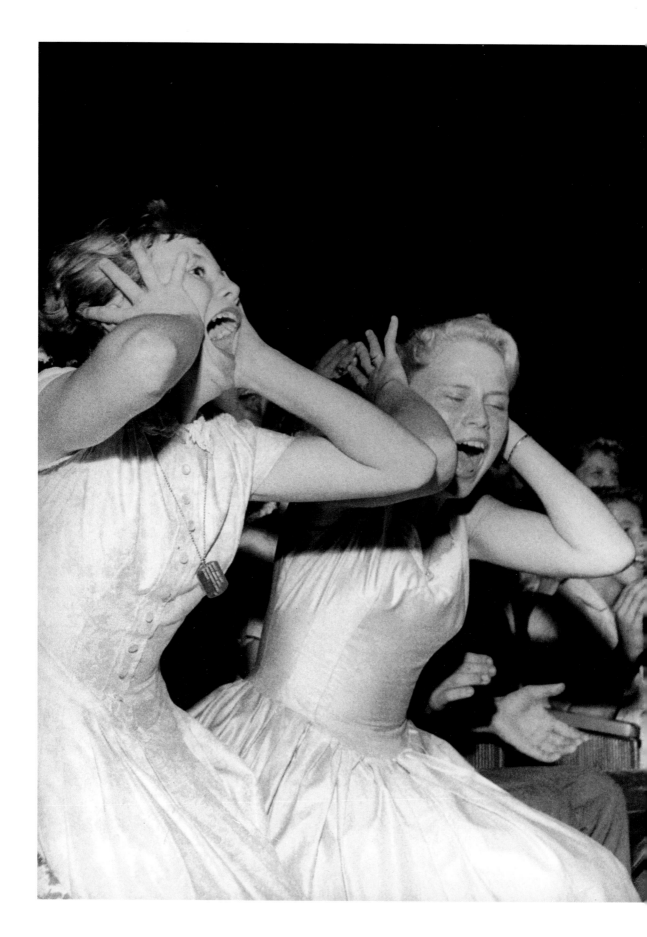

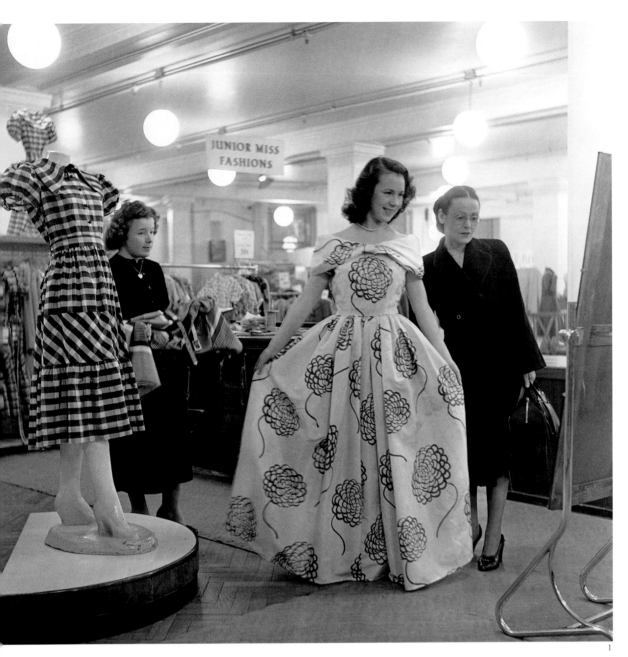

1

BLISS was it in the dawn of the 1950s to be a white in the US, but to be young was very heaven… The nation was untroubled by any doubt as to its right to rule the world, and the internal haemorrhaging that was to come from Vietnam and the Civil Rights Movement was still in the future. Right now, there was the emotional ecstasy of attending an Elvis Presley concert (2), or the deep happiness that came from choosing a dress for the Junior or Senior Prom (1).

SELIG, wer in den 1950er Jahren der USA weiß war; wer außerdem jung war, hatte den Himmel auf Erden … Noch war die Nation durch keinerlei Zweifel an der Rechtmäßigkeit, die Welt zu regieren, aus dem Gleichgewicht gebracht; und die internen Erschütterungen, die der Vietnamkrieg und die Bürgerrechts-bewegung bringen sollten, lagen noch in ferner Zukunft. Im Augenblick gab es nur die emotionale Ekstase bei einem Elvis-Presley-Konzert (2) oder das stille Glück bei der Wahl eines Abendkleides für die Junior- oder Senior-Proms (1).

HEUREUX celui qui avait la peau blanche aux États-Unis dans les années 50 ; s'il était, en outre, jeune, c'était le paradis terrestre ; la nation n'était pas encore divisée par le doute quant au bien-fondé de sa prétention à gouverner le monde ; et les dissensions intestines qui allaient déclencher la guerre du Vietnam ainsi que le mouvement des droits civiques étaient encore à des années lumières. Pour l'instant, seule l'extase lors d'un concert d'Elvis Presley (2) et le bonheur muet lors du choix d'une robe de soirée pour les juniors ou les seniors proms (1) comptaient.

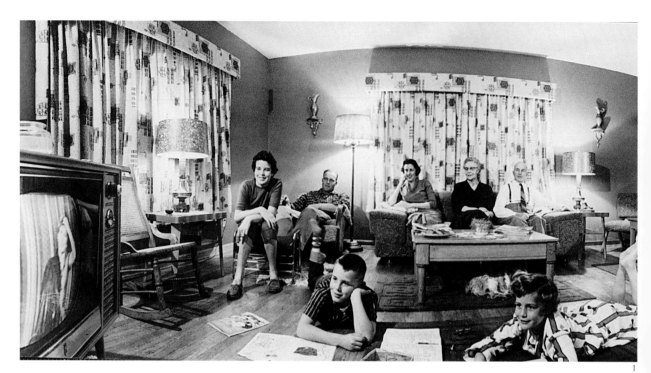

1

For millions of Americans, the dream became reality in the golden years that followed World War II. The boost to the nation's economy had put an end to the Depression of the 1930s, and it seemed the earth and the fullness thereof, which included watching the *Ed Sullivan Show* on TV (1), was there for the taking by 'God's own people'. Americans' standards of living were envied around the world – the gas-guzzling cars, the huge refrigerators, steaks the size of paving slabs, the rocking chair on the porch, and the vast shakes and sodas for junior at the corner *drugstore* (2).

Für Millionen Amerikaner wurde der nationale Traum in den goldenen Jahren nach dem Zweiten Weltkrieg Wirklichkeit: Ein enormer Wirtschafts-aufschwung trat an die Stelle der Depression der 1930er Jahre, und es schien, als warteten die Reichtümer und Genüsse dieser Erde – dazu gehörte auch die *Ed Sullivan Show* im Fernsehen (1) – nur darauf, von »Gottes Volk« konsumiert zu werden. Der Lebensstandard der Amerikaner wurde rund um den Globus beneidet: große Autos, riesige Kühlschränke, Steaks so groß wie Betonplatten, ein Schaukelstuhl auf der Veranda und eine nahezu endlose Palette von Limonaden und Milchshakes für die Jugend im *Drugstore* um die Ecke (2).

Pour des millions d'Américains, le rêve national des années d'or devient réalité après la Seconde Guerre mondiale : un essor économique sans précédent succède à la dépression des années 30 et il semble que toutes les richesses et tous les plaisirs de cette terre – dont le *Ed Sullivan Show* à la télévision (1) – n'attendent que d'être consommés par le « Peuple de Dieu ». Le monde entier envie les Américains pour leur mode de vie : grosses voitures, réfrigérateurs gigantesques, steaks de la taille d'une raquette de tennis, un fauteuil à bascule sous la véranda et un choix pratiquement infini de limonades et de milk-shakes pour la jeunesse au *drugstore* du coin (2).

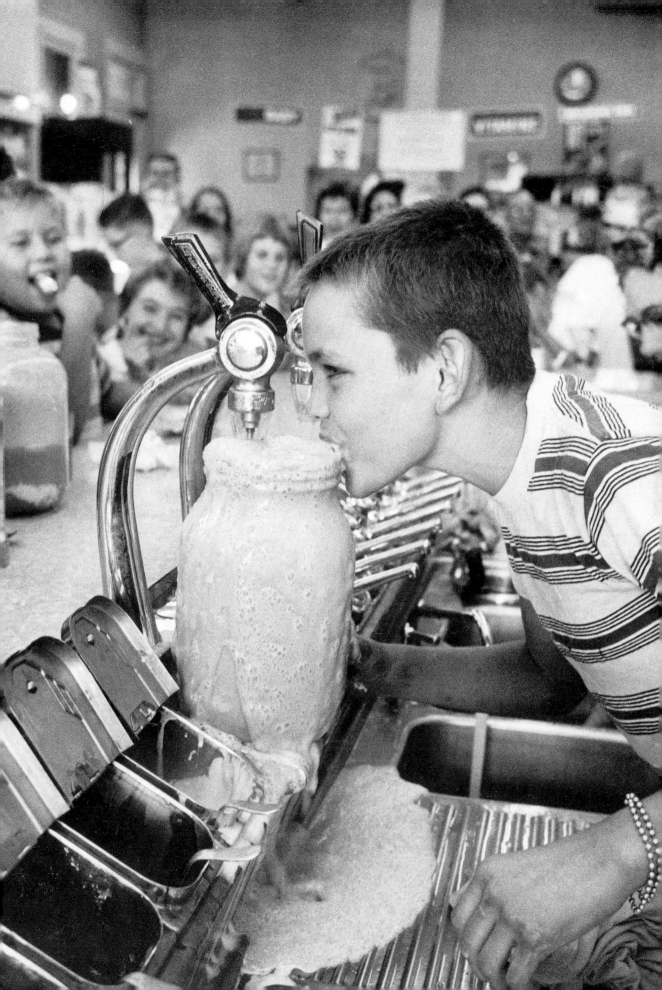

Cold War Era

WHEN the Iron Curtain came down after World War II, it divided the world into two immense *blocs*. The East was under the rule of Communism, much of it forcibly imposed by the Soviet Union. The West was under the sway of Capitalism, benignly represented by Coca-Cola, Wall Street and Hollywood. It was a world of threat, stand-off, posturing and brinkmanship – in Korea, Berlin and the Taiwan Strait. And all the while, in the shadow of these *blocs*, were other divided societies – in Malaya, the Indian sub-continent, the Middle East, Greece, Cyprus, much of Africa and all the countries across the world that were seeking to rid themselves at last of the scourge of colonial rule.

Culture and sport regularly broke through this Iron Curtain, though there were occasional boycotts of various world championships and even that greatest of all sporting symbols of the brotherhood and sisterhood of nations – the Olympic Games. Subversive literature was smuggled both ways, though pop music travelled a one-way street, heading eastwards from Motown and Liverpool and other points west. Among the West's greatest trophies was Rudolf Nureyev, who left his Leningrad choreographic home in 1961 to seek political asylum in Paris and then share his remarkable talent with Margot Fonteyn de Arias.

The newly-formed United Nations did what it could to keep the peace, but real power rested with those who had the Bomb. The rest of the world lived in its shadow, and, whether they approved or reviled it, everyone feared it.

NACH dem Zweiten Weltkrieg wurde der eiserne Vorhang herabgelassen und teilte die Welt in zwei *Blöcke:* Der Osten kam unter die Kontrolle der Kommunisten – ein großer Teil zwangsweise, durch die Macht der Sowjetunion. Der Westen geriet unter den Bann des Kapitalismus – dessen freundliche Seite durch Coca-Cola, Wall Street und Hollywood repräsentiert wurde. Zwischen den Blöcken herrschte eine Atmosphäre aus Drohung und Distanz, aus Polemik und einer Politik des äußersten Risikos – vor allem in Berlin, Korea und der Meerenge vor Taiwan. Währenddessen versuchten weitere zerrissene Gesell-schaften im Schatten dieser Blöcke, sich von der Geiß des Kolonialismus zu befreien – so in Malaysia, auf de indischen Subkontinent, im Nahen Osten, Griechenland, Zypern sowie in großen Teilen Afrik und in zahlreichen Ländern rund um den Globus.

Kultur- und Sportereignisse vermochten imm wieder, den Eisernen Vorhang zu durchbrechen – auc wenn hin und wieder Weltmeisterschaften und selb das größte Symbol der Brüderlichkeit der Nationen i Sport, die Olympischen Spiele, boykottiert wurde Subversive Literatur fand als Schmuggelware ihren W in beide Richtungen; nur die Popmusik zog vc Mowtown, Liverpool und anderen Orten des Weste in einer Einbahnstraße gen Osten. Eine der größt Trophäen für den Westen war Rudolf Nurejew, d 1961 seine choreographische Heimat in Leningra verließ, in Paris politisches Asyl suchte und sei bemerkenswertes Talent und seinen Erfolg fortan m seiner Tanzpartnerin Margot Fonteyn de Arias teilte.

Die neu gegründeten Vereinten Nationen taten all in ihrer Macht Stehende für den Erhalt des Friedens doch die wahre Macht lag in den Händen derer, die d Atombombe besaßen. Der Rest der Welt lebte in ihre Schatten, und jedermann – ob Befürworter od Gegner – fürchtete sie.

APRÉS la Seconde Guerre mondiale, le Rideau c fer tombe sur le monde, qu'il partage en deu immenses *blocs*: l'Est, placé sous le contrôle d communistes dans une certaine mesure par la force d choses, à cause du pouvoir de l'Union soviétiqu L'Ouest, lui, tombe sous le charme du capitalisme, dor le côté souriant est incarné par Coca-Cola, Wall Stree et Hollywood. Entre les blocs règne une atmosphè faite de menace et de distance, de polémique et d politique du risque extrême – notamment à Berlin, e Corée et dans le détroit de Taiwan. Pendant ce temp d'autres sociétés déchirées à l'ombre de ces blo cherchent à se libérer de la gangue du colonialisme par exemple en Malaisie, sur le sous-continent indie au Proche-Orient, en Grèce, à Chypre ainsi que dar de nombreuses régions d'Afrique et beaucoup de pa tout autour de la planète : le Rideau de fer s'entrouvr régulièrement pour des événements culturels et sporti

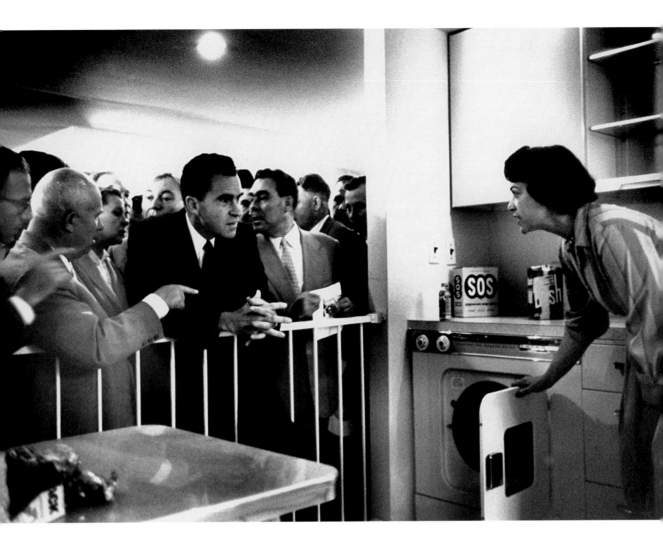

bien que des championnats du monde et même le
[p]lus grand symbole de la fraternité des nations au sein
[d]u sport, les Jeux olympiques, soient régulièrement
[b]oycottés. De la littérature subversive circulant sous le
[m]anteau parvient à s'infiltrer dans les deux directions ; il
[n]'y a que la musique pop qui, depuis Motown,
[L]iverpool et d'autres villes de l'Ouest, se déplace à sens
[u]nique vers l'Est. L'un des plus grands trophées de
[l']Ouest était Rudolf Noureïev, qui a quitté Leningrad,
[s]a patrie chorégraphique, en 1961, pour demander
[a]sile politique à Paris, où il partagea dorénavant son
[ta]lent exceptionnel et son succès avec sa partenaire de
[d]anse Margot Fonteyn de Arias.

Encore toutes jeunes, les Nations unies font tout ce
[q]ui est en leur pouvoir pour sauvegarder la paix – mais
[l]e véritable pouvoir est détenu par ceux qui possèdent la
[b]ombe atomique. Le reste du monde vit dans leur
[o]mbre et chacun – partisan ou adversaire – les craint.

SOVIET PREMIER NIKITA KHRUSHCHEV ENGAGES IN FINGER-
STABBING DEBATE WITH US VICE-PRESIDENT RICHARD NIXON AT
THE AMERICAN NATIONAL EXHIBITION IN MOSCOW, JULY 1959.

DER SOWJETISCHE PREMIERMINISTER NIKITA CHRUSCHTSCHOW
REDET WÄHREND DER AMERIKANISCHEN NATIONAL-
AUSSTELLUNG IN MOSKAU AUF DEN US-VIZEPRÄSIDENTEN
RICHARD NIXON EIN – JULI 1959

PENDANT L'EXPOSITION NATIONALE AMÉRICAINE DE MOSCOU,
LE PREMIER MINISTRE SOVIÉTIQUE NIKITA KHROUCHTCHEV
INTERPELLE LE VICE-PRÉSIDENT AMÉRICAIN RICHARD NIXON EN
POINTANT SON DOIGT VERS LUI – JUILLET 1959.

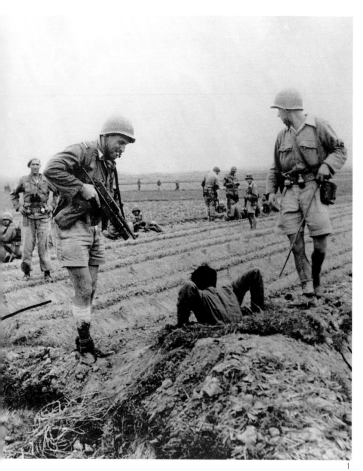

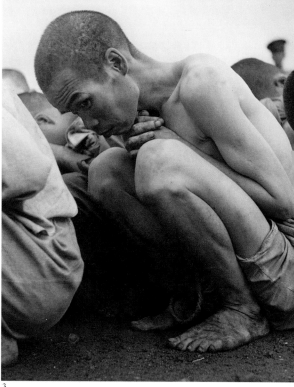

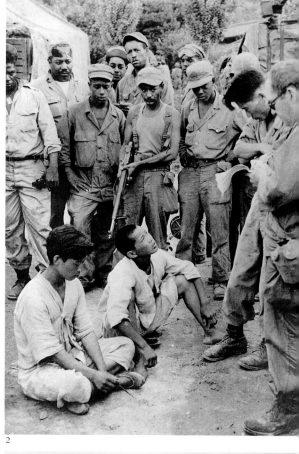

FRENCH and Vietnamese forces were already bogged down in southeast Asia when, following the crossing of the 38th Parallel by North Korean troops in 1950, the United Nations intervened on the side of South Korea to defeat the 'Communist Menace from the North'. Here French troops flush a 'rebel' from a foxhole (1), while others question Communist suspects (2). It was a British press photographer, Bert Hardy, who made waves with his pictures of refugees (4) and of the maltreatment of North Korean POWs under the banner of the UN flag (3).

DIE Fronten hatten sich in Südostasien bereits verhärtet, als nordkoreanische Truppen 1950 den 38. Breitengrad überschritten und die Vereinten Nationen auf seiten Südkoreas gegen die »kommunistische Bedrohung aus dem Norden« eingriffen. Hier holen französische Soldaten einen »Rebellen« aus einem Schützenloch (1), andere verhören verdächtige Kommunisten (2). Bert Hardy, ein britischer Pressephotograph, sorgte für Aufruhr, als er seine Bilder von Flüchtlingen (4) und von mißhandelten nordkoreanischen Kriegsgefangenen veröffentlichte (3).

LES forces françaises et vietnamiennes étaient déjà enlisées dans le Sud-Est asiatique quand les Nations unies intervinrent aux côtés de la Corée du Sud dans l'espoir d'écarter la « menace communiste du Nord ». Ici, les troupes françaises tirent un « rebelle » de son terrier (1), pendant que d'autres interrogent des suspects communistes (2). C'est un photographe de presse britannique, Bert Hardy, qui causa un grand trouble en publiant ces photos de réfugiés (4) et de prisonniers de guerre nord-coréens maltraités sous la bannière des Nations unies (3).

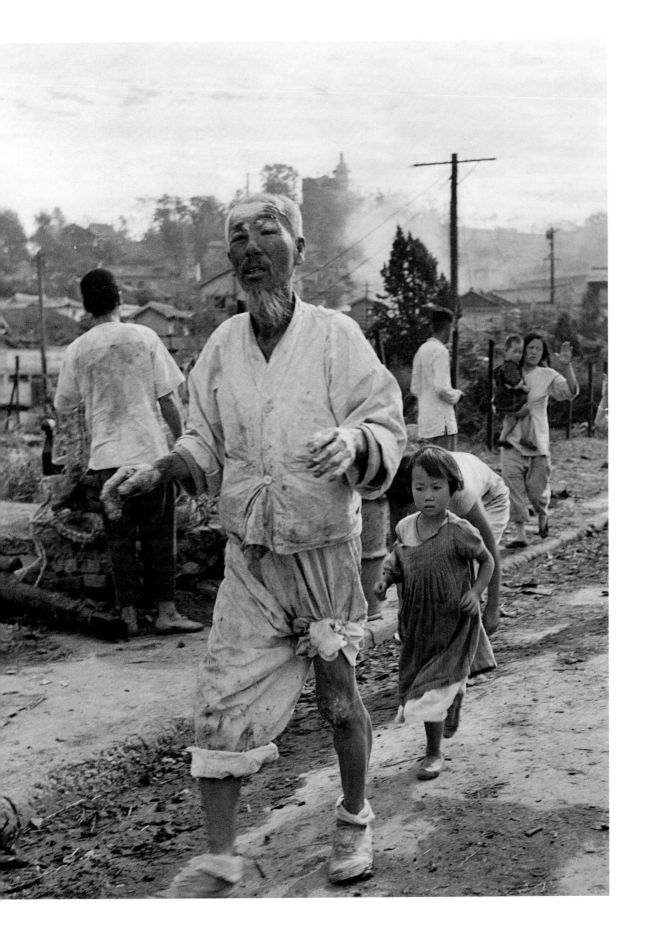

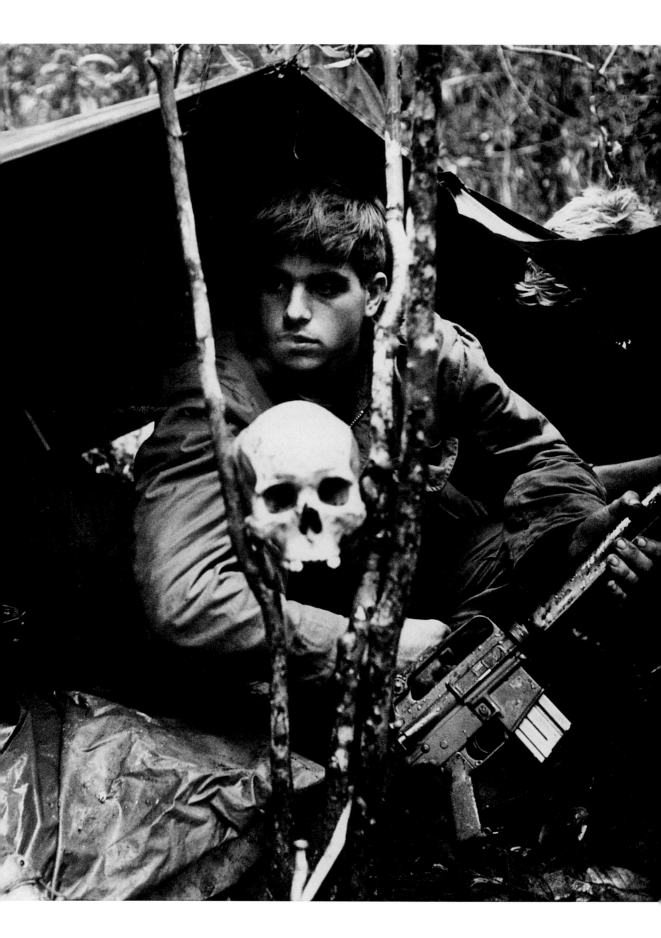

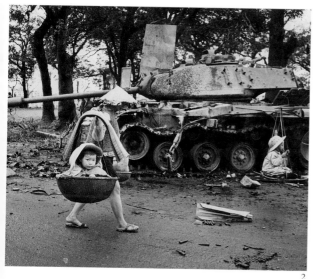

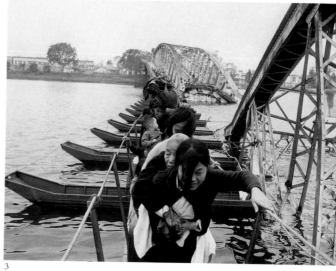

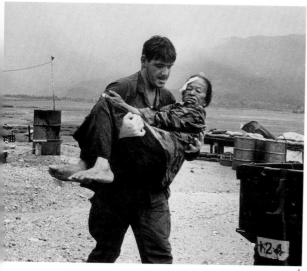

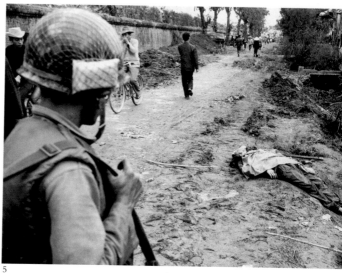

2 3

4 5

B Y spring 1965 President Johnson was sending the Marines into Vietnam to protect the US military base at Da Nang from increasingly stringent Viet Cong guerilla attacks. While a US soldier crouches at ease behind his automatic weapon and his skull trophy (1), a burnt-out tank lies abandoned by the road, a warning to the fleeing South Vietnamese refugees (2). A cyclist passes corpses in Hue, holding his nose to exclude the stench of death (5). By 1968 the Viet Cong Tet offensive had failed, but this was to be a classic instance of losing the battle to win the war. Not only was the US signally failing to win over the 'hearts and minds' of the South Vietnamese, but the Viet Cong were scoring one propaganda coup after another with pictures like these (2, 3, 4).

I M Frühjahr 1965 schickte Präsident Johnson die Marines nach Vietnam, wo sie die Militärbasis Da Nang vor den immer stärker werdenden Guerilla-Angriffen des Vietkong schützen sollten. Ein US-Soldat hat es sich mit seinem Gewehr und seinem Maskottchen bequem gemacht (1), und ein ausgebrannter Panzer liegt verlassen am Wegrand, eine Warnung für die vorbeiziehenden südvietnamesischen Flüchtlinge (2). Ein Radfahrer in Hué (5) hält sich die Nase zu, damit er die Leichen nicht riechen muß. 1968 war klar, daß die Tet-Offensive des Vietkong gescheitert war, doch war dies der klassische Fall einer Schlacht, die man verliert, um den Krieg zu gewinnen. Nicht genug, daß es den Amerikanern nicht gelang, »Verstand und Herz« der Südvietnamesen für sich zu gewinnen, der Vietkong errang mit Bildern wie diesen (2, 3, 4) einen Propagandasieg nach dem anderen.

D ÈS le printemps de 1965, le président Johnson envoyait les Marines au Viêt-nam assurer la protection de la base militaire américaine de Da Nang contre les attaques de la guérilla Viêt-cong de plus en plus virulentes. Tandis qu'un soldat américain s'accroupit derrière son arme automatique et le crâne qui est son trophée (1), un char d'assaut gît sur le côté de la route en guise d'avertissement aux réfugiés sud-vietnamiens qui fuient (2). Un cycliste dépasse des cadavres dans Hue, où règne l'odeur de la mort (5). Dès 1968 l'offensive Tet des Viêt-congs échouait, illustration du fait que perdre une bataille n'est pas perdre la guerre, bien au contraire. Non seulement les États-Unis se distinguèrent par leur incapacité à gagner les « cœurs et les esprits » des Sud-Vietnamiens, mais en plus la propagande des Viêt-congs marqua des points grâce à la diffusion d'images telles que celles-ci (2, 3 et 4).

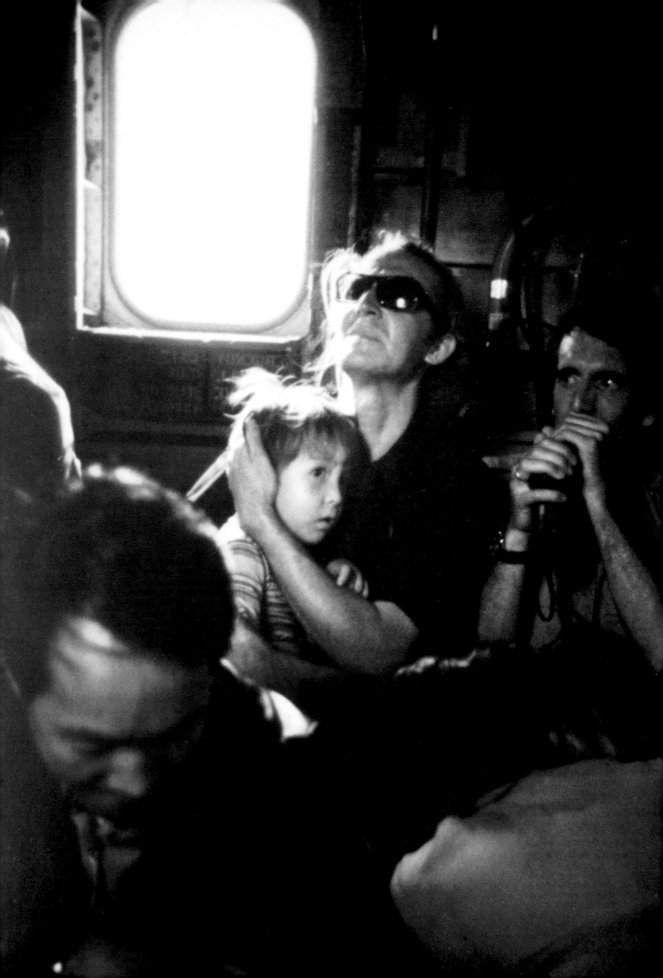

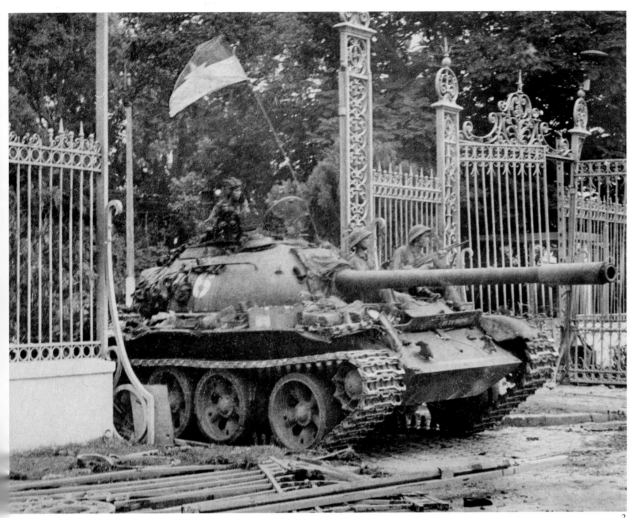

2

By the mid 1970s it was clear to President Nixon (and his successor Gerald Ford) that US victory in Vietnam was unachievable. The unthinkable had happened, and a citizen army of guerrillas, saboteurs and amateurs had defeated the greatest military power in the world. The US pulled out, leaving its South Vietnamese allies in an impossible situation. When the end came in April 1975, it was swift, dramatic and desperate. American civilians as well as military personnel had to be rescued by helicopter and flown to safety (1). On 30 April came the final *coup de grace*. Perched on a tank, soldiers of the North Vietnamese Army smashed their way into the grounds of the South Vietnam Presidential Palace in Saigon (2). It was all over bar the recriminations.

MITTE der 1970er Jahre wurde Präsident Nixon (wie auch seinem Nachfolger Gerald Ford) deutlich, daß der Vietnamkrieg nicht zu gewinnen war. Das Undenkbare war geschehen: Eine Volksarmee aus Guerillakämpfern, Saboteuren und Amateuren hatte die größte Militärmacht der Welt besiegt. Die USA zogen ab und ließen ihre südvietnamesischen Verbündeten in einer unmöglichen Lage zurück. Das Ende kam 1975 – und es kam heftig, dramatisch und verzweifelt. Amerikanische Zivilisten ebenso wie das Militärpersonal mußten mit Hubschraubern in Sicherheit gebracht werden (1). Am 30. April erfolgte der letzte Gnadenstoß: Soldaten der nordvietnamesischen Armee thronten auf ihrem Panzer, als er die Absperrgitter zum Gelände des südvietnamesischen Präsidentenpalastes niederwalzte (2). Alles war vorbei – bis auf die Vorwürfe.

VERS le milieu des années 70, le président Nixon (tout comme son successeur, Gerald Ford) prend conscience qu'il sera impossible de gagner la guerre du Vietnam. L'impensable s'est donc produit : une armée populaire constituée de guérilleros, saboteurs et amateurs a bel et bien fait plier la plus grande puissance militaire au monde. Les États-Unis se retirent et abandonnent leurs alliés sud-vietnamiens dans une situation impossible. La fin se produit en 1975 – et elle est brutale, dramatique et désespérée. Des civils américains et le personnel militaire doivent être évacués par hélicoptère (1). Le 30 avril, le coup de grâce est donné : des soldats de l'armée nord-vietnamienne trônent sur leur char d'assaut quand celui-ci renverse les grilles protégeant l'enceinte du palais du président sud-vietnamien (2). Tout est terminé – il ne reste plus que les reproches.

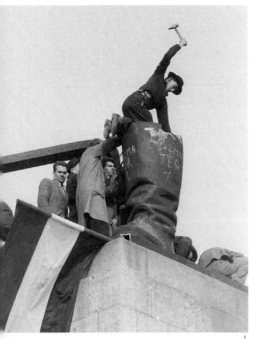

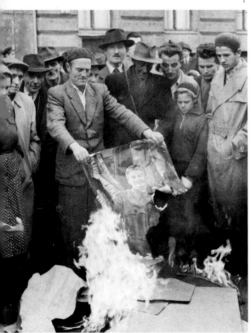

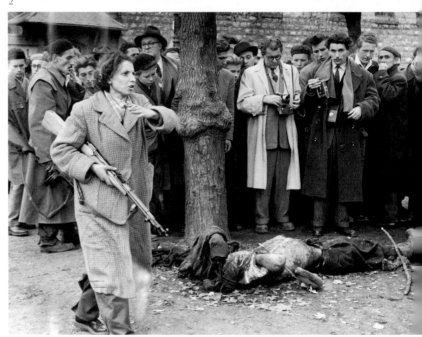

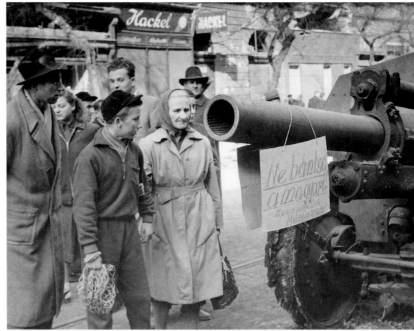

BUDAPEST, 12 November 1956: uprising. In the brief moments of hope that their country might break free of the Russian occupation, these men are furiously dismantling a giant statue of Stalin (1) while others burn his portrait in a pyre of Soviet propaganda (3). Even humour enters into it, as the Russian tank has a sign hung on it with an order not to fire (2). Suspected members of the AVO (Secret Police) are subjected to summary reprisal (4). Girls as young as fifteen (5) were trained to carry guns against the Russian invasion.

AUFSTAND in Budapest, 12. November 1956. In der Hoffnung, daß ihr Land sich vom russischen Joch befreien könne, reißen diese Männer ein Standbild Stalins nieder (1), während andere sein Porträt verbrennen (3). Es war ein Aufstand mit Galgenhumor, wie dieses Schild beweist, das einen russischen Panzer auffordert, nicht zu schießen (2). Mit Mitgliedern der Geheimpolizei AVO wurde indes kurzer Prozeß gemacht (4). Selbst 15jährige Mädchen (5) übten den Umgang mit Waffen gegen die russische Invasion.

BUDAPEST, 12 novembre 1956 : le soulèvement. Lors d'une brève lueur d'espoir, ces hommes sont en train de démanteler avec fureur une statue gigantesque de Staline (1) pendant que d'autres brûlent son portrait (3). L'humour n'est d'ailleurs pas absent ; ici, le blindé russe porte une pancarte où l'on peut lire l'ordre de ne pas tirer (2). Ceux que l'on soupçonne d'appartenir à l'AVO (police secrète) sont exécutés (4). Des filles de quinze ans (5) s'entraînent à porter des armes pour lutter contre les envahisseurs soviétiques.

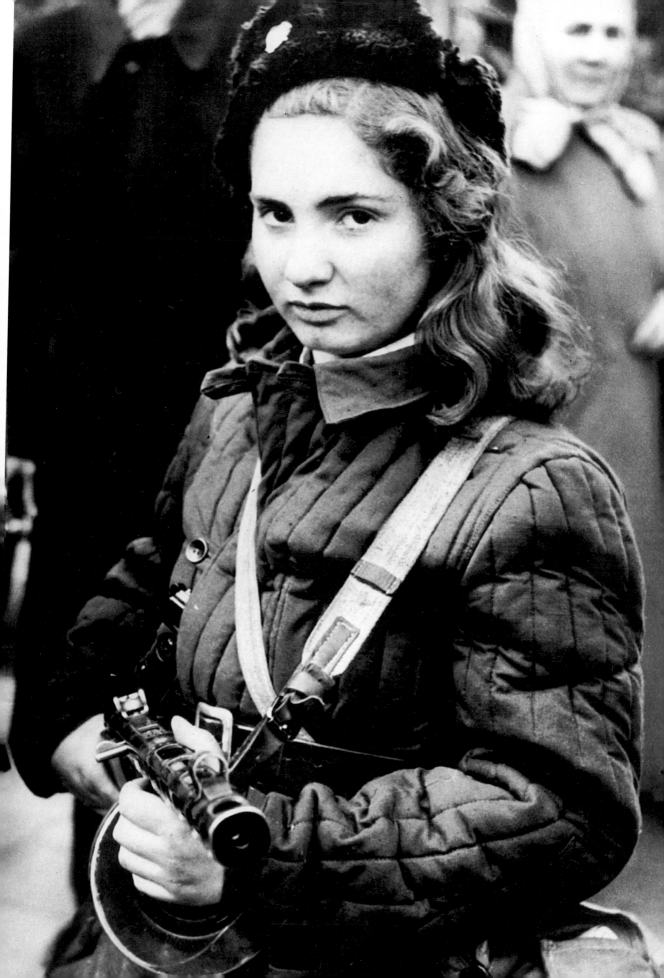

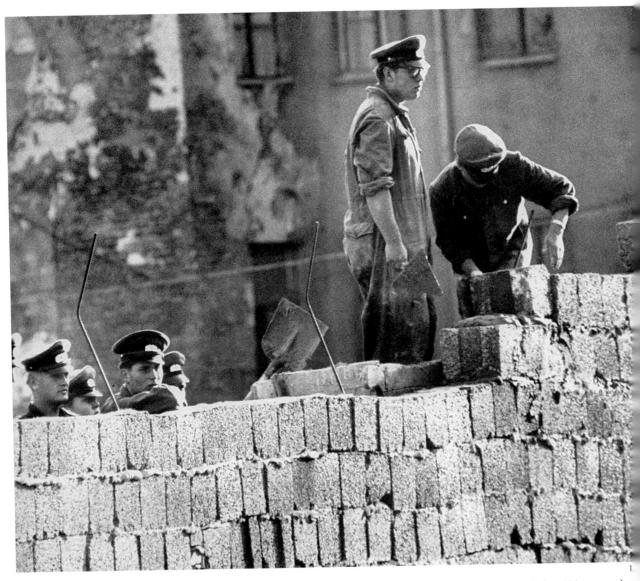

1

DURING the Cold War, it was always feared that Berlin would become the flashpoint. The city was divided, its western half governed by the West German administration – with backing from NATO powers – and its eastern half governed by the German Democratic Republic, backed by the Soviet Union. Back in the late 1940s, it had been enough to paint a line to differentiate between the two zones (3). In 1961 the division was clearly marked by the building of the Berlin Wall (1). The West saw the Wall as the East's attempt to stop its own people defecting. The East saw the Wall just as much as an attempt to keep Western ideas out. Either way, the Wall brought problems for Berliners (2), who had to find suitable positions from which to wave to friends and family on 'the other side'.

WÄHREND des Kalten Krieges wurde immer wieder befürchtet, Berlin könnte zum Brennpunkt der Auseinandersetzungen werden. Die Stadt war geteilt: Der Westteil wurde, mit Unterstützung der Natopartner, von der westdeutschen Regierung verwaltet, der Ostteil von der DDR-Regierung – mit Unterstützung der Sowjetunion. Ende der 1940er Jahre hatte es zunächst genügt, mit einer Linie auf dem Pflaster die Trennlinie zwischen den beiden Zonen zu markieren (3); 1961 wurde die Teilung mit dem Bau der Berliner Mauer zementiert (1).

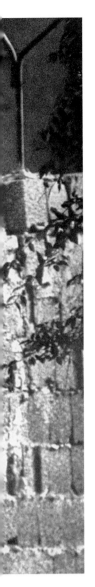

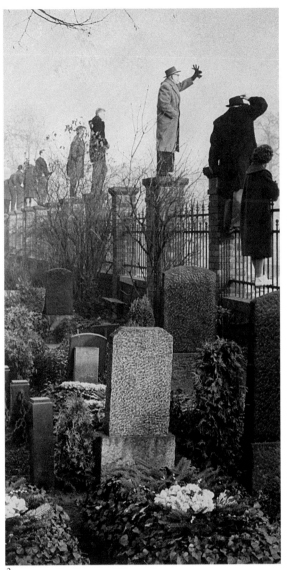

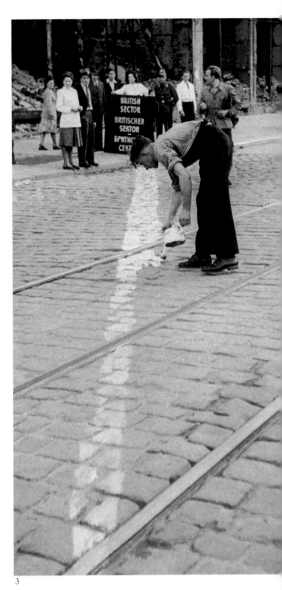

2

3

Der Westen betrachtete den Mauerbau als
verzweifelten Versuch der Regierung in
Ostberlin, ihre Bevölkerung daran zu
hindern, weiterhin in den Westen abzu-
wandern. Der Osten hingegen sah in der
Mauer vor allem einen »antikapitalistischen
Schutzwall«. Aus welchem Blickwinkel
man sie auch betrachtete – die Mauer
brachte von nun an den Berlinern eine
Menge Probleme; sie mußten stets
geeignete Plätze finden, von denen aus sie
Freunden und Verwandten »auf der
anderen Seite« zuwinken konnten (2).

PENDANT la guerre froide, on ne cesse
de craindre que Berlin puisse devenir le
pôle de conflits. La ville est divisée : la
partie occidentale de la ville est administrée
par le gouvernement ouest-allemand, avec
le soutien de ses partenaires de l'OTAN, et
la partie orientale, par le gouvernement de
la RDA – avec le soutien de l'Union
soviétique. À la fin des années 40, il avait
tout d'abord suffi de tracer sur les pavés la
ligne de démarcation entre les deux zones
(3) ; en 1961, la partition est concrétisée
avec la construction du Mur de Berlin (1).

L'Ouest considéra la construction du Mur
comme une tentative désespérée du
gouvernement de Berlin-Est pour
empêcher sa population de continuer à
s'enfuir à l'Ouest. L'Est, par contre, voyait
dans le Mur surtout un « rempart de
protection contre le capitalisme ». Quel
que soit le point de vue – le Mur causa dès
lors d'énormes problèmes aux Berlinois ;
ils durent toujours trouver des endroits
appropriés pour saluer leurs amis et leurs
parents restés de « l'autre côté » (2).

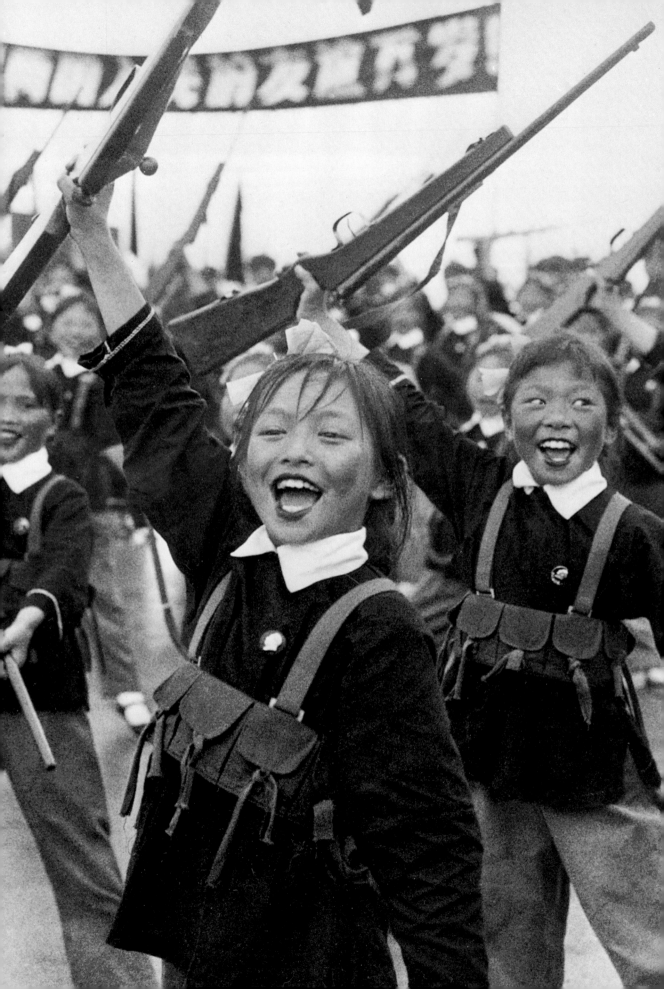

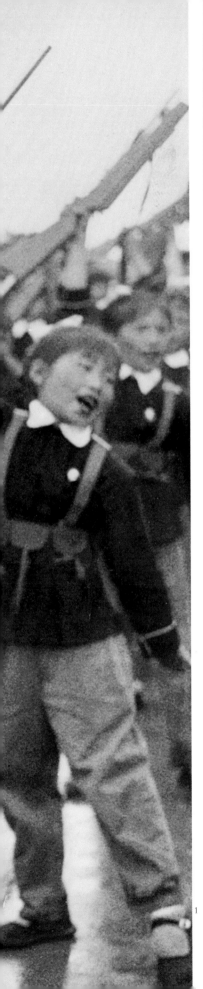

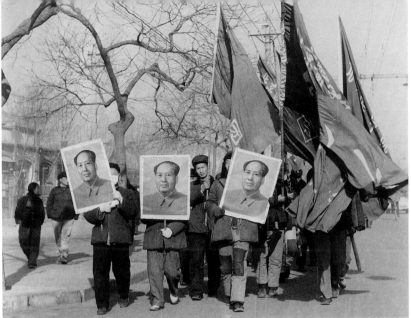

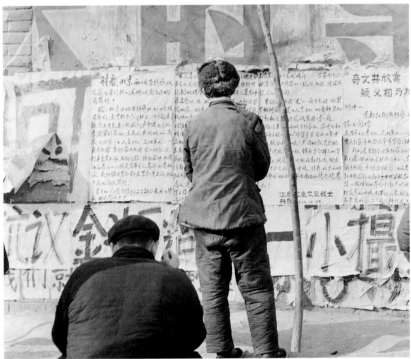

THE Communist Youth Movement in Hanking (1) learn how to handle weapons. In 1966, Mao proclaimed a Cultural Revolution. Thousands of students, organized into Red Guards, moved around the country as here in 1967 (2), bearing banners of Mao and copies of his Little Red Schoolbook. From the same period is an example of the Red Guards' 'wall to wall' poster campaign (3).

MITGLIEDER der kommunistischen Jugendbewegung in Hangking lernen an der Waffe (1). 1966 rief Mao die Kulturrevolution aus. Tausende von Studenten, zu Roten Garden organisiert, zogen mit Fahnen, Bildern Maos und der »Mao-Bibel« durchs Land (wie hier 1967, 2). Aus jener Zeit stammt auch das Bild von den Wandzeitungen der Roten Garden (3).

LES membres du Mouvement de la jeunesse communiste à Hanking (1) apprennent à manier des armes. Mao proclame la Révolution culturelle. Des milliers d'étudiants organisés en Gardes rouges voyagent dans tout le pays, comme ici en 1967 (2). Un exemple de la campagne d'affichage « mur à mur » des Gardes rouges (3).

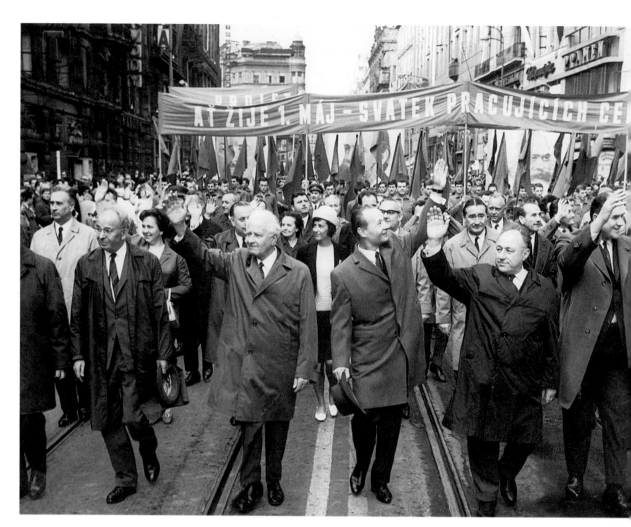

THE promising shoots of the Prague Spring (1) … On May Day 1968, Alexander Dubcek, First Secretary of the Czechoslovakian Communist Party (*third from right*), and General Ludvik Svoboda, President of Czechoslovakia (*third from left*), paraded through cheering crowds in Prague who were heralding their proposed liberal policies that included far-reaching economic and political reforms, and the abolition of censorship. Peaceful revolution was in the air.

VIELVERSPRECHENDE Anzeichen des Prager Frühlings (1): An der Parade zum 1. Mai 1968 nehmen der Erste Sekretär der kommunistischen Partei der Tschechoslowakei, Alexander Dubcek (*dritter von rechts*), und der Präsident der Tschechoslowakei, General Ludvik Svoboda (*dritter von links*), gemeinsam teil; die begeisterte Menge in den Straßen Prags heißt die angekündigten Liberalisierungen – zu denen weitreichende politische und wirtschaftliche Freiheiten ebenso gehören wie die Abschaffung der Zensur – willkommen. Eine friedliche Revolution lag in der Luft.

SIGNES avant-coureurs prometteurs du Printemps de Prague (1) : le Premier secrétaire du parti communiste de la Tchécoslovaquie, Alexander Dubcek (*troisième à partir de la droite*), et le président de la Tchécoslovaquie, le Général Ludvik Svoboda (*troisième à partir de la gauche*), participent en commun à la parade du 1er Mai en 1968 ; la foule enthousiasmée massée dans les rues de Prague se félicite des mesures de libéralisation annoncées – parmi lesquelles de vastes libertés politiques et économiques ainsi que l'abolition de la censure. Une révolution pacifique est dans l'air.

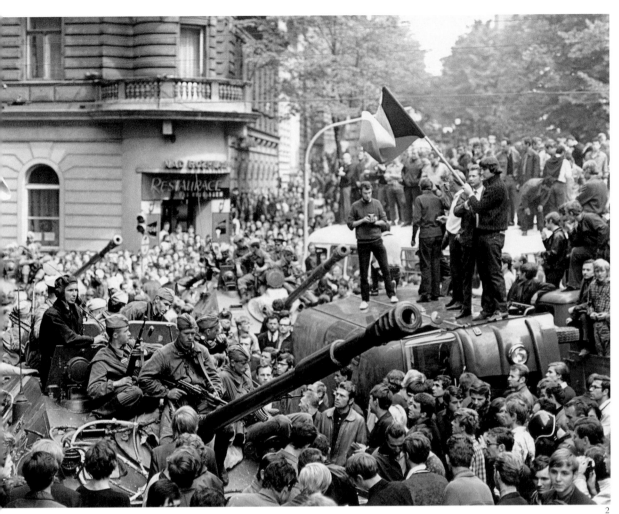

2

FOUR months later, a cold wind blew from the east. The Kremlin was not eased. Soviet tanks rumbled through the streets of Prague, restoring Soviet control. They brought the Prague Spring to an end, but not without a struggle. Czech freedom fighters, many of them young men and women, were largely unarmed, but were determined and, in this case, overturned one of the Soviet tanks (2), 21 August 1968.

VIER Monate später blies eisiger Wind aus dem Osten: Der Kreml war alles andere als begeistert – und sowjetische Panzer rollten über die Pflastersteinstraßen Prags und stellten die sowjetische Kontrolle wieder her. Sie erzwangen das Ende des Prager Frühlings – allerdings gegen erheblichen Widerstand: Die tschechischen Freiheitskämpfer, unter ihnen zahlreiche junge Männer und Frauen, waren in der Regel unbewaffnet, dafür um so entschlossener – und eroberten in diesem Fall (2) sogar einen sowjetischen Panzer – August 1968.

QUATRE mois plus tard, un vent froid souffle en provenance de l'Est : le Kremlin était tout sauf enthousiasmé – et les blindés soviétiques déferlent dans les rues pavées de Prague, rétablissant le contrôle soviétique. Ils imposent la fin du Printemps de Prague – mais malgré tout au prix d'une résistance considérable : les combattants de la liberté tchèques, parmi lesquels beaucoup d'hommes et de femmes encore tout jeunes, étaient en règle générale désarmés, mais d'autant plus déterminés et, dans le cas présent (2), ils ont même pris d'assaut un blindé soviétique – août 1968.

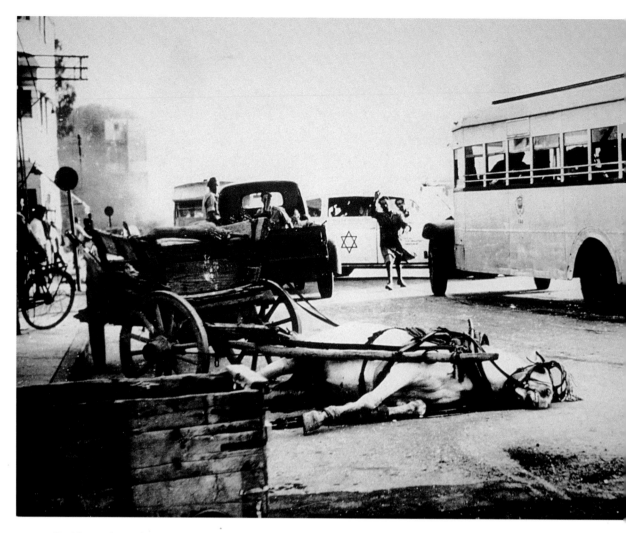

THE British mandate ended at midnight
14/15 May 1948. Immediately
Egyptian and Transjordan troops invaded
Palestine, and Egyptian planes bombed this
street in Tel Aviv (1). It took nearly 20
years, until 5 June 1967, for the Arab-Israeli
conflict to erupt into a full-blown war.
Israel, under the charismatic leadership of
General Moshe Dayan (4), emerged
triumphant. On 8 June, Egypt admitted
defeat (captured Egyptian troops, 2). A day
later, Israel began an all-out offensive hours
after Syria also accepted the ceasefire (3).
Yasser Arafat (5), leader of the Palestine
Liberation Organization, became the focus
of mass opposition.

DAS britische Mandat endete am 15. Mai
1948. Sofort begannen ägyptische und
transjordanische Truppen mit ihrer Invasion
Palästinas, und ägyptische Flugzeuge
bombardierten diese Straße in Tel Aviv (1).
Doch es dauerte fast zwanzig Jahre, bis am
5. Juni 1967 der israelisch-arabische
Konflikt zu einem Krieg auswuchs. Die

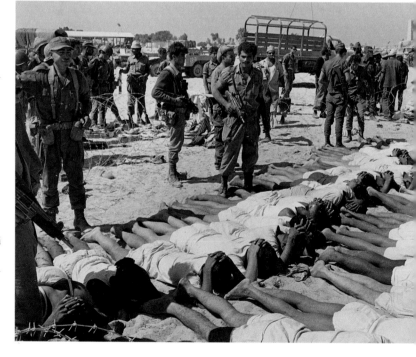

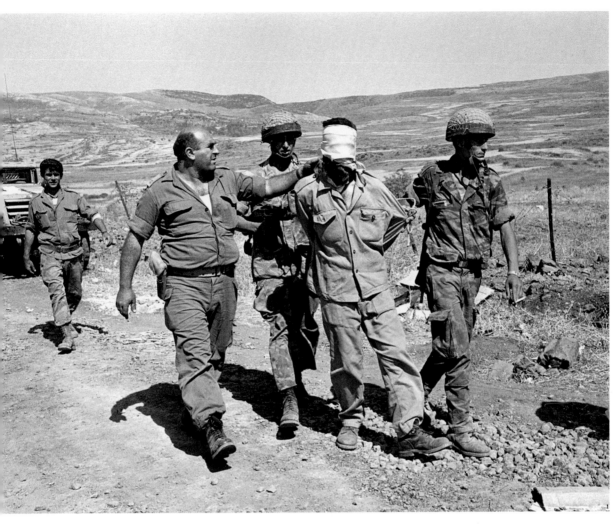

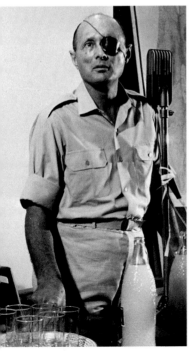

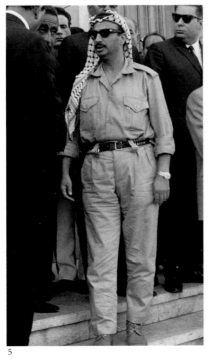

Israelis unter ihrem General Moshe Dayan
(4) waren siegreich. Am 8. Juni kapitulierten
die Ägypter (ägyptische Kriegsgefangene, 2).
Einen Tag darauf, nur Stunden nachdem
auch Syrien den Waffenstillstand akzeptiert
hatte (3), gingen die Israelis zum Groß-
angriff über. Der Palästinenserführer Yassir
Arafat (5) hatte viel Kritik einzustecken.

L E mandat britannique prit fin dans la
nuit du 14 au 15 mai 1948. Les troupes
égyptiennes et transjordaniennes envahirent
immédiatement la Palestine – des avions
égyptiens ont bombardé cette rue de Tel
Aviv (1). Il fallut près de vingt ans, jusqu'au
5 juin 1967, pour que la lutte israélo-arabe
se mue en conflit généralisé. Israël l'emporta
sous le commandement du général Moshe
Dayan (4). Le 8 juin, l'Égypte reconnut sa
défaite (2). Le lendemain, Israël entama une
offensive générale, des heures après que la
Syrie eut également accepté le cessez-le-feu
(3). Yasser Arafat (5), le chef de l'Organisation de libération de la Palestine, devint
l'objet d'une opposition massive.

5

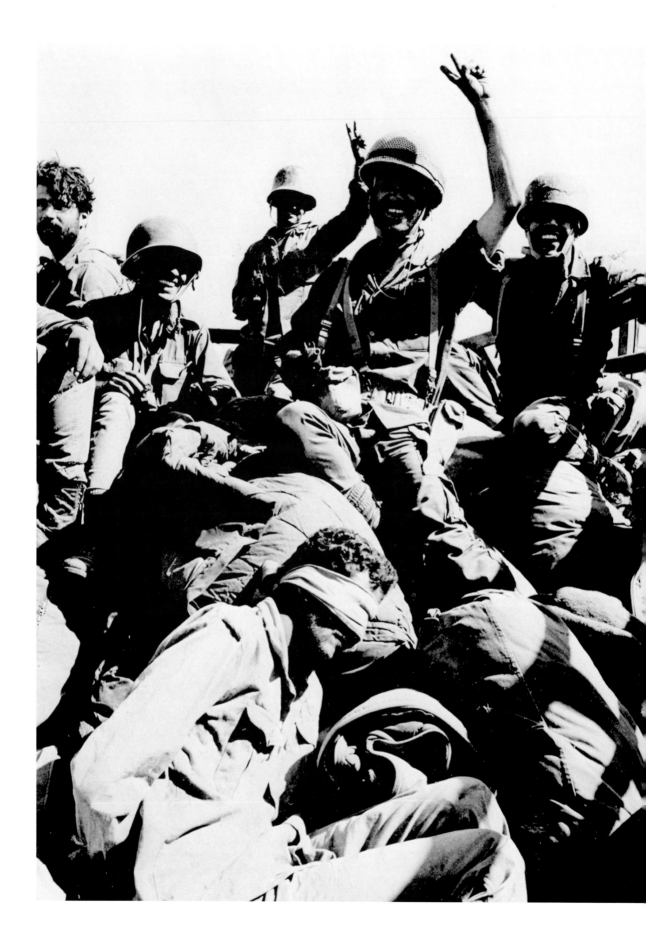

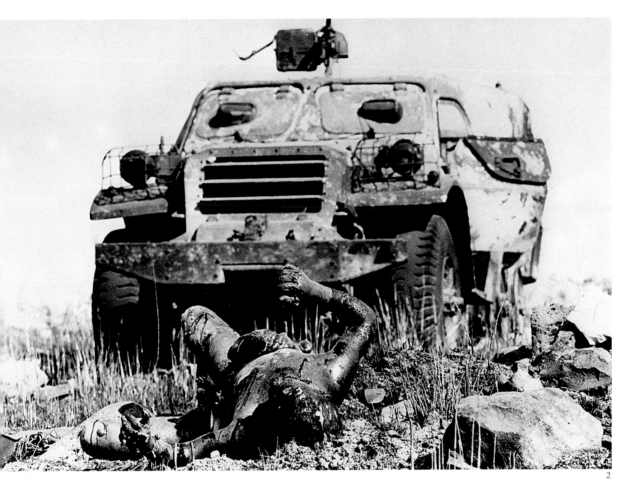

2

To the victor, glory and prisoners: Israeli troops had time to celebrate their occupation of the west bank of the Suez Canal during the Yom Kippur War, October 1973 (1). In the north, they were equally successful in their attack on the Golan Heights, where their napalm shells brought death in grotesque forms to Syrian soldiers (2). The war itself lasted only 18 days, before pressure from the US and the Soviet Union, and diplomacy by the UN brought an end to the fighting.

Für den Sieg: Israelische Truppen feiern die – als Antwort auf den ägyptischen Angriff im Oktober 1973 (Yom-Kippur-Krieg) erfolgte – vorübergehende Besetzung des westlichen Ufers am Suezkanal (1). Im Norden war Israels Antwort auf den gleichzeitigen syrischen Angriff durch die Besetzung der Golanhöhen ähnlich erfolgreich; hier brachten israelische Napalmbomben syrischen Soldaten den Tod in grotesker Gestalt (2). Der Krieg dauerte nur 18 Tage; Druck von Seiten der USA und der Sowjetunion sowie die Diplomatie der UN brachten die Waffen zum Schweigen.

Vive la victoire : des troupes israéliennes fêtent l'occupation provisoire de la rive occidentale du Canal de Suez (1) – réplique à l'attaque égyptienne d'octobre 1973 (guerre du Kippour). Dans le Nord, la réponse d'Israël à l'attaque syrienne simultanée a connu autant de succès avec l'occupation des hauteurs du Golan ; là-bas, des bombes au napalm israéliennes ont laissé des soldats syriens dans une posture grotesque après leur mort (2). La guerre n'a duré que 18 jours ; la pression des États-Unis et de l'Union soviétique ainsi que la diplomatie de l'ONU ont fait se taire les armes.

(Overleaf)
Soviet leader Leonid Brezhnev (fourth from right) and fellow Politburo members watching the Bolshevik anniversary parade in Red Square, Moscow, as the snow falls on Lenin's tomb on 10 November 1970. Crowds line up in the freezing snow at Red Square to visit Lenin's tomb in 1959 (inset).

(Folgende Seiten)
Der Führer der Sowjetunion, Leonid Breschnew (vierter von rechts), nimmt, zusammen mit weiteren Mitgliedern des Politbüros, aus Anlaß des Jahrestages der Oktoberrevolution am 10. November 1970 die Parade ab – während Schnee auf Lenins Grabmal fällt. Elf Jahre zuvor, 1959, steht eine Menschenmenge auf dem Roten Platz in eisiger Kälte Schlange, um Lenins Grabmal zu besuchen (Inset).

(Pages suivantes)
Le leader soviétique Leonid Brejnev (quatrième à partir de la droite) et ses collègues membres du Politburo assistent à la parade d'anniversaire bolchévique, sur la Place Rouge, à Moscou, lorsque les premières neiges tombent sur le mausolée de Lénine, le 10 novembre 1970. La foule fait la queue, les pieds gelés dans la neige, sur la Place Rouge, pour rendre visite au mausolée de Lénine, en 1959 (inset).

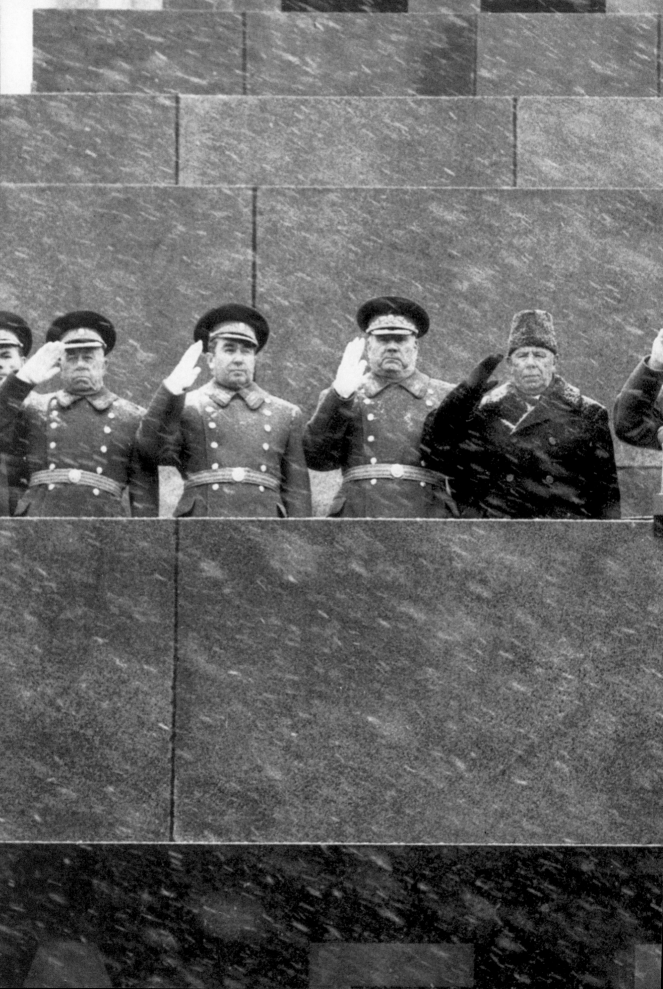

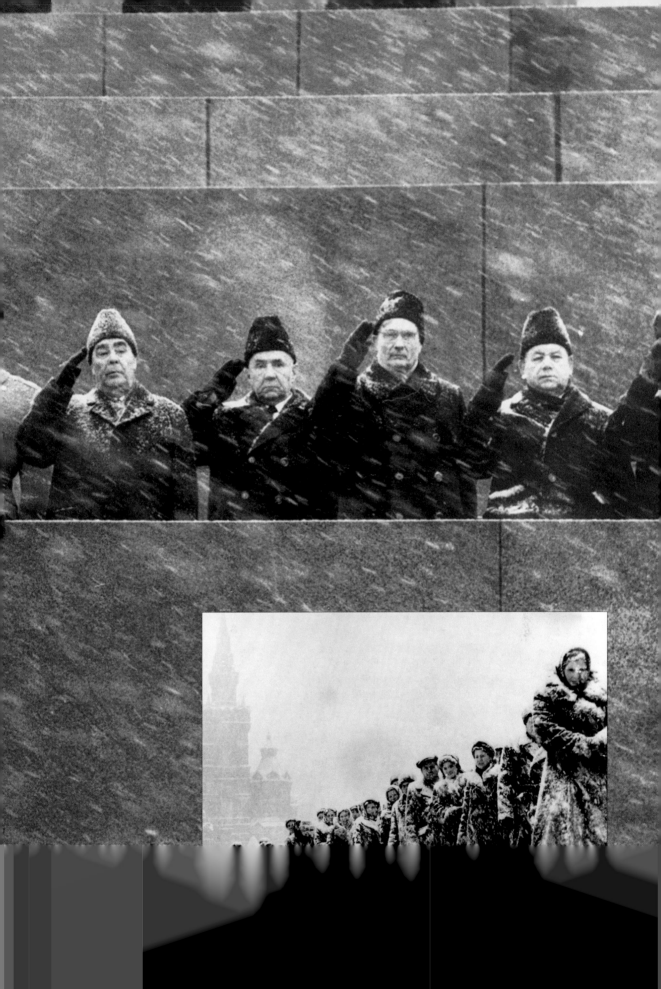

Civil Protest

IN South Africa the introduction of apartheid in 1948 (1) disbanded even the moderate Natives' Representative Council, leaving blacks no recourse but to work outside government dictates in order to pursue the mild but anti-segregationist policies of the Natives' Law Commission and to resist further forced deportations and cruel restrictions on their daily lives. In the United States (2), the foundation of the National Association for the Advancement of Colored Peoples (NAACP) threw into relief both the aspirations and the limitations of campaigns for a better deal for those whose living conditions continued, particularly in the Southern states, to show little improvement on those of their forefathers, imported into slavery.

The sheer scope of the 'Protest Movement', as it came to be called, was tremendous. Pastors such as the Reverend Frank Chikane and Archbishop Desmond Tutu in South Africa, Martin Luther King in the United States, militant separatist Black Moslems (Malcolm X) and Black Panthers (Bobby Seale, Eldridge Cleaver, Stokeley Carmichael), all had mass followings, protesting against not only local issues but highlighting a system of injustice against which many – particularly among the young – could unite in defiance. Against them were ranged fringe extremists like the Ku Klux Klan and the Afrikaner Brotherhood (A. W. B.) who sought to revive neo-Nazi visions of racial purity based on spurious biblical texts.

The whole western protest movement could be claimed to hinge on the strikes and sit-ins that culminated in all that went by the shorthand of 'May 1968', a time of spontaneous uprising in Paris and London, Rome and Berlin, Colombia and Berkeley. Solidarity with national liberation movements around the world; opposition to the Vietnam War and US 'neo-imperialism'; concern over the relevance of much that was taught in institutes of higher education: the basic upsurge of civil rights movements worldwide was deeply idealistic, frequently religious in its motivation and romantic in its expression.

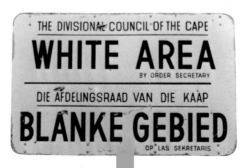

1

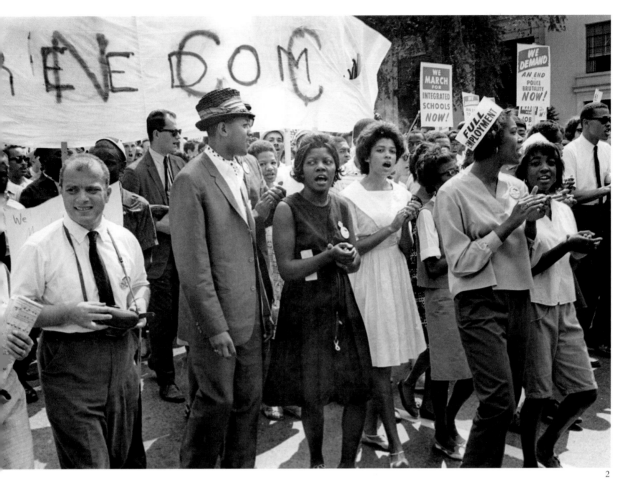

'INTRODUCTION de l'apartheid en Afrique du Sud en 1948 (1) entraîna la désagrégation du très modéré Conseil représentatif des indigènes. Dès lors, les Noirs n'eurent pas d'autre choix que celui d'agir en dehors du cadre imposé par les pouvoirs publics, d'une part pour suivre la Commission juridique des indigènes dans la voie antiségrégationniste toute modérée qui était la sienne, mais aussi pour résister à la multiplication des déportations forcées et aux vexations cruelles qu'ils subissaient dans leur vie quotidienne. Aux États-Unis (2), l'association nationale en faveur de la promotion des peuples de couleur (NAACP) suppléa aux limites des campagnes visant à améliorer le sort de ceux dont les conditions de vie, surtout dans les états du Sud, ne montraient guère d'amélioration par rapport à celles de leurs ancêtres amenés là en esclavage.

La portée du « Mouvement de protestation » comme on l'appela par la suite fut tout simplement immense. Il incluait des hommes d'église tels que le révérend Frank Chikane et l'archevêque Desmond Tutu en Afrique du Sud, ou encore Martin Luther King aux États-Unis, les militants séparatistes, Musulmans Noirs (les « Black Moslems » de Malcolm X) et Panthères Noires (« Black Panthers » – Bobby Seale, Eldridge Cleaver, Stokeley Carmichael) ; ils comptaient tous de nombreux fidèles parce que leur protestation, qui allait bien au-delà de problèmes locaux prétextes, portait sur un système injuste que beaucoup – surtout parmi les jeunes – défiaient en s'unissant. Ils avaient à faire aux éléments extrémistes de tous bords, tels le Ku Klux Klan et la Fraternité afrikaner (AWB) qui cherchaient à raviver les mythes néonazis de la pureté de la race fondés sur de faux textes bibliques.

On a pu dire de l'ensemble du mouvement de protestation occidental qu'il se joua dans les grèves et les occupations de locaux qui culminèrent dans ce qu'on appela « Mai 68 », époque de soulèvements spontanés à Paris, Londres, Rome, Berlin, Columbia et Berkeley. Solidarité avec les mouvements de libération nationale de par le monde, opposition à la guerre du Viêt-nam et au « néo-impérialisme » des États-Unis, vaste remise en question de la pertinence du contenu des programmes des établissements d'enseignement supérieur : au fond, les mouvements en faveur des droits civils qui avaient surgi partout à travers le monde étaient profondément idéalistes, fréquemment religieux dans leurs motivations et romantiques dans leur expression.

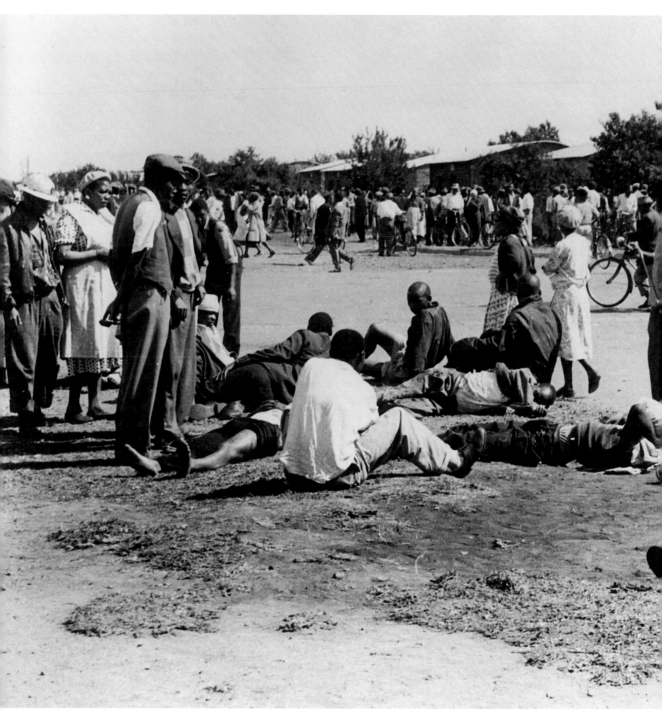

THE Sharpeville massacre, provoked by riots against the pass laws, took place in 1960 (1). Shortly afterwards Nelson Mandela, here photographed in discussion with a teacher (2), earned a reputation as the 'Black Pimpernel' for his resourcefulness in evading arrest. The 1964 Treason Trials sentenced him and eight others to life on Robben Island. Before his deportation he told the Pretoria courtroom: 'I do not deny that I planned sabotage. We had either to accept inferiority or fight against it by violence.' In Johannesburg, in June 1976, three days of uprising, leading to rioting and looting, left over 100 dead and 1,000 injured (3). Blacks were outraged at this response to an initially peaceful pupil-led protest, provoked when Afrikaans was suddenly made a compulsory subject on the school curriculum.

IM Jahre 1960 kam es nach Aufständen gegen die Paßgesetze zum Massaker vo Sharpeville (1). Später erwarb sich Nelson Mandela, hier im Gespräch mit einem Leh (2), seinen Ruf als »Schwarzer Pimpernell weil er sich so geschickt immer wieder de Verhaftung entzog. 1964 wegen Hochverr angeklagt, wurden er und acht andere zu lebenslanger Haft auf Robben Island verurteilt. Vor seiner Deportation sagte er: »l leugne nicht, daß ich sabotieren wollte. V

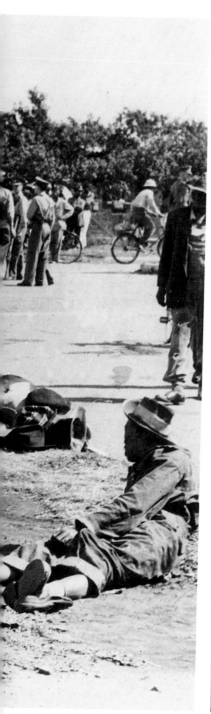

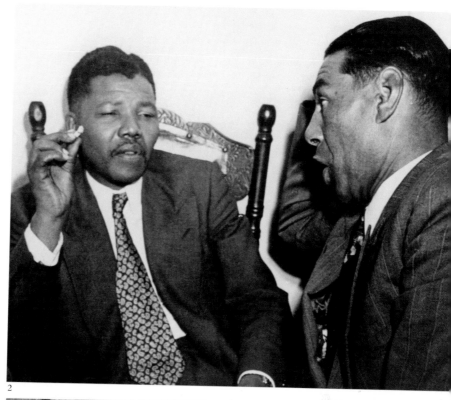

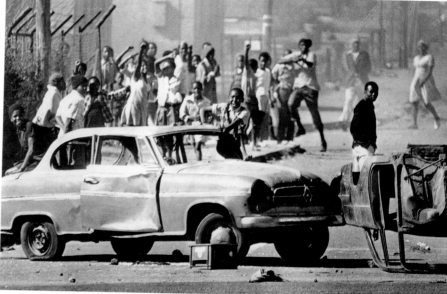

hatten nur die Wahl, unsere Benachteiligung
zu akzeptieren oder mit Gewalt dagegen
zu kämpfen.« Im Juni 1976 kam es in Johannesburg zu Aufständen und Plünderungen,
mit über hundert Toten und tausend Verletzten (3). Die Schwarzen waren empört
über die gewaltsame Reaktion auf einen
zunächst friedlichen Protest gegen ein Gesetz, das Afrikaans zum Pflichtfach in den
Schulen machte.

L E massacre de Sharpeville qui fit suite
aux émeutes déclenchées par les lois
entravant la libre circulation des Noirs eut
lieu en 1960 (1). Nelson Mandela, que l'on
voit ici photographié en discussion avec un
enseignant (2), y acquit peu de temps après
sa réputation de « Zorro Noir » tant il était
habile à échapper aux arrestations. Jugé
pour trahison en 1964, il fut condamné
avec huit autres personnes à la prison à
perpétuité sur Robben Island. Dans la salle

du tribunal à Prétoria il déclara : « Je ne
nie pas l'intention de sabotage. Soit nous
acceptions le statut d'infériorité soit nous le
combattions par la violence. » À Johannesburg, en juin 1976, trois jours de soulèvements se traduisent par mille blessés et plus
de cent morts (3). Les Noirs s'étaient sentis
outragés par cette mesure prise en réponse
à une protestation contre l'introduction
soudaine de l'afrikaans obligatoire à l'école.

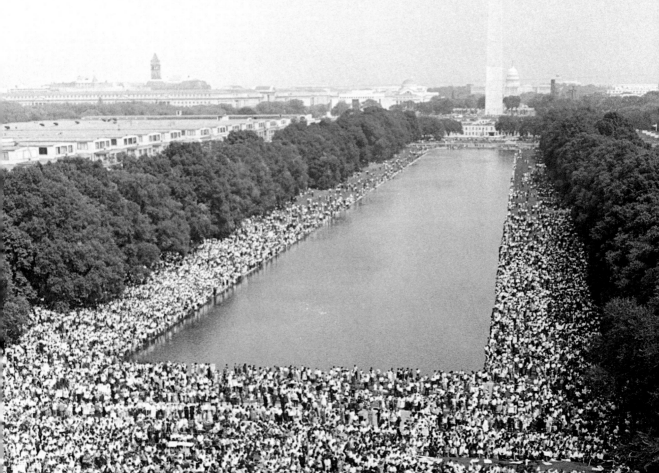

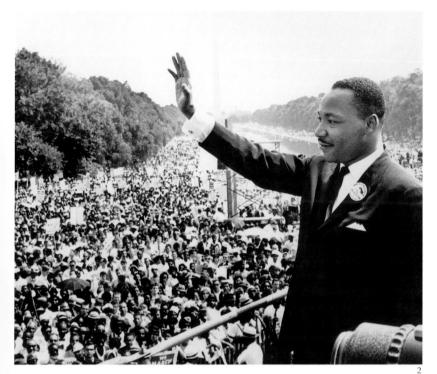

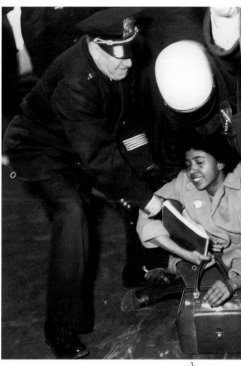

2

3

MARTIN Luther King addresses a crowd of a quarter of a million that included show business stars Marlon Brando, Burt Lancaster, Judy Garland and Bob Dylan (1, 2): 'I have a dream that one day this nation will rise up and live out the true meaning of its creed: "We hold these truths to be self-evident, that all men are created equal".' A year after President Lyndon Johnson signed the Civil Rights Act, he met with the six nuns leading the Civil Rights March from Selma, Alabama. The protest was in defiance of the police ban imposed after a gang of white supremacists attacked three liberal clergymen. One, the Rev. Reep, later died from his injuries. Pickets sitting down before the White House were bodily hauled away into police paddy wagons to be booked (3).

MARTIN Luther King spricht vor einer Viertelmillion Zuhörern, darunter die Stars Marlon Brando, Burt Lancaster, Judy Garland und Bob Dylan (1, 2): »Ich hatte einen Traum. Mir träumte, wie sich eines Tages diese Nation erheben wird und Wirklichkeit werden läßt, was sie sich auf die Fahnen geschrieben hat: Folgende Wahrheit halten wir für selbstverständlich: daß alle Menschen gleich geboren sind.« Ein Jahr nachdem Präsident Lyndon Johnson das Bürgerrechtsgesetz unterzeichnet hatte, traf er sich mit sechs Nonnen, den Führerinnen eines Protestmarsches, der von Selma, Alabama, ausging. Diese Demonstration setzte sich über das polizeiliche Verbot hinweg, das nach einem Überfall weißer Extremisten auf drei liberale Geistliche erfolgt war. Einer von ihnen, Reverend Reep, starb später an den Folgen seiner Verletzungen. Streikposten, die sich vor dem Weißen Haus niedergelassen hatten, wurden fortgezerrt und zum Verhör gebracht (3).

MARTIN Luther King harangue une foule d'un quart de millions de personnes et parmi elles des vedettes du spectacle tels que Marlon Brando, Burt Lancaster, Judy Garland et Bob Dylan (1 et 2) : « Je rêve du jour où cette nation se lèvera pour vivre pleinement le sens véritable du credo qu'elle a fait sien : nous tenons pour évidentes ces vérités comme quoi tous les hommes ont été créés égaux. » Un an après avoir paraphé la loi sur les droits du citoyen, le président Lyndon Johnson rencontra les six religieuses qui conduisaient en mars la marche en faveur des droits civils partie de Selma dans l'Alabama. Il s'agissait d'une protestation contre les mesures d'interdiction décidées par la police après l'attaque commise sur trois religieux libéraux par une bande de militants convaincus de la supériorité blanche. Un des religieux, le révérend Reep, devait plus tard décéder des suites de ses blessures. Les manifestants qui ont installé des piquets devant la Maison blanche sont traînés à l'intérieur des cars de police (3).

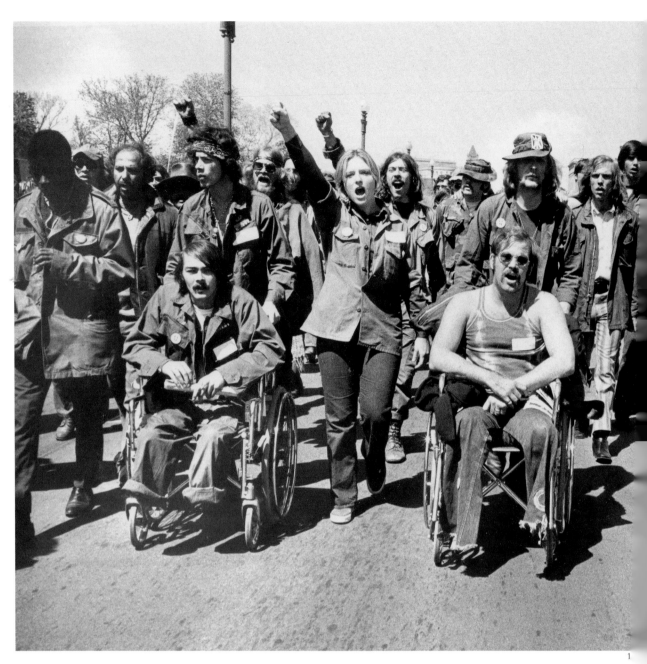

1

THE recriminations had already started back in the 1960s, with mass demonstrations in the States against the Vietnam War. What surprised the American administration was that anti-war sentiment ran high among businessmen like David Moss, a real-estate broker who sat down with thousands of others in October 1969 (2). The young continued to burn their draft cards, even on the steps of the Pentagon (3), but it was the Vietnam vets whose voices sounded most strongly against the war (1). The cost, the shame and the sorrow of the war had come home to the United States, and the American people were deeply moved.

ERSTE Vorwürfe wurden bereits in den 1960er Jahren laut – mit Massendemonstrationen gegen den Vietnamkrieg in den Vereinigten Staaten. Was die amerikanische Regierung dabei am meisten verwunderte, war die Tatsache, daß die Antikriegshaltung auch unter Geschäftsleuten weit verbreitet war – hier David Moss, ein Immobilienmakler, der sich im Oktober 1969 zusammen mit

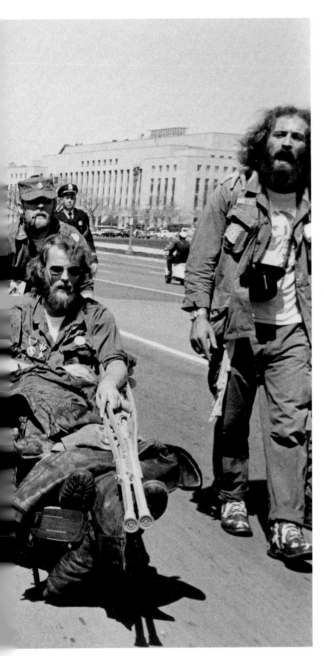

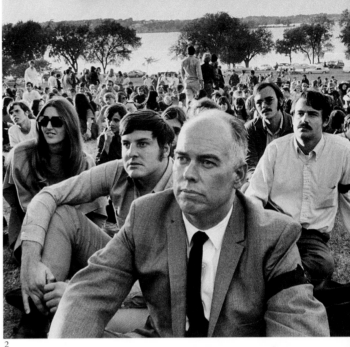

2

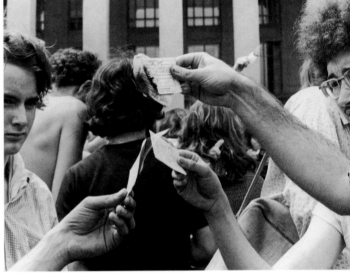

3

Tausenden von Demonstranten auf die Straße setzte (2). Die jungen Männer verbrannten ihre Einberufungsbescheide – sogar auf den Stufen des Pentagon (3). Die stärkste Stimme gegen den Krieg kam jedoch von den Vietnamveteranen. Die Kosten, die Scham und das Leid des Krieges waren in die USA zurückgekehrt – und die amerikanische Bevölkerung war tief erschüttert.

DE premiers reproches se sont fait entendre dès les années 60 – avec des manifestations de masse contre la guerre du Vietnam aux États-Unis. Ce qui a le plus étonné le gouvernement américain, c'est le fait que cette attitude antimilitarisme était aussi très répandue parmi les hommes d'affaire – ici, David Moss, un agent immobilier qui s'assoit dans la rue en octobre 1969 avec des milliers de manifestants (2). Des jeunes hommes brûlent leur ordre d'appel sous les drapeaux – et ce, jusque sur les marches du Pentagone (3). Mais ce sont cependant les vétérans du Vietnam qui s'opposent le plus violemment à la guerre. Les coûts, la honte et les souffrances de la guerre sont révélés aux États-Unis – et la population américaine se montre profondément ébranlée.

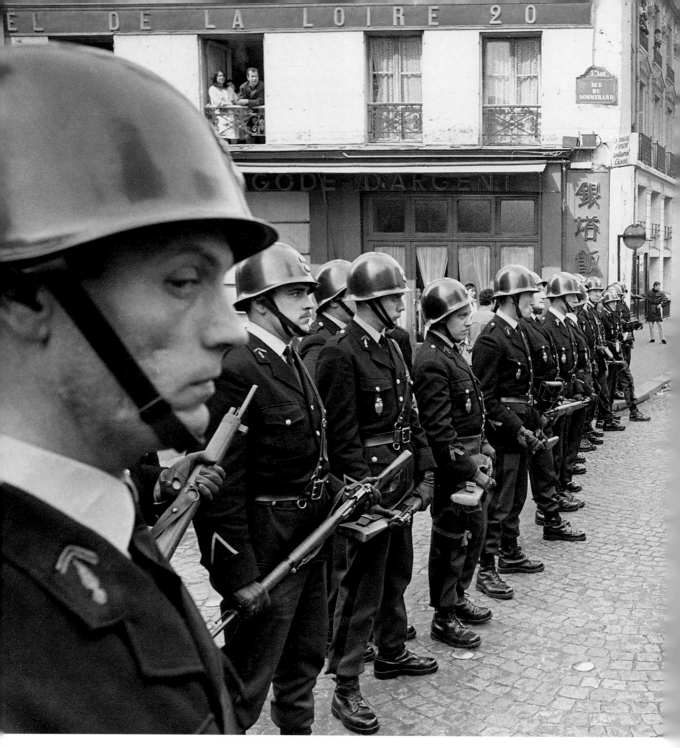

JEAN-PAUL Sartre did it. Simone de Beauvoir did it. In May 1968 it was hard to encounter anyone who *did not* have a part to play in *les événements* (1) or didn't at least claim they had, safely after the event. The Canadian writer Mavis Gallant kept a diary and observed that Sorbonne stone-throwing (4) brought forth the CRS with military responses of teargas (2) and baton charges (3): '… med. students kept out of it at the beginning, joined movement only as a reaction against the police… it wasn't safe for a doctor to help the wounded unless the doctor wore a helmet… wounded on stretchers beaten in a kind of frenzy. In Latin Quarter now, faces bruised, casts and bandages for what would seem to be ski accidents in another season, but these are fresh. Tendency of boys to behave like Old Soldiers: "I was on the barricades" like "I was in the Résistance"' (*Paris Notebooks 1968-86*).

JEAN-PAUL Sartre war dabei, Simone de Beauvoir war dabei. Im Mai 1968 war es schwer, jemanden zu finden, der *nicht* bei den *événements* dabeigewesen war (1). Die kanadische Schriftstellerin Mavis Gallant führte Tagebuch und beschreibt, wie sich die CRS von den Steinwürfen an der Sorbonne (2) zu martialischen Antworten mit Tränengas (3) und Schlagstöcken (4) hinreißen ließ: »Die Medizinstudenten hielten sich anfangs heraus und machten

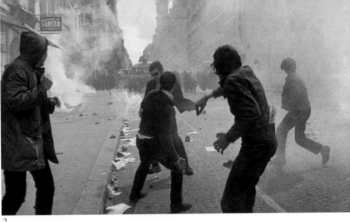

2

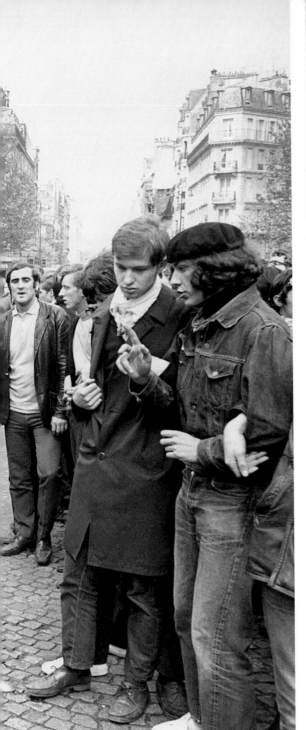

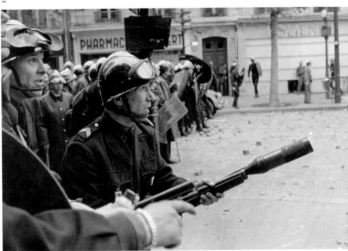

4

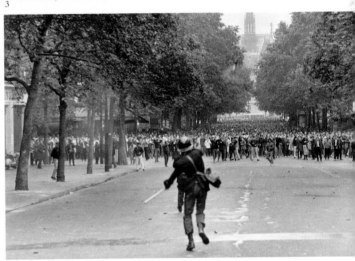

3

rst später aus Protest gegen die Polizei
it… selbst auf die Verwundeten auf ihren
ragen schlugen sie noch in einer Art
ausch ein. Jetzt bin ich im Quartier
atin, zerschundene Gesichter, Bandagen
nd Gipsverbände, zu anderen Zeiten hätte
an sie für die Opfer von Skiunfällen ge-
alten, doch die Verletzungen sind frisch.
ie Jungs führen sich auf wie alte Kämpfer:
ch war auf den Barrikaden‹, genau wie
e Alten einem ›Ich war bei der Résistance‹
rzählen«. (*Paris Notebooks*, 1968-86).

JEAN-PAUL Sartre y était. Simone de
Beauvoir aussi. En mai 1968, il était fort
difficile de rencontrer quelqu'un qui n'avait
pas joué un rôle dans les événements, ou
du moins qui le clamait très fort dès lors
que tout danger semblait écarté (1). L'écrivain canadien Mavis Gallant, qui tenait son
journal, observa les lanceurs de pavés de la
Sorbonne (4) face aux CRS armés de gaz
lacrymogènes (2) et de gourdins (3) : « Les
étudiants en médecine restèrent dès le début
à l'écart, ne se joignant au mouvement que

pour réagir contre la police (…) Il était
risqué pour un médecin d'aider les blessés,
sauf si le médecin portait un casque (…)
Maintenant, au Quartier latin, des visages
meurtris, des plâtres et des pansements
pour ce qui ressemble à des accidents de
ski survenus en une autre saison (…)
Tendance des garçons à se conduire en
vétérans : ‹ J'ai fait les barricades ›, comme
‹ J'étais dans la Résistance ›. »
(*Paris Notebooks* 1968-1986)

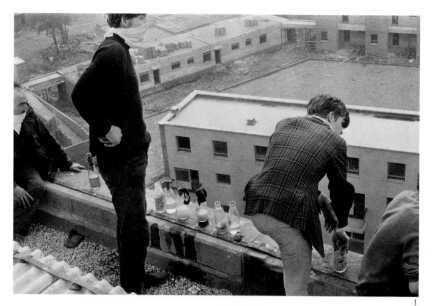

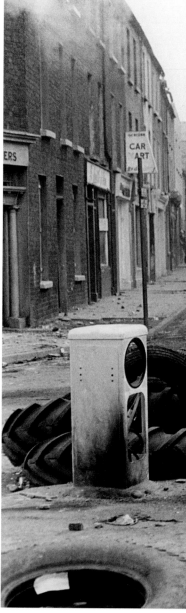

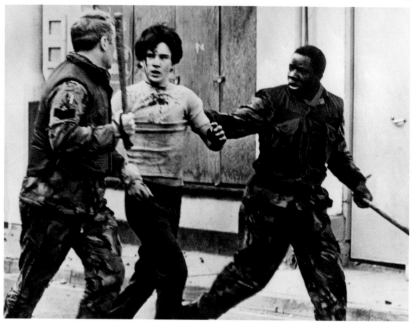

IN July 1969, shortly after the Protestants'
annual Orange Day parades, violence
erupted on the streets of Belfast and Londonderry (even the name was contentious,
Catholics preferring to leave off the English
prefix). Sympathies in the 'six counties'
of Northern Ireland were sharply divided
between the Protestant majority, who wanted
to retain rule from Westminster, and the
Roman Catholic minority, who wanted
union with Eire (Ireland). While the former
organized the paramilitary forces of the Ulster
Freedom Fighters and the Ulster Volunteer
Forces, the latter revived the military wing of
the Irish Republican Army and spawned a

radical new branch, the Irish National
Liberation Army. In August 1969 British
troops were sent in 'to keep the warring
factions apart' and 'restore the peace'
– the start of twenty-five further years
of 'troubles'.

A cheap weapon of choice was the
petrol bomb, often fired by youths (1).
Street barricades were hastily thrown up
from pallets and tyres (3). With youth
unemployment, especially among Catholics,
being the highest in the UK, many were
drawn into the street fighting almost as a
rite of passage to prove their manhood (2).

IM Juli 1969 kam es kurz nach den jähr-
lichen protestantischen Umzügen zum
Oraniertag zu Unruhen in Belfast und
Londonderry. Die Meinungen in den »sec
Grafschaften« Nordirlands waren streng
gespalten zwischen der protestantischen
Mehrheit, die weiterhin von Westminster
regiert werden wollte, und der katholisch
Minderheit, die eine Vereinigung mit der
Republik Irland forderte. Die Protestante
organisierten sich in den paramilitärischen
Truppen der Ulster Freedom Fighters und
Ulster Volunteer Forces, die Katholiken
ließen den militärischen Flügel der Irisch-
Republikanischen Armee wiederaufleben
und gründeten einen radikalen neuen Zw

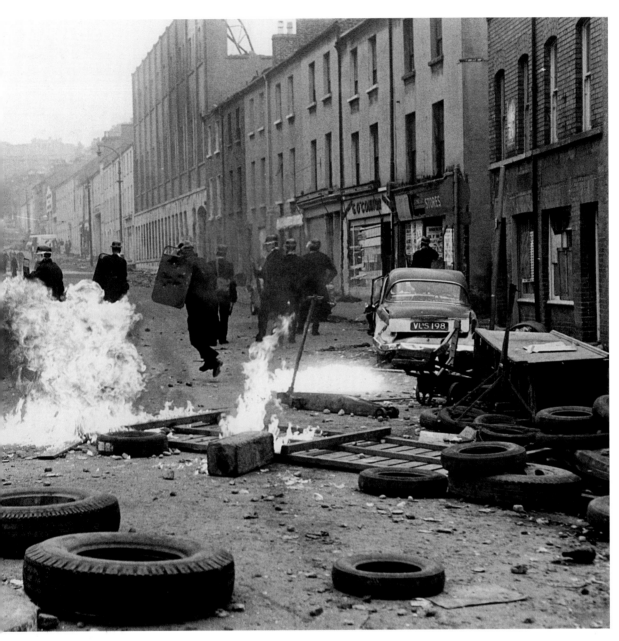

e Irisch-Nationale Befreiungsarmee. 1969 hickte London Truppen nach Nordirland, m Konfrontationen zwischen den sich kriegenden Parteien zu verhindern« und en Frieden wiederherzustellen« – der eginn von mittlerweile mehr als 25 Jahre ährenden Unruhen.

Eine beliebte, weil billige Waffe waren andbomben, die oft von Jugendlichen eworfen wurden (1). Barrikaden wurden aller Eile aus Paletten und Autoreifen er- chtet (3). Die Jugendarbeitslosigkeit, gerade ter den Katholiken, war die höchste in roßbritannien, und für viele waren die raßenkämpfe das einzige Mittel, mit dem e ihre Männlichkeit beweisen konnten (2).

EN juillet 1969, juste après les parades annuelles des protestants pour le Orange Day, la violence éclata dans les rues de Belfast et de Londonderry (pour lequel le nom même donnait lieu à des discussions : les catholiques préférant ignorer le préfixe anglais). Les sympathies dans les « six comtés » d'Irlande du Nord étaient nettement tran- chées entre la majorité protestante, qui dési- rait conserver la règle de Westminster, et la minorité catholique romaine qui désirait l'union avec l'Eire (Irlande du Sud). Alors que les premiers organisaient les forces paramili- taires de l'Ulster Freedom Fighters et les Ulster Volunteer Forces, les seconds faisaient renaître l'aile militaire de l'Armée républi- caine irlandaise et donnaient naissance à une

nouvelle branche radicale, l'Armée de libé- ration nationale irlandaise. En août 1969, le gouvernement britannique envoya des troupes dans le but de « séparer les factions guerrières » et de « rétablir la paix », ce qui n'eut pour autre résultat que de déclencher les « troubles » qui durent depuis vingt-cinq ans. Le cocktail Molotov, une arme bon marché, était souvent utilisé par les jeunes (1). Les barricades de rues étaient érigées à la hâte avec des caisses et des pneus (3). Les jeunes chômeurs, de plus en plus nombreux au Royaume-Uni, en particulier chez les catholiques, se mêlent aux combats de rue qui sont presque devenus un rite d'initiation à la virilité (2).

RIOT-SHIELDED British soldiers with a bleeding and unarmed protester (2). To many, the face of bigotry is that of the Reverend Ian Paisley, Ulster Unionist MP and a Protestant minister who sees the Pope as the anti-Christ. Here he is protesting away from home (1), at the celebration of a Catholic Mass at Canterbury Cathedral for the first time in 400 years in July 1970. A British soldier drags a Catholic protester (3) during the 'Bloody Sunday' killings on 30 January 1972 when 13 Catholic civil rights marchers were shot dead in Londonderry by the British army.

MIT Schilden geschützte britische Soldaten führen einen unbewaffneten, blutenden Demonstranten ab (2). Für viele die Bigotterie in Person: Reverend Ian Paisley, Parlamentsmitglied der Unionisten und protestantischer Geistlicher, für den der Papst der Antichrist ist. Hier (1) protestiert er in England, vor der Kathedrale von Canterbury, wo im Juli 1970 zum ersten Mal seit 400 Jahren eine katholische Messe zelebriert wurde. Ein britischer Soldat führt einen katholischen Demonstranten während des »Blutigen Sonntags« ab; an diesem 30. Januar 1972 wurden in Londonderry 13 katholische Bürgerrechtler von der britischen Armee erschossen.

LES soldats britanniques équipés d'une protection anti-émeute arrêtent un manifestant blessé et sans armes (2). Le visage de la bigoterie est pour beaucoup symbolisé par celui du Révérend Ian Paisley, unioniste de l'Ulster et ministre protestant qui considère le pape comme un militant de l'Antéchrist. Ici, il manifeste en Angleterre (1), en 1970, contre la célébration (la première depuis quatre siècles) d'une messe catholique à la cathédrale de Canterbury. Un soldat britannique pousse un manifestant catholique pendant le « Dimanche sanglant » ; ce 30 janvier 1972, à Londonderry, treize défenseurs de droits civiques catholiques ont été abattus par l'armée britannique.

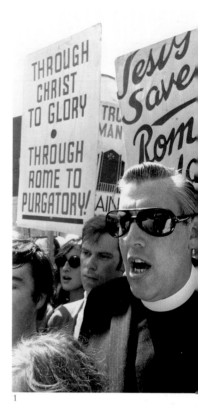

1

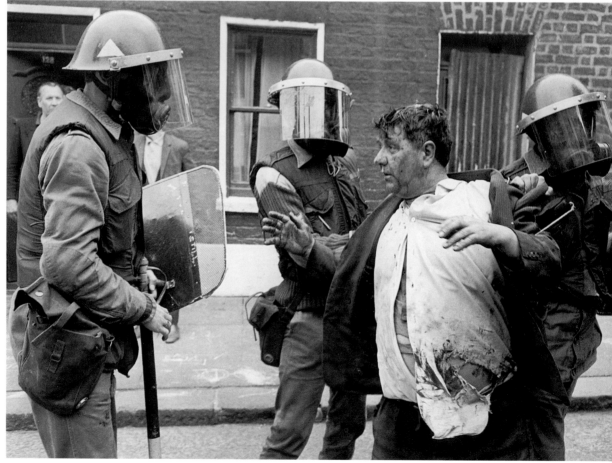

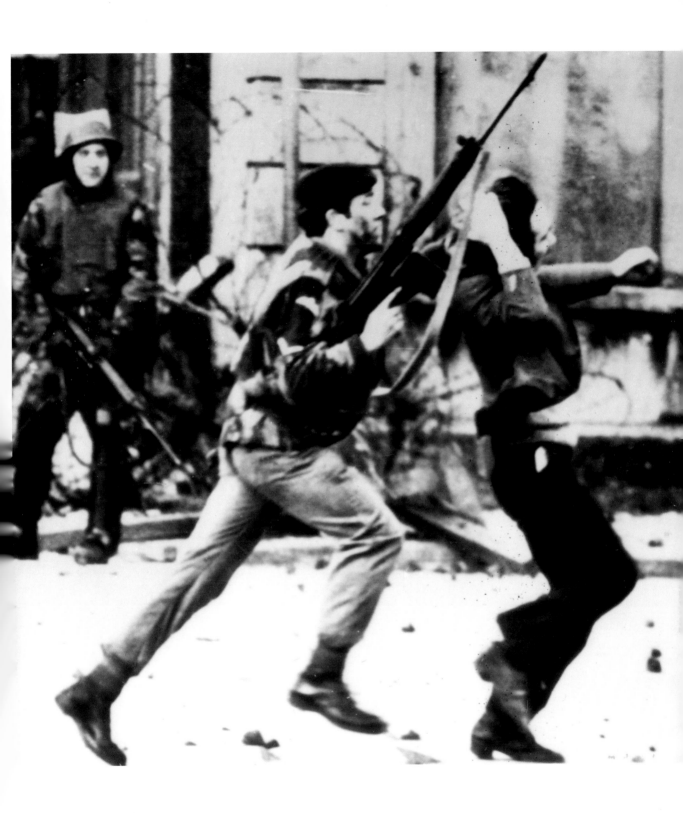

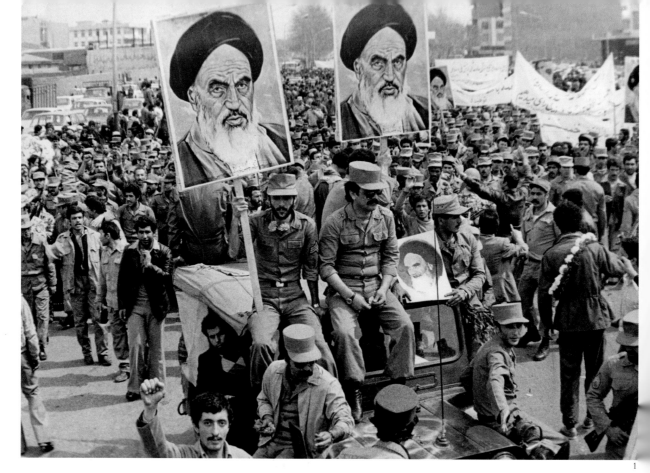

1

IT was with the Iranian Revolution of 1979 that a wave of politicized militancy swept through the Moslem world. Having forced their Shah into peripatetic exile, the Iranians called on other Moslem countries likewise to depose and replace their 'westernized' rulers. Called 'fundamentalism' by non-Moslems, the revolution was epitomized by the creation of a theocratic Islamic state by Ayatollah Khomeini (whose picture is carried through Tehran, 1) and by these women standing guard in Tehran (2) – women issued with modern weapons but directed to wear medieval clothing, with heavy penalties for uncovering their arms or hair.

IN der Folge der iranischen Revolution von 1979 ging eine Welle der Politisierung und Militarisierung durch die islamische Welt. Nachdem die Iraner den Schah in ein klägliches Exil gezwungen hatten, riefen sie ihre moslemischen Brüder auf, ihnen nachzueifern und ebenfalls ihre »verwestlichten« Herrscher abzusetzen. Sinnbilder dieser Revolution, die die Ungläubigen »Fundamentalismus« nennen und die einen theokratischen islamischen Staat begründete, sind der Ayatolla Khomeini (dessen Bild hier durch die Straßen Teherans getragen wird, 1) und diese Frauen, die in Teheran Wache halten (2) – Frauen, die moderne Gewehre, doch mittelalterliche Kleidung tragen, bei schwerer Strafe, wenn sie Arme oder Haar entblößen.

AVEC la révolution iranienne de 1979, le monde musulman fut traversé par une vague de militantisme politico-religieux sans précédent. Après avoir contraint leur Shah à errer en exil, les Iraniens exhortèrent les autres pays musulmans à déposer eux aussi leurs « dirigeants occidentalisés ». Taxée de « fondamentaliste » par les non-musulmans, la révolution se traduisit par l'instauration d'un État islamique théocratique avec l'ayatollah Khomeyni à sa tête (dont le portrait est arboré à travers les rues de Téhéran, 1). Ces femmes qui montent la garde à Téhéran (2), équipées d'armes modernes, sont cependant enjointes de s'habiller de façon médiévale au risque d'encourir de lourdes peines en cas de désobéissance.

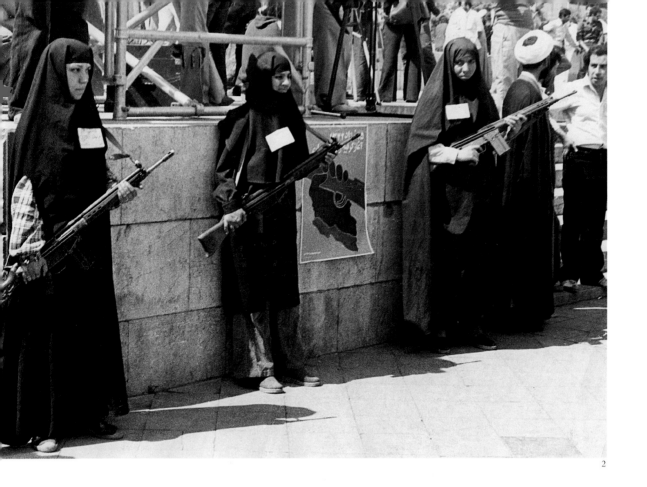

2

Cinema

CINEMA is essentially a twentieth-century phenom - enon, and although silent films are regarded nostalgically by buffs, the real heyday of the movies did not begin until the first 'talkie', Al Jolson's *The Jazz Singer*, came out in 1927. The Thirties saw a peak of activity, with the first colour films and the development of the Hollywood star system. Among the most luminous of the stars was Charlie Chaplin (1889-1977), reckoned the most popular film personality in the world for 25 years. Although he achieved great things as a writer, director, producer, musician and actor, it was as the last that he excelled. He created a character that was both entirely of its period and entirely his own: the Tramp. For this he borrowed Fatty Arbuckle's volum-inous trousers, one of Mack Swain's bushy moustaches (drastically trimmed), Ford Sterling's boatsized shoes (on the wrong feet), a tight jacket and a tiny derby, and the little Tramp emerged, forever down-at-heel, out of luck and on a collision course with the unwieldy world around him. This still from 1928 (1) shows Chaplin as he epitomized silent cinema, introducing pathos and humour to an adoring audience.

The decades of the Thirties and Forties could boast such highly stylized screen goddesses as Marlene Dietrich, Bette Davis and Greta Garbo. One other Nordic beauty boasted far more natural attributes, and contributed a lengthy variety of performances with many of the major directors of the day. Ingrid Bergman, known equally for her luminous loveliness and her 'immoral' (i.e. Swedish) love-life (for which a US senator denounced her as Hollywood's Apostle of Degradation), made her best films early on. Here she relaxes at the Tower of Lond with director Alfred Hitchcock in 1948 before maki *Under Capricorn*, a film that commenced the dow ward spiral of her career (2).

Dietrich was Paramount's answer to MGM's Gr Garbo – both embodied the alluring and ambiguo spirit of the Thirties, and both had relatively lit success beyond it. While dancing in a revue Dietri was spotted by the director Josef von Sternbe (overleaf, 1). He immediately cast her to play the part the cabaret singer and *femme fatale* Lola opposite En Jannings as the ultimately destroyed professor in his and her – most famous film, *The Blue Angel* (1930).

Brigitte Bardot was a generation younger, a blon sex kitten to Dietrich's sophisticate. Known in h native France as Bébé, after both her initials and h babydoll looks, Bardot (overleaf 2) caused hea scratching when she paraded through the crowds at t 1956 Cannes Film Festival.

There were threats to Cinema's very existence television moved into most homes during the 1950s a 1960s, but wide screen, surround sound and the mul plex saw Hollywood return to financial triumph couple of generations later while, on the other side the world, Bollywood emerged as the twin pillar of t new golden age. It was time, once again, to roll out t red carpets and hold back the crowds of worshipp who gathered at movie premieres. Scre gods and goddesses never had it so goo for films now came in series – fi *Rockys*, six *Star Wars*, eight *Har Potters*. Who could ask for anythi more?

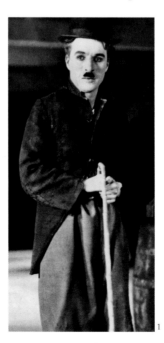

1

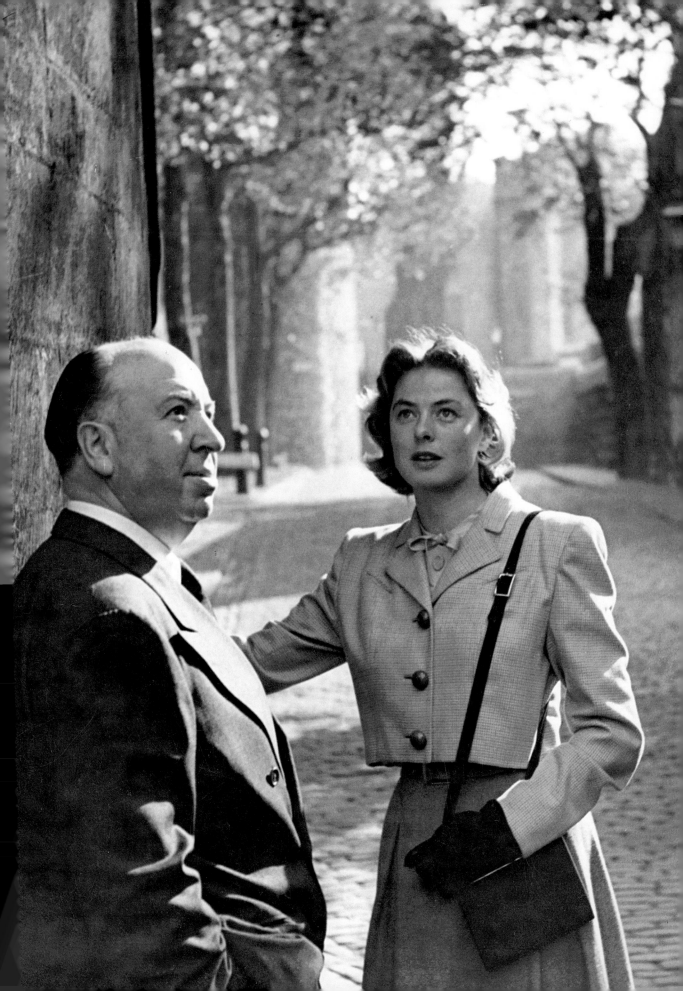

DAS Kino ist im Grunde ein Phänomen des 20. Jahrhunderts, und auch wenn Stummfilme ihre nostalgischen Verehrer haben, begann doch die eigentliche Blütezeit des Films erst mit dem ersten »talkie«, *Der Jazzsänger* mit Al Jolson von 1927. Ein erster Höhepunkt waren die 30er Jahre mit der Entwicklung des Farbfilms und der Etablierung des Hollywood-Starsystems. Zu den größten Stars dieser Ära zählte Charlie Chaplin (1889-1977), knapp 25 Jahre lang weltweit der beliebteste Filmschauspieler überhaupt. Auch als Drehbuchautor, Regisseur, Produzent und Komponist von Filmmusiken leistete er Großes, doch vor allem war er natürlich ein begnadeter Schauspieler. Er schuf eine Gestalt, die Inbegriff ihrer Zeit und auch Inbegriff von Chaplin selbst war: den Tramp. Dazu borgte er sich von Fatty Arbuckle die zu weiten Hosen, von Mack Swain den struppigen Schnurrbart (drastisch getrimmt), von Ford Sterling die unförmigen Schuhe (und vertauschte rechten und linken), nahm eine enge Jacke und einen winzigen Bowler, und schon war der kleine Tramp geboren, stets abgerissen, der ewige Verlierer, immer auf Kollisionskurs mit der allzu schwierigen Welt. Dieses Standphoto von 1928 (vorherige Seite, 1) zeigt uns Chaplin, wie er zum Inbegriff des Stummfilms wurde, zu einem Mann, der wie kein anderer dem Publikum Humor und Melancholie nahebrachte – und das Publikum liebte ihn dafür.

Die 30er und 40er Jahre glänzten mit hochstilisierten Filmgöttinnen wie Marlene Dietrich, Bette Davis und Greta Garbo. Eine andere nordische Schönheit gab sich im Vergleich dazu wesentlich natürlicher und spielte die verschiedensten Rollen unter einigen der bedeutendsten Regisseuren ihrer Zeit: Ingrid Bergman, für ihre strahlende Schönheit wie für ihren »unmoralischen« (sprich schwedischen) Lebenswandel bekannt (für den ein amerikanischer Senator sie »Hollywoods Apostel der Schamlosigkeit« nannte), drehte ihre besten Filme zu Anfang ihrer Karriere. Hier macht sie mit dem Regisseur Alfred Hitchcock einen Ausflug in den Londoner Tower, vor Beginn der Dreharbeiten zu *Sklavin des Herzens* (1948); das war der Film, mit dem der Niedergang ihrer Karriere begann (vorherige Seite, 2).

Die Dietrich war Paramounts Antwort auf MGMs Greta Garbo – beide verkörperten den Typus der geheimnisvollen und verführerischen Frau der 30er Jahre, und beide kamen über diese Rolle nie hinaus. Dietrich wurde von Regisseur Josef von Sternberg (1) in einer Revuetruppe entdeckt. Er gab ihr auf Anhieb die Rolle der Nachtclubsängerin und *Femme fatale* Lola, die in seinem – und ihrem – berühmtesten Film,

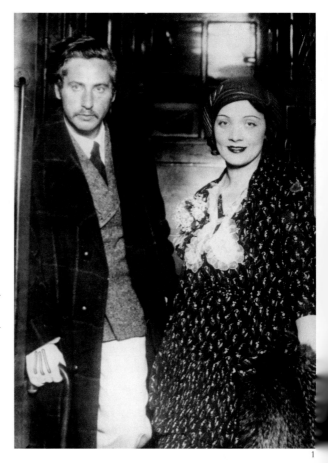

1

Der blaue Engel von 1930, Emil Jannings ins Verderben stürzt.

Brigitte Bardot war der Star der nächsten Generation, eine sexy Blondine, ungleich unkomplizierter als die Dietrich. Zu Hause in Frankreich nannte man sie »Bébé«, ein Spiel mit ihren Initialen und ihrem Auftreten als naive Kindfrau. Hier stolziert sie ketten- und hüftschwingend zum Filmfestival in Cannes 1956 (2).

Als in den 50er und 60er Jahren das Fernsehen Einzug in die Wohnzimmer hielt, war das Kino bedroht. Doch Riesenleinwände, Surround-Sound und Multiplex Kinos sorgten einige Jahrzehnte später dafür, daß Hollywood erneut triumphierte. Ein zweiter Stützpfeiler dieses neuen goldenen Zeitalters entstand auf der anderen Seite der Welt: Bollywood. Man rollte wieder die roten Teppiche aus, an denen die Fans standen und ihre Stars bejubelten. Leinwandgötter und -göttinnen hatten es noch nie so gut, denn Filme gab es jetzt in Serie: fünf *Rockys*, sechs *Star Wars*, acht Mal *Harry Potter*. Was wollte man mehr?

LE cinéma est essentiellement un phénomène du XXe siècle, et bien que les experts contemplent les films muets avec un brin de nostalgie, le véritable âge d'or du Septième Art n'a commencé qu'avec *Le Chanteur de jazz,* de Alan Crosland, premier film parlant, sorti en 1927 avec la voix de Al Jolson. Les années 30 ont connu un sommet d'activité avec les premiers films en couleurs et le développement du *star-system* à Hollywood. L'un des monstres sacrés fut Charlie Chaplin (1889-1977), considéré pendant près d'un quart de siècle comme la plus grande vedette populaire au niveau planétaire. Bien qu'il réalisât de grandes choses en tant qu'écrivain, réalisateur, producteur et musicien, il excellait surtout dans son activité de comédien. Il a créé une personnage qui correspondait à la fois parfaitement à cette époque et à lui-même : le clochard. Pour cela, il emprunta les vastes pantalons de Fatty Arbuckle, la moustache touffue de Mack Swain (radicalement taillée), les chaussures démesurées de Fors Sterling (portées sur le « mauvais » pied), une veste étroite et un chapeau melon minuscule. Le petit clochard était né, toujours déguenillé, malchanceux et en perpétuel affrontement avec le monde alentour. Cette photo de 1928 (pages précédentes, 1) montre Charlie Chaplin au temps du muet, quand il présentait le tragique et le comique à un public qui le vénérait.

Les années 30 et 40 peuvent s'enorgueillir de divinités du grand écran aussi sophistiquées que Marlene Dietrich, Bette Davis et Greta Garbo. Une autre beauté nordique, qui possédait des atouts beaucoup plus naturels et interpréta des rôles très divers avec nombre des plus grands réalisateurs de l'époque, Ingrid Bergmann, était aussi connue pour son charme lumineux que pour sa vie amoureuse « immorale » (un sénateur américain la dénoncera d'ailleurs comme un agent de la dégradation hollywoodienne). Elle fit ses meilleurs films en début de carrière. Ici, elle se détend devant la Tour de Londres en compagnie d'Alfred Hitchcock, en 1948, avant de tourner *Les Amants du Capricorne,* un film qui amorce le début de son déclin (pages précédentes, 2).

Marlene Dietrich était la réponse de la Paramount à la Greta Garbo de la MGM. Elles incarnaient toutes deux l'esprit séduisant et ambigu des années 30, et toutes deux connurent relativement peu de succès plus tard. Le réalisateur Josef von Sternberg découvrit Marlene Dietrich alors qu'elle se produisait comme danseuse dans une revue (1). Il l'engagea immédiatement pour lui faire jouer le rôle de Lola, chanteuse de cabaret et femme fatale qui donne la réplique à Emil Jannings,

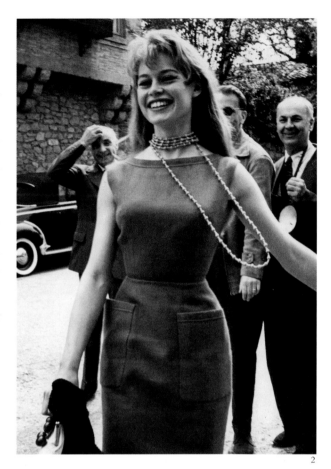

2

le professeur qu'elle finira par détruire, dans ce qui fut peut-être – pour lui comme pour elle – leur plus grand film, *L'Ange bleu* (1930).

La génération suivante fut celle de Brigitte Bardot, jeune blonde ingénue et sexy à l'opposé de la froide sophistication d'une Dietrich. Connue sous les initiales de B. B., Bardot fit chavirer la Croisette lors du Festival de Cannes, en 1956. Dans les années 1950 et 1960, l'existence même du cinéma sembla un temps menacée par la généralisation de la télévision dans les foyers, mais le format panoramique, le dolby stéréo et le multiplex participèrent deux décennies plus tard au retour triomphant de la machine hollywoodienne, alors qu'à l'autre bout du monde, Bollywood s'affirmait comme le second pilier de ce nouvel âge d'or. Le temps était venu de dérouler une nouvelle fois les tapis rouges et de refouler ces hordes d'admirateurs, qui se bousculaient à chaque première. Les dieux et déesses du Septième Art ne s'étaient jamais aussi bien portés, alors que leurs films se déclinent aujourd'hui en sagas – cinq *Rocky,* six *Star Wars,* huit *Harry Potter.* Que pouvions-nous espérer de mieux ?

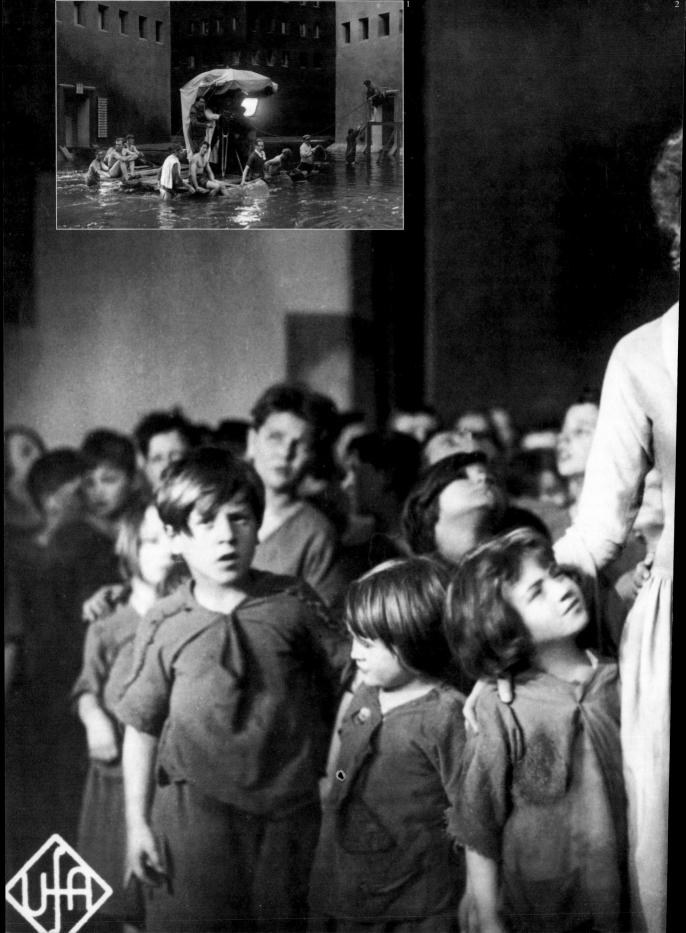

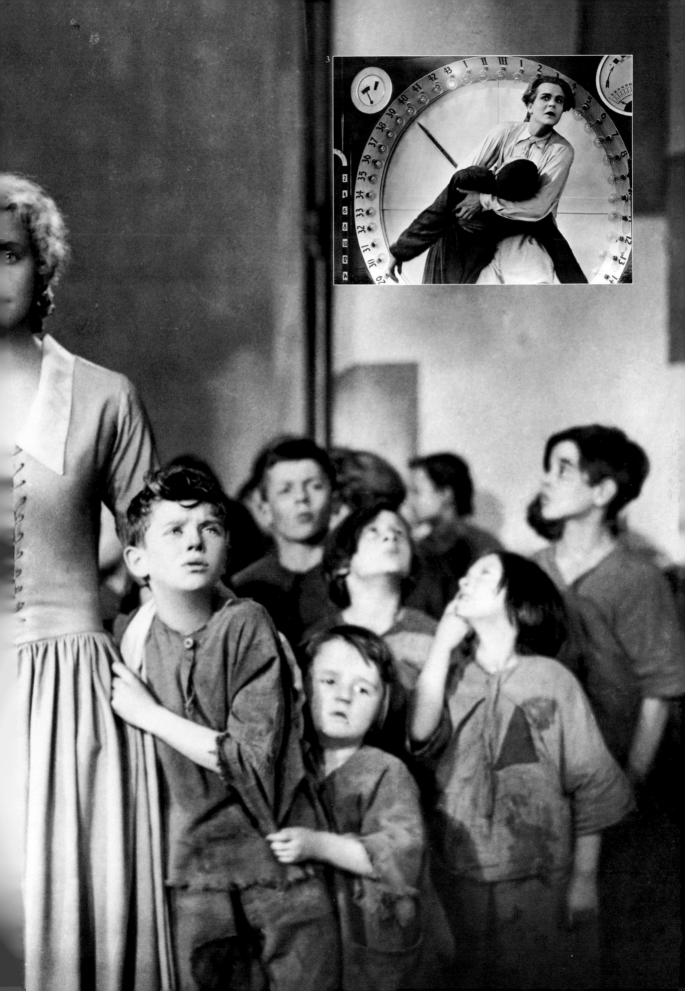

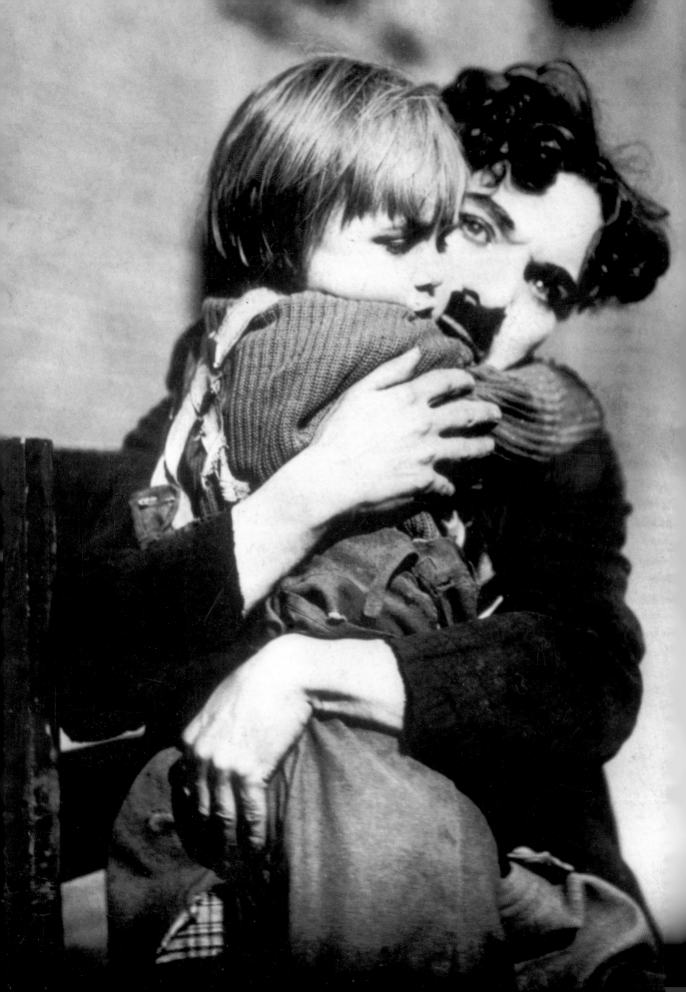

(previous pages)

PERHAPS the most famous film made by Fritz Lang was *Metropolis* (1926), which played on the fundamental fears of a post-industrial age. In it time becomes all-controlling and the clock cannot be turned back (3); the demands of the market-place led to child slavery (2); and a flood threatens an apocalyptic finale (1).

(Vorherige Seiten)

DER berühmteste Film Fritz Langs ist wohl *Metropolis* (1926), in dem er die tiefsitzenden Ängste eines postindustriellen Zeitalters zum Thema macht. Zeit wird zum alles beherrschenden Faktor, und keiner kann die Uhr zurückdrehen (3); die Anforderungen des Marktes versklaven die Kinder (2); und eine große Flutwelle droht mit einem apokalyptischen Finale (1).

(Pages précédentes)

LE film le plus célèbre de Fritz Lang est certainement *Métropolis* (1926), qui joue sur les craintes fondamentales de l'ère post-industrielle. C'est le temps qui contrôle tout et il est impossible de reculer les aiguilles de l'horloge (3) ; sur la place du marché les enfants sont vendus comme esclaves (2), et une inondation menace de l'apocalypse finale (1).

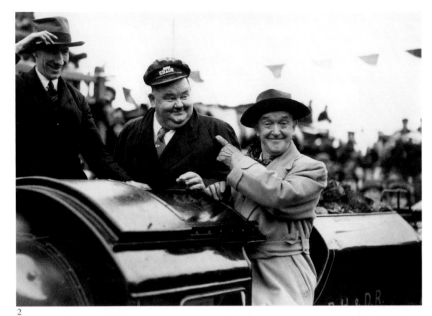

MANY considered the King of the Silent Comedy to be Charlie Chaplin, with his mixture of slapstick and pathos, as in *The Kid* (1). Others worshipped the mad antics and touching relationship of Stan Laurel and Oliver Hardy (2). But Buster Keaton (3) was in a class of his own, zigzagging his way through a world that constantly bewildered him.

FÜR viele war Charlie Chaplin der König des Stummfilms – mit seiner Mischung aus Slapstick und Pathos wie etwa in dem Film *The Kid* (1). Andere vergötterten die Possen und die rührend-komische Beziehung von Stan Laurel und Oliver Hardy (2). Buster Keaton jedoch war eine Klasse für sich – er lief im Zickzack durch eine Welt, die ihn permanent in Staunen versetzte.

POUR beaucoup, Charlie Chaplin était le roi des films muets – avec son mélange de slapsticks et de pathétisme comme, par exemple, dans le film *The Kid* (1). D'autres adoraient les blagues et la relation aussi émouvante que comique entre Stan Laurel et Oliver Hardy (2). Buster Keaton, quant à lui, était une classe à part – il marchait en zigzag dans un monde qui l'étonnait en permanence.

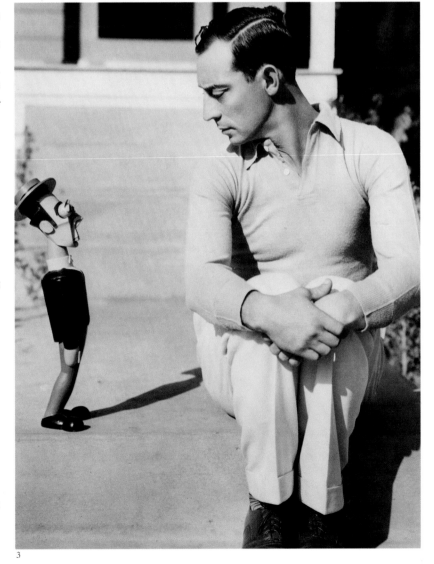

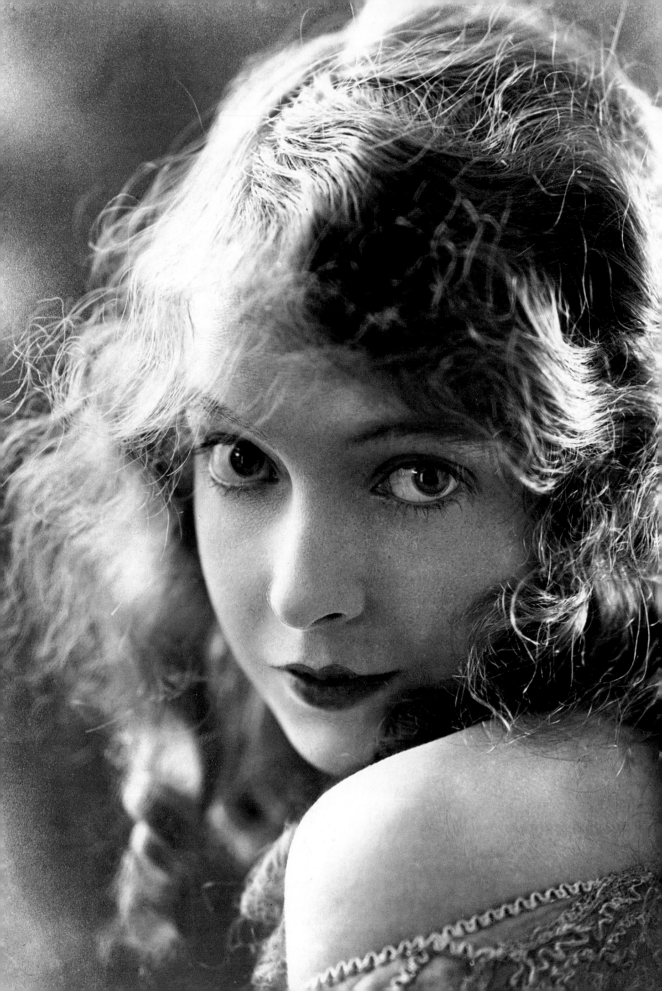

ILLIAN Gish (1) and Rudolph Valentino (2) were legends of the silent
screen. Gish started as a child actress and
often played alongside her sister, Dorothy,
until the latter's death in 1968. However,
her later films never had the impact of such
epic masterpieces as *Birth of a Nation* (1914)
and *Orphans of the Storm* (1922). Her most
prolific year was 1926 when she played
tragic lead roles in both *La Bohème* and *The
Scarlet Letter* for MGM. Valentino also
started young, alternating professional
dancing with sidelines as (among other
things) a gardener and a thief. The film that
turned him into the hottest property of
the 1920s was *The Four Horsemen of the
Apocalypse* (1921), grossing over $4.5 m.
For five years, Valentino made films with
titles like *The Sheikh* (1921) and *Blood and
Sand* (1922) that established his reputation
as a sultry and exotic screen lover. His
sudden death in 1926, from a perforated
ulcer brought on by overwork, brought
street riots at his funeral and even female
suicides.

ILLIAN Gish (1) und Rudolph Valentino (2) waren Legenden des Stummfilms. Gish stand schon als kleines Mädchen
auf der Bühne, oft zusammen mit ihrer
Schwester Dorothy, die 1968 starb. Doch
ihre späteren Filme erreichten nie wieder
die Kraft von *Die Geburt einer Nation*
(1914) und *Orphans of the Storm* (1922). Ihr
produktivstes Jahr war 1926, als sie bei
MGM die tragischen Hauptrollen in *La
Bohème* und in *Der scharlachrote Buchstabe*
spielte. Auch Valentino begann jung und
verband Auftritte als Tanzprofi mit Neben-
verdiensten als (unter anderem) Gärtner
und Dieb. Der Film, der ihn zum größten
Star der 20er Jahre machte und über viereinhalb Millionen Dollar einspielte, war
Die vier apokalyptischen Reiter von 1921.
Fünf Jahre lang drehte Valentino einen Film
nach dem anderen, mit Titeln wie *Der
Scheich* (1921) oder *Blood and Sand* (1922);
mit seinem Schmollmund wurde er zum
Inbegriff des exotischen Liebhabers auf
der Leinwand. Sein plötzlicher Tod 1926 –
ein Magengeschwürdurchbruch, die Folge
einer rastlosen Arbeit – führte zu erschüt-
ternden Szenen bei der Beerdigung, und
manche Frauen begingen sogar Selbstmord
deswegen.

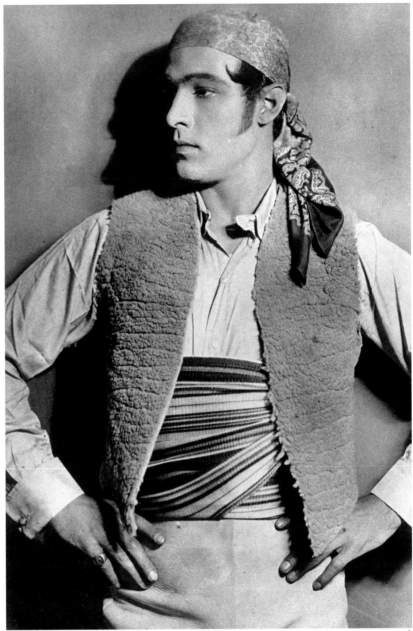

2

ILLIAN Gish (1) et Rudolf Valentino
(2) font partie de la légende du cinéma
muet. Lilian Gish fut actrice dès l'enfance
et joua souvent aux côtés de sa soeur Dorothy
jusqu'à la mort de celle-ci, survenue en
1968. Cependant, ses derniers films n'ont
jamais eu l'impact des chefs-d'œuvre épiques
comme *Naissance d'une nation* (1914) et *À
travers l'orage* (1922). 1926 fut son année la
plus féconde : elle y joue de grands rôles
tragiques dans *Au temps de la Bohême* et *La
Lettre rouge* pour la MGM. Valentino débuta
aussi très jeune dans le métier, alternant
la danse professionnelle avec des activités
secondaires dans le jardinage et le cambrio-
lage. Le film *Les Quatre Cavaliers de l'Apocalypse* (1921) en a fait la star des années 20
et il généra à lui seul une recette de plus
de 4,5 millions de dollars. Pendant cinq ans,
Valentino tourna des films aux titres prometteurs comme *le Cheik* (1921) et *Arènes
sanglantes* (1922) qui lui firent à l'écran une
réputation d'amant, sensuel et exotique. Il
mourut brusquement en 1926 d'un ulcère
dû au surmenage. Au cours de ses funérailles, on assista à des émeutes dans les rues
et des femmes se suicidèrent.

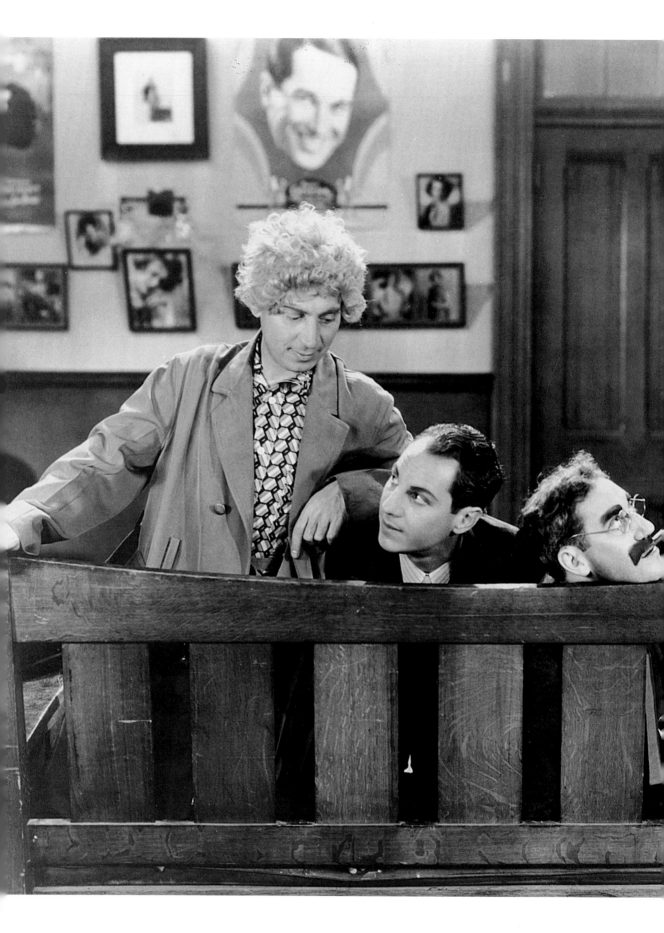

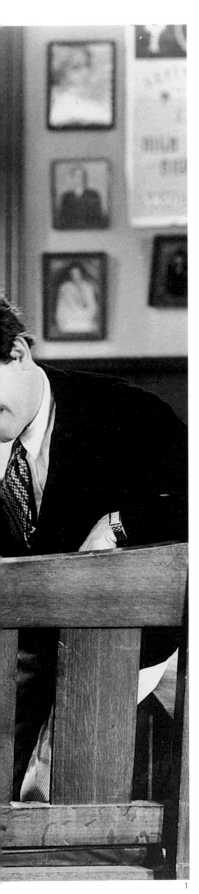

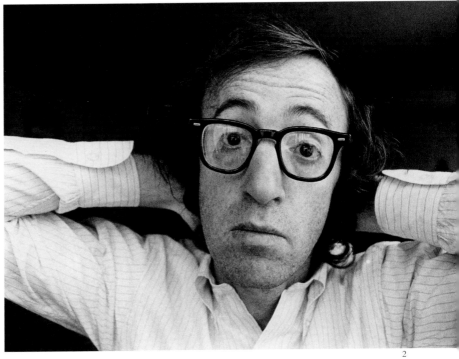

THE Marx Brothers were not only the most variously talented comedy team in Hollywood but the precursors of the zany 'Jewish humour' of later US comedians such as Mel Brooks and Woody Allen (2, photographed here in 1971). Groucho's droopy slouch, eyebrows and moustache; Chico's Italianate gobbledy-gook and magical piano-playing; Harpo's silly wig, dumb insolence and – of course – harp, with fourth brother Zeppo as a foil in the earlier movies, were fought over by the major film companies. While they made *Monkey Business*, *Horse Feathers* and *Duck Soup* (1) with Paramount, they added *A Night at the Opera*, *A Day at the Races*, *At the Circus* and *Go West* to MGM's list, being criticized by supremo Irving Thalberg for being 'too funny'. Love interest was his solution, often in the somewhat surprising person of Margaret Dumont at her most stately.

DIE Marx Brothers waren seinerzeit die wohl begabteste Truppe in Hollywood, die Urahnen des kuriosen »jüdischen Humors« späterer amerikanischer Komiker wie Mel Brooks oder Woody Allen (2, hier in einer Aufnahme von 1971). Die großen Studios rissen sich um Groucho mit seinem schleichenden Gang, den buschigen Augenbrauen und dem aufgemalten Schnurrbart, Chico mit seinem italienischen Akzent und magischen Klavierspiel sowie um Harpo mit der albernen Perücke, dem stummen Starrsinn und – wie der Name schon sagt – seiner Harfe, wobei anfangs der vierte Bruder,

Zeppo, noch für ein wenig ausgleichende Normalität sorgte. *Die Marx Brothers auf See*, *Horse Feathers* und *Die Marx Brothers im Krieg* (1) drehten sie für Paramount, während *Die Marx Brothers in der Oper*, *Ein Tag beim Rennen*, *At the Circus* und *Go West* das Repertoire von MGM zierten. Der dortige Boß, Irving Thalberg, fand sie »zu lustig«, und so kamen Liebeshandlungen hinzu, oft mit der pompösen Margaret Dumont.

LES Marx Brothers n'étaient pas seulement les comédiens aux talents les plus variés de Hollywood, ils furent aussi les précurseurs de « l'humour juif », type d'humour loufoque dont Mel Brooks et Woody Allen (2, photographié ici en 1971) seront les futurs représentants. L'allure avachie de Groucho, ses sourcils et sa moustache ; le charabia à l'italienne de Chico et son inimitable talent de pianiste ; la perruque impossible de Harpo, son insolence idiote et – évidemment – sa harpe, et Zeppo, faire-valoir dans les premiers films. Les plus grandes compagnies se battirent pour les engager. Pendant qu'ils tournaient *Monnaie de singe*, *Plumes de cheval* et *la Soupe au canard* (1) pour Paramount, ils ajoutaient *Une nuit à l'opéra*, *Un jour aux courses*, *Un jour au cirque* et *Chercheurs d'or* à la liste de MGM, critiqués par le grand chef Irving Thalberg parce que « *too funny* ». Pour remédier à cela, il eut l'idée de les rendre souvent amoureux, ce qui peut surprendre, de Margaret Dumont dans sa plus grande majesté.

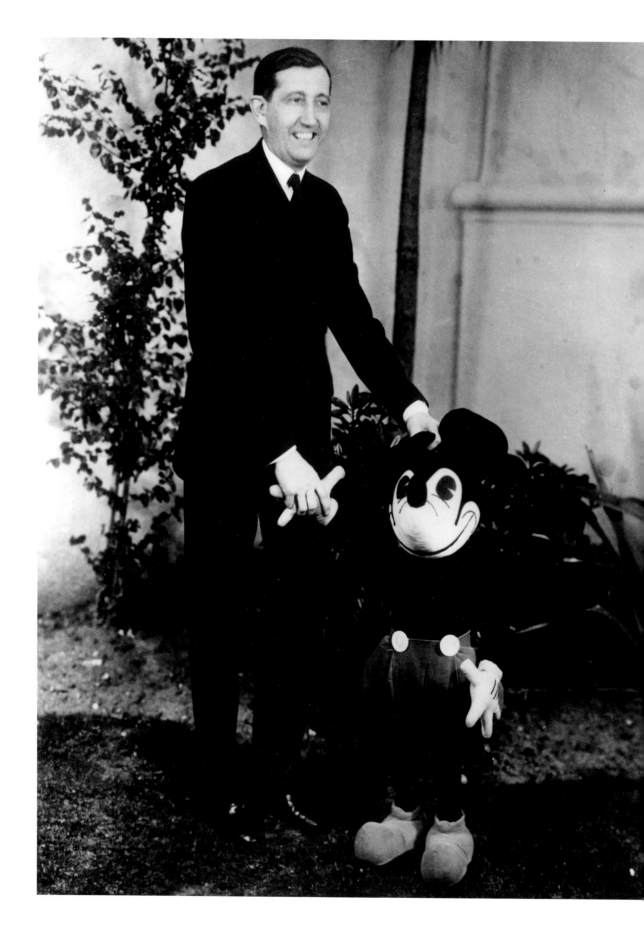

UNITED Artists was founded by arguably the four greatest silent film giants in 1919: Douglas Fairbanks, Mary Pickford, D. W. Griffith and Charlie Chaplin (2), with the invisible assistance of US Treasury Secretary William McAdoo. Mack Sennett, nicknamed 'The King of Slapstick', produced – among others – W. C. Fields, but his company hit the rocks for a second and final time in 1937. This photo was taken on the Sennett film lot just before it was torn down, at a visibly dismal last lunch shared by Marion Davies, Will Haines, King Vidor, Ulric Bush and Eileen Percy (3). Mickey Mouse takes Walt Disney for a walk (1). Disney (1901-66) was not necessarily the most innovative but he was certainly the most businesslike of film animators. Mickey Mouse was born in 1928 and greatly helped Disney's company to win its 19 Oscars.

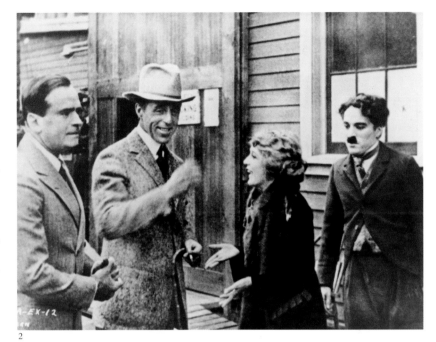

IM Jahre 1919 taten sich vier der einfluß-reichsten Persönlichkeiten der Stummfilmzeit zusammen – Douglas Fairbanks, Mary Pickford, D. W. Griffith und Charlie Chaplin – und gründeten die Filmgesell-schaft United Artists (2), wobei William McAdoo vom US-Schatzamt hinter den Kulissen entscheidend mitwirkte. Mack Sennett, der »König des Slapstick«, produzierte unter anderem W. C. Fields, doch 1937 mußte seine schon zuvor in Schwierigkeiten geratene Firma endgültig Konkurs anmelden. Unser Bild zeigt die gedrückte Stimmung bei einem Abschiedsessen auf dem Gelände der Sennett-Studios, unmittelbar bevor sie abgerissen wurden (3). Mit von der Partie sind Marion Davies, Will Haines, King Vidor, Ulric Bush und Eileen Percy. Micky Maus bei einem Spaziergang mit Walt Disney (1). Disney (1901-1966) war vielleicht nicht der innovativste unter den Trickfilmzeichnern, aber er hatte zweifellos den besten Geschäftssinn von allen. Micky Maus kam 1928 zur Welt und trug seinen Teil zu den 19 Oscars bei, die die Disney-Studios errangen.

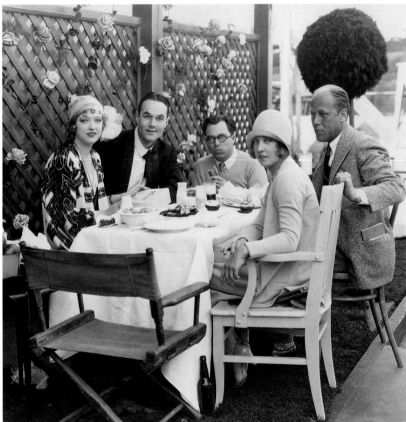

UNITED Artists a été fondée par les plus formidables géants du muet en 1919 : Douglas Fairbanks, Mary Pickford, D. W. Griffith et Charlie Chaplin (2) avec l'assistance invisible du secrétaire du ministère des Finances, William McAdoo. Mack Sennett, « le roi du slapstick », produisit – entre autres – W.C. Fields, mais sa compagnie fit naufrage une seconde et dernière fois en 1937. Cette photo a été prise sur le terrain des studios Sennet, juste avant qu'ils ne fussent rasés. On y assiste à un dernier repas visiblement lugubre avec Marion Davies, Will Haines, King Vidor, Ulric Bush et Eileen Percy (3). Mickey Mouse emmène Walt Disney en promenade (1). Disney (1901-1966) ne fut pas nécessairement le plus inventif, mais certainement le plus efficace des animateurs du cinéma. Mickey Mouse, né en 1928, a beaucoup aidé la compagnie de Walt Disney à gagner ses 19 Oscars.

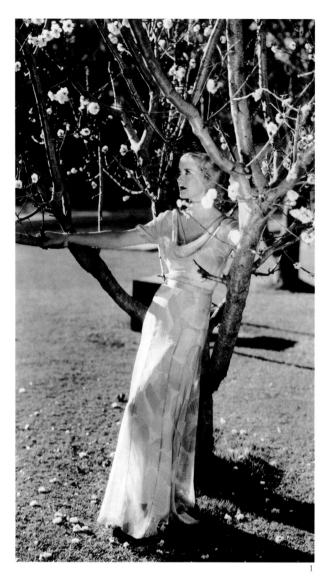
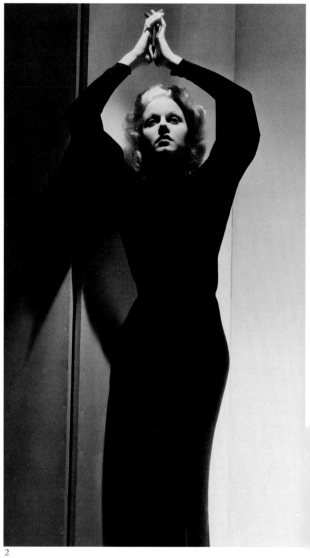

1   2

BETTE Davis, Jean Harlow and Greta
Garbo were all known as the vamps of
the 1930s. The first became Hollywood's
most enduring female star (1). Her
tempestuous personality gave her a dark
reputation, enhanced by a career renewed in
the 1960s by the psychological thrillers
Whatever Happened to Baby Jane? and *The
Nanny*. Harlow was the 'blonde bombshell'
whose locks were more platinum and
cleavage more exposed than any other
actress's (2). Paired with Clark Gable in five
films, she played tough, funny and sexy
through the 1930s. Her sudden death, aged
only 26, made her last film *Saratoga* (1937)
a huge box office success. Garbo's seductive
but intelligent dreaminess made her 'the
standard against which all other screen
actresses are measured' (3). *Queen Christina,
Ninotchka, Grand Hotel* and *Camille* afforded
her most famous parts.

BETTE Davis, Jean Harlow und Greta
Garbo galten als die drei Vamps der
30er Jahre. Bette Davis war wegen ihrer
Temperamentsausbrüche gefürchtet (1). In
den 60er Jahren erlebte sie mit Thrillern
wie *Whatever Happened to Baby Jane?* und
The Nanny noch einmal eine Blütezeit.
Harlow war die »Sexbombe«, die platin-
blondere Locken und tiefere Ausschnitte
hatte als jede andere Schauspielerin (2). In
fünf Filmen mit Clark Gable spielte sie
in den 30er Jahren ihren zähen, gewitzten
und aufreizenden Frauentyp. Ihr plötzlicher Tod mit nur 26 Jahren machte aus
ihrem letzten Film *Saratoga* (1937) einen
Kassenschlager. Die verführerische, doch
kluge Verträumtheit der Garbo macht
sie zum »Standard, an dem alle anderen
Schauspielerinnen sich messen müssen« (3).
Königin Christina, Ninotschka, Grand Hotel
und *Die Kameliendame* waren ihre größten
Rollen.

BETTE Davis, Jean Harlow et Greta
Garbo : les vamps des années 30. La
première devint la vedette féminine à battre
le record de longévité à Hollywood (1).
Son caractère ombrageux lui fit une mauvaise réputation qu'un nouveau départ dans
les années 60 avec les thrillers psycho-
logiques *Qu'est-il arrivé à Baby Jane ?* et
La Nanny ne fit qu'accentuer. Harlow était
la « bombe blonde », aux boucles les plus
platinées et au décolleté le plus large du
cinéma d'alors (2). Avec Clark Gable, durant
les années 30, elle joua dans cinq films qui
la montrèrent solide, amusante et sexy. Sa
mort soudaine, à l'âge de 26 ans, fit de son
dernier film, *Saratoga* (1937), un énorme
succès au box-office. Le caractère rêveur,
séduisant, mais intelligent de Garbo firent
d'elle « la norme à laquelle sont mesurées
toutes les autres actrices » (3). *La Reine
Christine, Ninotchka, Grand Hôtel* et *Camille*
lui offrirent ses plus grands rôles.

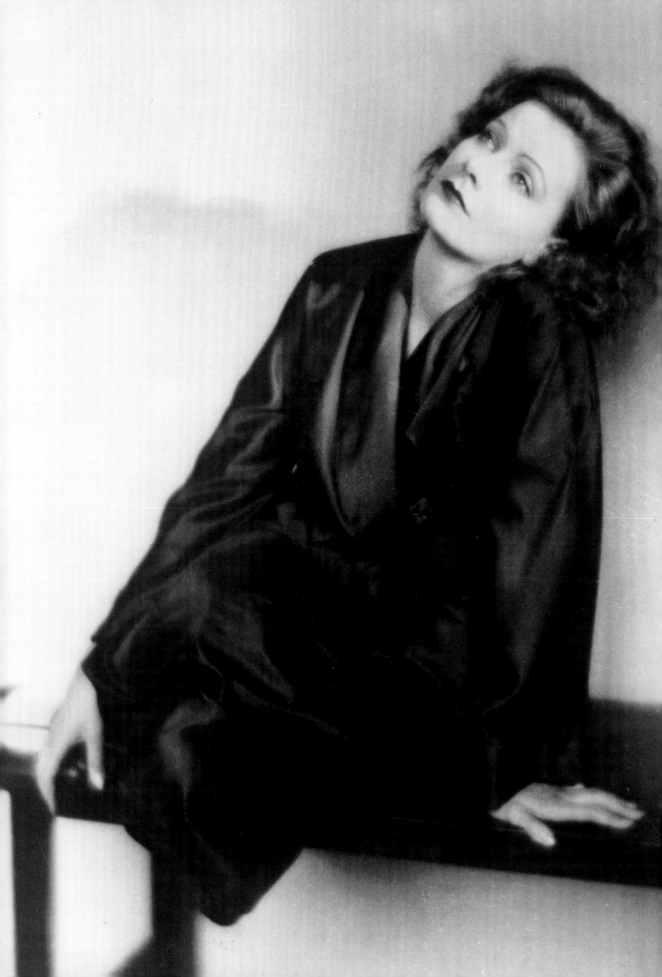

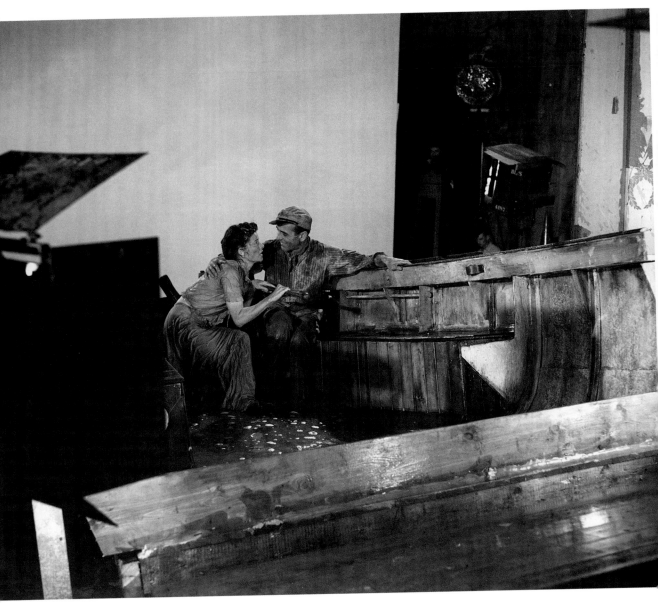

HUMPHREY Bogart and Katharine Hepburn, not up the Zambesi but at Britain's Isleworth studios during the filming of a storm-lashed scene from *The African Queen* (1). As soon as this last scene was shot, Bogart bailed out and scrambled on board the Île de France to sail for home with wife Lauren Bacall and son Stevie.

Some years before, in 1938, Hepburn proved she was no slouch, practising an acrobatic feat for *Holiday* with Cary Grant (2). Audrey Hepburn on set, discussing what must be her most unlikely role as the Cockney flower-seller Eliza in *My Fair Lady* with director George Cukor in 1964 (3).

HUMPHREY Bogart und Katharine Hepburn fahren den stürmischen Sambesi hinauf, und zwar in den englischen Isleworth-Studios während der Aufnahmen zu *African Queen* (1). Als diese letzte Szene im Kasten war, hielt Bogart nichts mehr: Er ging an Bord der Île de France und fuhr mit Ehefrau Lauren Bacall und Sohn Stevie nach Hause. Ein paar Jahre zuvor, 1938, bewies

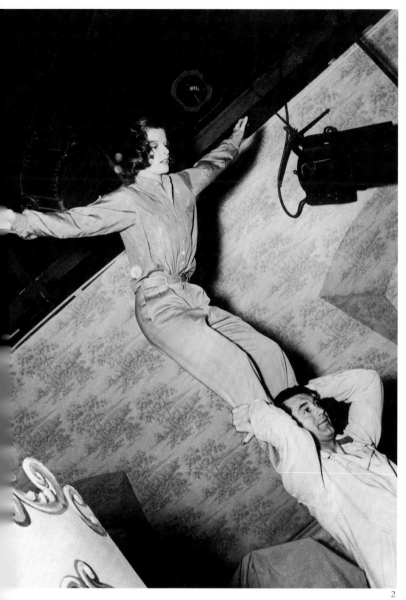

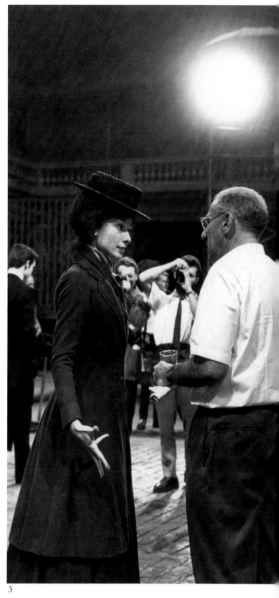

2

3

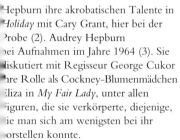
…Hepburn ihre akrobatischen Talente in
…Holiday mit Cary Grant, hier bei der
…Probe (2). Audrey Hepburn
…bei Aufnahmen im Jahre 1964 (3). Sie
…diskutiert mit Regisseur George Cukor
…ihre Rolle als Cockney-Blumenmädchen
…Eliza in My Fair Lady, unter allen
…Figuren, die sie verkörperte, diejenige,
…die man sich am wenigsten bei ihr
…vorstellen konnte.

Humphrey Bogart et Katharine
Hepburn ne remontent pas le Zam-
bèze, ils sont aux studios de Britain's
Isleworth où se tourne la scène d'orage
d'African Queen (1). À peine cette dernière
scène fut-elle en boîte que Bogart s'éclipsa
et grimpa à bord de l'Île de France pour
rentrer chez lui avec sa femme Lauren

Bacall et son fils Stevie. Quelques années plus
tôt, en 1938, Hepburn avait prouvé sa bonne
condition physique, réalisant dans Vacances, avec
Cary Grant, des prouesses acrobatiques (2).
Audrey Hepburn en scène, discutant de ce qui
sera son rôle le plus invraisemblable, la vendeuse
de fleurs populaire, Eliza, dans My Fair Lady,
réalisé par George Cukor en 1964 (3).

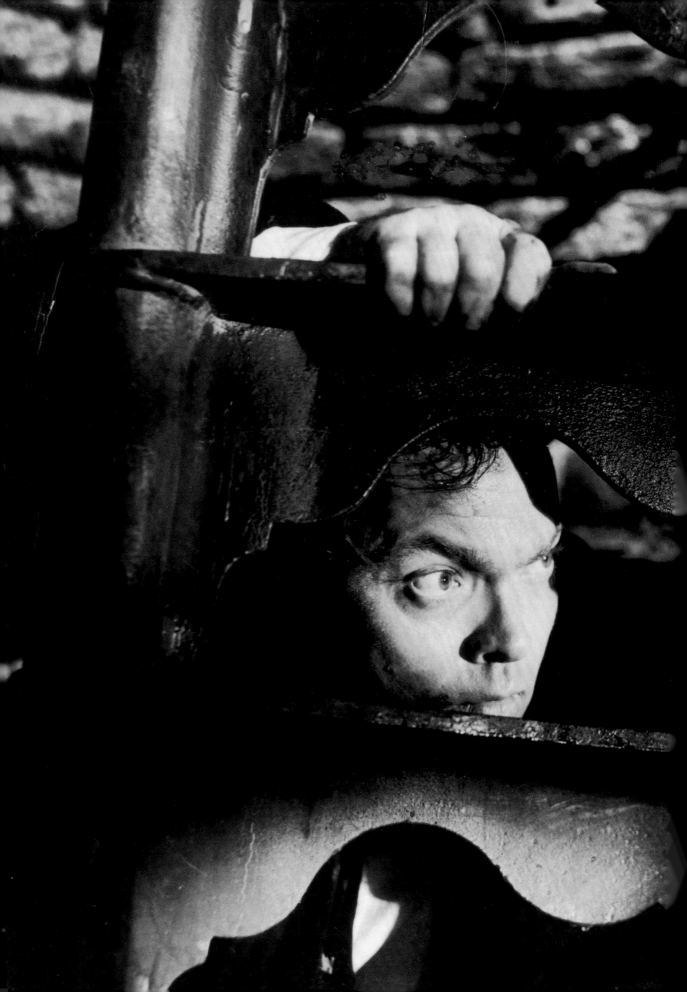

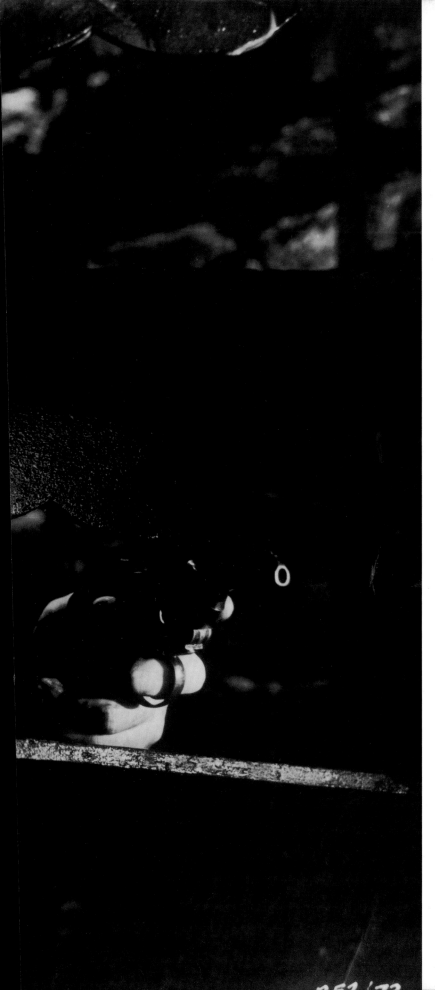

ORSON Welles as Harry Lime in
Carol Reed's adaptation of Graham
Greene's story *The Third Man*. Made in
1949, it was one of the few films to tackle
directly the sensitive theme of war racket-
eering by Allied Forces and the growing
rift between east and west Europeans in the
divided city of Vienna. Its most famous
scenes were set at the top of the Ferris
wheel in the Prater Gardens and inside the
city's underground sewers.

ORSON Welles als Harry Lime in
Der dritte Mann. Carol Reeds 1949
entstandener Film nach einer Vorlage von
Graham Greene war einer der wenigen,
die sich wirklich mit dem heiklen Thema
des Schwarzhandels der Alliierten in der
geteilten Stadt Wien und mit der immer
größer werdenden Kluft zwischen Ost-
und Westeuropa auseinandersetzten. Die
berühmtesten Szenen spielten auf dem
Riesenrad im Prater und in den Abwasser-
kanälen der Stadt.

ORSON Welles interprétant Harry Lime
dans l'adaptation cinématographique
par Carol Leed du livre de Graham Greene,
Le Troisième Homme. Réalisé en 1949, ce
fut un des rares films à attaquer de front le
sujet délicat des activités criminelles des
forces alliées durant la guerre, et la fissure
croissante entre les Européens de l'Est et de
l'Ouest à Vienne, cité en pleine division.
Les scènes les plus célèbres ont été prises au
sommet de la Grande Roue dans les jardins
du Prater et dans les égouts souterrains de
la ville.

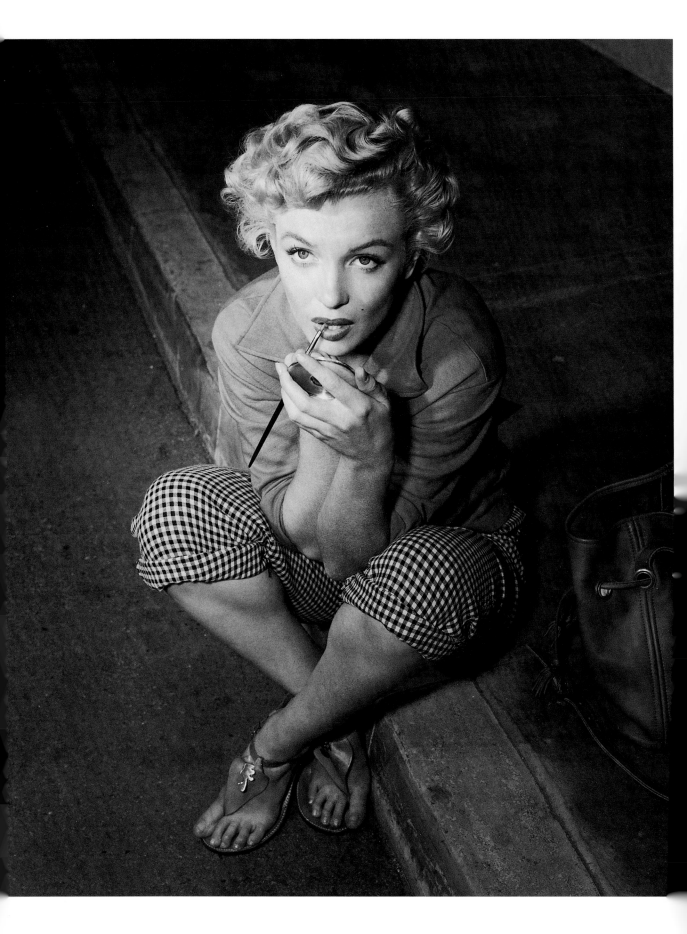

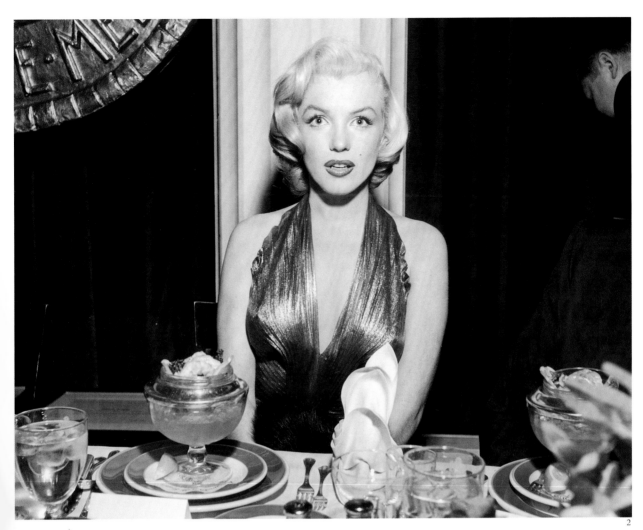

2

MARILYN Monroe conserved her little-girl-lost vulnerability (1), dying, aged 36, of a drugs overdose before age would have caused her to outlive it. Her fragile sexiness and breathy singing are best seen and heard in *Gentlemen Prefer Blondes* and *How to Marry a Millionaire* (both 1953); *The Seven Year Itch* (1955); *Bus Stop* (1957) and *Some Like It Hot* (1959). Seeking to go beyond her dumb blonde/gold-digger roles, in 1961 she starred in *The Misfits*, written for her by her last husband, Arthur Miller. In her life and in her films, Monroe needed direction. Too often, what she experienced was exploitation. Too much took her by surprise, as the camera seems to have done at the Photoplay Gold Medal Awards Dinner in 1953 (2).

MARILYN Monroe bewahrte den Ausdruck der Verletzlichkeit eines kleinen verirrten Mädchens (1) bis zu ihrem Tod im Alter von 36 Jahren; sie nahm sich das Leben – bevor das Leben ihr die Jugend genommen hätte. Beides, ihr fragiler Sexappeal und ihr gehauchter Gesangsstil, wurden zum Markenzeichen der Monroe und können am besten in den Filmen *Wie angelt man sich einen Millionär?* und *Blondinen bevorzugt* (beide aus dem Jahr 1953) sowie in *Das verflixte siebte Jahr* (1955) und in *Manche mögens heiß* (1959) bewundert werden. Mit dem Film *Nicht gesellschaftsfähig* aus dem Jahre 1961, zu dem ihr letzter Ehemann, Arthur Miller, das Drehbuch schrieb, versuchte Marilyn Monroe, aus dem Kassenschlager-Klischee des blonden Dummchens auszubrechen. In ihren Filmen, aber auch im Leben, suchte sie immer wieder nach Orientierung; allzuoft war jedoch, was sie erlebte, reine Ausbeutung. Und immer wieder wurde sie überrascht – so wie hier von der Kamera beim Dinner zur Verleihung der Photoplay-Goldmedaille im Jahre 1953 (2).

JUSQU'À sa mort à l'âge de 36 ans, Marilyn Monroe conservera toujours l'expression de vulnérabilité d'une petite fille effarouchée (1) ; elle se donne la mort – avant que la vie ne lui prenne sa jeunesse. Tous les deux, son sex-appeal fragile et ses chansons à la voix vaporeuse deviennent le symbole de Monroe, que l'on peut admirer à la perfection dans les films *Comment épouser un millionaire ?* et *Les hommes préfèrent les blondes* (tous deux de 1953) ainsi que dans *Sept ans de réflexion* (1955) et dans *Certains l'aiment chaud* (1959). Avec le film *Les désaxés*, de 1961, pour lequel son dernier époux Arthur Miller a écrit le scénario, Marilyn Monroe s'efforce de rompre avec le cliché à l'emporte-pièce de la belle blonde évaporée qui en a fait une vedette du box-office. Dans ses films, mais aussi dans la vie, elle a toujours cherché à s'y retrouver ; mais, la plupart du temps, ce qu'elle a vécu a été de la pure exploitation. En étant toujours surprise – comme ici par la caméra lors du dîner à l'occasion de la remise de la médaille d'or Photoplay, en 1953 (2).

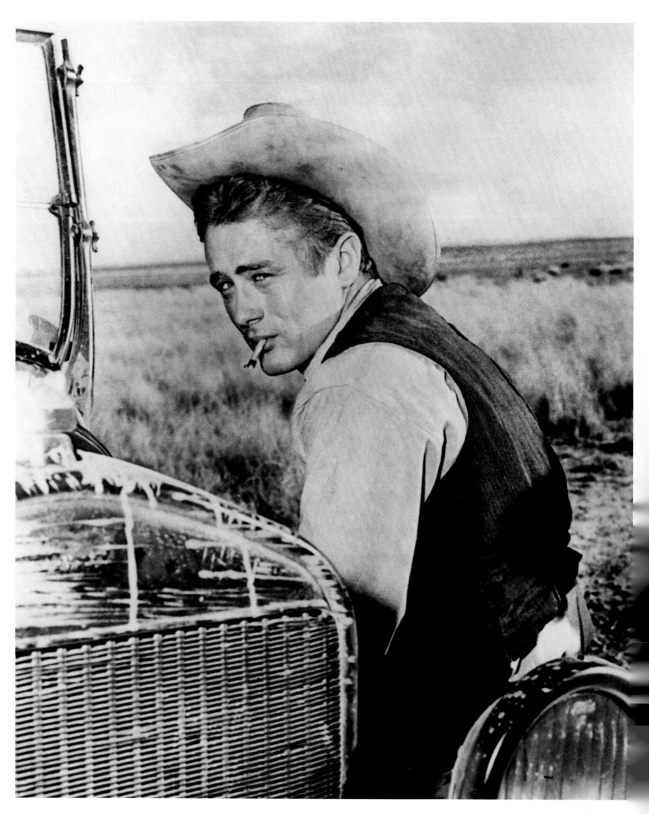

CLARK Gable's reputation as King of Hollywood came with *Gone With the Wind* in 1939 (4). Later Hollywood heroes were James Dean (1) and the longer-lived Marlon Brando, seen here relaxing on the set of *Desiree* in 1954 (5). Burt Lancaster's pin-up was taken while shooting *A Child is Waiting* with Judy Garland in 1966, at the height of his beef-cake popularity (3). His films became subtler and more inventive as he aged, ranging from Louis Malle's *Atlantic City* in 1980 to Bill Forsythe's *Local Hero* in 1983. Gregory Peck was caught during the filming of *The Million Pound Note* in 1953 (2).

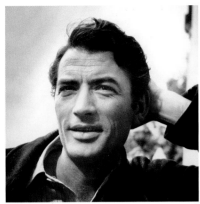

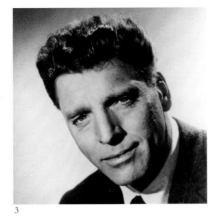

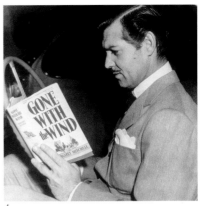

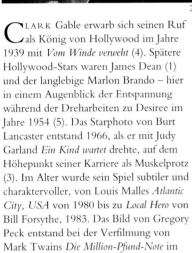

CLARK Gable erwarb sich seinen Ruf als König von Hollywood im Jahre 1939 mit *Vom Winde verweht* (4). Spätere Hollywood-Stars waren James Dean (1) und der langlebige Marlon Brando – hier in einem Augenblick der Entspannung während der Dreharbeiten zu Desiree im Jahre 1954 (5). Das Starphoto von Burt Lancaster entstand 1966, als er mit Judy Garland *Ein Kind wartet* drehte, auf dem Höhepunkt seiner Karriere als Muskelprotz (3). Im Alter wurde sein Spiel subtiler und charaktervoller, von Louis Malles *Atlantic City, USA* von 1980 bis zu *Local Hero* von Bill Forsythe, 1983. Das Bild von Gregory Peck entstand bei der Verfilmung von Mark Twains *Die Million-Pfund-Note* im Jahre 1953 (2).

EN 1939 Clark Gable devint le roi de Hollywood avec *Autant en emporte le vent* (4). Parmi les héros de Hollywood plus jeunes étaient James Dean (1) et l'inoxy-dable Marlon Brando – ici durant un moment de détente pendant le tournage de *Désirée*, en 1954 (5). La photo de Burt Lancaster a été prise pendant le tournage de *Un enfant attend* avec Judy Garland en 1966. À l'époque, il était l'un des rois du « beefcake » (3). À mesure qu'il vieillissait, ses films devinrent plus subtils et plus inventifs, allant d'*Atlantic City* de Louis Malle, en 1980, à *Local Hero* de Bill Forsythe en 1983. Gregory Peck a été saisi sur le vif en 1953 pendant le tournage de l'adaptation du livre de Mark Twain, *Un pari de milliardaires* (2).

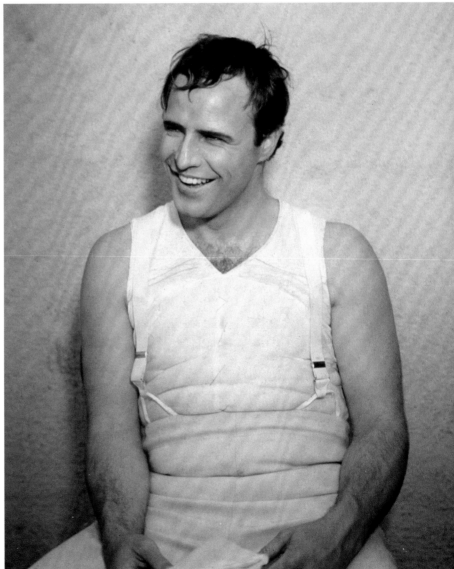

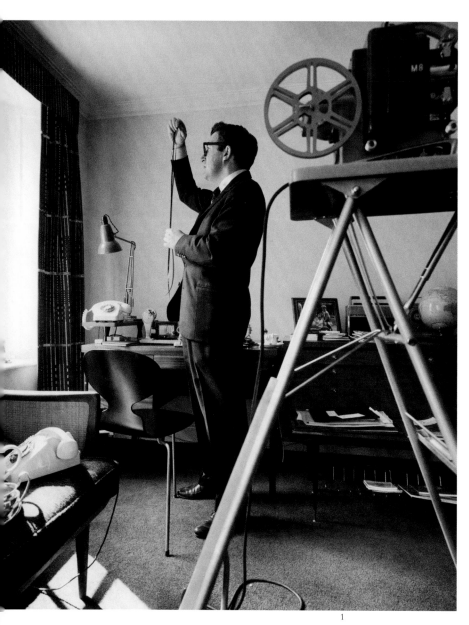

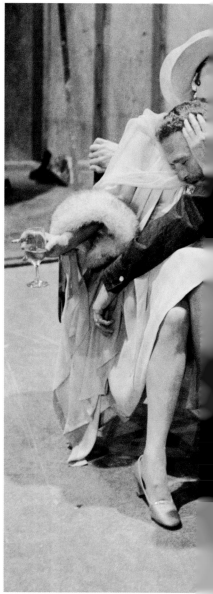

THE decline of the cinema, in terms of both the quality of its product and the size of its audience, was halted and reversed in the late 1960s and 1970s. The new generation of stars that had emerged in the 1950s came of age and turned in some their best performances. Peter Sellers (1) left his home movies and black-and-white knockabout short films for Hollywood and *The Pink Panther*. Paul Newman headed west with *Butch Cassidy and the Sundance Kid* and John Huston's *The Life and Times of Judge Roy Bean*, and found solace in the arms of Ava Gardner (2). Dustin Hoffman graduated to make *John and Mary* in 1969 (3).

NACH einem ersten Niedergang – sowohl, was die Qualität der Filme als auch, was die Größe des Publikums betraf – ging es in den 1960er und 1970er Jahren mit dem Kino bergauf. Eine neue Generation von Schauspielern aus den 1950er Jahren kam nun in ihre besten Jahre und bot ihr Bestes: Peter Sellers (1) verließ seine Heimkino- , Schwarzweiß- und Kurzfilm-Formate und ging nach Hollywood und zum *rosaroten Panther*; Paul Newman ging nach Westen, zu *Butch Cassidy und Sundance Kid* und zu John Hustons Film *Das war Roy Bean*; dort fand er Trost in den Armen Ava Gardners (2). Nach seiner »Reifeprüfung« spielte Dustin Hoffman 1969 in *John and Mary* (3).

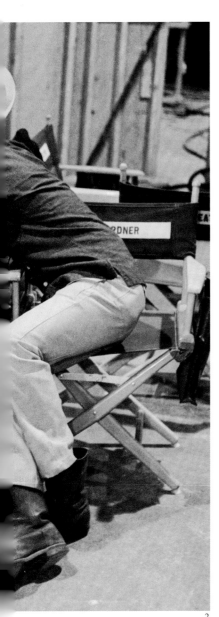
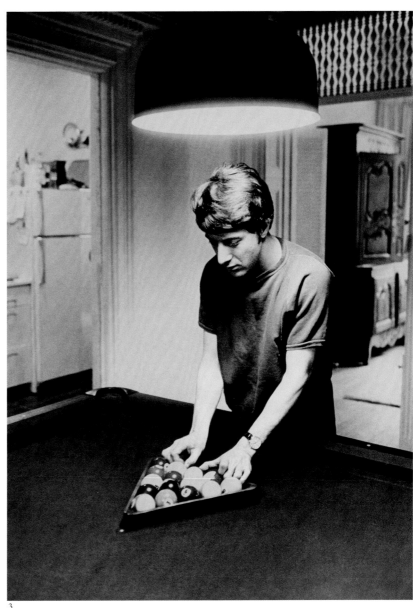

2   3

APRÉS une première défaite – aussi bien en ce qui concerne la qualité des films que l'accueil du public – le cinéma commence à remonter la pente dans les années 60 et 70. Une nouvelle génération d'acteurs des années 50 est maintenant à son apogée et donne le meilleur d'elle-même : Peter Sellers (1) abandonne ses formats de cinéma intimiste, films en noir et blanc et courts-métrages pour rejoindre Hollywood et *La panthère rose* ; Paul Newman prend la direction de l'Ouest, vers *Butch Cassidy et le Kid* ainsi que le film *Juge et hors-la-loi,* de John Huston ; là-bas, il trouve réconfort dans les bras d' Ava Gardner (2).

En 1969, Dustin Hoffman, devenu célèbre avec *Le lauréat,* joue dans *John and Mary* (3).

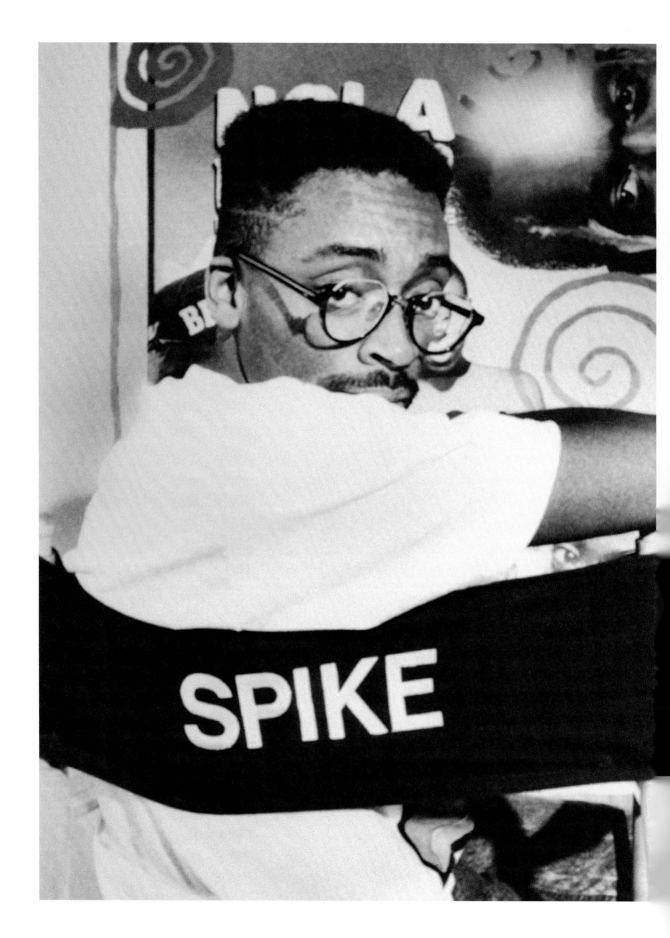

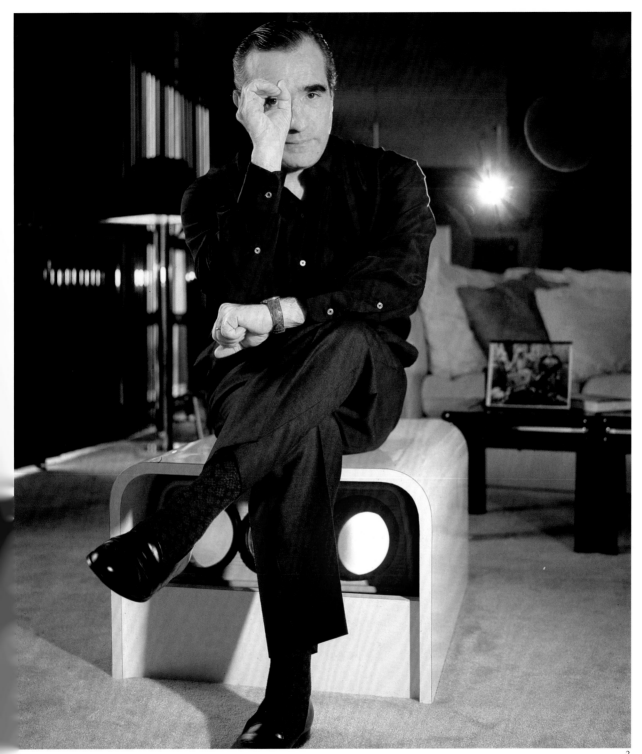

2

Nᴇᴡ York directors regained fame and prestige in the 1980s and 1990s, among them Spike Lee, photographed at home in 1989 (1), the year of *Do the Right Thing*; and Martin Scorsese, also at home in 1991, the year of *Cape Fear*.

Nᴇᴡ Yorks Filmemacher gewannen in den 1980er und 1990er Jahren Ruhm und Prestige zurück; unter ihnen war Spike Lee, hier 1989 in seinem Haus (1) – in dem Jahr, in dem sein Film *Do the Right Thing* herauskam – sowie Martin Scorsese (2) – ebenfalls zu Hause, im Jahre der Filmpremiere von *Cape Fire*: 1991.

Dᴀɴs les années 80 et 90, les cinéastes new-yorkais recouvrent célébrité et prestige ; parmi eux, Spike Lee, ici dans sa maison (1) en 1989 – l'année durant laquelle il a produit son film *Do the Right Thing* – ainsi que Martin Scorsese (2) – également chez lui, l'année de la première du film *Les nerfs à vif* : 1991.

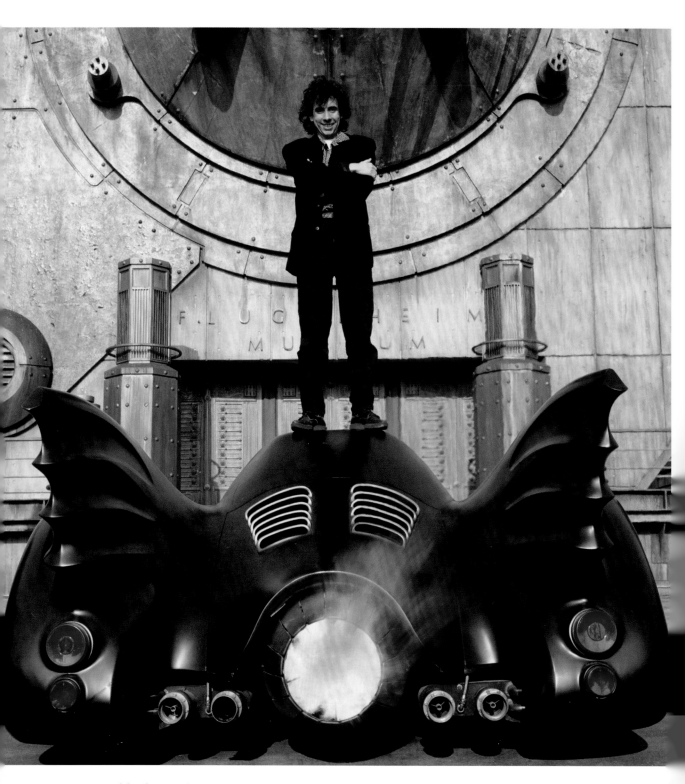

MAKING life safer in Gotham City, Tim Burton, director of *Batman*, stands on the top of the Batmobile at Pinewood Studios in January 1989 (1).

So wurde das Leben in Gotham City sicherer: Tim Burton, Regisseur des Films *Batman*, posiert auf einem Batmobil für die Kamera (1) – 1989 in den Pinewood Studios.

VOILÀ de quoi rendre la vie plus sûre à Gotham City : Tim Burton, metteur en scène du film *Batman*, pose sur une Batmobil pour les caméras (1) – en 1989 dans les studios de Pinewood.

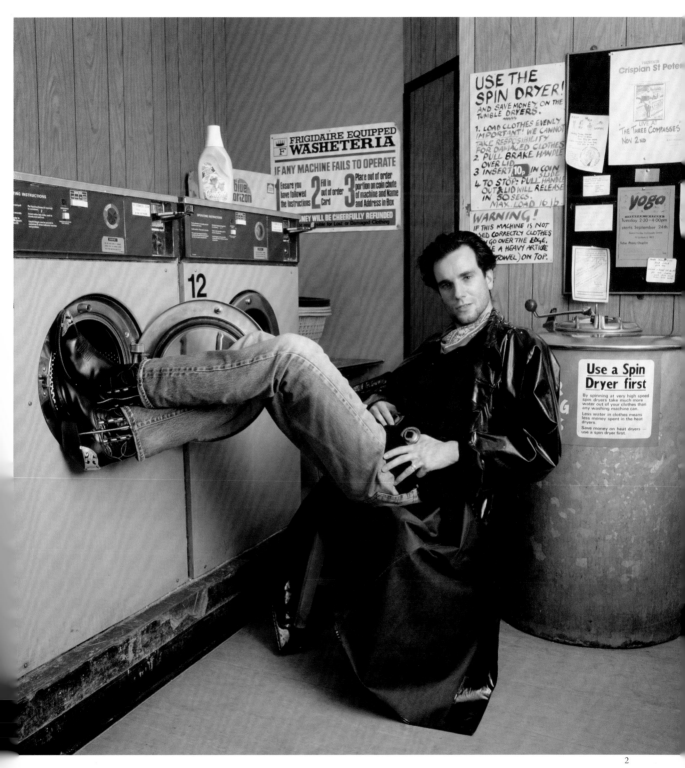

2

BRITISH actor Daniel Day-Lewis (2), who played Johnny in the Stephen Frears 1985 film *My Beautiful Laundrette*, poses in a less glamorous setting.

DER britische Filmschauspieler Daniel Day-Lewis (2) – der in Stephen Frears Produktion *Mein wunderbarer Waschsalon* aus dem Jahre 1985 die Rolle des Johnny spielte – hier in einer weniger glamourösen Umgebung.

L'ACTEUR de cinéma britannique Daniel Day-Lewis (2), qui a joué le rôle de Johnny dans la production *My beautiful laundrette* de Stephen Frears, en 1985 – ici dans un environnement avec beaucoup moins de paillettes.

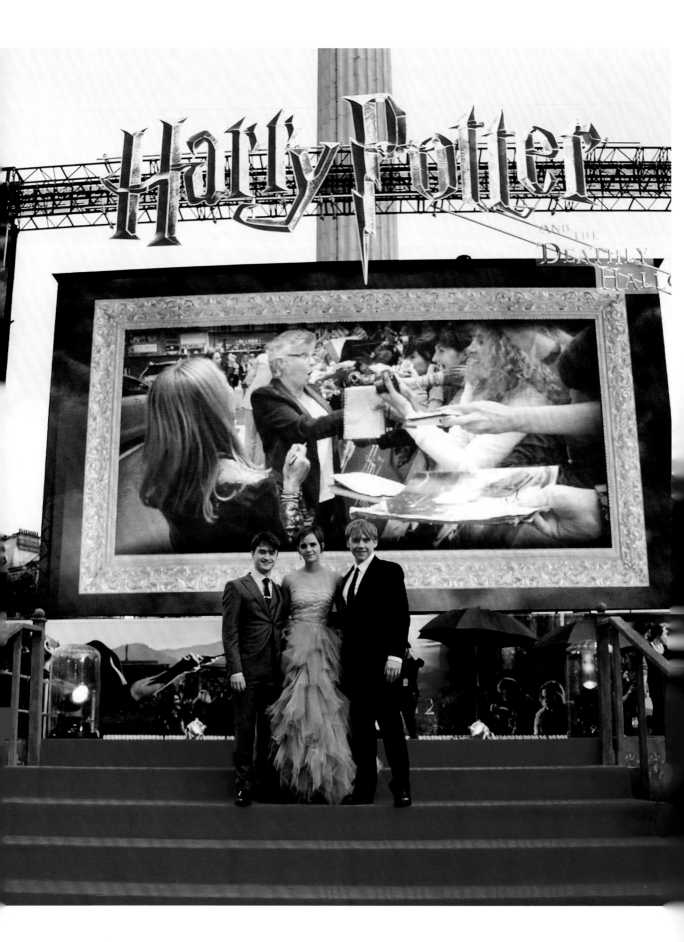

THE RENAISSANCE of the cinema industry continued apace in the early part of the 21st century, fuelled partly by new technology (IMAX screens, computer generated visual effects, and a return to 3D), and partly by world-wide distribution of films on a grand scale. (1- left to right) Daniel Radcliffe, Emma Watson and Rupert Grint, stars of the record breaking *Harry Potter* series of films, attend the World Premiere of *Harry Potter and the Deathly Hallows Part 2* in Trafalgar Square, London, 7 July 2011. The film grossed $7.7 billion, and the series provided the financial backbone for Warner Bros. between 2001 and 2011. A smiling fan stands beneath a poster in New Delhi, India, advertising *Om Shanti Om*, one of the most successful Bollywood films of 2007 (2). A Chinese audience watches a 3D film in a newly-opened IMAX cinema in Wuhan, Hubei Province, 8 February 2007 (3). The cinema was part of China's ambitious plans to build one of the largest entertainment industries in the world.

DIE RENAISSANCE der Filmindustrie ging auch nach der Jahrtausendwende weiter, vorangetrieben unter anderem von neuer Technologie (IMAX-Kinos, computeranimierte Effekte, 3-D-Technik) und von der weltweiten Verbreitung großer Film-Events. (1, v.l.n.r.) Daniel Radcliffe, Emma Watson und Rupert Grint, Stars der alle Rekorde brechenden Harry-Potter-Filmreihe, bei der Weltpremiere von *Harry Potter und die Heiligtümer des Todes 2* in London, 7. Juli 2011. Der Film spielte 7,7 Milliarden Dollar ein; die Reihe war zwischen 2001 und 2011 die Haupteinnahmequelle von Warner Bros. (2) Ein Fan vor einem Poster in Neu-Delhi, Indien, das für *Om Shanti Om* wirbt, einen der erfolgreichsten Bollywoodfilme des Jahres 2007. (3) Ein chinesisches Publikum schaut im neuen IMAX-Kino in Wuhan, Provinz Hubei, einen 3-D-Film an, 8. Februar 2007. Kino war Teil des chinesischen Plans, eine der größten Unterhaltungsindustrien der Welt aufzubauen.

LA RENAISSANCE de l'industrie du cinéma se poursuivit à un rythme rapide au tout début du XXIe siècle, alimentée en partie par l'introduction de nouvelles technologies (écran IMAX, effets

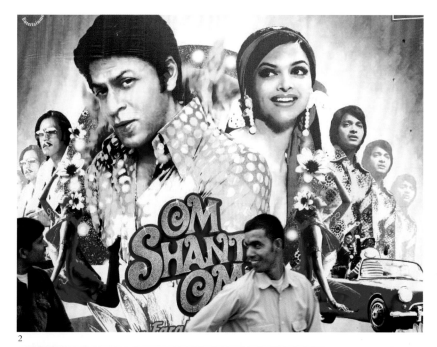

2

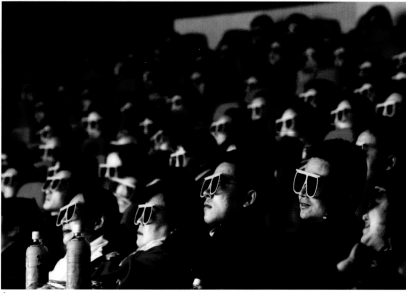

3

spéciaux générés par ordinateur et retour à la 3D), mais aussi par une distribution des films à l'échelle planétaire. Les stars de la saga Harry Potter, Daniel Radcliffe, Emma Watson et Rupert Grint (1 – de gauche à droite) assistent à la première mondiale de *Harry Potter et les reliques de la mort* – partie 2, à Trafalgar Square, Londres, le 7 juillet 2011. Le film rapporta près de 7,7 milliards de dollars et les bénéfices tirés de la saga, entre 2001 et 2011, contribuèrent à asseoir les finances de Warner Bros. À New Dehli, en Inde,

un fan pose sous l'affiche de *Om Shanti Om*, un des triomphes de Bollywood, en 2007 (2). Public chinois à la projection d'un film en 3D, dans une nouvelle salle IMAX de Wuhan, province du Hubei, inaugurée le 8 février 2007 (3). Le cinéma faisait partie de l'ambitieux programme de la Chine, décidée à bâtir l'une des plus grandes industries des medias et des loisirs au monde.

Arts and Entertainment

THE world of music was revolutionised in the 20th century by the invention of the phonograph and its subsequent development into the gramophone, the record-player, the stereo, the hi-fi, the CD player and finally the iPod. By the early 1930s it was possible to hear, whenever you liked, in your own home: Sir Edward Elgar conducting his violin concerto with the phenomenally gifted young Yehudi Menuhin as soloist, or the Duke Ellington orchestra *Rocking in Rhythm*; or Maurice Chevalier warbling any one of a dozen ballads of the boulevards. Music became all-pervasive, to the point when it was hard to escape. In shop, station concourse, or even the elevator, music invaded the conscious and the subconscious.

Parallel technical developments brought masterpieces of high art or popular entertainment within the reach of many. Books became talking books and ebooks; ballets pirouetted on videos and DVDs; struggling comedians became television celebrities. Popular music slimmed down to Pop Music, with legends created with the release of each new Chart List – The Stones, Michael Jackson, Nina Simone, Bob Dylan, Dolly Parton, Madonna, Lady Gaga and, above them all, Elvis – the King Who Never Died.

A few big theatres closed: a great many small ones opened. It was an era that encompassed the Broadway musical, the off-Broadway provocative play, *agit-prop*, cabaret, the Fringe Festival, the experimental – which meant that any evening at the theatre promised an equal chance of delight or disappointment. A cross-pollination between television and live theatre allowed the stars of TV soaps to tread the boards and face live audiences.

Then there was dance, never so popular as it was in the 1920s and 1930s, when the Western World bunny-hopped, Black-Bottomed, Charlestoned and quick-stepped its way across the well-sprung floors of the local *palais-de-danses*, around the bumpy boards of club-houses, between the tables of restaurants and through the dimly lit fug of many a nightclub. If all else failed, husband and wife stayed in, switched on the radio, rolled back the carpet and let themselves go in the comfort of their own home. There were dance marathons, tap-dancing competitions, formation dancing teams, ballroom dancing extravaganzas, and dance schools franchised coast-to-coast by Arthur Murray. And there was Fred Astaire, lithe and debonair, smiling, firing off his feet in syncopation, and making the impossible look comparatively easy.

On stages across the world, the Bolshoi, the *Ballets Russes*, New York City Ballet, Sadlers Wells and dozens of other companies twirled and leapt, pirouetted and snaked their way through the choreography of Fokine, Ashton, Martha Graham, Merce Cunningham, Balanchine, Twyla Tharp, Baryshnikov and Joaquin Cortez. Diaghilev was unique – a man and a monster who had limited agility but unlimited vision, and whose team of composers and designers (Stravinsky, Satie, Cocteau and Picasso) changed the face of ballet.

It was the Age of the Maestro: great conductors from Furtwängler to von Karajan, and from Beecham to Bernstein (opposite, conducting the New York Philharmonic). And it was also the Age of the Pioneer, exemplified by Stockhausen (see page 596)

And, most revolutionary of all, by the very late 20th century, there was entertainment that you could hold in your hand – the video game, crude in its early days, but a rapid developer into an astonishing new art form, mainlining on violence but with the thrill of inviting viewers to put their own lives at virtual reality risk.

DIE Welt der Musik erlebte im 20. Jahrhundert eine Revolution – beginnend mit der Erfindung des Phonographen und der daran anschließenden Entwicklung von Grammophon, Plattenspieler, Stereo und HiFi (High Fidelity) sowie CD-Player und schließlich dem iPod. Zu Beginn der 1930er Jahre wurde es möglich, zu Hause – wann immer man wollte – Sir Edward Elgars Violinkonzert mit den jungen, äußerst begabten Yehudi Menuhin als Solisten zu hören; oder das Duke-Ellington-Orchester mit *Rocking in Rhythm*; oder Maurice Chevalier mit einem seiner Dutzenden von Balladen über die Pariser Boulevards. Musik durchdrang den gesamten Alltag – bis zu dem Punkt, an dem es beinahe unmöglich wurde, ihr zu entkommen. In Geschäften, in Bahnhofshallen, ja selbst in Fahrstühlen eroberte die Musik das Bewußtsein und das Unterbewußtsein gleichermaßen.

Parallel brachten andere technische Entwicklungen weitere Meisterwerke aus Kunst und Unterhaltung in Reichweite des alltäglichen Kulturgenusses. Bücher begannen zu sprechen oder wurden zu E-books, Ballettvorführungen wurden auf Video und DVD gebannt, der Entertainer aus dem Varieté wurde zum Fernsehstar. Es wurde die größte Kulturrevolution aller Zeiten, bei der Fans – selbst eine Erfindung des 20. Jahrhunderts – tagtäglich das Beste von den Rolling Stones, Micha

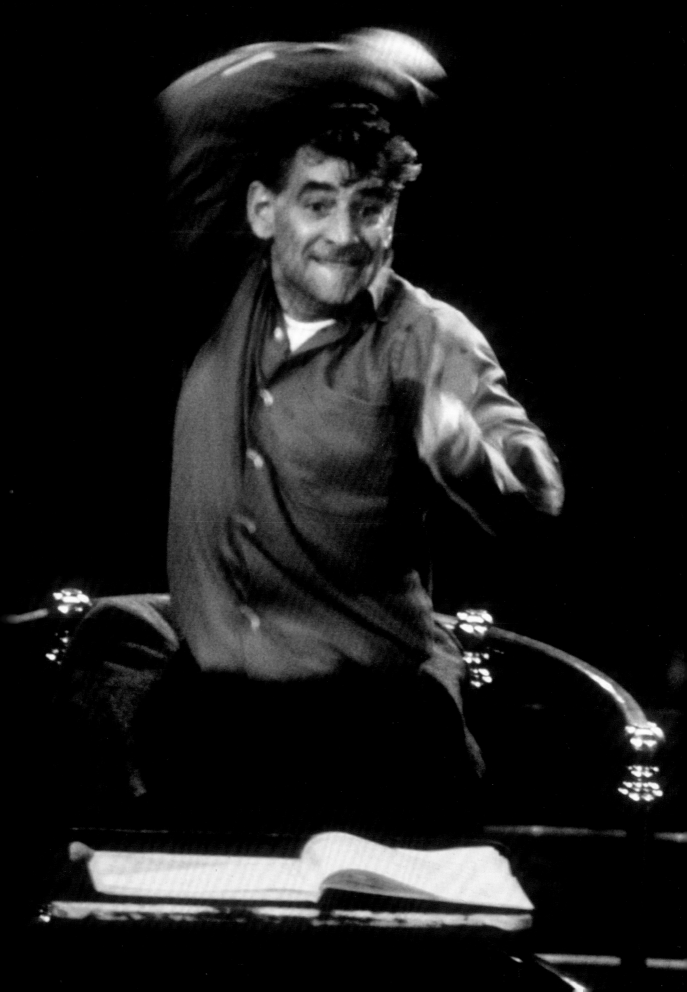

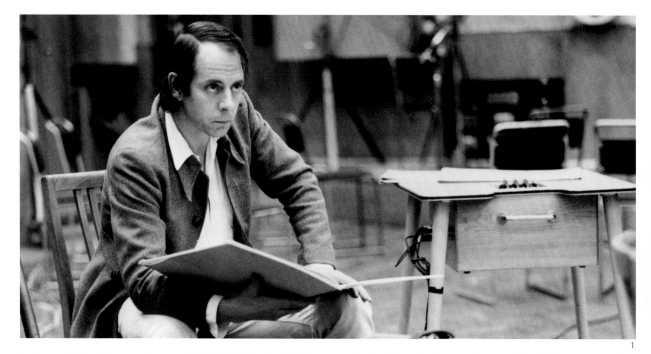

1

Jackson, Nina Simone, Jacques Brel, Bob Dylan, Dolly Parton, Madonna, Lady Gaga und, über allen thronend, König Elvis hören konnten.

Einige bedeutende Theater schlossen ihre Pforten; zahlreiche kleine Bühnen öffneten die ihren; es wurde das Zeitalter der Broadway-Musicals, der provokativen Off-Broadway-Produktionen, des Agit-Prop, des Cabaret und des »Fringe«-Festivals, des Experimentellen – was hieß, daß ein Abend im Theater entweder großartig oder enttäuschend sein konnte – sowie der Komiker. Eine gegenseitige Befruchtung zwischen Fernsehen und Theater erlaubte es den Stars aus TV-Serien, vor Livepublikum auf der Bühne zu stehen.

Und da war der Tanz: selten so populär wie in den 1920er und 1930er Jahren, als alle – westliche – Welt zum Bunnyhop, Black Bottom, Charleston und Quickstep über das glänzende Parkett der Tanzpaläste, die Bohlenbretter der Tanzclubs, zwischen den Tischen der Restaurants und im Dämmerlicht zahlreicher Nachtclubs schob und das Tanzbein schwang. Und wenn nichts anderes ging, blieben Männer und Frauen zu Hause, schlugen den Teppich zurück und ließen sich in den eigenen vier Wänden tüchtig gehen. Tanzmarathons, Steptanz-Wettbewerbe und Formationstanz-Kurse schossen landauf, landab ebenso aus dem Boden wie Gesellschaftstanz-Veranstaltungen und Arthur-Murray-Tanzstudiofilialen. Und dann war da Fred Astaire – geschmeidig, charmant und lächelnd trommelte er mit den Füßen alle möglichen Rhythmen und Synkopen auf den Boden und ließ dabei das Unmögliche lächerlich einfach erscheinen.

Auf den Bühnen der Welt drehten sie ihre Pirouetten und wirbelten, sprangen und schlängelten sich die Tänzer des Bolschoi, der Ballets Russes, des New York City Ballet, Sadlers Wells und zahlreiche andere Tanzkompanien durch die Choreographien von Michail Fokine, Frederick Ashton, Martha Graham, Merce Cunningham, George Balanchine, Twyla Tharp, Michail Barischnikow und Joaquin Cortez. Dabei war Sergej Diaghilew einzigartig: ein Mann, ein Monster – mit zwar begrenzter Beweglichkeit, jedoch grenzenloser Vision –, dessen Team aus Komponisten und Designern (Strawinsky, Satie, Cocteau und Picasso) das Gesicht des Balletts veränderten.

Es war das Zeitalter der Maestros – der großen Dirigenten, von Furtwängler bis von Karajan; von Beecham bis Bernstein (vorige Seite, beim Dirigieren des New York Philharmonic Orchestra). Und es war das Zeitalter musikalischer Pioniere wie Karlheinz Stockhausen (oben).

Und schließlich, gegen Ende des 20. Jahrhunderts, kam eine Form von Entertainment auf, die man in der eigenen Hand hielt und die man nicht nur passiv erlebte: das Computerspiel. In den Anfangsjahren noch primitiv, wurde es schnell zu einer erstaunlichen neuen Kunstform, die zwar oft auf Gewalt setzte, aber auf die User eben auch den Reiz ausübte, ihr Leben virtuell aufs Spiel zu setzen.

Au XXᵉ siècle, le monde de la musique est le théâtre d'une révolution – qui commence avec l'invention du phonographe, suivie de celles du gramophone, du tourne-disques, de la stéréo et de la hi-fi (haute-fidélité) ainsi que du lecteur de CD et, enfin, du iPod. Au début des années 1930, il devient possible d'écouter chez soi – à chaque fois qu'on le désire – le concert de violon de Sir Edward Elgar donné par un jeune soliste aux dons extraordinaires, Yehudi Menuhin ; ou l'orchestre de Duke Ellington avec *Rocking in Rhythm* ; ou Maurice Chevalier avec l'une de ses douzaines de ballades au sujet des boulevards parisiens. La musique imprègne la totalité du quotidien – à tel point qu'il devient pratiquement impossible de lui échapper. Dans les magasins, les halls de gare, voire les ascenseurs, la musique conquiert la conscience, mais aussi, en même temps, l'inconscient.

Simultanément, d'autres progrès de la technique transposent d'autres chefs-d'œuvre de l'art et du divertissement dans le domaine de la culture au quotidien. Les livres commencent à parler et se déclinent en e-books, les représentations de ballet sont proposées en vidéo et en DVD, les comédiens se bousculent pour devenir des stars de la télé. La musique populaire se recentre sur la pop music, avec la sortie de *best of* des légendes du genre – comme les Rolling Stones, Michael Jackson, Nina Simone, Bob Dylan, Dolly Parton, Madonna, Lady Gaga, et le plus grand de tous, Elvis – le King éternel.

Quelques théâtres mythiques ferment leurs portes ; d'autres petites scènes ouvrent les leurs ; c'est l'époque de la comédie musicale de Broadway, des productions provocantes off-Broadway, de l'Agit-Prop, du cabaret, du festival « Fringe » et du théâtre expérimental – chaque soirée théâtrale pouvait dès lors se transformer en une source d'enchantement ou de déception. Une pollinisation croisée entre télévision et théâtre vivant permet aux stars de séries du petit écran de fouler les planches et d'affronter le public en direct.

Il y a aussi la danse : rarement aussi populaire que dans les années 1920 et 1930, quand tout le monde occidental ondule sur le parquet brillant des palais de danse, sur les planches en bois des clubs de danse, entre les tables des restaurants et dans la lumière tamisée d'innombrables night-clubs ou frétille sur les rythmes du bunnyhop, black bottom, charleston et quickstep. Et, quand rien d'autre ne va plus – hommes et femmes restent chez eux, roulent le tapis et dansent jusqu'à épuisement entre leurs quatre murs. Marathons de danse, concours de claquettes et cours de danse en formation poussent comme des champignons dans tous les pays, aussi vite que les manifestations de danse mondaine et les filiales des studios de danse d'Arthur Murray. Et il y a, surtout, Fred Astaire – souple et élégant, souriant, le virtuose des claquettes, faisant paraître presque évident ce qui jusqu'alors semblait impossible.

Sur les scènes du monde entier, ils décrivent leurs pirouettes et tourbillonnent, sautent et virevoltent : ce sont les danseurs du Bolchoï, des Ballets russes, du New York City Ballet, de Sadlers Wells, ainsi que de nombreuses autres compagnies de danse présentant les chorégraphies de Michel Fokine, Frederick Ashton, Martha Graham, Merce Cunningham, George Balanchine, Twyla Tharp, Mikhaïl Barychnikov et Joaquin Cortez. Parmi eux, Serge Diaghilev était absolument unique : un homme, un monstre – avec une mobilité certes limitée, mais une vision, portée par une équipe de compositeurs et d'artistes (Stravinsky, Satie, Cocteau et Picasso) qui allaient métamorphoser le visage du ballet. C'était l'âge des maîtres, celui de grands chefs d'orchestre, de Furtwängler à von Karajan, de Beecham à Bernstein, dirigeant ici l'orchestre philharmonique de New York *(voir page suivante)*. C'était aussi l'âge des pionniers, comme en témoignait Stockhausen *(voir page 596)*.

Enfin, plus révolutionnaire que tout, la fin du XXᵉ siècle vit apparaître un loisir qui « tenait dans la main » – le jeu vidéo, rudimentaire à ses balbutiements, mais dont le développement rapide donna naissance à une nouvelle et étonnante forme d'art, à l'univers souvent violent, mais qui invitait les joueurs à se confronter au grand frisson de la réalité virtuelle.

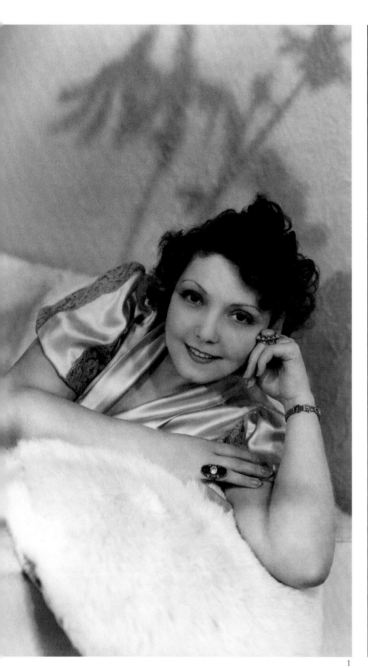

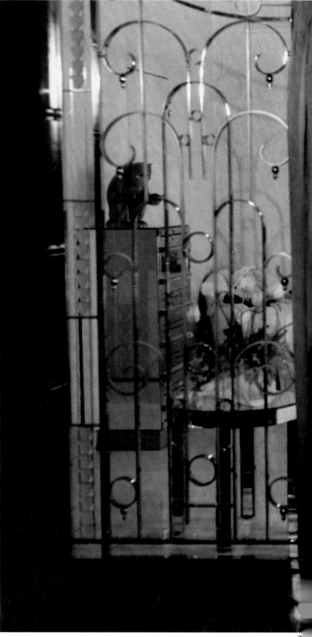

The delightful and popular Spanish mezzo-soprano Conchita Supervia imported the famous 1930s studio photographer Sasha for these 'informal' shots at her home in Mayfair (1). In fact the theatricality of the wrought-iron gates and drapes (2) well suited the disposition of the singer, whose principal roles included Carmen and the coloratura Rossini roles (Rosina, Cinderella).

DIE bezaubernde und beliebte spanische Mezzosopranistin Conchita Supervia ließ den berühmten Studiophotographen der 30er Jahre, »Sascha«, kommen, der diese »informellen« Aufnahmen in ihrem Haus im Londoner Stadtteil Mayfair machte (1). Eigentlich passen die schmiedeeisernen Gitter und die Vorhänge (2), die etwas Theatralisches haben, gut zu einer Sängerin, zu deren größten Rollen Carmen und die Koloraturen bei Rossini (Rosina, Aschenbrödel) gehörten.

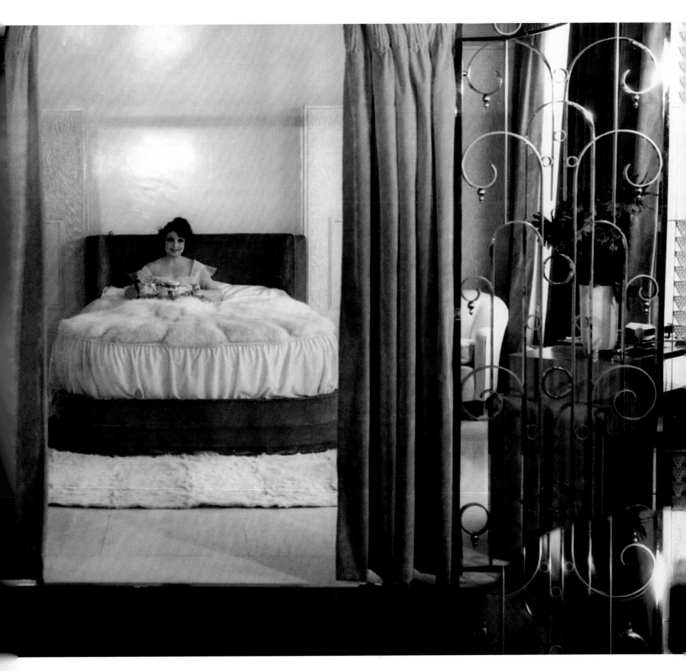

ONCHITA Supervia, la ravissante et populaire mezzo-soprano espagnole, introduisit le célèbre photographe en atelier des années 30, Sasha, dans son appartement à Mayfair où il réalisa ses prises de vues « informelles » (1). En fait, le côté théâtral des barrières en fer forgé et des draperies (2) est bien en accord avec le tempérament d'une cantatrice qui a interprété entre autres Carmen et les rôles à vocalises de Rossini (Rosina, Cendrillon).

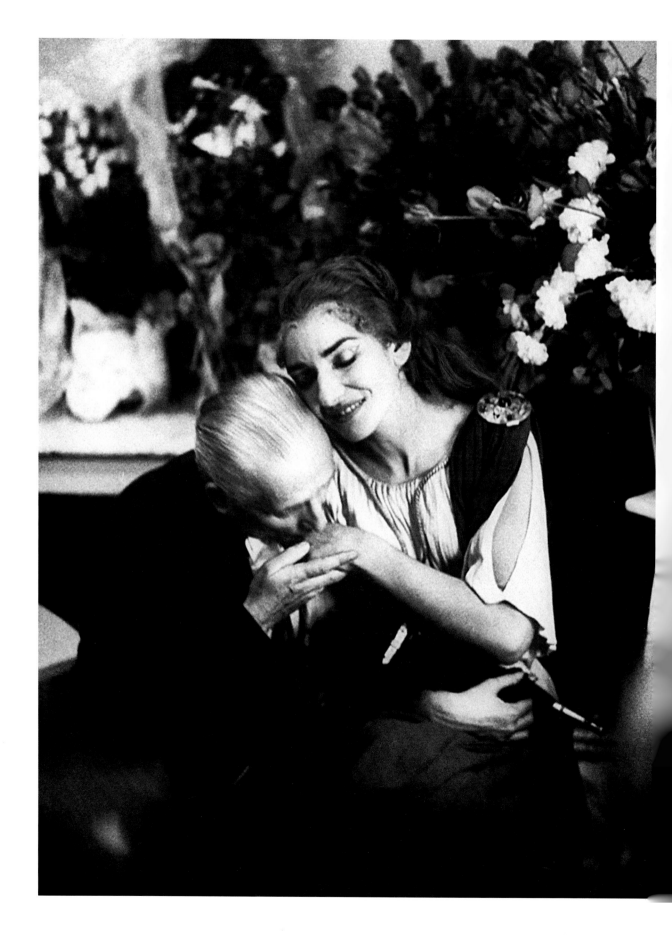

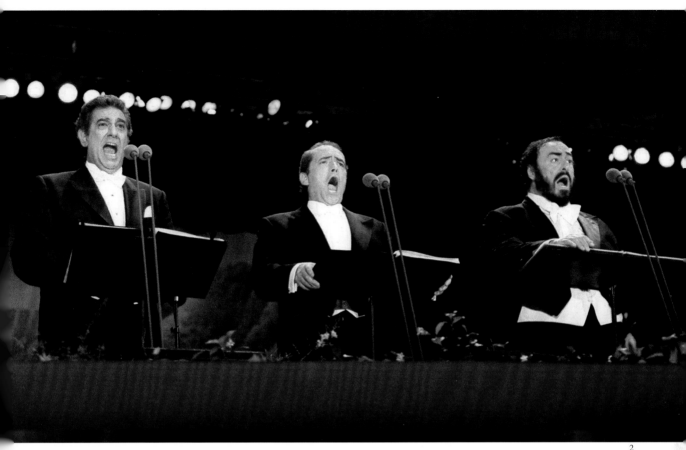

THROUGHOUT the second half of the 20th century, opera gradually ceased to be the exclusive property of the highly cultured or the pretentious *dilettante*. The wonderful voice and the dramatic intensity of Maria Callas (1), together with the mass marketing of great recordings, attracted millions of new *aficionados* to opera houses around the world. The real revolution, however, came some 40 years later with the record industry's creation of a phenomenon known as 'The Three Tenors' (2) – (*left to right*) Placido Domingo, José Carreras and Luciano Pavarotti – here performing at the closing ceremony of the Olympic Games, Dodger Stadium, Los Angeles, 16 July 1994. For a long while, in elevator, in clothing store or on TV, it seemed impossible to escape 'Nessun dorma' or 'O Sole Mio'.

IN der zweiten Hälfte des 20. Jahrhunderts hörte die Oper auf, das exklusive Vergnügen der Gebildeten und der Angeber zu sein. Die wundervolle Stimme und dramatische Intensität der Maria Callas (1) lockten – zusammen mit der erfolgreichen Vermarktung ihrer großartigen Aufnahmen – Millionen von neuen Fans in die Opernhäuser der Welt. Die wahre Revolution auf diesem Gebiet kam jedoch rund 40 Jahre später – mit der erfolgreichen Erfindung eines Phänomens seitens der Schallplattenindustrie und Tonstudios, das als *Die drei Tenöre* (2) Kulturgeschichte schrieb – Placido Domingo, José Carreras und Luciano Pavarotti (*von links nach rechts*) – hier bei der Abschlußzeremonie der Olympischen Spiele im Dodger-Stadion in Los Angeles am 16. Juli 1994. Für eine lange Weile danach schien es nahezu unmöglich, in Fahrstühlen, Boutiquen oder auch im Fernsehen ihrem »Nessun dorma« oder »O sole mio« zu entkommen.

DURANT la seconde moitié du XXᵉ siècle, l'opéra cesse d'être le plaisir exclusif de l'intelligentsia et des crâneurs. De concert avec la commercialisation lucrative de ses remarquables enregistrements, la voix merveilleuse et l'intensité dramatique de Maria Callas (1) attirent des millions de nouveaux adeptes dans les opéras du monde. La véritable révolution dans ce domaine se produit cependant une quarantaine d'années plus tard – avec l'invention – plébiscitée par le public – d'un phénomène de l'industrie du disque et des studios d'enregistrement qui est entré dans l'histoire de la culture sous le nom des *Trois Ténors* (2) – Placido Domingo, José Carreras et Luciano Pavarotti (*de gauche à droite*) – ici lors de la cérémonie de clôture des Jeux olympiques au Dodger-Stadium de Los Angeles, le 16 juillet 1994. Pendant une longue période, il semble alors quasiment impossible d'échapper à leurs mélodies « Nessun dorma » ou « O sole mio » dans les ascenseurs, les magasins ou, aussi, à la télévision.

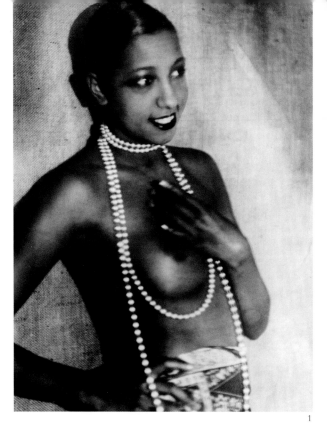

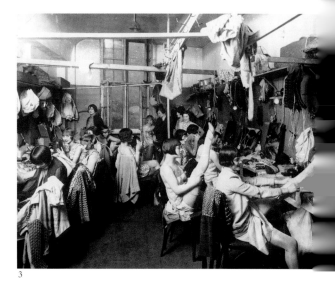

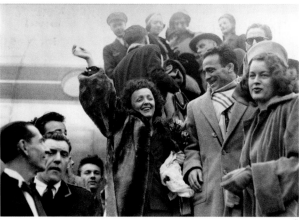

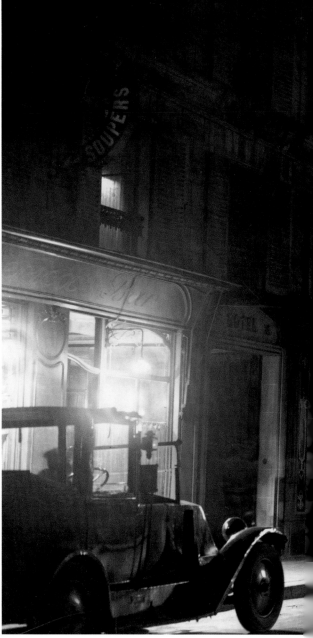

Fʀᴇɴᴄʜ night-life always had a certain *je ne sais quoi*. The Folies Bergère in 1929 was so grand and glamorous that it (and Maurice Chevalier) transferred direct to Hollywood's silver screen (4). Inside, the girls all acquired the same bobbed hairstyle – and the same high-kicking technique for pulling up their stockings (3). Josephine Baker was a legend in her two lifetimes: firstly as a dancer who brought her colour to the European stage and sexily sent up every racist prejudice with her oiled body, bouncing bananas and jungle seductions (1); secondly as the 'mother of a hundred' deprived and abandoned children she adopted and cherished. Edith Piaf's impoverished background; her past as a prostitute; her addiction to morphine and alcohol to help overcome the physical and emotional scars, all would have rendered her the quintessential victim, had it not been for her voice (2). Its tremendous power, combined with her fragile frame dressed always in black, made period songs like *La Vie en Rose* and *Non, je ne regrette rien* into her personal anthems.

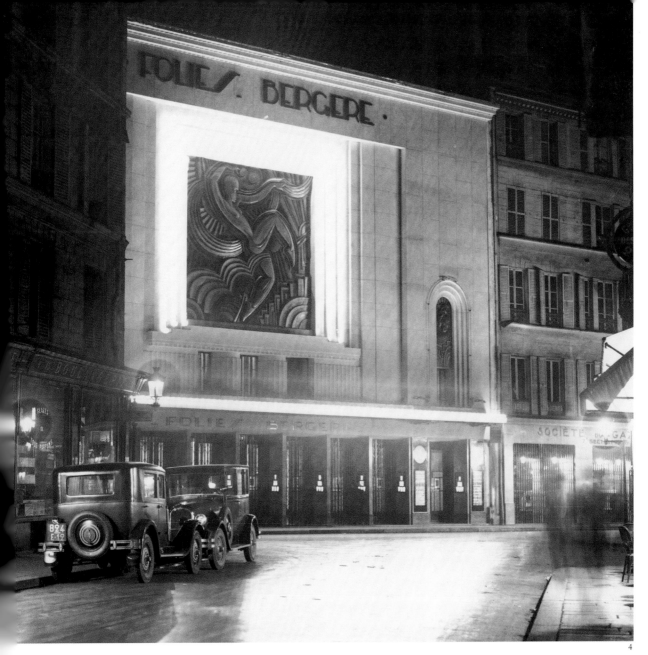

4

DAS Nachtleben in Frankreich hatte schon immer ein gewisses *je ne sais quoi*. Die Folies Bergère waren 1929 so grandios, daß man sie (und Maurice Chevalier) schnurstracks nach Hollywood verfrachtete (4). Drinnen hatten die Mädchen alle die gleiche Kurzhaarfrisur – und die gleiche Technik, um die Strümpfe anzuziehen (3). Josephine Baker wurde gleich zweimal zur Legende, in den zwei Leben, die sie führte: zuerst als Tänzerin, die Farbe auf die Bühnen Europas brachte und allen rassistischen Vorurteilen mit ihrem geölten Körper, den hüpfenden Bananen und ihrer Dschungelerotik die Spitze nahm (1), zum zweiten als Mutter von hundert verlassenen Kindern, die sie adoptierte und aufzog. Edith Piaf schien zum Opfer geboren, bei den ärmlichen Verhältnissen, aus denen sie kam, ihrer Vergangenheit als Prostituierte, ihrer Morphium- und Alkoholsucht; doch ihre Stimme rettete sie (2). Die enorme Kraft dieser Stimme, die in einem solchen Kontrast zu der zerbrechlichen, stets in Schwarz gekleideten Gestalt stand, machte Lieder wie *La vie en rose* oder *Non, je ne regrette rien* zu ihren ganz persönlichen Hymnen.

EN France, la vie nocturne possède un certain « je-ne-sais-quoi ». En 1929, le prestige et l'attrait des Folies Bergère était tels qu'on les transposa directement (avec Maurice Chevalier) sur le grand écran hollywoodien (4). À l'intérieur, les filles avaient toutes la même coupe au carré et une technique identique pour enfiler leur bas (3). Joséphine Baker fut deux fois légendaire : une première fois, en tant que danseuse de couleur en tournée européenne, elle ridiculisa tous les préjugés racistes avec son corps luisant, ses bananes bondissantes et ses attraits exotiques (1) ; une seconde fois en adoptant une centaine d'enfants abandonnés. Le milieu misérable d'où était issue Édith Piaf, son passé dans la prostitution, sa dépendance à l'alcool et à la morphine qui l'aidait à faire face aux problèmes physiques et émotionnels, tout cela aurait fait d'elle la quintessence de la victime s'il n'y avait pas eu sa voix (2). Celle-ci émanait de sa fragile silhouette toujours vêtue de noir. Grâce à elle, son nom est indissolublement lié à des chansons comme *La vie en rose* et *Non, je ne regrette rien*.

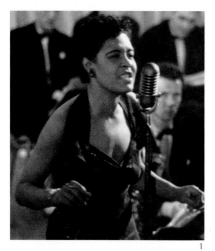

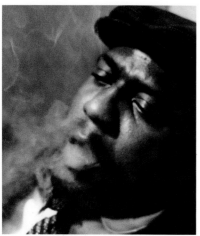

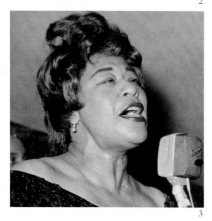

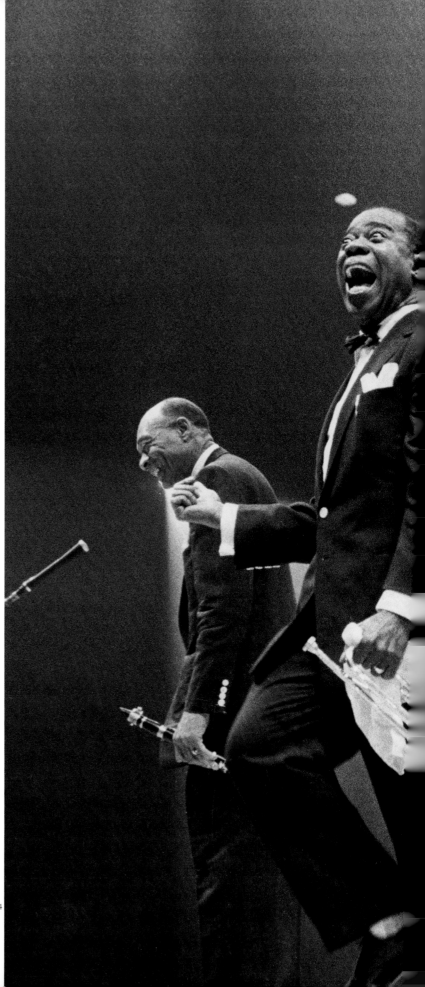

B{ILLIE} Holiday (1); Ella Fitzgerald in 1962 (3); Thelonious Monk (2); Louis Armstrong in the 1960s (4).

B{ILLIE} Holiday (1); Ella Fitzgerald, 1962 (3); Thelonious Monk (2); Louis Armstrong in den 60er Jahren (4).

B{ILLIE} Holiday (1) ; Ella Fitzgerald en 1962 (3) ; Thelonious Monk (2) ; Louis Armstrong dans les années 60 (4).

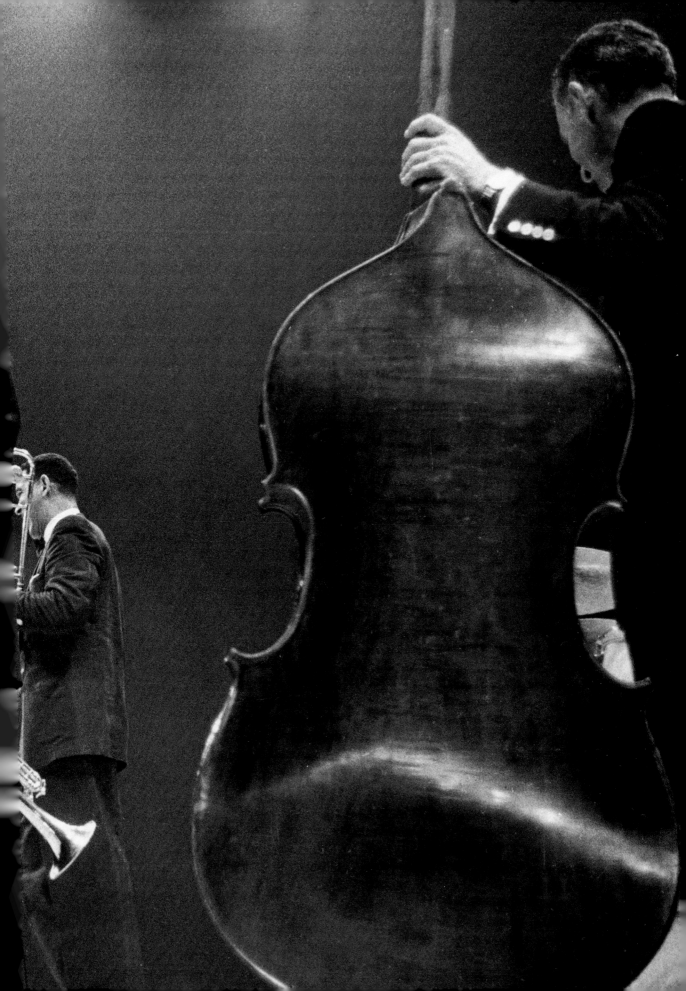

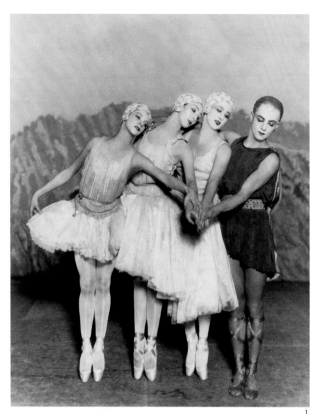

1

A NNA Pavlova (1881-1931) devint la plus célèbre représentante du ballet académique, se fixant dans cette maison (Ivy Lodge) de Golders Green à Londres (3). Le cygne posant à ses côtés est une lourde allusion au *Cygne* de Mikhaïl Fokine, qu'elle créa en 1905. Parmi les autres Russes qui ont compté à cette époque dans le monde du ballet, on note ici la présence de Serge Lifar posant ici avec les muses (1) dans *Apollon Musagète* et Serge Diaghilev (à droite), avec Jean Cocteau (2). En 1909, Diaghilev fonda la troupe des Ballets russes à Monte-Carlo et les fit connaître en Occident, réunissant les plus grands talents de la danse et de la musique de l'époque : Pavlova, Nijinsky, Fokine, Massine, Balanchine, Stravinsky et Prokofiev.

A NNA Pavlova (1881-1931) became the world's most famous exponent of classical ballet, basing herself in this house (Ivy Lodge) in London's Golders Green (3). The carefully posed swan is a heavy allusion to her signature solo, Mikhail Fokine's *Dying Swan* of 1905. Other important Russians in the world of dance at this time included Serge Lifar, posed with the muses (1) in *Apollon Musagète*, and Serge Diaghilev (on the right), with Jean Cocteau (2). In 1909 Diaghilev founded the Ballets Russes in Monte Carlo. From here, he brought Russian ballet to the west, introducing all the star composers, choreographers and dancers of the period: Pavlova, Nijinsky, Fokine, Massine, Balanchine, Stravinsky and Prokofiev.

A NNA Pawlowa (1881-1931) war die weltweit berühmteste Tänzerin des klassischen Balletts, und dieses Haus, Ivy Lodge im Londoner Golders Green, war ihr Hauptquartier (3). Der Schwan im Vordergrund steht für die Rolle, die sie zu ihrem Markenzeichen machte, Michel Fokines *Sterbenden Schwan* von 1905. Andere bedeutende Russen in der Welt des Tanzes waren damals Sergej Lifar, hier (1) mit den Musen in *Apollon Musagète* zu sehen, und Sergej Diaghilew (rechts), mit Jean Cocteau (2). 1909 hatte Diaghilew seine Ballets Russes in Monte Carlo gegründet. Von dort aus exportierte er russisches Ballett in den Westen und machte alle bedeutenden Komponisten, Choreographen und Tänzer der Zeit damit vertraut: Pawlowa, Nijinsky, Fokine, Massine, Balanchine, Strawinsky und Prokofieff.

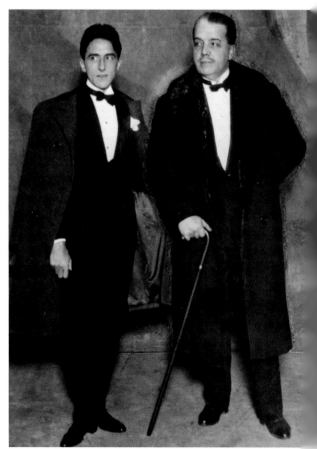

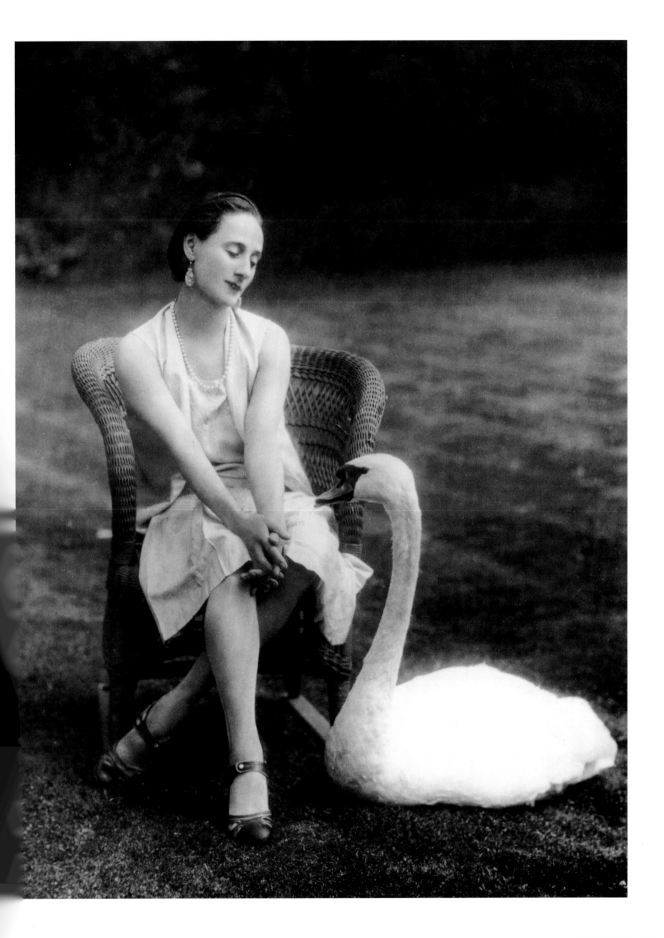

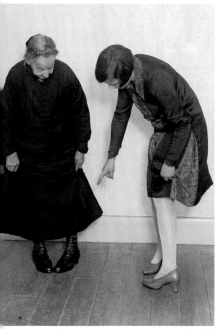

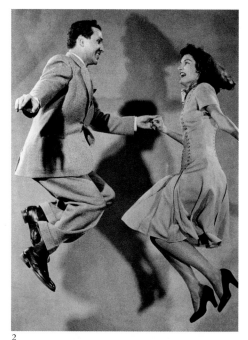

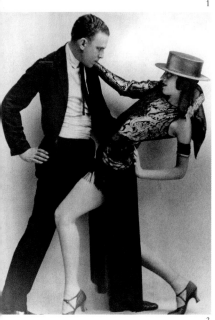

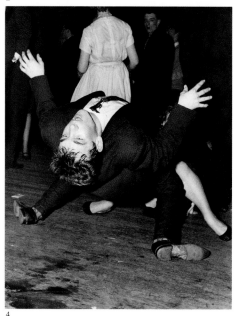

1   2

3   4

DIE Tanzstile wurden im Laufe des Jahrhunderts immer lockerer. Im Jahre 1927 nimmt Mrs. Harradine aus Wood Green, Nord-London, Unterricht im Black Bottom (1). Auch mit 87 Jahren möchte sie, wie sie sagt, auf dem laufenden bleiben, damit sie mit den jüngeren Familienmitgliedern Schritt halten kann. Eine andere Variante war der »Affentanz«, so genannt, weil Miss Jola Cohen aus Chicago und Arthur Murray sich die Schritte von der Äffin La Bella Pola beibringen ließen (5). Fred Astaire unterrichtet in seinem Atelier an der New Yorker Park Avenue gleich hundert Tanzlehrer in seinen Techniken. Zwei von ihnen demonstrieren den typischen Astaire-Tanz, eine Mischung aus Jitterbug, Foxtrott und einem geheimnisvollen »Jersey Bounce« (2). Das ist natürlich »der Astaire«. Latin Lovers wie Ramon Navarro führten einen »neuen Tango« ein, und im Londoner Piccadilly-Hotel eifern Josephine Head und Albert Zapp ihm nach (3). In den 60er Jahren kam es, wie es kommen mußte: Als es nicht mehr weiter voranging, konnte es nur noch rückwärts gehen (4) – und zwar bis ganz nach unten. Wer im Glenlyn Ballroom Dancing Club keinen Twist tanzt, der ist rettungslos verloren.

LA danse s'échauffe et s'agite au cours du siècle. Pour rester à la page à 87 ans et danser le Black Bottom en 1927, Mme Harradine, de Wood Green, au nord de Londres, écoute les instructions (1) pour demeurer, comme elle dit, « en paix avec les plus jeunes membres de la famille ». Une autre variation était la « danse du singe » – appelée ainsi depuis que le singe, La Bella Pola, avait appris un pas ou deux à Miss Jola Cohen de Chicago et Arthur Murray lui-même (5). Fred Astaire a transmis sa technique à cent instructeurs dans son propre studio de Park Avenue à New York. Deux d'entre eux font une démonstration de sa danse qui allie le jitterbug, le fox-trot et un énigmatique « bond de Jersey » (2). C'est, bien sûr, la « Astaire ». Des « latin lovers », à la façon de Ramon Navarro, ont remis le tango au goût du jour. Au Piccadilly Hotel de Londres, Josephine Head et Albert Zapp s'y exercent intensément (3). Durant les années 60 arriva ce qui devait arriver : quand tout mouvement vers l'avant a été fait, on ne peut plus qu'aller vers l'arrière (4) – à plat sur le dos. Au club de danse de Glenlyn, vous êtes vieux jeu si vous ne dansez pas le twist.

DANCE styles loosened up and shook down through the course of the century. Anxious to get with it and do the Black Bottom in 1927, 87-year-old Mrs Harradine of Wood Green, North London, takes instruction (1) in order, she says, 'to keep pace with the younger members of the family'. Another variation was the 'Monkey Dance', so-called since the monkey La Bella Pola taught Miss Jola Cohen of Chicago and Arthur Murray himself a step or two (5). Fred Astaire's technique is passed on to 100 instructors at his own studio on Park Avenue, New York. Two of them demonstrate his signature dance, which combines jitterbug, fox-trot and a mysterious 'Jersey bounce' (2). It is, of course, 'the Astaire'. Latin lovers like Ramon Navarro created a taste for a 'new-fangled tango'. At the Piccadilly Hotel, London, Josephine Head and Albert Zapp are in hot pursuit of it (3). The 1960s brought the predictable outcome: when every forward move has been made, there's nowhere to go but back (4) – flat on your back. At the Glenlyn Ballroom Dancing Club, if you're not in a Twist you're a Square.

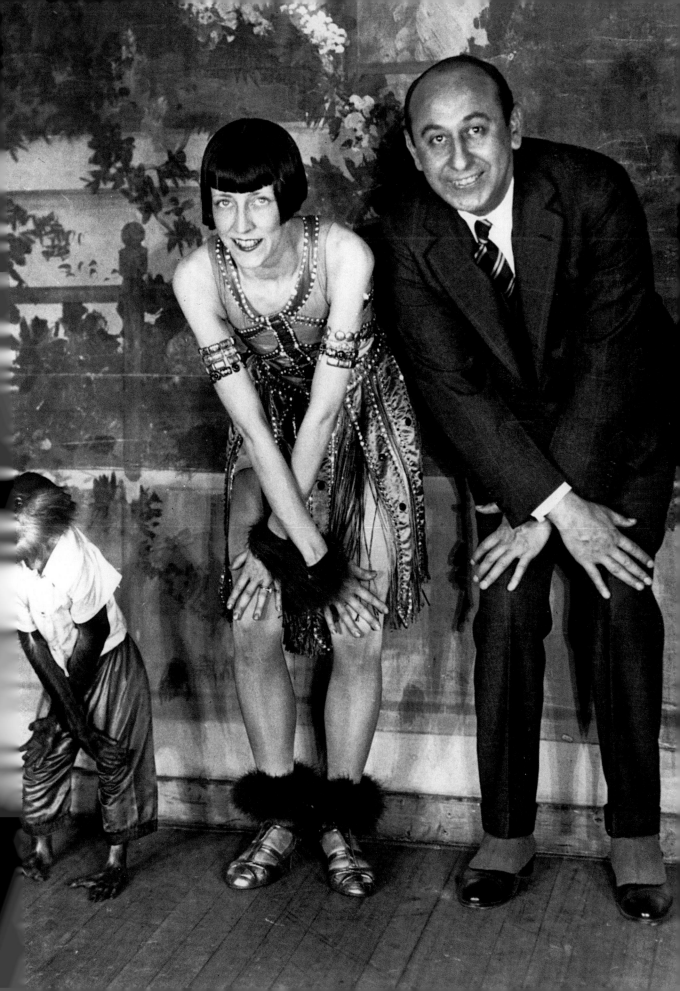

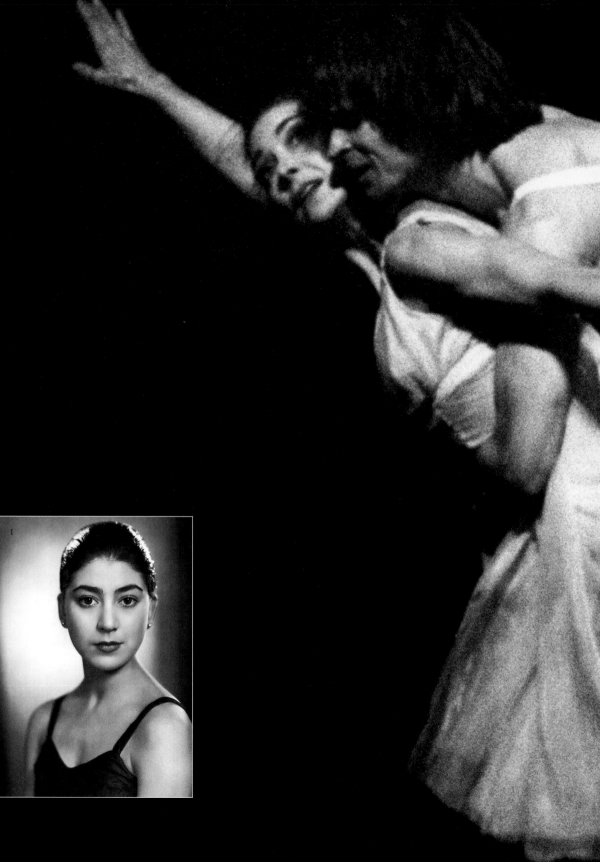

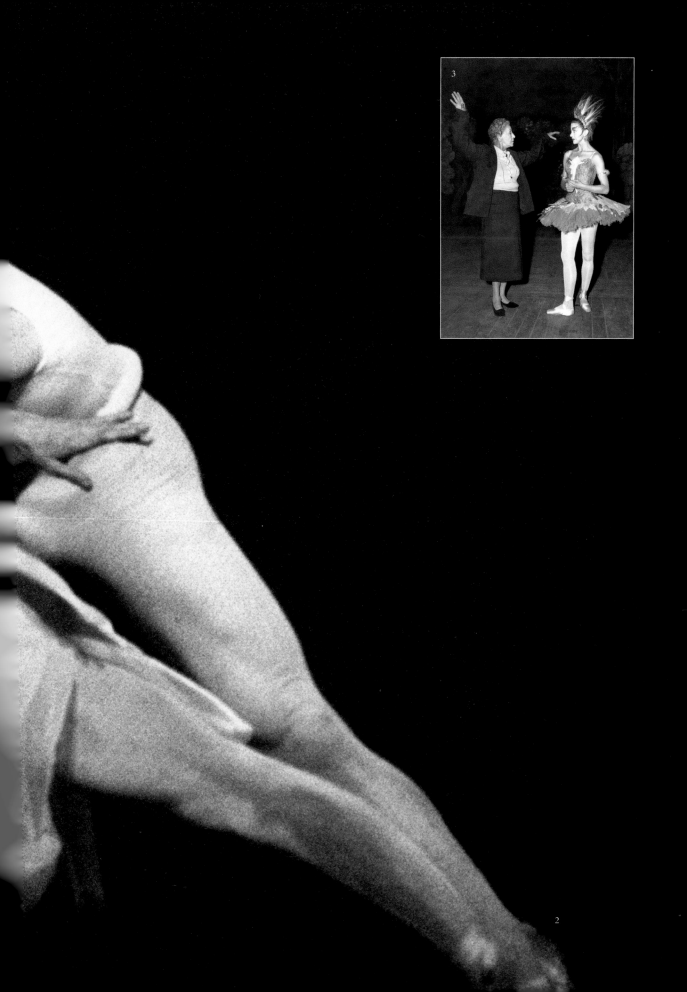

2

3

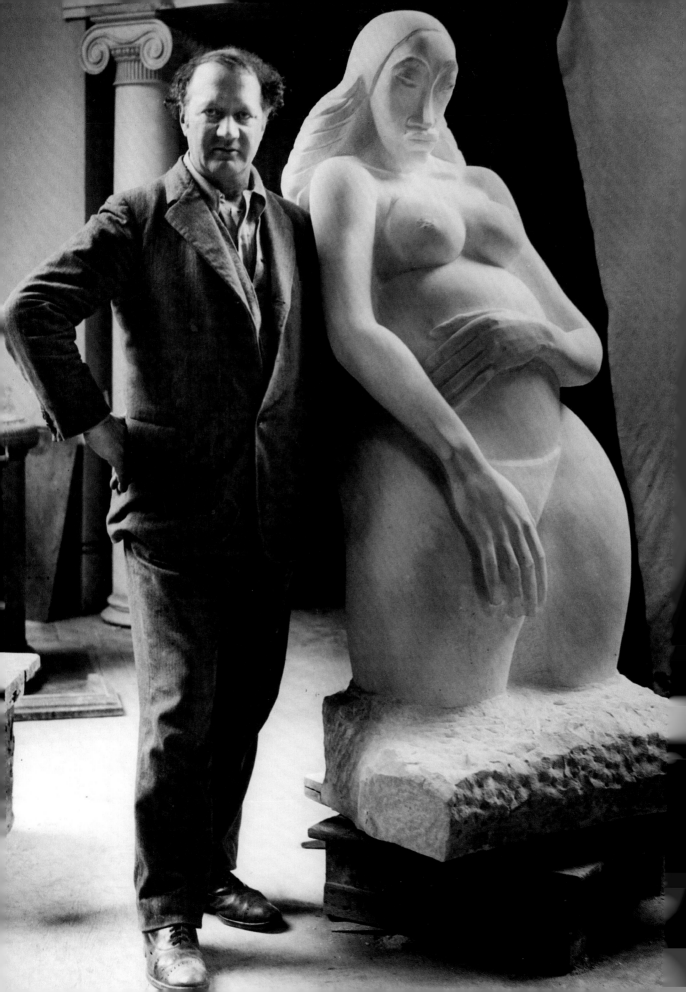

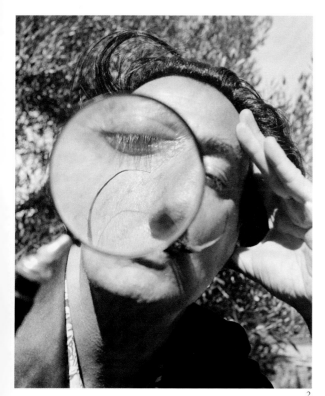

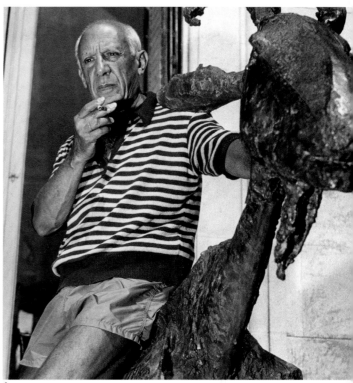

2 3

EPSTEIN, Dalí and Picasso: three prolific and international giants of twentieth-century art. Jacob Epstein was known mainly for majestic works such as that of St Michael the Archangel, over the portico of the new Coventry Cathedral, or this Earth Mother statue (1). An anonymous ditty ran: 'I don't like the family Stein;/There is Gert, there is Ep, there is Ein./Gert's writings are punk,/Ep's statues are junk,/And nobody understands Ein.' Dalí and Picasso were both Catalan, but had absolutely nothing in common. The former (2) was a truculent eccentric with a genius for publicity and moustaches, an exponent of Dada and Surrealist art. Having left Spain after the Guernica bombing that was to give rise to one of his most famous works, Picasso based himself in the South of France. Here he is meditating on his sinister carving of a goat (3) – a sculpture apparently light-years away from Picasso the Cubist, or of the Blue, Pink, abstract or later periods.

EPSTEIN, Dalí und Picasso: drei Giganten der internationalen Kunst des 20. Jahrhunderts. Jacob Epstein war vor allem für seine majestätischen Werke, wie den Erzengel Michael über dem Portikus der neuen Kathedrale von Coventry und seine Erdmutter (1), bekannt. Unser alter Freund Anonymus verspottet in einem Verslein die Marotten des großen Bildhauers: »Ich mag sie nicht, die Familie Stein, / Nicht die Gert, nicht den Ep, nicht den Ein. / Gerts Bücher sind schal, / Eps Statuen 'ne Qual, / Und Einstein versteht kein Schwein.« Dalí und Picasso waren beide Katalanen, doch das war auch ihre einzige Gemeinsamkeit. Dalí war ein hundertprozentiger Exzentriker mit einem Talent für Publicity und Schnurrbärte, ein Vertreter von Dada und Surrealismus (2). Picasso verließ Spanien nach der Bombardierung Guernicas, die ihm das Thema für eines seiner berühmtesten Bilder lieferte, und lebte seitdem in Südfrankreich. Hier sitzt er nachdenklich auf seinem Ziegenbock (3) – eine Skulptur, die Lichtjahre von Picassos kubistischer, blauer, rosa und abstrakter Periode entfernt ist.

EPSTEIN, Dalí et Picasso : trois géants du XXᵉ siècle, célèbres dans le monde entier. Jacob Epstein était connu surtout pour ses œuvres majestueuses comme l'archange saint Michel, érigée sur le portique de la nouvelle cathédrale de Coventry, ou la Grande Mère (1). Une mélodie anonyme dit irrévérencieusement : « Je n'aime pas la famille Stein / Il y a Gert, il y a Ep, il y a Ein / Les écrits de Gert sont moches / Les statues de Ep sont cloches / Et nul ne comprend Ein. » Le seul trait commun entre Dalí et Picasso était leur origine catalane. Dalí (2) faisait figure d'excentrique au caractère rebelle et était doué d'un sens génial de la publicité. Quant à Picasso, qui avait quitté l'Espagne à la suite du bombardement sur Guernica, il allait engendrer l'une de ses plus célèbres toiles. On le voit ici méditer sur sa sinistre chèvre sculptée

(Previous pages)

AFTER her first *Giselle* in 1937 (1), Margot Fonteyn (1919-1991) rapidly became a world star. Here she is in one of the roles she made her own: Stravinsky's *Firebird*, for which she was coached by Tamara Karsavina, the original Firebird (3). Her later career was revitalized by her partnership with Rudolf Nureyev (2).

(Vorherige Seiten)

MARGOT Fonteyn (1919-1991) wurde mit ihre ersten *Giselle* 1937 (1) zum Weltstar. Hier ist sie in einer ihrer Leib- und Magenrollen zu sehen, Strawinskys *Feuervogel*, für den sie Unterricht von Tamara Karsawina bekam (3). Später gab die Partnerschaft mit Rudolf Nurejew ihrer Karriere neuen Schwung (2).

(Pages précédentes)

APRÈS son premier *Giselle,* en 1937 (1), Margot Fonteyn (1919-1991) devint vite une star internationale. On la voit ici dans *L'Oiseau de feu* de Stravinsky, tandis qu'elle écoute les conseils de Tamara Karsavina, l'Oiseau de feu original (3). Sa carrière connut un nouvel essor grâce à Rudolf Noureev (1938-1993) (2).

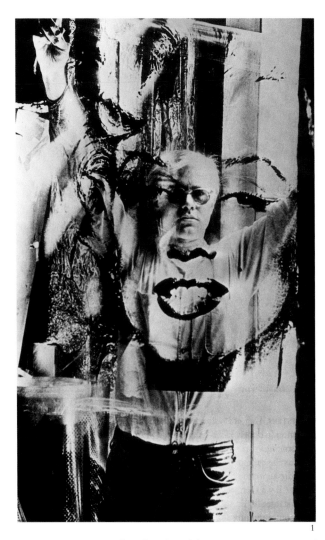
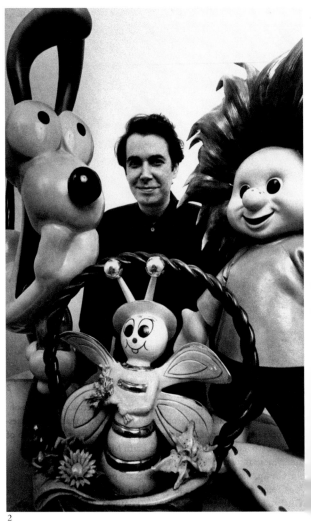

1   2

THOUGH some stood on the edge of the crowd and wondered if they were being asked to admire the Emperor's new clothes, painting and sculpture increasingly hit the headlines and demanded high prices in the last decades of the 20th century. One of the pioneers of what became known as Concept Art was Andy Warhol, whose Marilyn Monroe exhibition was staged in New York City in 1967 (1). Twenty years later, fellow American Jeff Koons produced his *Wild Boy and Puppy* (2).

OBWOHL manche am Rande der Menge blieben und sich fragten, ob hier des Kaisers neue Kleider zu bestaunen waren, kamen Malerei und Bidlhauerei zunehmend in die Schlagzeieln und erzielten in der letzten Dekade des 20. Jahrhunderts Preise in schwindelnder Höhe. Einer der Pioniere von dem, was als *Konzeptkunst* bekannt wurde, war Andy Warhol (1) – dessen Ausstellung über Marilyn Monroe im Jahre 1967 in New York eröffnet wurde. 20 Jahre später schuf sein amerikanischer Kollege Jeff Koons die Skulpturen *Wild Boy and Puppy* (2).

Bien que certains restent en marge de la foule et se demandent s'il s'agissait ici d'admirer « les nouveaux habits de l'empereur », la peinture et la sculpture occupent de plus en plus fréquemment les manchettes des journaux et, durant la dernière décennie du XXe siècle, leurs œuvres atteignent des prix qui donnent le vertige. L'un des pionniers de ce que l'on appelle *l'Art concept* est Andy Warhol (1) – dont son exposition dédiée à Marilyn Monroe a été inaugurée en 1967 à New York. Vingt ans plus tard, son collègue américain Jeff Koons crée les sculptures *Wild Boy and Puppy* (2).

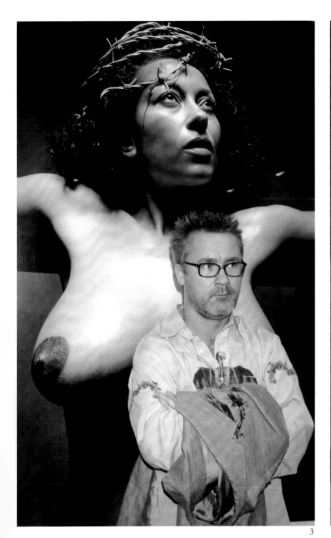
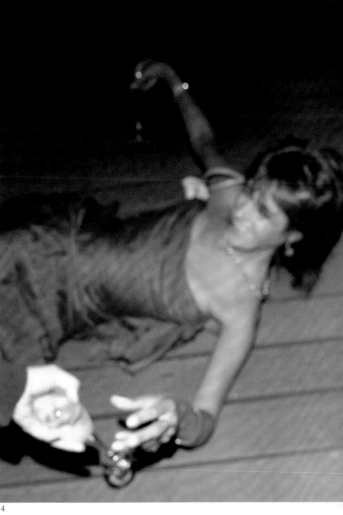

3 4

BRIT Art came to the fore in the 1990s, backed and promoted by Charles Saatchi, who championed the cause of many hitherto unknown young artists. Damien Hirst shocked his way to fame and fortune with such works as *The Physical Impossibility of Death in the Mind of Someone Living* and *Mother and Child Divided* (known by some as 'that shark thing' and 'that cow thing'), and his later *Stations of the Cross* (3). Tracey Emin failed to make her bed, and had the misfortune to fall at the *GQ Magazine* Awards in London, 2 September 2003 (4).

BRITISCHE Kunst kam in den 1990er Jahren in die vorderste Reihe – nicht zuletzt durch die Unterstützung durch Charles Saatchi, der sich zum Fürsprecher und Förderer vieler bisher unbekannter junger Künstler machte. Damien Hirst schockierte auf seinem Weg zu Ruhm und Erfolg mit solchen Werken wie *The Physical Impossibility of Death in the Mind of Someone Living* und *Mother and Child Divided* (auch bekannt unter den Titeln *Das Hai-Ding* und *Das Kuh-Ding*) sowie seines späteren Werkes *Stations of the Cross* (*Stationen des Kreuzes*) (3). Tracey Emin hatte weniger Erfolg und dazu das Pech, bei der Verleihung der GQ Magazine Awards in London hinzufallen (4) – 2. September 2003.

DURANT les années 90, l'art britannique se propulse sur les devants de la scène – aussi et surtout grâce au soutien de Charles Saatchi, qui se fait l'avocat et le mécène de nombreux jeunes artistes inconnus jusqu'à ce jour. Dans sa route qui le mène à la célébrité et au succès, Damien Hirst choque avec des œuvres comme *The Physical Impossibility of Death in the Mind of Someone Living* et *Mother and Child Divided* (connus également sous les titres *Le truc avec le requin* et *Le truc avec la vache*) ainsi qu'avec son œuvre ultérieure *Stations of the Cross* (le chemin de croix) (3). Tracey Emin a moins de succès et, comble du malheur, chute lourdement lors de l'attribution des GQ Magazine Awards à Londres (4) – 2 septembre 2003.

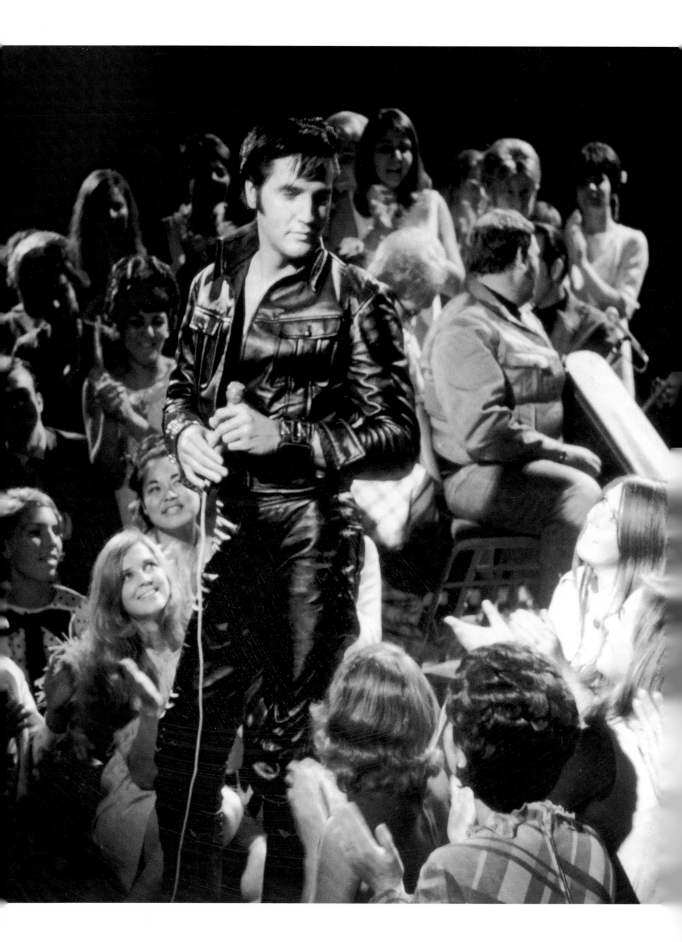

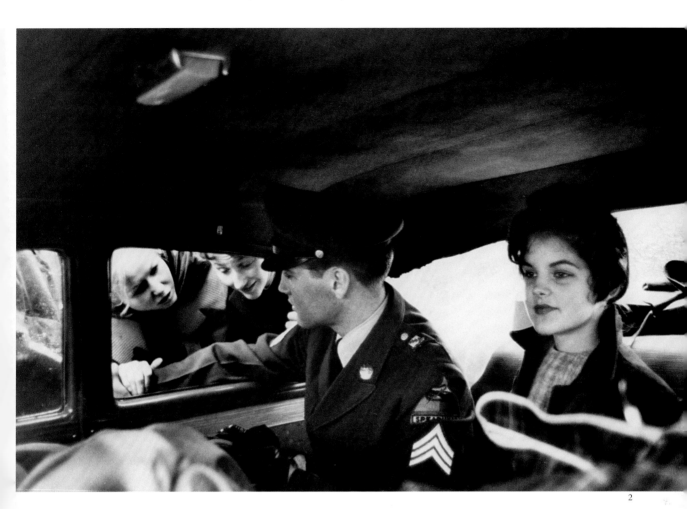

2

ELVIS Presley's career came in four parts. In the beginning, he was the sensation of the age – wild, sexy, moody, stirring up a whole heap of teenage furore. He hit the charts and he hit Hollywood. When he was drafted into the US Army in the late 1950s, The King went off to serve his country in Germany and to begin his romance with 14-year-old Priscilla Beaulieu (2). On his return, he made more films, more records, and continued to wow millions. Then came a lull, and a break in the live tours. In 1968 he made *Elvis Presley's Comeback Special* for TV (1). Some wondered if The King still had it: he silenced all doubters. From then on, however, it was all downhill.

ELVIS Presleys Karriere verlief in vier Etappen. Zunächst war er die Sensation seiner Generation – wild, sexy und launisch – und brachte damit die Teenager zum Kochen. Er stürmte die Charts – und Hollywood. Als er in den späten 1950er Jahren zum Militärdienst herangezogen wurde, leistete »The King« seinen Dienst für das Vaterland in Deutschland und begann eine Romanze mit der 14-jährigen Priscilla Beaulieu (2). Als er nach Amerika zurückkam, produzierte er noch mehr Filme, noch mehr Platten und riß ein Millionen-publikum mit. Dann kam eine Flaute – und eine Unterbrechung seiner Live-Auftritte. Im Jahre 1968 produzierte er fürs Fernsehen *Elvis Presley's Comeback Special* (1). Manche fragten sich, ob »The King« noch immer das gewisse Etwas habe – und er brachte alle Zweifler zum Schweigen. Doch von da an ging's bergab …

LA carrière d'Elvis Presley se déroule en quatre étapes. Il est tout d'abord la sensation de sa génération – sauvage, sexy et imprévisible – et mène ainsi les teenagers au bord de l'apoplexie. Il part à l'assaut du hit-parade – et d'Hollywood. Quand il doit faire son service militaire, à la fin des années 50, « The King » accomplit son service pour la patrie en Allemagne et commence sa romance avec Priscilla Beaulieu (2), âgée de 14 ans. À son retour en Amérique, il produit encore plus de films, encore plus de disques et se fait des millions d'adeptes. Puis suit une période de marasme – et une interruption de ses concerts sur scène. En 1968, il produit pour la télévision *Elvis Presley's Comeback Special* (1). Certains se demandent si « The King » a encore ce je ne sais quoi – mais il réduit tous ses détracteurs au silence. Pourtrant, viendra bienôt la chute brutale…

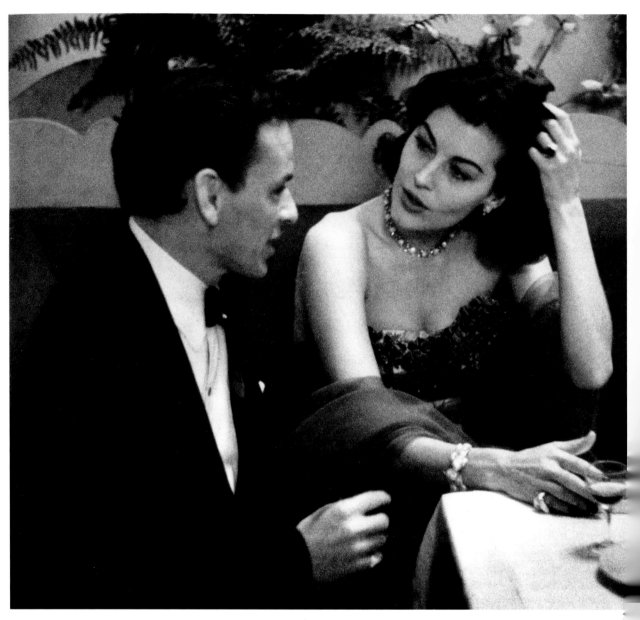

AT the beginning of the 1950s the career of Frank Sinatra was in comparative decline. He was no longer the idol of the bobbysoxers and MGM had no plans to star him in further musicals. His private life was happy enough – he was about to marry Ava Gardner (1) – but, musically, something new was needed. It came through the medium of Capitol Records, a great arranger named Nelson Riddle, and a terrific studio orchestra (2). Fifty years later, experts agree that *Songs for Swinging Lovers* remains one of the greatest albums of all time.

ZU Beginn der 1950er Jahre befand sich die Karriere des Frank Sinatra auf einem vergleichsweise absteigenden Ast: Er war nicht länger das Idol der Backfische, und MGM hatte nicht vor, weitere Musicals mit ihm in der Hauptrolle zu produzieren. Privat war er einigermaßen glücklich – und kurz davor, Ava Gardner zu heiraten (1); doch musikalisch brauchte er eine Erfrischungskur. Die kam in Gestalt der Produktionsfirma Capitol Records, eines großartigen Arrangeurs namens Nelson Riddle und eines fantastischen Studioorchesters (2). Und noch 50 Jahre später sind sich Experten einig: *Songs for Swinging Lovers* ist und bleibt eines der größten Alben, die je produziert wurden.

AU début des années 50, la carrière de Frank Sinatra semble bien compromise : il n'est plus l'idole des teenagers et MGM n'a pas l'intention de produire d'autres comédies musicales avec lui dans le rôle principal. En privé, il est à peu près heureux – et s'apprête à épouser Ava Gardner (1) ; mais, sur le plan musical il a bien besoin de se remettre en question Cela se produit sous la forme de la société de production Capitol Records, d'un arrangeur remarquable baptisé Nelson Riddle et d'un fantastique orchestre de studio (2). Et, cinquante ans plus tard, les experts sont unanimes : *Songs for Swinging Lovers* est et reste l'un des albums les plus sublimes jamais produits.

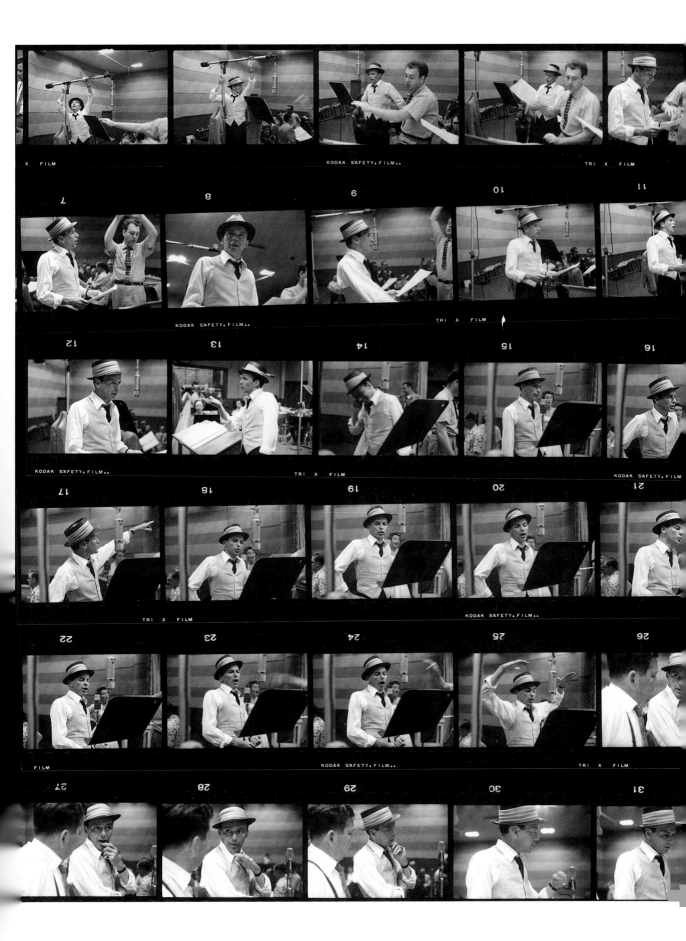

IN the 1960s, some pop music widened its horizons and sharpened its political attitude. Dylan and Joan Baez blazed a trail, but their folk-song output was aimed at an already committed audience of liberals and progressives. Scott Walker was different. Discovered by Eddie Fisher in the late 1950s, Walker began his career as a typical teen-idol singer from the same mould as Fabian or Frankie Avalon, but switched to darker material that mixed folk, pop and the ascerbic songs of cabaret, releasing his fourth album under his real name – Noel Scott Engel.

IN den 1960er Jahren wurde in einigen Bereichen der Popmusik der Horizont erweitert und die politische Botschaft zugespitzt. Bob Dylan and Joan Baez waren die Fackelträger auf dem Weg, doch ihre Folksongs richteten sich an ein Publikum, das bereits liberal und progressiv eingestellt war. Anders dagegen Scott Walker: Er wurde von Eddie Fisher in den späten 1950er Jahren entdeckt und begann seine Karriere als typisches Teenager-Idol von der Sorte eines Fabian oder Frankie Avalon; doch dann wechselte er zu dunkleren Tönen und mischte Folk, Pop und bittere Kabarettsongs – und brachte sein viertes Album unter seinem eigentlichen Namen heraus: Noel Scott Engel.

DANS les années 60, l'horizon s'élargit dans certains domaines de la musique pop et les messages politiques deviennent plus incisifs. Bob Dylan et Joan Baez sont les porte-drapeaux de cette direction, mais leurs folksongs s'adressent à un public qui est d'ores et déjà libéral et a un esprit progressif. Il en va différemment de Scott Walker : découvert par Eddie Fisher vers la fin des années 50, il entame sa carrière comme idole typique des teenagers dans le style d'un Fabian ou d'un Frankie Avalon ; mais il adopte bientôt une tonalité plus profonde et mélange folk, pop et des chansons de cabaret acerbes – et publie alors son quatrième album sous son véritable nom : Noel Scott Engel.

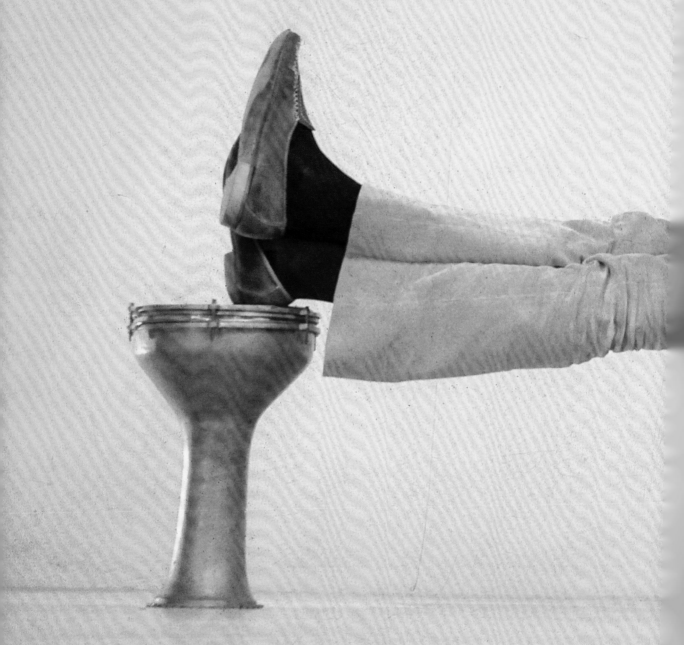

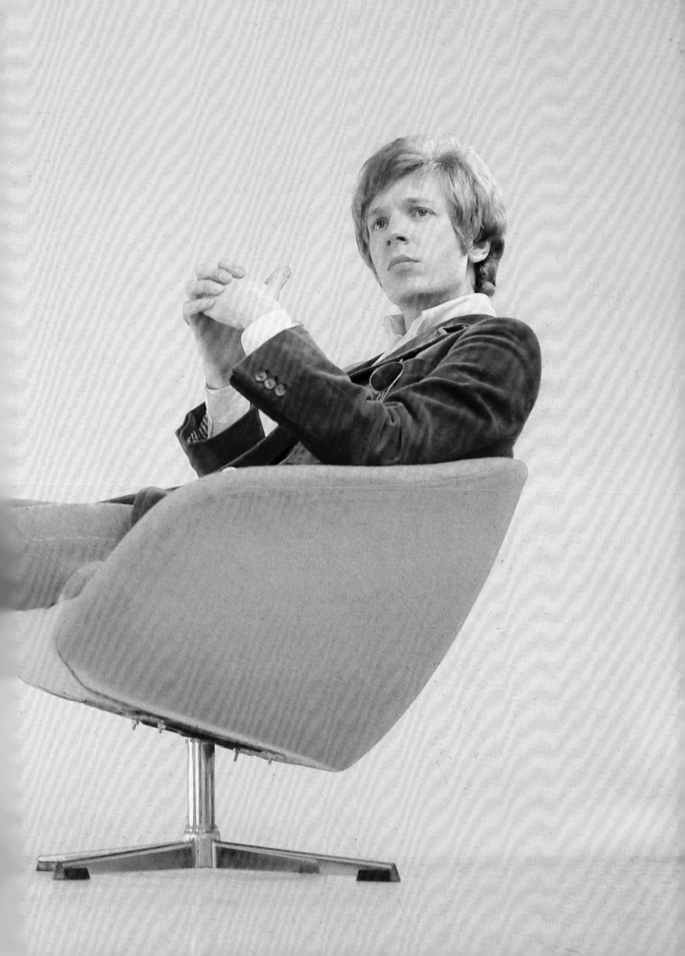

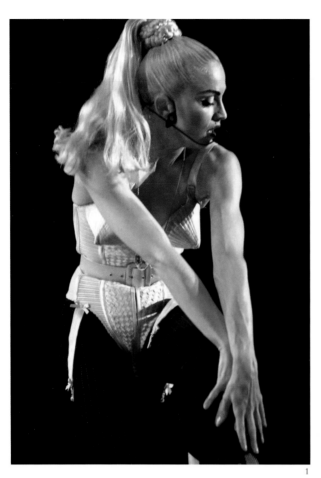
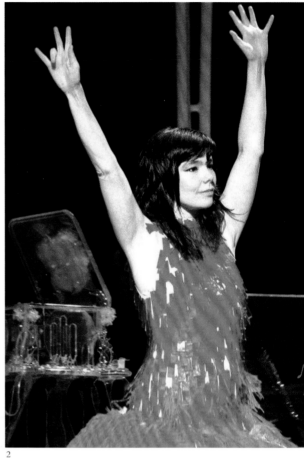

1   2

THE DAYS when middle-aged and even smoke-encrusted voices dominated the popular music charts were long gone. Madonna built on her phenomenal success in the 1980s and embarked on her Blond Ambition World Tour in 1990 (1). More than a decade later later, on 4 November 2001, the Icelandic singer Björk was performing at the Liceo Theater, Barcelona (2) as part of her world tour to promote the album *Vespertine*, which featured, among other things, experimental sounds and the poems of e. e.cummings. In the wake of Madonna came a host of female singers singing, dancing and gyrating their way to the top of the popular music charts. Lady Gaga hangs upside down to give her all onstage during the iHeart Radio Music Festival in the MGM Grand Garden Arena, Las Vegas, Nevada, USA, 24 September 2011 (4). One of the best of the bunch: Amy Winehouse performs at Shepherds Bush in London, 29 May 2007, just one month after the release of *Back to Black* (3). Her tragic death four years later, at the age of 27 robbed the music world of one of the finest soul, jazz and R&B singers of all time.

DIE ZEITEN, in denen ältere Herrschaften und rauchige Stimmen die Pop-Charts dominierten, waren lange vorbei. Madonna baute auf ihrem phänomenalen Erfolg der 80er Jahre auf und begab sich 1990 auf ihre *Blond-Ambition*-Welttournee (1). Mehr als zehn Jahre später, am 4. November 2001, trat die isländische Sängerin Björk im Rahmen ihrer Welttournee im Liceo in Barcelona auf (2), um ihr Album *Vespertine* zu promoten. Auf diesem sind unter anderem experimentelle Sounds und die Gedichte von e.e. cummings zu hören. Im Kielwasser von Madonna sangen und tanzten sich zahlreiche Sängerinnen an die Spitze der Charts. Lady Gaga gibt alles und hängt kopfüber auf der Bühne der MGM Grand Garden Arena in Las Vegas, Nevada, beim iHeart Radio Music Festival am 24. September 2011 (4). Eine der besten all dieser Sängerinnen, Amy Winehouse, tritt am 29. Mai 2007, einen Monat nach der Veröffentlichung von *Back to Black*, im Londoner Shepherd's Bush auf (3). Ihr tragischer Tod mit nur 27 Jahren vier Jahre später nahm der Musikwelt eine der besten Soul-, Jazz- und R&B-Sängerinnen aller Zeiten.

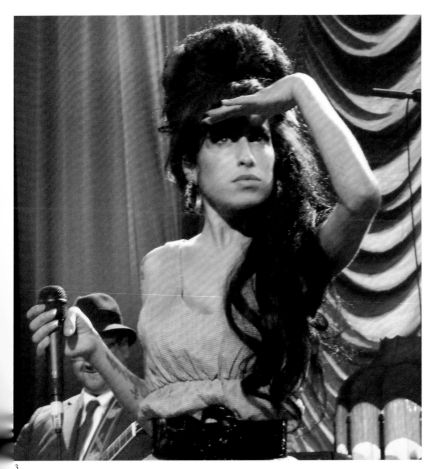

FINI LE TEMPS où les hit-parades résonnaient des voix matures, parfois même rocailleuses, des chantres de la musique populaire. Dans les années 1980, Madonna s'applique à bâtir son incroyable succès, avant de s'embarquer dans un *Blond Ambition* World Tour, en 1990 (1). Plus d'une décennie après, le 4 novembre 2001, la chanteuse islandaise Björk se produit sur la scène du Teatro del Liceu, à Barcelone (2), lors de sa tournée mondiale, dans le cadre de la promotion de *Vespertine*, un album mêlant entre autres sons expérimentaux et poèmes de E. E. Cummings. Dans le sillage de Madonna émerge une nuée d'artistes féminines, à la fois chanteuses et danseuses, qui à leur tour se hissent au sommet des charts. Lady Gaga n'hésite pas à chanter tête renversée, lors du iHeart Radio Music Festival, sur la scène du MGM Grand Garden Arena de Las Vegas, dans le Nevada, États-Unis, le 24 septembre 2011 (4). Étoile montante de cette nouvelle vague, Amy Winehouse chante au Shepherds Bush à Londres, le 29 mai 2007, un mois avant la sortie de *Back to Black* (3). Sa mort tragique quatre ans plus tard, à seulement 27 ans, prive le monde de la musique de l'une des plus grandes chanteuses de soul, jazz et R&B de tous les temps.

3

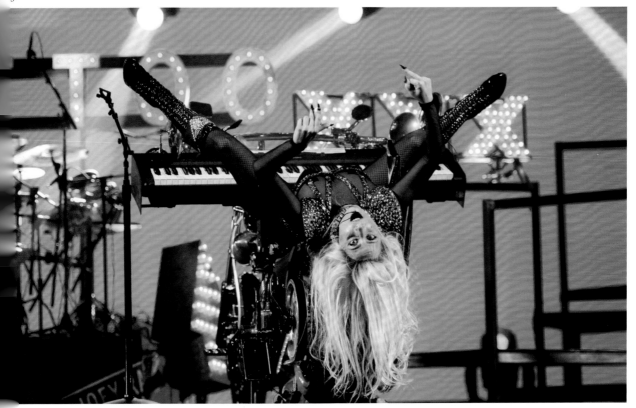

The Sixties and Seventies

THE decade opened with a bang, with Africa dominant. In 1960 Harold Macmillan's 'wind of change' speech unintentionally inaugurated a period of unprecedented bloodshed, which started when unarmed civilians attending a public meeting at Sharpeville were mown down as armed police opened fire without warning. That, of course, did most to radicalize both African and world opinion against apartheid. In the United States too the Civil Rights Movement was taking off, partly inspired by a time of rising expectations with Kennedy's presidential nomination in 1960. He won against Nixon, by only 120,000 votes, and promised in his inaugural speech that: 'The old era is ending. The old ways will not do.'

Kennedy's assassination in 1963 did not stem the tide of America's rise to the heights. In 1961 the US had put a chimpanzee named Ham into space; the Russians followed with their dog Laika – and, ahead of the US, their man, Yuri Gagarin. The Space War gradually turned into Star Wars: a hundred million viewers tuned in their television sets in 1969 to watch Neil Armstrong land on the moon, taking 'one small step for man, one giant leap for mankind'.

From August 1964, the US became heavily embroiled in the Vietnam war. By 1965 international protest was growing. In Washington candle-lit vigils were held outside the White House; in London 250,000 demonstrated before the US Embassy. 'Agent Orange', used in the war to defoliate trees and starve the local population, was perhaps one of the instigators of the backlash against environmental warfare.

Outstripping everything in popularity was 'Beatlemania', however fierce the defendants of the altogether rawer and raunchier Rolling Stones. The Beatles starred at the Royal Command Performance and walked away with their CBEs: by 1964 they were the country's most popular tourist attraction. Beatlemania was said to be primarily female, primarily below the belt. Even stay-up stockings sported pictures of the Fab Four.

London was swinging (1): more specifically, King's Road, Chelsea, was swinging to the sounds of British and West Coast bands and the fashions of Mary Quant, Ossie Clark and Barbara Hulanicki ('Biba'). Despite a radical student movement – causing the closure of numerous European universities, particularly in Britain, Germany and France – and the Black Power movement

in the United States, there was a mood of positive optimism abroad.

DAS Jahrzehnt begann mit einem Paukenschlag, ganz besonders in Afrika. Harold Macmillans Rede von 1960, in der er von einem »frischen Wind« sprach, löste unbeabsichtigt eine Welle beispielloser Bluttaten aus, die damit begann, daß unbewaffnete Zivilisten, Teilnehmer einer öffentlichen Versammlung in Sharpeville, von der Polizei niedergemäht wurden, die ohne Vorwarnung das Feuer eröffnete. Mehr brauchte es nicht, um Afrika und die ganze Welt auf die Barrikaden gegen die Apartheid zu bringen. In den Vereinigten Staaten kam die Bürgerrechtsbewegung in Gang, nicht zuletzt beflügelt von den großen Erwartungen der Nominierung Kennedys als Präsidentschaftskandidat im Jahre 1960. Mit nur 120 000 Stimmen Vorsprung setzte er sich gegen Nixon durch. In seiner Antrittsrede erklärte er: »Die alten Zeiten sind vorbei. Aber die guten Traditionen nicht.«

Die Ermordung Kennedys im Jahre 1963 konnte den Aufstieg der USA zu neuen Höhen nicht aufhalten. 1961 hatten die Amerikaner einen Schimpansen namens Ham in den Weltraum geschickt; die Russen folgten mit ihrer Hündin Laika – und vor den Amerikanern mit dem ersten Menschen im Weltraum, Juri Gagarin. Aus dem Wettlauf im Weltall wurde allmählich ein Sternenkrieg: 100 Millionen Menschen saßen 1969 an ihren Fernsehgeräten, um Neil Armstrong auf dem Mond zu sehen, wie er »einen kleinen Schritt für einen Menschen, doch einen großen Sprung für die Menschheit« machte.

Vom August 1964 an engagierten die Vereinigten Staaten sich verstärkt im Vietnamkrieg. 1965 kam es weltweit zu Protesten. Vor dem Weißen Haus in Washington wurden Mahnwachen gehalten; in London demonstrierten 250 000 vor der amerikanischen Botschaft. Das Entlaubungsmittel »Agent Orange«, das die Einheimischen dem Hungertod preisgab, war mitverantwortlich dafür, daß eine Kampagne gegen ökologische Kriegführung in Gang kam.

Populärer als alles andere war die »Beatlemania«, so sehr sich die Verehrer der handfesteren Rolling Stones auch ins Zeug legten. Die Beatles waren es, die vor der Queen auftraten und mit Orden dekoriert wurden; schon 1964 waren sie Großbritanniens größte Tourstenattraktion. Von der Beatlemania, heißt es, waren hauptsächlich die weiblichen Fans betroffen, und sie wirkte eher unter der Gürtellinie. Selbst halterlose Strümpfe zierten das Bild der »Fab Four«.

Es war die Zeit des »Swinging London« (1); genauer gesagt, war es die King's Road in Chelsea, die zu den Klängen britischer und kalifornischer Bands swingte, mit Mode von Mary Quant, Ossie Clark und Barbara Hulanicki (»Biba«). Trotz Studentenunruhen – die zur zeitweiligen Schließung zahlreicher Universitäten führten, vor allem in England, Deutschland und Frankreich – und der Black-Power-Bewegung in den Vereinigten Staaten war es ein durch und durch optimistisches Jahrzehnt.

LES années 60. La décennie s'est ouverte sur un véritable coup de tonnerre en Afrique du Sud. En 1960, le discours du Britannique Harold Macmillan à propos d'un certain « vent de changement » inaugura une époque d'épanouissement sans précédent, qui, paradoxalement, débuta à Sharpeville par un massacre. En effet, la police sud-africaine ouvrit le feu sans sommations sur des civils désarmés qui assistaient à un meeting public. Tout cela contribua évidemment beaucoup à durcir l'opinion africaine et mondiale contre l'apartheid.

Au États-Unis, c'est porté par une époque riche d'espoirs, dont l'élection de Kennedy à la présidence, que démarra le Mouvement pour les droits civils. Le nouveau président n'obtint que 120 000 voix de plus que Nixon et déclara dans son discours d'ouverture : « L'ère ancienne est révolue. Les vieilles méthodes ne fonctionnent plus. »

En 1963, son assassinat ne freina en rien l'ascension américaine. Dès 1961, les États-Unis avaient envoyé dans l'espace un chimpanzé du nom de Ham ; les Russes leur emboîtèrent le pas en lançant leur chienne Laïka sur orbite et, précédant les États-Unis dans ce domaine, il lancèrent Youri Gagarine. La guerre de l'espace se mua progressivement en guerre des étoiles : en 1969, pas moins de cent millions de téléspectateurs assistèrent à la sortie de Neil Armstrong sur la Lune et l'entendirent prononcer le fameux « petit pas pour un homme, pas de géant pour l'humanité » qui restera dans la postérité.

À partir du mois d'août 1964, les États-Unis furent étroitement mêlés à la guerre du Viêt-nam. Dès 1965, on assista à une vive recrudescence des protestations internationales. À Washington, on organisait des veillées aux chandelles devant la Maison Blanche ; à Londres, 50 000 personnes manifestèrent devant l'ambassade des États-Unis. L'agent orange, un défoliant utilisé pendant

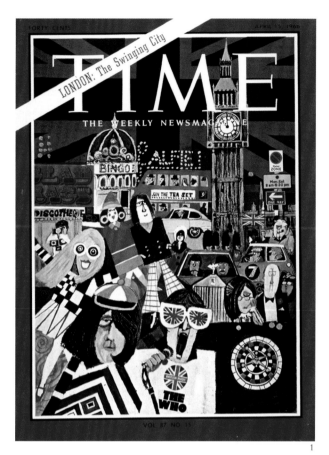

1

la guerre, destiné à affamer la population locale, inspira peut-être les campagnes contre les armes de guerre menaçant l'environnement.

Aussi populaires qu'ils fussent, les Rolling Stones, dans l'ensemble plus crus et plus sensuels que les Beatles, ne parvinrent jamais à égaler l'enthousiasme provoqué par la « beatlemania ». Les Beatles furent les vedettes de la Royal Command Performance avant de devenir « Compagnons de l'Ordre de l'Empire britannique » ; en 1964, ils incarnaient la principale attraction touristique de la nation britannique. On a prétendu que la « beatlemania » était surtout le fait des filles. Même les bas-jarretelles arboraient les portraits des quatre célèbres garçons.

Londres (1), ou plus spécialement King's Road, Chelsea, dansait au rythme des groupes britanniques et occidentaux, et s'habillait à la mode de Mary Quant, Ossie Clark et Barbara Hulanicki, « Biba ». En dépit d'un mouvement lancé par des étudiants radicaux – qui causa la fermeture provisoire de nombreuses universités européennes, en particulier en Grande-Bretagne, en Allemagne et en France – et du mouvement du Black Power aux États-Unis, on sentait en Occident un sentiment d'optimisme positif.

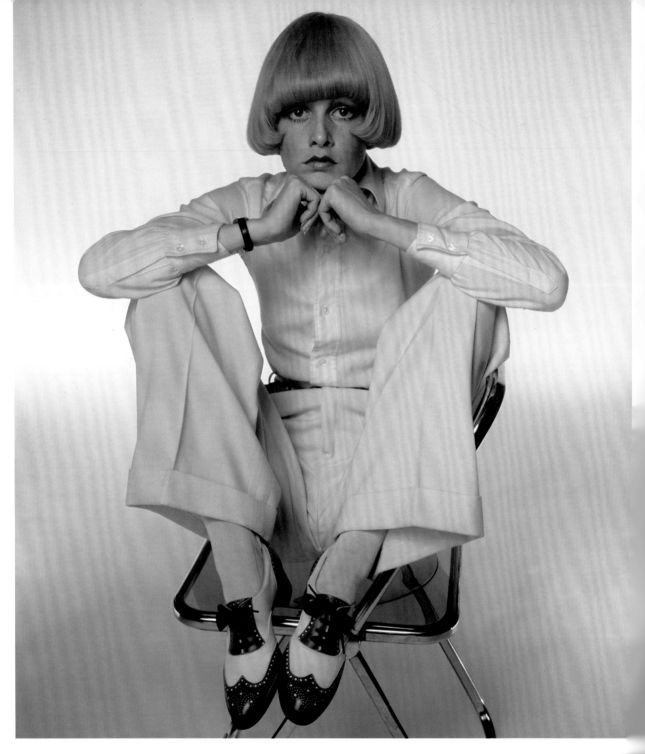

Two studies of one of the most famous fashion models of the 1970s, Twiggy, taken by her friend and lover, the photographer Justin de Villeneuve. Twiggy models a pair of shoes made for her by George Cleverley, hitherto exclusively a shoemaker for men (1). This Justin de Villeneuve 1972 portrait of Twiggy (2) was retouched by Klaus Voorman, creator of The Beatles *Revolver* album cover.

ZWEI Studien eines der berühmtesten Models der 1970er Jahre, Twiggy – aufgenommen von ihrem Freund und Liebhaber, dem Fotografen Justin de Villeneuve. Twiggy zeigt ein Paar Schuhe, die George Cleverley – ein Schuhmacher für Herrenschuhe – eigens für sie anfertigte (1); dieses Twiggy-Portrait des Fotografen Justin de Villeneuve aus dem Jahre 1972 wurde von Klaus Voorman – dem Coverdesigner des Beatles-Ablums *Revolver* – retuschiert.

DEUX études de l'un des mannequins plus célèbres des années 70, Twiggy photos prises par son ami et amant, le photographe Justin de Villeneuve. Twiggy présente une paire de chaussures que George Cleverley – un cordonnier spécialiste des chaussures pour hommes – a fabriquées spécialement pour elle (1) ; ce portrait de Twiggy signé du photographe Justin de Villeneuve, qui remonte à 1972, a été retouché par Klaus Voorman – le cover-designer de l'album des Beatles *Revolver*.

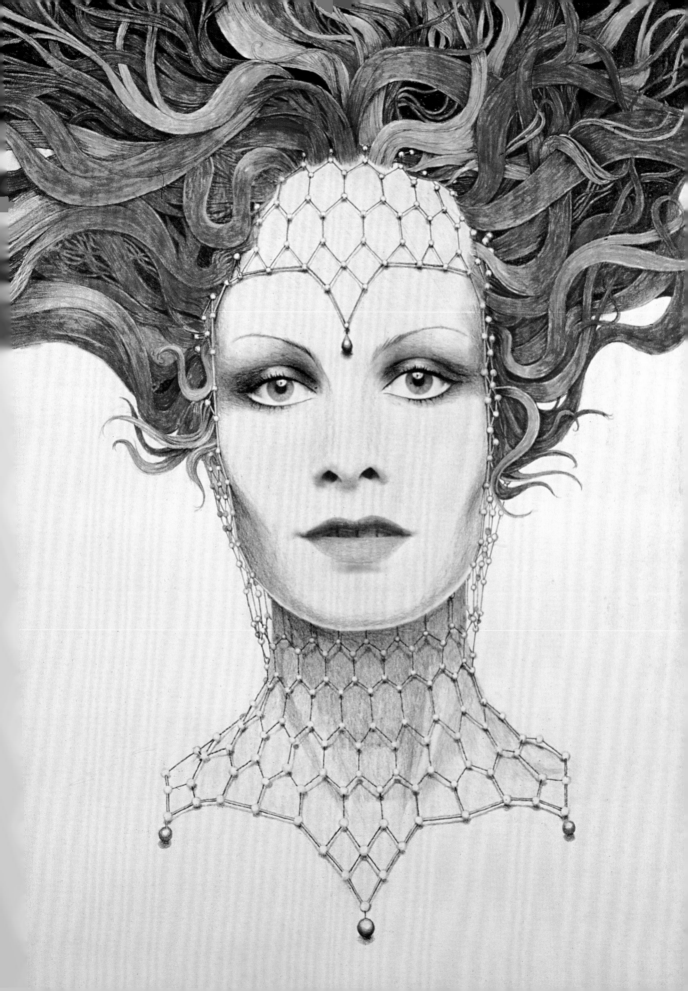

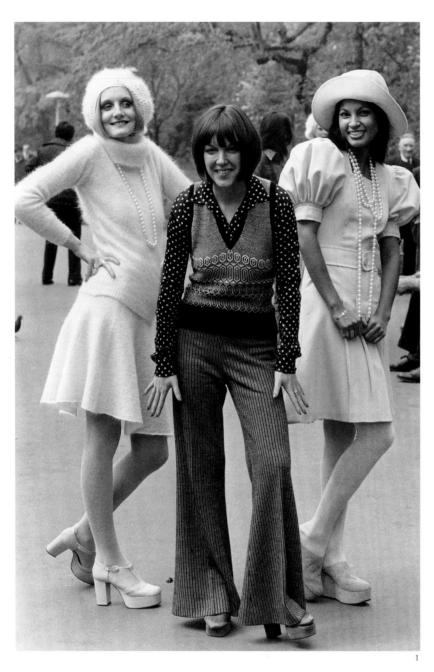

1

MARY Quant was fashion's contribution to 'Swinging London' (1). Even the staid *Time* magazine noted that: 'In a decade dominated by youth, London has burst into bloom. It swings: it is the scene'. Noted for swinging skirts and flares at near-High Street prices, and for her angular, heavily fringed haircut, Quant also attracted publicity when her husband trimmed her pubic hair into a heart-shape. Sandie Shaw (2), better known as a Eurovision Song Contest winner (with *Puppet on a String* in 1964), also launched a fashion boutique in 1967. Her perennially bare feet contrast with Quant's clumpy platform soles.

MARY Quant war der Beitrag der Modewelt zum »Swinging London« (1). Selbst die hausbackene Zeitschrift *Time* vermerkte: »In einem Jahrzehnt, das von der Jugend beherrscht wird, ist London erblüht. Es swingt: hier ist was los.« Quant war für ihre schwingenden Röcke und Schlaghosen bekannt, die sie zu Preisen verkaufte, die kaum über denen der Kaufhäuser lagen, und für den kantigen Haarschnitt mit dem tief in die Stirn gezogenen Pony. Sie erregte auch Aufsehen damit, daß ihr Mann ihr das Schamhaar herzförmig rasierte. Sandie Shaw (2), eher als Siegerin des Eurovision-Schlagerwettbewerbes bekannt (1964, mit *Puppet on a String*), eröffnete 1967 ihre eigene Modeboutique. Der Kontrast zwischen den nackten Füßen – ihrem Markenzeichen – und Mary Quants klobigen Plateausohlen könnte nicht größer sein.

MARY Quant était une haute figure de la mode au « Swinging London » (1). Même le *Time*, plutôt collet monté, notait : « Dans une décennie dominée par la jeunesse, Londres s'est épanoui. Il se balance : il est la scène. » Rendue célèbre par ses jupes courtes et ses pantalons à pattes d'éléphant, à des prix presque High-Street, mais également pour sa coiffure en casque à lourde frange, Mary Quant bénéficia des retombées publicitaires, lorsque son mari arrangea les poils de son pubis en forme de cœur. Sandie Shaw (2), que sa première place au concours de l'Eurovision de la chanson en 1964, avec « *Puppet on a String* a rendue célèbre, ouvrit aussi une boutique de mode en 1967. Ses pieds, perpétuellement nus, contrastent avec les massives semelles à plateau de Mary Quant.

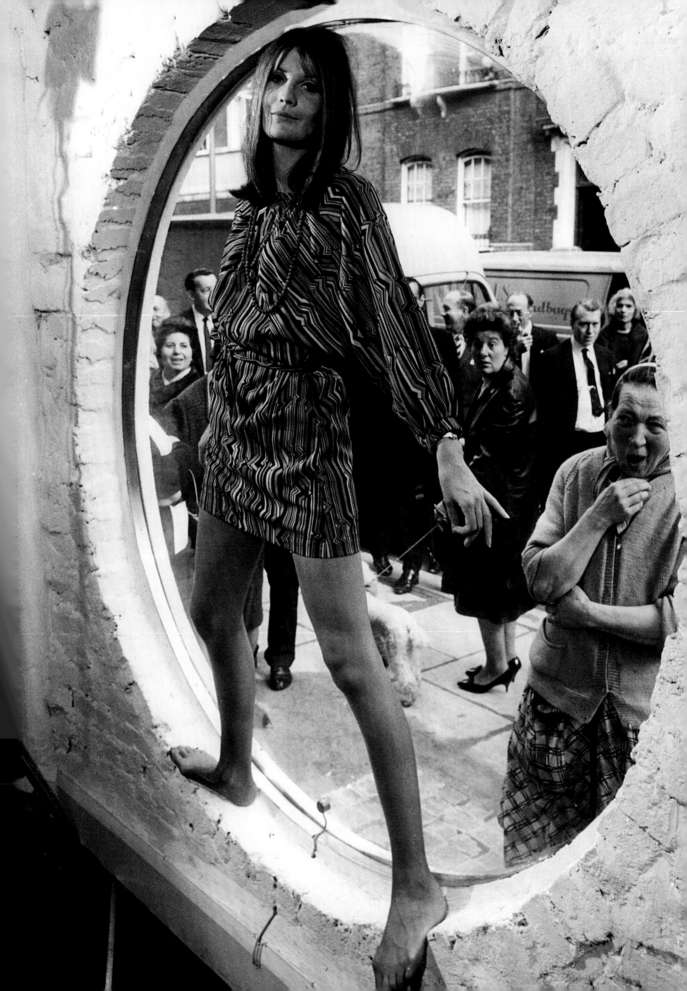

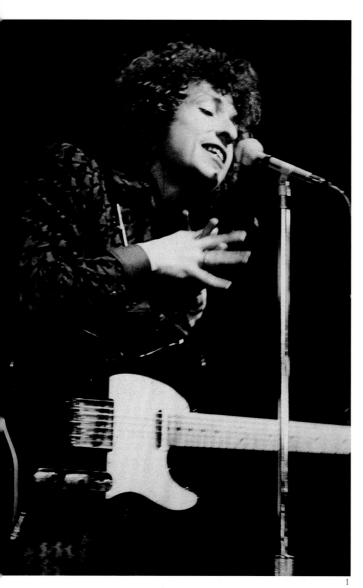

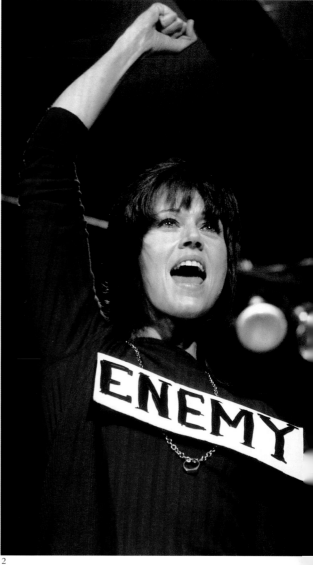

1 2

THE new troubadours of the late 1960s and 70s toured the world to make their protests. Bob Dylan provoked protest from his folk-fans and was labelled 'Judas' when he appeared with an electric guitar at the Olympia, Paris in 1966 (1). John Lennon and his second wife, the Japanese film-maker Yoko Ono, mock another established tradition in appearing on the Eamonn Andrews Show. While Eamonn gets to lie in the bed they made famous by taking to it for world peace, they occupy a sheet sleeping-bag at its feet (3). Critics of Jane Fonda and her support for the Vietcong gave her the *soubriquet* 'Hanoi Jane'. Here she addresses an anti-war rally in Washington DC, 12 May 1970 (2).

DIE neuen Troubadoure der 1960er und 1970er Jahre zogen mit ihren Protest-songs durch die Welt. Bob Dylan provo-zierte den Protest seiner Folkanhänger und wurde als »Judas« beschimpft, als er 1966 im Olympiastadion in Paris mit einer elektri-schen Gitarre auftrat (1). John Lennon und seine zweite Frau, die japanische Fluxus-Künstlerin Yoko Ono, verspotten in der Eamonn Andrews Show wieder einmal eine ehrwürdige Tradition. Eamonn liegt in dem Bett, das sie mit ihren Friedensdemonstra-tionen weltberühmt machte, und die beiden sitzen in einem Schlafsack ihm zu Füßen (3). Jane Fonda wurde wegen Ihrer Unterstützung des Vietcong von Kritikern abfällig »Hanoi-Jane« genannt. Hier spricht sie auf einer Antikriegsdemonstration in Washington DC am 12. Mai 1970 (2).

LES nouveaux troubadours des années 19 et 1970 partent en tournée dans le mon entier pour faire entendre leurs chansons de protestations. Bob Dylan provoque un jour colère de ses adeptes, amoureux de folk ; ils traitent de Judas quand il monte en scène, 1966 à l'Olympia à Paris, avec une guitare électrique (1). John Lennon et sa seconde épouse, la réalisatrice japonaise Yoko Ono, apparaissent dans le Eamonn Andrews Sho Tandis qu'Eamonn se couche dans le lit support de la campagne du couple en faveu de la paix dans le monde, ils se sont enrou ses pieds dans un drap blanc (3). À cause d critiques, Jane Fonda est surnommée avec mépris « Hanoï-Jane » ; on lui reproche de soutenir le Viêt-cong. Ici, elle tient un disc lors d'une manifestation contre la guerre à Washington DC, le 12 mai 1970 (2).

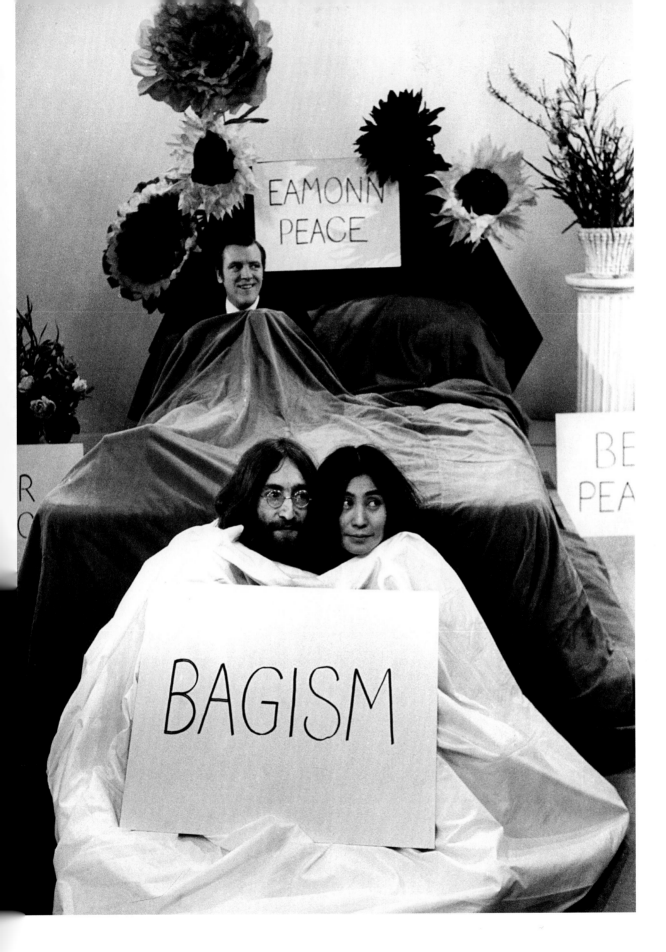

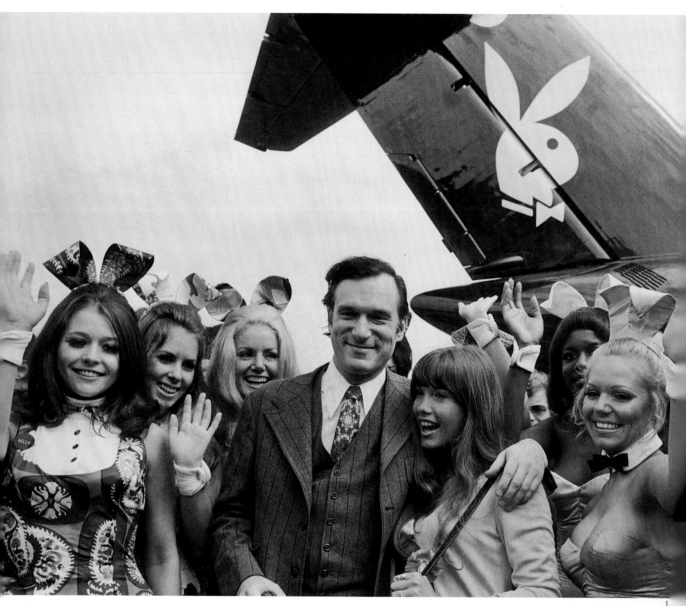

The 1960s were little if not exuberantly heterogeneous. While Stateside 'women's libbers' burnt their bras (even if only once and for a press-orchestrated publicity stunt), Hugh Hefner, head of the Playboy empire, stuffed his 'bunny girls' into ever-tighter, upward-thrusting corsets (1). An historic moment was reached in Vienna when, 16 years after the city's partition in 1945, President Kennedy exchanged hand-shakes with Prime Minister Khrushchev (2). The 1963 Profumo scandal brought down a minister and, subsequently, a govern-ment. Prostitute Christine Keeler was said to have bowed to the machinations of society doctor Stephen Ward, who used extensive connections to procure her high-class clients. Here she is seen waiting outside the courtroom at his trial (4).

She made a comeback of sorts at a 1969 photocall for photographer David Bailey's book *Goodbye baby and Amen*, alongside model Penelope Tree and singer Marianne Faithfull (3).

Das Bemerkenswerteste an den 60er Jahren war ihre Widersprüchlichkeit. Während in Amerika Feministinnen ihre BHs verbrannten, steckte Hugh Hefner, Chef des Playboy-Imperiums, seine »Bun-nies« in immer engere Korsetts (1). Ein historisches Ereignis fand in Wien statt, wo Präsident Kennedy sechzehn Jahre nach der Teilung der Stadt dem russischen Premierminister Chruschtschow die Hand reichte (2). Der Profumo-Skandal von 1963 brachte in England einen Minister und am Ende eine ganze Regierung zu Fall.

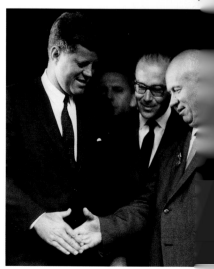

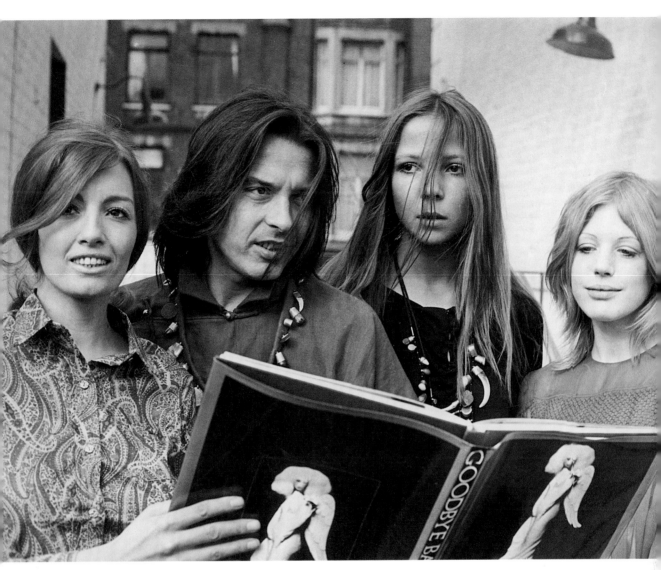

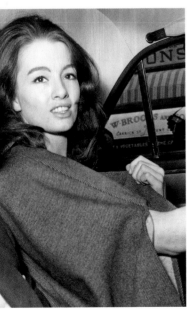

Es heißt, die Prostituierte Christine Keeler sei dem Arzt der High Society, Stephen Ward, gefällig gewesen, und dieser habe seine vielfältigen Kontakte spielen lassen, um ihr Kunden aus der besten Gesellschaft zu vermitteln. Hier wartet sie beim Prozeß gegen Ward vor dem Gerichtssaal (4). 1969 hatte sie eine Art Comeback, als der Photograph David Bailey der Presse sein Buch *Goodbye Baby and Amen* präsentierte. Die beiden anderen sind Model Penelope Tree und Sängerin Marianne Faithfull (3).

L ES années 60 n'ont pas connu la même évolution dans chaque pays. Alors qu'aux États-Unis, les adeptes du Women's Lib brûlaient leurs soutiens-gorge (en fait un seul devant les photographes et journalistes invités), Hugh Heffner, à la tête de l'empire Playboy, affublait ses Bunnys de corsets moulants qui mettaient en valeur leurs attributs (1). Vienne vécut un moment historique quand, seize ans après le partage de la ville, le président Kennedy échangea une poignée de main avec Khrouchtchev, alors Premier ministre de l'Union soviétique (2). En 1963, le scandale Profumo ne causa rien moins que la démission d'un ministre et la chute d'un gouvernement. La prostituée Christine Keeler était mêlée aux intrigues de Stephen Ward, médecin de la bonne société lui fournissant une clientèle haut gamme. On la voit ici pendant son procès, attendant devant le tribunal (4). Elle revint en 1969, en posant pour l'album du photographe David Bailey, *Goodbye Baby and Amen*, aux côtés du mannequin Penelope Tree et de la chanteuse Marianne Faithfull (3).

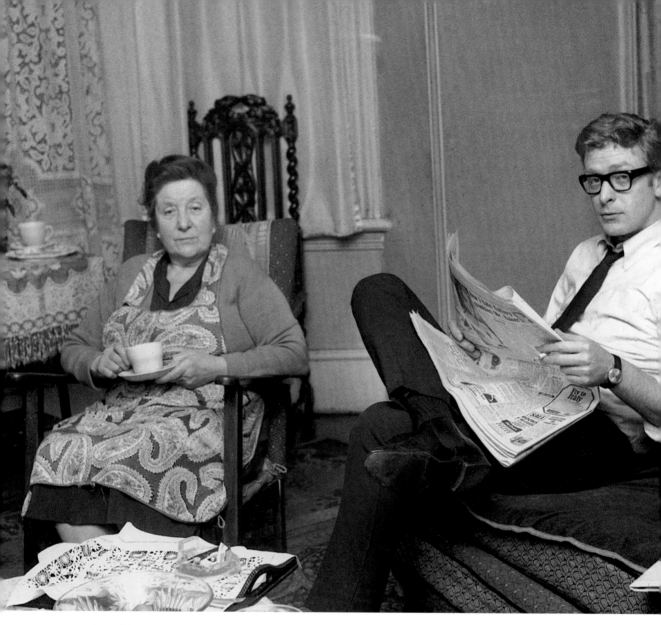

FILM faces of the 1960s. Michael Caine, at home with his mother and brother in 1964 (1), the epitome of a working-class lad made good who still loved his mum. His flat South London accent and square specs were as much a part of his act as the tough-guy parts he played. Polish film director Roman Polanski married Californian starlet Sharon Tate in January 1968 (2). Nothing in the sinister oddness of his fantasy world anticipated the horror that resulted. In August 1969, Tate and their unborn child along with four friends were murdered by maniac cult leader Charles Manson and three female accomplices. And in Venice for the 1963 Film Festival, British stars Julie Christie and Tom Courtenay captured the look and spirit of a decade in the hugely successful *Billy Liar* (3).

FILMSTARS der Sechziger. Michael Caine, zu Hause mit Mutter und Bruder im Jahre 1964 (1), ganz der brave Sohn aus einfachem Hause. Der Südlondoner Akzent und die breiten Brillengläser waren ebenso eine Rolle, die er spielte, wie der harte Typ, den er so oft verkörperte. Der polnische Regisseur Roman Polanski heiratete das kalifornische Starlet Sharon Tate im Januar 1968 (2). Doch auch die abseitigsten Phantasien seiner Filme

bereiteten niemanden auf das vor, was kommen sollte. Im August 1969 wurden Sharon Tate und ihr ungeborenes Kind zusammen mit vier Freunden von dem wahnsinnigen Sektenführer Charles Manson und drei Anhängerinnen ermordet. 1963, beim Filmfestival in Venedig, waren die britischen Stars Julie Christie und Tom Courtenay ganz auf der Höhe des Jahrzehnts, und ihr Film *Billy Liar* war ein großer Erfolg (3).

VISAGES de cinéma des années 60. Michael Caine, posant en modèle de garçon de la classe ouvrière et de fils aimant, chez lui avec sa mère et son frère en 1964 (1). Son parler, dépourvu de intonations du sud de Londres, et ses lunettes démodées revêtaien une grande importance dans les rôles d'homme confirmé qu'il devait interpréter. C'est en janvier 1968 que le réalisateur polonai Roman Polanski, épousa la petite actrice californienne Sharon Ta (2). En août 1969, alors que Sharon Tate était enceinte, un nomm Charles Manson, gourou d'un culte satanique, et trois femmes complices, assassinèrent l'actrice et quatre de ses amis. En 1963, au Festival de Venise, les vedettes britanniques Julie Christie et Tom Courtenay surent capter l'allure et l'esprit d'une décennie dans *Billy Liar* (3), un énorme succès.

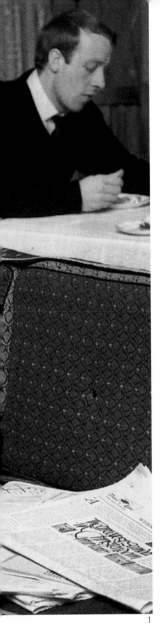

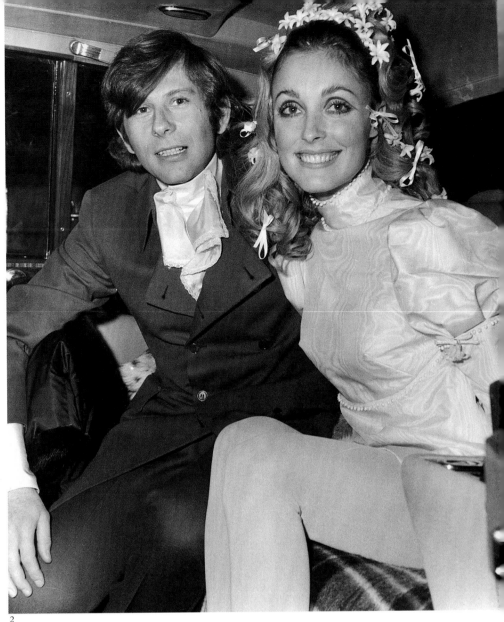

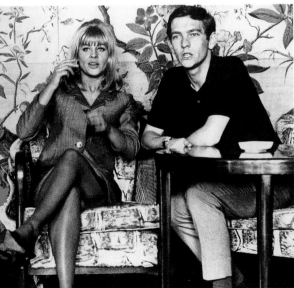

(Overleaf)

THE Hippie Dream – a sunny day, flutes and guitars, and wood smoke. This is the dawning of the Age of Aquarius in Windsor Great Park, England.

(Folgende Seiten)

DER Traum eines jeden Hippie: ein sonniger Tag, Flöten und Gitarren und knisterndes Holzfeuer ... Da kann das Zeitalter des Wassermanns kommen – hier im Windsor Great Park, England.

(Pages suivantes)

LE rêve de tout hippie : une journée ensoleillée, des flûtes et des guitares avec un feu de bois qui crépite ... l'époque du Verseau peut venir – ici à Windsor Great Park, en Angleterre.

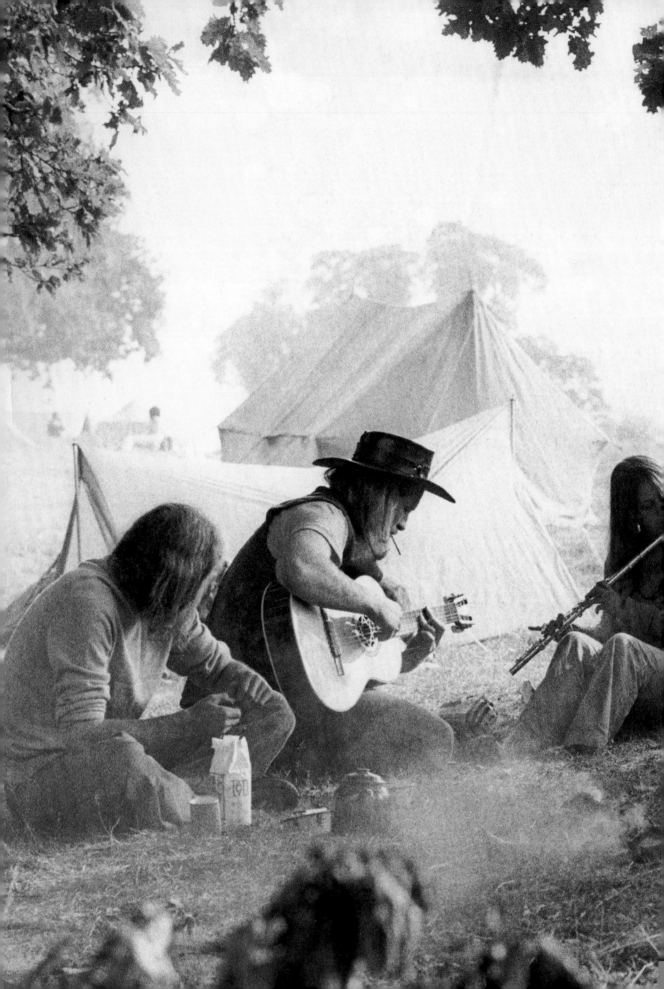

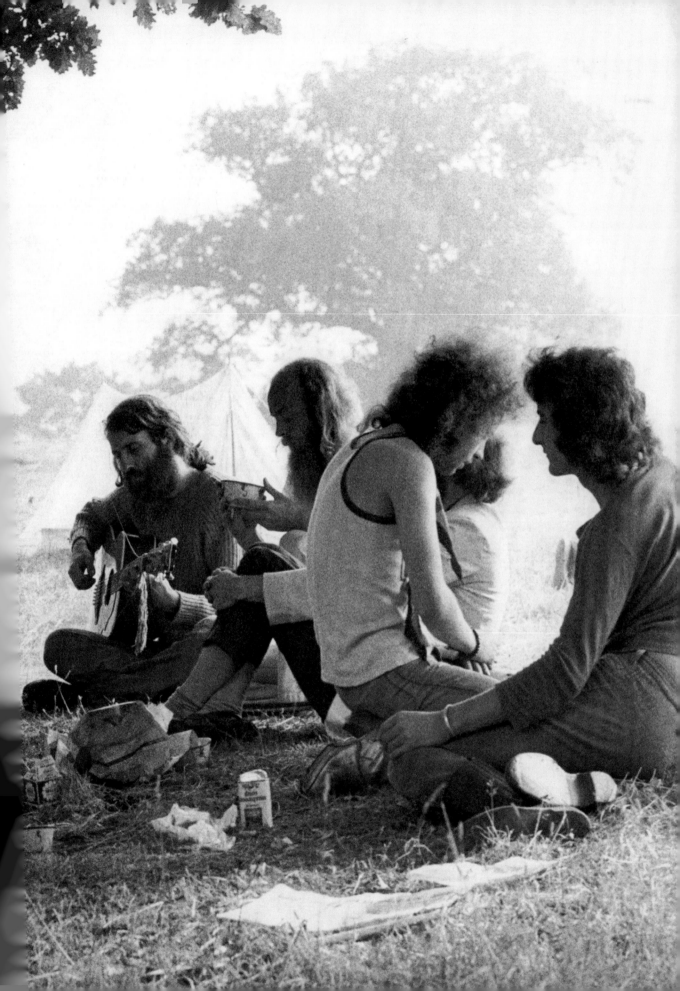

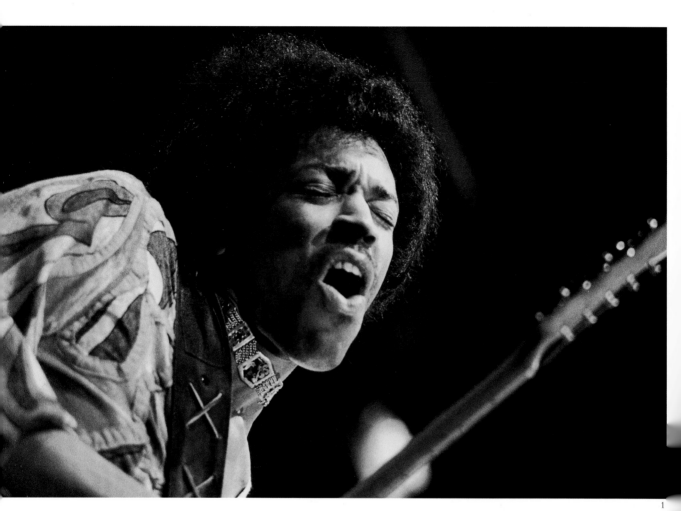

JIMI Hendrix rocks out a guitar solo at the Isle of Wight Festival, 1970 (1). Mary Wilson, Diana Ross and Cindy Birdsong in 1968 attained stardom as The Supremes (2). In 1967, the Rolling Stones enhanced their 'bad boys' image: Mick Jagger and Keith Richards sentenced for drug offences (3).

JIMI Hendrix spielt ein Gitarrensolo beim Festival auf der Isle of Wight 1970 (1). Mary Wilson, Diana Ross und Cindy Birdsong 1968, als sie schon als Supremes berühmt waren (2). Die Rolling Stones 1967: Mick Jagger und Keith Richards werden wegen Drogenbesitzes verurteilt (3).

JIMI Hendrix jouant un solo de guitare, lors du Festival de l'Ile de Wight, 1970 (1). Mary Wilson, Diana Ross et Cindy Birdsong en 1968, qui devinrent plus tard les Supremes (2). En 1967, Mick Jagger et Keith Richards, des Rolling Stones, furent condamnés pour usage de stupéfiants (3), accentuant leur image de mauvais garçons.

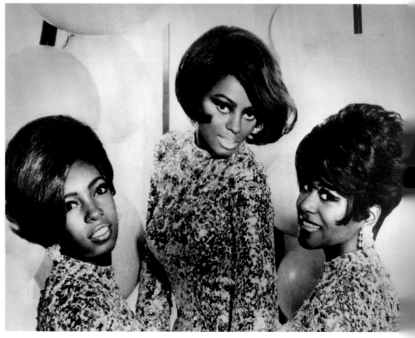

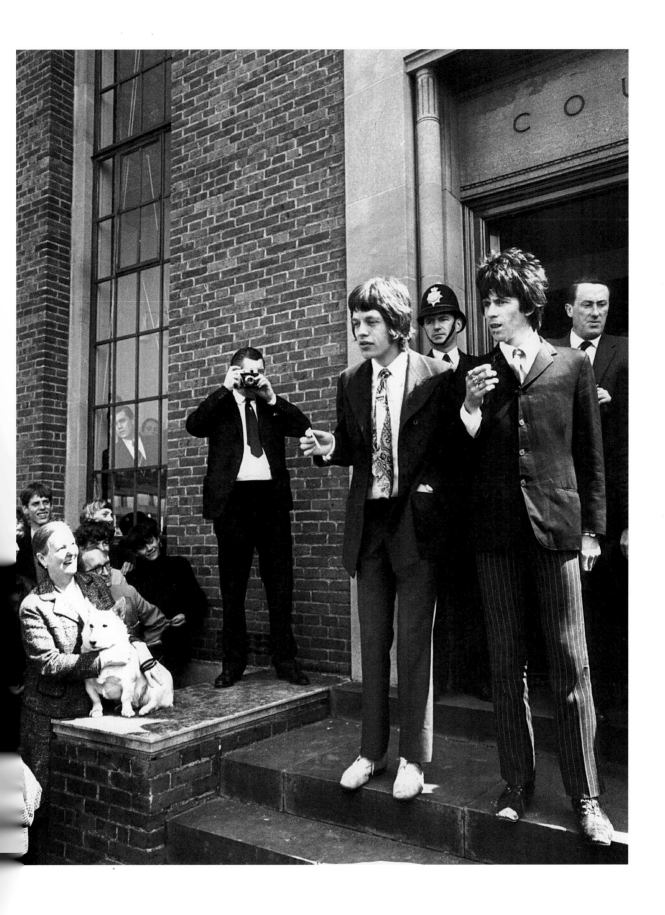

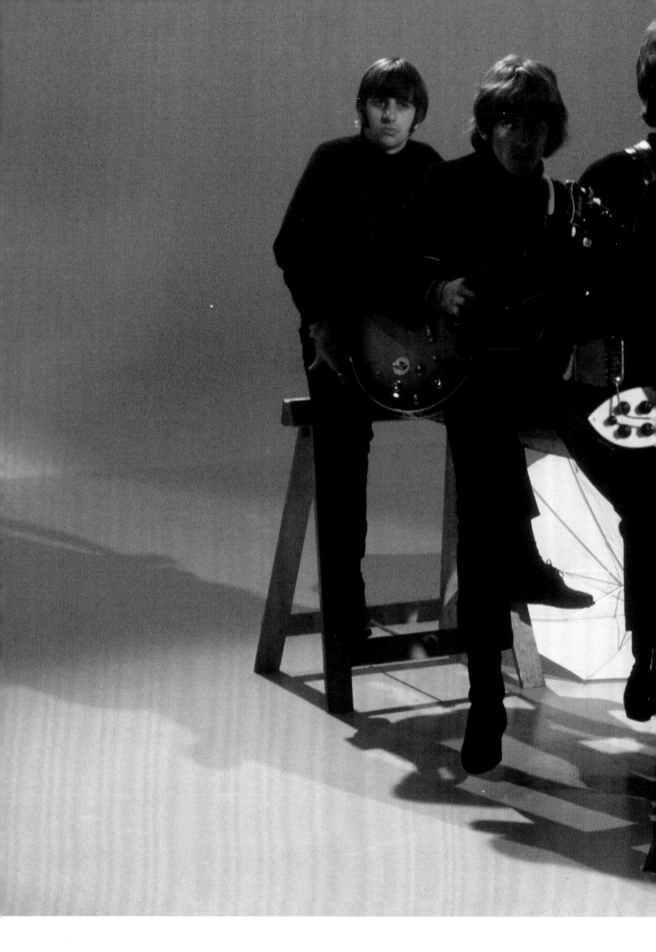

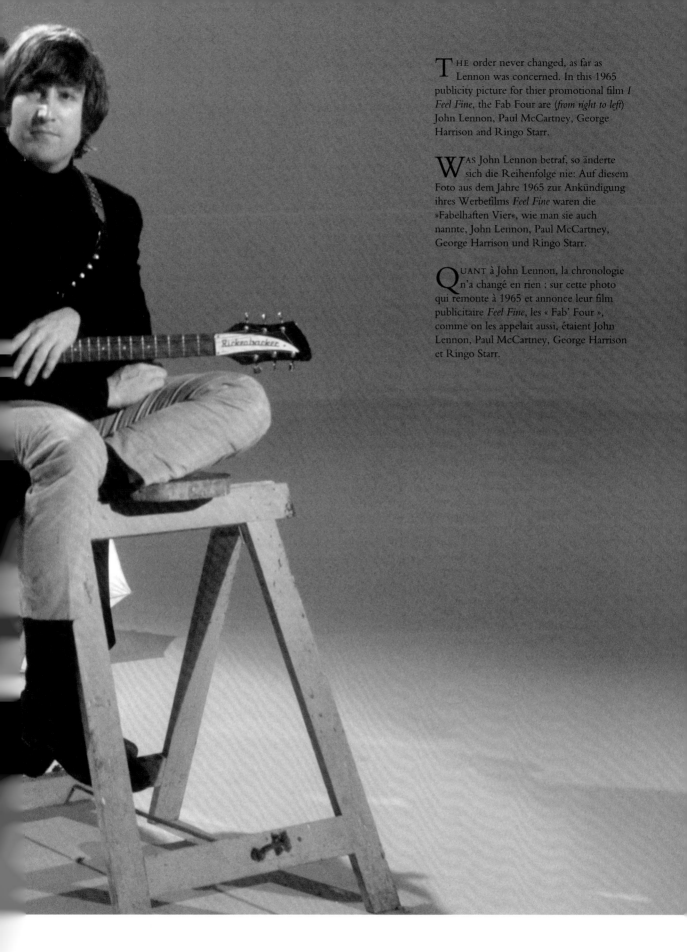

THE order never changed, as far as Lennon was concerned. In this 1965 publicity picture for thier promotional film *I Feel Fine*, the Fab Four are (*from right to left*) John Lennon, Paul McCartney, George Harrison and Ringo Starr.

WAS John Lennon betraf, so änderte sich die Reihenfolge nie: Auf diesem Foto aus dem Jahre 1965 zur Ankündigung ihres Werbefilms *Feel Fine* waren die »Fabelhaften Vier«, wie man sie auch nannte, John Lennon, Paul McCartney, George Harrison und Ringo Starr.

QUANT à John Lennon, la chronologie n'a changé en rien ; sur cette photo qui remonte à 1965 et annonce leur film publicitaire *Feel Fine*, les « Fab' Four », comme on les appelait aussi, étaient John Lennon, Paul McCartney, George Harrison et Ringo Starr.

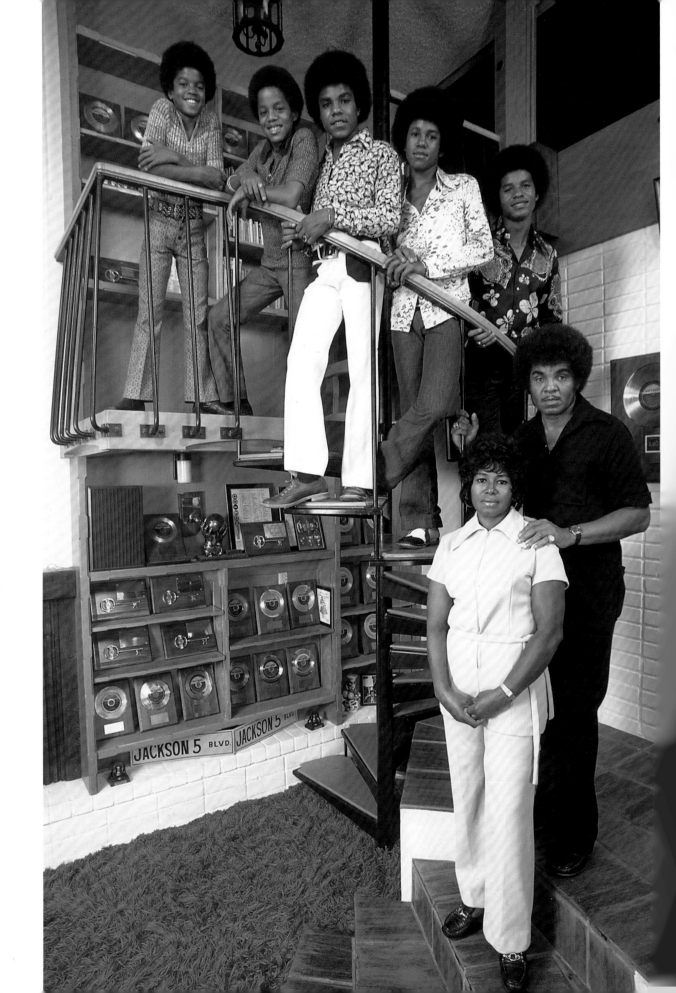

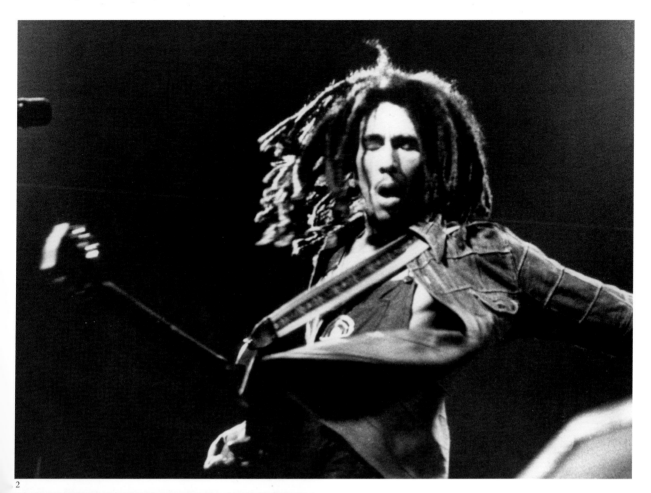

2

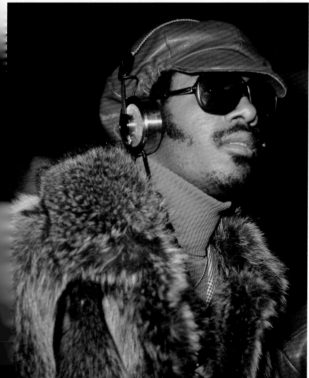

THE Jackson Five at home in 1971 (1): (*from top of stairs*)
Michael, Marlon, Tito, Jermaine, Jackie and Mr and Mrs
Joseph Jackson. By January 1974 Little Stevie Wonder (3) had
already won a clutch of Grammy Awards and was planning to
retire from the business and work with handicapped children in
Africa. A year later Bob Marley (2), master of reggae, was riding
high: 'Laugh and make the world laugh,' he said, 'so me dig it, so
me live'.

THE Jackson Five« – zu Hause im Jahre 1971 (1): Michael,
Marlon, Tito, Jermaine, Jackie und die Eltern, Joseph Jackson
und seine Frau (*von links oben*). Im Januar 1974 hatte Little Stevie
Wonder (3) bereits einen Korb voller Grammy Awards gewonnen
und plante, sich aus dem Musikgeschäft zurückzuziehen und mit
behinderten Kindern in Afrika zu arbeiten. Im Jahr darauf wollte
Bob Marley (2) hoch hinaus: »Laugh and make the world laugh«
(Lach' und lass die Welt lachen), sagte er, »so me dig it, so me live«
(etwa: Das ist mein Credo, so lebe ich).

THE Jackson Five » – chez eux en 1971 (1) : Michael, Marlon,
Tito, Jermaine, Jackie et les parents, Joseph Jackson et sa
femme (*à partir de la gauche en haut*). En janvier 1974, Little Stevie
Wonder (3) a déjà gagné toute une ribambelle de Grammy Awards
et projette de se retirer du monde de la musique pour travailler
avec des enfants handicapés en Afrique. L'année suivante, Bob
Marley (2) s'apprête à faire carrière : « Laugh and make the world
laugh » (Rire et fait rire le monde), « so me dig it, so me live » (à
peu près : c'est mon credo, c'est comme ça que je vis).

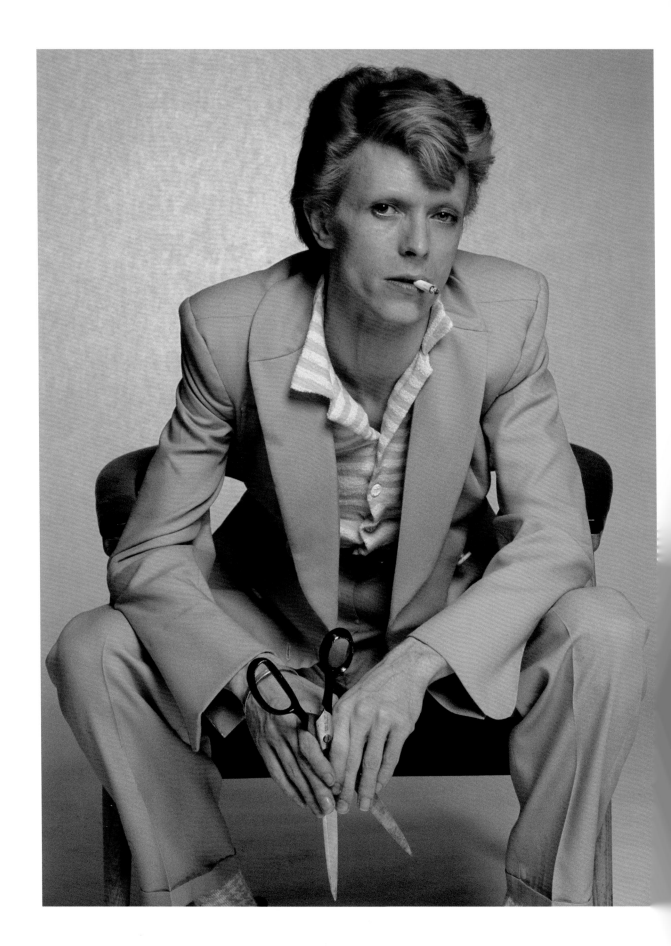

A MONG many pop cult schools in the
1970s was Glam Rock, personified by
David Bowie (1) in 1974, the year he set
off for the US to stage his revue *The 1980
Floor Show*, a work based on George
Orwell's *1984*. Bowie had an on-off
friendship with Iggy Pop (2), whose style
was harsher, meaner, and in the case of
The Stooges, more self-destructive.

E INE der zahlreichen Strömungen
innerhalb der Popkultur der 1970er
Jahre war der »Glam Rock«, personifiziert
durch David Bowie (1), der im Jahre 1974
in die USA ging, um dort seine Revue
The 1980 Floor Show zu produzieren; sie
basierte auf George Orwells Roman *1984*.
David Bowie verband eine wechselhafte
Freundschaft mit Iggy Pop (2), dessen Stil
rauher und bissiger war – und, im Fall der
Band »The Stooges«, auch
selbstzerstörerischer.

L 'UN des nombreux courants de la
culture pop des années 70 est le « Glam
Rock », personnifié par David Bowie (1),
qui se rend en 1974 aux États-Unis pour y
produire sa revue *The 1980 Floor Show* ;
elle s'inspirait du roman *1984* de George
Orwell. David Bowie a cultivé une amitié
qui a connu bien des hauts et des bas avec
Iggy Pop (2), dont le style était plus frustre
et plus mordant – et, dans le cas du groupe
« The Stooges », aussi, plus autodestructeur.

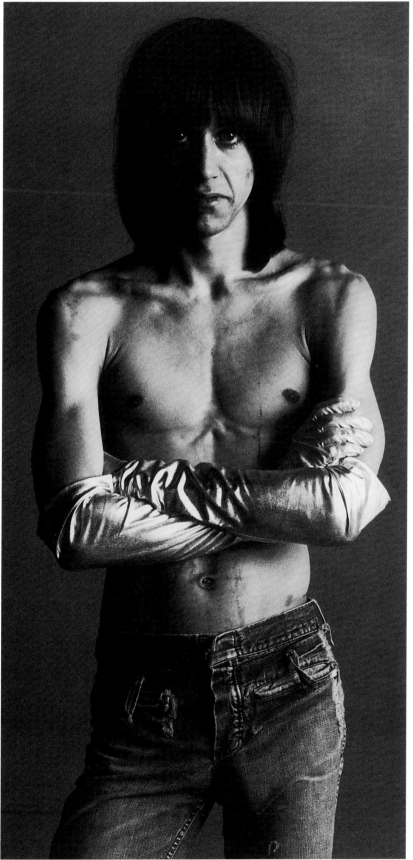

2

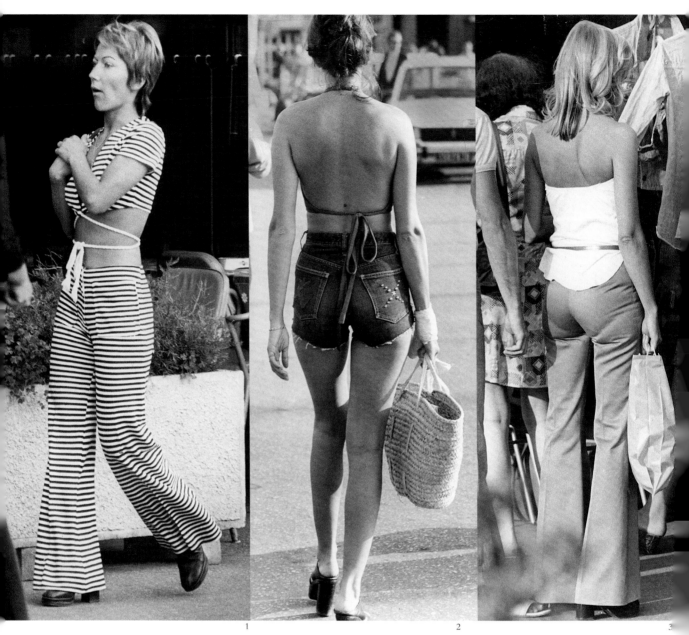

1   2   3

ST-TROPEZ, made famous by its yachts and by Brigitte Bardot's residence there, continued to flaunt fashion's bottom line into the 1970s. Buttock-cutting jeans (3), studded mini-shorts (2) and a scarf (4) – at times only a string – were rare concessions to dress when leaving the nudist beaches for the boutiques and cafés lining the boardwalks. The striped outfit (1) has more lasting appeal than the outrageous platforms (5) or the babydoll smock and bell-bottoms (6).

ST. TROPEZ – bekannt für seine Jachten und dafür, daß Brigitte Bardot sich dort niedergelassen hatte – machte auch in den 70er Jahren noch Mode. Hautenge Hüfthosen (3), nietenbewehrte, ultrakurze Shorts (2) und ein Tuch (4) – manchmal sogar nur ein String – waren die einzigen

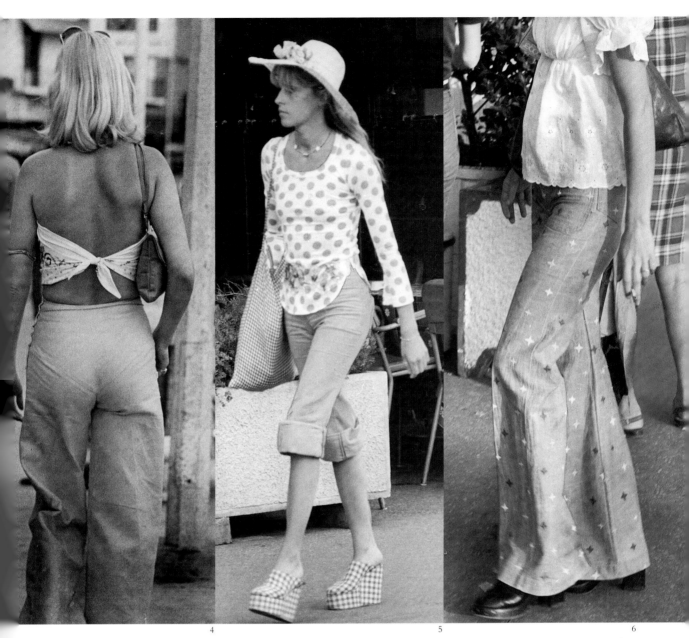

4   5   6

Zugeständnisse, die man machte, wenn man von den Nacktbadeständen zu den Boutiquen und Straßencafés herüberkam. Der Streifenanzug (1) kann heute eher noch überzeugen als die verrückten Plateausohlen (5) oder die Babydoll-Bluse mit Schlaghosen (6).

SAINT-TROPEZ, fameuse pour ses yachts et la maison de Brigitte Bardot, continua, au cours des années 70, à montrer l'essentiel. Des jeans coupés au ras des fesses (3), des mini-shorts cloutés (2) et un foulard (4) – qui tenait plus de la ficelle à l'époque – étaient les rares concessions faites par ceux qui quittaient les plages nudistes pour les boutiques et les cafés qui s'alignaient le long des trottoirs. Les vêtements à rayures (1) présentent un attrait plus durable que les semelles à plateau incroyablement hautes (5) ou les blouses babydoll et autres pantalons à pattes d'éléphant (6).

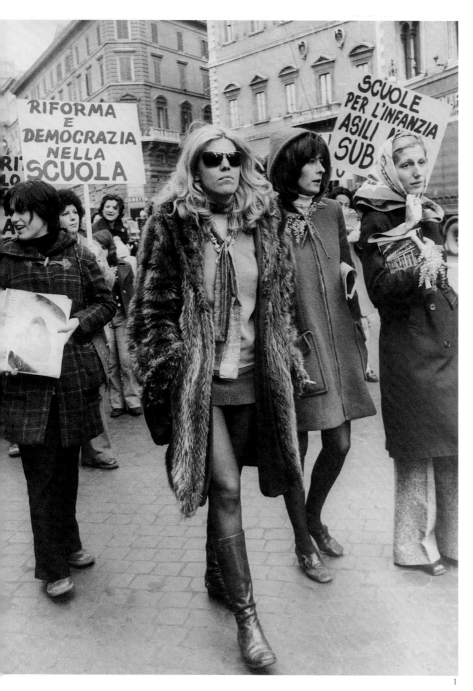

DEMONSTRATIONS had their fashions too. While feminist marches in the United States and Britain could not fail to be reported as packed with 'dungarees-wearing, burly lesbians', the Italians had their own inimitable style, linking sunglasses and furs with demands for preschool provision and curriculum reform (1). Meanwhile rock'n'roll revivalists (2) and Notting Hill carnival celebrants (3) show a perhaps surprising convergence of glamorous and androgynous intentional vulgarity.

DEMONSTRATIONEN hatten ihre eigenen Moden. In den angelsächsischen Ländern konnte man sich darauf verlassen, daß in einem Bericht über einen feministischen Protestmarsch von »kräftigen Lesben in Latzhosen« die Rede sein würde, während Italienerinnen stilvoller in Sonnenbrille und Pelz auftraten, wenn sie für Kindergärten und Schulreformen demonstrierten (1). Es mag erstaunen, wie beim Rock 'n' Roll-Revival (2) und beim Karneval in Notting Hill (3) Glamour und ein androgyner, bewußt vulgärer Stil zusammenkommen.

LES manifestations suivent également la mode. Alors que les marches féministes aux États-Unis et en Grande-Bretagne ne manquaient pas d'être attribuées à des « lesbiennes bien charpentées vêtues de salopettes », les Italiennes, avec un style inimitable, défilaient en manteaux de fourrure, arborant des lunettes de soleil pour réclamer davantage d'écoles maternelles et une réforme des programmes d'études (1). Pendant ce temps, ceux qui faisaient revivre le rock'n'roll (2) et qui célébraient le carnaval de Notting Hill (3) montraient, curieusement peut-être, la même vulgarité provocatrice, séduisante et androgyne.

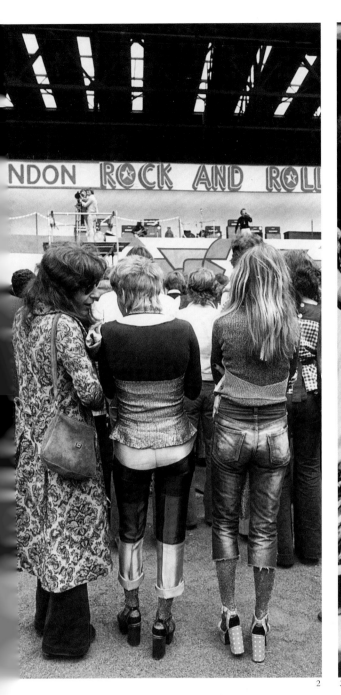

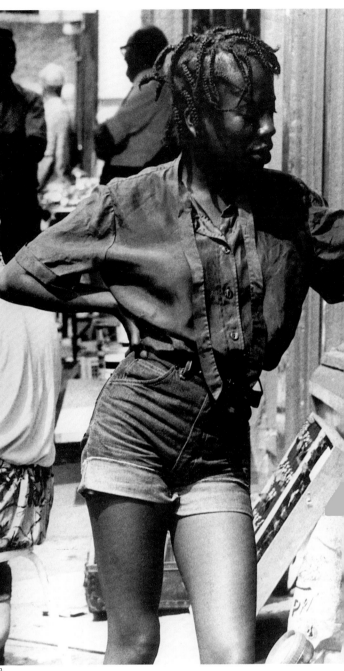

2 3

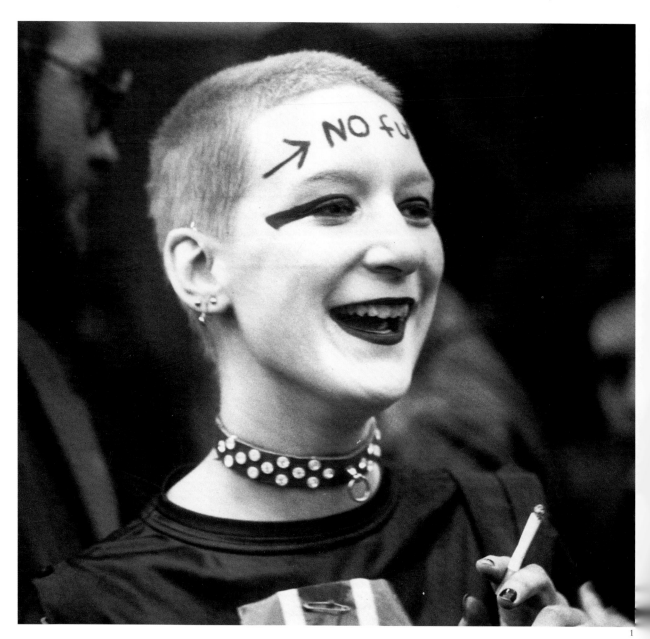

1

P UNK was huge in the 1970s, in music, in fashion and in attitude. One of those attending a Jam and Clash gig at the Rainbow Theatre in London, 14 May 1977, spread the message with the words 'NO FUTURE' painted on her forehead (1). Malcolm McLaren, manager of the Sex Pistols, and Vivienne Westwood (2), designer and owner of the SEX boutique on Chelsea's King's Road, were leading apostles of the Punk creed.

P UNK war absolut »in« in den 1970ern – sowohl in der Musik als auch in der Mode und nicht zuletzt in der Haltung vieler Jugendlicher. Eine der Besucherinnen und Besucher eines Auftritts der Gruppe »Jam and Clash« am 14. Mai 1977 im Rainbow Theatre in London verbreitete die Botschaft »No future«, indem sie sich diese auf die Stirn schrieb (1). Führende Apostel der Punkbewegung: Malcolm McLaren, der Manager der Gruppe »Sex Pistols«, und Vivienne Westwood, Designerin und Besitzerin der SEX-Boutique auf der Modemeile King's Road im Londoner Stadtteil Chelsea (2).

L E punk avait vraiment la cote dans les années 70 – aussi bien pour la musique que pour la mode, mais aussi et surtout en raison de l'attitude de nombreux jeunes. L'une des fans à un concert du groupe « Jam and Clash », le 14 mai 1977 au Rainbow Theatre de Londres, proclame le message « No future », qu'elle s'est peint sur le front (1). Deux prophètes du mouvement punk : Malcolm McLaren, le manager du groupe « Sex Pistols », et Vivienne Westwood, styliste et propriétaire de la boutique SEX, sur l'avenue de la mode King's Road, dans le quartier londonien de Chelsea (2).

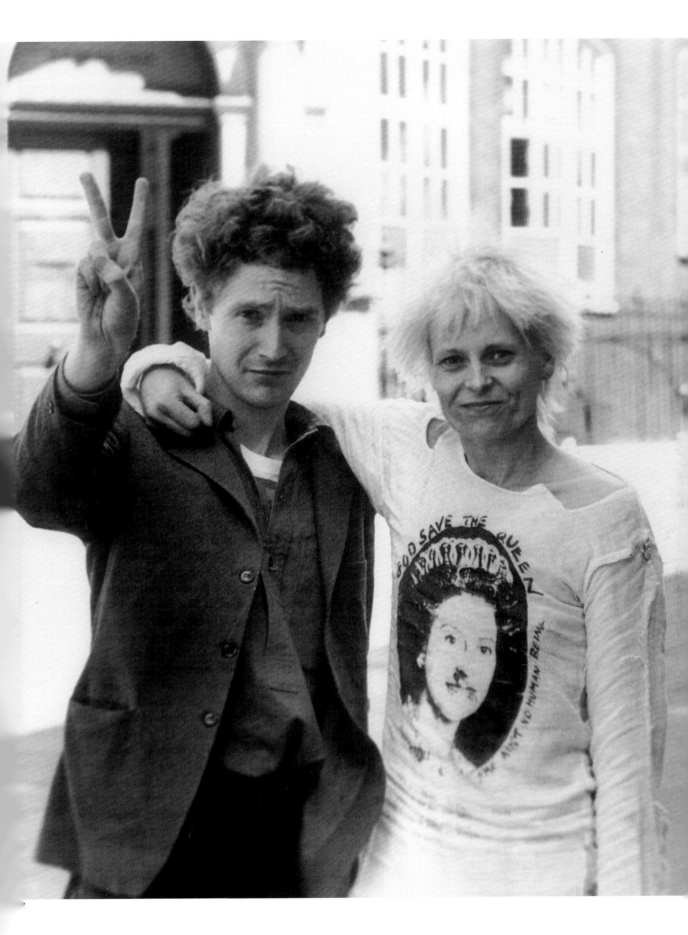

Space

IMMEDIATELY after World War II, the German designer of the V1 and V2 rockets, Wernher von Braun, with his team of designers and engineers, surrendered to the Americans. During the 1950s and 1960s, until the Apollo 8 moon landing in 1969, von Braun continued to direct space operations in the States. However, it was a Soviet spaceman named Yuri Gargarin who became the first to 'boldly go' in the wake of an assortment of monkeys, dogs and chickens beyond what the hit TV series *Star Trek* called 'the Final Frontier'. Just one month later, in May 1961, Gargarin was followed by the first American spaceman, Commander Alan B. Shepherd Jnr.

For a while, the conquest of space proceeded smoothly and easily, though at enormous expense. John Glenn, Valentina Tereshkova and many other pioneers flew their missions but never left their ships, unlike Edward H. White II in 1965 (1). Glory finally came on 21 July 1969, with the Apollo 11 mission to the moon and Neil Armstrong's 'giant leap for mankind' on its surface. In true *Star Wars* style, however, the Great Unknown struck back when the Challenger ship exploded shortly after lift-off on 28 January 1986, killing the entire crew. Entire programmes of space exploration were cancelled, but new generations of telescopes and space probes brought new knowledge and a staggering wealth of images to the watchers of the skies back on earth.

UNMITTELBAR nach dem Zweiten Weltkrieg lieferte sich der deutsche Erfinder der V1- und V2-Raketen, Wernher von Braun, mit seinem gesamten Team von Ingenieuren und Entwicklern den Amerikanern aus. Während der 1950er und 1960er Jahre – bis zur Mondlandung der Apollo 8 im Jahre 1965 – leitete von Braun die Raumfahrtunternehmen der Vereinigten Staaten. Es war jedoch der sowjetische Astronaut Juri Gagarin, der als erster Mensch nach einer Reihe von Affen, Hunden und Hühnern sich dorthin wagte, wo gemäß der beliebten TV-Serie *Star Trek* die »letzte Grenze« lag.

Nur einen Monat später, im Mai 1961, folgte Gagarin der erste amerikanische Astronaut, Commander Alan B. Shephard Jr. Eine Zeit lang verlief die Eroberung des Weltraums ruhig und ausgeglichen, wenn auch mit enormem finanziellem Aufwand. John Glenn, Walentina Tereschkowa und zahlreiche andere Pioniere flogen ihre Missionen, ohne jedoch jemals ihr Raumschiff zu verlassen. Nicht so Edward H. White II im Jahre 1965 (1). Der Triumph erfolgte endlich am 21. Juli 1969 mit der Mission der Apollo 11 und Neil Armstrongs »großem Schritt für die Menschheit« auf die Mondoberfläche. In regelrechter Manier eines »Kriegs der Sterne« schlug jedoch das Große Unbekannte zurück, als am 28. Januar 1986 die Challenger kurz nach dem Start explodierte und die gesamte Besatzung dabei ums Leben kam. Ganze Raumfahrtprogramme wurden daraufhin abgebrochen. Doch eine neue Generation von Weltraumteleskopen und Raumfahrtsonden brachte neue Erkenntnisse – und phantastische Bilder aus den Himmeln zurück auf die Erde.

IMMÉDIATEMENT après la Seconde Guerre mondiale, l'inventeur allemand des fusées V1 et V2, Wernher von Braun, se livre aux Américains avec toute son équipe d'ingénieurs et de savants. Pendant les années 1950 et 1960 – jusqu'à l'alunissage d'Apollo 8 en 1965 –, von Braun dirige les grandes aventures spatiales des États-Unis. Mais c'est pourtant l'astronaute soviétique Iouri Gagarine qui, après une ribambelle de singes, de chiens et de poulets, a le courage d'aller, comme premier être humain, là où, selon le populaire feuilleton télévisé *Star Trek*, se trouve la « dernière frontière ».

Un mois plus tard seulement, en mai 1961, Gagarine est suivi par le premier astronaute américain, le commandant Alan B. Shephard Jr. Pendant un certain temps, la conquête de l'espace suit un rythme calme et équilibré, faisant oublier qu'elle coûte des sommes… astronomiques. John Glenn, Valentina Tereschkova ainsi que de nombreux autres pionniers accomplissent leurs missions sans jamais quitter cependant leur vaisseau spatial. Ce n'est pas le cas d'Edward H. White II, en 1965 (1). Le triomphe est finalement obtenu le 21 juillet 1969, avec la mission Apollo 11 et le « grand pas pour l'humanité » de Neil Armstrong sur le sol de la lune. Dans le plus pur style d'une « guerre des étoiles », la Grande Inconnue frappe cependant lorsque, le 28 janvier 1986, la navette Challenger explose quelques secondes après le départ et se désintègre, faisant passer de vie à trépas la totalité de son équipage. Des programmes spatiaux entiers sont stoppés net. Mais une nouvelle génération de télescopes spatiaux et de sondes spatiales procurent de nouveaux enseignements – et ramènent sur la terre des clichés fantastiques du ciel.

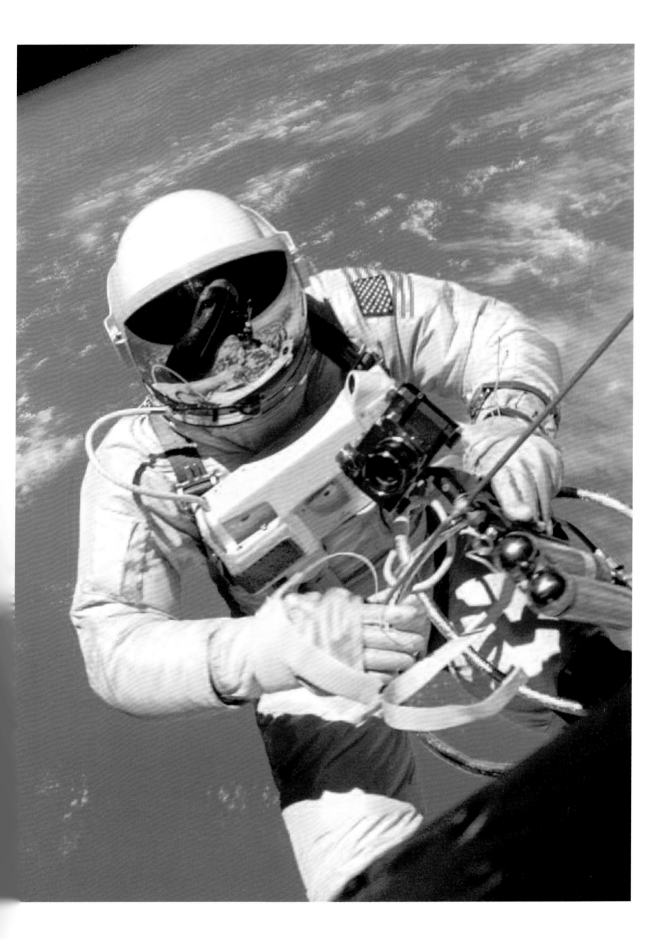

O N 12 April 1961, the Russian Yuri Gagarin (1) took his first space flight on board the *Vostok I*. The race to get the first man into space was terrific, given the intensity of Cold War competition as to which side had the more sophisticated technology. Gagarin orbited the earth in the 4.5 ton spacecraft for 108 minutes, reaching a height of 190 miles. He then fired braking rockets and the aircraft returned to earth by parachute. The USSR scored another 'first' when it put the first woman – Valentina Tereshkova – into orbit, travelling further than the longest-journeying US astronaut (2). Tereshkova and cosmonaut Valery Bykovsky joined hands in a Red Square salute – and a heroes' welcome back to earth – with Prime Minister Khrushchev (3). An old, illiterate sheep-farmer, who looks as though he were born before the invention of the newspaper, has the cosmonauts' story read to him (4).

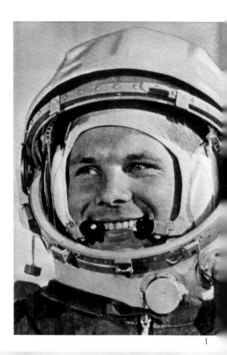

1

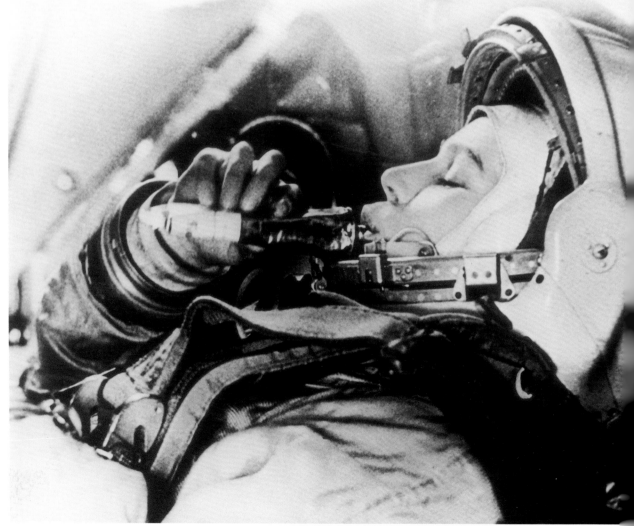

A M 12. April 1961 unternahm der Russe
Juri Gagarin (1) mit der *Wostok I* den
ersten bemannten Weltraumflug. Das Wettrennen darum, wer den ersten Menschen
ins Weltall brachte, war bei der großen
Rivalität der beiden Machtblöcke im Kalten
Krieg ungeheuer gewesen, denn schließlich
ging es darum zu zeigen, welche Seite die
technisch überlegene war. Gagarin umrun-
dete die Erde in dem viereinhalb Tonnen
schweren Flugkörper 108 Minuten lang
und erreichte dabei eine Höhe von 300 Kilometern. Dann zündete er die Bremsraketen,
und die Raumkapsel kehrte an einem
Fallschirm zur Erde zurück. Zum zweiten
Mal gewann die Sowjetunion das Wettrennen, als sie die erste Frau in den Weltraum schickte – Walentina Tereschkowa,
die weiter ins All hinausflog als der erfolg-
reichste amerikanische Astronaut (2). Der
russische Premierminister Chruschtschow
reicht ihr und Valery Bykowsky beim
Heldenempfang, der ihnen bei ihrer
Rückkehr auf dem Roten Platz bereitet
wurde, die Hand (3). Dieser Schafhirte, der
nicht lesen kann, läßt sich vom Triumph
der Kosmonauten vorlesen (4).

L E 12 avril 1961, le Russe Youri Gagarine (1) réalisa son premier vol dans
l'espace à bord du *Vostock 1*. La course
qu'occasionna l'envoi du premier homme
dans l'espace s'avéra fantastique. C'était
une façon de montrer de quel côté se trouvait la technologie la plus sophistiquée.
Gagarine resta en vol orbital pendant cent
huit minutes à l'intérieur d'un vaisseau
spatial de 4 tonnes et demie à une altitude
de 327 kilomètres. Il mit ensuite le feu aux
fusées de freinage avant d'atterrir en parachute. L'URSS releva un nouveau défi
avec. Valentina Terechkova, dont le voyage
dura plus longtemps que ceux des cosmonautes américains (2). Elle et Valery
Bykovsky sont salués comme des héros sur
la Place rouge. On les voit ici donner la
main au Premier ministre Khrouchtchev
(3). Un vieux berger illettré se fait lire la
saga des cosmonautes (4).

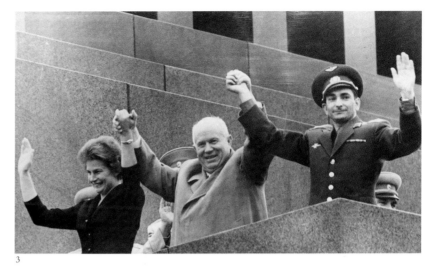

3

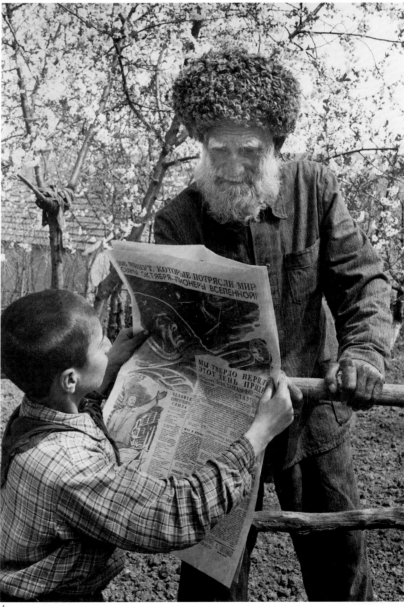

4

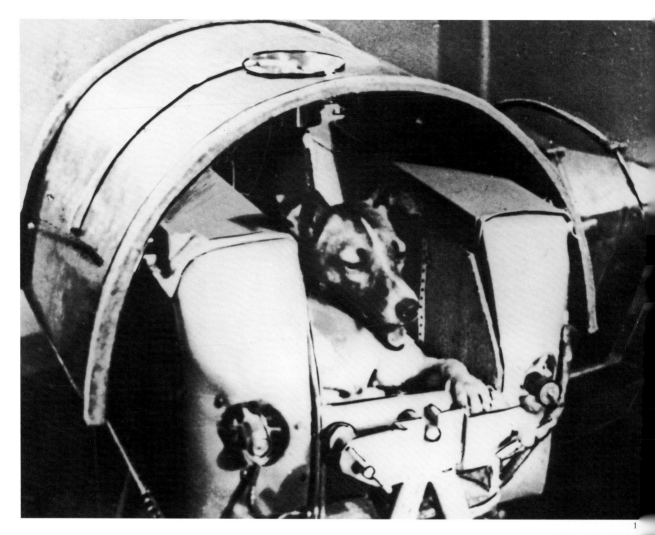

BEFORE the human guinea-pigs, the animal ones. In the 1950s animals were sent into space to see how they withstood flight conditions. Laika, the satellite dog in *Sputnik III* (1), achieved international fame – and indignation, when it was discovered that, mission accomplished, her food would be poisoned to prevent her dying slowly of starvation while still in orbit. In 1959, the US sent Sam (2), a 7-lb Rhesus monkey, 55 miles into space on a Project *Mercury* capsule. As late as 1970, NASA was performing an 'Orbiting Frog Otolith', placing two bullfrogs in a weightless environment for a period of days (3).

VOR den menschlichen Versuchskaninchen kamen die Tiere. In den 50er Jahren wurden Tiere in Raumkapseln ins All geschossen, um zu sehen, wie sie den Flug überstanden. Laika (1), die Hündin von *Sputnik III*, brachte es zu weltweiter Berühmtheit – und Empörung, als bekannt wurde, daß sie nach ihrer Mission vergiftet würde, damit sie nicht in der Erdumlaufbahn verhungerte. 1959 schickten die Amerikaner den Rhesusaffen Sam an Bord einer *Mercury*-Kapsel in den Weltraum (2). Und noch 1970 gab es bei der NASA den »Erdumlauffrosch Otolith«: Zwei Ochsenfrösche wurden der Schwerelosigkeit ausgesetzt (3).

LES cobayes animaux ont précédé les cobayes humains. Au cours des années 50, on envoie des animaux dans l'espace afin d'observer leur comportement face aux conditions de vol. La chienne Laïka, dans *Spoutnik III* (1), connut le succès international. En 1959, à 89 kilomètres d'altitude, dans une capsule du projet *Mercury*, les États-Unis envoyèrent Sam dans l'espace (2), un singerhésus 7-lb. En 1970, la NASA procède au « Orbiting Frog Otolith » : deux crapaudsbœufs sont envoyés dans l'espace où ils resteront plusieurs jours en apesanteur (3).

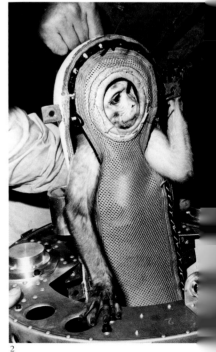

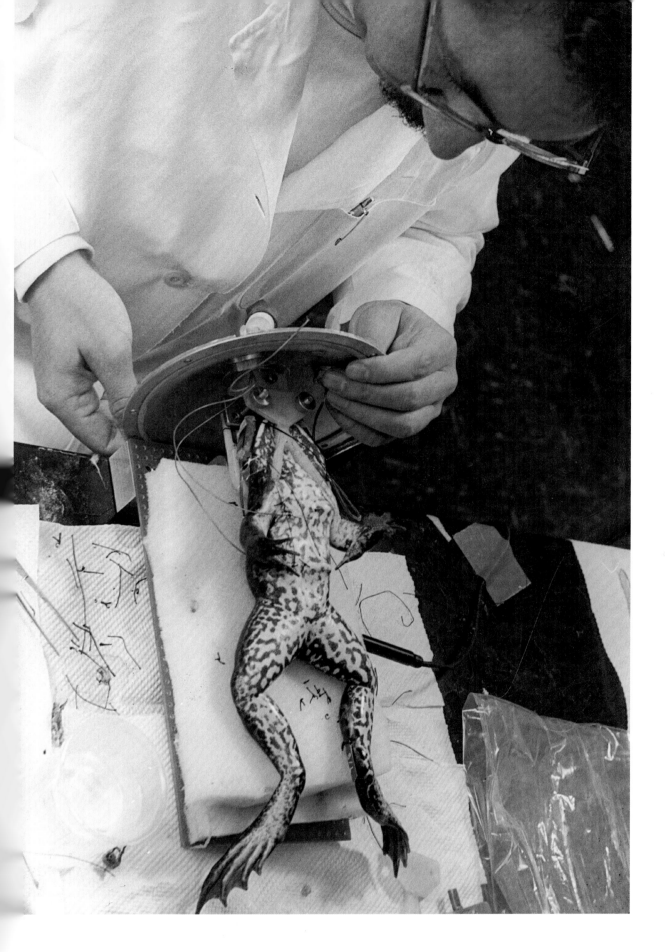

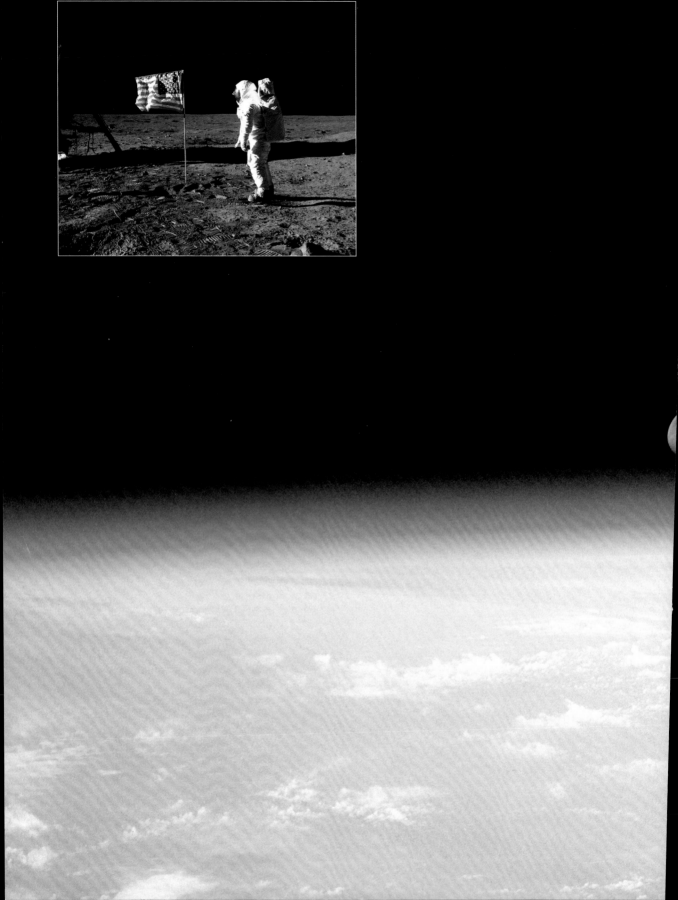

EARTHRISE: The Moon sets over the rim of the earth, an image taken from the Shuttle *Discovery* Mission STS-70 in July 1995. (*inset*) The Man on the Moon – Buzz Aldrin poses with the Stars and Stripes at the highpoint of the Apollo 11 mission, 20 July 1969.

ERDAUFGANG: Der Mond erscheint am Horizont der Erde – das Photo entstand im Rahmen der Shuttle-Mission STS-70, *Discovery*, im Juli 1995. Der Mann im Mond – Buzz Aldrin posiert auf dem Höhepunkt der Apollo 11-Mission neben der amerikanischen Flagge (*Inset*) – 20. Juli 1969.

LA lune se lève : la lune apparaît à l'horizon de la terre – la photo a été prise à l'occasion de la mission de la navette spatiale STS-70, *Discovery*, en juillet 1995. L'homme dans la lune – Buzz Aldrin pose à côté du drapeau américain, à l'apogée de la mission Apollo 11 (*inset*) – 20 juillet 1969.

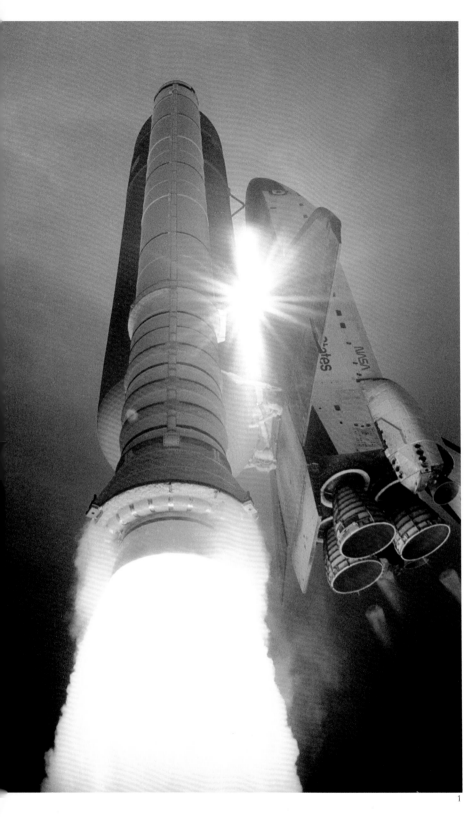

1

THE US space shuttle *Challenger* exploded 72 seconds after take-off on 28 January 1986, to the horror of watching millions (3). Among the crew of seven who died was Christa McAuliffe, a school-teacher selected as the first woman to fly in a new 'citizens in space' programme (2). The flight had already been postponed five times, three of them due to bad weather. Before blast-off, icicles had to be chipped from the shuttle by hand. These were the first US casualties in space, dealing a devastating blow to a programme already in serious difficulties from drastically over-running its budget. Five years later, *Atlantis* blasted off on 2 August 1991, with happier results (1).

AM 28. Januar 1986 explodierte das amerikanische Raumschiff *Challenger* nur 72 Sekunden nach dem Start – zum Entsetzen von Millionen von Zuschauern (3). Eine der sieben Besatzungsmitglieder war Christa McAuliffe, ein Lehrerin, die im Rahmen des neuen Programms »Bürger im Raum« als erste Frau mitflog. Der Flug war zuvor bereits fünf Mal verschoben worden, drei Mal wegen schlechten Wetters. Unmittelbar vor dem Start wurden noch Eiszapfen mit den Händen vom Raumschiff entfernt. Das waren die ersten amerikanischen Opfer im Raum; und das Unglück versetzte dem Raumfahrtprogramm – das bereits in erheblichen Schwierigkeiten aufgrund eines völlig überzogenen Budgets steckte – einen herben Rückschlag. Fünf Jahre später, am 2. August 1991, hob die *Atlantis* ab – mit weitaus glücklicherem Ergebnis (1).

Le 28 janvier 1986, la navette spatiale américaine *Challenger*, explose 72 secondes seulement après le décollage – sous les yeux horrifiés de millions de spectateurs (3). L'un des sept membres d'équipage était Christa McAuliffe, une enseignante et la première femme à participer à un tel vol dans le cadre du nouveau programme « Des citoyens dans l'espace ». Le vol avait auparavant déjà été reporté à cinq reprises, dont trois fois à cause du mauvais temps. Immédiatement avant le décollage, il avait encore fallu enlever à la main des morceaux de glace accrochés à la navette spatiale. Ce furent les premières victimes américaines de l'espace et la catastrophe porta un rude coup à un programme spatial qui rencontrait déjà des difficultés considérables en raison d'un budget complètement dépassé. Cinq ans plus tard, le 2 août 1991, décolle *Atlantis,* avec un résultat beaucoup plus heureux (1

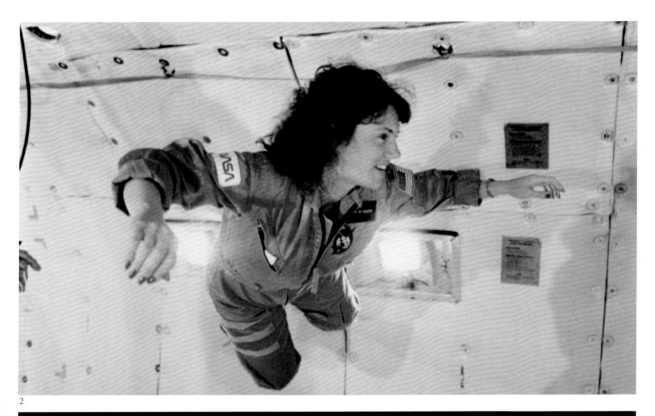

2

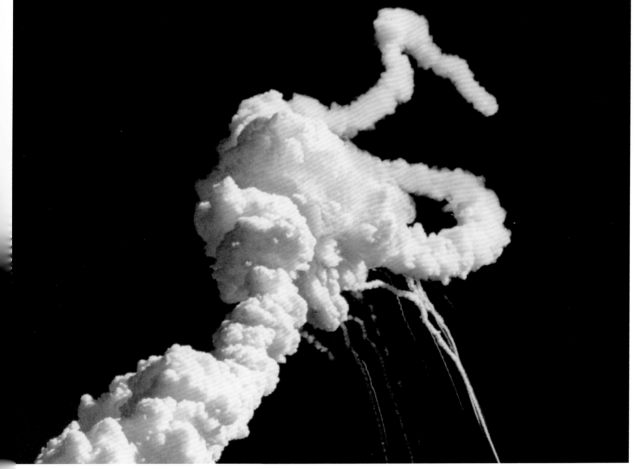

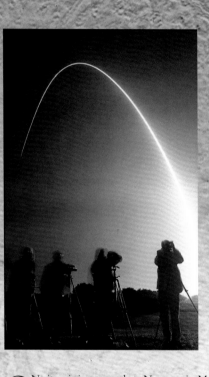

ON its mission to explore Neptune in May
1980, *Voyager 2* captured this image of Triton.
(*inset*) Cameramen capture the launch of the Mars
Pathfinder spacecraft over Cape Canaveral, Florida,
4 December 1997.

AUF seiner Mission zur Erkundung des Planeten
Neptun schickte das Raumschiff *Voyager 2* im
Mai 1980 dieses Bild vom Neptun-Mond Triton zur
Erde. Kameraleute filmen den Start des Raumschiffs
Pathfinder auf dem Weg zum Mars (*Inset*) – am
4. Dezember 1997 in Cape Canaveral, Florida.

LORS de sa mission d'exploration de la planète
Neptune, *Voyager 2* envoie à la terre, en mai
1980, cette photo de Triton, une lune de Neptune.
Des cameramen filment le décollage du vaisseau
spatial *Pathfinder* qui s'envole vers Mars (*inset*) –
le 4 décembre 1997 à Cap Canaveral, en Floride.

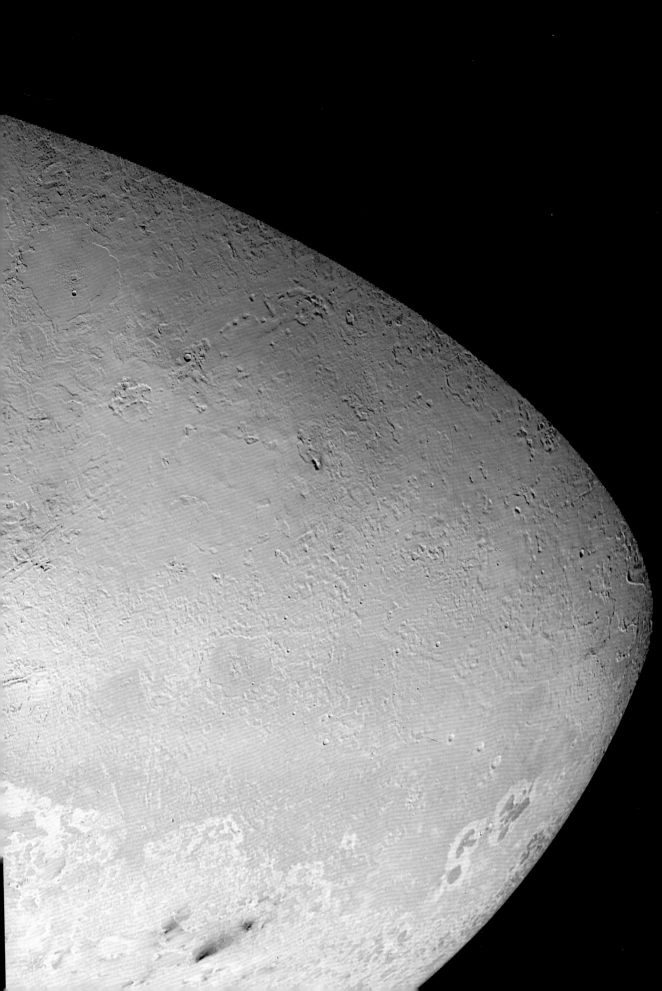

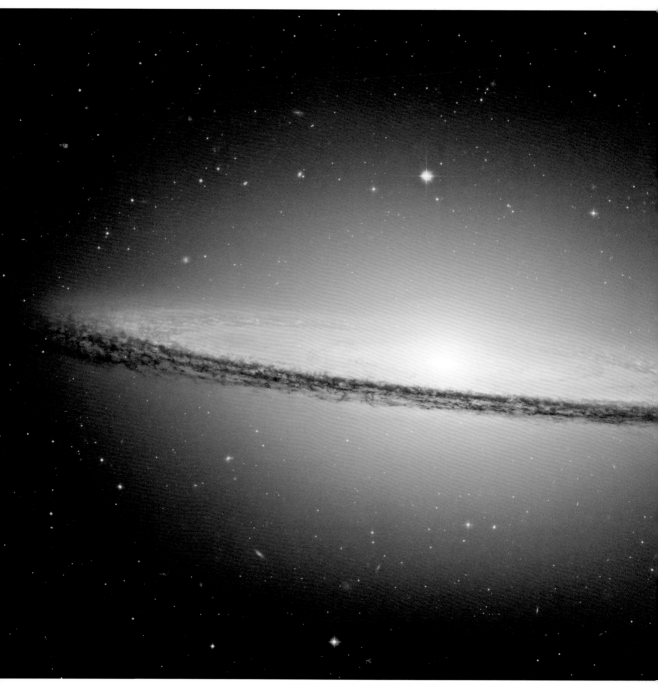

THE Hubble Space programme was a joint project of ESA and NASA. When the telescope was launched on 24 April 1990 to make its 20-year journey, not even its most optimistic supporters would have dreamed of the discoveries it would make, or the quality of the images it would produce, such as the Sombrero Galaxy (1), the red supergiant Star V838 (2) and a gas pillar in the Eagle Nebula (3).

DAS »Hubble«-Weltraumteleskop war ein gemeinsames Projekt von ESA und NASA. Als das Teleskop am 24. April 1990 auf die Umlaufbahn zu seiner 24 Jahre dauernden Reise gebracht wurde, hätten sich nicht einmal die optimistischsten Befürworter des Projekts träumen

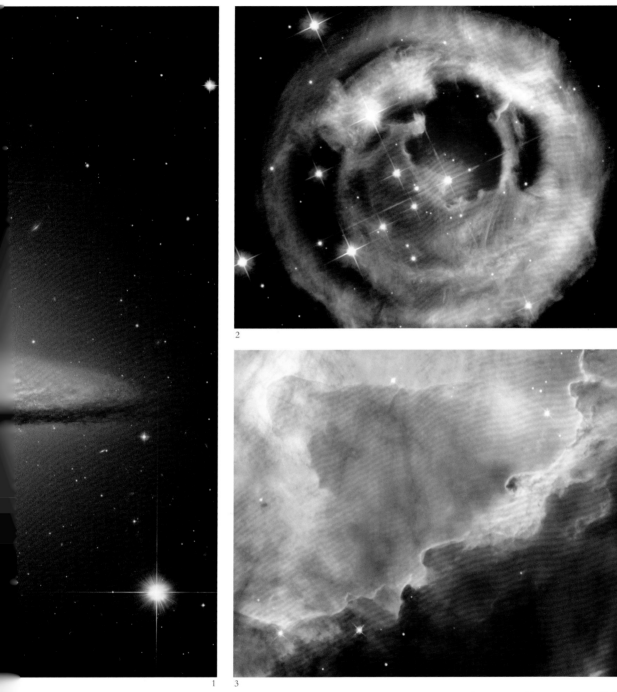

1

2

3

lassen, welche Entdeckungen damit möglich wurden und welche Qualität, welche Klarheit die Bilder haben würden, die es einfing – zum Beispiel von der Sombrero Galaxie (1), dem gigantischen roten Stern V838 (2) oder von dem Gaskissen im Adler-Nebel.

LE télescope spatial « Hubble » était un projet commun à l'ESA et à la NASA. Quand le télescope a été mis sur orbite, le 24 avril 1990, pour son voyage qui doit durer 24 ans, même les partisans les plus optimistes de ce projet n'auraient jamais osé imaginer quelles découvertes allaient

ainsi devenir possibles ni quelle qualité, quelle clarté auraient les photos qu'il allait prendre – par exemple de la galaxie Sombrero (1), la gigantesque étoile rouge V838 (2) ou des coussins de gaz dans le nuage d'Adler.

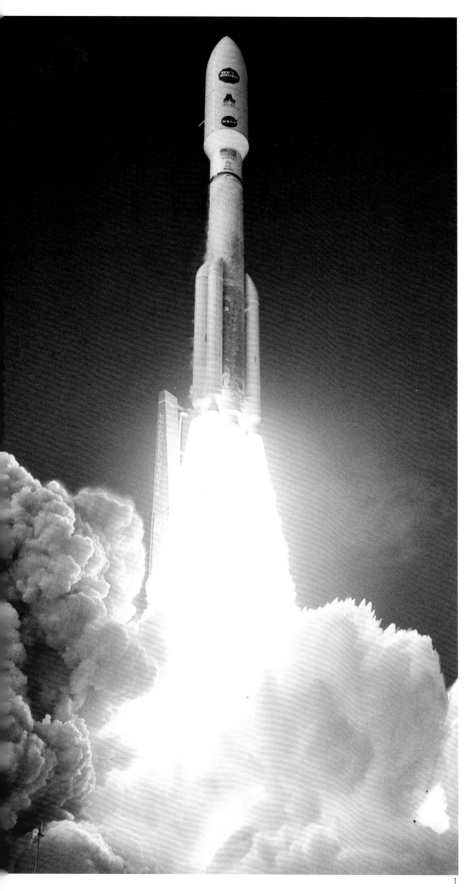

THE DREAMS of the 1960s, to build cities on Mars or the Moon before the end of the 20th century had not been fulfilled. But while there was still money in the kitty, agencies and scientists kept on seeking to explore the vastness of space. With more than 2 million pounds of thrust behind her, *Atlas V* lifts off from the Kennedy Space Center at Cape Canaveral, Florida, 19 January 2006 (1). It was one of the most ambitious missions of all time – ahead lay Mars, Jupiter and Pluto. A staggering image of the 4000 metre high cliffs and of Echus Chasma, one of the largest water source regions on Mars, taken from the European Space Agency's *Mars Express*, 25 September 2005 (2). The end of a great space era, as the US Space Shuttle *Atlantis* is about to touch down at the Kennedy Space Center, 11 July 2011 (3). This completed the final mission in NASA's 30 year Shuttle Programme.

DIE TRÄUME der 60er Jahre, noch vor dem Ende des 20. Jahrhunderts auf dem Mars oder dem Mond Städte zu bauen, hatten sich nicht erfüllt. Aber solange noch Geld in der Kasse war, erforschten Institutionen und Wissenschaftler weiterhin die Unendlichkeit des Alls. Mit mehr als 800 Tonnen Schub im Rücken startet die Atlas V am 19. Januar 2006 vom Kennedy Space Center, Cape Canaveral, Florida (1). Es war eine der ehrgeizigsten Missionen aller Zeiten, zum Mars, Jupiter und Pluto. Ein faszinierendes Bild von 4000 Meter hohen Klippen und der Echus Chasma, einer der größten Regionen des Mars, in denen man Spuren von Wasser fand, aufgenommen vom *Mars Express* der ESA am 25. September 2005 (2). Das Ende einer Ära: Das Space Shuttle *Atlantis* landet am 11. Juli 2011 auf dem Kennedy Space Center und beendet damit die letzte Mission des 30 Jahre währenden Shuttle-Programms der NASA (3).

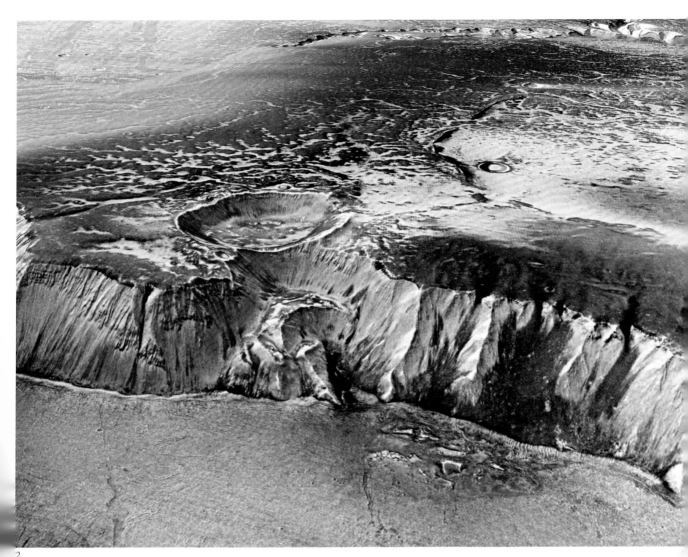

2

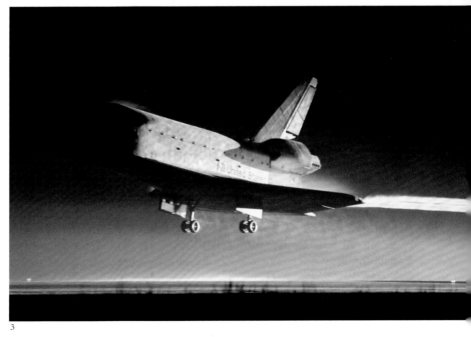

3

L ES RÊVES des années 1960, de bâtir des cités sur Mars ou sur la Lune avant la fin du XXe siècle, n'ont pu voir le jour. Mais alors que les caisses sont encore pleines, agences spatiales et scientifiques s'emploient à explorer l'immensité de l'espace. Sous l'effet d'une poussée de plus 900 tonnes, *Atlas V* s'arrache de son pas de tir du centre spatial Kennedy de Cape Canaveral, en Floride, le 19 janvier 2006 (1). Sa mission était l'une des plus ambitieuses de tous les temps – avec pour objectif Mars, Jupiter et Pluton. Un cliché stupéfiant, réalisé par la sonde spatiale européenne *Mars Express* le 5 septembre 2005, montrant des falaises de 4 000 m d'altitude bordant la vallée d'Echus Chasma, une des plus vastes et anciennes retenues d'eau de Mars (2). Avec le retour de la navette spatiale américaine *Atlantis* au centre spatial Kennedy, le 11 juillet 2011, une page de la conquête spatiale se tourne et met fin au programme spatial, lancé il y a 30 ans par la Nasa (3).

Sport

IN the second half of the 20th century, sport became big business. Television brought top class athletes from all fields of play into the homes of hundreds of millions, and sponsorship kept them in the limelight. The number of tournaments soared. The pots of gold for being the best golfer, tennis player, jockey, marathon runner or racing driver swelled. The wages of footballers, baseball players and basketball stars reached dizzy heights.

The Olympic movement attempted to keep its games free from drugs and the clamouring commercialism that pervaded other sports, but was not always successful. At the Atlanta Games in 1996, one sponsor festooned the stadium with a legend monstrously at odds with the Olympic spirit: 'You don't win silver,' it said, 'you lose gold'. It didn't matter – there were still millions all over the world who believed it was the 'taking part' that mattered.

For sport became a mass activity. More people than ever hurled themselves into running, swimming, kicking a ball about, hang-gliding, surfing, throwing darts, volleying and smashing, chipping from a bunker, or simply screaming from the terraces. Sport raised money for good causes, promoted world peace, improved the health and fitness of billions, and plunged as many into depression or filled them with joy as the fortunes of their heroes ebbed and flowed.

IN der zweiten Hälfte des 20. Jahrhunderts wurde der Sport zum großen Geschäft. Die Fernsehtechnologie brachte Spitzenathleten sämtlicher Disziplinen zu Hunderten von Millionen Zuschauern direkt ins Haus. Sponsoren sorgten im Weiteren dafür, daß die Topleistungen dieser Athleten permanent im Rampenlicht standen. Die Zahl der Turniere stieg beträchtlich. Die Goldtöpfe für den besten Golfer, Tennisspieler, Jockey, Marathonläufer oder Rennfahrer füllten sich, und die Gagen für die Stars unter den Fußballern, Basketballern und Baseballspielern erreichten schwindelnde Höhen.

Die Olympische Bewegung versuchte, sich weitestgehend von Drogen wie vom verführerischen Kommerz fernzuhalten, die andere Sportveranstaltungen heimsuchten – nicht immer jedoch mit Erfolg. Während der Spiele in Atlanta im Sommer 1996 verbreitete das Spruchband eines Sponsors ein dem olympischen Geist auf groteske Weise widersprechendes Motto: »Du gewinnst nicht Silber«, stand dort zu lesen, »du verlierst Gold«. Doch das richtete keinen weiteren Schaden an –

Millionen rund um den Erdball hielten den olympischen Gedanken des »Teilnehmen ist alles« aufrecht.

Denn Sport wurde ein Massensport. Mehr Menschen als jemals zuvor warfen sich ins Laufen, Schwimmen, Kicken, Drachenfliegen, Surfen, ins Darts-Werfen, ins Chippen oder einfach in die Begeisterung auf den Zuschauertribünen. Der Sport trieb Spenden für einen guten Zweck ein, engagierte sich für den Weltfrieden, verbesserte Gesundheit und Fitneß von Millionen Menschen und stieß ebenso viele in Depression oder auch in Siegestaumel – je nachdem, welche Richtung das Glück ihrer Helden gerade nahm.

DURANT la seconde moitié du XXᵉ siècle, le sport devient un gros business. La télévision amène les meilleurs athlètes de toutes les disciplines jusqu'au domicile de centaines de millions de téléspectateurs. Les sponsors, de leur côté, font tout pour que les performances spectaculaires de ces athlètes occupent en permanence les feux de la rampe. Le nombre des tournois ne cesse d'augmenter. Le montant des primes que peut emporter le meilleur joueur de golf ou de tennis, le jockey, le coureur de marathon ou le pilote de course est toujours plus élevé et les gages versés aux stars parmi les footballeurs, joueurs de basket-ball ou de baseball atteignent des hauteurs qui donnent le vertige.

Le mouvement olympique a pourtant cherché à s'isoler le plus possible de cette drogue qu'est la tentation du commerce qui gangrène d'autres manifestations sportives – mais pas toujours avec succès. Pendant les Jeux olympiques d'Atlanta, durant l'été 1996, le slogan d'un sponsor proclame d'une façon qui contredit grotesquement l'esprit olympique : « Tu ne gagnes pas l'argent, tu perds l'or. » Mais le dommage reste limité – des millions de spectateurs sur toute la planète continue de croire à l'idée olympique, qui veut que le principal soit de participer.

Le sport est devenu un activité de masse. Avec plus d'enthousiasme que jamais auparavant, on s'adonne au jogging, à la natation, aux jeux de ballon, au deltaplane, à la planche à voile, au volley, au golf ou, tout simplement, on se cantonne au rôle de spectateur sur les tribunes. Le sport génère des dons pour la bonne cause, s'engage pour la paix dans le monde, améliore la santé et la forme physique de millions d'individus, mais, en précipitant d'autres dans la dépression ou, encore, dans l'ivresse de la victoire – selon le sort que la chance a réservé aux héros.

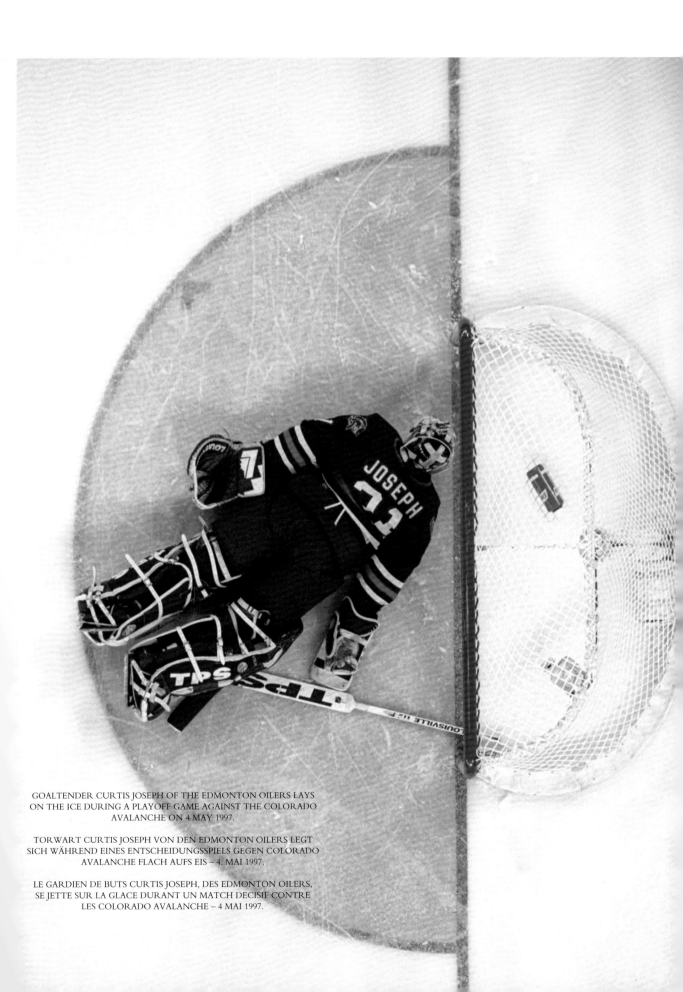

GOALTENDER CURTIS JOSEPH OF THE EDMONTON OILERS LAYS
ON THE ICE DURING A PLAYOFF GAME AGAINST THE COLORADO
AVALANCHE ON 4 MAY 1997.

TORWART CURTIS JOSEPH VON DEN EDMONTON OILERS LEGT
SICH WÄHREND EINES ENTSCHEIDUNGSSPIELS GEGEN COLORADO
AVALANCHE FLACH AUFS EIS – 4. MAI 1997.

LE GARDIEN DE BUTS CURTIS JOSEPH, DES EDMONTON OILERS,
SE JETTE SUR LA GLACE DURANT UN MATCH DECISIF CONTRE
LES COLORADO AVALANCHE – 4 MAI 1997.

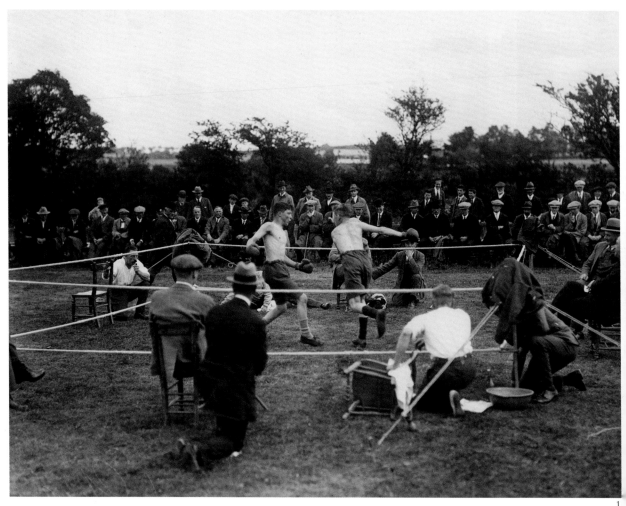

1

IN the years following World War I, there was considerable pressure on boys and young men to assert their manhood. They were the first generations to have escaped the slaughter, and though Cornwall was a long way from Flanders, thumping each other in a field near Bodmin in July 1922 (1) cannot have been much fun. After World War II, sport was a little more graceful, as Guy Amouretti revealed at the World Table Tennis Championships in Wembley (2), 30 December 1950.

IN den Jahren unmittelbar nach dem Ersten Weltkrieg sahen sich Jungen und heranwachsende Männer unter dem Druck, ihre Männlichkeit unter Beweis zu stellen. Dies war die erste Generation, die dem großen Schlachten entkommen war – und obwohl Cornwall nicht in Flandern lag, wird auch hier der Spaß, sich auf einem Feld in der Nähe von Bomin zu schlagen, nur gering gewesen sein (1) – Juli 1922. Nach dem Zweiten Weltkrieg wurde der Sport zunehmend anmutiger – wie Guy Amouretti bei der Tischtennis-Weltmeisterschaft in Wembley vorführt (2) – 30. Dezember 1950.

DURANT les années qui ont immédiatement suivi la Première Guerre mondiale, garçons et jeunes gens estimaient devoir afficher leur virilité. Il s'agissait de la première génération qui avait échappé aux grandes batailles de la guerre – et, bien que la Cornouailles ne soit pas les Flandres, ici aussi, se battre dans un champ proche de Bomin, n'était pas un amusement (1) – juillet 1922. Après la Seconde Guerre mondiale, le sport gagne de plus en plus en élégance – comme le prouve ici Guy Amouretti, lors des championnats du monde de tennis de table à Wembley (2) – 30 décembre 1950.

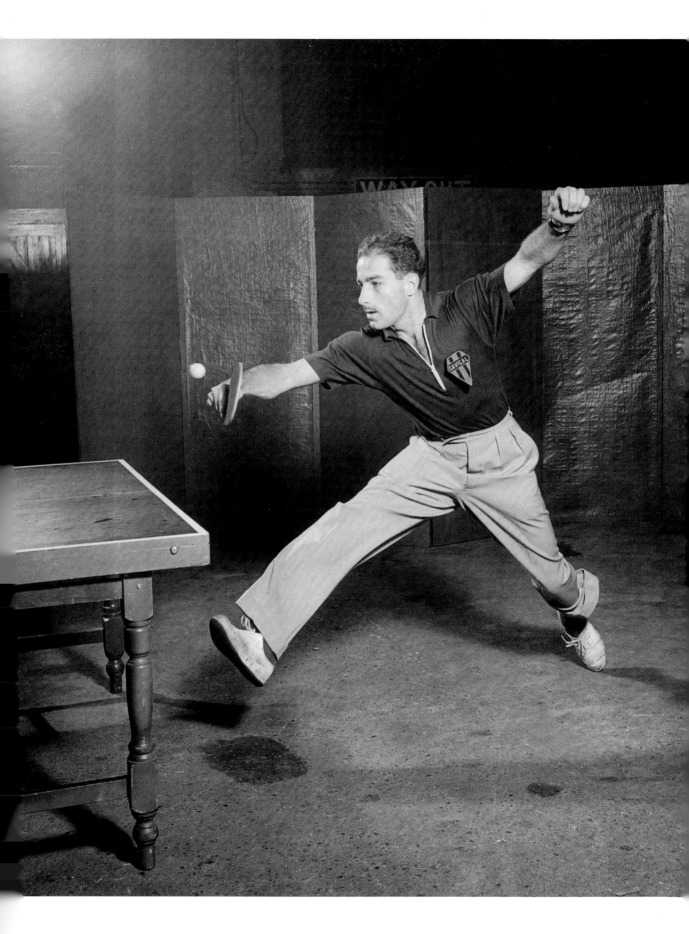

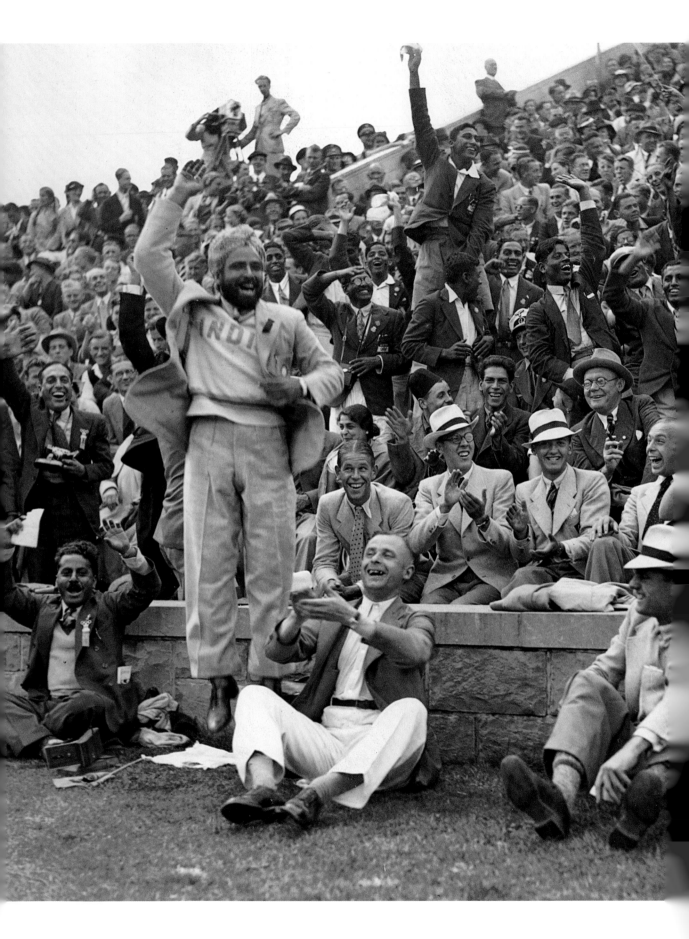

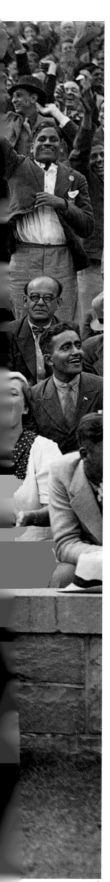

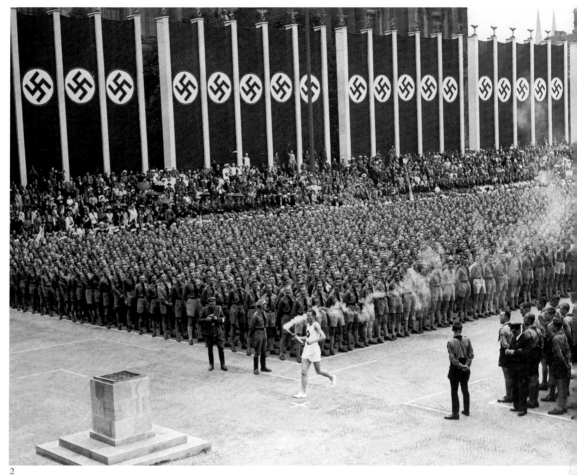

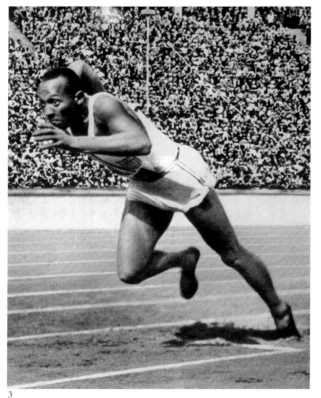

THE 1936 Olympic Games: those cheering wear logos as diverse as India and Brazil (1). The Olympic torch is run into the stadium beneath ranked banners of swastikas surmounted with eagles (2). Jesse Owens, star of the Games and Hitler's *bête noire*, takes off at the start of the Men's 200 Metres, one of four gold medals he won (3).

OLYMPISCHE Spiele 1936: begeisterte Zuschauer, darunter Inder und Brasilianer (1). Das olympische Feuer wird vor adlergekrönten Hakenkreuzflaggen ins Stadion getragen (2). Jesse Owens, der »schwarzer Panther« und Star der Spiele in Hitlers Berlin, beim Start des 200-Meter-Laufs der Männer – bei dem er eine seiner vier Goldmedaillen davontrug (3).

LES Jeux olympiques de 1936 : ceux qui acclament portent des inscriptions aussi diverses que « Inde » et « Brésil » (1). La flamme olympique traverse une rangée de croix gammées et d'aigles (2). Jesse Owens, star des Jeux de 1936 et « bête noire » de Hitler, au départ du 200 mètres hommes qui allait lui permettre de remporter l'une de ses quatre médailles d'or (3).

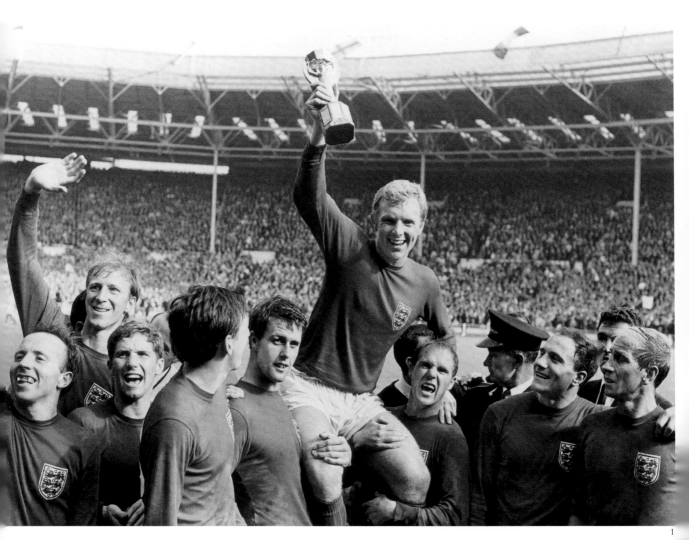

1

ENGLISH football captain Bobby Moore being chaired after England's victory over West Germany in the 1966 World Cup Final, which had 50 per cent of the British population tuned in (1). Moore, a West Ham United player, won 108 caps in his career – more than any other professional. At the final of the Soccer World Championships in 1974, West Germany won 2-1 against Holland to become World Champions. Here team member Franz Beckenbauer is embraced by coach Helmut Schön at the end of the match (2). Brazilian player Zito celebrates scoring a second goal in his country's International against Czechoslovakia, played in Santiago, Chile, in 1962 (3). Brazil went on to win 3-1. Pele, the most famous Brazilian player of all time, displaying the trophy (4) after he helped Brazil win the 1970 World Cup in Mexico.

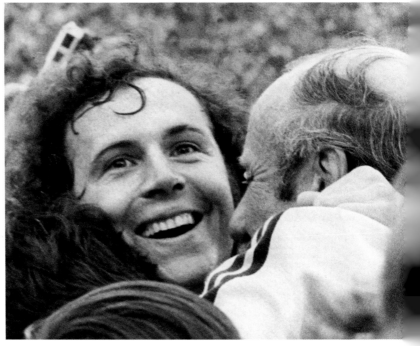

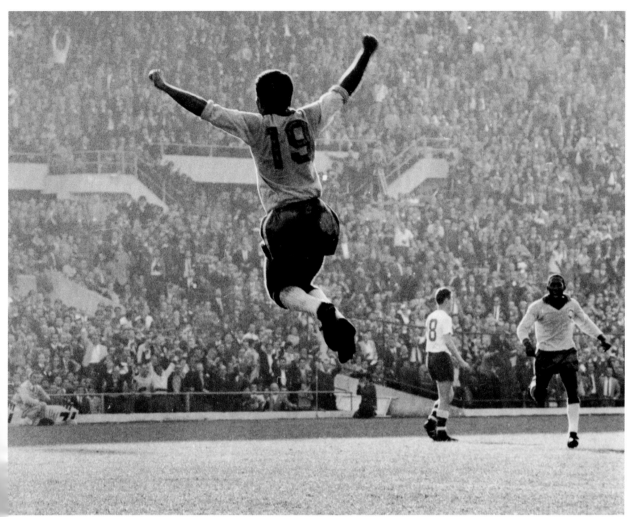

3

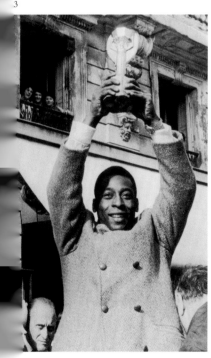

DER Kapitän der englischen Mannschaft, Bobby Moore, wird nach dem Sieg über Westdeutschland im Endspiel um den Weltmeisterschaftstitel 1966, ein Spiel, bei dem die Hälfte der britischen Bevölkerung an den Fernseh- und Radiogeräten saß, auf die Schultern gehoben (1). Moore, der für West Ham United spielte, wurde im Laufe seiner Karriere 108mal für die Nationalmannschaft aufgestellt – mehr als jeder andere Profifußballer. Im Endspiel der Weltmeisterschaft des Jahres 1974 gewann Westdeutschland gegen Holland 2:1. Hier wird Franz Beckenbauer am Ende des Spiels von Trainer Helmut Schön umarmt (2). Der brasilianische Spieler Zito freut sich im Länderspiel gegen die Tschechoslowakei, 1962 in Santiago de Chile, über sein zweites Tor (3). Brasilien gewann 3:1. Der Brasilianer Pelé, der berühmteste Fußballspieler aller Zeiten (4), hebt stolz den Weltmeisterschaftspokal des Jahres 1970, den die Brasilianer in Mexiko gewannen.

LE capitaine de l'équipe anglaise de football, Bobby Moore, est porté en triomphe après la victoire de l'Angleterre sur l'Allemagne de l'Ouest à la finale de la Coupe du monde en 1966, qui fut suivie à la radio par 50 % de la population britannique (1). Moore remporta 108 trophées au cours de sa carrière – plus que tout autre joueur professionnel. À la finale du championnat du monde, en 1974, l'Allemagne de l'Ouest battit la Hollande 2 à 1 et devint ainsi championne du monde. On voit ici le joueur Franz Beckenbauer embrassé par l'entraîneur Helmut Schön à la fin du match (2). Le joueur brésilien Zito, fou de joie après son deuxième but au cours de la rencontre avec la Tchécoslovaquie. C'était à Santiago, au Chili, en 1962 (3). Le Brésil continua sur sa lancée en l'emportant 3 à 1. Pelé, le joueur brésilien le plus célèbre de tous les temps, (4), après la victoire du Brésil lors de la Coupe du monde de Mexico en 1970.

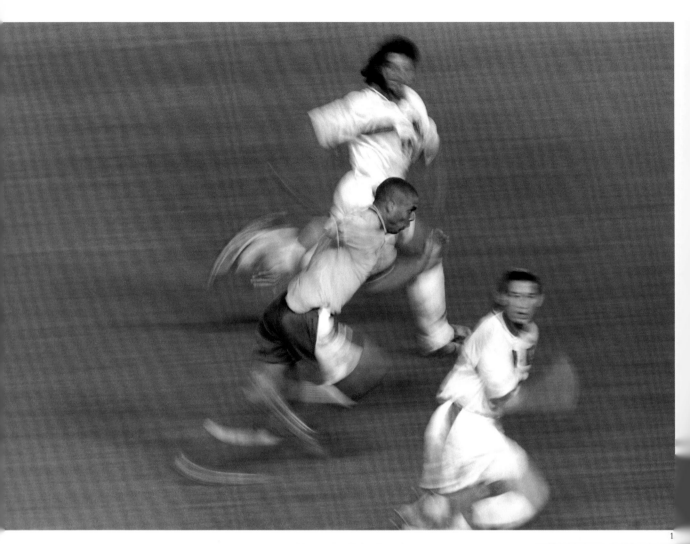

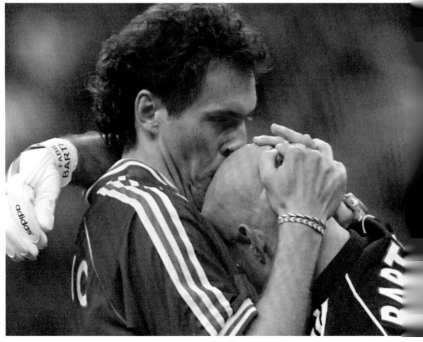

FOOTBALL'S World Cup was the dream of two Frenchmen, Jules Rimet and Henri Delaunay. The idea came to them in 1904, but they had to wait until 1930 before the first competition was held. Since then, each successive World Cup has produced bigger crowds, more excitement, and greater moments. The feet of a god… Diego Maradona of Argentina takes on more than half the Belgian team in a qualifying match in the World Cup, Spain, 1982 (3). The taste of victory… Jürgen Kohler, captain of West Germany, raises the World Cup after a penalty shoot-out gives his team victory over Argentina, Rome, 8 July 1990 (4). Ronaldo of Brazil (1) burns his way through the Moroccan defence in a qualifying match during the World Cup finals in Nantes, 16 June 1998. Brazil won 3-0. The Cup comes home… Laurent Blanc and Fabian Barthez celebrate French victory in the Final at the Stade de France, 12 July 1998 (2).

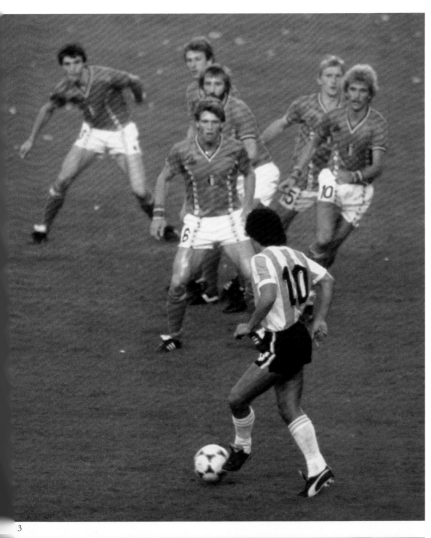

3

EINE Fußballweltmeisterschaft – das war der Traum zweier Franzosen: Jules Rimet und Henri Delaunay. Die Idee hatten sie bereits im Jahre 1904, doch mußten sie noch bis 1930 warten, bis die erste Weltmeisterschaft ausgetragen wurde. Seither hat jede Fußballweltmeisterschaft noch größere Menschenmengen angezogen, größere Aufregung verbreitet – und noch großartigere Sportmomente beschert. Die Füße eines Gottes: Argentiniens Diego Maradona nimmt es im Laufe eines Qualifikationsspiels zur Weltmeisterschaft in Spanien mit mehr als dem halben belgischen Team auf (3) – 1982. So schmeckt der Sieg: Jürgen Kohler, Kapitän der Mannschaft der Bundesrepublik, hebt den Weltmeisterschaftspokal, nachdem sein Team durch einen Strafstoß gegen Argentinien gewann (4) – Rom, 8. Juli 1990. Ronaldo aus Brasilien stürmt während eines Weltmeisterschafts-Qualifikationsendspiels durch die marokkanischen Verteidigungslinien – Nantes 16. Juni 1998; Brasilien gewann damals mit 3 zu 0. Der Pokal kommt nach Haus: Laurent Blanc und Fabian Barthez feiern den französischen Sieg im Endspiel (2) – im Stade de France, 12. Juli 1998.

UN championnat du monde de football – tel était le rêve de deux Français : Jules Rimet et Henri Delaunay. Ils avaient déjà eu cette idée en 1904, mais ils durent attendre jusqu'en 1930 pour pouvoir organiser la première Coupe du monde. Depuis, chaque championnat du monde de football draine un public toujours plus nombreux, suscite toujours plus d'émotions et donne lieu à des souvenirs sportifs encore plus remarquables. Les pieds d'un dieu : lors d'un match de qualification pour la Coupe du monde en Espagne, l'Argentin Diego Maradona dribble plus de la moitié de l'équipe de Belgique (3), en 1982. L'ivresse de la victoire : Jürgen Kohler, le capitaine de la Mannschaft de la République fédérale d'Allemagne, brandit la coupe du monde que son équipe vient de gagner après un penalty contre l'Argentine (4) – Rome, 8 juillet 1990. Au cours d'un match de qualification pour la Coupe du monde, Ronaldo, le Brésilien, fait éclater les lignes de défense marocaines – Nantes, 16 juin 1998 ; Le Brésil gagne alors par 3 à 0. La coupe rentre à la maison : Laurent Blanc et Fabien Barthez célèbrent la victoire de la France en finale (2) au Stade de France, le 12 juillet 1998.

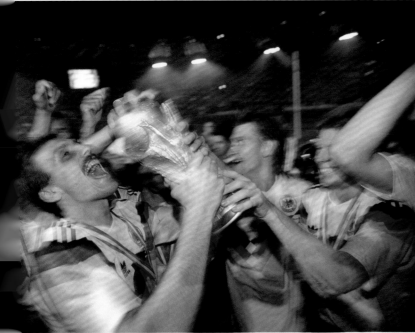

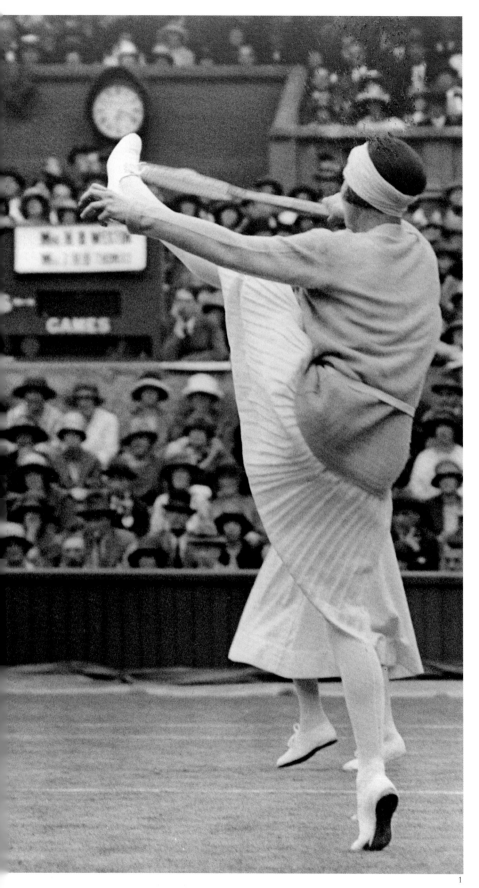

Suzanne Lenglen in play at the Wimbledon Lawn Tennis Championships, which she won in 1925 (1). Fred Perry, playing here in the men's semifinals in 1936, won the men's singles for the third year running (2). In 1975, US player Arthur Ashe made tennis history to become the first black Wimbledon champion (3). Björn Borg's double-handed grip served to confuse the opposition as to whether he was coming in for a forehand or backhand shot. Here he is in action against Yugoslav Nicky Pilic in 1977 (4). He was unbeaten at Wimbledon between 1976 and 1980. Martina Navratilova (5) went on to win the Wimbledon women's singles nine times before retiring in 1994 after missing the much sought-after tenth record-breaking triumph.

Suzanne Lenglen in voller Aktion beim Tennisturnier in Wimbledon, das sie im Jahre 1925 gewann (1). Fred Perry, hier im Halbfinale der Herren 1936, gewann den Pokal drei Jahre in Folge (2). 1975 machte der Amerikaner Arthur Ashe Tennisgeschichte als erster schwarzer Wimbledonsieger (3). Björn Borgs doppelhändiger Griff verwirrte den Gegner, der nie wußte, ob er Vor- oder Rückhand spielen würde. Hier sieht man ihn 1977 im Match gegen den Jugoslawen Nicky Pilic (4). Zwischen 1976 und 1980 konnte ihn keiner in Wimbledon schlagen. Martina Navratilova (5) gewann das Damen-Einzel neunmal; 1994 beendete sie ihre Karriere, nachdem ihr der zehnte Triumph, mit dem sie einen neuen Rekord aufgestellt hätte, nicht geglückt war.

Suzanne Lenglen, vainqueur au championnat de tennis à Wimbledon en 1925 (1). Fred Perry, qu'on voit ici disputer les demi-finales messieurs en 1936, remporta le simple messieurs pour la troisième année consécutive (2). En 1975, le joueur américain Arthur Ashe fut le premier champion Noir vainqueur à Wimbledon (3). Björn Borg, dont le jeu à deux mains désorientait ses adversaire. Le voici en action en 1977 contre le Yougoslave Nicky Pilic (4). Il resta invincible à Wimbledon de 1976 à 1980. Martina Navratilova (5) y remporta neuf fois le simple dames. Jusqu'à sa retraite, en 1994, elle ne parviendra pas à battre le record du monde en remportant la dixième victoire nécessaire.

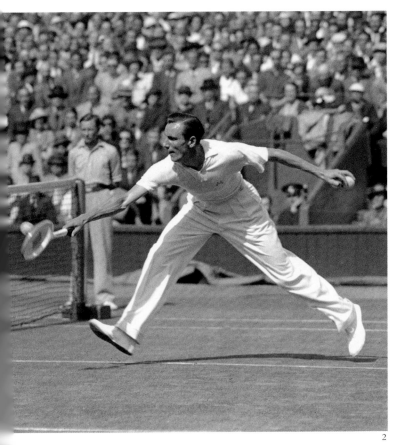

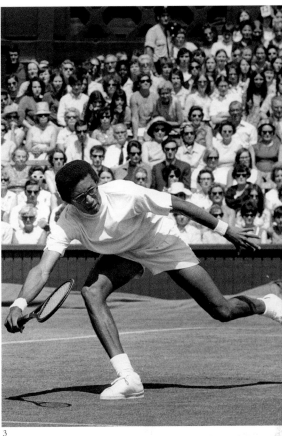

2 3

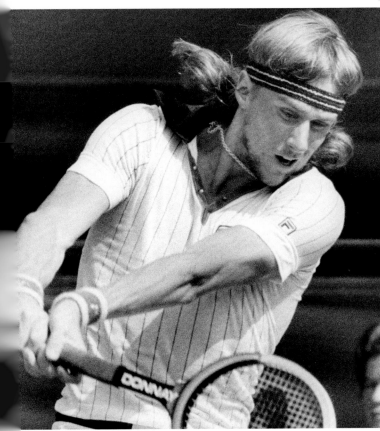

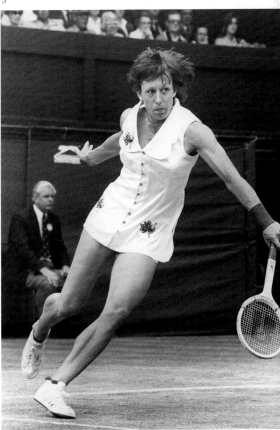

4 5

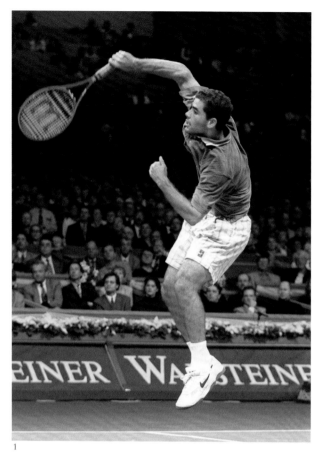

1

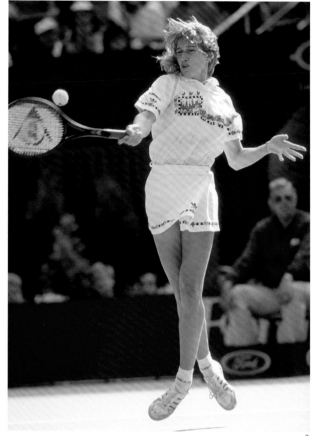

2

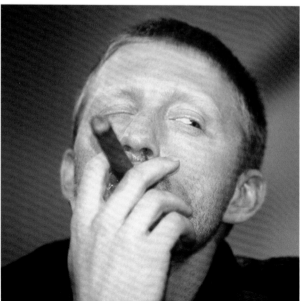

4

P OWER grace, agony and intense satisfaction – tennis at the highest level had it all. Pete Sampras (1) was the super-efficient champion in Hanover in 1996. Steffi Graf (2) combined balletic skills with speed and precision at Melbourne in 1989. Roger Federer (4) could not bear to lose a single point, let alone the match, when he was beaten by Andre Agassi in the US Masters at Key Biscaine, Florida in 2002. And Boris Becker (3) enjoyed every puff on his cigar when being interviewed in December 1995.

K RAFT, Anmut, Höllenqualen und äußerste Befriedigung – in seinen Höhepunkten bot Tennis all das. Pete Sampras war der Durchstarter und Sieger in Hannover im Jahre 1996 (1). Steffi Graf wußte ballerinenhafte Anmut mit Schnelligkeit und Präzision zu verbinden (2) – hier in Melbourne im Jahre 1989. Roger Federer hielt es nicht aus, auch nur einen Punkt in Rückstand zu geraten – geschweige denn, das Match gegen Andre Agassi bei den amerikanischen Meisterschaften in Key Biscaine zu verlieren (4) – Florida 2002. Und Boris Becker genoß jeden einzelnen Zug an seiner Zigarre (3) – während eines Interviews im Dezember 1995.

F ORCE, grâce, souffrances indicibles et satisfaction infinie – telles sont les multiples facettes du tennis à son apogée. Pete Sampras qui a fait une carrière météorique, gagne à Hanovre en 1996 (1). Steffi Graf restera célèbre pour son art de combiner la grâce d'une ballerine à la rapidité et à la précision (2) – ici à Melbourne en 1989. Roger Federer a horreur de perdre, ne serait-ce qu'un point – et a fortiori le match, comme ici contre André Agassi, lors du championnat des États-Unis à Key Biscaine (4) – Floride 2002. Et Boris Becker savoure chaque bouffée de son cigare (3) – pendant une interview en décembre 1995.

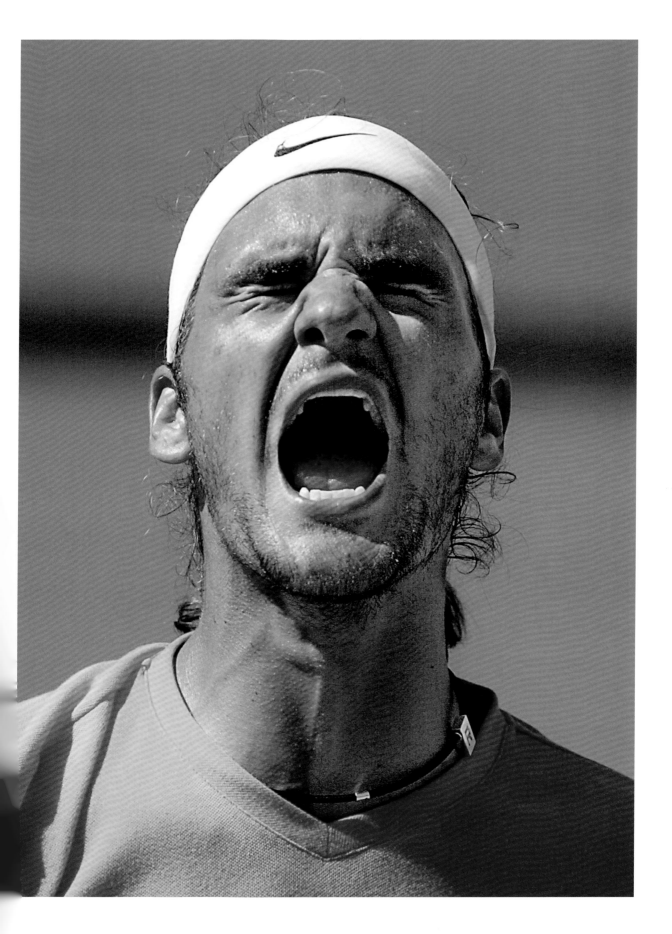

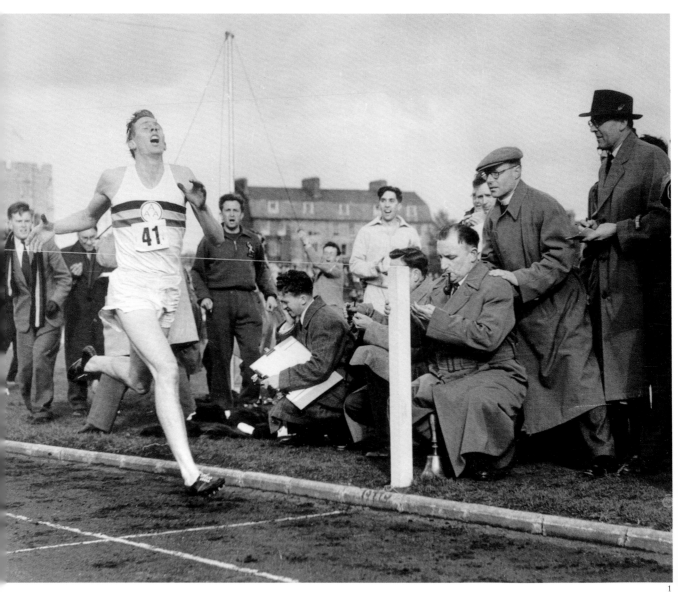

1

TRAINING, fitness, diet and sheer will-power led to an unending series of new world records across the board in athletics. One of the most famous was the first Four-Minute Mile, run by Roger Bannister on a wind-swept field at Iffley Road, Oxford on 6 May 1954 (1) – with just one cameraman (Norman Potter) present. There were plenty to witness Bob Beamon of the United States add 58 centimetres to the world Long Jump record at the Mexico City Olympic Games, 18 October 1968 (2).

TRAINING, Fitneß, Diät und pure Willenskraft führten zu einer Serie neuer Weltrekorde in zahlreichen leichtathletischen Disziplinen. Einer der berühmtesten war der erste Meilenlauf von vier Minuten, den Roger Bannister auf einem windigen Feld in Oxford, Iffley Road, am 6. Mai 1954 darbot (1) – nur ein einziger Photograph war damals dabei: Norman Potter. Weit mehr Zeugen hingegen hatte Bob Beamon aus den USA, als er bei den Olympischen Spielen in Mexico City 58 Zentimeter über den bisherigen Weltrekord im Weitsprung hinaus sprang (2) – 18. Oktober 1968.

ENTRAÎNEMENT, bonne forme physique, diététique et une volonté de performance absolue se traduisent par une série de nouveaux records du monde dans de nombreuses disciplines de l'athlétisme. L'un des moments les plus célèbres a été le premier mile couvert en moins de quatre minutes, record établi par Roger Bannister sur une piste battue par les vents à Oxford, Iffley Road, le 6 mai 1954 (1) – un seul et unique caméraman était présent ce jour-là : Norman Potter. L'Américain Bob Beamon, par contre, avait beaucoup plus de témoins quand, aux Jeux olympiques de Mexico City, il bat l'ancien record du monde de saut en longueur de pas moins de 58 cm (2) – 18 octobre 1968.

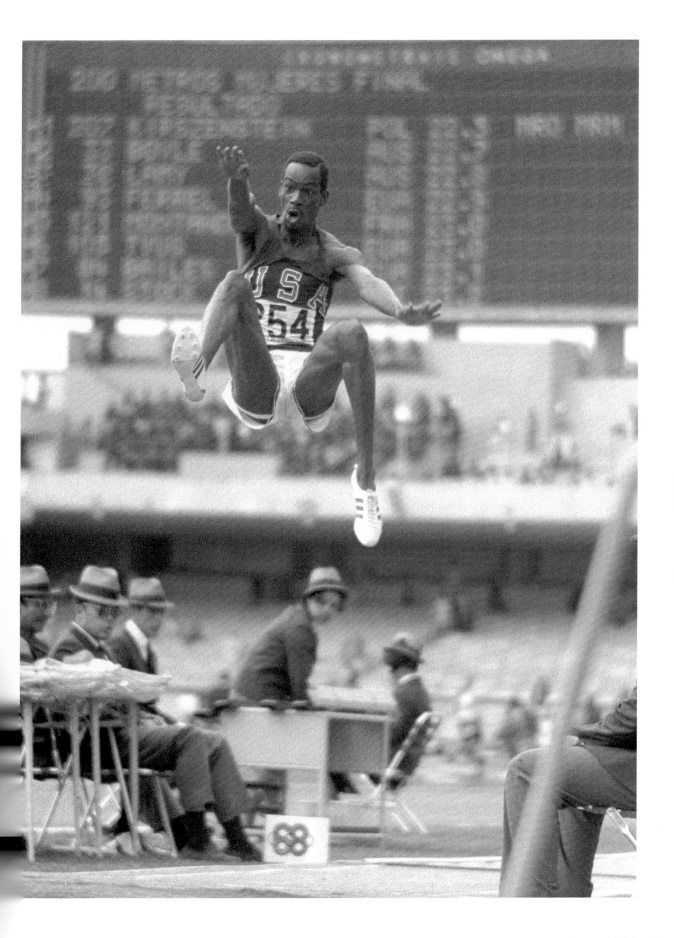

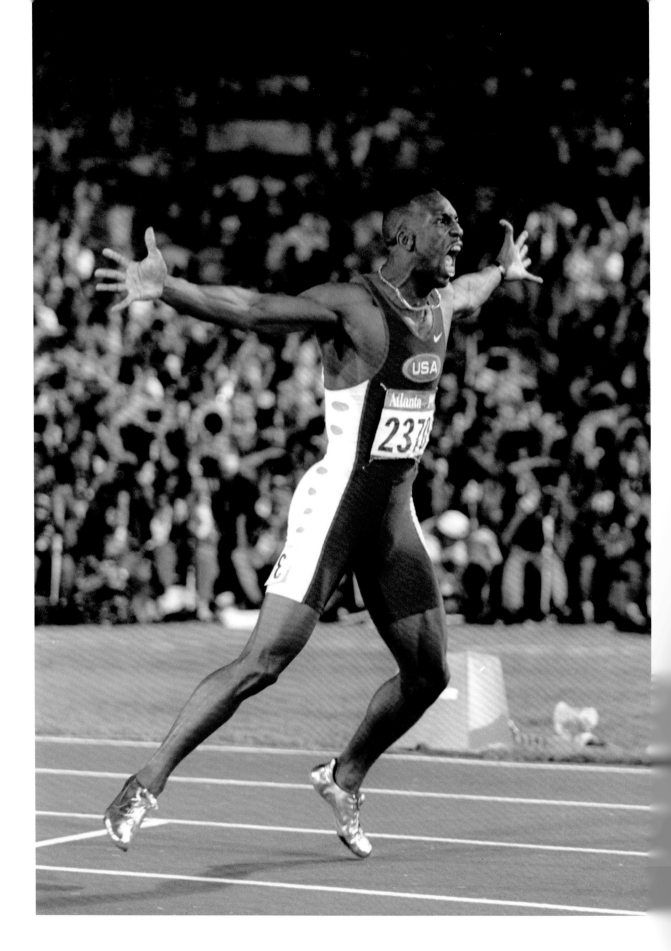

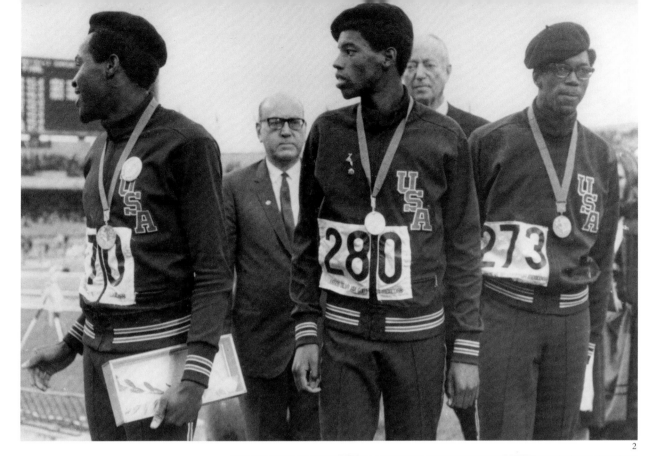

2

At the Olympics, the most important thing was not always the 'taking part'. For Michael Johnson at Atlanta, August 1996 (1), it was a new world record in the 200 metres. For Carl Lewis (3) in the 4 x 100 metre relay at Los Angeles in 1984, it was gold and another world record. For three 400-metre medal-winners at the Mexico City in 1968 (2), however, it was solidarity with Tommie Smith and John Carlos and their Black Power salute – (*left to right*) Lee Evans, Larry James and Ron Freeman.

Teilnahme« war bei den Olympischen Spielen das Entscheidende. Sie brachte Michael Johnson im August 1996 in Atlanta den neuen Weltrekord im 200-Meter-Lauf. Carl Lewis bescherte sie im Jahre 1984 in Los Angeles die Goldmedaille und einen neuen Weltrekord im Staffellauf über 4 x 100 Meter (3). Für drei Medaillengewinner beim 400-Meter-Lauf in Mexiko City im Jahre 1968 hingegen bedeutete die Teilnahme auch Solidarität mit Tommie Smith und John Carlos sowie ihr Gruß der Black Panther Bewegung: (*von links*) Lee Evans, Larry James und Ron Freeman (2).

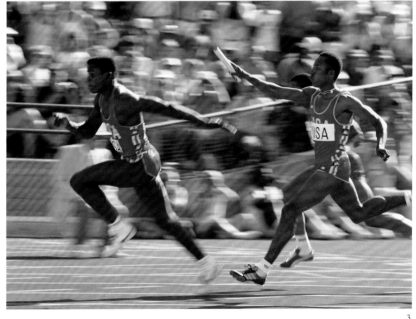

3

Juste participer est ce qui prime aux Jeux olympiques. Cela n'empêche pas moins Michael Johnson, en août 1996 à Atlanta, de battre le nouveau record du monde du 200 mètres. Et cela rapporte à Carl Lewis, en 1984 à Los Angeles, la médaille d'or et un nouveau record du monde en relais quatre fois cent mètres (3).

Pour les trois médaillés du 400 mètres de Mexico City, en 1968, la participation est, par contre, un moyen d'afficher leur solidarité avec Tommie Smith et John Carlos et de transmettre l'idée du mouvement des Black Panthers : (*à partir de la gauche*) Lee Evans, Larry James et Ron Freeman (2).

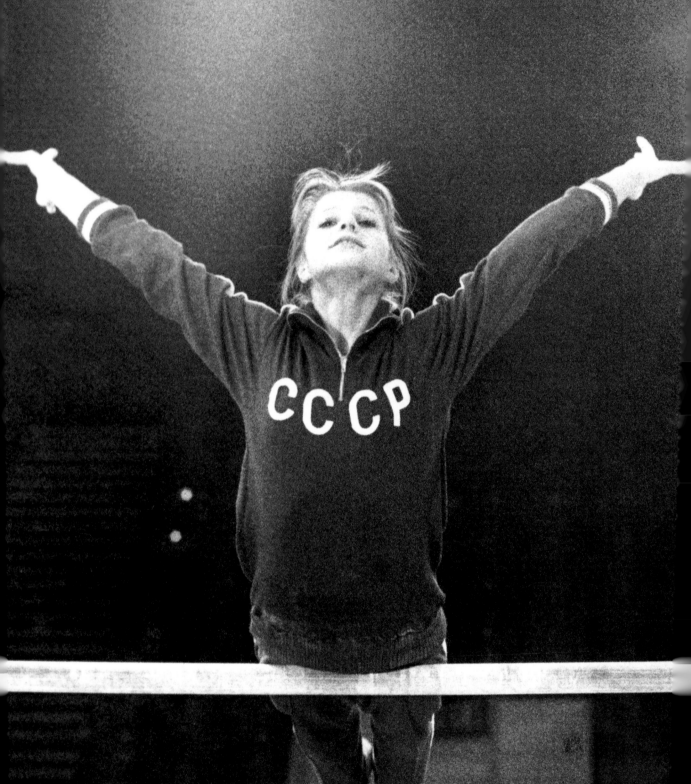

RUSSIAN Olga Korbut, aged 20 here in 1975, rehearsing for the World Gymnastics Championships (1), following her successes in the 1972 Olympic Games. A generation later, Anastasia Liukin of the USA goes through her paces on the Uneven Bars at the same championships in November 2005 in the Rod Laver Arena, Melbourne, Australia (2).

DIE Russin Olga Korbut, hier 1975 mit zwanzig Jahren (1), trainiert nach ihrem großen Erfolg bei den Olympischen Spielen für die Leichtathletik-Weltmeisterschaft. Eine Generation später absolviert im November 2005 Anastasia Liukin aus den USA bei denselben Meisterschaften in der Rod Laver Arena in Melbourne, Australien, ihren Parcours am Stufenbarren (2).

LA Russe Olga Korbut, alors âgée de vingt ans en 1975, se prépare ici aux championnats du monde d'athlétisme (1), après ses succès aux Jeux olympiques. Une génération plus tard, en novembre 2005, l'Américaine Anastasia Liukin accomplit son parcours aux barres asymétriques lors des championnats organisés à la Rod Laver Arena, à Melbourne, en Australie (2).

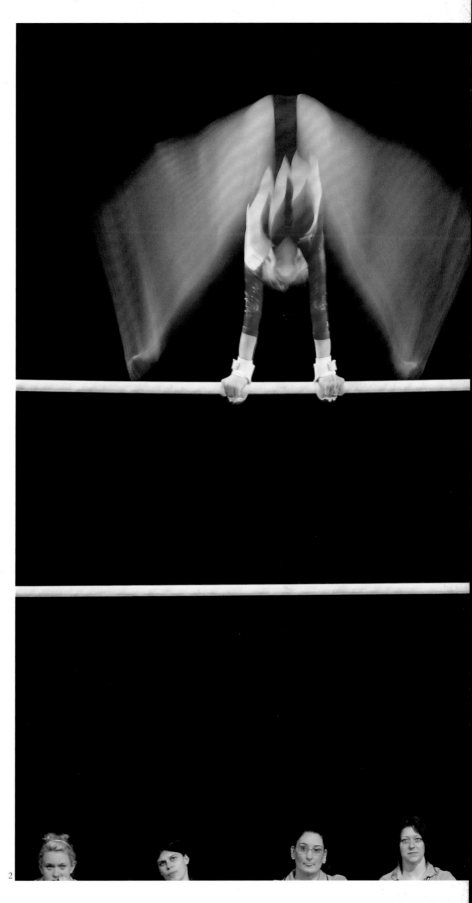

2

Mr and Mrs Joe Louis take a stroll in 1936 (1). The following year he won the World Heavey weight Championship, holding it until 1949, the longest reign ever. In July 1951, Sugar Ray Robinson was caught by photographer Bert Hardy, practicing at a gym in Paris shortly before his British match against Randolph Turpin (2). Robinson lost nine out of 15 rounds and needed 14 stitches over his eye. This US heavyweight is the only champion ever to win under two names – first as Cassius Clay in 1964, then, after his conversion to Islam, as Muhammed Ali ten years later. He never missed an opportunity to say that he was the 'greatest' – and he probably was. In May 1965 he KO'd Sonny Liston in the first round at Lewiston, Maine (3). Mike Tyson's mouth was as big as Ali's but used to more brutal effect when he bit Evander Holyfield's ear (4) in their title fight on 28 June 1997.

Mr. Joe Louis und Gattin machen einen Spaziergang, 1936 (1). Im folgenden Jahr wurde Joe Louis Weltmeister im Schwergewicht und hielt diesen Titel bis 1949, länger als jeder andere. Der Photograph Bert Hardy hielt Sugar Ray Robinson im Juli 1951 beim Training in einer Pariser Sporthalle fest, kurz vor seinem Kampf gegen Randolf Turpin in England (2). Robinson verlor neun von fünfzehn Runden und mußte über dem Auge mit vierzehn Stichen genäht werden. Dieser amerikanische Schwergewichtler ist der einzige Champion, der unter zwei verschiedenen Namen den Titel gewann: zuerst 1964 als Cassius Clay, und dann, nach seiner Bekehrung zum Islam, zehn Jahre später als Muhammed Ali. Er ließ nie eine Gelegenheit aus zu verkünden, daß er der Größte aller Zeiten sei – und wahrscheinlich war er das tatsächlich. Im Mai 1965 schlug er Sonny Liston in Lewiston, Maine, in der ersten Runde k.o. (3). Mike Tysons

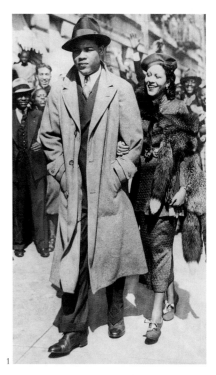

1

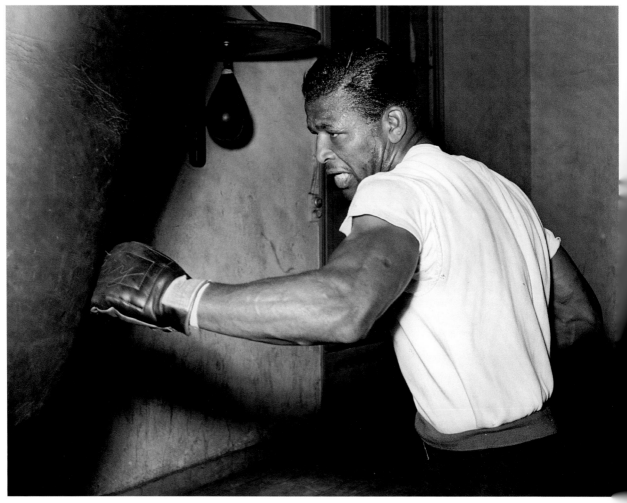

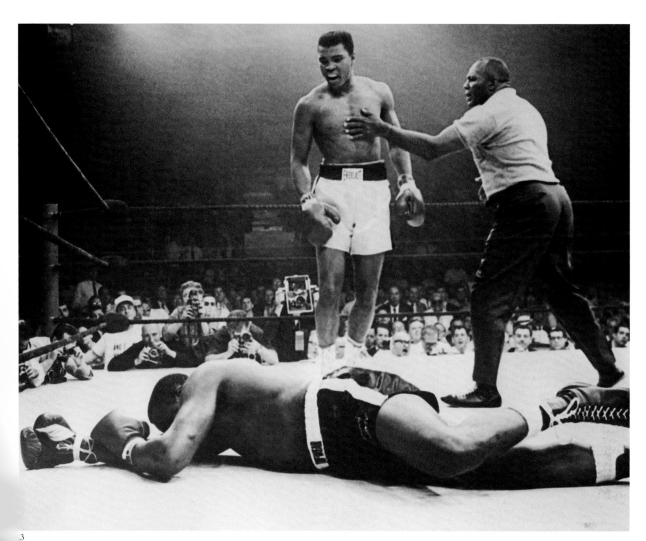

3

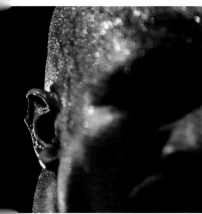

Eₙ 1936 se promènent Mme et M. Joe Louis (1). Il remportait l'année suivante le championnat du monde des poids lourds pour conserver son titre jusqu'en 1949, un record en matière de longévité. En juillet 1951, Sugar Ray Robinson est surpris par le photographe Bert Hardy tandis qu'il s'entraîne dans une salle de gymnastique parisienne peu de temps avant le match qui doit l'opposer à Randolf Turpin (2). Robinson perdit neuf rounds sur quinze et dut recevoir quatorze points de suture à l'arcade sourcilière. Ce poids lourd américain est le seul champion à avoir remporté la victoire sous deux noms : d'abord en tant que Cassius Clay en 1964, puis, dix ans plus tard, après sa conversion à l'Islam, sous celui de Mohammed Ali. Il ne perdait jamais une occasion de répéter qu'il était le plus grand champion de tous les temps, ce qui était probablement vrai.

En mai 1965, il met KO Sonny Liston à Lewiston, dans le Maine, lors du premier round (3). La bouche de Mike Tyson était au moins aussi grande que celle de Mohammed Ali, mais lui l'utilisa avec une brutalité sans précédent quand, lors de son combat contre Evander Holyfield, le 28 juin 1997, il le mordit et lui arracha l'oreille droite (4).

...und war mindestens so groß wie ...uhammed Alis; er benutzte ihn jedoch ...eitaus brutaler, als er im Titelkampf gegen ...vander Holyfield am 28. Juni 1997 dessen ...chtes Ohr abbiß (4).

THE mass appeal of sport in the age of television was often the product of the medium itself. By the end of the 20th century, television was bringing the top games, championships, World Cup competitions and Olympic Games into hundreds of millions of homes across the world. In terms of popularity, some sports were made by TV coverage, among them snooker, darts, bowling, and motocross. Basketball had long been a hugely popular sport in the United States, television took it to the far corners of the globe. Purists often moaned – the game wasn't the same, commercialism had ruined it, all people wanted were highlights, the new audience didn't appreciate the finer points, etc. It didn't matter. More people played and more people watched than ever before. And even those ignorant of the finer points would have appreciated the duel between Hakeem Olajuwon of the Houston Rockets and Shaquille O'Neal of Orlando Magic at The Summit, Houston, 14 June 1995 (1).

DIE Anziehungskraft, die der Sport im Fernsehzeitalter auf die Massen ausübte, war nicht selten ein Produkt des Mediums selbst. Am Ende des 20. Jahrhunderts brachte das Fernsehen Spitzenspiele, Meisterschaften und Weltmeisterschaften sowie Olympische Spiele Millionen von Zuschauern rund um den Globus direkt ins Haus. Was die Popularität betraf, so erzielten manche Sportarten diese vor allem durch ständige Fernsehübertragungen – dazu gehörten Snooker, Darts, Bowling und MotoCrossing. Basketball – in den USA seit langem eine äußerst populäre Sportart – wurde mit Hilfe des Fernsehens bis in die letzten Winkel der Erde übertragen. Puristen klagten, das Spiel sei nicht mehr dasselbe, der Kommerz habe alles ruiniert; alles, was die Leute sehen wollten, seien die Höhepunkte eines Spiels und das neue Publikum habe keinen Sinn für die leiseren Momente usw. Doch das tat dem Basketballsport keinen Abbruch: Immer mehr Menschen spielten – und mehr Menschen als je zuvor sahen dabei zu. Doch selbst, wer gegenüber den leiseren Momenten des Spiels eher ignorant blieb, genoß das Duell zwischen Hakeem Olajuwon von den Houston Rockets und Shaquille O'Neal von Orlando Magic beim Entscheidungsspiel am 14. Juni 1995 in Houston (1).

IL n'est pas rare que l'attrait exercé par le sport à l'ère de la télévision soit un produit du médium lui-même. À la fin du XXᵉ siècle, la télévision fait entrer directement au domicile de dizaines de millions de téléspectateurs du monde entier les plus grandes rencontres sportives, les championnats et les Coupes du monde ainsi que les Jeux olympiques. En termes de popularité, cela permet ainsi à certaines disciplines sportives de s'imposer surtout grâce aux retransmissions télévisées permanentes – ce qui est le cas du snooker, du billard, des fléchettes, du bowling et du motocross. Par le biais de la télévision, le basket-ball – depuis longtemps un sport extrêmement populaire aux États-Unis – est retransmis jusqu'aux coins les plus éloignés de la planète. Les puristes se plaignent que le jeu n'est plus le même, que le commerce a tout ruiné ; tout ce que les gens veulent voir, disent-ils, ce sont les temps forts d'un match, et ce nouveau public n'aurait aucun penchant pour les moments moins médiatiques. Or cela ne porte en rien préjudice au basket : de plus en plus de gens se mettent à y jouer – et de plus en plus de gens qu'auparavant, à le regarder. Mais même celui qui reste hermétique aux moments les plus intimistes d'un match saura apprécier le duel entre Hakeem Olajuwon, des Houston Rockets, et Shaquille O'Neal, d'Orlando Magic, lors du match décisif du 14 juin 1995 à Houston (1).

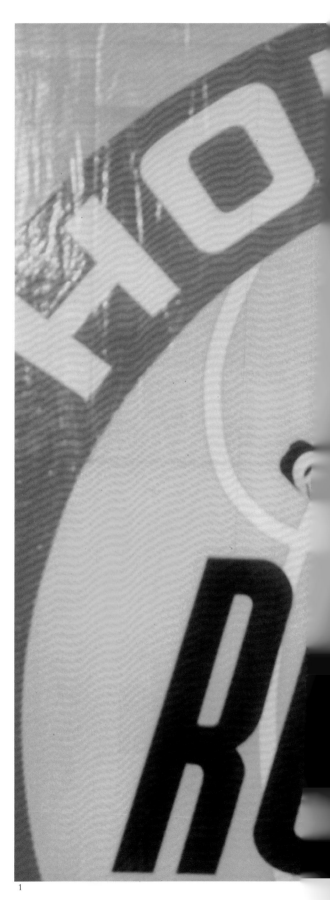

1

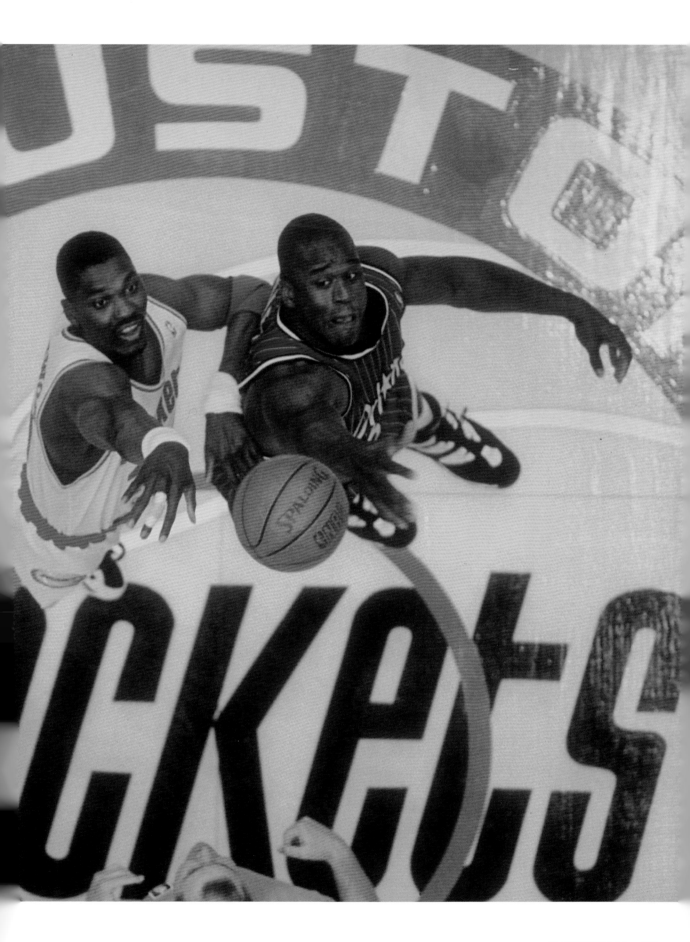

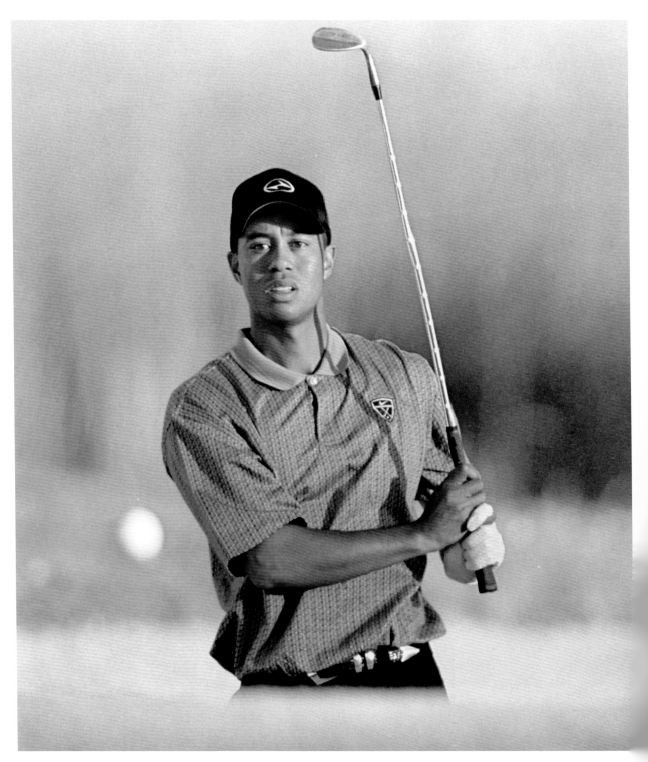

KEEPING their eyes on the ball... Tiger Woods chips from a bunker at the 12th in the 'Showdown at Sherwood', 2 August 1999 (1). Jonty Rhodes hangs on in the One-Day International against England, Edgbaston, 1998 (2).

IMMER den Ball im Auge behalten: Tiger Woods schlägt beim Finale in Sherwood den Ball bei der 12 in den Bunker (1) – 2. August 1999. Jonty Rhodes hält den Ball beim Internationalen Cricketturnier gegen England (2) – Edgbaston 1998.

NE jamais perdre la balle du regard : lors de la finale à Sherwood, Tiger Woods envoie la balle dans le bunker au 12ème trou (1) – 2 août 1999. Jonty Rhodes attrape la balle lors du tournoi international de cricket contre l'Angleterre (2) – Edgbaston, 1998.

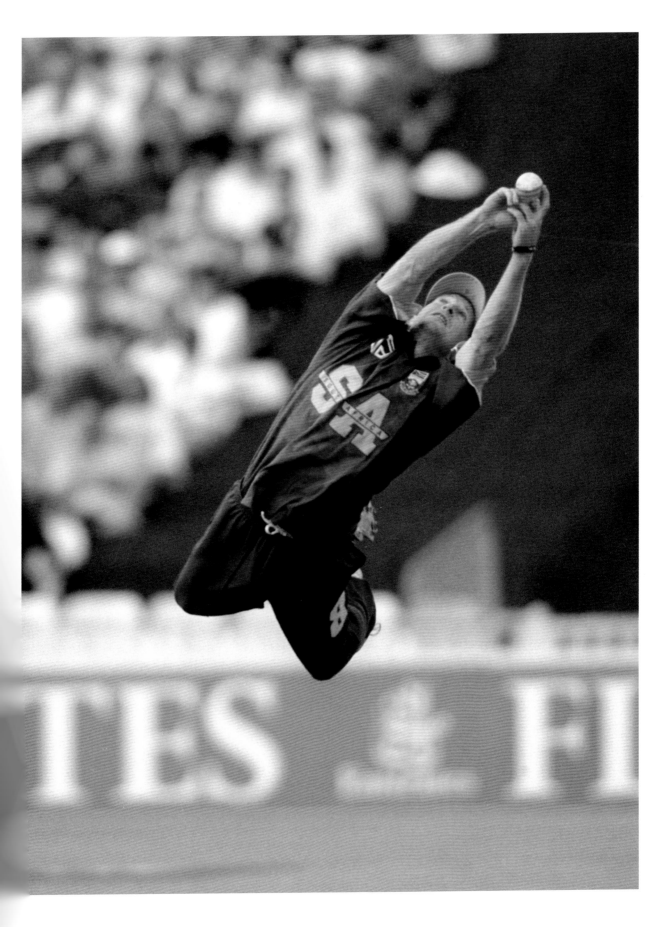

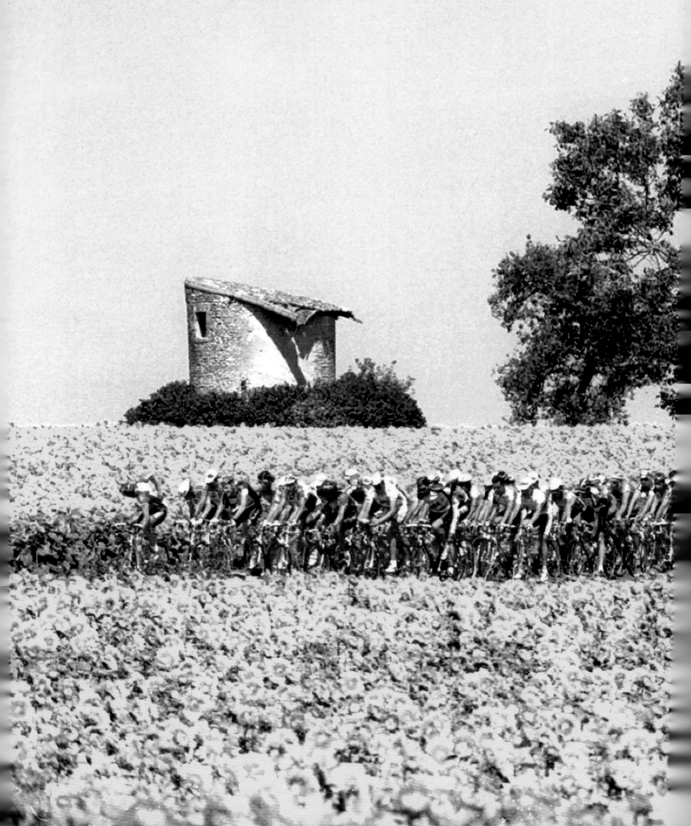

PARTICIPANTS on the eighth stage of the *Tour de France* speed between fields of sunflowers near Poitiers, 10 July 1994.

TEILNEHMER der achten Etappe der *Tour de France* spurten in der Nähe von Poitiers zwischen Sonnenblumenfeldern hindurch – 10. Juli 1994.

LES coureurs de la huitième étape du Tour de France défilent entre les champs de tournesols près de Poitiers – 10 juillet 1994.

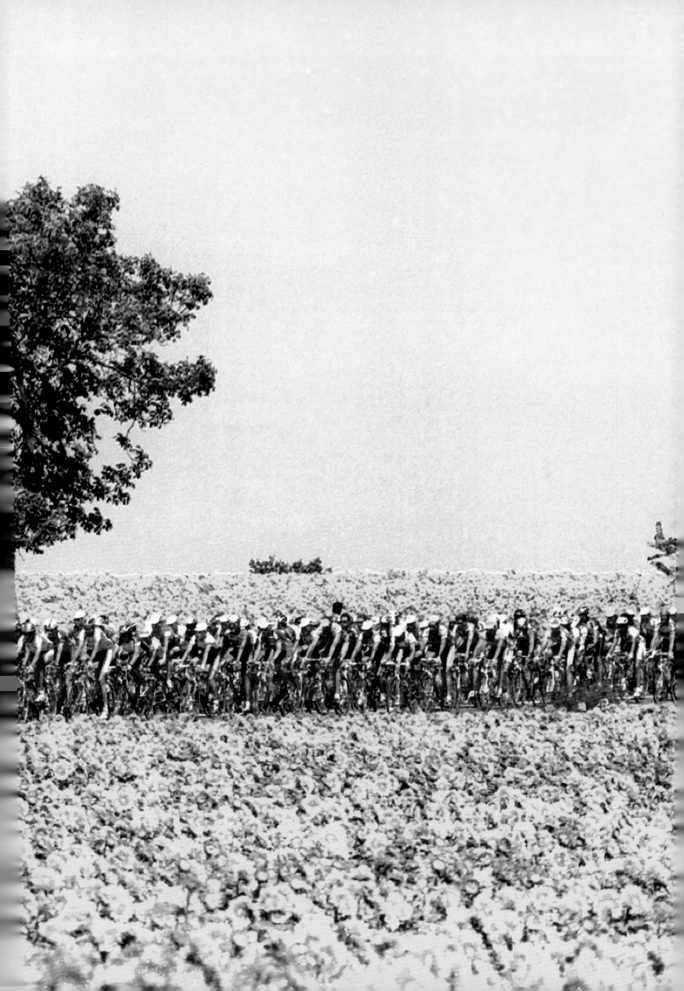

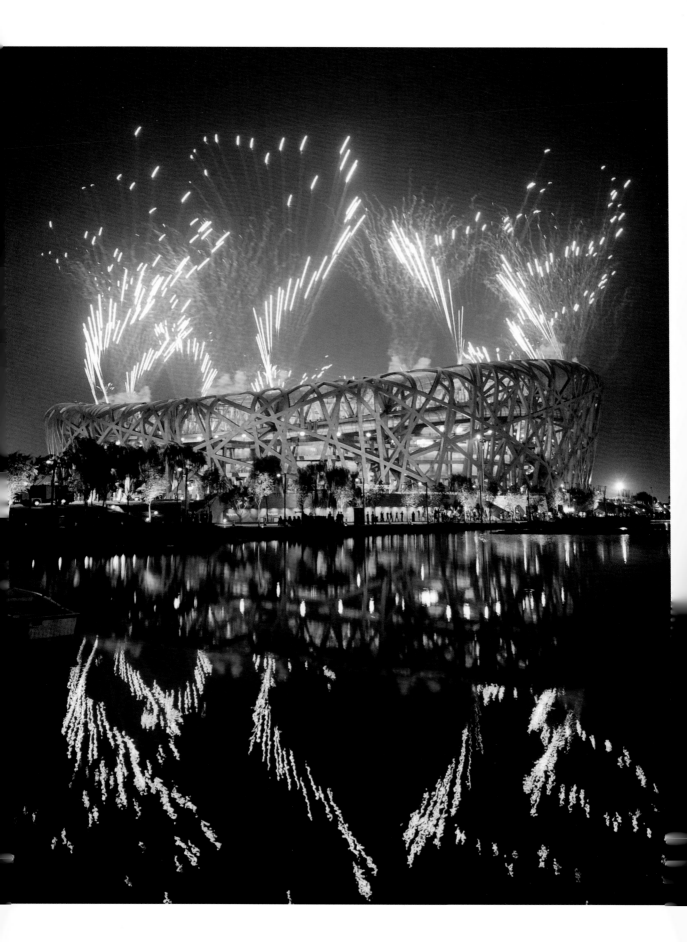

THE BEIJING OLYMPIC GAMES were always planned as a showcase for China, host nation and rapidly becoming one of the most powerful economies in the world, and from start to finish, the Games lived up to expectations. The Olympic party comes to an end as a massive display of fireworks lights up the sky above the Birds Nest, the Beijing National Stadium, during the closing ceremony to mark the end of the Beijing Olympic Games, 24 August 2008 (1). A stunning reflection of Michael Phelps on his way to winning the Men's 200 Metre Butterfly Final at the national Aquatics Centre on 13 August 2008 (2). It was one of eight gold medals won by Phelps at the Games. The Squat of Triumph… Jamaican sprinter Usain Bolt enjoys the aftermath of his sensational gold medal performance in the Final of the Men's 200 Metres at Beijing, 20 August 2008 (3). His time of 19.30 seconds was a new World Record.

DIE OLYMPISCHEN SPIELE waren schon immer als Vorzeigeprojekt des Gastgeberlandes China geplant, das rasch zu einer der mächtigsten Wirtschaftsnationen der Welt wurde, und die Erwartungen wurden nicht enttäuscht. Die olympische Party neigt sich dem Ende zu, mit einem großen Feuerwerk über dem »Vogelnest«, dem Nationalstadion in Peking, während der Abschlußzeremonie, 24. August 2008 (1). Eine verblüffende Spiegelung des US-Schwimmers Michael Phelps, der am 13. August 2008 im nationalen Schwimmzentrum gerade dabei ist, das Finale der Herren über 200 Meter Schmetterling zu gewinnen (2), eine der acht Goldmedaillen, die er in Peking holte. Die Kniebeuge des Triumphs: Der jamaikanische Sprintstar Usain Bolt genießt den Nachklang seines sensationellen Gold-Rennens im 200-Meter-Finale der Herren in Peking am 20. August 2008 (3). Mit 19.30 Sekunden lief er einen neuen Weltrekord.

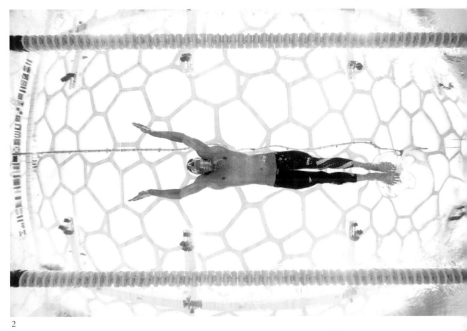

2

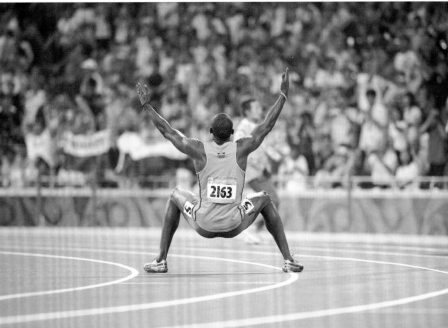

3

LES JEUX OLYMPIQUES de Pékin n'eurent d'autre objectif que d'offrir une vitrine à la Chine, nation organisatrice, rapidement devenue l'une des plus puissantes économies au monde. Du début à la fin, les Jeux se montrèrent à la hauteur de cette attente. Le 24 août 2008, la cérémonie de clôture des Jeux olympiques de Pékin s'accompagne d'un impressionnant spectacle pyrotechnique embrasant le ciel au-dessus du stade national de Pékin, surnommé le « nid d'oiseau » (1). Un instantané étonnant, montrant Michael Phelps en plein effort, s'apprêtant à remporter la finale du 200 m papillon masculin, dans le bassin du centre national de natation de Pékin, le 13 août 2008 (2). Une des huit médailles d'or remportées par Phelps lors de ces Jeux. La posture du triomphe… Le sprinteur jamaïcain Usain Bolt savoure son extraordinaire performance lors de la finale du 200 m masculin à Pékin, le 20 août 2008 (3). Avec un temps de 19''30 il établissait un nouveau record du monde.

The 1980s and 1990s

AT TIMES, it seemed the world was holding a closing-down sale, with the slogan 'Everything must go' – the Soviet Empire, the Berlin Wall, apartheid, socialism, old fashioned notions of liberty and democracy, religious toleration, prudent banking methods, the theory of evolution, the Playboy Club, the traditional roles of men and women, and a great deal more. In this restlessness, there were exciting new marriages and courtships: between black and white in South Africa; between North and South Korea; between France and Britain in the Channel Tunnel; and between East and West Germany. At the same time, there were terrifying divorces and family feuds. The old Yugoslavia blew itself apart. Civil wars that divided the Lebanon, Afghanistan, Zimbabwe, Angola and the Sudan. Street-fighting created a ghost town in Grozny, capital of Chechnya.

While traffic clogged the world's motorways, information raced along the super-cyber highways, creating an internet community that it was impossible to police. The mobile phone brought feelings of greater security to women and children, and banal conversation to every train and bus in the developed world. With the appropriate gadget, it became possible to slip an entire library of books, CDs and films into one's pocket. With a slim laptop, it eventually became compulsory to work as many hours a day as galley slaves and pyramid builders of old.

There were gluts of oil, lakes of wine, mountains of butter, and entire countries of famine. The gap widened between rich and poor, or as they were now called: the haves and have-nots. There were Yuppies and Nimbies and Dinkies – discernible sub-groups among the upwardly mobile Bright-Young-Things.

Supermarkets began to sell Fairtrade tea and coffee, presupposing that there must therefore be such a thing as un-Fairtrade tea and coffee. People marched and shouted, and sacrificed their lives in support of animal welfare and human rights. Laboratories and operating theatres performed new miracles – cloning a sheep and transplanting the heart of a baboon into a human being. In Poland, a trade unionist became a national hero. Wonders would never cease.

The dance went on and on. Hip-hop dancers did it on their hands and heads. The good times rolled over and over. Markets crashed and markets recovered. There were more people with more money than the world had ever known. In Europe and North America new golf courses gulped down supplies of water – not yet considered an endangered resource. Cars and boats and private jets burnt up vast quantities of oil – already considered a commodity worth sending young men and women to fight and die for.

But the belief was growing among some that a terrifying end might be in sight. 'Pollution' became an increasingly sinister word. Around the coastlines of the world, the sea was throwing up crude and unpleasant flotsam. Dust and smog and plain bad air choked the centres of many great cities. The major sources of power, including the dear old Sun, all posed a threat to human health and the environment – as the disaster at Chernobyl so dreadfully revealed. Forward thinkers suggested turning to renewable sources of energy – notably wind and wave – but many in authority answered that there really wasn't time to become involved in such things.

And time itself became a priceless commodity in its own right.

AN UNNAMED RESCUER RACES TO SAVE A BABY'S LIFE IN THE
CHRISTIAN QUARTER OF BEIRUT, 22 MAY 1985.

EIN UNBEKANNTER RETTER RENNT UM DAS LEBEN EINES BABYS
IM CHRISTLICHEN VIERTEL IN BEIRUT – 22. MAI 1985.

UN INCONNU COURT POUR SAUVER LA VIE D'UN BÉBÉ DANS LE
QUARTIER CHRÉTIEN DE BEYROUTH – 22 MAI 1985.

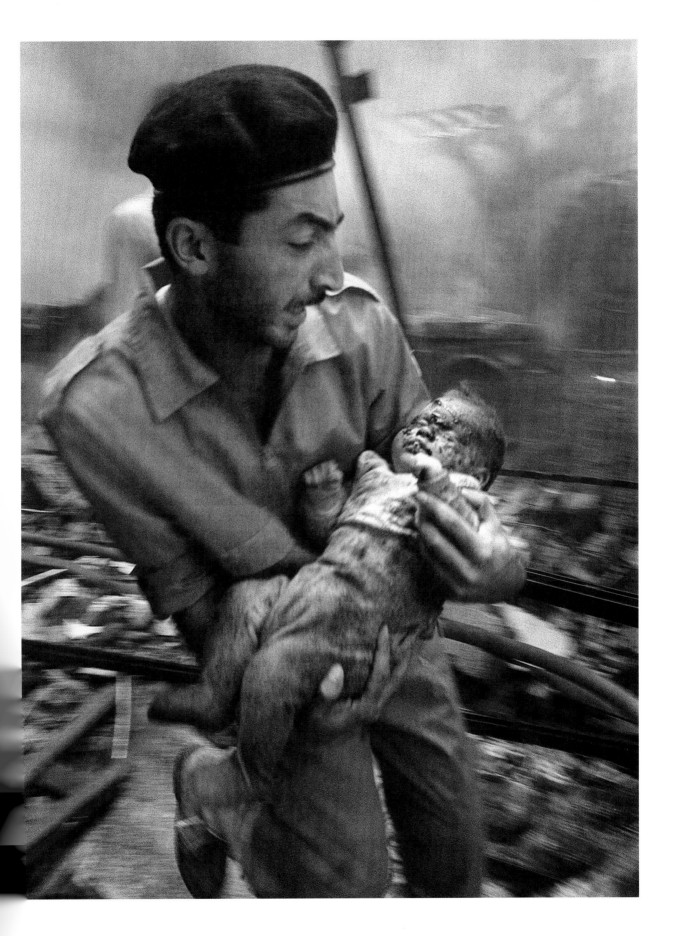

Es gab Zeiten, da schien die Welt einen totalen Ausverkauf abzuhalten, unter dem Motto »Alles muß raus« – das sowjetische Imperium, die Berliner Mauer, die Apartheid, der Sozialismus, das traditionelle Verständnis von Freiheit und Demokratie, religiöse Toleranz, besonnene Bankgeschäfte, die Theorie der Evolution, der Playboy-Club, die traditionellen Geschlechterrollen und vieles mehr. Diese unruhigen Zeiten ermöglichten aber auch eine Reihe aufregender Flirts und Ehen: zwischen Schwarzen und Weißen in Südafrika, zwischen Nord- und Südkorea, zwischen Frankreich und England im Tunnel durch den Ärmelkanal ... und zwischen Ost- und Westdeutschland. Zugleich gab es jede Menge furchterregende Scheidungen und Familienkriege: Das ehemalige Jugoslawien brach auseinander; Bürgerkriege zerrissen die Länder Libanon, Afghanistan, Zimbabwe, Angola und Sudan; Straßenkämpfe verwandelten Grosny, die Hauptstadt Tschetscheniens, in eine Geisterstadt.

Während der Verkehr überall in der Welt die Autobahnen verstopfte, rasten Informationen über Datenbahnen durchs weltweite Netz und schufen eine Internetgemeinschaft, die nicht mehr zu kontrollieren war. Das mobile Telefon brachte Frauen und Kindern ein Gefühl größerer Sicherheit – und banale Gespräche in jeden Bus und jede U-Bahn der westlichen Welt. Mit entsprechenden Geräten ließen sich ganze Bibliotheken von Büchern, CDs oder Filmen in der Hosentasche verstauen, und mit einem schlanken Laptop konnte man bald nicht anders als möglichst viele Stunden am Tag zu arbeiten – nicht anders als Galeerensklaven und die Pyramidenarbeiter der alten Welt.

Es gab Ölschwemmen, Weinfluten, Butterberge, und ganze Länder verhungerten. Die Kluft zwischen Arm und Reich (oder zwischen Wohlhabenden und Habenichts, wie sie jetzt genannt wurden) wurde immer größer. Und da waren die Yuppies und die Nimbies (Akronym für engl. »nicht in meinem Garten!« und die Dinkies (Akronym für engl. »Doppelverdiener ohne Kinder«) – erkennbare Untergruppen der aufstrebenden und mobilen strahlenden Jugend.

Supermärkte begannen, sogenannte Fairtrade-Produkte, wie Tee und Kaffee, zu verkaufen – damit wurde vorausgesetzt, daß es folglich auch »unfair« gehandelte Waren gab. Menschen demonstrierten und skandierten Losungen gegen Tierversuche und für Menschenrechte – und opferten dafür sogar ihr Leben. In Laboratorien und Operationssälen wurden Wunder vollbracht – wie das Klonen eines Schafes und die Transplantation eines Affenherzes in einen Menschen. In Polen wurde ein Gewerkschafter zum Nationalheld. Wunder gab es immer wieder.

Und es wurde in vollem Schwung weiter getanzt. Hip-Hopper tanzten auf Händen und Köpfen. Märkte brachen zusammen und erholten sich wieder. Es gab mehr Menschen mit mehr Geld als jemals zuvor. In Europa und Nordamerika schluckten neu angelegte Golfplätze jede Menge Wasser, das noch nicht als gefährdeter Rohstoff erkannt war. Autos, Boote und private Flugzeuge verbrannten Unmengen von Benzin – als Rohstoff, für den junge Männer und Frauen in den Kampf und in den Tod geschickt wurden, war das Öl durchaus bereits bekannt.

Unter einigen jedoch wuchs das Unbehagen, das alles könnte ein schreckliches Ende nehmen. »Verschmutzung« wurde zur zunehmend unheilvollen Vokabel. Entlang der Küsten der Welt warf das Meer rohes und häßliches Treibgut an Land. Staub, Smog und schlicht schlechte Luft erstickten das Zentrum so mancher Metropole. Alle wichtigen Energiequellen, einschließlich der guten alten Sonne, bedrohten die Gesundheit von Mensch und Umwelt – wie die Katastrophe von Tschernobyl auf schreckliche Weise demonstrierte. Zukunftsorientierte schlugen vor, sich erneuerbaren Energien zuzuwenden, allen voran Wind und Wellen; doch viele von denen, die das Sagen hatten, reagierten darauf mit Abwehr: Man habe wirklich keine Zeit, sich mit so etwas zu beschäftigen!

So wurde die Zeit selbst zu einem unschätzbar wertvollen Gut.

CERTAINES époques nous ont donné l'impression que le monde entier était en solde selon la devise « Tout doit partir ! » – l'empire soviétique, le Mur de Berlin, l'apartheid, le socialisme, les notions démodées de liberté et de démocratie, la tolérance religieuse, les méthodes bancaires guidées par la prudence, la théorie de l'évolution, le Playboy Club, les rôles traditionnels joués par l'homme et la femme, et bien d'autres choses encore, mais cette époque d'une grande fébrilité a aussi permis toute une série de flirts et de mariages excitants : entre Noirs et Blancs en Afrique du Sud, entre Corée du Nord et Corée du Sud, entre France et Angleterre avec le tunnel sous la Manche ... et entre Allemagne de l'Est et Allemagne de l'Ouest. Simultanément, nous avons assisté à d'horribles divorces et guerres intestines : l'ancienne Yougoslavie s'est effondrée tel un château de cartes ; des guerres civiles ont déchiré des pays comme le Liban, l'Afghanistan, le Zimbabwe, l'Angola et le Soudan ; les combats de rue ont transformé Grosny, la capitale de la Tchétchénie, en une ville fantôme.

Alors que le trafic engorgeait les autoroutes du monde entier, les informations circulaient à la vitesse de l'éclair sur les autoroutes des données grâce aux réseaux planétaires, créant une communauté d'internautes qui échappa désormais à tout contrôle. Le téléphone mobile a donné aux femmes et aux enfants un sentiment de plus grande sécurité – nous faisant participer à des conversations banales dans tous les bus et métros du monde développé. Avec l'appareil correspondant, on pouvait désormais transporter avec soi des bibliothèques entières de livres, CD ou films et, avec un mince ordinateur portable, rien ne nous empêcha désormais de travailler le plus grand nombre possible d'heures chaque jour – dignes descendants des esclaves ramant dans les galères et des ouvriers élevant les pyramides en Égypte.

Nous avons vu défiler des raz-de-marée de pétrole, inondations de vin et montagnes de beurre alors même que la famine sévissait dans de nombreux pays. Le fossé entre pauvres et riches (ou entre nantis et va-nu-pieds, comme on les appelait désormais), ne cessa de se creuser. Puis ce fut l'ère des yuppies, nimbies (acronyme anglais signifiant « Pas dans ma cour ! ») et autres dinkies (acronyme également anglais, pour « couple actif sans enfants ») – sous-groupes aisément identifiables d'une jeunesse ambitieuse et mobile à l'avenir rayonnant.

Les superettes ont commencé à vendre des produits qualifiés de « Fairtrade », par exemple le thé et du café – sous-entendant par là qu'il y avait aussi, logiquement, des marchandises méritant le qualificatif de « non équitable ». La population descendit dans la rue, scandant des slogans contre les essais sur les animaux et pour les droits de l'homme – offrant même leur vie pour cela. Dans des laboratoires et salles d'opérations, on réalisait des miracles – par exemple le clonage d'un mouton et la transplantation d'un coeur de singe dans un être humain. En Pologne, un syndicaliste est devenu héro national. Des miracles se sont reproduits avec une étonnante régularité.

Et l'on continua de danser sans perdre son élan. Les fans du hip-hop dansaient sur les mains et la tête. Les marchés s'effondraient et se redressaient. Il y avait plus d'êtres humains avec plus d'argent que jamais auparavant. En Europe et en Amérique du Nord, des terrains de golf flambant neufs gaspillaient l'eau, que l'on ne considérait pas encore comme une matière première en danger. Automobiles, bateaux et avions privés brûlaient des quantités stupéfiantes d'essence et de kérosène – le pétrole était déjà parfaitement connu comme matière première pour laquelle de jeunes hommes et femmes furent envoyés au combat et à la mort.

Parmi ceux-ci, certains commencèrent à avoir mauvaise conscience que tout cela pourrait se terminer dans l'horreur. « Pollution » devint un vocable de plus en plus funeste. Le long des côtes du monde entier, la mer rejeta des cadavres et épaves hideux. Poussière, smog et air nauséabond étouffaient le centre de maintes métropoles. Toutes les sources d'énergie importantes, y compris notre bon vieux soleil, commencèrent à menacer la santé de l'homme et l'environnement – comme la catastrophe de Tchernobyl l'a prouvé de façon effarante. Les futurologues proposèrent que l'on se consacrât aux énergies renouvelables, en tout premier lieu au vent et aux vagues ; mais beaucoup parmi ceux qui en avaient le pouvoir réagirent par la négative : avait-on vraiment le temps de s'occuper de telles balivernes ?

Ainsi, le temps lui-même est-il devenu un bien précieux inestimable.

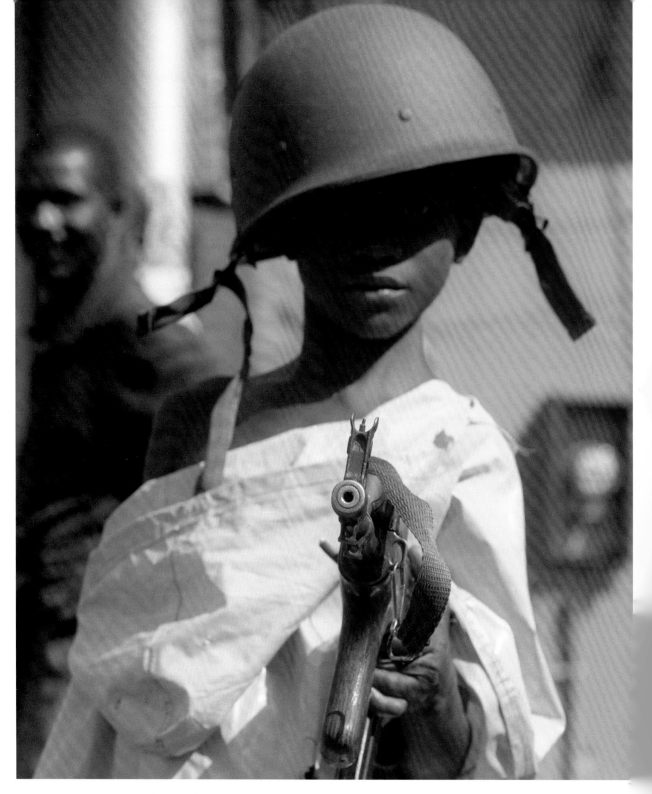

A THIRTEEN-YEAR-OLD boy (1) plays with his deadly toy on the streets of Monrovia, 21 May 1996. There were reckoned to be over 40,000 schoolchildren who had left the classroom for the battleground. Christophe Simon's chilling portrait of an execution in Monrovia, 8 May 1996 (2). In Simon's own words: 'The Krahn man was caught by a patrol of armed NPFL men... he was made to run, shot in the back, then dragged down the street and stripped down to his socks and underwear... the boss man finished him off.' Two women victims of the civil war in the Sudan walk in the grounds of the International Red Cross hospital at Lokichokio in Kenya, 11 October 1998 (3).

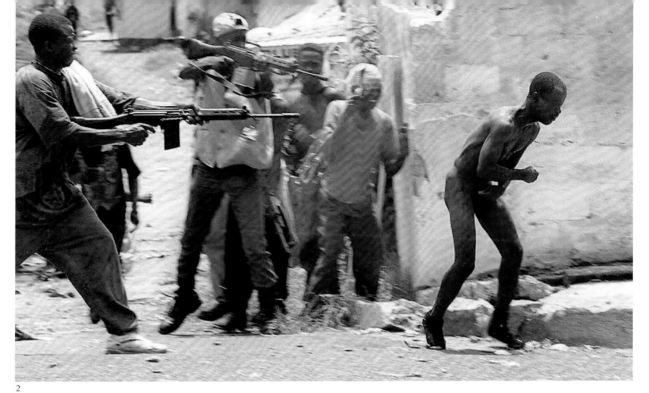

2

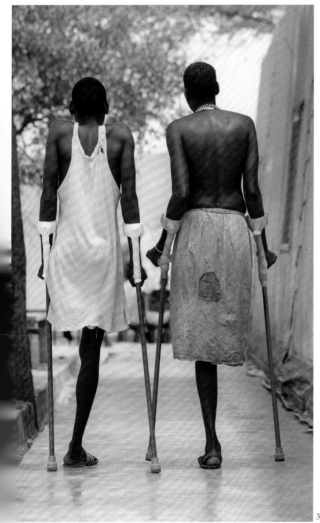

Ein 13jähriger Junge spielt in Monrovia, Liberia, auf der Straße mit seinem tödlichen Spielzeug – 21. Mai 1996 (1). Über 40 000 Schulkinder, so wurde geschätzt, hatten die Schule gegen das Schlachtfeld eingetauscht. Christoph Simons grauenerregendes Portrait einer Exekution in Monrovia – 8. Mai 1996 (2). Simons eigener Bildkommentar: »Der Mann, ein Krahn (eine der Ethnien Liberias), wurde von einer bewaffneten Truppe der NPFL (Nationale Patriotische Front Liberias) aufgegriffen ... Er mußte die Straße entlanglaufen und wurde dabei in den Rücken geschossen; man schleppte ihn weiter, riß ihm die Kleider bis zu Socken und Unterwäsche vom Leib ... Der Boß der Truppe erledigte ihn.« Zwei Opfer des Bürgerkrieges im Sudan auf dem Weg zum Krankenhaus des Internationalen Roten Kreuzes in Lokichokio, Kenia – 11. Oktober 1998 (3).

Monrovia, Libéria : un gamin de 13 ans erre dans la rue avec son jouet mortel – 21 mai 1996 (1). Selon certaines estimations, plus de 40 000 enfants ont quitté l'école pour les champs de bataille. L'horrible portrait, par Christoph Simon, d'une exécution sommaire à Monrovia – 8 mai 1996 (2). Commentaire personnel de Simon : « L'homme, un Krahn (l'une des ethnies du Libéria), a été attaqué par un groupe d'hommes en armes du NPFL (Front patriotique national du Libéria) ... Obligé à courir le long de la rue, on lui tira alors dans le dos ; on continua de le traîner, lui arracha les vêtements du corps, sauf les socquettes et les sous-vêtements ... le patron du groupe le liquida. » Deux victimes de la guerre civile au Soudan se rendant à l'hôpital de la Croix Rouge Internationale, à Lokichokio, au Kenya – 11 octobre 1998 (3).

3

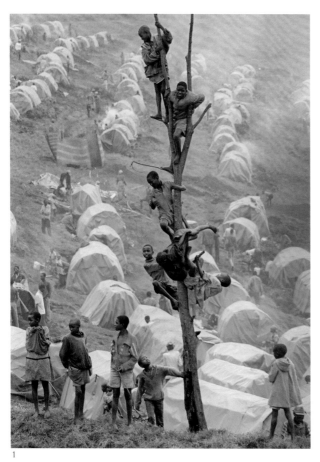

1

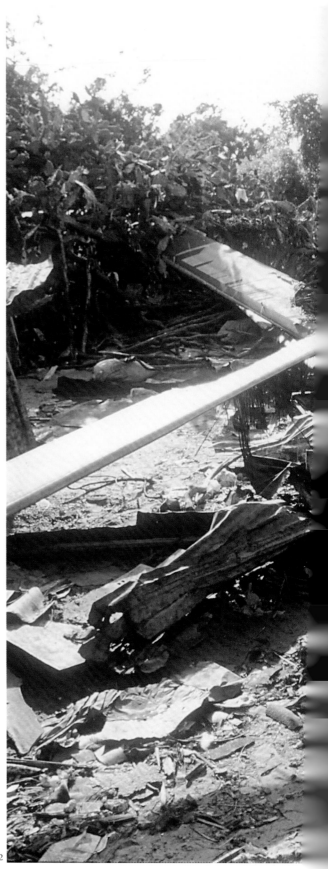

2

Under the protection of French soldiers, children play at the Niashishi Camp in Southern Rwanda, 30 June 1994 (1). The burnt-out remains of an American Blackhawk helicopter (2), shot down by troops of the Somali warlords, litter the ground near Mogadishu, 14 October 1993. Blackhawk helicopters were used for reconnaissance purposes and to destroy ammunition dumps.

Kinder spielen unter dem Schutz französischer Truppen im Niaschischi-Lager in Ruanda – 30. Juni 1994 (1). Die ausgebrannten Überreste eines amerikanischen »Blackhawk«-Hubschraubers in der Nähe von Mogadischu – 14. Oktober 1993 (2); er wurde von somalischen Kriegsherren abgeschossen. »Blackhawk«-Hubschrauber wurden zu Erkundungsflügen und zur Zerstörung von Munitionslagern eingesetzt.

Enfants jouant sous la protection de militaires français dans le camp de Niashishi, au Rwanda – 30 juin 1994 (1). Les restes calcinés d'un hélicoptère « Blackhawk » américain à proximité de Mogadiscio – 14 octobre 1993 (2) ; il a été abattu par des chefs de guerre somaliens. Les hélicoptères « Blackhawk » étaient utilisés pour des vols de reconnaissance et pour détruire des entrepôts de munitions.

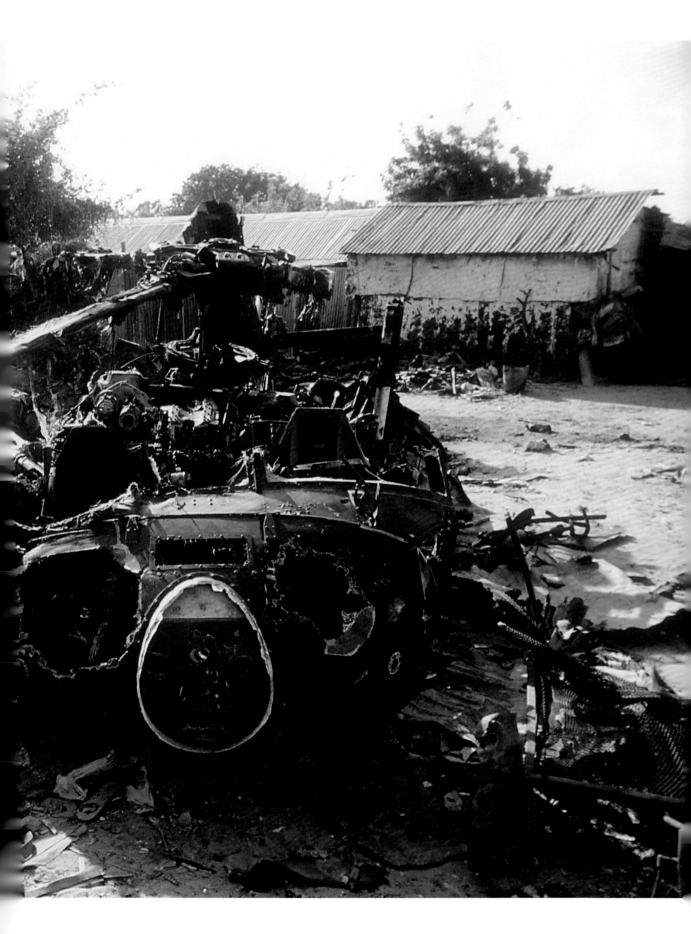

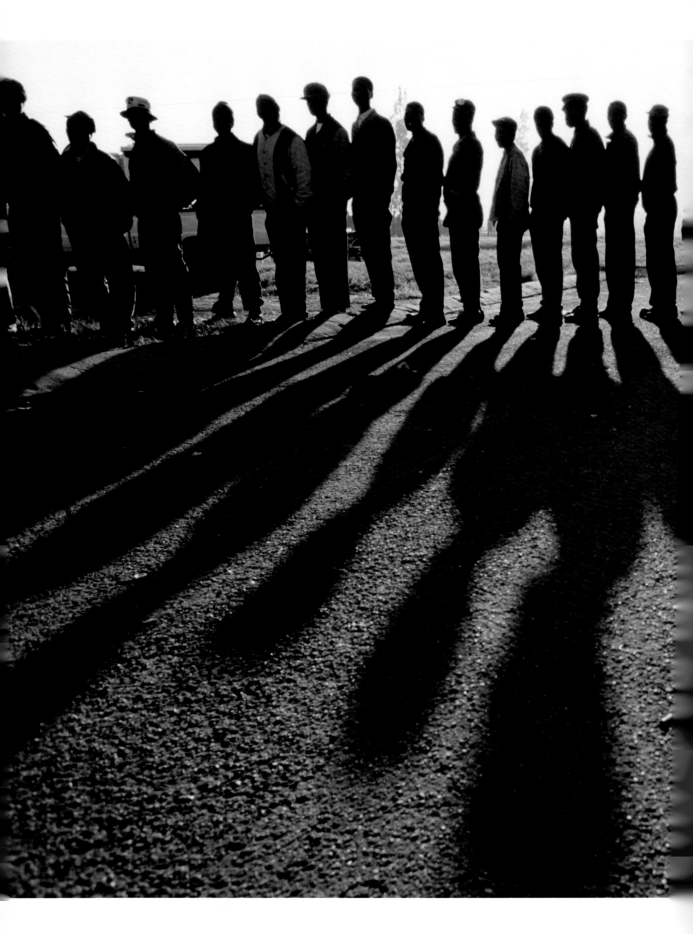

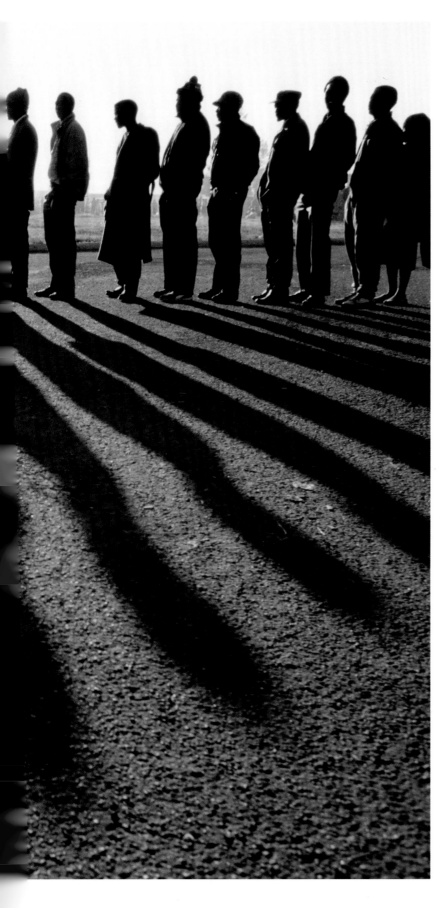

IN dawn's early light, voters queue to play their part in making history at the first truly democratic, multi-racial presidential election in South Africa, April 1994, just four years after Nelson Mandela's release from jail. Mandela's victory in the election was a vital step on the road to peace, truth and reconciliation.

IM Morgengrauen warten Wähler auf den historischen Augenblick, um erstmals ihre Stimme bei den wirklich demokratischen, multiethnischen Präsidentschaftswahlen Südafrikas abzugeben – im April 1994, nur vier Jahre nach Nelson Mandelas Haftentlassung. Mandelas Sieg bei diesen Wahlen war ein entscheidender Schritt auf dem Weg zu Frieden, Wahrheit und nationaler Aussöhnung.

À L'AUBE, des électeurs attendent le moment historique pour remettre leur voix lors des premières élections présidentielles multiethniques vraiment démocratiques d'Afrique du Sud – en avril 1994, quatre ans seulement après la sortie de prison de Nelson Mandela. La victoire de Mandela lors de ces élections a été une étape décisive dans la voie de la paix, de la vérité et de la réconciliation nationale.

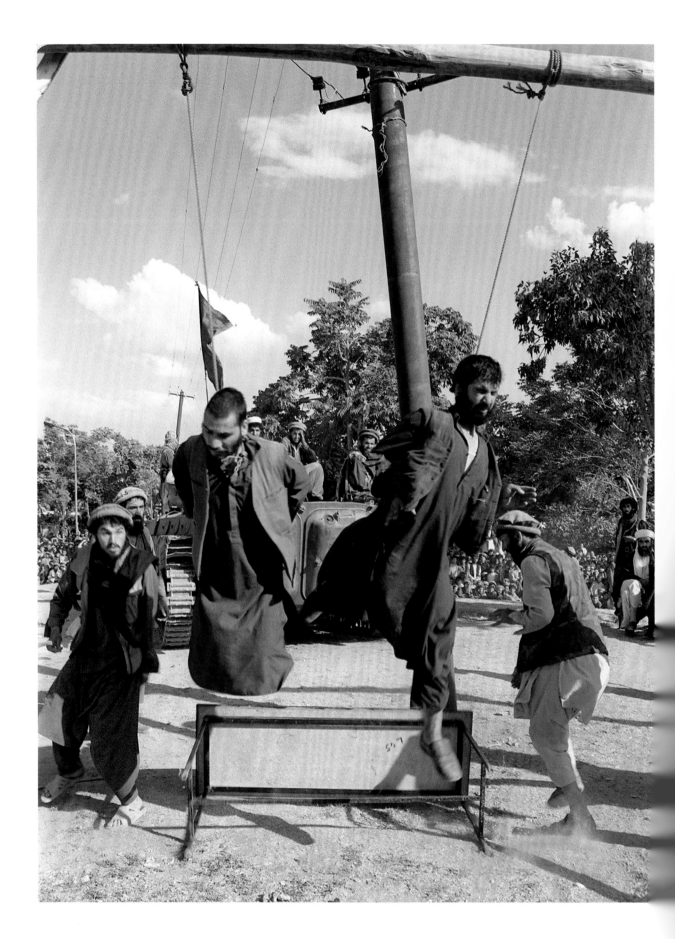

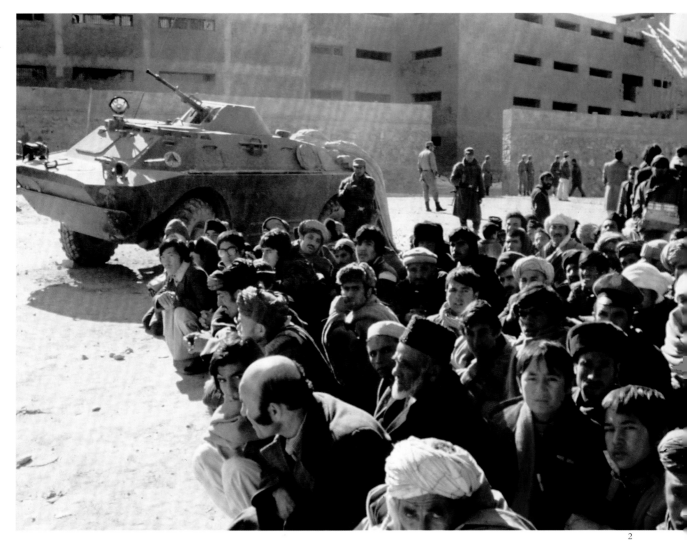

2

ROUGH justice in Afghanistan. A crowd of 5,000 watches as two Shoora-e-Nazar hangmen remove the table and execute two men found guilty of robbery, rape and murder, Kabul, 7 September 1992 (1). A dozen years earlier, tense crowds crouch outside Pulicharki Prison in Kabul, awaiting the release of prisoners, 14 January 1980 (2). The Soviet-backed regime of Babrak Karmal set 126 prisoners free, but the crowd later attacked the prison and released another 12 inmates.

RAUHE Justiz in Afghanistan: Eine Menge von 5 000 Menschen sieht zu, wie zwei Shoora-e-Nazar-Henker den Tisch umstoßen und zwei Männer exekutieren, die des Raubes, der Vergewaltigung und des Mordes schuldig befunden wurden – 7. September 1992 (1). Zwölf Jahre zuvor hockt eine gespannte Menge vor dem Pulicharki-Gefängnis in Kabul und wartet auf die Entlassung von Gefangenen – 14. Januar 1980 (2). Das von der Sowjetunion unterstützte Regime Babrak Karmals entließ 126 Gefangene; doch die Menge stürmte das Gefängnis und befreite zwölf weitere Insassen.

JUSTICE impitoyable en Afghanistan : une foule de 5 000 personnes observe deux bourreaux de Shoora-e-Nazar renverser la table et pendre deux hommes confondus de vol, viol et assassinat – 7 septembre 1992 (1). Douze ans plus tôt, une foule impatiente est accroupie devant la prison de Pulicharki, à Kaboul, attendant la libération de prisonniers – 14 janvier 1980 (2). Le régime de Babrak Karmal, soutenu par l'Union soviétique, libéra 126 prisonniers ; mais la foule prit d'assaut la prison et libéra douze autres de ses occupants.

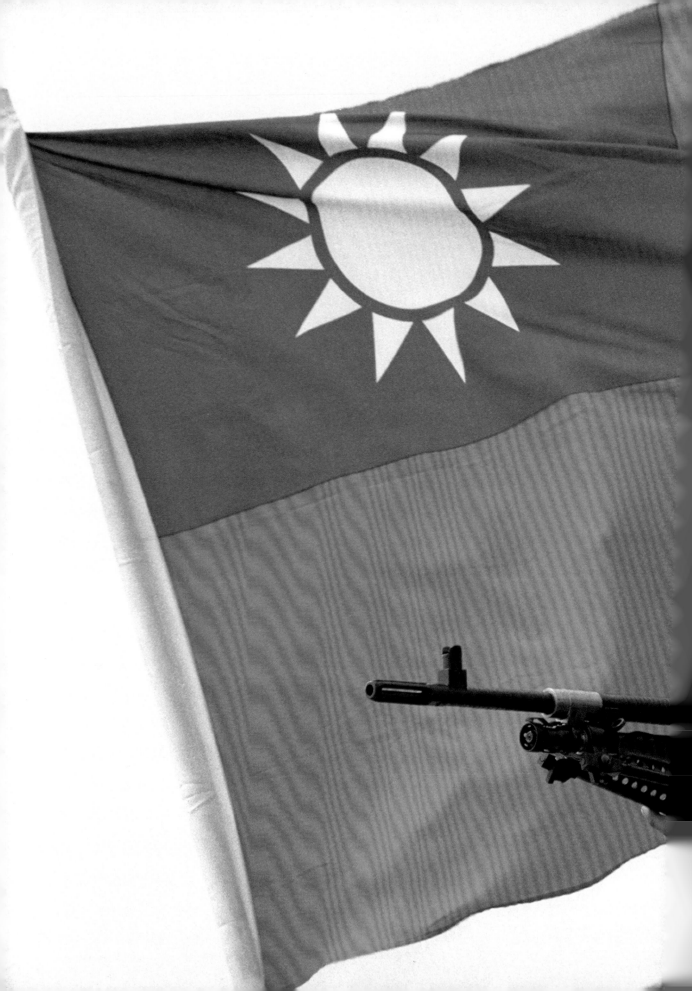

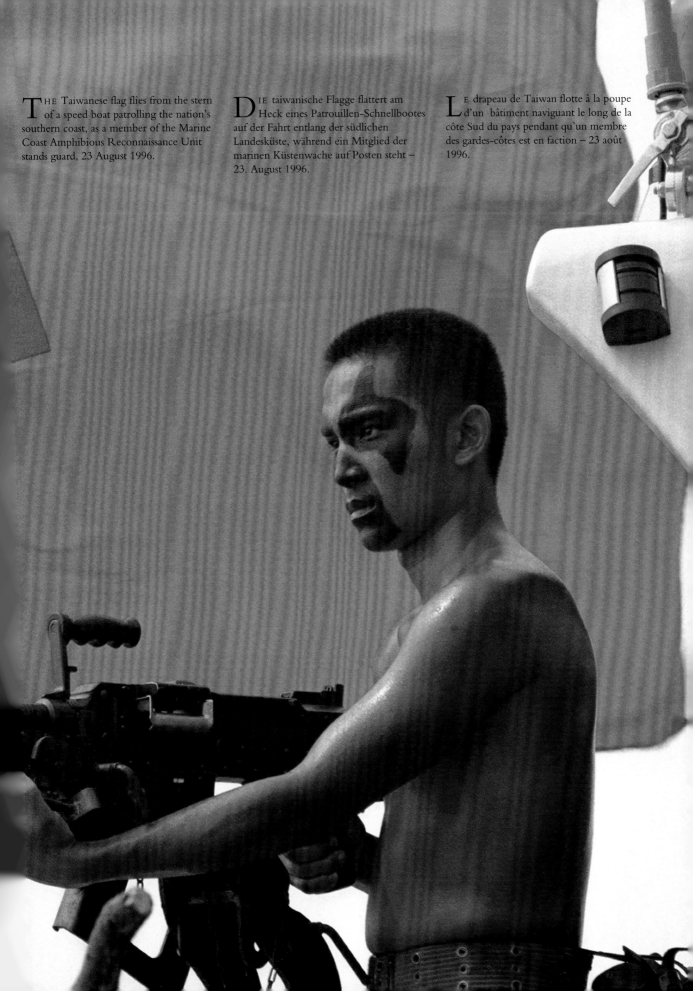

THE Taiwanese flag flies from the stern of a speed boat patrolling the nation's southern coast, as a member of the Marine Coast Amphibious Reconnaissance Unit stands guard, 23 August 1996.

DIE taiwanische Flagge flattert am Heck eines Patrouillen-Schnellbootes auf der Fahrt entlang der südlichen Landesküste, während ein Mitglied der marinen Küstenwache auf Posten steht – 23. August 1996.

LE drapeau de Taiwan flotte à la poupe d'un bâtiment naviguant le long de la côte Sud du pays pendant qu'un membre des gardes-côtes est en faction – 23 août 1996.

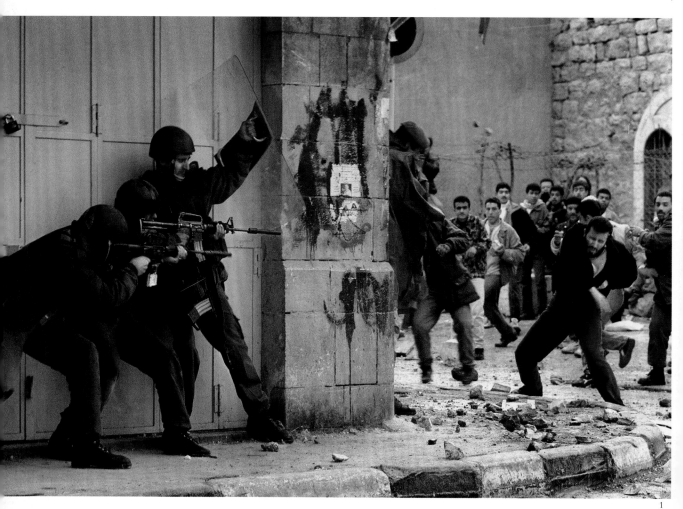

1

THE West Bank city of Hebron, holy to both Muslims and Jews, was a desperately dangerous place in the 1990s. In the city some 500 Israelis lived among 100,000 Palestinians. On 9 April 1997 tension exploded into violent rioting. One of the Palestinian rioters is shot while stoning Israeli soldiers (1). A young Palestinian poses for the camera with his AK-47, March 1987, at his home in the Shatila refugee camp in another war torn city - Beirut (2). In 1982, the Camp had been the site of one of the worst massacres of refugees in the civil war that tore Lebanon apart.

HEBRON im Westjordanland war in den 1990er Jahren ein äußerst gefährlicher Ort; hier befindet sich das Grab Abrahams, eine für Juden und Muslime gleichermaßen heilige Stätte. In der Stadt lebten unter 100 000 Palästinensern rund 500 Israelis. Am 9. April 1997 (1) entlud sich die Spannung in gewaltsamen Aufständen. Einer der palästinensischen Aufständischen wird, während sie israelische Soldaten mit Steinen bewerfen, erschossen. Ein junger Palästinenser posiert im März 1987 mit seiner AK-47 für die Kamera (2) – zu Haus im Flüchtlingslager Schatila, in einer weiteren vom Krieg zerstörten Stadt: Beirut. In diesem Flüchtlingslager ereignete sich eines der schlimmsten Massaker während des libanesischen Bürgerkrieges.

DURANT les années 1990, Hébron, en Jordanie occidentale, était un endroit extrêmement dangereux ; ici se trouve le tombeau d'Abraham, un lieu saint autant pour les juifs que pour les musulmans. Dans la ville, environ 500 Israéliens vivaient parmi 100 000 Palestiniens. Le 9 avril 1997 (1), la tension se déchargea lors de soulèvements violents. L'un des révoltés palestiniens fut abattu pendant qu'il jetait des pierres sur les soldats israéliens. Mars 1987, un jeune Palestinien posa avec sa mitraillette AK-47 pour le photographe (2) – chez lui, dans le camp de réfugiés de Shatila, une autre ville détruite par la guerre : Beyrouth. Dans ce camp de réfugiés a été perpétré l'un des massacres les plus horribles de la guerre civile libanaise.

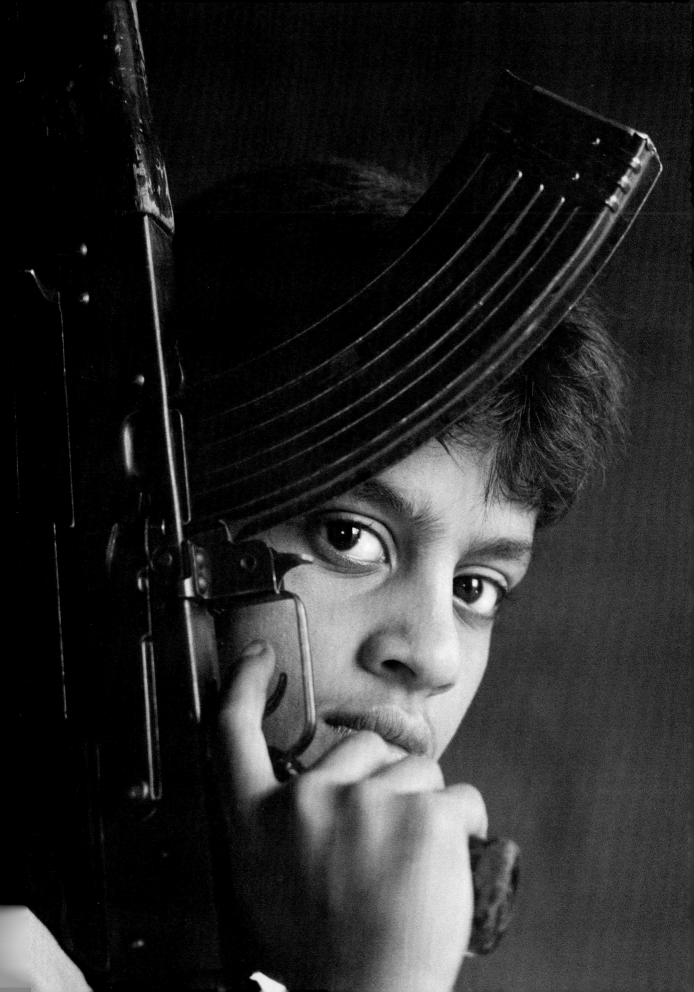

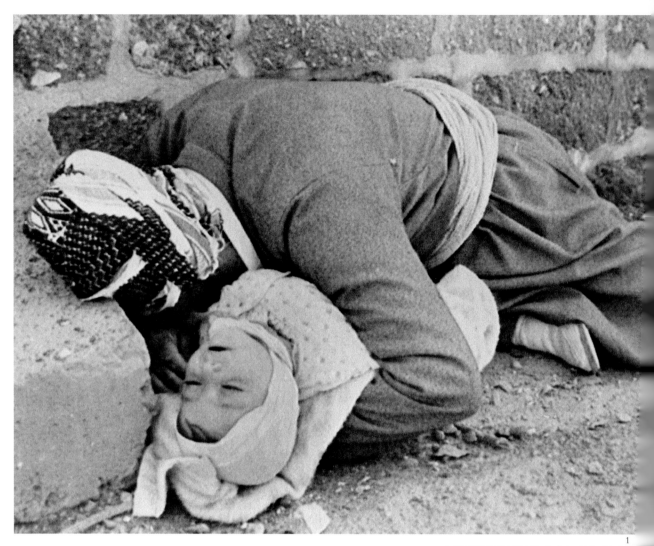

1

CHANGE of order in Iran and Iraq. A Kurdish father and his baby lie on the street, victims of an Iraqi chemical attack on Halabja, 17 March 1988 (1). After 15 years in exile, the Ayatollah Ruhollah Khomeini receives a rapturous welcome in Tehran, 1 February 1979 (2). Blindfolded Iranian POWs are paraded before news reporters in a camp north of Basra, 18 March 1985 (3). The Iran-Iraq war had already lasted over three and a half years. Donald Rumsfeld (extreme left) clinches a deal with president Saddam Hussein, 20 December 1983 (4).

A WHIRLPOOL of pilgrims to Mecca perform the 500-year-old ceremony of the *Tawaf* (sevenfold circling of the Ka'bah), see pages 716–717.

REGIMEWECHSEL in Iran und Irak: Ein kurdischer Vater mit seinem Baby im Arm – beide wurden Opfer des Gasangriffes auf Halabja – 17. März 1988 (1). Nach 15 Jahren Exil wird Ayatollah Ruhollah Khomeini in Teheran stürmisch empfangen – 1. Februar 1979 (2). Kriegsgefangene werden in einem Lager nördlich von Basra Nachrichtenreportern mit verbundenen Augen vorgeführt – 18. März 1985 (3). Der Krieg zwischen Iran und Irak (Erster Golfkrieg) dauerte bereits über dreieinhalb Jahre an; Donald Rumsfeld (links im Bild) schließt ein Abkommen mit Saddam Hussein – 20. Dezember 1983 (4).

EIN STROM von Mekka-Pilgern beim *Tawaf*, dem 500 Jahre alten Ritual der siebenmaligen Umrundung der Kaaba (siehe Seiten 716–717).

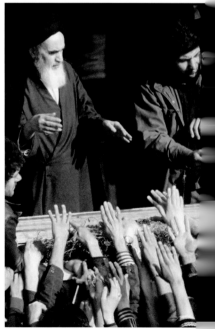

2

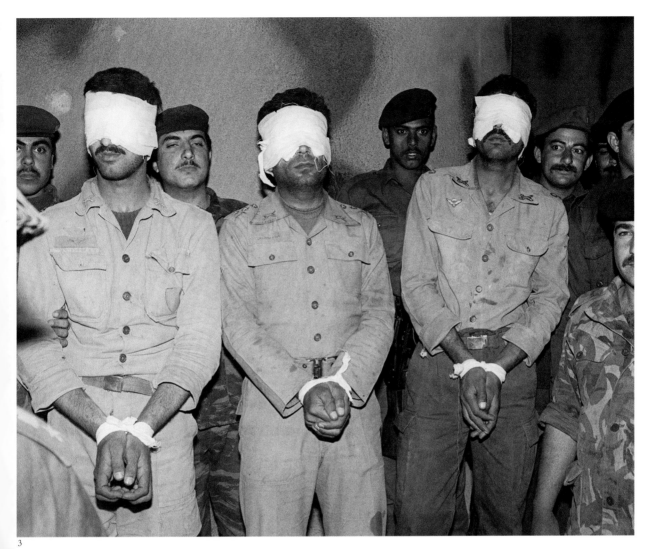

3

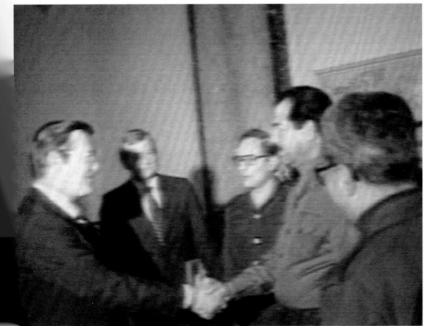

CHANGEMENT de régime en Iran et
en Irak : un père kurde avec son bébé
dans les bras – tous les deux victimes de
l'attaque aux gaz sur Halabja – 17 mars
1988 (1). Après quinze ans d'exil,
l'ayatollah Ruhollah Khomeiny est
accueilli frénétiquement à Téhéran –
1 février 1979 (2). Des prisonniers de
guerre aux yeux bandés sont présentés à
des correspondants de guerre dans un camp
au nord de Basra – 18 mars 1985 (3). La
guerre entre l'Iran et l'Irak (la première
guerre du Golfe) durait déjà plus de trois
ans et demi ; Donald Rumsfeld (à gauche
sur la photo) conclut un accord avec
Saddam Hussein – 20 décembre 1983 (4).

FOULE DE PÈLERINS à La Mecque
lors du tawaf, un rituel de circum-
ambulation vieux d'un demi-millénaire,
consistant à faire sept fois le tour de
la Kaaba (voir pages 716–717).

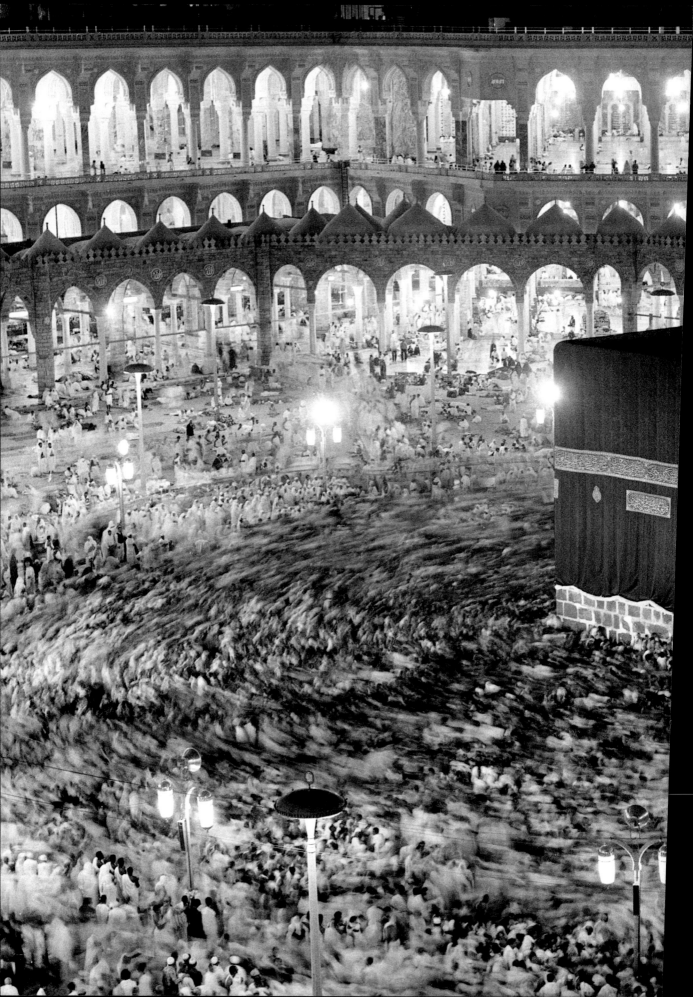

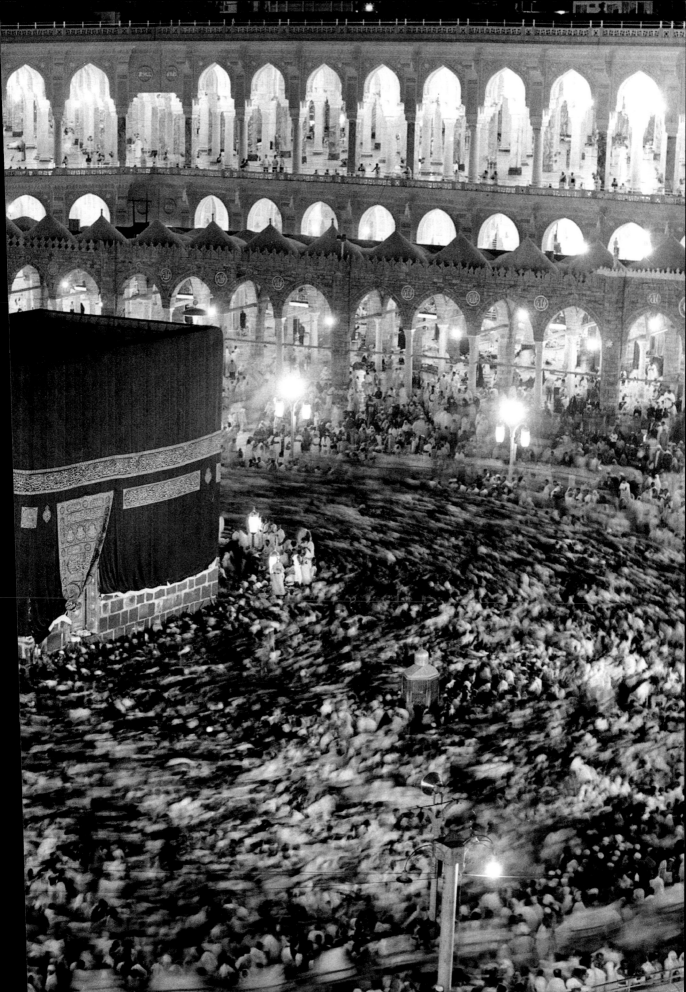

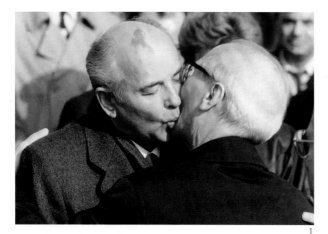

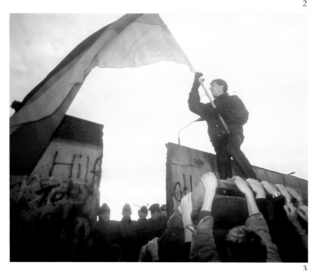

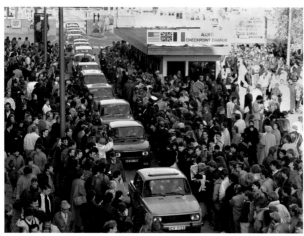

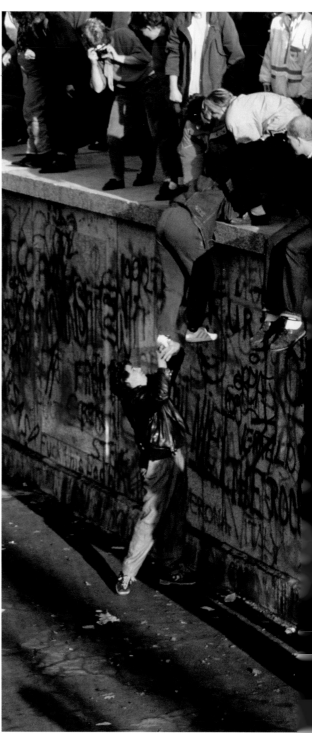

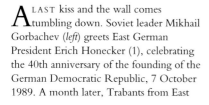

A LAST kiss and the wall comes tumbling down. Soviet leader Mikhail Gorbachev (*left*) greets East German President Erich Honecker (1), celebrating the 40th anniversary of the founding of the German Democratic Republic, 7 October 1989. A month later, Trabants from East Germany queue at Checkpoint Charlie to gain entrance to West Berlin (2). Excited crowds climb the Berlin Wall (4) as others begin its destruction, and (3) the German flag waves above what is about to become a united Berlin, 11 November 1989.

E IN letzter Kuß – und die Mauer fällt. Der sowjetische Führer Michail Gorbatschow (*links im Bild*) begrüßt das Staatsoberhaupt der DDR, Erich Honecke während der Feiern zum 40. Jahrestag der Staatsgründung – 7. Oktober 1989 (1). Einen Monat später stehen Trabanten am

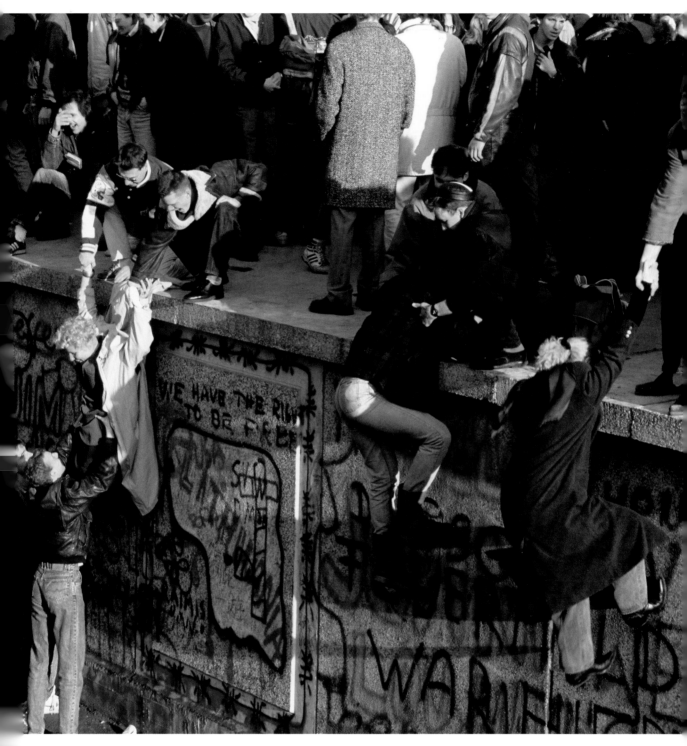

Checkpoint Charlie Schlange und warten darauf, nach Westberlin zu fahren (2). Eine erregte Menge erklimmt die Berliner Mauer (4), während andere bereits mit ihrem Abriß beginnen; und die deutsche Fahne flattert (3) über dem Beginn der Wiedervereinigung Berlins – 1. November 1989.

ULTIME baiser – et le Mur tombe. Le leader soviétique Mikhaïl Gorbatchev (*à gauche sur la photo*) accueille le chef d'État est-allemand Erich Honecker pendant les cérémonies du 40ème anniversaire de la fondation de la République démocratique allemande – 7 octobre 1989 (1). Un mois plus tard, des Trabant font la queue à

Checkpoint Charlie en attendant de rouler dans Berlin-Ouest (2). Une foule excitée grimpe sur le Mur de Berlin (4) pendant que d'autres commencent à l'abattre et que le drapeau allemand (3) flotte sur les débuts de la réunification de Berlin – 11 novembre 1989.

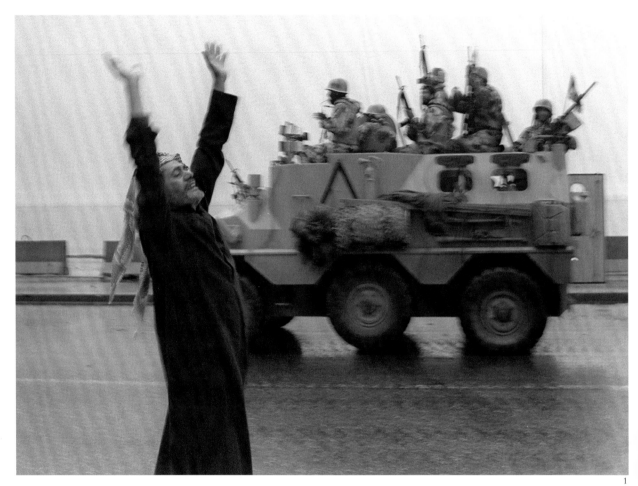

IN August 1990 Iraqi forces seized control of Kuwait. President George Bush (3) made a whirlwind tour of Europe and the Middle East, enlisting support for a US led war of liberation, and returned home to sell the war to his people. In the Gulf War that followed, the US and her allies gained a swift victory – a Saudi personnel carrier is greeted ecstatically by Kuwaiti citizens (1) as it rolls into Kuwait City, 27 February 1991. American Air Force F-15 C fighters fly over a Kuwaiti oilfield that has been set on fire by retreating Iraqi soldiers (2).

IM August 1990 eroberten irakische Truppen das Nachbarland Kuwait. US-Präsident George Bush (sen., 3) unternahm in Windeseile eine Reise durch Europa und den Nahen Osten, um Unterstützung für eine von den USA geführte Befreiung des Landes zu gewinnen; anschließend verkaufte er den Krieg der Bevölkerung zu Hause. In dem darauffolgenden Zweiten Golfkrieg erzielten die USA und ihre Verbündeten einen raschen Sieg: Ein saudi-arabisches Truppenfahrzeug wird auf der Fahrt durch Kuwait City von einem Bürger der Stadt stürmisch begrüßt – 27. Februar 1991 (1). F-15 C Jagdbomber der amerikanischen Luftwaffe fliegen über ein kuwaitisches Ölfeld, das von irakischen Truppen auf ihrem Rückzug in Brand gesetzt wurde (2).

EN août 1990, les troupes irakiennes envahissent le Koweït voisin. Le président américain George Bush sen. (3) entreprend en coup de vent un voyage en Europe et au Proche-Orient afin d'obtenir l'appui pour une guerre de libération du pays, dirigée par les États-Unis ; ensuite, il doit vendre la guerre à la population de son pays. Durant la guerre du Golfe qui s'ensuivra, les États-Unis et leurs alliés remportent une victoire éclair : un transport de troupes saoudien est accueilli frénétiquement par un citoyen de la ville lors de sa traversée de Koweït city – 27 février 1991 (1). Des chasseurs F-15 C de l'armée de l'air américaine survolent un champ pétrolifère koweitien incendié par les troupes irakiennes en déroute (2).

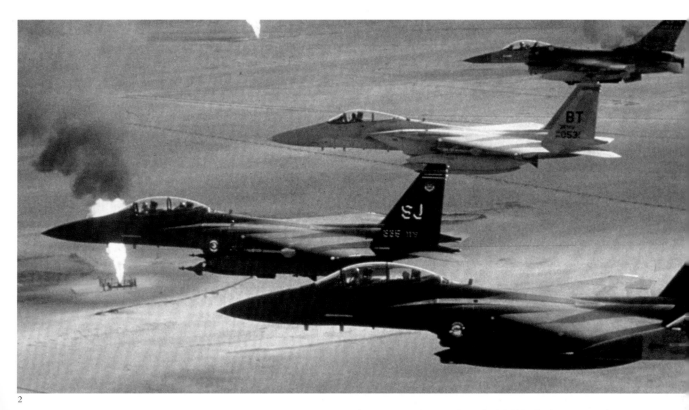

2

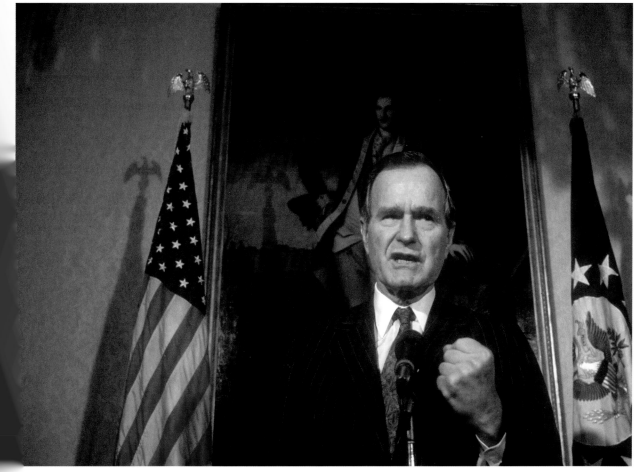

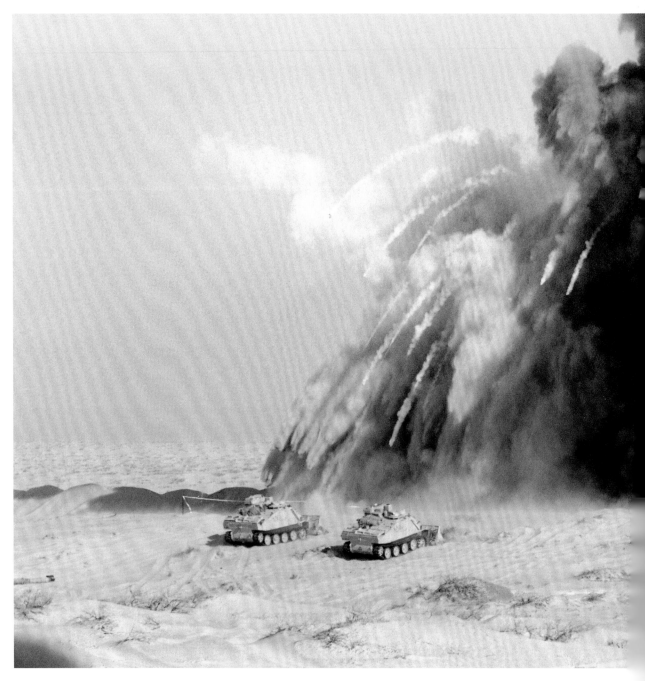

THE retreating Iraqi troops in the Gulf War left behind a series of minefields and booby-traps. British engineers from the 7th Armoured Brigade blow up a mine shield in the Saudi-Arabian desert, 7 January 1991 (1). On Day One of the Desert Storm Gulf War ground campaign, a US Marine takes stands guard over an Iraqi prisoner, 25 February 1991 (2).

DIE irakischen Truppen hinterließen bei ihrem Rückzug zahlreiche Minenfelder und versteckte Bomben. Britische Ingenieure der 7. Waffenbrigade zünden einen Minenring in der saudi-arabischen Wüste – 7. Januar 1991 (1). Am Tag Eins der alliierten Militäroperatio »Desert Storm« übernimmt ein Soldat der US-Marine die Wache über einen iraki-schen Gefangenen – 25. Februar 1991 (2).

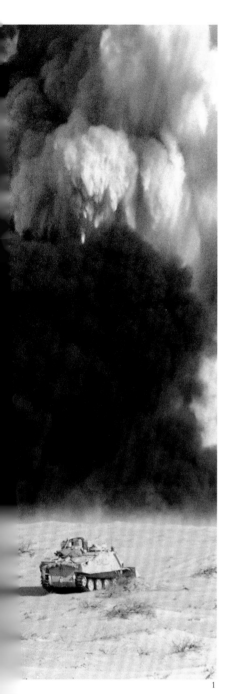

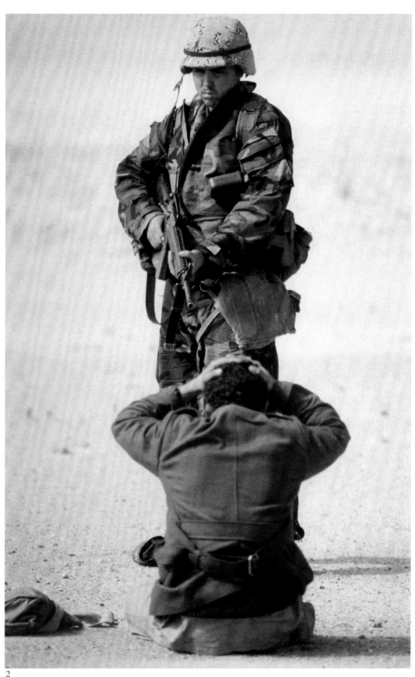

1 2

L ORS de leur retraite, les troupes
irakiennes ont laissé de nombreux
champs de mines et bombes enterrées. Des
ingénieurs du génie britanniques de la
septième brigade font sauter un anneau de
mines dans le désert d'Arabie saoudite –
7 janvier 1991 (1). Le jour 1 de l'opération
militaire alliée « Tempête du désert », un
soldat de la marine américaine surveille un
prisonnier irakien – 25 février 1991 (2).

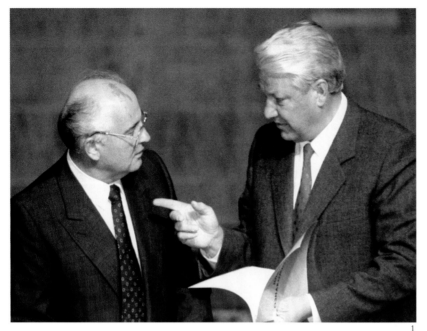

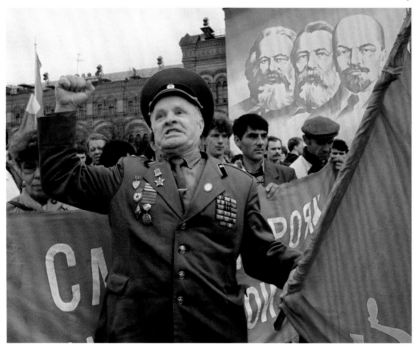

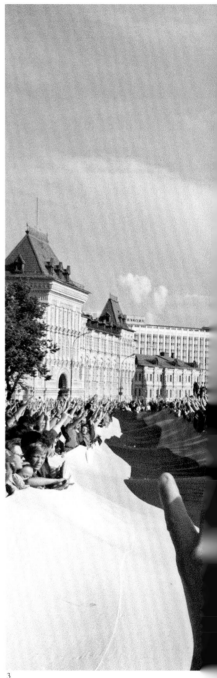

B Y the beginning of the 1990s, the Soviet Union had virtually disintegrated and there was a danger that Russia might tear itself apart. Following the collapse of an attempting *coup* by hardline Communists, Mikhail Gorbachev (*left*) meets with President Boris Yeltsin at the Russian Parliament to discuss where to go next (1), August 1991. Those behind the *coup* had included Soviet Vice-President Gennady Yanayev and KGB chief Vladimir

Kryuchkov – neither of whom carried much popularity. When they fell, there was considerable rejoicing in Red Square (3), where the Russian flag was paraded in place of the old Hammer and Sickle. Though the old order had pretty much died, at the traditional May Day Parade in Moscow in 1990, one seasoned campaigner from the Red Army gives the Communist salute (2), while others hold banners depicting Marx, Engels and Lenin.

Z U Beginn der 1990er Jahre war die Union der Sowjetrepubliken faktisch bereits auseinandergefallen, und es bestand ᵈ Gefahr, daß Rußland endgültig auseinander brach. Nach der Vereitelung eines versuchtᵉ Staatsstreiches durch konservative Kommunisten trifft Michail Gorbatschow (*links im Bild*) mit Präsident Boris Jeltzin im russischen Parlament zusammen, um über ᵈ nächsten Schritte zu beraten – August 1991 (1). Zu den Initiatoren des Staatsstreichs gehörten der sowjetische Vizepräsident Gennadi Janajew und der KGB-Chef

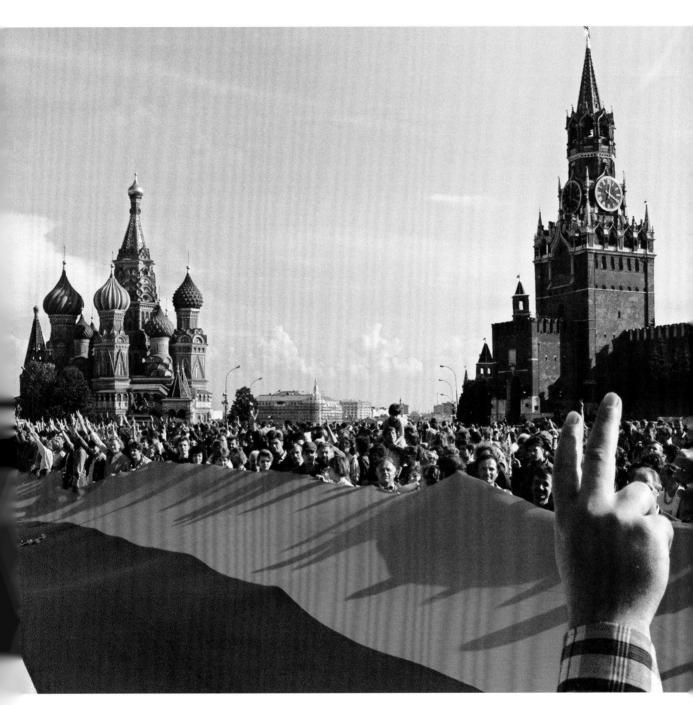

Wladimir Kryuchkow – beide genossen kaum Ansehen in der Bevölkerung. Als ihr Vorhaben fehlschlug, herrschte unverhohlene Freude auf dem Roten Platz (3), wo die Menge anstelle der Fahne mit Hammer und Sichel die russische Nationalflagge hielt. Obwohl die alte Ordnung bereits am Boden lag, salutiert ein betagtes Mitglied der roten Armee bei einer traditionellen Ersten-Mai-Demonstration 1990 in Moskau mit dem kommunistischen Gruß (2), während die Demonstranten im Hintergrund Plakate mit Marx, Engels und Lenin hochhalten.

DÈS le début des années 1990, l'Union des Républiques soviétiques était de facto en totale déliquescence et le risque que la Russie se désintègre définitivement était réel. Après l'échec de la tentative de coup d'État fomenté par des communistes conservateurs, Mikhaïl Gorbatchev (*à gauche sur la photo*) rencontre le président Boris Eltsine au Parlement russe pour se consulter sur la suite des événements – août 1991 (1). Deux des initiateurs du coup d'État étaient le vice-président soviétique, Gennadi Janajev, et le patron du KGB, Vladimir

Kryuchkov – deux hommes sans charisme aux yeux de la population. Leur chute cause une joie non dissimulée sur la Place Rouge (3), où la foule, à la place du drapeau avec le marteau et la faucille, brandit les couleurs nationales russes. Bien que l'ordre ancien soit déjà en cendres, un vieillard membre de l'Armée rouge fait le salut communiste lors du défilé traditionnel du 1er Mai 1990 à Moscou (2) tandis que des manifestants, à l'arrière-plan, brandissent des affiches avec des portraits de Marx, Engels et Lénine.

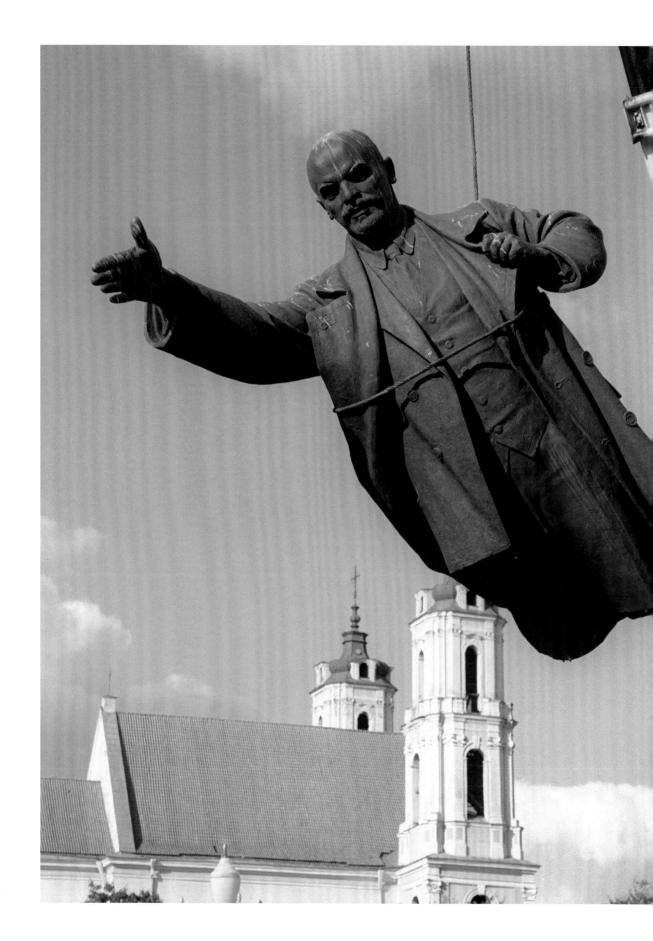

EVENTS moved swiftly throughout the old Soviet satellite states. The vast statue of Lenin is removed from Vilnius, capital of Lithuania, 23 August 1991 (1). Cheers greet the dismantling of the statue of Felix Dzerzhinsky in the square named after him in Warsaw, 17 November 1989 (2) – Dzerzhinsky had been the founder of *Cheka*, the Soviet's first secret service. Transition was less peaceful in Grozny, where a bitter war began between Chechen fighters and the Russian army (3).

AUCH in den ehemaligen Satellitenstaaten der Sowjetunion schritten die Ereignisse rasch voran. In Vilnius, der Hauptstadt Litauens, wird eine riesige Leninstatue demontiert – 23. August 1991 (1). Die Menge applaudiert beim Abriß der Statue von Felix Dzerzhinsky auf dem nach ihm benannten Platz in Warschau, Polen – 17. November 1989 (2). Dzerzhinsky war Gründer der Tscheka, der ersten sowjetischen Geheimpolizei. Weniger friedlich ging es in Grozny zu, wo ein erbitterter Kampf zwischen tschetschenischen Kämpfern und der russischen Armee einsetzte (3).

DANS les anciens États satellites de l'Union soviétique aussi, les événements se précipitent. À Vilnius, la capitale de la Lituanie, une gigantesque statue de Lénine est abattue – 23 août 1991 (1). La foule applaudit la chute de la statue de Felix-Dzerzhinsky dans le parc éponyme à Varsovie, en Pologne – 17 novembre 1989 (2). Dzerzhinsky était le fondateur de la Tcheka, la première police secrète soviétique. La transition a été moins pacifique à Groznyï, où une lutte armée a opposé les combattants tchétchènes à l'armée russe (3).

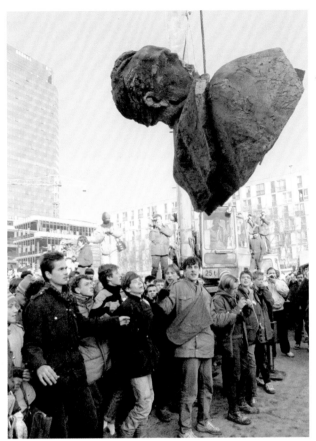

2

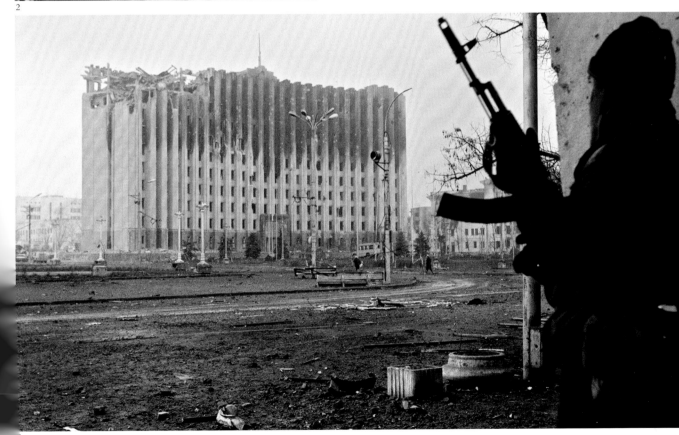

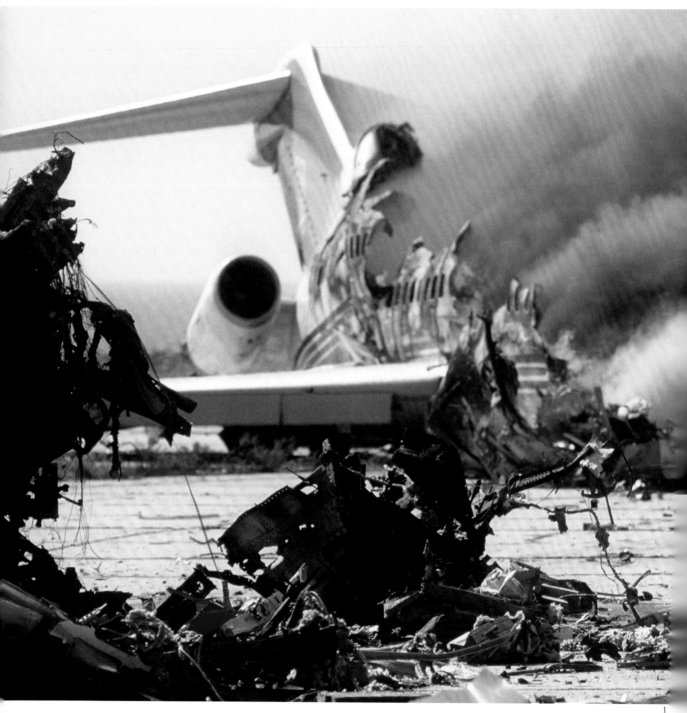

1

ONE of the greatest tragedies in the 1980s was the bitter and prolonged civil war conducted in Beirut. It began in 1975, with fighting between Palestinians and right-wing Phalangists in a city that was split between Christians and Muslims, and between groups taking different sides in the struggle between the Israelis and the Palestinians. Ten years later, a Lebanese Shi'ite Muslim stands guard over the remains of a hijacked Jordanian Boeing 727 at Beirut Airport, 11 June 1985 (1). A woman breaks down after a car bomb explodes in the mainly Muslim area of West Beirut, 8 August 1986 (2), and (3) a Muslim family huddle under a bridge in West Beirut during an artillery duel between opposing sides, 20 August 1985(3).

EINE der größten Tragödien der 1980er Jahre war der erbitterte und endlose Bürgerkrieg in Beirut; er begann 1975 mit Kämpfen zwischen Palästinensern und rechtsgerichteten Phalangisten in einer Stad deren Bevölkerung sich in Christen und Muslime teilte – sowie in Gruppen, die in der Auseinandersetzung zwischen Israel un den Palästinensern auf verschiedenen Seiter standen. Zehn Jahre später hält ein schiitischer Muslim bei den Überresten ein

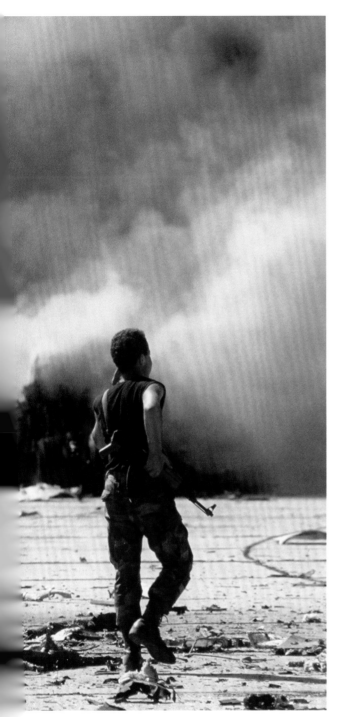

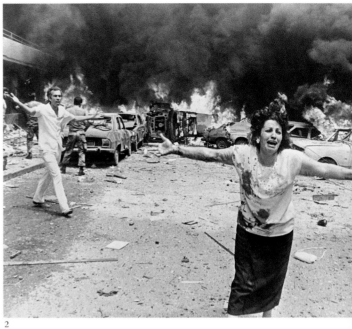

2

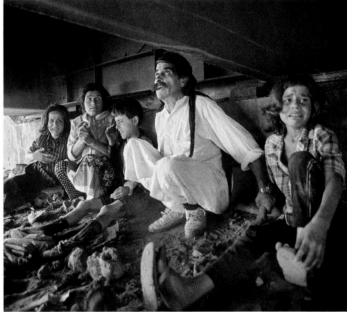

3

gekidnappten jordanischen Boeing 727 auf dem Flughafen in Beirut Wache – 11. Juni 1985 (1). Eine Frau bricht nach der Explosion einer Autobombe in dem vor allem von Muslimen bewohnten Stadtteil Westbeirut zusammen – 8. August 1986 (2); und eine muslimische Familie kauert während eines Artillerieduells zwischen gegnerischen Kampfeinheiten verzweifelt unter einer Brücke in Westbeirut – 0. August 1985 (3).

ACHARNÉE et interminable, la guerre civile à Beyrouth a été l'une des plus grandes tragédies des années 1980 ; elle a commencé en 1975 par des combats entre les Palestiniens et les Phalangistes de droite dans une ville où la population était divisée en chrétiens et musulmans – ainsi qu'en factions qui se tenaient de différents côtés dans la lutte entre Israël et les Palestiniens. Dix ans plus tard, (1), un musulman chiite libanais monte la garde

près des restes d'un Boeing 727 jordanien sur l'aéroport de Beyrouth – 11 juin 1985 (1). Une femme tombe en syncope après l'explosion d'une voiture piégée dans le quartier de Beyrouth-Ouest habité surtout par des musulmans – 8 août 1986 (2) ; pendant un duel d'artillerie entre des unités adverses, une famille musulmane désespérée cherche abri sous un pont à Beyrouth-Ouest – 20 août 1985 (3).

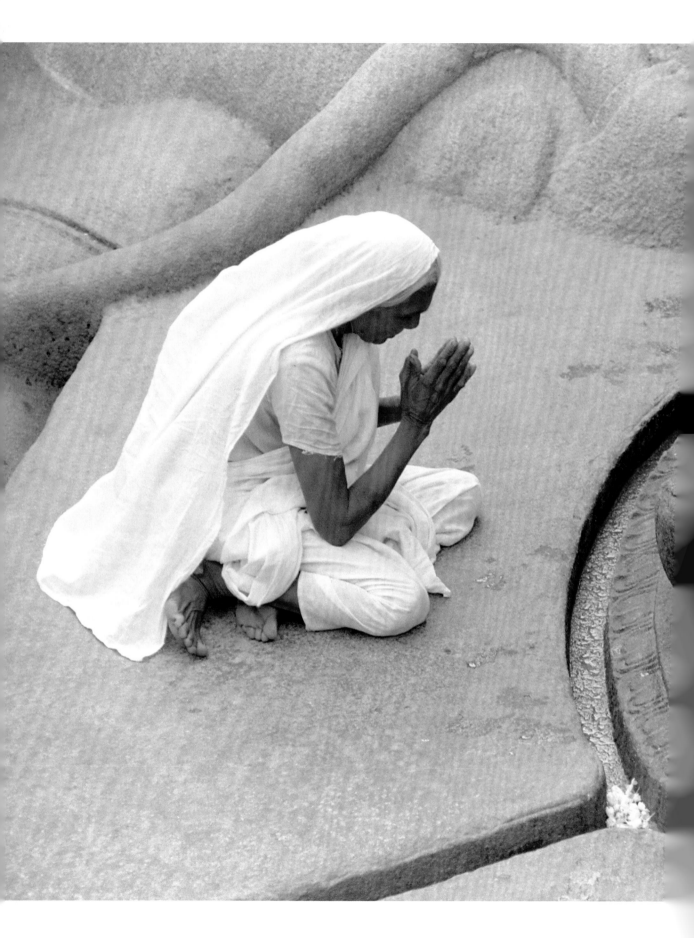

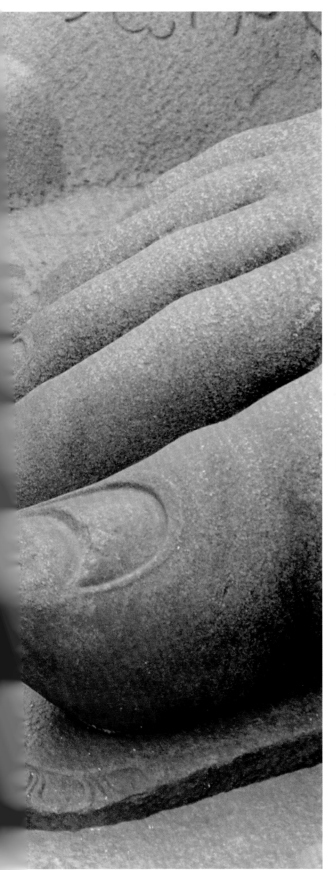

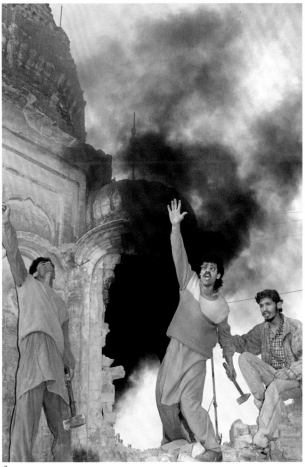

2

DEVOTION and destruction… A Jain woman prays before the stone feet of the idol Gomateshwar in Shravanabelagola, southern India, 19 December 1993 (1). The woman was taking part in a ceremony held every 12 years, where the 58 foot granite statue is sprinkled with milk, sugar cane juice, sandalwood paste and turmeric. Muslims celebrate after setting fire to a Hindu temple in Rawalpindi, Pakistan, 7 December 1992 (2).

VEREHRUNG und Vernichtung: Eine Jaina betet zu Füßen einer Gomarteschwarstatue in Schrawanebelagola, Südindien – 19. Dezember 1993 (1). Die Frau nahm an einer alle zwölf Jahre stattfindenden Zeremonie teil, bei der die 18 Meter hohe Statue mit Milch, Zuckerrohrsirup, Sandelholz und Kurkuma (Gelbwurz) besprenkelt und bestäubt wird. Muslime jubeln, nachdem sie einen Hindutempel in Rawalpindi, Pakistan, in Brand gesetzt haben – 7. Dezember 1992 (2).

DÉVOTION et destruction : une femme de l'ethnie Jaina prie aux pieds d'une statue de Gomarteshwar, à Shrawanebelagola, Inde du Sud – 19 décembre 1993 (1). Elle participe à une cérémonie organisée tous les douze ans lors de laquelle la statue de 18 mètres de haut est arrosée de lait, de sirop de canne à sucre, de bois de santal et de curcuma. Des musulmans laissent éclater leur joie après avoir incendié un temple hindou à Rawalpindi, au Pakistan – 7 décembre 1992 (2).

1

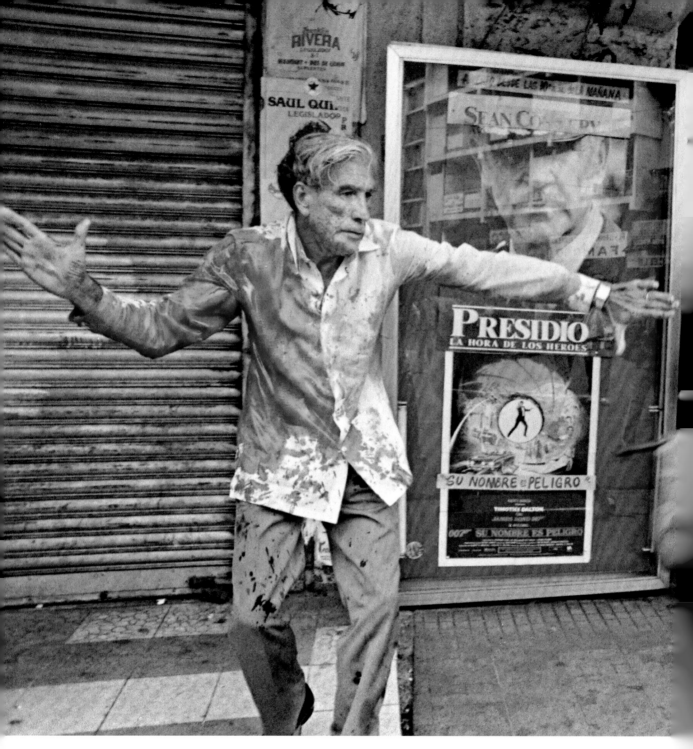

THERE was much happening in their 'back yard' to concern American citizens in the 1980s and 1990s. Vice Presidential candidate Guillermo Endara is attacked by a member of the Dignity Brigade, Panama City, 10 May 1989 (1). Ford's candidacy was strongly backed by the United States. A US Military Policeman protects a man suspected of throwing a hand grenade into a pro-Aristide rally, Port-au-Prince, Haiti, 29 September 1994 (2). "Muchachos" train

in a National Liberation Front camp in north east Salvador, 9 April 1982 (3).

Es war einiges los in Amerikas »Vorgarten«, das in den 1980er und 1990er Jahren die US-Bürger in Atem hielt. Der Vizepräsidentschaftskandidat Guillermo Endara nach einem Angriff eines Mitglieds der Brigade Dignitá in Panama City – 10. Mai 1989 (1). Endaras Kandidatur wurde von den USA massiv unterstützt. Ein US-Militärpolizist schützt einen Mann in Port-

au-Prince, Haiti, der verdächtigt wird, eine Handgranate in eine Demonstration von Aristideanhängern geworfen zu haben – 29. September 1994 (2). Ein Gefolge von »Muchachos« in einem Lager der Nationalen Befreiungsfront im Nordosten El Salvadors – 9. April 1982 (3).

Il y avait du « pétard » dans le « jardin » des États-Unis, qui a laissé les citoyens américains haletants dans les années 1980 e 1990. Le candidat à la vice-présidence

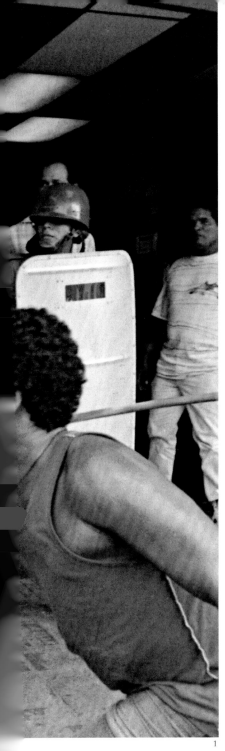

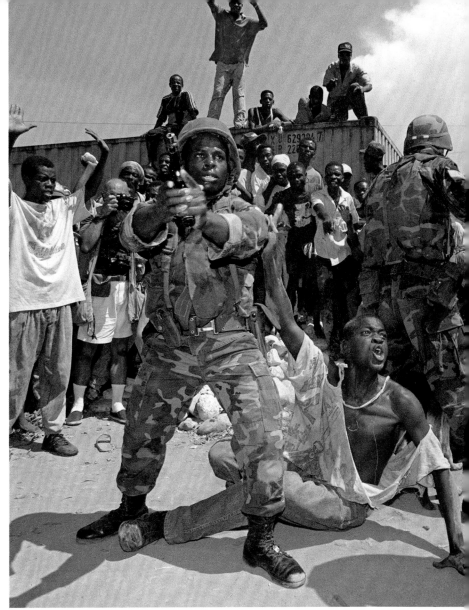

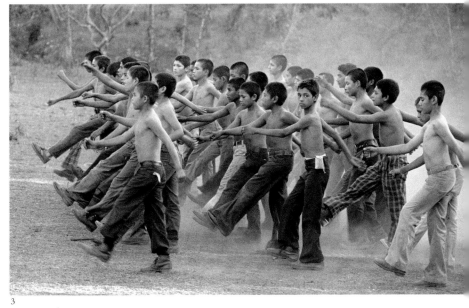

Guillermo Endara, après une attaque d'un membre de la brigade Dignità, à Panama City – 10 mai 1989 (1). Les États-Unis avaient soutenu bec et ongles la candidature d'Endara. À Port-au-Prince, à Haïti, un MP américain protège un homme accusé d'avoir lancé une grenade dans une manifestation de partisans d'Aristide – 29 septembre 1994 (2). Un défilé des « Muchachos » dans un camp du Front national de libération, dans le nord-est d'El Salvador – 9 avril 1982 (3).

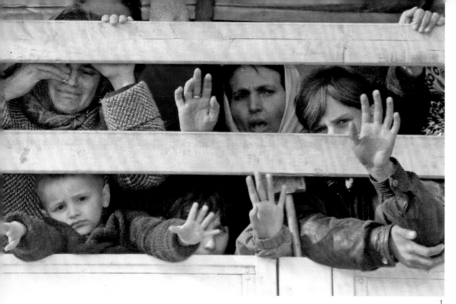

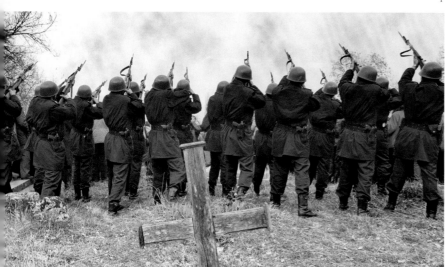

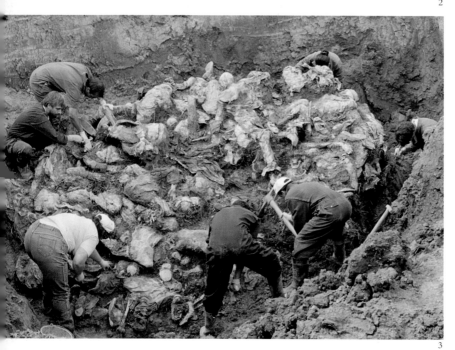

THE first serious war to take place on the European land mass since World War II broke out in the 1990s, following the partition of the old Yugoslavia. It was bloody and bitter, cruel and savage. Muslim refugees wave from a UN truck as they are escorted from Srebrenica, then besieged by Serbs and the scene of a massacre in 1995 (1). Forensic experts from the International War Crimes Tribunal examine the remains of some of the 7,000 killed in the massacre (3). A Serbian honour guard fires a salute at the funeral of a Serb policeman killed by the Albanian Liberation Army, near Pristina, 26 March 1998 (2). A young member of the Kosovo Liberation Army patrols the streets of Prizren, just a few miles from the Albanian border, 18 June 1999 (4).

DER erste ausdrückliche Krieg auf dem europäischen Festland nach dem Zweiten Weltkrieg brach in den 1990er Jahren in der Folge des Auseinanderfallens der ehemaligen Republik Jugoslawien aus. Es war ein blutiger und erbitterter, ein grausamer und barbarischer Krieg. Muslimische Flüchtlinge winken aus einem UN-Fahrzeug, das sie aus dem von Serben belagerten Srebrenica herausbringt (1). Die Stadt wurde 1995 zum Schauplatz eines Massakers. Gerichtsexperten des Internationalen Kriegsverbrechertribunals in Den Haag untersuchen Überreste einiger der 7000 Opfer des Massakers (3). Eine serbische Ehrenwache feuert Salutschüsse zum Begräbnis eines serbischen Polizisten ab, der in der Nähe von Pristina durch die Albanische Befreiungsarmee getötet wurde – 26. März 1998 (2). Ein junges Mitglied der Kosovarischen Befreiungsarmee patrouilliert auf den Straßen in Prizren, Kosovo, nur wenige Kilometer von der albanischen Grenze entfernt – 18. Juni 1999 (4).

LA première véritable guerre sur le territoire européen depuis la Seconde Guerre mondiale a éclaté dans les années 1990 à la suite de l'effondrement de l'ancienne République de Yougoslavie. Une guerre sanguinaire et acharnée, cruelle et barbare. Des réfugiés musulmans saluent depuis un véhicule de l'ONU qui les évacue de la ville de Srebrenica assiégée par les Serbes (1). La ville a été le théâtre d'un massacre en 1995. Des experts de la police scientifique du Tribunal international des criminels de guerre de La Haye analysent des restes de quelques-unes des 7000 victimes du massacre (3). Une garde d'honneur serbe tire une salve de coups de feu à l'occasion des funérailles d'un agent de police serbe tué à proximité de Pristina par l'Armée de libération albanaise – 26 mars 1998 (2). Un jeune membre de l'Armée de libération du Kosovo patrouille dans les rues de Prizren, au Kosovo, à quelques kilomètres seulement de la frontière albanaise – 18 juin 1999 (4).

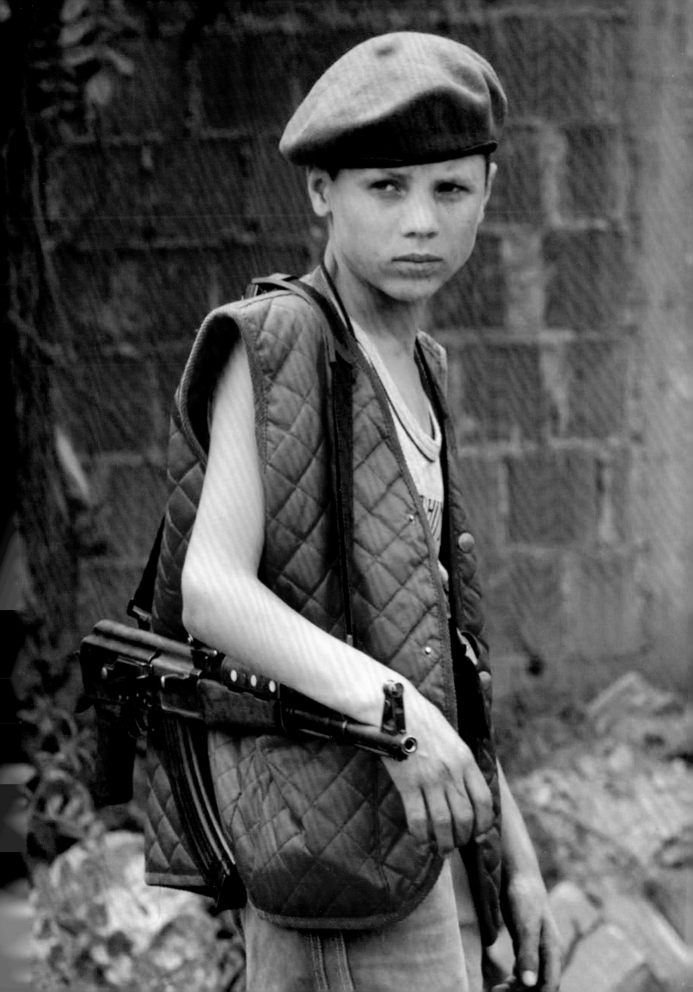

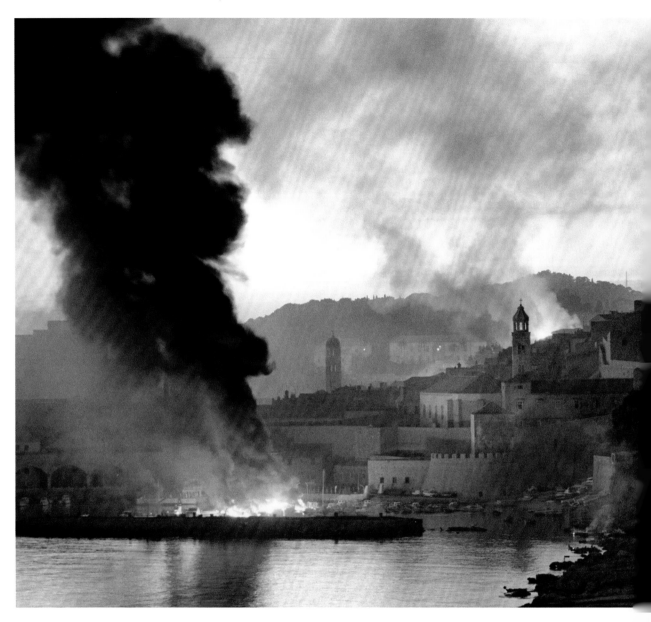

THE fighting spread throughout most of the former Yugoslav Republic. In the south, thousands of refugees fled to the old walled city of Dubrovnik, which came under bombardment (1) from the Yugoslav Federal Army, 12 November 1991. Sarajevo was among the worst hit cities. A Bosnian sniper returns fire after Serbs fired on a peace demonstration, 6 April 1992 (2). The Dayton Agreement was an attempt to bring peace. It was signed at the Wright-Patterson Air Force Base, near Dayton, Ohio (3), by (from left to right at table) President Slobodan Milosevic (Serbia), President Alija Izetbegovic (Bosnia-Herzegovina) and President Franjo Tudjman (Croatia) on 21 November 1995. The watchful *eminence gris* in the background is US Secretary of State Warren Christopher.

DIE Kämpfe breiten sich in nahezu der gesamten ehemaligen Republik Jugoslawien aus. Im Süden suchten tausende Flüchtlinge Schutz hinter den alten Stadtmauern Dubrovniks; die Jugoslawische Republikanische Armee nahm daraufhin die Stadt unter Bombenbeschuß – 12. November 1991 (1). Sarajewo gehörte zu den Städten, die am schlimmsten getroffen wurden. Ein bosnischer Heckenschütze erwidert das Feuer, nachdem Serben auf eine Friedensdemonstration geschossen haben – 6. April 1992 (2). Die Vereinbarung von Dayton sollte Frieden bringen; sie wurde auf der Wright-Patterson-US-Airforce-Basis in der Nähe von Dayton im US-Bundesstaat Ohio von Präsident Slobodan Milosevic (Serbien), Präsident Aljia Izetbegovic (Bosnien-Herzegowina) und Präsident Franjo Tudjman (Kroatien) (im Bild von links nach rechts) am 21. November 1995 unterzeichnet (3). Als wachsame graue Eminenz im Hintergrund: US-Staatssekretär Warren Christopher.

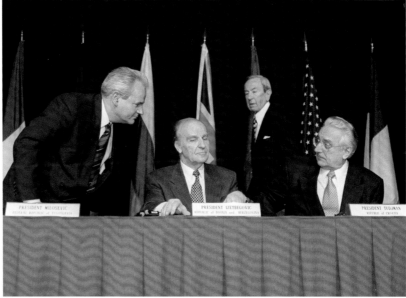

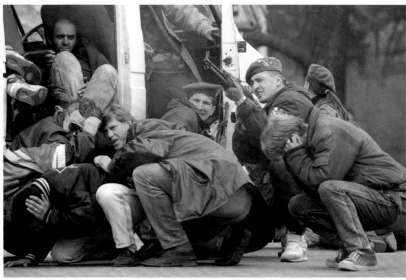

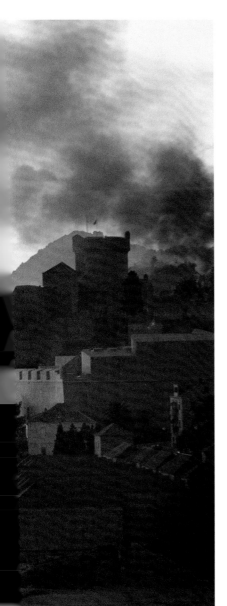

1 2

LES combats font tache d'huile dans presque toute l'ancienne
République de Yougoslavie. Dans le Sud, des milliers de
réfugiés cherchent protection derrière les murailles antiques de
Dubrovnik ; à la suite de quoi, l'armée républicaine yougoslave
n'hésite pas à bombarder la ville – 12 novembre 1991 (1). Sarajevo
est l'une des villes les plus gravement touchées. Un sniper
bosniaque réplique après que les Serbes ont tiré sur une
manifestation en faveur de la paix – 6 avril 1992 (2). L'accord de
Dayton est censé amener la paix ; il est signé sur la base de l'armée
de l'air américaine Wright-Patterson, à proximité de Dayton, dans
l'État fédéré américain de l'Ohio, par le président Slobodan
Milosevic (Serbie), le président Aljia Izetbegovic (Bosnie-
Herzégovine) et le président Franjo Tudjman (Croatie) (de gauche à
droite sur la photo), le 21 novembre 1995 (3). En tant
qu'éminence grise attentive qui a tiré les ficelles : le secrétaire
d'État américain Warren Christopher.

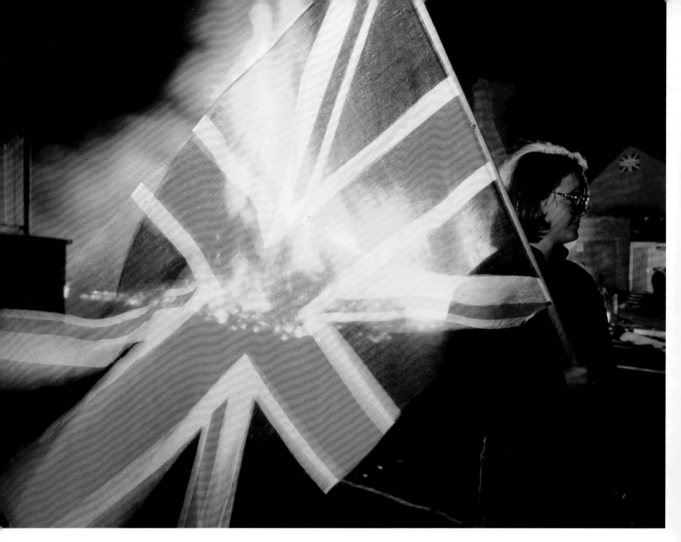

S EEN by some as another outpost of the British Empire, Northern Ireland remained a divided and unhappy community for much of the 1980s and 1990s. There were several major attempts to find sufficient compromise between Loyalists and Republicans to establish lasting peace, but the essential ingredient of goodwill was too often missing. From the early 1980s onwards, the government of the Irish Republic showed greater involvement in the future of Northern Ireland, and the 1985 Anglo-Irish Agreement hinted that power-sharing between the two sides might be a real possibility. But Prime Minister Margaret Thatcher declared herself 'Rock Firm' for the continued union of Northern Ireland with the rest of Britain, and her successor, John Major, said he was 'Four Square' behind the Union.

V ON manchen als ein weiterer Außenposten des britischen Imperiums betrachtet, blieb Nordirland in den 1980er und 1990er Jahren über weite Strecken ein geteiltes und tief unglückliches Land. Es gab mehrere ernsthafte Versuche, einen tragfähigen Kompromiß zwischen Loyalisten und Republikanern als Grundlage für einen dauerhaften Frieden zu finden; doch die entscheidende Komponente des guten Willens fehlte allzu oft. Seit den frühen 1980er Jahren zeigte die Regierung der Republik Irland zunehmend Engagement für die Zukunft Nordirlands; und das anglo-irische Abkommen im Jahre 1985 legte die Hoffnung nahe, daß eine Teilung der Macht zwischen den beiden Seiten ein gangbarer Weg sein könnte. Doch Premierministerin Margret Thatcher deklarierte »felsenfest« den Verbleib Nordirlands im Verbund mit Großbritannien – und ihr Nachfolger, John Major, stellte sich »standhaft« hinter die Union.

D ANS les années 1980 et 1990, l'Irlande du Nord, que certains considéraient comme un autre poste extérieur de l'Empire britannique, est resté longtemps un pays divisé et profondément malheureux. Ce ne sont pourtant pas les tentatives sérieuses qui ont manqué comme une base d'une paix durable pour élaborer un compromis viable entre Loyalistes et Républicains ; mais la composante décisive, la bonne volonté, a trop souvent fait défaut. Depuis le début des années 1980, le gouvernement de la République d'Irlande a fait preuve de plus en plus d'engagement pour l'avenir de l'Irlande du Nord et l'accord anglo-irlandai de 1985 a suscité l'espoir qu'un partage du pouvoir entre les deux parties pourrait être une méthode praticable. Mais la Dame de fer, le Premier ministre britannique Margaret Thatcher, a déclaré « solide comme un roc » que l'Irlande du Nord continuerait d'appartenir à l'alliance avec la Grande-Bretagne – et son successeur, John Major, s'est rallié corps et âme à l'Union.

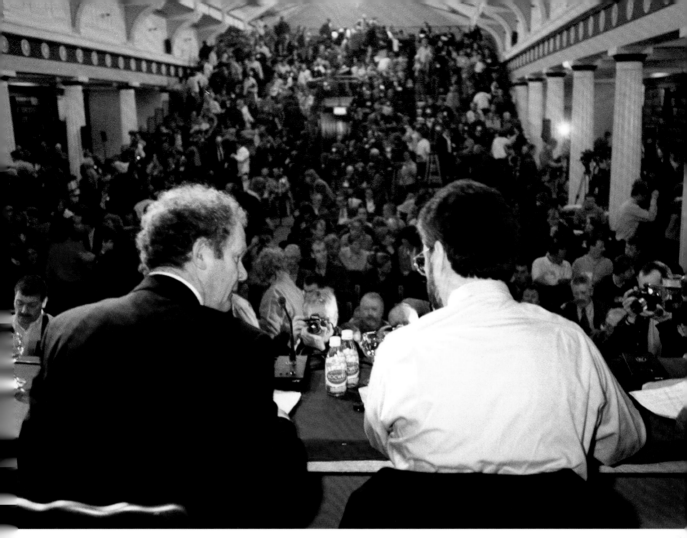

A GREAT deal of real optimism was generated by the IRA's announcement of a ceasefire in 1994, but the old sectarian rivalries arched their backs and the mixture of quibbling and fighting continued. A woman carries the flag of the Union in August 1989 (opposite), while fires burn in the violence that followed the annual march of the Apprentice Boys in the city that still bore two names – Derry to the Republicans, Londonderry to the Orangemen. In 1998 came the drafting of another peace agreement. (above) In a packed hall, Sinn Fein leaders Gerry Adams (right) and Martin McGuinness (left) prepare to address the Sinn Fein Annual Party Conference on which the fate of the Good Friday Agreement depended, 18 April 1998. Backed by the new Labour Government, and endorsed by a referendum of the people, it constituted the greatest hope for a lasting peaceful settlement.

E RNEUT große Hoffnung erzeugte die Waffenstillstandserklärung der IRA im Jahre 1994; doch die alten sektiererischen Rivalitäten setzten sich hinter ihrem Rücken durch, und die Querelen und Kämpfe setzten sich fort. Eine Frau trägt den Union Jack im August 1989, während die Feuer auflodern (linke Seite), die im Anschluß an den jährlichen Marsch der »Apprentice Boys« (einer protestantischen Vereinigung) durch die Stadt gezündet wurden, die noch immer zwei Namen trägt: Derry für die Republikaner, Londonderry für die »Orangemen« (Oranierorden). Im Jahre 1998 wurde ein weiteres Friedensabkommen aufgesetzt. In einer überfüllten Halle bereiten sich der Führer der Sinn Fein, Gerry Adams (oben im Bild rechts), und Martin McGuinness (Sinn-FeinAbgeordneter und Verhandlungsführer) auf die Eröffnung der jährlichen Parteikonferenz vor, von der das weitere Schicksal des sogenannten Karfreitagabkommens abhing – 18. April 1998. Unterstützt durch die neue Labourregierung in London und getragen durch ein Volksreferendum, stellte dies die hoffnungsvolle Basis für ein dauerhaftes Friedensabkommen dar.

L A déclaration de cessez-le-feu de l'IRA, en 1994, suscite de nouveau un grand espoir, mais les vieilles rivalités sectaires continuent de couver en catimini tandis que les querelles et les luttes se poursuivent. Une femme porte l'Union Jack, en août 1989, tandis que font rage les incendies (page de gauche) allumés à la suite du défilé annuel des « Apprentice Boys » (une association protestante) à travers la ville qui porte aujourd'hui encore deux noms : Derry pour les Républicains, et Londonderry pour les « Orangemen » (ordre d'Orange). En 1998, un autre accord de paix est conclu. Un avant-projet d'accord de paix est signé dans une salle absolument comble, où les leaders du Sinn Fein, Gerry Adams (en haut à droite sur la photo), et Martin McGuinness (député du SF qui préside aux négociations) s'apprêtent à inaugurer la conférence annuelle du parti du Sinn Fein, dont allait dépendre le destin de l'accord dit du Vendredi saint – 18 avril 1998. Soutenu par le nouveau gouvernement travailliste à Londres et confirmé par un référendum, il a constitué une base prometteuse pour un accord de paix durable.

The Health of the Planet

Towards the end of the old Millennium, the world was shaken by doubt. It seemed the sins of our industrial forefathers were being visited on new generations of scientists, environmentalists, farmers, and entire populations – to the extent that even politicians became concerned. There was increasingly alarming evidence that the resources of the planet were finite, that damage already done to the atmosphere was possibly irreparable, and that global warming was reaching menacing levels.

For every action, however, there is an opposite reaction. However finite they might be, it was still immensely profitable to exploit the world's resources. The rapid economic growth of China, India and the Pacific Rim, combined with the raw new capitalism of Russia, brought new markets, new goods, and new labour forces into play. East met West in a variety of guises – McDonald's in Moscow, Nike in Beijing, Russian entrepreneurs in Western Europe and the United States, vast quantities of Chinese manufactured hi-tech gadgets and gizmos in shops around the world. But doubt continued to nag away – was such profligate use of energy and raw materials wise?

Few could be sure. Arguments were fierce and protracted on issues such as carbon emissions, GM crops, world trade, Fairtrade, world debt, famine relief and many more. Should we rein in our consumerism, or should we trust to luck and nature to clear up our mess? At the Kyoto Summit in 1998, many were persuaded that limits had to be imposed, but the 'many' did not include the biggest players on the scene. Industrial giants sought to buy up the quotas of pollution allowed less developed countries, alleging that higher temperatures, melting ice caps and climatic changes were merely temporary aberrations in the world's age-old shifting patterns of ice and fire. It was mere coincidence that Nature was unleashing a whole host of disasters.

So they came: earthquakes, floods, drought, hurricanes and tsunamis. By such means, Mother Nature slaughtered millions of her children and rendered millions more homeless. There were cynics who dismissed as insignificant the protests of those forward-thinkers who wished to take precautions to pull us back from the brink of destruction. Recycling campaigns, the 'Go Green' initiative, alternative sources of energy, and steps to improve air quality were pioneered by a few dreamers but were championed by masses. Volunteers worked to clear the oil spills in Alaska and the Gulf of Mexico; to halt the runaway exploitation of the rain forests of South America and south-east Asia. Rescuers fought their way through the choking gas of Bhopal, braved the radioactive horrors of Chernobyl and Fukushima, and tore away the rubble of Kobe and Port-au-Prince to rescue survivors of the earthquakes.

And then there was AIDS, a late 20th century version of the Black Death, spread terrifyingly by love and lust from one continent to another – baffling as to its origins, and believed at various times to threaten a tenth, a quarter, a half of the world's population. To some it was a manifestation of the Wrath of God: to others it was simply one of those inexplicable disasters that imperil the world from time to time. Whatever the cause, this plague spread faster than wildfire, born aloft in standard class air flights for tourists and first class jet-setting for the agents of globalization.

The eyes and ears of the world's tired and poor and hungry turned from one sage to another, searching for someone they could trust. Scientists and politicians, economists and entrepreneurs gave conflicting advice. Some cried 'advance', others 'retreat', and both sides produced evidence to back up their conflicting theories.

A LONDON TAXI PASSES A BILLBOARD BACKING THE INTERNATIONAL DAY OF PROTEST AGAINST THE OIL GIANT EXXON (KNOWN IN BRITAIN AS 'ESSO') AND THE US PRESIDENT GEORGE W. BUSH, 11 JULY 2001 (1). YOUNG STUDENTS RUN ON WHAT IS LEFT OF THE RUNNING TRACK AFTER AN EARTHQUAKE HIT THE KUNGFU HIGH SCHOOL IN WUFENG, TAICHUNG, TAIWAN, 22 OCTOBER 1999 (2).

EIN LONDONER TAXI VOR EINER PLAKATWAND ZUM INTERNATIONALEN PROTESTTAG GEGEN DEN ÖLGIGANTEN EXXON (ESSO) UND DEN US-PRÄSIDENTEN, GEORGE W. BUSH – 11. JULI 2001 (1). JUNGE STUDENTEN LAUFEN ÜBER DIE AUFGEBROCHENE RENNBAHN, NACHDEM EIN ERDBEBEN DIE KUNGFU-SCHULE IN WUFENG GETROFFEN HAT – TAICHUNG, TAIWAN, 2. OKTOBER 1999 (2).

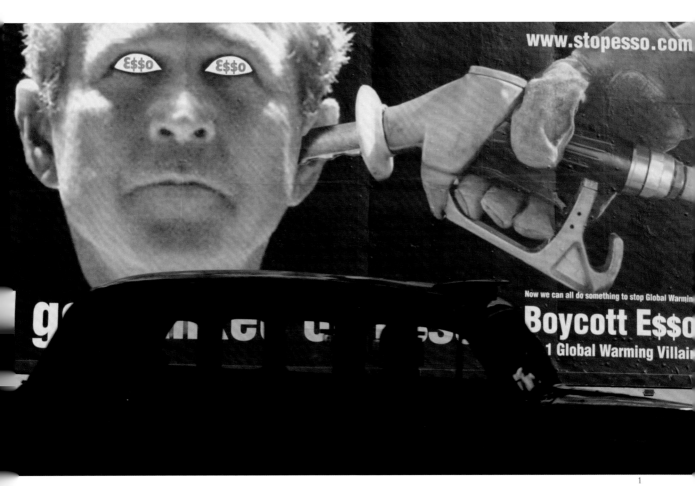

ZUM Ende des alten Jahrtausends wurde die Welt von Zweifeln erschüttert. Eine neue Generation von Wissenschaftlern, Ökologen, Bauern, Reisenden, ja, ganzer Bevölkerungen schien die industriellen Sünden der Vorväter neu in Augenschein zu nehmen – bis selbst Politiker begannen, sich des Themas anzunehmen. Sichtbar wurden zunehmend alarmierende Anzeichen dafür, daß die Ressourcen der Erde nicht unerschöpflich, daß die Schäden, die der Atmosphäre bereits zugefügt wurden, möglicherweise irreparabel waren und daß die globale Erwärmung ein bereits bedrohliches Ausmaß angenommen hatte.

Doch auf jede Aktion folgt eine Reaktion. Wie begrenzt auch immer die Energiequellen der Erde sein mochten – ihre Ausbeutung war nach wie vor äußerst profitabel. Das rapide Wachstum der Ökonomien Chinas, Indiens und der pazifischen Anrainerstaaten sowie der neue ungebremste Kapitalismus Rußlands brachten neue Waren, neue Märkte, neue Arbeitskräfte ins Spiel. Die Maxime »Ost trifft West« erhielt so zahlreiche neue Facetten: McDonald's in Moskau, Nike in Peking, russische Unternehmer in Westeuropa und in den USA, Unmengen von Geräten und Krimskrams »Made in China« in Geschäften rund um den Erdball. Doch die Zweifel nagten weiter: War dieser verschwenderische Umgang mit Energien und Rohstoffen noch vernünftig?

Zu wenige waren sich ihrer Sache sicher. Die Diskussionen wurden erbittert geführt und auf Themen wie Abgase, gentechnisch verändertes Getreide, Welthandel, »Fairtrade«, Staatsverschuldung, Hungerhilfe und vieles mehr ausgeweitet. Sollten wir unseren Konsum einschränken oder auf Glück und Natur vertrauen, die unseren Müll schon schlucken werden? Bei der Umweltgipfelkonferenz 1998 in Kyoto, Japan, waren viele bereit, Beschränkungen einzuführen – doch unter diesen vielen fehlte der größte Spieler auf dem Feld. Industriegiganten suchten nach Wegen, Entwicklungsländern Abgaskontingente abzukaufen und unterstellten damit, die gestiegenen Temperaturen, schmelzende Pole und klimatische Veränderungen seien

UN TAXI LONDONIEN DEVANT UN MUR D'AFFICHES Á L'OCCASION DE LA JOURNÉE INTERNATIONALE DE PROTESTATION CONTRE LE GÉANT PÉTROLIER EXXON (ESSO) ET LE PRÉSIDENT AMÉRICAIN, GEORGE W. BUSH – 11 JUILLET 2001 (1). DES ÉCOLIERS COURENT SUR UNE PISTE D'ATHLÉTISME DÉTRUITE APRÈS QU'UN TREMBLEMENT DE TERRE A TOUCHÉ LEUR ÉCOLE DE KUNG-FU, DANS LE WUFENG – TAICHUNG, TAIWAN, OCTOBRE 1999 (2).

nur temporäre Erscheinungen im ewigen Auf und Ab von Eis und Feuer auf der Erde – und daß die Natur eine wahre Flut von Katastrophen losließ, sei reiner Zufall.

Und so sahen sie aus: Erdbeben, Überschwemmungen, Dürre und Tsunamis. Durch sie brachte Mutter Natur Millionen ihrer Kinder um und machte weitere Millionen obdachlos. Es gab zynische Stimmen, die die Proteste derer, die etwas tun wollten, um uns vor der nahen Zerstörung zu retten, als bedeutungslos abtaten. Recycling-Kampagnen, grüne Inititativen, alternative Energien und Schritte zur Verbesserung der Luftqualität wurden von wenigen Träumern angestoßen, doch schon bald machten die Massen mit. Freiwillige halfen, die Ölteppiche vor Alaska und im Golf von Mexiko zu beseitigen oder den Raubbau in den Regenwäldern Südamerikas und Südostasiens aufzuhalten. Retter kämpften sich durch die giftigen Gase von Bhopal, trotzten den radioaktiven Schrecken von Tschernobyl und Fukushima und halfen, aus dem Schutt von Kobe und Port-au-Prince Überlebende der Erdbeben zu bergen.

Und dann kam AIDS – die Pest des ausgehenden 20. Jahrhunderts – und verbreitete sich auf furchterregende Weise durch Liebe und Lust von einem Kontinent zum nächsten; seine Herkunft gab der Menschheit ein Rätsel auf, und zeitweise hielt man ein Zehntel, ein Viertel, ja, die Hälfte der Weltbevölkerung für von der Krankheit bedroht. Manche sahen in ihr den Ausdruck von Gottes Zorn; für andere war sie eine der unerklärlichen Schrecken, die die Welt dann und wann heimsuchen. Ganz gleich, was man als Ursache ansah: Die Seuche verbreitete sich schneller als ein Buschfeuer – nicht zuletzt mit Hilfe der Billigflüge von Millionen Touristen und des Jetset von Businessagenten der Globalisierung.

Die Augen und Ohren der Müden, Armen und Hungrigen der Welt irrten von einem Weisen zum nächsten auf der Suche nach jemandem, dem sie vertrauen konnten. Wissenschaftler und Politiker, Ökonomen und Unternehmer widersprachen sich in ihren Ratschlägen. Einige riefen »Vorwärts«, andere »Zurück!«, und beide Seiten hatten Beweise für die Richtigkeit ihrer Theorien.

VERS la fin de l'Ancien Millénaire, le monde a été pris de doutes. Une génération nouvelle de scientifiques, écologistes, paysans, mais aussi des populations entières, se mirent à stigmatiser les péchés industriels commis par nos grands-pères – jusqu'à ce que les hommes politiques eux-mêmes se penchent sur cette question. Des signes alarmants que les ressources de la terre ne sont pas inépuisables, que les dommages déjà causés à l'atmosphère sont éventuellement irréparables et que le réchauffement de la planète a déjà pris une ampleur menaçante se firent de plus en plus visibles.

Mais à chaque action sa réaction. Aussi limitées que puissent être les sources d'énergie terrestres – les exploiter continue d'être extrêmement lucratif. La croissance rapide de l'économie en Chine, en Inde et dans les États riverains du Pacifique ainsi que le nouveau capitalisme sauvage en Russie nous firent découvrir de nouvelles marchandises, de nouveaux marchés, de nouveaux salariés. Ainsi la devise « l'Est à la rencontre de l'Ouest » a-t-elle pris nombre de facettes nouvelles : McDonald's à Moscou, Nike à Pékin, des industriels russes en Europe occidentale et aux États-Unis et de véritables raz-de-marée d'appareils et de gadgets « made in China » dans les magasins de toute la planète. Mais les doutes continuent de nous ronger : ce gaspillage d'énergies et de matières premières est-il encore raisonnable ?

Rares sont ceux qui étaient sûrs de leur affaire. Les discussions furent menées sur un ton acerbe et s'étendirent à des thèmes tels les gaz d'échappement, les céréales génétiquement modifiées, le commerce mondial, le commerce « équitable », l'endettement de l'État, la lutte contre la faim dans le monde et bien d'autres choses encore. Devions-nous restreindre notre consommation et nous fier à la chance et à la nature pour que cette dernière nous débarrasse de nos montagnes de déchets ? Lors du sommet mondial sur le climat, en 1998 à Kyoto, au Japon, beaucoup étaient déjà prêts à introduire des restrictions – mais, parmi ces nombreuses bonnes volontés, ne figurait pas l'acteur n° 1. Les géants de l'industrie cherchèrent des moyens d'acheter les quotas de pollutions permis aux pays en développement, laissant ainsi entendre que la hausse des températures, la fonte de la banquise et les changements climatiques n'étaient que des phénomènes temporaires dans les allers et retours de la glace et du feu sur la terre – et, si la nature déclenchait un véritable raz-de-marée de catastrophes, cela n'était, selon eux, qu'un pur hasard.

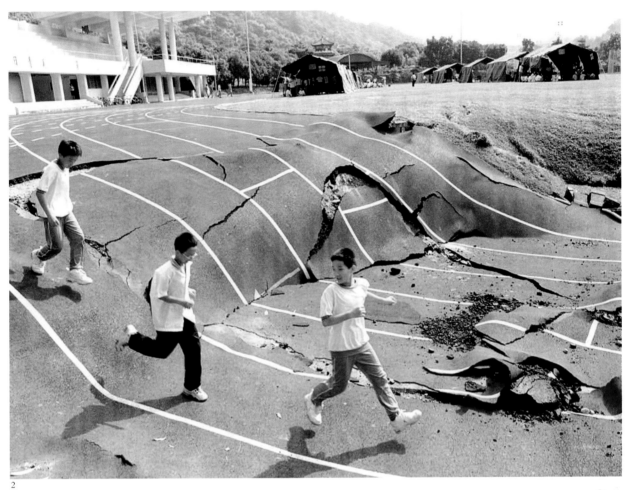

2

Un hasard qui ressemblait à cela : séismes, inondations, sécheresses, tornades et tsunamis. C'est ainsi que Mère Nature emporta des millions de ses enfants et en condamna des millions d'autres à l'errance. Les cyniques considéraient comme infondées les protestations de ces visionnaires qui souhaitaient nous soustraire à une destruction imminente. Campagnes de recyclage, initiatives vertes, sources d'énergies alternatives et mesures d'amélioration de la qualité de l'air étaient initiées par quelques doux rêveurs, mais défendues par les masses. Des volontaires œuvraient à dépolluer les eaux de l'Alaska et du golfe du Mexique touchées par les marées noires, à freiner la surexploitation des forêts tropicales humides d'Amérique du Sud et du Sud-Est asiatique. Des secouristes ont bravé les gaz toxiques de Bhopal, défié les horreurs radioactives de Tchernobyl et de Fukushima, fouillé les décombres de Kobe et de Port-au-Prince pour venir en aide aux victimes des séismes.

Et c'est alors qu'est survenu le SIDA – la peste de la fin du XXe siècle – qui s'est propagé de façon horrible, *via* l'amour et le plaisir, d'un continent à l'autre ; son origine a soulevé une énigme pour l'humanité et, parfois, on a cru qu'un dixième, un quart, voire la moitié de la population mondiale était menacée par la maladie. Certains y virent l'expression de la colère de Dieu ; pour d'autres, c'était l'une des horreurs inexplicables qui frappent le monde de temps à autre. Quelle qu'en ait été la cause pour chacun : l'épidémie s'est propagée plus vite qu'un incendie de savane – aussi et surtout à cause des vols à bas prix de millions de touristes et du jet-set du monde des affaires depuis la mondialisation.

Les yeux et les oreilles d'un monde fatigué, misérable et affamé, se tournaient d'un sage à un autre, à la recherche de celui en qui croire. Scientifiques et politiciens, économistes et entrepreneurs ne parlaient pas le même langage. Alors que certains nous intimaient l'ordre « d'avancer », d'autres conseillaient de « faire machine arrière », alors que chacun produisait ses propres preuves pour argumenter des théories contradictoires.

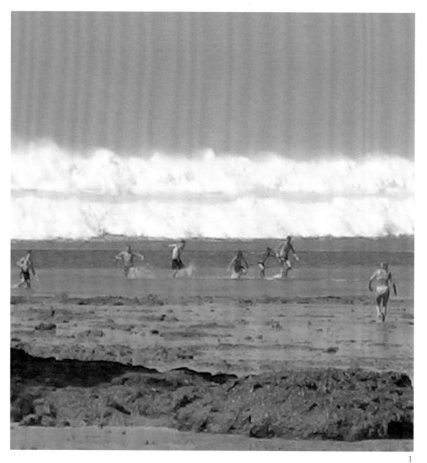

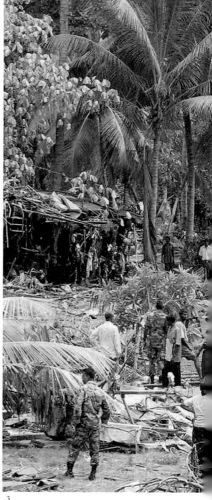

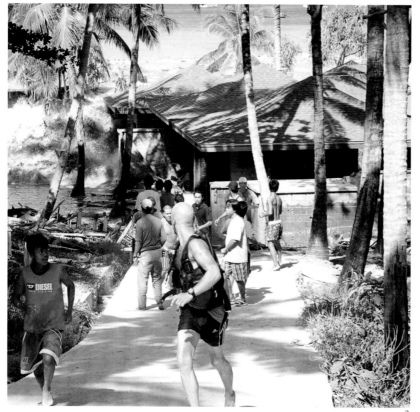

WHEN six tsunami waves raced across the Indian Ocean on 26 December 2004, entire fishing villages, tourist resorts and seaside towns were destroyed. The waves were created by the Sumatra–Andaman underwater earthquake, measuring over 9.0 on the Richter Scale. It was a disaster on an horrendous scale, and one that came without warning. The first wave surges towards Hat Rai Lay Beach, Thailand (1), and comes ashore at Koh Raya (2). The photographer survived. Boats were flung ashore, trees uprooted, and trains lifted like toys from the track and deposited in the jungle, as in Seeni-game, near the tourist centre of Hikkaduwa, Sri Lanka (3). Three days later, Indonesians queued for gasoline at Banda Aceh, 30 December 2004 (4). Over 180,000 people lost their lives and a year later, thousands more were still missing. In Thap Lamu, Thailand, and in many other places, bulletin boards were posted with pictures of unidentified victims of the disaster (5).

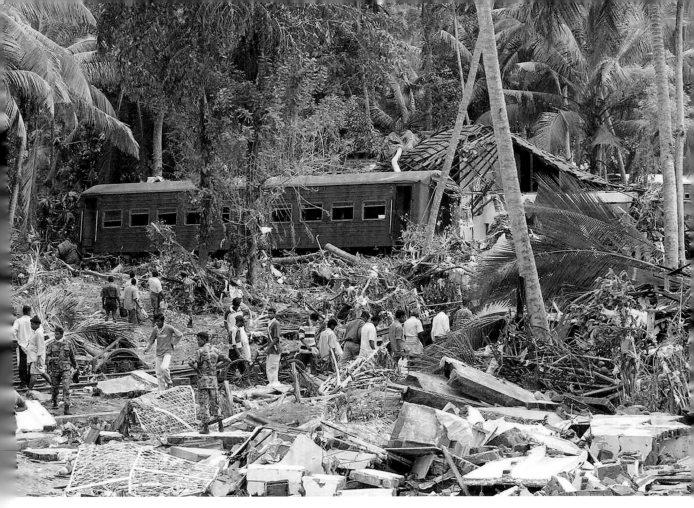

ALS am 26. Dezember 2004 sechs Tsunamiwellen durch den Indischen Ozean rasten, wurden ganze Fischerdörfer, Touristenanlagen und Hafenstädte zerstört. Die Flutwellen entstanden durch das Unterwassererdbeben zwischen Sumatra und den Andamanen, das eine Stärke von mehr als 9.0 auf der Richterskala aufwies. Es war eine Katastrophe von entsetzlichen Ausmaßen - und eine, die ohne Vorwarnung hereinbrach. Die erste Welle rollt auf Hat Rai Lay Beach, Thailand zu (1) und überflutet Koh Raya (2). Der Photograph überlebte.

Boote wurden an Land geworfen, Bäume entwurzelt, Eisenbahnwaggons wie Spielzeug aus den Schienen gerissen und in den Dschungel geschleudert – wie in Sinigame auf Sri Lanka, in der Nähe des Touristenortes Hikkaduwa (3). Drei Tage später stehen Indonesier in Banda Aceh für Benzin Schlange – 30. Dezember 2004 (4). Mehr als 180 000 Menschen starben, und ein Jahr später wurden noch Tausende vermißt. In Thap Lamu, Thailand, wurden - wie in zahlreichen anderen Orten – Anschlagtafeln mit Photos von bisher nicht identifizierten Opfern der Katastrophe öffentlich aufgestellt (5).

LORSQUE six vagues du tsunami ont traversé l'océan Indien le 26 décembre 2004, villages de pêcheurs, équipements touristiques et villes portuaires ont été totalement détruits. Le raz-de-marée a été déclenché par un tremblement de terre sous-marin entre Sumatra et l'archipel d'Andaman, qui avait une puissance de plus de 9,0 sur l'échelle de Richter. La première vague arrive à Hat Rai Lay Beach, en Thaïlande (1), et inonde Koh Raya (2). Le photographe a survécu.

Des bateaux ont été jetés à terre, des arbres, déracinés, des wagons de chemin de fer, arrachés des rails comme des jouets et projetés dans la jungle – ici à Sinigame, au Sri Lanka, à proximité de la station touristique Hikkaduwa (3). Trois jours plus tard, des Indonésiens font la queue pour obtenir de l'essence à Banda Aceh – 30 décembre 2004 (4). Plus de 180 000 personnes ont péri et, un an plus tard, on comptait encore des milliers de disparus. À Thap Lamu, en Thaïlande – comme dans de nombreuses autres localités – des panneaux ont été dressés dans les rues pour recevoir les photos de victimes de la catastrophe jusque-là pas toujours identifiées. (5).

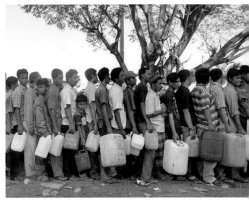

4

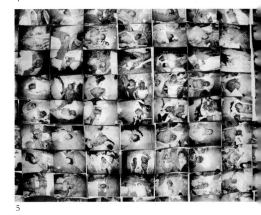

5

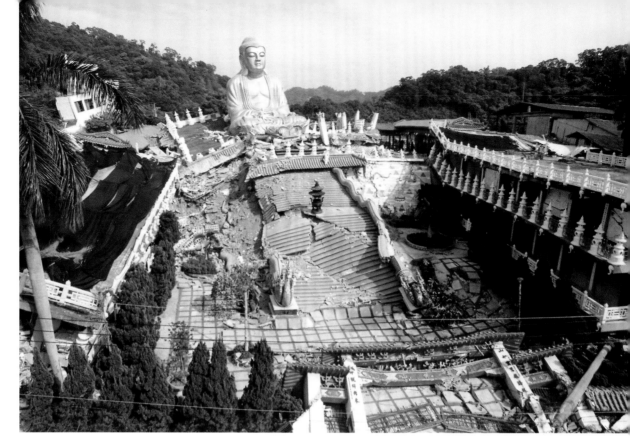

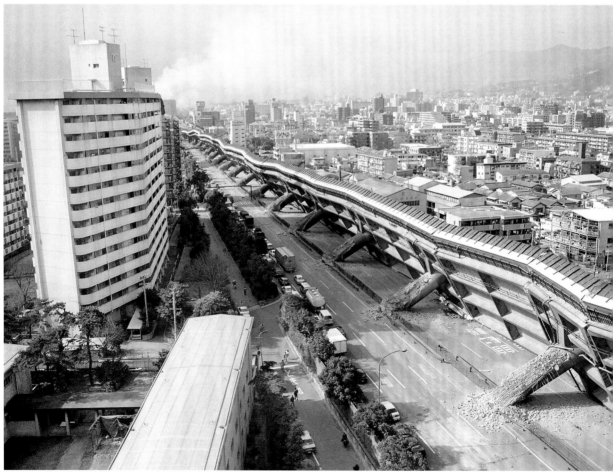

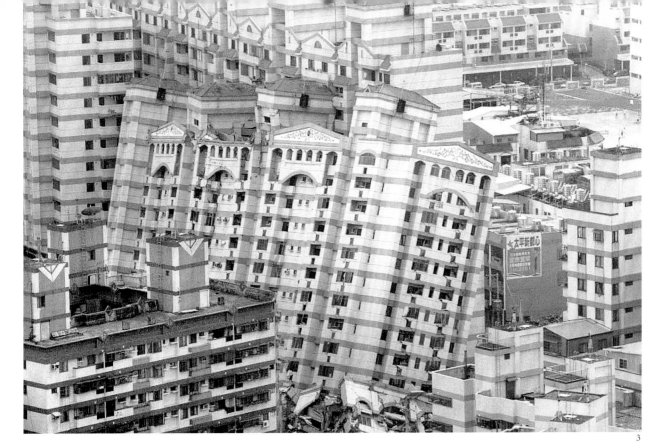

3

THE world was shaken by many
earthquakes in the 1990s, seen by
some as a sign of impending apocalypse, by
others as a sign that all was not well with
the health of the planet. A Buddhist temple
collapses (1) and residential buildings lean
drunkenly in the city centre (3) four days
after a quake hit Wufeng, central Taiwan
on 21 September 1999. A previously
elevated highway lies on its side in
Nishinomiya, western Japan, 17 January
1995 (2). A 9-year-old Israeli girl is rescued
by Israeli Army Medics from the rubble of
Cinarcik, Turkey on 21 August 1999 (4).

DIE Welt wurde in den 1990ern durch
zahlreiche Erdbeben erschüttert.
Manche sahen in ihnen Anzeichen für die
heraufziehende Apokalypse, andere
werteten sie als Indiz dafür, daß es mit der
Gesundheit des Planeten nicht zum Besten
stand. Ein buddhistischer Tempel bricht
zusammen (1), und ganze Wohnblocks
stehen, wie betrunken zur Seite geneigt,
mitten im Zentrum von Wufeng, Taiwan
(3) – vier Tage, nachdem ein Erdbeben die
Stadt am 21. September 1999 erschütterte.
Eine erst vor kurzem errichtete Autobahn
liegt umgestürzt mitten in Nishinomiya,
Westjapan – 17. Januar 1995 (2). Das
neunjährige israelische Mädchen wird von
israelischen Armeeärzten aus den Trümmern von Cinarcik, Türkei, gerettet –
21. August 1999 (4).

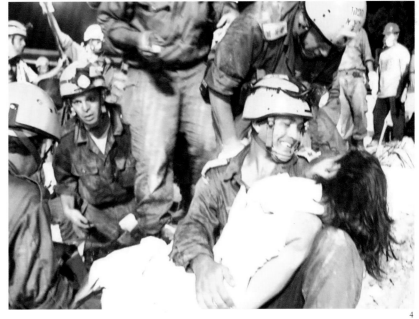

4

DANS les années 1990, le monde a été
ébranlé par une succession de
tremblements de terre. Certains y ont vu
un indice précurseur d'une apocalypse
imminente alors que d'autres ont considéré
que la santé de la planète n'était pas au
mieux. Un temple bouddhiste s'effondre
(1) et des blocs d'immeubles entiers
chancèlent, tel un ivrogne, dans le centre
de Wufeng, à Taiwan (3) – quatre jours
après qu'un tremblement de terre a secoué
la ville, le 21 septembre 1999.
Une autoroute inaugurée peu de temps
auparavant s'est effondrée comme un
château de cartes à Nishinomiya, dans
l'ouest du Japon – 17 janvier 1995 (2).
Une fillette israélienne de neuf ans est
sauvée par des médecins militaires israéliens
des ruines de Cinarcik, en Turquie –
21 août 1999 (4).

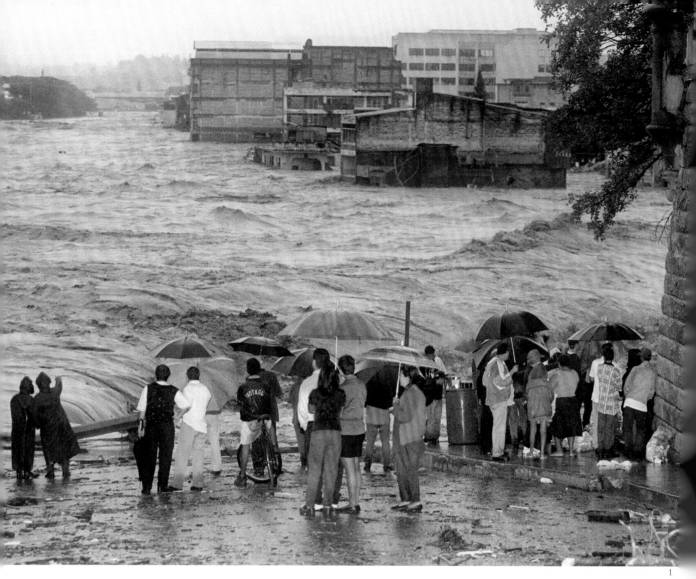

1

THE elements show their destructive power in the Nervous Nineties. Swollen by heavy rain from Hurricane Mitch, the floodwaters of the Choluteca river swirl through Tegucigalpa, Honduras, 31 October 1998 (1). On the other side of the world, a year later, a farmer rescues his pig after torrential rain battered Yonchon in central Korea in August 1999 (3). After the flood, the fire – smoke, ash and scalding steam erupt from the Guagua Pichincha volcano, just 10 kms (six miles) from Quito, capital of Ecuador, 7 October 1999 (2).

DIE Elemente zeigten in den nerven-aufreibenden Neunzigern ihre zerstörerischen Kräfte. Der Choluteca-Fluß schwoll durch heftige Regenfälle nach dem Wirbelsturm Mitch mächtig an. Seine Fluten ergießen sich in die Stadt Tegucigalpa, Honduras – 31. Oktober 1998 (1). Am anderen Ende der Welt rettet im Jahr darauf ein Bauer nach sturzbach-artigen Regenfällen in Yonchon, Korea, sein Schwein – August 1999 (3). Nach dem Hochwasser das Feuer: Rauch, Asche und siedend heißer Dampf brechen aus dem Guagua-Pichincha-Vulkan hervor, nur zehn Kilometer von Quito, der Hauptstadt Ecuadors, entfernt – 7. Oktober 1999 (2).

DURANT ces furieuses années 90, les éléments affichent leur force destructrice. Après l'ouragan tropical Mitch, le Choluteca a gonflé de manière impressionnante après de brutales chutes de pluie. Ses eaux se déversent sur la ville de Tegucigalpa, au Honduras – 31 octobre 1998 (1). À l'autre extrémité du monde, l'année suivante, un paysan sauve son cochon après des chutes de pluie catastro-phiques à Yonchon, en Corée, – août 1999 (3). Après les inondations, le feu : de la fumée, des cendres et de la vapeur d'eau brûlante s'échappent du volcan du Guagua-Pichincha, à neuf kilomètres seulement de Quito, la capitale de l'Équateur – 7 octobre 1999 (2).

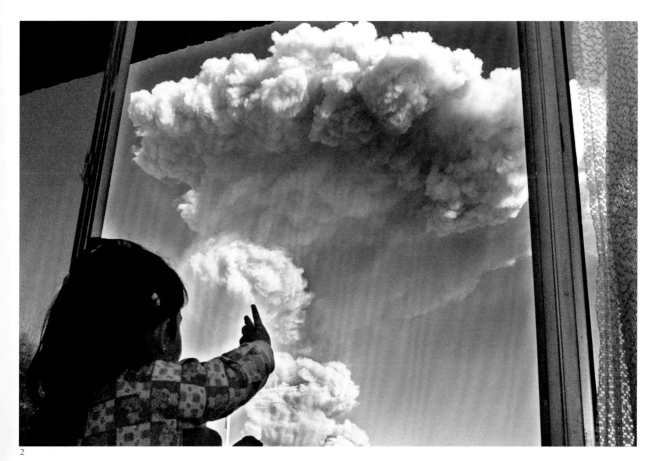

2

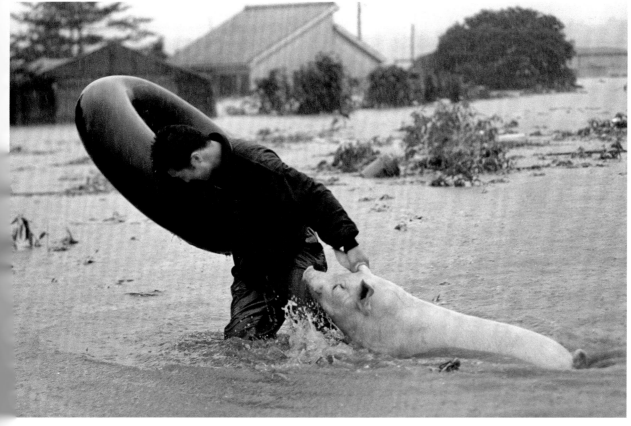

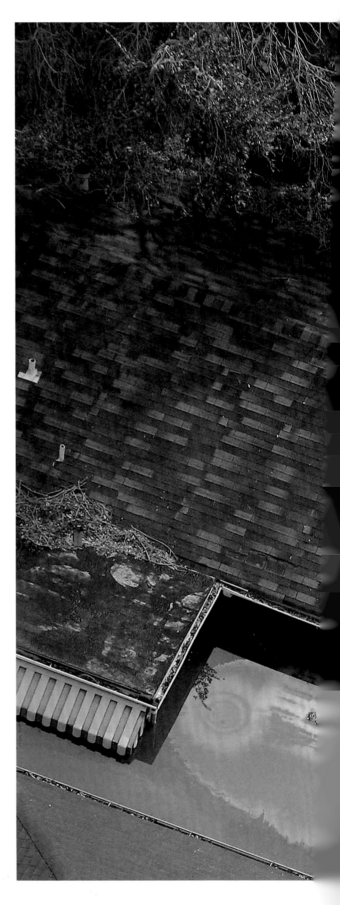

FOR several years it had been forecast that the levees protecting New Orleans from abnormally high tides would prove inadequate. In August 2005, the approach of Hurricane Katrina caused alarm, but the authorities saw no reason to take extreme measures. Then, on 30 August, Katrina hit the city, and a surging tide breached the levees around Lake Ponchartrain. Within hours, 80 per cent of the city was under water. Some citizens managed to flee in time, others were sent back. Thousands were trapped and forced to climb to the upper storeys or roofs of buildings (right) to await rescue by boat or helicopter. The predominately black areas of New Orleans were hardest hit, and the disaster threatened a political crisis for the Bush administration when many victims died simply from thirst and exhaustion. In all, Katrina was responsible for over $115 billion worth of damage.

JAHRELANG wurde vorausgesagt, daß die Dämme der Stadt New Orleans bei außergewöhnlich hohen Fluten nicht halten würden. Im August 2005 wurden die Behörden durch das Herannahen des Wirbelsturms Katrina zwar alamiert, ergriffen jedoch keine drastischen Maßnahmen. Dann brach am 30. August Katrina über die Stadt herein – und damit eine unaufhaltsame Flut durch die Dämme um Lake Ponchartrain. Innerhalb weniger Stunden waren 80 Prozent der Stadt unter Wasser. Einigen Bürgern gelang es, rechtzeitig zu fliehen; andere wurden zurückgeschickt. Tausende waren in der Stadt gefangen und gezwungen, in den oberen Stockwerken oder auf Dächern (Bild rechts) Zuflucht zu suchen und dort auf Rettung durch Boote oder Hubschrauber zu warten. Die überwiegend von Schwarzen bewohnten Teile der Stadt waren am härtesten betroffen; und die Katastrophe führte für die Bush-Administration beinahe zu einer Regierungskrise, als zahlreiche Bewohner der Stadt durch Durst oder Erschöpfung starben. Insgesamt verursachte der Wirbelsturm Katrina Schäden in Höhe von über 115 Milliarden US-Dollar.

PENDANT des années, on n'avait cessé de répéter que les digues de la ville de la Nouvelle-Orléans ne résisteraient jamais en cas d'inondations d'une hauteur exceptionnelle. Bien qu'alarmées par la proximité de l'ouragan Katrina, en août 2005, les autorités n'ont cependant pas pris les mesures qui s'imposaient. C'est alors que, le 30 août, Katrina se déverse sur la ville – et, avec lui, des masses d'eau submergent les digues du lac Ponchartrain. En quelques heures seulement, 80 pour cent de la ville se retrouvèrent sous l'eau. Certains habitants réussirent à s'enfuir à temps alors que d'autres durent retourner chez eux. Des milliers se retrouvèrent prisonniers dans la ville et contraints de chercher leur salut dans les étages supérieurs ou sur les toits (photo à droite) et, là, d'attendre d'hypothétiques bateaux ou hélicoptères salvateurs. Ce sont les quartiers de la ville habités en majorité par les noirs qui ont été les plus touchés et, pour l'administration Bush, la catastrophe a failli déclencher une crise gouvernementale à la suite de la mort de soif et d'épuisement de nombreux habitants de la ville. Au total, l'ouragan tropical Katrina a causé des dommages de plus de 115 milliards de dollars US.

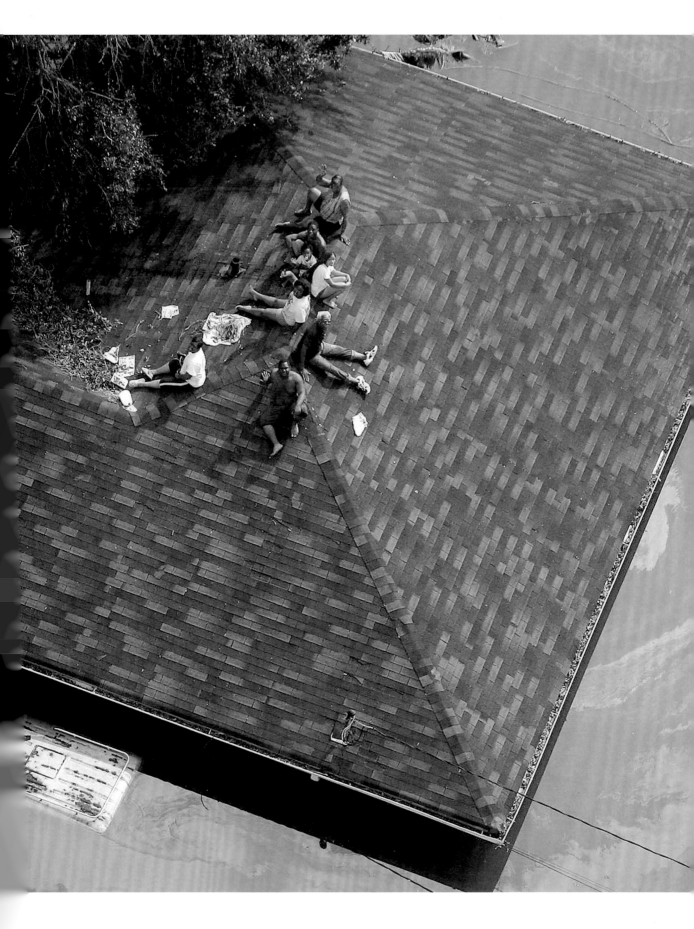

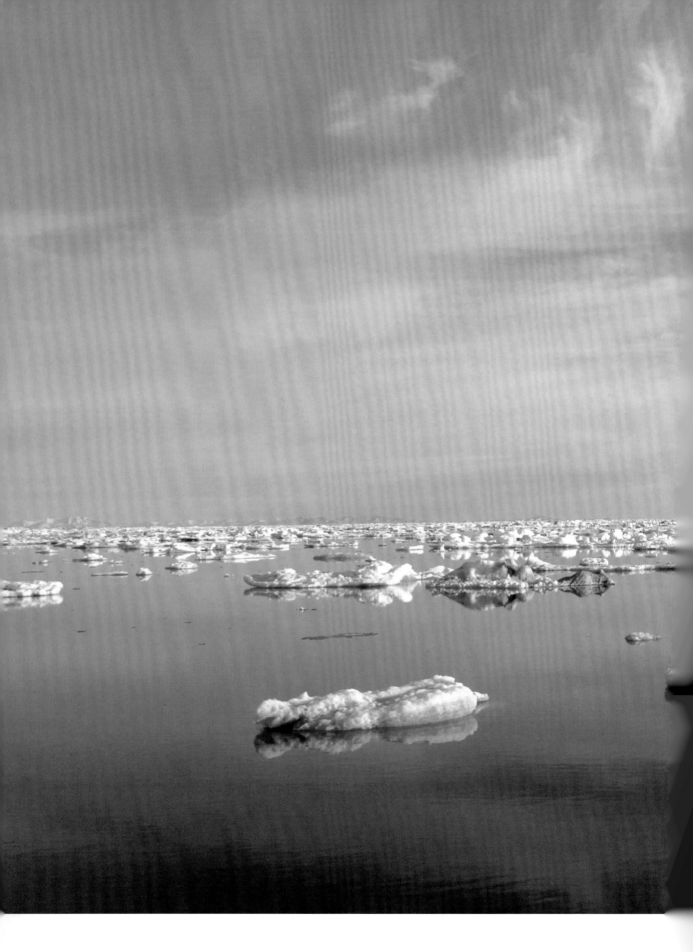

SMALL icebergs float in the Chukchi Sea, Alaska, 9 June 2005. In the past, this sea would have been a frozen expanse of ice many feet thick, but climate change brought problems to the 591 Inupiat Eskimos living in the small village of Shishnmaref nearby. The economy of the area is based on seal hunting, previously done on ice. By the 21st century, however, the hunters had to haul their boats across dangerously thin ice and work their way between the icebergs in pursuit of the seals.

KLEINE Eisberge treiben in der Tschuktschensee, Alaska – 9. Juni 2005. In der Vergangenheit lag über diesem Meer eine gefrorene, mehrere Meter dicke Eisdecke. Der Klimawandel wurde für die 591 Inuit in dem nahegelegenen Eskimodorf Shishnmaref zur existentiellen Gefahr: In dieser Region hängen Wirtschaft und Überleben von der Seehundjagd ab, die bisher auf dem Eis erfolgte. Mit Beginn des 21. Jahrhunderts jedoch mußten die Jäger ihre Beute über zunehmend dünneres Eis transportieren und ihre Boote auf der Jagd zwischen treibenden Eisbergen hindurchmanövrieren.

DE petits icebergs flottent dans la mer de Tchoukotka, en Alaska – 9 juin 2005. Autrefois, une banquise de plusieurs mètres d'épaisseur couvrait cette mer. Les changements climatiques représentent un danger mortel pour les 591 Inuits qui vivent dans le village esquimau tout proche de Shishnmaref : dans cette région, l'économie et la survie dépendent de la chasse aux phoques, qui se déroulait jusque-là sur la glace. Depuis le début du XXIe siècle, cependant, les chasseurs doivent transporter leur butin sur une glace toujours plus mince et manœuvrer leurs bateaux entre les icebergs en dérive.

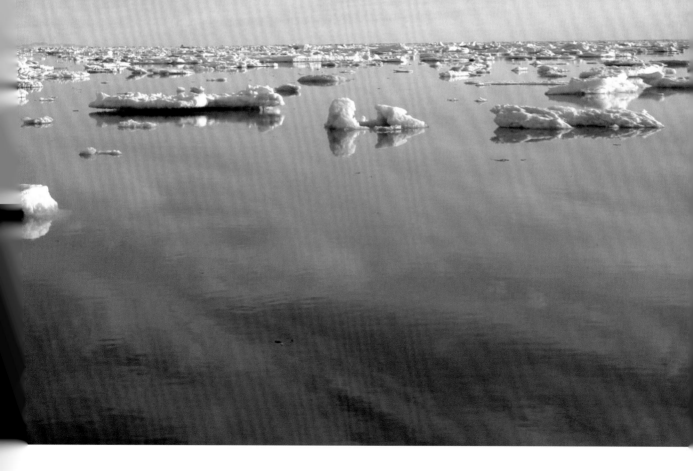

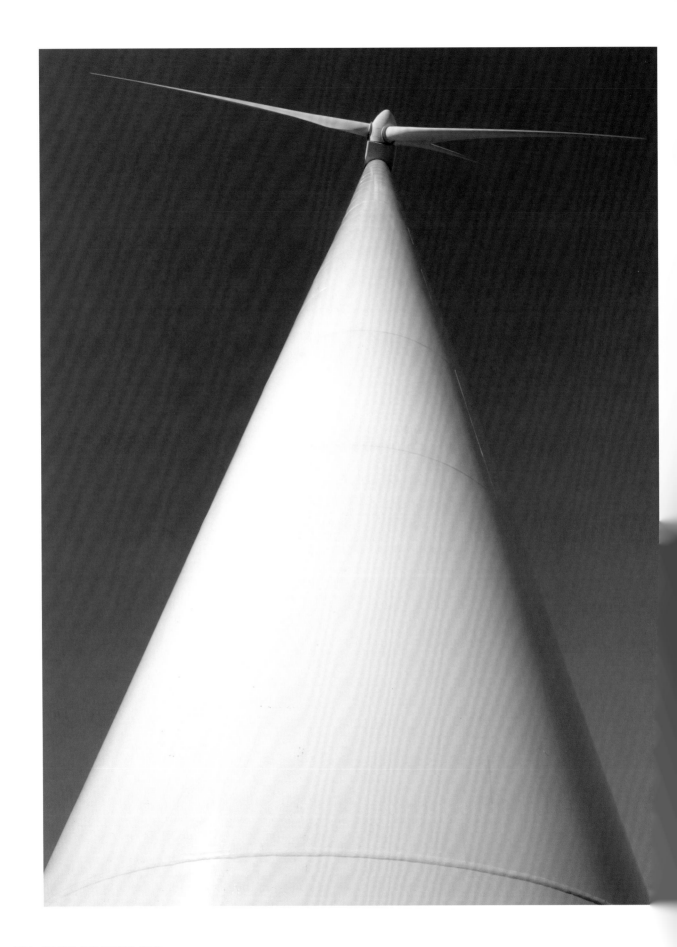

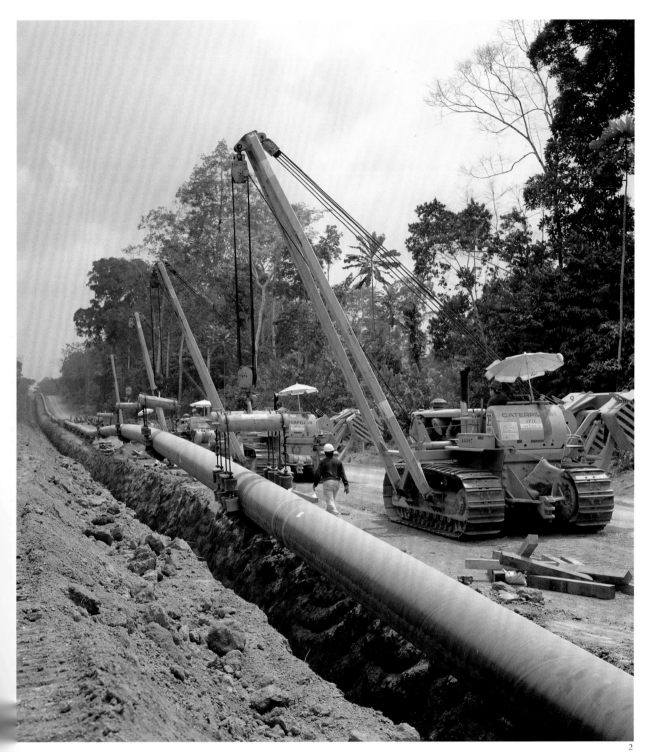

2

THOSE hunting for old sources of energy had to travel further and further in the 21st century. Workers prepare to bury a 660-mile oil-pipeline from Chad to the Gulf of Guinea in March 2002 (2). Renewable sources of energy on the second largest wind farm in the world at Higueruela, Spain, 25 November 2004 (1).

WER traditionelle Energiequellen suchte, mußte seit Beginn des 21. Jahrhunderts immer weitere Strecken hinter sich legen. Arbeiter verlegen eine Ölpipeline von Tschad bis zum Golf von Guinea – März 2002 (2). Erneuerbare Energiequellen im zweitgrößten Windenergiepark der Welt in Higueruela, Spanien – 25. November 2004 (1).

AU début du XXIᵉ siècle, à la recherche de sources d'énergie traditionnelles, on doit couvrir des distances toujours plus longues. Des ouvriers posent un oléoduc menant du Tchad au Golfe de Guinée – mars 2002 (2). Sources d'énergie renouvelables dans le deuxième plus grand parc d'énergie éolienne au monde à Higueruela, Espagne – 25 novembre 2004 (1).

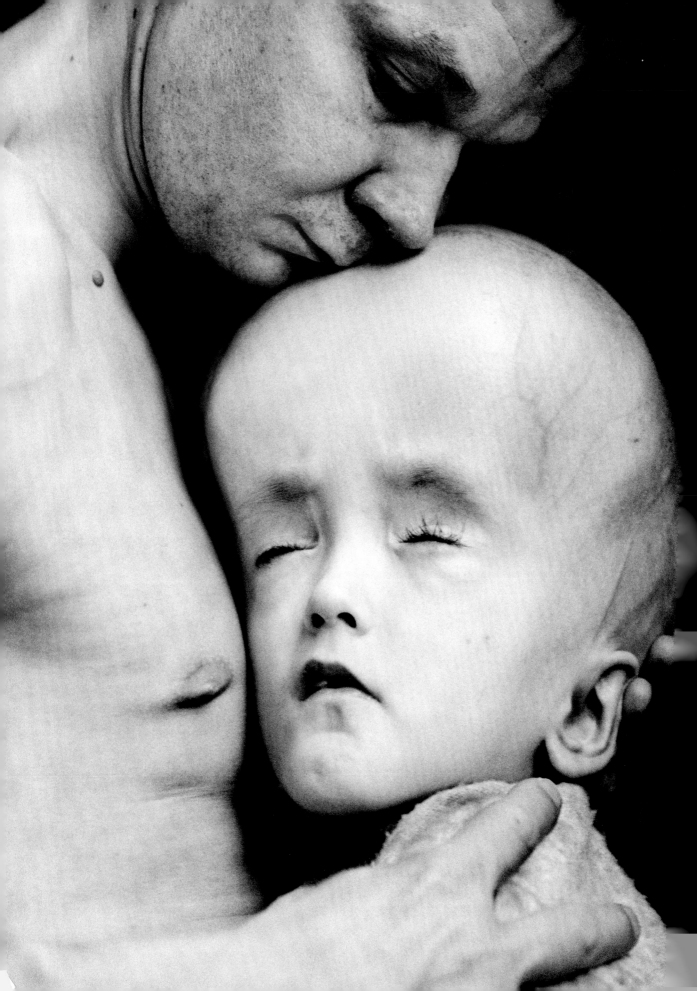

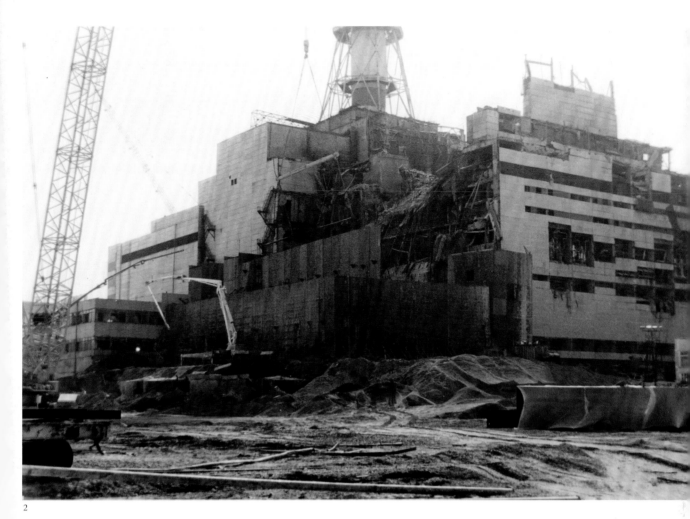

2

ON 28 April 1986 a devastating
explosion, 90 times more powerful
than the Hiroshima bomb, took place at
the Chernobyl nuclear plant in Russia.
Over 99 per cent of nearby Belarus was
contaminated by radioactivity. It was 10
years before repair work could begin (2).
In Belarus and the Ukraine, birth defects
increased by 250 per cent. Vitali
Prokopenko holds his nine-year-old
daughter Sasha, born in 1997 (1).

AM 28. April 1986 ereignete sich eine
verheerende Explosion im Atomkraftwerk in Tschernobyl, Rußland, die 90mal
stärker als die Bombe auf Hiroshima war.
Über 99 Prozent der Fläche Weißrußlands
wurden radioaktiv verseucht, und es
dauerte zehn Jahre, bis mit den Reparatu-
rarbeiten begonnen werden konnte (2). In
Weißrußland sowie in der Ukraine stieg
die Rate der Geburtsschäden um über
250 Prozent. Vitali Prokopenko mit seiner
neun Jahre alten Tochter Sascha, die 1997
geboren wurde (1).

LE 28 avril 1986 se produit une
dramatique explosion dans la centrale
nucléaire de Tchernobyl, en Russie, une
explosion 90 fois plus puissante que la
bombe d'Hiroshima. Plus de 99 pour cent
de la surface de la Biélorussie ont été
contaminés par la radioactivité et il a fallu
attendre dix ans pour que l'on puisse
commencer à la réparer (2). En Biélorussie
et en Ukraine, le taux des dommages
congénitaux a augmenté de plus de
250 pour cent. Vitali Prokopenko, avec sa
fillette Sacha âgée de neuf ans, qui est née
en 1997 (1).

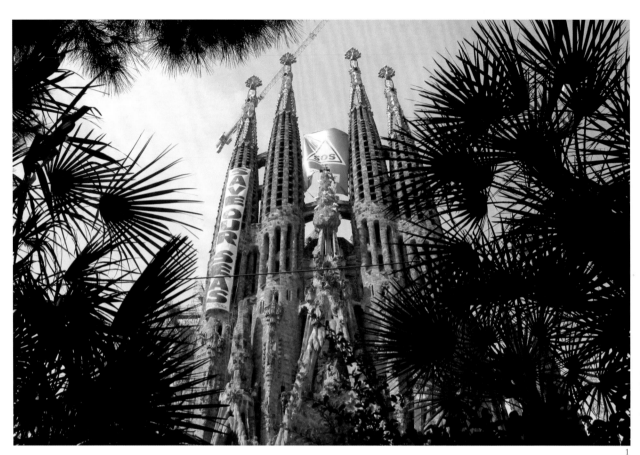

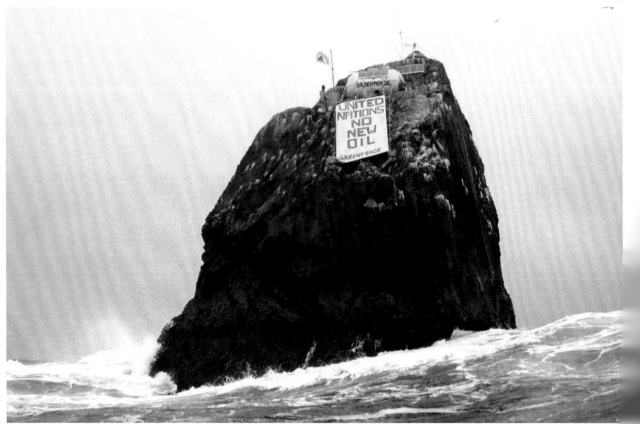

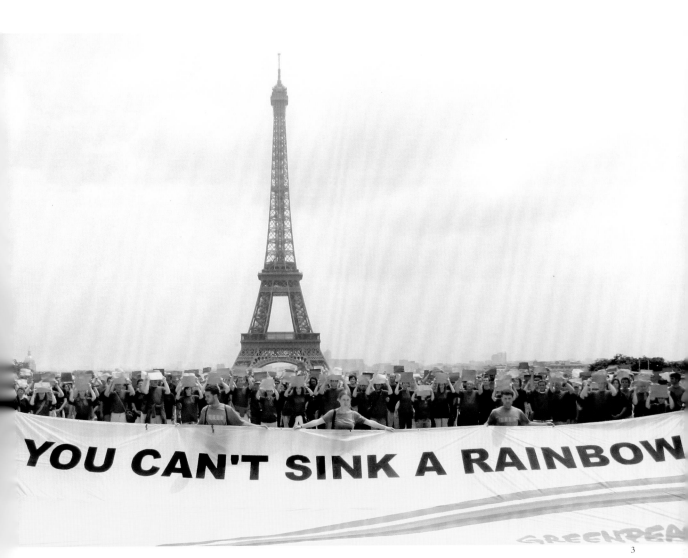

YOU CAN'T SINK A RAINBOW

3

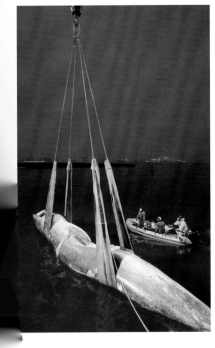

Among those many activists fighting to save the planet were the Greenpeace warriors, who waged a worldwide campaign. Their operations included: climbing the Sagrada Familia Cathedral in Barcelona (1) on 4 June 2004; occupying Rockall in the North Atlantic, 22 June 1997 (2); attempting to hoist a dead whale out of the harbour at Tonnenhof, Germany on 18 January 2006 (4); and demonstrating in Paris (3) to mark the 20th anniversary of the sinking of the *Rainbow Warrior* by French agents in New Zealand, 10 July 2005.

Unter den zahlreichen Aktivisten im Kampf für die Erhaltung unseres Planeten trat die Gruppe »Greenpeace« mit weltweiten Kampagnen hervor. Ihre Aktionen umfaßten unter anderem: die Ersteigung der Kathedrale Sagrada Familia in Barcelona – am 4. Juni 2004 (1); die Besetzung von Rockall im Nordatlantik – am 22. Juni 1997 (2); den Versuch, einen toten Wal im Hafen von Tonnenhof, Deutschland, aus dem Wasser zu heben – am 18. Januar 2006 (4); die Demonstration in Paris zur Erinnerung an die Versenkung ihres Schiffes *Rainbow Warrior* durch französische Agenten in Neuseeland – am 10. Juli 2005.

Parmi les nombreux activistes luttant pour la sauvegarde de notre planète, le groupe « Greenpeace » s'est signalé par ses campagnes mondiales. Des actions qui englobent notamment l'escalade de la cathédrale de la Sainte-Famille, à Barcelone – le 4 juin 2004 (1), l'occupation du Rockall, dans l'Atlantique Nord – le 22 juin 1997 (2), la tentative de hisser hors de l'eau une baleine morte, dans le port de Tonnenhof, en Allemagne – le 18 janvier 2006 (4), la manifestation organisée à Paris pour commémorer le naufrage de son bateau *Rainbow Warrior*, dynamité par des secrets français en Nouvelle-Zélande – le 10 juillet 2005.

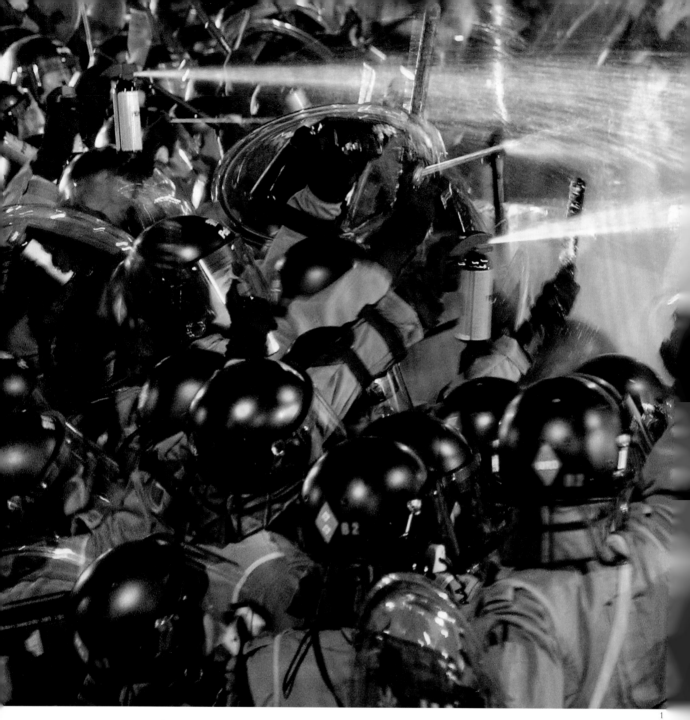

1

CONCERN for the planet, and discontent at its global abuse by many conglomerates, led to increasingly violent confrontations between activists and authorities. Riot police spray anti-World Trade Organization demonstrators in Hong Kong, 17 December 2005 (1). Calgary bicycle police stand guard outside a branch of Starbucks during the G-8 summit meeting 60 miles away, 25 June 2002 (2).

DIE Sorge um den Planeten und der Unmut über den weltweiten Raubbau mit ihm führten zunehmend zu gewalttätigen Auseinandersetzungen zwischen Umweltaktivisten und der Staatsgewalt. Polizisten gehen in Hong Kong mit Sprühdosen gegen Demonstranten vor, die gegen die Politik der Welthandelsorganisation protestieren – 17. Dezember 2005 (1). Vor einem Café der amerikanischen Kaffeehauskette »Starbucks« in Calgary, Kanada, halten Polizisten mit Fahrrädern während des 100 Kilometer entfernt tagenden G-8-Gipfels Wache – 25. Juni 2002, (2).

LA préoccupation pour la planète et la colère causée par son exploitation à l'échelle mondiale entraînent de plus en plus souvent des conflits violents entre activistes écologistes et forces de l'ordre. À Hong-Kong, des policiers s'attaquent avec

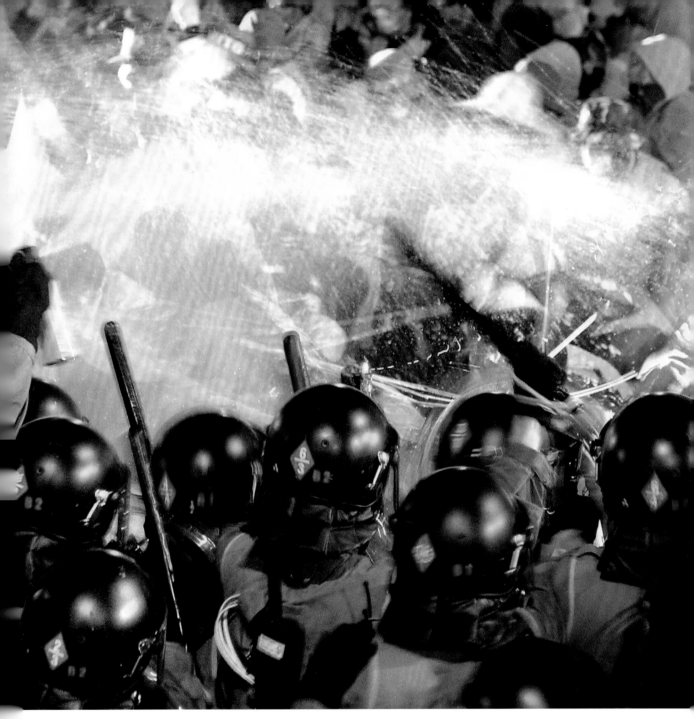

des pulvérisateurs à des manifestants qui protestent contre la politique menée par l'Organisation mondiale du Commerce – 17 décembre 2005 (1). Devant un établissement de la chaîne de salons de café américaine « Starbucks », à Calgary, au Canada, des agents de police en bicyclette montent la garde pendant le sommet du G8 organisé à 100 kilomètres de là – 25 juin 2002 (2).

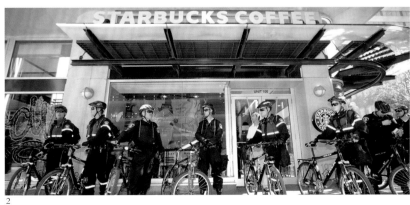

2

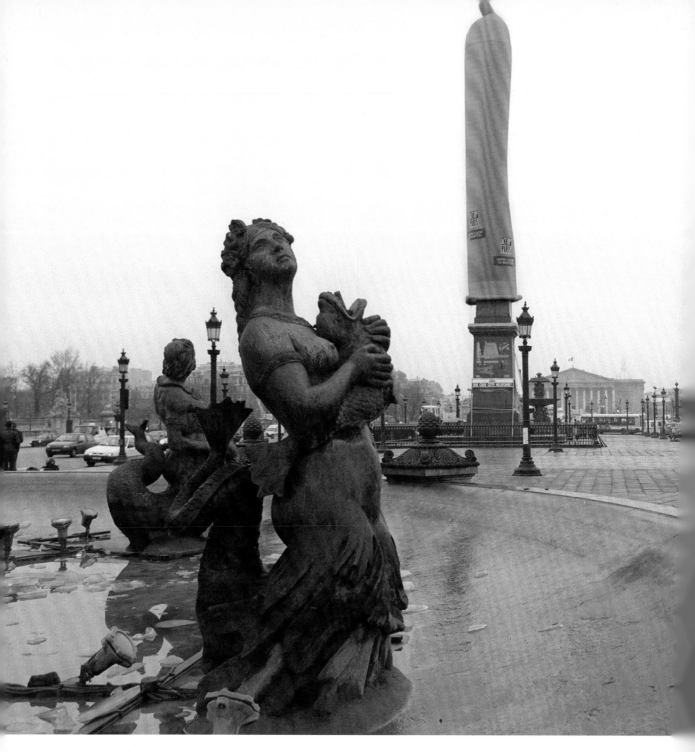

AIDS was the plague of the age. The French group Act-Up display a giant condom on World Aids Day 1993 (1) in Paris. A man ravaged by AIDS receives treatment at a Zambian hospice, 2003 (2). The Reverend John Nduati (centre background) seeks to cure AIDS by the 'Word of God' in Nairobi, Kenya (3). More practically, Mechai Viravaidya hands out condoms and instructions to go-go dancers at a Thai nightclub in 1990 (4).

AIDS wurde zur Pest des Zeitalters. Die französische Gruppe »Act-Up« zeigt zum Welt-Aids-Tag 1993 ein gigantisches Kondom (1). Ein von Aids gezeichneter Mann wird in einem Hospiz in Sambia behandelt – 2003 (2). Reverend John Nduati (im Hintergrund, Bildmitte) möchte Aidskranke in Nairobi, Kenia, durch »Gottes Wort« heilen (3). Praktischer geht Mechai Viravaidya vor und händigt Go-Go-Tänzerinnen in einem Nachtclub in

Thailand Kondome mit Gebrauchsanweisungen aus – 1990 (4).

LE SIDA est devenu la peste des temps modernes. Le groupe français « Act-Up » présente un gigantesque préservatif à l'occasion de la journée mondiale du SIDA en 1993 (1). Un homme avagé par le SIDA est soigné dans un hôpital en Zambie – 2003 (2). Le révérend John Nduati (à l'arrière-plan, au centre) souhaite guérir des

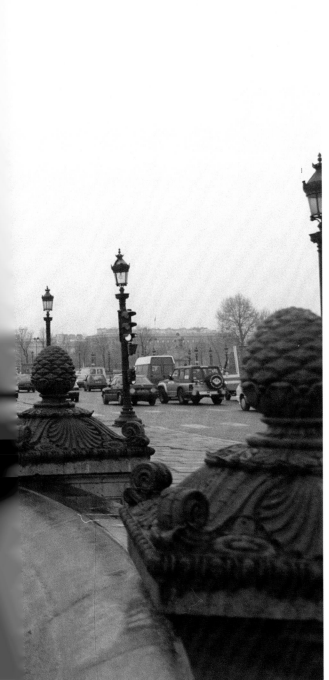

1

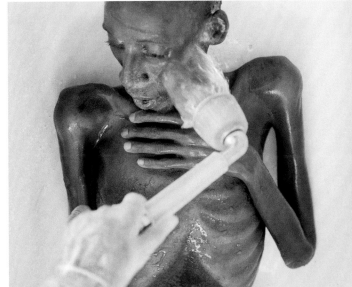

2

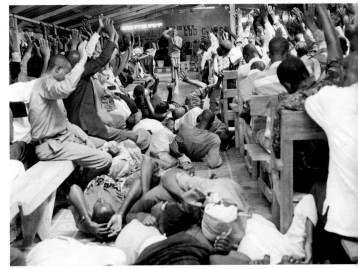

3

malades du SIDA à Nairobi, au Kenya, par
la « Parole de Dieu » (3). Mechai
Viravaidya est plus pragmatique et remet à
des go-go-girls d'une boîte de nuit de
Thaïlande des préservatifs accompagnés
d'un mode d'emploi – 1990 (4).

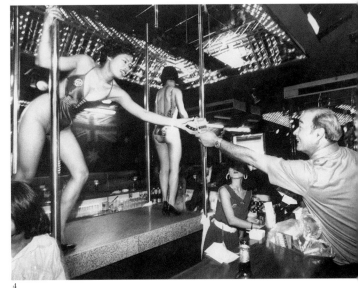

4

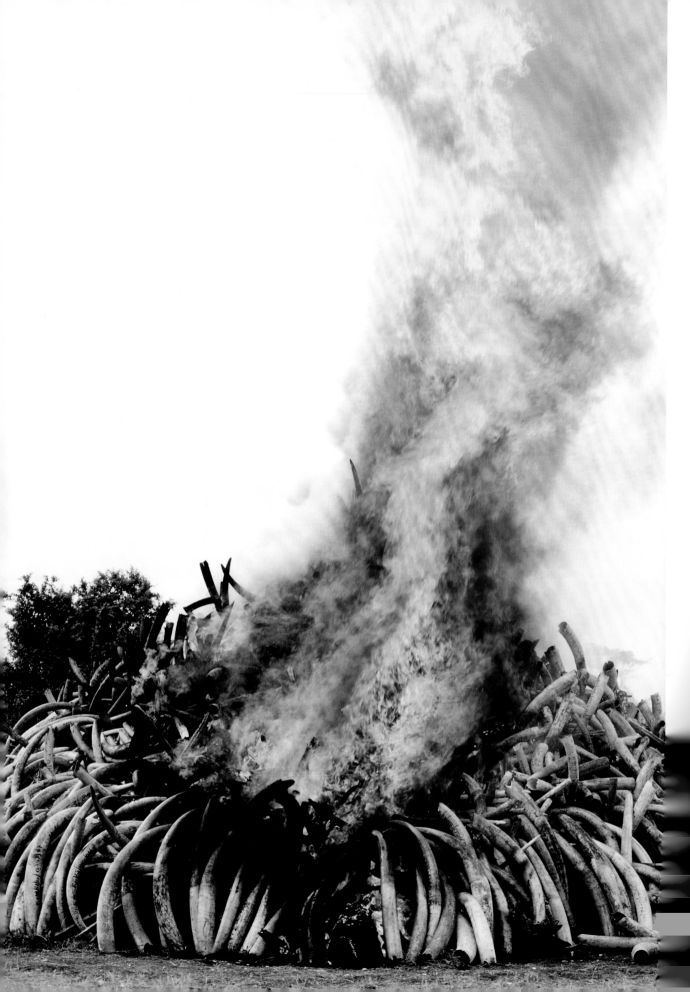

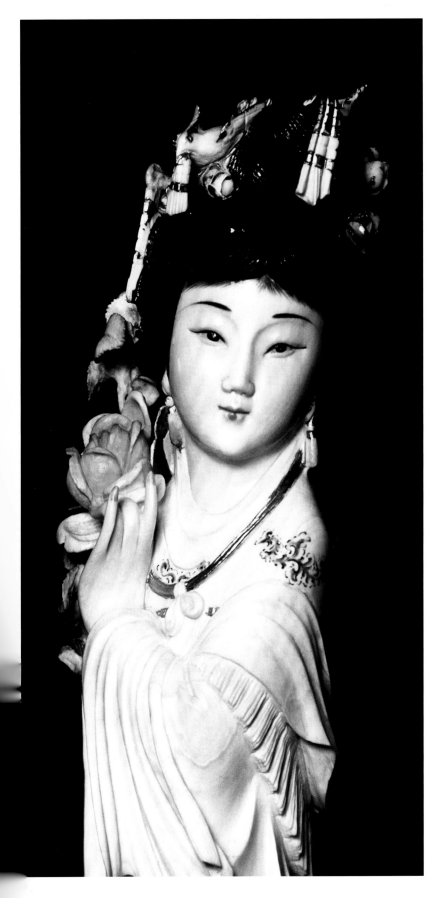

There was also growing concern with wildlife threatened with extinction – for the orang-utan, the white rhino, the Siberian tiger and a host of other creatures. The plight of the elephant was especially harrowing, as hundreds were killed for their tusks. This pile of ivory, confiscated from poachers and burnt by Kenyan Game Wardens in July 1989 had an estimated value of $3 million (1). Illicit ivory, in the form of this statue, reached the Hong Kong market in the same year (2).

DIE Sorge um bedrohte Tiere wuchs ebenfalls – etwa um den Orang-Utan, das weiße Rhinozeros, den sibirischen Tiger und eine Reihe weiterer Tierarten. Das Schicksal des Elephanten war besonders erschütternd: Hunderte wurden einzig wegen ihrer Stoßzähne getötet. Dieser Berg von Elfenbein wurde von kenianischen Wildwächtern im Juli 1989 beschlagnahmt und in Brand gesetzt; sein geschätzter Wert: drei Millionen US-Dollar (1). Illegales Elfenbein – aus dem diese Statue gefertigt wurde – erreicht im selben Jahr den Elfenbeinmarkt in Hong Kong (2).

LA préoccupation pour les animaux en danger a également cru – par exemple pour l'orang-outang, le rhinocéros blanc, le tigre de Sibérie et une série d'autres espèces animales. Le destin de l'éléphant est particulièrement émouvant : ici, des centaines ont été tués pour leurs seules défenses. Cette montagne d'ivoire a été confisquée par des gardiens de parcs kenyans en juillet 1989 et incendiée ; sa valeur estimée : trois millions de dollars US (1). L'ivoire illégal – qui a servi à fabriquer cette statue – atteint la même année le marché de l'ivoire à Hong-Kong (2).

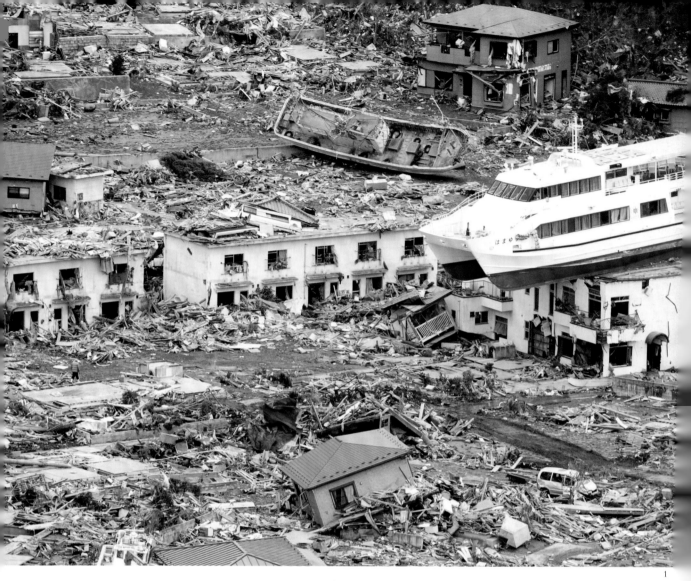

1

Natural disasters displayed the raw power of nature; mechanical disasters revealed the occasional but terrible outcome of human error. Following an earthquake registering 9.0 on the Richter Scale, the 10 metrehigh tsunami that hit the coast of Japan not only destroyed the Fukushima nuclear power station, but also reduced the city of Otsuchi to rubble. A ship built for sight-seeing tours is perched precariously on the roof of a house in Otsuchi, 15 March 2011 (1). One of the three million Haitians made homeless by the 2010 earthquake brings water to her tent in the largest refugee camp in Port-au-Prince, 6 February 2010 (3). Two years later, thousands of Haitian families were still homeless, and other disasters in other parts of the world had intervened. A brown pelican struggles onto East Grand Terre Island, Louisiana, USA after being coated with oil sludge following the Deepwater Horizon oil well explosion, 4 June 2010 (2). This picture was taken two months after the disaster, when oil was still coming ashore along the entire coast of Louisiana.

Naturkatastrophen führten uns die rohe Gewalt der Natur vor Augen; technische Katastrophen enthüllten die manchmal schrecklichen Ergebnisse menschlichen Versagens. Nach einem Erdbeben der Stärke 9 auf der Richterskala zerstörte der zehn Meter hohe Tsunami, der auf die japanische Küste traf, nicht nur das Atomkraftwerk Fukushima, sondern machte auch die Stadt Otsuchi dem Erdboden gleich. Ein Ausflugsschiff balanciert auf dem Dach eines Hauses in Otsuchi, 15. März 2011 (1). Eine der drei Millionen Haitianer, die beim Erdbeben 2010 obdachlos wurden, bringt im größten Flüchtlingscamp in Port-au-Prince Wasser zu ihrem Zelt, 6. Februar 2010 (3). Zwei Jahre später waren Tausende haitianischer Familien immer noch heimatlos, und die Aufmerksamkeit schweifte zu neuen Katastrophen anderswo auf der Welt. Ein von braunem Ölschlamm bedeckter Pelikan rettet sich am 4. Juni 2010 auf East Grand Terre Island in Louisiana, USA, nach der Explosion der Ölbohrplattform Deepwater Horizon (2). Das Foto wurde zwei Monate nach der Katastrophe gemacht, als das Öl noch immer die gesamte Küste Louisianas verschmutzte.

Si les catastrophes naturelles témoignent de l'extraordinaire puissance de la nature, les accidents aux conséquences terribles pointent la défaillance humaine. Après un séisme de magnitude 9 sur l'échelle de Richter, la vague de 10 m qui s'abattit sur les côtes japonaises détruisit non seulement la centrale nucléaire de Fukushima, mais réduisit aussi la ville d'Otsuchi à l'état de ruines. Un bateau conçut pour admirer

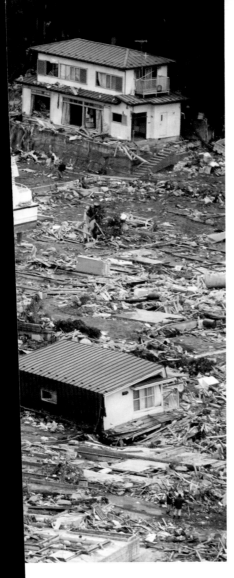

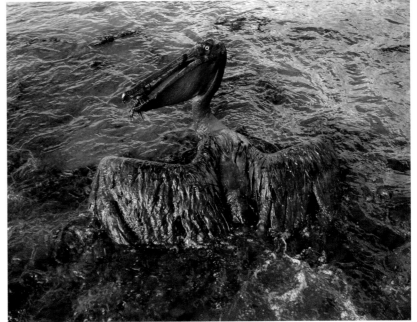

les fonds marins se retrouva en équilibre
précaire le toit d'une maison d'Otsuchi,
le 15 mars 2011 (1). Une Haïtienne, parmi
les trois millions de sans-abri laissés par
le séisme qui ébranla le pays en 2010,
rapporte de l'eau sous sa tente, dans le plus
grand camp de réfugiés de Port-au-Prince,
le 6 février 2010 (3). Deux ans plus tard,
des milliers de familles haïtiennes sont
toujours privées d'un toit, et bien d'autres
désastres ont depuis frappé d'autres régions
du monde. Un pélican brun lutte pour
sa survie sur East Grand Terre Island, en
Louisiane, États-Unis, englué de pétrole,
suite à l'explosion de la plateforme offshore
Deepwater Horizon, le 4 juin 2010 (2).
Cette photographie a été prise deux mois
après la catastrophe, alors que des nappes
de pétrole continuaient à souiller des
kilomètres de côtes en Louisiane.

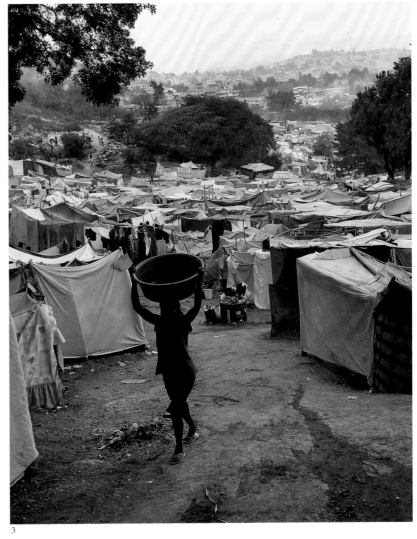

9/11 and After

THE TERRORIST ATTACK of 11 September, 2001 sent shock waves throughout the United States. This crime against humanity was committed on American soil, in the heart of New York and in and around Washington DC. Moreover, when the second plane hit the South Tower of the World Trade Center, millions were watching on TV. Within an hour, global satellite links had beamed reports and images around the world, and on the Internet debate was raging. Never before had a major historical event received live media coverage on this scale. Long before it was clear what was happening, hundreds of millions of onlookers were watching its effect unroll. The images they saw and the reports they heard that day were uncensored and unedited; some of the images so horrifying that they have seldom been seen since.

It was hardly surprising that the incumbent President was initially lost for words. Eventually, he found the phrase he had been searching for, and declared 'War on Terrorism', an old enemy hideously transformed. The modern terrorist may have been the direct descendant of the fanatics of old, who threw bombs at royal carriages or fired their pistols at passing despots, but the targets now were innocent men, women and children, and the weapons used against them were those of mass destruction. This was a different kind of war, and the world in which it was being waged would never be the same again. Old alliances were tested, with some disappointing results to both sides. The Western World, that had stood foursquare against the old USSR for 40 or more years, lost its unanimity of purpose in the War on Terrorism. What was at stake was the survival of civilization, but there were differences of opinion as to what that civilization might be.

The new terror spread like a plague. Within a frighteningly short time, there had been bomb outrages in Madrid, London, Bali, Baghdad, Afghanistan, Pakistan, Egypt, Saudi Arabia, Sri Lanka, Turkey and more than twenty other countries. Some places suffered repeated attacks. Some terrorists acted alone, some in co-ordinated groups. Most terrifying of all was the suicide bomber, prepared to walk into a shop or bar, or board a bus or train, and leave this world in a moment of chaos and destruction.

In such circumstances, it seemed nowhere was safe, and that few aspects of daily life could remain unaffected. The issue of homeland security became supremely important. Police and other agencies were given unprecedented new powers. Old liberties that had protected the individual for centuries were sacrificed in the name of the general good. Going to work or school, visiting a gallery or museum, passing through an airport or shopping mall entailed proving who you were and that you had a right to be where you were. Armed guards on the streets and messages piped regularly over PA systems about 'this time of heightened security...' became daily reminders that that in this new age, the world was likely to be – in old war terms – indefinitely at 'battle stations'.

For many desperate politicians and fervent religious leaders, the letting of blood seemed the only way to cure the sickness from which the planet was suffering. Nations went to war – in the Middle East, on the north-west frontier of the Indian sub-continent. But it wasn't the politicians or the clerics who died; as ever, that was to be the fate of the soldiers and civilians caught in the crossfire of history.

Die Terroristenangriffe des 11. September 2001 sandten Schockwellen durch die gesamten USA. Dieses Verbrechen gegen die Menschheit wurde auf amerikanischem Boden verübt, im Herzen New Yorks sowie in und um Washington DC. Darüber hinaus sahen Millionen von Menschen am Fernseher zu, wie das zweite Flugzeug in den Südturm des World Trade Centers raste. Innerhalb einer Stunde sendeten weltweite Satellitenverbindungen Berichte und Bilder rund um die Welt, und im Internet hatten die Debatten über »9/11« bereits begonnen. Nie zuvor wurde ein historisches Ereignis dieser Größenordnung von einer Live-Berichterstattung solchen Ausmaßes begleitet. Lange bevor überhaupt klar wurde, was sich ereignete,

A US MARINE COVERS THE HEAD ON THE STATUE OF SADDAM HUSSEIN
IN AL-FARDOUS (PARADISE) SQUARE, BAGHDAD, 9 APRIL 2003.

EIN US-MARINE BEDECKT DEN KOPF EINER STATUE VON SADDAM HUSSEIN
AUF DEM AL-FARDOUS-PLATZ (PARADIESPLATZ) IN BAGDAD, 9. APRIL 2003.

UN MARINE RECOUVRE LA TÊTE DE LA STATUE DE SADDAM HUSSEIN Á
AL-FARDOUS (PARADIS) SQUARE, BAGDAD, 9 AVRIL 2003.

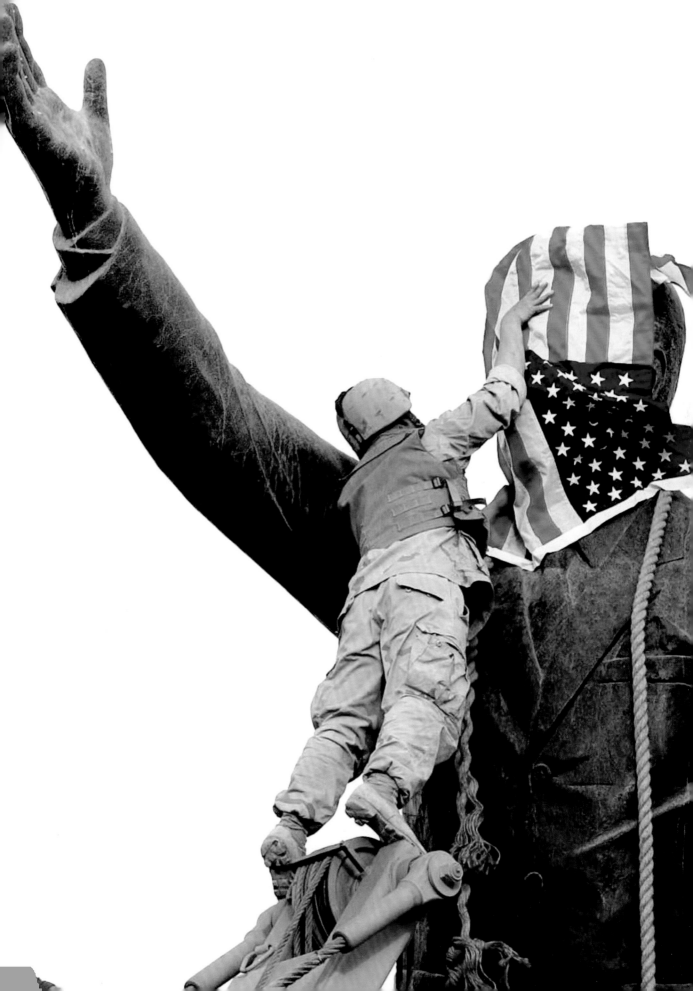

sahen Hunderte von Millionen Zuschauern rund um den Globus bei dem Geschehen zu. Die Bilder, die die Welt zu sehen bekam, waren unmittelbar und unzensiert – manche Bilder waren so entsetzlich, daß sie seither nicht mehr gezeigt wurden.

Kaum verwunderlich, daß dem amtierendem Präsidenten zunächst die Worte fehlten. Doch dann fand er den Satz, den er gesucht hatte und erklärte den »War on Terrorism«, den Krieg gegen Terror: der alte Feind in neuer, schrecklicherer Gestalt. Denn der moderne Terrorist konnte der direkte Nachfolger des Fanatikers früherer Zeiten sein – der Kutschen in die Luft sprengte und mit Pistolen auf Despoten schoß; nur, daß jetzt unschuldige Männer, Frauen und Kinder das Ziel und die Waffen solche der massenhaften Tötung waren. Dies war eine andere Art von Krieg, und die Welt, in der er geführt wurde, würde niemals mehr sein wie bisher. Alte Allianzen kamen auf den Prüfstand – und erlebten Enttäuschungen auf beiden Seiten. Die westliche Welt, die über 40 Jahre lang wie ein Block gegen die ehemalige Sowjetunion zusammengestanden hatte, verlor ihre Einmütigkeit im Krieg gegen den Terror. Was auf dem Spiel stand, war nicht weniger als das Überleben der Zivilisation; doch darüber, was diese Zivilisation ausmachte, herrschten unterschiedliche Auffassungen.

Der neue Terror verbreitete sich wie ein Lauffeuer. Binnen erschreckend kurzer Zeit gab es weitere Bombenanschläge in Madrid, London, Bali, Bagdad, Afghanistan, Sri Lanka, der Türkei und in mehr als 20 weiteren Ländern. Einige Orte wurden gar mehrfach attackiert. Manchmal agierten die Terroristen einzeln, beim nächsten Mal in koordinierten Gruppen. Der furchterregendste von allen war der Selbstmordattentäter – der bereit war, in ein Geschäft oder ein Café zu gehen, in einen Bus oder Zug zu steigen und diese Welt in Chaos und Zerstörung hinter sich zu lassen.

Unter solchen Umständen schien die Welt nirgendwo mehr sicher zu sein, und kaum ein Aspekt des täglichen Lebens blieb davon unberührt. Die Frage der inneren Sicherheit erhielt oberste Priorität. Polizei und Sicherheitskräften wurden bisher nicht gekannte Befugnisse eingeräumt; jahrhundertelang garantierte Freiheiten zum Schutz des Individuums wurden dem Gut der allgemeinen Sicherheit geopfert. Der Weg zur Arbeit oder zur Schule, in eine Galerie oder ein Museum, durch einen Flughafen oder ein Einkaufszentrum hatte zur Folge, beweisen zu müssen, wer man war und daß man ein Recht hatte, dort zu sein, wo man war. Bewaffnete Wächter in den Straßen und ständige Durchsagen über Lautsprecheranlagen über »Maßnahmen zur erhöhten Sicherheit« erinnerten in diesem neuen Zeitalter täglich daran, daß die Welt wohl für immer – in den Worten alter Kriege – in »Gefechtsstellung« bleiben würde.

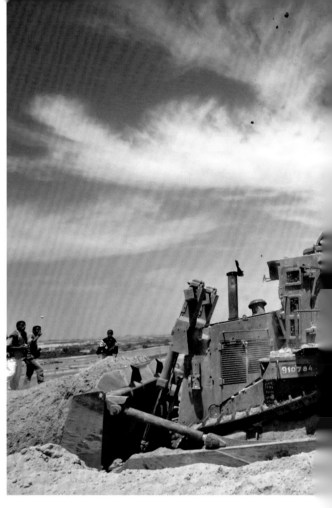

PALESTINIAN YOUTHS HURL ROCKS AT AN ISRAELI ARMY BULLDOZER NEAR THE BEIT LAHYEA REFUGEE CAMP, 20 APRIL 2004.

EIN PALÄSTINENSISCHER JUGENDLICHER BEWIRFT EINEN BULLDOZER DER ISRAELISCHEN ARMEE IN DER NÄHE DES FLÜCHTLINGSLAGERS BEIT LAYHEA MIT STEINEN, 20. APRIL 2004.

DES JEUNES PALESTINIENS LANCENT DES PIERRES CONTRE UN BULLDOZER DE L'ARMÉE ISRAÉLIENNE PRÈS DU CAMP DE RÉFUGIÉS BEIT LAHYEA, 20 AVRIL 2004.

L'attaque terroriste du 11 septembre 2001 a déclenché une onde de choc à travers tous les États-Unis. Ce crime perpétré contre l'humanité a été commis sur le sol même de l'Amérique, au cœur de New York, à et autour de Washington DC. Pire, quand le deuxième avion a percuté la tour Sud du World Trade Center, des millions d'êtres humains étaient rivés à leurs écrans de télévision. En l'espace d'une heure, les satellites qui gravitent autour de la planète ont diffusé reportage et photos dans le monde entier, et, sur Internet, le débats sur le 11 septembre ont commencé. Jama auparavant, un événement historique majeur n'ava fait l'objet d'une telle couverture médiatique. Bien ava que l'on sache ce qui s'était réellement passé, d

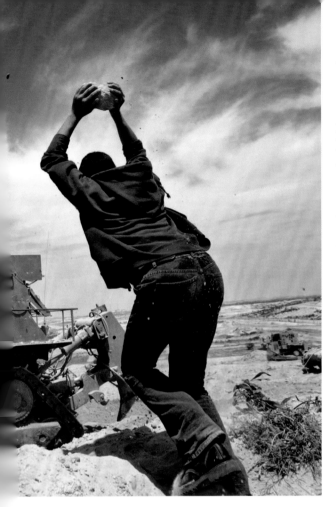

centaines de millions de téléspectateurs assistaient au déroulement de l'événement. Les images qu'ils découvrirent et les commentaires qu'ils entendirent ce jour-là étaient inédites et n'avaient pas été censurées ; des images reflétant pour certaines une telle horreur, qu'elles furent rarement rediffusées depuis.

Il n'y a rien de surprenant à ce que le président en exercice n'ait, tout d'abord, su que dire. Finalement, il a trouvé les mots qu'il cherchait et il a déclaré la guerre au terrorisme, un vieil ennemi qui s'était révélé sous une forme hideuse. Car, si le terroriste moderne est le descendant direct des fanatiques de jadis qui jetaient des bombes au passage des carrosses royaux ou tiraient des coups de pistolets sur des despotes défilant devant eux, les cibles d'aujourd'hui étaient des innocents, des femmes et des enfants, et les armes utilisées contre eux étaient des armes de destruction massive. Il s'agissait d'un nouveau type de guerre et le monde dans lequel elle se déroulait ne serait plus jamais le même. De vieilles alliances se virent mises à l'épreuve, avec, parfois, les résultats décevants des deux côtés. Le monde occidental, qui avait serré les coudes pendant quarante ans ou plus contre l'ex-URSS, perdit alors toute sa cohésion et sa solidarité face à la Guerre au Terrorisme. Si ce qui était en jeu, c'était la survie de la civilisation, il

y avait toutefois de profondes divergences d'opinions quant à ce que l'on devait entendre par civilisation.

Cette terreur d'un nouveau genre s'est répandue comme un feu de prairie. Coup sur coup, des attentats à la bombe ont été commis à Madrid, Londres, Bali, Bagdad, en Afghanistan, au Pakistan, en Égypte, en Arabie Saoudite, au Sri Lanka, en Turquie et dans plus de vingt autres pays. Certains lieux ont fait l'objet d'attaques répétées. Parfois, les terroristes ont agi seuls, parfois au sein de groupes coordonnés. Les plus terrifiants de tous, ce sont les attentats suicides, lorsqu'un individu n'hésite pas à pénétrer dans un magasin ou un bar ou à monter à bord d'un autobus ou d'un train et à quitter ce monde en semant le chaos et la destruction.

Dans de telles circonstances, on ne se sent en sûreté nulle part et rares sont les aspects de la vie quotidienne qui peuvent y échapper. Pour chacun, la question de la sécurité de son propre pays a pris une importance suprême. La police et les diverses administrations se sont vues conférer de nouvelles prérogatives sans précédent. De vieilles libertés qui avaient protégé l'homme durant des siècles ont été sacrifiées pour le salut de la collectivité. Aller au travail ou à l'école, visiter une galerie ou un musée, pénétrer dans un aéroport ou un centre commercial, tout cela implique désormais de devoir produire la preuve de son identité et du droit d'être là où l'on est. Des hommes en armes dans les rues et des messages émis régulièrement par haut-parleurs invoquant « notre époque de sécurité accrue… » nous rappellent chaque jour que, en cette nouvelle époque, le monde est en passe de devenir – pour reprendre une vieille terminologie guerrière – pour un temps indéfini un « champ de bataille ».

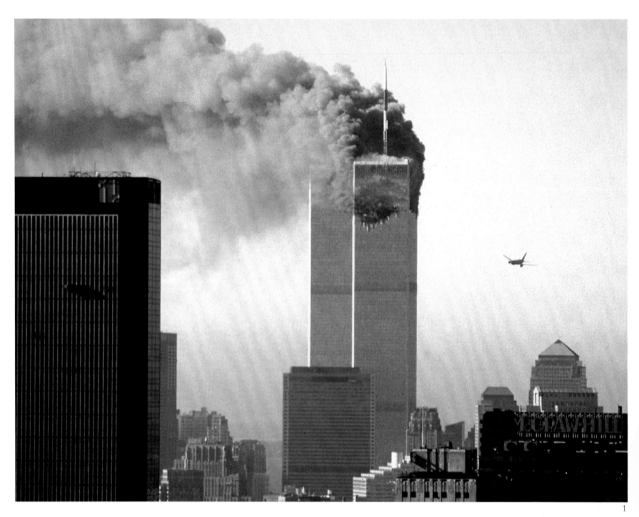

1

THE War comes home. With smoke already pouring from the North Tower of the World Trade Center (1), hijacked American Airlines Flight 175 approaches the South Tower at a speed of 590 mph (940 kph). The North Tower had been hit by the terrorists' first plane some 16 minutes earlier, at 08:46 AM. Until this point it was still reckoned by many that what had happened to the North Tower was some ghastly accident. Then came the realization of the true horror, as seconds later (2) AA Flight 175 hit the South Tower between the 78th and 84th floors and explodes, sending glass and debris raining down on to the streets below. Millions saw the crash live on TV. Far worse was soon to follow.

DER Krieg kehrt heim: Während aus dem Nordturm des World Trade Centers bereits der Rauch hervorquillt (1), nähert sich die gekidnappte Maschine des American-Airlines-Fluges 175 dem Südturm mit einer Geschwindigkeit von 940 km/h. Der Nordturm wurde von dem ersten Flugzeug der Terroristen bereits 16 Minuten früher getroffen, um 8 Uhr 46. Bis zu diesem Zeitpunkt dachten viele noch, bei dem, was im Nordturm passiert war, handele es sich um einen schrecklichen Unfall. Wenige Sekunden später offenbarte sich der wahre Horror, als AA-Flug 175 den Südturm zwischen dem 78. und 84. Stockwerk traf und explodierte. Glas und Trümmer regneten auf die Straßen herab. Millionen Menschen sahen live am Fernseher zu; und schon bald sollte noch weitaus Schlimmeres folgen.

LA guerre arrive aux États-Unis : alors que de la fumée s'échappe déjà de la tour Nord du World Trade Center (1), l'avion du vol 175 d'American Airline, lui aussi détourné, se rapproche à une vitesse de 940 km/h de la tour Sud. La tour Nord a déjà été touchée par le premier avion des terroristes seize minutes auparavant, à 8 h. 46. Jusqu'à ce moment-là, beaucoup pensaient encore que ce qui s'était passé dans la tour Nord était un terrible accident. Quelques secondes plus tard, la véritable horreur se dévoile à eux lorsque le vol 175 d'AA percute la tour Sud entre le 78ème et le 84ème étage et explose. Des débris de verre et de béton pleuvent dans les rues environnantes. Des millions d'êtres humains y assistent en direct à la télévision, mais, très bientôt, ils verront des scènes encore plus atroces.

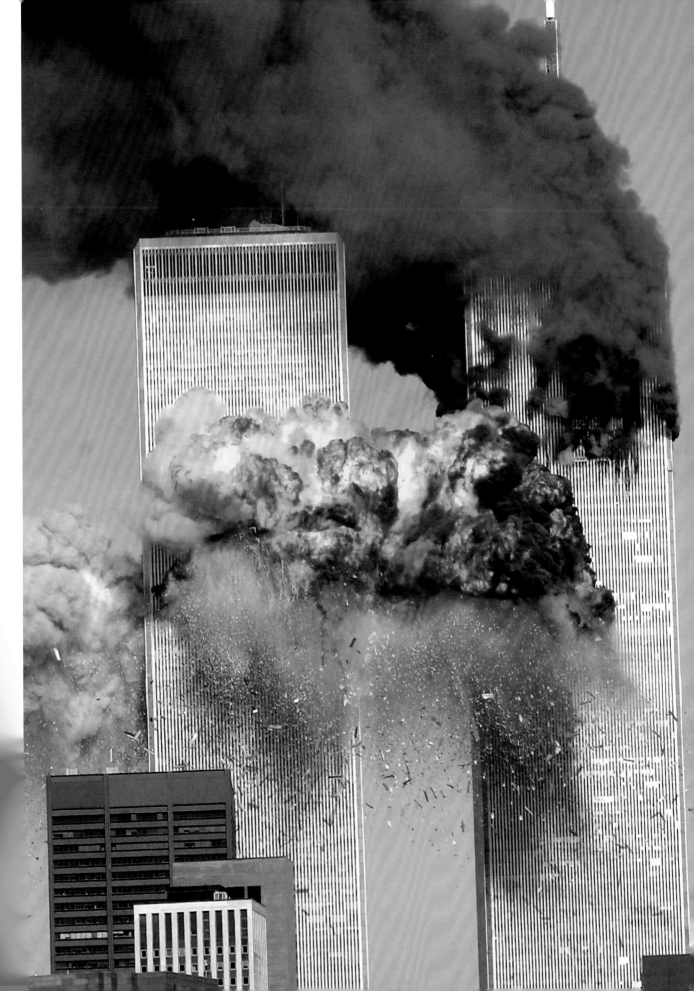

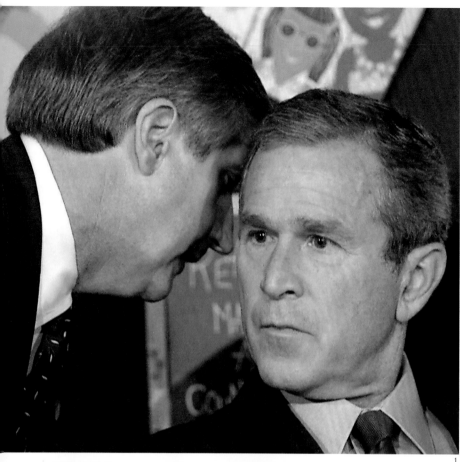

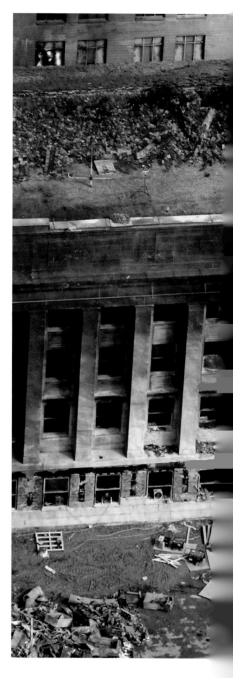

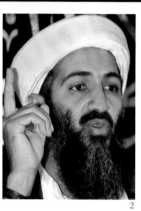

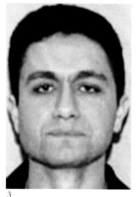

2   3

Aᴺ early morning lesson at the Emma E. Booker Elementary School, Sarasota, Florida is interrupted (1). White House Chief of Staff Andrew Card (*left*) tells President George W. Bush that the United States is under attack. The Saudi connection – Osama bin Laden, leader of al-Qaeda, and the man responsible for the overall strategy of the attacks on the World Trade Center (2). A Florida Department of Motor Vehicles ID photo of Mohammed Atta (3), who spent six

months undergoing training to be a pilot at Huffman Aviation, Venice, Florida from July to December 2000. It was Atta who flew AA Flight 11 into the North Tower. Five days later, rescue workers and engineers sift through the rubble of the west face of the Pentagon (4) , which had been hit by the third hijacked plane, AA Flight 77. All 64 people on board the plane were killed, together with 125 members of the Pentagon staff.

Eɪɴᴇ Schulstunde am frühen Morgen in der Emma E.-Booker-Grundschule in Sarasota, Florida wird unterbrochen (1). Andrew Card, Chef des Weißen Hauses (*im Bild links*) informiert den Präsidenten George W. Bush darüber, daß die Vereinigten Staaten angegriffen werden. Die Verbindung zu den Saudis – Osama bin Laden, Chef der Terrorgruppe Al-Qaida und der Verantwortliche für den Gesamtplan des Anschlags auf das World Trade Center (2). Ein Foto von Mohammed Atta der Abteilung für

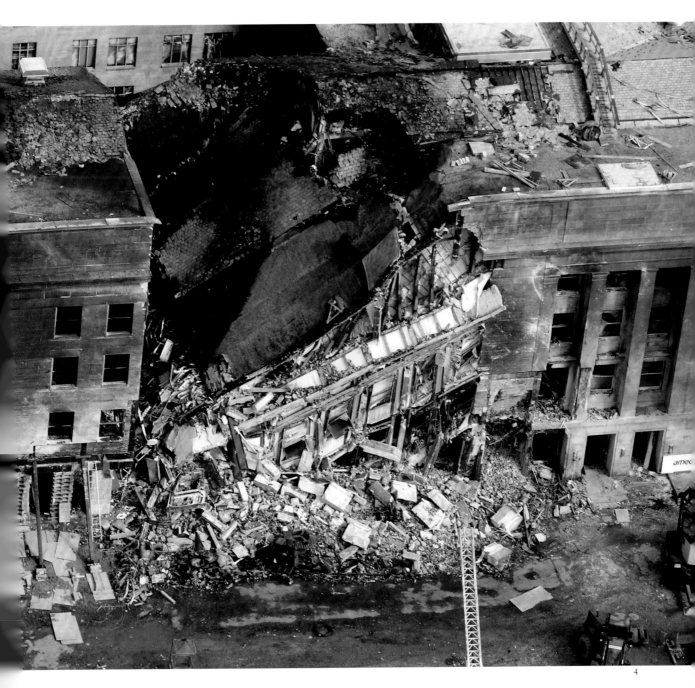

4

Fahrzeughalter in Florida (3); er nahm sechs Monate an einem Pilotentraining bei Huffman Aviation in Venice, Florida, teil – von Juli bis Dezember 2000. Atta steuerte den AA-Flug 11 in den Nordturm. Fünf Tage später durchkämmen Rettungsarbeiter und Ingenieure die Trümmer der Westseite des Pentagon (4) in Washington, das von dem gekidnappten AA-Flug 77 getroffen wurde. Alle 64 Insassen des Flugzeugs starben, ebenso 125 Mitglieder des Personals im Pentagon.

U̶N cours d'école, tôt le matin, à l'école primaire Emma E.-Booker de Sarasota, en Floride, est interrompu (1). Andrew Card, le patron de la Maison Blanche (*à gauche sur la photo*), informe le président George W. Bush que les États-Unis ont été attaqués. Il y a un lien entre les Saoudiens et Osama ben Laden, chef du groupe terroriste El-Qaida et responsable du plan général de l'attentat perpétré contre le World Trade Center (2). Une photo de Mohammed Atta, du département des licences automobiles de Floride (3) ;

pendant six mois – de juillet à décembre 2000 – il a suivi des cours de pilotage près de Huffman Aviation, à Venice, en Floride. Atta pilotait le vol 11 d'AA qui a percuté la tour Nord. Cinq jours plus tard, des sauveteurs et des ingénieurs inspectent les ruines de la façade Ouest du Pentagone (4) à Washington, qui a été percutée par le vol 77 détourné d'AA. La totalité des 64 occupants de l'avion ont péri, de même que 125 membres du personnel du Pentagone.

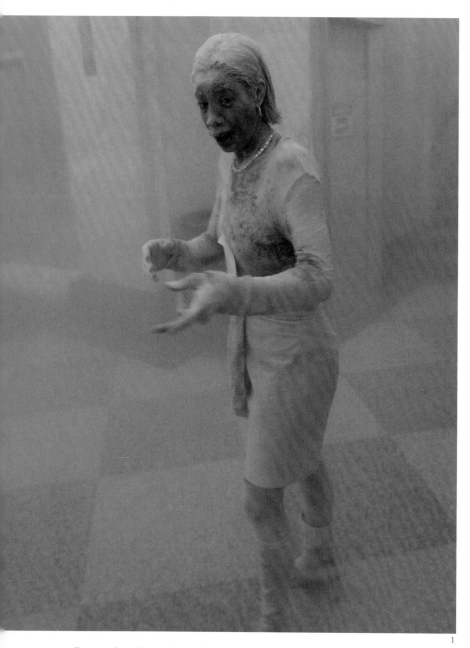

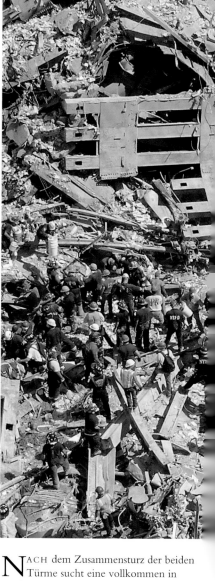

1

Following the collapse of both Towers, a woman covered in dust seeks refuge in a nearby office block (1). She had been caught in the clouds of pulverized concrete and gypsum dust that enveloped the streets.

Four days later, rescue workers continue the desperate work of search for survivors and casualties from the wreckage at Ground Zero, 15 September 2001 (2).

Nach dem Zusammensturz der beiden Türme sucht eine vollkommen in Staub eingehüllte Frau Schutz in einem nahegelegenen Büroblock (1). Sie geriet in eine Wolke aus pulverisiertem Beton und

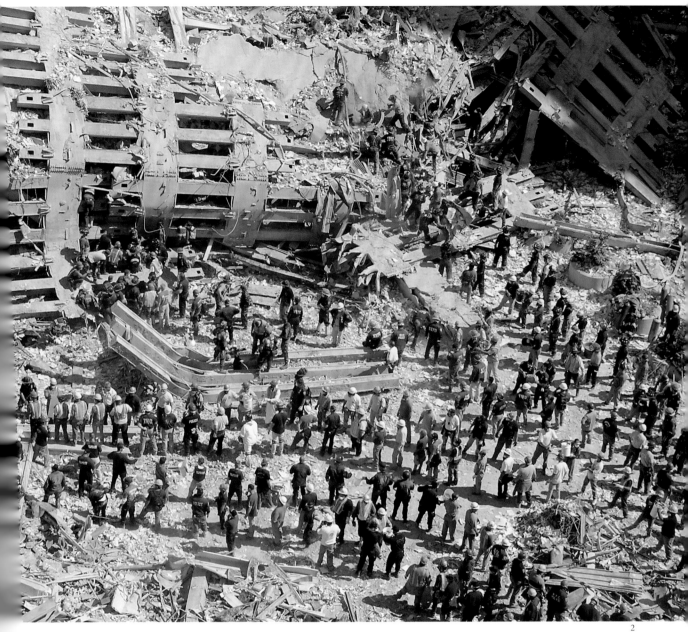

2

Gips, der die Straßen einhüllte. Vier Tage später arbeiten sich Rettungsmannschaften auf der Suche nach Überlebenden verzweifelt durch die Trümmer von »Ground Zero« – 15. September 2001 (2).

APRÈS l'effondrement des deux tours, une femme complètement recouverte de poussière cherche un abri dans un bloc de bureaux tout proche (1). Elle s'est trouvée enveloppée dans un nuage de béton et de plâtre pulvérisés qui a envahi les rues comme une nappe de brouillard. Quatre jours plus tard, des équipes de sauveteurs inspectent désespérément les ruines de « Ground Zero » à la recherche de survivants – 15 septembre 2001 (2).

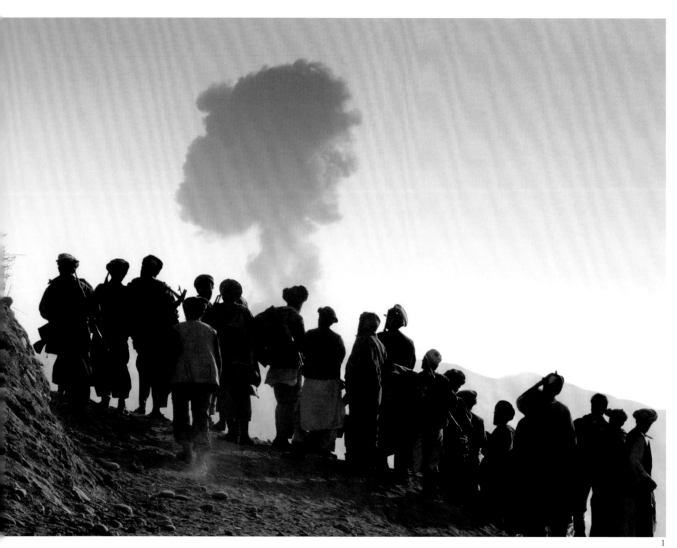

1

FRIENDLY fire. Warriors of the Afghan Northern Alliance (1) observe the effects of US B-52 bombers on Taliban positions in Khanabad, Afghanistan, 22 November 2001. The Northern Alliance had joined forces with American troops on the frontline between Kunduz and Talogan. Victims of the war... Afghan women (2), whose husbands have been killed in the war, wait for a distribution of food in Kabul by workers from the Co-operative for Assistance and Relief Everywhere (CARE), 23 January 2002. At that time, relief agencies reckoned that there were between 30,000 and 50,000 widows with little or no means of support in Kabul alone.

FREUNDLICHES Feuer: Kämpfer der Afghanischen Nordallianz beobachten die Auswirkungen der Angriffe von US B–52-Bombern auf Stellungen der Taliban in Khanabad, Afghanistan – 22. November 2001 (1). Die Nordallianz bildete, zusammen mit amerikanischen Truppen, eine Frontlinie zwischen Kunduz und Talogan. Opfer des Krieges – afghanische

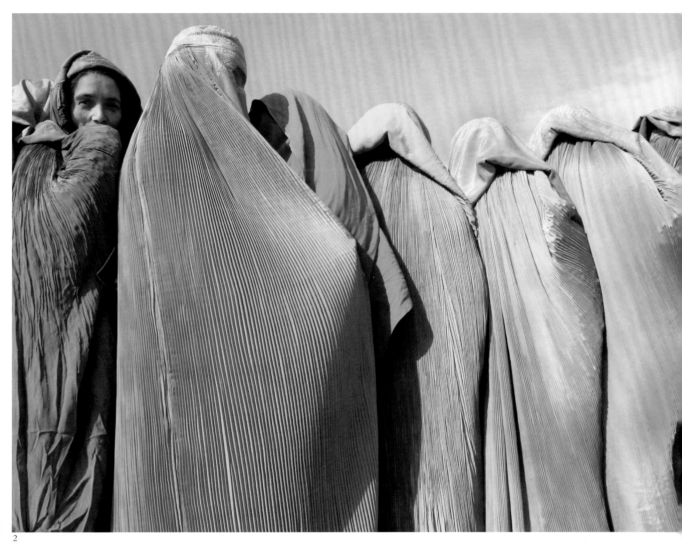

2

Frauen, deren Männer im Krieg getötet wurden, warten in Kabul auf die Verteilung von Lebensmitteln durch CARE-Mitarbeiter (der 1946 in den USA gegründeten Vereinigung zur Organisation von Hilfssendungen) – 23. Januar 2002 (2). Zu dieser Zeit gingen Hilfsorganisationen von rund 30 000 bis 50 000 hilfsbedürftigen Witwen allein in Kabul aus.

Feu allié : des combattants de l'Alliance du Nord afghane observent les répercussions des attaques de bombardiers américains B-52 sur des positions des Taliban à Khanabad, en Afghanistan – 22 novembre 2001 (1). De concert avec les troupes américaines, l'Alliance du Nord constitue en quelque sorte une ligne de front entre Kunduz et Talogan. Les victimes de la guerre (2) – des femmes afghanes dont le mari a péri au combat attendent, à Kaboul, la distribution de denrées alimentaires par des collaborateurs de CARE (l'association, fondée en 1946 aux États-Unis, pour l'organisation d'envois de secours) – 23 janvier 2002. À cette époque, les organisations humanitaires tablaient sur environ 30 000 à 50 000 veuves dans le besoin dans la seule ville de Kaboul.

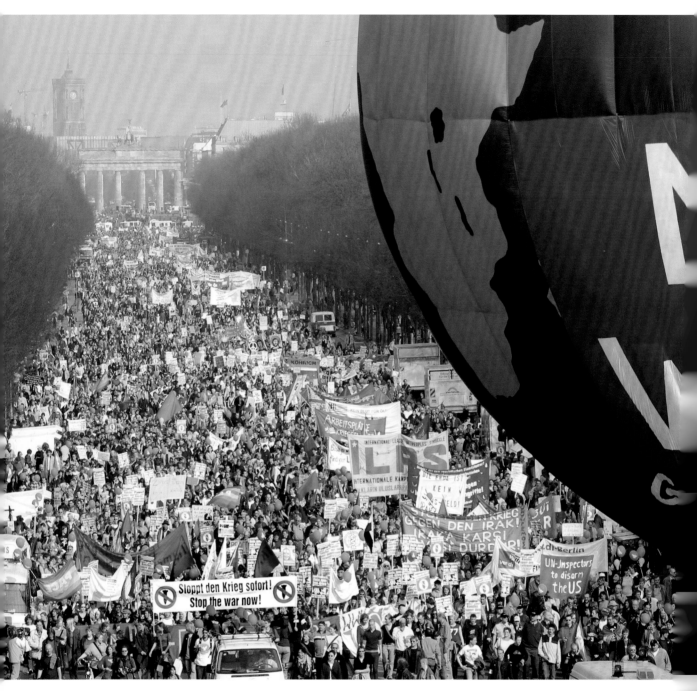

EUROPEAN protests at the US-led
invasion of Iraq in 2003.
Demonstrators march from the
Brandenburg Gate to the Victory Column
in the heart of Berlin, 29 March 2003 (1).
British protesters (2) topple an effigy of US

President George W. Bush in Trafalgar
Square, London, 21 November 2003.
Pro- and anti-war feelings were strong
especially in Britain, a country seen by
many as a staunch ally of the United States.

EUROPÄISCHE Proteste gegen die von d
USA geführte Invasion im Irak 2003. De
Zug der Demonstranten im Herzen Berlins
geht vom Brandenburger Tor zur Siegessäul
29. März 2003 (1). Britische Demonstranter
bringen ein Bildnis des US-Präsidenten

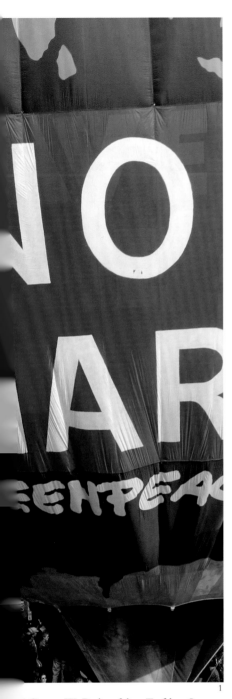

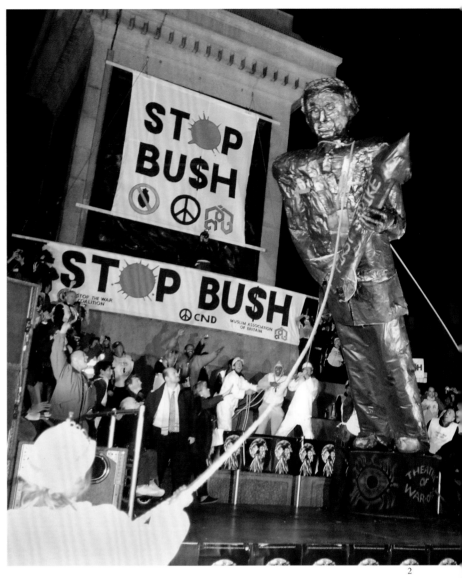

MANIFESTATION, en Europe, contre l'invasion de l'Irak par les États-Unis, en 2003. Le défilé des manifestants, au coeur de Berlin, va de la Porte de Brandebourg à la Colonne de la Victoire – 29 mars 2003 (1). Des manifestants britanniques renversent une effigie du président américain George W. Bush à Trafalgar Square, à Londres – 21 novembre 2003 (2). La Grande-Bretagne, surtout – pays qui, aux yeux de beaucoup, était un partenaire fiable des États-Unis – s'est divisée en partisans et adversaires de la guerre.

George W. Bush auf dem Trafalgar Square in London zu Fall – 21. November 2003 (2). Vor allem Großbritannien – ein Land, das für viele als verläßlicher Partner der USA galt – teilte sich in Befürworter und Gegner des Krieges.

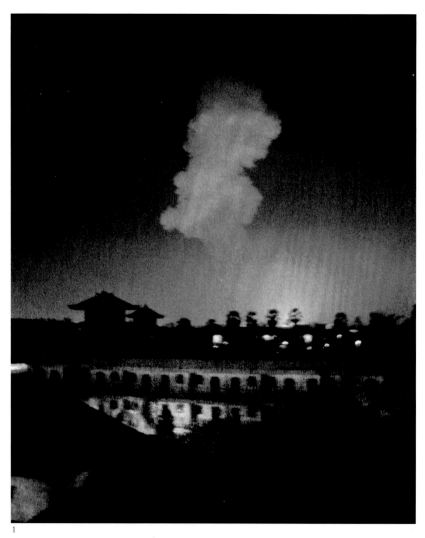

1

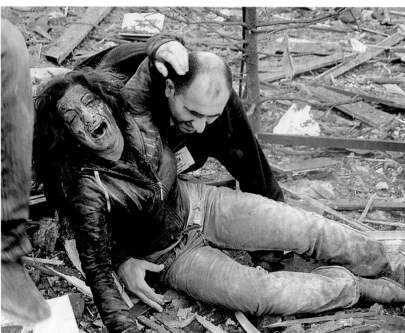

2

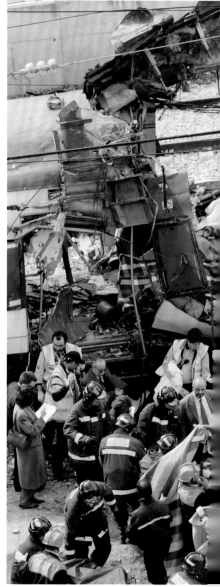

3

THE War spreads… (1) Smoke rises
above the tourist area of Kuta in Bali
after a suicide bomber attacks a nightclub,
killing at least 25 people, 12 October 2002.
One of the hundreds of people injured in
bomb blasts outside the British Consulate
and a British bank in Istanbul, Turkey, 20
November 2002 (2). Twenty-eight people
were killed. Bodies of victims of the
Madrid bombings are carried from the
wreckage of a train near Atocha Station, 11
March 2004 (3). Three bombs were
detonated almost simultaneously at the
height of the morning rush hour. Brian
Haw updates his one-man newsdesk of
protest in London's Parliament Square
following the tragic killing of Jean Charles
de Menezes by British security forces on 22
July 2005 (4).

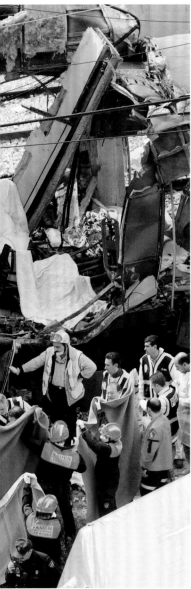

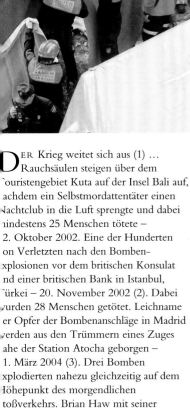

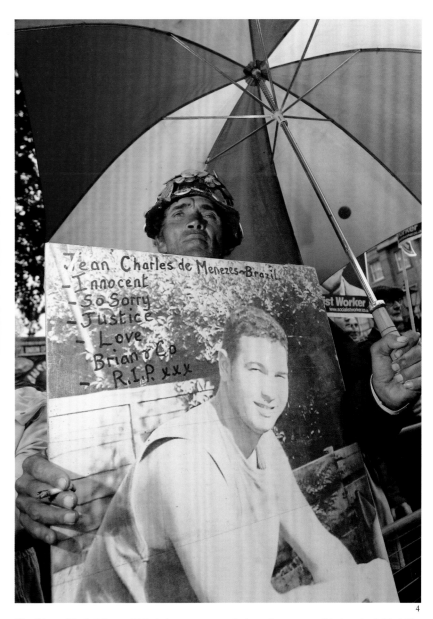

4

DER Krieg weitet sich aus (1) …
Rauchsäulen steigen über dem
Touristengebiet Kuta auf der Insel Bali auf,
nachdem ein Selbstmordattentäter einen
Nachtclub in die Luft sprengte und dabei
mindestens 25 Menschen tötete –
2. Oktober 2002. Eine der Hunderten
von Verletzten nach den Bomben-
explosionen vor dem britischen Konsulat
und einer britischen Bank in Istanbul,
Türkei – 20. November 2002 (2). Dabei
wurden 28 Menschen getötet. Leichname
der Opfer der Bombenanschläge in Madrid
werden aus den Trümmern eines Zuges
nahe der Station Atocha geborgen –
1. März 2004 (3). Drei Bomben
explodierten nahezu gleichzeitig auf dem
Höhepunkt des morgendlichen
Stoßverkehrs. Brian Haw mit seiner

Ein-Mann-Nachrichtentafel bei einer
Protestkundgebung auf dem Parliament
Square in London – nach dem tragischen
Tod von Jean Charles de Menenez durch
britische Sicherheitsbeamte am 22. Juli
2005 (4).

LA guerre fait tache d'huile (1) … des
colonnes de fumée s'élèvent au-dessus
du quartier touristique de Kuta, sur l'île de
Bali, après qu'un attentat suicide a ravagé
une boîte de nuit, causant la mort d'au
minimum 25 personnes – 12 octobre 2002.
L'une des centaines de blessés après des
explosions de bombes devant le consulat de
Grande-Bretagne et une banque
britannique à Istanbul, Turquie –
20 novembre 2002 (2). 28 personnes ont
péri à cette occasion. Des cadavres des

victimes des attentats à la bombe à Madrid
sont extraits des restes calcinés d'un train
près de la gare d'Atocha – 11 mars 2004
(3). Trois bombes ont explosé presque
simultanément à l'apogée du rush-hour
matinal. Brian Haw met à jour son tableau
d'informations personnel lors d'une
manifestation à Parliament Square, à
Londres – après la mort tragique de Jean-
Charles de Menenez, abattu par des agents
de sécurité britanniques le 22 juillet 2005
(4).

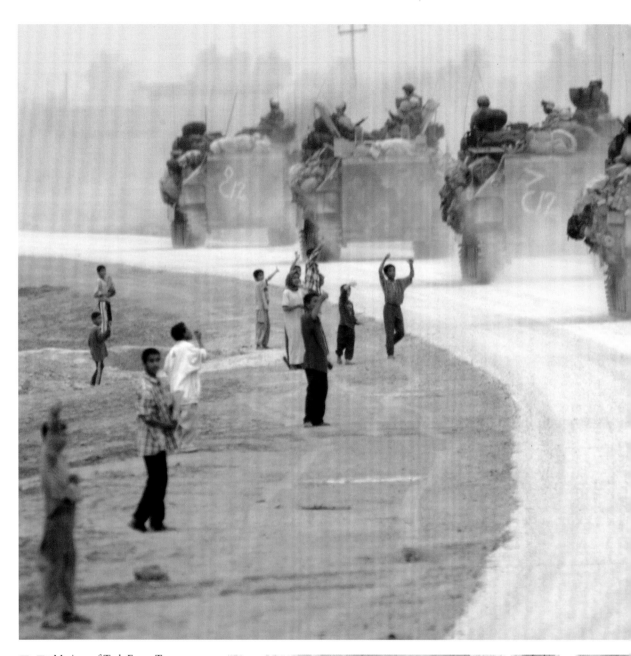

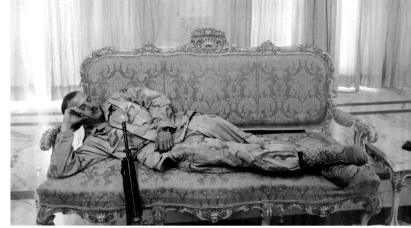

Us Marines of Task Force Tarawa are greeted as liberators by young Iraqis (1) as they move through central Iraq, 7 April 2003. A week later, US Army Sergeant Roscoe Archer (2), of the Third Infantry Division, rests his weary feet and body on a couch in the Presidential Palace, Baghdad. The massive statue of Saddam Hussein (3) is wrenched from its pedestal in al-Fardous Square, Baghdad by a US Marine vehicle, 9 April 2003. It was seen as a highly symbolic moment, but the fall of the dictator did not put an end to the war.

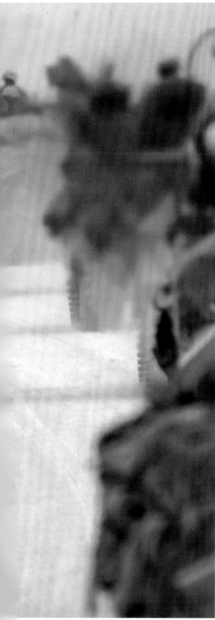

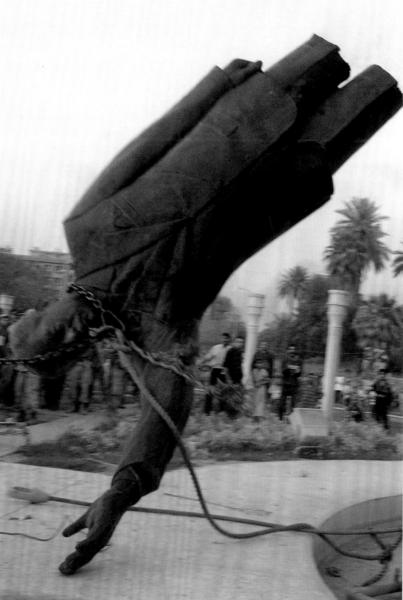

1

3

US-Marinesoldaten der Spezialeinheit Tarawa werden auf dem Weg durch das Landesinnere von jungen Irakern als Befreier begrüßt – 7. April 2003 (1). Eine Woche später streckt US-Sergeant Roscoe Archer von der Dritten Infantrie-Division seine wunden Füße und müden Glieder auf einer Couch im Präsidentenpalast in Bagdad aus (2). Die kolossale Statue Saddam Husseins wird auf dem al-Fardouz-Platz in Bagdad mit Hilfe eines US-Marinefahrzeugs vom Sockel geholt – 9. April 2003 (3). Dies war ein überaus symbolischer Augenblick – doch der Fall des Diktators bedeutete keineswegs das Ende des Krieges.

DE jeunes Irakiens acclament des marines américains de l'unité spéciale de Tarawa qui se rendent dans l'intérieur du pays – 7 avril 2003 (1). Une semaine plus tard, le US-Sergeant Roscoe Archer, de la troisième division d'infanterie, allonge ses pieds blessés et ses membres épuisés sur un divan dans le palais présidentiel de Bagdad (2). A l'aide d'un véhicule de la marine américaine, la colossale statue de Saddam Hussein, sur la place al-Fardouz de Bagdad, est abattue de son socle – 9 avril 2003 (3). Aussi symbolique qu'ait été cet instant – la chute du dictateur ne signifie en aucun cas la fin de la guerre.

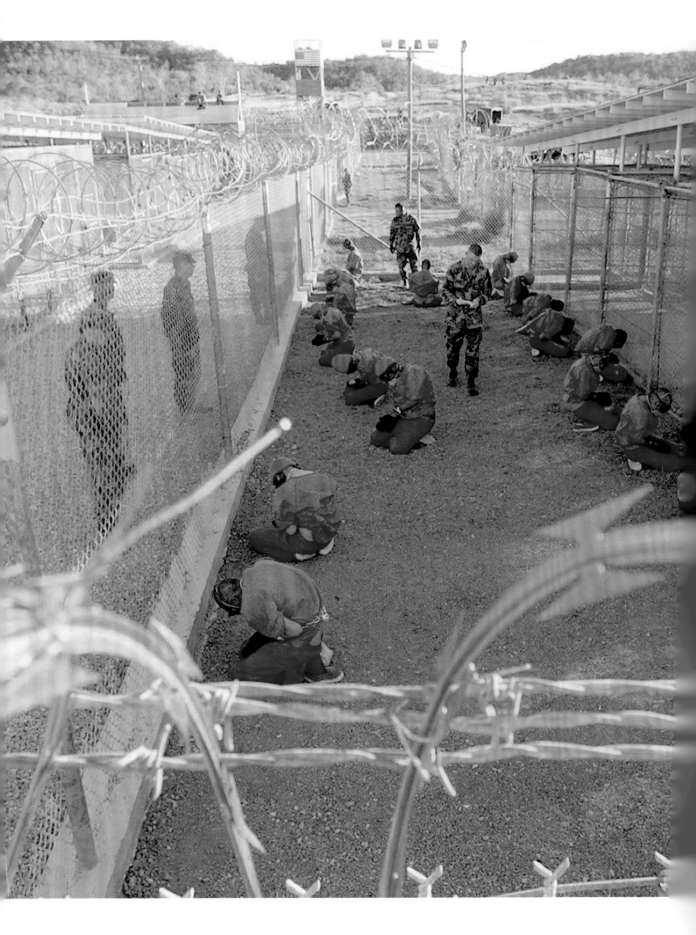

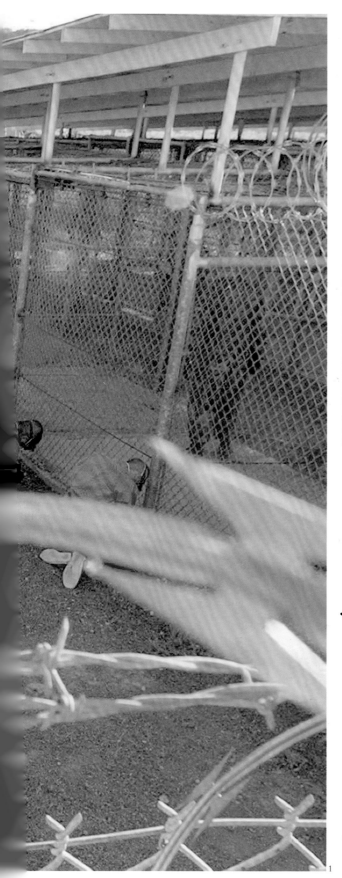

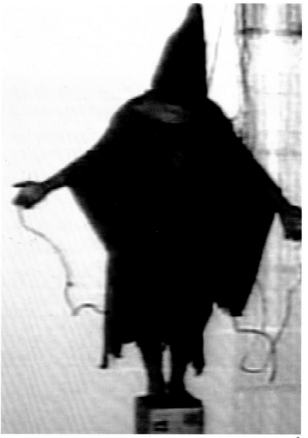

B EYOND the reach of Justice. American military police survey their suspected Taliban prisoners (1) at Camp X-Ray on the US Naval base at Guantanamo Bay, Cuba, 11 January 2002. A still from an Al-Arabiya TV broadcast shows a hooded Iraqi prisoner at the notorious Abu Ghraib prison, standing on a box with wires attached to his hands. The authenticity of the shot could not be proved (2). The damage it did to US prestige could hardly be measured.

J enseits des Zugriffs der Justiz überwachen amerikanische Militärpolizisten als Talibanmitglieder verdächtigte Gefangene im Camp »X-Ray« auf der US-Marinebasis Guantanamo Bay in Kuba – 11. Januar 2002 (1). Ein Standfoto des Fernsehsenders Al-Arabiya zeigt einen mit einer Kapuze verhüllten irakischen Gefangenen in dem berüchtigten Gefängnis Abu Ghraib, der auf einer Kiste steht und an den Händen elektrisch verkabelt wurde (2). Die Authentizität dieses Fotos konnte nicht geklärt werden. Der Schaden, der dem Ansehen der USA aus seiner Veröffentlichung entstand, läßt sich ebenfalls nicht endgültig ermessen.

D ans un espace de non-droit, des MP américains surveillent des prisonniers soupçonnés d'être membres des Taliban au camp « X-Ray » de la base de la marine américaine de Guantanamo Bay, à Cuba – 11 janvier 2002 (1). Une photo de la chaîne de télévision Al-Arabiya représente un prisonnier irakien encapuchonné, dans la sinistre prison d'Abu Ghraib, qui se tient debout sur une caisse, les mains ligotées par des câbles électriques (2). L'authenticité de cette photo n'a jamais pu être prouvée. De même, il n'est pas possible d'évaluer définitivement le préjudice que sa publication a causé au prestige des États-Unis.

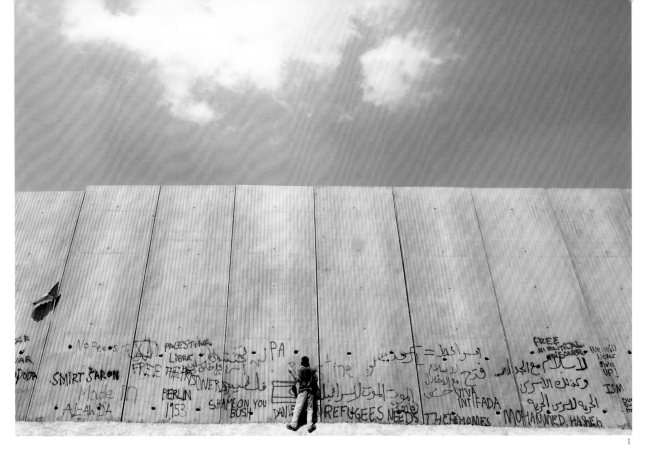

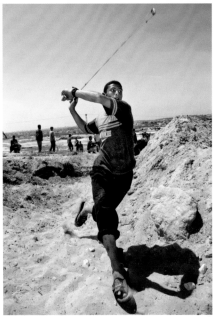

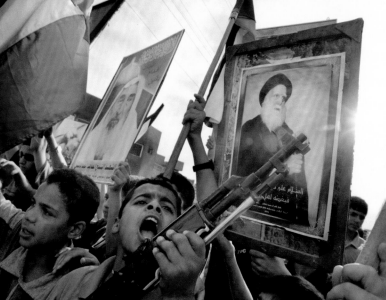

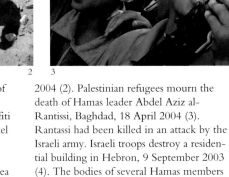

PROTEST and violence remain part of everyday life in the Middle East. A Palestinian adds his contribution to graffiti on the 8 metre high barrier built by Israel on the West Bank to prevent militants launching attacks (1). A modern David takes on Israeli tanks near the Beit Lahyea Refugee Camp in the Gaza Strip, 20 April 2004 (2). Palestinian refugees mourn the death of Hamas leader Abdel Aziz al-Rantissi, Baghdad, 18 April 2004 (3). Rantassi had been killed in an attack by the Israeli army. Israeli troops destroy a residential building in Hebron, 9 September 2003 (4). The bodies of several Hamas members were subsequently found in the ruins.

PROTEST und Gewalt bleiben Teil der alltäglichen Erfahrung im Nahen Osten. Ein Palästinenser ergänzt seinen Beitrag zu den Graffiti auf der acht Meter hohen Mauer, die Israel errichtete, um Angriffe militanter Palästinenser aus dem Westjordanland auf israelisches Gebiet zu verhindern (1). Ein moderner David (mit Steinschleuder) attackiert einen israelischen Panzer nahe des Flüchtlingslagers Bei

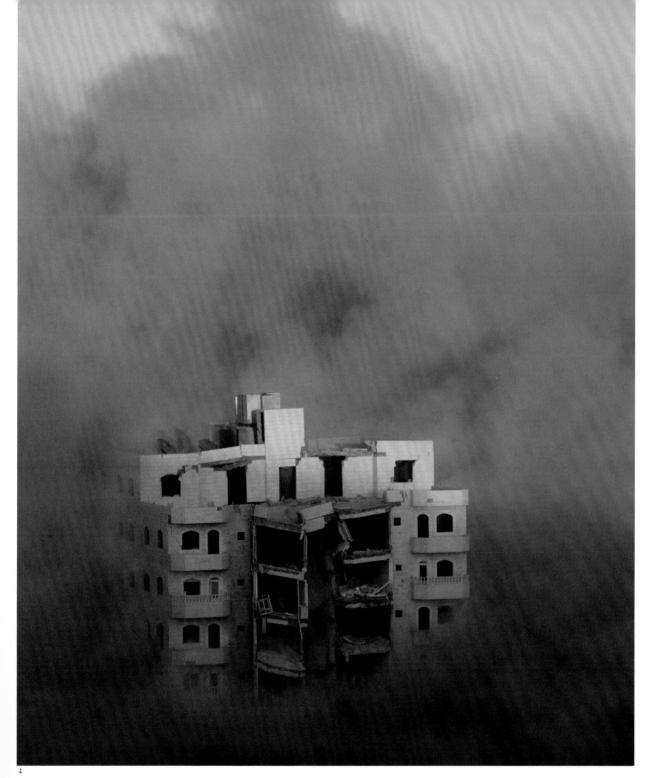

4

Lahyea im Gasastreifen – 20. April 2004 (2). Palästinensische Flüchtlinge in Bagdad trauern um den Tod des Hamasführers Abdel Aziz al-Rantissi – 18. April 2004 (3). Rantissi wurde bei einem Angriff der israelischen Armee getötet. Israelische Truppen zerstören ein Wohnhaus in Hebron – 9. September 2003 (4). Mehrere Hamasmitglieder wurden anschließend tot aus den Trümmern geborgen.

MANIFESTATIONS et violence continuent de faire partie du quotidien au Proche-Orient. Un palestinien complète son tag sur le mur de huit mètres de haut qu'Israël a édifié pour empêcher des attaques de Palestiniens militants en provenance de Jordanie occidentale contre le territoire israélien (1). Un David moderne (avec un lance-pierres) attaque un blindé israélien près du camp de réfugiés de Beit

Lahyea, dans la Bande de Gaza – 20 avril 2004 (2). Des réfugiés palestiniens de Bagdad manifestent leur tristesse à l'occasion du décès du leader du Hamas, Abdel Aziz al-Rantissi – 18 avril 2004 (3). Rantissi a été tué lors d'une attaque de l'armée israélienne. Des troupes israéliennes détruisent une maison d'habitation à Hébron – 9 septembre 2003 (4). Plusieurs membres du Hamas ont ensuite été retrouvés morts dans les ruines.

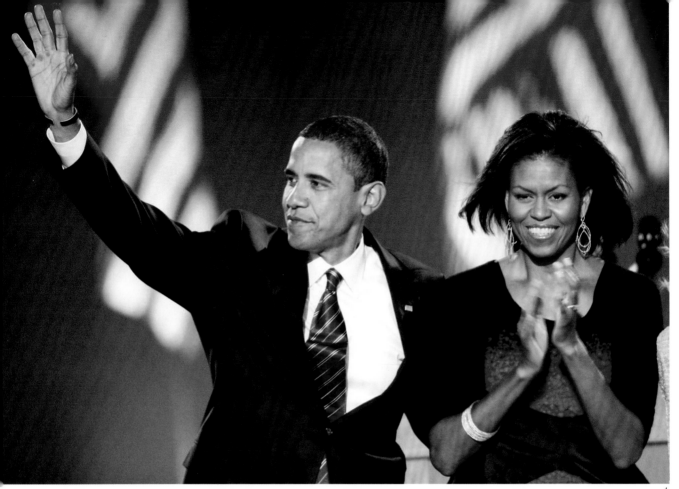

1

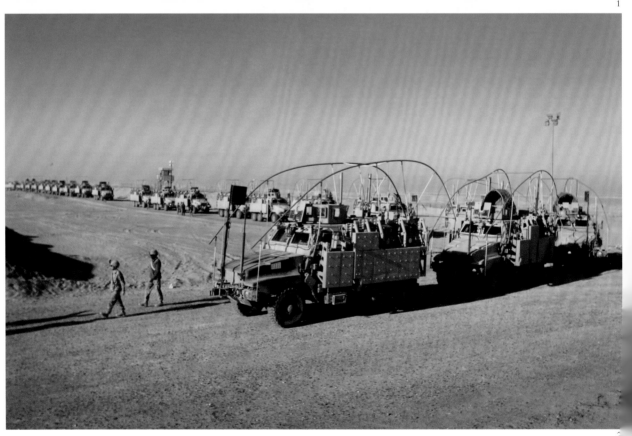

THE WAR against terrorism declared by President George W. Bush in the wake of the attack on the Twin Towers, rumbled on into the presidency of Barack Obama, seen here with his wife Michelle acknowledging the cheers of supporters in Grant Park, Chicago after his victory speech, 4 November 2008 (1). The aims of the war became less clear as the years passed in the dust and horror of battle zones in Iraq and Afghanistan, but one constancy was to track down and kill Osama bin Laden. Members of the US National Security team follow the progress of the mission to kill bin Laden, 1 May 2011 (3). The mission's success was front page news around the world – Australian press coverage of the death of bin Laden on 3 May 2011 (4). Their duty done in the Iraq War, US troops from the 1st Cavalry Division prepare to leave Kuwait City after eight years of service, December 8, 2011 (2).

DER »WAR ON TERRORISM«, den Präsident George W. Bush nach dem 11. September ausgerufen hatte, erstreckte sich bis in die Präsidentschaft Barack Obamas. Hier freut sich Obama mit seiner Frau Michelle über den Jubel im Grant Park, Chicago, nach seiner Siegesrede am 4. November 2008 (1). Mit den Jahren wurden die Ziele des Krieges im Staub und Schrecken der Kampfzonen im Irak und in Afghanistan immer undurchsichtiger, aber ein Ziel blieb klar: Osama bin Laden zu finden und zu töten. Präsident Obama, Außenministerin Clinton und andere verfolgen am Bildschirm die Tötung bin Ladens, 1. Mai 2011 (3). Der Erfolg der Mission machte weltweit Schlagzeilen – hier australische Zeitungen vom 3. Mai 2011 (4). Nach Erfüllung ihrer Pflicht im Irakkrieg und acht Dienstjahren verlassen die US-Truppen des 1. Kavallerieregiments Kuwait City, 8. Dezember 2011 (2).

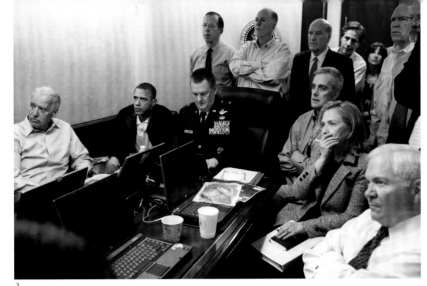

3

LA GUERRE contre le terrorisme, déclarée par le président George W. Bush aux lendemains de l'attaque contre les Twins Towers, s'invita dans la présidence de Barack Obama, photographié ici en compagnie de sa femme Michelle, répondant aux applaudissements de la foule de supporters réunis à Grant Park, à Chicago, après sa victoire, le 4 novembre 2008 (1). Certes, les raisons de cette guerre apparaissaient moins évidentes, après des années passées dans la poussière et l'horreur des zones de combats en Irak et en Afghanistan, mais l'objectif demeurait inchangé, traquer et abattre Oussama Ben Laden. Une équipe composée de membres de l'agence de sécurité nationale américaine supervise l'opération visant à neutraliser Ben Laden, le 1er mai 2011 (3). Le succès de la mission fait la une des journaux de la planète – entre autres de la presse australienne, annonçant la mort de Ben Laden, le 3 mai 2011 (4). Leur travail accompli en Irak, les troupes américaines de la 1re division de cavalerie se préparent à quitter Koweït City, après huit ans de service, le 8 décembre 2011 (2).

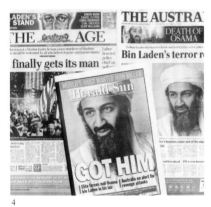

4

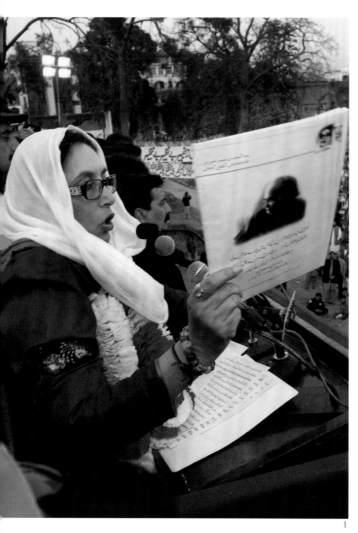

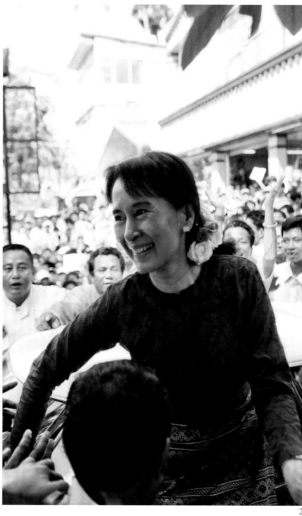

IN THE EARLY YEARS of the 21ˢᵗ century, there were signs that women were breaking through one of the toughest glass ceilings – that over the world of politics. The United States produced successive female Secretaries of State; for the first time France had a female presidential candidate; and Ellen Johnson Sirleaf became President of Liberia. But perhaps the greatest breakthroughs took place in southern Asia, with a mixture of tragic and heroic results. Just before her assassination, Benazir Bhutto reads from her election manifesto as she addresses supporters at a campaign rally in Rawalpindi, Pakistan, 27 December 2007 (1). Moments later, she was assassinated. After being released from house arrest, Aung San Suu Kyi arrives at her National League for Democracy headquarters in Yangon, Burma, 14 November 2010. Ahead lay another eighteen months of waiting before she was elected to the Burmese Parliament (2).

IN DEN ERSTEN JAHREN des 21. Jahrhunderts durchstießen immer mehr Frauen die stärkste der gläsernen Decken: die der Politik. Die USA hatten nacheinander mehrere weibliche Außenminister, Frankreich zum ersten Mal eine Präsidentschaftskandidatin; Ellen Johnson Sirleaf wurde die Präsidentin Liberias. Doch der größte Durchbruch geschah wohl in Südasien, mit heroischen, aber auch tragischen Ergebnissen.
Nur Minuten vor ihrer Ermordung liest Benazir Bhutto bei einer Wahlveranstaltung in Rawalpindi, Pakistan, aus ihrem Wahlprogramm, 27. Dezember 2007 (1). Yangon, Birma: Nach dem Ende ihres Hausarrests trifft Aung San Suu Kyi im Hauptquartier ihrer Nationalen Liga für Demokratie ein, 14. November 2010. Vor ihr lagen weitere 18 Monate des Wartens, bevor sie ins birmesische Parlament gewählt wurde (2).

AU COURS des premières années du XXIᵉ siècle, des signes montraient que les femmes étaient en train de briser un des remparts les plus solides – celui qui les séparait du monde de la politique. Les États-Unis avaient par deux fois nommé des femmes au poste de secrétaire d'État, pour la première fois en France une femme se présentait à l'élection présidentielle et Ellen Johnson Sirleaf accédait au poste de présidente du Liberia. Mais la plus grande avancée se produisit en Asie du Sud, mêlant le tragique à l'héroïsme. Peu de temps avant son assassinat, Benazir Bhutto dévoilait son programme électoral à une foule de supporters, lors d'une étape de sa campagne à Rawalpindi, au Pakistan, le 27 décembre 2007 (1). Peu de temps après, elle fut assassinée. Après la levée de sa mise en résidence surveillée, Aung San Suu Kyi arrive au quartier général de Ligue nationale pour la démocratie, à Rangoun, en Birmanie, le 14 novembre 2010 (2). Il lui faudra attendre encore dix-huit mois pour être élue au Parlement birman.

THE COLLAPSE of Lehman Brothers was merely the prelude to the revelation of dodgy financial speculation on a vast scale across the world. President Obama speaks at Federal Hall National Memorial, New York City on 14 September 2009, a year after the Lehman Brothers debacle (1). Nearly two years later, police use water hoses to drive protesters surrounding the Greek Parliament from Syntagma Square, Athens, 15 June 2011. Inside the building, the Greek government was trying to push through emergency measures to deal with the financial crisis (2).

DER ZUSAMMENBRUCH der Lehman-Brothers-Bank war nur der Auftakt zu Enthüllungen waghalsiger, schiefgegangener Finanzspekulationen, weltweit und von immensem Ausmaß. Präsident Obama spricht im Federal Hall National Memorial, New York, am 14. September 2009, ein Jahr nach dem Lehman-Debakel (1). Fast zwei Jahre später: Die Polizei geht auf dem Syntagma-Platz in Athen mit Wasserwerfern gegen Demonstranten am griechischen Parlament vor, 15. Juni 2011. Drinnen versucht die griechische Regierung, Notfallmaßnahmen zur Bewältigung der Finanzkrise durchzudrücken (2).

LA FAILLITE de Lehman Brothers ne fut que le prélude des révélations d'une dangereuse spéculation financière à l'échelle mondiale. Le président Obama prononce un discours au Federal Hall National Memorial, à New York, le 14 septembre 2009, un an après l'effondrement de Lehman Brothers (1). Près de deux ans plus tard, la police armée de canons à eau disperse la foule des manifestants réunis aux abords du Parlement grec, sur la place Syntagma, à Athènes, le 15 juin 2011. À l'intérieur du bâtiment, le gouvernement grec tente de faire adopter des mesures d'urgence pour lutter contre la crise financière (2).

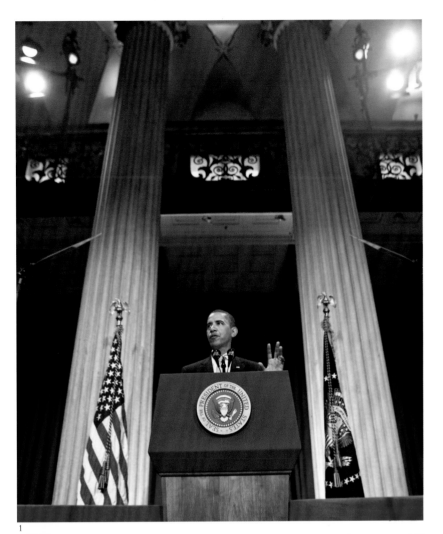

1

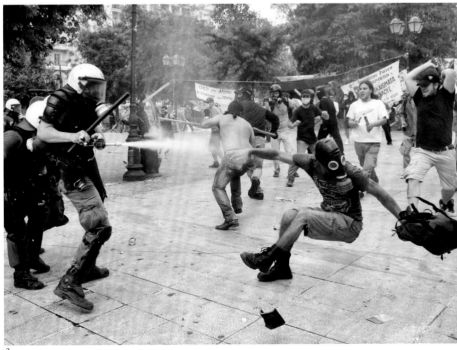

2

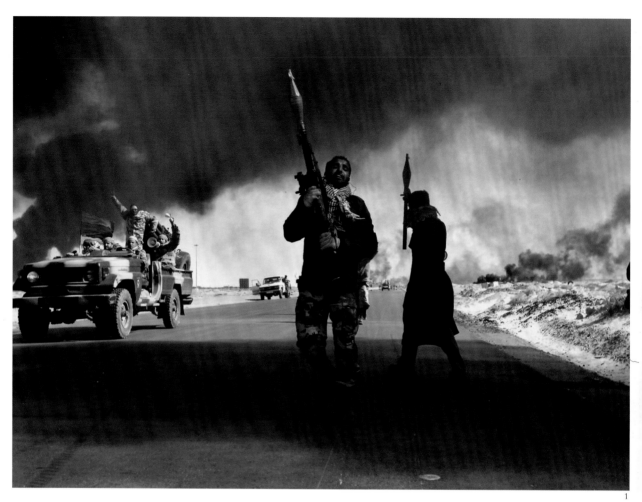

1

THE STRUGGLE to oust Muammar Gaddafi from Libya waged to and fro throughout much of 2011. Libyan freedom fighters retreat into the desert after being driven from the town of Ras Lanuf by Gaddafi loyalists, 11 March 2011 (1). At this time it was believed that Gaddafi had been wounded but was still alive. Women demonstrators for peace take part in an anti-Assad protest in Binnish, Syria, 9 April 2012 (2). An eye-witness described events prior to the protest: "Everywhere we went we saw burned and destroyed houses… and heard from people whose relatives had been killed…" The great day has arrived, Mubarak has resigned. Delighted Egyptians march across the Nile Bridge from Tahrir Square, 12 February 2011 (3). The brooms were used to clean up the Square after the protest.

DER KAMPF gegen Muammar al-Gaddafi in Libyen tobte fast das ganze Jahr 2011 hindurch. Libysche Freiheits-kämpfer ziehen sich in die Wüste zurück, nachdem sie von Gaddafi-Getreuen aus der Stadt Ras Lanuf vertrieben wurden, 11. März 2011 (1). Zu dieser Zeit dachte man, Gaddafi sei verwundet, aber noch am Leben. Friedensdemonstrantinnen bei einer Anti-Assad-Demonstration in Binnish, Syrien, 9. April 2012 (2). Ein Augenzeuge beschreibt die Ereignisse vor dem Protest: »Überall, wo wir hingingen, sahen wir abgebrannte und zerstörte Häuser … und hörten von Leuten, deren Angehörige getötet wurden …«. Der große Tag ist da: Mubarak ist zurückgetreten. Erfreute Ägypter marschieren vom Tahrir-Platz über die Qasr-el-Nil-Brücke, 12. Februar 2011 (3). Die Besen wurden zum Fegen des Platzes nach den Demonstrationen benutzt.

LA BATAILLE engagée pour chasser Mouammar Kadhafi de Libye s'éternise tout au long d'une grande partie de l'année 2011. Les combattants libyens pour la liberté se retirent dans le désert, après avoir été chassés de la ville de Ras Lanouf par les forces loyalistes de Kadhafi, le 11 mars 2011 (1). À cette époque, on pensait que Kadhafi avait été blessé, mais qu'il était encore vivant. Des manifestants pour la paix prennent part à une manifestation anti-Assad à Binnish, en Syrie, le 9 avril 2012 (2). Un témoin décrit la situation avant la manifestation : « Partout où nous nous rendons, nous voyons des maisons brûlées et détruites… nous entendons des gens dont les proches ont été massacrés… » Le grand jour est arrivé, Moubarak a abdiqué. Les Égyptiens en liesse traverse le pont Qasr El-Nil, depuis la place Tahrir, le 12 février 2011 (3). Les balais furent utilisés pour nettoyer la place après la manifestation.

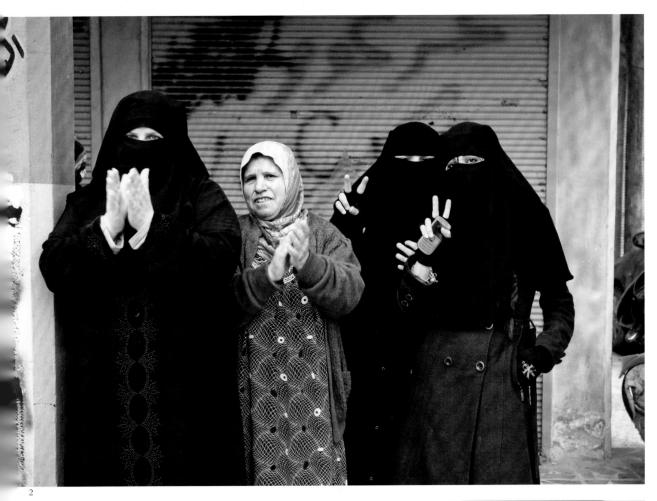

2

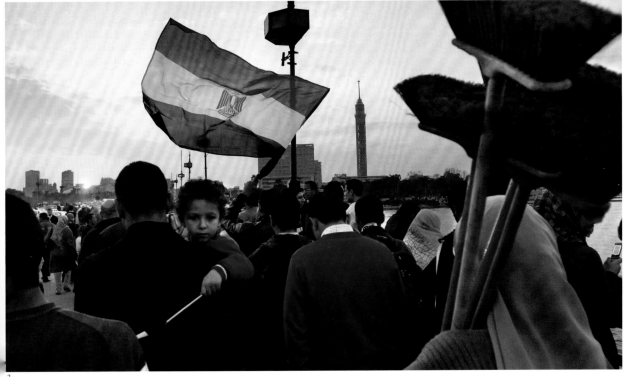

3

Index

gettyimages

Picture Acknowledgements

Even with 70 million images to choose from amongst the vast archives and collections of Getty Images the editors' task for this project was daunting. Much thanks go to our colleagues at Agence France Presse, to Michelle Franklin and Jeff Burak at Time & Life Pictures, to Mitch Blank at Getty Images in New York and to Jennifer Jeffrey at Getty Images in London.

We are grateful to the Royal Geographical Society for providing Frank Hurley's photo of Shackleton's *Endurance* on page 376 and also to Redferns for their shot of Scott Walker on page 620-1. All other pictures are courtesy of the various collections either held or represented by Getty Images. Those requiring further attribution are indicated as follows

Key:

t top **m** middle **b** bottom **l** left **r** right **i** inset

AFP Agence France Presse, **FSA** Farm Security Administration, **LOC** Library of Congress **NA** National Archives, **NYT** New York Times, **T&LP** Time & Life PicturPictures

393tr Anne Frank Fonds – Basel/Anne Frank House
385 Charles Conrad Jr./NASA
407 Schostal Archiv/Imagno
411b American Stock
412 Margaret Bourke-White/T&LP
414t Arthur Rothstein/FSA/LOC/T&LP
414b FSA/LOC
415 Dorothea Lange/FSA/LOC
468 NA/T&LP
476b Georgi Zelma/Slava Katamidze Collection
479 Evgueni Khaldi
480 Leonard McCombe/T&LP
516-17, 517r Margaret Bourke-White/T&LP
520 Robert W Kelley/T&LP
522 AY Owen/T&LP
523 Carl Iwasaki/T&LP
525 Howard Sochurek/T&LP
528, 529tl, tr, bl Terry Fincher
530 Dirck Halstead/T&LP
531 AFP
534, 535l Robert Lackenbach/T&LP
538 AFP
539 Libor Hajsky/AFP
540 Terry Fincher
542 AFP
543 Gabriel Duval/AFP
552 Michael Abramson/T&LP
553tr Leonard McCombe/T&LP
559 Thompson/AFP
582 John Kobal Foundation
583 Murray Garrett
586 John Sadovy/T&LP
587l, r Terry O'Neill
588 Michael Abramson/T&LP
589 Ted Thai/T&LP
590-1 Terry O'Neill
592 Dave Benett
593t Tauseef Mustafa/AFP
593b China Photos
600 Gordon Parks/T&LP
601 Lester Cohen
614l Santi Visalli Inc

614r Henry Grossman/T&LP
615l Dave Benett
615r David Westing
616 Frank Driggs Collection
617 James Whitmore
622l DMI/T&LP
622r Carlos Alvarez
623t Gus Stewart/Redferns
623b Kevin Mazur/WireImage
625 T&LP
626-7 Justin de Villeneuve
630l RDA
630r Bill Ray/T&LP
640-1 Robert Whitaker
642 John Olson/T&LP
644 Terry O'Neill
645 Jack Robinson
653 James McDivitt/NASA
658 NASA
658i Neil Armstrong/NASA
660 NASA
661t Keith Meyers/NYT/NASA
661b NASA
662 NASA
662i Bruce Weaver/AFP
664 NASA and The Hubble Heritage Team (STScI/AURA)
665t NASA, ESA and HE Bond (STScI)
665b NASA, ESA and J Hester (ASU)
666 Business Wire
667t ESA
676b Omar Torres/AFP
681 Eliot Schechter/AFP
692 Vince Bucci/AFP
696 Franck Fife/AFP
697b Bill Frakes/Sports Illustrated
699 Faddoul/AFP
702 Joel Robine/AFP
703t Christophe Simon/AFP
703b Eric Feferberg/AFP
704 Pascal Guyot/AFP
705 Scott Peterson
706 Tom Stoddart Archive
708 Sohail Nashir/AFP
709 Hans Paul/AFP
710 Tao Chuan Yeh/AFP

712 Wendy Sue Lamm/AFP
713 Tom Stoddart Archive
714t Irna/AFP
714b Gabriel Duval/AFP
715t Jean-Claude Delmas/AFP
718t DPA/AFP
718m EPA/AFP
718b Stephen Ferry
719 Tom Stoddart Archive
720 Bob Pearson/AFP
721b Diana Walker/T&LP
722 Patrick Baz/AFP
723 Todd Buchanan/T&LP
724t Sergei Guneyev/T&LP
724b Andre Durand/AFP
725 Anatoly Sapronyenko/AFP
726, 727t Wojtek Druszcz/AFP
727b Michael Estafiev/AFP
728 Joel Robine/AFP
729t Khalil Dehaini/AFP
729b Kamel Alamaa/AFP
730 Douglas E Curran/AFP
731 Saeed Khan/AFP
732 Ron Haviv/AFP
733t Bob Pearson/AFP
733b Dominique Faget/AFP
734t Pascal Guyot/AFP
734m Joel Robine/AFP
734b Odd Andersen/AFP
735 Christophe Simon/AFP
736 Peter Northall/AFP
737t John Ruthroff/AFP
737b Mike Persson/AFP
738 Tom Stoddart Archive
739 Alan Lewis/AFP
741 Sion Touhig
743 Sung Chih-Hsiung/AFP
744t AFP
744b John Russell/AFP
745t Jimin Lai/AFP
745m Choo Youn-Kong/AFP
745b Paula Bronstein
746t Chenghui Hsu
746b Jiji Press/AFP
747t Johnson Liu/AFP
747b IDF/AFP
748 Yuri Cortez/AFP
749t Martin Bernetti/AFP
749b Kim Jae-Hwan/AFP

751 Vincent Laforet/AFP
752 Gilles Mingasson
754 Denis Doyle
755 Tom Stoddart Archive
756 Tom Stoddart Archive
757 Zufarov/AFP
758 Pedro Armestre/AFP
758b David Sims/AFP
759t Jean-Pierre Müller/AFP
759b Danny Gohlke/AFP
760 Jung Yeon-Je/AFP
761b Paul Richards/AFP
762 Gerard Julien/AFP

763t, m Tom Stoddart Archive
763b Taro Yamasaki/T&LP
764-5 Tom Stoddart Archive
766 The Asahi Shimbun
769 Mirrorpix
770-1 Abid Katib
772 Seth McCallister/AFP
773 Spencer Platt
774tl Paul J Richards/AFP
774bl AFP
774br Mai/T&LP
775 Tech. Sgt. Cedric H Rudisill/DoD
776 Stan Honda/AFP
777 Mario Tama
778 Jean-Pierre Ksiazek/AFP
779 Paula Bronstein
780 Kurt Vinion
781 Patrick Barth
782t AFP
782b Vatan
782-3 Christophe Simon/AFP
783r Bruno Vincent
784t Joe Raedle
784b Mario Tama
785r Ramzi Haidar/AFP
786 Shane McCoy/Mai/T&LP
787 AFP
788t David Silverman
788bl Abid Katib
788br, 789 Paula Bronstein
791t The White House
791b William West/AFP
793t Bloomberg
793b Louisa Gouliamaki/AFP
795t John Cantlie

www.gettyimages.com